ANTICLERICALISM
IN LATE MEDIEVAL AND EARLY MODERN EUROPE

STUDIES
IN MEDIEVAL AND
REFORMATION THOUGHT

EDITED BY

HEIKO A. OBERMAN, Tucson, Arizona

IN COOPERATION WITH

THOMAS A. BRADY, Jr., Berkeley, California
E. JANE DEMPSEY DOUGLASS, Princeton, New Jersey
MANFRED SCHULZE, Tübingen
DAVID C. STEINMETZ, Durham, North Carolina

VOLUME LI

PETER A. DYKEMA AND HEIKO A. OBERMAN (EDS.)

ANTICLERICALISM IN LATE MEDIEVAL
AND EARLY MODERN EUROPE

ANTICLERICALISM
IN LATE MEDIEVAL
AND EARLY MODERN EUROPE

EDITED BY

PETER A. DYKEMA

AND

HEIKO A. OBERMAN

E.J. BRILL
LEIDEN • NEW YORK • KÖLN
1993

The paper in this book meets the guidelines for permanence and durability of the Committee on Production Guidelines for Book Longevity of the Council on Library Resources.

BR
735
.A58
1992

Library of Congress Cataloging-in-Publication Data

Anticlericalism in late medieval and early modern Europe / edited by
Peter A. Dykema and Heiko A. Oberman.
  p.   cm.—(Studies in medieval and Reformation thought, ISSN
0585-6914; v. 51)
  Text in English and German.
  Proceedings of an international colloquium held Sept. 20-22, 1990
at the University of Arizona, Tucson, Ariz.
  Includes bibliographical references (p.   ) and indexes.
  ISBN 9004095187 (alk. paper)
  1. Anti-clericalism—Europe—History—Congresses. I. Dykema,
Peter A. II. Oberman, Heiko Augustinus. III. Series.
BR735.A58   1992
274'.05—dc20   92-21783
                                                                      CIP

ISSN   0585-6914
ISBN   90 04 09518 7

PRINTED IN THE NETHERLANDS

CONTENTS

III. REFORM AND REFORMATION: THE CALL FOR CHANGE

ANTICLERICALISM AS AN AGENT OF CHANGE

Rarely do conferences deserve to be recorded for posterity to their full extent; notoriously their 'proceedings' are graveyards for exceptional — and hence bibliographically elusive — contributions. However, the international Colloquium convened by the Division for Late Medieval and Reformation Studies from September 20-22, 1990 at the University of Arizona under the title "Anticlericalism in Late Medieval and Early Modern Europe", not only responded to a widely-felt need for consultation and confrontation but was, from its very inception, geared towards designing a manual which should encompass the best of present wisdom on this central and sensitive issue.

To say that the term 'anticlericalism' functioned in the past widely as a stop-gap is not completely accurate, because it is too innocuous: this particular stop-gap made historians 'stop to gape', wielding the power of the seemingly self-evident. The term has not merely been used in an unsophisticated fashion but has actually been misleading by distorting the dynamics of the period of reform and reformation.

In a curious, indirect, and unintended fashion it cemented the wall of separation between intellectual and social history, which for so long has blocked advances — particularly noticeable in the whole field of medieval, renaissance and reformation studies. Church historians, traditionally the main bearers of intellectual history in the reformation era, tended to use the term 'anticlericalism' to satisfy the requirement of at least some treatment of the so-called non-theological factors. The social historians, on the other hand, were inclined to subsume under anticlericalism the 'revolt of faith' as a shorthand for the religious fervor of the time and as an explanation for the impact of theological ideas which appeared too abstract to the modern observer.

This volume documents the extent to which a new sense of interdependence between fields of necessary specialization provides access to the phenomenon of anticlericalism in its many variations. The very title of this preface is intended to draw attention to the fact that the negative connotation of the prefix 'anti' has distorted and disguised the underlying programmatic call for renewal of institutions in church and society. Above all, the perimeters of our investigation had to be drawn in a way that would allow for different perspectives on anticlericalism, namely in *time, place* and *carrier*. Thus important contributions from specialists covering the entire period from the late middles ages to the seventeenth century alert us to the differences in tone of anticlericalism as fermenting and fomenting in 1400, 1500 and 1600.

As far as geographical differences and 'place' are concerned, we should be increasingly sensitive to possible variations between the Low Countries and Italy, between Europe south and north of the Alps and between rural areas and urban centers.

The third perspective, that of the 'carriers', is perhaps the most significant in that a classification according to social groups throws the sharpest possible light on the fragility of the term 'anticlericalism', once we are prepared to look behind expressions and actions to the sometimes overlapping targets and 'cradle-groups' or 'carriers'. Viewed in this fashion we encounter papal, episcopal, monastic, and clerical anticlericalism. Moreover, we learn to distinguish between shades of anticlericalism as articulated by men and by women, at the court and in the city council, among the peasants and among the privileged professionals.

The nineteenth-century emphasis on the prefix and, in its wake, the ensuing negative view of anticlericalism, obscures both the variety in types and the variety in goals which our sources so eloquently advance. But beyond the importance of adjusting the rhetoric of interpretation to the irregular, ragged edges in the historical record, the suggested, more sophisticated and nuanced use of this central operative term opens up as many windows which allow us to look through expressions of frustration, discontent, and resentment to alternative visions of what its proponents expected and desired to be a 'modern and just society'.

At the end of the Conference and as an important form of summary of its deliberations, a redefinition of 'anticlericalism' was circulated and amended, which can now be said to represent the 'common sense' of the participants:

> Anticlericalism is a collective term, gaining currency in the nineteenth century as a one-sided negative designation. Properly understood, it describes attitudes and forms of behavior which in late medieval and early modern Europe engendered literary, political or physical action against what were perceived as unjust privileges constituting the legal, political, economic, sexual, sacred or social power of the clergy. Significantly different according to place, time and social background, anticlericalism could focus on papal, episcopal, sacerdotal, monastic, ministerial or intellectual power-structures.

> These grievances and actions emerged from a long tradition of medieval critique directed against the first *ordo*. Around the time of the reformation, anticlericalism's programmatic goal was to reform and discipline the clergy. In the post-reformation era we note the reversal of this tendency: now the clergy, as state-officials, turned their efforts more assertively than before to the problem of disciplining the laity; church and state cooperated to (re)form the laity into subjects. This gave rise to a new type of anticlericalism.

*   *   *

The Conference could not have been convened had it not been for the immediate, sustained, and substantial support by the former President of the University of Arizona, Henry Koffler. Further, this volume could not have been published so expeditiously and in its present form had the vice-president of Brill Publishers in Leiden, Drs. Elisabeth Venekamp, not encouraged me to place it in the series "Studies in Medieval and Reformation Thought".

But in between the essential support for the convocation of the Conference at the beginning, and the completion of its codification at the end, stands one person to whom I owe a word of special thanks: Pete Dykema, the Conference Director. This title covers the practical dimensions of overseeing the planning and execution of the Conference. But Pete Dykema is at the same time a perceptive contributor to this volume as well as the meticulous editor of a collection of bilingual contributions which by its very nature taxes to the utmost the ingenuity of the cultural go-between.

I do not doubt that the entire Division for Late Medieval and Reformation Studies took pride in hosting some fifty leading scholars from both sides of the Atlantic. Yet the privilege of witnessing the growing awareness of interdependence among formerly opposing or competing 'Schools' and 'School-heads' in a terrain deeply scarred by old and new ideological conflicts will be of lasting significance for all who participated.

Heiko A. Oberman
University of Arizona
Tucson, Arizona
January 6, 1992

I. THE LATE MEDIEVAL SETTING

ANTIKLERIKALISMUS IM DEUTSCHEN MITTELALTER[*]

KASPAR ELM

Freie Universität Berlin

I

Wenn man sich mit den üblichen Hilfsmitteln einen ersten Überblick über Art und Ausmaß des Antiklerikalismus im deutschen Mittelalter verschaffen will, macht man eine überraschende Entdeckung. Einschlägige Enzyklopädien wie der *Brockhaus* und *Meyers Konversationslexikon* reden zwar von der Antikomintern und der Anti-Corn-Law-League, nicht aber vom Antiklerikalismus. Auch das *Evangelische Staatslexikon* und das *Staatslexikon* der Görres-Gesellschaft, die *Theologische Realenzyklopädie*, ja selbst das *Lexikon des Mittelalters* verzichten auf ein eigenes Lemma "Antiklerikalismus". Dort wo man, wie im *Lexikon für Theologie und Kirche*, den Antiklerikalismus erwähnt, begnügt man sich mit der Feststellung, es handele sich bei ihm um Bestrebungen, die Kirche daran zu hindern, dort Einfluß zu gewinnen, wo der Staat seine notwendige Funktion habe.[1] Wenn man auf die historische Bedeutung des Antiklerikalismus eingeht, ist weder von der Reformation noch vom Mittelalter die Rede, sondern so gut wie ausschließlich von dem zwischen 1871 und 1887 geführten Kulturkampf. So belehrt wird man sich nicht wundern, daß das Wort "Antiklerikalismus" im *Deutschen Wörterbuch* der Brüder Grimm überhaupt nicht auftaucht, nach Ausweis jüngerer Wörterbücher der deutschen Sprache vielmehr erst im 19. Jahrhundert Eingang ins Deutsche gefunden hat.[2] Daß es falsch wäre, diese Beschränkung als eine deutsche Besonderheit anzusehen, bestätigen Enzyklopädien und Lexika anderer Länder und Sprachen, die sich mit ähnlichen Definitionen begnügen, den Gebrauch des Wortes erst für die Anfänge des 19. Jahrhunderts nachweisen können und als Beispiel für Antiklerikalismus lediglich die Französische Revolution, das Risorgimento und die im 19. bzw. 20. Jahrhundert in katholischen Ländern wie Frankreich,

---

[*] Es handelt sich um den deutschen Text des am 20. September 1990 vor einem größeren Publikum gehaltenen Vortrages, in dem nicht mehr als Erwägungen über Eigenart, Bedeutung und Deutung des Antiklerikalismus im Mittelalter — speziell in Deutschland — angestellt wurden. Die ursprüngliche essayistische Fassung wurde beibehalten und lediglich um die erforderlichen Nachweise ergänzt.

[1] *Lexikon für Theologie und Kirche*, 2. Aufl. (Freiburg i. Br., 1957), 1: 639-40.

[2] *Duden. Das große Wörterbuch der deutschen Sprache*, 2. Aufl. (Mannheim, 1977), 1: 164. *Brockhaus-Wahrig. Deutsches Wörterbuch* (Wiesbaden, 1980), 1: 272.

4 KASPAR ELM

Belgien, Spanien und Mexiko getroffenen antikirchlichen Maßnahmen anführen.[3] Wie kann man sich diese Blickverengung erklären? Sollte es in Mittelalter und Frühneuzeit keinen Antiklerikalismus gegeben haben? War man in Deutschland dagegen besonders gefeit? Handelt es sich bei ihm um ein Phänomen, das sich allein auf die katholischen Länder beschränkt und dort, wo sich die Reformation durchsetzte, ohne Bedeutung ist? Solche Fragen zu stellen, heißt sie zu verneinen. Der Grund für das Schweigen der Enzyklopädien und Lexika muß woanders liegen. Der Begriff Antiklerikalismus und die Bedeutung, die man ihm in Sprachgebrauch und Lexikographie gibt, sind — und das ist wohl die einzig richtige Erklärung — eindeutig von Phänomenen des 18. und des 19. Jahrhunderts und nicht etwa des Mittelalters oder der frühen Neuzeit abgeleitet worden. Will man den wie in der Neuzeit so auch im Mittelalter gegenüber Kirche und Klerus geäußerten Widerspruch erfassen und richtig beurteilen, wird man daher, wenn nicht auf den anachronistischen Begriff "Antiklerikalismus", dann doch auf den Bedeutungsinhalt, den ihm das 18. und 19. Jahrhundert gegeben haben, verzichten müssen, sonst läuft man Gefahr, lediglich Geist vom eigenen Geist und nicht dem zu begegnen, was das Mittelalter zum Ausdruck bringen wollte, wenn es die in allen Lebensbereichen präsente Kirche, ihre Institutionen und Repräsentanten, der Kritik unterzog.[4]

II

Wenn man, was sicherlich auch für das Mittelalter erlaubt ist, unter Antiklerikalismus die Kritik versteht, die Laien an dem Leben und der

[3] J. A. Simpson, E. S. C. Weiner, *The Oxford English Dictionary*, 2. Aufl. (Oxford, 1989), 1: 522. P. Imbs, *Trésor de la langue française. Dictionnaire de la langue au XIXe et du XXe siècle (1789-1960)*, Bd. 3 (Paris, 1974), 137-8. *Vocabulario della lingua Italiana* (Rom, 1986), 1: 209. M. Alonso, *Enciclopedia del Idioma Española (Siglos XII al XX)* (Aquilar, 1958), 1: 383. *The New Encyclopaedia Britannica* (Chicago, 1985), 1: 450-1. *Grand Dictionnaire Encyclopédique Larousse* (Paris, 1982), 1: 531.

[4] A. Mellor, *Histoire de l'anticléricalisme français* (Paris, 1966). J. Devlin, *Spanish Anticlericalism* (New York, 1966). M. Themelly, *L'anticlericalismo nel Risorgimento 1860-1870* (Manduria, 1966). J. H. Fichter, "Anticlericalism in the American Catholic Culture", *The Critic* 21 (1963): 11-15. J. Salwyn Shapiro, *Anticlericalism: Conflict Between Church and State in France, Italy and Spain* (Princeton, 1966). J. Sánchez, *Anticlericalism: A Brief History* (Notre Dame, 1972). Auch der von J. Marx herausgegebene Sammelband, *Aspects de l'anticléricalisme du Moyen Age à nos jours. Hommage à Robert Joly*, Problèmes d'histoire du christianisme 18 (Bruxelles, 1988), beschäftigt sich, von einer einzigen Ausnahme (Vgl. Anm. 26) abgesehen, lediglich mit dem Antiklerikalismus des 18. und 19. Jahrhunderts, ohne jedoch von ihm ein "abgerundetes Bild" liefern zu können (*Deutsches Archiv für Erforschung des Mittelalters* 46 [1990]: 561).

Amtsführung der mit ihrer geistlichen Leitung betrauten Weltkleriker und Ordensleute übten, findet man dafür wie im 19. und 20. Jahrhundert auch im Mittelalter so viele Belege, daß man sie kaum überblicken kann. Seit der Christianisierung wurde allenthalben in Europa — Deutschland eingeschlossen — die *vita clericorum et monachorum* an den Forderungen des Neuen Testaments, den Lehren der Kirchenväter und den Ordensregeln, am Vorbild der Heiligen und den Vorschriften des Kirchenrechts, vor allem aber an den eigenen Worten gemessen. Wie überall ging es auch in Deutschland in massiven Anklagen, in Spottgedichten und Satiren, mit Bildern und Schaustellungen um den sittlichen Lebenswandel, die Einhaltung der Gelübde, um Privilegien und ungerechtfertigten Reichtum, um Unbildung und Nachlässigkeit bei der Erfüllung der Standespflichten. Schon im frühen, erst recht aber im hohen und späten Mittelalter verfestigten sich die Einzelvorwürfe zu einer generellen Ablehnung der Kleriker und Mönche als Vertreter einer Gegenwelt und Repräsentanten eines Lebensstils, von der sich der *miles* und der *civis* sowie, mit deutlicher Zuspitzung bei den Humanisten, auch der *doctus* distanzierten, wobei die Schärfe, mit der Priester und Mönche zum Gegenstand von Spott und Verachtung gemacht wurden, erkennen läßt, daß diese Distanzierung nicht nur eine Angelegenheit des Intellekts war, sondern tief im Unterbewußtsein einer nicht selten von den Geistlichen, was Geisteskraft und Wortgewalt, Raffinesse und Geschmack, Sensibilität und Verführungskunst angeht, deklassierten Männerwelt wurzelte.[5]

Für den Antiklerikalismus, der sich weniger am Verhalten einzelner Kleriker und Religiosen als vielmehr an der privilegierten Rechtsstellung, der sozialen Überlegenheit, politischen Macht und wirtschaftlichen Stärke des geistlichen Standes entzündete, gilt das Gleiche. Anlässe zur Kritik an den geistlichen Institutionen und ihren Praktiken gab es in Deutschland wie überall in Europa. Ihr Inhalt und die Art, in der sie geübt wurde, unterschieden sich nur in Nuancen von den anderswo geäußerten Vorwürfen. Wie die gegen einzelne Individuen gerichtete Kritik setzte sie schon in der Frühzeit der Christianisierung ein. Man kann aus den Kapitularien Karls des Großen den Protest der eben bekehrten Sachsen gegen die Zehntforderungen des fränkischen Klerus und die mit der Mission und Einbeziehung in das

---

[5] Im Blick von der Reformation aus auf das Spätmittelalter: R. W. Scribner, "Anticlericalism and the Reformation in Germany", in ders., *Popular Culture and Popular Movements in Reformation Germany* (London, 1987), 243-56. H.-J. Goertz, *Pfaffenhaß und groß Geschrei. Die reformatorischen Bewegungen in Deutschland 1517-1529* (München, 1987). Eine Reihe von einschlägigen Quellen in Auswahl: Gerald Strauss (Hrsg.), *Manifestations of Discontent in Germany on the Eve of the Reformation* (Bloomington, 1971).

Frankenreich einhergehenden Einschränkungen der Freiheit heraushören.[6]
Wenige Jahrhunderte später berichten Adam von Bremen, Helmold von
Bosau und Thietmar von Merseburg vom Widerstand der Slawen zwischen
Elbe und Oder, die sich mit Gewalt gegen die mit dem neuen Glauben
verbundenen Zwangsmaßnahmen auflehnten.[7] Das sind nur einige Glieder
in der langen Kette des Widerspruches und Widerstandes, mit denen sich das
"Land" gegen die Forderungen des Klerus und der geistlichen Herren wandte
und ihre Praktiken im Umgang mit alter Gewohnheit und gutem Recht
anprangerte.[8] Sie findet ihre Fortsetzung in Erscheinung wie dem Aufstand
der Stedinger gegen den Erzbischof von Bremen und der Rolle des
Deutschen Ordens als Landesherrn,[9] verdichtet sich, wie zahlreiche
gravamina, planctus, Reformpläne und Reformtraktate deutlich machen, im
15. Jahrhundert und erreicht am Vorabend der Reformation in Ritterbünden,
Klosterstürmen und Bauerntumulten, vor allem aber in den Bauernkriegen,
auf deren antiklerikalen Charakter mehr als einmal hingewiesen worden ist,
ihren Höhepunkt.[10]

---

[6] E. Müller-Mertens, *Karl der Große, Ludwig der Fromme und die Freien. Ein
Beitrag zur Sozialgeschichte und Sozialpolitik des Frankenreiches*, Forschungen zur
mittelalterlichen Geschichte 10 (Berlin, 1962). J. Semmler, "Zehntgebot und
Pfarrtermination in der Karolingerzeit", in H. Mordek (Hrsg.), *Aus Kirche und Reich.
Studien zu Theologie, Politik und Recht im Mittelalter. Festschrift für Friedrich
Kempf* (Sigmaringen, 1983), 33-44.

[7] J. Herrmann (Hrsg.), *Die Slawen in Deutschland. Geschichte und Kultur der
slawischen Stämme westlich von Oder und Neiße vom 6. bis 12. Jahrhundert. Ein
Handbuch* (Berlin, 1986), 402-4.

[8] S. Epperlein, *Bauernbedrückung und Bauernwiderstand im hohen Mittelalter. Zur
Erforschung der Ursachen bäuerlicher Abwanderung nach Osten im 12. und 13.
Jahrhundert, vorwiegend nach den Urkunden geistlicher Grundherrschaften*,
Forschungen zur mittelalterlichen Geschichte 6 (Berlin, 1960). W. Eggert, "Rebel-
liones servorum", *Zeitschrift für Geschichtswissenschaft* 23 (1975): 1147-64.

[9] L. Deike, *Die Entstehung der Grundherrschaft in den Hollerkolonien an der
Niederweser*, Veröffentlichungen aus dem Staatsarchiv der Freien Hansestadt Bremen
27 (Bremen, 1959). M. Burleigh, "Anticlericalism in Fifteenth-Century Prussia: the
Clerical Contribution Reconsidered", in C. Benson, C. Harper-Bill (Hrsgg.), *The
Church in Society in the Century before the Reformation* (Suffolk, 1985), 38-47.

[10] H. A. Oberman, "Tumultus rusticorum: Vom 'Klosterkrieg' zum 'Fürstensieg",
in ders. (Hrsg.), *Deutscher Bauernkrieg 1525*, 157-72 (= *ZKG* 85 [1974]: 301-16). R.
Endres, "Zur sozialökonomischen Einstellung des 'gemeinen Mannes'. Der Kloster-
und Burgensturm in Franken 1525", in H. U. Wehler (Hrsg.), *Der deutsche
Bauernkrieg 1524-1526, Geschichte und Gesellschaft*, Sonderheft 1 (Göttingen, 1975),
70-5. H. J. Cohn, "Anticlericalism in the German Peasants' War 1525", *PaP* 83
(1979): 3-31. Ders., "Reformatorische Bewegungen und Antiklerikalismus in
Deutschland und England", in W. J. Mommsen u.a. (Hrsgg.), *Stadtbürgertum und
Adel in der Reformation. Studien zur Sozialgeschichte der Reformation in England
und Deutschland*, Veröffentlichungen des Deutschen Historischen Instituts London
5 (Stuttgart, 1979), 309-29.

Mit dem Aufkommen der Stadt als einer eigenen Rechts-, Sozial- und Wirtschaftsordnung entstand wie überall in Europa so auch in Deutschland ein "Konfliktpotential", das neben der bäuerlichen und adeligen eine spezifisch bürgerliche Variante des Antiklerikalismus entstehen ließ. Hier wie dort waren es die Standesprivilegien, die politische und wirtschaftliche Machtkonzentration, der Wissensvorsprung und die Lebensführung, die Anlaß zu Spannungen gaben, die angesichts der höheren Dynamik der städtischen Gesellschaft und der größeren Vielfalt der sich in ihr ausbildenden Interessen nicht nur häufiger auftraten, sondern sich auch sehr viel heftiger entluden. Das begann mit den alltäglichen Auseinandersetzungen um die Leistung und Befreiung von städtischen Abgaben, um die Behauptung von Immunität und den Erwerb des Bürgerrechts, führte zum Streit über das Bildungs- und Schulmonopol sowie das Spitalwesen, schloß die Konkurrenz in Handwerk, Handel und Gewerbe ein und kulminierte in den Kämpfen zwischen Stadtgemeinden und geistlichen Stadtherrn, die in den meisten Fällen zur Folge hatten, daß der Bischof seine Bischofsstadt verließ und außerhalb ihrer Mauern seine Residenz aufschlug.[11] Bei aller Interdependenz zwischen Geistlichkeit und Bürgertum und trotz der Tatsache, daß die Kirche nicht selten zum öffentlichen Versammlungsort und das Rathaus zum Gotteshaus wurden, entwickelten sich in den deutschen Städten des Mittelalters Animositäten gegen die Standesvorrechte adeliger Chorherren und Mönche, die Pfründenhäufung der Prälaten, die Nachlässigkeit des Pfarrklerus, die Sittenlosigkeit, Geldgier und Streitsucht der Mendikanten, die in Volkslied und Volksbuch, Chroniken und Annalen ihren Niederschlag fanden, ja nicht selten in elementaren, mit blasphemischen Äußerungen in Gang gesetzten und häufig von Kirchen- und Sakramentenschändungen begleiteten blutigen Übergriffen, den Pfaffenstürmen, zum Ausbruch kamen.[12]

---

[11] A. Störmann, *Die städtischen Gravamina gegen den Klerus am Auggang des Mittelalters und in der Reformationszeit*, RGST 24-26 (Münster, 1916). J. Sydow, "Bürgerschaft und Kirche im Mittelalter. Probleme und Aufgaben der Forschung", in ders. (Hrsg.), *Bürgerschaft und Kirche*, Stadt in der Geschichte 7 (Sigmaringen, 1980), 9-25. E. Isenmann, *Die deutsche Stadt im Spätmittelalter 1250-1500. Stadtgestalt, Recht, Stadtregiment, Kirche, Gesellschaft, Wirtschaft* (Stuttgart, 1988), 225-30. B.-U. Hergemöller, *"Pfaffenkriege" im spätmittelalterlichen Hanseraum*, Städteforschung Reihe C: Quellen 2, 1-2 (Köln, 1988).

[12] O. Kopelke, *Beiträge zur Geschichte der öffentlichen Meinung über die Kirche in den deutschen Städten von 1420-1460* (Halle, 1910). H. Schmidt, *Die deutschen Städtechroniken als Spiegel des bürgerlichen Selbstverständnisses im Spätmittelalter*, Schriftenreihe der Hist. Komm. bei der Bayer. Akad. d. Wiss. 3 (München, 1958). R. Barth, *Argumentation und Selbstverständnis der Bürgeropposition in städtischen Auseinandersetzungen des Spätmittelalters*, Kollektive Umstellungen und sozialer Wandel 3 (Köln; 1974).

Wie mit der Entstehung der Stadt war auch mit der Ausbildung der Landesherrschaft eine Wendung gegen den Sonderstatus der Kleriker und Ordensleute verbunden. Die Einschränkung ihrer Rechte und Privilegien, die Integration geistlicher Grundherrschaften sowie die möglichst weitgehende politische Instrumentalisierung von Kirche und religiösem Leben waren Maxime, die der von der Grundherrschaft über die Territorialbildung bis zum Fürstenstaat führenden Entwicklung des "modernen Staates" in Deutschland zugrundelagen. Klagen über den Mißbrauch der geistlichen Autorität, die Vernachlässigung der seelsorgerischen Pflichten und den Mißbrauch der für Kult und Seelsorge zur Verfügung stehenden Einkünfte und Besitzungen begleiteten wie ein *tonus rectus* die vielfältigen Maßnahmen, die die Konsolidierung des Territoriums zum Ziel hatten. Die bei großzügiger Verwendung des Begriffes zweifellos als antiklerikal zu bezeichnenden Vorwürfe und Anklagen gegen die Sonderstellung des Klerus dienten nicht selten als Alibi für die Inanspruchnahme der Vogteirechte und des *ius reformandi*, der Patronatsgewalt und des Nominationsrechtes für politische Zwecke, waren aber auch — daran kann kein Zweifel bestehen — Ausdruck landesherrlicher Sorge um die Sicherung des religiösen Lebens, die Förderung des Schul- und Fürsorgewesens sowie der Verhinderung des Ärgernisses, das von pflichtvergessenen Klerikern und nichtregulierten Ordensleuten ausging und sowohl dem Ansehen der Obrigkeit als auch dem öffentlichen Wohl schadete.[13]

Die Kritik der Bauern und des Adels, der Städte und der Fürsten richtete sich nicht allein gegen den Episkopat und den Ortsklerus, gegen Mönche, Kanoniker und Mendikanten, sie wandte sich zunehmend auch gegen den Papst und die römische Kurie. Sie richtete sich gegen den päpstlichen Fiskalismus, der auch vor den spirituellen Bereichen keinen Halt machte, gegen die Stellenbesetzungs- und Pfründenpolitik der Kurie, gegen Mißbrauch im Ablaßwesen, gegen Verweltlichung und Politisierung der geistlichen Autorität. Hand in Hand damit ging ein antirömischer Affekt, der am Ende des 15. Jahrhunderts apokalyptische Züge annahm und damit weit über die bekannten *Invectiva in Romam*[13a] des frühen und hohen Mittelal-

---

[13] I. W. Frank, "Kirchengewalt und Kirchenregiment in Spätmittelalter und früher Neuzeit", *Innsbrucker Historische Studien* 1 (1978): 33-60. D. Stievermann, *Landesherrschaft und Klosterwesen im spätmittelalterlichen Württemberg* (Sigmaringen, 1989). M. Schulze, *Fürsten und Reformation. Geistliche Reformpolitik weltlicher Fürsten vor der Reformation*, Spätmittelalter und Reformation, Neue Reihe 2 (Tübingen, 1990).

[13a] J.A. Junck, "Economic Conservatism, Papal finances and the medieval satires on Rome", *Mediaeval Studies* 23 (1961): 334-51. J. Benzinger, *Invectiva in Romam. Romkritik im Mittelalter vom 9. bis 12. Jahrhundert*, Historische Studien 404 (Lübeck-Hamburg, 1968). R. Hiestand, "'Dominum papam appellando canem cum omnibus cardinalibus singulis'. Zum Widerstand gegen Rom im Hochmittelalter", in K. Herbers, H.H. Kortüm, C. Servatius (Hrsgg.), *Ex ipsis Rerum Documentis.*

ters hinausging. Die Gereiztheit über den Hochmut, mit dem die Italiener und andere "Welsche" auf die Barbaren von jenseits der Alpen herabblickten, war jedoch keineswegs das eigentliche Charakteristikum dieser in allen Ständen Deutschlands verbreiteten Spielart des Antiklerikalismus. In fast allen Fällen, in denen es zu einer expliziten Kritik an Papsttum und Kurie kam, wurde die Ursache für die beklagten Mißstände am Haupt der Kirche weniger bei den Personen und erst recht nicht bei der Institution selbst gesucht. Es war vielmehr das gestörte Verhältnis zwischen den Universalmächten, zwischen Papst und Kaiser, Kirche und Reich, das die Päpste und die Kurie ihre eigentliche Aufgabe zum Schaden von Kirche und Christenheit vergessen ließ.

Diese Beobachtung trifft nicht nur auf die *Gravamina deutscher Nation*, die *Reformatio Sigismundi* und die Reformschrift des Oberrheinischen Revolutionärs zu, sie gilt auch für die literarischen Bundesgenossen Ludwigs des Bayern, den über die Mißachtung des Kaisertums erzürnten Alexander von Roes, für die antipäpstliche Propaganda Friedrichs II., die kaiserfreundliche Chronistik des 12. Jahrhunderts und die den Investiturstreit begleitenden *Libelli de lite* der antigregorianischen Partei.[14] Sie alle haben jene Klage gemeinsam, die Friedrich Barbarossa 1157 in einem Schreiben an die deutschen Fürsten anstimmte: "Wir sehen uns mit tiefster Bekümmernis des Herzens gezwungen, Eurer Liebe zu klagen, daß von dem Haupte der Heiligen Kirche, der Christus das Zeichen seines Friedens und seiner Liebe aufgeprägt hat, der Samen des Bösen und das Gift einer verderblichen Seuche auszugehen scheinen, und befürchten sehr, daß, wenn Gott es nicht verhütet, dadurch der ganze Leib der Kirche befleckt, die Einheit gesprengt und zwischen Königtum und Priestertum eine Spaltung herbeigeführt wird."[15] Wie sehr das gestörte Verhältnis zwischen Kaiser und Papst auch dann noch bei den Deutschen Verdrossenheit gegenüber Klerus, Episkopat, vor allem aber gegen das Papsttum hervorzurufen vermochte, als der Papst

---

Beiträge zur Mediävistik. Festschrift für Harald Zimmermann zum 65. Geburtstag (Sigmaringen, 1991), 325-34.

[14] H. Koller (Hrsg.), *Reformation Kaiser Siegmunds*, MGH Staatsschriften des Mittelalters 6 (Stuttgart, 1964). A. Franke (Hrsg.), *Das Buch der hundert Kapitel und der vierzig Statuten des sogenannten oberrheinischen Revolutionärs*, LÜAMA A 4 (Berlin, 1967). O. Berthold u.a. (Hrsgg.), *Kaiser, Volk und Avignon. Ausgewählte Quellen zur antikurialen Bewegung in Deutschland in der ersten Hälfte des 14. Jahrhunderts*, LÜAMA A 3 (Berlin, 1960). H. Grundmann, H. Heimpel (Hrsgg.), *Alexander von Roes, Schriften*, MGH Staatsschriften des Mittelalters 1,1 (Stuttgart, 1958). H. Wieruszowski, *Vom Imperium zum nationalen Königtum. Vergleichende Studien über die politischen Kämpfe Kaiser Friedrichs II. und König Philipps des Schönen mit der Kurie*, Beihefte der *HZ* 30 (München, 1933). C. Mirbt, *Die Publizistik im Zeitalter Gregors VII.* (Leipzig, 1894). C. Erdmann, "Die Anfänge der staatlichen Propaganda im Investiturstreit", *HZ* 154 (1936): 491-512.

[15] H. Appelt (Hrsg.), *Die Urkunden Friedrichs I. 1152-1158*, MGH. Diplomata 10,1 (Hannover, 1975), 314, Nr. 186.

längst aus der Reichsverfassung hinausgedrängt war und das Kaisertum
seinen universalen Charakter weitgehend verloren hatte, machte der Mainzer
Kanzler Martin Mayer 1457 gegenüber Enea Silvio Piccolomini deutlich, in
dem er alle Beschwerden, die die Deutschen gegen den Hochmut der
römischen Päpste, Kardinäle und Protonotare vorzubringen hatten, darauf
zurückführte, daß diese "unser einst ruhmreiches Volk, das durch seine
Tüchtigkeit und sein Blut das Römische Imperium erworben hat und Herr
und König der Welt gewesen ist, nunmehr so an den Bettelstab gebracht,
geknechtet und zinspflichtig" gemacht haben, daß es "im Staube liegend sein
Los, seine Armut" zu beklagen hat.[16]

III

Für den im 18. bzw. 19. Jahrhundert geprägten Begriff "Antiklerikalismus"
ist die Vorstellung konstitutiv, daß dieser seine Ursache im spannungsrei-
chen Verhältnis von Klerikern und Laien habe und im Grunde genommen
nichts anderes sei als die Opposition einer Mehrheit von Laien gegen eine
zahlenmäßig kleinere, auf die Sicherung des Monopols der Heilsvermittelung
bedachten Priesterschaft, die sich unberechtigterweise in die ureigensten
Angelegenheiten der Laien einmische. Genausowenig wie die von Gratian
mit der Feststellung: *duo sunt genera Christianorum* formulierte Prämisse
von der Dualstruktur der mittelalterlichen Gesellschaft unbesehen hingenom-
men werden kann, kann es als selbstverständlich gelten, daß der Antiklerikalismus ausschließlich eine Sache der Laien gewesen sei.[17] Wider-
sprüche gegen Amtsmißbrauch und Kritik an ungerechtfertigten Vorteilen
gab es auch im Klerus selbst, wobei freilich die Motive für diese Opposition
keineswegs immer die gleichen waren. Soziale Inferiorität, wirtschaftliche
Benachteiligung und strenge Disziplinierung ließen den Niederklerus, die
Konversen und Laienbrüder gegen Adels- und Bildungsprivilegien, die
Pfründenhäufung und das Wohlleben der Prälaten, Äbte und Prioren zu
Felde ziehen,[18] während umgekehrt Bischöfe und Superioren die schlechte

---

[16] Enea Silvio Piccolomini, *Deutschland. Der Brieftraktat an Martin Mayer und
Jakob Wimpfelings "Antwort und Einwendungen gegen Enea Silvio"*, übersetzt und
erläutert von A. Schmidt, Die Geschichtsschreiber der deutschen Vorzeit 104 (Köln,
1962), 34. Immer noch heranzuziehen ist: B. Gebhardt, *Die Gravamina der deutschen
Nation gegen den römischen Hof*, 2. Aufl. (Breslau, 1895).
[17] C. 12, q. 1, c. 7. E. Friedberg (Hrsg.), *Corpus iuris canonici* 1 (ND Graz, 1959),
678. Vgl. O. G. Oexle, "Die funktionale Dreiteilung als Deutungsschema der sozialen
Wirklichkeit in der ständischen Gesellschaft des Mittelalters", in W. Schulze (Hrsg.),
Ständische Gesellschaft und Mobilität, Schriften des Historischen Kollegs München,
Kolloquien 12 (München, 1988), 19-51.
[18] D. Kurze, "Der niedere Klerus in der sozialen Welt des späteren Mittelalters",
in K. Schulz (Hrsg.), *Beiträge zur Wirtschafts- und Sozialgeschichte des Mittelalters.
Festschrift für Herbert Helbig zum 65. Geburtstag* (Köln, 1976), 273-305. J. Batany,

Lebensführung, den geringen Bildungsstand und die Nachlässigkeit von Vikaren und Kaplänen, Rektoren und Konversen brandmarkten und mit den ihnen zur Verfügung stehenden Instrumenten der Disziplinierung wie Visitationen und Synoden, Strafkapitel und Klosterhaft zu beseitigen versuchten.[19]

Diese vorwiegend sozial bzw. sozialpsychologisch motivierten, von Kritik und Vorwürfen begleiteten Spannungen, die man als Ausdruck eines innerkirchlichen Klassenantagonismus bezeichnen könnte, sind jedoch nicht gemeint, wenn von einem klerikalen Antiklerikalismus gesprochen wird. Es geht dabei vielmehr um die Reaktionen, die die im Frühchristentum einsetzende Ausbildung einer Hierarchie und die dadurch entstandene Dichotomie von Klerus und Laien hervorrief. Es waren — das wurde bereits gesagt — die Laien, die in erster Linie die negativen Folgen dieser innergemeindlichen Differenzierung zum Gegenstand der Kritik machten und immer wieder, vor allem im Spätmittelalter, in Bruderschaften und anderen semireligiösen Gemeinschaftsformen den urkirchlichen Zustand wiederherzustellen versuchten.[20] Es waren aber auch Angehörige des Klerus selbst, die den Prozeß der Verfestigung und Abgrenzung, der Monopolisierung und Distanzierung rückgängig zu machen bestrebt waren, im Rekurs auf die *ecclesia primitiva* und die *vita evangelica* die Befreiung von den Bindungen an die Welt forderten und in der Hinwendung zu Amt und Gemeinde dem Ideal des *pastor bonus* zu entsprechen versuchten.[21] Die "Selbstreinigungs-

---

"Les convers chez quelques moralistes des XIIe et XIIIe siécles", *Cîteaux* 20 (1969): 241-59. J. S. Donnelly, *The Decline of the Medieval Cistercian Laybrotherhood*, Fordham University Studies, History Series 3 (New York, 1949).

[19] Dazu vgl. u.a.: N. Coulet, *Les visites pastorales*, Typologie des sources du Moyen Age occidental A IV 1 (Turnhout, 1977) und J. Leinweber, "Provinzialsynode und Kirchenreform im Spätmittelalter", in R. Bäumer (Hrsg.), *Reformatio Ecclesiae. Festgabe für Erwin Iserloh* (Paderborn, 1980), 113-27.

[20] M. D. Chenu, "Moines, clercs, laïcs au carrefour de la vie évangélique (XIIe siècle)", *RHE* 49 (1954): 59-88. R. Zerfass, *Der Streit um die Laienpredigt. Eine pastoral-geschichtliche Untersuchung zum Verständnis des Predigtamtes und seiner Entwicklung im 12. und 13. Jahrhundert*, Untersuchungen für praktische Theologie 2 (Freiburg i.Br., 1974). K. Schreiner, "Laienbildung als Herausforderung für Kirche und Gesellschaft", *ZHF* 11 (1984): 257-354. *I laici nella "Societas Christiana" dei secoli XI e XII*, Miscellanea del Centro di Studi Medioevali V. Pubbl. dell'Univ. Catt. del S. Cuore, Contr. III, Varia 5 (Milano, 1968). A. Vauchez, *Les laics au Moyen Age. Pratiques et expériences religieuses* (Paris, 1987). G.G. Meersseman, *Ordo Fraternitatis. Confraternite e pietà dei laici nel medioevo*, 3 Bde., Italia Sacra 24-26 (Rom, 1977).

[21] Neben den grundlegenden Beiträgen in *La vita comune del clero nei secoli XI e XII*, Miscellanea del Centro di Studi Medioevali III. Pubbl. dell'Univ. Catt. del S. Cuore III, Sc. stor. 2-3 (Milano, 1962). K. Bosl, *Regularkanoniker (Augustinerchorherren) und Seelsorge in Kirche und Gesellschaft des europäischen 12. Jahrhunderts*, Bayer. Akad. der Wiss., Phil.-hist. Kl. Abh. NF 86 (München, 1979). H. Fuhrmann,

kräfte" und der "Besserungswille" des Klerus reichten freilich nicht aus, um die stetigen, sich in religiösen Bewegungen verdichtenden Reformbemühungen, den Kampf gegen Simonie und Konkubinat, die Durchsetzung der *vita communis* für Domkapitel und Stiftsklerus, die Gründung regulierter Chorherrenorden, reformierter Chorherrenkongregationen und Regularpriestervereinigungen zu erklären. Es war das im Laufe des 4. Jahrhunderts entstandene und sich alsbald auch im Westen ausbreitende Mönchtum, das, aus dem *status laicorum* hervorgegangen, zur Herausforderung für den Klerus und die sich in der neuen Ordnung des Imperiums etablierende Kirche wurde, das Leben der Apostel und der Urkirche in Erinnerung rief und den Willen zur *perfectio* auch im Klerus weckte.[22] Wie nachdrücklich und intensiv es die durch Entstehung, Geschichte und Selbstverständnis definierte Aufgabe, Unruheherd wie Reformkraft zu sein und die Utopie einer rein geistlichen Kirche wachzuhalten, erfüllte, kann und braucht hier nicht nachgewiesen zu werden.[23] Die Wirkungen der Reformzentren von Gorze und Cluny, die Reformorden des 12. Jahrhunderts, die Bettelorden des Hochmittelalters und die spätmittelalterlichen Observanzbestrebungen, die für die Mönchstheologen und Geschichtstheoretiker des Mittelalters Stadien der Heilsgeschichte und Garantien für das Wirken des Hlg. Geistes waren, markieren zugleich auch neue Stufen im Verständnis vom Wesen der Kirche und der Aufgabe des Klerus, die, wer wüßte das nicht, von heftigen Diskussionen, wütenden Auseinandersetzungen und gelegentlich rabiaten Streitigkeiten zwischen Klerikern und Ordensleuten, Mönchs- und Priestertum, gekennzeichnet waren und am Ende, auch das braucht nicht eigens betont zu werden, zu jenen Querelen ausarteten, die als sprichwörtliches

---

Papst Urban II. und der Stand der Regularkanoniker, Bayer. Akad. der Wiss., Phil.-hist. Kl. Siztungsberichte 1984, 2 (München, 1984). J. Laudage, *Priesterbild und Reformpapsttum im 11. Jahrhundert*, Beihefte zum *Archiv für Kulturgeschichte* 22 (Köln, 1984). M. Fois, "Il contesto ecclesiastico ed ecclesiale italiano alla nascità dei chierici regolari", *Archivum Historiae Pontificiae* 27 (1989): 401-18.

[22] G. B. Ladner, *The Idea of Reform. Its Impact on Christian Thought and Action in the Age of the Fathers* (Cambridge, Mass., 1959). Ph. Rousseau, *Ascetics, Authority, and the Church in the Age of Jerome and Cassian* (Oxford, 1978). A. Guillaumont, *Aux origines du monachisme chrétien. Pour une phénoménologie du monachisme*, Spiritualité orientale et vie monastique 30 (Abbaye de Bellefontaine, 1979). D. König, *Amt und Askese. Priesteramt und Mönchtum bei den lateinischen Kirchenvätern in vorbenediktinischer Zeit*, Regulae Benedicti Studia, Suppl. 12 (St. Ottilien, 1985).

[23] Knappe Überblicke: D. Knowles, *Christian Monasticism* (London, 1969). K. S. Frank, *Grundzüge der Geschichte des christlichen Mönchtums*, Grundzüge 25 (Darmstadt, 1975). C. H. Lawrence, *Medieval Monasticism. Forms of Religious Life in Western Europe in the Middle Ages*, 2. Aufl. (London, 1989).

Mönchsgezänk zum Ärgernis wurden und zu neuem Antiklerikalismus Anlaß gaben.[24]

IV

Es ist sicherlich nicht falsch, im Antiklerikalismus des Mittalters vorwiegend einen systemimmanenten Protest zu sehen, der seinen letzten Grund in der Sorge für die Kirche und der Angst um das Heil der Seelen hat, sich in Klage und Gebet äußert und Bekehrung und Reform herbeiführen will. Dennoch kennt auch das Mittelalter den fundamentalen Protest gegen die hierarchische Struktur der Kirche, den sakramentalen Charakter des Priestertums und den Anspruch des Klerus auf das Monopol der Heilsvermittlung, den man als das eigentliche Wesensmerkmal des modernen Antiklerikalismus anzusehen gewohnt ist.

Auch wenn es im frühen und hohen Mittelalter im Reich, abgesehen von einzelnen Persönlichkeiten, keine dauerhaften häretischen Strömungen gegeben hat und, wie man weiß, kirchenkritische Massenbewegungen erst im 14. Jahrhundert auftraten, konnte sich der deutsche Klerus, spätestens seit dem ausgehenden 11. und dem beginnenden 12. Jahrhundert, keineswegs vor Zweifel an der Gottgewolltheit seiner Ämter und dem sakramentalen Charakter seiner geistlichen Funktionen sicher fühlen. Die an das orthodoxe Kirchen- und Sakramenteverständnis rührende Predigt eines Tauchelm von Antwerpen, Heinrich von Lausanne und Petrus von Bruys blieb nicht ohne Echo im Westen des Reiches.[25] Und schon 1156 mußte der rheinische Prämonstratenser Eberwin von Steinfeld, der als einer der ersten die Ankunft der Katharer registriert hatte, Bernhard von Clairvaux um Unterstützung gegen die wortgewaltigen Ketzer bitten.[26] Waldensische Ideen und Gemeinden fanden im 13. Jahrhundert den Weg in die Diözese Passau, nach Mitteldeutschland und Böhmen und bereiteten hier, wie man annimmt, den Boden für die Unruhen und Aufstände des 15. Jahrhunderts, die die Kirche

---

[24] Vgl. z.B. die Kritik an den Franziskanern: C. Erickson, "The Fourteenth-Century Franciscans and Their Critics", *Franciscan Studies* 35 (1975): 107-35, 36 (1976): 108-47. P. R. Szittya, *The Antifraternal Tradition in Medieval Literature* (Princeton, 1986). Für Deutschland im Überblick: N. Hecker, *Bettelorden und Bürgertum. Konflikt und Kooperation in deutschen Städten des Mittelalters*, Europäische Hochschulschriften XXX, 146 (Frankfurt, 1985).

[25] H. Grundmann, *Religiöse Bewegungen im Mittelalter*, Eberings Historische Studien 267 (Berlin, 1935; ND 1961). J. B. Russell, *Dissent and Reform in the Early Middle Ages* (Berkeley, 1965).

[26] A. Borst, *Die Katharer*, Schriften der MGH 12 (Stuttgart, 1953). G. Despey, "Hérétiques ou anticléricaux? Les 'Cathares' dans nos régions avant 1300", in J. Marx (Hrsg.), *Aspects de l'anticléricalisme* (Vgl. Anm. 4), 23-33.

und Gesellschaft Deutschlands stärker als je zuvor und nachhaltiger als anderswo im Mitleidenschaft zogen.[27]

V

Die im 19. Jahrhundert in Deutschland im Anschluß an Reformation und Aufklärung zustandegekommene Vorstellung von Charakter und historischer Bedeutung des Antiklerikalismus als Gegenreaktion gegen eine unberechtigte Beeinflussung, wenn nicht gar Bevormundung von Staat und Gesellschaft, ist, auch wenn sie längst noch nicht als irrelevant bezeichnet werden kann, keineswegs mehr vorherrschend. Gegenwärtig ist es nicht mehr möglich, mit der gleichen Entschiedenheit wie im 19. Jahrhundert die Fiskalisierung, Juridifizierung und Bürokratisierung der Kurie, den Nepotismus von Päpsten und Kardinälen, die Auseinandersetzungen zwischen Mönchen und Klerikern, das zweifelhafte wirtschaftliche Gebaren, die Unbildung und Unsittlichkeit des Klerus als moralische Abirrungen von Individuen zu verdammen oder als Verfallssymptome von Institutionen abzutun.[28] Stärker als zuvor neigt man dazu, sie in den Kontext ihrer eigenen Zeit zu setzen und angesichts der damals herrschenden politischen, sozialen und ökonomischen Bedingungen als verständliche, wenn nicht gar unvermeidliche Erscheinungen einzuschätzen.[29] Die von Hegel vorgenommene, von

---

[27] M. Schneider, *Europäisches Waldensertum im 13. und 14. Jahrhundert. Gemeinschaftsform, Frömmigkeit, sozialer Hintergrund*, Arbeiten zur Kirchengeschichte 51 (Berlin, 1981). D. Kurze (Hrsg.), *Quellen zur Ketzergeschichte Brandenburgs und Pommerns*, Veröffentlichungen der historischen Kommission zu Berlin 45 (Berlin, 1975). A. Patschovsky (Hrsg.), *Quellen zur Geschichte der böhmischen Inquisition im 14. Jahrhundert*, MGH.QG 11 (Weimar, 1979). P. Segl, *Ketzer in Österreich. Untersuchungen über Häresie und Inquisition im Herzogtum Österreich im 13. und beginnenden 14. Jahrhundert*, Quellen und Forschungen aus dem Gebiet der Geschichte NF 5 (Paderborn, 1984).

[28] Das ganze Ausmaß des Antiklerikalismus des 19. Jhs. lassen Schriften wie E. Leistner, *Wie das Volk über die Pfaffen spricht. Neuer Kloster- und Pfaffen-Spiegel enthaltend Sprüchworter, geschichtliche Aussprüche und Volksredensarten über Klöster und geistliche Orden, Rom und die Klerisei* (Lahr, 1877), vor allem aber der seit 1868 mit dem Untertitel "Historische Denkmale des Fanatismus in der römisch-katholischen Kirche" erscheinende "Pfaffenspiegel" von O. von Corvin, der in zahlreichen Ausgaben in weit über einer Million Exemplaren verbreitet wurde, erkennen.

[29] J. Löhr, *Methodisch-kritische Beiträge zur Geschichte des Klerus besonders der Erzdiözese Köln am Ausgang des Mittelalters*, RGST 17 (Münster, 1910). J. Lortz, "Zur Problematik der kirchlichen Mißstände im Spätmittelalter", *Trierer theologische Zeitschrift* 58 (1949): 1-26, 212-27, 257-79, 347-57. K. Elm, "Verfall und Erneuerung des Ordenswesens im Spätmittelalter", in *Untersuchungen zu Kloster und Stift*, Veröffentlichungen des Max-Planck-Instituts für Geschichte 68, Studien zur Germania Sacra 14 (Göttingen, 1980), 188-238.

Treitschke und anderen preußisch-kleindeutschen Historikern zugespitzte Gegenüberstellung von katholisch-mittelalterlicher Rückständigkeit und protestantisch-neuzeitlichem Fortschrittswillen, die dem Antiklerikalismus des Mittelalters in einer Art Umwertung der Werte den Rang eines entscheidenden Movens auf dem Wege des Fortschritts und der Aufklärung verlieh und ihm eine Konsistenz und Homogenität unterstellte, die er nie besessen hat, kann angesichts der Ernüchterung durch die politisch-sozialen Entwicklungen der letzten Jahrzehnte längst nicht mehr mit der Zustimmung rechnen, der sie sich noch zu Beginn dieses Jahrhunderts erfreute.[30] Gleiches gilt für das der Politik, dem Nationalbewußtsein und der Geschichtswissenschaft des 19. Jahrhunderts zugrundeliegende Axiom, daß nämlich nach der Erringung der religiösen Freiheit durch die Reformation und der geistigen Freiheit durch die Aufklärung mit der Gründung des deutschen Nationalstaates die staatliche Freiheit und die endgültige Emanzipation der Gesellschaft und Kultur aus den Bindungen einer überlebten Religion erreicht sei.[31] Die Deutung des Antagonismus zwischen Kaiser und Reich, des "uralten Machtstreites zwischen König- und Priestertum", wie ihn 1876 R. Virchow während des Kulturkampfes in einer Rede vor dem Preußischen Landtag bezeichnet hat, als eines Emanzipationsprozesses von kirchlicher und klerikaler Beeinflussung, der in der Bildung des säkularen Nationalstaats seinen Abschluß fand, vermag immer weniger zu überzeugen.[32] Wie die Auseinandersetzung zwischen Bischof Ambrosius und Kaiser Honorius erscheinen vielen Beobachtern der Investiturstreit, der im 13. und 14. Jahrhundert geführte Kampf zwischen Kaiser und Papst und die Konflikte des 19. Jahrhunderts nicht mehr als Stadien der Emanzipation des Staates und der säkularen Kultur, sondern als die immer wieder notwendig werdenden Reaktionen der Kirche auf das Übergewicht der Laien, gegen absolutistische und totalitäre Übergriffe, als der Kampf um die *libertas ecclesiae*, der zugleich auch als Kampf für die Freiheit des Geistes

---

[30] E. Gans, K. Hegel (Hrsgg.), "Vorlesungen über die Philosophie der Geschichte", in H. Glockner (Hrsg.), *Georg Wilhelm Friedrich Hegel, Sämtliche Werke* 11 (Stuttgart, 1949), 519ff. H. v. Treitschke, "Luther und die deutsche Nation", in K. M. Schiller (Hrsg.), *Heinrich von Treitschke. Aufsätze, Reden und Briefe* (Meersburg, 1929), 1: 233-49.

[31] E. W. Zeeden, "Die katholische Kirche in der Sicht des deutschen Protestantismus im 19. Jahrhundert", *HJ* 72 (1953): 433-56. F. W. Kantzenbach, "Protestantische Geisteskultur und Konfessionalismus im 19. Jahrhundert", in A. Rauscher (Hrsg.), *Probleme des Konfessionalismus in Deutschland seit 1800*, Beiträge zur Katholizismusforschung, Reihe B: Abhandlungen (Paderborn, 1984), 9-28.

[32] Stenographischer Bericht über die Verhandlungen des Preußischen Landtags, 28. Sitzung am 17. Januar 1873, 1: 629-35. Vgl. dazu G. Franz, *Kulturkampf. Staat und katholische Kirche in Mitteleuropa von der Säkularisation bis zum Abschluß des Preußischen Kulturkampfes*, (München, 1954), 9.

verstanden wird.[33] Auch wenn man nicht eine Vereinfachung durch eine andere ersetzen will, ist ein Resultat dieser Diskussion als unumstritten festzuhalten: die Tatsache nämlich, daß es die neuere kirchen- und verfassungsgeschichtliche Forschung ablehnt, weiterhin die politischen und kirchlichen Organisationsformen des hohen und späten Mittelalters und die ihnen zugrundeliegenden Ordnungsvorstellungen mit denen des Bismarckreiches auf der einen und des Ultramontanismus auf der anderen Seite gleichzustellen.[34]

Damit nicht genug: Gegenüber der Auffassung, der mittelalterliche Antiklerikalismus trage primär emanzipatorischen Charakter und habe sowohl den geistigen als auch den sozialen und ökonomischen Fortschritt zur Folge gehabt, wird in zunehmendem Maße die konservativ reformerische Tendenz des deutschen Spätmittelalters betont. "Es gab Kritik an der Kirche und an den Klerikern, ja es gab Haß gegen den Klerus, aber nicht, weil man der Kirche kalt gegenüberstand, sondern weil man die Kirche liebte. ... Die Kirche war den Deutschen nicht kirchlich genug", wie H. Heimpel die von ihm und anderen eingenommene Position beschreibt,[35] deren Berechtigung H. Grundmann für das hohe und frühe Mittelalter bestätigt, wenn er feststellt, daß die Deutschen den Protest, der sich in Frankreich und Italien gegen die Kirche und ihre Institutionen richtete, verinnerlichten und im Geiste arm wurden, um gegen die reiche Kirche zu protestieren.[36] Wie immer man diese von der Annahme einer besonderen Eigenart der Deutschen ausgehenden Einschätzungen auch beurteilen mag, ja selbst dann, wenn man so weit geht, nicht nur den Deutschen, sondern dem ganzen Mittelalter die Fähigkeit und den Willen zu einer Kritik im modernen Sinne abzusprechen,[37] bleibt festzuhalten, daß solche Erwägungen eine weitaus

---

[33] W. Kasper, "Zur Lage des deutschen Katholizismus heute. Stellungnahme eines Theologen", in U. v. Hehl, K. Repgen (Hrsgg.), *Der deutsche Katholizismus in der zeitgeschichtlichen Forschung* (Mainz, 1988), 84.

[34] G. Tellenbach, *Libertas, Kirche und Weltordnung im Zeitalter des Investiturstreites*, Forschungen zur Kirchen- und Geistesgeschichte 7 (Stuttgart, 1936). Ders., "'Gregorianische Reform'. Kritische Besinnungen", in K. Schmid (Hrsg.), *Reich und Kirche vor dem Investiturstreit. Vorträge beim wissenschaftlichen Kolloquium aus Anlaß des achtzigsten Geburtstags von Gerd Tellenbach* (Sigmaringen, 1985), 99-113.

[35] H. Heimpel, "Das deutsche fünfzehnte Jahrhundert in Krise und Beharrung", in *Die Welt zur Zeit des Konstanzer Konzils, Reichenau-Vorträge im Herbst 1964*, Vorträge und Forschungen 9 (Konstanz, 1965), 15.

[36] H. Grundmann, "Die geschichtlichen Grundlagen der deutschen Mystik", *Deutsche Vierteljahrschrift für Literaturwissenschaft und Geistesgeschichte* 12 (1934): 400-28. Jetzt: Ders., *Ausgewählte Aufsätze*, Schriften der MGH 25,1 (Stuttgart, 1976), 243-68, 258.

[37] R. Koselleck, *Kritik und Krise. Eine Pathogenese der bürgerlichen Welt* (Freiburg, 1959). Vgl. dazu jedoch K. Schreiner, "'Correctio Principis'. Gedankliche Begründung und geschichtliche Praxis spätmittelalterlicher Herrscherkritik", in F.

differenziertere Sehweise erkennen lassen, als sie noch vor wenigen Jahren bei der Beurteilung des Spätmittelalters zu beobachten war. Was traditionellerweise als Antiklerikalismus gedeutet wurde, gilt heute als Hinweis auf die selbstverständlichen Spannungen innerhalb eines komplizierten, aber dennoch locker strukturierten Systems, das sich der Beurteilung nach modernen oder auch nur posttridentinischen Kategorien entzieht. Vieles von dem, was bisher als Dekomposition und Deviation verurteilt wurde, wird heute als Ausdruck von Lebenskraft und Erneuerungswillen positiv eingeschätzt. Die Kirchen- und Ordensreform, die devoten und mystischen Strömungen und die Forderung nach der Laienpredigt, die man als innerkirchlichen Antiklerikalismus bezeichnete, als man sich noch von der Kirche des Mittelalters ein Bild machte, das dem Integralismus des 19. Jahrhunderts entsprach, gelten im Lichte eines neuen Kirchenverständnisses als Ausdrucksformen, ja als substantielle Elemente einer in allen Bereichen der Wirklichkeit präsenten Kirche.[38]

VI

Historiker, die anthropologische und ethnologische Methoden mit historischen verbinden, verweisen auf die bis in die Anfänge der menschlichen Kultur zurückgehende Verwurzelung der Vorstellung von einer Zweiteilung der Gesellschaft in Priester und Gläubige und gehen davon aus, daß deren gegenseitiges Verhältnis stets von einem Nebeneinander von Verehrung und Ablehnung, Unterwerfung und Widerspruch bestimmt gewesen sei. Die Mentalitätsforschung ist davon überzeugt, daß dieser Dualismus weniger eine Wirklichkeit als vielmehr eine "réalité d'ordre psychologique" war und die Spannung zwischen Klerikern und Laien "n'existe jamais que par l'idee qu'on s'en fait",[39] wobei zu berücksichtigen ist, daß sich nicht nur die Laien ihr Bild von den Klerikern, sondern auch die Kleriker ein solches von den Laien machen, neben dem Antiklerikalismus also auch ein klerikaler "Antilaizismus" vorausgesetzt werden kann, wofür sich als Kronzeuge Bonifaz VIII. mit seiner berühmten Bulle *Clericis laicos* anführen läßt.[40] Es gibt Theologen, die im Sinne des Pauluswortes *Oportet et haereses esse* im Antiklerikalismus keineswegs nur einen Schaden für die Kirche, sondern

---

Graus (Hrsg.), *Mentalitäten im Mittelalter. Methodische und inhaltliche Probleme*, Vorträge und Forschungen 35 (Sigmaringen, 1987).

[38] K. Rahner, *Strukturwandel der Kirche als Aufgabe und Chance* (Freiburg, 1972). F. X. Kaufmann, J. B. Metz, *Zukunftsfähigkeit. Suchbewegungen im Christentum* (Freiburg, 1987).

[39] M. Bloch, *Liberté et servitude personelles au Moyen Age, particulièrement en France: Contribution à une étude des classes* (Paris, 1933). Jetzt in ders., *Mélanges historiques* 1 (Paris, 1983), 286-355, 355.

[40] C. Mirbt, K. Aland (Hrsgg.), *Quellen zur Geschichte des Papsttums und des römischen Katholizismus* 1 (Tübingen, 1967), 457.

ein notwendiges Pendant zu ihrer Verkündigung sehen: "Die Existenz eines
Standes der Gottgeweihten fordert heraus, weil sie die Geschlossenheit des
Weltlichen durchbricht und dessen souveräne Selbstgenügsamkeit ständig in
Frage stellt. Der Priester ist ihm eine Absurdität, weil sein Amt nicht durch
die Kategorien des Profanen gerechtfertigt werden kann und sich auf einen
Grund außerhalb der Welt beruft; in der Welt ausgeübt, ist es doch kein
Weltgeschäft."[41]

Man kann von solchen Beobachtungen halten, was man will, man kann
sie ernst nehmen oder als wenig hilfreich für die Erkenntnis historischer
Vorgänge abtun. Dennoch sollte man sie nicht unberücksichtigt lassen. Der
Antiklerikalismus ist kein Problem, das allein die Mediävisten beschäftigt,
er ist zu wichtig, als daß man ihn ausschließlich denjenigen überlassen
sollte, die sich am häufigsten mit ihm beschäftigen, nämlich den Kirchen-
und Reformationshistorikern. Wie bei anderen historischen Phänomenen, die
bis heute Erregung auslösen können und zu Ablehnung oder Parteinahme
provozieren, sollten auch in seinem Falle alle Stimmen gehört und alle
Argumente gewürdigt werden, die Distanz schaffen und zu einer ab-
gewogenen Beurteilung des Antiklerikalismus im späten Mittelalter und der
Reformationszeit, die hier im Mittelpunkt des Interesses stehen, verhelfen
können.

---

[41] G. Montesi, "Über den innerkirchlichen Antiklerikalismus", *Wort und Wahrheit*
8 (1953): 645.

LATE MEDIEVAL ANTICLERICALISM:
THE CASE OF THE NEW DEVOUT

JOHN VAN ENGEN

University of Notre Dame

Anticlericalism is a nineteenth-century phenomenon, a political program to dis-establish and secularize the church's power and privileges. But anticlerical attitudes date from the establishment of Christianity in the west, and grew apace with the institutionalization of Christendom. The more fully the church reached into the lives of the European peoples, the more forcefully anticlerical attitudes came to expression. By the high middle ages Europeans took for granted smouldering resentments directed against monks, friars, bishops, priests, and clerics who claimed this-worldly privileges by way of an other-worldly office. For its part this clerical caste frequently displayed attitudes we might call "anti-laicism", religious contempt for lay people said to think mostly about their bellies and their genitals and their honor with no receptivity to a higher eternal good. While in countless individual cases relations between clergymen and lay people must have been good, even charitable, and mutual respect high, some mistrust, some natural rivalry, was built into the very structure of things. So long as Europe was conceived as Christendom, a society of the baptized, there were necessarily those who christened and those who received christening, those ordained to represent the Lord Christ in their acts and words and those expected to accept such representatives as sent by the Lord Christ. The Reformation movement toppled many structures specific to the medieval clerical estate, but it could not alter this underlying dynamic, and it did not remove all forms of anticlericalism.

For the medieval historian, resentment and critique of the clergy indicate relatively little in themselves. Of interest are the forms of expression that critique may take. Were clergymen merely lampooned, which is to say, mocked and parodied in verse and song and story,[1] or were they socially and legally restricted in some way, even physically attacked? And who led those attacks, peasants, burghers, knights, or rival clerics? Whenever a religious movement attained an institutional status surpassing and threatening the privileges of others, critique was sure to follow. Satire commonly sprang up within the first generation; legal or physical threats, if ever, came subse-

---

[1] The best orientation here remains Paul Lehmann, *Die Parodie im Mittelalter* (Munich, 1922; 2nd rev. ed., Stuttgart, 1963); and John A. Yunck, *The Lineage of Lady Meed*, Publications in Medieval Studies 17 (Notre Dame, 1963).

quently. So it was with Cluny, the first medieval monastic house to acquire an organization comparable to that of a modern religious congregation; then with the Roman curia as it centralized law and administration in the twelfth century; then with the Cistercians as their economic power, built up in the name of poverty, dominated ever larger patches of the countryside; then with village curates as their parish obligations, tithes, and stole fees intruded into the lives of every Christian; then with the mendicant friars as their spiritual mission (and their begging for money) infiltrated all the towns of Europe; then with the Avignon papacy as its administration in exile laid claim to every benefice in Christendom — and so on through a long list.

It is not difficult to identify actions and attitudes sprung from critique of the clergy; it is far more difficult to know how best to interpret them. Was this medieval anticlericalism generated by a resentful and destructive impulse or by an ameliorating and reforming impetus? Or indeed by some mixture of the two with all the range of ambiguity in between? Is it even right to label such outbursts, whether verbal or physical, "anticlericalism"? The word is nineteenth-century, after all, with no real medieval equivalent. Authorities understood full well that clergymen might be bullied or physically attacked, and they legislated severely against it — thereby provoking more resentment and strife over "benefit of clergy". But were such incidents sparked by true anticlericalism? More sharply put, was true anticlericalism even *thinkable* in the middle ages? If most people could not imagine a world without God, could they imagine a world without God's mediators or representatives? They could resent and criticize monks and priests; could they imagine simply doing without them or even doing away with them?

Medieval Christendom's religious inheritance proved ambivalent on the status of a divinely sanctioned clerical caste. The Hebrew Scriptures opened a great gulf between the unnameable Almighty beyond creation and the world of creation with all its named creatures including priests and the Chosen People. God gave the law through Moses and in Aaron established a priesthood. Yet when the Almighty put words into the mouth of a hapless prophet, like Isaiah or Jeremiah, he could cut down all pretention with a divine sword, even that of the priests and the keepers of the law. This prophetic impulse, this scathing critique even — or especially — of those who claimed to speak and act in God's name, reemerged repeatedly in medieval Christendom. But it was always counterbalanced by the incarnational impulse, the New Testament vision of the Word taking flesh, of the untouchably holy present and represented in human persons and acts. In the Epistle to the Hebrews Christ was even represented as incarnating a new priesthood with himself as chief priest and chief sacrifice. In medieval Christendom, this incarnational impulse nearly always prevailed, embodied in a church that reached down into every aspect of human and social life — even when the fleshly representatives of the holy were themselves less than holy and their position in society resented.

For the historian, then, the question is not whether "anticlerical" attitudes were in evidence during the middle ages, but how they should be interpreted and under what conditions frictions endemic to historic Christendom might generate a spark capable of igniting an explosion. Medieval historians have done remarkably little systematic work on this subject, which is to say, on either side of it: How medieval people thought, or were expected to think, about their clergy as God's divinely-appointed mediators,[2] or alternatively, how deeply critical and resentful they could become, to the point of attacking or legally restricting them.[3] On this subject the later middle ages offer intriguing possibilities for study, rich not only in sources but also in ironies. Lay people, whether kings, princes, city magistrates, or local lords, defended their own interests ever more vigorously and publicly, restricting the growth of religious foundations and resisting clerical privileges, even as religious institutions (and the clerical guidance that came with them) abounded, catching up ever more people in their nets and encompassing every facet of human life. Most later medieval Europeans held in tension, it seems, two fundamental convictions: That the church, her teachings, and her ministrations offered the necessary and exclusive way to everlasting beatitude, and that the organs of the church, including much of her clerical establishment, had become a burden at the very least, when not deeply corrupt and corrupting.

But what were people to do about it? To throw themselves cynically into the chase as ambitious clerics, or mutter about the church as embittered lay people? Some — like Will in *Piers Plowman* — attempted to find ways of standing over against this clerical caste, of getting some angle of vision, some purchase, on this dilemma. He was a literary visionary.[4] Catherine of Siena was a female ascetic visionary and epistolary preacher. Carthusians, the most austere of the religious, expanded as never before on the edges of cities and wrote as never before for an expanding circle of serious readers. Historians, including Reformation historians, have yet to exploit all the materials generated in the later middle ages by groups determined both to improve and to stand over against the established clerical estate. The

---

[2] See, for instance, Johannes Laudage, *Priesterbild und Reformpapsttum im 11. Jahrhundert* (Cologne, 1984), and D. Catherine Brown, *Pastor and Laity in the Theology of Jean Gerson* (Cambridge, 1987).

[3] Perhaps the most systematic work, still useful for all its material, though skewed by an attitude that reflected nineteenth-century anticlericalism, was that by Georges Lagarde, *La naissance de l'ésprit laïque au déclin du moyen age* (Paris, 1934-46), 6 vols. See also Joseph Strayer, "The Laicization of French and English Society in the Thirteenth Century", in his *Medieval Statecraft and the Perspectives of History* (Princeton, 1971), 251-65.

[4] See now Wendy Scase, *Piers Plowman and the New Anticlericalism* (Cambridge, 1989), one of the few recent contributions to this topic. Her argument for a "new" anticlericalism in this period requires closer examination.

purpose of this study is to focus upon one such group, the Modern Devout in the Netherlands (with a shorter complementary piece to follow on the Lollards in England), thereby indicating the range of possibility within the medieval church as well as the ambiguity of interpreting medieval forms of anticlericalism.

Adherents of the *Devotio Moderna* venerated Master Geert Grote (1340-84) as their founder. Within a generation the movement comprised four distinguishable branches, the Augustinian canons and canonesses of the Windesheim Chapter together with the unprofessed Brothers and Sisters of the Common Life.[5] The Augustinians, though closely related in spirit and in personnel to the Brothers and Sisters, took vows and had many of their males ordained. Even among them, however, a critical distrust of established and non-"observant" houses persisted, as Johan Busch recounted at length in his *Liber de reformatione monasteriorum*.[6] But for the purposes of studying anticlerical attitudes these canons and canonesses will be left to one side, as will in large measure the Sisters of the Common Life. Their status — inside, outside, or over against the "clerical" establishment —, though contested and intriguing, never became problematic in quite the same way as the Brothers' nor did it require choices about sacerdotal status.[7]

About the year 1374 Geert Grote, patrician's son from Deventer, perpetual student (sixteen years off and on at university), and ambitious cleric (applied for five benefices and secured two) experienced a great turnaround at age thirty-four. He repudiated his extended and undisciplined youth, adopted a penitential way of life (to the scorn of his fellow townspeople in Deventer), spent time in retreat among Carthusian hermits, turned his father's mansion into a hospice for poor women, and eventually secured a license to preach. He resisted ordination to the priesthood (though he was made a deacon in order to preach), severely criticized the secular clergy of Utrecht for their immorality, and in time had his license suspended by the clerics he had

---

[5] The best general orientation to the entire movement remains R. R. Post, *The Modern Devotion*, SMRT 3 (Leiden, 1968), though the questions raised by Albert Hyma, *The Christian Renaissance*, 2nd ed. (Hamden, Conn., 1965) still deserve serious consideration. For more recent essay-length introductions (with more complete bibliographies) see Willem Lourdaux, "De Broeders van het Gemene Leven", *Bijdr.* 33 (1972): 372-416; Kaspar Elm, "Die Brüderschaft vom gemeinsamen Leben. Eine geistliche Lebensform zwischen Kloster und Welt, Mittelalter und Neuzeit", *OGE* 59 (1985): 470-96; A. G. Weiler, "Recent Historiography on the Modern Devotion: Some Debated Questions", *AGKKN* 27 (1985): 161-75; and my introduction to *Devotio Moderna: Basic Writings* (New York, 1988).

[6] *Des Augustinerpropstes Iohannes Busch Chronicon Windeshemense und Liber de reformatione monasteriorum*, ed. Karl Grube (Halle, 1886; repr., 1968), 379-799.

[7] By far the best orientation to the Sisters now in Gerhard Rehm, *Die Schwestern vom gemeinsamen Leben im nordwestlichen Deutschland*, Berliner Historische Studien 11 (Berlin, 1985).

enraged. He died a deacon, appealing to the pope for support against the clerics of Utrecht.[8]

Just as he had resisted ordination to the priesthood, though not to the diaconate or the status of preacher, so he remained secular ("in the world") and declined to take vows — the natural course of action in the middle ages for most people who had experienced such a conversion. The reasons for his resistance are plain: Common wisdom held that most of those who took vows were hypocrites, and Grote was determined not to join their number. In an early letter he counseled a good friend who had apparently promised to join the Franciscans. The friend grew worried because in the Low Countries the Friars Minor were not yet reformed (that is, Observant), and began to wonder whether his inclination might not have arisen from the "whispering of the Devil" (*susurrium diaboli*). Master Geert agreed that it probably had, offering to prove the Devil's power to do so — that is, to move the will falsely toward a would-be religious house — with "many authorities". William of Salvarvilla, as it turned out, never joined the Franciscans.[9] So too Johan Busch claimed in his epilogue that in the entire province (meaning, all the dioceses subject to Cologne) hardly a house existed in those days where the narrow way was walked rather than the broad, the three vows genuinely kept, or the spiritual life nurtured, with the exception of the Carthusians and an occasional Cistercian house.[10] Entering a monastery or priory was therefore not the way to perfection.

But what else could Grote do? About his own turnaround or conversion, as others came to call it, he said little directly. But in his "Resolutions and Intentions but not Vows" (preserved for us by Thomas of Kempen), Master Geert betrayed much indirectly about his state of mind during the turmoil of his spiritual reorientation.[11] These notes to himself catch the man

---

[8] The 500th anniversary of Grote's death in 1984 produced a number of commemorative volumes and essays, of which the best was the exposition catalogue, *Moderne Devotie: Figuren en Facetten* (Utrecht-Deventer, 1984). For Grote himself, the starting points must be Post (n. 5 above), 51-196; Theodore van Zijl, *Gerard Groote, Ascetic and Reformer (1340-84)* (Washington, D.C., 1963); and Georgette Epiney-Burgard, *Gérard Grote (1340-84) et les débuts de la dévotion moderne* (Wiesbaden, 1970).

[9] *Gerardi Magni Epistolae* 10, ed. W. Mulder (Antwerp, 1933), 37. Henceforth *Epistola*, followed by the letter number and page reference.

[10] Busch, *Liber de origine moderne devocionis* 47, ed. Grube (n. 6 above), 372-73.

[11] This recognized by Epiney-Burgard (n. 8 above), 37-50; van Zijl (n. 8 above); and also by R. W. Southern, *Western Society and the Church in the Middle Ages* (Harmondsworth, 1970), 334-36. The text was included by Thomas in his *Dialogus noviciorum* 2.18, *Opera Omnia*, ed. M. J. Pohl (Freiburg, 1922), 7: 87-107. Since this is the only copy to have come down to us, and Thomas is known to have edited materials he transmitted, we cannot be sure of the exact text of Grote's own "resolutions". I provided an English translation in my *Basic Writings* (n. 5 above), 65-75.

"thinking out loud" (or on paper) about how to proceed. Read positively, his resolutions disclose someone groping toward a plan of spiritual action; read negatively, they indict the clerical estate he had known and pursued the past sixteen years. His first resolution, or very first note to himself, was "to desire no more benefices" — he soon gave up both — and "to serve no cardinal or churchman with a view to gaining benefices", which he equated, quite simply, with "temporal gain", not spiritual office. After renouncing benefices, he moved on to renounce astrology, another pursuit that commonly brought advancement and income to fourteenth-century clerics[12] — and to which Master Geert may have been extraordinarily attached as a part of his desperate spiritual quest. One legend held that he later burnt his astrological books in the city's public square.

Next he resolved to turn his face against the pursuit of learning, the mark *par excellence* of the cleric; its pursuit, Grote noted to himself — or we might say, of himself —, wholly corrupted natural goodness with enflamed desires for gain or fame. It is, he observes, "the rarest thing for someone given to medicine, canon law, or civil law (the lucrative arts) to be found upright, or balanced in reason, or just, or tranquil, or of genuine insight." As for the liberal arts, and the public disputations that go with them in Paris, these too, Master Geert judges in retrospect, aim only at fame or renown. The time spent pursuing them "could better be spent in prayer or reading a devotional author." All these things, the liberal arts, medicine, and canon law, he had done and now resolved to curtail or to pursue no further. But his indictment went further: In this new penitential state he also resolved never to seek a degree in theology, for, he noted down, it is of use only to those "who want gain or benefices or fame." And he added to himself: It's a "carnal subject" which, if pursued, would tend to "draw you away from the salvation of your neighbor" and also "from prayer, purity of mind, and contemplation."

Evident in all this is the white-hot fervor of the convert, of a man who had just spent sixteen formative years as a cleric pursuing benefices, learning, and the lucrative arts. The charges he made against the late medieval clerical establishment were commonplace, but they were now turned sharply against himself and his sixteen mis-spent years, time he once described, borrowing prophetic language, as given over to fornicating on every hilltop and under every spreading tree. Pursuit of the clerical life and its attendant privileges had become a sore point with him, a source of distress, and it remained so during his ten last years. Two letters in particular (roughly seventy-five have been preserved) focus attitudes found scattered all through his writings.

---

[12] See Lynn White, Jr., "Medical Astrologers and Late Medieval Technology", in his *Medieval Religion and Technology* (Berkeley, 1978), 297-316.

The first is to the same man who had considered joining the Franciscans. An old school friend from days together in Paris, now the archdeacon of Brabant for the diocese of Liège, William of Salvarvilla was apparently just as determined as Geert Grote to lead a more fruitful life, and he now proposed to go east on a preaching tour as a kind of missionary to the schismatic Greeks.[13] Master Geert strongly demurred. If he truly possessed the gifts of a preacher, Grote urged, he should expend this rare talent "among the lost sheep of Israel, that is, the French, Italians, and Germans." Today, he explained, there are few or none who preach from the fervor of the spirit (*feruorem spiritus*), who know the righteousness of God by which God speaks to the heart or the Holy Spirit anoints and kindles it to rise upward. They all preach useless sermons, full of introductions and divisions and recapitulations. "This is not a learning or preaching that comes down from the father of lights but something earthly, bestial, diabolic (*terrena, animalis, dyabolica*)." Grote continued in this fashion for a page or two. Then he declared: "The battle is here" (*hic ... locus est belli*). With nearly all Europe infected from this kind of sermon-making, medicine must be applied to the head from which it derives (Paris) and the supporting neck (the Roman curia). The chief Pharisees, those who most distort Scripture and the simple faithful, are the professed religious and the professional jurists who know nothing of simple piety or justice. They have taken nearly all Europe captive with philosophy, and it has become the source of all heresies.[14]

Master Geert proposed an alternative vision, a new spiritual challenge for his friend: The simple and ignorant poor, shunned by the mighty and the learned, should be embraced, for the farther they are from these "heights", the more stripped of this false learning, the more receptive they are to the real word of God.[15] Like Christ retiring to the Mount of Olives, he should seek out silence at night, should work and live mostly in rural villages, but on feastdays and special occasions return to the royal city to take on the pharisees, scribes, pontiffs, and princes.[16] Master Geert cited yet more

---

[13] *Epistola* 9, ed. Mulder, 23-36. On Salvarvilla, see W. Mulder's recapitulation of the evidence in *OGE* 5 (1931): 186-211.

[14] *Epistola* 9, ed. Mulder, 25-30.

[15] "Scitis namque quod agrestibus innocentibus et simplicibus modicum est subsidium a doctis nostris theologis, et minus in locis capitalibus ut prope curiam et Avenionem et Parisius, non permittente ad alciora uocacionem quam in locis simplicibus uel elongatis. Unde michi uisum est simplices pauperes et abiectos et ignaros magno feruore et labore amplecti debere, qui et quanto nudiores ab altis fastigiis tanto uerbi Dei receptibiliores sunt. Et sic uidetur michi quod incipiendum esset Parisius et tuba canendum et bellum uirilitatis omnibus Dei inimicis indicendum qui Dei ueritatem in iniusticia detinent." *Epistola* 9, ed. Mulder, 30-31.

[16] "Demum puto semper ad montem Oliveti nocte per silencium uos retrahendum; item ad uillas campestres interpolatis diebus et pro maiori parte exemplo Christi

reasons for staying in Europe, above all, the difficulty of converting these easterners whose language and customs William does not know. Think how difficult it is in your own land to call back to "mystical theology" (*misticam theologiam*) or to apostolic innocence or to the bounds of justice the "vain and curious philosopher", the "pompous jurist", the "seeming theologian".[17] And there were practical considerations too: Can you even be released by your ordinary (the bishop of Liège), Master Geert asks at the end — indicating that for all his critique he wholly presupposed the legal hierarchy. If I were consultant to that bishop, he writes (as he plainly was at times to other local prelates), I would advise him to insist on your help with his own people who are many and broken and needy.[18] Master William did not go east, just as he had not joined the Franciscans.

Yet another of Grote's letters, preserved and widely read, touched upon the relationship of priestly to devotional life. It was addressed to a young cleric from Zwolle named Johan ten Water. This man had come to associate with the "devout", the men and women moved by Grote's preaching to gather in informal circles. But then he took it into his head, at the encouragement of city authorities, to leave their group, pursue higher learning, and advance to the priesthood. The urban magistrate (the richer and mightier men of Zwolle: *prioribus dicioribusque oppidi*) probably saw in him a young man full of zeal, capable of becoming an honest curate; Grote saw apostasy. It was the Devil, he wrote to him in a fiery letter, who turned you away from your good intentions under the guise of study, away from the Lord and good resolutions in order to descend into all manner of carnal, worldly, and vain desires.[19] Grote confronted him squarely with death and the last judgement, and in his final arguments became insultingly personal. It's the Devil who has spurred you on to worldly learning, the Devil who says a priest must know and learn many things.[20] You will know much if you perceive that you are not up to it and will never be up to it; the thing for you is godly charity, not worldly learning. The learned man with an evil will is the worst of men, worse still than the drunk or the unfaithful. Grote's

---

eundum et immorandum, et in festis et in certis causis ad urbem regiam contra pharizeos, scribas, pontifices et principes reuertendum." *Epistola* 9, ed. Mulder, 31.

[17] "Quamque sit difficile, curiosum et uanum et leuem dictum philosophum retrahere, quantumque arduum sit pomposum iuristam ad iusticie metas, uel apparentem theologum seu prophanum ad apostolicam innocenciam, ad misticam theologiam ... ." *Epistola* 9, ed. Mulder, 33.

[18] *Epistola* 9, ed. Mulder, 35.

[19] *Epistola* 29, ed. Mulder, 124-31. The letter was preserved and the case discussed by Johan Busch as well, *Liber de viris illustribus* 52-53, ed Grube (n. 6 above), 149-56.

[20] "Dicit enim inimicus: oportet multa scire presbiterum et discere. Multa scis si te cognoscis, quia non potes." *Epistola* 29, ed. Mulder, 130.

letter ended with an emotional plea for him to return to the circle of the
devout and to forego university learning ("my whole heart bursts for you").

The move this young cleric was about to make, from devotional life to
learning and the priesthood — the exact reverse of Grote's own —, had
touched the rawest of nerves. In the event Master Geert's plea was
successful. Johan Busch reproduced the letter and then told the story. Johan
ten Water gathered with friends at a *vinarium*, and after drinking for a time
asked them all to ride with him out to Windesheim. When they arrived
amidst much joking and noise-making, he announced to their astonishment
that he was staying and they were free to return. The fathers at Windesheim
hesitated at first to receive him, owing to the wealth of his family; then they
thought he might better make profession at one of their newer and poorer
houses, where the family's wealth might prove a boon. In the end he was
accepted, and within the order this Johannes advanced to the priesthood and
eventually served as a father-confessor to sisters. The ironies of the Devouts'
position begin to emerge from this story, as from Grote's letters: Keep the
young cleric from higher learning but advance him as a father-confessor to
sisters; keep his corrupting wealth away or bend it to the needs of a house
in genuine need.

Far more evidence could be adduced about Grote's view of the clergy, in
whose ranks, it must be remembered, he remained, though never ordained
a priest.[21] With respect to monasteries and the religious, he recommended
people to houses whose strictness he trusted, while warning people away
from lax houses and encouraging some at least to live religiously outside
vows like himself. As for the secular clergy in the diocese of Utrecht, the
sharp critique he delivered against them paralleled in many particulars the
points made by other clerical reformers such as Nicholas of Clamange[22]
and Conrad of Megenberg.[23] With the outbreak of schism in 1378 such
pamphlets and reform proposals only increased in number and urgency.
Grote himself distinguished between the church as it was in his day, which
he labeled a "ruin" (*ruinam ecclesie que late et undique patens est*: same
word as Nicholas of Clamange), and the church as it was in truth.[24] But as
a person trained mostly in law and medicine rather than philosophy and
theology, he rarely took on theological issues as such. No sermons or
scriptural commentaries were preserved, or possibly even written down, and
his preaching apparently took the form of ardent moral homilies. He focused
ever more intensely upon the spiritual life. Questioned about the schism in

---

[21] There is a nuanced account citing some of the major sources in Epiney-Burgard
(n. 8 above), 205-47.

[22] Alfred Coville, *Le traité de la ruine de l'Eglise de Nicholas de Clamanges et la
traduction française de 1564* (Paris, 1936).

[23] Konrad von Megenberg, *Planctus ecclesiae in Germaniam*, ed. R. Scholz, MGH
Staatsschriften des späteren Mittelalters 2 (Leipzig, 1941).

[24] See *Epistola* 20, ed. Mulder 72-77, here 74.

the papacy, Master Geert eventually prepared a formal legal reply (*Epistola* 21), but he declared himself in a preceeding letter far more concerned about the "schism in the soul".

Master Geert never repudiated the sacerdotal priesthood in any formal or theological sense. On the contrary, he set its standards so high as to be nearly unattainable. In the late fourteenth century, reformers saw everywhere the same vices that had preoccupied the Gregorian Reformers: simony and concubinage. After his conversion Master Geert continued to write *consilia* or juristic advice, and two at least turned on whether collation to a curate had involved simony.[25] In the second Grote argued that a young man should give up a curate obtained for him through the influence of his sisters, even though his parents were poor and desperately needed the material support their son could have offered. From Grote's strict reading of the law there were too many irregularities here (including the man's age and the sisters' entreaties). In this land (*in hac terra*) in these times (*istis temporibus*), Master Geert observed, almost no one is instituted to a curate or prebend without a financial arrangement (*pactis pecuniarum*), and to do so is to become caught up in diabolic simony and the devil's own net (*cum dyabolicis symoniacis symoniace se commisceant et dyaboli laqueis se inuoluant*).[26] More fundamental still than the legal niceties of what constituted simony was another question, that of spiritual intention. In his first and longer *consilium* Master Geert had gone into detail about simony and its legal features; now he offered a fuller teaching on curates. He required of them five spiritual qualifications: First, that they have the right intention (that is, not be moved by career or financial considerations), 2) that they be illumined by the learning of God, 3) that they have lived and now live a good and examplary life, 4) that they surpass others in inward love and living, and 5) that they spurn earthly and mundane matters.[27] Grote drew his own consequences from an ideal of pastoral office set so high and

---

[25] The first is called *De locatione ecclesiarum* and was edited by J. Clarisse in the *AKeG* 8 (1837): 119-52; it requires more extensive analysis than can be attempted here. The second, closely related and used here, was edited among the letters (no. 73, ed. Mulder, 310-21), though it was clearly a *consilium*, as evidenced by some of the titles affixed: "Consilium siue responsio magistri Gherardi Groot cognominati, cuidam iuueni data, cui collata fuit ecclesia quedam curata ad instanciam sororum suarum." And again: "Lege istam epistolam, quisquis ad curam animarum festinas, et quod periculosum sit anhelare ad prebenda uel officium cui annexa est cura animarum perpende!" (ed. Mulder, 310).

[26] *Epistola* 73, ed. Mulder, 312-313.

[27] "Item omnis uolens digne intrare curam animarum iudicio consciencie ex diuinis et naturalibus legibus tenetur: primo habere intencionem rectam, secundo tenetur esse illuminatus Dei scientia, tercio tenetur et uixisse et uiuere uita bona et exemplari, quarto tenetur amore interno et uita alios precellere, quinto terrena et mundana contempnere." *Epistola* 73, ed. Mulder, 313.

from so fierce a repudiation of any simoniacal maneuver: When this young man (with whom others plainly had sympathy) acceded to this benefice with temporal considerations in mind (his parent's poverty), he *committed mortal sin* and became separated from God, whence the Devil, not God, had inspired his taking up the cure of souls.[28]

This position might have remained buried in a few *consilia* or confined to a circle of followers had Master Geert not spelled it out in detail before Utrecht's assembled clergy. The most renowned preacher in the diocese by the early 1380's, far surpassing any mendicants (with whom there were tensions), he was asked in the summer of 1383 to address the diocesan clergy gathered in synod. Grote took as his text Is. 52:11: "Depart, Depart, Go out from thence, Touch not what is unclean; be ye clean that bear the vessels of the Lord." Armed with this text, he called upon priests, clerics, and all people of good will or right intention to separate themselves from the polluted concubinate clergy (the focarists = those who have a female companion at the hearth). He launched an attack upon his fellow clerics that bore not a trace of mercy or humor. "Behold, he shouted (and we can visualize the accompanying gesture), the fornicating priest. Here we have two words. I honor and greatly love the 'priest'; I hate and properly abominate the 'fornicator'."[29] Grote's attack found a surprising resonance: No less than twenty-five manuscript copies have survived of the large and difficult treatise he developed out of this sermon. No less importantly, within weeks, by October at the latest, his preaching license was suspended. The clergy would hear no more from this deacon who preached radical moral revolt and separatism. He spent the last year of his life elaborating his position in writing and appealing to Rome for support.

The heart of his stance, worked out eventually in twenty-six points, he enunciated in his first declaration or *dictum*: That a manifest fornicator was *ipso facto* suspended, and his masses and sacred rites to be shunned (*euitari*).[30] Notorious fornicators who kept women publicly, morever, were *ipso facto* excommunicated, and their women to be forcibly restrained, even "frightened with frequent excommunications".[31] Master Geert knew better than to fall into the Donatist heresy, and his twenty-sixth or final *dictum*

---

[28] "Item, quando sic temporalia querit iuuenis et ad beneficium sic accedit, non est dubium, eum mortaliter peccare ipso ingressu et a Deo separari. Unde istius introitus pocius dyabolus est agitator quam Deus ... ." *Epistola* 73, ed. Mulder, 314.

[29] The sermon has not come down to us in its original form, but as a large treatise in which Grote defended his "twenty-four points (*dicta*)" (actually twenty-six) with an elaborate canonistic apparatus still awaiting proper analysis. Th. and J. Clarisse provided a remarkably reliable edition a century and one-half ago: *AKeG* 1 (1829): 364-79, 2 (1830): 307-95, 8 (1837): 5-107; text cited here 1 (1829): 372. For question of editions and dating, see Epiney-Burgard (n. 8 above), 236ff.

[30] Clarisse, *AKeG* 2 (1830): 307.

[31] Clarisse, *AKeG* 2 (1830): 380, 389.

explained correctly that any priest who intended to confect the sacrament, even a suspended or degraded one, did so. But the whole force of his sermon and argument ran in the contrary direction, urging good clerics and lay people to "come out from among" these polluted priests. At its controlling center, here as in the case of the simoniac young man, was Grote's conviction, stated in his second *dictum*, that anyone who attended the mass of a known fornicator (presumed of most with hearth companions) committed mortal sin (*peccat mortaliter*). The laity were therefore — his third *dictum* — to shun such "focarists" even when their prelates upheld them (*licet prelati ecclesie eos sustineant, adhuc sint uitandi, nec propter hoc subditi excusantur*)[32] Acted upon literally, Grote's call would have provoked something tantamount to a revolt against the secular clergy of his day in the name of a pure sacramental priesthood.

There is no evidence that it did. On the contrary, some at least tried to answer Master Geert argument for argument from the canon law.[33] And only a year later he died of the plague, with his appeal to Rome still unanswered. But the impulse to create communities of spiritual people, especially spiritual clerics, only increased in him and his followers during these last months of his life. In June 1383, thus at nearly the same time as his sermon in Utrecht, he and others established a common endowment to support "two or three inward-looking poor priests who would serve God in separation from the world" (*tween of drien gueden ynnighen armen priesters die mit afghesceydenheit van der werlt Gode dienden*). They were to be chosen from among the most humble (*oetmoedichsten*) and holy (*god-lichsten*), to serve as a mirror to other people (*een spieghel anderen menschen*), and to live in Deventer, there to hear the confessions of those converted to God.[34] Historians have treated this charter as the first docu-mentary evidence toward the founding of the Brothers of the Common life, and indeed (though not legally until 1465) these properties ended up among their holdings. But read chronologically, this document, prepared under the auspices of city magistrates, bears witness no less accurately, indeed more so, to Master Geert's radical vision in 1383 of a purified spiritual priesthood set off from the world. During those same last months, according to Thomas of Kempen, Grote also resolved to found a community of canons regular (which is to say, priests living an ordered spiritual life) according to the

---

[32] Clarisse, *AKeG* 2 (1830): 330, 335.

[33] The evidence of it was presented by Titus Brandsma, "Drie onuitgegeven werkjes van Geert Groote", *OGE* 15 (1941): 5-61.

[34] This charter was edited most recently by C. van der Wansem, *Het ontstaan en de geschiedenis der Broederschap van het Gemene Leven* (Leuven, 1958), 181.

model provided by John of Ruusbroec, who had himself left the collegiate church in Brussels to found his community in the woods at Groenendael.[35]

Grote died of the plague at age forty-four, and historians can only speculate on what might have happened had he lived twenty-five years longer. Would he have become absorbed into the later medieval religious world of observants and inspired preachers like Bernardino of Siena? Or would his severe critique of the secular clergy and his separatist impulse have driven him ever more to the margin and beyond? The answer, to judge from the Brothers of the Common Life, entails something of both. The Brothers and Sisters certainly belonged to that larger world of renewal and observantism in the later middle ages,[36] as their personal connections, their preferred reading (Bernardino, for example), and the diffusion of their own works plainly attested. Yet by refusing to take vows or to assume the status of a religious order they also remained something of an oddity, not fitting with the laity, or the religious, or the secular clergy.

The Brothers seemed nearest in status to the secular clergy. Not in Deventer, but in other places including Zwolle, their communities were known locally as "the clerks' house". Florens Radewijns, who inherited Grote's mantle at Deventer and after whom that house was subsequently named, held a modest vicarage in the great collegiate church of St. Lebwin's. His task was to sing the hours and to say mass at the altar of St. Paul's, but his vocation was to gather around him interested clerics, student-clerics, and lay people, and to guide them in the spiritual life. Out of these informal gatherings in houses (*vergadering* or *congregatio* in a *huis* or *domus*, in the original languages) came the Brothers in Deventer, Zwolle, and many other towns. Their way of life — clerics and lay people who acted much like religious — blurred all the ordinary distinctions, eliciting criticism from nearly every group, especially in the mid 1390's when their communities first emerged as something distinct. To the religious, especially the mendicants, they seemed "impersonators" or even rivals. Friars·

---

[35] It may be worth citing Thomas's way of putting it: "Habuit etiam in proposito edificandi monasterium clericorum ordinis canonicorum regularium, uolens quosdam de idoneis clericis sibi adherentibus ad religionis habitum promouere, ut aliis deuotis essent in exemplum, et aduentantibus deforis clericis uel laicis bone conuersationis iter ostenderet. Ad hunc ordinem regularium instituendum precipue inductus fuit propter singularem reuerentiam et amorem uenerabilis domini Iohannis Rusebroec...." Thomas of Kempen, *Dialogus noviciorum* 2.15, ed. Pohl (n. 11 above), 7: 77-78. On the "southern" or "Brabantine" origins of the Modern Devotion, see my "A Brabantine Perspective on the Origins of the Modern Devotion: The First Book of Petrus Impens's *Compendium Decursus Temporum Monasterii Bethleemitice*", in *Studies voor Willem Lourdaux* (Leuven, 1992).

[36] For this world, see Kaspar Elm, "Verfall und Erneuerung des Ordenswesens im Spätmittelalter. Forschung und Forschungsaufgaben", in *Untersuchungen zu Kloster und Stift*, Veröffentlichungen des Max-Planck-Instituts für Geschichte 68, Studien zur Germania Sacra 14 (Göttingen, 1980), 188-238.

challenged their right to live the common life without taking vows, a
principle fought out in legal *consilia* during the 1390's and finally resolved
at the Council of Constance in 1417.[37] To secular clergy caught up in
making a living from their church offices, or as Will said of contemporary
clergymen in *Piers Plowman*, to "synge for symonye",[38] these brothers
seemed a constant reproach, the ever-present "holier-than-thou's". To lay
people who expected of their clergymen only the ordinary services (or, for
the cynical, the common disservice), these men seemed either holy or
fanatic. The story is told of Egbert, from a well-off local family and later
rector in Deventer (1450-83), who as a young man once walked though the
public square in the modest garb of the devout with his head down and
bearing a plate of food to someone. He nearly stumbled into one of his
female relations without seeing or greeting her. "What for a lollard is this
who walks around in this fashion?" she snipped, and knocked the plate from
his hands. He merely picked it up and walked on[39] — no doubt bolstering
in her mind the sense that these were indeed outlandish fanatics.

The Brothers knew that theirs was a distinct way of life, a *status* that fit
no existing categories. However complex the world of the later medieval
secular "clerk", certainly more so than anything suggested by a single broad
division between clergy and laity, the Brothers represented yet something
else. They lived and acted as observant religious, as disciplined clerics, and
as pious laymen; they were at once all and none of these. It is little wonder
that Albert Hyma could make them out as proto-Calvinists and R.R. Post as
good Catholics, even ultramontane. The Brothers were not anticlerical in any
Reformation or secular sense. But they were born of Master Geert's call for
the devout to come out from among polluted clergymen, and their whole
way of life, including their vocation to serve student-clerics[40] and Sisters,
yielded in effect an alternative structure. The Brothers never defended it as

---

[37] This still requires fuller analysis. The most important defense produced by the
Brothers themselves came from Gerhard Zerbolt of Zutphen in his *Super modo
vivendi devotorum hominum simul commorantium* edited by Albert Hyma in *AGU* 52
(1926): 1-100, and which I am re-editing for *Corpus Christianorum* with Marc
Haverhals (Leuven). The most important legal *consilia* may be found in L. Korth,
"Die ältesten Gutachten über die Brüderschaft des gemeinsamen Lebens", *Mitteilungen aus dem Stadtarchiv Köln* 5 (1887): 1-27; and P. Fredericq, *Corpus documentorum inquisitionis pravitatis Neerlandicae* (Ghent, 1896), 2:153-85.

[38] Derek Pearsall, *Piers Plowman by William Langland: an edition of the C-Text*
(Berkeley, 1978), 33.

[39] *Vita Egberti* 1 (in my forthcoming new edition) = G. Dumbar, *Analecta seu
vetera aliquot scripta inedita* (Deventer, 1719), 163.

[40] See now G. Epiney-Burgard, "Die Wege der Bildung in der Devotio Moderna",
in *Lebenslehren und Weltentwürfe im Übergang vom Mittelalter zur Neuzeit*
(Göttingen, 1989), 181-200.

something different from the existing church, only as a "modest" way of life for the converted or the devout.

For the New Devout, as for nearly all medieval Christians, the priestly office represented the pinnacle of the spiritual universe. The lowliest priest and the pope in Rome were one in their power to confect the body of Christ and to rule in the confessional over his mystical body. The pressure on religious men to assume the priestly office was nearly irresistable: The Benedictines became clericalized (meaning, ordained in increasing numbers) from the ninth century onwards (probably originating, certainly fostering, the private mass), Franciscans were drawn into clerical and priestly roles within a generation after their founding, and secular clerics were most prized in the later middle ages as "chantry priests" (hired chiefly to say mass). Conversely, professed religious who could not assume the priestly office, above all, women and illiterate lay brothers, were thereby relegated to a lesser position in the spiritual universe, with rare exceptions. How the Devout regarded the priesthood, therefore, shaped, or became an emblem for, their stance toward the entire clerical establishment.

The devout Brothers, trained in many instances from early days as "student-clerics" with larger prospects, resisted promotion to the priesthood, following in the footsteps of Master Geert Grote the deacon. Rudolph of Muiden, author of an important early account of the house in Deventer, ascribed to Grote the views that obtained within the Brothers' house: Considering the great dignity of the priesthood, he dared not be ordained in fear of his conscience.[41] John Cele, schoolmaster in Zwolle and close companion to Grote, taught Scripture to his schoolboys and preached to lay men and women, attracting many of them to his spiritual teachings. This elicited a protest from the local curate, which in turn angered Master Geert, who claimed that this curate (also an acquaintance) had power over parishoners only in the confessional (*nisi in foro consciencie*) with no right to interfere in this spiritual teaching and preaching (*rapiens sibi potestatem super homines quam non habet*) — a point he then made directly to the curate himself (*Et sibi hoc scripsi*). The obvious canonical solution, that Cele be ordained, this schoolmaster refused: The office was so high, surpassing even angelic power, and he a man still so caught up in the earthly ways of this world that it would be sheer presumption; he would persist as a spiritual teacher in a humble estate (*in humili statu*: very quickly a code word for the Brothers' chosen "estate"). This same outlook he passed on to his schoolboys (according to Johan Busch, who was one of them and gave this account), namely that the sacerdotal office was highly dangerous,

---

[41] "Deinde ordinatus dyaconus cepit predicare vulgo uerbum Dei; nam non audebat ex timore consciencie effici presbiter, considerans magnam dignitatem ordinis sacerdotalis." Rudolphus, *Vitae fratrum* 1.5 = Dumbar, *Analecta*, 5.

even pernicious, especially for those whose lives did not correspond to the office.[42]

What Grote and Cele taught and practiced, the Brothers came to appropriate within and to institutionalize. According to Peter Hoorn, Rudolph's continuator at Deventer and longtime librarian there (1440's-1479), Godfrey the rector (1410-50) wished himself wholly blind and deprived of both legs and arms so as to render himself unfit for the priestly office — an outlook for which he cited authorities including Geert Grote.[43] In the memorial *vitae* kept in their houses, the Brothers took special note of those, whether clerical or lay, who never aspired to the priesthood. A certain Arnold lived in the house in Deventer for thirty-one years, always a simple cleric, never seeking advancement to the priesthood.[44] Another clerical brother served the student-clerics in Deventer, never seeking promotion for himself, "though he was sufficiently lettered [in Latin]."[45] A man who studied for a time in Deventer's schools and even served as the house's procurator (second in command charged with all economic affairs) "gloried" that he was not promoted; he died and was buried in the humble estate of the brothers.[46] A brother who died in 1453 actively resisted the efforts of an uncle, dean of St. Severinus in Cologne, to have him promoted and well endowed; the man rejoiced to die in this abject estate — which is described here, most interestingly, as "clerical or rather semi-lay".[47]

---

[42] The entire account, including Grote's letter, appears at the end of Johan Busch's *Liber de viris illustribus* 69, ed. Grube (n. 6 above), 211, with this explanation as Busch had himself learned it from Cele: "Considerans autem magister Iohannes sacerdocii statum fore altissimum et angelicam supergredi potestatem, nimis esse terribile, hominem secularem moribus incompositum, multis peccatis et uiciis subiacentem, a terrenis actibus et affectibus ad diuina et celestia nondum totum suspensum, angelicam necdum uitam terrenis actibus ducere ualentem, et huiusmodi excellentissimum in ecclesia militante statum aliquatinus aspirare; sacerdos fieri non presumpsit nec ad sacros ordines promoueri, sed in humili statu ecclesie deliberauit permanere. De statu uero sacerdocii ex scripturis diuinis doctorumque sentenciis multa nobis dicere et pronunciare consueuit, ostendens ualde fore periculosum et animabus sanctis nimis perniciosum instare pro sacerdocio, illis tamen permaxime quibus uita cum nomine et sanctitas in effectu minime correspondent ... ."

[43] *Vitae fratrum* 64.1 = Dumbar, *Analecta*, 115.

[44] *Vitae fratrum* 58 = Dumbar, *Analecta*, 83.

[45] "... fuit receptus ad domum nostram, ubi permansit usque ad finem uite sue, seruiens Domino in humilitate et subiectione in statu clericali sine promocione ad sacros ordines, quamuis tamen esset sufficientis literature." *Vitae fratrum* 61 = Dumbar, *Analecta*, 85.

[46] "Inclinatus multum ad humilia, quare gloriabatur quod ipse non fuit promotus ad sacerdocium, sed in humili et abiecto statu in hora mortis sue posset inueniri et in sepulchro fratrum nostrorum sepeliri." *Vitae fratrum* 42 = Dumbar, *Analecta*, 67.

[47] "Habebat auunculum qui erat decanus ecclesie sancti Seuerini in Colonia et ualde pluralis in prebendis. Hic multum laborabat eum promouere ad sacerdocium et

Inside the house, though something of a clerical-lay distinction persisted (about which more later), this was seriously blurred by lay brothers who could read and give spiritual guidance on the one hand and clerics who did lay work as cooks or tailors on the other. Thus a brother who made it through the second highest class in school was content to do lay work for fifty-two years while other junior brothers were promoted.[48] Yet of a lay brother active in the kitchen and other such jobs, but a competent scribe, his memorialist noted that he never was tempted "to seek further learning and other shameful things" (*temptacionem acquireret amplius discendi et probrandi*), remaining content in his humble estate.[49]

Each of these brothers — and many more that might be cited from Deventer and other houses — had appropriated for himself this ethos. But such a distinctive outlook on the priestly office so cut against the grain in the late middle ages that objection was inevitable. Here too the Brothers were forced to defend their stance, something scholars have not perceived in context. It was Gerard Zerbolt of Zutphen (†1398) who emerged as the community's most learned defender, filling one-hundred pages in his best-known legal defense.[50] In another treatise he criticized the extragavant clothing of late medieval clerics and defended the Brothers' own simplicity.[51] And when someone challenged the Brothers' stand on promotion to the priesthood, Gerard responded with a fifty-five page letter-treatise[52] intended to refute this man who had, as he put it, "an inordinate desire for ecclesiastical orders and the office of preaching." This young man, described as a cleric in minor orders of only moderate education (*mediocris literature*), wondered whether he should remain in this "status" (suggesting

---

bonis dotare ecclesiasticis. Sed ipse ualde strenuiter abiecit consilium auunculi sui, magis eligens abiectus esse in domo Dei et cohabitare pauperibus. Unde et circa mortem gloriabatur quod in tam humili statu clericali, quin pocius semilaycali, deberet mori." *Vitae fratrum* 65 = Dumbar, *Analecta*, 121.

[48] "Nam dum fuisset competenter bonus clericus, uidelicet in Dauentriensi schola secundarius, pacientissime tulit hiis laycalibus se implicari officiis, perseuerans, ut dictum est, in illis annis quinquaginta-duobus, nunquam aspirans ad alciora cum uideret iuniores et, ut ita dicam, filios filiorum suorum de anno in annum promoueri ad sacerdocium." *Vitae fratrum* 72.1 = Dumbar, *Analecta*, 139.

[49] *Vita Mathiae* 4, in Brussels, Royal Library 8849-59, 61v. The unusual word "*probrandi*" means "do shameful things", here linked with "learning" (*discendi*).

[50] On Zerbolt, see Th. M. van Rooij, *Gerard Zerbolt van Zutphen, Leven en Geschriften* (Nijmegen, 1936); W. Lourdaux, "Gérard Zerbolt de Zutphen", *Dictionnaire de Spiritualité* 6: 284-89; and G. H. Gerrits, *Inter Timorem et Spem: A Study of the Theological Thought of Gerard Zerbolt of Zutphen*, SMRT 37, (Leiden, 1986) with a complete bibliography.

[51] D. J. M. Wüstenhoff, *Het tractaat 'De pretiosis vestibus'* (Ghent, 1890).

[52] Albert Hyma, "Het *Scriptum pro quodam inordinate gradus ecclesiasticos et praedicationis officium affectante*", *NAKG* 20 (1927): 178-231. There is a summary in Dutch in van Rooij (n. 50 above), 222-41.

he was himself from the circles of the devout) or aspire to the priesthood and the office of preaching in order to bear the fruits of holy living among more people. Gerard, though himself eventually ordained, mustered a whole series of arguments against it.[53]

First, while a person ought to choose for himself the contemplative life, rule over the souls of others and any external charge must be left to the judgement of another; to it a person should never aspire himself. This was not a pious platitude, but something the brotherhood put seriously into practice. Each house had a specified number of priests, and brothers were "chosen" by other brothers (*electione fratrum*) for promotion; this was a duty or honor they did not decide upon for themselves. In the earliest days this was a genuine election, which depended upon consensus and a plurality of votes (*per plures uoces*), sometimes painfully arrived at, to judge from an extant letter on the subject.[54] In later practice this "election" may often have followed the rector's lead; at least that is how it was depicted as happening after Gerard's own early death of plague in 1398.[55] The brothers worried exceedingly — as Grote had for Johan ten Water — about any brother with higher aspirations, whatever the stated motives.

While to refuse promotion to higher orders might be licit or illicit, according to the circumstances (ch. 2), the desire for holy orders (ch. 3, longest in the tractate) was "always wrong" (*semper viciosus*), in Gerard's view: First, because men do so out of "ambition and arrogance"; second, because they fail to perceive how difficult the priestly charge truly is; third, because they obviously fail to "reverence the terrible and marvelous depths of the sacraments" or they would "fear to approach rather than push themselves forward." Even those properly called and truly fit should assume this dignity only with fear[56] — the same theme sounded in those years by John Cele in Zwolle. It is, Gerard observes, "far safer to serve the Lord in a lesser estate than in some elevated office or order, for higher dignities do

---

[53] The work, remarkably enough, has survived in six manuscripts: van Rooij (n. 50 above), 347-48. Here Hyma's edition is used (n. 52 above).

[54] *Epistolae fratrum* 7 = Dumbar, *Analecta*, 109-11.

[55] "Et quia tantum duo presbiteri remanserant in domo uiui, scilicet ipse dominus Florencius et frater Henricus Bruyn, ut compleretur numerus quaternarius pres-biterorum, in proxima quadragesima fecit dominus Florencius duos clericos in sacerdotes ... ordinari pro domo." *Vitae fratrum* 23 = Dumbar, *Analecta*, 49. But even if Florens took the lead, there was still an "election" procedure, as attested by later *vitae*.

[56] "Satis ergo apparet quod si eciam quis ydoneus esset uocatus a Deo tanquam Aaron, uel superiorum coactus imperio, attamen deberet cum timore, tremore et reuerencia accedere per huiusmodi sacramenti summam excellenciam et officii huius ordinis terribilem dignitatem. ... Unde presumptuosum est ut neque uocatus quis proprio motu et ambicioso affectu se ingerat et ad gradum alciorem anhelet, eciam si dignus fuerit, maxime autem cuius uita tali ordini non respondet." *Scriptum*, ed. Hyma (n. 52 above), 191.

not put vices to flight but rather put them on display."[57] The danger, moreover, is not only for the person but for the whole church: Ambitious desire for the priesthood on the part of so many unworthy individuals, Gerard asserts, is the reason "the sacrament of orders is held in contempt, the church's ministers vilified, the sacraments profaned and, as it were, trampled underfoot by the laity as something vile, even as they are consoled in their evil ways by the example of the privileged."[58]

Some, he goes on, mask their ambition with pious phrases, that for instance, these ministers and orders are the glory of the church. But if so, he objects, the standards ought to be made stiffer and the candidates more strictly examined; then few would be found suitable, especially in our day.[59] In fact from this multitude of ministers there comes upon the Christian religion not glory but shame.[60] The exact same point was argued many years later in the chronicle for the Brothers' house at Hildesheim. An interdict, its chronicler argues, can actually serve to bring us back to our inner spiritual senses, to turn us away from this multiplicity of priests and altars.[61]

In sum, however worthy the office or the spiritual work, to seek a curate or a benefice or some greater dignity, Gerard insisted, is always wrong

---

[57] "Sed eciam multo tucius est in inferiori statu Domino seruire quam in gradu uel dignitate sublimiori. Dignitates enim non solent uicia fugare sed illustrare." Ibid., 192.

[58] "Istud autem periculum non solum respectu ordinem suscipientis sed eciam inde graue periculum contingit tote ecclesie quod ambicioso affectu indigni accedunt. Inde enim sacramentum ordinis contempnitur, inde ministri ecclesie uilipenduntur, inde sacramenta nostra prophanantur et quasi uilia a laycis conculcantur, et honoris exemplo in malo confortantur." Ibid., 193. He repeats the same point, obviously an important one for him, on the next page: "Unde enim in ecclesia tanta indisciplinacio, unde nunc quod simul ministri ecclesie, ministeria officia, et sacra eorum tam parum reputantur a laycis, ne dicam uilipendunt, nisi a multitudine male ministrancium, indigne et sine reuerencia et sanctitate accedencium, sine deuocione ministrancium?"

[59] "Dicunt ergo primo quod decus uniuersalis ecclesie consistit in ordine et multitudine ministrorum et graduum dignitate. Si autem, adeo difficulter deberent ad sacros ordines accedere atque districte examinari, pauci reperirentur ydoney, presertim nostris temporibus ... ." Ibid., 193.

[60] "Unde et huiusmodi ministris ecclesie non tam decus nascitur quam obprobrium christiane generatur religioni." Ibid., 195.

[61] R. Doebner, ed., *Annalen und Akten der Brüder des gemeinsamen Lebens im Lüchtenhove zu Hildesheim* (Hannover, 1903), 149-50: "Ecce totus pene mundus plenus est sacerdotibus, altaribus ecclesie replentur et habunde cumulantur! Et quicumque fundare poterit altare pro paupere, ut aiunt, sacerdote — ne dixerim pro amicis, filio uel nepote — gloriatur quasi de anime sue certa redempcione uel salute. Sicque fit ut pro multitudine altarium copia requiratur sacerdotum, quorum, ut communiter, confusa et numerosa improbitate et necessitate non parum derogatur clericali honestati. ... Et sicut sacerdotibus paucis et dignis melius seruiretur Christi famulis, sic forte non absurde concluderetur de paucis legendis missis. Cum quanta, putas, auiditate ac deuocione frequentaretur missa, si fieret non nisi una?"

(*semper est uiciosum*), can never be rightly desired (*indigne appetitur*). Nor does a person's merit or progress consist in the dignity of his sacerdotal rank; it comes only from charity and secondarily from purity and the inner virtues.[62] The Brothers implicitly shifted the plane of action and judgement to the inner moral life, whatever their protests about the dignity of the sacerdotal hierarchy. Their Customary — in which Gerard may have had a hand — begins with the same language and likewise includes chapters on charity, humility, obedience, and the like as the heart of their way of life.[63] A single brief chapter deals with mass, and explains that they ordinarily "hear" it everyday (*Missam cottidie consueuimus audire*), with no special provisions for the priesthood or for saying mass.[64] On this point Gerard took refuge in the doctors of the church, who, he says, exhort us not to seek higher orders but humility and charity — like "those of us choosing a lower estate (*statum bassum*) as less dangerous."[65]

As for the desire to preach and benefit others (ch. 4), Gerard responds that in the contemplative life — or as he puts it, not running around to convert others and pervert yourself — one may on occasion seek to aid those persons one meets with friendly admonition and fraternal correction, as well as aid and counsel both spiritual and temporal.[66] But an "inordinate desire to preach and help others" is essentially a form of temptation. After refuting certain passages alleged from Scripture (ch. 5) and certain examples drawn from the saints (ch. 6), he concludes: only the strong and the perfect should take up the office of preaching (*opus forcium et perfectorum est officium predicacionis, a uiris perfectis arripiendum*). But what of that strong desire to preach, including a certain spiritual restlessness, which so many clerics claim for themselves (including apparently this one)? Such inner drives, he

---

[62] "... nequaquam profectus noster uel meritum consistit in sublimitate graduum, nec meritum nostrum in ordine digniori, sed principaliter in caritate, secundario uero in puritate et in interioribus actibus uirtutum aliarum; non enim in sublimitate graduum sed in amplitudine caritatis acquiritur regnum Dei." *Scriptum*, ed. Hyma (n. 52 above), 197.

[63] "Sit igitur summum et cottidianum studium et exercitium nostrum proficere in cordis puritate, ut uidelicet primo omnium discamus nosipsos cognoscere, uicia et passiones anime sine dissimulatione diiudicare, et eas totis uiribus niti extirpare, gulam domare ..." (etcetera, through the virtues and vices). M. Schoengen, *Jacobus Traiecti alias de Voecht, Narratio de inchoatione domus clericorum in Zwollis* (Amsterdam, 1908), 241.

[64] Schoengen, 243.

[65] "Hinc est quod sancti doctores ... non nos hortantur ad altos gradus sed humilitatem et caritatem uite, quantum ex nobis est semper statum bassum et locum inferiorem utpota minus periculosum eligentes." *Scriptum*, ed. Hyma (n. 52 above), 198.

[66] Ibid., 204.

points out (ch. 7), may well come from the Devil rather than the Spirit.[67] Indeed this diabolic yearning to preach arises most often from an arrogant desire to show off learning, or an envious desire to become a prelate oneself, or simply an idle desire to break tedium (ch. 8).

After addressing this man's supposed call to the offices of priest and preacher, Gerard takes up yet another question, making it clear that this young man was indeed from the circles of the New Devout and Gerard's epistolary response had become in fact an apology for their outlook on the priesthood and their whole way of life. "What point is there, this young cleric objects, to baking, brewing, copying books, and such manual labor? I count this estate for little with all its exercises if it does not profit others with preaching."[68] With striking effect, Gerard immediately cites Bernard's letter to Robert who had similarly objected to the Cistercian's manual labor and fled to the Cluniac's office. His entire chapter (10) then defends spiritual exercises as essential and as the way of the fathers (meaning, the Desert Fathers) even if they do not lead to preaching. The person who plunges into preaching without preparing himself by way of these exercises is doubly unfruitful, to himself and to others.[69] It requires a long time and much exercise before the heart is sufficiently grounded in virtue and contempt of the world to go out into the world preaching and not deviate to the left or right. In sum, only daily exercise in the virtues and lengthy self-examination can prepare one for the state of perfection necessary for assuming the priesthood.[70]

Finally — and here again we see evidence of a certain sobriety or this-worldly common sense in the midst of an other-worldly ideal — a person must examine carefully his natural gifts and aptitudes, for it does not seem likely that God would call anyone to a certain office who lacks the gifts requisite for that office (ch. 12). This closing chapter, combined with the opening description of the young man as "modestly educated", suggests that Gerard did not believe him equipped to become a preacher, quite apart from his youth and his inordinate desire to leave the humble circle of the New Devout. There is in this letter no send-off, no final word to a brother cleric.

---

[67] "Unde ualde stultum esset semper tali instinctui uel interne mocioni inherere uelud reuelacioni spiritus sancti. Hoc est inicium dyabolice decepcionis et ad decipiendum precipuum instrumentum ... ." Ibid., 211.

[68] "Quid est, inquit, pinsere, braxare, libros scribere, et similia manibus laborare? Parum, inquit, reputo statum in suis exerciciis si non proficiat aliis predicando." Ibid., 219.

[69] "Sed hoc indubitanter uerum est, quod parum est eius predicacio reputanda, eciam si aliis proficiat, si non se ipsum piis exerceat operibus. Qui enim bene docet et male uiuit, quid aliud faciat nisi ut doceat quomodo ipse sit contempnandus? Vacare ergo sibi semper est tucius, sed est multis fructuosius." Ibid., 222.

[70] Hyma, 227-28. The implication throughout is that this man is still only a "beginner".

It had become for Zerbolt a treatise in its own right justifying the Brothers'
attitudes toward their own estate and the sacerdotal office.

The attitudes and practices represented by Gerard in this treatise of the
mid 1390's pervaded the subsequent *vitae*, the quasi-official edifying
memoires of the departed brothers. They recall relatively little about
specifically priestly practices. All their emphasis falls upon the brothers'
virtues, especially their chastity, humility, obedience, and charity, but also
their devotion to the community and its spiritual discipline. What these
brothers aimed to avoid above all, as they are depicted in these *vitae*, was
the arrogance and privilege associated with the priestly caste, whether
religious or secular. Yet the Brothers did not — despite Gerard's treatise —
wholly avoid priestly roles. Promoted only by the mutual election of their
fellow brothers, they exhorted and admonished one another, they confessed
and trained the students under their charge, and they confessed and taught
the sisters to whom they were assigned — this itself judged "lowly" work
in most professed religious orders. The Brothers even preached. But they did
not call it that. From the beginning they offered "collations" to students and
townspeople on Sunday afternoons and feastdays. Few of these have
survived, but they appear to have been simple explanations of scriptural
passages combined with moral exhortation. In time these collations began
to draw upon the brotherhood itself for *exempla*, the exemplary stories
meant to teach these virtues.[71] But quite unlike all the famous observant
leaders, such as Bernardino in Italy or John Brugman in the Netherlands, the
Brothers never led preaching tours, and they never projected themselves into
positions of ecclesiastical power.

Yet they did not wholly eliminate from their consciousness or their
practice the social and ecclesiastical divisions that contemporaries took for
granted. This ambiguity has plagued historical interpretation, with some
scholars inclined to find at work a proto-protestant undermining of the
sacerdotal hierarchy and others (especially Post) that system still fully
operative. The reality is more nuanced. Lay brothers appear in the first
official document for the house at Deventer as *cum aliquibus familiaribus*,
that is, as servants to the eight clerics and four priests; and in the customary
ascribed to Deventer the lay brothers appear as a kind of appendage to the
original clerical community.[72] This traditional attitude, with its attendant

---

[71] See my "The Virtues, The Brothers, and the Schools: A Text from the Brothers
of the Common Life", *Revue Bénédictine* 98 (1988): 178-217.

[72] van der Wansem (n. 34 above), 189. The Customary says it quite plainly:
"Domus hec nostra ... ad hoc fundata ... est, ut ad exemplum ecclesie primitiue deuoti
presbiteri et clerici cum nonnullis paucis laicis in ea uiuant in communi de labore
manuum, uidelicet opere scripture, et de redditibus siue bonis ecclesiasticis uitam
transigant mediocrem ... ." Hyma, *The Christian Renaissance* (n. 5 above), 442.
Intriguingly, the parallel version from the house in Zwolle omits the phrase "cum
nonnullis paucis laicis" but describes as the agents of this communal life "deuoti uiri,

categorization, never wholly disappeared: the cook, the taylor, the brewer, and all the others, though necessary and full members of the community, were perceived as different from — and in some sense attached to — the clerics who had received some measure of education before entering. This could provoke tensions: Among the virtues of the lay brother Matthew, Peter Hoorn (priest and librarian) noted about 1460 that he got on easily with his clerical brothers in genuine love and friendship, harboring none of the rancor or discord that the laity often show toward the clergy.[73] In a remarkable aside, found in a late *vita* (1492), the writer noted that extra caution was required in accepting laymen into the house.[74] But this traditional attitude on the part of clerics represented only one side of the story. All the Brothers, even a priest-librarian like Peter Hoorn, helped out in baking, brewing, and even the field and garden work.[75] These houses of the common life managed to achieve, relative to their times, a remarkable degree of leveling between clerics and laymen. There was never any open conflict or public disturbance, as in the case of many uprisings of lay brothers in monastic or convent settings. That same librarian who outstripped others in carrying wood and beams says of the lay brother Matthew that he outstripped many of his clerical brothers in his copywork and scrapbook, offering apt spiritual guidance to others from his reading.[76] So too lay brothers were memorialized in *vitae* that were fully as long and caring as any of the priests', sometimes more so. Indeed this layman Matthew was the only brother, outside Grote and Florens, for whom two were written, one by Peter Hoorn (already cited) and one in a separate quire by another priest friend (Peter of Ghent, still unpublished).

If in their view of the priesthood (at once exalted and sober) the Brothers reacted sensitively to its common vilification (both by lay people and by zealous reformers), there were still other ways in which this novel way of life implicitly addressed the charges brought most often against the clerical establishment. I will focus on three: jurisdiction, property, and learning.

---

presbiteri et clerici", thus placing devout laymen at the beginning of the commune: Schoengen (n. 63 above), 240.

[73] "Item dilectione et amore cordetenus iunctus erat clericis fratribus suis, nec iuxta morem laycorum leuiter discordabat ab eis, nec auersiuum seu rancorosum affectum gerebat ad eos; sed econtra multum beniuole concorditer et cum gracia conuersatus est cum ipsis." *Vitae fratrum* 69.1 = Dumbar, *Analecta* (n.39 above), 126.

[74] "... eo quod in laicis suscipiendis abundancior cautela sit necessaria ... ." *Vita Alberti* 1 = Brussels, Royal Library, 8849-59, f. 252^r.

[75] He was said to be, for instance, "ad cespites et ligna portanda in domo promptissimus"; see *Vita Petri Hoorn* 3 = Dumbar, *Analecta*, 150.

[76] "Unde factus est ita illuminatus ut circa uiciorum remedia et uirtutum exercicia tam lucida sciret dare consilia ac apta scripturarum testimonia allegare, ac si non laycus sed clericus uideretur esse." *Vitae fratrum* 69.1 = Dumbar, *Analecta*, 126.

First, the matter of jurisdiction. The special privilege known as benefit of clergy riled late medieval people like few others in their relations with clergymen. The issue was fought out on the large scale by kings and popes, but it increasingly gave rise on the local scale to palpable tensions and specific actions, especially in cities. The insistence during the Reformation that clerics be made citizens was one powerful manifestation of this resentment. On this point the Brothers and Sisters offer an interesting test case. Sisters' houses originated under civil, or local urban, jurisdiction. City magistrates ordinarily issued the founding charter, retained oversight rights with respect both to economic affairs and the internal moral order, and could in the last resort reclaim the house and its properties. Indeed the founding documents issued in the name of civil magistrates often served simply as statutes or in place of statutes.[77] These were women living a religious life who had not escaped civil jurisdiction, nor were their properties exempted from the cities' rents and rules, except by the magistrates' own decision. When, for instance, strife arose in Deventer over whether the Sisters could freely leave the house to visit friends and relatives (which had apparently generated scandal), the issue was fought out before the magistrates of the city.[78] This retention of urban oversight may well account for the uncommon popularity of Sisters' houses throughout the northwestern part of the German Empire in the fifteenth century.

The Brothers represent a slightly different and more confusing case. The earliest document for the house in Deventer (1391) was issued by the city's magistrates (*Wy scepen ende raedt der stad van Deventer*), and it has much the same character and provisions as other city-controlled religious corporations, such as hospices or alms houses. Two members of the council were included in the regime set up to rule the house and its clerics (*ende daer wille wy toe voeghen twee van onsen rade, dien dies vorsz. regierders des huyses toe spreken moeghen alse sies behoeven*). The document lists a series of expectations (equivalent to the sisters' statutes), with the provision that the magistrates can intervene if the house falls into the hands of unqualified clerics. The councilmen have given their consent in order to increase the worship and praise of God in their city (*opdat die dienst, lof ende ere onses lieven Heren Goedes altoes wassen ende vermeerdert moge weerden in onser stad ende oeck mede in den lande*), and have freed the inhabitants of this house from normal watch and neighborhood duties (*vrij wesen sollen van onser stad wake en buerwercke*) so that these devout priests and clerics — and here the Brothers have evidently communicated or formulated their own self-conception — may exercise themselves more

---

[77] See Rehm (n. 7 above), 110-12, 225-29, who is the best on this point.
[78] *Vita Egberti* 10 = Dumbar, *Analecta*, 171-72.

fully in the virtuous and inner life (*hem in meerre innicheit ende doegheden in den dienste ons lieven Heren oefenen moeghen*).[79]

What appears so simple in the final document was achieved in reality only by tough bargaining. Deventer's magistrates had indeed feared that they would lose property and jurisdiction to this house of clerics, and the Brothers' patron, a noblewoman, had to intervene together with her influential nephews in order to secure the agreement before the council. The life of this Lady Swedera van Runen further explains that the magistrates resisted her gift of the house to these clerics because "the councilmen and citizens of Deventer were harsh and unfavorable to clerics."[80] An updated confirmation of this agreement issued nearly six years later in Latin (November 1396) made no mention of the city council, though its role was apparently presumed and established by the former document.[81] Five years later, or ten years after the founding of the house (1401), the bishop of Utrecht officially approved this communal and devotional way of life without designating its devotees precisely as "clerics".[82] A generation later (1431) Pope Eugene IV extended full protection to them, and his letter spoke plainly of clerics, albeit ones who act like religious without being professed.[83] Even if the Brothers, many of them clerics or student-clerics before joining the house, obtained ecclesiastical status for themselves and their houses, they remained, as unprofessed or "secular" persons, fully a part of the city, living on ordinary city streets and regulating their affairs with city magistrates. However extraordinary their devotional lives and household commune, these Brothers and Sisters remained visible in the city, keeping up contacts with friends and relatives, purchasing supplies at the market, selling their books and their textiles, going out to work in their gardens and fields.

---

[79] This important document (dated 31 January 1391) is printed in van der Wansem (n. 34 above), 183-7.

[80] "Mer die scepene ende die borgers van Deventer weren den geesteliken luden also hart ende ongustich Ende en woldens niet toe laten dat sie enyge besittinge hebben solden." D. A. Brinkerink, ed., *Van den doechden der vuriger ende stichtiger susteren van Diepen veen* (Leiden, 1904), 44. In an unedited Latin version of this life, the text reads: "Quod [the proposed exchange, granting a house to the Brothers] tamen cum scabini et consules Dauentrienses percepissent (quia minus fauorabiles erant piis et Deo deuotis) admittere hanc permutacionem recusabant. Quapropter ... ." The text goes on to refer to the magistrates' document cited in the preceeding paragraph ("quemadmodum scabinates littere et instrumenta super his confecta testantur"). Brussel, Royal Library MS 8849-59, f. 187^r.

[81] van der Wansem (n. 34 above), 188-90.

[82] The document pertains to both brothers and sisters, and seems to take in everyone without bringing them under "clerical" jurisdiction: "... super statu quarundam personarum nostrae dioecesis sexus utriusque quae diuisim uiri et diuisim mulieres insimul in suis domibus commorantur ... ." Schoengen (n. 63 above), 512.

[83] Schoengen (n. 63 above), 515-18.

Both Brothers and Sisters, just as importantly, remained part of the local parish system, with all its expectations and obligations. In the bishop's approval for their way of life, he explicitly required that they remain subject to their ordinary curates.[84] One of the first agreements ordinarily worked out by a new house of Brothers was with its parish curate; in the case of the house at Louvain this document still exists.[85] Moreover, the Brothers' statutes and customaries spell out how they are to go to church, and how to conduct themselves in the midst of the other parishioners.[86] Sisters and Brothers obtained separate chapels, removing them from parish networks, only a hundred years or so after their founding, thus on the eve of the Reformation. Just as they remained outside the special status of the professed religious, so they remained inside the obligations of the ordinary urban parish. On one of the most sensitive sources of anticlerical resentments, therefore, benefit of clergy with all its attendant privileges and abuses, the Brothers and Sisters self-consciously adopted a position much closer to, though not entirely within, the lay world of late medieval towns.

Priestly status and jurisdictional privilege: If on both these points the Devout struck a compromise position, still within the clerical world, yet closer to the lay, they adopted their most distinctive stance on the item that generated the most resentment, clerical property, income, and wealth. Probably nothing irritated the laity quite so deeply as the wealth of the clergy, the endowments they accrued, the fees they incessantly charged, the income they demanded in return for their spiritual offices. The Brothers repudiated all the usual arrangements for clerical income as unsatisfactory and contrary to the model of the early church. Thus in contrast to the begging friars whose door to door quest for gifts increasingly drew down the ire and mockery of late medieval city-dwellers, the Brothers earned their income by the work of their own hands. They stated this purpose at the outset of their Customary, reinforced it with a section on "manual labor"

---

[84] "ecclesie praelatis et curatis humiliter subiuncti et reuerenter obedientes, quibus, ut tenentur, dumtaxat sua peccata ad minus semel in anno confiteantur ... ." Schoengen (n. 63 above), 514.

[85] See Willem Lourdaux, *Moderne Devotie en Christelijk Humanisme: De geschiedenis van Sint-Maarten te Leuven van 1433 to het einde der XVIe eeuw* (Louvain, 1967) 30f.

[86] "Missam cottidie consueuimus audire, ad quam audiendam propter uniformitatem omnes simul, licet non pariter, transimus, et ea finita redimus. ... In ecclesia non solemus ad populum conuersi stare uel sedere, ne distrahamur mente, sed magis ab impedimentis liberum, prout oportunius ualemus, locum querere et nos prosternere, ut eo intentius possimus cor nostrum ad Deum dirigere." Schoengen (n. 63 above) 243, 244. The statutes published by Hyma in *The Christian Renaissance* (n. 5 above), 445 are confusing on this point because while they retain the latter sentence they also stipulate "gathering in our church" (*signo tempestiue conuenimus in ecclesia nostra*), which may well reflect some later time when the house had acquired its own church (in Deventer, after 1500).

(emphasizing its usefulness in spiritual discipline), and put it into practice chiefly by copying books for pay, secondarily by caring for their own fields and gardens. A procurator at Deventer, John of Hattem (†1485), prepared a remarkable record in a single quire to document the fact that the brothers there had "purchased" with their own incomes all their "fields and revenues" and that these were not the "gift of any outside person" (*non de largicione alicuius hominis externei*).[87] Of the Sisters too, including those who became professed canonesses at Diepenveen, it is remembered that they not only earned their way by work in textiles but helped in the gardening and even in the building of their convent. In contrast to the well-endowed monastic houses, moreover, the Brothers set a statutory limit to their income, this to be regulated by their procurator, so they would always need to work for their daily bread; what exceeded that amount was to be re-distributed, one-third toward the library, two-thirds to the poor.[88]

The Brothers were closest in legal status to secular clerics, and here the contrast was sharpest and most deliberate: Where secular clerics could accrue personal income and property while living legally under benefit of clergy, the Brothers pledged themselves, on the model of the early church (Acts 4:32), to a common life without benefit of the religious vow of poverty. The religious orders, especially the Dominicans, cried foul, and this point was consistently the first taken up in the legal apologias (also in the customary). The Brothers made their case, winning approval for their way of life, and the "Common Life" emerged as one of their most distinctive features, lending them the name by which they are known to this day. How this common life originated and how it was perpetuated outside the recognized system of religious corporations deserves a thorough study in itself.[89] The system was an ingenious one by which upon entry brothers deeded their properties or inheritance to the *provisores* of the house (present and future) as a gift made *inter uiuentes* with no right of reclamation, and

---

[87] This document (The Hague, Royal Library, 70 H 75, ff. 151-62) will also be in my forthcoming *The Brothers of the Common life at Deventer: An Edition of Texts*, and its contents analyzed in an accompanying volume entitled *Handwritten Quires and Fraternal Devotion*.

[88] "Preterea quia fragilitas et miseria nostra uidetur exigere competentem prouisionem uictualium et aliorum necessariorum, ne tamen nos uel posteri nostri mensuram sufficiencie excedant et tot redditus sibi accumulent ut non necesse habeant manuum suarum adiumento uictum querere ... , idcirco proponimus firmiter quod nobis et posteris nostris quod in annuis perpetuis redditibus summam centum nobilium pro personis domus nostre nequaquam uolumus excedere. Sed si contingat post hoc aliqua bona ad nos deuolui, possumus unam terciam partem de hiis ad librariam nostram deputare, cetera pauperibus uolumus erogare." Hyma, *The Christian Renaissance* (n. 5 above), 468. The text that has come down from Zwolle is virtually the same: Schoengen (n. 63 above), 267.

[89] I am preparing an essay on this subject.

then made out a will with their fellow brothers named mutual heirs and testators.[90] The documents were enforced. When a brother left the community, the Brothers had to decide — as an act of charity, not of legal obligation — whether to provide him with some small gift or income in return for that which he had forfeited by joining the common life.[91] Thus the Brothers remained outside the world of corporate religious wealth and yet within a world of shared goods and poverty which they believed was mandated by the first Christian community in Jerusalem. Though some of the brothers came to the community from wealthy families and brought substantial legacies with them, both Brothers and Sisters were highly suspicious of wealthy converts (as illustrated above in the story of Johan ten Water). In this "modest" way of life, the Brothers and Sisters aimed at the community of goods which had long been the ideal for religious, but in a form that was devoid of either prestige or corporate wealth.

Spiritual office set the clergy apart, together with the legal and economic benefits that accompanied it. But there was one last characteristic of the clerical estate: learning and language, or literacy and latinity. From the twelth century onwards, "cleric" often meant simply someone literate in Latin, or alternatively someone who had been to university and read its prescribed books. With such literacy and latinity came a certain social power, as recent scholars have emphasized. While this was not inevitably resented — princes attracted clerics into their chanceries, lay people counted on local priests and clerics to draw up their legal documents — the combination of literacy, latinity, and social privilege, rooted ultimately in the knowledge of a sacred language and sacred books, could easily provoke resentment when its ends seemed self-serving, as they often did. Here too, the New Devout, while never repudiating literacy or latinity and thus remaining within the "clerical" estate broadly conceived, worked out a

---

[90] The key phrase, taken from a document prepared at Zwolle in 1455, reads: "idcirco prouisores, presbyteri et clerici ac familiares antenominati omnia et singula bona sua mobilia et immobilia ... et ea qua in futurum omni tempore contigerint obtinere, donauerunt ac tradiderunt ... sibi inuicem donatione inter uiuos, ita quod singula et omnia bona premissa erunt eis indifferenter communia, et manebunt perpetuis temporibus pro deuotis presbyteris et clericis presentibus et per eos et eorum successores sub ista forma resignationis bonorum suorum ad communionem sue societatis et dictorum bonorum assumendis." Schoengen (n. 63 above), 408. The most accessible documents on this legal form of the common life may be found in Schoengen (n. 63 above), 274-78, 405-24. The house at Alberghen has also left good records but most remain unpublished (in the provincial archive for Overijssel in Zwolle).

[91] Thus in John of Hattem's Register: "Sed post recessum suam ex gracia [that is, they were not legally bound to do do!] dedimus sibi circa centum quinquagenta florenos renenses in ualore, scilicet in pecuniis et byblia." So on leaving this brother received gratuitously coins and a book in return for his original gift, probably property which had since been sold.

distinctive approach which continues to puzzle scholars and is often labeled simply anti-intellectual. Its true contours come far more sharply into focus when viewed against the backdrop of later medieval anticlerical attitudes.

Brothers and Sisters knew and shared the sharp critique directed against the self-serving learning of the university elite. Master Geert himself set the tone here, and the Brothers remained no less skeptical of advanced learning on two counts: Socially it aimed only at gain or fame, and intellectually it ruined devotion. Thomas of Kempen captured the tone set in the 1390's when he said near the beginning of the book now called *The Imitation of Christ*: "What good is it to dispute profoundly about the Trinity if you lack humility and so displease the Trinity? Truly, deep words do not make a person holy and righteous, but a virtuous life makes one dear to God. I would rather feel compunction than know its definition. If you were to know the whole Bible by heart, and the sayings of all the philosophers, what would it profit you without the love and grace of God?"[92] He simply reiterated a sentiment found in the sayings of Florens Radewijns (from whom he had learned it): "To study much profits little unless someone studies to emend his life and to order it with all diligence toward good conduct (*bonos mores*), for the Devil knows much of Scripture and yet it profits him nothing," or again "a modest spirit is far better than much learning without devotion, for the purchase of beautiful words [one way to describe the clerical enterprise] is very easy but the making [or, uncovery: *inuentio*] of good works is difficult."[93] Yet to hedge clerical learning with such powerful moral and devotional strictures was not to rule out literacy or even advanced latinity. While the Brothers never sent their members off to university or founded a house of studies at a university, their houses in university towns, chiefly Louvain and Tübingen, participated in and contributed to the life of clerical learning there while retaining a distinctive devotional emphasis.[94] Here too a saying of Florens Radewijns, himself a master from Prague, pointed the way: "Worldly learning is very alluring. Let a man beware, therefore, lest he become too drawn toward its teachings. Let

---

[92] "Quid prodest tibi alta de Trinitate disputare, si careas humilitate, unde displiceas Trinitati? Vere alta uerba non faciunt sanctum et iustum, sed uirtuosa uita efficit Deo carum. Opto magis sentire compunctionem quam scire eius definitionem. Si scires totam bibliam exterius et omnium philosophorum dicta, quid totum prodesset sine caritate Dei et gracia?" *De imitatione Christi* 1.1, ed. Pohl (n. 11 above), 2: 6.

[93] "Parum prodest multum studere, nisi quis studeat uitam suam emendare et cum omni diligentia ad bonos mores ordinare, nam diabolus multa scit de scripturis et tamen nihil ei prodest." "Melius est modicum spiritus quam multa scientia sine deuotione, nam pulchrorum uerborum ualde leuis est emptio sed operum bonorum difficilis inuentio." Thomas, *Dialogus noviciorum* 3, ed. Pohl, 7: 206, 207.

[94] See especially Lourdaux (n. 85 above) for Louvain: and for Tübingen, Heiko A. Oberman, *The Harvest of Medieval Theology* (Cambridge, Mass., 1963) and *Masters of the Reformation* (Cambridge, 1981).

him study rather to pass through them as a means to God, and stand
unmoved in their midst."[95] Learning was a means, not an end. In keeping
with that conviction the Brothers took as one of their major tasks the care
for schoolboys. While in some instances they helped teach the lessons, their
main purpose was to bend literacy and latinity from early on in these young
student-clerics toward their proper devotional ends.[96]

Both Brothers and Sisters assumed and fostered the basic literacy
necessary for their devotions, their reading of the hours, their keeping of a
book of spiritual commonplaces (*rapiarium*), their attendance at mass, and
their copying of books. Fundamental to their spiritual discipline was private
reading in their own room, the kind of "devotions" that sound more
"modern" than most medieval forms of communal or liturgical worship.
Thus in another of his sayings Florens instructed the devout: "Force yourself
to remain in your room and read in a book. Accustom yourself until it
becomes pleasing to you, hard to go out and joyful to enter."[97] But the
books read in their rooms and the snippets copied into their "scrapbooks"
were all to serve the ends of the devotional life. When the brothers at
Deventer built a new and larger house (1441), the rector (Godfrey, 1410-50)
insisted that the library be accessed only through the librarian's adjoining
room so as to control which brothers read which books. He did not want the
Brothers reading books on the virtues treated in the fashion of the modern
schoolmen (*sancti Thome et ceterorum similium modernorum scolastice de
obediencia et materiis similibus tractancium*).[98] The pattern was consistant
and persistent. It could be found already in the reading program established
for himself around 1375 by the newly converted Geert Grote,[99] and it
obtained still in the suggested readings for novices and more advanced
devout recorded at the house in Louvain in 1526.[100] The level and style
of literacy aimed at by these Brothers and Sisters came much nearer to the
practical learning that was on the increase among their lay relatives in the
towns. This was not the theoretical learning of elite clerics, but the practical
learning of a humbler estate, learning not aimed at advancement or self-
enrichment but at spiritual devotion, a kind of spiritual book-keeping, we
might say.

The Brothers also broke with the exclusive use of Latin common to the
clerical estate. During his last months of enforced suspension from

---

[95] "Scientia secularis est ualde allectiua. Caueat ergo homo ne nimis afficiatur ad
illas, sed per illas quasi per medium studeat transire ad Deum. Maneat in medio
stare." Thomas, *Dialogus noviciorum* 3, ed. Pohl, 7: 202.

[96] Epiney-Burgard (n. 40 above).

[97] "Assuesce et coge te in camera manere et in libro legere, donec sit tibi dulce,
et graue exire et cum gaudio intrare." Thomas (as in n. 95 above), 201.

[98] *Vitae fratrum* 64.4 = Dumbar, *Analecta*, 117.

[99] Epiney-Burgard (n. 8 above), 51-103 has done an excellent analysis of this.

[100] Lourdaux (n. 85 above), 106-07.

preaching, Grote translated certain liturgical hours into Middle Dutch. These became the prayer book for the Sisters and the non-Latinate Brothers, as well as for devout laity beyond the houses of the common life; more than 800 manuscript copies are said to survive.[101] From the beginning the Brothers used the vernacular in their public reading of Scripture and in their collations or homilies, and they also made vernacular devotional books available to the Sisters and to other interested people. This too came under attack already in the 1390's and was vigorously defended by Gerard Zerbolt of Zutphen, first in Latin as part of his larger apologia and then, appropriately enough, in a vernacular version as well.[102] He argued from the fathers of the church that "the laity do well in giving themselves over to the study of the holy writings, especially books that are devout and edifying."[103] There follow many reasons and authorities (fourteen in all, though unnumbered) which allow for the reading and possessing of sacred books in the vernacular. What Gerard defended, the Devout practiced. Dirk of Herxen, longtime rector at Zwolle, prepared a lengthy book of readings in the vernacular.[104] Brother Johannes Scutken († 1423), librarian of the vernacular books at Windesheim, prepared a translation of the New Testament and the parts of the Old used in pericopes.[105] *Vitae* which the Brothers in Deventer wrote in Latin were translated for Sisters and lay people into Middle Dutch, and in turn *vitae* which the Sisters wrote for themselves in Middle Dutch were translated into Latin. In addition, numerous devotional works circulated in the vernacular among both Brothers

---

[101] See *Moderne Devotie* (n. 8 above), 93ff. for examples and a full bibliography.

[102] *Super modo vivendi*, ed. Hyma (n. 37 above), 56-71. This also circulated as an independent work in Latin: Albert Hyma, "The *De libris teutonicalibus* by Gerard Zerbolt of Zutphen", *NAKG* 16 (1921): 107-28; and Carl J. Jellouschek, "Ein mittelalterliches Gutachten über das Lesen der Bibel und sonstiger religiöser Bücher in der Volkssprache", in *Aus der Geisteswelt des Mittealters* (Munich, 1935), 1181-99. For the Middle Dutch version, see J. Deschamps, "Middelnederlandse vertalingen van Super modo vivendi (7de hoofdstuk) en De libris teutonicalibus van Gerard Zerbolt van Zutphen", *Handelingen van de Koninklijke Zuidnederlandse Maatschappij voor Taal- en Letterkunde en Geschiedenis* 14 (1960-61): 67-108, 15 (1961-62): 175-220. The question is: "Queritur utrum sit licitum sacros libros in vulgari editos seu de latino in vulgari translatos legere uel habere." And Gerard's answer is: "quod huiusmodi libros legere, dummodo heresim non contineant uel errores, et maxime si de plana materia aperte pertractent et a libris sanctorum tam stilo dictaminis quam concordia sensus non discordent, est licitum et meritorium."

[103] "Ergo sequitur quod bene faciunt layci dando se ad studium scripturarum, precipue circa libros deuotos et edificationis." *Super modo vivendi*, ed. Hyma (n. 37 above), 57.

[104] Utrecht, Universiteitsbibliotheek 3 L 16; see *Moderne Devotie* (n. 8 above), 139-42.

[105] See C. C. de Bruin, "De Moderne Devotie en de verspreiding van de volkstaal-bijbel", *OGE* 59 (1985): 344-56 with bibliography.

and Sisters, even as Gerard's own *Spiritual Ascensions*, which became the
basic devotional guide among the Devout, was translated almost immediately
into Middle Dutch.[106] Thus while most of the Brothers were conversant in
Latin and tended themselves to read and write in Latin, they worked with
and promoted the vernacular for sacred purposes, consciously giving up that
linguistic singularity or superiority which set clerics apart.

The Brothers of the Common Life, in sum, adopted a peculiar middling
status for themselves halfway between the religious and the lay, working out
distinctive forms of life at precisely those points where anticlerical reactions
were most aroused (sacerdotal status, legal privilege, material wealth, Latin
learning). But the skeptical reader may well ask in conclusion how
consciously this was done; or differently put, how much has been read back
into this movement in the light of our question. The answer here too must
be nuanced, and it discloses an increasing self-consciousness about theirs as
an independent *status* or form of life.

Thomas of Kempen, himself a professed regular, claimed that Geert Grote
intended to found a house of canons regular in order to offer an example to
the other devout (n. 35 above) — something that sounds very much like the
way professed religious conceived of themselves throughout the middle ages.
By contrast Rudolph, a contemporary of Thomas and a Brother in the house
at Deventer, had another explanation: Fearing persecution, the Brothers
established a regular branch for a few (*aliquibus*) so that "many devout"
might find "protection" or even "hiding" under the professed.[107] Whether
or not the Devout had such a strategy from the outset, it is what actually
happened. The professed canons regular at Windesheim issued a document
in 1396 declaring that the way of life adopted by the unprofessed brothers
in Deventer (their colleagues only a few years earlier) was acceptable.[108]
In a letter from the mid 1390's Florens Radewijns complained that too
many, even in those early days, were tempted by the religious option — for
him, plainly, not the main point of their movement.[109]

In the document from Windesheim (24 November 1396) and in the one
issued by the brothers at Deventer only seven days earlier (17 November
1396), the Devout described their way of life, *first*, as for those not suited
to the rigors of professed life, and *additionally* as for those differently

---

[106] van Rooij (n. 50 above), 313-12, 381-82 lists twelve complete manuscripts and
several fragments, as well as two printed editions before 1500.

[107] "Ista fuit causa mouens ad instituendum religiosos, quia in simplici communi
uita timebant sustinere persecuciones ab emulis, ut sic aliquibus existentibus religiosis
multi fratres deuoti non professi religione tuerentur seu laterent sub professis
religionem." *Vitae fratrum* 3.1 = Dumbar, *Analecta*, 13.

[108] van der Wansem (n. 34 above), 190-2.

[109] *Epistolae Florentini* 6 (in my forthcoming edition), from Johan Busch, *Liber de
viris illustribus* 15, ed. Grube (n. 6 above), 43.

inspired who chose to pursue the life of virtue in this house-community.[110] In later accounts too the Brothers continued to say, especially in defensive situations, that theirs was a way of life for those either unfit for the religious life or still in preparation. But the second reason, that this *status* represented their own vocation, their own religious choice, plainly gripped them most, though they remained hesitant to claim it outright. They were proud, for instance, that Peter Hoorn, longtime librarian at Deventer, was content with this *status*, and had rebuffed those who tempted him to join the professed religious.[111]

Only in documents that come from the 1450's, a good two generations after their founding, do some brothers argue for their position outright. Gabriel Biel places this matter at the outset of his little treatise on the common life, arguing that the term "religion" is used properly of all those who imitate Christ and the Jerusalem community and only by extension, or even improperly (*abusiue et improprie*), of the professed.[112] An anonymous apology makes the same point: Their way of life, the basic Christian *religio* established by Christ himself, requires no further approval of the pope and no additional institutionalization as a professed religion (i.e. religious order).[113] Both made the argument from a defensive stance: It

---

[110] First the words of the brothers from Deventer: "... qui quibusdam obstaculis prepediti ad ingressum religionis non sunt idonei, uel aliter secundum suam uoluntatem inspirati religionem ingredi non proponunt, sed in ipsa domo perseueranter usque ad finem uolunt in diuino seruitio permanere, ac in humilitate, castitate, ceterisque uirtutibus uiuentes ... ." Then the description seven days later by the professed at Windesheim: "... adhuc plurimi in seculo remanserunt qui quibusdam corporis uel anime defectibus prepediti religionem ingredi non ualebant, aut certe alterius propositi aut aliter diuinitus inspirati (nam diuersa sunt dona et modi uocationum) religionem ingredi non ualebant seu non intendebant ... ." van der Wansem, (n. 34 above), 189, 191.

[111] "Et tanto amore domui nostre et exerciciis est colligatus ut nunquam post ingressum per inconstanciam vacillaret; sed si aliquando siue monachi siue quicumque alii eum ad alium ordinem siue uite modum niterentur attrahere, non sine rubore ab ipso recedebant. Omnium enim qui se a domo nostra retrahere conabantur manus pii zeli dente momordit." *Vita Petri Hoorn* 1 = Dumbar, *Analecta*, 149.

[112] W. M. Landeen, "Gabriel Biel and the Devotio Moderna in Germany", *Research Studies* 28 (1960): 79-80.

[113] "Religio enim christiana que prior et maior est omnium religionum approbatissima est, utputa a Christo summo legislatore instituta et approbata et a fidelibus deinceps obseruata, nec indigens aliqua approbatione sedis apostolice. ... Ad quam obseruanciam consiliorum Christi non requiritur quod superadditur alia religio, cum in christiana religione perfectissime obseruata sunt et obseruari possunt. ... [consilia euangelica] ... que perfecte ymmo perfectissime in ipsa christiana religione adhuc sine assumpcione facticie religionis impleri possunt. Longe enim hoc erat a mentibus sanctorum patrum qui religiones instituerunt tantipendere suas regulas quasi ad ipsa solum limitaretur et retorqueretur obseruancia consiliorum Christi ... ." Emmerich, Gymnasialbibliothek MS 5, f. 61v, 64r-v. For providing me with a photocopy of this

was still taken for granted everywhere that the way to be "religious" was to profess religion. Yet by claiming priority for a "Christian religion" instituted by Christ and exemplified in the Jerusalem community these brothers had taken an important step toward justifying a way of life that was not religious or clerical or lay.

But was it possible in the middle ages to maintain such a peculiar *status* and not be driven either into heresy or profession? The Brothers and Sisters never questioned any points of doctrine, and were never charged with heresy after the opening disputes about the common life. But in the course of the fifteenth century they acquired ever more of the features of a religious order: endowments (even if they came from the work of their own hands), statutes that became relatively common among them, a colloquy at which the heads of all houses met annually, visitations from the heads of other houses, more lands and buildings making their houses look ever less like an ordinary "house", and eventually churches of their own. The pressures to assume the form of a religious order were great, and the canons soon far outnumbered the Brothers, despite the original plan to have it the other way around; Sisters, by contrast, were to far outnumber the canonesses. At the time of the Reformation, Brothers' houses were generally closed down like other religious corporations. Yet the Brothers flourished most in the second half of the fifteenth century, and into the sixteenth century they retained their distinctive form of life. To conclude, the Brothers knew in their hearts, indeed in their very bones, the anticlericalism that rippled through late medieval towns, in whose centers they continued to live. They did not question the sacerdotal hierarchy, though they kept at a distance from it, and their writings rarely referred to popes or bishops or ecclesiological disputes. For themselves they limited the number of priests in their houses, and encouraged an ethos in which laymen, clerics, and priests lived in common with laymen devising their own copybooks and spiritual exercises and priests working in gardens and fields. They did not question the theology of the eucharist, though they thought the multiplication of priests and altars in their day had lowered rather than raised its dignity. They came to enjoy ecclesiastical status; yet they remained, through most of their history, within the confines of their local parishes, and they worked cooperatively with local city magistrates. They used civil law, not the law and vows of a religious corporation, to establish a common life which was to guarantee poverty and community at the same time. Though conversant in Latin, they worked in the vernacular with those whom they sought to encourage in devotion. Thus they devised a way to live religiously in accordance with the New Testament and the Desert Fathers, while avoiding the "diabolical and overweening ambition" to enjoy the privileges and wealth of the clerical estate.

---

manuscript, I am deeply indebted to Kaspar Elm. This *Apologia* will be included in my new edition of texts.

ANTICLERICALISM AMONG THE LOLLARDS

JOHN VAN ENGEN

University of Notre Dame

The Lollards resemble the New Devout in several noteworthy features. Both originated with zealous and somewhat crabbed secular clerics who died prematurely in 1384. Both founders, themselves trained and active as clerics, enveighed against the clerical establishment of their day in clerical Latin and public sermons. Both founders in turn spawned movements among the people that flourished in the generation following their deaths (1380's-1410's), though the exact relationship of the Lollards and the New Devout to the teachings and intentions of John Wyclif and Geert Grote remains a matter of scholarly dispute. Both movements repudiated the evils of the Christian church in their day and aimed to establish an "authentic" Christian community. Both placed great emphasis upon teaching the word of God in the people's own language, be it in the clandestine gatherings of the Lollards or in the public collations of the Devout. And both formed alternative communities in which, among other things, the distinction between clergymen and laypeople shrank in importance, even if it did not disappear altogether.

There were, to be sure, also great differences. Wyclif was a master of theology, Grote a master of arts with extensive training in law. The Devout drew their adherents ever closer to a semi-religious way of life (common property, a customary, daily hours of prayer, a superior to be obeyed, and the like), while the Lollards drew theirs toward a semi-lay way of life (marriage, local organization and teaching, the vernacular throughout). The Devout, it might be said, put in place an alternative that outdid the established clergy (achieving community of life and spiritual discipline apart from vows), while the Lollards appropriated for "every good Christian" clerical functions they saw as compromised (preaching, teaching, and so on). The Devout, like their founder, largely avoided theological issues, venerating the eucharist and respecting the hierarchy, even if their writings said relatively little about either topic. The Lollards, like their founder, took on theological topics, and perpetuated views of the eucharist, of vows, and of the hierarchy that were quickly adjudged heretical. The turning point for each came at the Council of Constance: The Devout were exonerated from charges of heresy and their way of life approved, the Lollards and the Hussites definitively condemned.

No brief article, especially one essentially reliant on the work of others, can attempt a thorough analysis of the part played by anticlericalism in the

shaping of Lollard thought and practice. It can, however, raise again the
question broached earlier: What were the limits and the possibilities of
anticlericalism within the medieval worldview? Wyclif and the Lollards
plainly tested those limits far more vigorously than did the New Devout. For
by questioning transubstantiation, whatever the original philosophical
motivation, and then sacramental confession, Wyclif and the Lollards struck
at the heart of that power thought peculiar to priests. And by questioning the
clerical claim to property and linking property-holding to a "state of grace"
rather than church office, they undermined the claims to material power
which lay at the heart of much clerical privilege and much anticlerical
irritation.

For all the differences between a theologian and a lawyer, an Englishman
and a Netherlander, a man seeking patronage and advancement and a man
repudiating it, there were several themes common to their critique of the
clerical establishment. Both identified simony, the corruption of spiritual
office by material considerations, as the crucial factor, Wyclif devoting a
whole book to it; and both contended that simony was mortal sin, rendering
those clerics guilty of it unfit to administer the sacraments.[1] Whatever
subtle qualifiers each inserted to parry the charge of Donatism, the thrust
was clear and so perceived by contemporaries, friend and foe alike:
"Simoniac priests", lost in mortal sin, were to be avoided. Both Grote and
Wyclif, moreover, dreamed of a new order of "poor priests" who would lead
an authentic Christian community, for Grote probably the original impulse
toward gathering the New Devout, for Wyclif — though this is less clear —
the core of his earliest Lollard disciples.[2] Both Grote and Wyclif, secular
clerics all their lives, also turned against the professed religious orders, the
ordinary medieval option for a model community. Grote set about to work
out his own religious way, as had John Ruusbroec before him, while Wyclif
actively campaigned against the "private religions" and the "possessioners".[3]
The result, inevitably, was that monks, and especially friars, emerged as
their most severe critics. Both likewise launched powerful invectives against
a propertied church. Geert Grote, more modestly, gave up his own property
and fostered a community of property for poor priests and clerics; John
Wyclif vigorously attacked clerical wealth and any lordship exercized by
those outside a state of grace. The political settings for their critiques of

---

[1] See Friedrich de Boor, *Wyclifs Simoniebegriff. Die theologischen und kirchen-politischen Grundlagen der Kirchenkritik John Wyclifs* (Halle, 1970).

[2] This has never been properly investigated owing to the fascination with the broader lay Lollard movement; see the interesting and apposite hints in Michael Wilks, "*Reformatio regni*: Wyclif and Hus as Leaders of Religious Protest Movements", in *Schism, Heresy and Religious Protest*, ed. D. Baker, Studies in Church History 9 (London, 1972), 109-30, esp. 124-27.

[3] For the long tradition of hostility on the part of secular clerics, see Penn Szittya, *The Antifraternal Tradition in Medieval Literature* (Princeton, 1986).

property and the priesthood — not to say the political stakes — differed vastly as well. Geert Grote worked with city magistrates in a modest town and had connections to the court of one bishop; John Wyclif became caught up in the court intrigues of John of Gaunt, was associated in the minds of some with a peasant rebellion, and tried to influence the ecclesiastical policies of an entire kingdom. Both, finally, spent the last year of their lives out of favor and devoting, it seems, more attention to vernacular materials, Grote by translating devotional and prayer books, Wyclif — though this is less clear — by fostering his teachings in the vernacular.[4]

Intriguing as these comparisons may be, Wyclif and Grote nonetheless stood in a long line of clerics attacking other clerics, whether that arose from group rivalries (evident especially in the attack on the religious), personal idiosyncracies (both often described as "cranky"), or reform impulses — with something of all three doubtless at work. But the teachings of these two secular clerics found a large and persistent resonance among the people. Whatever that owed to the inspiring vision of an authentic Christian community, it drew as well upon a darker side which included latent anticlerical resentments.

Eleven years after Wyclif's death, during a session of parliament, several Lollards reportedly tacked to the doors of the hall at Westminster a kind of pamphlet or manifesto, written in the vernacular, containing twelve denunciations of the English church. These Lollards described themselves as "poor men, treasurers of Christ and his apostles" and ascribed the "blind and leprous" condition of the church to "the doing of arrogant prelates, borne up by the curried favors of the religious, who have multiplied to become a great and onerous burden to the people of England."[5] Most texts in which orthodox churchmen singled out the irregularities of Lollards began with their suspect view of the eucharist and confession. In this public manifesto directed by Lollards to the people of the realm, however, the first issue taken up was the church's temporal wealth: When the English church began to grow senile (or, mad: *dote = delirare*) with temporal goods like her stepmother in Rome, the Lollards declared, faith, hope, and charity took flight from her. This general conclusion, it went on, was confirmed — calling in effect upon the people themselves — by experience and custom. The Lollard manifesto next raised for public discussion the priesthood itself: This priesthood from Rome with all its rites and blessings, said to be greater in power than the angels, is "of little power" and not the priesthood instituted by Christ. The manifesto lashed out, third, at clerical celibacy,

---

[4] See now Margaret Aston, "Wyclif and the Vernacular", in *From Ockham to Wyclif*, ed. A. Hudson, M. Wilks (Oxford, 1987), 281-330.

[5] See the Middle English text edited by Anne Hudson, *Selections from English Wycliffite Writings* (Cambridge, 1978), 24, with commentary on 150-51. There is a Latin version (probably a translation of the English original) in W. W. Shirley, ed., *Fasciculi zizaniorum* (London, 1858), 360ff., that lacks this introductory paragraph.

another practice that set the clerical caste apart, contending that it was not
mandated by Scripture and — invoking again the people's prejudices — that
it engendered only "sodomy", for which reason all the professed (*the privat
religions, begynneris of this synne*) deserved to be dispensed with (*anullid*).
Only in fourth place did it take up the eucharist as an object of idolatry.

Whether the Lollards were themselves driven by anticlerical convictions,
or hoped only to draw more effectively on the people's resentments, their
ordering of the church's ills plainly presupposed the kind of critique to be
found in *Piers Plowman* and said to represent a "new anticlericalism"
widespread in that era.[6] Attempts to explain or account for this "anticlericalism" in simplistic social categories, however, have not proved
convincing. In the first generation many Latinate scholars[7] and a number of
noblemen[8] supported the Lollard vision of an authentic Christian community, though they were never successful in winning the support of the
royal court, a critical difference perhaps with what transpired in Bohemia.[9]
Only after the Oldcastle Rebellion and increased repression did the Lollards
assume ever more the role of the hunted and the dispossessed little
people.[10] During the first generation theirs was a radical position but one
that resonated among many people of different social and ecclesiastical
stations, drawing in common on that bundle of resentments scholars have
lumped together as anticlericalism.

To contend that "confession should be made only to God and to no priest,
for no priest has power to remit sin", as did at one time Hawisia Moone of
Norwich,[11] may have arisen from a fresh reading of Scripture on the part
of the Lollard leaders and in fact revived a dispute waged among twelfth-
century theologians. But its appeal was to eliminate one of the least liked
and potentially most embarrassing duties imposed by the church, that of
annual confession at Lent. Sins needed confessing, to be sure, but to God
and in the heart, not to a priest in the sight of all in some corner of a parish
church. Similarly, to contend that "only consent of love between a man and
a woman, without any verbal contract or church solemnization, ... is

---

[6] See Wendy Scase, *Piers Plowman and the New Anticlericalism* (Cambridge,
1989).

[7] See now Anne Hudson, "Wycliffism in Oxford 1381-1411", and Maurice Keen,
"The Influence of Wyclif", in *Wyclif in his Times*, ed. A. Kenny (Oxford, 1986), 67-
84, 127-46.

[8] K. B. McFarlane, *Lancastrian Kings and Lollard Knights* (Oxford, 1972), to
compare with W. T. Waugh, "The Lollard Knights", *Scottish Historical Review* 11
(1913-14): 55-92.

[9] M. Wilks (n. 2 above), 109-30.

[10] J. A. F. Thomson, *The Later Lollards 1414-1520* (London, 1965).

[11] Norman Tanner, ed., *Heresy Trials in the Diocese of Norwich, 1428-31* (London,
1977), 140.

sufficient for the sacrament of marriage"[12] was to repel the steadily encroaching intrusion of churchmen into this most basic of human arrangements.

If indeed negative resentments fueled the Lollard movement, their effects would likely be felt most quickly in material matters. Lollards were commonly charged with refusal to pay tithes and other fees accruing to local curates. Thus Hawisia Moone also foreswore the position that "every man may lawfully withdraw and withhold tithes and offerings from priests and curates and give them to the poor people, which is more pleasing to God."[13] In a vernacular pamphlet designed to help Lollards answer the sixteen most common charges brought by bishops, they were instructed to answer that they were indeed bound to pay tithes "to that end that curates do their office as God has commanded them. And if they live as curates should and expend the goods of the church to the worship of God on themselves and other poor people, then the tithes would be paid out to the poor and needy, for they themselves would be poor."[14] This reply may represent something of a fudge, for in many texts the monies given to curates were described simply as alms, voluntary gifts in support of the ministry. So their position was reported at the Blackfriars Council already in 1382.[15] The point for the Lollards was not the removal of support — as in most modern forms of anticlericalism — but the removal of obligation and of required support for undeserving priests. Parsons were to be supported as parsons but also and especially because they were poor and faithful and worked for their living.[16] Whether then tithes and other spiritual incomes were "owed" in the case of a poor and faithful priest, or represented purely voluntary gifts removable and transferable at the will of the people, apparently remained under dispute among the Lollards themselves.[17] But the appeal of the Lollards's position to anticlerical resentment was plain. Theirs was not just a positive vision of voluntary support offered to the likes of Chaucer's "povre persoun ... that Cristes gospel trewely wolde preche, ... ful looth ... to cursen for his tithes ... ." Their stance projected a vision of lifting from the people's shoulders forever this hated material burden, casting off the galling obligation to support even undeserving clerics.

---

[12] Tanner (n. 11 above), 140.

[13] Tanner (n. 11 above), 141.

[14] Hudson (n. 5 above), 21.

[15] "Item quod decime sunt pure eleemosyne, et quod parochiani possunt propter peccata suorum curatorum eas detinere et ad libitum aliis conferre." *Fasciculi* (n. 5 above), 280-81.

[16] Thus from a sermon quoted by Anne Hudson, *The Premature Reformation* (Oxford, 1988), 343.

[17] Materials on this point gathered by Hudson (n. 16 above), 337-46.

This was still more true of the position on clerical property which the Lollards inherited from Wyclif, namely, that all temporal goods or lands possessed by the clergy and not attached directly to their spiritual offices were necessarily illicit, an abomination which temporal lords were encouraged to remove. This too the Archbishop of Canterbury understood already in 1382.[18] And this too Hawisia Moone foreswore, namely, "that the temporal lords and temporal men may lawfully take all possessions and temporal goods from all men of holy church and from all bishops and prelates, both horse and harness, and give their goods to poor people, and [that] the temporal men are bound thereto on pain of mortal sin."[19] Within the Lollard movement this grew into a full scale demand for disendowment, which circulated among the people just after 1400 as a bill proposed to parliament, whether or not it was ever formally presented.[20] The proposed bill ended in fact with an appeal that "these worldly clerics, bishops, abbots, and priors which are such worldly lords be forced to live off their spiritual incomes" and perform their spiritual offices.

However radical the demand for disendowment might appear (and for it too there were earlier precedents), and however novel-sounding their stands on marriage and confession (at least for the fourteenth century, not the eleventh), these Lollard teachings still spared the priesthood as such. But in their public manifesto of 1395 an attack on the received priestly office constituted their second main point. Both the Devout and the Lollards, reacting to the steady emphasis since the twelfth century on office and privilege, insisted upon a radical "moralization" of what constituted a good priest. But whereas the Devout simply resisted choosing the priesthood for themselves and placed most emphasis upon personal progress in virtue, Lollards set about redefining the priesthood. Bishops accused them of teaching that "there should be but one rank of priesthood in the church of God, and every good man is a priest and has the power to preach the word of God" and "that priests were not ordained to say masses or matins but only to teach and preach the word of God." In the answers Lollards were taught to give to such charges, they professed to recognize one priestly office with various powers of jurisdiction (essentially the orthodox position

---

[18] "Item asserere quod est contra sacram scripturam quod uiri ecclesiastici habeant possessiones temporales." and "Item quod domini temporales possint, ad arbitrium eorum, auferre bona temporalia ab ecclesiasticis habitualiter delinquentibus, uel quod populares possint ad eorum arbitrium dominos delinquentes corrigere." *Fasciculi* (n. 5 above), 279, 280. See Michael Wilks, "Predestination, Property, and Power", in *Papers of the Ecclesiastical History Society*, ed. G. J. Cuming, Studies in Church History 2 (London, 1965), 220-36, and "Royal Patronage and Anti-Papalism from Ockham to Wyclif", in *From Ockham to Wyclif*, 135-63.

[19] Tanner (n. 11 above), 141.

[20] For the Middle English text, see Hudson (n. 5 above) 135-37, with her commentary on 203-07.

since the later twelfth century), and limited this preaching power to husbands within their households.[21] But more radical charges (and views) plainly emanated from their circles, as evidenced by the record of heresy trials in Norwich. Hawisia Moone came to renounce the position that "every man and every woman being in good life out of [mortal] sin is as good priest and has [as] much power of God in all things as any ordained priest, be he pope or bishop", along with its moral counterpart, "that he only that is most holy and most perfect in living on earth is a true [verry] pope, and these mass-singers that are called priests are no priests but lecherous and covetous men and false deceivers of the people."[22] So too the public manifesto of 1395, in railing against an "idolatrous" view of the eucharist, explained: "For we suppose that in this way every man and woman true to God's law may make the sacrament of the bread without any such miracle."[23]

All these charges and countercharges have produced a scholarly debate on whether lay men and women actually acted in priestly capacities within these Lollard communities.[24] They doubtless did on some occasions, above all in teaching, though it remains hard to distinguish reality from rumor and innuendo. What deserves notice, however, and bears comparison with the New Devout, is this emphasis upon teaching, and especially teaching Scripture in the vernacular language in their own groups or "conventicles". Here again there is not so much a repudiation as an intense alternative appropriation of priestly functions — though there appears to be no Lollard counterpart to the Devout's concern with ordered prayer. Equally similar is the consistent moralization, of rejecting immoral priests and of raising faithful or virtuous lay people nearly to the same status as priests, in communal practice among the Devout, in principle apparently among the Lollards. Penitential practices, central to medieval notions of the religious life, offer a good point of comparison. Within the ordered life of their houses the Devout imposed upon themselves austere forms of penance that made them look virtually like religious. Lollards, again to follow Hawisia Moone, rejected any obligatory penance laid on them by a priest, "for sufficient penance for all manner of sins is for every person to abstain from lying, backbiting [achtersprake was a big item among the Devout as well] and evil-doing, and no man is bound to do any other penance."[25]

Finally, and in keeping with their position on enjoined penances (which usually fell under the auspices of canon law), the Lollards also attacked the law itself, that other bastion of clerical privilege. Though Wyclif was

---

[21] Hudson (n. 5 above), 19, 22.

[22] Tanner (n. 11 above), 142, 141.

[23] Hudson (n. 5 above), 25.

[24] See Hudson (n. 16 above), 326-26 for a review of the evidence, and Margaret Aston, "Lollard Women Priests?" *JEH* 31 (1980): 441-61.

[25] Tanner (n. 11 above), 141.

himself a secular cleric subject to and protected by the canon law, he and
the Lollards increasingly contrasted "man's law" with God's law, setting
Scripture (or their reading of it) against the canon law of the church.[26] But
except when engaged in such defensive maneuvers, they seem generally to
have bothered less with reigning in the clergy's legal privileges than with
eliminating their intrusions into lay life, as in the cases of marriage and
penance. Thus Hawisia Moone had once held "that it is no sin for any
person to do the contrary of the precepts of holy church" and that "the
censures of holy church, the sentences and cursings and suspensions given
by prelates and bishops, were not to be dreaded or feared, for God blesses
the cursings of bishops."[27] In a more apologetic form, the Lollards
explained that only God's censure was binding, not that falsely done by
prelates,[28] a much milder point and one frequently asserted by lay powers
in the later middle ages when the power of excommunication was so widely
misused. All the same, these Lollards had cast off the yoke of clerical
authority imposed on them by way of the church's law.

To indicate the role of anticlerical resentments in Lollardy's appeal, this
brief essay began with their own public manifesto. It will end, fittingly, by
examining the public response of state and church, which is to say, their
perception of the nature of this threat. Monks and friars generated doctrinal
analyses and refutations of Lollard teachings in abundance, and they nearly
always began with the eucharist or some other exposed doctrinal point such
as predestination or ecclesiology, an approach true already of the Blackfriars' Council of 1382.[29] But the two main public responses, the royal
statute of 1401[30] and the archepiscopal statutes of 1407/09,[31] took a
different line in attacking these sectarians: They both objected first and
foremost to the Lollards' appropriation of the preaching office. The main
threat to the religious well-being of the realm, as the royal statute relays it
from the bishops, is that these "sectarians" have "usurped the office of
preaching contrary to divine and church law" and under a guise of sanctity
are "preaching and teaching, publicly and privately", all manner of new and
heretical doctrines. They hold illicit gatherings, they keep schools, they write
books, and they instruct the people in sedition, even attacking the laws and
liberties of the English church.[32] What exactly should be concluded from

---

[26] Hudson (n. 16 above), 378-80. Compare M. Hurley, "Scriptura sola: Wyclif and
his Critics", *Traditio* 16 (1960): 275-352.

[27] Tanner (n. 11 above), 142.

[28] Hudson (n. 5 above), 19, 21.

[29] See *Fasciculi* (n. 5 above), 275-82.

[30] *Statutes of the Realm*, 2: 125-28.

[31] D. Wilkins, *Concilia Magnae Britanniae et Hiberniae* (London, 1737; repr.,
1964), 3: 314-19.

[32] "... contra legem diuinam et ecclesiasticam predicacionis officium temere
usurpantes, diuersas nouas doctrinas et opiniones iniquas hereticas et erroneas, eidem

these charges has kept scholars digging and debating for a long time.[33] But even allowing for a measure of rhetorical exaggeration, the magnates of the realm perceived the Lollards not only to have threatened the faith but also to have appropriated the clerical instruments of the faith, the preaching and teaching, the gatherings, the schools, the books, the laws — indeed all that belonged to and protected the clerical monopoly. And so the royal statutes provided that no one might preach without prior permission of the diocesan bishop, nor might anyone teach or write without submitting their views to the determinations of holy church, nor might they keep in their possession heterodox books, and so on. The king, at the urging of the bishops, had taken up the defense of the faith, as, to be sure, he represented his purposes in this statute: Those caught and refusing to recant were to be burnt in a high place before the people, "that such punishment may strike fear to the minds of others, whereby no such wicked doctrine and heretical and erroneous opinons, nor their authors and fautors in the said realm and dominions against the catholic faith, christian law, and determination of the holy church be sustained or in any wise suffered." But in so doing this statute also reasserted — now, ironically, with the power of secular courts — the power and control of the clerical caste charged with overseeing the faith.

Six years later the Archbishop registered his views and purposes even more plainly in a synodical statute consisting of twelve provisions (as in n. 31 above). His first forbade any lay or religious person to assume for themselves the office of preaching, in either Latin or the vernacular, without diocesan permission, a mandate elaborated in two additional statutes treating such unauthorized preaching. His fourth and fifth provisions went on to forbid any preaching, teaching, or disputing about the sacraments and especially about the eucharist which was contrary to the accepted teachings of holy church. Again the substantive or theological issue at stake was manifest but the archbishop's way of dealing with the perceived problem was to stop all those who have taken to preaching and teaching about it in unauthorized ways — which might include in this case some sympathetic

---

fidei ac sanctis determinacionibus ecclesie sacrosancte contrarias, peruerse et maliciose infra dictum regnum in diuersis locis sub simulate sanctitatis colore predicant et docent hiis diebus publice et occulte, ac de huiusmodi secta nephandisque doctrinis et opinionibus conuenticulas et confederaciones illicitas faciunt, scolas tenent et exercent, libros conficiunt atque scribunt, populum nequiter instruunt et informant, et ad sedicionem seu insurrectionem excitant quantum possunt, et magnas dissenciones et diuisiones in populum faciunt, ac alia diuersa enormia auditui horrenda indies perpetrant et committunt in dicte fidei catholice et doctrine ecclesie sacrosancte subuersionem diuinique cultus diminucionem, ac eciam in destructionem status iurium et libertatum dicte ecclesie anglicane. ..." *Statutes* (n. 30 above), 2: 126.

[33] See, for instance, Margaret Aston, "Lollardy and Sedition", *PaP* 17 (1960): 1-44; and Hudson (n. 16 above), 180-200 on the schools.

clerics as well as lay Lollard leaders. The next two provisions aimed to halt the circulation of books: no book of Wyclif's was permitted prior to a careful examination of its contents, and no English translation of Scripture issuing from Wyclif and his circle. The next provision forbade disputing about the laws of the church. And this statute ended with the Archbishop making inquisitional arrangements to seek out these sectarians. For the archbishop as for the king, what needed stopping was the unauthorized appropriation of clerical functions, preaching, teaching, books, laws and the like, through which novel and erroneous teachings had infected the English church.

But we must return, to conclude, to our comparison. Why were Lollards condemned "to be burned in a high place" and driven underground, while the New Devout survived initial resistance to become a part of the established scene in the Low Countries? And did the difference in their treatment have anything to do with the limits of anticlericalism in the medieval world? Two crucial points first, and then some tentative remarks on the last question. From the outset Wyclif and the Lollards were perceived to preach "new and heretical" teachings, most often associated with views on the eucharist, the heart of lay and priestly devotion in the middle ages, and as well on the divine plan of salvation (predestination with attendant shifts in ecclesiology). The Devout, despite recurrent rumblings and rumors, were never charged with any substantive heresy, and were themselves at pain to distance their houses from the suspicion of heresy. Had friars in the Low Countries been able to charge the Devout with error on some point of doctrine, their movement would doubtless have been seriously undermined. Thus, where the Devout argued successfully in the end that vernacular books and scriptures only helped foster devotion, English bishops regarded these English books chiefly as vehicles for spreading heresy and dissent among the people. Second, Wyclif and the Lollards took on, intentionally, the central powers of church, state, and learning in an entire kingdom. The Devout operated largely in one diocese, in a de-centralized political setting (where they could flee to the next diocese or principality in times of trouble), apart from any university (until the later developments in Louvain and Tübingen), and without consciously challenging any major authorities. This meant that the struggle was virtually over for the Devout once they had gained a friendly hearing in the episcopal court at Utrecht (which happened in 1401, the same year as the royal statute was issued against the Lollards).

Yet, even if doctrinal fears and local political circumstances played a decisive role in outlawing the Lollards, the outspoken anticlericalism of the Lollard party, their outright attacks on both clerical property and priestly prerogatives, transgressed the limits of what the established order, either lay or clerical, could tolerate. This, beyond their precise teachings, was at once their appeal and their undoing. Not only bishops and friars but kings and noblemen too were threatened by these religious enthusiasts who took into their own hands all the elements — preaching, teaching, writing, presiding over the sacraments, determining rites and rules — over which a divinely sanctioned clerical caste had presided for generations. On the other hand, those who harbored age-old resentments against the clerical combination of material privilege and spiritual presidence, or who came to doubt the divine sanction for it, or who rebelled against the abusive character and practices of those presiding, found in the Lollards an inspiring vision of a more authentic religious community. For precisely these reasons, both taken together, the debate about Lollardy in its first generation proved much more widespread and confused, as recent scholars have demonstrated, than many earlier protrayals of sharp division, of heresy and repression.

But for all the force and appeal of anticlerical themes, the Lollard community had its own leaders, its own purified curates or "poor priests". For even though Lollards attacked clerical property and priestly prerogatives, they did not eliminate priestly roles as such. Someone still had to preach and teach the Scriptures, even if they did so in the vernacular; someone still had to lead the eucharistic celebration, even if it was some "good" man or woman not ordained by a simoniac bishop; and these good curates or poor priests had still to receive material support, whether it was reckoned voluntary or obligatory. There is every reason to believe, moreover, that something of a priestly caste developed and persisted among the outlawed Lollards as well, indeed was necessary to guarantee their continuity. Thus anticlerical themes played a role in Lollard history that was both crucial and ironic: It contributed to the strength of Lollardy's persistent appeal in the face of persecution and as well to the violence of the reaction when church and state felt threatened by all those who would alienate clerical property and re-appropriate priestly roles; yet it never eliminated, or intended to eliminate, a role for legitimate priestly mediators in medieval Christendom.

THE CHURCH AND ITS CRITICS IN TIME OF CRISIS

FRANTIŠEK GRAUS[*]

edited and translated by
DOROTHEA A. CHRIST

Basel, Switzerland

I

In Part Two of his book Pest — Geissler — Judenmorde, *František Graus claims that the sense of crisis in the fourteenth century was closely linked to the church. What is "the church"? It is the community of the baptised, represented by the ecclesiastical hierarchy and headed by the pope. Although its influence was far-reaching, the church was not the only power to shape human ideas and desires. A series of other significant "parallel systems" existed alongside the church. Graus uses this terminology to avoid pejorative expressions like "superstition". He emphasizes the lack of uniformity within the church as well as within society. Different groups had diverse expectations and views of the church, and thus criticised and attacked the institutional hierarchy from a wide range of perspectives. For what reasons might one be both subject to and critical of the church? First Graus analyses the "Functions and Contradictions of the System" (Chapter 1). The foundations of faith are the Bible and the traditions of the church, but these themselves are full of contradictions. Graus highlights the contrast between the Old and the New Testaments which could not be resolved — even by allegorical exegesis. The doctrine of salvation clashes with the idea of the fallen world. Despite the actions of the historical Jesus, the world still awaits eternal salvation, continually threatened by judgement and by Satan.*

[*] František Graus died on May 1, 1989. His work on late medieval culture and society has not yet been made available to an English reading public. The editors have invited Dr. Dorothea A. Christ, one of the last students of Professor Graus, to translate these key passages and to include the introductions which place them within the broader context of Graus' work. With the kind permission of Vera Graus and the publishing house of Vandenhoeck & Ruprecht, the translated selections and comments here serve together as a continous essay. The excerpts have been edited yet citations to literature relevant for the theme of this volume have been retained. For complete documentation and bibliography the reader may refer to *Pest — Geissler — Judenmorde. Das 14. Jahrhundert als Krisenzeit*, Veröffentlichungen des Max-Planck-Instituts für Geschichte 86 (Göttingen, 1987; 2nd rev. ed., 1988), 86-93, 144-53.

How does the believer deal with the dilemma of election (personal salvation); with the relationship between the church of the chosen and the visible church? Views of God are similarly inconsistent. Is he judge or father? Is he omnipotent — the only power to conquer Satan — and omniscient — the only one to know who will be saved or condemned? Or is God merciful and therefore unable to banish the majority of his children to hell? The problem of justice emerges here, and it is not only divine justice which comes into focus. Why are Christians tortured and murdered? Why do Christian armies lose battles against pagans, why do crusades fail? Fundamental discrepancies in the foundations of the church also appear when one considers the relationship between ecclesiastical and worldly powers. Christ claims a kingdom not of this world yet his followers are members of a visible church and subjects of earthly kingdoms, which Christ himself established. The poverty of Jesus clashes with the opulence of the church; the church must decide between the poor child in the cradle or the king of kings. A compromise between the institutional, official church and the divine mandate of Christ's disciples was necessary. The dogma of apostolic succession gave stability to the church, but it often attracted criticism from those who claimed to have a "divine calling". This kind of polarisation also pertains to depictions of women, due to the key roles both Eve and Mary played in the Biblical description of salvation history. Church teaching regarding their images oscillated accordingly between adoring worship and malicious caricature.

The most obvious contradictions were found in the lives of clerics, whose actions refuted their own teaching. They provoked criticism while undercutting the assertion that the church rules over all souls. Here Graus calls upon the "parallel systems" which also claimed the allegiance of the populace. He includes Judaism, various heresies, so-called superstitious practices ("popular piety"), courtly love, magic, and a new appreciation for the Aristotelian philosophy of antiquity. Finally, apart from faith and the "parallel systems" there is also the simple absence of faith.

In the fourteenth century, there certainly was not yet a philosophical formula for atheism, as in the Enlightenment.[1] Certain ideas and practices were widespread, generally known and accepted — but apart from this there was a frequently documented "lack of faith", which could develop into numerous shades and practices of atheism. The philosophers of the Enlightenment were not the first to maintain that clerics invented the devil and hell in order to terrify believers. This assertion had already been made by the "heretics" of

---

[1] Lucien Febvre underlines this rightly in *Le problème de l'incroyance au XVIe siècle. La reliqion de Rabelais*, L'évolution de l'humanité 53 (Paris, 1942). Febvre, on the whole, seems to have overestimated the "religiosity" of the time.

the fourteenth century.[2] The late medieval world of faith was not uniform, but often contradictory; the church always perceived itself as endangered and threatened. Inherent contradictions and the lack of uniformity in the basics of belief were not mere games for those concerned but rather part of their life. During the fourteenth century only some of the inconsistencies were clear. Individual periods can be differentiated by identifying those discrepancies which reached popular consciousness and how intensely a change in consciousness was felt. Despite all the immanent contradictions within church teaching, the entire medieval system of ideals, which could be burdened in a variety of ways, was for the longest time hardly threatened; it completely dominated the thoughts and experience of many people. The reason for this lies not only in the greatly varied means by which the ecclesiastical hierarchy exercised power, but also in its monopoly over preaching (propaganda),[3] and in the intricate system of the late medieval inquisition, all of which were all used and displayed unscrupulously. These mechanisms, which could stifle doubts about basic dogma at their root and could neutralise or divert criticism, along with the flexibility of the system and its built-in "safety-valves", accounted for the secure longevity of the church.

The obvious defects of the church — the contradiction between the preaching and the life-styles of numerous clerics, monks and nuns — were not the only sources of criticism. People were also amazed that God would allow all of this to happen; they thought it a miracle that God's judgement had not yet fallen upon the church.[4] Rarely did the church use force to counter this kind of criticism. Instead a system of particular and different ideas was created in order to divert and channel discontent: the ideal monk or nun in contrast to the slovenly priest, the pious layman juxtaposed to the "impious" Jew, the God-given feudal lord against the wicked heretic — all concrete stereotypes that were always at hand and which "lived" in harmony together; many more could be added to these. In many ways, the church was

---

[2] "... nec debes timere dyabolum nec infernum nec purgatorium, quia vere nichil sunt in natura, set excogitata per clericos et sacerdotes ad timorem hominum, set homo habens conscienciam est ipse dyabolus et infernus et purgatorium, se ipsum tormentando." Thus argued the Brethren of the Free Spirit according to John of Brünn in the first half of the fourteenth century; Wilhelm Wattenbach, ed., *Über die Secte der Brüder vom freien Geiste* (Berlin, 1887), 532-3.

[3] Rolf Zerfass, *Der Streit um die Laienpredigt*, Untersuchungen zur praktischen Theologie 2 (Freiburg, 1974). About the significance of the monopoly of preaching see part three of Jean Delumeau, *Le péché et la peur. La culpabilisation en Occident XIIIe-XVIIIe siècle.* (Paris, 1983).

[4] This idea is argued anecdotally in a tale by Boccaccio (*Decameron* I,2), where the Jew Abraham is ready to be baptised after he has visited Rome: The Christian God must be exceptionally merciful, because he has not destroyed Rome yet. About the distribution of similar ideas see below in connection with the criticism of the church in the fourteenth century.

very flexible. When alien elements of thought could not be eradicated, the church was able to integrate them through sometimes rudimentary adaptation.[5] In this process the church left room for free play, sometimes even creating it, as in the case of the brotherhoods, which became the typical organizational model for the later Middle Ages.[6] The church, moreover, proved flexible and able to integrate differing perspectives beyond matters of popular piety: in the area of medieval learning, Aristotelianism was adapted just as humanism would be later. In judging these movements, it must not be forgotten that theologians, not philosophers, formulated the decisive theses which shook up late medieval church and society.

Relativising all worldly contradictions was a good start toward deactivating them,[7] but even the sometimes acid criticism of the church served as a safety valve which allowed accumulated discontent to dissipate. Because historians have, again and again, interpreted this criticism out of context,[8] it is necessary to characterise it, if only by way of an outline. This sketch will allow us to judge late medieval criticism of the church more objectively.

Since the high Middle Ages, at the latest, calls for reform of the church from top to bottom had never ceased.[9] True "topoi" of criticism came into

---

[5] A textbook case for this is the long contested celebration of the 1st of January. Eventually, the day was celebrated as the *Circumcisio domini*. About the question as to whether the saints were the "successors" of pagan gods, see František Graus, *Volk, Herrscher und Heiliger im Reich der Merowinger* (Prague, 1965), 171-96.

[6] Graus deals with these fraternities in connection with the upheavals in the cities, *Pest — Geissler — Judenmorde*, 450-1.

[7] This relativisation included not only the shift of the "decision" into the other world (parable of Lazarus) and the expectation of the last judgement or the second coming of Christ, but — in literature — the use of old tales about the happy poor and the unhappy rich.

[8] The ahistoric interpretation started as early as the antipapal polemics of the sixteenth century, in which the authors consciously used an ideal church as a basis for criticism.

[9] About such critics see Paul Grabein, "Die altfranzösischen Gedichte über die verschiedenen Stände der Gesellschaft" (Diss., Halle, 1893); Josef F. Falk, "Etude sociale sur les chansons de geste" (Diss., Uppsala, 1899), 56-70; Paul Sebillot, *Le Folk-lore de France*, vol. 4 (Paris, 1907), 230ff; Paul Lehmann, *Die Parodie im Mittelalter*, 2nd ed. (Stuttgart, 1963); Ernst Nitz, "Die Beurteilung der römischen Kurie in der deutschen Literatur des 13. und der ersten Hälfte des 14. Jh." (Diss., Berlin, 1930); Jeanne Ponton, *La religieuse dans la littérature française* (Laval, 1969); Heinz Mettke, "Kritische Züge in einigen Dichtungen des 12. und 13. Jahrhunderts", *Wissenschaftliche Zeitschrift (Jena)*, Gesellschafts- und sprachwissenschaftliche Reihe 20 (1971): 513-26; Helga Schüppert, *Kirchenkritik in der lateinischen Lyrik des 12. und 13. Jahrhunderts*, Medium Aevum 23 (Munich, 1972). Almost all literary history handbooks and many more specific papers in the field of literary history deal with the particular problems concerning criticism of the church and clergy.

being, were passed from generation to generation and adapted differently.[10] At the same time, new reports appeared, such as tales concerning priests' concubines and lusty priests chasing honorable wives. Stories and invectives of this kind are ubiquitous in medieval literature, whether written by laymen or clerics. Everyone in the church was criticised, beginning with the pope, about whom people were ready to believe the worst.[11] The cardinals were the next to be attacked, after whom came the whole Roman curia and then the Romans. What can be expected of a city founded on fratricide, where Caesar was murdered as well as saints Peter and Paul, and where the papacy had been corrupted.[12] The prelates are worse than the Jews and the pagans,[13] their way of life is wicked, the oppression of their subjects monstrous. The lower clergy are uneducated, slovenly and live with concubines. The priests are greedy and avaricious and care more for their own bellies than for the souls entrusted to them. A soul in hell might well wonder that there were still priests on earth: he had thought that all of them had already arrived in hell.[14] Similarly, monks and nuns are completely corrupt. In short, a negative image of the church develops in which all members of the church have their place; no-one finds grace in the eyes of such strict critics.[15] The church is "now" full of filth and stench,[16] corrupt

---

[10] The "Devil's letters" are an example. They are written by the lord of Hell and directed to the pope or clergy, containing a satirical praise of their behavior. These letters probably appeared as early as the eleventh century. See Gianni Zippel, "La lettera del Diavolo al clero, dal sec. XII alla Riforma", *Bullettino dell'Istituto storico italiano per il medio evo* 70 (1958): 125-79 and Lehmann, *Die Parodie*, 58ff. In the fourteenth century they were fairly widespread (ibid., 61ff.). The use of this genre, however, reveals very little about the attitude of its author, as the "Devil's letter" by Peter d'Ailly proves (see Zippel, 126). Regardless of all calls for reform he was loyal to the church.

[11] See Johann Josef Ignaz Döllinger, *Die Papstfabeln des Mittelalters* (Munich, 1863). Here is also the widely spread — and commonly believed — tale about the "popess" Johanna. See also J. Reinhold, *Zeitschrift für romanische Philologie* 37 (1913): 171ff., about the crimes of a pope from Ganelon's family. The "Liber generationis Jesu Christi" mentions a pope fathered by the devil; see Lehmann, *Die Parodie*, 257, cf. 57-8.

[12] La Bible Guiot, see Charles V. Langlois, *La vie en France au moyen âge de la fin du XIIe s. au milieu de XIVe s.*, 2nd ed., 4 vols. (Paris, 1924-28), 2: 68. See Lehmann, *Die Parodie* for the polemics in medieval novels. For the high Middle Ages see Josef Benzinger, *Invectiva in Romam. Romkritik im Mittelalter vom 9. bis zum 12. Jahrhundert*, Historische Studien 404 (Lübeck, 1968).

[13] Prologue to Eudes de Cheriton, *Fabulae*, in *Les Fabulistes*, ed. L. Hervieux, 5 vols. (Paris, 1893-99), 4: 174.

[14] An *exemplum* of the thirteenth century. Albert Wesselski, *Mönchslatein* (Leipzig, 1909), 168-9, nr. 131; for parallels see 247.

[15] An example of this systematic criticism is the work of the Franciscan Gilbert of Tournai for the Council of Lyon in 1274: *Collectio de scandalis ecclesiae*, ed. Autbertus Stroick, *AFH* 24 (1931): 33-62. As an appendix, so to speak, follows the

and devastated. This view was relatively widely held, yet still the church prevailed.

The above mentioned criticism penetrated a wide range of genres in medieval literature. We find evidence of it in the poems of wandering vagrants as well as in courtly literature, in parodies and treatises as well as in sermons and farces.[17] Novels and stories portray priests, their mishaps and heroic deeds.[18] It is difficult to find a genre in medieval literature where criticism of church and clerics is absent. From the pope to the chaplain, sins and failures are counted, described often in a very concrete, even drastic way. Vice was ridiculed and condemned.

If we pay attention to *what* is criticised, we soon notice that there is a characteristic limitation: the ideas and the teaching of the church are not attacked — on the contrary, they form the foundation for all criticism. The clerics' way of life is scourged — their licentiousness, their luxury and avarice (simony is a watchword in this context), their laxity in fulfilling their duties. In literature each of these aspects can be developed and presented in manifold ways. However, it is obvious that this criticism accepts and defends the basics of church-doctrine. In the final analysis, therefore, this criticism conforms to the teachings of the church and does not occasion persecution (unless by those who felt personally offended). This "inner censorship" stops — by the choice of its starting point — all truly threatening criticism in its tracks. Critics stepping over these bounds and directly attacking the foundations of the church were called heretics and mercilessly persecuted.[19]

---

scolding of the secular orders.

[16] Jacques de Vitry in his exemplum. Thomas F. Crane, *The Exempla or illustrative Stories from the Sermones vulgares of Jacques de Vitry*, Publications of the Folk-Lore Society 26 (London, 1890), 9. "Ecce quot monstris hiis diebus ecclesia Dei occupatur, quot sordibus imprimatur, quot fetoribus inficitur ut quocumque te vertas fetorem sentias, sicut dicitur de symia que jacebat inter scrophas et, dum ex parte una sentiret fetorem, convertebatur ad aliam et nichilominus intollerabilem fetorem sentiebat ..."

[17] Marie-Thérèse Lorcin, *Façons de sentir et de penser: les fabliaux français* (Paris, 1979), 18lff.

[18] Examples: parts of the *Roman de renart*; synopsis by John Flinn, *Le Roman de renart dans la littérature française et dans les littératures étrangères au moyen âge* (Toronto, 1963). *Der Pfaffe Amis* by Stricker, in *Erzählungen und Schwänke*, ed. Hans Lambel, Deutsche Classiker des Mittelalters 12 (Leipzig, 1883). The fifteenth century produced tales of the clever priest who repeatedly outwits the members of his parish; "Der Pfaffe von Kahlenberg", in Hans Rupprich, *Das Wiener Schrifttum des ausgehenden Mittelalters* (Vienna, 1954), 84ff.

[19] A known example of criticism against Rome and the church — with explicit heterodox aspects — is the *Sireventès* by Guilhem Figueira, written in the twenties of the thirteenth century; ed. with French translation by René Nelli, *Ecrivains anticonformistes du moyen-âge occitan* (Paris, 1977), 2: 244-59. A textbook case for the heretisation of a critic is Hus.

Moreover, such criticism of the church was deactiviated when integrated into a general critique of the world. It was commonly held that all things were subject to a slow but steady deterioration.[20] Moral relations continuously worsen, people become more malicious. The world is similar to a stormy sea, where the small are devoured by the large and everything further deteriorates. The world is described as "upside down"[21] and, in the fifteenth century, as mad.[22] In this earthly "Valley of Tears" where truth has no place, where might, caprice, injustice, falsehood and deceit reign[23] — there, necessarily, the church is not good: it is in need of God's grace. Typically, numerous polemics against clerics are connected to a general attack which includes not only the sins and mistakes of prelates and other members of the church: the offenses of the laity also are described graphically, beginning with the king or emperor and ending with the peasant. Each "estate" has its vices, just like the clergy. The devil has married his "daughters", the different vices, to the individual "estates", and thus each of them has its specific sins.[24]

The church managed, through toleration of essentially conformist criticism (later often misinterpreted due to ahistorical arrangement), to nip potentially dangerous views in the bud. This way, Christians were "immunised", so to

---

[20] This idea is strongly connected to the common view of the "aging world", that has its starting point in the fourth book of Esra 5:50 ff., often considered a part of the Bible. About the distribution of these ideas see Walther Rehm, "Kulturverfall und spätmittelalterliche Didaktik", *Zeitschrift für deutsche Philologie* 52 (1927): 289-330; Dimitri Scheludko, "Klagen über den Verfall der Welt bei den Trobadors", *Neuphilologische Mitteilungen* 44 (1943): 22-45; Amos Funkenstein, "Heilsplan und natürliche Entwicklung", *Dialog* 5 (1965): 28-9, 37ff.

[21] About the motive of the world "turned upside down" see E. R. Curtius, *Europäische Literatur und lateinisches Mittelalter*, 3rd ed. (Bern, 1961), 102ff.; Philippe Menard, *Le rire et le sourire dans le roman courtois en France au Moyen Age 1150-1250* (Geneva, 1969), 379ff. As a typical and well-known example, here the opening words of the *Songe du vergier* I,1 (1378), ed. M. Goldast, *Revue du Moyen Age Latin* 13 (1957): 9. "Maintefois me suis esmerveillé de ce que je voy que le temps est ainsi comme du tout changé et destourné, car nous voyons visiblement que justice est ensevelie, et les lois naturelles, divines, canoniques, et civiles, et generalement toute bonne police sont contre raison et nature destournez ...", an often heard opinion.

[22] A typical example: Jean Molinet's *Les eages du monde*, in *Les faictz et dictz de Jean Molinet*, ed. Noël Dupire (Paris, 1937), 2: 588-96.

[23] These ideas were treated in the widely known, strongly schematised genre of grievances (*gravamina*) in the late Middle Ages.

[24] See Jacques de Vitry, ed. Crane (n. 16 above), 101, 235-6. Jacques de Vitry wrote sermons for the "ordines" as well. So far they are only partially edited; see Johannes Baptista Pitra, *Analecta novissima ... Continuatio* (Paris, 1888), 2: 344-442. For the standardized attribution of sins from the fourteenth century, see the fable by Polycarp in Konrad Burdach, *Vom Mittelalter zur Reformation* (Berlin, 1926), 3.2: 520.

speak, against a variety of doubts. Most important, the church was able to make itself indispensable by means of a symbiotic relationship with secular institutions and a consistent ritualisation of life. Even very "lax" believers were accompanied from cradle to grave by the sacraments of the church, a system which was consciously expanded.[25] Even when disaster struck, people could beg for heavenly mercy in prayer processions, hoping to turn away the danger. In everyday life the saints protectively accompanied humans, and the sacraments of the church offered a spiritual safety net not available from by any other institution. In short, the church and its institutions were part of everyday life, regardless of the strength of an individual's faith. Moreover, local life was embedded in church-dominated communities, especially monasteries (even in the most corrupt monastery traces of an ordered life remained);[26] the laity belonged to parishes or to one of the many brotherhoods influenced by the church. Holy Days, the highlights of the year, and theatrical performances were shaped by the church. Even though the late Middle Ages saw a certain trend toward independence in this area, there was no great breakthrough yet.[27]

The omnipresence of the various, absolutely heterogenous forms of church life explains why the majority understood only "criticism from within the church". It is absolutely no coincidence that the great movements of the late Middle Ages expressed themselves "religiously" and appeared as non-conformist church criticism. Only in the confines of the church could contradictions become truly conscious. Only claims phrased in familiar everyday language and images could evoke or "trigger" enthusiasm or disdain. In this way, the whole system was seemingly uniform — yet in truth, it was full of internal contrasts and contradictions, which although veiled, could not be resolved. These contradictions were at the same time a decisive opportunity for further development; as soon as they were recognised, they provoked positive or negative reactions within the existing system of ideas and behavior. However, they also threatened to become starting points for nonconformist criticism — all the more since the whole "world" itself was full of contradictions and increasingly full of social tension. Ecclesiastical ubiquity and claims to universality linked the church inextricably to all forms of power. The church formulated doctrine concerning just and unjust rule, fair prices and wages, permissible and impermissible forms of credit — in short, almost all phenomena which we call social or societal. The church had to voice an opinion about human

---

[25] Especially by the Fourth Lateran Council (1215). An example is the obligation to confess once a year, intended as a way to discipline the laity.

[26] This can be seen in various popular parodies of monastery life up into the sixteenth century.

[27] An overview of the development is given by David Brett-Evans, *Von Hrotsvit bis Folz und Gengenbach. Eine Geschichte des mittelalterlichen deutschen Dramas*, 2 vols., Grundlagen der Germanistik 15/18, (Berlin, 1975).

insecurity, as well as about the oppression of the poor and the problem of rebellion against unjust rule. All these elements formed an immensely complex system, inextricably linking theoretical foundations to societal life. This inevitably involved the clergy in social conflicts, and often drove critics to argue basic social issues in "ecclesiastical" language.

II

In Part Two, chapter 2, Graus discusses medieval social theory and its opponents. Chapter 3 deals with the "Church in Crisis". Graus outlines the main causes, both within and outside the church: the failure of the crusades, the expansion of discipline and legislation, social tensions within the church, schism, the supremacy of the papacy and antagonism to worldly powers. He then describes the reactions to these phenomena: a growing unrest and frustration regarding the unreliability of former certainties, which caused an "almost hectic search for new possibilities" and a desire to find "culprits who could take the blame for everything". Chapter 4 explains how this search for reassurance and scapegoats altered the intellectual and social "climate".

If one asked who was responsible for the obvious breakdown apparent everywhere, the answer seemed clear: the corrupt church was at fault. In concrete terms, this meant the clergy, for they had sinned against the fundamental divine commandments. Critical voices raised accusations against the whole church.[28] The clergy were responsible for the downfall of Christianity, and even for the disasters afflicting humankind.[29] These statements were accompanied by somber prophecies about a persecution of the clergy. The expectation that all members of the first *ordo* would be persecuted was integral to apocalyptic ideas. In earlier centuries such a persecution was to usher in the Antichrist and the battle against Christ's church. Now, in the later Middle Ages, the view had shifted. The prophesied eradication of the clergy tended to be seen as a just punishment of their sins and failures.

---

[28] As an example see Matthäus of Krakau, in *Quellen zur böhmischen Inquisition im 14. Jahrhundert*, ed. Alexander Patschovsky, MGH.QG 11 (Weimar, 1979), 110-13, 318-23; Nicolas de Clamanges, *De ruina et reparacione ecclesiae* (ca. 1400/01), in *Le traité de la ruine de l'église de Nicolas de Clamanges et la traduction française de 1564*, Alfred Coville (Paris, 1936); *Die Chronik des Johannes von Winterthur*, ed. Friedrich Baethgen, MGH.SS NS 3 (Berlin, 1924), 238f.; Heinrich of Herford, *Liber de rebus memorabilibus*, ed. A. Potthast (Göttingen, 1859), 265-8.

[29] Very explicit is the *Prophetia* by John of Rupescissa, ed. E. Brown, *Appendix ad Fasciculum rerum expetendarum et fugiendarum ...* (London, 1690), appendix 2, 498.

Prophecies about an imminent judgement of all clerics are not peculiar to the late Middle Ages. Occasionally they appeared even earlier. At this time, however, apocalyptic voices multiplied and grew in intensity and urgency. At the end of the thirteenth century an orthodox southern Italian prophecy expecting the persecution,[30] as well as the "heretical" speculations of the so-called "Apostolic Brethren",[31] found consolation in the belief that the clergy were soon to be robbed, even eradicated. Clerics would hide their tonsure in order to avoid recognition, an effective and widespread motif in literature. Referring to uprisings and heresies, it was often claimed that rebels had threatened the clergy. This accusation was raised, for example, against the leader of the Flemish peasant revolt,[32] as well as against the heretical Beguines.[33] Conrad of Megenburg feared a persecution of the first *ordo* in connection with the wave of pogroms in 1336-1338.[34] A contemporary of his contended that on this occasion 1,500 peasants in the Alsace had sworn to kill all idlers such as bishops, clerics, monks, nuns and scholars.[35] Such fears were not confined to literary sources. On March 3, 1345, the bishop of Strasbourg and several nobles formed an alliance amongst themselves and the cities for five years in order to prevent unrest. The source explicitly names "phaffen, sú werent geistlich oder weltlich" (i.e. all members of the clergy), other Christians or Jews as causes of unrest.[36] In 1349 flagellants were likewise accused of murdering clerics.[37] These fears continued to be expressed after the first wave of the plague had passed.

---

[30] Emil Donckel, "Visio seu prophetia fratris Johannis", *Römische Quartalschrift* 40 (1932): 376.

[31] Bernard Gui, *De secta illorum que se dicunt esse de ordine Apostolorum*, ed. A. Segarizzi, *Historia fratris Dulcini Heresiarche di anonimo sincrono e De secta ...*, Rerum Italicarum Scriptores, vol. 9, part 5 (Città di Castello, 1907), 20-1.

[32] Jacques Peyt, who never went to church, was said to have declared that he wanted to see each and every priest hang. This evil heretic would have robbed and expelled all priests, if he had not been murdered first: *Chronicum comitum Flandrensium*, ed. J. J. de Smet, *Corpus Chronicorum Flandriae*, vol. 1 (Brussels, 1837), 202.

[33] Bernard Gui, *Manuel de l'inquisiteur*, ed. G. Mollat, Classiques de l'histoire de France au moyen-âge 8-9 (Paris, 1926-27), 1: 148ff.

[34] Graus uses the name "Armlederaufstand" here; see Konrad of Megenberg, *Klagelied der Kirche über Deutschland (Planctus ecclesiae in Germaniam)*, ed. Horst Kusch, LÜAMA A-1 (Leipzig, 1956), 56-7, v. 600ff.

[35] Concerning the events of 1340 (sic), Conrad Derrer of Augsburg noted: "... quod circa Renum in Alsacia coniurabant 1500 rusticorum, quod vellent occidere omnes comedentes panem ociosum ut episcopos, clericos, monachos, moniales, scholares"; G. Leidinger, "Aus dem Geschichtenbuch des Magisters Konrad Derrer von Augsburg", *Zeitschrift des historischen Vereins für Schwaben* 31 (1904): 24-5.

[36] *Urkundenbuch und Akten der Stadt Straßburg I. Urkundenbuch der Stadt Straßburg*, 7 vols. (Strasbourg, 1879-1900), 5: 132-3, nr. 130.

[37] See Graus, part one, 55-6.

The idea of an imminent persecution of the priests can be found later in John of Rupescissa,[38] the *Sibillenboich*,[39] and Jean de Bassigny.[40] During the war between the cities, 1397-1400, the people of Würzburg are said to have threatened to rob the clergy as they would rob the Jews.[41] At the same time, the prophecies of a general persecution of clerics reappeared.[42]

Animosity and fear increased in the following century, which saw the decimation of the "orthodox" clergy in Bohemia by the Hussites. A satire recommended to the Council of Constance that cardinals, archbishops and prelates be captured and drowned in the Rhine, as a strong medicine for the church.[43] From Basel, Julian Cesarini wrote to the pope in 1432; if all hopes for improvement disappeared, the laity would justly rise up against the church as the Hussites had done (which everyone was already considering, according to Cesarini).[44] In 1449 the "Meistersinger" Ulrich Wiest of Augsburg wrote: "O Lord, I cry out to you, I have heard and one reads in prophecies, that the clergy will be beaten,"[45] and in 1476 the peasants went to Niklashausen singing: "Let's complain to God in heaven, kyrie eleison, we are not allowed to kill the clerks, kyrie eleison."[46]

The conviction that the clergy would soon be in danger was common; it was hailed with glee by some of the laity and feared by the potential

---

[38] *Prophetia*, ed. E. Brown (n. 29 above), appendix 2, 494-503, about the years 1356 and 1370. These prophecies were included in a fifteenth-century Czech version, where they indeed became reality during the time of the Hussites.

[39] *Sibillen boich* (ca. 1361), v. 483ff; in *Geistliche Gedichte des XIV. und XV. Jh. vom Niederrhein*, ed. Oskar Schade (Hannover, 1854), 313f.

[40] R. E. Lerner, "The Black Death and Western European Eschatological Mentalities", *AHR* 86 (1981): 547.

[41] "Vom Würzburger Städtekrieg", in *Die historischen Volkslieder der Deutschen vom 13. bis 16. Jahrhundert*, ed. Rochus v. Liliencron, vol. 1 (Leipzig, 1865), 171, nr. 40, v. 505-24.

[42] Karl Koehne, ed., "Die Weissagung auf das Jahr 1401", *Deutsche Zeitschrift für Geschichtswissenschaft*, NF 1 (1897): 360-1.

[43] Lehmann, *Die Parodie* (n. 9 above), 68.

[44] Joannis de Segovia, *Historia* II,15, in *Monumenta conciliorum generalium seculi decimi quinti. Consilium Basiliense SS*, vol. 2 (Vindobonae, 1873), 99. Cesarini's purpose was to prevent the break-up of the council.

[45] "Ain hupsch liedt von den alumûssen", *Epochen der deutschen Lyrik*, vol. 2, ed. E. and H.-J. Kiepe (Munich, 1972), 242-46, v. 27ff.

[46] Klaus Arnold, *Niklashausen 1476. Quellen und Untersuchungen zur sozial-religiösen Bewegung des Hans Behem und zur Agrarstruktur eines spätmittelalter-lichen Dorfes*, Saecula Spiritalia 3 (Baden-Baden, 1980), 281, nr. I/68, Arnold follows George Widman's *Chronica*; cf. 215, nr. I/23 where the song is a little different. See also the chronicle by Adrien de But about the expected persecution of clerics at that time, *Chronique relatives à l'histoire de Belgique sous la domination des ducs de Bourgogne*, ed. Kervyn de Lettenhove, vol. 1 (n.p., 1870), 305ff.

victims.[47] Before the Hussites, actual riots against the clergy (apart from
the usual conflicts in cities and villages[48]) were exceptional. Only the "Pastoureaux" in 1251 could, in a later phase of the movement, be called openly
anticlerical.[49] During the first wave of the Black Death monks (perhaps
priests, too) were occasionally accused of having poisoned wells and,
therefore, of responsibility for the pestilence. Despite such accusations there
was no true persecution.[50] Only during the Hussite uprising (when supporters of the chalice for the laity were persecuted and punished by the
church as impenitent heretics), did the Taborites attack with fire and sword
"orthodox" priests who would not turn to the "truth of the Gospel".[51]
Partisans of the church assumed the long awaited and prophesied persecution
of the clergy by Antichrist was at hand. Clerics were made responsible for
the downfall of the church. They, in turn, looked for scapegoats within their
own ranks and repeatedly blamed heretics for threats and conflict. As we
know, the persecution of heretics did not stop in the late Middle Ages.
During the Hussite Wars the fear of heretics increased even more, and
Hussite sympathisers could easily make the acquaintance of the inquisitors.

According to contemporaries, it was not only the church of Christ which
was corrupt — the whole world was mad. Full of falsehood and deceit, it
was growing ever more vicious. The clergy could not be exclusively to
blame, the Prince of Darkness must have had other helpers as well. An old

---

[47] Bernard Gui about the "pastoureaux" raging against the clerics: "Universus
autem populus eis favebat, aliqui quia haec fieri et ad bonum finem proventura
sperabant, plurimi autem et pene universi quia de persecutione clericorum gaudebant,"
in *Recueil des historiens des Gaules et de la France par Dom Martin Bouquet*, ed.
L. Delisle, 24 vols. (Paris, 1869-1904), 21: 697. There are many late medieval
accounts about the hostility of laymen against clerics.

[48] Graus deals with hostility against clerics within the context of social unrest in
cities and villages in part four.

[49] The following sources tell in detail about the raging of the "Pastoureaux":
Annales de Burton, ed. H. R. Luard, in *Annales Monastici*, vol. 1, Rerum Britannicarum medii aevi scriptores 36 (London, 1864), 290ff; Bernard Gui, *Recueil* (n. 47
above), 21: 697; *Les grandes chroniques de France*, ed. J. Viard, 10 vols. (Paris,
1920-23), 7: 162ff; *Matthaei Parisiensis Chronica Majora*, ed. H. R. Luard, Rerum
Britannicarum medii aevi scriptores 57 (London, 1880), 246ff.; *Chronica universalis
Mettensis add.* MGH.SS 24 (Hannover, 1879), 522. It is striking that geographically
very distant authors describe the persecutions so thoroughly — they are trying to
underline the "depravity" of the insurgents.

[50] About these accusations see Graus, *Pest — Geissler — Judenmorde*, 307.

[51] The radical Adamites extended their hatred to all priests — even to the
Taborites' priests. According to Žižka's letter to the people of Prague (1421), they
had called the Taborite priests "impersonate devils" (d'ábly vtĕlenými). "Lauren-
tius/Vavřinec von Březová", *Fontes rerum Bohemicarum*, 5: 519.

tradition of ecclesiastical literature called women Satan's allies,[52] for Eve was already in alliance with Satan when Adam fell. Fear of women and of their special powers and qualities was not peculiar to Christianity: it is present in different cultures in manifold forms. In Christianity this fear became ideology very early, but it never dominated. It was balanced by the glorification of woman in ecclesiastical literature and particularly in pious thought: Eve was overcome by Mary,[53] — or in the language of the theologians — the salvation of the world, once lost because of one woman, was recovered with the help of another. The secular veneration of women did not stop either, and in the period of courtly love, her praises were sung in many different ways. One could easily compile high and late medieval anthologies which praise as well as condemn women. Each trend developed a specific stereotype which was elaborated and passed on in a whole cycle of stories;[54] neither can be considered typical for any period.

Nevertheless, a certain shift among so-called intellectuals seems to have taken place during the late Middle Ages; a contempt for women, peculiar to this group and seemingly based on intellectual criteria, gained ground in part due to attempts by women to play an independent role in the religious and spiritual world of the time.[55] Late medieval polemic against women accused them not only as quarrelsome, jealous, deceitful and cunning, but also as intellectual stumbling blocks for men. This attitude is clearly visible in the success of the Lamentations of Matheolus,[56] and in a different way,

---

[52] Tertullian's dictum is well known: "Vivit sententia Dei super sexum istum in hoc saeculo: vivat et reatus necesse est. Tu es diaboli ianua; tu es arboris illius resignatrix; tu es divinae legis prima desertrix; tu es quae eum suasisti, quem diabolus aggredi non valuit; tu imaginem Dei, hominem, tam facile elisisti; propter tuum meritum, id est mortem, etiam filius Dei mori habuit." *De cultu feminarum* I,2. Cited from the edition of Maria Turcan in *Sources chrétiennes*, vol. 173 (Paris, 1971), 42.

[53] Ernst Guldan, *Eva und Maria. Eine Antithese als Bildmotiv* (Graz, 1966).

[54] On the one hand there are numerous variations of the tale of the innocent wife, who is unjustly suspected to be unfaithful; on the other hand there are many stories about women who always find an opportunity to betray and cheat on their husbands. I do not want to deal with the already rather extensive literature about the issue of women in the Middle Ages. The literature often shows far too uniform a picture. Before general judgements can be made, the analysis of specific tropes in literature is indispensable, for in praise as well as in damnation of women literary stereotypes are particularly frequent.

[55] Especially striking are the attempts of the female Dominican mystics and of the Beguines.

[56] A.-G. van Hamel, ed., *Les lamentations de Matheolus et le Livre de leesce de Jehan le Fèvre, de Resson*, Bibliothèque de l'Ecoles des Hautes Etudes 95/96 (Paris, 1892, 1905). Also C. V. Langlois (n. 12 above), 2: 241-90. The latin poem of the late thirteenth century was only turned into a "bestseller" in the fourteenth century, by way of the translation by Jehan Le Fèvre.

the "Roman de la Rose".[57] For intellectuals, women were obstacles to man's spiritual journey: women were scorned and yet always desired. During the Middle Ages, this male need was particularly symbolised by the Master of Wisdom, Aristotle, who let beautiful Phyllis saddle and ride him like a mule.[58] (How the position of women during this period actually changed, or whether there was a discernible shift at all, cannot be established clearly. The already extensive literature about the "female problem" is generally not very productive. Comprehensive judgments are contradictory and, so far, depend on a relatively small range of sources.)

Women could be scorned and attacked, and indeed, late medieval voices hostile to women grew louder and increasingly "intellectual". However, both hostility towards women and the demonisation of women remained within a relatively limited sphere. More generally, intolerance and uncertainly in society increased. Prejudice against outsiders certainly increased in the fourteenth and fifteenth centuries,[59] particularly regarding homosexuals[60] but they were certainly not the only targets. The change in tolerance towards practioners of magic was especially significant. The condemnation of magical practices was ancient — the Old Testament tells of both the persecution and the miraculous power of witches,[61] and the magician Simon was known from the Acts of the Apostles.[62] During the following centuries magic was continuously condemned, and at the same time used in a variety of situations.[63] Although sorcerers and witches were constantly consulted, they also were abused and condemned. (It is a widespread misinterpretation that magic was an exclusively "female" issue. In all

---

[57] The representation of women in this novel, especially the jealous husband raging against all women, gave reason for protest as early as the fifteenth century. Christine de Pisan defended the women against the unjust accusations. See Eric Hicks, *Le débat sur le Roman de la rose*, Bibliothèque du XVe siècle 43 (Paris, 1977). In Chaucer's *Canterbury Tales* the polemics against women are frequent, too, but so is the defense; Paul Meyer, "Mélanges de Poésie française", *Romania* 6 (1877): 499ff.

[58] See Stith Thompson, *Motif-Index of Folk-Literature*, 6 vols., 2nd ed. (Copenhagen, 1955-58), col. 1215.

[59] František Graus, "Randgruppen der städtischen Gesellschaft im Spätmittelalter", *ZHF* 8 (1981): 385-437.

[60] See the fundamental work by John Boswell, *Christianity, Social Tolerance and Homosexuality: Gay People in Western Europe from the Beginning of the Christian Era to the Fourteenth Century* (Chicago, 1980). Boswell rightly claims (269ff.) that intolerance against homosexuals became the rule only in the late Middle Ages.

[61] The witch of Endor 1 Sam. 28. Prohibition of magic and fortune-telling is to be found in the books of Moses: Ex. 22:18; Lv. 20:6,27; Dt. 18:10.

[62] Acts 8.

[63] For the development of the term *Superstitio artis magicae* to Thomas Aquinas, see Dieter Harmening, *Superstitio. Überlieferungs- und theoriegeschichtliche Untersuchungen zur kirchlich-theologischen Aberglaubensliteratur des Mittelalters* (Berlin, 1979), 217-58.

periods both women and men practised magic, and late medieval and early modern witchtrials were directed against men as well as women[64] — the rate of women sentenced rose only gradually.)

The image of magic began to change fundamentally in the fourteenth century.[65] Witchcraft was demonised ever more explicity. In the high Middle Ages sorcerers still could play a positive role in literature — a representation that is almost unthinkable in the late Middle Ages. The good fairies of the preceding period became revolting goblins and witches, who appeared as lovely fairies only to deceive. This demonisation was based not only on biblical prohibitions, but also on the old idea of an alliance between the Antichrist and his prospective instructors, the magicians. In the late medieval period, magic and heresy were often equated. The inquisition began to take a close interest in magic.[66] Soon thereafter, the secular authorities followed this path, eagerly persecuting and burning sorcerers and witches. Accusations of magical practices were still used occasionally in political trials and this brought about a clear change in the overall picture: sorcerers and witches were consistently and closely linked to Satan, to whom they swore a special oath.[67] They were his underlings and tools; they celebrated their gatherings and festivals together with the Prince of Darkness (as in accusations against heretics, imagination went wild here in the invention of numerous details concerning such orgies). These festivals

---

[64] About the high rates of men condemned as sorcerers in the late Middle Ages, see Pierre Braun, "La sorcellerie dans les lettres de rémission du trésor de chartes", in *Etudes sur la sensibilité. Actes du 102e Congrès national des Sociétés savantes*, Section de philologie de d'histoire jusqu'à 1610 (Paris, 1979), 2: 257-78, or the tentative synopsis of the known witch trials 1300-1499 in Richard Kieckhefer, *European Witch Trials: Their Foundations in Popular and Learned Culture, 1300-1500* (London, 1976), 106-47. The fifth book of the *Formicarius* by Johannes Nider (available in numerous old-prints only) deals extensively with magic, and male sorcerers prevail.

[65] Though there are many rather important, more recent studies on magic, the fundamental work by Joseph Hansen (esp. his sources) remains indispensable: *Zauberwahn, Inquisition und Hexenprozess im Mittelalter und die Entstehung der grossen Hexenverfolgung*, Historische Bibliothek 12 (Munich, 1900). Among the more recent works the following are particularly noteworthy: Jeffrey Burton Russell, *Witchcraft in the Middle Ages* (Ithaca, 1972); Norman Cohn, *Europe's Inner Demons* (London, 1975); R. Kieckhefer, *European Witch Trials*.

[66] As early as 1320; Joseph Hansen, *Quellen und Untersuchungen zur Geschichte des Hexenwahns und der Hexenverfolgung im Mittelalter* (Bonn, 1901), No. 4, 4. Later the papal bull *Summis desiderantes* was fundamental (ibid., No. 36, 24ff.). In earlier times the inquisition had dealt only with magic when heresy was suspected, following the explicit order of pope Alexander IV (ibid., No. 1, 1). Up to the fifteenth century, the opposition of the learned did not stop completely.

[67] For women, sexual intercourse is perhaps the confirmation of the pact.

were called magicians' and witches' "Sabbaths",[68] a frankly symptomatic name.

The complete demonisation of magic,[69] i.e. the final victory of the old idea that magic practices were effective (only with the help of the devil), was not limited to theological and legal circles. This idea penetrated the greater population, becoming a dominant factor. When in need, people still called out to magicians for help, but fear of them increasingly prevailed. The devil was everywhere; humankind was continuously threatened by him and by disasters. The Devil Incarnate was ever-present and his allies were next door: magicians and witches were always ready to harm and harass their neighbors. The persecution of witches and sorcerers had long ceased to be the exclusive preserve of ecclesiastical and worldly authorities. A considerable number of those dying at the stake, if not the majority, were the victims of their dear neighbors.[70]

The complete demonisation of witches and sorcerers signals a change in point of view, in mentality. We meet this change in several places in late medieval sources. The world, the course of events, became less and less intelligible; the traditional roles of the *ordines* were confused (most notably concerning the clergy). Disasters appeared as the contemporary "writing on the wall". Somber prophecies held sway as the world seemed to worsen daily and people grew more vicious. The church, which should have been a bulwark providing shelter for the oppressed, obviously failed and could barely help itself. In such a time of uncertainty, when traditional values were threatened, it was not surprising that people searched for scapegoats — or at least for allies of the Enemy. The burden of blame was placed on the corrupt clergy. Priests were generally scorned. There was hardly a crime of

---

[68] The idea of the witches' gathering was old, see Alfons Hilka, *Historia septem sapientum*, Sammlung mittellateinischer Texte 4 (Heidelberg, 1912), 12-13. The oldest source we know so far for the name "witches' sabbath" is from 1335; Julio Caro Baroja, *Les sorcières et leur monde* (Paris, 1972), 105. About the etymology of the word (originally, it meant Jewish sabbath as well as riot, row) see Pierre-François Fournier, "Etymologie de sabbat 'Réunion rituelle de sorcières'", *Bibliothèque de l'Ecole des Chartes* 139 (1981): 247ff. Carlo Ginzburg, "Présomptions sur le sabbat", *Annales ESC* 39 (1984): 341-54, esp. 342f., suggested, that the link between witches and Jews was connected to the tales about the poisoned wells (1348-1350). However, one must note that the quite numerous and detailed accounts about "Jewish conspiracies" of the same years do not mention sorcerers or witches at all.

[69] This was nearly "dogmatised" in the notorious "Hammer of the Witches" (*Malleus maleficarum*, 1487) by the Dominicans Heinrich Institoris and Jakob Sprenger.

[70] See the fundamental work of Robert Muchembled, *La sorcière au village XVe-XVIIIe siècle*, Collection Archives 84 (Paris, 1979). For the late Middle Ages there is abundant material in Pierre-François Fournier, *Magie et sorcellerie, essai historique accompagné de documents concernant la magie et la sorcellerie en Auvergne* (Moulins, 1979), esp. the supplemental documents.

which they were thought incapable — and yet without them, late medieval society would have been as bereft as a village without a church. Despite all the opposition and hostility, despite all the recurring fears, no persecution of the clergy occurred in the fourteenth century. People sought and found other "enemies", other emissaries of Satan, such as magicians and witches, who, however, first had to be found and "convicted". In connection with the threats of persecution against the clergy,[71] a group traditionally linked to the church appear in the sources.[72] The Middle Ages knew the Synagogue as the opponent and indispensable companion of the Church Triumphant.[73] "Unbelieving Jews" lived in the midst of the "believing Christians". Their otherness did not have to be found or proved — it was obvious at first sight. To many of their contemporaries, the Jews were the ideal scapegoat for all evils. Thus, in the middle of the fourteenth century, the Jews fell victim to the most extensive wave of pogroms of the Middle Ages.

---

[71] In 1251 the "Pastoureax" fought against the clerics just as against the Jews, whereas the second movement of the "Pastoureaux" in 1320 was directed only against the Jews. During fights of citizens against clerics there were frequent riots against the Jews. For 1324 in Nordhausen, see E. G. Förstermann, *Friedr. Chrn. Lesser's Historische Nachrichten von den ehemals kaiserlichen und des heil. röm. Reichs freien Stadt Nordhausen gedruckt daselbst im J. 1740 umgearbeitet und fortgesetzt* (Nordhausen, 1860), 251ff.; or in 1397-1400 in Würzburg, see n. 41 above.

[72] Examples: Nicolas de Clamanges, *De ruina et reparacione ecclesiae*, ed. A. Coville (n. 28 above), 146 n. 30, calls the church "infelix soror Synagoge"; the pipe-player of Niklashausen called the clerics more obstinate than the Jews; ed. K. Arnold, *Niklashausen* (n. 46 above), 196, nr. I/8, also 103.

[73] For pictorial representations see Wolfgang Seiferth, *Synagoge und Kirche im Mittelalter* (Munich, 1964).

THE HUSSITE CRITIQUE
OF THE CLERGY'S CIVIL DOMINION

FRANTIŠEK ŠMAHEL

Director, Institute of History, Prague

In Hussite Bohemia, the land of the first reformation, of long-term religious conflicts, and finally, of two legally established confessions, manifestations of anticlericalism necessarily took sharper forms than they did in neighbouring territories. In their unending quarrels over the true faith, the rival confessional parties had abused each other and had banished and even burned priests. The reputation and standing of the spiritual estate was in consequence generally damaged, and the laity began to question the clergy's social role and precedence among the estates.[1] The confiscation of church property went hand in hand with the reversal of the old privileges of the upper clergy. One of the four basic demands of the Czech reformation was carried out to the word and to the letter: the Bohemian Province of the church was deprived of roughly four-fifths of its property and, in short, stripped of its temporal powers.[2]

The roots of this process in the Bohemian lands can be traced far back into the fourteenth century and to the sharp rise in the power and prestige of the Bohemian monarchy in the reign of Charles IV. Prague became the seat of a newly-established archbishopric and imperial residence as well as the site of the first university in central Europe. All these developments were part of a rapid movement to "catch up" with the more advanced southern and western regions of Christian Europe. In these regions emphasis on fiscal procedures, conspicuous wealth and other abuses characteristic of a worldly church had long been familiar aspects of everyday experience, but in Bohemia their novelty inflamed opinion and stirred up opposition. After Rome and Avignon, Prague quickly became the third clerical city of Christendom. One in every twenty of its forty thousand inhabitants was a

---

[1] For detailed treatment of the period in English see Frederick Heymann, *John Žižka and the Hussite Revolution* (New York, 1955; 2nd ed., 1969), and F. M. Bartoš, *The Hussite Revolution 1424-1437* (Boulder, Colo., 1986). The most important recent work is Howard Kaminsky, *A History of the Hussite Revolution* (Berkeley, 1967). A bibliographical study guide with particular references to resources in North America is Jarold K. Zeman, *The Hussite Movement and the Reformation in Bohemia, Moravia and Slovakia* (Ann Arbor, 1977).

[2] See František Šmahel, *La révolution hussite, une anomalie historique* (Paris, 1985), 105-10.

member of the spiritual estate. The overgrown network of church institutions extended even into the countryside. Local sample studies show that in districts selected for research there were more than twice the number of clergy in the pre-Hussite period than at any time thereafter, despite a gradual several-fold increase in the overall population. The number of regular clergy and those in special orders came to exceed the needs of the country and so became an obstacle to the development of its economic potential. From this point of view some reduction became inevitable.[3] In towns where the mendicant orders had established themselves, the problem was evident well before the mid-fourteenth century. In these towns, there were series of scandalous disputes between the friars and the parish clergy as both groups competed for the rewards of pastoral care.

It is relatively safe to say that a tiny minority of clerics were siphoning off almost a third of the country's entire yield of land rents. The huge estates of the monasteries and the Prague archbishopric irritated the aristocracy and gentry, many of whom were from impoverished families. While they themselves simply plundered church estates, their sons actually seized and broke these estates up, either in apparent support for the demands of the reformers or under the transparent pretext of defending the threatened property. We can say that, although the Bohemian church with its riches, extensive privileges and political influence seems at first sight to have forged a state within a state, it was in fact of colossus with feet of clay. This had become strikingly evident during the conflicts between members of the ruling dynasty and high-ranking representatives of the church hierarchy beginning in the 1380s. When Wenceslas IV proceeded against the rebellious Archbishop John of Jenstein and his vicars, he encouraged other enemies of the church and indirectly offered them an example.[4] Meanwhile, robber barons and knights raided monasteries, and some yeoman in South Bohemia threatened his parish priest with death if he "spoke a word against him in his sermons."[5]

Thus, the church in Bohemia had begun to show cracks well before the storm of the Hussite revolution. But without the reforming ideology which sprang from New Testament fundamentalism, the attitude of the lay public toward the far from exemplary clergy would not have broken the bounds of moralistic critique. We have a rare surviving visitation record left by a Prague archdeacon, who personally visited about three hundred parishes in Prague and its environs between 1379 and 1382. From this source, it appears that clerical offenses against morality and decency were taken for granted

---

[3] Šmahel, *La révolution hussite*, 110-12, with references to studies in Czech.

[4] For details, Gerhard Losher, *Königtum und Kirche zur Zeit Karls IV*, (Munich, 1985); Zdeňka Hledíková, "Kirche und König zur Zeit der Luxemburger", in *Bohemia sacra*, ed. Ferdinand Seibt (Düsseldorf, 1974), 307-14; and Ruben E. Weltsch, *Archbishop John of Jenstein 1348-1400* (The Hague, 1968), 40-78.

[5] František Šmahel, *Dějiny Tábora* 1-1 (České Budějovice, 1988), 160.

by parishioners.[6] Some three or four decades later no priest in Hussite districts could get publicly drunk, gamble, practice usury or keep a concubine without punishment. In the intervening period the demands of the reformers had been spread, via the pulpit, from the university to the town and even to the villages. But for the common people to be spiritually and intellectually capable of receiving the reformed ideals, it was necessary that they be more deeply Christianised. In this respect, the Hussite movement succeeded only partially. The arguments of the academic reformers were received principally by the educated. Simple people were guided by simplified rules and articles of belief, more or less strengthened by the charisma of a preacher, the magical quality of the spoken word, or the collective sensibility of the crowd. For example, the third article of the Military Ordinance of the undefeated Hussite commander Jan Žižka proclaimed it a duty to bring the clergy to a life worthy of Christ and his apostles, and with the help of God, to seize on His behalf the endowments and property of simoniacs. The list of methods for the reform of the wicked of all estates, the clergy not excepted, is noteworthy: the reprobate should be punished by beating, flogging, burning, hanging, drowning and other means.[7] In the fulfillment of this article the higher principle of God's Law combined with military command and with the spontaneous impulses and emotional responses of "God's Warriors".

The anticlericalism of the Hussite reformation was directed against bad priests who neglected God's Law. Only exceptionally did it extend to a negative attitude toward the clergy as a whole. This was natural, since in any case those who demanded the radical purification of a worldly church were themselves clergy. All the Hussite reformers made high demands on the clerical office. Certainly, the Prague professor John Hus, like his Oxford teacher Wyclif, recognised the right of the priest to preach the Word of God without the prior permission of bishop or Pope, but at the same time he acknowledged the distinction between priest and layman, the holiness of the priestly office (*sacramentum ordinis*) and the hierarchical nature of church organisation. According to Hus, a good priest is a servant of Christ and "in his spiritual office he is, therefore, of greater dignity than the secular king. The king however, being anointed equally as the priest, is of greater dignity in the secular rule than the priest."[8] Hus was merciless in his criticism of unfit and, above all, of simoniac priests. Under certain conditions he was

---

[6] See Ivan Hlaváček, "Beiträge zum Alltagsleben im vorhussitischen Böhmen. Zur Aussagekraft des Prager Visitationsprotokolls von 1379-1381 und der benachbarten Quellen", *Jahrbuch für fränkische Landesforschung* 34-35 (1974-75): 865-82.

[7] The English translation of the Military Ordinance of Žižka's New brotherhood in Heymann, *John Žižka*, 492-7.

[8] Václav Flajšhans, ed., *Mag. Io. Hus Sermones in Bethlehem, 1410-1411*, 4 (Prague, 1942), 334. On this point see Matthew Spinka, *John Hus' Concept of the Church* (Princeton, 1966), 302f.

even willing to follow the example of the early church and admit the election of bishops and parish priests. In the case of bishops he most probably had in mind election carried out by the clergy of the diocese, and in the case of parish priests, the transfer of rights of patronage to the whole parish community.[9] But it must be added that, even for Hus, the fundamentals of priesthood remained in the power of the keys, committed to the clergy by God, and in the mystery of the act of consecration. In Hus' defence of the sixteenth erroneous article of John Wyclif, sacramental authority is seen as very much relative to the fitness of priests. But even here Hus' position is more cautious than that of his Oxford teacher, because he understands disqualification purely in a moral sense.[10] It is in the same sense that we need to take his assertion that a poor husbandman can have greater dignity before God than a bishop. In Hus' eyes only the Papacy lacked significant justification, although Hus, unlike his associate Jakoubek of Stříbro, did not go so far as to perceive in the Popes the incarnation of Antichrist.[11]

The very foundation of a privileged spiritual estate was the target of old and new manifestations of so-called "popular heresy". Already in 1408 the Vicar General of the Prague Archbishopric denounced as heresy the opinion of one suspect priest that not only the clergy, but also the laity could preach. This was not necessarily a heresy of Waldensian provenance, since shortly afterwards Master Jerome of Prague preached frequently in Prague and the countryside, although he was not an ordained priest.[12] According to an anonymous report written between 1414 and 1416, self-styled people's preachers from the area around Sezimovo Ústí were pouring scorn on priestly vestments, devotional objects and symbols; offering the people the sacrament outside the mass; irresponsibly shortening and changing the liturgy; holding services in barns; replacing altars with simple barrels; and christening children in streams and fishponds.[13] In the lobbies of the Council of Constance anti-Hussite pamphlets spread the news that —

---

[9] Jiří Daňhelka, ed., *Magistri Iohannis Hus Opera Omnia*, Tomus 4 (Prague, 1985), 257-8. Many other similar passages by Vlastimil Kybal, *M. Jan Hus. Učení* 2.1 (Prague, 1926), 311-29, 394-401.

[10] Jaroslav Eršil, ed., *Magistri Iohannis Hus Opera Omnia*, Tomus 22 (Prague, 1966), 205f. For the discussion see Paul De Vooght, *L'Hérésie de Jean Huss* 2 (Louvain, 1975), 729-78.

[11] Paul De Vooght, *Jacobellus de Stříbro (†1429), premier théologien du hussitisme* (Louvain, 1972), 3-7, 32-6.

[12] See Václav Novotný, *M. Jan Hus. Život a učení* 1.1 (Prague, 1919), 240-1. Most notable the defense of preaching by laymen, in the "De quadruplici missione" by Nicholas of Dresden, ed. Jan Sedlák, in *Studie a texty* 1 (Olomouc, 1914), 95-117.

[13] For an anonymous account of radical activities in the castle of Kozí Hrádek and around the castle and in the town of Ústí-nad-Lužnicí see Kaminsky, *A History of the Hussite Revolution*, 166f.; Šmahel, *Dějiny Tábora* 1.1, 210f.

horribile dictu — "the most precious sacrament of the blood of Our Lord is being carried around Bohemia in bottles, and cobblers are hearing confession and are giving the sacred body of the Lord to others."[14]

The shortening of the mass and all other church ceremonials in the radical Taborite communities meant that the clergy, dressed in their simple coats, were indistinguishable from the laity. Earlier, and indeed in all Hussite groups, the reintroduction of the Chalice had lessened the distance between the priest and the layman. For with the aid of both sacraments, both could now communicate with Jesus Christ and with the sphere of the supernatural. Those who went furthest in this respect were the Taborites and Pikards. In the joyful age of the Holy Ghost which had, according to these believers, already begun, Christ was spiritually present among his followers on Taborite soil, and he supped with them at every meal; in no way was he confined in a piece of bread or a drop of wine. When every layman could thus so easily join with Christ in spirit, it followed that the priest lost his importance as intermediary.[15]

For a completely different reason the modest squire, Peter of Chelčice, one of the most penetrating of fifteenth-century thinkers, challenged the privileges of the clergy as an estate. Chelčický categorically denied the validity of the church's teaching on the triple division of society, since he found nothing in St. Paul's Epistle to the Romans (13:1f.) which would support the claims of the aristocracy and clergy to worldly power. Hence he de facto placed the clergy on the same level as the common people. But he did so only within the notion of an ideal state and he argued in moral rather than political terms, for nothing was more repugnant to him than violence of any kind.[16] Chelčický's challenge, however, was refused and ignored in Hussite Bohemia, where even for the theologians of the Taborite "Party of Order" (such as Kaminsky), the division of society into three estates was an unchangeable reality in harmony with the law of God.[17]

From the time of Hus onward the ideal remained of harmonious cooperation among the three estates in the spirit of feudal justice. It must, however, be added that all Hussite thought, whether or not influenced by Wyclif's doctrine of predestination, displayed a dualistic conception of the church and Christian society. This conception suggested the existence of two parallel societies each including every rung of the estates. In the most

---

[14] "Petri de Mladoniowicz Relatio de magistro Johanne Hus", ed. Václav Novotný, in *Fontes rerum Bohemicarum* 8 (Prague, 1932), 45-8.

[15] For details, Kaminsky, *A History of the Hussite Revolution*, chap. 9.

[16] Howard Kaminsky, "Peter Chelčický: Treatises on Christianity and the Social Order", *Studies in Medieval and Renaissance History* 1 (1964): 4-179, esp. 107-36; Murray L. Wagner, *Petr Chelčický: A Radical Separatist in Hussite Bohemia* (Scottdale, Penn., 1983), 94-8; Wojciech Iwańczak, *Ludzie miecza, ludzie modlitwy i ludzie pracy* (Kielce, 1989), chap. 3.

[17] Kaminsky, *A History of the Hussite Revolution*, 397ff.

radical version of this conception, the social body which had succumbed to the Antichrist was destined for complete destruction. Accordingly, in the revolutionary wave, the Taborite warriors mercilessly exterminated the opponents of God's Law from the ranks both of the regular and spiritual clergy. But with the emergence in the Taborite brotherhood of the Pikard heresy, which blasphemously denied the Hussite sacrament of the Chalice, there began a remorseless fight among factions in which the majority of free-thinkers were slaughtered or finished up at the stake. In less than a year the number of priests and preachers among the Taborites had fallen by more than half.[18]

Not only their manifestos, but also at the public hearing of the Council of Basel, spokesmen of the Hussite federation consistently put forward articles demanding a church divested of wealth and worldly power. A resolution of the Diet of Čáslav, which confirmed the importance of the Four Hussite Articles in June 1421, legalised the seizure and confiscation of church property on Bohemian soil. At Basel this resolution was extended to apply to the entire Roman Catholic community. It is not surprising that the demand of secularization of all the clergy's civil dominion, which according to F. G. Heymann was the most politically significant and far reaching of the Four Articles of Prague, should have called forth protracted theoretical discussion of the definition of ownership (possessio), use (usum rei) and worldly authority (dominium civile). Insofar as some controversy surrounded the question of who was to have lordship over church goods, this was resolved by a theoretical compromise acceptable to both sides.[19] But in practice the debate changed nothing, for the confiscated estates were not returned.

Already in the pre-Hussite period radical preachers had stepped out of the sphere of purely spiritual duties and had become popular leaders. The place of the Taborite clergy was at the battle front, where some of them even wielded the sword. The spiritual leaders of the Taborite and other Hussite armies habitually intervened in military affairs, became officers in town halls and municipal organisation and so influenced public opinion. It is therefore hardly surprising that their opponents hastened to present this behaviour in an unflattering light. In a pamphlet attacking the Taborite priests, the Prague university Master John Příbram colourfully described how they "themselves exercise worldly power in contravention of the Third Article", how they controlled the pillaged church goods like "kings and emperors", and how

---

[18] For details, Šmahel, *Dějiny Tábora* 1.1, 314-6.
[19] See Heymann, *John Žižka*, 153-4; and for other references most recently Johannes Helmrath, *Das Basler Konzil 1431-1449. Forschungsstand und Probleme* (Cologne, 1987), 353-72.

they sat in judgment over the townspeople and the neighbouring squires and husbandmen.[20]

Thus in Hussite Bohemia, the secular power of the clergy had been pushed out of the door only to return rapidly by the window. Representatives of the Utraquist Consistory, led by the elected archbishop Jan of Rokycany, did not agree to give up power and influence over the lords and town authorities. Rokycana sided with his clergy against justified complaints, pilloried his secular opponents from the pulpit, and frequently interfered in municipal affairs. The public agents whose guardianship was affected by this behaviour took an entirely different view. The article against the civil dominion of the clergy was, in fact, a noose around the necks of the Hussite clergy, which in the first half of the fifteenth century some officials of the Hussite King George of Poděbrady would begin to tug.[21]

In a small treatise written by the Sub-Chamberlain Vaněk Valečovský (†1472) and entitled "Against Priestly Rule", the trumpet of anticlericalism was again sounded, and this time directed against the Utraquist clergy. Valečovský was a soldier of gentry origins, who by his own account had honoured the sacrament in both kinds from childhood, for which he had suffered considerably. While he got on well with the Roman Catholic clergy, he found nothing to praise among the Taborite or Utraquist priests. In the treatise, which he put together in the Autumn of 1453, Valečovský took the Taborite clergy as his first target. To his no less intemperate criticism of the Utraquist clergy he than brought a whole range of examples from his own experience. To believe Valečovský, we must accept that Rokycana's priests were ruled by "irresponsibility, pride, arrogance, avarice, drunkenness, sodomy and other beastly abuses". The Utraquist church was suffering from a critical shortage of priests and so the morally blameless archbishop had to turn a blind eye to the vices of his clergy. But the Sub-Chamberlain undoubtedly exaggerated in his criticism. It cannot be a coincidence that the old Bohemina Annals, in the necrology, contain the comment on Valečovský that he would have happily seen every priest in the stocks.[22]

This squire in royal service provoked the anger of both clerical parties, for on the facade of his Prague house he had painted an allegory of the church in the likeness of a wagon hitched to two teams. The painting was completed sometime before 1461. A contemporary interpretation of this allegory survives in a manuscript of the Czech Brethren:

---

[20] John Příbram, "Život kněží táborských", ed. Josef Macek, in *Ktož jsú boží bojovníci* (Prague, 1951), 284-5.

[21] See Frederick Heymann, "The Hussite-Utraquist Church in the Fifteenth and Sixteenth Centuries", *ARG* 52 (1961): 1-16; and above all Rudolf Urbánek, *České dějiny. Věk poděbradský* 3.3 (Prague, 1930), 595-989.

[22] For Valečovský's career, see Urbánek, *České dějiny* 3.3, 72-85. The text is published most recently by Jaroslav Bidlo, in *Akty Jednoty bratrské II* (Brno, 1923), 242-54.

This carriage shows the Church Errant in this world, and the wretched people sitting in it would happily travel to the Kingdom of God. But they cannot, for priests have harnessed horses to opposing ends of the wagon, and they drive and draw the cart each in his own direction. Therefore, the wagon remains in the same place, and the people sitting in it quarrel so fiercely that they incite and plague each other like madmen, without saying anything to the drivers.[23]

There could be no better illustration of anticlerical reaction in Hussite Bohemia. Moreover, this allegory of double and conflicting faiths, as conceived by Valečovský of Kněžmost, had not lost its relevance even on the eve of the German reformation, for in 1518 it was printed at the Nuremberg press upon the Map of Bohemia by Nicholas Klaudyan.[24]

---

[23] See Bidlo, *Akty II*, 255. For discussion about this painted allegory, see Urbánek, *České dějiny* 3.3, 74-5.

[24] For the map by Nicholas Klaudyan with the allegory of the church, Mirjam Bohatcová, "Höltzlův jednolist s Klaudiánovou mapou Čech", *Strahovská knihovna* 14-15 (1979-80): 39-47.

ANTICLERICALISM IN LATE MEDIEVAL GERMAN VERSE

ALBRECHT CLASSEN

University of Arizona, Tucson

One of the most dramatic events of the later Middle Ages was the "fall" of the Catholic Church and the emergence of the Reformation.[1] The decline of the only Christian church had been anticipated for hundreds of years, but it became acutely noticeable only in the fifteenth century. The phenomenon of anticlericalism, common in one form or another throughout the medieval period, reflects this perception as it reached a peculiar pitch during the same century.[2] We have a plethora of literary and historical documents testifying to this process. The incrustation of simony and the inextractable intertwining of worldly and clerical spheres were two major targets of criticism which the church of that age experienced on an almost daily basis, and this perhaps since the late twelfth century.[3] From the time of the late fourteenth century, the most vocal criticism was addressed toward the contenders for the supreme clerical position and to the schism which threatened the religious and political unity of Europe and the church. Despite the various conciliar movements, a real reform was apparently not possible.[4] Not surprisingly, Luther had his stunning success, contrary to his own intentions and expectations, because of deep-seated popular resentment against the clergy

---

[1] It proves to be problematic to label the 'Reformation' as an age quite separate from the previous century in theological, intellectual and historical terms; cf. Stephan Skalweit, *Der Beginn der Neuzeit*, Erträge der Forschung 178 (Darmstadt, 1982), 108f. For a broader discussion of the epoch, see Reinhart Herzog and Reinhart Kosellek, eds., *Epochenschwelle und Epochenbewußtsein*, Poetik und Hermeneutik 12 (Munich, 1987).

[2] See the definition by José Sánchez, *Anticlericalism: A Brief History* (Notre Dame, 1972), 7ff.

[3] Helga Schüppert, *Kirchenkritik in der lateinischen Lyrik des 12. und 13. Jahrhunderts*, Medium Aevum 23 (Munich, 1972); Eberhard Nellmann, "Spruchdichter oder Minnesänger?", *Walther von der Vogelweide. Hamburger Kolloquium 1988 zum 65. Geburtstag von Karl-Heinz Borck*, ed. J.-D. Müller, F. J. Worstbrock (Stuttgart, 1989), 37-59, here 55ff.

[4] Erich Meuthen, *Das fünfzehnte Jahrhundert*, Oldenbourg Grundriß der Geschichte 9 (Munich, 1980), 75ff.

and due to social conflicts inherent within this religious — yet increasingly secular — institution.[5]

Among other important factors stimulating the rise of anticlericalism, we might also mention the emergence of humanism in the late fourteenth and fifteenth centuries with its debilitating effect on the Catholic Church and its dogmatic and orthodox teachings.[6] Much of the anticlericalism voiced by the Renaissance philosophers addressed intellectual questions, and, therefore, did not become part of the mainstream popular criticism against the church. Nevertheless, even these "new" teachings were based on an old tradition of attacks on Catholic theology coming from the ranks of university scholars.[7] But taking all forms of anticlericalism together, the Lutheran Reformation appears to be the culminating point of many different strands in the transition from the Middle Ages to the early modern age.

The distinction between laity and priesthood, still clear-cut in the high Middle Ages, corroded during the fourteenth and fifteenth centuries. The decreasing difference between the two social groups became more noticeable in the later Middle Ages and provided rich material for a large body of satirical texts,[8] such as Giovanni Boccaccio's *Decameron*, the Stricker's *maeren* or Sebastian Brant's *Narrenschiff*, Poggio Bracciolini's *Fazetie* or Chaucer's *Canterbury Tales*, to mention only a few.[9]

But the criticism of the two major pillars of medieval society — clergy and chivalry — was not unique to the fifteenth and sixteenth centuries, nor

---

[5] Peter Moraw, *Von offener Verfassung zu gestalteter Verdichtung. Das Reich im späten Mittelalter 1250 bis 1490*, Propyläen Geschichte Deutschlands 3 (Berlin, 1985), 405f.

[6] See Hans Baron, *The Crisis of the Early Italian Renaissance: Civic Humanism and Republican Liberty in an Age of Classicism and Tyranny*, vol. 1 (Princeton, 1955), 284.

[7] See, for example, the heated debate over the proper reception and interpretation of Aristotle, Averroes, and Avicenna in the late thirteenth century in Paris. In 1277, Bishop Etienne Tempier condemned 219 theses which various teachers at the university had allegedly developed and proclaimed in public. Whether reflecting the true opinion of Siger of Brabant, Albertus Magnus, Boethius of Dacia, among others, or simply reflecting what Tempier, Thomas Aquinas, and Bonaventura read into their opponents' writings, these condemned opinions demonstrate the beginning of a fully-fledged anticlericalism in the late Middle Ages. See *Aufklärung im Mittelalter? Die Verurteilung von 1277*, ed. Kurt Flasch, Excerpta Classica 6 (Mainz, 1989).

[8] Ute Monika Schwob, "Formen der Laienfrömmigkeit im spätmittelalterlichen Brixen", *Volkskultur des europäischen Spätmittelalters*, ed. P. Dinzelbacher, H.-D. Mück, Böblinger Forum 1 (Stuttgart, 1987), 159-75, here 160f.; Ronald Pepin, *Literature of Satire in the Twelfth Century. A Neglected Mediaeval Genre*, Studies in Mediaeval Literature 2 (Lewiston, 1988).

[9] Wolfgang Beutin, "Zur Problematik des Antiklerikalismus in der europäischen Erzählliteratur um 1400", *Jahrbuch der Oswald-von-Wolkenstein-Gesellschaft* 4 (1986/87): 81-94.

was it limited to German and Italian poetry. The Spanish debate poem *Elena y María* from 1280 reveals that there existed a long-standing anticlerical tradition in medieval literature.[10] Walther von der Vogelweide, and with him many political and didactic poets of his age such as Thomasin von Zerclaere, imparted harsh criticism both against the Papacy and the lower clergy, against the members of the institution and the church itself.[11]

Here I intend to survey fifteenth-century German lyric poetry in light of its anticlerical stance. My purpose is to investigate how the various authors spoke out against the church, how they defined their criticism, how they expressed their antipathy and whether we can speak of a literary genre under the heading 'lyric anticlericalism'.

First I suggest to examine the historical-intellectual context of anticlericalism in order to establish a conceptual framework for the poems under discussion. Although the fifteenth century provided the platform upon which the Reformation could develop in the early sixteenth century, it was not simply an age of conflict and unrest, when opposing forces were preparing the battleground for the Reformation.[12] Rather the opposite can be observed. It has been said that the fifteenth century was one of the most pious ages within the history of the Christian church. For instance, the largest number ever of religious fraternities were founded in Hamburg after 1450. Pilgrimage assumed a new dimension and was directed not only towards the traditional goals such as Jerusalem, Rome or Santiago de Compostella, but also towards many locales within central Europe where miracles allegedly had been witnessed. The number of dedications to saints or Christ himself, expressed in the form of altar pieces, paintings or capellas rose considerably during the century.[13] However, Johan Huizinga warns us against identifying the surge in piety with a strong support for the Catholic Church:

> Of all the contradictions which religious life of the period presents, perhaps the most insoluble is that of an avowed contempt of the clergy, a contempt seen as

---

[10] Julio Rodríguez-Puértolas, *Poesía de protesta en la edad media castellana. Historia y antología*, Biblioteca románica hispánica 6 (Madrid, 1968), 16f.

[11] *Die Gedichte Walthers von der Vogelweide*, ed. Karl Lachmann, 13th rev. ed. by Hugo Kuhn (Berlin, 1965), L. 11, 6ff.; L. 25, 11ff.; L. 34, 1ff. Thomasin von Zerclaere, *Der welsche Gast*, ed. F. W. von Kries, vol. 1, GAG 425/I (Göppingen, 1984), v. 13407ff. For a brief survey of anticlerical poetry in twelfth and thirteenth-century Germany, cf. Olive Sayce, *The Medieval German Lyric 1150-1300. The Development of its Themes and Forms in their European Context* (Oxford, 1982), 428f.

[12] For a history of social unrest see Peter Blickle, *Unruhen in der ständischen Gesellschaft 1300-1800*, Enzyklopädie Deutscher Geschichte 1 (Munich, 1988).

[13] P. Moraw, 403.

an undercurrent throughout the Middle Ages, side by side with the very great respect shown for the sanctity of the sacerdotal office.[14]

John Hus and John Wyclif, although not directly related in their reformist endeavors, were the most outspoken defenders of splinter groups which were strongly condemned by church officials, although they did not succeed in suppressing them.[15]

Not only the church but the state as well was under heavy attack from many sides and considered to be on the brink of collapse, as the Emperor Sigismund acutely observed upon assuming power as King in 1410: "leider in Tutschen und Welschen landen durch daz kunigrich von Arlatt in Savoy und an allin enden zerrissen virfallin und allir siner zugehorungen stete sloße lande ... so gar entwert ist daz im widerbrengung sere note were ... "[16] In other words, the awareness of a crisis extended far beyond daily problems with the parish priest or a bishop as a political opponent, but rather was perceived as a threat to the whole society of late medieval Europe.

What did this mean for late medieval literature? How did the poets vocalize these general and all-affecting trends? How did they depict the church and its representatives? I suggest to concentrate on fifteenth-century German poetry only because this focus will enable us to perceive continuity and discontinuity within one body of texts which were relatively closely related to one another. Certainly, a large number of poets were building on a broad literary tradition rather than relying on specific exchanges, adaptations and receptions, even though this form of consensus-building among the poets should not be excluded. In other words, the poets reflected their own personal experiences and at the same time they drew upon popular opinions. The theme of anticlericism had developed over centuries and thus could easily be expanded and altered by each individual writer at a time when the collapse of the church seemed to be imminent.

The South Tyrolean singer Oswald von Wolkenstein (1376/77-1445) served for a number of years as diplomat, translator for and political representative of Emperor Sigismund. He was fully aware of the devastating effects which the schism had on the structure of the church because he was a first-hand witness of the deliberations which Sigismund carried out both at the Council of Constance (1414-1418) and during his extensive journey through France, Aragón and England in which the Emperor aimed at settling the fight among the three competing Popes.[17] Instead of dealing with the concrete political events and the religious conflict, however, Oswald simply

---

[14] Johan Huizinga, *The Waning of the Middle Ages*. First published in 1924 (Garden City, NY, 1954), 178.

[15] E. Meuthen, 74ff.

[16] Quoted from: Heinz Angermeier, *Die Reichsreform 1410-1555. Die Staatsproblematik in Deutschland zwischen Mittelalter und Gegenwart* (Munich, 1984), 31.

[17] Albrecht Classen, *Zur Rezeption norditalienischer Kultur des Trecento im Werk Oswalds von Wolkenstein (1376/77-1445)*, GAG 471 (Göppingen, 1987), 33.

mentions the schism and deliberately ignores its wider implications for the church. He perceives Sigismund's endeavors as a form of hunting with Pope Benedict XIII as the prey which needs to be lured into the hunter's net:

> Der ainen vogel vahen müss,
> das er im nicht emphliege,
> der tü im richten, locken süss,
> domit er in betriege.[18]

Whereas the Emperor expressed deep concerns about the split of the Catholic Church and undertook all efforts he could to heal this rift, Oswald observes the events only from the distance and with amusement.[19] For the poet, the priorities have changed. Although the prime object is the future of one of the opposing Popes, the poet does not treat him with any particular attention and instead focuses on political events and the military and cultural situation in Perpignan. He only marginally touches upon the negotiations between Sigismund and the Pope's emissaries and representatives:

> Künig Sigmund teglich zumal
> sich arbait, achzehn wochen
> mit bäbsten, bischoff, cardinal;
> und wĕrn si erstochen,
> der seinen falsch darinn erzaigt
> und zu der scisma was genaigt,
> ich wolt si all verklagen,
> mit pfeiffen auf ainem wagen.
>
> (Kl 19, 57-64)

But even this attitude of a comedian betrays that the ordinary lay person, here the noble poet, does not perceive any particular importance in the dealings with the church. Any contact with a bishop, cardinal or even the Pope himself (59) is not to be evaluated in any other way as those with secular dignitaries. Those representatives of the church, however, who are considered guilty of wrongdoing are no longer sacrosanct and should be indicted in the public. Oswald laughs at Pedro Luna (Benedict XIII's given name), attacks him for his greediness and threatens that from now on those who had been subservient to him will pick up their flutes and play their tunes to which the Pope will have to dance:

---

[18] *Die Lieder Oswalds von Wolkenstein*, 3rd rev. ed., ed. H. Moser, N. R. Wolf, N. Wolf, ATB 55 (Tübingen, 1987); quotations from Oswald's songs are taken from 1st ed. (1962), ed. K. K. Klein (=Kl) et al., giving the song and verse numbers, here 19, 17-20. For a modern German translation cf. Wernfried Hofmeister, *Oswald von Wolkenstein. Sämtliche Lieder und Gedichte. Ins Neuhochdeutsche übersetzt*, GAG 511 (Göppingen, 1989).

[19] Cf. Anton Schwob, *Oswald von Wolkenstein. Eine Biographie*. 3rd ed., Schriftenreihe des Südtiroler Kulturinstitutes 4 (Bozen, 1979), 112ff.

> die vor an dich *geloubet* hand,
> die pfeiffent dir mit grillen
> zu tanz auff ainer tillen.

(Kl 19, 134-136)

From a larger perspective these few verses indicate, so personal they seem
to be, that the late medieval lay individual, represented here by our poet, has
become liberated and freed from his traditional submission under the
church's control. Whereas before the clerical dignitaries had assumed the
supreme role within society, they are now criticized and laughed at. In fact,
the poet as entertainer claims more attention from his audience than Pope
Benedict XIII himself, who is under political siege as Sigismund is trying
to convince him to resign from office:

> Weib und ouch man mich schauten an mit lachen so;
> neun personier kungklicher zier, die waren da
> ze Pärpian, ir babst von Lun, genant Petro,
> der Römisch künig der zehent und die von Praides.

(Kl 18, 45-48)

But Oswald was too concerned with his own life to deal with political and
clerical matters on a broader philosophical level. In his song "Wer machen
well sein peutel ring" (Kl 45), where he presents a picture of daily events
at the Council of Constance, all his attention is focused on entertainment,
prices, food, women and music, whereas the larger issues, the schism and
the reform of the church, are only touched upon to provide a historical
framework for his song. The same applies to the song "O wunnikliches
paradis" (Kl 98), where the poet's erotic adventures occupy the attention,
while the clerical debate is entirely neglected. Oswald has obviously
discarded the traditional respect for the members of the higher church
administration and sarcastically refers to a bishop as a comic figure when
he reports of everyday affairs and problems. In "Sich manger freut" (Kl 102)
the painter Hans is attacked by a group of Hungarian street robbers while
he is enjoying a prostitute in a brothel. He comments about his dire
situation:

> ain bischof solt ich machen,
> darauss so wurden Unger vier,
> die kind der teufel nem.

(Kl 102, 58-60)

Indicating that 'to act like a Bishop' means to make love with a prostitute.
    Oswald's relationship with the clergy seems to have been special,
however, because he had close contacts with the Bishop of Brixen and was
a member of his political entourage for a number of years.[20] When he later

---

[20] A. Schwob, *Oswald von Wolkenstein*, 91ff.

fell out with him because of disagreements over political decisions, the poet ignores his episcopal rank and identifies him as his opponent in military terms.[21] The tensions culminated in a personal attack in which Oswald punched the Bishop on his nose. Ulrich Putsch II related this detail in his diary and thus confirms the historical truth of the poet's statement. Yet later developments in Tyrol brought both men back into a close political alliance, which indicates that the conflict itself was of a purely political nature and could be healed easily if an agreement was made.[22] Here, however, as in many other incidences, the highest ranking member of the regional clergy is not exempted from the poet's sharp criticism. Oswald characterizes all clerics as guilty of adultery and fornication, and he blames Ulrich in particular for having a courtesan at hand whom he provides with rich gifts (Kl 104, 31). As a consequence of his sinful behavior, which would find multiple parallels among nuns, monks and priests, the Bishop has a special place reserved for him in hell:[23]

> Das sibent gadem ist beswärt
> mit grosser zagknuss, ewiklich dorinn bewärt,
> da sein vermärt böss nunnen, münch und pfaffen.

(Kl 32, 55-57)

But apart from his satire Oswald had more serious points of complaint against the clergy, the heaviest being that they misused their power as spiritual leaders and assumed legal positions inappropriate for God's representatives here on earth. His criticism is directed against the church laws and clerics functioning as lawyers:

> ain bös gewonhait in der welt:
> die gaistlich sein und weltlich recht
> regieren mer wann ritter und knecht
> und wellen nutzen baide swert,
> wie habent die so güten wërt?

(Kl 112, 144-148)

---

[21] This role the Bishop shared with Oswald's other neighbors, the alpine farmers, who all hated the Wolkensteiner for his impetuousness and ruthlessness in economic and military terms. At one point, however, both the local peasants and the clerical dignitary seemed to have won considerable influence over Oswald since he complains: "Nu mir der pawer ist gevar,/ und auch gen Brixsen nicht wol tar" (Kl 104, 21f.). See my study "Der Bauer in der Dichtung Oswalds von Wolkenstein", *Euphorion* 82/2 (1988): 150-67.

[22] Dirk Joschko, *Oswald von Wolkenstein. Eine Monographie zu Person, Werk und Forschungsgeschichte*, GAG 396 (Göppingen, 1985) 103f.

[23] This is the complete reversal of the description of Saint Anno in the *Annolied* from ca. 1080/85 or 1105 where the Bishop of Cologne finds a seat reserved for himself in heaven. Whether Oswald was familiar with this poem is entirely uncertain; for the *Annolied* see: *Das Annolied*, ed. Eberhard Nellmann (Stuttgart, 1975).

All deviations from traditional law are described as elements undermining society at large. The ideal of medieval order, as Oswald envisions it, cannot be upheld if even the clerics begin to assume worldly attitudes and they cheat and rob their neighbors just like any other ordinary person: "als wenn der abpt die würfel tragt,/ die brüder spilen all hin nach/ zu lieb dem herren wüster sach." (Kl 112, 32-34). But Oswald goes one step further in his statement that clerics should not be allowed to exert worldly rule at all: "wo gaistlich herschen leut und lant,/ da wirt mer ungeleichs erkant,/ wann fürsten, den das zu gebiert" (Kl 112, 157-159). The clergy were assigned by God the role of praying for themselves, the knights and the peasants and to secure for them all a place in heaven (167ff.).[24] Moreover, Oswald blames the priests for more conflicts and trouble in society than any other social class:

> mer unfrid kompt der welde blos
> von priesterschaft und ir genoss,
> wann susst von allen laien pschicht.
>
> (Kl 112, 182-4)

Because he has witnessed the situation of the church in Rome, he claims to speak from experience: "si machen kunnen krump und slecht/ ... / lernt man zu Rom, wie vil man wil" (192-4) and thus places himself in a tradition which would have tremendous effects on Martin Luther not quite a hundred years later. But already at the beginning of the fourteenth century the debaucheries of the members of the Roman Papacy were well known and found many critics all over Europe.[25] Oswald reflected a popular notion and could expect to find approval among his audience in his criticism of the church. The more conservative his outlook, the more his listeners must have prodded him along to continue with his poem.

Of course, reality was different, and many church institutions had adapted to the needs of their time. When a reformer energetically tried to impose rigid rules, he normally encountered stiff opposition from the local nobility above all, who also complained about the church's laxness and deviation from traditional ideals. Even Oswald's own daughter Maria experienced a conflict with Bishop Nicholaus of Cusa, because she saw her existence in the St. Claire convent in Brixen not so much as a personal dedication to God, but rather as a form of institutional procurement for unmarried women. She fought bitterly against the attempts to force her and other rebellious women to adjust to a new set of rules.[26]

---

[24] The same attititude is expressed in his song "Ir bäbst, ir kaiser, du pawman" (Kl, 113).

[25] Will Durant, *Glanz und Zerfall der italienischen Renaissance*, Kulturgeschichte der Menschheit 8 (Frankfurt, 1981; first published in English, 1953), here 135ff.

[26] D. Joschko, 106f. He seems to side with the reform-minded Bishop, although the St. Claire convent did not suffer at all from a negative reputation. For the literary

Her father, however, considered the church to be an institution of old reputation which should not be touched, although its clergy did not hold to the moral standards of the old days. The most common accusation levied against priests or monks in fifteenth-century poetry, denounced them for blatant sexuality either within the convents or outside. Oswald also confirms this impression in his *Trinklied* (Kl 84) — "Wol auff, wir wellen slauffen" — because there he admonishes his friends to return home early enough from the tavern to prevent anyone, including monks or priests from paying a visit to their wives and to commit adultery with them: "das laien, münch und pfaffen/ zu unsern weiben staffen" (Kl 84, 6f.).[27] The humorous tone indicates, however, that the breach of the clerical vows was considered a much lesser crime than the assumption of worldly power, greed and luxury on the part of the clergy. In "Ach got, wër ich ain bilgerin" (Kl 90) Oswald even confirms that he himself used the disguise of a pilgrim to win the love of a woman and thus approves, at least to some extent, that members of the clergy do seek erotic adventures despite their commitment to God's service and vows of chastity.

Oswald was not the most relentless critic of the church, because he had other concerns and expressed them in his poetry quite clearly. Nevertheless, his lyric oeuvre reveals some of the basic points of criticism which were constantly raised against the clergy in the later Middle Ages. How did other fifteenth-century poets react to the declining morality of the church? Did they perceive the same malaise as Oswald, or did they experience different problems with the church than he? We need to consider, in particular, whether a different class background induced poets to see the church in a light other than the aristocratic singer. Although we often know too little to determine the poets' biography, I hope to reach a definite conclusion regarding their treatment of anticlericalism in the late Middle Ages in the German speaking countries.

One of the most vocal critics of clerical vices in poetic terms seems to have been an anonymous author called "Pfaffenfeind" who composed a

---

aspect of Maria's correspondence cf. A. Classen, "Footnotes to the Canon: Maria von Wolkenstein and Argula von Grumbach", in *The Politics of Gender in Early Modern Europe*, ed. J. R. Brink, A. P. Coudert, M. C. Horowitz, Sixteenth Century Essays & Studies 12 (Kirksville, Mo., 1989), 131-47.

[27] For an interpretation of this song in the tradition of 'Trinklieder' cf. Wilfried Schwanholz, *Volksliedhafte Züge im Werk Oswalds von Wolkenstein. Die Trinklieder*, Germanistische Arbeiten zu Sprache und Kulturgeschichte 6 (Frankfurt, 1985), 270ff. I cannot agree with Lambertus Okken and Hans-Dieter Mück, who perceive in this criticism an attack on all people who are not members of the peasant class, *Die satirischen Lieder Oswalds von Wolkenstein wider die Bauern. Untersuchungen zum Wortschatz und zur literarhistorischen Einordnung*, GAG 316 (Göppingen, 1981), 464.

diatribe against the church in 1431.[28] He reflects on the battle between the city of Magdeburg and its Archbishop over legal matters and property issues. Since the Hussites had made dangerous incursions into lower Saxony, Magdeburg was afraid of future attacks and began to fortify the city walls and buttresses. This necessitated, however, the infringement upon the Bishop's land and buildings, and soon both parties were embroiled in long lasting warfare which was settled only in 1435 and which, ironically, destabilized the city more so than the Hussites ever could.[29]

The poet complains about the church's presumptious attitude, because it is not able to protect the city from the Hussite attacks and at the same time undermines its position within the German empire:

> Der krieg sich angefangen hat,
> darzu gaben die pfaffen raht,
> das ist ganz offenbare,
> beschirmn nicht wol die christenheit
> und geben bôse lahre, ja lahre.

$$(3, 1-5)$$

Moreover, the animosity between city and Bishop revealed where the true interests of many a citizen rested. Instead of supporting the poor with alms, a man called Sadelman dedicated all his wealth to the church and its fight with the city: "het ers an arme leute gelegt,/ kem seiner seel zu masse, zu masse" (5, 4f.). Many other people followed his example, but the poet stresses it would lead them — just as the clerics — only to hell: "gottsdienst han sie gekrenket./ ihrn seeln gemacht ein bôses bad" (10, 3f.). Already here in life they have signed a pact with the devil: "sie dienen dem teufel frû und spat" (13, 4) and committed all kinds of horrible crimes, the most notable being the rape of virgins and exploitation of the common man. The poet's attack assumes a higher pitch when he characterizes the priests as street robbers ("strassenreuber", 14, 2) who have abandoned all honor and virtue. Consequently he appeals to Duke Günther and other worldly rulers to provide Magdeburg with protection from the vicious church, for which God would give them a reward (17ff.). A significant rift between the church and laity is opening here and the parties are seen as enemies here on earth. God, however, is declared to be the judge over the dispute, which indicates an early concept of reformist thought: "erbarm dich des, herr Jhesu Christ,/ hilf das gar bald vertreiben" (24, 4f.). The singer no longer accepts the role of

---

[28] Quotes of this poem from Thomas Cramer, ed., *Die kleineren Liederdichter des 14. und 15. Jahrhunderts*, vol. 3 (Munich, 1982), 9ff.; cf. Frieder Schanze, "Pfaffenfeind", *Die deutsche Literatur des Mittelalters. Verfasserlexikon*, 2nd ed. by Kurt Ruh et al. (henceforth, Ruh, *Verfasserlexikon*), vol. 7, section 2 (Berlin, 1988), col. 550f.

[29] The historical context is outlined by Rochus von Liliencron, *Die historischen Volkslieder der Deutschen vom 13. bis 16. Jahrhundert* (Leipzig, 1865; repr. Hildesheim, 1966), 1: 340f.

the church as mediator, since the latter transgressed the traditional role assigned to it by God. Only direct appeals to God and self-reliance can help in this situation.

The war declaration and preparation indicate, however, that the city went ahead with its independent governmental decision and rejected any influence peddling by the nobility: "Der adel thut daran nicht recht,/ das sie der stadt absagen schlecht" (47, 1f.). As so often in such cases, the religious dispute soon turned out to be nothing else than a smoke screen for a major political struggle over who governed Magdeburg. But the poet continues unabated with his animosity against the hostile clergy which explains why at the end the poet names himself "Pfaffenfeind" ('enemy of the priests') (63, 4). We observe an intricate combination of political, religious and ideological conflicts expressed in this song. It seems to demonstrate the dangerous and potent recipe underlying the coming tensions between the reformers and the traditional Catholic Church and which would lead to the collapse of both the church and the Hapsburg dominance over Germany.

Another powerful expression of anticlericalism can be found in the song "Priester, du usserweltes vasß" by one Alblin.[30] He attacks the priests because they are supposed to be God's most cherished recipients of his wisdom and mercy, and yet they prove to be blind, greedy and evil. The priests are invested with a vision of the divine light, and yet they are unable to perceive it: "du trest daz liecht und bist doch blint" (1, 7). They are chosen by God to be his emissaries, and yet they need to be reminded of their own duties: "darzû haut er dich usserkorn" (2,5). In a variant of the song we notice an even stronger moral appeal to the priests to correct their ways: "ir sulet euch bedencken pas,/ so want got pey euch tougen."[31] Alblin also says that the priests read from the Bible, but he observes that they do it only perfunctorily: "got gebúrt in schneller sag,/ mit worten das beschichte" (2, 3f.). Criticism and nostalgia for the ideals of the priestly function are combined in this song as it expresses clearly the popular attitude towards the clergy. This vacillated between admiration and respect for God's representatives on earth ("sit du nûn gottes tempel bist", 2, 14) on the one hand, and, on the other, critical observation of deviance from the right path: "und pflig des schatzes wol" (2, 17). In other words, the lay poet decrees himself to be a necessary watchdog for the class of priests, not because God has asked him to do so, but because the priests have obviously abandoned the traditional ideals and are in need of admonishment.

Anticlericalism was, quite obviously, a very political issue and it reflects a number of motives which the various authors pursued. Depending on the individual situation a poet could, of course, assume the very opposite

---

[30] All quotes from Cramer, ed., *Die kleineren Liederdichter*, 1: 36ff.; cf. Burghart Wachinger, "Alblin", in Ruh, *Verfasserlexikon*, vol. 1, section 1 (Berlin, 1977/78), col. 155f.

[31] Stanza one in cgm 1019 (D), here quoted from Cramer, ed., 1: 37, v. 1f.

position and give praise to the cleric in question. To illustrate this case I refer to a song written in favor of Abbot Ulrich from St. Gallen who had successfully opposed the nearby Swiss city of St. Gallen and the Appenzell canton in the late 1470s in their attempt to place him under their political control. The anonymous poet characterizes the abbot as a "himelfürsten sant Gallen knecht"[32] and praises him as: "Du bist gekrönet mit der eren flût/ als ain ritter, der durch criste globen/ sin bestes mit dem swerte tût." (34-6) Another poet, however, with all certainty a citizen of St. Gallen, attacks the cleric bitterly, accusing him of all possible evil acts. He is "ain roter man,/ der vil unglück machen kan",[33] he has proven his disloyalty (12, 1f.) and has revealed his evil intentions against the city (13, 2). His dangerous impact on the country would be felt if he were allowed to carry out his plans to build a fortress-like church next to the monastery: "so mûß das land verderben!" (16, 5).

The following two songs assume, however, the very opposite attitude and charge St. Gallen and its allies with treason against the well-meaning abbot. The exchange of arguments is based on identical accusations against each other, for instance, when one poet says "Die von sant Gallen und ir mithaften/ die haten ainen list erdächt" (nr. 176, 7, 1f.), whereas the other rejects the accusation by defending the abbot as: "den hetens unbillich beschwert" (nr. 176, 9, 7).

Obviously these songs reveal their political nature, because even when we cannot detect a concrete historical event as an underlying motive, we may safely assume that the poet felt a personal antipathy against a cleric and vented his anger against clerics in general, thus creating a stereotype which occurs in a myriad of forms all over Europe in the later Middle Ages. Considering that even many Latin texts contained this theme, we can exclude the notion that only vernacular poets, and especially those who strove for popular appeal, stood out as the clerics' enemies.[34] But we also have to understand that the church, being the most visible public institution in the Middle Ages, attracted, quite naturally, the most attention and was easily made a scapegoat for many evils of that time.

Certainly, not every priest in the fifteenth century can be described as a greedy and vile person, and yet the clerical estate as a whole received the

---

[32] Quoted from R. von Liliencron (n. 29 above), 2: 163, v. 3.

[33] Liliencron, 2: 277, 10, 1f.

[34] See the critical songs against the church and the clergy in *Die Sterzinger Miszellaneen-Handschrift. Kommentierte Edition der deutschen Dichtung*, ed. Manfred Zimmermann, Innsbrucker Beiträge zur Kulturwissenschaft, Germanistische Reihe 8 (Innsbruck, 1980), 53. For Latin poems condemning the clergy, see "Propter Syon non tacebo" in *Carmina Burana. Texte und Übersetzungen*, ed. Benedikt Konrad Vollmer. Bibliothek des Mittelalters 13 (Frankfurt, 1987), nr. 41, 100ff. Also, "Vtar Contra uitia carmine rebelli", nr. 42, 110ff.; "Roma, Tue mentis oblita sanitate", nr. 43, 118ff.

most criticism because of its official claim to moral and ethical superiority over the rest of the population. Occasional clashes between this claim and economic, moral and religious realities were easy prey for any poet interested in composing anticlerical songs. The *Spruch* "Secht umb, ir heren, was ruschet in der hecken" by Frauenzucht-Bernkopf, written in 1437 on the occasion of the feud between Michel of Wertheim on the one side and Bishop John II of Würzburg and Archbishop Dietrich of Mainz on the other, provides ample evidence for this observation.[35] Disregarding the political context of the song, we observe a sharp attack on the clergy at large. The poet has heard from the population that the priests have assumed an attitude of arrogance ("ubermüt", 17, 2). He therefore declares that the time has come to mete out punishment: "die zit si do hie, daz man sú sülle stroffen" (17, 3) in order to gain peace again with God: "got welle uns fride schaffen" (17, 5). Whereas before the man on the street ("gemeine man", 18, 1) had been deceived by the priests' pretense of well-meaning, now he realizes the double standards in morality and the clergy's purely worldly goals: "das ir nit stellent wan uf zitliche gewinne" (18, 3).

Traditional values such as *mâze* ('moderation' in Middle High German) have been lost to them, since they do not even care for God's love: "achtent ir gar klein und uf götlich *minne*" (18, 5). The following stanza contains a rather surprising statement, because, as the poet highlights, even the Jews have a more pleasant character than the priests. The latter always take money from their flock, whereas the former bring money to them in form of credits: "wanne ein jude die pfennig bringet" (19, 3). But Frauenzucht-Bernkopf is willing to differentiate where it might be necessary. He does not want to be labelled as an enemy of the priesthood in general, because otherwise he could not be called a Christian at all: "ich were nit cristen" (21, 1). He only wants to chide the clergy and point them into the right direction.

Moreover, not all clergy are liable for those crimes he had charged them with: "man vindet ir fil, die sollich sin nit wissen" (21, 5). In other words, the poet makes an attempt at portraying the clergy not as a uniform body of evil-doers, but as a diverse group of both good and evil people. The fact, however, that some do commit crimes weighs more than the case of lay people since the clergy are invested with God's service, and thus subject to more intense scrutiny than lay members of the church.

One of the most problematic and most-often satirized aspect of the clergy's deviation from its traditional path of moral rectitude is the role which many high-ranking church functionaries played in politics and warfare. We noticed this in the case of the poet "Pfaffenfeind", and the same

---

[35] The following quotes are from Th. Cramer, ed. (n. 28 above), 1: 218ff.; historical information is given on p. 456; Cf. Liliencron, 1: nr. 73, 357ff. Ulrich Müller, "Frauenzucht, genannt Bernkopf", in Ruh, *Verfasserlexikon*, vol. 2, section 3 (Berlin, 1979), col. 883f.

emerges in a large number of other political songs as well. In the war of the Palatinate, Count Elect Frederick I fought against Count Ulrich of Württemberg, Margrave Karl of Baden and the Bishops Georg of Metz and a Bishop of Speyer, and defeated them in the battle of Seckenheim on June 30, 1462.[36] Two poets, among others, treated the events in their work: Gilgenschein and Hans von Westernach. Both resorted to anticlerical images which however do not differ basically from those coined for attacking the political opponents. In other words, both Count Ulrich, Margrave Karl and the two Bishops are treated alike; all are portrayed as despicable characters. Gilgenschein advises the Bishop of Metz that he would have done better if he had stayed home and performed his church service: "werst du daheim verliben/ und drügst ein korock an,/ das dir vil besser were."[37] The Bishop of Speyer is accused of being false and deceiving ("falschen dücken", 11, 3), and all war lords receive harsh criticism for their desires to overthrow the traditional ruler of the Palatinate: "mit gewalt on alles recht" (4, 7).

However, the poet does perceive some differences among the clergy and recommends Georg of Metz to follow the examples set by his own subordinate priests: "het ein mesz gelesen,/ als ander pfaffen driben!" (6, 6f.). In each of these cases the political thrust is aimed at restoring the previous order characterized by the three classes of *oratores*, *bellatores*, and *laboratores*. But in addition the poet idealizes the concept of a political order dominated by an old noble family. Thus a nostalgic aspect enters the song and fuels the anticlerical statements even more. Consequently Gilgenschein ends his poem with a praise of Count Frederick: "O edeler Fürst gerecht" (13, 1) and with a self-presentation in the last stanza: "Gilgenschein ist ers genent" (14, 1).

In the case that local supporters of the bishops might find his songs objectionable, the poet points out in "Wölt ir hören ein nuwes geticht" (p. 249ff.) that the real source of all evils does not rest with the bishops, but with the Pope in Rome. The poet claims that the Pope supports the wrong people and issues bulls against those who side with the 'right' party: "er wil dem unrechten bigestan" (7, 2) and "Wer dem rechten wil bigestan,/ der bapst der dut ine in den ban" (8, 1f.).[38] Together with the Emperor the

---

[36] I have discussed the historical context and particularly the poetic descriptions of the events by Hans von Westernach in a previous article, "Hans von Westernach: *Der Pfalzgraf hieß da ziehen baß*. Politische und militärische Dichtung des deutschen Spätmittelalters", *Amsterdamer Beiträge zur älteren Germanistik* 26 (1987): 133-51.

[37] Quoted from Th. Cramer (n. 28 above), 1: 249, 12, 3-5; cf. Thomas Cramer, "Gilgenschein", in Ruh, *Verfasserlexikon*, vol. 3, section 1 (Berlin, 1980), col. 44.

[38] Some of Gilgenschein's verses are direct borrowings from the critic of the twelfth and thirteenth centuries, Walther von der Vogelweide; for example "darumb kein strasz mocht werden fri/ uf wasser noch uf lande" (7, 4f.), which is closely modelled on Walther's "untriuwe ist in der sâze,/ gewalt vert ûf der strâze:/ fride unde reht sint sêre wunt." Quoted from: *Die Gedichte Walthers von der Vogelweide*,

Pope aims at destroying the traditional law and thus Christendom at large: "sie wolten das recht verkeren./ darumb cristen glaub undergat" (9, 3f.). Rescue from the catastrophic downfall of medieval Europe seems possible only if Count Frederick of the Palatinate takes up his weapons and defeats the evil forces: "Schick den lewen in das felt,/ richt uf din banner und gezelt/ vor witwen und vor weisen" (11, 1-3). In other words, a conservative political viewpoint here merges with the concept of anticlericalism since the poet demands the restoration both of the traditional church and the German Empire.

Turning to Hans von Westernach, another poetic chronicler of the war of the Palatinate, we notice a different tone of voice and yet the same critical stance regarding the involvement of the clergy.[39] Particularly his satirical comments about the Archbishop of Mainz' bellicose strategy stand out. Assuming that a Bishop should only be seen as a servant of God and perform the liturgy, the military event suddenly assumes a religious appearance:

"asperges" thet er singen,
das weihwasser wol geben kan
er mit seinr scharpfen klingen,
haut uf die naß
und gab ablas,
das mancher kam von leben
und ihm die seel hopft auf dem gras;
solch buß die thet er geben!

(6, 2-9)

Hitting with the sword and cutting off the limbs of his opponents is compared with the benediction in mass. The practice of indulgence is alluded to when he cuts off noses ("und gab ablas"). Finally, he compares the act of killing his enemies to that of confession and absolution: "solch buß die thet er geben." However, Hans von Westernach does not embark on an explicitly anticlerical campaign in writing his war-song, although he clearly plays on this tradition and is well versed in satirical and sarcastic commentary on the behavior and role of the clergy.

In his second song "O welt, bedenk die alt und neu geschicht"[40] Hans confirms that all worldly institutions are bound to fail and to collapse under their own weight. Referring to Babylon, Troy, Jerusalem, Rome and Constantinople he outlines a historical-moral philosophy of doom (stanzas 1-8). Here the nobles are the recipient of his harshest criticism: "Der adel

---

ed. Karl Lachmann, Hugo Kuhn (n. 11 above), 10 (= L. 8:24-26).

[39] Quoted from Th. Cramer, ed. (n. 28 above), 1: 328ff.; cf. Ulrich Müller, "Hans von Westernach", in Ruh, *Verfasserlexikon*, vol. 3, section 2/3 (Berlin, 1981), col. 463f.

[40] Quoted from Th. Cramer, ed. (n. 28 above), 1: 341ff.

am meisten schuldig ist" (15, 1), because they are supposed to uphold social ideals and courtly ethics and yet have given in to robbery and highway crimes.[41] But the clergy is seen in terms almost as negative. Appealing to the Pope, Hans requests that the priests should not only preach good deeds, but that they also should provide a model for their flock: "doch heissends auch güt ebenpild tragen" (19, 4). The poet's source of irritation is his daily experience that word and action within the church have nothing in common:

> ann welicher prediger wer so frum und stet,
> was er lert und gebutt, daz ers auch tet? (20, 1f.)

But worse still, the renewed Roman law (the decretals) which gained entrance to the law books since the eleventh and twelfth centuries,[42] allowed the clergy and the princes to impose their arbitrary decisions upon the laity: "damitz uns leien überfüren" (22, 4) and thus to embark upon their most detestable departure from Christian values and ideals. Hans considers these changes in jurisdiction as the most heinous alteration of the traditional distribution of power between the people and the worldly and ecclesiastical governments, but he has no other recourse than God himself: "Das lauß ich zü got, dem herren, ston" (24, 1). The poet as critic thus aims both at nobility and clergy, and he perceives the two social groups as liable for the moral decline of his time.

The same attitude can be observed in the *Minnerede* of Heinzelin von Konstanz.[43] He also places knighthood and priesthood in the same boat and charges them with misconduct and betrayal of the ideals entrusted them by God. In "Ei, mir begunde missehagen" (p. 393ff.) two maidens discuss the amorous qualities of a priest and a knight and compare their qualities, strengths, and weaknesses. The criticism of priests, who comply with their service duties only because of monetary recompense, is of special interest to us. One of the girls stresses:

---

[41] Werner Rösener, "Zur Problematik des spätmittelalterlichen Raubrittertums", in *Festschrift für Berent Schwineköper zu seinem siebzigsten Geburtstag*, ed. H. Maurer, H. Patze (Sigmaringen, 1982), 469-88; Dagmar Rauter, "Zur wirtschaftlichen und sozialen Lage der Ritterschaft im spätmittelalterlichen Kärnten", *Österreich in Geschichte und Landeskunde* 29/6 (1985): 353-76.

[42] R. C. Van Canegem, "The 'Reception' of Roman Law: A Meeting of Northern and Mediterranean Tradition", *The Late Middle Ages and the Dawn of Humanism outside Italy. Proceedings of the International Conference Louvain May 11-13, 1970*, ed. G. Verbeke, J. Ijsewijn, Mediaevalia Lovaniensia Series 1 Studia 1 (Louvain, 1972), 195-204.

[43] Only little is known of this poet, see Edward Schröder, "Heinzelin von Konstanz", *Zeitschrift für das deutsche Altertum und deutsche Literatur* 53 (1912): 395; F. Höhne, *Die Gedichte des Heinzelin von Konstanz und die Minnelehre*. (Ph.D. diss., Leipzig, 1894). The poems are here quoted from Th. Cramer (n. 28 above), 1: 375ff.; Ingeborg Glier, "Heinzelin von Konstanz", in Ruh, *Verfasserlexikon*, vol. 3, section 2/3 (Berlin, 1981), col. 936-938.

si sint der pfafheit zu gezelt
um niht wen um ir pfeflich gelt.

....

ich mein, di enklein
sint pfaffen als du merkest mich wol.

(II, 315-321)

But neither do the knights deserve a better name for they befoul the ideals
of traditional chivalry with their acts and words (323ff.).[44] Even as the
contemporary knights do not have any resemblance with Parcifal (sic!)
(327), the members of the clergy have failed in their profession and do not
deserve the name of priests: "si halten alle den orden niht" (330). Heinzelin
differentiates, however, between ordained and unordained priests, because
he perceives a better fulfillment of the clerical vows within the higher
echelons of the church hierarchy:

jo mein ich solicher pfaffen niht,
di man di messe sprechen siht,
ich mein, di pfaffen sint genant
und doch nit hoher wihe hant.

(311-314)

Obviously the common man could observe more closely the moral
weaknesses of those clerics with whom they were in constant contact. And
it is possible, although not necessarily true, that ethical ideals were much
better adhered to among the higher ranks of the clergy than at the bottom.

Heinrich obviously reflects only the viewpoint of the laity which dealt
with the clergy on a daily routine and thus, in his poem, leaves out any
criticism of the higher church hierarchy. Hans von Westernach had no
reason to do so and ridiculed the Bishops just as much as the Dukes in their
role as military leaders, but he employed the genre of war poetry and
touched upon anticlericalism only marginally.[45]

A very illuminating group of songs can be found among the Sangsprüche
of the courtly poet Michel Beheim, whose massive lyric oeuvre has
heretofore received only marginal attention from modern scholars.[46] Born

---

[44] Robert L. Kindrick, "The 'Unknightly Knight': Teaching Satires on Chivalry",
The Study of Chivalry. Resources and Approaches, ed. H. Chickering, T. H. Seiler
(Kalamazoo, Mich., 1988), 663-82.

[45] On war poetry, see Albrecht Classen, "German Military Verse in the 15th
Century", Archiv für das Studium der neueren Sprachen und Literaturen 225 (1988):
12-27.

[46] See, however, the seminal study by William C. McDonald, "Whose Bread I
Eat": The Song-Poetry of Michel Beheim, GAG 318 (Göppingen, 1981); Frieder
Schanze does not do justice to the enormous breadth of Beheim's poetic themes and
artistic skills, Meisterliche Liedkunst zwischen Heinrich von Mügeln und Hans Sachs,
2 vols., MTU 82 (Munich, 1983), 1: 191ff. See also my monograph Die autobiogra-
phische Lyrik des europäischen Spätmittelalters. Studien zu Hugo von Montfort,

in 1416 and murdered sometime after 1474, he experienced the whole spectrum of political events typical of the fifteenth century.[47] Hence it is not surprising to encounter a number of songs in which Beheim also deals with the church and the clergy. In "ain beispiel von ainer eptissin",[48] for example, the poet ridicules the nuns as being totally driven by lust and adduces an abbess who slept with a man in her cell. Early in the morning, on her way to the church, she mistakenly takes his underwear as her veil and thus reveals her erotic adventure to the rest of the convent:

Die swang sy auff und wont, daz ez ir weile wer.

die nunnen wurden lachen,
da sie die eptissin so spötiglichen sahen gen,
in dem kor treten her.

(nr. 269, 25-28)

But Beheim does not criticize only the women among the clergy, he also lambasts the priests who are to be blamed for similar misbehavior:

Den priestern in dem tempel
die eptissin wal zu geleichen ist.
die geben pös exempel,
was sy uns wern, das dün sie selb.

(33-36)

The poet does not claim innocence for himself and the rest of the laity, but he feels unjustly admonished by priests for sins which they themselves carry out on a daily practice: "Geitikait sie uns weren/ und suchen doch vil pösser, valscher list" (37f.). In "von miet und gab der richter" (nr. 184) Beheim highlights donations to the church. The clergy seem to take in more than they could ever give back in the form of prayers or other religious services (31ff.). Similar to the high Middle Ages when the monastic orders were criticized by reformers who then in turn founded their own institutions, the poet emphasizes the dangers of money and wealth which undermine the priests' virtues and their oaths to God: "wann sie sein streites mer/ Wann des friden peger" (nr. 352, 102f.). But Beheim also perceives the root of the problem in the fact that the Pope and his Cardinals were greedy politicians who no longer pursued religious ideals (nr. 109, 61ff.). In his prophetic song

---

Oswald von Wolkenstein, Antonio Pucci, Charles d'Orléans, Thomas Hoccleve, Michel Beheim, Hans Rosenplüt und Alfonso Alvarez de Villasandino, Amsterdamer Publikationen zur Sprache und Literatur 91 (Amsterdam, 1991), 347-424.

[47] Ulrich Müller, "Beheim, Michel", in Ruh, *Verfasserlexikon*, vol. 1 (Berlin, 1978), cols. 672-80.

[48] Quoted from *Die Gedichte des Michel Beheim*, ed. Hans Gille, Ingeborg Spriewald, 3 vols., Deutsche Texte des Mittelalters 60, 64, 65 (Berlin, 1968-1972), 2: 423ff., nr. 269.

"von propheceyen sagt das" (nr. 116) about Emperor Frederick III, he severely attacks the church in Rome:

> der romischen phaffheite
>   Wirt er czerstoren ir geteusch
> durch symoney und ir unkeusch.
> der romisch sal wirt vallen.

(130-133)

Beheim also compares the clergy to mice which eat away all food and take the money of the laity (135f.). Beheim's basic poetic strategy consists in contrasting the appearance of the clergy with reality, and obviously he included almost all members of the church hierarchy in his condemning verses (see nr. 445: "von der welt ungerechtikait"). Klaus Grubmüller observed that "hier ... sichtbar [wird], wie bei Beheim Töne angeschlagen sind, die dann erst in den Auseinandersetzungen der Reformation vollends zur Wirkung kommen."[49]

Poets such as Hans Rosenplüt, traditionally known for their *Fastnachtspiele* and *maeren*, followed the lead of anticlerical singers and employed the same motive in their work. In one of his *Priameln*, Rosenplüt projects the image of the bad priest and then outlines the characteristics of an ideal representative of the clergy. According to his opinion a priest should not be illiterate, nor drink too much alcohol and should fulfill his duty by giving sermons and acting as a confessor. Obviously Rosenplüt's experience within Nuremberg — he is an urban poet — reflected the debilitating effect of secularization on the late medieval priesthood because, as he says about bad priests:

> und an der peicht seß und slief,
> wann man im peicht von sünden tieff,
> und nit west, was ein todsünd wer:
> der wer nit ein gutter peichtiger.[50]

As a contrast and with tongue-in-cheek he recommends the clergy to be thoroughly familiar with all aspects of daily life. A good priest should have worked hard as a laborer, as a social worker for blind people or as the head of a brothel ("und ein jar ein wirt wer in eim frauen hauß", p. 249, 3). Only then would he be able to fathom all aspects of human existence and thus to assume responsibly the function of a priest: "do würt gar ein guter peichtiger

---

[49] Klaus Grubmüller, *Meister Esopus: Untersuchungen zu Geschichte und Funktion der Fabel im Mittelalter*, MTU 56 (Zurich, 1977), 433.

[50] Here quoted from Hermann Maschek, ed., *Lyrik des späten Mittelalters*, Deutsche Literatur. Reihe Realistik des Spätmittelalters 6 (Leipzig, 1939), 248, v. 9-12. I disregard Maschek's verse count, because he begins on the top of each page anew. After this article was completed, a new edition of Rosenplüt's poems appeared which I could not consult in time for this study: Hans Rosenplüt, *Reimpaarsprüche und Lieder*, ed. Jörn Reichel, ATB 105 (Tübingen, 1990).

aus" (p. 249, 4). Those clergymen, however, who did not keep the secrets which they had heard in the confessional were betraying their vows (referring to evil priests in general): "und ein priester, der aus der peicht sagt" (p. 250, 14).[51] Rosenplüt did not refrain, however, from criticizing the laity as well, because his poem contains a whole list of various sinners and criminals who populate the city. In fact, his worldview was negative in general, and the decline of morality among the clergy is fully paralleled by the loss of ethical standards throughout society. A statement such as "und ein pfarrer, der sich an nichte kert/ und allweg tut, waz er sein scheflein lert,/ und eins dem andern helt, waz es geret" (p. 252, 31-33) is an exception and represents an ideal of worldly order which seems, in Rosenplüt's eyes, to have evaded man and to be beyond his reach in the later Middle Ages.

Even in his didactic-political songs, Rosenplüt incorporates anticlerical criticism. Thus, for instance, in his "Von den Türken",[52] the attack of the Turks on Europe is seen as God's punishment for the many evils which have corrupted all of society. Apart from the Emperor, whom the poet blames for negligence and idleness in the face of the life-threatening situation (stanza 14, 22ff. and 35ff.), Rosenplüt criticizes the nobility for its lack of manhood (stanza 28, 1), womanhood for its lack of virtue (28, 2), young women for their lack of virginity (28, 3), scholars for their lack of humbleness (29, 1), and the clergy for their lack of modesty: "die meßigkeit von den geistlichen sleichet" (29, 2). On a broader level, in Rosenplüt's eyes the time has come for the Antichrist,[53] because all traditional values and morals have been abandoned or have become topsy-turvy. But strangely enough the apocalypse has not yet begun, to his utter surprise:

> Die gotlich lieb ist als der sne zugangen,
> fur got lobt man die weißen spangen,
> der glaub hat sich zudrumet;
> der Entchrist hat nicht rechten sin,
> daß er nicht iezunt kumet

(stanza 31).

Even when the poet reports on some seemingly courageous and virtuous bishops who meet the expectations of their congregation and are willing to fight the Hussites (for instance in song nr. 68, p. 332ff.), the historical outcome of the battle at Tauß in 1431 proved the opposite. Rosenplüt

---

[51] Scholarship has not focused on this aspect of Rosenplüt's oeuvre at all. See Jörn Reichel, *Der Spruchdichter Hans Rosenplüt. Literatur und Leben im spätmittelalterlichen Nürnberg* (Stuttgart, 1985); Hansjürgen Kiepe, *Die Nürnberger Priameldichtung. Untersuchungen zu Hans Rosenplüt und zum Schreib- und Druckwesen im 15. Jahrhundert*, MTU 74 (Munich, 1984).

[52] Quoted from Liliencron (n. 29 above), 1: 503ff., nr. 109.

[53] Richard Kenneth Emmerson, *Antichrist in the Middle Ages: A Study of Medieval Apocalypticism, Art, and Literature* (Seattle, 1981).

stresses, in the vein of a war reporter, that the individual leaders of the imperial army and the troops of the various dukes, princes and bishops declared their staunch support of the fight against the Czech opponents:

> Do sprach zu den fursten der cardinal:
> "welcher unter euch ein aufbruch macht,
> der sol entert werden und gesmacht
> und von seinem cristenlichen namen getriben
> und in des babst echtbuch geschriben
> als ein vermaledeiter man!"

(v. 130-135)

But as soon as the Hussites approached the German army there was no halt to the general retreat, lead by the bishops and dukes ("und westen nicht, daß die fursten hin fluhen", 253). As an aside, no army was ever able to defeat the Czech troops, and peace came about only after lengty negotiations in 1433.

Whereas before we observed either critical attitudes towards the clergy as a whole or towards individual members of the church hierarchy, here bishops are seen only as part of the broad group of nobles who all fail in their role as representatives of God and the Emperor. Rosenplüt's criticism does not single out the church functionaries, but his opinion of their behavior is as low as his view of the disreputable noblemen. Other songs or *Reimpaarreden* from the same singer confirm his generally pessemistic outlook of life and his nostalgic view of a past in which all people submitted to a divinely structured *ordo*:

> Selig ist der nicht auss ordenung tritt
> Alle creatur pleiben jn jrem stant
> Darein sy got an ersten wantt.[54]

Anticlericalism, as observed in the poems discussed above, merges here in Rosenplüt's oeuvre with a general complaint about the decline of morality, ethics, values and society at large.[55] He imagines an ideal world in which both clergy and laity adhere to the traditional values, but he observes that neither priests nor ordinary citizens demonstrate any tendency to do so in the present. In his *Priameln* the poet laments the changes and thus admonishes his fellow citizens to return to the old order, but obviously to no avail. Since people follow the new fashion, don themselves with luxurious items and reveal purely egoistic instincts, even their subordination under the church is failing:

---

[54] Quoted from Karl Euling, "Zwei ungedruckte Rosenplütsche Sprüche", *Zeitschrift für deutsches Altertum und deutsche Literatur* 32 (1888): 436-45, here 440, v. 150-152.

[55] Rosenplüt's poem "Eine Lügendichtung" corroborates this observation, see Karl Euling, "Eine Lügendichtung", *Zeitschrift für deutsche Philologie* 22 (1890): 317-20.

und die alten recht wart verkeren
und die priesterschaft nimmer wolt haben in eren
und niemant mer auf den pan wolt achten,
den ettwann die frummen pebst machten,
und die reichen die armen wurden versmehen
und der paurn wart spotten und anpleen.[56]

Thus a broad catalogue of criticism against insufficient law, the rampant disrespect of the priesthood and the papacy, and the contempt which the rich feel for the poor and for the peasants forms a general complaint about shortcomings in the city and in society at large.[57]

This late fifteenth-century poet serves as the best example to show us from where many poets received their inspiration. Anticlericalism was only one way to express discomfort with life, although it highlighted the general plight in the most dramatic way. Sinful behavior was not a novelty in the catalogue of vices discussed both in didactic and theological texts. But the decline of the church and its clergy proved to be the last drop of water to make the glass spill over.

Jörg Schilknecht, one of the many late medieval poets of whom we know only little, expresses this opinion in a particularly skilfull manner, because he contrasts the present situation with that of the biblical past. He explains the origin of priesthood as descending from Noah's son Shem,[58] but now has reason to complain about its present appearance. The clergy is possessed by greed ("aüaricia", 4, 5), hatred and envy (4, 7), and is occupied with a constant battle to establish a pecking-order within the church: "münch, pfaffen itz mit haß und neid/ all auf ein ander picken" (4, 7f.). As a consequence of this deterioration the poet foresees the demise of the world: "in der welt müs es ubel stan,/ seindt das geistlich geschlechte/ itz furt scholir und graüe ... / als ritter und ... chnechte" (3, 7-10). But neither the scholars at the universities (stanza 5ff.) nor the nobility are innocent of vices (stanza 8ff.). To top it off, taxes and toll fees are blamed for an economic decline all over the country (stanza 10), whereas the lawyers — here characterized as theologians who have not given their vows — undermine justice through their use of the newly revived Roman law (stanza 11). Other aspects are peoples' hostility towards each other (12), disloyalty (13), usury (14), the merchants and their high prices fueling a constantly climbing inflation (15ff.), and finally and all embracing, sinfulness and vice:

---

[56] Quoted from H. Maschek (n. 50 above), 252, 21-26.

[57] J. Reichel (n. 51 above), 219: "Schließlich ist bemerkenswert, daß auch die Bauern, die Hintersassen der Stadt, in den Sprüchen Rosenplüts ... Berücksichtigung finden."

[58] Quoted from Th. Cramer (n. 28 above), 3: 182ff., here stanza 2, v. 7.

Was unratz in der welt aufstat
smacht alles unser sundenthat,
damit wir uns verschulden.
iderman hat mit sunden meil,
verdint ... wol seinen teil.

(17, 1-5)

In other words, the clergy proves to be as guilty as any other social class or group within late medieval society.

The poets discussed so far were filled with fear, discomfort and unease regarding the social, economic and political changes transforming the traditional world, and preparing the battle ground for the forthcoming Reformation. It is quite natural that they first condemned the clergy and nobility, because both social groups were supposed to live up to specific standards of conduct, and both had failed to do so. Schilknecht admits, in the final stanza, however, that it is not the priests alone, but all people who have lost their ideals and lead an egocentric, selfish existence. Jörg Schiller, writing at about the same time, summarizes this observation in his verses: "Darumb steht es auf erd nicht wol,/ die welt steckt aller laster vol",[59] and thus dismisses the clergy from being solely responsible for all sins in this world. He does not, however, reinstitute the priests into their formerly elevated position, but rather appeals to his audience simply to return to an honorable life: "wer mit mir dienen wil Fraw Ehr,/ von laster zu der tugent ker" (9, 18f.).

In our last example, the poet Suchensinn presents a literary debate between a woman and a priest over the question who assumes a higher rank before God.[60] Contrary to expectations fed by theological considerations,[61] the woman is given victory, because:

ee himmel, erde wart gedicht,
wip was bi gottz angesicht.
redet kein priester anders icht,
der fluch kan es verrichten.

(p. 296, 5, 10-13)

The theological authority of the clergy has obviously lost its legitimacy since lay poets could ridicule basic tenets and concepts held by the representatives of the church without fearing any persecution.

---

[59] Quoted from Th. Cramer (n. 28 above), 3: 206, 9, 1f.

[60] Cramer (n. 28 above), 3: 293ff.; cf. Erich Liermann, "Suchensinn", *Die deutsche Literatur des Mittelalters. Verfasserlexikon*, ed. Karl Langosch, vol. 4 (Berlin, 1953), col. 307-310.

[61] For the misogynist tradition, see Katherine M. Rogers, *The Troublesome Helpmate: A History of Misogyny in Literature* (Seattle, 1966); Edelgard DuBruck, "Introduction", *New Images of Medieval Women. Essays Toward a Cultural Anthropology*, ed. E. DuBruck, Mediaeval Studies 1 (Lewiston, 1989), 1-18.

Wherever we investigate poetic treatment of fifteenth-century clergy, we always discover critical, sometimes even hostile commentaries. Very few of the poets discussed showed the slightest signs of sympathy with the clergy, although exceptions are noticeable in a few cases dealing with individual clerics. Some, however, such as Rosenplüt, express hope that life will change in every sense once people have begun to return to a traditional and — synonymous for the poet — virtuous lifestyle. Then the church would be able to recover from its demise as well. But it remains only a hope. In most cases money and early forms of capitalism are seen as auxiliary forces which have caused the downfall of the clergy and the church as an institution,[62] but these do not exculpate the priests from their moral decline.

As a conclusion, we can make three observations. First, almost all major and minor poets of the fifteenth century deliberately make an attempt to incorporate the topic of anticlericalism in their oeuvres. And second, virtually no poet can be identified who defended the clergy in concrete terms. We notice occasional efforts to project an ideal concept of priesthood, but even then reality clashes with the conservative ideal. Third, the Catholic church had long lost its broad support among the general population and the poets of that time provided the spark which was to explode the whole church structure. It is interesting that satirical criticism of the clergy thus emerges as a particular topic which, although it did not dominate late medieval German poetry, obviously had a tremendous appeal among the population at large and was often repeated and adapted by a large number of singers, both of high and low rank. The anticlerical sentiment was not limited to any social class, and both urban and noble poets expressed similar views of the church and its clergy because they had become common targets for criticism. The clergy was considered a prime culprit of social disorder, lost virtues, and disregard of the traditional *ordo*. Although Martin Luther's attack on the church was aimed at bringing about nothing else than a reform, he caused almost immediately the crumbling of the decayed institution. Fifteenth-century lay poets can also be credited with contributing to the church's downfall because of their effective anticlericalism and for laying the groundwork for the political and theological upheavals in the sixteenth century.

---

[62] Cf. especially Balthasar Wenck and his song "Wend ir schwigen und betagen", in Th. Cramer, ed. (n. 28 above), 3: 426ff., here 444.

ANTIKLERIKALISMUS UM DEN VIERWALDSTÄTTERSEE 1300-1500: VON DER KRITIK DER MACHT DER KIRCHE

PETER BLICKLE

Universität Bern

In der Nacht des Dreikönigstages 1314 ereignete sich ein äußerst denkwürdiger Vorgang. Bauern aus Schwyz fielen im Kloster Einsiedeln ein, verwüsteten und plünderten Kirche und Konventsgebäude und verschleppten die Mönche nach Schwyz, wo sie elf Wochen lang gefangengehalten wurden.[1] Derart spektakuläre "Klosterstürme" hat es in Europa in der Regel nur im Zusammenhang mit Revolutionen gegeben, und entsprechendes Aufsehen hat denn auch dieser Vorgang nicht nur in der Innerschweiz, sondern weit darüber hinaus erregt. Immerhin gehörte Einsiedeln zu den bedeutendsten Wallfahrtsstätten Europas, und seine Vögte waren die Habsburger, die sich gerade anschickten, neben ihrer Hausmacht in Süddeutschland im Osten des Reiches die Grundlagen für ihre spätere Weltmachtstellung zu legen.

Der Klostersturm vom 6. Januar 1314 ist für mittelalterliche Verhältnisse einmalig gut dokumentiert. Für den Überfall selbst verfügt man über den in Gedichtform gehaltenen Augenzeugenbericht Rudolfs von Radegg, der die Einsiedler Klosterschule leitete. Er hat die Vorgänge von der Erstürmung des

---

[1] In den Anmerkungen werden folgende Abkürzungen verwendet:

Gfr. = *Der Geschichtsfreund, Mitteilungen des Historischen Vereins der Fünf Orte Luzern, Uri, Schwyz, Unterwalden und Zug,* Bd. 1ff. (Einsiedeln/Stans, 1843ff.).

QW = *Quellenwerk zur Entstehung der Schweizer Eidgenossenschaft,* Abt. 1: Urkunden, 3 Bde. (Aarau, 1933-1964); Abt. 2: Urbare und Rödel bis zum Jahre 1400, 4 Bde. (Aarau, 1941-1957); Abt. 3: Chroniken, 4 Bde. (Aarau, 1947-1975).

UB Zug = *Urkundenbuch von Stadt und Amt Zug vom Eintritt in den Bund bis zum Ausgang des Mittelalters. 1352-1528* (Zug, 1964).

Zürcher Stadtbücher = H. Zeller-Werdmüller, Hans Nabholz (Hrsg.), *Die Zürcher Stadtbücher des XIV. und XV. Jahrhunderts,* 3 Bde. (Leipzig, 1899-1906).

Die hier beschriebenen Vorgänge behandeln: Leo Wirth, *Ein Vorspiel zur Morgartenschlacht. Der Marchenstreit in der Urschweiz. Rudolf von Radeggs Gedicht 'Capella Heremitarum' in der Uhr'schen Übersetzung* (Aarau, 1909); Andreas Riggenbach, *Der Marchenstreit zwischen Schwyz und Einsiedeln und die Entstehung der Eidgenossenschaft,* Geist und Werk der Zeiten 15 (Zürich, 1965).

Klosters bis zur Entlassung der Mönche aus der Schwyzer Gefangenschaft miterlebt und wohl noch im gleichen Jahr seinen Bericht geschrieben.[2]

> Unterdessen[3] durchstürmen zahlreiche Scharen [von Schwyzern] das Kloster/ Und verheeren das Haus; da ist im Schafstall der Wolf./ [...]/ Dieser begehrt keine Schlüssel zum Schlafgemach, Sälen und Zellen,/ Ohne Schlüssel erbricht selber die Türen sofort/ [...]/ Unsere Bücher, Kleider und Betten tragen von dannen/ Sie und anderes mehr, was nur gebraucht werden kann./ Sie verschleppen, was wir gesammelt und schonlich verwendet,/ Und das Heilige selbst treten mit Füßen sie frech/ [...]/ Mit gewaltigen Sparren erkühnen sie sich und mit Äxten/ Einzuhauen das Tor, das zum Tempel hin führt./ [...]/ Die zerstreuten Hostien stampfen mit Füßen sie; diese/ Gottesschänd'rische Tat schreit zu dem Himmel empor./ [...]/ Und die Gebeine der Heil'gen, die im Frieden da ruhten,/ Welche jeder Christ, wie es sich ziemt, verehrt,/ Wagen sie zu berühren mit besudelten Händen,/ Sie zu entreißen der Ruh' und auf die Erde zu streu'n./ [...]/ Dann nach toller Tat, durch Getränk auf's Höchste erhitzet,/ Da sie gesoffen ohn' Maß unsern spärlichen Wein,/ Taumeln sie alsbald umher nach genossenem Weine,/ Schänden den Tempel des Herrn mit ihrem/ Unrat sodann.

Sind die geschilderten Vorgänge Ausdruck einer "antiklerikalen" Haltung der Schwyzer Bauern?

I

Zur Bewertung des Ereignisses muß man in Rechnung stellen, daß die Konflikte zwischen den Schwyzern und ihrem benachbarten Kloster alt waren:[4] strittige Nutzungsrechte um Forsten und Allmenden hatten immer wieder zu massiven, fehdeähnlichen Auseinandersetzungen mit den Vögten des Klosters geführt. Doch nach 1300 hatten Abt und Konvent zu neuen, bislang nicht üblichen Mitteln gegriffen. Über das geistliche Gericht in Konstanz erreichten sie die Exkommunikation des Landammanns von Schwyz und von 15 seiner Gefolgsleute wegen angeblicher Übergriffe auf die Weiden, Wiesen und Wälder des Klosters.[5] Die Gebannten wehrten sich

---

[2] Zur Biographie L. Wirth, *Vorspiel* (wie Anm. 1), 42-8.

[3] Der folgende Text nach der Übersetzung von Franz Uhr, die von L. Wirth (wie Anm. 1), 92-5, wiedergegeben wird. Das lateinische Original ediert in *QW* 3/4, 161-224 (ebd., 226-67 eine zweite neuhochdeutsche Übersetzung); die lateinische Vorlage für den hier auszugsweise abgedruckten Text, 186-9.

[4] Für die Vorgeschichte A. Riggenbach, *Marchenstreit* (wie Anm. 1), 71-89. Heinrich II. hatte 1018 Einsiedeln den um das Kloster liegenden Forst verliehen. Spätestens hundert Jahre später setzen die Streitigkeiten um die Nutzungsrechte ein. Der Konflikt gründete in einer grundsätzlich schwer lösbaren Rechtsunsicherheit: zwar stiftete die Verleihung eines Forstes einen Obereigentumsanspruch, schloß aber ältere Nutzungsrechte nicht unbedingt aus.

[5] Die einschlägigen Belege *QW* 1/2 Nr. 499, 243f.; Nr. 552, 265f.

durch eine Appellation an den Papst, offensichtlich waren ihnen die über sie verhängten Kirchenstrafen keineswegs gleichgültig.

Die Schwyzer waren noch kaum von der Exkommunikation freigesprochen, wurden sie auf Betreiben Einsiedelns 1318 neuerlich mit den kirchlichen Strafmitteln verfolgt: zahlreiche Schwyzer kamen in den Bann, und die Pfarreien im Tal wurden mit dem Interdikt belegt.[6] Nur durch massiven politischen Druck auf die Habsburger, die gerade einen Krieg von geschichtlicher Bedeutung gegen die Innerschweizer verloren hatten, nämlich die Schlacht von Morgarten 1315, gelang es den Bauern, die Aufhebung der Kirchenstrafen zu erzwingen.[7] Was sie nicht davor schützte, bei den nächsten Auseinandersetzungen um Nutzungsrechte mit dem Kloster zwei Jahrzehnte später wieder mit Bann und Interdikt belegt zu werden.[8]

Die kirchlichen Strafen zogen ihre weiteren Kreise, weil die Nachbarn und Verbündeten der Schwyzer nicht jeden Verkehr mit ihnen einstellen konnten oder wollten — was sie nach Kirchenrecht hätten tun müssen —, damit aber gleichfalls Bann, Exkommunikation und Interdikt verfielen. Jahrelang ruhte in großen Teilen der Innerschweiz in der ersten Hälfte des 14. Jahrhunderts das religiöse Leben: die Kirchen blieben den Gläubigen verschlossen, den Toten die Bestattung in der geweihten Erde des Friedhofs verwehrt. 1350 anläßlich der Aufhebung von Exkommunikation und Interdikt mußten 12 Kirchen und deren Altäre neu konsekriert werden.[9]

Bann und Interdikt wurden über die Schwyzer in allen Fällen auf Betreiben des Klosters Einsiedeln verhängt, und immer dienten als rechtliche Begründung die gewaltsam erzwungenen Nutzungsrechte an den Alpen und Wäldern im klösterlichen Forstbann.

Um Sicherung weltlicher Ansprüche kirchlicher Institutionen ging es meistens, wenn Strafen des geistlichen Gerichts verhängt wurden. Die Urner wurden gebannt, weil sie mit den Visconti, den Erzfeinden der Kurie, Handel trieben.[10] Kaum hatten sie sich 1375 aus der Exkommunikation gelöst,[11] wurde wegen Zehntstreitigkeiten mit dem Fraumünster in Zürich über die ganze Talschaft das Interdikt verhängt.[12] Die Beispiele ließen sich

---

[6] *QW* 1/2 Nr. 960, 490ff.; Nr. 971, 498. Eine größere Zahl von Schwyzern kommt in den Bann, die Pfarreien Schwyz, Steinen, Muotatal und Arth werden mit dem Interdikt belegt. Vgl. ergänzend den Kommentar von J. Brändli in *QW* 3/4, 23 und Carl Pfaff, "Pfarrei und Pfarreileben. Ein Beitrag zur spätmittelalterlichen Kirchengeschichte", in *Innerschweiz und frühe Eidgenossenschaft* (Olten, 1990), 203-81, hier 280.

[7] *QW* 1/2 Nr. 989, 506-10, bes. 509.

[8] Erschließbar aus *QW* 1/3 Nr. 860, 537ff. oder Nr. 861, 539.

[9] Vgl. *QW* 1/3 Nr. 892, 563f.; Nr. 895, 565; Nr. 896, 565; Nr. 897, 566; Nr. 899, 567; Nr. 900, 567 und Nr. 901, 567.

[10] C. Pfaff (wie Anm. 6), 280.

[11] *Gfr.* 4 (1847): Nr. 32, 299ff.

[12] *Gfr.* 8 (1852): Nr. 62-69, S. 71-8.

vermehren.[13] Ein "antiklerikaler" Interpretationen gänzlich unverdächtiger Schweizer Mediävist hat in einer umfassenden Kirchengeschichte der Innerschweiz erst neulich folgende Bilanz gezogen: "Ohne Bedenken verhängten Päpste, Bischöfe und andere Würdenträger geistliche Strafen über einzelne Personen, ganze Orte und Länder. Mit Bann und Interdikt sollten politische Gegner in die Knie und Steuerschuldner zur Zahlung gezwungen werden."[14]

Die Gläubigen fürchteten sich vor den kirchlichen Strafen — daran ist wohl kaum zu zweifeln. Das belegen einmal die immer hektisch betriebenen politischen Aktivitäten, um aus Bann und Interdikt wieder entlassen zu werden.[15] Das zeigen aber auch einzelne vorbeugende Maßnahmen in den Städten und den Ländern selbst. Der Zürcher Rat verbot allen seinen Bürgern jeglichen Geschäftsverkehr mit Exkommunizierten, weil zu befürchten war, "das man ane gottes dienst sin muos", falls sie in die Stadt kommen sollten.[16] Daß man auf die Heilsmittel der Kirche nicht verzichten konnte und wollte, belegt die Beobachtung, daß beispielsweise Küßnacht einen fremden Geistlichen anstellte, wiewohl die Pfarrei mit dem Interdikt belegt war und der Leutpriester alle sakramentalen und liturgischen Handlungen eingestellt hatte.[17] Bürgermeister und Rat von Zürich verfügten 1339 aus demselben Grund,

> das alle pfafheit ze Zůrich si sin geistlich oder weltlich, die von unser stat gevarn sint, her wider in unser stat suln varn hinnen ze dem palme abende, also das si an dem selben palme abende und von dannen hin steteclich, gottes dienst mit offenner kilchtůr haben sul.[18]

Die geistlichen Gerichte — Kleriker also — brachten mit den ihnen zur Verfügung stehenden Strafmitteln immer wieder das kirchlich-religiöse Leben zum Erliegen, die Gesellschaft wehrte sich dagegen, so gut sie konnte. Durch die Schaffung neuen Rechts auf der Ebene der Städte, der Länder und der Eidgenossenschaft insgesamt sollten die Kompetenzen des geistlichen Gerichts zurückgedrängt, wo nicht ganz ausgeschaltet werden.

---

[13] Gelegentlich dringen selbst die Päpste darauf, mit Bann und Interdikt zur Erzwingung von Zahlungen zurückhaltend umzugehen. Vgl. *QW* 1/2 Nr. 610, 308; Nr. 1020, 523.

[14] C. Pfaff (wie Anm. 6), 280. Einige ausgewählte Beispiele zur Abstützung seien genannt: *UB Zug* Nr. 106; Nr. 177; Nr. 346; Nr. 348.

[15] Viele der oben genannten Belege aus dem *QW* bezeugen das. Auf die Wiederholung der Einzelbelege wird verzichtet.

[16] Friedrich Ott (Hrsg.), "Der Richtebrief der Bürger von Zürich", *Archiv für Schweizer Geschichte* 5 (1847): 212.

[17] Thomas Stocker, "Die ältesten kirchlichen Verhältnisse der Gemeinde Küßnach zu dem Gotteshause Engelberg", *Gfr.* 24 (1869): 246-300, bes. 253-270. Vgl. ergänzend auch Gall Heer, *Aus der Vergangenheit von Kloster und Tal Engelberg 1120-1970* (Engelberg, 1975), 115f.

[18] *Zürcher Stadtbücher* 1/1, Nr. 171, 71.

Nach dem ersten Zusammenschluß der drei Länder Uri, Schwyz und Nidwalden von 1291 und dessen Ausdehnung auf Luzern 1332 kam es in den Jahren 1351 und 1352 zu einer stattlichen Erweiterung der Eidgenossenschaft in Form eines komplizierten Bündnissystems.[19] Neue Länder traten bei, aber auch Städte wie Zürich, Bern und Zug. Die vielen in diesem Zusammenhang entstandenen "Bundesbriefe" haben einen weitgehend gleichen Wortlaut und verfolgen damit auch gleiche Ziele. Zu ihnen gehört vorrangig auch die Zurückdrängung der Kompetenzen des geistlichen Gerichts.

> Es sol ouch kein leye den andern, so in dirre buntnisse sind, umb kein geltschuld uff geistlich gericht laden, wan jederman sol von dem andern recht nemen an den stetten und in dem gericht, da der ansprechig dann seshafft ist und hingehôret.[20]

Der Artikel verbietet allen Laien, das geistliche Gericht wegen Schuldforderungen in Anspruch zu nehmen, vielmehr wird für solche Fälle der Wohnort des Beklagten der ordentliche Gerichtsstand; das geistliche Gericht soll sich künftig, wie es präzisierend in einem der Bundesbriefe heißt, beschränken auf Fälle "umb ê und wûcher".[21] "Laien", so heißt es in den Bundesbriefen von 1351/52, sollen das geistliche Gericht wegen weltlicher Angelegenheiten nicht anrufen. "Pfaffen" sollen das auch nicht mehr tun, verfügt eine "Ordenung vnd gesetzten" der Orte Zürich, Luzern, Zug, Uri, Schwyz und Unterwalden von 1370.

> Waz ôch pfaffen in ûnser Eydgnosschaft, in stetten oder in lendern, wonhaft sint, die nicht burger, lantlütt noch eydgnossen sint, die sûlent kein frômdes gericht, geistlichs noch weltlichs, sûchen noch triben gen nieman, so in disen vorgenanten stetten und lendern sint, wan si sûlent von iechlichem recht nâmen an den stetten und vor dem richter, da er gesessen ist, es wer dann umb ein e oder umb geistlich sachen, an all geverd.[22]

Wer sich diesen Bedingungen nicht unterwirft, wird aus der Gemeinschaft ausgeschlossen — er wird nicht anders behandelt als ein Friedbrecher.

---

[19] Die Text sind abgedruckt in *QW* 1/3,1 Nr. 942, 600-18; Nr. 989, 658-77; Nr. 995, 682-700; Nr. 1037, 742-63. Zu vergleichen ist auch die sechsjährige Einung von Zürich mit dem Landvogt von Sundgau, Elsaß und Breisgau, sowie mit dem Landvogt von Schwaben, Aargau und Thurgau, *QW* 1/3 Nr. 913, 577-82.

[20] *QW* 1/3, 1 Nr. 942, 611. Die gleichen Textstellen in den anderen Bundesbriefen werden hier nur noch mit Seitenzahlen aufgeführt: 581, 668f., 692f., 756f.

[21] *QW* 1/3, 1 Nr. 1037, 757.

[22] Hans Nabholz, Paul Kläui (Hrsg.), *Quellenbuch zur Verfassungsgeschichte der Schweizerischen Eidgenossenschaft und der Kantone von den Anfängen bis zur Gegenwart*, 3. Aufl. (Aarau, 1947), 33-6. Die umfassendste Interpretation bei Ferdinand Elsener, "Der eidgenössische Pfaffenbrief von 1370. Ein Beitrag zur Geschichte der geistlichen Gerichtsbarkeit", *Zeitschrift der Savigny-Stiftung für Rechtsgeschichte* 75, Kanonistische Abteilung 44 (1958): 104-80.

> Welcher pfaff aber do wider tût, da sol dů statt oder daz land, do der selb pfaff
> wonhaft ist, verhûten und versorgen mit aller ir gemeind, daz dem selben
> pfaffen nieman essen noch trinken gâb, huse noch hofe, gen im mit kôff noch
> verkôff noch kein ander gemeinsamy mit im hab.

Die Kompetenz der "fremden" Gerichte will die im Jahre 1370 noch
vergleichsweise junge Eidgenossenschaft eingrenzen. Und unter den als
besonders fremd empfundenen Gerichten steht das geistliche ganz vorne.
Den Klerikern soll ihr gesonderter Gerichtsstand möglichst genommen
werden, sie sollen der örtlichen Gerichtsbarkeit unterworfen werden, ja das
Ziel ist eindeutig, auch die Geistlichen den in der Innerschweiz geltenden
Stadt- und Landrechten zu unterstellen, sie zu Eidgenossen zu machen.[23]

Das hier auszugsweise referierte Dokument trifft auch andere Bestimmungen, doch daß seine vorrangige Bedeutung in der Beschneidung des
geistlichen Gerichts und der gerichtlichen Exemtion der Kleriker liegt, sagt
bereits sein Name—"Pfaffenbrief" heißt diese Satzung seit alters. Welchen
verfassungsrechtlichen Stellenwert der Pfaffenbrief in der Schweizer
Geschichte einnimmt, wird erst so recht deutlich, wenn man hinzufügt, daß
es zahlreiche "Bundesbriefe", also Abmachungen zwischen drei oder
mehreren Orten, gegeben hat, kaum aber "Verfassungsbriefe", das heißt für
alle eidgenössischen Orte gleichermaßen verbindliche Beschlüsse.[24] Mehr
als eine Handvoll Verfassungsbriefe gibt es nicht. Daß der erste Verfas-
sungsbrief der Schweiz die Kompetenz des geistlichen Gerichts und damit
die Strafgewalt der Geistlichen deutlich einschränkt, zeigt, was man der
Kirche nicht zuzubilligen bereit war.[25]

Die Bestimmungen der Bundesbriefe und Verfassungsbriefe wurden durch
Beschlüsse der städtischen Magistrate oder der Landsgemeinden vorbereitet
oder ergänzend gesichert. Schon 1316 hatte der Zürcher Rat verfügt, "swelch
burger deheinen usman gegen Kostenze ladet ane des rates urloup, der sol

---

[23] "Wer mit husrôchi mit sin selbers lip oder mit sinem gesind sitzen und wonhaft
sin wil in dekeinen disen vorgenanten stetten und lendern, er si pfaff oder ley, edel
oder unedel, die der herzogen von Österrich rat oder dienst gelopt oder gesworn hand,
die alle sůlent ôch loben und sweren ûnser der vorgenanten stetten und lendern nutz
und ere ze fůrdern und mit gûten trůwen ze warnen vor allem dem schaden, so si
vernement, daz dien vorgenanten stetten oder lendern gemeinlich oder sunderlich
dekeine wis brâsten oder schaden bringen môcht, und sol si da vor kein ander eyd,
den si ieman getan hand oder noch tâtin, nût schirmen an all geverd."

[24] Vgl. Johann Jakob Schollenberger, *Das Bundstaatsrecht der Schweiz. Geschichte
und System*, 2. Aufl. (Berlin, 1920), 10. Vgl. auch die jüngste Verfassungsgeschichte
von Hans Conrad Peyer, *Verfassungsgeschichte der alten Schweiz* (Zürich, 1978), 32.

[25] Selbst in der geschlossenen Grundherrschaft des Klosters Engelberg kam in der
ersten Hälfte des 15. Jahrhunderts die Forderung auf, daß die Äbte "die tallüt von
allen geistlichen gerichten schirmen süllent." Vgl. Alfred Bruckner, "Zur Rechts- und
Wirtschaftsgeschichte des Tales Engelberg", *Gfr.* 99 (1946): 25.

geben V ß";[26] in Luzern wurde das gleiche Delikt mit der doppelten Bußenhöhe geahndet.[27] Schwyz versuchte mit den ihm möglichen Mitteln, auch die Ehegerichtsbarkeit von Konstanz möglichst nicht wirksam werden zu lassen. Die Landsgemeinde setzte 1419 mittels eines Landsgemeindebeschlusses fest, Ehevorhaben seien dem Landammann anzuzeigen, und zwar mit der ausdrücklichen Begründung, damit unnötige Prozesse vor dem geistlichen Gericht zu vermeiden.[28] Das waren alles andere als papierene Normen ohne Realitätsgehalt. Als der Urner Ueli Ritt 1447 vier Landsleute vor dem geistlichen Hofgericht in Konstanz verklagte, wurde er gezwungen, unter Berufung auf die eidgenössischen Bünde und das Urner Landrecht die Klage zurückzuziehen.[29]

Durch die Stadtrechte und die Landrechte wurden auch die Geistlichen gezwungen, die weltlichen Gerichte anzuerkennen und das geistliche Gericht möglichst zu meiden. In allen weltlichen Angelegenheiten unterstehen die Priester dem Stadtrecht, hatte Zürich schon zu Beginn des 14. Jahrhunderts dekretiert.[30] Glarus verfügte in der Mitte des 15. Jahrhunderts, "es sol kein priester nieman uff dehein geistlich gericht laden noch trieben",[31] vielmehr sollen alle Rechtsansprüche von Klerikern durch ein Schiedsgericht bereinigt werden. Zur Symmetrie dieser Verfügung gehörte es, die Geistlichen zu zwingen, die von den lokalen und regionalen Gerichten gefällten Urteile anzunehmen, anderenfalls "so sol man in von stund an urlob geben",[32] wie dieser Landesverweis schmeichelhaft umschrieben wird.

Naturgemäß beschränkten sich solche Maßnahmen nicht allein auf den Weltklerus, vielmehr suchte man auch die Klöster vom geistlichen Gericht abzuschneiden — verständlicherweise nach den Erfahrungen, welche die Schwyzer mit dem Kloster Einsiedeln, die Urner mit dem Fraumünster in Zürich gemacht hatten. Das Frauenkloster in Schwyz mußte eigens einen urkundlichen Revers ausstellen, "stoß oder mißhellung" mit den Schwyzer

---

[26] *Zürcher Stadtbücher* 1/1, Nr. 111, 44. Republikation 1333; ebd., Nr. 142, 58. Ergänzend zur praktischen Durchführung; ebd., Nr. 145, 59. Besondere Hilfe gegenüber Bürgern, die vor das Konstanzer Gericht gezogen werden, verspricht die Stadt 1318; ebd., Nr. 35, 15.

[27] Peter Xaver Weber (Hrsg.), "Luzerns ältestes Ratsbüchlein (ca. 1300-1402)", *Gfr.* 65 (1910): 1-55, hier 17. Vgl. für Zug, *UB Zug*, Nr. 160, 73f.

[28] Martin Kothing (Hrsg.), *Das Landbuch von Schwyz* (Zürich-Frauenfeld, 1850), 46f. Vgl. auch den Eintrag, ebd., 48, wo Altersgrenzen für Heiratsabreden festgelegt werden und eine gewisse Öffentlichkeit der Verlobung verankert wird, übrigens in Absprache mit dem Bischof von Konstanz.

[29] *UB Zug*, Nr. 898, 466.

[30] *Zürcher Stadtbücher* 1/1, Nr. 45, 18f. Vgl. für frühere Vereinbarungen zwischen Konstanz und Zürich hinsichtlich des Gerichtsstandes der Geistlichen in der Stadt, Rudolf Pfister, *Kirchengeschichte der Schweiz*, 1. Bd. (Zürich, 1964), 460.

[31] Fritz Stucki (Hrsg.), *Die Rechtsquellen des Kantons Glarus*, 2. Bd., *Einzelbeschlüsse bis 1679*, Sammlung Schweizerischer Rechtsquellen 7 (Aarau, 1984), 591.

[32] F. Stucki (wie Anm. 31), 592.

Landleuten ausschließlich "vor dem amman vnnd dem geschwornen gericht zu Schwytz" auszutragen, das geistliche Gericht als die für ein Kloster zweifellos zuständige Instanz wurde ausdrücklich als möglicher Gerichtshof ausgeschlossen.[33] Selbst strittige Rechtsansprüche zwischen einem Kloster und einem Pfarrer konnten nach dem Urteilsspruch von Zürcher und Zuger Räten nicht mehr vor dem bischöflichen Gericht in Konstanz verhandelt werden, sondern gehörten fortan vor ein von beiden Parteien paritätisch besetztes Schiedsgericht.[34]

Mit diesen kursorischen Hinweisen auf Schiedsgerichte ist ein äußerst interessantes Problem erreicht, das bislang als solches noch gar nicht erkannt wurde. Offenkundig nämlich wird das geistliche Gericht zunehmend durch Schiedsgerichte verdrängt, und bei ihnen handelt es sich in der Regel um Laiengerichte, mehrheitlich bestehend aus vier Mitgliedern. In den Streitigkeiten zwischen der Kirchgemeinde Altendorf und dem Kloster St. Johann als Inhaber des Kirchensatzes um die Besetzung der Pfarrei ließen sich die Urteile des geistlichen Gerichts in Konstanz offensichtlich nicht durchsetzen, wohl aber die eines weltlichen Gerichts.[35] Gleiche Vorgänge wiederholen sich anderwärts,[36] so daß die Vermutung einige Evidenz für sich hat, das geistliche Gericht in Konstanz habe im Verlauf des 15. Jahrhunderts seine Zuständigkeit für die Innerschweiz weitestgehend verloren.[37] Schrittweise, aber konsequent haben die Städte- und Länder-Orte die geistliche Gerichtsbarkeit in der Innerschweiz ausgeschaltet.

Diktiert wurde eine solche Politik zweifellos auch von dem Bedürfnis der Eidgenossen, einen geschlossenen Rechtsraum durchzusetzen, fremdes Recht auszuschalten, fremde Gerichte in der Innerschweiz nicht mehr wirksam werden zu lassen. Daß jedoch Mißbräuche des geistlichen Gerichts eine solche Entwicklung eingeleitet hatten, legt schon die Chronologie nahe. Der

---

[33] M. Kothing (wie Anm. 28), 56ff.

[34] *UB Zug* Nr. 2261, 1081f. Wenigstens anmerkungsweise sei darauf verwiesen, daß sich auch mindere Formen der kirchlichen Gerichtsbarkeit offensichtlich kaum mehr behaupten konnten. In Luzern tritt das städtische Gericht konkurrierend neben und schließlich wohl vor das Kanzelgericht: Vgl. C. Pfaff (wie Anm. 6), 251. Vgl. auch als besonders frühen Beleg *QW* 1/2 Nr. 290, 140.

[35] Die Belege bei Regula Hegner, *Geschichte der March unter schwyzerischer Oberhoheit*, Mitteilungen des Historischen Vereins des Kantons Schwyz 50 (Einsiedeln, 1953), 205ff.

[36] R. Hegne (wie Anm. 35), 212f. Gerold Meyer von Knonau (Hrsg.), "Die Urkunden der Abtei Zürich bezüglich auf das Land Uri; von 853-1525", *Gfr.* 8 (1852): 3-100, hier Nr. 42, S. 49ff.

[37] Fälle von Ladungen vor das bischöflich-konstanzische Gericht kommen nur mehr vereinzelt vor, ganz selten wird das geistliche Gericht ausdrücklich vorbehalten. Dazu *UB Zug*, Nr. 1299, 671; Nr. 1684, 840. Dennoch wären für endgültige Urteile erst die noch vorhandenen Akten des geistlichen Gerichts aufzuarbeiten bzw. die nicht edierten Urkundenbestände in den Innerschweizer Archiven vornehmlich für die Zeit des späteren 14. und des 15. Jahrhunderts durchzuarbeiten.

exzessive Umgang mit Bann und Interdikt liegt zeitlich vor den legislatori-
schen Maßnahmen der Eidgenossen, diesem Zustand ein Ende zu machen.
Der "Pfaffenbrief" von 1370 hat nachweislich die mißbräuchliche
Inanspruchnahme des geistlichen Gerichts in zwei Fällen zum Anlaß.[38]

Aus dem geistlichen Gericht zog die Kirche ausgangs des Mittelalters
keinen politischen Nutzen mehr. Doch dabei allein sollte es nicht bleiben.
Die Kirche verlor in der Innerschweiz überhaupt ihre weltliche Herrschaft.

II

Noch um die Mitte des 13. Jahrhunderts unterschied sich das Gebiet um den
Vierwaldstättersee von seiner politischen Organisation her wenig von
anderen Regionen des Reiches. Adelige und kirchliche Herrschaften
überstiegen an Bedeutung erheblich die kleinen, noch unbedeutenden
Freienverbände unter dem Schutz des Reiches. Das änderte sich in den
folgenden 150 Jahren dramatisch, und zwar vornehmlich zu Lasten der
Klöster.

Die Bauern in der Innerschweiz haben zuerst die Steuerprivilegien der
Klöster mißachtet. Wiederholt mußte König Heinrich in den 1230er Jahren
den Urnern verbieten, das Kloster Wettingen zu besteuern.[39] Offensichtlich
hatte er damit wenig Erfolg, denn die Steuerforderungen wurden im
Gegenteil auch auf andere Klöster ausgeweitet, so etwa auf das reichsunmit-
telbare Frauenkloster in Zürich für dessen Liegenschaften in Uri.[40] Ähnliche Vorgänge wiederholten sich in der zweiten Hälfte des 13. Jahrhunderts
in Schwyz.[41] Unbeeindruckt von königlichen Verboten hatten Landammann
und Landleute von Schwyz das Zisterzienserinnenkloster Steinen besteuert
und aus dieser Praxis 1294 die verallgemeinernde Konsequenz gezogen, die
Güter der Klöster genauso zu Anlagen heranzuziehen wie jene der Landleute. "Wenn die klöster", so heißt der Landsgemeindebeschluß von 1294,

so in vnnßerm Lanndt sindt, Nitt welltendt hellffen tragen schaden, gemeinen
kosten, stür vnnd ander gewerffe Mitt dem Lannde Nach Irem gutt vnnd alls ein

---

[38] Knapp Rudolf Pfister, *Kirchengeschichte der Schweiz*, 1. Bd. (Zürich, 1964),
460ff. Die Beispiele breit belegt bei Josef Schürmann, *Studien über den eidgenössischen Pfaffenbrief von 1370*, Beiheft zur Zeitschrift für Schweizerische Kirchengeschichte 6 (Freiburg i. Ü., 1948), 67-87.

[39] *QW* 1/1 Nr. 345, 161; Nr. 349, 164. In gewissem Widerspruch dazu ebd., 38.

[40] Das geht aus einem Klagerodel des Klosters hervor. Vgl. G. Meyer v. Knonau
(wie Anm. 36), 73.

[41] *QW* 1/1 Nr. 1155, 520ff.; Nr. 1178, 532f.; Nr. 1582, 722f. *QW* 1/2 Nr. 191, 88-
99. Vgl. auch Fritz Wernli, *Die Entstehung der schweizerischen Eidgenossenschaft.
Verfassungsgeschichte und politische Geschichte in Wechselwirkung*, Studien zur
mittelalterlichen Verfassungsgeschichte 6 (Wildhaus, 1972), 35.

anderer Lanndtman, alls dann söllendt sy miden Holltz, velld, wasßer, wunn vnnd weyd des Landes.[42]

Güter, für die keine Steuern entrichtet wurden, verfielen dem "weltlichen Bann" und waren damit nicht mehr lebensfähig.

In diesem Landsgemeindebeschluß, dessen Bedeutung sich auch darin ausdrückt, daß er noch im 16. Jahrhundert in das neu angelegte Schwyzer Landbuch, die verbindliche Rechtskodifikation, aufgenommen wurde, kommt auch das Rechtsempfinden einer bäuerlichen Gesellschaft zum Ausdruck, daß derjenige, der Nutzungsrechte am Allgemeinen habe, auch die allgemeinen Lasten mittragen müsse.

In der Besteuerung der Kirche kommt, wenn man so will, ein rechtsegalitäres Denken der einfachen Leute zum Ausdruck. Das Attribut "antiklerikal" hingegen verdient die schleppende Zahlung rechtmäßiger Abgaben an die geistlichen Korporationen. Spätestens seit der ersten Hälfte des 14. Jahrhunderts beschweren sich alle in der Innerschweiz begüterten Klöster darüber, wie schwer die ihnen zustehenden Abgaben einzubringen seien. Das Fraumünster in Zürich klagt

> um die Meyeraemter, dass sie [die Urner] vns der entwert haben, daruor wir grossen Schaden haben empfangen. [...] Ouch ist es vm die Vell [Erbschaftsab-gaben], dass sie vns die nit geben vnd weren, als von alter her an vns kommen ist. [...] Ouch brechend sie vns ein Zehend ab,

und so setzt sich die Litanei der Gravamina fort.[43] Ähnliche Beschwerden kennt man von den anderen Klöstern — überliefert sind mehrere solcher Klagen von den Mönchen aus Einsiedeln und Wettingen.

Die Abgabenrenitenz der Bauern einerseits und der politische Druck auf die Klöster andererseits haben — andere Gründe gibt es kaum — dazu geführt, daß der Klosterbesitz in der Innerschweiz schließlich in der zweiten Hälfte des 14. Jahrhunderts im allgemeinen ganz in den Besitz der Bauern bzw. der Länder überging. Schwyz und Uri haben zur Durchsetzung des Eigentums an Liegenschaften unterschiedliche Wege gewählt.

Die Schwyzer hatten ihren Beschluß, die Klostergüter zu besteuern, mit der Maßgabe verknüpft, generell keinen Verkauf von Liegenschaften an Auswärtige mehr zu erlauben.[44] Dem entsprachen die Veräußerungsverbote an die Tote Hand in den Schweizer Städten und Ländern.[45] In der

---

[42] *QW* 1/2 Nr. 89, 40. Das Zitat nach M. Kothing (wie Anm. 28), 58.

[43] G. Meyer v. Knonau (wie Anm. 36), 72.

[44] *QW* 1/2 Nr. 89, 40.

[45] *Zürcher Stadtbücher* 1/1, Nr. 157, 64. M. Kothing (wie Anm. 28), 58. 1363 und 1382 verbieten Nid- und Obwalden den Verkauf von Liegenschaften an Klöster und Auswärtige. Vgl. Theophil Graf, "Die Nidwaldner Landesgesetze gegen die Tote Hand", *Beiträge zur Geschichte Nidwaldens* 17 (1944): 7-19. Carl Deschwanden, "Die Rechtsquellen von Nidwalden. Altes Landbuch von Nidwalden", *Zeitschrift für Schweizerisches Recht* 6 (1857), II Rechtsquellen: 80.

Fluchtlinie solcher Maßnahmen lag als Fernziel die Beseitigung jeder feudalen Herrschaft.

Das Kloster Einsiedeln verlor seine Besitzungen im Tal Schwyz um die Mitte des 14. Jahrhunderts.[46] Das Kloster Engelberg mußte 1366 seinen gesamten Besitz in Schwyz verkaufen.[47] Auf dem Weg des Landsgemeindebeschlusses wurde 1389 jede Art von Grundherrschaft definitiv abgeschafft: Niemand darf Lehen vergeben oder nehmen; alle auswärtigen Grundherren haben ihre Güter innerhalb von zwei Jahren an die Landleute zu verkaufen, und zwar gegen eine Kapitalisierung der Abgaben im zeitüblichen zwanzigfachen Betrag, "und tetint si des nit, so sol das guot, das si in vnserm land hant, vns, den landlüten, vervallen sin."[48] Diese legalistisch verbrämte Zwangsenteignung traf zwar alle Grundherren, da es jedoch adeligen Grundbesitz de facto nicht mehr gab, richtete sich der Beschluß doch vorrangig, wenn nicht ausschließlich gegen die Klöster.

Die Allodifizierung klösterlicher Besitzungen in Uri erfolgte nahezu gleichzeitig. 1359 verkaufte das Kloster Wettingen seine Besitzungen in Uri zum Preis von 8448 Gulden an das Land.[49] Nach Auskunft des Wettinger Urbars gingen jährlich 50 Pfund an Abgaben ein; bei einer üblichen Kapitalisierung hätte der Kaufpreis bei 1000 Pfund liegen müssen. Vermutlich hat Uri für die Wettinger Rechte einen "politischen Preis" bezahlt — auch wenn man in Rechnung stellt, daß nicht nur Abgaben, sondern auch Herrschaftsrechte abgelöst wurden —, und das würde den Rückschluß erlauben, daß die Urner gewissermaßen "um jeden Preis" die Abhängigkeiten von den Klöstern loswerden wollten.

Nachdem Wettingen seine Rechte verkauft hatte, konnten sich offensichtlich auch die anderen Klöster nicht mehr halten: die Güter der Klöster Rathausen, Kappel und Frauenthal gingen an das Land über.[50] Auch bei diesen Ablösungsgeschäften läßt sich der Verdacht nicht ganz ausräumen, Uri habe überhöhte Preise gezahlt.[51]

---

[46] *QW* 2/2, 110 (Einkünfteverzeichnis). Die Einsiedler Rechte dürften mit der Bereinigung des Marchenstreits 1350 erloschen sein; vgl. *QW* 1/3 Nr. 879, 550-6. Eine förmliche Kaufurkunde fehlt. Thomas Faßbind, *Geschichte des Kantons Schwyz. Von desen ersten Gründung bis auf die helvetische Staatsumwälzung,* 1. Bd. (Schwyz, 1832), 41, gibt an, Schwyz habe die letzten Einsiedler Rechte 1353 für 75 Pfund Stäbler erworben.

[47] G. Heer (wie Anm. 17), 111.

[48] M. Kothing (wie Anm. 28), 273.

[49] Urkunde abgedruckt in *Gfr.* 41 (1886): 110f.

[50] Ausführlich Paul Kläui, "Bildung und Auflösung der Grundherrschaft im Lande Uri, *Historisches Neujahrsblatt Uri* 12/13 (1957/58): 40-89, bes. 78.

[51] Paul Kläui vermerkt im Kommentar zu seiner Edition der Rödel und Urbare von Rathausen (*QW* 2/3, 339f.), die Ablösungssumme übersteige den Wert der kapitalisierten Zinsen um das Sechsfache. Er schließt daraus auf den Zukauf durch das Kloster zwischen 1270 und dem Verkaufsdatum, was m.E. wegen der durchgängigen Tendenz, die Grundherrschaften zurückzudrängen, eher unwahrscheinlich ist.

Dem politischen Drängen auf eine umfassende Allodifizierung des Landes Uri konnte auf die Dauer auch das Reichskloster Zürich nicht erfolgreich widerstehen. Dessen ansehnlicher Besitz, der noch um 1370 auf 80 Hofstätten und 160 Güter und zahlreiche Gotteshausleute veranschlagt wurde und organisatorisch über drei Meierhöfe verwaltet wurde, scheint nach dem eingangs zitierten Klagerodel nur mehr wenig eingebracht zu haben. In dieser Zeit kämpfte das Kloster mit Bann und Interdikt um die Sicherstellung seiner Rechte, freilich letztlich erfolglos. Zwischen 1418 und 1428 gingen die Herrschaftstitel des Zürcher Fraumünsters an Uri über.[52]

Etappenweise, einsetzend mit der Besteuerung der Klöster, gefolgt vom Verbot des Güterkaufs an die Tote Hand bis zur mehr oder minder gewaltsamen Ablösung der grundherrlichen Rechte der Klöster, in deren Folge auch die leib- und gerichtsherrlichen Rechte obsolet wurden, entziehen die Innerschweizer der Kirche ihre weltliche Herrschaft. Es handelt sich dabei um einen Prozeß, der zeitlich mit der Zurückdrängung des geistlichen Gerichts parallel läuft und um 1400 im wesentlichen abgeschlossen gewesen sein dürfte. Zeitlich später liegt ein dritter bemerkenswerter Vorgang, als dessen Ergebnis schließlich die Pfarreien mehr oder minder in der Verfügungsgewalt der Gemeinden sind.

III

Am 31. Juli 1426 wurde von einem Notar ein Instrument aufgenommen, das folgende Vereinbarungen zwischen dem Pfarrherrn und Ammann und Rat von Zug festhielt:[53] Der Pfarrherr unterliegt der Residenzpflicht in Zug, bestellt er für die Zeit seiner Abwesenheit einen Vertreter, ist dazu die Zustimmung der Gemeinde erforderlich; gleiches gilt übrigens auch für den "Helfer" (Vikar), den er anzustellen hat. Zu den Amtspflichten des Pfarrherrn gehört das tägliche Messelesen, die gewissenhafte Ausführung der Seelenmessen, die Begleitung bei Prozessionen und Wallfahrten. Für die ordentliche Versorgung der Gemeinde mit den Sakramenten sind er und sein Helfer gleichermaßen zuständig; weil der Pfarrherr selbst ein Haus außerhalb der Stadtmauer bewohnt, darf der Helfer in der Nacht die Stadt nicht verlassen — offenbar wollte man ihn innerhalb der Mauern haben, falls es notwendig werden sollte, Kranken und Alten die Sterbesakramente zu spenden. Diese "Dienstaufgabenumschreibung" hat beim Amtsantritt seines Nachfolgers Christian Brenner 1461 noch ein paar kleine Ergänzungen erfahren:[54] dieser verspricht, zur Durchsetzung seiner eventuellen Rechtsansprüche nur das städtische Gericht anzurufen und "erlich unn mit miner

---

[52] Zur Rekonstruktion des Prozesses vgl. Paul Kläui, "Die Meierämter der Fraumünsterabtei in Uri", *Historisches Neujahrsblatt Uri* NF 10/11 (1955/56): 7-34.

[53] *UB Zug* Nr. 680, 336-9.

[54] *UB Zug* Nr. 1035, 524.

mûtter huszehaben, die wil sÿ in leben ist, unn mit keiner andren fröwen, mit der ich von unseren verlumdet sin möchte."

Was die Zuger Gemeinde will, läßt sich aus diesen beiden "Spanbriefen", wie in der Schweiz solche Vereinbarungen über das "Pflichtenheft" der Geistlichen heißen, gut ablesen. Man will mit den Heils- und Gnadenmitteln der Kirche ordentlich versorgt werden, mit der täglichen Messe, der Taufe und den Sterbesakramenten, und dafür ist die Residenz eines Priesters unentbehrlich. Diese Bedürfnisse werden sichergestellt durch eine Art "Wahlkapitulation".[55] Eine solche setzt zwingend voraus, daß die Gläubigen eine positivrechtlich anerkannte Mitsprache bei der Bestellung ihrer Seelsorger haben. Sie beschränkt sich in Zug 1426 noch auf den Helfer, 1461 jedoch ist auch der neue Pfarrer von der Stadt gewählt. Die Wahl aller Priester durch die Pfarrgemeinde sicherte den Gläubigen die Möglichkeit, die Kirche auf ihre Bedürfnisse auszurichten und konnte so zum naheliegenden Ziel gemeindlicher Kirchenpolitik werden.

Das kleine Landstädtchen Zug ist kein Einzelfall; ein ähnlicher Spanbrief — schmucklos und knapp, wie ihn Bauern lieben — liegt für die Pfarrkirche in Andermatt im Ursental von 1481 vor. Der Pfarrer, Johannes Geußer, verspricht den "frommen tallúte zu vrsern", die ihn auf die Pfarrei gewählt haben, den Gottesdienst selbst zu versehen oder anderenfalls das Amt wieder aufzugeben, bei kürzerer Abwesenheit zuvor die Erlaubnis des Ammanns einzuholen und die Bauern nicht vor fremde Gerichte zu bringen; das geistliche Gericht kann ausdrücklich nur dann angerufen werden, wenn es um Ehre, Amt, Leib und Leben des Pfarrers geht.[56] Die vorliegende Wahlkapitulation ist rechtlich etwas dubios, weil den Talleuten von Ursern ein Nominationsrecht nicht zukam.[57] Doch gerade das deutet eine Tendenz an, die nämlich, daß es für einen Kandidaten auf eine Pfründe in der Innerschweiz kaum noch Wege gab, die Interessen der Pfarrgemeinden zu umgehen.

"Das kanonische Recht, die päpstlichen Dekretalen, die Akten von Synoden und Konzilien sahen [...] nirgends ein Recht der Pfarrgenossen auf Mitsprache vor."[58] Um so bemerkenswerter ist es, daß es sich in der Innerschweiz auf ungemein breiter Front hat durchsetzen lassen.[59]

---

[55] Die lateinische Bezeichnung der Spanbriefe heißt hübscherweise "litterae electoriales". Vgl. Eduard Schweizer, "Das Gemeindepatronat in den Urkantonen", *Zeitschrift für Schweizerisches Recht* 46 (1905): 1-80.

[56] *Gfr.* 44 (1889): 119.

[57] Daß es deswegen mit dem Kirchherrn, dem Kloster Disentis, Spannungen gegeben hatte, bestätigt eine Urkunde von 1484, die dann allerdings auch das Wahlrecht der Talleute bestätigte. Regest in *Gfr.* 8 (1852): 140.

[58] C. Pfaff (wie Anm. 6), 215.

[59] Für die Erschließung des edierten Materials und das Verständnis von kirchenrechtlichen Zusammenhängen war die Arbeit meines Fribourger Kollegen Carl Pfaff (wie Anm. 6) wichtig, und ich danke ihm für die bereitwillige Zurverfügungstellung

Am Vorabend der Reformation verfügen die Kirchgemeinden oder politischen Gemeinden der Innerschweiz über Nominations- oder Präsentationsrechte auf rund 30 Pfarreien.[60] In anderen Worten, um das Gesagte schärfer zu profilieren: alle Seelsorgerstellen in den heutigen Kantonen Uri, Schwyz, Nid- und Obwalden und viele in den benachbarten Gebieten (in Ursern, Glarus und Zug) werden entweder durch die Kirchgemeinde oder die politische Gemeinde — die Stadt beziehungsweise das Land (und entsprechend von Ammann und Rat) — vergeben.[61]

Aufschlußreich ist die zeitliche Ebene. Im 15. Jahrhundert wächst die Zahl jener Pfarreien rasch, für deren Besetzung die Gemeinden ein irgendwie geartetes, bindendes Vorschlagsrecht durchsetzten.

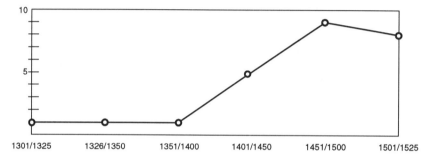

Erwerb von Nominations- und Präsentationsrechten durch die Gemeinden und Orte in der Innerschweiz (in 25 Jahresdurchschnitten)

---

des Manuskripts seiner mittlerweilen erschienenen Arbeit. Einen knapperen Überblick bietet Dietrich Kurze, *Pfarrerwahlen im Mittelalter. Ein Beitrag zur Geschichte der Gemeinde und des Niederkirchenwesens*, Forschungen zur kirchlichen Rechtsgeschichte und zum Kirchenrecht 6 (Köln-Graz, 1966), 308-14. Alle Arbeiten gehen zurück auf Eduard Schweizer, "Das Gemeindepatronatsrecht" (wie Anm. 55). Wichtige Anregungen, für die Erklärung der "Gemeindereformation" die kommunalen Einflußmöglichkeiten auf die Pfarreien und Niederpfründe im Spätmittelalter zu berücksichtigen, verdanke ich Rosi Fuhrmann (Mainz). Vgl. zuletzt Rosi Fuhrmann, "Dorfgemeinde und Pfründstiftung vor der Reformation. Kommunale Selbstbestimmungschancen zwischen Religion und Recht" in *Kommunalisierung und Christianisierung. Voraussetzungen und Folgen der Reformation 1400-1600*, ZHF Beiheft 9 (Berlin, 1989), 77-112. Neuerdings auch dies., *Pfarrei und Kaplanen*, Diss. Phil. Bern 1992.

[60] Die Daten sind aus der allgemeinen und der ortsgeschichtlichen Literatur zusammengezogen. Eine ausführliche Übersicht bei C. Pfaff (wie Anm. 6); knapp und übersichtlich Joseph Frei, "Die Pfarrwahlbulle Papst Julius' II.", *Gfr.* 89 (1934): 165-93, bes. 184f.

[61] Für Einzelheiten der rechtlichen Verhältnisse vgl. J. Frei, (wie Anm. 60), 183f.

Die Strategien und Techniken der Bürger und Bauern, auf die Besetzung der geistlichen Stellen Einfluß zu gewinnen, waren sehr unterschiedlich: politischer Druck auf den Kirchherrn oder den Patronatsherrn, Kauf und schließlich vereinzelt auch kriegerischer Erwerb von Patronaten gehören dazu.[62] Ich beschränke mich jeweils auf ein Beispiel, um das zu belegen.[63]

Ein mittels politischen Drucks durchgesetztes Pfarrerwahlrecht kennt — um einen von vielen Fällen herauszugreifen — die Gemeinde Steinen[64] im Land Schwyz. Die Pfarrei wurde von den Habsburgern als Patronatsherren vergeben, 1337 begegnet dort als Lehensträger ein Ritter Kraft der Biber, vermutlich ein Laie, der folglich die Pastorierung der Gemeinde einem Dritten übertragen mußte. Seelsorger soll, so versprach Kraft der Biber der Gemeinde 1337, nur werden, wer "dem bessern und dem meren teile gevallet."[65] Üblicherweise konnte der Kirchherr, in diesem Fall Kraft der Biber, dem Patronatsherrn, in diesem Fall den Habsburger Grafen, einen Geistlichen seiner Wahl zur Investitur durch den Bischof vorschlagen. Dieses Recht wurde dem Kirchherrn hier beschnitten; und das blieb in Zukunft nicht nur so, sondern erfuhr auch noch eine zusätzliche Erweiterung zugunsten der Kirchgemeinde. 1348 mußte sich nämlich der neue Kirchherr verpflichten, falls er die Priesterweihe empfangen sollte, selbst die sakramentalen und liturgischen Handlungen vorzunehmen, und zwar solange die Gemeinde mit seiner Amtsführung einverstanden war. Falls nämlich dem "merteil der selben undertan dûchte, das ich inen unfûglichen were, da sol aber der merteil der selben undertanen einen nemen, der dem besseren und dem merten teile under inen wol gevallet."[66] Der etwas im Unklaren bleibende Sinn dieser Urkunde läßt sich entziffern, wenn man annimmt, der amtierende Geistliche, der Leutpriester, hätte ein bescheidenes Einkommen bezogen, weil die Einkünfte aus der Pfründe ja auch der Versorgung des Kirchherrn dienen mußten. Gute Kandidaten zu bekommen, war somit wohl nicht einfach, Zustiftungen der Gemeinde mußten möglicherweise das Interesse erst wecken. "Besang" der Kirchherr selbst seine Kirche, entfielen für die Gemeinde solche zusätzlichen Aufwendungen. Offensichtlich will die

---

[62] Die Vorgänge im einzelnen quantifizierend zu erfassen, ist angesichts der noch nicht ganz befriedigenden Forschungen nicht möglich. Vornehmlich liegt das in den recht komplizierten kirchenrechtlichen Verhältnissen begründet, die nicht immer hinreichend berücksichtigt werden. Der empirisch noch abzustützende Eindruck geht dahin, daß die Kategorie "politischer Druck" überwiegt, gefolgt vom Kauf, während Zuwächse aus kriegerischen Ereignissen stark zurücktreten und Schenkungen schließlich nahezu vernachlässigt werden können.

[63] Belege für die Repräsentativität werden in Anmerkungen gegeben. Vollständigkeit ist angesichts des gegenwärtigen Forschungsstandes nicht zu erreichen.

[64] Vgl. C. Pfaff (wie Anm. 6), 228, der diesen Fall vergleichsweise ausführlich beschreibt.

[65] *QW* 1/3 Nr. 165, 116.

[66] *QW* 1/3 Nr. 768, 476.

Gemeinde von Steinen, daß derjenige, der die Pfründe innehat, auch die *cura animarum* besorgt. Das war ja auch der ursprünglich gemeinte Zusammenhang von Pfründe und Amt, von *beneficium* und *cura*. Er blieb dort erhalten, wo es Gemeinden gelang, den Kirchensatz (das Patronat) zu kaufen, wie 1483 "ammann und gemein kilchgenossen zu(o) gersow."[67] Oft ließen sich solche Ziele auch schon mit geringeren finanziellen Aufwendungen erreichen. Die Kirchgenossen von Silenen in Uri erwarben von der Patronatsherrin der Kirche, der Reichsäbtissin des Fraumünsters in Zürich, gegen Zahlung von 80 fl. die Zehntrechte. Damit war das Kloster der Baupflicht für die Kirche enthoben, die fortan die Gemeinde übernehmen mußte; möglicherweise wurde ihr dafür das Recht eingeräumt, den Leutpriester für die Pfarrei vorzuschlagen.[68] Gleiche Konstruktionen wurden in den nächsten Jahren für alle ans Fraumünster gehörenden Kirchen in Uri getroffen, so daß die Gemeinden ein verbindliches Vorschlagsrecht für die Leutpriester gegenüber der Äbtissin erlangten.[69]

Die Pfarreien Alpnach, Sachseln und Giswil in Obwalden waren bis 1415 in habsburgischen Besitz und 1434 vom Kaiser als konfisziertes Gut des geächteten Herzogs Friedrich von Habsburg den Obwaldnern zugesprochen worden; 1461 schließlich hatte das Land nach bischöflicher Zustimmung die Patronatsrechte auf die drei Pfarrein urkundlich absichern können.[70]

Separationen von Filialkirchen von der Mutterpfarrei belegen besonders deutlich das Interesse der Menschen nach einer besseren seelsorgerischen Betreuung. Immer ist die bessere Versorgung mit Messen und Sakramenten das Motiv zur Separation; immer ist die Separation kostenaufwendig. Die Separation von Spiringen von der Mutterpfarrei Bürglen ist ein durchaus repräsentativer Vorgang. Zunächst legte eine Delegation der Gemeinde dem Bischof von Konstanz dar, daß wegen Hochwasser, Eis und Schnee die Mutterpfarrei Bürglen von den Gläubigen nicht immer besucht werden könne.[71] Die Sterbenden müßten auf die letzte Ölung verzichten, die Toten könnten nicht bestattet werden. Dem Antrag der Gemeinde auf eine eigene Kirche mit Friedhof wurde nach einem Augenschein durch zwei Chorherren entsprochen. Haus, Hofstatt und Garten für den Priester, den Bauplatz für Kirche und Friedhof, die Aufwendungen für die Lichter in Kirche und an Altären sowie für den Altar- und Kommunionwein müssen die Gemeinde-

---

[67] Bezirksarchiv Gersau, Urkunde Nr. 12. Eine Kaufsumme wird nicht genannt.

[68] Vgl. P. Kläui (wie Anm. 52), 28f.

[69] P. Kläui (wie Anm. 52), 28f. Das Patronat erwerben auch die Gemeinden Weggis (C. Pfaff [wie Anm. 6], 213) und Kerns (Ephrem Omlin, *Die Geistlichen Obwaldens vom 13. Jahrhundert bis zur Gegenwart* [Sarnen, 1984], 45.)

[70] Vgl. Hermann Christ, Johannes Schnell (Hrsg.), "Die Rechtsquellen von Obwalden. Das älteste Landbuch", *Zeitschrift für schweizerisches Recht* 8 (1860), II Rechtsquellen: 65f. C. Pfaff (wie Anm. 6), 231. Ergänzend E. Omlin (wie Anm. 69), 27, 37f., 56f.

[71] Vgl. C. Pfaff (wie Anm. 6), 216.

mitglieder aufbringen.[72] Daraufhin belasteten 71 Inhaber von Gütern ihre Grundstücke mit Ewigzinsen, und ein kompliziertes System von Bürgschaften sollte den wirklichen Eingang der notwendigen Gelder sichern.[73]

Ein letzter Blick muß noch auf die Gemeinden geworfen werden, die sich mit bemerkenswerter Hartnäckigkeit gegen die Folgen der Inkorporation wehrten. Die Pfarrei Stans war 1270 dem Kloster Engelberg inkorporiert worden. Gegen den damit verbundenen Anspruch, die Kirche durch einen Mönch versorgen zu lassen, wehrten sich die Kirchgenossen. Der Bischof sah sich 1318 gezwungen, trotz formaler Bestätigung der Inkorporation, den Abt zu verpflichten, den Leutpriester und seinen Helfer aus den Einkünften der Pfarrei zu versorgen, was eigentlich zwingend die Besetzung der Pfarrei mit einem Weltgeistlichen voraussetzt. Eine dauerhafte Lösung scheint das nicht gewesen zu sein. Eigenmächtigkeiten der Stanser müssen den Bischof veranlaßt haben, die Pfarrei mit dem Interdikt zu belegen. Erst ein Schiedsgericht der eidgenössischen Schirmorte unter Beteiligung Nikolaus' von der Flüe half die Ansprüche der Stanser durchsetzen.[74] Seitdem konnte von einer inkorporierten Pfarrei nicht mehr die Rede sein, selbst das Patronatsrecht Engelbergs war merklich geschmälert.[75]

Residenz des Seelsorgers ist das Leitmotiv aller kirchenpolitischen Aktivitäten der Bauern und Bürger auf der Pfarreiebene. Die Residenz soll die Vermittlung des Heils sicherstellen. Residenz ließ sich offenbar nur erreichen, wenn die Gemeinde ein verbindliches Recht zur Bestellung des Seelsorgers durchsetzte. Damit verloren Pfründenhäufung und Inkorporation ihre schädliche Wirkung für die *cura animarum*.

IV

Die Bauern und die Bürger der Innerschweizer Orte haben in einer zweihundertjährigen Auseinandersetzung mit der Kirche dreierlei erreicht, was sich sonst im Reich wohl nirgendwo hat durchsetzen lassen:

(1) Die Pfarrerwahl durch die kirchliche oder die politische Gemeinde,

---

[72] Detailliert *QW* 1/1 Nr. 1620, 738-45.

[73] Separiert werden des weiteren Ufenau (*QW* 1/2 Nr. 458, 219f.; Nr. 460, 221), Sisikon (Pfaff, wie Anm. 6, 218), Menzingen (*UB Zug* Nr. 1245, 650; Nr. 1209, 631), Illgau (Pfaff, wie Anm. 6, 218; *Gfr.* 7 [1849]: 137-40), Beckenried (Anton Odermatt, "Die Pfarrkirche in Beggenried", *Gfr.* 46 [1891]: 109-91, bes. 156-73) und Morschach (*QW* 1/2 Nr. 283 und 284, 113f.)

[74] Druck der Quelle bei Robert Durrer, *Bruder Klaus. Die ältesten Quellen über den seligen Nikolaus von der Flüe, sein Leben und seinen Einfluss*, 1. Bd. (Sarnen, 1921), 17ff.

[75] Ähnliche Maßnahmen gegen die Besetzung der Pfarreien mit Ordensgeistlichen sind belegt für Altendorf (vgl. R. Hegner, wie Anm. 35, 205), Lachen (ebd., 209), Wangen (ebd., 211ff.), Küssnacht (*Gfr.* 24 [1869]: 253-70; G. Heer [wie Anm. 17], 115f.) und Kerns (*Gfr.* 21 [1866]: Nr. 7, 207-13).

(2) die Beseitigung der weltlichen Herrschaft der Klöster und
(3) die Einschränkung der Kompetenzen des geistlichen Gerichts und
deren Übernahme durch weltliche Gerichte.

Pfarrerwahl, Beseitigung der weltlichen Herrschaft der Kirche und Einschränkung der Kompetenzen des geistlichen Gerichts gehören zweifellos zu
den zentralen Forderungen der Reformatoren und ihrer Anhänger. Städte und
Dörfer rücken die Pfarrerwahlforderung an die Spitze ihrer Gravamina; die
Beseitigung der weltlichen Herrschaft der Klöster gehört zu den herausragen-
den Forderungen des Bauernkriegs, und deren Säkularisation in der Stadt
gehört zum geläufigen Erscheinungsbild der 1520er Jahre; Klagen gegen die
Kompetenzanmaßungen des geistlichen Gerichts und seinen exzessiven
Einsatz von Bann und Interdikt begünstigen in starkem Maße schon die
Bundschuhaufstände.

Daraus läßt sich folgern, daß es in der Innerschweiz keinen "Refor-
mationsbedarf" gab oder, weniger scharf formuliert, die Bedingungen für die
Rezeption der Reformation erheblich ungünstiger waren als in anderen
Regionen Mitteleuropas. Aus der Gegenüberstellung der konkreten Situation
der Kirche in der Innerschweiz und den Forderungen an die Kirche in der
Reformationszeit läßt sich auch etwas zur Präzisierung des Begriffs
"Antiklerikalismus" beitragen. Die Wurzeln des Antiklerikalismus lägen
danach einerseits in der zunehmenden weltlichen Macht der Kirche und
andererseits in ihrer Unfähigkeit, sich den Wertvorstellungen der Gesellschaft anzupassen und das heißt, ihre Tätigkeit auf die *cura animarum* zu
konzentrieren. In der Innerschweiz gab es jedenfalls in der Reformationszeit
keine erkennbaren antiklerikalen Äußerungen. Zweihundert Jahre zuvor war
das durchaus noch anders. Bevor die Schwyzer in der Dreikönigsnacht 1314
das Kloster Einsiedeln stürmten, hatten diejenigen, die auf Betreiben des
Abtes von Einsiedeln vom Konstanzer Bischof exkommuniziert worden
waren, eine beachtliche Prämie ausgesetzt: 400 Pfund wollten sie demjenigen zahlen, der ihnen den Abt tot, verstümmelt oder gefangen ausliefern
würde.[76]

---

[76] *QW* 1/2 Nr. 960, 490ff.

LEONARDO BRUNI
AND THE 1431 FLORENTINE COMPLAINT
AGAINST INDULGENCE-HAWKERS:
A CASE STUDY IN ANTICLERICALISM

GORDON GRIFFITHS

University of Washington, Seattle

The complaint[1] addressed to Pope Eugenius IV by the secular government of Florence deserves inclusion in a handbook on anticlericalism for its sharp invective, but also because it reveals the scope of anticlericalism in that time and place.

The Florentine letter begins in a neutral tone with the information that a knight of the Order of St. John of Jerusalem had recently come into the city, accompanied by a large number of scribes. By the third sentence, however, the author of the letter adopts a sarcastic tone as he comes to describe the cleric who was to preach the indulgence as "one who would pay little attention to the spirit but a great deal to the money." The preacher's "strange and astonishing assertions ... that the knight had the power to confer plenary indulgence from both sin and penalty (*culpa et pena*) upon anybody who was willing to offer a subsidy", and the wholesale hawking of salvation for cash, produced great indignation amongst "good and thoughtful men", who are contrasted by the author with "the ignorant and especially the women from all over the city", who were gathered in such numbers as to create the atmosphere of a market-place. In this crowd there was no antagonism toward the clerics; the author is at pains to point the contrast between the credulity of the ignorant crowd, in which he suggests that there was a preponderance of women, and the "good and thoughtful men" who had brought the problem to the attention of the Signoria.

As for the clerics engaged in the selling of the indulgences, the author says merely that they were a pleasure-seeking lot, who, while promising salvation to others, were giving "no thought whatever to their own salvation."

The anticlericalism in this case, then, is a sentiment prevalent among men in the ruling circles of society, and directed, not against the clergy in

---

[1] See Document I below. I do not believe that this has ever been published, despite the fact that, especially when its probable composition by Leonardo Bruni is taken into account, it offers an opportunity to compare Renaissance and Reformation attitudes toward the abuse of indulgences.

general, or even against the mendicant orders in particular, but against those among them who abused their office.

When a letter was to be sent to the pope by the Signoria of Florence, the task of composition would be assigned to the Chancellor. Since December 1427, this had been Leonardo Bruni. His experience would be particularly useful in this case, for he had previously served as secretary to a series of popes between 1405 and 1415. He was probably aware that Boniface IX in 1402 had revoked all grants of the power to offer indulgences that contained the phrase *culpa et pena* (though he was subsequently persuaded to issue fresh ones).[2] We know that Bruni had to make himself cognizant of papal policy in the matter because it was to Bruni that Pope Gregory XII turned to draft the powers he wished to confer upon Giovanni Dominici, his Cardinal Legate to Poland and Hungary in 1409. One of these conferred upon the Legate the power to authorize the granting of plenary indulgences at the moment of death to some thousand persons of both sexes, *provided*, however, that they had confessed their sins with a contrite heart.[3] There is no reference to *culpa et pena*, nor is the requirement of contrition forgotten.

Later in the year 1409 Bruni left Gregory and became secretary to Alexander V who was elected at the Council of Pisa. Alexander did grant plenary absolution *a pena et culpa* to members of the Council, qualified only by the requirement that it be *in forma ecclesie*.[4] Bruni was still in the papal service when in 1412 John XXIII granted the indulgence that provoked the famous protest of John Hus over the alleged power to forgive both *culpa et pena*.[5]

In 1415 Bruni accompanied John XXIII to the Council of Constance which, while rejecting the challenges of Wyclif and Hus to the power of granting indulgences,[6] did propose that all granted since the Council of Vienne (1312) be annulled. The newly-elected Martin V promised at least to revoke all concessions to churches of the power to grant plenary remission of *culpa et pena*.[7]

---

[2] Henry Charles Lea, *A History of Auricular Confession and Indulgences in the Latin Church* 3 vols. (Philadelphia, 1896). Part II, on *Indulgences*, opens with an introductory chapter that traces the history of the controversy over the claim to relief from *culpa et pena* since the thirteenth century (3: 54ff.). For the reference to Boniface IX, 3: 67.

[3] See Document II below.

[4] Lea, 3: 67.

[5] Lea, 3: 68.

[6] Bernhard Poschmann, *Penance and the Annointing of the Sick*, tr. F. Courtney, S.J. (New York, 1964), 230, citing Denzinger, *Enchiridion Symbolorum* (ed. 28, Freiburg i. Br., 1952), 622 and 676. For Leo X's insistence on the power: 740a and 757-762.

[7] Lea, 3: 70.

From his own experience, then, Bruni was familiar with the terms prescribed by a pope of this era for the guidance of a preacher of indulgences. What did he see in the assertions of the preacher in Florence in 1431 that was "strange and astonishing?" It was the knight's claim to possess the power to confer plenary indulgence with respect to both *culpa et pena*. No such power had been included in the letter that Bruni had drafted for Gregory XII, nor was any such power conferred by Martin V upon the knight. Such a power could be exercized, according to current doctrine, only by the pope in Rome.[8]

When the Signoria summoned the knight and demanded to see the papal documents authorizing the preaching, Bruni says,

> we found what we had previously suspected: that the limited and restrained authorizations that this knight had obtained from the Apostolic See, were being transformed, through the mouth of his venal and mercenary preacher, into promises that were unlimited and unbelievable.

The Florentine complaint was thus not against the pope, but against the knight and those who who had exceeded the powers the pope had given them.

The complaint of the Renaissance Humanist in 1431 thus was not the same as that expressed eighty-six years later by Martin Luther in his Ninety-Five Theses, many of which challenge the claim to be able to remit *culpa et pena* (See especially Theses 5, 6, 21, 36, 70, 76). Papal restrictions regarding indulgences had in the interval been attenuated, notably by Julius II in *Liquet omnibus* (11 January 1510), which makes no mention of repentance or confession as conditions, and which was drawn up in such a way as to permit the pardoners to claim the power to offer relief from both *culpa et pena*.[9] Luther could not content himself with Bruni's complaint that the traffickers were exceeding papal guidelines. Instead (with certain qualifications) Luther questions whether such a power is possessed even by the pope in Rome.

In 1436, five years after the episode we have described, another letter to the pope regarding the preaching of indulgences in Florence appears in the correspondence of the Chancery, but this time not to complain against the practice, but to ask the pope to confirm the indulgences granted by his predecessors to the "first and principal church in our city", the Baptistry.[10] There is no inconsistency here, for the Florentines in 1431 had not expressed any objection to the lesser indulgences often granted, as in this case, for the benefit of a church.

---

[8] Augustin Fliche and Victor Martin, eds., *Histoire de l'Eglise* (Paris, 1934-), vol. 14.2, 817.

[9] Lea, 3: 75.

[10] See Document III below.

Bruni was of course not in a position, either as papal secretary or as Chancellor of Florence, to express his personal opinion. Though we may reasonably suspect that certain turns of phrase in the complaint against the indulgence-hawkers were the personal contributions of this master of humanist rhetoric,[11] we must assume that he was faithfully expressing the attitude of the members of the Signoria.

Thus far we have emphasized the restricted scope of the anticlerical sentiment expressed in the 1431 letter, but perhaps it should also be seen as an example of anticlericalism in the wider sense of conflict between the Church and the secular authority. There is a hint of this in the defensive note in the passage of the complaint in which the Signoria protests that "we are not the ones who have been violating apostolic authority." Yet they had had the presumption to forbid the further preaching of the indulgences on the part of the knight and his assistants, armed though they were with letters from the pope. And evidently the pope had received complaints against the Signoria's action.[12]

To justify the interference of the secular authority in what was clearly a spiritual matter, the Signoria was fortunate to have at its disposal the literary talents of Leonardo Bruni.

---

[11] After leaving the papal service, and before taking up his duties as Chancellor, Bruni had written a diatribe Against Hypocrites (*In Hypocritas*). This opens with Bruni's encountering two hypocrites. He will not name them, but in his description of their hairshirts and of their lowered eyes, he obviously intended us to understand that they were mendicants. Pretence, he says, is what he detests, wherever it may be found, among seculars as well as among the regular clergy. Despite this disclaimer, however, the diatribe clearly belongs amongst attacks on the mendicant orders. For the dating of *In Hypocritas* to 1417-1418, see Ludwig Bertalot, *Quellen und Forschungen* 28 (1938): 277-8, where he cites Bruni's letter to Guarino of 1 April 1418 (*Ep.*, ed. Mehus, Lib. IV, no. 14).

[12] In the past, would-be preachers of indulgences had to obtain the written authorization of the bishop of Florence: "Omnes questuarii, qui suis privilegiis vel indulgentiis in nostra civitate vel dyocesi uti voluerint, antequam eis utantur, coram nobis vel nostro vicario de ipsis fidem facere teneantur." Constitutions of the Bishop of Florence, 1310, p. 285, 11. 30-34, quoted by Richard C. Trexler, *Synodal Law in Florence and Fiesole, 1306-1518* (Vatican City, 1971), 90. This provision was tightened under the constitutions issued by Bishop Francesco da Cingoli in 1327, where it is stated "quod nullus questiarius in aliqua ecclesiarum civitatis et diocesis Florentie ad predicandum et questum querendum admittatur, nisi cum litteris nostro sigillo munitis ... Qui contrarium fecerint, nostro arbitrio puniantur." *I Capitoli del Comune di Firenze* 2, ed. Guasti and Gherardi (Florence, 1893), 44.

DOCUMENT I

The Florentine Complaint to Eugenius IV
Against Indulgence-Hawkers
(Presumably composed by Leonardo Bruni, 20 July 1431)

Sanctissime ac Beatissime Pater, post humilem recommendationem ...

Venit nuper in urbem nostram miles quidam ordinis Sancti Iohannis Ierusalemitani cum satis magno numero ministrorum. Erant vero hi omnes fere scriptores litterarum. Conduxerat preterea mercede pecuniaria predicatorem quendam ex ordine minorum, hominem loquacem, lingua exercitata, et qui parum de spiritu, plurimum de pecunia cogitaret.

Hic, multitudine populi congregata, cum superiori de suggesto litteras explicaret, sigillasque ostenderet, inaudita quedam ac mirabilia populi auribus ingerebat, ut omnem sedis apostolice potestatem pene in hunc militem trransfusam translatamque asseveraret. Nam et indulgentiam plenissimam culpe et pene, ut illius verbis utamur, affirmabat ipsum militem concedendi potestatem habere quibuscumque subsidium sibi offerentibus. Et usurarios omnes absolvendi et dispensandi in multiplicibus variisque et arduissimis casibus. Horum singula verbis extolendo, hortabatur quod haberent homines nostri facultatem in celum ascendendi ut pecuniam traderent ac se ipsos a damnatione redimerent.

Hec dicebantur ab illo magna voce atque clamore. Quibus verbis imperiti homines presertimque mulieres tota urbe concursu mirabili confluebant. Ut esset instar mercatus cuiusdam, cum alie pecuniam, alie vestem, alie pannum, alie argentum illis deferrent. Egregii vero mercatores ac nundinatores gratiarum nichil penitus recusantes, omnia capiebant.

In templis autem scamna erant posita quibus scriptores illi litteras conficiebant sigillasque imprimebant permaxime, passimque coram omnibus omnia venditabant.

Quo videntes boni et graves viri plurimum indignabantur. Cum igitur ex querela multorum ad nos delata fuissent, vocammus militem illum postulammusque ut unde hec tam grandia profitentur nobis exhibeat. Ille vero litteras attulit, quas legi examinarique fecimuus diligenter, repperimusque id quod prius quoque nostris mentibus insidebat, hunc militem, cum moderata quedam et castigata a sede apostolica obtinuisset, immoderata tamen et incredibilia per illum predicatorem suum venalem atque conductitium profiteri.

Concessio enim facta fuerat a domino Martino et per Vestram Beatitudinem confirmata. Unis in litteris erat facultas concedendi indulgentiam in mortis articulo euntibus personaliter in subsidium contra infideles vel mittentibus aliquem loco sui vel tribuentibus centesimam partem omnium bonorum suorum. Aliis in litteris facultas erat absolvendi usurarios modo peniterent modo desisterent omnino in posterum facerentque restitutionem ablatorum omnium. Eodem modo in ceteris litteris rationabilia quedam et moderata continebantur. Sed professio istorum aliusmodi erat.

In prima enim gratia deligendi in mortis articulo, que satis faciliter per sedem apostolicam concedi consuevit, nomen "culpe et pene" pretexebatur et quasi rarum aliquid et nunquam alias fere concessum laudabatur. Et nulla centesime bonorum ratione habita pro quibuscumque pecuniis vendebatur. In absolutionem vero usurariorum hoc unum profitebantur: absolvere posse et pecuniam capere; qualitates vero et circumstantie que permulte sunt apposite tacebantur.

Eodem modo in ceteris, mirabilis erat asseveratio atque inductio ad pecunias tradendas. Ex quibus, cum videremus aperte decipi simplices homines mulieresque, et imperitam turbam circumveniri, redundareque totam hanc rem in damnum civitatis, inhibuimus militi ac ministris eius illa profiteri.

Si ergo aliter relatum est Beatitudini Vestre, quicumque retulat, a vero recessit. Non enim ii sumus qui autoritati apostolice refringemur. Sed totum factum est a nobis ut fraudibus et deceptionibus evidentissimis obviaretur.

Tacemus vero referre que sit vita, qui mores istorum qui hec profitentur, que prandia, que sumptuositas, que voluptates. Monstro quippe videri potest persimile hoc qui salutem animabus aliorum se profitentur afferre, ita vivere ut nichil unquam de salute propria cogitasse videantur.

Quocirca, Beatissime Pater, Vestre Beatitudine humiliter supplicamus, ut hanc rem intellegere dignetur, ac remedium adhibere, nobisque super his aliquid significare de intentione Beatitudinis Vestre.

Dat. Florentie die XX Julii 1431.

SOURCE: Florence, Archivio di Stato, *Missive* 33: fols. 45r-46v.

Holy and Blessed Father, our humble salutation ...

Recently there came to our city a certain knight of the Order of St. John of Jerusalem, with quite a large number of assistants. Almost all of these were in fact letter-writers. Especially to raise money he had brought with him a certain preacher of the Franciscan Order, a loquacious man with a well-practiced tongue, and one who would pay little attention to the spirit, but a great deal to money.

When a great crowd of people had gathered, and while this man, standing on a raised platform, exhibited the letters and displayed the seals, he would assail the people's ears with certain strange and astonishing assertions to the effect that just about all the power of the Apostolic See had been transfused and transferred into this knight. For he would affirm that the knight had the power to confer plenary indulgence for both guilt and punishment (*culpa et pena*), to use his very words, to anybody who was willing to pay him the money, and the power, too, to offer absolution and dispensation to all usurers in their multiple problems, and even in their most difficult cases.

After describing particular examples, he would urge that our citizens, to gain the opportunity of ascending to heaven, pay over the money and so ransom themselves from damnation.

These things were proclaimed by him in a loud and noisy voice. In response to such words, the ignorant and especially the women from all over the city converged in such an astonishing concourse that it had the look of a sort of market place, with some of the women offering money, others clothing, others cloth, others silver. No gratuities were wholly rejected by these really upright merchants and traffickers, who took everything that was offered.

In the churches, benches had been placed, on which the scribes were composing the letters and impressing their seals wholesale and selling them indiscriminately to all comers.

Sights like these produced the greatest indignation amongst men of substance and influence. When, therefore, on the complaint of many of them, the matter was laid before us, we summoned that knight and demanded that he show us his authority for making such bold promises. He was able in fact to produce letters, which we caused to be carefully read and examined, and we found what we had previously suspected: that the limited and restrained authorizations that this knight had obtained from the Apostolic See, were being transformed, through the mouth of his venal and mercenary preacher, into promises that were unlimited and unbelievable.

The grant had in fact been made by Martin V, and then confirmed by Your Holiness. In one letter was the power of granting an indulgence on the point of death in aid of those going in person on crusade against the infidels, or of those sending someone in their place, or of those contributing the hundredth part of their wealth. In another letter was the power of absolving usurers if they were penitent, would completely desist from the practice in future, and would make restitution of all their ill-gotten gains. The other letters contained similarly reasonable and carefully limited provisions. But the promises offered by these fellows were quite a different matter.

For in the first case, of opting (for an indulgence) on the point of death, what has customarily been quite readily granted by the Apostolic See, the words "culpa et pena" were put forward and boasted of as something quite unusual and almost never granted before. Furthermore, it was sold for whatever payment could be obtained, without any mention of the hundredth part of the property.

As for absolution of usurers, they limited themselves to one point: to be able to grant absolution and to accept cash for it, while they remained silent about the various conditions and circumstances specified (in the apostolic letter).

Similarly in the other letters, the claims made and the inducements advanced for the handing over of money were simply amazing.

Consequently, when we saw that they were clearly deceiving simple men and women, and captivating the ignorant mob, and that this whole business was getting so far out of hand as to threaten the damnation of the city, we forebade the knight and his assistants to continue making these professions.

If, therefore, Your Holiness has received any different report, whoever conveyed it was departing from the truth. For we are not the ones who have been violating apostolic authority. Whatever we have done has been to prevent the most obvious frauds and deceptions.

We shall say nothing about the conduct and morals of the men who have been making these professions: about their banquets, their extravagance, their pleasures. It certainly seems monstrous that those who are promising salvation to the souls of others are themselves living in such a way as to suggest that they are giving no thought whatever to their own salvation.

Wherefore, Holy Father, we humbly beg that Your Holiness may condescend to look into this matter, and bring apropriate remedy to bear, and give us some indication of Your Holiness' intentions.

Given at Florence, 20 July 1431.

DOCUMENT II

Grant by Gregory XII to Giovanni Dominici
of the Power to Authorize Indulgences
(drafted by Leonardo Bruni, 8 January 1409)

Gregorius, *etc.*, Dilecto filio Johanni, titulo Sancti Sixti Presbitero Cardinali, Apostolice Sedis Legato Salutem *etc.* Cum te ad Ungarie, Polonie et nonnullas alias partes pro arduis Sancte Romane ecclesie negotiis cum plene legationis officio presentialiter destinemus,

Nos, volentes tibi illa concedere per que hominibus dictarum partium te possis reddere gratiosum, circumspectioni tue concedendi mille personis utriusque sexus ut confessorum quem ipsem duxerint eligendum omnium peccatorum suorum de quibus corde contrite et ore confesse fuerint semel tantum in mortis articulo plenam remissionem concedere valeat in forma *etc.*,[13] cunctis per nos opponi consuetis, plenam et liberam auctoritate apostolica tenore presentium concedimus facultatem.

Dat. a Rimini, VIo Idus Januarii, Pontificatus Nostre Anno Tertio.

L. de Aretio   De Curia
                                                        P. de Vicicomitatu

SOURCE: Archivio Segreto Vaticano, Reg. Vat. 337, fol. 57r.

Gregory to his beloved son, John, cardinal titular priest of St. Sixtus and Legate of the Holy See, Greeting, etc. Since we are sending you presently to parts of Hungary, Poland and various other parts on the arduous business of the Holy Roman Church with full legatine authority,

Being desirous of granting what may enable you to make yourself welcome to the people of the said parts, by our apostolic authority by the tenor of these presents we grant you plenary and free power to grant, according to your discretion, to a thousand persons of both sexes, that the confessor of their choice may grant plenary remission of all their sins that they have orally confessed and with a contrite heart, once only, on the point of death, in accordance with the rule customarily required by us.

Given at Rimini, 8 January 1409, in the third year of our Pontificate.

---

[13] For a discussion of this formula, see Lea, 3: 67.

DOCUMENT III

A Florentine Supplication to Eugenius IV
to Confirm Indulgences to the Florentine Baptistry
(presumably drafted by Leonardo Bruni, 15 June 1436)

Beatissime Pater, post humilem recommendationem, *etc.*:

Sepius iam supplicatum fuit Beatitudini Vestre per antecessores nostros, Priores Artium et Vexilliferem Justitie qui tunc erant in officio, ut dignaretur Sanctitas Vestra indulgentias quasdam per Romanos Pontifices ecclesie Beati Johannis Baptiste concessas, de speciale gratia confirmare. Super qua quidem re, benignum et gratissimum a Beatitudine Vestra reportarunt responsum cum firmissima spe huius gratie concedende. Et certe, Beatissime Pater, cum veneratio singularis totius populi nostri sit erga illam ecclesiam utpote primam et principalem nostre civitatis, nichil gratius universo populo nostro facere possit Vestra Sanctitas, quam illi ecclesie grandia ac precipua indulta exibuere: pro inextinguibile memoria Vestre Beatitudiinis et pro consolatione populi nostri. Qui ad eam ecclesiam precipua ut diximus veneratione concurrit.

Quocirca, Beatitudini Vestre humiliter supplicamus ut dignetur Vestra Beatitudo annuere supplicationibus et postulationibus super his Beatitudini Vestre porrectis. Quod ad singularissimam gratiam ac sempiterni beneficii memoriam adscribemus.

Dat. Florentie, die XV Junii 1436.

SOURCE: Florence, Archivio di Stato, *Missive* 35, fol.48v.

Blessed Father, with humble salutation *etc.*:

Your Blessedness has already been requested several times by our predecessors in office as Priors of the Guilds and Standard Bearer of Justice[14] to condescend by your special grace to confirm certain indulgences granted by Roman pontiffs to the church of St. John the Baptist. Regarding which they reported that the response of Your Blessedness had been benign and most gratifying, and that there was high hope that the grace would be granted. Certainly, Blessed Father, since a special veneration is felt by our whole people toward this church, being the first and foremost in our city, Your Holiness could do nothing that would be more gratifying to our whole people than to present that church with great and special privileges, as a permanent memorial to Your Blessedness and as a consolation to our

---

[14] The collective executive body of the city of Florence was composed of eight "Priors of the Guilds" and the "Standard Bearer of Justice".

people, who are, as we have said, united in their feeling of special veneration for that church.

Wherefore we humbly beg Your Blessedness to condescend to listen to the supplications and requests addressed to Your Blessedness regarding these matters. We shall ascribe it to a very special grace and regard it as the memorial of an eternal beneficence.

Given at Florence, 15 June 1436.

II. THE TRANSITION
TO EARLY MODERN SOCIETY

ANTICLERICALISM AND THE CITIES

BOB SCRIBNER

Clare College, Cambridge University

There are two ways of viewing anticlericalism: first, as a *mentalité* or psychological stance, with emotional and affective dimensions; and second, as a form of behavior, involving particular types of action expressing hostility to the clergy, action which could range from verbal abuse and harassment, over physical attack, breach of the peace and forms of ritualized behavior, to officially approved confrontations and political impositions. My interest in this paper is threefold: to ask how attitudes turn into behavior; to explore, in particular, the psychology or psychological processes whereby an anticlerical mentality leads to certain forms of action broadly called "evangelical"; and to analyse how these forms of action play their part in evangelical movements effecting religious change in urban communities. I shall presuppose a definition of anticlericalism which I have adumbrated elsewhere: that anticlericalism involves a perception of, and reaction to, the power wielded by the clergy as a distinctive social group, power which expressed itself in the economic, political, legal, social, sexual and sacred spheres of daily life.[1]

I

Let me begin my discussion of anticlericalism in the cities with a testimony from someone who experienced it firsthand:

> During Vespers on the day of Christ's birth, when the Magnificat was to have been sung, I, Jacob Megerich, pastor in Our Lady's Church, according to praiseworthy ancient custom was incensing St. Stephen's altar ... As I went on to St. George's altar a great murmur arose from the Lutheran women and men [in the church]. They made a great disturbance and charged forward. They drove me into the sacristy with great violence and there reviled and scolded me with many words of abuse, beat me about the head and shoulders with their fists, kicked me in my side and threw me down onto my hip, pelted me with stones in the sacristy, smashed and tore out the window panes, damaged the picture on

---

[1] See "Anticlericalism and the German Reformation", in Robert W. Scribner, *Popular Culture and Popular Movements in Reformation Germany* (London, 1987), 243-56; originally in German as "Antiklerikalismus in Deutschland um 1500", in *Europa 1500. Integrationsprozesse im Widerstreit*, ed. F. Seibt, W. Eberhardt (Stuttgart, 1987), 368-82.

the retable, overturned the altar light, broke off and carried away the candles on the altar. They carried on with this mischief and violence from 4 am to 6 am. If the Mayor Hans Keller and six town councillors had not arrived, I would have been struck dead in the sacristy. I had to promise the Lutherans that I would afterwards present myself before the worthy town council and dispute with the preacher Christoph Schappeler. They led me forcibly as a prisoner from my church, one of three priests, with the intention that I, master Hans Tieffenthaler and the reverend Ulrich Cammerer should all be placed in the thieves' tower and kept there overnight. But the mayor had us taken to his house under his protection and had us treated honorably and with dignity, indeed, he had us guarded under the protection of two city constables until 11 am on St. Stephen's Day. Then he discussed with us until midday how to deal with the matter of the disputation and other things.[2]

This incident, which occurred in Memmingen on 25 December 1524, reveals not only the vehemence and turbulence of anticlerical feeling during the emergence of the reform movements in Germany. It also shows its strategic importance for the progress of those movements. The context of the attack on the hapless Memmingen pastor is informative. Christoph Schappeler, preacher in St. Martin's church in Memmingen since 1513, had been engaged since the summer of 1523 in increasingly bitter polemics with Megerich over evangelical reforms. Schappeler, who encouraged private

---

[2] The text of Megerich's statement given in J. Miedel, "Zur Memminger Reformationsgeschichte. Der Tumult in der Frauenkirche", *Beiträge zur bayerischen Kirchengeschichte* 1 (1895): 172-3: "Item an dem Tag, de gebuert Christi unnder der Vespel so man das magnificat hat gesungen, bey St Stephanos altar da dann patrocinium ist gewesen, habe ich Jacob megerich Pfarherr zu unnser frawen, die altar gereichet nach löblichen alter gewonheit, So ich herab bin khomen zu St Jeorgen altar hat sich ein gros murmeln erhebt von den luterischen weyb und man, darnach gross auffruhr unnd auf geläuff ist worden. Und mich in die Sacristey geiagt und getrieben mit grosser ungestumligkhait daselb mit vil Schmech worten gelestert und gescholten, mit fausten geschlagen, ann mein haubt und auff die Schultern, mich auch mit den fuessen an mein seiten und auff die huff gestossen, mit steinen zu Mir inn die Sacristei geworffen, die glässer zerrissen und erschlagen, die bildlin an dem tafeln gebrochen, die amplen erworffen, Kertzen auff dem altar abgebrochen und hinweg getragen, Sollich unfuhr und gewalt von 4 bies 6 getriben und gehalten. Unnd wo Hanns Keller der burger meister und 6 des Raths nit khommen, so ware ich in der Sacrystei erschlagen worden, habe denn Lutterischen miessen verhaissen, darnach ann st steffanstag vor einem Ersamen Rath mich zu stellen unnd mit dem prediger Cristoff Schappeler disputieren, haben mich mit gewalt gefangelich aus meiner Kierchen gefuert, selb dritt priester, der meinung, man solte mich unnd maister hanns tieffenthaler unnd Herr ulrichen Cammerer die nacht inn den Diebsthurm gelegt und behalten han: aber der Burgermeister hat unns in sein haus unnd gewarsamkheit fueren lassen, uns Ehrlich und redlich gehalten, doch mit 2 Statknechten lassen hüeten und wol bewaren, biss an St steffans tag umb die 11. stundt, darnach mit unns gehandelt bis inn die 12. stundt, wie wy in dem handel weiter würden hatten, mit disputieren und anderen sachen."

reading and discussion of the Bible, had gathered a large popular following, which became irreconcilably hostile to the strictly orthodox pastor when he occasioned the imposition of an episcopal ban over the evangelical preacher in February 1524. The progressive collapse of the old religious observance was brought to a head on 7 December 1524, when Schappeler distributed communion under both kinds in St. Martin's. The parishioners of Our Lady's church sought the same from their pastor and on 16 December sent a deputation to the town council demanding communion under both kinds and German baptism, insisting that if Megerich refused he should be made to dispute with Schappeler about right doctrine and ceremonies. The town council temporized, provoking the evangelical party into taking the law into its own hands. The disputation held at the town hall on 2-7 January 1525 revolved around central issues of evangelical reform: auricular confession, invocation of the Virgin Mary and the saints, the tithe, the sacrificial character of the Mass, purgatory, how to celebrate communion and the nature of the priesthood. By all accounts, it was no contest; Schappeler won hands down and the town council began to institute formal measures of religious reform: the abolition of the Mass, the subjection of the clergy to civic control, the allowance of clerical marriage, reordering of clerical benefices and the appointment of Schappeler as the head of a "local church" — a church, as Megerich described it, independent of pope and emperor. The tumult in Our Lady's church on Christmas Day had served to precipitate an ecclesiastical revolution.[3]

II

The phenomenon of anticlericalism during the German Reformation is indisputable, whether in such tumultuous manifestations as it took in Memmingen or in more restrained forms. The problem for the historian is

---

[3] On the Reformation in Memmingen and especially these events, besides Miedel (as note 2), see Eugen Rohling, *Die Reichsstadt Memmingen in der Zeit der evangelischen Volksbewegung* (Munich, 1864), 79f., 92f., 112-16; Friedrich Dobel, *Memmingen im Reformationszeitalter* (Memmingen, 1877), 32f., 41f., 56-64; Wolfgang Schlenck, "Die Reichsstadt Memmingen und die Reformation", *Memminger Geschichtsblätter* (1969): 30-43; Martin Brecht, "Die theologische Hintergrund der Zwolf Artickel der Bauernschaft in Schwaben von 1525", *ZKG* 85 (1974): 174-208, esp. 39-41, who does not use Miedel's article; Barbara Kroemer, "Die Einführung der Reformation in Memmingen", *Memminger Geschichtsblätter* (1980): 67-112, esp. 103f. Sebastian Lotzer, in his pamphlet defending the tumultuous events in Memmingen, *Entschuldigung ainer Frummen Christlichen Gemaine zu Memmingen ... von wegen der emporungen so sich bey uns begeben* (1525), emphasized the cathartic nature of the tumult with his comment: "ist on zweyfel alles von Got also angesehen gewesen, damit die sach zu ainer rechtfertigung keme", in Alfred Goetze, ed., *Sebastian Lotzers Schriften* (Leipzig, 1902), 84.

to evaluate its significance for the nature and progress of the Reformation. Here it often appears that the stance of any given historian on the question of significance rests on certain assumptions, indeed we might say certain convictions, about the nature of the Reformation. These convictions become hermeneutic points of departure for the assessment and evaluation of the phenomenon and the role it is *allowed* to play. That is, the importance of anticlericalism is inexplicable apart from the historiography of the Reformation, the way in which each age reinterprets, indeed reshapes, the Reformation in terms of its own interests. I fear that we cannot escape this trap, even within the reevaluative framework represented by this volume. However, we may come to a better understanding of the significance of anticlericalism if we ask how the anticlerical mentality influenced behavior, and then how this behavior in its turn shaped the process of reform, that is, the actual restructuring of religious cult and institutions. In this sense we are dealing primarily with a *political* question, for we are seeking to understand forms of public action.

First, it should be said that anticlerical outbursts during the Reformation were probably no different in their individual intensity from those found previously. The anticlerical *Pfaffensturm* was a recurrent feature of late-medieval urban life and exemplified violent passions that were more than comparable with those aroused by evangelical feeling.[4] Let us take one example chosen at random. In the Pomeranian town of Kolberg civic struggles with the episcopal chapter and the Bishop of Kammin reached back to the conciliarist conflicts of the early fifteenth century. The Bishop was a conciliarist, while the town council of Kolberg supported the deposed pope Eugenius IV (1431-1447, dep. 1439). It gained thereby various privileges limiting the powers of ecclesiastical courts within the town, and restricting the effects of ecclesiastical bans or interdicts. It was also in conflict with the chapter over the saltworks and usage of the town harbor. However, it was a clash over a case before the ecclesiastical court that lead the town mayor, Hans Schlief, to appear in the cathedral one Sunday in 1442 and to disrupt Mass by abusing the bishop as a heretic, a traitor, and a profane perjurer. The mayor went on to have the bishop's chaplain and notary seized and the episcopal palace stormed and sacked. Later, the houses of the cathedral canons were stormed and in 1461 Hans Schlief showed his stubborn unrepentance not only by disrupting the procession held by the Antonine monks in honor of their patron saint, but also by mishandling the

---

[4] For examples in Würzburg, see Karl Trüdinger, *Stadt und Kirche im spätmittelalterlichen Würzburg* (Stuttgart, 1978), esp. 24, 75, 77, 143; and in Osnabrück, Minden and Rostock, see Bernd-Ulrich Hergemöller, *"Pfaffenkriege" im spätmittelalterlichen Hanseraum. Quellen und Studien zu Braunschweig, Osnabrück, Lüneburg und Rostock* (Cologne, 1988), 1: 83, 88, 93-96, 225-6, who also points out (88) that such incidents were perceived by the clergy not as isolated incidents but as part of a long chain of hostility.

holy relics. The Antonine order was expelled from the town for the next thirty years.[5]

Such examples could be multiplied from all parts of Germany and illustrate how far anticlericalism can be understood as a reaction to the various kinds of power wielded by the clergy. In as far as the reform movements of the sixteenth century were an attempt to remove or reduce that power, anticlericalism was both a natural precondition and a precipitant of those movements. However it would be misleading to posit any kind of natural antipathy between city governments and the clergy, or even between burghers and clergy as an automatic stimulus to, or accelerator of, reform. The rich and informative research of recent years on pre-Reformation urban ecclesiastical life and institutions reveals a more complex picture and suggests the need for a more differentiated approach to Reformation anticlericalism.[6]

Some of the complexities are revealed in the history of a town such as Erfurt, which had a strong anticlerical tradition. Here the clergy's tax-exempt milling, brewing and winemaking were very popular with the common citizenry, which was able to avoid civic excises by frequenting clerically-owned mills and inns, and in clashes of 1490 and 1502-3 over clerical exemptions, the citizenry sided with the clergy rather than the town council. Indeed, it was the council's lack of tactical skill that drove the citizenry into an alliance with the clergy in the upheavals that shook the city in 1509.[7] The outbursts that made Erfurt a byword for anticlericalism in the early 1520s may have owed as much to more machiavellian tactics by the council than to any instinctive hatred of the clergy by the citizenry. The case reveals that simplistic dichotomies between clergy and layfolk are not very helpful for uncovering the social complexity of clerical-lay relations. The social interface between parish clergy and burgher elite in towns such as Hannover or Mainz, or between mass priests and burgher families in towns like Neustadt an der Orla may have had a double effect. On the one hand, it may have aroused social hostility from lower urban classes who resented a

---

[5] H. Riemann, *Geschichte der Stadt Kolberg* (Kolberg, 1924), 219-20, 231-3, 240.

[6] See, for example, Dieter Demandt, *Stadtherrschaft und Stadtfreiheit im Spannungsfeld von Geistlichkeit und Bürgerschaft in Mainz 11.-15. Jahrhundert* (Wiesbaden, 1977); Kaspar Elm, ed., *Stellung und Wirksamkeit der Bettelorden in der städtischen Gesellschaft* (Berlin, 1981); Norbert Hecker, *Bettelorden und Bürgertum. Konflikt und Kooperation in den deutschen Städten des Spätmittelalters* (Frankfurt, 1981); Hubert Höing, *Kloster und Stadt. Vergleichende Beiträge zum Verhältnis Kirche und Stadt im Spätmittelalter* (Münster, 1981); Bernhard Neidiger, *Mendikanten zwischen Ordensideal und städtischer Realität* (Berlin, 1981); Ernst Voltmer, *Reichsstadt und Herrschaft. Zur Geschichte der Stadt Speyer im hohen und späten Mittelalter* (Trier, 1981).

[7] Robert W. Scribner, "Reformation, Society and Humanism in Erfurt ca. 1450-1530", University of London, Ph.D. Diss., 1972, 1: 40.

combination of clerical and elite wealth: the Neustadt mass priests had considerable wealth in hereditary property and annuity incomes and in 1525 provoked the special attention of the rebel band composed of Neustadt citizens and peasants from surrounding villages.[8] On the other hand, the close association of ruling elite and parish clergy in many towns may have facilitated the introduction of evangelical preaching. A third of the leading reformers were sons of town councillors, urban patricians or wealthy merchants, many of them subsequently became preachers in their home towns, and were no doubt helped by their social connections.[9]

Similarly, urban relations with monastic orders, and especially with the mendicants, were far from straightforward. In some places such as Augsburg, Frankfurt or Speyer, the religious orders supported the town in its conflicts with ecclesiastical overlords during the fifteenth century, and helped to breach ban and interdict by celebrating religious services as usual. In Frankfurt the mendicant orders, who stood on the town's side against the Archbishop of Mainz, were exempted from agreements touching the clergy and treated as if they were citizens. In Braunschweig, the Friars Minor were virtually a civic institution, with close links to the town council, their church serving as a civic church.[10] We require a more systematic overview than we have had hitherto of the relations between religious orders and their host towns both before and during the Reformation before we can draw up a final balance sheet on this point.[11] However, it is certain that the relationship of mendicant friars to the urban evangelical movements was quite complex. Around forty percent of leading evangelical preachers were members of religious orders, and there is more than a strong suspicion that at least their initial attraction arose from their identity as monks or mendicants. Part of Luther's popularity stemmed from his public persona as a friar bringing the Bible to the people, and it seems likely that mendicant preaching styles could account for the effectiveness of many a popular evangelical preacher.

---

[8] See Rudolf Herrmann, "Die Messpriester in einer Thüringer Kleinstadt vor der Reformation und ihr Verhältnis zum Bauernkrieg", *Zeitschrift des Vereins für thüringische Geschichte* 34 (NF 26) (1926): 1-64, esp 27. On Hannover, Siegfried Müller, *Stadt, Kirche und Reformation. Das Beispiel der Landstadt Hannover* (Hannover, 1987), 37, who establishes that 80% of the Hannover clergy came from resident burgher families.

[9] Robert W. Scribner, "Preachers and People in the German Towns", in *Popular Culture and Popular Movements*, 131. Examples are Ambrosius Blarer and Johann Zwick in Konstanz, Kaspar Cruciger in Leipzig, Andreas Cellarius in Rottenburg/Necker and Adam Weiss in Crailsheim.

[10] Hecker, *Bettelorden und Bürgertum*, 95f., 110; Hergemöller, *"Pfaffenkriege"*, 1: 49.

[11] The useful study by Hecker (as note 6) is limited by its lack of attention to changing periodization, treating the thirteenth to fifteenth centuries as a unified whole, without differentiating changes in emphasis or specific problems occasioned by variations of historical context.

The same is true of the secular clergy, where an effective parish priest could, because of his standing in the community, play a key role in effecting evangelical reform. Many examples from all parts of Germany come readily to mind, such as Heinrich Brun in Aurich, Heinrich von Bünau in Elsterberg in the Vogtland, Tilemann Platner in Stolberg, Wolfgang Vogel in Bopfingen or Adam Weiss in Crailsheim. The question requires systematic region by region exploration if we are fully to understand how far the urban evangelical movements were, as I understand them to be in great part, an attack on the old church led from within, by the established clergy themselves.

This is a view of anticlericalism as a form of "self-hatred", a notion that has complex ramifications. We might point to the clergy as a "sexual anomaly", a view so cleverly exploited by the propaganda of the *Epistolae obscurorum virorum*,[12] or to the agonies experienced by those clerics who were the sons of priests, and therefore "whore's bastards".[13] There was also clerical agonizing over the hypocrisy of their sexual behavior, especially by conscientious clerics who felt they were unable to remain celibate but who knew that they could buy their way out of the offence. Their pressing moral problem was how to preserve integrity in such a situation.[14] Evangelical theology pointed out the existential nature of this self-hatred, that it was the sincere agonizing of those striving to be truly Christian but frustrated by the constraints of an all too human institution out of tune with Christ's injunctions. Above all, because it was the failings of the clergy that condemned the church to corruption and mankind to divine anger, the clergy's self-hatred involved what might be called an apocalyptic *Angst*, a

---

[12] Not only in its continual emphasis on the unchastity of the monks and friars, but also in its tale of the women brought into the Dominican monastery in Strassburg disguised as friars, "so that for a long time they passed as monks, and went to market and bought fish from their husbands, the fishermen", until the ruse was uncovered by students who sought to administer a beating to a monk and his "monkess" and who thereby "uncovered her shame." See Ulrich von Hutten, et al., *On the Eve of the Reformation. "Letters of Obscure Men"*, trans. Francis Griffin Stokes, with an Introduction by Hajo Holborn (New York, 1964), 97.

[13] Cf. the example of Erasmus Alberus, who expressed his personal relief as the bastard son of the priest, that "now the child of a pious evangelical priest is not called a whore's child, but an honourable child. For this good deed we can never thank God enough." Cited in E. Körner, *Erasmus Alberus* (Leipzig, 1910), 3.

[14] Cf. the example of Justus Jonas, who wrote to Johannes Lang on 8 November 1521: "Nescio an dominus vocet ad ducendam uxorem. Hac tenus quid carnis ignes sint nescivi, ut in aurem tibe dicam, nam serio cupio, ut pro me ardentissime ores. Aegre me reprehendo, aegre sudans me reprimo, quin scortationis impetu auferar. At dominus servabit (spero), quod in me peccatore miserrimo planavit", *Der Briefwechsel des Justus Jonas*, ed. G. Kawerau, vol. 1 (Halle, 1884), ep. 69, p. 95. Jonas married shortly thereafter, on 9 February 1522, *Contemporaries of Erasmus*, ed. P. G. Bietenholz (Toronto, 1986), 2: 246.

fear that the world would be condemned because of their failings. This apocalyptic anxiety the evangelical message was able successfully to resolve for those who accepted its implications, offering in the "preacher of the Word" a resolution especially to their personal dilemmas, thus enabling the self-hating cleric to attain a new dignity freed from the causes of self-hatred.

III

I do not intend these qualifying comments to suggest that anticlericalism was no more than a precondition, perhaps necessary but not sufficient, for the unfolding of the reform movements of the sixteenth century. Nor do I accept the view that it was no more than a marginal concomitant of these movements. We could easily fall into this error if we regarded it as merely an instinctive form of behavior used to express the exasperation of those who demanded evangelical preaching but who found their demands blocked by a recalcitrant clergy — anticlericalism as irate reflex, so to speak. That was admittedly the case in some towns where the council was lukewarm in its support of the evangelical party or where it took up a negatively neutral stance. Aschersleben provides an interesting example, where the town council was caught between hostility towards the city pastor, Johann Weber, and the determination of the city's overlord, the Archbishop of Mainz, to tolerate no evangelical preacher. Acting on appeals from the citizenry, the council at its own expense in 1524 appointed a preacher to deliver a daily sermon. However he was quickly removed following threats from the Archbishop of Mainz, leaving Weber in control of the town's religious life. Dislike of Weber was such that many refused to attend church and took to the tavern instead, and the council was forced to close the *Ratskeller* until the sermon was over.

From Michaelmas 1525 the citizenry began a consistent campaign against this hated priest, standing before his parsonage each day singing slanderous songs and showering him with abuse, affixing libels to his door, blocking the entry with skulls and a bier, pelting the house with stones, breaking open the wooden shutters on his bedroom and hurling a rock through the unprotected window. He enjoyed little nocturnal peace during that time, and his complaints to the town council and the Elector of Mainz proved as fruitless as his attempts to sleep. On the feast of the Visitation of the Virgin, 2 July 1527 a mob tried unsuccessfully to break into his house, defeated only by the thickness of the door and the strength of its locks. As a result of such hostility, Weber found it impossible to find a sexton, and he and his chaplain had to carry out all the duties in the parish church themselves. On the night of Sunday, 17 August, another mob stood outside chanting abuse and the refrain "Death to monks and priests, in the Devil's name!" They defecated on his doorstep and smeared their ordure on the locks and doorhandle. Weber had now had enough, and the next day he tendered his resignation to the Archbishop.[15]

The effect of Weber's removal was, nonetheless, relatively minor. The town council, which had acquired the *ius patronatus* in 1526, seized the opportunity to appoint an evangelically-minded successor, the schoolmaster Jacob Lentz, who had formally introduced evangelical ideas into Aschersleben in 1524 by disseminating them to his pupils. However, when Lentz died only two years' later, he seems to have been succeeded by an orthodox priest and Aschersleben had to wait until 1536 before it saw another evangelical preacher, and until 1540 for the first administration of communion under both kinds. Thus, anticlericalism had served only to vent anger and frustration and, although I do not wish to suggest that this anger was unstructured or unpurposive, it had no cathartic effect within the town comparable to that in Memmingen. It proved to be no more than an episode, and the fate of religious reform was determined by other long-term political and diplomatic matters. Anticlericalism was certainly not a marginal phenomenon in this instance, for evangelical militants invested a good deal of channelled energy into it; rather, among many other considerations it simply failed to be the decisive factor.

IV

The contrast of the two cases Memmingen and Aschersleben is nonetheless informative, for it indicates that anticlericalism should be seen as an ideological resource which was drawn upon in varying ways to effect the purpose of spreading evangelical ideas and bringing about reform. Its role in the dissemination of ideas is undeniable, especially its propagandist function, about which I have written elsewhere.[16] By identifying the orthodox clergy as "enemies of the Gospel" it overcame a major psychological hurdle in winning adherents to the cause of reform. To have directly attacked popular devotional forms and practices as false and impious would have aroused popular resistance, but to depict them as devices invented by the clergy to line their own pockets was an effective propagandist first step in demolishing the basis of Catholic cult and practice. To emphasize that the clergy were hypocrites and deceivers was a propagandist aid to seeing them as agents of the devil and representatives of the Antichrist. To focus upon their presence in a community as threatening to salvation was to personalize

---

[15] For these events and the following paragraph, G. Liebe, "Das Entlassungsgesuch des Pfarrers Johann Weber zu Aschersleben 1527", *Zeitschrift des Vereins für Kirchengeschichte der Provinz Sachsen* 7 (1910): 126-8; E. Strassburger, *Geschichte der Stadt Aschersleben* (Aschersleben, 1906), 179-92.

[16] Robert W. Scribner, *For the Sake of Simple Folk: Popular Propaganda for the German Reformation* (Cambridge, 1981), 37-58.

and concretize the sense of eschatological crisis evoked by Reformation propaganda. Thus, the clergy represented a perverted moral order, the world upside-down, the physical presence of the Antichrist in the streets and dwellings of town and village. This provided a stimulus to the central purpose of evangelical propaganda, the call to action, to remove the danger to spiritual (and material!) well-being and to begin with the true preaching of the Word.

We rarely have the opportunity to see such propaganda in action in a concrete urban setting, but in the case of Annaberg we have extant several libels (*Schmähbriefe*) from 1523, which reveal how anticlerical feeling and propagandist imagery could be linked to evangelical criticism.[17] One was an attack on Tetzel, exhorting him under threats and abuse to acknowledge biblical truth, but others were directed against the Franciscan Guardian, Franciscus Seiler, and against the parish priest Wolfgang Gulden. One attacked Gulden's sermons for their views on good works, a second abused the Bergmeister Johann Ruling for expelling an evangelical preacher, a third defended the preacher in St. Anna, Johann Loewasser, against Gulden's attacks and denounced the weak-kneed attitude of council and commune. It contained a scarcely veiled threat of a *Pfaffensturm* with the statement that if this evangelical preacher was also expelled, "then the old would have to depart with the new." The fourth threatened Seiler with punishment for betraying the expelled preacher, heaping abuse on him as a false prophet, a venal hypocrite and a wolf among the sheep. A cartoon affixed to the pulpit in the parish church depicted a fox in priest's vestments and denounced the unnamed target as a false prophet, a thief and a murderer.

These items formed part of a wider public campaign of anticlerical propaganda by the sizeable evangelical party in Annaberg (comprised of perhaps fifty to eighty persons). The campaign was characterized by Duke George of Saxony in a subsequent condemnation of "seditious muttering, speaking, singing and writing". He prohibited further polemical attacks on religious ceremonies, the use of *Schandtlied, Spruch oder Reym* directed against anyone of secular or clerical estate, and the dissemination of any abuse whether sung, spoken, uttered, rhymed or printed. What is interesting here, apart from the manipulation in concert of the many forms of oral communication, is the punitive tone: for misleading or deceiving the people the offending clerics deserve punishment. This link of unpunished transgres-

---

[17] The texts in HSA Dresden, loc. 9827, "Die Stadt Annaberg, 1497-1528", vol. 1, 156ff. They are mentioned briefly in Felician Gess, *Akten und Briefe zur Kirchenpolitik Herzog Georgs von Sachsen*, vol. 1 (Leipzig, 1905), 520, note 2, and are discussed in detail, but with an incomplete and imperfect version of the letters, in O. B. Wolf, "Zur Geschichte der Reformation in Annaberg", *34. Bericht über das königliche Realgymnasium zu Annaberg* (Annaberg, 1886), 6-9. The evangelical movement in Annaberg requires a modern investigation, but for the following discussion I have relied largely on Wolf's account, while conscious of its defects.

sion and popular justice lay at the heart of urban disturbances of the period, and evangelical anticlerical propaganda established the same nexus.

Anticlericalism used in this way, albeit as a subtle psychological strategem, was largely a negative instrument, wielded to create fear and loathing, playing on emotions and arousing anxieties. This was sometimes realized only too well by the orthodox side, who also occasionally invoked it in polemical warfare against evangelical preachers. In Altenburg the provost of the Bergerkloster, who held the *ius patronatus* over the parish churches of St. Nicholas and the monastic church of St. Bartholomew, fought a long struggle with the town council about the irregular appointment of an evangelical preacher in St. Bartholomew, a post previously filled by the parish priest of St. Nicholas, Heinrich Koler. In 1522 Koler was forcibly ejected and first Gabriel Zwilling, then Wenzeslaus Linck was installed in his place. In February 1524, responding to an incorrect rumor, the provost thought that he had secured a perfect propaganda coup against Linck with the claim that the preacher had charged a Gulden to perform an evangelical burial and had charged fees to perform other religious services. The provost denounced Linck to the town council and the Elector of Saxony, and a special hearing was arranged before the town council at which Linck not only successfully defended himself but forced the provost to apologize for reacting to hearsay without any proof. The provost's loss of moral authority was probably not as great as Linck's would have been had the rumor proved true and the evangelical preacher been unmasked as a hypocrite.[18]

A similar tactical invocation of anticlerical passions, but with a more serious outcome occurred in Leisnig in 1522, where the parsonage was stormed by an angry crowd. The district official investigating the incident was offered the following explanation by the town council, speaking in the name of "mayor, council and commune". They blamed the self-interested conduct of the Leisnig preacher, who was renowned for his diatribes from the pulpit and whose hectoring style was allegedly inspired by a desire to increase incomes by preaching up the necessity for offerings, requiems, anniversaries, vigils, and the creation of new confraternities. After the commune had complained to the town coucil about his preaching, he had changed tack and tried to deflect hostility towards the mendicant orders and provost (who was also the parish priest) by inflammatory preaching which instigated the storming of the provost's house.[19] This version of events may have been concocted by the council to lay the blame for the outbreak on the shoulders of the orthodox clergy. Whatever the truth of the matter, the

---

[18] Cf. the documents published in J. Löbe, "Mitteilungen über den Anfang und Fortgang der Reformation in Altenburg", *Mitteilungen der geschichts- und altertümsforschenden Gesellschaft des Osterlands* 6 (1863-66): Nr. LVIII, 91-3.

[19] HSA Weimar, Reg L1, 532.

incident seems to have enabled the commune to take charge of the parish and to lay claim to the right to elect its own pastor.[20]

Fear of violent outbursts caused by inflammatory preaching or by preaching wars (*ungleiche Predigt*) was a danger of which magistrates were only too aware in the emotionally charged atmosphere created in many towns by the evangelical movements. It is epitomized in an incident in Zwickau in 1520, when a clerical critic of Thomas Müntzer slipped into the back of St. Catherine's church in order to spy on his opponent's sermon. Recognized and denounced by Müntzer, he had to take to his heels with an angry crowd in hot pursuit. He was hunted through the streets and pelted with stones and dung so that he barely escaped with his life.[21] In the case of Altenburg, it was the provost who invoked the danger of disturbance caused by evangelical preaching, during negotiations with the town council held before the Elector of Saxony's commissioners in April, 1522. The town council was concerned to show that its irregular appointment of Zwilling would lead to no disturbance, while the provost raised the spectre of cessation of the Mass, the tearing down of altars, the destruction of churches and the plundering of clerical property. The provost's prediction proved to be accurate when on 1 June 1522, the pastor of St. Nicholas, Heinrich Koler, was forcibly prevented from ascending the pulpit. Several men with drawn knives forced him back into the sacristy and threatened that if he attempted to preach, he would be ejected from the pulpit and stoned. The pastor was later interrupted while celebrating Mass and a crowd forced a way into the church, where Zwilling was forcibly installed as preacher.[22]

There certainly seems to have been a direct connection between evangelical preaching and anticlerical disturbance in Eilenburg, one of the earliest Saxon towns to take radical measures of religious reform, where communion was distributed under both kinds on New Year's Day 1522, the communicants being allowed to take the communion wafer in their own hands. The town council write to the Elector Frederick the Wise expressing its concern about the preacher's attacks on orthodox ceremonies and the "great strife and discord among the common people in word and deed" (*vil zwitracht und gezcayncke mit wortten und wergken in gemeynen volgke*) caused by the distribution of communion. It probably also had in mind the storming of the parsonage about which the provost of the Petersberg complained on 13 January, and which led to the arrest and long imprisonment of thirteen culprits, some of them children.[23] This almost certainly influenced the cessation of innovations and the suspension of evangelical

---

[20] See G. Kawerau, Introduction to *Ordnung eines gemeinen Kasten 1523*, in *WA* 12. 3.

[21] P. Wappler, *Thomas Müntzer in Zwickau und die "Zwickauer Propheten"*, 2nd ed. (Gütersloh, 1966), 32-3.

[22] Löbe (as note 18), Nr. XXI, 62-3.

[23] HSA Weimar, Reg N 47 and Reg Ii 106.

preaching, which had become linked in the council's mind with the threat of disturbance and even rebellion against secular authority.[24]

In such cases it is admittedly difficult to distinguish between traditional anticlerical passions and the anger provoked by frustrated evangelical militancy, although I have argued elsewhere that it is misleading to do so, for direct evangelical action was often no more than a reenactment of traditional modes of behavior.[25] What is important is that both sides in the polemical battle realized the potency of anticlerical feeling as an ideological resource, and as our last examples here have shown, that it could also be a stimulus to direct action.

V

I now want to address the contribution of anticlericalism to the dynamic of evangelical movements considered as a form of political action. In general, we can say that anticlericalism fed disillusionment with the old church and led to a hollowing-out of its moral authority. It also played its part in a build-up of militancy fired by a mixture of evangelical fervor and hatred of the unreconstructed clergy. Psychologically, this made it easy to throw off inhibitions about certain kinds of direct or even violent action, especially in a society with a low threshold of violence. Many evangelical preachers had a flair for confrontation, as in the case of the evangelical preacher in Neustadt a.d. Orla, who stage-managed a showdown on Sunday, 11 October 1523 by leading a crowd of followers into the parish church during the sermon, which he disrupted by interjections, confutations and abuse. He challenged the orthodox preacher to climb down from the pulpit and let him have a go, for he knew more about Scripture. The tumult was such that the orthodox preacher adjudged it safer to retreat. The incident repeated itself two weeks later, on Sunday, 25 October, when the evangelical preacher staged a confrontation with the vicar of the parish church, this time accompanied by a jeering crowd who followed the unfortunate priest through the streets, so that he went in fear of his life. The town council watched these developments impassively, giving the impression that it was not too displeased with the turn of events, possibly hoping that direct action would lead to the expulsion of the orthodox clergy without it having to soil its hands.[26]

---

[24] This can be inferred from the plea sent by Gabriel Dies [Zwilling] to the town council sometime in 1522, pleading to be allowed to preach to the community again and disclaiming any intention of causing disturbance or advancing the cause of the Gospel with the sword, HSA Weimar, Reg Ii 104.

[25] Robert W. Scribner, "Ritual and Reformation", in *Popular Culture and Popular Movements*, 103-22.

[26] HSA Weimar, Reg N 27.

By a combination of incitement by evangelical militants and inaction by the authorities, one could easily proclaim open season on the clergy in any urban community, opening the way to the kinds of cathartic activity I have analysed elsewhere when speaking of the links between reformation and ritual or carnival and reformation: the reshaping of traditional rituals and popular cultural forms as a means of freeing oneself from the enchantment of the old religion, whether demonstratively, educatively, expressively or as a quasi-sacramental rite of passage.[27] Attacks on the clergy, a frequent form of youth group behavior well before the Reformation, could become a stylized youthful fashion, as it seems to have been in many towns and in the Saxon countryside in 1523, when a masked mob plundered the manse in the parish of Dittersdorf. The Saxon official who investigated this incident feared that the gang responsible had formed a league, and that if any of them were arrested for it, the others would take reprisals. Since no formal complaint had been laid, he had held back from any arrests and hoped that as soon as the winter had passed the society (evidently a carnival society and probably composed of youths) would dissolve.[28]

Few such outbreaks were as lacking in consequences, and the political dimension in *Pfaffen- und Klostersturme* cannot be overlooked. There were several variants to what we might call the "politics of evangelical anti-clericalism": manipulation, opportunism, militant pressure, and creation of evangelical solidarity. I shall illustrate each of these in turn, conscious that these four variants do not exhaust all that could be said under this rubric.

5.1 Manipulation

Secular authorities eager to proceed with formal measures of reform but blocked by an intractable clergy or immovable legal rights often resorted to manipulation and opportunism to effect their purposes. The classic case of manipulation of anticlerical feeling remains Erfurt, where two major attacks against the clergy in 1521 and 1525 were skillfully exploited by the town's leaders, first to subdue the clergy and then in 1525 to confiscate clerical wealth and sweep away episcopal lordship, orthodox cult and its organizational underpinnings. The entire course of events in 1525 was instigated and guided by the Lutheran mayor of Erfurt, Adolarius Huttener, in the interests of civic independence and religious reformation.[29] Huttener was at least willing to cloak the events in the guise of a peasant and civic revolt. In Zerbst, the authorities made no such pretence. In 1522 violent behavior in the form of a "carnival visitation" was used by evangelical

---

[27] Robert W. Scribner, "Reformation, Carnival and the World Turned Upside-Down", in *Popular Culture and Popular Movements*, 71-102.

[28] HSA Weimar, Reg L1, 173.

[29] Robert W. Scribner, "Civic Unity and the Reformation in Erfurt", in *Popular Culture and Popular Movements*, 185-216, esp. 210ff.

militants to drive out a hated priest, Johann Wilbolt, the chaplain of St. Nicholas, an action transparently connived at by the town council which treated it merely as carnival high spirits.[30] In 1526 it did not even bother to disguise its involvement, when the mayor led a crowd of citizens in a storm of the Zerbst Franciscan friary.[31]

5.2 Opportunism

Less spectacular were the many cases of political opportunism, where civic authorities exploited the possibilities presented by anticlerical outbursts, as occurred most notoriously in Torgau on 25 March 1525, when the Franciscans suffered two stormings of their church and friary in the same night. There is strong but inconclusive evidence in this well-documented case that the town council had conspired to have the friary stormed. Incontrovertible, however, is the speed with which the council seized its chance to halt celebration of orthodox ceremonies, to take charge of the Franciscans' cash and valuables, and to force any friars who wished to remain in the town to put off their habits and wear secular clothes.[32]

It is worth mentioning, however, that such civic opportunism was not always applied in the interests of evangelical reform. In Regensburg, a town council reluctant to make any overt evangelical commitment was nonetheless ready to take its chances in early May 1525, when the peasant rebellion was riding on the crest of a wave of success. On 18 April Johann Hiltner, the leading advocate of reform in Regensburg, wrote from Amberg to tip the town council the wink by reporting "what happened to the cathedral canons' houses in Bamberg until they subjected themselves [to civic authority]."[33] He thought the moment right openly to implement reform and to subject the clergy, and hurried back to take charge. The council moved quickly, setting up a series of negotiations with the clergy on 3, 4, 6, 9 and 10 May. The clergy were confronted with a united front of all communal bodies, the Kammerer, the small and large councils and a citizen committee. They were told baldly that they had contributed little to aid the town in its poverty and

---

[30] On Zerbst, cf. Friedrich Westphal, "Ein Fastnachtsspiel zu Zerbst", *Der alte Glaube* 5 (1904): 586-90; H. Becker, "Reformationsgeschichte der Stadt Zerbst", *Mitteilung des Vereins für Anhaltische Geschichte und Altertumskunde* 11 (1910): 240-460, esp. 273-5.

[31] Becker, "Reformationsgeschichte der Stadt Zerbst", 381.

[32] See HSA Weimar, Reg N 840 (Schriften betr. die Sturmung des Barfusser Closters zu Torgau). See also P. F. Doelle, *Der Klostersturm von Torgau im Jahre 1525*, *Franziskanische Studien* Beiheft 14 (Münster i. W., 1931), with numerous documents as Beilage, 86-124, correcting the earlier account by Agnes Bartscherer, "Wahres und Sagenhaftes vom Klostersturm und der Auflösung des Barfüsserkonvents in Torgau", *Zeitschrift des Vereins für Kirchengeschichte der Provinz Sachsen* 22 (1926): 52-73.

[33] HSA München, Gemeiner Nachlass, Kart. 40/4, fol. 117.

financial difficulties, and would have to accept civic burdens the same as others: excise, taxation and watch-duty.[34] Meanwhile all the town gates were kept shut and closely guarded, two hundred citizens stood under arms, and neither the clergy nor their servants were allowed to leave the town.[35] The council gained what it sought, but a memorandum written shortly afterwards on the question of appointing an evangelical preacher advised against it on the grounds that it was impolitic.[36] Regensburg failed fully to exploit its opportunity and remained by its former policy of creeping, covert religious reform.[37]

5.3 Militant Pressure

The politics of anticlericalism was not, however, always a matter of machiavellian authorities exploiting the passions of wide-eyed evangelical militants. Sometimes the reverse was the case, when godly militants wielded the threat of anticlerical outbursts like a club over the heads of reluctant authorities. This occurred most notably in Lüneburg at the end of the 1520s, where citizens frustrated by the town council's unwillingness to appoint an evangelical preacher first refused to concede an extraordinary levy of taxation unless the council agreed to allow them a preacher. When the town council equivocated and played for time, there followed growing muttering about direct action to expel the orthodox clergy, causing the council to give in and allow the appointment of an evangelical preacher in the church of St. Nicholas, the focal point of evangelical opinion in Lüneburg.

The concession was minimal, however: apart from permitting Mass in German all other ceremonies were to be observed. The new preacher, Friedrich Henning, was not unsympathetic to the evangelical cause but was not Lutheran enough for his parishioners, and had to endure his congregation disrupting the Mass by singing evangelical hymns and interrupting the distribution of communion with German psalms. Despite promises to allow the singing of German psalms in Lent, the impatience of the congregation could not be stilled and the disturbances spread to other churches. A mock eucharistic procession staged by apprentices during Fastnacht 1530 led the council to threaten exile for the culprits. The citizenry threatened mass revolt if this were to occur and a committee of a hundred evangelical citizens was formed to demand complete unqualified evangelical preaching. The council conspired to seize the leaders of this committee, but the plan was betrayed

---

[34] Ibid., fols. 9-25 for the negotiations.

[35] Ibid., letter of Dr. Mathes Linck, Vicarius, to the Episcopal Administrator, 3 May 1525.

[36] Ibid., fols. 96-98.

[37] For the wider picture of the situation in Regensburg, L. Theobald, *Die Reformationsgeschichte der Reichsstadt Regensburg* (Munich, 1936); Carl Theodor Gemeiner, *Reichsstadt Regensburgische Chronik* (Regensburg, 1824), 4: 445-556.

and two hundred evangelical citizens assembled together in a house for their own protection.

There followed months of negotiation in which the citizen committee won concession after concession from the town council by threats of direct action against the clergy during major liturgical events such as the Palm Sunday ceremonies or the Easter procession. Two weeks after Easter, the council's resistance collapsed and no less than seven evangelical preachers were appointed in rapid succession. By the feast of the Ascension 1530, the committee was strong enough to have the Mass prohibited and it thenceforth held the initiative. Progressively, it forced the town council to prohibit priests from Lübeck, Hamburg or Bremen holding secret masses and proceeded to have the monastic houses closed, especially the Michelskloster, which had a strong following in the orthodox citizenry. When the town council tried on St. Bartholomew's Eve 1530 to take a firm stand and to resist the closure of the Marienkloster, there was open murmuring that the friars would have to leave or be expelled. The following day, the threat was put into practice, and the Franciscans were forced to leave Lüneburg. The creation of a *Kirchenordnung* marked the complete abolition of old ceremonies, but several years elapsed before the orthodox party in the town was subdued.[38]

The threat of *Pfaffensturm* or *Klostersturm* was clearly a political ploy used in Lüneburg as part of a wider strategy to force the civic authorities to give ground. With each concession, the town council's position became weaker, the threat of direct action more potent, until the threat to expel the clergy was sufficient to effect that very result. Anticlericalism here became a functional means to the end of radical reform. It operated in a similar way in our fourth variant, by creating solidarity among evangelical believers confronting long-term immoveable barriers to their aims for reform, so that all their hopes for an evangelical church order seemed to be frustrated or negated. Here an ever-present *Feindbild* was necessary to maintain solidarity and preserve militancy.

5.4 Creation of evangelical solidarity

The most striking example of this variant is found in Magdeburg, which had a long tradition of conflict between the clergy and city government. Magdeburg was a triplet city, with the Altstadt, the Neustadt and the Sudenberg each being governed by its own council, although the council in the Altstadt usually took the lead in civic politics during the Reformation. Evangelical ideas had been present in Magdeburg since 1521 and the

---

[38] See Olaf Mörke, *Rat und Bürger in der Reformation. Soziale Gruppen und kirchlicher Wandel in den welfischen Hansestädten Lüneberg, Braunschweig und Göttingen* (Hildesheim, 1983), 97-121; Ludwig Wallis, *Abriss der Reformations-Geschichte Lüneburgs* (Lüneburg, 1831).

growing evangelical party waged a doughty struggle to obtain permanent preachers against the stubborn opposition of the orthodox clergy. A series of decisive confrontations took place in 1524, including a tumult to force the release of a man imprisoned for selling printed copies of Luther's hymns on the market square, the storming of the St. Agnes convent in the Neustadt and several acts of iconoclasm, culminating in a cathartic upheaval of the Feast of the Assumption, 15 August 1524. This involved an iconoclastic riot fostered by inflammatory preaching and lead to the cessation of Catholic ceremonies. The threat of further attacks on monastic properties was used to force the Altstadt council to permit evangelical ceremonies — the evangelical Mass and the distribution of Communion under both kinds. The commons made the running in this movement, led by the provost of Our Lady's Chapter and other priests, especially two Augustinian friars and the parish priest of St. Peter. The evangelical movement spread from the Altstadt to the two other sections of the city, but more complete success was inhibited by orthodox complaints to the Reichskammergericht and by the irreconcilable stance of the dean and chapter of the cathedral.[39]

A further attempt was made in 1525 to drive the process of reform forward by attacks on clerical houses, but the Altstadt council now became afraid of social unrest and applied the brakes to check momentum. However there were still anticlerical outbursts at Christmas 1525, followed by disruption of the Palm Sunday procession in 1526.[40] However, this led only to a concord between the Archbishop and the town, so that an attempt in 1528 to stage a disputation between Nicolaus von Amsdorf and a Catholic preacher foundered on the Altstadt council's reluctance to encourage anything that might stir up popular feeling.[41] Nonetheless, there was a string of incidents throughout 1528 involving attacks on Catholic priests, and open harassment of the dean and cathedral chapter continued into the 1530s. In the years 1539 to 1541, the Archbishop was able to produce a long catalogue of disputes between clergy and city over the previous two decades, and in 1543 the Altstadt council made yet another attempt to

---

[39] For this rather summary account of the events in Magdeburg, I have drawn on the archival materials in HSA Magdeburg, Rep. A2, nos. 617, 618, 625, 625a, 625b, 626. See also the accounts in F. Hülsse, "Die Einführung der Reformation in der Stadt Magdeburg", *Geschichtsblätter für Stadt und Land Magdeburg* 18 (1883): 209-369; "Die Historia des Möllenvogtes Sebastian Langhans", in *Chroniken der Deutschen Städten*, vol. 17, 141-208.

[40] HSA Magdeburg, Rep. A2, 652b for the storming of clerical houses in 1525; Rep. A2, 617, fols. 205-6 for the events of Christmas 1525 and Palm Sunday 1526; and Rep. A2, 618, fol. 1 on the latter events.

[41] HSA Magdeburg, Rep. A2, 66, fol. 30; Rep. A2, 618, fols. 11-14.

dislodge the cathedral chapter, the major obstacle to a complete evangelical reform of the town.[42]

With the situation still unresolved, the city faced the events of the Schmalkaldic War and the subsequent catastrophe of the Interim. We can certainly argue that the evangelical militancy evidenced by Magdeburg on that occasion was related to the protracted struggle to win evangelical control of the town. For over two decades, the emotions of the evangelical party were kept constantly near boiling point in their struggle against an immoveable and intractable clergy, a situation ideally suited to create and maintain intense solidarity among the most fervent evangelical believers. It is not surprising that evangelical militants in Magdeburg were willing to entertain revolution rather than lose ground by admitting the Interim.

VI

Let me sum up. I have sought to examine anticlericalism in two ways: first, as a set of attitudes linked to emotional and psychological states; second, as a form of behavior conducive to certain forms of direct action. My exposition has sought to show how both components played a part in evangelical movements as they developed towards their critical point, i.e. towards a dramatic break with the old religion, repudiation of orthodox cult and the adoption of the radically new. I have sought to emphasize that there was no crude or direct causal connection between anticlericalism and these developments. The connections are to be found at two rather different levels: in changing attitudes and in turning attitudes into political behavior. The latter I regard as crucial for the success of such evangelical movements. Therefore we must not think of anticlericalism as a knee-jerk reaction, but as a resource consciously employed in political strategies. Anticlericalism was an ideological resource which had a functional political role, a tool used as a means towards an end. Without exhausting all that could be said on this subject, I have held up to scrutiny a few of these functional variants. In as far as such forms of political action necessary to actualize evangelical reform were unthinkable without anticlericalism, we can say it was functionally necessary for their success. Certainly there were towns which adopted evangelical reform without recourse to anticlericalism in this way, just as we must recognize that there was a wide range of other issues affecting reform in any city which cannot be mentioned here.

I have sought not to reduce anticlerical to any simple set of causal relationships, but to uncover the rich layers of feeling and action attached to the phenomenon. Let me simply conclude with an example that shows that we should not attempt to take too abstract a view of what anti-

---

[42] HSA Magdeburg, Rep. A2, 625a, "Allerley Späne und eingrieffe der Magdeburger wieder das Ertzstifft ..."; Rep. A2, 618, fols. 70, 77-79.

clericalism involved, for its most salient feature was that it often stirred up baser emotional instincts while invoking a morally elevated cause. During the introduction of the Reformation in Jägerndorf in Silesia in 1535, Margrave George of Brandburg granted to his court joiner, Hans Unvertorben, the possession of the chapel belonging to the Franciscan convent for his own use as a private house. Unvertorben went to the convent, dressed as the pope, accompanied by a crowd of folk dressed as Catholic clerics. Here he demanded entry and presented himself to the Franciscans as if he were the pope, insisting that his foot be kissed in homage. He then forced the friars to mum themselves as devils, who were immediately driven from the town to the accompaniment of scornful mockery. At the city gates, he ascended the tower and bade them farewell with a "kind of blessing" over the populace. In response to this "blessing", the crowd ran into the church and destroyed all its altars.[43] The tone of this incident we could describe in just three words: revenge was sweet. We may thus end (as historians often do) where we began, with the reflection that many unspeakable things are done in the name of Christian zeal.

---

[43] For the incident, Johann Soffner, *Geschichte der Reformation in Schlesien* (Breslau, 1886), 451.

"YOU HATE US PRIESTS":
ANTICLERICALISM, COMMUNALISM,
AND THE CONTROL OF WOMEN
AT STRASBOURG IN THE AGE OF THE REFORMATION

THOMAS A. BRADY, JR.[1]

University of California, Berkeley

"You laymen hate us priests, and it is an old hatred between you and us."[2] This anguished cry comes from a work called "The Ants", a cycle of sermons preached by Johann Geiler von Kaysersberg (1445-1510) at Strasbourg and published posthumously by his Franciscan disciple, Johannes Pauli.[3] It has become well known to the current generation of reformation scholars through Francis Rapp's study of conditions in the diocese of Strasbourg between 1450 and 1525.[4] Rapp's book provides a sturdy backdrop to this study of anticlericalism at Strasbourg, which aims to examine some aspects of the problem of anticlericalism and the social integration of the clergy at Strasbourg before and during the reformation era.

Recent literature on the Holy Roman Empire in the sixteenth century offers a rich variety of reformations: "people's", "princes'", "urban", "magisterial", "radical", and "communal". Against this proliferation works a tendency to reunify the movement, most recently attempted by Hans-Jürgen Goertz, who unites the various streams of reform during the 1520s

---

[1] Abbreviations specific to this paper:
AEKG = Archiv für elsässische Kirchengeschichte/Archives de l'Eglise d'Alsace
AMS = Archives Municipales de Strasbourg
AST = Archives du Chapître de St.-Thomas de Strasbourg
BSCMHA = Bulletin de la Société pour la Conservation des Monuments Historiques d'Alsace

[2] Johann Geiler von Kaysersberg, Die Emeis: Dis ist das buch von der Omeissen, und auch Herr der könnig ich diente gern (Strasbourg: Johann Grüninger, 1516), 28b: "Ir leyen hassen uns pfaffen / und ist auch ein alter hass zwischen euch und uns."

[3] On these sermons, see Eugen Breitenstein, "Die Autorschaft der Geiler von Kaysersberg zugeschriebenen Emeis", AEKG 13 (1938): 149-98; id., "Die Quellen der Geiler zugeschriebenen Emeis", AEKG 15 (1941/42): 141-202. On the problematical texts of Geiler's sermons in general, see Luzian Pfleger, "Zur handschriftlichen Überlieferung Geilerscher Predigttexte", AEKG 6 (1931): 195-205.

[4] Francis Rapp, Réformes et reformation à Strasbourg. Eglise et société dans le diocèse de Strasbourg (1450-1525), Collection de l'Institut des Hautes Etudes Alsaciennes 23 (Paris, 1974), 419.

under the rubric of anticlericalism.[5] What all these streams had in common, Goertz writes, was the aim "to break off the top of the medieval pyramid of estates."[6] Inspired by his work in Anabaptist studies, Goertz argues that the aim to integrate the clergy into the lay community halted part-way in the Protestant cities and lands and found its full realization only among the radical sects, supremely among the Hutterite communities in Moravia, which at last abolished the distinction between clergy and laity. Although he does not claim that anticlericalism was the sole cause of the reformation,[7] Goertz does regard it as the common, radical font from which the various streams of reformation poured forth to differentiate themselves and to moderate their respective forces as they spread.[8] The radical reformation was not Protestant-ism radicalized; Protestantism was the reformation de-radicalized.

Goertz's interesting thesis is open to several qualifications. Not only is it unclear why all other social groups should have united in the desire to "break off the top of the medieval pyramid of estates", but there is no real evidence that the actors thought of their actions in this way, nor for the existence of such a unified idea of society.[9] The notion of society as a social pyramid with the clergy at the top was but one of many competing conceptions in late medieval thought. Just as common was the notion of dual, coordinated hierarchies, lay and clerical, which were sometimes integrated into a single pyramid. A good example is the "tree of society" (*Ständebaum*) in the famous woodcut of 1519/20 by the Petrarch Master, which shows pope with emperor and kings and cardinals and bishops with princes and nobles; priests and monks, who are not shown, would pre-sumably rank with the merchants and artisans.[10] This and other contem-

---

[5] Hans-Jürgen Goertz, *Pfaffenhaß und groß Geschrei. Die reformatorischen Bewegungen in Deutschland 1517-1529* (Munich, 1987). Heiko A. Oberman has also identified anticlericalism as the initial rallying cause of the reformation movement, in "The Gospel of Social Unrest: 450 Years after the so-called Peasants' War of 1525", now in his *The Dawn of the Reformation: Essays in Late Medieval and Reformation Thought* (Edinburgh, 1986), 155-78, originally published in 1976.

[6] Goertz, *Pfaffenhaß*, 260: "die Spitze der mittelalterlichen Ständepyramide ab-zubrechen."

[7] This is noted by Tom Scott, "Historiographical Review: The Common People in the German Reformation", *Historical Journal* 34 (1991): 183-92, here at 192.

[8] Goertz, *Pfaffenhaß*, 245, 250.

[9] Goertz takes the classic scheme of three estates seriously, though he does not repeat the error of Robert H. Lutz, who tried to identify the "Common Man" with the third estate in the classic, triadic scheme. See Thomas A. Brady, Jr., *Turning Swiss: Cities and Empire, 1450-1550*, Cambridge Studies in Early Modern History (Cambridge, 1985), 32 note 86, for references.

[10] The woodcut is often reproduced, notably in Adolf Laube, Max Steinmetz, and Günter Vogler, eds., *Illustrierte Geschichte der deutschen frühbürgerlichen Revolution* (Berlin, 1974), 219.

porary concepts cast doubt on the thesis of a single pyramid capped by the clergy.

These qualifications aside, the Goertz thesis holds far more promise than does the proposition that the virulent anticlericalism of the 1510s and 1520s erupted in direct response to clerical degeneracy. The burden of proof for this hoary favorite now lies with those who believe that the later Middle Ages witnessed a pronounced decline in clerical standards of personal behavior and learning. A younger version of this view holds that reformation anticlericalism reflects the grave psychological burdens that late medieval religion placed on the average Christian. There is no sign that the thesis of "burdensome religion" is likely to succeed where that of "corrupt clergy" has faltered.[11]

Such theses lack power to explain the fearfully explosive power of anticlericalism in the early reformation movement, because they all assume that the new anticlericalism arose as a reaction to the clergy alone, not as a critique of society as a whole. Far more persuasive is the view of Günter Vogler, that the new anticlericalism served as a powerful but transitory unifier of a wide variety of groups and their interests, and that its historical function was to facilitate both this union for action and the transitions from particular to general grievance and from religious to social criticism. "The movement's heterogeneity", he writes, "began to be more clearly discernible when it was recognized that adherents intended to apply the reform teachings to secular life and the social realm."[12] Vogler cites a telling remark by Karl Marx about the need for a revolutionary moment to take on the guise of a general emancipation and to find a general enemy:

---

[11] The basis for such views has been eroding for some time. See, in general, Francis Oakley, "Religious and Ecclesiastical Life on the Eve of the Reformation", in *Reformation Europe: a Guide to Research*, ed. S. Ozment (St Louis, 1982), 5-32. See also Lawrence G. Duggan, "The Unresponsiveness of the Late Medieval Church: A Reconsideration", *SCJ* 9 (1978): 2-26; id., "Fear and Confession on the Eve of the Reformation", *ARG* 75 (1984): 153-75, who questions the corruption thesis and the burden thesis respectively. The latter was cast in its current form by Steven E. Ozment, *The Reformation in the Cities* (New Haven, 1975), 22-32. James M. Stayer has recently written: "If we accept that the abuses of the clergy caused the Reformation, then we are returning to the nineteenth-century interpretation of the field. ... I am loathe to do that because there are too many evidences of institutional, intellectual and spiritual vitality in the pre-Reformation clergy to accept that it simply collapsed by itself." James M. Stayer, "Anticlericalism: A Model for a Coherent Interpretation of the Reformation", unpublished (my thanks to him for a copy of this paper).

[12] Günter Vogler, "Imperial City Nuremberg, 1524-1525: The Reform Movement in Transition", in *The German People and the Reformation*, ed. R. Po-chia Hsia (Ithaca, 1988), 33-51, here at 37.

> If the revolution of a people and the emancipation of a particular class [*Klasse*] of bourgeois society are to coincide, so that one group [*Stand*] stands for all social groups, then the contrary is also true: a particular group must be despised by all others, it must embody that which blocks the desires of the others. In this case, one particular social sphere [*Sphäre*] must be the locus for the notorious crimes of the entire society, so that the liberation of this sphere may appear to be a general self-emancipation.[13]

This notion, the revolutionary transformation of one social group from objects of criticism into a general scapegoat, has the great virtue of capturing the psychological difference between revolutionary and ordinary times. It helps us to understand, for example, why the reformation movement in Germany often demonized the clergy in images and language which also seemed appropriate to Jews and Turks.[14] Based on these insights, we might see reformation anticlericalism as part of the mentality of a revolutionary situation, not as a reasoned response to escalating clerical corruption.[15] The explanation focuses less on inherent, religious characteristics of the clergy as a social group than on their relationships to the broader distinctions between wealth and poverty, power and impotence, and respectability and despicability. The dying years of our own century offer an especially good vantage point from which to understand how a specific, easily identifiable, clearly privileged group might, given the right conditions, come to be identified as the overriding source of all social ills, particularly if the group had long been the object of widespread criticism and suspicions of unwarranted power and privileges.

If this view has merit, it is fair to ask how the Empire's clergy got itself into this vulnerable position. Here we are helped by R.W. Scribner's recent proposal that the pre-reformation decades witnessed a "disintegration" of the clergy's power, which he classifies as economic, social, political, legal, sexual, and sacral, from the greater web of social and spiritual power.[16]

---

[13] Karl Marx, "Kritik der Hegelschen Rechtsphilosophie. Einleitung", in Karl Marx, *Werke*, ed. Hans-Joachim Lieber, 6 vols., 2nd ed. (Darmstadt, 1962), 1: 501. Vogler ("Imperial City Nuremberg, 1524-1525", 48) cites Karl Marx and Friedrich Engels, *Werke*, vol. 1 (Berlin, 1981), 388.

[14] A phenomenon noted by Heiko A. Oberman, *Wurzeln des Antisemitismus: Christenangst und Judenplage im Zeitalter von Humanismus und Reformation* (Berlin, 1981), 148.

[15] The same analysis could be applied to the furious, public outburst of antipapalism in Germany during the 1510s, one cause of which was surely Emperor Maximilian's violently antipapal propaganda during the Italian Wars. See Hermann Wiesflecker, *Kaiser Maximilian I. Das Reich, Österreich und Europa an der Wende zur Neuzeit*, 5 vols. (Munich, 1971-86), 5: 172-78, 462-65.

[16] R. W. Scribner, "Anticlericalism and the Reformation in Germany", in R. W. Scribner, *Popular Culture and Popular Movements in Reformation Germany* (London, 1987), 243-56; id., "Antiklerikalismus in Deutschland um 1500", in *Europa 1500*.

This idea of "disintegration" ought to supply a starting point for detailed, comparative studies of how the clergy's position and influence was changing in relation to other groups who wielded power in one form or another. The virtue of this line of thought is that it recognizes the weakening of clerical power before the reformation, whereas both Goertz's view of anticlericalism as laicization and the older response-to-corruption thesis require just the opposite assumption — which contradicts most of what we know. It also fits much better with the known intensification of popular religious devotion in Central Europe during these decades.[17] The evidence for this upswing is abundant. Recently, for example, there has been uncovered a movement to supply the villages of southwestern Germany with something like a people's *Eigenkirche*, well before the Protestant reformers came on the scene.[18] This movement illustrates the popular appropriation of religious life, especially in the regions gripped by what Peter Blickle has called the "communal reformation". Even where perfectly orthodox, as it normally was, the move tended to push the clergy out of some long-held positions, powers, and privileges.[19] This happened earliest where popular political forces were free to act, as in Central Switzerland, where the reduction of clerical power long before the reformation removed the reasons for religious communalism to demonize or marginalize the clergy.[20] Does this mean that communalism could coexist with the other forms of clerical power identified by Scribner, such as their sacral and sexual powers? If so, then the role of the Protestant reformation as the culmination of the communal reformation becomes all the more episodic.

The problem of clerical integration and disintegration, therefore, is central to the study of anticlericalism before and during the reformation. The following pages explore texts which help to document, first of all, how one

---

Integrationsprozesse im Widerstreit: Staaten, Regionen, Personenverbände, Christenheit, ed. F. Seibt, W. Eberhard (Stuttgart, 1987), 368-82.

[17] The older views are examined by Francis Oakley, *The Western Church in the Later Middle Ages* (Ithaca, 1979), 127-30, but the entire subject has been transformed by Scribner's studies on religion and ritual, which are collected in his *Popular Culture and Popular Movements in Reformation Germany*.

[18] See Rosi Fuhrmann, "Die Kirche im Dorf. Kommunale Initiativen zur Organisation von Seelsorge vor der Reformation", in *Zugänge zur bäuerlichen Reformation*, ed. P. Blickle, Bauer und Reformation 1 (Zurich, 1987), 147-86; id., "Dorfgemeinde und Pfründstiftung vor der Reformation. Kommunale Selbstbestimmungschancen zwischen Religion und Recht", in *Kommunalisierung und Christianisierung. Voraussetzungen und Folgen der Reformation 1400-1600*, Beiheft 9 der Zeitschrift für Historische Forschung (Berlin, 1989), 77-112. Her studies put the subject on an entirely new footing.

[19] Peter Blickle, *Gemeindereformation. Die Menschen des 16. Jahrhunderts auf dem Weg zum Heil* (Munich, 1985).

[20] See Peter Blickle, "Antiklerikalismus um den Vierwaldstädtersee 1300-1500", in this volume.

clergyman struggled with the problem of clerical integration, and what he anticipated and did not anticipate about its solution. Then come texts from the heart of the early reformation at Strasbourg, which show that the consequences of the movements' drive for clerical integration differed for clergy of the two genders, men and women. These documents appear in proper context, if we set them against the backdrop of Rapp's conclusions about reforms and reformation in the diocese of Strasbourg.

I

The works of the Strasbourg historian Francis Rapp make us better informed about clerical life and reputation in the diocese of Strasbourg, 1450-1530, than in any other of the some fifty-five dioceses of the Holy Roman Empire.[21] Rapp's most important conclusion is that the clergy of the diocese of Strasbourg between 1450 and 1525 were not more ignorant, avaricious, or loose-living than their predecessors of the fourteenth century had been.[22] Although there was no general decline, Rapp nonetheless discovers at least two important changes in clerical life during this long era, neither of which could have been accurately predicted from the literature. First, his study of clerical personnel shows a major loss of familiarity and increasing estrangement between the people of the diocese and their clergy. The clergy as a whole was recruited increasingly from outside the diocese — roughly Lower Alsace and Middle Baden — especially from Swabia, Bavaria, and the lands west of the Vosges, which means that the axis of clerical recruitment ran not along the Rhine Valley but perpendicular to it. Of 529 parish priests in the era 1450-1520 whose place of origin is known, 400 came from other dioceses.[23] The same pattern is observable among the upper clergy, especially in the cathedral chapter, which, despite the heavy

---

[21] Rapp, *Réformes*; id., "Préréformes et humanisme. Strasbourg et l'Empire (1482-1520)", in *Histoire de Strasbourg des origines à nos jours*, vol. 2, ed. G. Livet, F. Rapp (Strasbourg, 1981), 177-254; id., "Les strasbourgeois et les universités rhénanes à la fin du Moyen Age et jusqu'à la Réforme", *Annuaire des Amis de Vieux-Strasbourg* 4 (1974): 11-22; id., "Les clercs souabes dan le diocèse de Strasbourg à la veille de la Réforme", in *Landesgeschichte und Geistesgeschichte. Festschrift für Otto Herding zum 65. Geburtstag*, ed. K. Elm, E. Gönner, E. Hildenbrand, Veröffentlichungen der Kommission für geschichtliche Landeskunde in Baden-Württemberg, series B, 92 (Stuttgart, 1977), 265-79.

[22] Rapp, *Réformes*, 430-34.

[23] Rapp, *Réformes*, 313. It is worth noting that analysis of the registers of new citizens shows a similar pattern for this period (ibid., 314). The pattern of heavy Swabian and Bavarian immigration continued into the later sixteenth century. See Jean-Pierre Kintz, *La société strasbourgeoise du milieu du XVIe siècle à la fin de la Guerre de Trente Ans 1560-1650. Essai d'histoire démographique, économique et sociale* (Paris, 1984), 112.

representation from Alsace and the Ortenau (Middle Baden) in the fourteenth century, admitted no canon from these lands after 1455. In the other collegial chapters at Strasbourg, the proportion of natives also declined, at St. Thomas, for example, from nearly 30% to 7%. In the urban religious houses, too, the local elites, once the dominant force in the religious houses and especially in the mendicant orders, lost this position to outsiders. The sole exception to this trend involved the mendicant women's houses of the Observance, which the native elite continued to control.[24] Not surprisingly, these houses offered the stoutest resistance to the Protestant reformation, a consequence, no doubt, of the fact that the nuns' resistance "dramatized and focused the divisions within the elite."[25] The overall pattern for the years from 1450 to 1520 is neatly summed up by Rapp: "almost nothing remained of these familiar relations between the local notables and the clergy."[26] The colonization of the clergy, especially from Swabia and Bavaria, accelerated the process of estrangement of clergy from laity. Against this process the canon law was helpless, for the legal separation of the clergy from the laity had been devised for a society in which the familiar bonds between the two groups were very close, too close, for the church's comfort.

Rapp's second major discovery is that after the agrarian depression of the fourteenth century nearly ruined the convents, foundations, and much of the benefice system, the clergy recovered through investment in agriculture and its products. By the mid-fifteenth century, clergymen and clerical corporations were playing a massive role in the financing, collection, storage, marketing, and export of foodstuffs, especially grain, from Lower Alsace and the Ortenau to poorer, neighboring regions.[27] This process accelerated a weakening of the benefice system, chiefly through commercialization and pluralism, which left large numbers of poorly paid, insecure vicars ("arme dorfpfäfflin") in the rural parishes and reduced, in general, the social status and prestige of the clergy.[28]

From Rapp's book emerges a portrait of a clergy increasingly colonized by place-seekers from other regions, the fortunate of whom shared in the profits from the burgeoning trade in foodstuffs, while the less lucky slipped into the proletariat of rural vicars. The clergy of the pre-reformation era, therefore, were socially more alien and less prestigious, but economically better off — and thus more competitive with the laity — than their predecessors had been. This situation might have been helped, had the governance of the church in this diocese not broken down. During the first half of the fifteenth century, however, the mercantile elite of Strasbourg had

---

[24] Rapp, *Réformes*, 284-87.

[25] Lyndal Roper, *The Holy Household: Women and Morals in Reformation Augsburg* (Oxford, 1989), 210.

[26] Rapp, *Réformes*, 451-52.

[27] Rapp, *Réformes*, 435-41.

[28] Rapp, *Réformes*, 265-79, 298-99, 306-18.

tried, and failed, to take over the finances of the diocese and prince-bishopric of Strasbourg.[29] Their failure left a spirit of rivalry between Strasbourg's civic elite and the whole apparatus of episcopal governance, and all subsequent efforts at clerical reform smashed against the connivance between the native lay elites and the middling and upper clergy, who formed an unloving partnership to skim the rich agriculture of Lower Alsace and the Ortenau.

Rapp's findings allow us to hazard an explanation of the clergy's fate at Strasbourg during the reformation. The clergy had rescued itself from financial disaster during the depression by enhancing its activities in moneylending and trading in foodstuffs; these operations made the clergy more exposed to criticism and resentment from the common people, especially the peasants; the native elites, who protected from reform a clergy with whom they shared strong economic interests but ever weaker social solidarity, sacrificed their clergy to the popular movements of the 1520s. Whether this picture can be applied as a model to other regions and dioceses, remains to be seen, but for the moment it may underpin an investigation of some aspects of clerical integration at Strasbourg before and during the reformation.

II

Johann Geiler von Kaysersberg (1445-1510), who was cathedral preacher at Strasbourg from 1478 until his death, is widely recognized as an acute diagnostician of the problems of Christian life in general, and of clerical life in particular, during the generation before the onset of the Protestant reformation.[30] This reputation is very old, for the historical consciousness

---

[29] Martin Alioth, *Gruppen an der Macht: Zünfte und Patriziat in Straßburg im 14. und 15. Jahrhundert. Untersuchungen zu Verfaßung, Wirtschaftsgefüge und Sozialstruktur*, 2 vols., Basler Beiträge zur Geschichtswissenschaft 156 (Basel, 1988), esp. 502-4. Alioth has completely undermined the conventional view of Strasbourg's political history in the later Middle Ages, a classic statement of which is in Philippe Dollinger, "La ville libre à la fin du Moyen Age (1350-1482)", in *Histoire de Strasbourg* (n. 21 above), 99-175. The rivalry between magistrates and bishops is dramatized in Thomas A. Brady, Jr., "Rites of Autonomy, Rites of Dependence: South German Civic Culture in the Age of Renaissance and Reformation", in *Religion and Culture in the Renaissance City*, ed. S. Ozment, Sixteenth Century Essays & Studies 11 (Kirksville, Mo., 1989), 9-24.

[30] The best introduction to Geiler's career is by Francis Rapp, "Jean Geiler de Kaysersberg (1445-1510), le prédicateur de la cathédrale de Strasbourg", in *Grandes figures de l'humanisme alsacien. Courants, milieux, destins*, ed. F. Rapp, G. Livet, Publications de la Société Savante d'Alsace et des Régions de l'Est, Collection "Grandes Publications" 14 (Strasbourg, 1978), 25-32, plus many sections of Rapp, *Réformes*. Still worth consulting is Charles Guillaume Adolphe Schmidt, *Histoire*

of Protestant Strasbourg long revered Geiler as chief forerunner to the city's reformation. Caspar Hedio, for example, a Protestant who was Geiler's successor but one as cathedral preacher of Strasbourg, remarked in 1526 that

> the more I read Dr. Kaysersberger, the more he pleases me, for when I read his writings, I find that he identified and understood the problem quite well. The time, however, was not yet ripe.[31]

A generation later, the Protestant town architect Daniel Specklin (ca. 1536-89) fixed Geiler's reputation by including in his *Collectanea* a notice about Geiler's sermon before the Emperor Maximilian I at Strasbourg during the Bavarian War of 1504.

> At the end of his sermon, Dr. Kaysersberger referred once again to the problem of reform. If, he said, pope, bishop, emperor and king will not reform our unspiritual, insane, godless way of life, God will raise up one who will do it and will reestablish our ruined religion. I hope to see the day and to become his disciple, but I am too old. Many of you, however, will live to see it, and please remember me then and what I said.[32]

Emperor Maximilian, Specklin notes at another place, "also experienced Dr. Luther's reformation and surely must have thought often about Dr. Kaysersberger."[33] Protestant Strasbourg acknowledged its indebtedness to Geiler for his attacks on the problem of reform before, in their view, the time was ripe. Their respect for him as a diagnostician of reform corroborates the Strasbourg laity's affection for him in his own day, and if this stature possessed a theological basis, it lay in his adaptation of mystical

---

littéraire de l'Alsace à la fin du XVe et au commencement du XVIe siècle, 2 vols. (Paris, 1879; repr., Nieuwkoop, 1966), 1: 337-461.

[31] Jacob von Gottesheim, "Les éphemerides de Jacques de Gottesheim, docteur en droit, prébendier du Grand-Choeur de la Cathédrale (1524-1543)", ed. Rodolphe Reuss, *BSCMHA*, 2nd ser., 19 (1898): 271. See also ibid., "1527. Dominica post Valentini, 17. Februarii, D. Caspar hedio fecit concionem merdianam, praedicavit de cadaveribus sepeliendis etra urbem, extulit Dominum Joannem Keyserpergium, ..." See, too, the testimony of Otmar Nachtigall, in the preface to his *Dye gantz Euangelisch Hystorie wie sie durch die vier Euangelisten, yeden sonderlich, in kriechischer sprach beschrieben, in ain gleychhellige unzertaylte red ordenlich verfasst* (Augsburg, 1525): "Ich hab in meiner kinthayt von Doctor kaysersberger in seinen predigten zu Strasburg gethon, vnd sonst in seynem hauss ayns tayls, also vil haylsamer lere empfangen, die mir darzu geholffen, das man mich zeycht, ich sey kain weltmensch."

[32] Daniel Specklin, "Les Collectanées", ed. Rodolphe Reuss, *BSCMHA*, 2nd ser., 14 (1889): no. 2190. Specklin, Strasbourg's first municipal architect, wrote a two-volume chronicle, of which only fragments survive. Johannes Ficker and Otto Winckelmann, *Handschriftenproben des 16. Jahrhunderts nach Straßburger Originalen*, 2 vols. (Strasbourg, 1902-5), 2: 99.

[33] Specklin, "Les Collectanées", no. 2167.

theology to lay piety, not in the degree to which he did or did not anticipate Luther's teaching on justification.[34]

Geiler's opinions and programs are contained in the huge corpus of his sermons, which is now once again attracting the kind of scholarly attention it deserves.[35] His social ideas, including his ecclesiology, have attracted only scattered attention.[36] This neglect is all the more remarkable, because not only does Geiler pronounce on many particular issues of the day, such as anticlericalism and clerical social integration, but his general social outlook diverged radically from those of the Alsatian humanists among whom he is often numbered.[37] For Geiler stood close to the movement that Peter Blickle has called "the communal reformation".[38]

Geiler's relationship to religious communalism, which frames his other social views, including his program for the clergy, is suggested by three aspects of his thought. First, he believed that human laws must be judged by divine laws, which sounds much like the fundamental principle of religious communalism, the supremacy of the "godly law".[39] Geiler broaches the question in the preface to his "21 Articles" of 1500:

> These articles state the customs, statutes, and usages of the city of Strasbourg. One must approach them cautiously and consult godfearing, honorable, wise, and learned experts in Imperial, canon, and divine law, to see whether these customs, usages, and statutes are not opposed to Christian principles and God's laws. Otherwise the city's rulers and inhabitants might, through their observance

---

[34] This last is the question pursued by E. Jane Dempsey Douglass, *Justification in Late Medieval Preaching. A Study of John Geiler of Keisersberg*, SMRT 1 (Leiden, 1966; 2nd ed., 1989), who judges — correctly, I believe — that Geiler was no proto-Lutheran. A new and fruitful approach to this subject, Geiler's relationship to the reformation, is opened up by Herbert Kraume, *Die Gerson Übersetzungen Geilers von Kaysersberg: Studien zur deutschsprachigen Gerson-Rezeption* (Munich, 1980). It has been expanded to Geiler's whole mystical theology in an unpublished dissertation by Georges Herzog, "Mystical Theology in Late Medieval Preaching: Johann Geiler von Kaysersberg (1445-1510)", (Boston University, 1985).

[35] The fullest discussion of the literature on Geiler is by Herzog, "Mystical Theology", 19-31.

[36] See, for example, Jakob Strieder, *Studien zur Geschichte kapitalistischer Organisationsformen. Monopole, Kartelle und Aktiengesellschaften im Mittelalter und zu Beginn der Neuzeit*, 2nd ed. (Munich, 1935), 189-92.

[37] Rapp, *Réformes*, 150-70, develops very clearly the contrast between Geiler's reform program, based on preaching, and the "programme médiocre" of Jakob Wimpheling and the other local humanists.

[38] Peter Blickle, *Gemeindereformation. Die Menschen des 16. Jahrhunderts auf dem Weg zum Heil* (Munich, 1985).

[39] Blickle, *Gemeindereformation*, 59-67. An investigation of this theme should begin with Geiler's views on natural law. See Peter Bierbrauer, "Das Göttliche Recht und die naturrechtliche Tradition", in *Bauer, Reich und Reformation. Festschrift für Günther Franz zum 80. Geburtstag*, ed. P. Blickle (Stuttgart, 1982), 210-34.

of such statutes, customs, and usages, fall from God's grace and into eternal damnation of their souls.[40]

Geiler's godly law is not yet the godly law of the Peasants' War, which would tie the concept to the "pure gospel" and localized it in the Bible.[41] God's laws, for example, do not yet stand in judgment on the laws of Empire and church.[42] Geiler nonetheless teaches a recognizable form of the ideal of godly law, which monitors, corrects, and even vacates human law.

A second connection between Geiler and communalism is his republicanism. In the absence of adequate restraints, Blickle has noted, communal political organization tended to evolve into republican forms of governance well before any full-blown republican theory emerged in the German-speaking world.[43] The German cities, at least as compared with those of Italy and the Netherlands, proved poor nurseries of political theory of any kind, including republicanism.[44] There may be political ideas, however, where there is no true theory, and Geiler's political ideas took a decidedly republican turn. In his sermons on "The Ants", for example, he examines the governments of several species of animals to shed light on human society. This is a convention, of course, the best known contemporary example of which may be the remark of Ottaviano Fregoso (†1524) of Genoa in Baldesar Castiglione's *Book of the Courtier*: "deer, cranes and many other birds, when they migrate, always choose a leader whom they follow and obey; and bees, almost as if they had discourse of reason, obey their king with as much reverence as the most obedient people on earth."[45] Like Fregoso's opponent, Pietro Bembo (1470-1547), Geiler chooses the republican side of the argument, though unlike the Venetian he accepts the analogy between animal and human government. In his sermon cycle on "The Ants", Geiler compares human society to that of the ants, whom he sets in the political context of the animal kingdom as follows:

---

[40] Johann Geiler von Kaysersberg, *Die ältesten Schriften*, ed. Léon Dacheux (Freiburg i. Br., 1882; reprint, Amsterdam, 1965), 3.

[41] Blickle, *Gemeindereformation*, 62-64.

[42] See, *Gemeindereformation*, 67, where Blickle warns against seeing in the godly law too radical a negation of tradition, that is, of the "old law". I follow Vogler, "Imperial City Nuremberg, 1524-1525", 38-39, in seeing biblicism as a sign of the movement's radicalization.

[43] Peter Blickle, "Communalism, Parliamentarism, Republicanism", trans. T. A. Brady, Jr., *Parliaments, Estates and Representation* 6 (1986): 1-13.

[44] See Heinz Schilling, "Gab es im späten Mittelalter und zu Beginn der Neuzeit in Deutschland einen städtischen Republikanismus? Zur politischen Kultur des alteuropäischen Stadtbürgertums", in *Republiken und Republikanismus im Europa der Frühen Neuzeit*, ed. H. Koenigsberger, Schriften des Historischen Kollegs, Kolloquien 11 (Munich, 1988), 101-44, here at 142, with whose argument I agree.

[45] Baldesar Castiglione, *The Book of the Courtier*, trans. Charles Singleton (Garden City, N.Y., 1959), 304.

> There are two sorts of animals. Some, such as bears and lions, are solitary. Other animals live together, such as doves and chickens, which fly together in a flock. ... Sheep, too, move about in large flocks. We humans must be together. A man can never be self-sufficient, we all need one another ("man is a political animal"). The ants, too, live together, for these small creatures live together with large numbers in one anthill with no leader, no prince, and no teacher.

Whereas some animals, such as cranes and herring, have leaders, "the ants have no king", says Geiler, overlooking the fact that ants do have queens. Over them, as over humanity, stands only God, for "we know very well that God is the common ruler of all creatures, and there can be no government on earth without the commune."[46]

His view of the Swiss Confederacy, the most important example of communally based political autonomy, forms Geiler's third connection to communalism. Geiler had been born at Schaffhausen, a free city which joined the Confederacy in 1501. At that time, after the Swabian War of 1499, the Alsatian humanists turned against the Swiss, who had long been allies of the Alsatian communes, and supported the House of Austria and the idea of imperial monarchy.[47] Geiler, by contrast, understood why the Swiss had gone to war with the emperor. They were victims of bad government and arrogant rulers, he thought, just as the poor, especially poor women, are the victims of arbitrary and uncaring urban magistrates.

> And when a poor widow or a poor woman comes, they [the officials] say to her: "Do you think that we've nothing more to do than deal with you?" ... Then she's referred to the ammeister or sent to [privy council of] the XV, and so forth. The judges are supposed to help them, and most of all under communal governments, such as rule Strasbourg, Mainz, and Nuremberg, the widows and orphans should be relieved of lengthy judicial procedures. Sometimes a suit goes for thirty years. What created Switzerland? It was the arbitrariness of the officials and their failure to give expeditious justice. Read the histories!

The closing passage is nothing less than an adaptation to the free city — the officials named have Strasbourg titles — of the saying, "Question: What makes Switzerland grow? Answer: The lords' greed", which we find, among

---

[46] Geiler, *Die Emeis* (1516), xii^v-xiii^v.

[47] The chief example is Wimpheling. See Guy Marchal, "Bellum justum contra judicium belli. Zur Interpretation von Jakob Wimpfelings antieidgenossischer Streitschrift 'Soliloquium pro Pace Christianorum et pro Helvetiis ut respiscant ... ,' (1505)", in *Gesellschaft und Gesellschaften. Festschrift zum 65. Geburtstag von Professor Dr. Ulrich Im Hof*, ed. N. Bernard, Q. Reichen (Bern, 1982), 114-37. On this movement in general, see Dieter Mertens, "Maximilian I. und das Elsaß", in *Die Humanisten in ihrer politischen und sozialen Umwelt*, ed. O. Herding, R. Stupperich, Mitteilungen der Kommission für Humanismusforschung 3 (Boppard, 1976), 177-200.

other places, on the title page of the great programmatic pamphlet of the Peasants' War, *An die Versamlung gemainer Pawrschafft* (1525).[48]

Once Geiler's communalist stance is recognized, it can be seen to underpin most of his ideas about society and government. Whether he speaks of nobles or peasants, the message is the same: government exists for the sake of the community, not the community for the sake of government. It is not that he merely contrasts the ideal of nobility with the reality, though he does that,[49] or that he abhors the nobility's characteristic arrogance, as in this passage from his cycle of sermons based on *The Ship of Fools* by his friend, the city attorney Sebastian Brant (1459-1521):

> The fifth bell means to take pride in one's nobility. O, you foolish black horse, you, you take pride because the peacock's feathers made your father and your ancestors noble because of their virtues; but you are ennobled by your vices. You foolish black horse, they were noble and you are not.[50]

He lashes out, too, at the rich burghers' longing to be thought noble and the obsessive inflation of titles. He cites, for example, the proverb, "Whoever is rich, wants honor (i.e., nobility)", the aptness of which is documented by the sigh of Hans Armbruster in *der Brandgaße*, "he whom God has made rich, also wants honor."[51]

The greatest of the nobles were the princes, and in the German cycle based on Brant's *Ship of Fools*, Geiler exposes their foolishness:

> The sixth bell means to pursue one's own interest. What prince is not guilty of this bell? They all pursue their own goals, not one of them pursues God's goals. ... Nor have they any sympathy with their neighbors. If my side of the wall is cool, they say, I'm doing all right.[52]

Such rulers, Geiler predicts, will come to a bad end:

> They will be devoured one-by-one, like the oxen who were eaten by the wolf, because they wouldn't help one another. Everyone wants to rule himself, and some even abandon the jurisdiction of the [Holy] Roman Empire. Just so, when one brand after the other is pulled out of the stove [*felix*], the fire goes out. A

---

[48] "Wer mehret Schweiz? Der Herren Geiz." *"An die Versammlung gemeiner Bauernschaft." Eine revolutionäre Flugschrift aus dem deutschen Bauernkrieg (1525)*, ed. Siegfried Hoyer, Bernd Rüdiger (Leipzig, 1975). The author is unknown, though Christian Peters has made a case for Andreas Bodenstein von Karlstadt. Christian Peters, "An die Versammlung gemeiner Bauernschaft (1525)", *Zeitschrift für bayerische Kirchengeschichte* 54 (1985): 16-28.

[49] See, for example, the quotes from his *Nauicula sive speculum fatuorum* (Strasbourg, 1510), by Léon Dacheux, *Un réformateur catholique à la fin du XVe siècle, Jean Geiler de Kaysersberg* (Paris, 1876), 210 note 1, which measure the reality against the ideal.

[50] Geiler, *Narrenschiff* (Strasbourg, 1520), 182^v.

[51] Geiler, *Navicula penitentie* (Strasbourg, 1511), fol. VI E.

[52] Geiler, *Narrenschiff* (Strasbourg, 1520), 195^r; and there, too, the following quote.

ruler should pursue the common good, for which purpose he was elected. Therefore, he should be content with his salary and seek no more.

Here Geiler interprets Swiss disobedience to the Holy Roman Empire — of which he does not approve — as an understandable reaction to the princes' selfish greed.

Geiler tends to believe that princes and their spiritual counterparts, bishops, form the main source of the world's ills, especially in the burghers' world. He writes:

> Now look at the prelates, how they behave in the cities in both spiritual and temporal affairs, and you see how they wear the bell. Don't you see how the prelates and princes through their bad example are the cause and source of destruction of the whole earth? They mislead the poor sheep who follow them.[53]

In keeping with this attitude, when he wishes to present images of spiritual authority, Geiler chooses familiar types. He speaks, for example, of "Christ, the community's merchant", by which he means — as we can infer from his violent views against usury and usurers — one who serves the commune in an important way.[54]

Geiler once preached an entire sermon cycle in which he interpreted in a religious sense the status and duties of a village headman (*Dorfmeier*). The headman is distinguished, Geiler says, by the fact that he is elected by, and responsible to, the commune.

> The custom is that a headman is elected by the commune and receives from it authority and power over the commune. Even though he is installed by the village's seigneur, his authority comes originally from the commune, which elected his predecessors. And whoever is elected by the commune, is elected for the commune's sake and not for his own sake. Therefore, whoever is in authority ought to consider that he belongs to the commune, not the commune to him. He therefore should not raise himself over those who elected him, the officials who act for the commune.[55]

Geiler's belief in the rightness of popular election ran very deep, and, like the author of *An die Versamlung gemainer Pawrschafft*, he felt election of rulers far superior to hereditary rule. In the sermons on the *Ship of Fools*, for example, he says,

> The fifth bell means to elect rulers for their family and their nobility. This is a sign of great foolishness, to fill offices out of friendship and because of nobility, and to disregard the pious and the wise. All Germany is filled with this

---

[53] Ibid., 106ᵛ.

[54] Geiler, *Das Buoch Arbore humana* (Strasbourg, 1521), fol. 43ʳ⁻ᵛ; id., *Brösamlein* (Strasbourg, 1517), 47ᵛ-48ʳ; id., *Narrenschiff* (Strasbourg, 1520), 185ʳ⁻ᵛ; id., *Das Evangelibuch* (Strasbourg, 1515), 30ᵛ.

[55] Geiler, *Das Buoch Arbore humana* (Strasbourg, 1521), fol. 135ʳ.

foolishness, for bishops are elected not for their chastity or their holiness; magistrates are not elected for their wisdom, but because of their nobility and their families. Thus come fools, mischievous and stupid men, into the government.[56]

These texts illustrate the degree to which Geiler's communal ideal consisted not just of formal characteristics, such as election, but also of a deep antipathy for the domination of the world by inherited power.[57] There is very little substantive difference between his social ideal and that of the author of *An die Versamlung gemainer Pawrschafft*, the radical pamphlet of 1525.

And what of the clergy, Geiler's own estate? Geiler's ideal could be inferred from what I have said above, but that is not necessary. In one place he speaks of "a common person, who serves the whole community, such as a bishop, a priest, an ammeister", which makes the priest and bishop officers of the civic church.[58] Further on in the same text, he reinforces his point:

> The Son of Man is not come to be ministered to but to minister. All rulers, temporal and spiritual, should hear this and should believe not that the commune belongs to them, but they to the commune. The communes exist not for their sake, but they for the commune's sake. They are the commune's servants.

The most striking dramatization, however, of Geiler's ideal of the clergy's integration into communal life comes in his cycle of sermons on the ants.[59] Geiler compares Christian society to an anthill, an image not unknown to modern anticommunist polemics, though there the similarity ends. Following Aristotle, he says, one may divide people into three groups: "One part consists of the working folk, the 'artisans', as we call them, such as tailors, cobblers, etc. The second is the burghers, and the third is the nobles." The first group, the workers, he compares with those ants who carry bodies to the graves. They are the vast majority, and each has his task: "These are the artisans, of which there are many kinds on this earth. This kind makes shoes, another farms, another can't farm, and I must preach." Each employs his craft to nourish himself and his children, with something left over, "so that he can also help the poor."

The second group is like the ants who carry in the food, for it does much good by teaching.

> These are the clergy, who should live by alms, sing, read, and praise God, since they can't chop and plough or make shoes. We don't do these things that we

---

[56] Geiler, *Narrenschiff* (Strasbourg, 1520), 194ᵛ-95ʳ.

[57] See his portrayal of the ideal and the reality of the nobles, in Geiler, *Narrenschiff* (Strasbourg, 1520), 182ᵛ; id., *Navicula sive speculum fatuorum* (Strasbourg, 1510), Turb. LXXVI C, F, and G.

[58] Geiler, *Postille*, part II, 5, quoted by Dacheux, *Un réformateur catholique*, 544 note 2.

[59] Geiler, *Die Emeis*, 8ᵛ-9ᵛ.

should do, but we get our sustenance nonetheless, for the wine and corn is packed into our cellars. This is all given to us so that we might celebrate the Mass and do our other duties, not so that we can collect three or four whores apiece, as the proud college boys at the bishop's court do.

Geiler's clerical ideal contains no hint of lordship, for "thus we clergy, monks, priests, and nuns eat up your work. You nourish us, so we should repay temporal with spiritual goods. To have much property, however, such as rents and dues, wine and grain, and then fail to offer spiritual goods in return, this angers the people." The laity should not respond, "we should take half the property which the priests have. Why should they have so much property? They have too much." Truly, Geiler sighs, "many priests do have too much, but you shouldn't for that reason take it away. I don't know where it will end, if you start taking away from all who have too much. It would injure many people. If you took the priests' property, God knows, what would happen then." Rather, give "the priests and the convents their proper incomes, and otherwise watch carefully and see that they live correctly and perform the duties for which they hold and enjoy what they have."

Behind Geiler's plea lies less a desire to defend property rights in general than a vision of the clergy's necessary contribution to the common good. It is the prayers and sacramental functions of the clergy, he believes, which link the communities spiritually with one another. The clergy "do much good, not only for themselves but also for all others. It is so, for when they and you are in the state of grace, whatever a friend of God does, the others all share in it." The chief, but not exclusive, role in maintaining the spiritual interdependence of communities, falls to the clergy. "When a priest at Rome says Mass in the state of grace", Geiler says, "you benefit from his action. And when you here at Strasbourg pray the Our Father in the state of grace, the priest at Rome benefits from it. That is *participium*." Recognizing that his hearers would meet this idea with skepticism, Geiler goes on: "You ask, 'how can that happen? How can someone at Rome share in what is done here'?" He tries to meet such questions with a version of the paramount metaphor of all corporatist-communal thinking.

> It happens just as with a human being, who has many organs. The limbs and organs are weak and ill, the fingers slack, the ears pointed, and the mouth pale. Then you eat a little soup or porridge, and though the stomach receives the porridge, all the organs benefit from it. The toes on your foot become strong; the fingers become red again; the mouth and all the organs become stronger. Each limb begins once more to move as it needs to. So, in like manner, when a just person does a good deed, the others all benefit from it.

This spiritual communalism, therefore, is neither created nor maintained exclusively by the clergy.

One final point illustrates the civic and communal character of Geiler's clerical ideal. The third group of persons is compared with the third sort of ants, who show the right way to others. Here Geiler places "the nobles, prelates, and especially bishops and doctors". The proper office of the bishop, he says, is "to preach and to teach the way to heaven. ... For this reason St. Paul tied the two offices, pastors and doctors, together, for their task is to herd the sheep as pastors and teach and instruct them as doctors." This passage proves that Geiler's is not just a new version of the tired old feudal triad of *oratores*, *bellatores*, and *laboratores*.[60] His clergy are divided among all three of the social groups: the preacher in the first; the priest in the second; and the bishop in the third. The legal unity of the clerical estates here yields to a division of labor which is both material and spiritual.

Geiler's benign view of the bishop as a kind of local patriarch may reflect conditions in the diocese and city of Strasbourg, where the bishop had access to his cathedral church only at the sufferance of the civic magistrates. To be sure, the Strasbourgeois were quite unaccustomed to seeing their bishop in a pastoral role, and when Bishop William of Honstein (r. 1506-41) came to Strasbourg at Corpus Christi 1508 and said Mass in the cathedral, Sebastian Brant rushed to the archives to discover precedents. He found that no bishop had said Mass at Strasbourg for 150 years.[61] On the other hand, the bishop was no lord in the city, and the magistrates reminded him of this fact as often as they thought necessary. When Bishop William came to be enthroned in 1507, for example, and complained of the restrictions they placed on his entourage, the magistrates set him straight. "It pertains to the Senate of the city of Strasbourg", they replied, "to order, mobilize, command, and forbid in their city, just as they please. Enough said."[62] At Strasbourg, therefore, the bishop's power was far weaker than, say, at Worms, where the bishop conducted a long feud against the city, and the clergy engaged in an especially humiliating exodus in 1499.[63]

In Geiler's vision, the clergy are servants, not lords. The church, the only necessary supra-communal body, is a structure of grace rather than of lordship, and its bonds are neither exclusively sacramental nor exclusively clerical. Geiler's vision is thus a kind of Christian clerical Guelfism, an alliance of local community and universal Church, and a far cry from the caesaropapist Ghibellinism of many German humanists.[64]

---

[60] See Thomas A. Brady, Jr., "Luther's Social Teaching and the Social Order of His Age", in *Martin Luther Quincentennial*, ed. G. Dünnhaupt (Detroit, 1985), 270-90.

[61] Sebastian Brant, "Bischoff Wilhelm von Hoensteins waal und einritt. Anno 1506 et 1507", in *Code historique et diplomatique de la Ville de Strasbourg*, ed. Louis Schneegans, 2 vols. (Strasbourg, 1845-47), 2: 296.

[62] Ibid., 296.

[63] Scribner, "Anticlericalism", 251.

[64] I have treated this theme — universal church and local autonomy — in a forthcoming study, "The Rise of Merchant Empires — a European Counterpoint". On

Finally, it is important to remind ourselves that this is a dream, a vision, an ideal, and while it reflected realities, it was not itself reality. Geiler was hardly faint-hearted about reform. In 1492, when he discussed with the bishop and the civic magistrates the prospects for reform in some of the worst religious houses, Geiler is said to have recommended as follows:

> We should take those nuns who not only are whores but who have secretly killed their own babies, stuff them in a sack, and throw them in the river. The monks and priests who are implicated or assisted in these crimes should be beheaded with a sword.[65]

Not only would the bishop not "lay a hand on consecrated persons", but "the nobles and magistrates, who had daughters, sisters, and other female relations and friends in the house, wouldn't act without papal permission", even though "Dr. Kaysersberger said he would take responsibility for the act before God, pope, emperor, and bishop." It was the same old story, clerical reform blocked by the powerful laity. By 1492 or so Geiler's belief in the possibility of reforming the secular clergy began to falter, and though he hoped longer for a reform of the regulars, by 1508, two years before his death, he had given up. He declared that "the best thing to do is to sit in one's own corner and stuff one's head into a hole, seeking only to follow God's commandments, to do good, and thereby to gain eternal salvation."[66]

Geiler was correct in believing that he would not live to see reform, but it did come within two decades of his death and at the hands of men who had known and admired him. One of them was Stettmeister Jacob Sturm (1489-1553), who had stood at Geiler's deathbed in 1510, and who in 1523

---

the German humanists' political loyalties, see John M. Headley, "The Habsburg World Empire and the Revival of Ghibellinism", *Medieval and Renaissance Studies* 7 (1978): 92-127; id., "Germany, the Empire and *Monarchia* in the Thought and Policy of Gattinara", in *Das römisch-deutsche Reich im politischen System Karls V.*, ed. H. Lutz (Munich, 1982), 15-33; Mertens, "Maximilian I. und das Elsaß" (n. 47 above), 177-200. We badly need a new understanding of the German humanists' political ideas and loyalties, which continue to be characterized vaguely as "patriotism" or "nationalism". See, for example, Noel L. Brann, "Humanism in Germany", in *Renaissance Humanism: Foundations, Forms, and Legacy*, ed. A. Rabil, Jr., vol. 2: *Humanism beyond Italy* (Philadelphia, 1988), 123-55, here at 137-41. By contrast, Quentin Skinner, *Foundations of Modern Political Thought*, 2 vols. (Cambridge, 1978), 1: 235, 238, recognizes the socially conservative, politically monarchist tendencies of northern humanism in general.

[65] Specklin, "Les Collectanées" (n. 32 above), no. 2164; and there, too, the quotes in the following sentence.

[66] Geiler, *Die Emeis,* 22ʳ. See Rapp, "Jean Geiler de Kaysersberg (1445-1510)" (n. 30 above), 29: "Jusqu'en 1492 à peu près, Geiler crut qu'une réforme du clergé séculier était possible." Rapp (ibid., 29-30) offers the clearest picture of Geiler's ideal of clerical reform.

abandoned both his own clerical career and the old faith.[67] In very many ways, the ecclesiastical reform undertaken by Sturm and his fellow magistrates between 1527 and 1534 realized Geiler's ideal of integrating the clergy in communal life.[68] The clergy surrendered their separate legal status and most of their property, and those who remained conformed very well to Geiler's ideal of pastoral office. The presidency of the Strasbourg's Church Assembly, for example, much resembled Geiler's ideal of the bishop as one who "teaches and shows the way to heaven."[69] The differences, however, were also great. The Protestant reformers stripped away the entire edifice of trans-local spiritual exchange, and they and the magistrates made war on the religious orders, both the lax and the strict, to which Geiler had felt a special attachment. Geiler had not foreseen that integration of the clergy might lead to a purely pastoral clergy and thus to the disappearance of the religious orders. Nor had he any inkling of the effect that integration might have on the most vulnerable sector of the clergy, the women.

III

"The female religious life", Lyndal Roper has written, "was understood through a metaphor at once social and sexual: the nun was the bride of Christ."[70] While the convents used the language of kinship — the nuns were "sisters" — they "created a series of relationships which were at odds with civic kin structures." The most important of such structures was the patriarchal household, the solidification of which — one of the major facts of contemporary urban life — cast even graver doubt on "an option which ensured that wifehood was not the only socially valued role for women." The nuns' chief role as part of the clergy, of course, was the one specified by Geiler for all clergy: their prayers and, for the priests, Masses conferred spiritual benefits on all Christians. The reformation's message concentrated sacral power in spoken words, it stripped the world of holy things and

---

[67] Jakob Wimpheling, *Opera selecta*, vol. 2: Jakob Wimpfeling and Beatus Rhenanus, *Das Leben des Johannes Geiler von Kaysersberg*, ed. Otto Herding and Dieter Mertens (Munich, 1970), 18, 84 lines 837-48; also in Joseph Anton Riegger, *Amoenitates literariae friburgenses* (Ulm, 1775-76), 124-25.

[68] François Wendel, *L'Eglise de Strasbourg, sa constitution et son organisation, 1532-1535*, Etudes d'histoire et de philosophie religieuses 38 (Paris, 1942); Miriam Usher Chrisman, *Strasbourg and the Reform: A Study in the Process of Change* (New Haven, 1967); William S. Stafford, *Domesticating the Clergy: the Inception of the Reformation in Strasbourg, 1522-1524* (Missoula, Mont., 1976); Lorna Jane Abray, *The People's Reformation: Magistrates, Clergy, and Commons in Strasbourg, 1520-1599* (New Haven, 1985).

[69] Abray, *People's Reformation*, 72-76, 159-60.

[70] Roper, *Holy Household*, 206; and there, too, the remaining quotes in this paragraph.

actions, and radically localized the sense of church, all changes which tended to strip the cloistered orders of their spiritual utility and to expose them to charges of parasitism. For the women, whose gender entered into all their relationships, the blow fell very early and doubly hard, for not only did Protestant city governments harass, bully, and even force them to dissolve, but the new, Protestant clergy had no place for them.[71] Whether its discipline was harsh and authoritarian or mild and affectionate, the patriarchal household received reinforcement from the reformation, both as symbol through the elimination of a rival way of life for women and through the repatriation of women who had chosen that way of life.

The convent of St. Nicolaus-in-Undis had been founded in the thirteenth century in one of Strasbourg's swampy suburbs, hence the reference in its name to "waves" or water, though the locals Germanized it to mean "among the dogs" (*zu den Hunden*).[72] In the later Middle Ages, St. Nicolaus-in-Undis and the eight other mendicant women's houses remained the province of the native elites, and the spread of the practices of the Observance among the six Dominican convents had renewed their reputation for austerity and strictness.[73] In 1522 one of the young women living at St. Nicolaus-in-Undis was fourteen-year-old Margarethe Kniebis, who had entered the house at the age of nine and now wanted to begin her novitiate.[74] This, Margarethe's father decided, was not to be.

Claus Kniebis was a wealthy, university-educated rentier, who had entered the Senate from the Smiths' Guild in 1512 and in 1519 gained the ammeistership, the commune's highest office.[75] In April 1522, while

---

[71] Merry E. Wiesner, "Nuns, Wives, and Mothers: Women and the Reformation in Germany", in *Women in Reformation and Counter-Reformation Europe: Public and Private Worlds*, ed. S. Marshall (Bloomington, 1989), 8-28, here at 9-10.

[72] Medard Barth, *Handbuch der elsässischen Kirchen im Mittelalter* (Strasbourg, 1960-63; reprint, Brussels, 1980), coll. 1386-88; Luzian Pfleger, *Kirchengeschichte der Stadt Straßburg im Mittelalter*, Forschungen zur Kirchengeschichte des Elsaß 6 (Colmar, 1941), 87; Adolph Seyboth, *Das alte Straßburg vom 13. Jahrhundert bis zum Jahre 1870* (Strasbourg, 1890), 222.

[73] Socially, Strasbourg's mendicant women's houses probably resembled the much better documented Augsburg convents, on which see Roper, *Holy Household*, 207-9.

[74] This story comes from AMS, II 7/20, fols. 26ʳ-29bisᵛ; noticed with an excerpt in *Humanisme et Réforme à Strasbourg. Exposition organisée par les Archives, la Bibliothèque et les Musées de la Ville* (Strasbourg, 1973), 51-52, no. 108; partly printed by Jean Lebeau and Jean-Marie Valentin, eds. *L'Alsace au siècle de la Réforme 1482-1621. Textes et documents* (Nancy, 1985), 193. The text is printed in this volume in Katherine G. Brady and Thomas A. Brady, Jr., eds., "Documents on Communalism and the Control of Women at Strasbourg in the Age of the Reformations", no. 1. In subsequent references, this edition is referred to as "Documents", with document number and lines.

[75] Thomas A. Brady, Jr., *Ruling Class, Regime, and Reformation at Strasbourg, 1520-1555*, SMRT 22 (Leiden, 1978), 326-27; Jean Rott, "Un recueil de correspon-

representing Strasbourg in the Imperial Diet at Nuremberg, Kniebis had begun to move toward the reformation movement, which may or may not have inspired him, once back home, to intervene in his daughter's plans. On 22 June he came with his mother's brother, Hug Meyer, who was a priest and a vicar in the cathedral chapter, to St. Nicolaus-in-Undis for an interview with his daughter and with the prioress, Ursula von Mörßmünster.[76] Kniebis refused the proposal that Margarethe be allowed to enter the novitiate, and before she might even think about it, two or three years hence, "his wish is that she live in his house for a time and test herself in the world."[77] Margarethe reminded her father that "I've said to you many times that I don't want to leave, that I don't want to be in the world. If you force me, God will forgive me, for my will is never again to be in the world." Kniebis grew angry and retorted, "even if you don't want to leave, you must leave. You must leave, even if you do so in the Devil's name." "In his name I won't leave," Margarethe responded, "but in God's name and in obedience to God's will. For you brought me into this house and offered me to God with your own hands." Now the prioress intervened and proposed that the novitiate be put off, with the provincial's permission, until Margarethe turned seventeen, and that meanwhile she should continue to live in the community. No, Claus Kniebis replied, that would not do, and he would come to fetch her home in two day's time.

Next day the prioress decided to write to Margarethe's mother, Ottilia Rot, and "ask her humbly to play the loyal mediator among the father's anger, the daughter, and us."[78] Two days later, she also wrote to Kniebis himself and pleaded "that he should forgive us, leave off his anger, and become our good friend." He replied that "he will do anything else we want, but he must take his daughter away." But he did not come, and Margarethe, as the prioress told her mother, "waited day after day, filled with anxiety

---

dances strasbourgeoises du XVIe siècle à la Bibliothèque de Copenhague (Ms. Thott 497,2°)", in *Bulletin philologique et historique (jusqu'en 1610) du Comité des Travaux Historiques et Scientifiques 1968*, (1971), 2: 749-818, here at 756-58; Jean Rott, "La Réforme à Nuremberg et à Strasbourg. Contactes et contrases (avec des correspondances inédites)", in *Homage à Dürer. Strasbourg et Nuremberg dans la première moitié du XVIe siècle*, Publications de la Société Savante d'Alsace et des Régions de l'Est, series "Recherches et Documents" 12 (Strasbourg, 1972), 91-142, here at 99-100. The studies by Rott are reprinted in Jean Rott, *Investigationes Historicae. Eglises et société au XVIe siècle. Gesammelte Aufsätze*, ed. M. de Kroon and M. Lienhard, 2 vols. (Strasbourg, 1986), 1: 250-52, 399-400.

[76] On Hug Meyer, see Brady, *Ruling Class*, 146 note 97.

[77] "Documents", no. 1; and there, too, the remaining quotes in this paragraph. Following the prioress' account, I have transposed the conversation into direct address. "Documents" refers to this volume, 209-28.

[78] Ibid.; and there, too, the remaining quotes in this paragraph and those in the following one.

and fear, until he should fetch her. ... Thus the child wasted away visibly in body and strength, because of her grief and sorrow."

Finally, on Friday after St. Martin's Day (14 November) — not two days but nearly five months after his first threat — Kniebis and his uncle, Hug Meyer, came once more to the convent. There ensued the final interview among them, Margarethe, and Ursula von Mörßmünster. The prioress turned to the young woman and said with sad, ritualized solemnity, "I would rather see you lying in a grave than see you go out into the world. But if he demands to have you, then I give you from my hand to his hand, from my care to his care." She reminded Margarethe to meditate on the brevity of life and on the last things in the hope, perhaps, that the woman could maintain something of her old spiritual life in her father's house. Then she turned to the ammeister and said,

> this is your daughter, whom I give from my hand into your hand, from my care into your care. Please God, that you care for her well. I give you a good, devout, innocent child. Please God, that you keep her so, and if you do not, then we are absolved of responsibility before God and before you.

Nine days later, on Sunday, 23 November 1522, Kniebis and his brother-in-law, Dr. Michael Rot, fetched Margarethe from the convent to her parents' home in Dragon's Street.[79]

We know something about this story's aftermath. Claus Kniebis became the political leader of the Evangelical movement, served again as ammeister in the year of the Peasant's War, 1525, and remained a strongly committed Evangelical until his death in 1552. He knew how to do well by doing good, for he, Dr. Rot, and their dependents were some of the few Strasbourgeois to enrich themselves from properties of the dissolved religious houses.[80] Margarethe Kniebis never returned to her convent. She resided at her parents' home until 1525, when at the age of nearly seventeen she was

---

[79] Seyboth, *Das alte Straßburg*, 178. Dr. Michael Rot (d. after 1533), who figures in the documents analyzed below, was active at Strasbourg by 1515, when he drafted an opinion for the regime about the reform of the civic hospital. Later, after the events narrated here and in the following paragraphs, he married a woman (name unknown), who died in 1555 and left some money to the hospital. During the early 1530s Rot served as churchwarden at New St. Peter's Church, and he helped to draft the church ordinance of 1534. Otto Wickelmann, *Das Fürgsorgewesen der Stadt Straßburg vor und nach der Reformation bis zum Ausgang des sechzehnten Jahrhunderts. Ein Beitrag zur deutschen Kultur- und Wirtschaftsgeschichte*, QFRG 5 (Leipzig, 1922; repr., New York, 1971), vol. 1: 25-26, and vol. 2: 260; Manfred Krebs and Hans-Georg Rott, eds., *Elsaß. Stadt Straßburg 1522-1535*, QFRG 27-28 (Gütersloh, 1959-60), vol. 2: 95, 135, 178-79.

[80] Brady, *Ruling Class*, 144-46.

married to Caspar Engelmann, a well-to-do cloth merchant.[81] She married
into her father's own set, the nouveaux-riches, mostly cloth merchants, who
played such a prominent role in Strasbourg's government during the
reformation generation.[82] As for the nuns at St. Nicolaus-in-Undis, despite
its discipline this redoubtable community lost many of its nuns just after the
great Peasants' War of 1525.[83] It nonetheless endured far into the post-
reformation era until the magistrates decided on 8 April 1592 to close it, and
its nuns were taken into the Dominican community of St. Mary Magdalene.[84] Of all the women's houses at Strasbourg, those of the Dominican
Observance survived the longest, despite the endless campaigns of
vilification by the Evangelical preachers and intermittent harassment by the

---

[81] Their marriage agreement, dated 12 September 1525, records her dowry of 300
fl. and his *Morgengabe* of 100 fl. Caspar, son of Christoph Engelmann (1494-1541),
a cloth merchant and senator, and Margarethe Surgant (1498-1540) of Thann in
Upper Alsace; he was Schöffe 1535 and Zunftmeister 1541 of the Guild zum Spiegel;
he and Margarethe Kniebis lived since February 1527 in a house they rented from the
chapter of St. Thomas; their son, Heinrich, was a Schöffe zum Spiegel 1563-73, and
he and his two brothers formed a firm to sell cloth; Caspar renounced his citizenship
on 21 July 1548 during the crisis of the Interim at Strasbourg. F.-J. Fuchs,
"Engelmann", *Nouvelle dictionnaire du biographie alsacienne*, vol. 7 (Strasbourg,
1986), 813; Karina Kulbach, "Ascendances des enfants d'André Sandherr (1672-
1737) et d'Anne Salome Oestringer, de Colmar", *Bulletin du Cercle Généalogique
d'Alsace*, 31 (1975): 63-70; AMS, KS 18, fol. 100ʳ, AMS, KS 19, fol. 115; AMS,
Corporation du Miroir, 5. Much of this information comes from F.-J. Fuchs of
Strasbourg, to whom my thanks.

[82] See Brady, *Ruling Class*, 183-84.

[83] The convent's manager (*Schaffner*) drew up ca. 1525 a list of "Volgende
Closterfraüwen sindt nach dem Bauren krieg auß dem Closter St. Claus in vndis
allhie zu Strasburg kommen vnd weltlich worden", which contains the following
names: Subprioress Margarethe Rötin, Susanna Pfaüren, Maria Gerhartin, Ursula
Ehingeren, Magdalena Stürmin, Margareth Böcklerin, Anna Heüsin, Anne Wurme,
Veronica Mehen, Juliana Bÿsin, Appolonia von Heÿdelberg, Paulina Furtherin, Ursula
Spitzlerin, N. Neuischin, Margreth von Waltzhut, Agneß Dolden, Elizabeth Hüsen,
Barbara Eppen, Elizabeth Beÿnen, Margen Stürmin, Maria Durbchen, Margreth
Müllerin. AMS, II 7/20, fol. 42ʳ.

[84] Francis Rapp, "La vie religieuse du couvent Saint-Nicolas-aux-ondes à Strabourg
de 1525 à 1592", *Études de sociologie religieuse*, Cahiers de l'Association
interuniversitaire de l'Est (1962), 1-16; Pierre Levresse, "La survie du catholicisme
à Strasbourg au XVIe siècle", in *Strasbourg au cœur religieux du XVIe siècle.
Hommage à Lucien Febvre*, ed. G. Livet, F. Rapp, Publications de la Société Savante
d'Alsace et des Régions de l'Est, Collection "Grandes publications" 12 (Strasbourg,
1977), 457-69, here at 462. Five other communities survived the reformation era
intact: the women's houses of St. Mary Magdalene and SS. Margarethe and Agnes;
and the men's houses of the Carthusians, the Knights of St. John, and the Teutonic
Knights. F.-J. Fuchs, "Les catholiques à Strasbourg de 1529 à 1681", *AEKG* 38
(1975): 141-69, here at 142-43.

regime, a process which began in 1525 under the eye of the ruling ammeister, Claus Kniebis.[85] The nuns' resistance, as Lyndal Roper has written of Augsburg, "dramatized and focused the divisions within the elite", from whose daughters the convents recruited.[86] The repudiation of their way of life by the reformers and followers split families at Strasbourg, as it did elsewhere. No case at Strasbourg is so well documented as that of the Poor Clares at Nuremberg under the redoubtable Caritas Pirckheimer (1467-1532).[87] We do know of other cases of removals, however, mostly carried out by prominent Strasbourgeois who repatriated their female relations. This happened, for example, to Clara Sturm, who was removed from the convent of SS. Margarethe and Agnes by her two brothers, Jacob and Peter, in 1524.[88] Both their father's family, the Sturms, and their mother's kinsmen, the Schotts, long enjoyed especially strong ties to the houses of the Dominican Observance.[89] The two younger Sturm brothers nevertheless removed Clara from her convent, where she had lived for sixteen years and was, unlike Margarethe Kniebis, almost certainly a professed nun. A number of other removals occurred, or were attempted, about the same time by men of equal rank.[90]

---

[85] See AMS, II 57/7, two letters from the prioress and community of SS. Margarethe and Agnes, another Dominican house, to Ammeister Kniebis concerning the replacement of their confessor by the wardens (*Pfleger*). On the struggle of the women's houses to maintain their religious life, see Fuchs, "Les catholiques à Strasbourg", 156-61.

[86] Roper, *Holy Household*, 210.

[87] The best study is still Gerta Krabbel, *Caritas Pirckheimer. Ein Lebensbild aus der Zeit der Reformation*, 5th ed., Katholisches Leben und Kirchenreform im Zeitalter der Glaubensspaltung 7 (Münster, 1982 [1940]), esp. 86-197; and see Klaus Guth, "Caritas Pirckheimer. Kloster und Klosterleben in der Herausforderung der Zeit", in *Caritas Pirckheimer. Eine Ausstellung der Katholischen Stadtkirche Nürnberg, Kaiserburg Nürnberg, 26. June-8 August 1982* (Munich, 1982), 13-29.

[88] Brady, *Ruling Class*, 351-53; Rapp, *Réformes*, 520. The convent, which dated back to the union of two communities of Dominican women, held out until the French Revolution. Barth, *Handbuch*, coll. 1369-70, 1381-84.

[89] Their aunt, Magdalena Sturm (†1520), and their sister, Margarethe (†1530), were nuns at St. Nicolaus-in-Undis; and two aunts and two uncles were buried at the men's Dominican house. AMS, II 7/20, fol. 42^r; and see Thomas A. Brady, Jr., "La famille Sturm aux XVe et XVIe siècles", *Revue d'Alsace* 108 (1982): 29-44, here at 32-33, for further documentation. Anna Schott, a great-aunt on the Schott side, had been a nun at SS. Margarthe and Agnes, and her family was said to have a "special love" for the Dominicans. Bibliothèque Nationale et Universitaire de Strasbourg, Ms. 1058, fol. 166^r; Charles Guillaume Adolphe Schmidt, *Histoire littéraire de l'Alsace* (n. 30 above), 2: 9 note 20, 29 note 78; Dacheux, *Un réformateur catholique*, 426-27.

[90] Other actions of this kind are known. Jacobe Spender, for example, was removed by her father, Jacob Spender († ca. 1525), from St. Nicolaus-in-Undis on 25 November 1522. AMS, II 7/20, fol. 29^r, noticed in *Humanisme et Réforme à Strasbourg*, 52; and on the father, a privy councillor, see Brady, *Ruling Class*, 210,

The story of Margarethe Kniebis captures in midstream the pressure placed on this sector of the clergy by the reformation movement and its consequences for familial relations. Although at first glance Kniebis' actions seem to be a predictable — given his commitment — rescue of his daughter from the monastic life, which Luther had decreed to be worse than useless, on closer scrutiny the document reveals Kniebis' action to have been more paternal than Protestant. He argued not that Margarethe's chosen way of life was worthless or harmful but that she was too young to take first vows, and that he wanted her to live in the world for a few years before deciding to remain in the convent for the rest of her life. Indeed, the prioress says that until he was angered, he consented to let her live in the community, though not to take vows.[91] Once angered, "he swore that he would fetch her in two days' time", and when he did fetch her, nearly five months later, she never returned. Perhaps this story catches the ammeister in religious midstream, when the new faith could prompt his doubts about his daughter's choice but did not yet grip him so firmly as to demand immediate action.

Other male patricians likely underwent similar experiences. Local law seems to have permitted them to remove kinswomen, even adults, from their convents, perhaps based on residual right of guardianship over the women. Once their communities no longer shielded them, the nuns perhaps came under a law of 1500 — protested to no avail by Johann Geiler — which provided that all widows "shall be given a guardian without their knowledge or will."[92] This law merely illustrates the progressive deterioration of women's legal rights in sixteenth-century Europe, including the Holy Roman Empire.[93] The fate of women from communities attacked or dissolved in the wake of the reformation movement, therefore, must be seen in this larger light. The attack on the women's communities represented not only a confessional act against Catholicism but also an affirmation of the patriarchal household's rights over women. This process enjoyed widespread

---

223, 379, 382, 391. Adolf von Mittelhausen, a noble senator, tried to remove his daughter from SS. Margarethe and Agnes in 1522. AST 37, fols. 48ʳ, 59ᵛ. Mathis Wurm von Geudertheim tried four times between September 1522 and February 1523 to force his sister, Anna, from the convent of St. Nicolaus-in-Undis, which she had entered in 1512. See Jean Rott and Gustave Koch, "De quelques pamphletaires nobles", in *Grandes figures de l'humanisme alsacien*, 135-45, here at 139-45 (reprinted in Rott, *Investigationes Historicae*, 2: 575-85).

[91] "Documents", no. 1; and the remaining quotes in this paragraph are from ibid.

[92] Geiler, *Die ältesten Schriften*, 19.

[93] Merry E. Wiesner, "Frail, Weak, and Helpless: Women's Legal Position in Theory and Reality", in *Regnum, religio et ratio. Essays Presented to Robert M. Kingdon*, ed. J. Friedman, Sixteenth Century Essays & Studies 8 (Kirksville, Mo., 1987), 161-69. On the economic basis of the deterioration, see id., *Working Women in Renaissance Germany* (New Brunswick, N.J., 1986), esp. 149-85, 187-98; Susan C. Karant-Nunn, "The Woman of the Saxon Silver Mines", in *Women in Reformation and Counter-Reformation Europe*, ed. S. Marshall, 28-45, here at 42-43.

popular support because of the widespread doubts about women's inability to manage either their properties or their sexuality.[94] By disrupting and dissolving the communal religious life of women, therefore, the reformation movement eased such doubts by promoting the consolidation of male authority over women's religious life. This improved domestication of women formed one aspect of the reformation's integration of the clergy.

IV

Authority and gender enter richly into another story about the relationships between the domestication of women and the integration of clergy. It, too, involves what Scribner calls the "sexual power" of the clergy.[95] Strasbourg certainly rivalled other major South German cities in its number of high- and loose-living clergymen, and the notorious clan of the Wolfs of Eckbolsheim contained some of the worst. Its head, Thomas Wolf, Sr. (1445-1511), was the son of rich peasants at Eckbolsheim, who studied at Erfurt, Basel, and Bologna.[96] Wolf collected benefices and books, conducted an active law practice, and consorted with humanists without being one. Upon his death, his fine house at New St. Peter's was sacked by his brother, Caspar, whose gang of mercenaries looted the plate and drank up the cellar. Wolf was the very type of the pre-reformation gentleman-clergyman, a "master-pluralist" who dabbled in all that was fashionable, lived well off the church, and performed as "an efficient opponent to the efforts of Bishop William III of Strasbourg to reform his clergy in 1509."[97] Wolf's brother, Andreas, married Katherine Meyer and had four sons by her, all clergymen. The best of the lot was Thomas, Jr. (1475-1509), who followed in his uncle's footstep as a pluralist, though he made a better mark as a humanist and, one assumes, lived more modestly, for he was a particular favorite of Geiler's.[98] The Wolfs who interest us here are two of his brothers, Johann Andreas and Cosmas, both canons of New St. Peter's

---

[94] Roper, *Holy Household*, 229. See ibid., 211-28, on the closing of convents, a process much better documented at Augsburg than at Strasbourg.

[95] Scribner, "Anticlericalism", 246-48.

[96] On the Wolf family, see also Schmidt, *Histoire littéraire*, 2: 58-60; Jean Rott, "The Library of the Strasbourg Humanist Thomas Wolf, Senior († 1511)", in *The Process of Change in Early Modern Europe* ed. P. Bebb and S. Marshall (Athens, Ohio, 1988), 33-58, here at 33-34; Rapp, *Réformes*, 292 note 63, 299-300, 302-4; Miriam Usher Chrisman, *Lay Culture, Learned Culture: Books and Social Change in Strasbourg, 1480-1599* (New Haven, 1982), 41, 61, 82.

[97] Rott, "The Library of the Strasbourg Humanist", 33, 35.

[98] According to Matern Berler, "Chronik", 114. This Wolf was a minor humanist and holder of four benefices, of whose career Chrisman (*Lay Culture*, 82) writes that "he spent more time collating the Latin inscriptions he had brought from student days in Italy than in pursuing questions of doctrine or theology."

at Strasbourg.[99] The brothers, themselves notable womanizers, became embroiled in the worst clerical scandal of the immediate pre-reformation years. The case involved one Johann Hepp of Kirchberg, a canon of St. Thomas at Strasbourg, who had seduced a young country girl, brought her to Strasbourg as his mistress, and then kidnapped her when she mysteriously fell ill; after her death he had been arrested by Strasbourg's regime and let go, whereupon he sued Strasbourg at Rome for violation of clerical immunity. The city's case was handled by Hans Murner, brother to the much more famous Franciscan writer and a terror to wayward clergymen. In 1509 his sister, Anna, had been seduced and left pregnant by Friedrich von Beyern, a chaplain at Old St. Peter's Church and bastard son of the late bishop of Strasbourg. Murner's involvement in the Hepp case brought him into conflict with the Wolf brothers, who took Hepp's part and who had, Murner believed, designs on a woman he called his kinswoman but whom the Wolfs called "his good little whore". After several threats and broken windows, on the nights of 21 and 22 January 1522, the matter came to blows in wild scenes staged in the cemetery of New St. Peter's Church. On the second night, Murner and three armored companions, who were armed with boar spears, ambushed the Wolfs and three others. In the petition which he submitted next day to his employers, Murner raged against "these unworthy, alleged clergymen", who constantly offend the citizens, "sparing no respectable man's wife or child."[100] This notorious case combined clerical concubinage, clerical crime, clerical violence, all protected by the web of clerical immunities and ecclesiastical jurisdiction, for eventually Murner was excommunicated at Rome, notice of which was posted at Strasbourg on Christmas Day 1519. The affair caused Nicolaus Wurmser (1473-1536), who was dean of the chapter of St. Thomas, to which the Wolfs belonged, to exclaim in his diary, "Oh, it is such a wondrous thing that the clergy are hated by everyone and have no defenders!"[101]

This tangled series of scandals, which unfolded in the last pre-reformation years, colored the mood at Strasbourg about clerical behavior and formed, therefore, part of the psychological background to the case of Drenss vs.

---

[99] This is based on Jean Rott, "Clercs et laïques à Strasbourg à la veille de la Réformation: Les tragiques amours du Chanoine Jean Hepp et ses procès (1512-1521)", *Annuaire des Amis de Vieux-Strasbourg* 9 (1979): 15-52; and id., "Pfaffenfehden und Anfänge der Reformation in Straßburg. Die Streitigkeiten des Johannes Murner mit den Brüdern Wolff und dem Jung Sankt Peter-Stift daselbst (1519-1522)", in *Landesgeschichte und Geistesgeschichte* (n. 21 above), 279-94 (reprinted in Rott, *Investigationes Historicae*, 1: 313-50, 351-67).

[100] Quoted by Rott, "Pfaffenfehden", 282.

[101] Rott, "Pfaffenfehden", 294 note 71: "Or res auditu mirabilis, quod clerus tanto odio est omnibus, ut nullum defensorem habeat!" On Wurmser, see Ficker and Winckelmann, *Handschriftenproben*, 2: 53.

Hedio. The gist of the case is related in a fragmentary minute of the Senate
& XXI of Strasbourg for 14 May 1524. It says that Augustin Drenss charges

> that Dr. Hedio has taken his sister in marriage, and this was done through the
> connivance of Sir Claus Kniebis and Dr. Michael Rot, who seduced the sister
> and her mother with smooth words, so that they were betrayed and humili-
> ated.[102]

The object of this complaint was the wedding of Dr. Caspar Hedio and
Margarethe Drenss on St. John the Baptist's Day 1524.[103] The clergyman
is the historian Caspar Hedio (1494-1552), a native of Ettlingen near
Karlsruhe, who had studied theology at Freiburg im Breisgau and served
successively as vicar at St. Martin's Church in Basel, cathedral preacher at
Mainz, and since September 1523 cathedral preacher at Strasbourg.[104] He
was, therefore, Geiler's successor but one in the cathedral's pulpit.

Augustin Drenss († 3 May 1552) was a substantial citizen. He came from
one of the Gardeners' guild's most prominent families, three of whom —
including Augustin — served the guild in the privy councils between 1483
and 1557.[105] Augustin, though a truck gardener, was also a moneylender,
and his father had been wealthy enough to serve the commune mounted.[106]
Augustin's wife was Aurelia Rot, whose sister, Ottilia, was married to Claus
Kniebis, and both were kinswomen of Dr. Michael Rot. Drenss vs. Hedio,
therefore, is a familial matter which got out of hand, one of those many
instances of the intermingling of private and public life.[107]

The case is unusually well documented. Besides Augustin Drenss' original
petition, we have the responses of Claus Kniebis, Dr. Michael Rot, and
Agnes Drenss, mother of Margarethe and Augustin, plus a final statement
by Drenss himself.[108] August Drenss came to the Senate for justice, and
he reminds the magistrates that, according to local law and ancient custom,

---

[102] "Annales de Sébastien Brant", ed. Léon Dacheux, BSCMHA, 2nd ser., 19
(1899): 95, no. 4521.

[103] Sebald Büheler, "La chronique strasbourgeoise", ed. Léon Dacheux, BSCMHA,
2nd ser., 13 (1888): 71.

[104] On Hedio, see Ficker and Winckelmann, Handschriftenproben, 2:60; Charles
Spindler, Hédion. Essai biographie et littéraire, theol. dissertation (Strasbourg, 1864).

[105] Brady, Ruling Class, 113, 181, 387.

[106] Ibid., 307. Augustin was the son of Agnes N. and Andres Drenss, who served
three two-year terms as senator from the Gardeners' Guild between 1482 and 1497;
Andres appears among the mounted burghers in the civic muster lists of his time.
Jacques Hatt, Liste des membres du grand sénat de Strasbourg, des stettmeistres, des
ammeistres, des conseils des XXI, XIII, et des XV du XIIIe siècle à 1789 (Strasbourg,
1963), 557; AMS, IV 86.

[107] Their marriage took place before October 1526. AMS, KS 19, fol. 292ᵛ. Aurelia
Rot and her daughter are called Dr. Rot's "mumen", that is, female relations in
undetermined degrees. AST, 69/3, fol. 8ᵛ.

[108] "Documents", nos. 2-6.

no one may entice or lead away a child from its father behind his back. Whoever is found to have assisted in such an act, whether by word or deed, is to be punished. If the child is fatherless, the guardian named according to the statute by you, my gracious lords, is to be regarded as standing in a father's place.[109]

Dr. Hedio, Drenss claimed, had nonetheless

decided and brazenly plotted to take as his wedded wife my sister, Margarethe Drenss, secretly, without the knowledge, and against the wills of the guardian and of myself, as I am told. And he did as follows. Michael Rot, doctor of medicine, invited my sister and her mother to his house to dine. Secretly and without their knowledge, as I have been told, he also invited Dr. Caspar Hedio. Then Sir Claus Kniebis, the ammeister, also arrived, and the two men smoothly told daughter and mother that vows should be exchanged, as common rumor said they already had been. My mother and sister, however, very properly demurred, replying that it was not right to do such a thing behind the backs of her guardian, brother, and friends.[110]

Kniebis and Rot, however, assured mother and daughter that they would fix the matter with him, Augustin, which they tried to do several days later. Meanwhile, Margarethe was staying in Dr. Rot's house, "even though there is no wife in his house." Drenss, however, refused his consent and told his mother, sister, and others that

my sister must give up the priest and marry a good, honest citizen, and I will dower her with 100 florins from my own property. For the doctor is a clergymen, and they are forbidden to marry not only by local law and custom, but also by the laws according to which Christendom has lived for a thousand years and more. From this marriage, too, will come considerable disadvantage to me and mine, not to mention the scandal. For a proper, conscientious Christian ruler cannot allow such an act, but must forbid and disallow it, for it is unthinkable that such a mischievous undertaking be permitted to cancel and cast aside both papal and imperial law. Otherwise, my sister would rightly be regarded as called a public sinner and a whore. If she bears children by the aforementioned doctor, and her mother and grandmother were already dead, the children could not inherit from either woman, for they would justly be regarded as bastards.[111]

Drenss, therefore, asked the magistrates to force Hedio "to desist from his undertaking and to have nothing to do with my sister or my relations, except at law." If that is not possible, he asks them to support his attempts to find redress in other courts,

for if it should happen, that it were considered proper and permissible for any priest or monk to take with impunity and by fraud and trickery a child or other

---

[109] "Documents", no. 2.
[110] "Documents", no. 2.
[111] "Documents", no. 2.

relation from a respectable citizen, without his knowledge and against his will, that would be a scandalous thing. What that might lead to, my lords can well imagine.[112]

So they might have, but the subsequent responses of Claus Kniebis, Caspar Hedio, and Agnes Drenss did not corroborate Augustin's allegations.

Kniebis responded angrily that "I, one of your ammeisters, had to listen to this petition, in which I and my brother-in-law are not a little insulted." Kniebis related that Caspar Hedio had just happened by, as he was told, "to have a friendly talk [with Dr. Rot] about all sorts of things, as scholars do", and after a while Agnes and Margarethe Drenss knocked at the door. As they were his kinswomen ("mumen"), Rot let them in and explained that about a month ago he had invited them to come "and see, how I keep house."[113] The conversation turned to the secret betrothal of Margarethe Drenss and Caspar Hedio three weeks before, which gossiping tongues were now spreading about, "so they thought it perhaps better to send for a good friend of the house, before whom they could say their vows." Several were asked, and Claus Kniebis, who was sitting at dinner, agreed to come, though he wasn't told why he was wanted. That he learned only at Dr. Rot's house, and "they proposed to me that, since they were already betrothed, to unite them in marriage publicly. Which I at first refused, protesting that some one else should do that, as I was not a priest."[114] They all persisted, however, so Kniebis

> talked to the mother and her daughter (whom I hadn't known before), shook hands with them and greeted them. Then I asked the daughter and Dr. Caspar separately whether each desired to wed the other. And after each said, "yes", I united them in marriage and wished them much happiness, peace, and grace.[115]

After the wedding dinner, mother, newlyweds, "and some others" begged Kniebis and Rot "to go to Augustin Drenss, their son, brother, and brother-in-law, and asked him in a most friendly way to give his consent to the marriage, which he had not approved."[116] Next day they did so, taking three others who were "our dear and good friends and kinsmen".[117]

---

[112] "Documents", no. 2.

[113] "Documents", no. 3.

[114] "Documents", no. 3.

[115] "Documents", no. 3.

[116] "Documents", no. 3. The mention of Drenss as "brother-in-law" does not mean that Kniebis' wife, Ottilia Rot, was present, for among those who went to get Augustin's consent was Mathis Rot, who may well have been brother to Ottilia, Aurelia, and Michael Rot.

[117] They took with them Drenss' kinsman, Jacob Drenss, and Lorentz Graff († 8/9 July 1553), XVer from Drenss' own Gardeners' Guild and described as Kniebis' "vetter". "Documents", no. 3. On Graff, see Brady, *Ruling Class*, 316.

Augustin's reply was curt and simple: he would go after Dr. Hedio, find him, and strangle him. Kniebis, fearing the worst, commanded Augustin "in the name of the Senate" to keep the peace, an act which Drenss later denounced as an attempt to exploit the ammeister's office for personal advantage.

Dr. Hedio, the bridegroom, also replied to Augustin Drenss' charges, mainly, he said, "because I must be unimpeded in my office, to which God has called me, for the advancement of his honor and of the salvation of many souls."[118] The marriage occurred, he asserted, "with the knowledge, will, and approval of the honorable Agnes Drenss, her mother and my dear mother-in-law." He confirmed the betrothal and the details of the wedding three weeks later, as related by Claus Kniebis, whose intervention with Augustin Drenss he justified. As for the allegation that clergymen may not marry, Hedio thought it known to everyone now,

> that the Lord God, who stands above all laws and all kings of the earth, never forbade marriage to anyone, but on many occasions approved it. But about five hundred years this divine ordinance was abolished through the arbitrariness and violence of Pope Gregory VII, who acted tyrannically and against God's law. This led to the ruin of [clerical] behavior, which can be accepted and approved by no Christian ruler who regards Christ as Lord set above all human legislators.[119]

The Word of God, he warned in the spirit of the glory days of the reformation movement,

> which abides eternally, through which were created heaven and earth, not only shatters the canon law but also dashes to the ground the whole world, Hell, and the Devil — indeed all who undertake anything against God's will.

Hedio then tempered this outburst with another defense of his right to marry, and then he ended his response.

Much the most interesting of the three responses to Augustin's charges came from his mother, for from Agnes Drenss we learn enough about the dynamics of will and interest to make sense of the story. Dr. Hedio, she affirmed, "courted my dear daughter, Margarethe, as a pious, upright gentleman ought to do."[120] He made his suit known to mother, daughter, son, and friends, to which Augustin had replied that "concerning the marriage, whatever pleased me and my daughter, would please him as well." As soon, however, as Augustin learned that the women were inclined to accept Hedio's suit, he "acted improperly through words and gestures." She attributed that to the "bad lads" whose company Augustin kept, "who oppose all that fosters God's Word and Christian uprightness, for, under-

---

[118] "Documents", no. 4.
[119] "Documents", no. 5.
[120] "Documents", no. 5.

standably enough, they hate the gospel." She hoped that sound preaching would soften her son's heart and make him recognize "that holy matrimony is permitted and even recommended by God to everyone, and that just because the clergy have been forbidden to marry, scandal and vice have flourished and flourish still."[121] The duty, however, of every good Christian to help see that "the divine, holy institution of marriage should drive out the improper, shameless way of life of some clergyman", was lost on Augustin.

Agnes was moved to her decision, she said, "by the daily, clear preaching of the gospel in this city of Strasbourg, which would not be allowed by Your Graces, or attended by so many respectable citizens, were it not truly divine and Christian."[122] The decision to accept Hedio's suit, therefore, was made by Agnes, for her daughter "while she was in my care she always obeyed my will."[123] Fortified by the advice of "quite a few of my relations, friends, and chums, all honorable and pious folk", Agnes Drenss decided "that this marriage will be pleasing to God and beneficial and useful to my dear daughter, and will in no way be shameful to my son", providing he followed good rather than evil counsellors.

Agnes' decision, we learn, lay behind her visit, Margarethe in tow, to Dr. Rot's house on St. George's Day, which she made without notifying the doctor. Upon finding Hedio there, Agnes "spoke with him about the gossip, and we two decided that, ... with my daughter's consent, which she had already given him, to arrange the wedding now in order to stop the gossip."[124] Now she asked their host to send for the ammeister to preside over the wedding. Like Hedio, Agnes Drenss was careful to say that Kniebis knew nothing of the matter until he arrived. The ammeister, "since our request was reasonable and in accordance with godly law, could not refuse", and he united them in marriage, wished them well, and stayed for the wedding dinner — having missed his own. There were no "smooth words", as Augustin alleged, nor any coercion, nor yet any pressure from Dr. Rot.

It was not the gospel alone, as we learn from Agnes Drenss, that made her and Margarethe so receptive to Hedio's suit. The daughter, she asserted, "is mine and not my son's, and we told him that after he had turned away so many previous suitors, he was rejecting this one purely because of his unbelief [unglauben] and the counsels of evil folk." In fact, "he cannot forbid us anything which we have not put in his power, so I think we have committed no grave sin." They did not consult Margarethe's guardian, true, but "we think we were not obliged to do so, having so many good relations and friends whose advice we followed." The long and the short of it was, "sooner or later, it had to happen."

---

[121] "Documents", no. 5.

[122] "Documents", no. 5.

[123] "Documents", no. 5.

[124] "Documents", no. 5.

Against this battery of responses, poor Augustin Drenss had few weapons left. Probably he recognized that as the magistrates had decided to protect other married priests, they would not make an exception of their cathedral preacher, especially if they had to injure an ammeister in order to do so. Drenss appealed to their belief that women, being weak, can easily be exploited, for anyone could see, he alleged in his final statement, that just as his mother "was used in the original affair, so is she further manipulated in this one, for if Dr. Caspar's response and those of my mother and others are compared, one can easily tell that they are all arrows from the same quiver."[125] The whole matter showed very clearly, "how the new Evangelical teaching has the aim to bring contention and division between father, mother, and children." Although he professed his willingness "to acknowledge and hold her as mother all my life, despite this new doctrine", he blamed Agnes for arranging this wedding in the absence of the guardian and the family's friends.[126] It was simply not true, Augustin said, "that I would approve no man for my sister." He'd found several good prospects for her, "but she would take only this one [i.e., Hedio]."[127]

The game was up, and Augustin Drenss knew it. He closed his second statement with a bitter comment on the illegality of what had happened.

> That priests and monks should once more be allowed to marry, is against both papal and imperial law. Nor, according to Your Graces' ancient customs and the usage of Christendom for many centuries, may the child of a priest, legitimate or illegitimate, inherit.

With this final shot, Drenss withdrew his complaint.[128]

The story behind Drenss vs. Hedio is less a tale of the reformation movement at Strasbourg than one of the Drenss family and the impingement of the reform on their relations. The movement bitterly split families, and though many of them later patched over their differences, as the Drenss family was to do, others never did.[129] The movement's point of entry into

---

[125] "Documents", no. 6.

[126] "Documents", no. 6.

[127] "Documents", no. 6: "dann ich gearbeit das sie den schaffner zu Sant Catharina oder Vältin des Schultheÿssen sun von Wangen zu der ee nemen."

[128] *Annales de Sébastien Brant*, no. 4521: "Hat Drens endlich revocirt."

[129] This was true, for example, of the family of Franz Frosch (1490-1540), a lawyer from Nuremberg who served as city attorney of Strasbourg from 1533 until his death. Three years later, his sister, Gertrud, came from Nuremberg to announce that in a codicil to his will her brother had stipulated that none of his property should go to his two brothers-in-law, who were members of religious houses. AMS, KS 48/I, fols. 61^v-62^r. These will have been members of the Scher von Schwarzenburg family, from which Frosch's wife, Felicitas, came. Jacob Bernays, "Zur Biographie Johann Winthers von Andernach", *Zeitschrift für die Geschichte des Oberrheins* 60 (1901): 30, 33, 35-38. On Frosch, see Ficker and Winckelmann, *Handschriftenproben*, 1: 23; Hans Winterberg, *Die Schüler von Ulrich Zasius*, Veröffentlichungen der Kommission

this story is Agnes Drenss, the story's key figure, whose energy and decision brought the entire affair to a head. She wanted her daughter, Margarethe, properly settled, while her son, Augustin, turned away suitors, either because he didn't want to pay her dowry or because he simply opposed his mother's authority over Margarethe. Perhaps he changed his mind about Hedio's suit — Agnes says that he originally did not oppose it — because of his mother's enthusiasm for preaching that conveniently attacked the rule of mandatory clerical celibacy. Marriage of priests, after all, had come to Strasbourg only half a year earlier, when on 18 October 1523 Anton Firn (†1545) announced his marriage, and on 3 December the pastor of the cathedral parish, Mathis Zell (1477-1548) publicly married a local woman, Katherine Schütz (1497/98-1562).[130] The magistrates vacillated well into the new year, though they continued to interpose themselves between bishop and priests even after the citation on 24 January of the priests to Saverne for disciplinary action. The bishop's letter of excommunication of married priests was published at Strasbourg on 3 April, but on 18 March the magistrates had taken the decisive step to block any further prosecution. This affair, which aroused great interest and partisanship at Strasbourg, was well advanced before the end of 1523, when Caspar Hedio arrived from Mainz to assume the cathedral pulpit. And at least five weeks before his wedding day (23 April), a Strasbourgeoise could marry a priest at Strasbourg with the assurance that her husband would not lose his benefice. And Dr. Michael Rot must have invited Margarethe Drenss and her mother to visit him just after the Senate & XXI had decided to block episcopal prosecutions of married priests.

This chain of events liberated Agnes Drenss from her son's will, or whims, and emboldened her to push forward the match between Margarethe and her betrothed. Not that this action was out of character, for her statement shows her to have been the real head of the Drenss household and to have had a very firm, untroubled conscience about what she had done. So much so that her son's allegation about her manipulation by Hedio, Kniebis, and Rot — women are weak, after all — was almost certainly false.

Augustin Drenss' motives are more difficult to construe, for though he insists on enforcement of the law and makes clear his dislike for "the new doctrine", his two statements contains very little in the way of positive comments on religion. Perhaps he wished to be saved Margarethe's dowry, perhaps he simply played the tyrant, though, if so, by his mother's account he did so desultorily. What is certain is that he saw this marriage as just another case of clerical misbehavior, another priest invading the sanctity of a burgher's home to get at his women. He wanted, ironically enough, what

---

für geschichtliche Landeskunde in Baden-Württemberg, series B, 18 (Stuttgart, 1961), 38-39.

[130] The most detailed account of these events and the bishop's magistrates' reactions is in Stafford, *Domesticating the Clergy*, 151-65.

the Protestant reformers wanted, a chaste, disciplined clergy, though he rejected their solution, clerical marriage.

Claus Kniebis' role in Drenss vs. Hedio is more difficult to judge. Augustin Drenss' complaint cannot have put him in much danger, given the recent movement of the Senate & XXI against the bishop, though it clearly angered him, especially the charge that he had misused his ammeistership in a private matter. Kniebis' role in the wedding nonetheless entered that zone of lawlessness which lay between the local regime's repudiation of episcopal jurisdiction over the clergy and marriage and its own' assumption of jurisdiction over marriage.[131] The transition hardly affected official views on what made a valid marriage, namely, the exchange of vows (*sponsalia*) in the absence of coercion or impediments.[132] According to the ritual ordinance then formally still in effect in the diocese of Strasbourg, this was supposed to take place outside the church, usually on the steps, to be followed by a Mass and blessing of the union in the church.[133] The Protestant marriage services, drafted by Diebold Schwarz (1485-1561) in 1524 and Martin Bucer in 1525, moved the central act into the church, as vows were now to be exchanged in church, before a clergyman, and as part of a wedding service.[134] In this, as in most other things pertaining to marriage, the Protestants made few radical changes.[135] According to canon

---

[131] François Wendel, *La mariage à Strasbourg à l'époque de la Réforme 1520-1692*, Collection d'études sur l'histoire du droit et des institutions de l'Alsace 4 (Strasbourg, 1928), 97-118. On this question in general, see Lyndal Roper, "'Going to Church and Street': Weddings in Reformation Augsburg", *PaP* 106 (February 1985): 62-101, here at 64-67, with full references; and id., *Holy Household*, 132-64.

[132] See Thomas M. Safley, "Civic Morality and the Domestic Economy", in *The German People and the Reformation*, ed. R. Hsia, 173-90, here at 175, for references.

[133] Wendel, *La mariage*, 214-19, prints the passages from this book and from Diebolt Schwarz's ritual. On the changes in the conception and liturgy of marriage, see René Bornert, *La réforme protestante du culte à Strasbourg au XVIe siècle (1523-1598): Approche sociologique et interprétation théologique*, SMRT 28 (Leiden, 1981), 553-69. On Diebold Schwarz, a local man, see Ficker and Winckelmann, *Handschriftenproben*, 2: 61.

[134] Bornert, *La réforme protestante du culte*, 561: "Le mariage est célébré à l'église."

[135] See Thomas M. Safley, *Let No Man Put Asunder: The Control of Marriage in the German Southwest, a Comparative Study, 1550-1600* (Kirksville, Mo., 1984); id., "Civic Morality and the Domestic Economy", 173-90. The researches of Safley and Lyndal Roper do not bear out the contention that the Protestant reformation transformed marriage. See, for this view, Steven Ozment, *When Fathers Ruled: Family Life in Reformation Europe* (Cambridge, Mass., 1983). Indeed, as Lyndal Roper has written, "the Protestant view of marriage approximated more closely to German townspeople's traditional notions of how a marriage was made" than the Catholic sacramental theory of marriage did. Roper, "'Going to Church and Street'", 65.

law, the only impediment to the validity of the Drenss-Hedio marriage was Hedio's status as a priest. The wedding's private setting nonetheless violated deep sensibilities of German townsfolk, who held that publicity, "going to church and street", contributed in an important way to a completed marriage.[136]

The rancor aroused by this affair seems to have faded away within a few years. Augustin Drenss converted to the new religion by 1529, when he was churchwarden (*Kirchenpfleger*) at St. Aurelia's, which was Bucer's first parish and a font of Strasbourg's reformation. Drenss entered the Senate from the Gardeners' Guild in 1536 and the privy council of the XV in 1542.[137] The restoration of peace between him and Margarethe is suggested by the fact that two of her eight children were boys named "Augustin", each whom died at the age of five.[138] She lived to be very old, and in her widowhood her guardian, prescribed by Strasbourg's law, was Nicolaus Hugo Kniebis, Claus' son.[139]

V

Taken together, the sources presented above yield some insights into the disintegration and reintegration of clerical power in one local setting. They show, for one thing, that the process went much deeper than the legal and political integration of the clergy — the priests became citizens and members of guilds — which is the only aspect of clerical integration that has been well studied.[140] Johann Geiler, who sensed the disintegration on all sides, also felt that the root of anticlericalism lay in the breakdown of the grand system of material and spiritual exchange that underlay universal church's existence as a grand community of sacramental grace and prayer. His explanation for the decay was the laity's perception that "the priests have too much", but his sole remedy, short of expropriation, was that the clergy must be urged to moderation and to more faithful devotion to service.

---

[136] Roper, "'Going to Church and Street'", 66-67. The campaign against clandestine marriage characterized all marriage legislation of the time. See Safley, "Civic Morality and the Domestic Economy", 175-76.

[137] AMS, KS 18, fol. 218ʳ, dated 26 April 1529, which mentions him as one of the "verordnete pfleger des wercks zu St. Aurelien". See Jean Rott, "Die 'Gartner', der Rat und das Thomaskapitel", in Jean Rott, *Investigationes Historicae*, 2: 177-80.

[138] Augustin in 1537 and Augustin Chrysostomus in 1542. Six of these children died before age fifteen. Wilhelm Horning, *Beiträge zur Kirchengeschichte des Elsasses vom 16.-18. Jahrhundert*, 7 vols. (Strasbourg, 1881-87), 7: 1-3.

[139] AMS, V 14/112 (1571).

[140] Bernd Moeller, "Kleriker als Bürger", in *Festschrift für Hermann Heimpel zum 70. Geburtstag zum 19. September 1971*, edited by the Max-Planck-Institut für Geschichte, 3 vols. (Göttingen, 1971-72), 2: 195-224; id., *Pfarrer als Bürger* (Göttingen, 1972).

His emphasis on communal service — bishop and priests are servants of the community — probably stood in tension with his sacramental conception of the common good, for it is clear from his anticipation of listeners' questions that stronger skepticism attached to the universal than to the local exchange of spiritual and material goods between clergy and laity. This, in turn, suggests that domestication, cutting the local church off from the greater church, might be the most effective path to integration. For this reason, it is surely correct to identify (with Scribner) the clergy's sacral power as the critical aspect of their power, and to say that the reformers' attack on the sacramental notion of the church made possible a provisional reintegration of the clergy through a whole series of measures.[141] These measures included suppression of the *privilegium fori* and spiritual jurisdiction, expropriation, abolition of mandatory celibacy, mandatory clerical citizenship, dissolution of the convents, and a great reduction in the numbers of clergy. Together they constituted perhaps the principal social change wrought by the Protestant reformation in the Holy Roman Empire, the magnitude of which is undiminished by our recognition that, after a decent interval, a new clericalism succeeded the old.[142]

The austere Geiler may well have underestimated, on the other hand, the importance of the clergy's sexual power and the burgher's longing to have it controlled. Both the facts and the obvious remedy had long been recognized, for example, by the anonymous priest who wrote in the late 1430s *The Reformation of the Emperor Sigismund*:

> It may be a good thing for a man to keep himself pure, but observe the wickedness now going on in the Church! Many priests have lost their livings because of women. Or they are secret sodomites. All the hatred existing between priests and laymen is due to this. In sum: Secular priests ought to be allowed to marry. In marriage they will live more piously and honorably, and the friction between them and the laity will disappear.[143]

---

[141] Scribner, "Anticlericalism", 249: "Sacred power can be taken as a measure of all other clerical pretensions, and can be seen as the ultimate fountain of all kinds of anticlericalism. ... What seems to have aroused most lay anger was three things: clerical claims to exercise a monopoly of sacred power; their demand that this be provided only in return for payment; and their readiness to deny their priestly services, often for light causes and often because of the inability of layfolk to pay." Much the same point — desacralization as the condition for radical change — is made on a grander scale by Carlos M. N. Eire, *War Against the Idols: The Reformation of Worship from Erasmus to Calvin* (Cambridge, 1986).

[142] Scribner, "Anticlericalism", 254-56.

[143] "The Reformation of the Emperor Sigismund", trans. Gerald Strauss in *Manifestations of Discontent in Germany on the Eve of the Reformation* (Bloomington, 1971), 14-15.

Luther and the other Protestant reformers accepted this diagnosis and its remedy, which they supplied with a theological justification.[144] They thus canonized in word and deed one traditional diagnosis of and remedy for anticlericalism, but it was not Geiler's diagnosis, nor his remedy. In this respect, the Strasbourg Protestants' respect for Johann Geiler rested on a very limited kinship between his imagined reform and their accomplished one. The Protestants shared Geiler's ideal of the clergy devoted to communal service but not his view of the clergy's role in the church as a community of sacramental grace and prayer. It was Luther, not Geiler, who opened the path to integration of the clergy through desacralizing them and their social role, and he thereby brought down the walls against reform that Geiler had attacked in vain. Luther's attack on this sacramental view of the church may well have constituted his most powerful contribution to the urban reformation; it was certainly his major contribution to overcoming late medieval anticlericalism.

As Geiler had hardly anticipated the coming desacralization of the clergy, he certainly could not have foreseen its effects on the regular clergy, men and women. The story of Margarethe Kniebis cannot be explained as a lay reaction to clerical abuses, for her father removed her from one of the strictest religious communities at Strasbourg, into which he had brought her some years before. Only Claus Kniebis' changed sensibilities explain this act, and the same may well be true of other removals, such as that of Clara Sturm. Here, again, the events must be seen in the light of the Protestant reformers' attacks on the religious orders in general and the women's houses in particular. Their attack succeeded in part, because their theology empowered the burghers' deep views about the proper place of women. As Luther put it in 1523, "a woman is not created to be a virgin, but to conceive and bear children."[145] He and the other reformers did not cause men to remove their kinswomen from convents so much as they legitimized action based on the burgher's sensibilities about relations between the genders.[146] Such sensibilities were by no means universal among the burghers, and particularly not among the upper class, whose daughters had long populated the urban convents. During the struggle over the house of the Poor Clares at Nuremberg, for example, male patricians reacted in different ways to pressure to remove their kinswomen from the convent. The patrician Christoph Kress (1484-1535), for example, bluntly told his fellow magistrates what he thought: "I have told my sister that if one cowl is not enough for her, she may wear three, one on top of other. And then we'll see who

---

[144] Ozment, *When Fathers Ruled*, 3-9.

[145] Quoted in Ozment, *When Fathers Ruled*, 17, from Martin Luther, *Ursach und anttwort das iungkfawen kloster gottlich verlassen mugen* (Wittenberg, 1523).

[146] The story thus confirms Roper's judgment that Protestant reformers brought the understanding of marriage, and of all matters of gender, closer to the burghers' own views. Roper, "'Going to Church and Street'", 65-70.

will try to forbid it or to take them away from her."[147] Next day, however, male members of the Ebner, Nützel, Tetzel, and Fürer families arrived at St. Clara's to fetch their daughters home. Some women, like Margarethe Kniebis, had to be forced to leave, but others were glad to go, sometimes — as with Felicitas Peutinger, who left St. Katherine's at Augsburg — against parental wishes.[148]

It has been argued that in this "liberation of women from cloisters", the Protestant reformers "were particularly concerned ... to free nuns from their cloisters, and allow them to rejoin society", because of the "reformers' own recent appreciation of the joys of marriage."[149] Perhaps, but our judgment ought to pay attention both to the views of the women who were subject to such "liberation" and to the fact that they were being "liberated" from one type of authority into the hands of another, the male authority of fathers, brothers, guardians, and husbands. This aspect is neatly expressed by Prioress Ursula von Mörßmünster's formula of re-commendation — "I give her from my hand to your hand, from my care to your care" — which laicized Margarethe Kniebis and reintegrated her into communal life by passing her back from a woman's authority to that of a man. The world of the burghers, especially Protestant burghers, had no place for female authority, even when women did not altogether lack power.[150]

This picture of the mutual reinforcement of the urban reformation, clerical integration, and the control of women is contradicted, but only apparently, by the story of Drenss vs. Hedio. One has only to recognize the connection between celibacy and the sacral power of the clergy, both for men and for women, in order to appreciate how their desacralization through the reformers made possible the control of their sexuality as part of their integration. Agnes Drenss and her son, Augustin, did not disagree about the

---

[147] Related in *Die "Denkwürdigkeiten" der Caritas Pirckheimer (as den Jahren 1524-1528)*, ed. Josef Pfanner, Caritas Pirckheimer Quellensammlung, vol. 2 (Landshut, 1962), 75 line 38-76 line 1. These men came from the political cream of Nuremberg's oligarchy. See Phillip N. Bebb, "Humanism and the Reformation: The Nürnberg *Sodalitas* Revisted", *The Process of Change in Early Modern Europe*, ed. P. Bebb and S. Marshall, 59-79, here at 65. On Kress, see Jonathan W. Zophy, "Christoph Kress, Nürnberg's Foremost Reformation Diplomat" (Ph.D. diss., Ohio State University, 1972).

[148] Roper, *Holy Household*, 210.

[149] Ozment, *When Fathers Ruled*, 9, 12-13; the first phrase quoted is a subhead in a chapter entitled, "In Defense of Marriage", which contains an eloquent defense of the Protestant reformers.

[150] I do not mean only that former monks could remain clergy and former nuns could not, though this is true (see Wiesner, "Nuns, Wives, and Mothers", 10). Rather, I mean the exclusively male character of civic language and political sensibility, on which see Lyndal Roper, "'The common man', 'the common good', 'common women': Gender and Meaning in the German Reformation Commune", *Social History* 12 (1987): 1-21, here at 2-5.

desirability of having a chaste clergy, only about how that goal was to be achieved. He called on the regime to enforce the canon, Imperial, and local laws; she referred to the new gospel as providing a remedy, marriage of the clergy, for the evil of which they both disapproved. They agreed on this, at least in principle, for in practice personal interests — the desires respectively to marry off the daughter and to save the dowry — may have weighed heavily with both mother and son. The actions of Agnes Drenss show that in the absence of a father, authority over dependent women could devolve on the mother rather than on the son, not only in practice — as we should expect — but also in the eyes of the magistrates. The case also illustrates the intertwining of private with public affairs, for though born of a familial dispute, Drenss vs. Hedio was also highly political, both because it involved the conflict over religion which then occupied the city, and because of an ammeister's involvement.[151] Agnes Drenss had her way against her son, Caspar Hedio got his bride, and only in the irregular form of the wedding does the story bear the stamp of the transition period when the gospel shattered laws. Otherwise, this story and its outcome fit the broad pattern of the urban reformation, in which the desacralization of the church opened the way to a settlement of the question of reform, which had so bedeviled Johann Geiler. It enabled the integration of the clergy into the commune through their conformity to the only social ideal — the patriarchal household — for which the burghers had thoroughgoing respect. With different results, naturally, for men and for women.

Do these materials and stories shed any light on the conclusions framed by Francis Rapp? Perhaps. For one thing, they suggest that the important changes of the pre-reformation had less to do with clerical behavior than with lay standards of behavior for the clergy, which were based on their standards for themselves. They were becoming intolerant not just of a clergy that misbehaved but of one that lived differently. If anything, the holiest nuns and the most austere priests threatened their own ideals more deeply than did dissolute nuns and whoring priests, for the success of a celibate way of life relativized and therefore devalued, by its very success, their own ideal of the harmonious and hierarchical household. To burghers who were ever more used to running their own affairs and having their own way, the very existence of wayward clergy eased the moral pressure placed on their own ideal way of life by the existence of another, stricter, harder way to salvation. This sensibility — relief at the clergy's imperfections — lies behind much of the anticlerical humor of the pre-reformation era. A wayward clergyman might arouse anger, but not spiritual intimidation. The reformation made such humor obsolete, at least in principle at Strasbourg and other reformed cities, as an old and extremely varied way of life was

---

[151] The dichotomy of public and private does not adequately express the consistent differences between male and female lives, at least not in early modern Europe. See ibid., 21; Wiesner, "Nuns, Wives, and Mothers", 9.

suppressed. With it went the old jokes, such as one composed by the young Peter Schott (1460-90), Jacob Sturm's great-uncle, who as a schoolboy at Sélestat is said to have penned these lines:

> These three things you should never let into your home:
> An old ape, a young priest, or wild bears.[152]

---

[152] "Alt aff, jung pfaff, dazu wilde Bären / Soll niemand in sein Haus begehren." Geiler, *Das Buoch Arbore humana* (Strasbourg, 1521), 91. The couplet is also quoted in *Works of Peter Schott (1460-1490)*, ed. Murray A. Cowie and Marian L. Cowie, 2 vols., University of North Carolina Studies in the Germanic Languages and Literatures 41, 71 (Chapel Hill, 1963-71), 1: 266, no. 234; and Schmidt, *Histoire littéraire*, 2: 4 note 7. On Schott, see *Works of Peter Schott*, 2: xxii-xxxi; Schmidt, *Histoire littéraire*, 2: 2-35.

DOCUMENTS ON COMMUNALISM
AND THE CONTROL OF WOMEN AT STRASBOURG
IN THE AGE OF THE REFORMATION

Edited by
KATHERINE G. BRADY
Berkeley, California
and
THOMAS A. BRADY, JR.
University of California, Berkeley

The following six documents support the study, "'You Hate us Priests': Anticlericalism, Communalism, and the Control of Women at Strasbourg in the Age of the Reformation", by Thomas A. Brady, Jr. They are edited according to the following guidelines.

– Only initial letters of sentences and proper nouns are capitalized; all other words begin in lower case.

– Punctuation follows the rules for modern German, and long sentences are often broken into shorter ones.

– All abbreviations are resolved.

– Except for verbs, words with prefix "zu" are normally put together.

– The distinctions between vowel "i" and consonant "j" and between vowel "u" and consonant "v" and "w" have been normalized.

– The letters "f" and "v" are interchangeable.

For analysis of the documents and information on the persons mentioned in them, readers are referred to the study they accompany. The editors express their gratitude to Dr. Jean-Yves Mariotte, Director of the Archives de la Ville de Strasbourg, for his kind assistance.

DOCUMENT NO. 1

Claus Kniebis removes his daughter, Margarethe, from the
Convent of St. Nicolaus-in-Undis,
Strasbourg, 1522

SOURCE: Archives Municipales de Strasbourg, II 7/20, fols. 26ʳ-29bisᵛ.
HAND: Ursula von Mörßmünster, prioress of St. Nicolaus-in-Undis.[1]

[fol. 27ʳ] Anno xvᶜ xxii uff den xᵐ ritter dag[2] ist Herr Claus Kniebis[3] bei
uns an der winden gewesen und bei siner dochter, Margreden,[4] die het in
frintlich gebetten, um gotts willen ir zu gönnen, das versuch jor an zu legen,
si sige im xiiii jor. Das hat er ir abgeslagen, geseit, wann si xvi oder xvii jor
alt werde, und nit e, si es echter zu der selben zit nach sin will oder
gutbeduncken. Er welle si aber ain zit lang vor in sinen huß in der welt
versächen und probieren. Het si sich vast übel gehebt, in ernstlich do fur
gebetten, zu im geseit zu vil molen, si well slechtlich nit hinuß, well nit in
der welt sin. Werde er si aber hinuß zwingen, welle si vor got entschuldiget
sin, müß dennocht ir will, nimmer me werden in der welt zu sin, und
derglichen vil und me wort. Do ist der vater erzürnt warden uber unß und
die dochter, het geseit, well si nit hinuß, so müß si hinuß. Si soll hinuß gon,
glich in ein tufel namen. Het si geseit, in dem namen well si nit hinuß, si
well in gottes namen, und umb gotts willen hin sin, in der meinung, er si
öch harin geben hab, und mit siner eigen hant selbs zu opfer gefürt. Und het
in aber frintlich gebetten, umb gotts willen er soll si hinlossen, und wir öch.
Und hab ich im zu geseit, ich woll im die dochter lossen still ston mit dem
versuch jor, bis si xiiii jar alt si. Do zwischen werden unser obren[5] komen,
will ich im sin meinung sagen, will er zu losse, si so lang bitz xvii jar
lossen gon, well ich gehorsam sin. Will er aber einanders, will ich aber
gehorsam sin und in das selb öch lossen wissen. Disse red geschach vor
dem, das er so erzürnt was, und [er] nam das an. Aber zu lest, do er also
erzürnt was, swür er, er wolt die dochter in zweien dagen holen. Es müst
also sin, und slechtlich nit anders. Bei dissen ist zu gegen geweß Her Hug
Meiger,[6] vicarius der hohen stift.

---

[1] The hand is an old-fashioned, late fifteenth-century hand, perhaps because of the
prioress' age, or perhaps because the nuns preserved an older style of writing.

[2] Ten Thousand Knights' Day, 22 June 1522.

[3] Ammeister Claus Kniebis (1479-1552).

[4] Margarethe, daughter of Claus Kniebis.

[5] I.e., the Dominican provincial.

[6] Hug Meyer, priest and vicar in the cathedral chapter, brother to Claus Kniebis'
mother.

Uff den abend des dags der vergangnen geschicht, schreib ich der frowen[7] ein brieflin, bat si demüticlich, ein getruwe mittlerin zu sin zwischen dem zorn des vaters, der dochter, und unser.

Do noch am dritten dag[8] hab ich dem herrn selbs geschriben, und die dochter auch, in demüticlich um gotts willen gebetten um verzühung, sinen zorn abzulossen und unser guten frint zu sin. Het er unß entboten, er wolle unß dun, alles das uns lieb ist. Er well aber slechtlich die dochter hinuß haben.

Uff dise wort ist die dochter genug betrüpt und ellend, von der x^m ritter dag untz uff Martini[9] het [sie] alledag mit engsten und schrecken gewartet, wenn er si holen welle. Denn er ir noch unß do zwischen chein ander antwort geben het, den i mol, iii oder iiii mol zwischen der zit unß entboten bei unsern schafner, er si noch des willens, sin dochter hinuß zu nemen, er well si nit bei unß haben. Also ist das kint ellend gangen, sich verjomert und betrübt, das si zusehenlich an iren lib und kreften abgenomen hett, das ich es jriencie[10] halb nin hab mögen sehen noch liden. Ist er öch do zwischen nie zu unß kommen haruß, das ichs hot mögen mit im reden.

Also hab ich siner frowen der dochter mutter uff zinstag S. Martins dag einen brief geschriben, wie die dochter sich verellende und betrüpt si, an iren lib abnemen, [und] si geboten, den herrn frintlich zu bitten, das er der dochter zu friden helf, wie den die copi des briefs lutet also gezeicht.[11] Also ist Herr Claus Kniebis dem schriben noch mit dem alten herrn, Herr Hug Maiger, kommen uff Fritag noch Martini,[12] het gesait, er hab in dem ...[13]

[fol. 27^v blank]

[fol. 28^r] Min liebs kint, do stat din vater. Der hat dich geben in dis closter, in meinung zu sin der will, das gevallen im die ere gottes und diner selen seliklich. In der selben guten meinung hant wir dich um gotts willen angenommen, und dich nun im fünften jor nit mit cleiner arbeit erzogen und gelert. Jetzt ist eß nimm der will dins vaters, das du solt bei unß sin, und will dich bei im duß haben. Und het unß getröwen, wo wir dich [nit] im gutwilliclich geben, well er etwas zu richt, das wir dich im müssen geben. Des tröwes und gewalts wollent wir nit warten sin, darumb wollent und müssen wir dich im geben. Ich wolt dich aber lieber sehen in ein grab legen, denn das ich dich müß sehen in die welt gon. So er dich aber je haben will, so gib ich dich uß miner hant in sin hant, uß miner sorg in sin sorge. Wir

---

[7] Ottilia Rot, sister to Dr. Michael Rot.

[8] 25 June 1522.

[9] St. Martin's Day, 11 November 1522.

[10] iwwerenzi = übrig, übereinzig. Charles Schmidt, *Wörterbuch der Straßburger Mundart* (Strasbourg, 1896), 54.

[11] Here a flower is drawn.

[12] 14 November 1522.

[13] The remainder of this paragraph is missing.

stossent dich nit uß und wellent dich öch unußgestossen haben, denn du hests nit verschuldet. Du waist, das dich der convent lieb und wert gehebt het, und noch. Ich bin dir vil hert gemess, das hab ich dir im besten gedon. Ich hab dich nit wellen betrügen oder verfüren, das ich dir zum ersten zäigte das süß, und so du gebunden wurdest, das bitter. Ich hab dir von erst wollen zäigen das bitter, ob es dich rüwen wolt. Das es dich ruwete, öb du gebunden wurdest, darumb solt du mir es nit fur übel. Und gesegne und behüt dich got, liebs kint. Und ich bitt dich, hab got alwegen vor ögen, gedenck die kürtze diß lebens, wie alle ding zergont als der röuch. Das end aller ding, so uff erden sint, ist der bitter dot. Der kant und blibt nit uß. Bedenck den spruch, daß wiß manns, do er spricht, mensch gedenck diner lesten stend, so gesindestu niemer. Schrib in din hertz die vier lesten ding, der wir warten sint, die unfelich kommen, und nit ußbliben, das ist der dot, das lest streng urteil gottes, die ewige fröid. Die gab der Her bereit hett, denen die in lieb haben, und die ewige verdampnuß, die denen bereit ist, die sich von got abwenden.

Das ist uwe dochter, die gib ich uch uß miner hant in uwer hant, uß miner sorg in uwer sorg. Nun welle got, das ir si wol versorgen. Ich gib uch ein gut, fromm, unschuldig kint. Got woll, das ir eß also behalten, und wo ir harnoch anders begegnen wurd, wellen wir vor got und vor uch entschuldiget sein.

[fol. 28ᵛ blank]

[fol. 29ʳ] Uff Sonndag noch Presentacionis Marie, ist Sant Clemens dag,[14] het der Kniebis sin dochter uß dem closter gerissen. Im geholfen Michel Rot.[15]

Uff S. katherinen dag Anno xxii hat Jacob Spender[16] sin dochter, Jacobe, uß dem closter genommen.

[fol. 29bisᵛ] Diß ist wie Her Klaus Kniebis sin dochter uß unßren kloster mit gewalt genomen hatt und wie mutter Ursel von Morschminster zur selben zit priorin und öch der convent sich dorin gehalten haben.

---

[14] St. Clement's Day, 23 November 1523.
[15] Dr. med. Michael Rot, brother-in-law to Claus Kniebis.
[16] Jacob Spender († ca. 1525), patrician of Strasbourg and member of the XXI.

DOCUMENT NO. 2

Drenss vs. Hedio: Petition of Augustin Drenss
[14 May 1524]

SOURCE: Archives du Chapître de St.-Thomas, Strasbourg, 69/2, fols. 5^r-6^r.
HAND: Augustin Drenss.

[fol. 5^r] Strengen, edlen, erenvesten, ersamen, frumen, fursichtigen, wisen, gnödigen herren. Wie wol durch euer, meiner gnödigen herren, ordnung, artickel und altem herkhomen bei hochen penen und strafen verboten, das do niemas khainem vater sin khind wider sinen willen und im zu ruck zu usseren zu verenderen oder zu entziechen. Und welcher do funden wurdt dar zu sollichem hilf oder rat thon hett, der soll deß gestraft werden. In welchem fall wo das khind vaterloß wer, ein vogt von euch, minen gnödigen herren, im geben nach inhalt dis artickel fur ein vater geacht soll werden. Uber sollichen artickel gar unangesechen hat kurtzer verschiner ziten Doctor Caspar Hedion, predicant im munster, understanden und im furgenomen, Margret Thrensin, meins schwoster, heimlich und on wissen und wider willen eins vogt und minen, als irs elichen bruders, im zu elichen gmahel, als mich anlangt, understanden anzumassen. Und das durch sollich mittel, es hat Michael Rott, doctor der artznei, benante miner schwoster sampt ir mutter in sin huß zu tisch geladen und darzu heimlich on wißen der mutter und der dochter, als ich wisen mag gehabt, und verhalten bestimpten Doctor Caspar Hedion. Darzu ouch beruft, hernach worden Herr Clauß Kniebis alt ammeister ouch khommen, die do mit glatten worten die dochter und mutter beredt, das do etwas zusagens und der handschlag als die red offenlich beschehen soll sin und wie wol gemelt min mutter und schwöster sich mit zimlichen worten ab ziechen wellen, sagende, das inen sollichs nit hinder irem vogt bruder und fruntschaft gepuren welle. Aber gemelten personen min lieb mutter und schwester nit von handen laßen wellen, besunder gesagt, es werde khein mangel haben, gemelter Herr Claus Kniebis und Doctor Michel wellendt sollichs bei mir abtragen. Als ouch an anderen tag darnach si baidt mit dem schafner in der Ellenden Herberg zu mir khomen und mich mit glatten worten uberreden wollen, hab ich mich gegen inen hören lassen, das kheiniß wegs darzu gehellen welle, mit mer worten etc. Uff sollichs gemelter Kniebis [fol. 5^v] mir den friden gepoten. Ist nit euwer, meiner herren, ordnung, gemelter Hedion were dann zu gegen gewesen. Aber in abwesen einer parthi ist frömdt zuhoren on geheiße der oberkheit, ein burger dem anderen frid zubieten.[17] Und uber sollich alles ist gedachts min schwester in gemeltz Doctor Michels huß, welher doch khein eefrow in sinem huß haben ist,[18] muß ich und mein fruntschaft zu diser zit gott befelchen. Sollich alles ist geschehen uber das ich bei meinem schweher, Mathis Rotten, und ander gemelten Doctor Rott, Hedion und Kniebis dar zugepötten und bitten lassen. Ouch ich zu meiner mutter, schwester und anderen, do mir sollichs furkhemen, gesagt, min swester solle der pfaffen mießig ston und sunst einen erlichen frummen burger nemen, so wil ich mines gutzs ir hundert gulden zu irem eigenthum fursetzen. Und diewill aber der doctor geisthlich und sollich ee nit allein nit landtlöfig und bruchlich funden, ouch wider alle recht geisthlich und weltlich, dero si die Cristenheit dusent jar und noch lenger gebrucht hat, und ouch daruß mir und den meinerm nit kleiner nachteil, schandt und schmach erwachsen möcht, dann wo ein ordenliche geburende oberkheit der Cristenheit sollich handel nit nach lassen wurd sunder verbiete und kheins wegs gestatten, als zu erachten, geschehen werd. Dann je nit gloublich, das durch frevel furnemen ettlicher und der wenig bepstlich und keiserlich recht umgestossen und zuruck geworfen mag werden. Als dan wurd billich mein swester wie ein offne sunderin und metz geacht und gehalten. Verer, wo sie bei benantem doctor khind uberkhomen wurdt und die mutter oder großmutter mit tod abgeen solten, mochten solliche khindt verlassens gutz mit kheinem rechten erben sin, darum dann sie billich als uneelich geacht wurden, Welches alles, gnödigen herren, nit zu kleinem nachteil, schmach und schanden mir und den minen dienen möcht. Und diewill dann sollich vermeint ee durch benanten doctor und ander als obluwt wider euwer, meiner gnödigen herren, ordnung und alten herkhomen gehandlet und furgenomen ist und nach allen [fol. 6ʳ] rechten sollich ee nit sin khan und mag, bitt ich undertenigklich, euch meine genödigen herren, ir wolt mich und die minen als euer gnaden burger zu guten und gnaden bedencken, und mit oft benanten doctor verschaffen, das er von solchem sinem furnemen abstandt miner swester und minem, anders dann mit dem rechten mussig gan. Wo aber sollich je sin nit möcht, der zuversicht ich doch zu euch, meinen herren, bin, bitt ich euer gnad, ir wolt mir nit zu wider sin sunder bewilligung thun, das ich an anderen orten vor geburenden richtern und fur die sollich hendell gehören mit dem rechten ersuchen mög. Dann solt es je do hin khomen, das ein jedem pfaffen und munch zimmen und geburen wolt, on witer ungeltnuß einem frumen biderman und burger sine khindt oder verwanten wider wissen und willen zu betriegen und zu bescheissen, wer sollich schimpflich zu hören. Und was dar uß erwachsen möcht, khunnen ir, meine gnödigen herren, wol ermessen. Hierin ich dan unzweifelter hoffnung und zu versicht

---

[17] The practice of "geboter Friede" was an admonition to keep the peace, that is, refrain from violence, until a matter could be settled at law or by arbitration.

[18] Dr. Michael Rot later married. His widow, whose name is unknown, died in 1555.

bin, ir, meine gnödigen herren, werden mir als einem burger beraten und beholfen sin, damit mein beger als obluwt der billicheit und rechten nach stathaben möge. Oder aber wo sollichs nit kheiner parthi zu beladen, wil ich anderweg dem rechten und billicheit nach an orten und enden, da sich sollichs geburt, zu rechtvertigen nit underlassen, euwer gnad zum aller hochsten anrufende etc.

Euer gnödigen wißheit undertöniger burger

Augustinus Trenß, burger zu Straßburg etc.

[fols. 6ᵛ, 7ʳ⁻ᵛ blank]

DOCUMENT NO. 3

Drenss vs. Hedio:
Response of Dr. Michael Rot and Ammeister Claus Kniebis
[ca. 14 May 1524]

SOURCE: Archives du Chapître de St.-Thomas, Strasbourg, 69/3, fols. 8^r-9^v.
HAND: Claus Kniebis.

[fol. 8^r] Strengen, erenvesten, fursichtigen, ersamen und wisen gunstigen heren. Euer ersamen wißheit hat uff nest vergangen pfingst aben[19] verlesen horen, ein vermeinte supplication, so durch Augustin Trensen ingeben, darin er den wurdigen der heiligen gotlichen schriften hochgelerten lerer, Doctor Casparn Hedion, sin schwoger, schwerlich verunglimpftet und verclaget etc. Darzu den hochgelerten Doctor Micheln Rot, min schwogern, und mich, Clausen Kniebiß etc., als ob wir zu etwas gescheften, die unß nit geburten, und im zu nit kleiner schmach, nachteil und schanden reichten geholfen, und darzu mit glatten worten sin muter und schwester beredt. Und uber daß si sich mit zimlichen worten abziehen wollen, sollen wir si nit von handen lossen wollen etc, alles inhalt gemelter siner vermeinten, erdichten, unworhaftigen supplication etc. So dann ich als ein altammeister bei euch, min herrn, gesessen und sollichs verlesen horen, darin min schwoger und ich unser eren nit klein (so dem also were) geschmecht, hat mir gebürt, sollichs zu verantwurten. Und hab uff daß mol mich protestiert vor euer wißheit, die schmach schriften, wie sich gebürt zu siner zit zu rechtvertigen, als ich von wegen mins schwogers und min uff hüt aber protestiert haben will, [MARGIN: protestiert mich ouch wes hie anzeigt wurt, keiner ander meinung, dann unß zu verantwurten und die worheit als vil wir wissen, dar zu thun, do mit euwer wißheit erfar, mit was fugen der gegentheil suppliciert]. Und uff daß ich die obigen sin vermeint unworhaftig supplication mit der worheit, als vil die unß belangt, verantwurdte, hab ich die zit der selbingen abgeschriften begert, die mir von euch, min herrn, gutlich zu gelossen, die ich dann als bald minem schwoger, als dem, den si ouch zum hochsten belangt, angezeigt. Der hat si dem obigen herrn Doctor Casparn, als dem principal beclagten, ouch nit wollen verhalten, und anzeigt, sich dem nach wissen zu richten etc. Und uff daß ir, min herrn, der worheit bericht werden, so hat es die gestalt und ist ergangen, als harnach volget. Namlich, sagt Doctor Michel, min schwoger, das er uff den selben tag den obgemelten Doctor Casparn weder frow Anges Trensen noch Jungfrow Margred, ire dochter, keins geladen als von Augustin ußerthalb der worheit

---

[19] Pentecost Eve, 14 May 1524.

angezeigt. Aber si nit on, es si Doctor Caspar in sin, Doctor Michels, als in [fol. 8ᵛ] sines guten und lieben frinds und gönners, huß komen, und als gelerte lute von allerlei frintlich gesprech gehabt. Und als si ein gut wile bieinander gewesen, on aller menschen schühe oder forcht, nit heimlich [MARGIN: als Augustin sagt] verhalten, ist im on wissen genante frow Agnes Trensen und Jungfrow Margred, ir dochter, an daß thor komen anklopfende. Die er, Doctor Michel, als sin mumen²⁰ ingelossen und frintlich entpfangen, die do gesagt (als ouch wor ist), er, Doctor Michel, habe vor iiii wochen do vor ungeverlich si geladen, si sollen eins zu jme komen und sehen, wie er huß halte etc. Daruff so konnen si wie er das begert witer, als nun si in Doctor Michels huß gewesen, haben si witer gesprech gehalten und einander angezeigt, wie vil red iren halben allenthalben in der stat sei von dem, als si ungeverlichen vor iii wochen einander mit der hand verheissen die ee. Und haben doch sollichs willen gehabt zu verbergen bitz noch Pfingsten. So aber also vil red do von sei, so dunckte si gut, daß si jemants guter frind beschicken und vor den selben sollichs offentlich ouch theten und bekanten etc. Doruff si etlich beschickt und under andern, so hat in dem nacht imbiß genanter min schwoger mich, Clausen Kniebiß, ouch selb erbeten, mit im in sin huß zu gon zu etlichen guten frinden und mir nit eroffnet, was ich thun solte. Also bin ich mit im gangen in sin huß. So bald ich darin komen, hab ich Doctor Casparn, Jungfrow Margreden, ir muter und andern, so ouch darzu beschickt, do funden, die mich bericht, warumb ich also beschickt, und mich gebeten, wie woll si der sach mit einander dohin eins und die ee einander gelobt, so bitten si mich, doch si zu samen zu geben ouch offentlich. Des ich mich gewidert und vermeint, es solt das einander thun dann ich, so ich doch nit priester were etc. Und doch uff ire begere mich bereden lossen, daß ich bewilligt, und die mutter und die dochter (die ich vormals nit kandte) angesprochen, inen die handt geboten und gegrußt, und also Doctor Casparn und die dochter jeglichs gefragt, ob es des andern zu der heiligen ehe begere etc. Und noch ire antwort als si beidersit jo sagten, zusamen geben und vil glücks friden und genod gewnscht etc. [fol. 9ʳ] Und sunst hab ich, Clauß Kniebiß, die mutter und die dochter weder mit glatten noch mit rüwen worten angesprochen, ouch gar nit zu thun oder zu lossen beredt, ouch si nit behalten oder si nit von handen lossen wollen (als er erdichtlich on worheit schriftlicht anzeigt), sunder nit anders dann wie hie vor angezeigt mit ire geredt. Was ouch gar nit not, dann die sach vorhin beschlossen gewesen (als si sagen). Nach disem sind wir gesessen zu tisch und bei einander das nachtmol frölich genomen, und noch dem nachtmol haben genanter Doctor Caspar, frow Agnes Trensin und ire dochter Doctor Micheln, min schwogern, und mich mit sundern fliß und ernst gebeten, daß wir und etlich andere mit unß sollen gon zu Augustin Trensen, iren sun bruder und schwoger, und

---

²⁰ That is, his kinswoman.

in uff das frintlichst ansuchen und bitten, das er sin willen (dann er des nit wol zu friden sei) darzu gebe und inen thu das inen liebe sei, daß wollen sei in alle weg ouch thun. Daß hab ich uff ir flissig bitt bewilligt und mich vor mols nit erboten, ouch nit do von geredt oder sei etwas vertrost, als er, Augustin, unworhaftiglich anzeigt. Uff den andern tag[21] bin ich mit Doctor Michel und den schafner in der herberg[22] hinuß gangen und uff der gartner stuben under wagner[23] funden die ersamen unser lieben und guten frind und vettern Lorentzen Grofen,[24] Mathis Roten[25] und Jacob Trensen.[26] Die haben wir bericht, wes wir willens, und si gebeten, unß ouch helfen, frintschaft zu behalten und machen etc. In dem haben wir Augustin obigen ouch beruft und mit im wie obstat vilfaltig geredt und umb gottes willen sin selbs, sins weibs, kinder, und fruntschaft willen, sin willen abzustellen. Darin er mit vil andern worten anzeigt, er were bedocht, des mochten wir Doctor Caspar sagen, er wolt im noch gon, so lang biß er Doctorn Casparn betrete, so wolte in erwürgen, oder er muste es im thun. Mit vil anderen, trotzigen, unfrindtlichen trow worten uber unser aller vil faltige bitt und ermanen, so wir theten, mit dem das wir im anzeigten, was im schand daruß [fol. 9ᵛ] erwachsen mochte etc. Als er aber daruff behart, gedocht ich, wo ein burger dem andern vor schaden sein mocht und in sunderheit vor todschlegen, das er sollichs zuthun schuldig, und zeigt im an. Die wil er also uff sinen furnemen verhart und dann ich sollichs horte, so were ich schuldig, daß (so vil mir moglich) zu furkomen und gebote im do mit in gegenwertig obgenanter siner und unser guten frind, nitzt in ungutem gegen Doctor Casparn, siner muter, und schwester ouch gegen den, so darin verwant weren, furzunemen mit der thät. Sunder hette er anspruch an jeman, solte er mit recht thun, friden halten, das gebiete ich im als euer, des Radts, als hoch in den friden zu gebieten hette etc. Uff sollichs er wider antwort gab, gebiete ich zum friden, so wolte er die nit halten etc. Uber sollich alles haben wir alle in mer gebeten, von sinem fursatz abzuston. Er verharret aber, wie er gesagt, dem nach zu komen, und haben also mussen ungethan abscheiden.

---

[21] 24 April 1524.

[22] Lux Hackfurt († 6 April 1554), since 15 August 1523 manager (*Schaffner*) of the municipal poor house. Johannes Ficker and Otto Winckelmann, *Handschriftenproben des 16. Jahrhunderts nach Straßburger Originalen*, 2 vols. (Strasbourg, 1902-1905), 2: 78.

[23] The guildhall of the Gartner unter Wagnern, one of three halls of the Gardeners' Guild.

[24] Lorentz Graff († 8/9 July 1553), gardener; married 1534 Katharina Apt; XVer from the Gardeners' Guild 1524-42; Evangelical by January 1524. Thomas A. Brady, Jr., *Ruling Class, Regime, and Reformation at Strasbourg, 1520-1555*, SMRT 22 (Leiden, 1978), 316.

[25] Obviously the physician's kinsman.

[26] This may be the Jacob Drenss, who as a clergyman studied at Heidelberg in 1512-14. Brady, *Ruling Class*, 308.

Also ist es und nit anders ergangen. So nun ir min herrn hören, daß diser handel gar nit ist, als er in anzeigt, und die so die obigen vermeint unworhaftig supplication erdicht. So ist uff diß mol Doctor Michels, mines schwagers, und min underthenig bitt und beger, Augustin Trensen als dem, der unß unbillich, schmechelich antast in siner vermeinten erdichten supplication und clag, absolvieren mit körung costens und in ein ewig stil schweigen uff legen, vor behalten Doctor Michel und mir zu gelegener zit dise injurii, wie recht und sich geburt zu rechtvertigen. Hie mit euer er, wißheit flissig anrufen, hoff ouch, euer wißheit werd Doctor Michel und mir glouben geben, als den die sich bitzhar (als wir hoffen) unverwißlich gehalten. Beger ouch zu meren bericht, wo not, alle, die ee do bei gewesen, deßhalb zu verhoren.

Euer strengen, fursichtigen, wisen gehorsamen burger
Doctor Michel Rot und
Clauß Kniebiß

DOCUMENT NO. 4

Drenss vs. Hedio: Response of Dr. Caspar Hedio
[ca. 14 May 1524]

SOURCE: Archives du Chapître de St.-Thomas, Strasbourg, 69/4, fols. 10ʳ-11ᵛ.
HAND: Caspar Hedio.

[fol. 10ʳ] Strengen, ernvesten, fursichtigen, ersamen und wisen gendigen herrn. Nach dem in kurtzverruckten tagen, Augustinus Trenß, mein lieber schwager, mir zu ruck und on alle verkündung, ein supplication euer gnaden uberantwort,[27] und verlösen hat lassen, darin er mich und andere treffeliche personen unbillich beclagt, und der massen euer gnaden anbracht, das weder mir noch in zu schweigen geburen wil. Dan wie wol ein jeden christen schmach oder lesterung umb der gerechtigkeit willen zu leiden befollen, sollen wir doch der onwarheit und boßheit mit unserm schweigen kein kraft oder zunemen nit gestatten. Namlich, so sollichs auch unsern nesten belangen ist, als in dieser handlung der ersame, fursichtige, und weise Her Claus Kniepse, altammeister, und der hochgelert Her Doctor Michael Rott unverdienet, wie dan euer gnaden vernemen werden, gezogen sindt. Und weiter, dieweil ich in meinem bevelch, zu dem ich durch gots berufung verordnet bin, gern onstroflich sein wolte, zu mherem furgang der ehr gots und vieler menschen seelen heil, hab ich angezeigte meins schwagers anclag, und mein und gemelter miner herrn veronglimpfen nach minem besten vermogen zu entschuldigen, und zu verantworten nit mogen underlassen, so vil mich von noten sin beduncken wil. Sag hiruff zum ersten, das mein wil oder gmüt nie gewesen, und noch nit sei, wider die gebot gots, uß denen ich wol weiß, das man vater und mutter gehorsam sin soll, noch euer, miner herren, als weltlicher oberkeit satzung, die wider gots gebot nit streben, zereissen oder zeubertreten. Darumb mir unbillichen zugelegt wurt, das ich wider inhalt euer gnaden artickel Junckfrow Margret zu den ehe erworben habe, dan es ist mit wissen, wollen, und gutem wolgefallen der ersamen frowen Agnesen Trensin, irer mutter, miner lieben schwiger beschehen, wolche darumb wol mag verhort werden. Ich wolte mich auch in mein hertz schemen, das man mit warheit von mir sagen mochte, wie ich jemans sein dochter oder kind mit list betrug oder alfantz[28] hette understanden zu entweren. Bin auch ungezweifelt, euer gnaden artickel möge in diesem fal der strenge nach nit verstanden werden, das von noten sei, ein bruder,

---

[27] Document No. 2.

[28] Deceit, trick (from MHG: *alevanz*).

schwester, oder vogt in einicher vermehelung zebegrussen, und si darumb zu ersuchen, vorab wo die mutter zu gegen [fol. 10ᵛ] und die dochter zu iren verstendigen jaren kommen ist, auch in ander werbungen von inen etwas hindernuß befunden were etc. Als aber Augustin, mein schwager, mit der lenge erzelet, mit was mittel die dochter wider iren willen mit glatten worten dahin berot sol sin durch Her Claus Kniepsen, Doctor Michaeln und mich, sag ich bei hohem glauben, das beden itzgenanten, min herrn und mir, sollichs ungillich zugemessen wurt. Dan vor und ehe ungeverlich fur iii wochen hat min schwiger vnd ir dochter mir zulößlich antwort und zur heiligen ehe bewilligung geben, mit diesem anhangk, das wir zu gelegner zeit unß des handels, als der gotlich und gerecht vor nimans nit zu bergen, offentlich vernemen lassen wolten. Wie dann uff Georgii²⁹ in bisein Her Claus Kniepsen und Doctor Michael, beider miner herrn, beschehen ist, on allen widerwillen der mutter und der tochter, des ich mich abermals uff ir verhor gezogen haben wil. Nach dem allen, als der handtschlag beschehen ist, hab ich fruntlicher meinung Her Claus Kniepsen und Doctor Michaeln gepeten, sich zu meinem schwager, Augustin, zu verfugen und dieser geschehener handlung gutig zu berichten, da mit zwischen unß frid und einigkeit, deren ich mich alles vermogen bevlissen, erhalten wurde. Was aber ungeschickter, unfruntlicher und heftiger trowwort er, min schwager, ußgestossen, ist nit von noten zuerzelen. Doch ist Her Niclaus Kniepß, als burger und des regiments vertrawter, in den friden zegepieten verursacht worden. Uber daß mein schwager schimpflicher weiß furbringt, wie Doctor Michael, unangesehen, das er kein eheweib hab, sin schwester und mein gemahel bei im uffenthalte, als ob Doctor Michael, so eins unredlichen gemüts were, das er schmach oder laster gedachte zuzufugen einer frommen dochter; und je nimans ist, der uff Doctor Michael mit der warheit etwas so arges gedencken oder in sin nemen mochte. Das aber Augustin mein schwager weiter meldet, mir als ein geistlicher, ein [fol. 11ʳ] eheweib zunemen nit gepuren wölle, angesehen das sollichs nit landleufig und geprauchlich, auch in geistlichen und wöltlichen rechten verboten ist etc. Das selbig der lenge nach zu entschuldigen, ist nit von nöten. Dan menglichen zu wissen, das got der Her, der uber alle recht und uber alle künig der erden ist, die ehe nie verboten, sunder jedes gelegenheit nach gepoten hat. Aber in derthalb vᶜ ongeverlich durch gewalt und mutwil Gregorii des Bapsts des sibenden³⁰ dise gotlich ordnung tyrannisch und wider gots recht und gbot gewert worden ist, zu grossem abbruch aller erbarkeit, wolchem on zweifel kein christliche oberkeit, die Christum fur ein haupt, und uber alle gesatzgeber haltet, anhangen und bestetigen mage. So sind wir nit frevele menschen in geringer zall, die das geistlich recht zuruck werfen etc., wie dan Augustin, mein schwager, anregt, oder andere die si

---

²⁹ St. George's Day, 23 April 1524.
³⁰ Pope Gregory VII (r. 1073-1085). He means, of course, about 500 years ago.

supplication mir zu dienst begriffen haben, sonder das wort gots, das in ewigkeit wert und bleiben wurt, dadurch himel und erden beschaffen sin, das verwurft nit allein geistlich recht sonder stosset zu boden auch die gantz welt, hell, und teufel, gewaltiglichen, namlich, so sich wider den rat gots uffzubouwen onderstön. Dorumb mich hochverwundert, so got der Her die ehe, die dan an kein person uff erden, in sunderheit gepunden ist, durch die gantz heilig geschrift, so hoch bevor hat und rümbt, das in min schwagers namen so schimpflich furgeben wurt, als ob sin schwester bei mir wie ein offne sunderin oder metz wonen solle. Darzu wer auch on not, das er so grosse sort trüge, wie das gut solte geteilt werden, dan so sich der fal, das got lang wenden wölle, begebe, weiß man wol vermög gemeiner recht und einer loblichen stat ordenung etc. Darumb gnediger herrn, angesehen das got der Her frei gelassen und jederman erlaubt, ja gepoten hat, wer sich nit enthalten mag, das er in die ehe komme, und ich als ein frummen man geburt, umb ein frummen tochter geworben, auch si mit [fol. 11ᵛ] willen, wissen und gehel ir beder, der mutter und tochter, zum ehegemahel erlangt, und darin dem gebot und bevelch gotts nach gehandlet. Dan der Her sagt, was got zusamen verfügt, sol der mensch nit scheiden oder trennen.[31] Item, verlasse der mensch vater und mutter und hang an seinem weib.[32] Und ich auch kein gepot euer, miner herrn, darin ubergangen, weiß ich minen gemahel min leben lang nit zu verlassen. Bin auch ungezweifelt, ir, min gnedigen herrn, als liebhaber gotlicher gepot und christlicher freiheit, werden mich bei dem, so got zugehört, als euern gehorsamen burger gnediglich handhaben und beschirmen. Und wo Augustin, mein schwager, je vermeinte, das ich unbillich und wider euer gnaden artickel gehandelt haben solte, das sich doch mit der warheit nimmer erfunden wurt, wil ich im vor euer gnaden zurecht sin, und erkante straf darumb erwarten und gehorsamlich leiden. Dan ich niemans sein kind beschissen hab oder noch zethon in willens bin, als dan mich meins schwagers supplication gern veronglimpfete. Wil hiemit euer gnaden undertheniglich gepeten haben, mit Augustin, meinem schwager, gutlich zuverschaffen, als er mich und andere der sachen halb ongeschmecht, ongeirt und bekummert lasse. Dan ich in fruntschaft, liebs und guts zubeweisen geneigt bin, wo ich das umb euer gnaden sampt und sunder beschulden oder verdienen konndte, wolt ich allerzeit onverdrossene fleiß erfunden werden.

    Euer strengen, fursichtigen, wißheit undertheniger
        burger und diener,
           Doctor Caspar Hedio, predicant im Münster zu
           Straßburg

---

[31] Matt. 19:6.
[32] Gen. 2:24.

DOCUMENT NO. 5

Drenss vs. Hedio: Response of Agnes Drenss
[ca. 14 May 1524]

SOURCE: Archives du Chapître de St.-Thomas, Strasbourg, 69/5, fols. 12ʳ-
13ᵛ.
HAND: Secretarial hand.

[fol. 12ʳ] Strengen, ernvesten, ersamen, weisen, gnedigen, gunstigen herren.
Mit besunder beschwerdt und hertzen leidt, als woll zuvermuten, hab ich
vernomen, wie mein son Augustin Trenß uß unwissend villeicht oder mher,
als ich woll acht, uß anreitzung und verhetzung etlicher ungotsferchtigen
unruwigen leudt, denen woll ein anderns were angestanden, wo si gott und
iren statt bedencken wolten, habe etliche theure und dapfere menner gegen
euer gnaden schwerlich zuverunglimpfen, sich undernomen und das
gesparter worheit, nemlich den ersamen weisen und die hochgelerten und
erbarn Her Niclaus Kniebis, alt Ammeister, und Doctor Michael Rodt, beide
mein lieben vettern, und Doctor Caspar Hedio, predicanten im Munster.
Nun, meinen lieben vertrauwten dochterman, do mit den nun euer gnaden
eigentlichen bericht,³³ wie die sach ergangen habe. Und dester fuglicher
alle uneinigkeit und zweitracht hinlegen moge, so sag ich unverholen vor
euer gnaden mit der warheit, das der hochgelert, christlich Doctor Caspar
Hedio, predicant im Munster, umb mein liebe dochter, Margaredt, gewarben
hat, wie das einem fromen, zuchtigen herren und man geburen mag, hat
[MARGIN: an mein son] mich und mein dochter geschickt, gemelten
meinen lieben vettern und herren, den hochgelerten Doctor Michael Rodt,
der on zweifel mein und meiner dochter wolfart nit weniger begert zu
furdern, dan eben mein son, und freilich vil mher dan alle sin rath geber.
Dem auch mein son zuantwort geben hat, was der ehe halb mir und meiner
dochter gefelligk und gelegen sei, sol im auch gefelligk und gelegen sein.
Daruff ich und mein dochter unß ein zeitlang zubedencken genomen haben.
So bald aber mein son gemergkt, das wir, ich und mein dochter, die in
meinem gewalt sich alweg nach meinem willen gehalten hat, ob angeboter
ehe nit groß scheueten, hat er sich ungepurlich genug ertzeigt mit worten
und geperden. Das hab ich do zu mol zu geben bösen jungen, die on das
allem dem entgegen sind, daß das gottlich wort und christlich erberkeit
vermag die auch der mossen leben, das sie nit on vrsach das licht des
evangelii hassen.³⁴ Und hab also die sach lossen anston, verhoffet durch die

---

³³ Document No. 3.
³⁴ This passage attests to the existence in mid-1524 of popular opposition to the
Evangelical preachers.

teglichen predigen des gotlichen worts wurt er, wie ich das genugsam erkent hab, ouch erkennen, das die heilig ehe jederman von got zugelossen [fol. 12ᵛ] und vergunt ist. Und freilich, die weil daher, das den geistlichen die ehe verpoten gewesen ist, so groß schand und laster furgangen ist, und noch furget, ein jeder frommer christ nit allein sinem vermogen dartzu helfen solt, das durch die gottlich und gebenedeite ehe das ungeschickt, unverschampt leben etlicher geistlichen abtreiben wurd. Diese erkantnuß hat aber villeicht durch teglich der gotlosen hinderhalten bei meinem son nit wollen komen. Do ich im dan genug hab vorgeben, vill meher dan ich als ein mutter schuldigk gewesen, und gesehen, das er uß keinem guten christlichen grundt wieder unß an getragene ehe gewesen ist, hab ich bewegt uß teglichen hellen predigen des evangelii, so in dieser loblichen Stat Straßburhgk geschehen, und aber euer gnaden frilich nit geschehen liessen, nach auch so ein merckliche erbare burgerschaft die horten, wo sie nit christlich und gotlich weren, mein dochter obgemeltem Doctor Caspar zu einem ehegemahel mit irem willen zugesagt, do zu mir auch nit wenig meiner verwanten frundt und sunst gute gunner — erbar, frumm, redlich leudt, die mein son noch jeman anders in kein weg schmehen mag mit der warheitt, geraten haben. Und bin auch ungetzwifelt, wie solche ehe gott gefelligk, also soll si auch fuglich und gantz nutzlich sein meiner lieben dochter, dero sich auch mein son gar nit dorft beschemen, so er gott vor augen wolt haben und mer folgen denen, die im guts gonnen in der warheit, dan denen die durch in villeicht etwas ungluck wolten anrichten. Und ist diß geschehen achtag nach Ostern.³⁵ Nach diesem, als ich kein besserung an meinem son sahe, dem ich doch gerne hette gehofirt, wo er nur nit so gar heßlich geton hette, ob dem, das doch gotlich und billich ist, sein wir, ich und mein dochter, uff Sant Jorgen tagen³⁶ gemelts Doctor Michaels unsers lieben vetterns hauß komen. Dan zumal on sein Doctor Michels wissen, der uns dan wol ein monat zu vor geladen hat, etwan ein mol zu im zu komen in sein hauß, do wir dan Doctor Caspar offentlich und nit heimlich gehalten in befunden. Und nach dem ich mit im fruntlich red gehapt [MARGIN: und wir vermerckt], das wir allenhalb im geschrei gewesen,³⁷ haben wir unß entschlossen, on Doctor Michaels zu thon, die weil wir doch einer verwilligung noch der zeit hoffen mechten bei meinem son und ich im [fol. 13ʳ] doch mit willen meiner dochter, si im schon zuvor zugeseit hatte, den handt streich zu thun und den leiten uß dem geschrei zuhelfen. Und die weil wir besorgten, das dan nun beschicht, hab ich Doctor Michael gepeten, das er Her Niclaus Kniepsen wolt vermogen, das er si oftgedochtem Doctor Caspar und mein dochter zusamen geb. Hab auch sust noch andern meinen lieben frunden etlichen geschickt, als aber die gescheft halben nit mochten komen. Und Her Nicolaus Knieps kam, den Doctor Michael von seinem essen beruft hat, und

---

³⁵ 4 April 1524.
³⁶ 23 April 1524.
³⁷ That is, there was gossip about their secret betrothal.

des handels auch nit bericht, biß das er in zu unß in sein hauß brocht hat, hab ich und Doctor Caspar in gepeten, er wolte sie zusamen geben und also ein zeug sein, der versprochenen und redlich uffgerichten ehe. Das er, die weil unser beger billich und gottlichem [MARGIN: rechten gemeß] nit kindte abschlagen, und hat sie also uff unser bitt zusamen geben, glucks gewunscht, und druff bei unß im nachtmol blieben, und mit einigem wort wider dartzu noch von geroten, ich schweig, das er mit glatten worten mich oder mein dochter solte hinder gangen sein, vil weniger getzwongen. Wie dan auch Doctor Michael der uber sein erste werbung, als wol gegen meinem son als gegen mir gethon, auch weder zu noch von geroten hat, dann allein das er alweg gestanden ist, wie er schuldig und ein jeder christ, das solche ehe gottlich und billich sei. Des ich selb ouch solchen grundt hab und weiß sampt meiner dochter, so haben wir auch bed solchen geneigten willen zu oftgemeltem Doctor Caspar also einem getruwen lerer der gantzen stadt, das so es nit geschehen were, muste es noch heute bei tag geschehen. Dan die dochter mein und nit meins sons ist. Wir haben in lang genug vor augen gehabt, etwa manchen erlichen werbern haben wir umb seindt willen abgeschlagen, so hat im dieser[38] allein uß ein unglauben und böser leut reitzung nit gefallen. Die weil dan er unß nit zuverbieten hat, ob wir dan schon uff sein verbot nit geben haben, acht ich wir haben nit hoch gesundet. Den vogt haben wir uß vrsach nit gefragt, acht wir seins auch nit schuldigk gewesen. Vill guter verwanter frundt haben wir gehabt, und irem roth gefolgt, hat unß auch in kein weg geruwen. Und sag frei und onverholen, wie vor, so es noch nit geschehen were, must es nach geschehen. Darumb, gnödige herren, ist am euer gnaden mein under- [fol. 13ᵛ] thenigk, demutige bitt, ir wollent dem unworhaftigen furtragen meins sons kein glauben geben, sonder wie ich die sach in der warheit ertzelt hab, also kein zweifel haben, es sei alles der massen ergangen. Und wollent verschaffen mit meinem son, das er mich mein liebe dochter und vertrauweten dochterman unbemuhet und on geschmecht lasse, sampt mein andern gnödigen hern und frunden, die er mit der unworheit unbillich euer gnaden furtragen hat. Doch im uff diß mol, wo er anders von seinem ungeschickten furnemen wolte abston seiner unwissenthalb, und des argen anreitzens des sich etlich böß leut, als ich gontzlich in glauben gut vrsach hab, gegen im iben, vertzeihen, das er also mit der unworheit meine lieben herren und frundt Her Niclaus Knieps, Doctor Michael und Doctor Caspar gegen euer gnaden zu unglimpfen understanden hat. Dan so er je in seinem ungeschickten unchristlichen furnemen wolte furfare und also frevenlich gotlichen gepot entgegen handelen, mich als sein mutter, deren er in billichen sachen als diese ehe ist gehorsamen soll, uß gotlichem rechten nit erkennen, so betzeug ich mich des offentlich hie vor euer gnaden, meinen gnödigen herren, das ich in auch nit hinfurt fur ein son erkennen wurde, das dan im und seinen kinden keinen

---

[38] I.e., Dr. Caspar Hedio.

frummen bringen wurdt. Diß hab ich die worheit zubetzeugen und zuent-
schuldigen, meine lieben herren und frundt, so mein son oder die, so im die
supplication begriffen mit der unworheit haben wellen ver unglimpfen, do
mit auch uneinichkeit und zweitracht mochte hingelegt und recht christliche
einigkeit uffgericht werden, im besten nit wollen bergen, mit anhangenden
bitt, euer gnaden wolle mich als ein witfrauwe sampt meiner dochter und
verwanten dochterman, euer gnaden burger altzeit in gnedigem befelch
haben.

    Euer strengen, fursichtigen wißheit alltzeit gehorsame
      burgerin,
        Agnes Trensin,
          Andres Trensen seligen verloßne witfrauwe.

DOCUMENT NO. 6

Drenss vs. Hedio: Second Petition of Augustin Drenss
4 June 1524

SOURCE: Archives du Chapître de St.-Thomas, Strasbourg, 69/6, fol. 14^{r-v}.
HAND: Augustin Drenss.

[fol. 14^r] Strengen, erenvesten, fursichtigen, ersamen, wisen, gnödigen
herren, demnach uff min warhaftig suppliciern und ingeprachte supplication[39] Herr Claus Kniebiß und Doctor Michel Rott, ouch mein lieb
mutter und Doctor Caspar, predicant, gegen supplicationes,[40] ire handlung,
so ich euch, min gnödigen herren, angepracht, zu beglimpfen angezeugt, laß
ich alles zu diser zit in sinem werd beston. In ansehung, das der gegenteil
muntlich und schriftlich furtreg nit rechtlichen wiß, als ich ouch nit in recht
ingebracht haben werd und will, und alles, so ich in miner supplication
ingepracht, doch mit protestation do zemal noch ietz nimandt damit
zuinjurieren besunder allein zu behilf miner noturft, ist selbs von miner
lieben mutter wie gehandlet ist, als mir angezeigt, gehort worden. Und als
gemelt min muter selbs durch ein geschrift verantwurt,[41] ist lichtlich
abzunemen, wie sie hindergangen ist. Sie im ersten handel da me angelegen
uberredt, vill mer in disem fall. Dan so Doctor Caspar verantwurtung und
stilus ouch dargegen miner muter und der andren fur ougen gnomen wirdet,
sindt pfill uß einem kocher. Diewill Her Claus Kniebiß ouch Doctor Michell
alle handlung gestandt, doch nit mit uff satz besunder mit einer hupschen
beschonung, pringt der handel selbs deßhalb ein claren verstandt. Und wie
wol jetz die neu evangelisch leer so vill wircken will, das vater und mutter
und ire khinder ouch eegemächt[42] und andre fruntschaft zu widerwertigkeit
und zertrennung khomendt, als jetz leider, gott erbarmß, zwischen miner
lieben einigen swester gewesen und miner lieben muter alß sie sich vor
eueren gnaden schriftlich hören lassen, sie wolle mich nit fur einen sun mer
haben, befunden wirdet, wil doch ich sie unangesehen dise neue leer fur ein
muter mein leben lang erkhennen und haben. Hoff, eß sie gotz gepot und
will. Dann wo sollichs nit were, wolte ich euere gnade wol witer wissen
anzuzeigen. Ich hette ouch geachtet, wo sach also schlecht ergangen, als
[der] gegenteil angezeigt hette, billich einigen frundt oder vogt von minem
vater oder mutter darzu beruft. Were wol alß erlich und billich, dann [der]
gegenteil niemandt dar bei gehept, dann die personen obbestimpt. Und das

---

[39] Document No. 2, Petition of Augustin Drenss.
[40] Documents 3, 4, and 5.
[41] Document No. 4, the petition of Agnes Drenss.
[42] Spouses (from MHG: *egemechide*).

euer gnaden mag erwegen, das [der] gegenteil gern etwaß wider mich inprechte, zeit er an, wie ich miner swester kheinen man zunemen vergunstigen. So doch das widerspill offenbar ist, dann ich gearbeit, das sie den schafner zu Sant Catharina[43] oder Vältin des Schultheissen sun [fol. 14ᵛ] von Wangen[44] zu der ee nemen. Diser[45] hat aber ir allein gefallen. Diewill dann, gnödige herren, luwt miner vor ingeprachter supplication verstanden nach der lenge gehort, das pfaffen und munch ee wider haben sollendt, weder bäpstlich und keiserlich satzung und recht ist, ouch euer, miner gnödigen herren, alten herkhomen, ouch in aller cristenheit vill hundert jar nie ingepruch gewesen, und namlich uff disentag khein erbfall den khinden, so von pfaffen, eß sei in oder vsserthalb der ee, zu gelassen wurdet. Mag euer gnaden wol erwegen, waß sollichs min geschlecht erlich frundtschaft, so lieb und leid vill jar mit diser statt erlitten, ein insehen haben, damit die neuerung mit mir und miner frundtschaft nit angefangen werde. Will also lut miner vorigen supplication als ein armer burger den handel zu erwegen und zu bedencken, und also eueren gnaden ergeben, mit namlich geding, waß sich mit der zit zu tragen möchte, das mir euere gnaden solliches mines ernstlichen anhaltes nit in vergeß stellen wellendt.

Euer wißheit undertäniger burger

Augustin Trenß

---

[43] Unidentified.
[44] Unidentified.
[45] I.e., Dr. Caspar Hedio.

ERSCHEINUNGEN DES ANTIKLERIKALISMUS IN SACHSEN VOR UND WÄHREND DER REFORMATION

KARLHEINZ BLASCHKE

Sächsisches Staatsarchiv, Dresden

Das Anliegen einer wissenschaftlichen Konferenz über Antiklerikalismus sollte darin bestehen, aus einem polemisch gefüllten und politisch-agitatorisch verwendeten Schlagwort einen wissenschaftlich verwendbaren, sachlichen Begriff zu machen. Dazu kann vor allem die Aufarbeitung der quellenmäßig bekannten Überlieferung dienen. Deshalb soll im folgenden aus dem Zusammenhang der sächsischen Reformationsgeschichte ein Beitrag zur Begriffsbestimmung geleistet werden, wobei für die Darbietung des Materials die zeitliche Abfolge als Ordnungsgrundsatz gewählt wird. Es wird versucht, auf diese Weise einige Tatsachen über den Gegenstand zusammenzutragen, ohne vorerst eine scharfe Definition des Begriffs im Auge zu haben. Vielmehr geht es zunächst darum, alles das zu erfassen, was an kritischen Erscheinungen, Haltungen und Maßnahmen gegen den Klerus bekannt ist.

Bereits in der Landesordnung des Herzogs Wilhelms III. für die thüringischen Landesteile des Kurfürstentums Sachsen von 1446 lassen sich Töne hören, die als kirchenkritisch angesehen werden können. Der Herzog erklärte es als seine Pflicht, für die Reformation der Klöster zu sorgen und sie zu redlicher, geistlicher Regierung zu bringen. Er tat das kraft seines weltlichen Herrscheramtes, ohne sich etwa auf eine päpstliche Bevollmächtigung zu berufen oder den Papst auch nur zu erwähnen. Die geistliche Gerichtsbarkeit wurde in ihre Schranken gewiesen, vor Übergriffen in die Zuständigkeit weltlicher Gerichte wurde gewarnt.[1]

Unter Kurfürst Friedrich II. (1428-1464) wurde diese kirchenpolitische Linie für das ganze Kurfürstentum Sachsen fortgesetzt. Das zeigt sich in seinen Maßnahmen zur Einschränkung des Ablaßhandels, die im Jahre 1458 bis zur Verhaftung eines päpstlichen Ablaßkommissars gingen.[2] Die klare Parteinahme der wettinischen Landesherren für die Observanten unter den Bettelorden muß in diesem Zusammenhang ausdrücklich erwähnt werden.

Auch nach der verhängnisvollen Landesteilung von 1485 wurde die traditionelle wettinische Kirchenpolitik fortgesetzt. Als gegen das Ende des 15. Jahrhunderts eine für beide wettinische Fürstentümer vorgesehene

---

[1] *Akten und Briefe zur Kirchenpolitik Herzog Georgs von Sachsen 1517-1527*, hg. von Felician Gess, 2 Bände (Leipzig, 1905 und 1917), 1: XXI.

[2] Karlheinz Blaschke, *Geschichte Sachsens im Mittelalter* (Berlin, 1990), 325.

Landesordnung vorbereitet wurde, kamen wieder alle die bekannten Vorwürfe und Klagepunkte gegen den Klerus zur Sprache.[3] Die Überlegungen wandten sich besonders gegen den Mißbrauch der geistlichen Gerichtsbarkeit, gegen das Verhalten des Weltklerus, dem Unkeuschheit, Trunkenheit und Verursachung von Lärm und Gezänk vorgehalten wurde, und gegen den unerlaubten Ausschank von Wein und Bier durch die Geistlichkeit, die außerdem Ausschreitungen und Schlägerei verursache. Dabei käme es gelegentlich zum Totschlag von Priestern, worauf dann die Kirche über den betreffenden Ort das Interdikt verhänge, was sich wiederum für die geistliche Betreuung der Gläubigen schädlich auswirkte.

In die Zeit unmittelbar vor Luthers Thesenveröffentlichung fallen zwei Ereignisse um den Ablaßprediger Tetzel, der noch unter den altgläubigen Verhältnissen auf scharfe Kritik stieß. In Görlitz wandte sich 1516 der streng katholische Stadtschreiber Johannes Haß gegen die törichten Predigten und die freche Art, wie Tetzel den Ablaß nur um des Geldes willen den Leuten "aufzumutzen" versuchte. Schließlich wurde ihm jede weitere Tätigkeit in der Stadt verboten.[4] Ein Jahr später wurde er in Halle/S. der Gotteslästerung bezichtigt, weil er gesagt hatte, er könne mit seinem Ablaß auch denjenigen von der Sünde befreien, der die heilige Jungfrau geschwängert habe.[5] Überhaupt rief die üble Art, in der damals das Ablaßgeschäft betrieben wurde, den Widerstand der Laienwelt bis hinauf auf die fürstliche Ebene hervor. Herzog Georg von Sachsen stand schon zu Beginn des Jahres 1517, als an Luthers Thesen gegen den Ablaß noch nicht zu denken war, in Verhandlungen und Korrespondenz, worin es darum ging, den Ablaß in seinem Lande nicht zuzulassen.[6] Er als der Landesherr war es auch, der in geistlicher Verantwortung für seine Untertanen für ordentlichen Gottesdienst sorgte, wo dieser gefährdet war.[7] 1518 griff die Landesherrschaft gegen den Pfarrer von Schneeberg ein, der wegen des Verhältnisses zu seiner Köchin und wegen der ihm zur Last gelegten Abtreibung eines Kindes bestraft werden sollte.[8]

Auch während der Wochen, in denen Herzog Georg im Frühjahr 1519 mit einer umfangreichen Korrespondenz die Leipziger Disputation vorbereitete, ließ er die schlimmen Verhältnisse unter dem Gemeindeklerus nicht aus den

---

[3] *Akten und Briefe* (wie Anm. 1) 1: LV ff.

[4] Karlheinz Blaschke, *Sachsen im Zeitalter der Reformation*, SVRG 185, Jahrgang 75 und 76 (Gütersloh, 1970), 108.

[5] *Die Reformation in Dokumenten*, hg. von Hans Eberhardt und Horst Schlechte (Weimar, 1967), 12f.

[6] *Akten und Briefe* 1: 3ff.

[7] *Akten und Briefe* 1: 14f.; Schreiben vom 28. Mai 1517 an den Pfarrer zu Senftenberg wegen Abstellung von Mißbräuchen bei Beichte und Abendmahl; 27. Juni 1517 an den Amtmann zu Schellenberg wegen Abschaffung der Beischläferinnen bei den Pfarrern zu Euba und Flöha.

[8] *Akten und Briefe* 1: 37, 43.

Augen. Er klagte es dem Bischof von Meißen, daß der Pfarrer zu Krum-
hermersdorf bei Zschopau wegen Trunkenheit seine geistlichen Pflichten
beim Abendmahl und bei der Beichte nicht hatte erfüllen können.[9] Im Jahre
darauf beklagte sich der Rat zu Leipzig über den Mißbrauch des geistlichen
Gerichts durch den dortigen Erzpriester, während der Rat zu Dresden den
Wein- und Bierschank der Geistlichen beanstandete.[10]

Solcherart war der Boden bereitet, auf dem Luthers neue Theologie im
Volke Verständnis und Zustimmung fand. Herzog Georg befand sich mit
seiner vielfach wiederholten Kritik am Zustand der Kirche und des Klerus
auf der gleichen Ebene wie Luther. Seine Beschwerden gegen die Geistlichkeit, die er für den Wormser Reichstag 1521 zusammengestellt hatte,
stimmmen nach Inhalt und Tendenz weitgehend mit Luthers Schrift *An den
christlichen Adel deutscher Nation* überein.[11] Die Vorwürfe gingen bis in
Einzelheiten, die ein anschauliches Bild vom Zustand des Klerus vermitteln,
sie setzten sich in den folgenden Monaten mit dem Einschreiten des Herzogs
gegen die bei den ersten Messen der Priester üblich gewordenen Schwel-
gereien, gegen den Verkauf der Sakramente um Geld und immer wieder
gegen das Brauen und Schenken der Geistlichen fort.

Im Sommer 1521 drückte der Herzog in einem längeren Schreiben an
Kardinal Albrecht seine Meinung aus, daß die Empörungen, die sich
allenthalben gegen "die Geistlichen und gemeine Klerisei" erhoben hatten,
von den Geistlichen selbst verursacht worden seien.[12] Er vertrat dabei nicht
nur den Standpunkt des Landesfürsten, dem es um die Wahrung seiner
Rechte gegenüber der Kirche ging, sondern machte sich zum Sprecher der
Laienwelt schlechthin, die er meinte gegen "unpriesterlichen, leichtfertigen
Handel und Mißbrauch" der Geistlichen schützen zu müssen. Diese
Äußerung ist umso bemerkenswerter, als sie von einem Fürsten kam, der zeit
seines Lebens treu und fest zur römischen Kirche und zum alten Glauben
stand und der die letzten zweiundzwanzig Jahre seines Lebens, wenn auch
vergeblich, unentwegt und unnachgiebig gegen die auf sein Land andrin-
gende Flut der Reformation ankämpfte.

So konnte es nicht ausbleiben, daß dieses reformatorische Gedankengut
sich auch in Georgs Herzogtum mit antiklerikalem Verhalten verband. Im
Frühjahr 1522 trat das bemerkenswerteste Ereignis dieser Art in der Stadt
Oschatz auf. Der dortige Kaplan Lukas Leder war das Ziel tumultartiger
Angriffe, die nachts vor seinem Hause stattfanden, wobei die Leute mit
zugehaltenen Nasen ein Schmählied auf ihn sangen und ihm im Laufe
mehrerer Tage dreimal die Fensterscheiben einwarfen. Er erhielt einen Brief
mit Anklagen wegen "Verräterei" und "Schalkheit", er wehrte sich, es kam
zu Handgemenge und Schlägerei, man beschuldigte ihn der Hurerei. Er

---

[9] *Akten und Briefe* 1: 82.
[10] *Akten und Briefe* 1: 116, 131.
[11] *Akten und Briefe* 1: 151ff.
[12] *Akten und Briefe* 1: 183ff.

selbst betrachtete sich als Opfer der "Martinianer", die es damals schon in einer nennenswerten Anzahl in der Stadt gab. Hier ging also das antiklerikale Verhalten fließend in die reformatorische Bewegung über oder war überhaupt ein wesentlicher Teil von ihr, in dem sie ihren ersten Ausdruck fand.[13]

Im Jahre darauf wurden einem altgläubigen Priester in der Bergstadt Annaberg anonyme Schmähschriften zugestellt, in denen er als unverschämter, ungelehrter Mann und verwunschener Gotteslästerer, als toller, grober, unsinniger Esel bezeichnet wurde, dem nun seine "Lügen" vorgehalten wurden. Besonders bemerkenswert ist die dabei aufgetretene Feststellung, die Laien könnten nun auch die Bibel lesen. Der Priester stand somit unter der Anklage, er habe die ihm anvertrauten Seelen falsch unterrichtet und ihnen des reine Wort Gottes vorenthalten. Antiklerikalismus und reformatorische Gesinnung flossen hier in eins zusammen.[14]

Im gleichen Jahre veranstalteten einige Bewohner der benachbarten Bergstadt Buchholz eine narrenhafte Prozession mit verfaulten Tüchern als Fahnen, Mistgabeln anstelle von Kerzen und einem aufgeschlagenen Schachbrett anstelle eines Gesangbuches. In einer Jauchentrage wurden die "Reliquien" des soeben heiliggesprochenen Bischofs Benno von Meißen vorgeführt: ein Pferdeschädel, einige Kuhknochen und zwei Pferdebeine. Am Markt hielt die Prozession an, ein "Bischof" predigte, ein "Papst" spendete Ablaß, ein Spottlied auf den Heiligen wurde abgesungen, und auf dem Höhepunkt der Ausgelassenheit wurde der 'Papst' mitsamt seinen Trägern in den Röhrkasten der städtischen Wasserleitung geworfen.[15]

Antiklerikales Verhalten zeigte sich auch während des Bauernkrieges 1525. Obwohl er sich in Sachsen auf örtlich begrenzte und nur kurzfristig auftretende Handlungen beschränkte und längst nicht die Ausmaße wie in Thüringen erreichte, führte er doch zu einigen Gewalttätigkeiten gegen den Klerus. Hunderte von Bauern stürmten das Kloster Grünhain im Westerzgebirge und die Pfarrhäuser in Königswalde bei Annaberg, Mildenau, Nenkersdorf bei Geithain, Schönbrunn bei Wolkenstein und Großrückerswalde.[16] Die Ursachen für diese Ereignisse sind im einzelnen nicht bekannt. Da von den mehr als tausend Pfarrhäusern in Sachsen nur die fünf genannten und von den zahlreichen Klöstern des Landes nur dieses eine betroffen war, wird man an örtliche, situationsbedingte Konflikte denken müssen, die aber doch erkennen lassen, wie leicht im gegebenen Fall eine allgemein kritische Einstellung gegenüber dem Klerus aufbrechen und zu Taten und Tätlichkeiten führen konnte.

---

[13] *Akten und Briefe* 1: 304-58 passim; *Die Reformation* (wie Anm. 5), 15f.

[14] Blaschke, *Sachsen im Zeitalter der Reformation*, 116.

[15] Blaschke, *Sachsen im Zeitalter der Reformation*, 116.

[16] *Akten und Briefe* 2: 235; *Akten zur Geschichte des Bauernkrieges in Mitteldeutschland*, hg. von Peter Walther Fuchs, Bd. 2 (Jena, 1942), 274ff., 566.

Wahrend bisher kirchenkritische bis eindeutig antiklerikale Einstellungen und Verhaltensweisen auf der Ebene der Landesherrschaft, des städtischen Bürgertums und der aufständischen Bauern betrachtet wurden, ist abschließend auf eine davon abweichende Art der Kritik einzugehen, die von der humanistischen Grundhaltung juristischer und theologischer Räte in einem von der Renaissance geprägten Denken ausging. Als die evangelischen Visitatoren im Frühjahr 1539 an den Dom zu Meißen kamen, um auch dort die Reformation einzuführen, fanden sie sechzig Vikare und zwanzig Kapläne vor, die in althergebrachter Weise die liturgischen Dienste verrichteten. Dieser geballten Masse von Klerikern hielten die von ihrer guten Sache überzeugten Visitatoren vor, es sei gegen alle Vernunft, wenn sie ihr Leben in Müßiggang zubringen wollten, denn niemand lebe für sich allein.[17] Man könnte hier vielleicht von einem intellektuell begründeten Antiklerikalismus sprechen, der auf einer neuzeitlich ausgerichteten geistlichen Ebene kein Verständis für mittelalterliche Religiosität im Rahmen einer Kirche hatte, in der Weltflucht und Kultgottesdienst auch ohne Beziehung zum tätigen Leben einen Sinn hatten und die Nützlichkeit des menschlichen Daseins in den gesellschaftlichen Zusammenhängen keinen herausragenden Wert darstellte.

Die dargelegten Tatsachen gestatten es nunmehr, die Frage nach den Ursachen des Antiklerikalismus zu stellen. Sie lassen sich auf fünf verschiedene Arten zusammendrängen.

Den Inhabern weltlicher Gewalt ging es um eine deutliche Abgrenzung ihrer Rechte und Befugnisse gegenüber Kirche und Geistlichkeit. Landesherren und Stadträte traten mit einem stärkeren Selbstbewußtsein auf. Sie waren nicht mehr bereit, die konkurrierende Ausübung öffentlicher Gewalt durch die Kirche zu dulden. In dieser Hinsicht kündigte sich schon lange vor dem Beginn der Reformation eine kirchenkritische Haltung an, die aus der allumfassenden mittelalterlichen Religiosität herauswuchs und den frühneuzeitlichen Staat vorzubereiten half. Diese auch in Sachsen anzutreffende Entwicklung ist in die allgemein im späten Mittelalter sich ergebende Gestaltung des Verhältnisses von Staat und Kirche einzuordnen, wie es grundsätzlich schon von Marsilius von Padua im frühen 14. Jahrhundert im Sinne einer klaren Trennung beider Gewalten vorgedacht worden war. Die Kirche hatte im Zeichen der religiösen Durchdringung des gesamten gesellschaftlichen und persönlichen Lebens während des hohen Mittelalters so sehr an Boden gewonnen und dabei auch Zuständigkeiten der weltlichen Herrschaft an sich gezogen, daß eine Gegenbewegung durchaus erklärlich war. Diese Bewegung lag im Zuge einer Entwicklung, die zum modernen Staat und zum Anspruch der weltlichen Obrigkeit auf die Gestaltung des gesamten öffentlichen Lebens führen sollte.

---

[17] Blaschke, *Sachsen im Zeitalter der Reformation*, 115f.

An zweiter Stelle ergab sich eine wirtschaftliche Konkurrenz ebenfalls dadurch, daß Geistlichkeit und Kirche in das Wirtschaftsleben handelnd eingedrungen waren, wo sie ihrer Bestimmung gemäß nicht hingehören. Stadtpfarrer mißbrauchten das ihnen zustehende Privileg, für den eigenen Bedarf Bier zu brauen, indem sie das Bier verkauften und damit die brauberechtigte Bürgerschaft in ihrem Erwerb schädigten. In der Sorge um ihr Seelenheil stifteten viele Bürger im Sinne eines guten Werkes Grundstücke an die Kirche, die dann als Besitz der toten Hand dem städtischen Grundstücksmarkt entzogen wurden. Die in der Steuer- und Gerichtsverfassung privilegierte Kirche durchlöcherte damit die verfassungsrechtliche Einheit des Stadtgebietes, was die Stadträte auf die Dauer nicht hinzunehmen bereit waren, weil ihr Bestreben gerade in die andere Richtung ging. Sie wollten die Stadt zu einem einheitlichen politischen Körper machen und mußten zu diesem Zweck all Sonderrechtsbereiche beseitigen.[18] Auf der landesherrlichen Ebene ergab sich im Blick auf den immer umfangreicher werdenden Ablaßhandel die wirtschaftspolitisch begründete Sorge, daß durch ihn ein allzu großer Abfluß des Geldes aus dem Territorium zustandekommen könnte.

Als dritter Gesichtspunkt tritt die Abwehr einer unmittelbaren Bedrückung auf, die von Angehörigen des Klerus ausging. Es gab offensichtlich Geistliche, die ihre gesellschaftlich führende, rechtlich privilegierte Stellung zur Ausübung einer Macht benutzten, die ihnen nicht zustand und die grundsätzlich im Gegensatz zur dienenden Rolle der Kirche stand, wie sie vom Evangelium her geboten ist. Gegen solchen unsachgemäßen Mißbrauch von Macht wandten sich ganze Gemeinden, einzelne Gruppen der Bevölkerung oder auch Einzelpersonen. Diese Beweggründe liegen also im Bereich des Subjektiven, des Charakterlichen und des Menschlich-Allzumenschlichen. Sie sind mit Rücksicht auf menschliche Schwächen, die stets auch unter der Geistlichkeit anzutreffen waren, in allen Zeiten der Kirchengeschichte und nicht nur vor und während der Reformation aufgetreten, erlangten hier aber in den besonderen Zeitverhältnissen einen ganz anderen Rang.

Ein vierter Beweggrund ist in der Sorge um das Seelenheil zu sehen, das in der Reihe der Werte einen der ersten Plätze einnahm, wie es für die Gesellschaft insgesamt und für den einzelnen Menschen galt. Von den Geistlichen wurde die Beförderung des Seelenheils, die zuverlässige Vermittlung der Gnade Gottes erwartet, was sie zu einem besonders heiligmäßigen Leben verpflichtete. Ein unwürdiger Kleriker war kein Garant der Heilsvermittlung. In dieser Hinsicht waren gerade die Mißstände in der Kirche und die vielfach bemerkte Nachlässigkeit und Liederlichkeit in der

---

[18] Vgl. hierzu: Karlheinz Blaschke, "Sonderrechtsbereiche in sächsischen Städten an der Wende vom Mittelalter zur Neuzeit", in *Civitatum Communitas. Festschrift für Heinz Stoob*, Städteforschung Bd. A 21, Teil 1 (Köln, 1984), 254-65.

Lebensführung der Kleriker nicht nur eine schwere Enttäuschung für die Laienwelt, sie gefährdeten geradezu die Erfüllung der Aufgaben, die man dem geistlichen Stande im Sinne einer gesellschaftlichen Arbeitsteilung gestellt hatte. Wer sich in diesem System seiner Aufgabe entzog, verfiel der gesellschaftlichen Kritik.

Schließlich ist hier nochmals die Beobachtung aufzunehmen, daß in den reformationszeitlichen Antiklerikalismus eine humanistisch-modernistische Strömung einfloß, die für ausgesprochen mittelalterliche Formen liturgisch-kultisch geprägter Frömmigkeit kein Verständnis hatte und deshalb dem Klerus in seiner traditionellen Funktion und Gestalt grundsätzlich ablehnend gegenüberstand. Von hier aus ergab sich eine Brücke zu Grundanliegen der Reformation mit ihrer humanistischen Verwurzelung.

Die Suche nach den Ursachen des kirchenkritisch-antiklerikalen Verhaltens hat somit ein Bündel von Erscheinungen erbracht, die sich wiederum auf drei Ebenen verteilen: die Landesherrschaft als Anwalt des werdenden modernen Staates, die Stadträte als Vertreter der bürgerlichen Gemeinden und den gemeinen Mann.

Damit entsteht aber die Frage, was Antiklerikalismus eigentlich ist und ob er sich einfach mit einer allgemein kirchenkritischen Einstellung deckt. Die Deutung der hier dargelegten Tatsachen führt zu einer Unterscheidung zwischen Kirchenkritik und Antiklerikalismus. Die unter (1) aufgeführten Beobachtungen aus der Ebene der Landesherrschaft gehören in einen normalen Säkularisierungsprozeß, der zum modernen Staat führte, auf lange Dauer eingestellt war und besonders stark die gesellschaftliche Struktur im Auge hatte. Hier ging es um prinzipielle Fragen, die sich auf die Kirche als Institution bezogen. Die unter (5) gekennzeichnete humanistische Einstellung ging von einem neuen Wertsystem aus, das gewisse rationale Züge an sich trug, und hatte die Überwindung der gesamten herrschenden Ordnung zum Ziel. Daher fällt es schwer, sie für eine Anti-Stellung innerhalb des gegebenen Systems zu beanspruchen, weil sie im Grunde genommen darüber hinauszustreben suchte.

So bleiben als echte Äußerungen eines "eigentlichen" Antiklerikalismus die unter (2), (3) und (4) genannten Erscheinungen. Hier ging es um unmittelbare Wechselwirkungen zwischen der Laienwelt und dem Klerus, hier wurden persönlich erlebte Defizite und Konflikte wirksam, hier richteten sich die Handlungen konkret, spürbar und handgreiflich gegen die Personen der Kleriker, nicht gegen die anonyme Institution der Kirche im ganzen oder gegen Teile von ihr. Antiklerikalismus in diesem Verständnis des Begriffs erwächst zwar in einer bestimmten zeitgeschichtlichen Umwelt, aber er ist in seinem tatsächlichen Geschehen als emotional, spontan, aggressiv und personenbezogen zu kennzeichnen. Ein Blick auf die ganze Kirchengeschichte kann zu der Feststellung führen, daß es einen Antiklerikalismus in dieser Qualifikation nur vor und während der Reformation gegeben hat, weil nur in dieser Epoche die Voraussetzungen dafür vorhanden waren. Nicht jede Art der Kirchenkritik, nicht jeder Angriff auf einen Geistlichen, sei es

Schmähung, Beleidigung oder Gewalttätigkeit, nicht jede antireligiöse Agitation ist schon Antiklerikalismus. Unter den besonderen Bedingungen des späten 15. Jahrhunderts ist aber eine weitverbreitete antiklerikale Grundhaltung in der Gesellschaft aufgekommen, auf der die Reformation mit ihrem großen Erfolg aufbauen konnte. Die Reformation hat diesem Antiklerikalismus den Boden entzogen, indem sie ein völlig neues Pfarrerbild schuf und den Status des Geistlichen, des studierten Theologen, in der Gesellschaft vollkomen neu bestimmte.

ANTICLERICALISM AND THE EARLY SPANISH INQUISITION

WILLIAM MONTER

Northwestern University

Despite its official title, this conference has essentially confined itself to the history of pre- and post-Reformation anticlericalism within the spacious boundaries of the Holy Roman Empire (which in theory stretched from the Low Countries via Switzerland into much of northern Italy, and retained formal connections with the kingdom of Bohemia). What has been missing from the picture are the varieties of anticlericalism to be found in the three great monarchies of western Europe during the fifteenth and sixteenth centuries.

Even upon superficial inspection, it seems apparent that these three monarchies present three very different pictures. Proceeding from north to south, and perhaps from the most to the least vigorously anticlerical, it is obvious that the kingdom of England had a long and broad anticlerical tradition, channeled by Wyclif into the movement known as Lollardy and still very much alive in the early Tudor era, as the classic works of A. G. Dickens long ago demonstrated.[1] Moreover, it seems obvious that British anticlericalism has direct ties to the early Protestant Reformation. In other words, English anticlericalism should provide the most useful and most important comparisons with the Germanic lands.

By contrast, the kingdom of France is virtually terra incognita for students of fifteenth and sixteenth-century anticlericalism. We can be reasonably certain that it flourished here in both literary forms and everyday life; *l'esprit gaulois* dominated late medieval French writing, the genius of Rabelais proves that it continued to dominate Renaissance French literature, and the example of Bishop Roussel reportedly dying from injuries suffered when a nobleman chopped down the pulpit from which he was preaching suggests a degree of direct anticlerical action rarely attained elsewhere, either in fact or fiction. However, the subject of anticlericalism has been virtually tabu for historians of sixteenth-century France ever since 1929, when Lucien Febvre published an all-too-successful article deriding the link between anticlericalism and the French Reformation as "a badly-put

---

[1] See his fundamental synthesis: A. G. Dickens, *The English Reformation* (London, 1964), esp. chaps. 2 and 5 and literature cited there.

question".[2] It is not certain that Febvre rejuvenated the study of the origins of the French Reformation (few major theses have been devoted to this topic in the past sixty years), but it is highly probable that he killed the study of French anticlericalism.

Finally we reach the kingdom of Spain, a proverbially dry and barren land, perhaps also for the historian of anticlericalism. Here the dominant theme of late medieval history is the gradual reconquest of the peninsula from the Moslems by Christian kings who tolerated a sizable Jewish minority among their subjects. Many things changed rather suddenly with the reign of the "Catholic kings", Ferdinand and Isabella, who conquered the Moslems and forbade the practice of Judaism in 1492 and the practice of Islam ten years later. Although the kingdom of Castile boasted of its freedom from heresy during the middle ages, its Queen created a royal Inquisition with papal blessing in 1478 in order to deal with disbelief among converted Jews; it was subsequently extended to deal with heresies among converted Moslems. What, if anything, do its early workings tell us about the problem of anticlericalism in Renaissance Spain?

The Spanish Inquisition spread quickly to all parts of Ferdinand and Isabella's lands. Although subsequent boasts about the extent of its activities were greatly exaggerated, there is no doubt that it condemned upwards of fifty thousand people in its first fifty years of activity; it actually executed close to two thousand living people, along with a larger number of cadavers and effigies. To put the element of persecution into comparative perspective, the Spanish Inquisition killed about twice as many "Judaizers" in the forty years after 1480 as the number of Anabaptists executed in the Empire (excluding the Netherlands) in the fifteen years after 1525.

As one would expect, the records of the early Spanish Inquisition are extremely incomplete. But they are also quite extensive. We possess files of correspondence between the governing council of the Holy Office and its Castilian branches dating back to about 1500, and correspondence with the Aragonese branches dating from about 1515. Mostly complete series of trials survive from the district of Cuenca, and partial trial records survive from two more important districts, Toledo and Valencia. Extensive early financial records — extremely valuable sources, often as informative as the trials themselves — also survive from Valencia and from the Sicilian tribunal at Palermo.[3] Miscellaneous bits of evidence survive from a variety of local

---

[2] Lucien Febvre, "Une question mal posée: Les origines de la Réforme française et le problème des causes de la Réforme", originally printed in *Revue historique* 161 (1929), reprinted at the head of a collection of Febvre's essays, *Au coeur religieux du XVIe siècle* (Paris, 1957).

[3] An excellent example of Valencian scholarship relying on these fiscal records is Ramon Ferrer Navarro, "Aspectos economicos de la inquisición turolense a fines del siglo XV", in *Ligarzas* 7 (1975); for an even more valuable work using Palermo fiscal records, see Pietro Burgarella, "Diego de Obregon e i primi anni del

sources; perhaps the most interesting are the eyewitness reports on Seville's *autos de fe* (1483-1524) scattered through notarial documents, collected by Klaus Wagner.[4] Enough is known — or at least, knowable — to offer a reliable outline of how this peculiar organization actually functioned.

Enough material survives, at any rate, to convince me that the relationship between the early Spanish Inquisition and the history of anticlericalism in Reformation Europe is a classical example of *une question mal posée*. An historically-trained anthropologist working on early modern Spain comments that "building a picture of rural Catholicism from [Inquisition] archives would be like trying to get a sense of everyday American political life from FBI files."[5] The early Spanish Inquisition concentrated obsessively on one form of religious deviation: "Judaizing", the relapse into (or survival of) practices of Mosaic law among converted Jews and their descendants. For anyone interested in the history of religious assimilation among members of two major faiths (Jews and later, Moslems) who rarely if ever abandon their original ritual practices, the history of the early Spanish Inquisition offers a veritable mountain of fascinating evidence. No place in Christendom except the monarchy of Ferdinand and Isabella ever tried to convert either Jews or Moslems en masse, let alone both. Given such a Utopian goal, of course they needed something like a royal Inquisition to keep the whole enterprise from becoming an unmitigated farce.

If the Spanish Inquisition was intensely anti-Judaic (and later, intensely anti-Moslem), it was not particularly interested in signs of anticlericalism. Instead of searching for traces of latent anti-Semitism among the virulent anticlericalism of the *Flugschriften* as Hsia has encouraged us to do, the historian of the Spanish Inquisition deals with the exact reverse situation. Given the conditions of Isabella's Castile, where *conversos* were so well-entrenched within both the state and the church, anti-Semitism found several of its most important targets among the clergy; clerics comprised several of the most prominent victims of the early Inquisition, and also provided some of its most important opponents.

The deeply anti-Semitic parish priest Andres Bernaldez, an eye-witness to Spain's first public *auto de fe* in 1481, provides our best source on the workings of the early Seville Inquisition. Summarizing the first eight years of its activities, Bernaldez claims that it burned more than eight hundred people (most of them, I believe, in effigy) and reconciled more than five thousand. When recalling the various victims who had been burned, Bernaldez listed only "three Mass-priests and three or four monks, all of *converso* lineage; and they burned a doctor who was a Trinitarian monk,

---

Sant'Uffizio in Sicilia (1500-1514)", in *Archivo storico siciliano*, 3d ser., 20 (1970).

    [4] Klaus Wagner, "La Inquisición en Sevilla (1481-1524)", in *Homenaje al profesor Carriazo*, 3 (Seville, 1973), 439-60.

    [5] William Christian Jr., *Local Religion in Sixteenth-Century Spain* (Princeton, 1981), 4.

named Savariego, who was a great preacher and a great liar, a deceptive heretic; I heard him preach about the Passion once on Good Friday."[6] Perhaps only a clergyman would be so attentive to the *trahison des clercs*. However, important clerics were among the early victims of the Inquisition in other cities as well: Toledo, for example.

Bishops of *converso* lineage disliked the new institution and did their best to delay or mitigate its actions. For example, Burgos, the capital of Old Castile, scene of anti-*converso* rioting in the mid-fifteenth century, never saw the Inquisition until 1491 and apparently recorded only one early *reconciliado*, who was a cathedral canon. The newly-conquered kingdom of Granada was soon given an Archbishop of *converso* ancestry who never disguised his dislike for the Holy Office and was himself arrested on its orders in 1506. In Cordoba, where serious rioting against the Inquisition occurred in 1506, the ringleader was a local abbot.[7] The reasons are not far to seek: apart from its greed and occasional bloodthirstiness, Spanish bishops had little love for the new Inquisition because it cut into areas of their traditional jurisdiction.

If *converso* clerics were prominent both as opponents and as victims of the early Inquisition (and of course they were equally prominent among its promoters), these facts tell us little about the connections, if any, between the Holy Office and Spanish anticlericalism. When prosecuting ordinary laymen, the Inquisition wanted evidence about Jewish practices, not anticlerical opinions, among the *converso* population. But what did they find? Inquisitorial evidence suggests that Spanish *conversos* during Isabella's reign were caught between Catholic demands and old Jewish customs, maintained more out of habit than conviction. Some remained genuinely Jewish in outlook and practices; Juan Luis Vives' uncle ran a clandestine synagogue in Valencia and was burned alive in 1501. Others had become genuinely Christian; St. Teresa of Avila's grandfather had voluntarily confessed Judaic practices in his childhood during a period of grace in 1485 and lived as an ordinary Catholic thereafter.[8] Most converted Jews who encountered the Inquisition fit somewhere in between these two extremes.

"Anticlerical" the converted Jews were not. But the experience of attempting to turn Christian (and encountering various forms of hostility from the self-styled "Old Christians") did make some of them quite cynical.

---

[6] Andres Bernaldez, *Memorias del reinado de los reyes catolicos*, ed. Gomez-Moreno and Carriazo (Madrid, 1962), 101.

[7] See Lucino Serrano, *Los reyes católicos y la ciudad de Burgos (desde 1451 a 1492)* (Madrid, 1943), 254, 285f. (this tribunal was closed down permanently a few years later); and Rafael Gracia Boix, *Colección de documentos ineditos para la historia de la Inquisición de Cordoba* (Cordoba, 1982), 89.

[8] Compare Angelina Garcia, *Els Vives: una familia de juheus valencians* (Valencia, 1986), and José Gomez-Menor, *El linaje familar de Santa Teresa y de San Juan de la Cruz* (Toledo, 1970).

As Jewish sources also recognized, these people were not likely to believe two religions; they were more likely to believe neither. A recent and persuasive look by John Edwards at the testimony against ordinary *conversos* during the 1490s in the eastern district of Siguenza confirms our most cynical speculations: if the experience of inquisitorial persecution turned a minority of *conversos* back into genuine Jews awaiting an imminent Messiah, it made even more of them into materialists disillusioned by both religions.[9]

If anticlericalism existed in Ferdinand and Isabella's Spain, one might expect to find strong traces of it in inquisitorial records. Although we can find plenty of evidence of non-Christian behavior, and some explicitly anti-Christian behavior, among ex-Jews (and later among ex-Moslems), it seems virtually impossible to find anticlerical behavior in these sources. But does the scarcity of genuinely anticlerical evidence in Spanish inquisitorial records mean that Castile was truly a land without anticlericalism? Probably not.

Bartolomé Bennassar, one of the best Hispanists alive today, insists in a major synthetic work that anticlericalism was rife among the highly devout Castilian peasantry. His first evidence, borrowed from Bataillon, is the extraordinary popularity of Erasmus' monastophobic *Enchiridion* in Renaissance Spain. His second and more persuasive piece of evidence comes from a collection of Castilian proverbs first published in 1627. It contains almost three hundred proverbs relating to the clergy, overwhelmingly hostile: "to have a clean home, build no dovecotes and avoid priests"; "a priest without children is a priest without testicles"; "no monk is fit to be a friend or unfit to be an enemy"; "Dominus vobiscum never died from hunger"; or "the love of a nun is the same thing as a fart."[10]

Please note that Bennassar's examples come from folklore, but not from legal records or printed satires directed principally against either regular or secular clergy. Spaniards were understandably cynical about clerical morality and greed, but they respected the office if not the man. The Spanish situation seems relatively close to the portrait of sixteenth-century Italian anticlericalism painted by Silvana Seidel Menchi: an "almost instinctive reaction to intimate (and excessive) familiarity", a verbal grumbling that almost never evolved into acts of direct personal hostility.

Moreover, unlike the situation in Italy, Castilian anticlericalism never encouraged the growth of heresy. As its Inquisitors boasted to the Pope in 1558, Protestantism had spread to almost every corner of Christendom; but "the province which by God's grace has been freest of this stain has been the very heart of Spain, thanks to the great care and vigilance of the Holy

---

[9] John Edwards, "Religious Faith and Doubt in Late Medieval Spain: Soria circa 1450-1500," *PaP* 120 (1988): 3-25.

[10] Bartolomé Bennassar, *The Spanish Character: Attitudes and Mentalities from the Sixteenth to the Nineteenth Centuries* (Berkeley, 1979), 97-102, esp. 98.

Office of the Inquisition."[11] They were basically correct. The great Marcel Bataillon, who revealed the enormous popularity of Erasmus' *Enchiridion* in Spain, also insisted that the *conversos* who so relished Erasmianism rarely if ever became genuine Protestants. Apart from a few foreign-trained autodidacts like Servetus, there really was no indigenous "Lutheranism", in Spain. The number of unrepentant Spaniards executed as Protestants by the Inquisition scarcely totalled fifteen men in all.

In more or less benign forms, anticlericalism was probably ubiquitous in Christendom in 1500. But a land without serious heretical movements in the middle ages was a land immune from Protestantism. Consider the large but sparsely-populated Duchy of Luxemburg, which straddled the linguistic frontier between French and German. Here the noun "vauldoise", Waldensian, appears in some texts between 1510 and 1550, but it invariably refers to women accused of witchcraft. Although Protestantism seems as inconsequential here as in Castile, anticlericalism abounded in the Duchy of Luxemburg; in the district of Bastogne, priests were involved in criminal cases almost every year from 1555 to 1616, usually as plaintiffs who had been beaten, stoned, or had their homes pillaged.[12] None of this applies to Spain, where clergy were rarely assaulted physically.

Most of western Europe seems very different from Luxemburg or Castile. France, England, or Italy look like counter-examples, where remnants of medieval heretical groups, Waldensians or Lollards, combined with literary portraits satirizing the clergy, generated significant public support for a Protestant movement by 1530. Anticlericalism may have been a necessary ingredient of the explosive mix which transformed so many beliefs and practices in Reformation Europe, but it was never sufficient to start the explosion.

---

[11] Henry Charles Lea, *A History of the Inquisition of Spain*, 4 vols. (New York, 1906-08), 3: 567.

[12] See M. S. Dupont-Bouchat, "La répression de la sorcellerie dans le duché de Luxembourg aux XVIe et XVIIe siècles", in Dupont-Bouchat, Frijhoff and Muchembled, eds., *Prophètes et sorciers dans les Pays-bas XVIe-XVIIIe siècle* (Paris, 1978), 63, 67, 71 n. 61, 73-4; compare G. Christophe, *Histoire de la Réforme protestante et de la Réforme catholique au Duché de Luxembourg jusqu'au milieu du XVIIe siècle* (Luxemburg, 1975).

A REPORT ON ANTICLERICALISM
IN THREE FRENCH WOMEN WRITERS 1404-1549

JANE DEMPSEY DOUGLASS

Princeton Theological Seminary

In the broad circle touched by French humanism in the late middle ages and the Reformation can be found a group of writers who may offer insight into a distinctive form of anticlericalism in that period. They are connected by their engagement in the *querelle des femmes*, a literary debate about the nature of women extending from the fourteenth to the seventeenth centuries.[1] From this diverse group of men and women, I have selected three women whose writings in French span the period from the late fourteenth century to the mid-sixteenth century: Christine de Pizan (or de Pisan), a late medieval Catholic woman; Marguerite of Navarre, a Catholic in the humanist reforming movement; and Marie Dentière, a nun who converted to Protestantism. Though it is not apparent in the writings which I will discuss that there is any direct literary dependence of one on another, there is some relationship among the writers. Marguerite of Navarre grew up in a household where writings of Christine were part of the family library.[2] Marie Dentière's second published work was an open letter to Marguerite of Navarre, with whom she claimed a close relationship.[3] Their writings show that they stood together among the defenders of women in the *querelle des femmes*, in a common tradition of thought.

One element in this tradition was the belief that the clergy had a mistaken understanding of women's nature and role, based on prejudice, inaccurate information from ill-informed authorities, and misreading of the Bible; and

---

[1] For the nature of the *querelle des femmes*, see for example Emile Telle, *L'Oeuvre de Marguerite d'Angoulême, Reine de Navarre, et la querelle des femmes* (Toulouse, 1937; repr. Geneva, 1969), chaps. 1-3; Joan Kelly, *Women, History, and Theory* (Chicago, 1984), chap. 4.

[2] Dorothy Moulton Mayer, *The Great Regent: Louise of Savoy 1476-1531* (London, 1966), 12. See also Mayer's claim that Marguerite's mother, Louise of Savoy, had "certainly" read Christine as a girl at the court of Anne de France, 9.

[3] *Epistre très vtile faicte et composée par vne femme Chrestienne de Tornay, Envoyée a la Royne de Nauarre seur du Roy de France ... Anuers. M.Vc.XXXIX* (actually Geneva, 1539). For a discussion of the authorship of both this work and her earlier anonymous one, *La Guerre et Deslivrance de la Ville de Genesve* (Geneva, 1536), see A. Rilliet, "Restitution de l'écrit intitulé: *La Guerre et Deslivrance de la Ville de Genesve (1536)*", in *Mémoires et documents publiés par la Société d'Histoire et d'Archéologie de Genève* 20 (1881): 309-84.

that clerics, profiting from their unjust sexual and social privilege, were causing women to be treated in a manner which belied women's God-given dignity. The writings of the three women represent a protest both against intellectual or theological positions and also against offensive and unjust behavior.

Christine de Pizan stands at the very beginning of the *querelle des femmes*. She objected vigorously to the misogyny of the *Roman de la Rose*, an immensely popular example of the literature of courtly love. Her protest helped to set off the protracted literary debate among men and women about the nature of women and their proper education and style of life.[4]

These issues were not abstract for her. Born in Venice to the family of a doctor and professor of astrology from the University of Bologna, she was taken to Paris as a child when her father received a court appointment there. There is some suggestion that Christine realized that the fires of the Italian inquisition may have played a role in that move, and that she was fearful of inquisitorial condemnations.[5] Though Christine was better educated than most of her female contemporaries, she was regretful that her parents had not given her the education a son would have received. She apparently had heard from her father about Giovanni Andreae, professor of canon law at the University of Bologna while her father was there, and his daughter, Novella, who was so learned that she sometimes taught his classes for him.[6] When Christine found herself suddenly a young widowed mother without financial resources, she became one of the very rare women of her era to support her household by writing.[7] Her influence was felt for centuries as her books were circulated and translated.[8]

Among her many books, *The Book of the City of Ladies*, composed between 1404 and 1407,[9] may be particularly useful for the topic of anticlericalism. It is in fact an extended response to *Lamentations*, a book written by the cleric Matheolus, which Christine found deeply disturbing because of its contempt for women and marriage.[10] She relates that having

---

[4] See Charity Cannon Willard, *Christine de Pizan: Her Life and Works* (New York, 1984), chap. 4.

[5] See Maureen Cheney Curnow, *The Livre de la Cité des Dames of Christine de Pisan: A Critical Edition* (Ann Arbor, 1975), 20-1.

[6] Curnow, 19-20.

[7] For biographical and bibliographical information, see Willard; Earl Jeffrey Richards, ed. and transl., *The Book of the City of Ladies* (New York, 1982), xix-li; Curnow, chap. 1.

[8] For the influence of her writings, see Willard, chap. 11; for that of *The Book of the City of Ladies*, specifically, see Curnow, chaps. 6-8.

[9] Curnow, 18. Richards chooses 1405, xxv.

[10] On Matheolus and Christine's specific treatment of his ideas, see Curnow, 227-35. Matheolus married unhappily, lost his ecclesiastical benefices, and is himself described by Curnow as "anticlerical", 229.

read a bit in this book, finding it distasteful, she began to reflect on the fact that all the male poets, philosophers, and orators, not just the author of this book, speak so badly of women, as though all women were full of vice.[11] She began to analyze her own character and that of women she knew from all walks of life, but she could not see how that judgment could possibly be true. Still, she had such deep respect for the knowledge of all the famous men, the scholars who proclaimed the evilness of women, that in humility she denied her own knowledge of herself and other women and recalled one after another the male authorities and their opinions.[12] In her sadness she began to wonder how such a worthy divine artisan could have made such a vile creature as woman. She despised herself and all women as "monstrosities in nature."[13] She lamented to God that God had made her a woman so full of abominations rather than a man, all of whose inclinations would be to serve God better, who would not err, who would have the perfection a male person is said to have. She asked God to forgive her failings in God's service because women were given fewer gifts.[14]

Suddenly Christine was roused from her despair by a vision of three crowned ladies who proved to be Reason, Rectitude, and Justice. They had come to answer her questions, to bring her to her senses and dispel her ignorance, to help her trust her identity as a woman and become confident of her capabilities, to teach her to distinguish truth from falsehood, and to instruct her in the history of valiant women in the ancient world and in the Bible as well as more recent times.[15] They also wished to assist her in building a city for worthy women where they will be protected from their assailants.[16]

As part of Christine's labor in building the city of ladies, she asks questions of Reason, using the pick of her understanding to cut away the dirt and rocks to build a proper foundation.[17] Dame Reason teaches Christine that neither nature nor reason is the source of the lies men tell about women. Rather the lies come from the men's own vices, like jealousy.[18] Christine inquires about the Latin book, *About the Secret of Women*,[19] (at that time

---

[11] Curnow, 616-7.
[12] Curnow, 618-9.
[13] Curnow, 620.
[14] Curnow, 621.
[15] See especially Curnow, 974ff.
[16] Curnow, 621-30.
[17] Curnow, 639.
[18] Curnow, 640-7.
[19] Curnow, 223-4, identifies this with the *Secreta mulierum*, "a semi-scientific treatise on gynecology", falsely attributed in Christine's day to Albertus Magnus and containing references to Aristotle. Curnow cites evidence that editions of this work did indeed commonly include the threat of excommunication to which Christine refers; but she believes that Christine has in her memory conflated this work with

commonly attributed to Albertus Magnus) which, she says, discusses the defects of women's natural bodies. She recalls that it tells how women's imperfect bodies result from inadequacy in the gestational process, producing a being of which Nature is ashamed. Reason points out that although the book has been attributed to Aristotle, to charge such a great philosopher with authorship of such lies is hardly credible. Women would immediately know that such teaching consisted of lies if they read it. Therefore the book indicates that some pope or other excommunicated any man who would read it to a woman or allow a woman to read it. This threat was intended to ensure that men would continue to be deceived by the book's lies and never know the truth.[20] In contrast to such views, Reason teaches Christine about the biblical understanding of the creation of woman in the image of God, and about the nobility of woman which follows from that creation.[21]

Dame Reason undercuts the authority of men's teaching in various other ways. She points out that men criticize each other. For example, Augustine and other doctors sometimes criticize Aristotle, despite their vast respect for his teaching.[22] She teaches Christine that one should never assume that the philosophers' words are infallible articles of faith. With regard to the poets, sometimes they say the opposite of what they mean and should be interpreted by the figure of *antiphrasis*; if some of Matheolus' points were to be taken literally, they would be "pure heresy".[23]

When Christine asks about men's despising of women's tears and loquaciousness, Reason points her to the Gospels. Jesus did not despise the tears of Mary Magdalene or Martha or the mother of the child who had died. And Augustine was converted by his mother's tears.[24] As for speech, Jesus commanded Mary Magdalene to be the first to proclaim his resurrection. Reason is certain that preachers who explain this command by saying that Jesus knew women would never keep quiet and thus would spread the news quickly are imputing blasphemy to Jesus, suggesting he would reveal perfection through a vice. Jesus also had mercy on the Canaanite woman who just would not stop talking, pleading for mercy on her sick daughter: "In the heart of a little woman of pagan stock, God found more faith than

---

another, since it does not contain all that Christine attributes to it. See 224, n. 46. Curnow, 224, suggests Christine "does not seem to know that it was indeed Aristotle who postulated that woman is an imperfect man." That may be true. But Christine often cloaks her attacks with a satirical naiveté which should not be taken at face value.

[20] Curnow, 649-50.
[21] Curnow, 651-3.
[22] Curnow, 623.
[23] Curnow, 624.
[24] Curnow, 657-9.

in all the bishops, princes, priests, and all the people of the Jews."[25] Reason points out the admirable example of the Samaritan woman who spoke on her own behalf to Jesus. Jesus did not disdain her, in contrast to contemporary pontifical bishops who do not deign to discuss anything with a simple little woman, let alone her own salvation.[26] Reason also commends the woman at the sermon of Jesus who could not keep quiet and called out boldly, "Blessed is the womb which bore you and the breasts which you sucked"; her words are recorded in the Gospel.[27]

Were we to tell the whole story of the city of ladies, it would be clear that the literary structure of this work gives far more attention to the positive praise of historical women (or at least women whom Christine believed to be historical) than to complaints about men.[28] Rarely are particular men even mentioned. Nonetheless the chief purpose of the book seems to be to challenge the contemporary scholastic understanding of the nature of women. In Christine's eyes it is too heavily dependent on Aristotle's view of women as misbegotten males[29] and therefore weak and inferior to men; it is too deficient in a biblical view of the creation of women in the image of God and in Christ's respect for women; and it is too ignorant of the capabilities and achievements of real women: the women of classical antiquity, of biblical times, and of Christian history down to her day, whose stories she relates.[30] The corollary, of course, is that scholastic teaching has an inflated view of the perfection and virtue of men and grants them unjust privilege over women. Christine relies more on gentle satire than heavy denunciation, but her point is clear.

Occasionally she criticizes the morals of the popes and clergy which have deteriorated from ancient sanctity since Constantine endowed the church with wealth, but this is a minor theme.[31] She pokes fun at the claims of exclusive male privilege to teach, especially about the nature of women — a subject about which they know so little. Though her arguments are aimed at male authorities more broadly than merely the clergy, we have seen that she clearly faults the pope's unjust use of his churchly authority to perpetuate malicious lies about women, she faults theology's reliance on ignorant secular authorities, and preachers' giving credence to prejudice

---

[25] Curnow, 659-62.

[26] Curnow, 662.

[27] Curnow, 663.

[28] See Curnow's summary, 235-8.

[29] See for example the discussion of Thomas Aquinas in Kari Elisabeth Børresen, *Subordination and Equivalence: The Nature and Role of Woman in Augustine and Thomas Aquinas* (Washington, D.C., 1981), 141-311.

[30] The references to women in Pt. I of *Le Livre de la Cité des Dames* are mostly to those of classical antiquity. Pt. II includes also some women of the Old Testament and Christian women. Pt. III focuses on Christian women.

[31] Curnow, 898.

against women by repeating it in the pulpit. In her view, authoritative teaching needs to be received in a much more critical spirit.

One senses humanist influence in this critical approach to the use of authorities. It also seems visible in her heavy use of figures from classical antiquity as examples of strong and capable women and in the broad literary context in which she works.[32] Furthermore it can be seen in her frequent appeal to the simple piety of the biblical characters over against the corrupt teaching authority of the church. Simple women in the Bible have more faith than contemporary bishops and priests, she thinks.

Our second writer, Marguerite of Angoulême, Queen of Navarre, reflects some of the same themes but in the context of events more than a century later. Daughter of a powerful woman regent of France, Louise of Savoy,[33] Marguerite was also deeply engaged in the life of the court of her brother, King Francis I of France.

Like Christine, Marguerite was far from submissive to ecclesiastical authority. But because Marguerite was a more public figure, this assertiveness had more immediate consequences. Deeply identified with the catholic reforming movements within France, especially that of Bishop Guillaume Briçonnet and his "Group of Meaux", she was supportive of the new humanistic concerns, though she never openly espoused Protestantism. She intervened when the Sorbonne attacked reforming leaders, though she was not always able to protect them from the Inquisition. At her court she sheltered many accused of the new protestant heresy, and she invited protestant pastors to preach. She even translated one of Luther's writings: a meditation on the Lord's Prayer.[34] In Marguerite's case, therefore, she is opposing the old clericalism but supporting reforming clergy.

Her own closest brush with the Inquisition, then flourishing in Paris, came at least partly as the result of publication of her mystical, spiritual poetic work, *The Mirror of the Sinful Soul*. Noel Béda at the theological faculty of the Sorbonne questioned its doctrinal orthodoxy in 1533. When the king made inquiries about the nature of the heresy, the charges against Marguerite were dropped, and the printer was sent to the stake because of publication without permission.[35]

---

[32] See Curnow's discussion of Christine's sources, 124-80.

[33] See Mayer's biography (n. 2 above), which gives considerable attention to Marguerite as well. For biography of Marguerite, see Pierre Jourda, *Marguerite d'Angoulême, Duchesse d'Alençon, Reine de Navarre (1492-1549)* (Paris, 1930).

[34] See Roland H. Bainton, *Women of the Reformation in France and England* (Minneapolis, 1973), chap. 1. For more extended discussion of Marguerite's religion, see Lucien Febvre, *Autour de l'Heptaméron: Amour sacré, amour profane* (n.p., 1944), especially for her relation to Briçonnet and other Catholic reformers and to Luther. He also notes the mixing of evangelical fervor with frank sexuality, not uncommon in Marguerite's day, 212-3.

[35] Bainton, 25-6.

The climate then seemed to improve slightly, and Marguerite published in 1536 a little farce, *The Inquisitor*.[36] The starring inquisitor is surely Béda, and at the outset he is satirized in most unflattering terms. He recognizes the strength of the new religion, that it is overshadowing the old, but he is resolved to kill it. He acknowledges that whereas ignorant people could be dealt with by fear, he cannot quiet the learned ones who know Scripture much better than he. He prides himself on sparing no one — unless a good bribe might be offered. "For it is better that an innocent man die cruelly as an example to everyone than that this error remain for a long time, turning our laws upside down."[37] In an encounter with happy children, singing the Marot version of Psalm 3, this cruel man learns about the new birth and justification by faith alone and is converted to a new person, happily joining the children in faith.[38] Here Marguerite conveys a hope that the old clericalism can still be transformed by the new, reforming understanding of faith and lose its inquisitorial, self-justifying mentality.

Subsequent resurgence of the persecution of reform destroyed that hope, and in the *Heptameron*,[39] published after her death, one sees bitter anti-clericalism. The work claims to be a collection of stories told over a period of several days by a group of noble French men and women who were marooned by floodwaters at an abbey. By the rules of the storytellers, the stories are supposed to be true. Marguerite has recorded the stories and also included revealing dialogue among the travelers about the meaning and significance of the stories.[40] The overarching theme is the relation between men and women in all its complexity, occasionally loving, often cruel or even murderous. Though both men and women are portrayed as both virtuous and sinful, the collection leaves the impression of a catalogue of

---

[36] *L'Inquisiteur*, in Marguerite de Navarre, *Théatre profane*, ed. Verdun L. Saulnier (Paris, 1946), 35-81.

[37] Saulnier, 49-50. The apparent quotations in Bainton, 26-7, are mostly summaries and paraphrases, seldom direct quotations.

[38] Whereas Bainton, 26, and others seem to regard this play as a sort of vengeance on Béda, Saulnier argues that it represents hope that a better day is coming. Since 1535 Béda is a little less intransigent, the children represent the new generation of young reformers, and Marguerite hopes for reconciliation, 38-41.

[39] Marguerite de Navarre, *L'Heptaméron*, ed. Michel François (Paris, n.d. [1943]). For discussion of questions of text and authorship, see François, i-xxviii; Marguerite de Navarre, *The Heptameron*, transl. and ed. P. A. Chilton (Penguin Books, 1984), 7-44. First published nine years after her death, the work has appeared in various forms and occasioned much discussion by literary critics. There is a consensus that the structure of the work was created by Marguerite and that the tales included are, as indicated within the work, probably contributions by others rather than creations of Marguerite.

[40] A useful but rather sketchy analysis of this dialogue can be found in Marie-Madeleine de la Garanderie, *Le dialogue des romanciers: une nouvelle lecture de L'Heptaméron de Marguerite de Navarre* (Paris, 1977).

ways in which men mistreat women, often brutally.[41] Quite a few of the stories celebrate strong, virtuous, and clever women who succeed in protecting their virtue against lustful men, and some also criticize those who are too trusting or timid.[42]

Two of the seventy-two stories[43] speak of pious priests; a few more tell of frustrated lovers who become good monks.[44] Seventeen focus on sinful clerics. In one story[45] some priests exploit a false claim of a miracle to enrich themselves. The other sixteen anticlerical stories deal in some way with immorality of the clergy related to their sexual exploitation of women.[46] The picture presented is not merely that of individual sinners but rather of a clergy fundamentally corrupted by futile and perverse rules of celibacy. A storyteller declares that the clerics' lack of opportunity for love of an honest woman renders them unspiritual, never loving anything but good wine and filthy chambermaids.[47]

One story tells of a seducing bishop,[48] but nearly all the rest concern friars, mostly Franciscans. The focus on disreputable Franciscans is quite self-conscious.[49] One sixteenth-century editor, Pierre Gruget, seems to have been particularly sensitive to this bias; he not only suppressed some passages which would have offended conservative religious minds, as did a previous editor, but he actually omitted completely from his edition of the *Heptameron* three of the stories which are particularly unflattering to the Franciscans.[50] Most offenses involve attempted or actual seductions. One Franciscan confesses frankly that the order will last forever because it is founded on the folly of women.[51]

Especially powerful is the theme of the betrayal of the family by clergy trusted by the family to support its integrity and spiritual health. Four stories involve Franciscans who exploit their trusted roles as spiritual advisors within a household out of uncontrollable desire for women. In each case the family had sought out a Franciscan as preacher and confessor with the

---

[41] Bainton's description, 33, of the book as a collection of tales of love written by Marguerite ignores the discussions of the literary critics and also the feminist edge of the work as a whole. For the latter, see Telle (n. 1 above).

[42] See stories 5 and 46, where women outwit those who would seduce them; François, 35-8, 308-9. See stories 46 and 72, where imprudent trust and timidity are pointed out; François 309-11, 424-8.

[43] Stories 19 and 35; François, 143ff., 255ff.

[44] Stories 19 and 64; François, 143ff., 383ff. See Chilton, 20-1, for discussion of this phenomenon.

[45] Story 65; François, 388ff.

[46] Stories 1, 5, 11, 22, 23, 29, 31, 33, 34, 41, 44, 46, 48, 56, 61, 65, 72.

[47] Story 19; François, 152.

[48] Story 1; François, 11ff.

[49] See for example François, 241, 285, 347.

[50] Stories 11, 44, 46; see Chilton, 8.

[51] Story 44; François, 302ff.

expectation of holiness and competent spiritual counsel. One confessor brutally killed servants and forcibly carried off the mistress of the house to keep her with other women he had kidnapped for his pleasure.[52] Another callously raped the family's daughter under pretext of disciplining her for laziness.[53] Still another Franciscan confessor attempted to use the privacy of the confessional to seduce a young girl, but she sensibly refused the "penance" he was attempting to impose, even when the priest then refused to give her absolution.[54]

The most fully developed of these four stories of Franciscan betrayal within the household links family tragedy to both the immorality and also the bad theology of a friar. Consulted by a trusting husband, the priest calculatingly twisted his advice about church sexual laws to provide himself with an opportunity for rape of the wife. The pious and quite innocent wife was so distraught by this violation, wrongly blaming herself, that she committed suicide, unintentionally killing her infant son in the process.[55]

This tale was told by Oisille, a respected and spiritual older woman who had been called upon, after others had engaged in much criticism of monks, to tell something good about "holy religion". She declined on the grounds that the storytellers had vowed to tell the truth, offering instead this story.[56] Oisille does not merely communicate her criticism of the monk's misuse of the church's teaching about sexual matters but also her disgust with ecclesiastical interference with marriage: marital rights are by the ordinance of God, not dependent on human permission.[57] Oisille further attributes the wife's despairing suicide to bad Franciscan theology, emphasizing confidence in good works and satisfaction for sin through austerity of life but ignorant of God's goodness and mercy, of grace and remission of sin through Christ's reconciling work.[58] Her listeners agreed that the former practice of inviting Franciscans into the household is disappearing because "people now know them so well that they fear them more than outlaws."[59] Oisille, responding to an attack on priests who insist on the importance of marriage bonds but then violate them, declared, "It is a great pity that those who are responsible for the administration of the sacraments play games with them in this way; they should be burned alive!"[60] Yet another listener

---

[52] Story 31; François, 237ff.
[53] Story 46; François, 308ff.
[54] Story 41; François, 283ff.
[55] Story 23; François, 186ff.
[56] François, 186.
[57] François, 189.
[58] François, 190-1.
[59] François, 193.
[60] François, 193.

cautioned that the priests should be treated with some respect because they
have the power to dishonor and burn others.[61]

What of the monks with whom the travelers have found refuge? The
narrator in the Prologue notes that the abbot was a rather bad man who
received the travellers only because he did not dare turn away such
influential people.[62] By the fifth day he was irritated that their presence
made it impossible for him to invite his women pilgrims as usual.[63] Twice
the monks were so engrossed in listening to the stories from behind the
hedge that they nearly missed vespers.[64] But regular community worship
did take place. The party of storytellers attended mass daily.[65] In fact,
though they are said to attend devotedly, their prayer commending their
spirits to God in order to receive word and grace to continue their "gathering", presumably the storytelling, does not suggest very deep devotion.[66]
They also attended vespers daily, often arriving late.[67] There is no indication of their receiving any non-liturgical spiritual guidance from the
monks, but neither is there any suggestion of hesitation to attend services
conducted by monks of dubious morality and spirituality.

Given the setting in a monastery, there seems to be an anticlerical
coloring to the fact their spiritual teaching comes from a woman, Oisille.
Oisille is pictured as a very deeply spiritual woman who reads the Bible at
the beginning of every day, contemplating the goodness of God and the
forgiveness of sin through Christ, and singing the psalms. In the evening
before dinner she again reads the Bible and prays for pardon.[68] The group
of travellers asked her permission to join her each morning before mass. She
began her day by preparing herself alone for at least half an hour before the
arrival of the others. The first five days she read to them from Romans each
morning for about an hour. By the fourth day it is clear that she was also
expounding the lesson to them in a way they found sound and devout as
well as interesting. On the fifth day the narrator speaks of a sermon more
profitable than any they have ever heard. The sixth day she read from the
Epistle of John, and the lesson lasted half an hour longer than usual without
their being conscious of it. The following day she read and expounded the
beginning of Acts, preceding the mass of the Holy Spirit, probably
Pentecost. On day eight she returned again to John. She kept them longer
than usual, and "it seemed that the Holy Spirit, full of love and sweetness,
spoke by her mouth. And, all having been inflamed by this fire, they went

---

[61] François, 193.
[62] François, 6.
[63] François, 282.
[64] François, 156, 234-5.
[65] François, 10, 87, 157, 236, 282, 328, 370, 421.
[66] François, 10, 87.
[67] François, 84-5, 156, 235, 280, 326, 369, 420.
[68] François, 7-8.

to hear the great mass."[69] The delight of the entire group in hearing the Scripture expounded by this pious woman is warmly described in the account of each morning. Oisille's devotion to the study of Scripture is presented as giving her confidence that she can distinguish between true and false preaching by monks and priests who are often lacking in devotion or may even be consciously teaching false doctrine. Only what is in Scripture is binding on the Christian.[70]

In the *Heptaméron* one sees little that is respectful of the clergy and much biting anticlericalism. The criticism of the clergy, by the nature of the work, is focused on their unjust and unlawful sexual exploitation of women and on the personal and communal tragedy which follows from that. Here one sees no hope, as in *The Inquisitor*, that the clergy will be transformed. So thoroughly corrupt is the clergy that Marguerite proposes a radically different vision, exactly the opposite of her present experience: a devout laywoman, inspired by the Holy Spirit, thoroughly grounded in Scripture and able to open it persuasively to others, teaching the evangelical theology of the reforming movements, becomes the symbol of renewed spiritual leadership for the church. There is some indication that Marguerite, like Christine, draws this vision from a new way of reading the Bible which makes clear that women in the ancient church carried leadership responsibility and were respected by Paul.[71]

Our last writer, Marie Dentière, was an abbess in Picardy who converted to evangelical faith, married a pastor, Antoine Froment, and found herself in Geneva preaching and trying to convert the nuns and other Genevan citizens to the evangelical faith in the years just prior to the city's commitment to the Reform in 1536.[72]

Later in 1536 Marie published the first protestant history of the reform of Geneva, a small book entitled *The War and Deliverance of the City of*

---

[69] François, 10, 87, 157, 236, 282, 328, 370, 421.

[70] François, 303-4.

[71] François, 394. La Garanderie has also briefly noted the ministry of Oisille, seeing her as "femme-pasteur", 76. Like La Garanderie, A. J. Krailsheimer notices the figure of Oisille and the crescendo of fervor through the week of biblical teaching. See "The *Heptaméron* Reconsidered", in *The French Renaissance and its Heritage: Essays Presented to Alan M. Boase*, ed. D. R. Haggis, et al. (London, 1968), 75-92, esp. 79, 83-8. He suggests an explanation for the puzzling reference to Pentecost when the story-telling supposedly takes place in the fall, 83-4.

[72] For a summary of biographical information, see Thomas Head, "Marie Dentière, a Propagandist for the Reform", in *Women Writers of the Renaissance and Reformation*, ed. K. M. Wilson (Athens, Ga., 1987), 260-7. Two brief excerpts from her writings follow in English translation, 270-80. See also Jane Dempsey Douglass, *Women, Freedom, and Calvin* (Philadelphia, 1985), chap. 5, esp. 100-4; Douglass, "Marie Dentière's Use of Scripture in her Theology of History", in *Biblical Hermeneutics in Historical Perspective*, ed. M. S. Burrows, P. Rorem (Grand Rapids, 1991), 225-42.

Geneva.[73] More a theological reflection on God's work in history than a full narrative of events, the theme of the book is the power of the Word of God to liberate the suffering faithful people of God no matter how hopeless their bondage seems. She celebrates the fact that the long bondage of Geneva to its overlords is over, and there is now full freedom to preach the Word of God and reform society according to it. In this work she portrays the priests linked to political tyrants as oppressors, those who oppose the Word of God and the freedom of God's people, guilty of outrageous crimes to protect their power: murder, rape, theft, burning of houses and even people.[74]

Marie relates that when William Farel came to Geneva to preach the Gospel in 1532, he was called before the City Council and forbidden to preach in the city. But the priests and monks then also called him into their council and became so enraged that they tried to kill him, prevented only by God's providential care. They also banished him, to fulfill the prophecy of Matthew 10 about the apostles being persecuted and cast out of the synagogues. This whole account is set in the literary framework of the biblical account of Jesus' trial, with the priests cast in the role of the Jews.[75]

It is not only evangelical preachers who are persecuted by the priests. Marie relates the story of a monk who preached during Advent of 1532, probably the Franciscan Christophe Bocquet. She believes he came to preach about Jesus and his word, and she is approving of him. But she tells how the other priests chased him out of town because his preaching threatened their power and their way of life.[76] The priests are portrayed as living luxurious, idle and immoral lives; in the spirit of the Magnificat, Marie exults that with the Reformation the poor will be cared for in the former homes of the clergy, and the priests will have to work for their living.[77]

In this first book by Marie, we have seen very strong anticlericalism in her treatment of the old clergy, the Catholic priests who preach bad theology, trying to shut God's power up in their "cupboards" on the altar,[78] making their idol-god their prisoner, and living useless lives. But she is very positive about clergy who preach the Word of God, the true Gospel of Jesus Christ, whether they are catholic or protestant.

Marie's second book, *A Very Useful Letter Prepared and Composed by a Christian Woman of Tornay, Sent to the Queen of Navarre, Sister of the King of France, Against the Turks, Jews, Infidels, False Christians,*

---

[73] Rilliet, "Restitution" (n. 3 above), 312, 314.

[74] *La Guerre* in Rilliet, for example 344-5, 347, 359.

[75] *La Guerre*, 349-50.

[76] *La Guerre*, 351.

[77] *La Guerre*, 365-7.

[78] *La Guerre*, 367-8.

Anabaptists, and Lutherans,[79] published in Geneva in 1539, presents an unexpected twist on this view. Here the anticlericalism is directed against the new Reformed pastors called to replace Calvin and his associates who were exiled. One has the impression that life in the city is not so different than prior to 1536; she speaks of tumult, debates, dissensions, divisions, robbery, murder and other crimes.[80] Marie sees the new pastors as weak, too compliant to civil authorities, avoiding in the name of pastoral concern taking position against idolatrous practices. Those who curry favor with the people are honored, she says, while those who serve and honor Christ, boldly preaching the Gospel, are persecuted and chased away.[81]

Marie has still another fundamental complaint against the pastors: "Those to whom God gives grace to wish to write, speak, preach, and announce what Jesus and the Apostles said and preached" are often rejected and reproved, especially by the "learned sages".[82] One thinks immediately, of course, of the banished pastors. Still the whole context suggests that she is speaking of women. She proceeds to say to Marguerite of Navarre, to whom the letter is addressed, that women should not hide in the earth what God has given them and revealed to them any more than men should. "And although it is not permitted to us to preach in public assemblies and churches, nonetheless it is not forbidden to write and admonish one another in all love."[83] And so she writes in the hope that women held in captivity and exiled from their countries will be encouraged and strengthened to follow the Gospel. Marie thinks that up to now the Gospel was so hidden that women were not supposed to say anything or "to read and understand anything from the Scriptures." But she writes in hope "that in the future women will no longer be so despised as in the past. For God changes his peoples' hearts for the better from day to day."[84]

Within this book is a brief section entitled, "A Defense for Women".[85] Very much in the tradition of the humanist *querelle des femmes*, Marie confronts the charge by adversaries but also by faithful people that "for women to write one another about Scripture is too bold."[86] She answers the charge by pointing out the bold role of women in Scripture itself. From the Old Testament she chooses Sarah, Rebecca, the mother of Moses who defied the law to protect her son, Deborah the judge, Ruth, and the Queen of

---

[79] I have worked from excerpts in Rilliet, 377-84; and in A.-L. Herminjard, *Correspondance des réformateurs dans les pays de langue française*, vol. 5 (Geneva, 1878), 295-304.

[80] *Epistre*, Herminjard, 5: 296-7.

[81] *Epistre*, Herminjard, 5: 299-304.

[82] *Epistre*, Herminjard, 5: 296-7.

[83] *Epistre*, Herminjard, 5: 297.

[84] *Epistre*, Heminjard, 5: 297-8.

[85] *Epistre*, Rilliet, 378-80.

[86] *Epistre*, Rilliet, 378.

Sheba. From the New Testament she points out again the Queen of Sheba, the Virgin Mary, Elizabeth, the Samaritan woman who preached Christ, and Mary Magdalene's proclamation of the resurrection. She concludes:

> If God has then given graces to some good women, revealing to them by his Holy Scriptures something holy and good, will they not dare to write, speak or declare it one to another for fear of deprecators of truth? Ah! It would be too boldly done to wish to stop them, and for us, too foolishly done to hide the talent given us by God, who grants grace to us to persevere till the end. Amen![87]

One hears here the voice of a woman whose gifts were willingly used by clergy for the conversion of the city but who was afterwards told to be silent. This experience provides a particular shape to anticlericalism. The book was in fact understood by the pastors to be anticlerical, and it was banned and confiscated.[88] This episode illustrates the collaboration of the "new" protestant clergy with the "new" city government to repress dissent.

All three of the women writers we have considered reflect some varieties of anticlericalism common to other sources. Anticlericalism in the writings of Marguerite and Marie has not gone unnoticed,[89] but those who notice it do not connect it with the women's role in the *querelle des femmes* and therefore miss elements which make it distinctive. Their special awareness of misogyny on the part of the priests, of improper theological teaching about women, and of the clerical role in limiting women's public roles in the community offers a particular contribution to the study of anticlericalism. These writers also illustrate significant continuity of concern about clerical injustice to women throughout the period studied.

---

[87] *Epistre*, Rilliet, 380.

[88] Herminjard, 5: 296, n. 2; 301 and 456-7.

[89] See for Marguerite: Chilton, 16; Jules Gelernt, *World of Many Loves: The Heptameron of Marguerite de Navarre*, (Chapel Hill, N.C., 1966), 101ff. For Marie, see immediately previous note.

ELEMENTS OF ANTICLERICAL SENTIMENT
IN THE PROVINCE OF HOLLAND UNDER CHARLES V

JAMES D. TRACY[1]

University of Minnesota, Minneapolis

Writing from Basel in August 1525, in one of the many letters to Willibald Pirckheimer that were not published during his own lifetime, Erasmus described the religious situation in his native land: "Maxima populi pars apud Hollandos, Zelandos et Flandros scit doctrinam Lutheri, et odio plusquam capitali fertur in monachos."[2] Erasmus was reasonably well informed about the affairs of the Low Countries,[3] even after he had departed for Basel in 1521, and it will be the argument of this paper that the people of the Habsburg Netherlands were indeed animated by a "more than deadly hatred of the monks". As elsewhere in Europe, anticlerical feeling was compounded of a variety of elements. These remarks will be confined to the single province of Holland, based on the sources I have had occasion to use for my work on the political history of the province. In terms of traditional complaints that were not redressed by the government of Charles V, at least not to the satisfaction of the laity, one can usefully distinguish between opposition to the tax exemptions which all clerical institutions enjoyed, both at the provincial and the local level (part 1), and opposition, especially in the towns, to what were seen as abuses of power by particular sectors of the clergy, such as local representatives of the bishopric of Utrecht, or urban convents, or mendicant friars (2). In addition, there was another perceived abuse of power that was quite distinctive to the Reformation era, insofar as enforcement of the Emperor's brutal decrees for the

---

[1] Abbreviations specific to this paper: Aud. = the collection "Papiers d'Etat et de l'Audience" at the Algmeen Rijksarchief in Brussels; AJ = Andries Jacobszoon, "Prothocolle van alle die reysen ... bij mij Andries Jacopss gedaen ...", covering the years 1523-1538, Gemeentearchief Amsterdam; RSH = Resolutiën van de Staten van Holland, 278 vols. (Amsterdam, 1795ff.), of which vols. 1 and 2 cover the years 1525-1560.

[2] P. S. Allen, Opus Epistolarum D. Erasmi, 12 vols. (Oxford, 1906-1958), 6: 155, Letter 1603, 27-29. As indicated by Allen, most of Erasmus' surviving letters to Pirckheimer appeared for the first time in Pirckheimeri Opera (Frankfurt, 1610). As one might expect in letters to a man who was clearly a confidant and kindred spirit, even though the two never met, Erasmus' comments to Pirckheimer are often marked by unusual candor.

[3] See James D. Tracy, The Politics of Erasmus: a Pacifist Intellectual and his Political Milieu (Toronto, 1978).

repression of heresy in his native provinces was seen as propping up a hated regime of clerical privilege (3).

I

The County of Holland was precocious in the development of its fiscal institutions,[4] but slower than England or France to employ statues of mortmain to discourage the erosion of the base of taxable property. According to R. R. Post, Duke Philip the Good, who brought Holland under Burgundian rule in 1428, was the first to introduce here the French practice of collecting a fee for letters of mortmain authorizing novel gifts to or purchases by religious institutions.[5] This regulation was often ignored, but it did permit Philip and other rulers to demand a share of the "fruits" from "recent acquisitions" that had not been registered. To be sure, Holland's monasteries were not so politically potent as those of Brabant,[6] nor so richly endowed as those of Friesland and Groningen.[7] Yet in 1474, when Duke Charles the Bold demanded from the clergy of his lands a tax equal to three years' income on properties acquired since 1414, it was Holland's clergy which, instead of bargaining for a better deal, refused to pay — until Charles threatened to confiscate the lands of any institution which dared appeal to Rome. Because of his success in this matter, one Protestant church historian of the seventeenth century speculated that he had earned his

---

[4] James D. Tracy, *A Financial Revolution in the Habsburg Netherlands: Renten and Renteniers in the County of Holland, 1506-1566* (Berkeley, 1985).

[5] R. R. Post, *Kerkgeschiedenis van Nederland in de Middeleeuwen* (Utrecht, 1957), 75-76; an ordinance of 1462 prohibited the creation of new cloisters without express ducal approval.

[6] In the States of Brabant, the abbots of twelve important monasteries made up the first estate; see Pieter Gorissen, *De Prelaten van Brabant onder Karel V: Hun Confederatie (1534-1544)* = *Standen en Landen* 6. The States of Holland never had a clerical estate, although at one time in the fifteenth century there were five abbeys which paid in the *bede* or subsidy as part of the noble estate: Post, *Kerkgeschiedenis van Nederland*, 85.

[7] L. J. Rogier, *Geschiedenis van het Katholicisme in de Noordelijke Nederlanden*, 2 vols. (Amsterdam, 1947), 1: 45-53; abbeys in the early sixteenth century controlled roughly a third of the land in Friesland, and a fourth in Groningen. By contrast, Jan De Vries, *The Dutch Rural Economy in the Golden Age* (New Haven, 1974), 42, finds that although great houses in Holland (like the Benedictine abbey of Egmond and the convent of Rijnsburg) owned a great deal of land, they played a much smaller role than similar institutions did in Friesland and Groningen; De Vries finds that ecclesiastical corporations as a group seldom owned more than 10% of the land in any Holland village, whereas figures might go as high as 38% for villages in the neighboring province of Utrecht.

sobriquet by facing down the clergy.[8] Yet if this Duke was at times able to cow his subjects into submission, the resurgence of local autonomy which followed the collapse of Charles's ambitious plans left his Habsburg successors in a much weaker position. Like towns and provinces,[9] the clergy too reclaimed its traditional privileges, so that in the early sixteenth century both clerics as individuals and religious instititions were exempt from both the *ordinaris bede* which Maximilian I or Charles V as Count of Holland could expect to collect from the province every year, and from the *extraordinaris beden* to which the States of Holland would consent in time of need.[10]

It need hardly be said that the exemption of clerical wealth from taxation would appear all the more conspicuous once Holland and other provinces were expected to pay the military costs of the Habsburg-Valois wars, which began almost as soon as Archduke Charles attained his majority (1514), and Francis I acceeded to the French throne (1515). (The exemptions enjoyed by towns and villages controlled by important nobles who were direct vassals of the Count were even more of a problem, but will not be discussed here.)[11] In April 1523, when the States agreed to raise an *extraordinaris bede* by levying, for the first time, provincial excise taxes, the deputies made it a condition of their consent that all persons must pay, including the clergy and others hitherto exempt. But collecting such novel impositions was not easy — the Franciscans and Poor Clares were among those refusing to pay — and in the end the States had to make good a large shortfall by resorting to the traditional schema of assessment, in which the clergy and the nobles paid nothing.[12] In subsequent months, the clergy agreed to make some contribution, though "without prejudice" to their immunities, and when an *extraordinaris bede* of 80,000 Holland pounds was levied in 1524 there was

---

[8] Post, *Kerkgeschiedenis van Nederland*, 80; Petrus Scriverius, *Oudt-Batavia*, as cited by Isaak Le Long, *Historische Beschryving van de reformatie der stad Amsterdam* (Amsterdam, 1729), 379.

[9] A. G. Jongkees, "Het Groote Privilege van Holland en Zeeland (14 Maart 1477)", in W. P. Blockmans, ed., *Het Algemene en de Gewestelijke Privileges van Maria van Bourgogne voor de Nederlanden* (Kortrijk, 1985), 145-235.

[10] The *ordinaris bede* was collected according to a system of repartition known as the *schiltal*, which was last revised in 1514-1515. An *extraordinaris bede* could be collected "according to the *schiltal*", or by other means, such as introducing provincial excise taxes, or by selling bonds or *renten* backed by the full faith and credit of the province.

[11] James D. Tracy, *Holland under Habsburg Rule: the Formation of a Body Politic, 1506-1566* (Berkeley, 1990), 135-8.

[12] AJ 23 April, 28 May, 17 July, 23 August, 7 September 1523; Table III, item h, in Tracy, "The Taxation System of the County of Holland during the Reigns of Charles V and Philip II, 1519-1599", *Economisch- en Sociaal-Historisch Jaarboek* 48 (1984): 72-117. The excise involved taxes on wine and beer in the towns, and on cattle and real property income in the countryside.

for the first time a separate "subsidy" of 5,000 pounds from the clergy.[13] Early in 1525 the Regent of the Netherlands (Charles V's aunt, Margaret of Austria) acceded to requests from the provincial states by ordering an inventory of clerical acquisitions since the last inventory (1515) for which there was no letter of mortmain; together with a subsequent *taxatie* in 1533, this record became the basis for the collection at regular intervals of clerical subsidies which could amount to as much as half the "fruits" of all benefices (not just "novel acquisitions") for a given year.[14] Yet these contributions, by consent of the clergy, and authorized by papal bulls, were still not part of the *beden* which bore more and more heavily on each province, and which, unlike the subsidies, were collected every year.

In the 1540s, when the government's underlying fiscal problems had only gotten worse, the Regent was Mary of Hungary, Charles V's sister, and her chief minister was Lodewijk van Schore, a *doctor utriusque juris* from Leuven, in whose distinctive hand there is an undated Latin memorandum laying out the basis in "natural law" for the clergy's obligation to contribute to the defense of the land. Under Schore's prodding, the states of the important provinces (including Holland) agreed (1543-1544) to try once again the expedient of provincial excise taxes, to used this time to fund a series of bonds or *renten* issued by the states of each province. At the insistence of the states, the Regent issued the necessary decrees "derogating" from the exemptions of the clergy and the nobles, so that they too would have to pay. In fact, the accounts for these new taxes, together with discussion in the States of problems that arose, indicates that payments did come in from religious houses that did not have to pay in the traditional *bede*. This breach of clerical privilege was not trivial, but one doubts that it was enough to overcome a legacy of resentment. As the Advocate of the States records, discussion of the new taxes opened with a session in which deputies from Holland's towns "cursed" the clergy and the exempt nobles.[15]

---

[13] AJ 26-28, 30 May 1524; Tracy, "Taxation System of Holland", Table III, item i.

[14] M. Rollin-Couquerque, A. Meerkamp van Embden, "Gouda Vroedschapsreso-lutiën betreffende Dagvaarten van de Staten van Holland", *Bijdragen en Mededelingen van het Historisch Genootschap te Utrecht* 37 (1916): 61-81, 38 (1917): 98-357, 39 (1918): 306-406; 5 February 1525; *RSH* 19 June 1525; Tracy, "Taxation System in Holland", Table III, item s; Assendelft to Hoogstraten, 26 October, 4 November 1533, 1 January 1534 (Aud. 1446/2b), and 31 August 1537 (Aud. 1524); Assendelft to Mary of Hungary, 23 October 1546 (Aud. 1646:3); Mary of Hungary to Cornelis Suys, 15 December 1552 (Aud. 1646:2). For an overview, Michel Baelde, "De Kerkelijke Subsidies in de Nederlanden onder Karel V (1532-1555)", *Revue Belge de Philologie et d'Histoire / Belgische Tijdschrift voor Filologie en Geschiedenis* 43 (1965): 1243-71.

[15] For the general context, Tracy, *A Financial Revolution*, Chapter III; accounts for the tenth penny on *renten* and real property income, Rijksarchief van Zuid-Holland, The Hague, "Staten van Holland", e.g. nos. 2278, 2284, receipts from e.g. "Prelaat van Egmond", "Carthusians of Utrecht". *RSH* 19 August 1543 (the quote); for

Taxes at the local and provincial levels were intimately linked, in that towns (and an increasing number of villages) had authorization from the government to levy various excise taxes or *accijnsen*, revenues of which were used to pay the town's or village's quota in the *ordinaris bede* as well as for other expenses. There are indications that clerical corporations could be made to contribute in special capital expenditures, such as the building or repair of town walls,[16] but townsfolk throughout the Netherlands resented the clergy's continuing exemption from local *accijnsen*. In the summer of 1525, efforts by the city of 's Hertogenbosch in Brabant to compel payment of the *accijnsen* by religious houses led to attacks by angry townsmen on the powerful chapter of St. John's church, as well as three cloisters that refused to pay; the disturbances were not quieted until the government sent in 1,110 mercenaries.[17] There was a similar disturbance in The Hague the previous year, and in the summer of 1525 there are references to protests against clerical exemptions in Antwerp (Brabant), Utrecht, and Roermond (Gelderland).[18] Erasmus was perhaps reacting to reports of these incidents in the letter to Pirckheimer cited above.[19]

If one could not, in the end, force the cloisters and the chapters to pay, the next best course was to prevent the establishment of new cloisters inside town walls. As part of his ordinance on mortmain in 1462, Philip the Good decreed that no new cloisters should be created without his express permission. In Amsterdam, which by 1500 had within its walls nineteen cloisters occupying about a third of the city, there were determined efforts to put this principle into practice. Nonetheless, the Obersvant Franciscan movement was flourishing in late fifteenth century Holland, and in 1462 its partisans in Amsterdam were able to secure approval for the building of an

---

continuing disputes about clerical exemption, 6-12 November 1543, 16 February 1553, and Council of Holland to the Secret Council, 27 June 1558, Rijksarchief van Zuid-Holland, "Hof van Holland", no. 381. For Schore's memorandum, Aud. 650: 527-528.

[16] Theodorus Velius, *Chronijk van Hoorn*, ed. Sebastiaan Centen (Hoorn, 1740), 173/4, 221; J. C. Overvoorde, J. N. Overburgt, *Het Archief van de Secretarie van de Stad Leiden, 1253-1575* (Leiden, 1937), "Regesten", 7 January 1519, 24 October 1520; A. J. Enschede, *Inventaris van het Oud-Archief van de Stad Haarlem* (Haarlem, s.d.), "Contracten", 16 May 1516.

[17] Aelbertus Cuperinus, *Chronicke*, in C. R. Hermans, *Verzameling van Kronyken, Charters en Oorkonden betrekkelijk de Stad en Meijerij van 's Hertogenbosch* ('s Hertogenbosch, 1848), 1: 70-71, 79-81, 90-91.

[18] AJ July 1524, 19 June 1525; Post, *Kerkgeschiedenis van Nederland*, 92-93.

[19] There would seem to be an obvious connection between what was happening in the Low Countries during these months and recent events in Germany, touched off by the Peasants' Revolt, but to my knowledge no one has yet attempted to map the progress of anticlerical protest along the Rhine and its branches into the Netherlands.

Observant friary (1462), and, after a long struggle, a convent of the Poor Clares (1509).[20]

Since religious orders always had friends in high places, cities could force cloisters to contribute only in circumstances in which they had the government, with its power to abrogate privileges, on their side. For example, the government and the cities had a common interest in finding buyers for the *renten* issued by the States of Holland, at a time when private investors were wary of committing their funds to these new instruments of public debt. Thus local magistrates were able to obtain permission to "constrain" wealthy monasteries to subscribe for some portion of the quota of *renten* sales allotted to each city.[21]

If the sums which cloisters had to immobilize in this way are added to the sums paid in clerical subsidies, and (after 1543) in the new provincial excise taxes, one might conclude that Charles V's government, responding to pressure from the States and the towns, made significant breaches in the wall of clerical immunity. Yet that potent if somewhat abstract person whom the sources refer to as *de gemeene man* had no knowledge of how much clerical subsidies amounted to, or what cloisters invested in *renten*, and from his perspective things must have seemed as they had always been. In the taxes that were most visible, and which bore most heavily on the average person[22] — that is, the urban *accijnsen* — the layman paid, and the cleric did not.

II

Complaints about the wealth of the clergy were not exhausted by the issue of taxation. The business activities of religious communities were often in direct competition with the laity, as elsewhere in Europe. When the States petitioned Margaret of Austria (1524) for better enforcement of mortmain laws, they also named certain cloisters that were engaged in weaving, baking, and brewing; Margaret's response stipulated that all such activities were banned, except for the direct support of conventuals, and that any products offered for sale should be confiscated. The issue did not end here, but it seems to have been overshadowed by a more general concern of

---

[20] Post, *Kerkgeschiedenis van Nederland*, 76; Tracy, *Holland under Habsburg Rule*, 150-151.

[21] "Goudse Vroedschapsresolutien", 26 March 1528; AJ 31 March 1528; Assendelft to Hoogstraten, 14 March 1531 (Aud. 1525), and to Mary of Hungary, 19, 22 October 1542 (Aud. 1646:3); Tracy, *Financial Revolution in the Habsburg Netherlands*, 126-127.

[22] The States, nervous about popular reaction to *accijnsen*, were careful to keep the new provincial excixe taxes on beer and wine in the towns at levels notably lower than the traditional urban excises.

Holland's towns with business activity outside town walls, especially in villages controlled by important nobles; their efforts in this regard were crowned with success in a 1531 ban on *buitennering*.[23] In a province where wealthy burgers would usually put some of their money in land, large purchases of land by certain cloisters were another issue. For example, when government commissioners made a circuit of the province in 1514 in order to revise the assessment of wealth on which the *ordinaris bede* was based, Amsterdam's magistrates complained that two local monasteries just outside the walls — the Carthusians and the Canons Regular of St. Augustine, or *Reguliers* — bought up land without caring about the price. (Interestingly, these same two houses were specifically mentioned whenever Amsterdam sought permission to "constrain" its cloisters to buy *renten*.)[24] When the main building of the *Reguliers* burned down in the summer of 1532, under suspicious circumstances, Amsterdam demanded that the Canons Regular not be allowed to rebuild on the site under any circumstances; to do so would be dangerous, the magistrates alleged, because during the most recent war with the Duke of Gelderland (a French ally), the Canons had made a secret private treaty with the Duke, so that their lands would not be damaged by marauding mercenaries. Mary of Hungary evidently found these arguments credible, because she "absolutely" prohibited the Canons from rebuilding on the spot, as they wished, forcing them to relocate in another house of the same order.[25]

To some degree, towns and the central government could also find common ground in resisting what both saw as abuses of power by bishops and their officials. In 1524, when the Prince-Bishop of Liège (Erard de la Marck) threatened to withdraw from negotiations over jurisdictional disputes, Margaret of Austria wrote Charles V that if he acceded to such demands, he would have "no more authority in Brabant than a village mayor". With encouragement from the government, deputies from the provincial states convened in a special meeting of the States General (March 1524) to discuss issues concerning their relations to the various bishoprics that had jurisdic-

---

[23] Aud. 1524: Council of Holland to Margaret of Austria, 2 June 1524, Margaret to the Council, 14 June 1524, and Margaret's decision (undated, leaves 81-84); J. ter Gouw, *Geschiedenis van Amsterdam* (Amsterdam, 1879-1893), 4: 111; E. C. G. Bruenner, *De Orden op de Buitennering van 1531* (Utrecht, 1918).

[24] Post, *Kerkgeschiedenis van Nederland*, 72-73.

[25] Assendelft to Hoogstraten, 19 January 1533 (Aud. 1525), 25 May 1533 (Aud. 1446/2b), Hoogstraten to Assendelft, 7 June 1533 (Aud. 1446/2b); see also the undated memorandum explaining Amsterdam's reasons for seeking the ban, Aud. 1446/2b, leaves 7-8. For the strong opposition in the States to secret treaties of this kind (often made by leading nobles), Tracy, *Holland under Habsburg Rule*, 85-87. Cf. Dirck van Bleswijck Everszoon, *Beschryving der Stad Delft* (Delft, 1667), 361: the house of the Canons Regular at Sion, outside Delft, burned under suspicious circumstances in January 1544.

tion in the Low Countries.[26] On the local level, towns in Holland turned to the comitial government in The Hague, in hopes of making headway with venal officials of the bishopric of Utrecht. For example, Amsterdam tried, without success, to secure the removal of the dean and provisor of Amstelland, because of his "evil living", which gave much credit to the Lutheran heresy. This man's immediate superior, the provost of Utrecht cathdral, when approached, said at first that he did not even want to hear about the matter unless he were first given 1,000 crowns.[27] In 1534, the towns of Hoorn and Enkhuizen and the village of Grootebrouck arranged, through the mediation of the Court of Holland in The Hague, an agreement with the dean of West Friesland, whereby the fees he was to charge for his services (letters of dispenation, absolution, etc.) in over a dozen cases were carefully defined; he was also to use his powers of excommunication as little as possible, and stop preventing pastors from marrying couples who had slept together, or demanding for this purpose a special letter of absolution *a clandestino*.[28] Many of the issues which pitted town governments against episcopal authority, such as the use of ecclesiastical penalties for frivolous reasons,[29] or attempts by officers of justice to arrest criminals who had taken "sanctuary" in a church,[30] will be familiar to students of other parts of Europe. What made this area somewhat different was that episcopal authority was exercised by princes of the church whose lands were not themselves under Habsburg control — e.g., Liège, or, until 1527, Utrecht — so that those who governed in Charles V's name did not have the leverage of, say, a king of England or of France. It is not surprising, then, that Habsburg officials were considering, as early as the 1520s, ideas for new diocesan boundaries. Ironically, it was the final implementation of these plans, under Philip II, that put wind in the sails of noble and popular opposition to the government, and to its draconian religious policy.[31]

---

[26] Margaret to Charles V, 21 February 1524, in K. Lanz, *Correspondenz des Kaisers Karls V*, 3 vols. (Leipzig, 1844-1846), 1: no. 49; AJ 24 January 1524.

[27] AJ 2, 25 October 1525; Ter Gouw, 4: 145, is uncertain whether the "Gerrit Pieters" named as dean and provisor was the same Gerrit Pieters who was then pastor of the Oude Kerk.

[28] Geraardt Brandt, *Historie der Vermaerde Zee- en Koop-Stadt Enkhuizen* (Hoorn, 1740), 72-79.

[29] Bleswijck, *Beschryving der Stad Delft*, 213; in 1497, the Nieuwe Kerk was laid under interdict for five weeks in the interest of a man in Utrecht "die groot was in den Hogen Hove", who held a *rente* backed the the States of Holland on which interest payments had fallen behind.

[30] Velius, *Chronyk van Hoorn*, 208-9; De Hoop Scheffer, *Geschiedenis van de Kerkhervorming*, 595-602.

[31] M. Dierickx, S.J., *De Oprichting der Nieuwe Bisdommen in de Nederlanden onder Filips II, 1559-1570* (Antwerp, 1950).

In the two generations prior to the Reformation, the most strenuous critics of luxury and moral decay among the clergy were often to be found Obervant Franciscan friars, like Jan Brugman in the Netherlands, whose popularity as a preacher apparently owed not a little to his habit of censuring his brethren of the cloth.[32] Holland was a veritable land of promise for observant movements among the mendicant orders, at least the Franciscans and Dominicans. In 1517, the stricter rules of what had been called the Holland Congregation of the Dominicans were made binding on the entire order, and Franciscan friars had seventeen houses in the province, all but one of which were affiliated with the Observance.[33] Yet precisely because many of these houses, as well as many convents of the Poor Clares, were established in the second half of the fifteenth century, when sentiment for placing limits on property under the dead hand was growing in Holland, they had, from the start, bitter foes as well as ardent partisans. Also, it sometimes seems to have been the Franciscans and the Poor Clares who took special exception to efforts by the government and the States to subject the clergy to new forms of taxation.[34]

III

Starting in the 1520s, there was a new and more urgent reason why mendicant friars, especially the Observant Franciscans, became targets of popular ire. No doubt because news of Luther's doctrines had touched a sympathetic chord among townsfolk, magistrates in several of Holland's towns began to favor popular preachers, often vice-curates, who combined forthright critique of the clergy with a theology that was at least "Protestantising" (in J. J. Woltjer's sense),[35] if not unambiguously Protestant. This tendency was especially clear in Amsterdam, the one town that was wealthy and influential enough to extract from the Stadtholder, in return for its support of the *beden*, a promise that a vice-curate denounced by church

---

[32] Willem Moll, *Johannes Brugman et het Godsdienstig Leven onzer Vaderen in de 15e Eeuw*, 2 vols. (Amsterdam, 1854); Moll draws heavily on the account of Brugman by the seventeenth century Remonstrant church historian Geraardt Brandt, *The History of the Reformation and Other Ecclesiastical Transformations in and about the Low Countries*, 4 vols. (London, 1720), 1: 26ff.

[33] Rogier, *Geschiedenis van het Katholicisme*, 1: 69-76; R. R. Post, *Kerkelijke Verhoudingen in Nederland voor de Reformatie* (Utrecht, 1954), 327-41; R. C. H. Roemer, *Geschiedkundig Overzigt van de Kloosters en Abdijen in de Voormalige Graafschappen van Holland en Zeeland*, 2 vols. (Leiden, 1854), 1: 213-26.

[34] AJ 28 May - 2 June 1523, the Franciscans and the Poor Clares sought exemption from the levy of 2 stuivers per vat of beer that was part of the provincial excise taxes then being collected.

[35] Woltjer, *Friesland in Hervormingstijd*, Chapter VI, "Protesatantiserenden en Protestanten".

authorities would be allowed to remain in his post.[36] To this new direction, and indeed to anything that smacked of heresy, the Franciscans were often the leading opponents. Thus when the President of the Council of Holland was summoned to the presence of Margaret of Austria, to answer for the Council's alleged laxity about heresy in Holland, it was on the basis of charges by the Franciscan Guardian in Brussels.[37] Attempting to check the growth of dissent in Amsterdam were a certain Friar Joseph, whom the magistrates were apparently allowed to expel, in return for their support of a *bede*, and, some years later, Friar Cornelis van Naarden, who was dismissed after officials in The Hague decided he was not doing much good.[38] To be sure, in the wake of an attack on Amsterdam's town hall in 1535 by radical Anabaptists, the magistrates who had backed the reformist preachers were supplanted by a new ruling faction whose leaders proclaimed their devotion to Catholic orthodoxy, and made a point of holding ceremonial banquets in the Franciscan friary — a circumstance which led Protestant historians of a later generation to describe the friary, with some exaggeration, as a second city hall.[39] In other words, just as at the time when the Observant movement was establishing itself in Holland, the friars had staunch defenders among layfolk as well as bitter critics. It seems clear, however, that the focus of debate had shifted, from questions of clerical immunity to the implementation of Charles V's *placards* against heresy.

Resistance to the *placards*, among officials and magistrates as well as ordinary folk, is one of the great themes of sixteenth century Low Countries history. The question has particular importance for the years just prior to the Revolt,[40] when Philip II insisted on rigorous enforcement of the laws, after a period of relative laxity in most provinces. Yet even the first of the *placards* (1521) was met by foot-dragging on the part of town governments. The Emperor was determined not to allow heresy to gain a purchase in his

---

[36] The preachers in question were the vice-curates Adrianus Cordatus and Pieter Quadratus, and Jan de Haes, preacher at the leprosarium chapel outside the walls. See the references to these men in the documents in A. F. Mellink, *Documenta Anabaptistica*, vol. 5 (Leiden, 1985), and the following correspondence of the Court of Holland: Assendelft to Hoogstraten, 26, 30 October 1533 (Aud. 1446/2b); memorandum of points made by Stadtholder Hoogstraten to Assendelft and Meester Vincent Corneliszoon, 20 Nov. 1533 (Aud. 1446/2b); Assendelft to Hoogstraten, 8, 11 November 1534 (Aud. 1529).

[37] Ter Gouw, *Geschiedenis van Amsterdam*, 4: 151.

[38] AJ 1 December 1527, and Assendelft to Hoogstraten, 21 December 1527 (Aud. 1524; Friar Joseph); Assdendelft to Hoogstraten, 11 November 1534 (Aud. 1529).

[39] Tracy, "A Premature Counter-Reformation: the Dirkist Government of Amsterdam, 1538-1578", *Journal of Religious History* 13 (1984): 150-67; Rogier, *Kerkelijke Verhoudingen in Nederland*, 188, 332-340.

[40] See especially J. J. Woltjer, "De Vredemakers", *Tijdschrift voor Geschiedenis* 89 (1976): 299-321, an interpretation of the decade 1566-1576 that has come to be accepted as a starting point for further scholarly discussion.

native provinces, as it had in Germany, and, so as to deprive local courts of all excuses for shilly-shallying, he promulgated in 1529 a heresy ordinance that was surely as brutal as any to be issued in Europe during the sixteenth century: those found guilty of any of a long list of actions prohibited by the *placards* were to be punished by death, without any possibility of mitigating the sentence.[41]

Charles's first thought was to create a territorial inquisition for the Low Countries, as his maternal grandparents (Isabella and Ferdinand) had done for the realms of Castile and Aragon. This plan had to be abandoned fairly quickly, because of fierce resistance in the States of Holland to actions by the Inquisitor, a lay jurist named Frans van Hulst,[42] but the scheme is instructive for present purposes even though it failed. The fact that Hulst had provoked the wrath of the States by his attempted violation of the privilege *de non evocando* (by which no Hollander could be tried outside the province) indicates the theme that would be uppermost in all subsequent resistance to the *placards*. There can be no doubt that popular opposition reflected a fierce attachment to local privileges that were in fact threatened by this intrusive exercise of sovereign power.[43] As the men of Delft said in a discussion of heresy laws a few years later in the States, "For the defense of our privileges, we must all stand together, even if it means sending to [Charles V in] Spain."[44]

As may be inferred from the fact that Hulst himself was not a cleric, Charles did not intend by his campaign against heresy to shield the privileges of the clergy from change or criticism.[45] But it seems his subjects did not make such fine distinctions. Indeed the context of Erasmus' comment to Pirckheimer, cited above, was a false rumor that Hulst had regained his standing with the Emperor; it was this circumstance that prompted the remark about the monks, "qui cum plerique sint mali, tamen pro his nunc belligerabimur" — sc. by the allegedly restored power of the inquisition. To what extent did Erasmus' countrymen see the matter in the

---

[41] Tracy, "Heresy Law and Centralization under Mary of Hungary", *ARG* 73 (1982): 284-308.

[42] The best account is still to be found in J. G. de Hoop Scheffer, *Geschiedenis der Kerkhervorming in Nederland van haar Ontstaan tot 1531* (Amsterdam, 1873); for pertinent sources, Paul Fredericq, *Corpus Documentorum Haereticae Pravitatis Neerlandicae*, 5 vols. (Ghent, 1889-1902).

[43] The contention of the *placards* (and of the most zealous of Charles V's officials) was that heresy was treason against God (*lèse majesté divine*), meaning that it was one of the rare "reserved" cases in which all judicial privileges to the contrary were of no effect.

[44] Tracy, *Holland under Hapsburg Rule*, Chapter VI.

[45] Charles was persuaded to dismiss the Inquisitor because Hulst had secured a papal commission, and threatened to conduct himself in disregard of his commission from the Emperor.

same light? In addition to the just-mentioned concern about privileges, there are at least indirect indications in the sources of further reasons for resisting the *placards*, including the likelihood that many in the Low Countries were repelled by the sheer cruelty of sentencing people to death for (say) possessing a Protestant bible, or participating in a conventicle.[46] The fact that popular anger was directed at the Franciscans for their leading role in the campaign against heresy suggests a linkage to earlier anticlericalism. Under Philip II, when resistance to the *placards* is increasingly visible in almost all parts of the Netherlands,[47] there are numerous popular attacks on the judicial machinery by which accused persons are held prisoner, or brought forth to the gibbet.[48] There are, in addition, incidents of violence in which opposition to religious repression seems to merge with older anticlerical themes. In 1557, for example, authorities in Brussels were disturbed by the light sentence which the town court of Enkhuizen (northern Holland) had meted out to certain members of the civic guard who presumed one night to rap on the pastor's door and summon him forth in the format used by minions of the law, and then stove in his door with a beam when he did not answer. Their grievance against the pastor seems to have been that he was instrumental in the removal of his vice-curate, a popular reforming preacher. But Enkhuizen's magistrates, in defense of their conduct, alleged that this was the sort of conduct one had to expect now and then from guardsmen who had a bit too much to drink.[49]

The important point about this episode is precisely that one cannot easily separate a rowdy if conventional resentment of the clergy from sympathy for the new doctrines. In light of the themes of this volume, which traces the movement from late medieval anticlericalism to new forms of opposition to the better disciplined clergy of the Reformation era, it may be pertinent to suggest a kind of transition from one stage to the other, in which proponents of the Reformation gain a wider hearing partly because the laws directed against them are seen precisely as a means of protecting the clerical power which they so effectively attack. In the Netherlands, and no doubt elsewhere as well, it was surely a transition stage of this kind which later gave moral force to the new anticlericalism. As those Protestants whom Dutch Calvinists would call "libertines" would argue, lay folk had not overthrown the tyranny

---

[46] See note 62 in chapter VI of Tracy, *Holland under Hapsburg Rule*.

[47] One can illustrate the point just as well from French-speaking towns in the south as from Friesland in the far north; see Charlie Steen, *A Chronicle of Conflict: Tournai, 1559-1567* (Utrecht, 1985), and J. J. Woltjer, *Friesland in Hervormingstijd* (Leiden, 1962).

[48] See especially the discussion of the volatile industrial district of West-Flanders in Johan Decavele, *De Dagraad van de Reformatie in Vlaanderen* (Brussels, 1975), 389-426.

[49] For sources on this incident: Tracy, *Holland under Habsburg Rule*, Chapter VII, note 95.

of the Catholic clergy merely in order to subject themselves to the authority of their Reformed successors.[50]

---

[50] See, for example, the opposition in Leiden in the 1570s and 1580s to Calvinist church discipline, as described in Olivier Fatio, *Nil Pulchrius Ordine: Contribution a l'Etude de la discipline Ecclesiastique aux pays Bas* (Leiden, 1971), and J. Kamphuis, *Kerkelijke Besluitvaardigheid: Over de Bevestiging van het Gereformeerd Kerkverband in de Jaren 1574 tot 1581/2* (Groningen, 1970).

CHARACTERISTICS OF ITALIAN ANTICLERICALISM

SILVANA SEIDEL MENCHI

Università degli Studi di Trento

I. INTRODUCTORY CONSIDERATIONS

A statement by Francesco Guicciardini, written around 1530, will serve to introduce the theme of Italian anticlericalism. It comes from the Florentine statesman's most private work, the *Ricordanze*, a distillation of his experience and reflection intended exclusively for his kin and descendants.

> Naturally I have always wanted to see the ruin of the Papal State. But as fortune would have it, I have been forced to support and work for the power of two popes. Were it not for that, I would love Martin Luther more than myself, in the hope that his sect might demolish, or at least clip the wings, of this wicked tyranny of the priests.[1]

Although this statement is so well known that it seems almost trite to cite it, one can hardly find a more explicit expression of the most distinctive characteristic of Italian anticlericalism in the early modern era: the disjunction between words and actions, the contradiction between conscience and comportment. The very same man who, in what might be called his spiritual testament, expressed his hatred of priests' "wicked tyranny" and declared himself a follower of Luther also devoted his life and talent to the service of two Medici popes, Leo X and Clement VII, playing a major role in the enhancement of his masters' reputations. In my view, this split between words and things, between declarations of principle and compromises in practice, lies at the heart of the relationship between clerics and the laity in early modern Italy.

The Italians certainly did not mince words. From the very beginning, Italian vernacular literature was marked by intransigent anticlericalism. Italians' literary production in Latin as well — indeed, humanism in general — has been presented by qualified modern interpreters like Riccardo Fubini as a process of secularization dominated by the anticlerical component.[2] Although this interpretation is open to discussion, there is no question that the greatest writers in Italy between the Trecento and the Cinquecento would

---

[1] Francesco Guicciardini, *Maxims and Reflections of a Renaissance Statesman*, trans. M. Domandi (New York, 1965), 125-6.

[2] Riccardo Fubini, *Umanesimo e secolarizzazione da Petrarca a Valla* (Rome, 1990).

find a place in any anthology of European anticlericalism. In his *Monarchia*, Dante Alighieri provided strong support for the German imperial ideology in its struggle against the Papacy, and in the *Commedia*, besides locating most of the popes of his day in hell, Dante took care to reserve a place for the most powerful of them, Boniface VIII, as well as his successor, Clement V, in the circle of the simoniacs.[3] The erotic tales of Boccaccio familiarized Europeans with the figure of the lusty friar or priest who achieved his lascivious ends "under the cover of religion and by means of Christ".[4] Such humanist anticlerical treatises as Poggio Bracciolini's oration against clerical vices delivered at the Council of Constance and Leonardo Bruni's invective *Contra hypocritas* fed aversion against the clergy in fifteenth-century Germany.[5] And in the sixteenth century, the *Zodiacus vitae*, a marvelous didactic poem by a Neapolitan humanist who prudently disguised his identity under the pseudonym Marcellus Paligenius Stellatus, was printed again and again in Protestant Germany, not only on account of its literary qualities but also because of the violence of its anticlerical tirades.[6]

The Council of Trent sought to cut off this current. But it was so ancient and illustrious that when the Counter Reformation popes set out to eradicate the anticlerical component of Italian literature through the Index of Prohibited Books, the majority of first-rank Italian writers — from Boccaccio to Machiavelli, from Petrarch to Guicciardini — were placed on the list. As a consequence, for centuries in Italian schools the masters of the Italian language were read in expurgated editions.

While literary culture spoke one language, social structures sent an entirely different message. Violent Italian literary anticlericalism was the product of a society that lived in a close, continuous relationship with the Church. In the communes of the thirteenth and fourteenth centuries the symbiosis between civil and ecclesiastical society manifested itself in what Luigi Donvito has called "civic religion".[7] Communes sought in religion an ideological support for their policies; the growth of ecclesiastical institutions was nourished by the same patriotism that inspired the safeguarding of communal liberties. In the construction of the cathedral, in the celebration of the patron saint's feast day, municipal pride was so closely linked with devotion, with loyalty to the Church, that any attempt to separate the two sentiments would be artificial. If the most important positions in the local church were always held by members of the families who exercised political

---

[3] Dante Alighieri, *Commedia*, Inferno, canto 19.

[4] Quoted from Marino Berengo, *Nobili e mercanti nella Lucca del Cinquecento* (Turin, 1965), 365.

[5] Fubini, *Umanesimo e secolarizzazione*, 303-38.

[6] Franco Bacchelli is preparing a critical edition of this work, which will include an essay on its publication history and influence.

[7] Luigi Donvito, "La 'religione cittadina' e le nuove prospettive del Cinquecento religioso italiano", *Rivista di storia e letteratura religiosa* 19 (1983): 431-74.

power, the reason lies not merely in the working out of some mechanical form of hegemony but also in the common outlook of laymen and clerics. The fact that the composition of the cathedral chapter usually mirrored the makeup of the city council resulted not only from the logic of the spoils system but also from the organic unity of family and class, and consequently of interests.[8]

In the fifteenth century the relationship between clerics and laity became even more complex because alongside the local church, and often at its expense, the Papacy increasingly made its weight felt. As a consequence, the intermingling of civil and ecclesiastical society became even more intimate: the oligarchies of the Italian states increasingly identified their interests with those of the Roman Curia. The control exercised by lay holders of political power in collaboration with Rome for the purpose of dominating the religious sphere, both its property and its ideals, was total. The election of a bishop, the conferral of some paltry rural benefice, fiscal exemption, the repression of religious dissent: all these matters were regulated in the context of a basic understanding between the Church and the rulers. This gave the ecclesiastical hierarchy the possibility of influencing civil society to a considerable degree. Even though the discourse between clerics and laymen was not unmarked by conflicts, the spirit of conciliation always managed to prevail, since both parties were committed to seeking a compromise that would serve their common interests.[9]

Political developments in fifteenth-century Florence were the most conspicuous product of this system. Control of ecclesiastical institutions was a determining factor in the rise of the Medici: their position in Florence was in large part a function of the authority which they, as bankers of the Holy See, enjoyed in Rome. As Roberto Bizzocchi has shown, Lorenzo de'Medici in particular enlarged the family's network of clients on the principle that control of the state carried with it control of the Church, and its corollary, that control of ecclesiastical structures could be translated into increased political influence.[10]

From the fifteenth century on, Italian men of letters profited greatly from the increased strength of the Church and its omnipresence in civil society. The office of secretary of apostolic letters in Rome was a prestigious, remunerative post which left its holder sufficient leisure to write the elegant Latin letters that were a humanist's passport to fame. Hence for almost fifty years Poggio Bracciolini held onto his position in that Curia whose vices he

---

[8] Giorgio Chittolini, "Stati regionali ed istituzioni ecclesiastiche nell'Italia centro-settentrionale del Quattrocento", in *La Chiesa e il potere politico dal Medioevo all'età contemporanea*, Storia d'Italia, Annali 9, ed. G. Chittolini, G. Miccoli (Turin, 1986), 147-93.

[9] Robert Bizzocchi, *Chiesa e potere nella Toscana del Quattrocento* (Bologna, 1987).

[10] Bizzocchi, *Chiesa e potere*, 82-98, 343-8.

so eloquently deplored. Carlo Dionisotti has calculated that of the one hundred or so most prominent writers in the first half of the sixteenth century, twenty were cardinals or bishops, twelve were members of religious orders, and another twenty supported themselves entirely or in part from the revenues of ecclesiastical benefices.[11] These figures are approximate, but their significance is clear: in Renaissance Italy, one of every two literary men was economically dependent on the Church.

With these considerations in mind, the contradiction between words and things with which I began makes sense. Clearly, Italian literary anti-clericalism should not be considered as the expression of a real need for change, nor as a sign of crisis, but rather as an almost instinctive reaction to intimate familiarity with the clergy and the Curia — a healthy blowing off of steam that served to reinforce the system which it claimed to challenge. In order to survive, the Italian system of total osmosis between Church and civil society needed a certain dose of anticlericalism, a control mechanism that drew attention to excesses and ensured that collective ethical sensibilities were not seriously violated. Men of letters took upon themselves to devise this mechanism. Far from being a catalyst for change, Italian anticlericalism was a stabilizing factor, a safety valve that guaranteed the equilibrium of the system and helped to perpetuate it for centuries.[12]

Now let us turn to two areas in which Italian anticlericalism manifested its stabilizing function: monacation in the absence of vocation and the city versus the inquisitor. These concrete, very limited themes are deliberately chosen in order to counterbalance the generalizations I have been putting forward up to this point.

II. MONACATION IN THE ABSENCE OF VOCATION

Richard Trexler has calculated that in 1336 nuns constituted 1.6% of the female population of Florence; in 1428-29 this percentage had risen to 2.5%; and by 1552 it had reached 13%.[13] On the basis of data from the Florentine *catasto*, David Herlihy and Christiane Klapisch-Zuber estimate that in 1427 there was one nun for every forty laypeople: 2.6% of the total population and 5% of the female population.[14] These data make it abundantly clear

---

[11] Carlo Dionisotti, "Chierici e laici", in *Geografia e storia della letteratura italiana*, 3rd ed. (Turin, 1977), 55-88.

[12] For the application of the "safety valve" theory in a different context, that of Carnival, see Peter Burke, *Popular Culture in Early Modern Europe* (New York, 1978), 201-4.

[13] Richard C. Trexler, "Le célibat à la fin du Moyen Age: Les religieuses de Florence", *Annales ESC* 27 (1972): 1329-50.

[14] David Herlihy and Christiane Klapisch-Zuber, *Les toscans et leurs familles* (Paris, 1978), 73-9.

that from the fourteenth century to the sixteenth, there was an enormous increase in the proportion of women entering convents. What we might call galloping monacation was not the result of an increase in the number of women who felt called to the religious life, but rather of the generalized use of convents as holding tanks for the left-overs from the marriage market.

To my knowledge, the earliest analysis of this practice dates back to 1562, when one Giovanni Andrea Ugoni published a work denouncing forced monacation.[15] Ugoni was well informed about this phenomenon because he was a member of the landed nobility, among whom the practice was widespread. That the dowries requested by convents were much lower than those demanded on the marriage market was a economic fact of life. Consequently patrician fathers sent some of their daughters to convents in order to preserve their financial resources for one or at the most two privileged daughters, who through a prestigious marriage would consolidate their families' social position. Ugoni suggested that among the aristocracy of northern Italy, the relationship between girls destined for the convent and those to be married was two to one.[16] This was a conservative estimate: documents of the period, as Giovanna Paolin has shown, attest to the presence of not only two or three but even four or five sisters in the same convent.[17] Future nuns were placed in convents when they were six or seven and took vows of perpetual chastity between the ages of ten and twelve — even before they knew the meaning and consequences of the word "chastity", according to Ugoni. Such silent violence committed against little girls produced restless and resentful young women who, as Ugoni put it, could hardly be expected to put up the least resistance to "the pricks of the flesh". On the contrary, he argued, girls forced to become nuns "seek out every opportunity to satisfy their voracious appetites, all the way into old age."[18] Ugoni's denunciation stood alone in Italy on the eve of the Counter Reformation. Nevertheless, the consequences of forced monacation for behavior in convents were well known to Italians. For two centuries the writers of *novelle* had challenged the conventional wisdom that convents

---

[15] Giovanni Andrea Ugoni, *Ragionamento di tutti gli stati dell'humana vita* (Venice: Pietro da Fine, 1562). After this article went to press, my attention was drawn to an analysis of forced monacation written about the same time as Ugoni's: the Bolognese noble Giovanni Boccadiferro's "Discorso sopra il governo delle monache", addressed to Giovanni Campeggi, Bishop of Bologna (Bologna, Biblioteca Comunale dell'Archiginnasio, MS B.778, 165-198), which is summarized in Mario Fanti's introduction to *Abiti e lavori delle monache di Bologna in una serie di disegni del secolo XVIII* (Bologna, 1972), 12-32. This work deserves more extensive analysis.

[16] Ugoni, 58. A particularly lucid analysis of the phenomenon of forced monacation is provided by Francesca Medioli, *L'"Inferno monacale" di Arcangela Tarabotti* (Turin, 1990), 112-22.

[17] Giovanna Paolin, *Lo spazio del silenzio*, in press.

[18] Ugoni, 50.

sanctified the city, that they were places devoted exclusively to prayer, and that within them chastity reigned. Thus they had anticipated Ugoni's revelations, but with an entirely different variety of violent language and a vivid imagination. That narrative line which we can call "eros in the convent" had contributed to one of the most monotonous motifs of anticlerical polemic: charges of lust and infringement of the rules. Boccaccio's story of the peasant who, pretending to be a deaf-mute, gets a job as a gardener in a Tuscan convent renowned for asceticism,[19] Sercambi's technically precise description of the lesbian activities of nuns in a convent in Arezzo,[20] Sacchetti's detailed account of the night spent by a mystical vagabond with three female inhabitants of a hermitage near Todi,[21] and many more such tales had placed the results of forced monacation before the eyes of everyone — not only the fathers of the girls destined for the convent in order to further patrimonial strategies, but also people who could hardly read. A printed miscellany in the Wolfenbüttel Library demonstrates that Boccaccio's tale of the gardener and the nuns was part of the repertory of stories sung in the piazza during fairs and recounted during gatherings on winter evenings.[22]

Notwithstanding this vast diffusion, the effects of the *novella*-writers' more or less moralistic denunciations were nil. The statistics presented by Trexler, Herlihy, and Klapisch-Zuber suggest that doubts about the moral tone in convents did not dissuade Florentine fathers from making their daughters nuns. More positive proof that "eros in the convent" was not a major concern of nuns' relatives is provided by evidence about their reactions to sexual scandals involving their daughters or sisters. As Bizzocchi has put it, they did not "care for excessive moral zeal". To be sure, a scandal had to be hushed up at any cost, but no one actually expected the nuns to be obligated "to observe the sort of renunciation of the world to which, in theory, they had dedicated themselves."[23] Imposition of a strict conventual regime was likely to provoke objections from the nuns and rebellion on the part of young girls destined for the convent. Hence, when the Tridentine reformers attempted to impose strict cloistering, the nun's resistance was very strong, and that of their relatives even stronger. Post-Tridentine bishops had to fight a real war against nuns' kinfolk.[24]

---

[19] Giovanni Boccaccio, *Decamerone*, giornata terza, novella prima.

[20] Giovanni Sercambi, *Novelle*, novella 32, "De libidine".

[21] Franco Sacchetti, *Trecentonovelle*, novella 101.

[22] Herzog August Bibliothek Wolfenbüttel, Lk Sammelband 64 (a collection of 92 poems aimed at a popular audience, most of them printed in Florence in 1567 and 1568), no. 19: *Istoria di Masetto da Lamporechio*; see Erhard Lommatzsch, *Beiträge zur älteren italienischen Volksdichtung* (Berlin, 1951), 3, Texte.

[23] Bizzocchi, *Chiesa e potere* (n. 9 above), 32-3; Paolin (n. 17 above).

[24] Paolin (n. 17 above); Gaetano Greco, "Monasteri femminili e patriziato a Pisa (1530-1630)", in *Città italiane del Cinquecento tra Riforma e Controriforma* (Lucca,

In this delicate equilibrium, the narrative line of "eros in the convent", I think, played a stabilizing role by furnishing negative examples. It gave the collective public conscience ample material for moralistic disdain and abundant opportunity for anticlerical outbursts, which in the end made absolutely no difference. In contrast, a real concern to bring about change rings out from the denunciation made by Giovanni Andrea Ugoni. He was too much concerned with identifying the social roots of the problem and seeking remedies for it to engage in easy moralizing or titillating anticlericalism. "Even if we had more daughters than Danaus' fifty, we really out to marry them all", he asserted.[25] Ugoni, a Protestant who at the time he wrote this book had been tried and condemned for heresy and sentenced to confiscation of his property and perpetual banishment, was among the few who genuinely sought to change the relationship between clergy and laity in Italy.[26]

III. THE CITY VERSUS THE INQUISITOR

Moralistic anticlericalism was not the only form of lay opposition to the clergy in early modern Italy. There was also what we might call institutional anticlericalism, which called into question and vigorously challenged the operations of certain ecclesiastical institutions. A particularly vivid manifestation of this second variety is the struggle of certain cities against the tribunals of the Roman Inquisition.

Two Italian cities of the sixteenth century, Naples and Lucca, opposed the introduction of the Inquisition into their territories. Venice, too, posed a certain degree of resistance to the tribunals. The secular authorities in these cities kept a close watch on developments elsewhere, and each encouraged the others by example. Naples, where there was an uprising against the Inquisition in 1510 and an armed rebellion in 1547, finally had to yield and submit to inquisitorial jurisdiction.[27] For the entire sixteenth century the small Tuscan republic of Lucca, fighting with the more subtle arms of

---

1988), 313-39.

[25] Ugoni (n. 15 above), 55.

[26] Silvana Seidel Menchi, "Der Protestantismus in Venedig im XVI. Jahrhundert", *NAKG* 70 (1990): 140-57.

[27] Luigi Amabile, *Il Santo Officio dell'Inquisizione a Napoli* (Città di Castello, 1892); Giovanni Romeo, "Una città, due inquisizioni: L'anomalia del Sant'Ufficio a Napoli nel tardo Cinquecento", *Rivista di storia e letteratura religiosa* 24 (1988): 42-67.

diplomacy, managed to avoid the introduction of the Inquisition.[28] In
Venice the Inquisition was finally introduced, but in a modified form.[29]

Beginning at the turn of the century, and particularly in recent years,
Italian historians operating from a lay perspective have investigated
intensively the phenomenon of resistance to the Inquisition by Renaissance
states, hoping to find the first signs of a secular conception of the state, a
precedent for the assertion of the autonomy of civil states vis-a-vis the
Church. Although I myself have contributed to this effort, I have come to
realize that the struggle of Italian cities against the Inquisition was
conducted entirely on the Church's ground and on its terms — that is,
within the paradigm of the inquisitorial system — and that it served in the
long run to consolidate that system.

Resistance against the Inquisition was one manifestation of jurisdictional
conflict between state and Church, which was always on the agenda in
Italian cities during the early modern era. The civil power, which had never
been enthusiastic about clerics' exemption from lay jurisdiction, took an
even dimmer view of an ecclesiastical tribunal, directed from Rome,
exercising jurisdiction over its subjects, both laity and clerics, and confis-
cating their goods.[30] Lay critics of inquisitors made frequent use of
anticlerical arguments drawn from the jurisdictional tradition. Here are a few
Venetian examples of statements by members of the government involved
in this struggle. 1519: The friars of the Inquisition "use their hoods to cover
every sort of egregious and nefarious crime ... confident that laymen and
temporal rulers ... have no power over them."[31] 1536: The sentence against
Girolamo Galateo, a philo-Protestant friar, "is totally unjust, like all the
sentences emitted by ecclesiastical judges, who never act justly."[32] 1564:
"The bishop's and inquisitor's mode of proceeding is unjust, impious, and
completely contrary to the intentions, laws, and ordinances of this dominion."[33]

Neither these nor other similar proclamations, however, called into
question the Inquisition as a system. In their resolute opposition to

---

[28] Simonetta Adorni-Braccesi, "La Repubblica di Lucca e l''aborrita' Inquisizione:
Istituzioni e società", in L'Inquisizione romana in Italia nell'età moderna: Archivi,
problemi di metodo e nuove ricerche, ed. A. Del Col, G. Paolin, Ministero per i beni
culturali e ambientali (Rome, 1991), 233-62.

[29] Andrea Del Col, "Organizzazione, composizione e giurisdizione dei tribunali
dell'Inquisizione romana nella repubblica di Venezia (1500-1550)", Critica storica
25 (1988): 244-94.

[30] Berengo, Nobili e mercanti (n. 4 above), 385.

[31] Del Col, "Organizzazione", 266.

[32] Del Col, "Organizzazione", 262.

[33] Silvana Seidel Menchi, Erasmo in Italia, 1520-1580 (Turin, 1987), 325. A
German translation will be published in the series Studies in Medieval and
Reformation Thought.

inquisitors, the people of Naples and the members of the government of Lucca did not intend to deny to legitimacy of violent repression of religious dissent. On the contrary, their object was to see that jurisdiction over crimes of heresy was assigned to the bishop of the city. The alternative, in other words, was not inquisition or no inquisition, but Roman Inquisition or episcopal inquisition. In fact, episcopal tribunals followed the same procedure as the Roman tribunal; the only difference was the greater sensitivity to the city's interests which the bishop, rightly or wrongly, was assumed to have.

This was a difference of degree, not of kind. Everywhere in Italy the philo-Protestant movement was stamped out, whether by the Roman Inquisition or by an episcopal inquisition. In the early 1550s the Roman Inquisition operated with particular rigor against the "heretics" of Naples, perhaps because of the revolution of 1547. In Lucca the government, in order to prevent the introduction of an inquisitor, created a lay magistracy, the *Officio sopra la religione*, which prosecuted heretics using procedures that were a carbon copy of those followed by the Roman Inquisition. The only benefit gained by the many Calvinists of Lucca from their government's opposition to the introduction of an inquisitor was that it was easier for them than for heretics in other cities to flee. A person denounced as a Calvinist received a discreet warning from the government — and in some cases no warning was necessary because the Calvinist sat on the city council. He then put his affairs in order and headed for Geneva. Once he was safely out of Lucchese territory, the council proclaimed him a heretic and banished him. As far as the individual was concerned, this system presented certain advantages. But from the objective point of view, the flight and banishment of the heretic resulted in precisely what the Inquisition wanted to accomplish: ridding Italy of heresy. Hence the Lucchese mode of operation was agreed on in Rome in 1558 between the Republic's ambassador and Michele Ghislieri, commissar general of the Roman Inquisition.[34] Consequently, by the end of the sixteenth century, Lucca was completely "purified".

The Republic of Venice had a certain degree of success in resisting the Inquisition. In two fundamental respects, the procedure adopted by the Venetian tribunal diverged from the norms of canon law. The property of those condemned was not confiscated, nor were their relatives excluded from public office. Furthermore, the Venetian government monitored the operation of the tribunal through the three elected patricians who participated in its deliberations and could therefore intervene to propose compromises that would prevent the emigration of philo-Protestant subjects.[35] Such govern-

---

[34] Adorni-Braccesi (n. 28 above), 244.
[35] Archivio di Stato di Venezia, Santo Ufficio, b. 23, *Contra Paulum Moscardum*, 1568.

mental intervention, however, was furtive and circumspect. Trial transcripts contain no trace of discussions between lay and ecclesiastical members of the tribunal, and, as Andrea Del Col has shown, the letters sent by the Council of Ten to the rectors of outlying territories concerning the operations of the Inquisition were highly confidential and surrounded with mystery.[36] Such secrecy is a clear sign of a bad conscience. Venetian statesmen, the rulers of the most anticlerical state in Italy, were not really comfortable about trying to challenge or limit the control exercised by the clergy over the opinions and consciences of their subjects. Even when they fought the Inquisition, their mentality was circumscribed by its logic.

The resistance of Italian cities to the Inquisition, therefore, was in no way innovative, for the right of the Church to prosecute heresy and the duty of the state to render the prosecution effective were never questioned. Institutional anticlericalism helped to cleanse the system of some abuses (such as inquisitors' appropriating the property of those convicted of heresy[37]) and helped it to function in a less arbitrary fashion, thus contributing to entrench it. If John Tedeschi is right, by the seventeenth century the tribunals of the Inquisition were functioning in an impeccable way — impeccable, that is, in terms of its own logic.[38]

IV. CONCLUSION

What conclusions can be drawn from the argument that the struggle against the clergy served to confirm and perpetuate the influence of the clergy? Must we adopt the position that the interpenetration of Church and civil society in Italy locked the relationship between clergy and laity into a static equilibrium, thereby preserving it from any and all shocks that could alter it?

The historical record appears to contradict this thesis. Between the end of the fifteenth and the beginning of the seventeenth century, the lay-clerical relationship experienced three potentially subversive shocks: in the Florence of Savonarola (1494-1498), in the Italian Protestant movement (circa 1520-circa 1580), and in the Venetian Interdict crisis (1606-1607). What role did anticlericalism play during these three critical moments?

My answer to this question is: little or none. In my view, the road to transformation of the relationship between clergy and laity was paved not

---

[36] Del Col, "Organnizzazione"; see also Del Col, "L'Inquisizione Romana e il potere politico nella Repubblica di Venezia", *Critica storica* 28 (1991): 219.

[37] Del Col, "Organizzazione", 254-5.

[38] John Tedeschi, "The Status of the Defendant before the Roman Inquisition", in *Ketzerverfolgung im 16. und frühen 17. Jahrhundert*, ed. H.R. Guggisberg, B. Moeller, S. Seidel Menchi, Wolfenbütteler Forschungen 51 (Wiesbaden, 1992), 125-46.

with polemics against the clergy but, on the contrary, with the clericalization of the entire society. The password of innovation, or of revolution, was not "fewer clergy, less Church", but rather "total clergy, total Church". To liberate society from the power of the Church, it was necessary to confer a sacral, ecclesiastical character on society. To free a city from the influence of the friars, as Erasmus put it, the entire city must be transformed into a monastery.[39]

That this was what happened in Savonarola's Florence has been made abundantly clear by Donald Weinstein.[40] That the same tendency underlay the struggle of the Venetian Republic against the Interdict of 1606 may be inferred, if I am not mistaken, from the studies of Gaetano Cozzi. Paolo Sarpi, the brain behind the Interdict controversy, started from the premise that the doge was pope in Venice, and he aimed at building a church that recognized no superior on earth other than the doge. The axiom according to which the doge was *princeps in ecclesia* as well as *princeps in republica* assumed a complete overlap of *respublica* and *ecclesia*.[41] Neither in Savonarola's Florence nor in Sarpi's Venice was anticlerical polemic absent, but the conception of the sacrality of civil society deprived the clergy of their monopoly on the sacred, consequently emptying anticlericalism of its meaning and relegating it to the wings of the stage.

A significant softening of the anticlerical polemic may also be seen in the Italian Reformation movement. The price paid by Italian Protestants in their struggle against the clericalization of society was high indeed. Hence one might expect that their anticlerical polemic would have been correspondingly violent. True, philo-Protestant Italians drew freely on the arsenal of anticlerical argument: they read and cited Petrarch's anticlerical sonnets, as well as the works of Ockham, Valla, and Machiavelli. But for them, resort to these anticlerical sources was mainly a way of attracting an audience and enlarging their ranks. Within the movement, anticlericalism played a minor role. For the layman who felt himself invested with the authority to absolve people of their sins, the issue of whether the parish priest charged fees for confession was not central. Whether the nuns in the local convent observed chastity was only marginally relevant to the man who considered his wife just as chaste as the Virgin Mary.

Translated by Anne Jacobson Schutte

---

[39] Desiderius Erasmus, *Opus epistolarum*, ed. P. S. Allen and H. M. Allen, III (Oxford, 1913), epistola 858, lines 560-569.

[40] Donald Weinstein, *Savonarola and Florence: Prophecy and Patriotism in the Renaissance* (Princeton, 1970).

[41] Gaetano Cozzi, "Stato e Chiesa: Vicende di un confronto secolare", in *Venezia e la Roma dei papi* (Milan, 1987), 11-56.

ARIOSTO ANTICLERICAL:
EPIC POETRY AND THE CLERGY
IN EARLY CINQUECENTO ITALY

THOMAS F. MAYER

Augustana College, Rock Island

Ludovico Ariosto's *Orlando Furioso* (final version 1532) is one of the longest poems in Italian.[1] That together with its constant rough and tumble, and pelting here and pelting there, puts a great deal of pressure on its characters' identities. Its eponymous "hero" loses himself in a fit of feral love madness; Ruggiero, the focus of the sub-plot about the founding of the house of Este, Ariosto's patrons, makes one blunder after another; and Astolfo, a clownish figure to be sure, first appears as an enchanted tree, takes an eccentric voyage to the moon, and another, concentric one around the earth.[2]

Some of this is satire, but virtually all of the poem trades in Ariosto's notorious irony, leaving the text and its readers suspended between established pieties.[3] Yet, for all this, two kinds of characters and one crucial attitude remain fairly constant, perhaps because they do not last long enough to suffer from the persistent inconsistency which plagues the larger characters. However that may be, the *Furioso* knows only two types of hermits and two of monks, evil and good (although the lines between them can be blurred and monks are mainly evil). Of secular clergy there is almost no word, except for several hearty whacks at the papacy and courtier prelates. Nor are they missed. Ariosto *anticlericale* chose his targets carefully.[4]

---

[1] My thanks to Heiko A. Oberman for the invitation to write this article and to the Interlibrary Loan staff of Augustana College. I owe my introduction to Ariosto to an NEH Institute "From Ariosto to Tasso", directed by Albert R. Ascoli and David Quint. Professor Ascoli read this piece carefully (and quickly); I hope it is less heavy-handed than it would have been without his advice.

[2] For the best treatment of Astolfo, who is also important to my interpretation, see Peter V. Marinelli, *Ariosto and Boiardo: The Origins of "Orlando Furioso"* (Columbia, Mo., 1987), passim.

[3] For the degree to which the poem accomplishes its suspensions, see Albert R. Ascoli, *Ariosto's Bitter Harmony: Crisis and Evasion in the Italian Renaissance* (Princeton, 1987), e.g., 342.

[4] I am aware of the vexed problem of the relation of author and text and have tried not to skip too blithely over the gap. Cf. above all Michel Foucault, "What is an Author?" in Paul Rabinow, ed., *The Foucault Reader* (New York, 1984), 118; Ascoli,

Ariosto's anticlericalism has not been the subject of much comment, aside from a seminal essay of Carlo Dionisotti, and both he and Emilio Zanette drew exclusively on the *Satire*.[5] Dionisotti used these autobiographical verse epistles as some of his strongest evidence for a "situazione ambigua fra laicato e stato ecclesiastico" which characterized the literary generation of the first half of the sixteenth century. This ambiguity arose in part from uncertainty about the benefits of marriage, at least in Ariosto's case. Dionisotti fairly reductively traced the "disenchanted" compromise which ended this moment to Ariosto's disappointed hopes for a curial career. Earlier, the *Furioso* had reflected "una situazione più aperta e ambiziosa". Certainly the anticlerical passages of the *Satire*, especially the extended attack on courtier clerics which occupies about half of the second satire, put things more bluntly than the *Furioso* usually does, but the overall treatment of the problem in the final edition makes much the same points as the *Satire*. Since Dionisotti wrote, scholarship has transformed the religious landscape of early sixteenth-century Italy, making it possible at least to raise the issue of the relation between Ariosto's anticlericalism and reform.

The *Furioso*'s anticlericalism, and its place in a long tradition going back at least as far as Dante and Boccaccio, shows most obviously in its dim view of the vast majority of monks.[6] Ariosto embedded a vicious attack on monasteries in one of the poem's most strongly parodic passages, the

---

Bitter Harmony, passim; and Jonathan Crewe, *Trials of Authorship: Anterior Forms and Poetic Reconstruction from Wyatt to Shakespeare* (Berkeley, 1990), 14, who calls Foucault's stance "an irrevocable critical advance".

[5] Carlo Dionisotti, "Chierci e laici", in *Geografia e storia della letteratura italiana* (Turin, 1967), 47-73, esp. 59-61. Emilio Zanette offers a similarly biographical reading of the anticlericalism of *Satira 2* as a product of family romance in *Personaggi e momenti nella vita di Ludovico Ariosto* (Naples, 1970), 502-13. I borrow my title from Zanette.

[6] Sorting out the relative weight of poetic tradition and Ariosto's immediate historical moment would go well beyond the scope of this paper, which mainly makes a case for the importance of his poem as an interpretation of some of his circumstances, without denigrating a more "intertextual" reading. On this score, it may be significant that the *Orlando Innamorato* of Ariosto's immediate predecessor in Ferrara, Matteo Mario Boiardo, contains virtually no anticlericalism. About the only passage concerns an inept friar who rather than trying to rescue Orlando according to his directions, instead tries to prepare him for death (I.6.16-38). Ariosto claimed to be continuing Boiardo's work. Matteo Maria Boiardo, *Orlando Innamorato*, trans. with intro. and notes by Charles Stanley Ross (Berkeley, 1989). Emilio Bigi compares the first of Ariosto's hermits to a Mohammedan *incantatore* in I.20.1-8 and 22.1-6, but Boiardo never called him a hermit or a friar. Ludovico Ariosto, *Orlando Furioso*, ed. Emilio Bigi (Bologna, 1982), I, 139. I cite Bigi's text throughout.

Archangel Michael's descent from heaven (14.76-97).[7] In response to Charlemagne's apparently heart-felt prayer for help for his forces besieged in Paris, God dispatches Michael both to order Silence to aid the Christian relief force coming from England and also to set Discord to work in the pagan camp. Michael naturally searches for Silence in monasteries of both friars and cloistered monks, "dove sono i parlari in modo esclusi,/ che 'l Silenzio, ove cantano i salteri,/ ove dormeno, ove hanno la piatanza, e finalmente è scritto in ogni stanza" (14.79; references are to canto and stanza). He also expects to find Peace, Quiet and Charity, but none is any longer in residence, and Piety, Humility, and Love have decamped, too. Astounded, the archangel discovers that Gluttony, Avarice, Wrath, Pride, Envy, Sloth and Cruelty have replaced them.

At least Michael can accomplish one of his missions, since he does meet Discord there, acting as patron saint of lawyers. Thus Michael is spared the trip to Discord's native habitat in Hell among the damned, instead finding her "in questo nuovo inferno/ (chi 'l crederia?) tra santi ufficii e messe". Michael, who does not make much of an archangel, thinks this odd (*strano*), but no more, perhaps thereby strengthening Ariosto's sarcasm at the expense of the monks. When Discord, taking Pride with her, prepares to leave the monastery, she leaves a substitute, Fraud, "a guerreggiare il loco, fin che tornasse, e a mantenervi il fuoco", while Pride appoints Hypocrisy her *vicaria* and *locum tenens* (18.26-7). But Discord cannot be relied upon; in canto twenty-seven Michael has to go back to the monastery where he finds her enjoying herself during elections as the monks pelt one another with their breviaries. Michael must give her a thorough beating, some of it with a crucifix, before she promises to execute his orders (37-8).[8]

In the course of looking for Silence, Michael takes Discord's advice to question Fraud, who sometimes keeps company with him. When asked how to find Silence, Fraud replies,

> ... Già costui solia
> fra virtudi abitare, e non altrove,
> con Benedetto e con quelli d'Elia

---

[7] Echoing Benedetto Croce, Thomas M. Greene argues on the basis of this passage that "the Christianity of the *Furioso* is not so much disbelieved as made insubstantial", and that Michael's mission represented an "Olympian toying with a beloved thing". Founded in part on an intertextual reading of the poem, this judgment seems to me to go too far, once the poem is placed in immediate context, and, indeed, to resemble the way an inquisitor might have read it. *The Descent from Heaven: a Study in Epic Continuity* (New Haven, 1963), 119-24.

[8] Is this beating an echo of Machiavelli's notorious advice on how to deal with Fortune in *The Prince*, chap. 25? Bigi (II, 1150) notes a distinction between Michael's two scenes with Discord. He calls the first a satire on ecclesiastical corruption, and this one a much broader parody of popular preachers who made "supernatural religion" too concrete.

[i.e., with Benedictines and Carmelites]
ne le badie, quando erano ancor nuove: ...
Mancati ... quei santi
che lo solean tener pel camin ritto,
dagli onesti costumi ch'avea inanti,
fece alle sceleraggini tragitto (14.88-9).

Thus Silence moves only in the circles of Treachery, Murder, and forgers, although if Michael is quick enough, he might catch Silence in the cave of Slumber. The monks have not only failed themselves, but their mission to the world has also broken down.

The point is reinforced a few pages later when Astolfo and his companions temporarily detour into the Holy Land. There

Purgati de lor colpe a un monasterio
che dava di sé *odor di buoni esempii*,
de la passion di Cristo ogni misterio
contemplando n'andar per tutti i tempii
ch'or con eterno obbrobrio e vituperio
agli cristiani usurpano i Mori empii.
L'Europa è in arme, e di far guerra agogna
in ogni parte, fuor che ch'ove bisogna (15.99; emphasis added).

The call for a new crusade runs throughout the *Furioso*, and apparently was seriously meant (see below). Its linkage here to observant monasticism in the east, which sets an example to laymen, drives home the failings of western monks.

Yet the *Furioso* does not present monasticism in an unrelievedly evil light. One male monastery apparently serves as an example to the others, and there are two ambiguous references to female convents. The house held up for imitation, Vallombrosa, almost provides the setting for both key actions in the dynastic plot.[9] Ruggiero meant to be baptized and to marry Bradamante there, and thereby found the Este. Vallombrosa is described as "una badia ricca e bella, né men religiosa, e cortese a chiunque vi venia" (22.36), that is, as both a religious and a chivalric institution. Unfortunately, another romance turning in the plot disrupts Ruggiero's intention. Later, when he does finally come to the point of baptism again, he regrets having been so cavalier the first time around, even if his decision is still heavily utilitarian (41.47; cf. Bigi, II, 1681 and 1684).

When Orlando attempts to persuade the disconsolate Fiordiligi to leave Brandimarte's tomb, he offers to build her a convent if she wishes to serve God (43.184); under the circumstances, unrelieved by the possibly comic strokes surrounding the death of another woman deprived of her lover,

---

[9] Bigi (I, 934n) theorizes that the name Vallombrosa is invented, despite the fame of the monastery; he suggests that it replaced Valspinosa — the house's name in the first two versions of the poem — for reasons of alliteration.

Issabella, this seems to reflect a relatively positive attitude. It may, however, be significant both that Orlando proposes the idea and also that he deems it necessary to create a new house. Earlier, a convent also figures in Issabella's story, when her hermit protector set out to take her to an unnamed nunnery outside Marseilles, which is described in terms similar to those applied to Vallombrosa as full of "sante donne ... ricchissimo ..., e di edificio bello" (24.92). This well-intended scheme misses fire, but the attitude to the monastery itself again seems positive. It is unfortunate (although perhaps not accidental) that Ariosto did not identify it. It might reinforce the clue provided by Vallombrosa.

Issabella's story offers one instance of the vital roles played by hermits in the *Furioso*. As in the case of the regular clergy, so a superficially ambiguous attitude to hermits, the most irregular kind, runs through the poem. The first two of them, both necromancers, behave very differently toward Angelica, the object of nearly everyone's desires. When she makes her first escape from pursuit, a hermit, "devoto e venerabile d'aspetto" and "di conscienza scrupulosa e schiva", assists her by conjuring a demon out of a book to lay a false trail for her pursuers (2.12-15).[10] His double in canto eight also "aids" Angelica's flight, but via an attempted rape and into the hands of captors who will eventually offer her as a sacrifice to the Orc (and after which Ruggiero will again attempt to rape her). The hermit is explicitly identified as demonic, but "a lei fingendo divozione quanta avesse mai Paulo o Ilarione", two famous anchorites. He succeeded in consoling Angelica "con alquante ragion belle e divote" before drugging her to sleep and failing in his assault on her only because of his aged debility (8.44-50, 61). The first of these encounters marks a straight and indispensable romance moment in the plot, the second a "comic" episode.

A third hermit exercises both plot functions at once, and while apparently good, he is probably meant to appear a ridiculous figure upon reflection. Astolfo, the "anti-hero", encounters him in Egypt. The hermit's location in one of the homes of anchoritism perhaps reinforces his significance. He warns Astolfo of a terrible giant in his path, and urges him to cross to the other bank of the Nile. Astolfo, who is also a holy fool, refuses, thinking only of the safety of subsequent travelers. Thus fails another romance diversion, within one of the grandest romance diversions in the poem. The valence of the episode comes into question when the hermit, in blessing Astolfo, prays that God send the Archangel Michael to protect him (15.42-8). Michael is an intensely conflicted figure at best, who has so far appeared only by making a complete mess of God's command to set Discord at work in the pagan camp outside Paris. His protection might not be worth much. Perhaps Astolfo does not need it.

---

[10] Cf. Bigi's note (I, 139) on the symbolic value of this hermit and a sketch of similar figures in chivalric literature.

The final hermit in this group might again seem to be the first "good" one. Coming upon a distraught Issabella just after the death of her lover Zerbino, he combines functions much as the last hermit did. He consoles Issabella, albeit disinterestedly, as he talks her out of suicide, and then fosters her escape. Nevertheless, his actions have sufficiently ambiguous results for both Issabella and himself to cast a cloud over his portrayal as a good hermit. His much lengthier introductory description immediately puts distance between him and his brother hermits thus far.

> Il venerabile uom, ch'alta bontade
> avea congiunta a natural prudenzia,
> et era tutto pien di caritade,
> [as the first necromancer had been also]
> di buoni esempi ornato e d'eloquenzia,
> alla giovan dolente persuade
> con ragioni efficaci pazienzia;
> et inanzi le puon, come uno specchio,
> donne del Testamento e nuovo e vecchio.

Unsurpisingly, this paragon proves his worth to be more than verbal by further persuading Issabella "come non fusse/ alcun, se non in Dio, vero contento" and that she should enter a nunnery. Again distancing himself from the rapist hermit, this one is physically strong enough, despite his age, to help Issabella lug Zerbino's corpse around for days and morally strong enough not to trust himself alone with her. Instead he sets off to take her to a convent outside Marseilles (24.87-93).

So far, so good. Alas, they encounter the archpagan Rodomonte several cantos later. Once more deploying his eloquence to best effect, the hermit provides "scudo e falda" for Issabella's chastity. Rodomonte for some reason suffers "con lunga noia quel monaco audace", before seizing him by the hair, spinning him twice around his head, and flinging him into the sea. The narrator professes not to know what became of the hermit, although he notes the possibility that he drowned "per non saper notare". The hermit's end is "comic", but Issabella's is less so. Having failed in her original attempt at suicide, she tricks Rodomonte into chopping her head off, with nearly immediate effect (it manages to call Zerbino's name three times as it rolls downhill; 29.4-27). Thus it seems the hermit's virtue served no higher end than to postpone Issabella's death and ensure his own.

The moral of the story of Ariosto's final hermit is much different. At the climax of the dynastic plot the holiest hermit of all converts Ruggiero, preparing the way for marrige to Bradamante, which depends on his embracing Christianity. Nevertheless, it is probably not an accident that Ruggiero finds himself subject to the hermit's good offices only *after* a shipwreck led his *conscienza* to fear that Christ was pursuing a vendetta against him. Promising to convert, Ruggiero is miraculously rescued and led, according to God's plan, to meet his hermit on top of a cliff. Ruggiero thus comes to the point of no return without human intervention. His hermit, unlike the others, is "di molta riverenzia e d'*onor* [the principal chivalric value] degno" (41.47-52; emphasis added). As Ruggiero approaches, the hermit calls out "Saulo, Saulo ... perché persegui la mia fede?" which the narrator glosses as the Lord's saving intervention with Paul.

Drawing on a complete revelation of Ruggiero which he had received the night before, the hermit faults him for thinking he can escape God (Ruggiero thus becomes Jonah, bizarrely enough) and then consoles him with the parable of the laborers in the vineyard. Once he had instructed Ruggiero in the faith, the hermit told him most of what God had shown him of Ruggiero's future, omitting only the fact that once he had married Bradamante Ruggiero had only seven years to live before dying by treachery (41.52-67). Rather than a duplicitous way to convert Ruggiero, this is probably meant to figure the value of the hermit's prudence. But nothing in the dynastic plot is simple.[11]

Ruggiero's hermit returns two cantos later to heal Oliviero, one of the Christian champions in the tricorner duel which marks Orlando's reappearance as defender of the church. Once again, the hermit had been forewarned, this time by the saints. Disdaining medicaments, he went into his chapel and prayed for Oliviero's recovery. Once blessed by the hermit, Oliviero's nearly severed foot was, naturally, better than ever. The narrator intrudes to expostulate "Oh virtù che dà Cristo a chi gli crede!" (43.192) leaving unclear whether this applies to the hermit, Oliviero or both. If to Oliviero, it removes the necessity of even the holy hermit's mediation. Then again, this language closely resembles that applied to Astolfo a few cantos earlier, when his prayer led to the transformation of rocks rolling downhill into enough fully equipped horses to mount 80,102 foot soldiers for his campaign against Biserta (38.33). This is undoubtedly more comic than Oliviero's healing, but humorous or no, Astolfo also needs no human mediation to get his herd. The restoration of Oliviero's foot is not the end of the episode. The wisest of the pagan kings, Sobrino, witnessed the "miracolo grande et evidente", and asks "*con cor di fede attrito,/* d'iniciarsi al nostro sacro rito" (emphasis added; see below). Once baptized, Sobrino also recovered his health through the hermit's prayer. During the subsequent *agape*, the hermit keeps up his sorely needed catechesis, although he does bow to persuasion and drinks wine and eats meat (43.188-96).

There can be no question about the importance of this explicitly figured love feast, nor of the hermit's domination of it. The proem to the next canto, in which the story continues, hammers home the point.

---

[11] Greene, *Descent from Heaven*, 123 calls Ruggiero's conversion "unconvincing", without demonstrating the point. Andrew Fichter, by contrast, hinges his interpretation of the *Furioso* as Christian epic in part on Ruggiero's transformation. Christian epic may also be a little strong — Ariosto was no Marco Girolamo Vida — but Fichter's analysis deserves consideration. *Poets Historical: Dynastic Epic in the Renaissance* (New Haven, 1982), chap. 3, esp. 99-102.

> Spesso in poveri alberghi e in picciol tetti,
> ... meglio s'aggiungon d'amicizia i petti,
> che fra ricchezze invidiose et agi
> de le piene d'insidie e di sospetti
> corti regali e splendidi palagi,
> ove la caritade è in tutto estinta,
> né si vede amicizia, se non finta.

Playing a consistent anti-courtier theme, Ariosto highlights the behavior of the "santo vecchiarel" in tying a permanent "nodo" of "amor vero" between Orlando and his companions, most of whom had fought one another at one time or another, "ch'altri non avria fatto [the *nodo*] in real corte." This unfeigned male bonding continues through stanza eighteen, and the hermit is called "prudente", "santo", "devoto", "monaco saggio", and finally Ruggiero's "mastro santo" in the true faith (44.1-18). Thus this hermit, anyway, transcends the limits and the failings of both religious and political institutions, acting directly under divine guidance.[12]

By comparison with the attention given to monks and hermits, the secular clergy hardly appear in the *Furioso*. Again by comparison to the superficial ambiguity in Ariosto's attitude to regulars and irregulars, the seculars never appear in a flattering pose, with one possible exception. This may not be entirely fair, since in fact most of the secular clergy never come on stage at all, save for one scene. In the funeral of Brandimarte, all the clergy process, both regulars and secular, but it would be difficult to make much of this very bit part (43.175). Instead, only prelates represent the secular clergy, and even that elite group comes down to almost the pope alone, usually Leo X. Very early on there is one harsh attack on courtier prelates when the evil giant Erfilla wears vestments "di quella sorte ch'i vescovi e i prelati usano in corte", except for their color (7.4). In the first two versions of the *Furioso* the target of this barb had been even clearer: the *romana corte*.[13] Later, Charlemagne assigns archbishop Turpin of Rheims, wearing full pontificals, to undertake the catechesis of the newly converted Marfisa (38.23). Turpin also joins in the fighting, and the poem quietly mocks his authority as historian throughout, but neither kind of portrait has anticlerical overtones.[14]

---

[12] There is one more holy hermit, with a very minor role. He helps to heal one of Bradamante's wounds by cutting her hair (25.24). That, however, earns him the sobriquet "servo di Iesù".

[13] Bigi, I, 298n.

[14] In 26.23 he is called "il buon Turpin, che sa che dice il vero,/ e lascia creder poi quel ch'a l'uom piace", and in 30.49 the narrator comments that "scrive Turpin, verace in questo loco." Sexism may be responsible for Marfisa drawing the prelate Turpin, rather than a hermit like the one Ruggiero — who turns out to be her brother — got.

The popes, mainly Julius II and Leo X, do not escape so lightly. Julius II comes in for criticism in 40.42 in the midst of an apostrophe to Alfonso d'Este, who, under attack by a "pontifice irato", refused to surrender his territory as Ludovico il Moro had turned his over to Louis XII, to his cost. Leo X attracts more attention. In canto seventeen a proem on tyranny as God's reward for sin introduces an extended call for a crusade to free Christians from the Turks and Moors. Drawing a contrast to the time when the Franks ruled "la sacra stanza/ dove in carne abitò Dio onnipotente", the narrator bemoans the fact that now "i superbi e miseri cristiani,/ con biasmi lor, lasciano [the holy places] in man de' cani."

> Dove abbassar dovrebbono la lancia
> in augumento de la santa fede,
> tra lor si dan nel petto e ne la pancia
> a destruzion del poco che si crede.
> Voi, gente ispana, e voi, gente di Francia,
> volgete altrove, e voi, Svizzeri, il piede,
> e voi, Tedeschi, a far più degno acquisto;
> che quanto qui cercate è già di Cristo.

Next the kings of France and Spain are upbraided for killing Christians instead of recovering Jerusalem and Constantinople, and so it goes for three more stanzas. Then comes Leo's turn.

> Tu, gran Leone, a cui premon le terga
> de le chiavi del ciel le gravi some,
> non lasciar che nel sonno si sommerga
> Italia, se la man l'hai ne le chiome.
> Tu sei Pastore; e Dio t'ha quella verga
> data a portare, e scelto il fiero nome,
> perché tu ruggi, e che le braccia stenda,
> sì che dai lupi il grege tuo difenda (17.73-9).

The attack on Leo is heightened by the portrait earlier in the same canto of another "pastor", the monstrous Orco who ravaged Norandino's bridal party (17.32).[15] Machiavelli offered the same advice about Leo's behavior, but more temperately!

Similarly Machiavellian echoes hang over part of the explication of Merlin's allegorical carvings. One depicted a beast with ass' ears, the head and teeth of a wolf, the claws of a lion and the rest pure fox. He was shown wreaking havoc all over Europe, but he had saved his worst for the court of Rome "che v'avea uccisi cardinali e papi:/ contaminato avea la bella sede/ di Pietro, e messo scandol ne la fede." This beast, which turns out to be avarice, is eventually slain by a coalition made up of Francis I, Maximilian, Charles V, Henry VIII, and a "Leon" with the numeral "X" on his back

---

[15] I am grateful to Professor Ascoli for pointing out this parallel.

(26.31-6). This whole passage, and hence the transparent reference to Leo, is at least ironic, if not more broadly drawn.

This self-subversion of Leo's portrait characterizes most of the *Furioso*'s anticlericalism, making it as hard to decipher as the rest of the text. How can Leo be both the lion who helps to kill avarice, and one of its victims? How can he be both shepherd, and the one who yanks Italy by the hair? Ariosto's anticlericalism is undoubtedly complicated, but perhaps not indecipherable. His text offers two clues to his attitude to the clergy, which can then be put into a larger context of a possible set of religious beliefs.

The variegated functions of the hermits suggest one line of analysis. The necromantic hermits were distinguished from one another neither by their place in the plot nor, obviously, by their addiction to necromancy. Predicting the future was not itself objectionable, indeed prophecy is one of the devices which holds the *Furioso*'s plot together, and the best of the hermits, Ruggiero's, engages in it at length. Perhaps Ariosto meant to draw a distinction between the black arts and divinely inspired prophecy, even if Ruggiero's hermit says much the same thing as Merlin, one of the two chief prophets and the son of a demon. Instead, their actions lead to the assignment of different values to the two hermits: the first helps Angelica, while the second causes her great harm. The same point helps to clarify the ambiguity surrounding Issabella's hermit. He may have suggested either the wrong kind of "holy" action, withdrawal, or perhaps within the wrong kind of monastery, by comparison again to Ruggiero's hermit who pushes him finally into permanent, holy action in the world. There may also be a parallel between Issabella's hermit and Ruggiero's, and Ruggiero's own, gradual education, in which he fails both the first test after his instruction from Logistilla, and also to carry out his original intention to convert.[16]

It is probably not an accident that Ruggiero's hermit acts outside all the institutions in the poem, whether of chivalry, monasticism, formal religion, or the court. The Christian love he foments can come to fruition, thinks Ariosto, only from a place apart from all of them, through the mediation of a holy hermit in direct contact with God, whose own designs he merely forwards.[17] If this hermit is meant to be taken at face value, then great importance attaches to Ariosto's praise of the monastery of Vallombrosa and of the eastern house in which Astolfo and his companions undergo penance. Vallombrosa, the only monastery named in the poem, was, like most eastern monasteries, as nearly eremitic as a communal institution could be, and like its near neighbor Camaldoli, a place of strict observance. Thus it seems that

---

[16] Ascoli treats Ruggiero's education by Logistilla in depth in *Bitter Harmony*, chap. 3, esp. section iii.

[17] Nevertheless, one measure of the distance between Ariosto and Tasso is the much greater importance accorded to Peter the Hermit as a leader of the first crusade in *Gerusalemme liberata*.

Ariosto put forward an exemplary clerical life, which should hold both for the clergy and the laity.[18]

But even this paragon may not be entirely necessary. It must be stressed that God worked Ruggiero's conversion without human assistance, once Ruggiero had repented. Similarly, in at least three places laymen pray, and more or less rapidly have their wishes granted, again without clerical intervention. Two of these prayers may be in part parodic, or at least they occur in the midst of parodies. When Charlemagne prays for divine assistance in 14.69ff., God responds by sending the bumbling Michael, whose assistance only takes effect fifteen cantos later. We have already noted Astolfo's petition which produced an avalanche of horse-rocks and the language in which it was described. But if the narrator's comment on Astolfo's prayer may parody it and undercut some of the force of Ariosto's later praise in very similar terms for Ruggiero's hermit's prayer for Oliviero's foot, the apparent sincerity of *those* terms might also be turned back onto Astolfo's prayer.

Irony, then. Still, one of these prayers is offered by a laymen, one by an irregular cleric. The point that no one other than the individual offering the prayer need have anything to do with it seems to be underlined at the

---

[18] It may prove important that Vallombrosa was a historical place and the rest of Ariosto's monasteries probably fictitious, but too little work has yet been done on how Ariosto "processed" history (at the same time as he may sometimes have attempted to write it) in order to pursue the implications of this distinction. Little is likewise known about Vallombrosa and its congregation in the early sixteenth century. At the close of the previous century it underwent a schism triggered by a new group of "observant" houses modelling themselves on the reform stemming from the Benedictines of Santa Giustina in Padua. This suggests some measure of laxity in the rest of the order. The abbot elected in that crisis, Biagio Milanesi, was a great patron of culture, which may partly explain Ariosto's interest in the monastery. (Then again, if the observants held some of the same theological views as their Benedictine brothers, that could have been a more important lure for Ariosto, given my suppositions about his religious beliefs. On the traditional but still Pauline theology of Santa Giustina, see Barry Collett, *Italian Benedictine Scholars and the Reformation* [Oxford, 1985].) At the same time, Milanesi in particular and the order as a whole were subjected to an unrelenting Medici vendetta which led finally to Milanesi's deposition and replacement by a Medici outsider who held the generalcy for twenty-five years. Perhaps in an effort to dilute any further interference, the order changed its constitution in 1540 to make the abbot general's term one year only. Caught between the pressures of rigorists within and state-building without, all may not have been quite as the intensely eremitic image of Vallombrosa would seem to say. For a brief sketch of the later history of the order see R. N. Vasaturo, et al., eds., *Vallombrosa nel IX centenario della morte del fondatore Giovanni Gualberto* (Florence, 1973) and D. F. Tarani, *L'ordine vallombrosano* (Florence, 1921), which includes useful lists of abbots general and of houses (for which see also the map in H. Jedin, et al., eds., *Atlas zur Kirchengeschichte* [Freiburg, 1987]). There was none in Ferrara, and not many in the whole of the Val padana.

beginning of the siege of Biserta. For the only time in the poem, aside from
Charlemagne's prayer

> Come veri cristiani Astolfo e Orlando,
> che senza Dio non vanno a rischio alcuno,
> ne l'esercito fan publico bando,
> che sieno orazion fatte e digiuno; ...

> E così, poi che le astinenzie e i voti
> devotamente celebrati foro,
> parenti, amici, e gli altri insieme noti
> si cominciaro a convitar tra loro,

thus echoing the scene at Ruggiero's hermit's love-feast a little earlier. All
this simple, Christian behavior is undertaken at the orders of two laymen.
Meanwhile, inside Biserta,

> ... *i sacerdoti santi*
> supplicando col populo dolente,
> battonsi il petto, e con dirotti pianti
> chiamano il lor Macon che nulla sente.
> Quante vigilie, quante offerte, quanti
> doni promessi son privatamente!
> quanto in publico templi, statue, altari,
> memoria eterna de' lor casi amari!

> E poi che dal Cadì fu benedetto,
> prese il populo l'arme, e tornò al muro (40.11-14; emphasis added).

Despite (because of?) this massive clerical intervention, Biserta is doomed.
The explicit parallel is striking between infidel preparations, dependent on
the clergy (including the Imam [Cadì]), and Christian, which make no
mention even of their presence.

The clergy, then, aside from the monks of Vallombrosa and the Near East,
and a few hermits, have virtually no role in *Orlando Furioso*, and especially
not at critical moments.[19] Laymen manage their own religious affairs
perfectly capably, with the aid of the odd prophet, even possibly un-
Christian ones.[20] These twin emphases on lay control and on prophecy
appear to fit Ariosto's poem neatly into the context of the *religione cittadina*
of Ferrara. It appears that Ariosto's beliefs especially overlapped with the

---

[19] The absence of anticlericalism in the lunar episode (34.68- 35.30) poses a large
unresolved problem. Ariosto's poem ironizes virtually every other dimension of
human and divine existence in this extended tale. See David Quint, *Origin and
Originality in Renaissance Literature: Versions of the Source* (New Haven, 1983),
81-92 and Ascoli, *Bitter Harmony*, 285-304.

[20] Ariosto's ideas about secular supremacy probably have something to do with his
complicated attitude to the Empire, on which see most recently Alberto Casadei, *La
strategia delle varianti. Le correzioni storiche del terzo "Furioso"* (Lucca, 1988).

dukes' commitment to secular control of religious observance.[21] This they maintained in part through patronage of the strictest religious orders, above all Observant Dominicans, the order of Savonarola. Some of his followers, including the native Ferrarese Francesco Silvestri, were active in Ferrara and the ducal court about the time the first edition of the *Furioso* appeared, but I have not yet found any direct links to Ariosto.[22] Unsurprisingly, the dukes and their subjects, together with their near neighbors in Mantua, assigned great importance to prophecy as an alternative, but acceptable, source of religious authority.[23]

These coincidences in turn open the almost unasked question of Ariosto's relation to reform. Although it is much too early for more than preliminary observations, Ariosto's attitudes may have been rooted in a loosely evangelical religion, like that of some of his Venetian contemporaries, the so-called *spirituali*, which would also come to prominence in the Academy of Modena in the decade after Ariosto's death.[24] Perhaps Ariosto found in Pietro Bembo, now thought to have been a key *spirituale* from early on, more than a neo-platonic target, a linguistic model, and a close friend.[25] Marcantonio Flaminio, one of the authors of *Il Beneficio di Cristo* and a major force in Valdesian spiritualism later, joined Bembo among those

---

[21] Adriano Prosperi, "Le istituzioni ecclesiastiche e le idee religiose", in *Il Rinascimento nelle corti padane* (Bari, 1977), 125-163, esp. 128 where Prosperi cites one of Ariosto's letters as evidence that he was a "fedele interprete" of the duke's ideology of temporal superiority. Cf. the conclusion of the essay (162) where Prosperi provides evidence against Dionisotti's claim for Ariosto's biographically rooted "suspension" — his descendants deployed exactly the same strategy on the score of benefices in the 1590s as Ariosto had in the 1510s and 1520s.

[22] After having been prior at Mantua in 1513 and at Ferrara in 1516, Silvestri rose to become general of the Dominicans a decade later. Gabriella Zarri, "Pieta e profezia alle corti padane: le pie consigliere dei principi", in *Corti padane*, 201-37, 223ff. and note 69 for other Savonarolans active in the area. For Savonarola's own prophecies and their survival after his death see Donald Weinstein, *Savonarola and Florence: Prophecy and Patriotism in the Renaissance* (Princeton, 1970), especially chap. 10.

[23] Zarri, passim; for the situation at the eastern end of the Val padana in Venice at roughly the same time, see most recently Bernard McGinn, "Circoli gioachimiti veneziani (1450-1530)", trans. R. Rusconi, *Cristianesimo nella storia* 7 (1986): 19-39.

[24] There is now a large literature on the Academy of Modena, much of it the work of Massimo Firpo. See esp. "Gli 'spirituali', l'Accademia di Modena e il formulario di fede del 1542: controllo del dissenso religioso e nicodemismo", *Rivista di storia e letteratura religiosa* 20 (1984): 40-111. Cf. Albano Biondi, "Streghe ed eretici nei domini estensi all'epoca dell'Ariosto", *Corti padane*, 165-99, esp. 183ff., which also contains a good deal of material on popular anticlericalism.

[25] Ascoli, *Bitter Harmony*, 89, 99, 111-13, 116, 222-3, and Paolo Simoncelli, "Pietro Bembo e l'evangelismo italiano", *Critica storica* 15 (1978): 1-63.

welcoming Ariosto's ship to shore near the end of the *Furioso* (46.13-15).[26] It may then not be irrelevant that one of Bembo's Paduan friends, Marco Mantova, combined anticlericalism and resistance to hierocratic pretensions with fideism.[27] Finally, there may be an analogue to the appeal of Camaldoli to Venetians in Ariosto's praise for Vallombrosa, but its links to Ferrara, if any, remain to be uncovered.[28]

In addition to these contextual hints, Ariosto's text could support this theory, especially in its constant references to *fede* (as in Sobrino's conversion), *benefizio*, and grace, sometimes explicitly contrasted with merit, as in Drusilla's defiant death in 37.73-4, as well as the poem's denigrating of clerical mediation in salvation. Perhaps most suggestive, Ariosto paralleled Ruggiero's conversion to that of Paul, a primary inspiration behind the highly amorphous *spirituali*. It also seems likely that the *Furioso* contains a good dose of Erasmus, who likewise made Paul one of his principal champions.[29]

Generalizations from one case have little value, but the enormous popularity of the *Furioso* in the sixteenth century make it worth comparing its attitudes to one of the most important recent analyses of anticlericalism. Whatever its social, political or personal springs, the *Furioso* fits only some of the six categories of anticlericalism detailed by R. W. Scribner.[30] Its political dimension shows clearly, especially in attacks on Leo X and on courtier prelates, as it does in the poem's nearly direct support for lay control of much religious observance. The stronger form of personal responsibility for salvation brings the *Furioso*'s attitudes under the head of sacred anticlericalism, although without reference to the economic dimension of clerical monopoly of sacred power. Similarly, anticlericalism's sexual aspect recurs, as in the attempted rape of Angelica set against the self-control of Issabella's hermit. Making Discord both chief denizen of monasteries

---

[26] Massimo Firpo, "Valdesianesimo ed evangelismo: alle origini dell''Ecclesia Viterbense'", in *Libri, idee e sentimenti religiosi nel Cinquecento italiano* (Modena, 1987), 53-71, and in Massimo Firpo, *Tra alumbrados e "spirituali:" studi su Juan de Valdés e il valdesianesimo nella crisi religiosa del '500 italiano* (Florence, 1990), 155-84, and passim for Flaminio.

[27] Thomas F. Mayer, "Marco Mantova and the Paduan Religious Crisis of the Early Sixteenth Century", *Cristianesimo nella storia* 7 (1986): 41-61.

[28] See esp. James Bruce Ross, "Gasparo Contarini and his Friends", *Studies in the Renaissance* 17 (1970): 192-232; Felix Gilbert, "Religion and Politics in the Thought of Gasparo Contarini", in T. K. Rabb and J. E. Seigel, eds., *Action and Conviction in Early Modern Europe* (Princeton, 1969), 90-116 (also in *History: Choice and Commitment* [Cambridge, Mass., 1977], 247-67); and Giuseppe Alberigo, "Vita attiva e vita contemplativa in un'esperienza cristiana del XVI secolo", *Studi veneziani* 16 (1974): 177-225.

[29] Ascoli, *Bitter Harmony*, passim, esp. 335-6.

[30] R. W. Scribner, "Anticlericalism and the Reformation in Germany", in *Popular Culture and Popular Movements in Reformation Germany* (London, 1987), 243.

and also patron of lawyers takes aim at the monk's legal authority. Yet the social side of anticlericalism and most of its economic overtones are almost entirely absent. That may well be traced both to Ariosto's own ambiguous position "fra laicato e stato ecclesiastico", and to his dependence on income from his benefices until very late in his life. Thus the *Furioso*'s irony may have served to protect Ariosto from its own unmasking which could have threatened his hard-won position. Nevertheless, the *Satire* clearly depict Ariosto as a "chierico anticlericale"; his greatest poem, perhaps not by chance, displays a narrator and characters who hold very similar opinions.

SIXTEENTH-CENTURY ITALIAN SPIRITUALI
AND THE PAPACY

ELISABETH G. GLEASON

University of San Francisco

Asking why Italy "did not accomplish a reformation like that which occurred in Germany", Jakob Burckhardt pointed to "a plausible answer" which maintained that the Italian mind "never went further than the denial of the hierarchy, while the origin and vigor of the German Reformation was due to its positive religious doctrines, most of all to the doctrines of justification by faith and of the inefficacy of good works."[1] However, modern scholarship on sixteenth-century Italian religious history points in an altogether different direction. The doctrine of justification by faith had many adherents in Italy, but very few people were willing to deny the hierarchy, and especially the papacy. This was the case even after the writings of Northern reformers and their rejection of the Catholic ecclesiastical hierarchy became known to many educated Italians. Why Italian advocates of church reform by and large did not attack the existing structure of ecclesiastical institutions is a complex question, a small aspect of which I would like to consider in my paper.

We know that Luther's criticism of clerical abuses did not reach an indifferent or uncomprehending Italian milieu. On the contrary, the ideal of a purified church as opposed to the reality of the actual corrupt one has deep roots in Italian medieval culture and continued vigorous throughout the Renaissance period. It surfaced not only among fringe groups like Waldensians, Spiritual Franciscans, or self-appointed wandering prophets,[2] but in sermons of many mainstream popular preachers and in works of Benedictine and Augustinian monastic writers.[3] The ideal pure and holy church of Savonarola's mystical and millenarian visions was kept alive by his followers long after his death.[4] However, once the upheaval of the Reformation began, one group in particular advocated reform of the church:

---

[1] *The Civilization of the Renaissance in Italy* (Oxford, 1945), 280.

[2] Ottavia Niccoli, *Prophecy and the People in Renaissance Italy* (Princeton, 1990), esp. chs. 1 and 4.

[3] Barry Collett, *Italian Benedictine Scholars and the Reformation* (Oxford, 1985), esp. chs. 3 and 4.

[4] Donald Weinstein, *Savonarola and Florence* (Princeton, 1970), ch. 10; Paolo Simoncelli, *Evangelismo italiano del Cinquecento* (Rome, 1979), ch.1.

the so-called *spirituali*,[5] a term used already in the 1520s in contrast to *carnali* or *mondani* to designate devout, austere Christians who wanted to base their religion on a biblical and patristic foundation. By and large they shared a recognizable set of religious attitudes, now often called Italian Evangelism,[6] foremost among which was adherence to the doctrine of justification by faith and the desire for peace and concord among all Christians. Yet, despite their irenic ideas, they made little impact on Italian Catholicism. One of the reasons for this was the equivocal position of their most conspicuous figures concerning the nature and limits of papal power.

In modern Italian historiography religious dissenters have received much scholarly attention, enlivened by the wider debates concerning lay and ecclesiastical culture since the Risorgimento. The *spirituali*, too, as critics of established practices and ideas have on the whole had a good press. Although they played a role in Italian religious history for fifty years beginning with the 1520s, they formed a recognizable group at the papal court only during a short time, from 1536-1542, when the politically astute Pope Paul III gave them high visibility by appointing several of their members to the college of cardinals. Among them were Morone, Bembo, Fregoso, Badia, Carafa, Sadoleto, and the two most prominent spokesmen of the *spirituali*, Contarini and Pole. Almost all of these men minced no words about clerical abuses and the depth of resentment that the behavior of the clergy had created among the common people. Yet they dealt only tangentially with the most basic structural questions regarding ecclesiastical institutions. The shape of their thought on this subject defies easy generalizations.

One of the first members of this group to plead for disciplinary control over dissolute clergy was Gianpietro Carafa, later Pope Paul IV, who in a *Memorial* of 1532[7] appealed to Clement VII to rid the church of sowers of scandal, whether they be heretics or immoral clergy. This was to be accomplished by strict enforcement of disciplinary measures without regard to person. Carafa predicted the direst consequences for the church unless she brought her house in order, and proposed a remedy for the present crisis in the foundation of a new order under strict papal control, modelled on the

---

[5] For the use of the term in contemporary sources, see Gigliola Fragnito, "Gli «spirituali» e la fuga di Bernardino Ochino", *Rivista Storica Italiana* 84 (1972): 780-1, reprinted in her *Gasparo Contarini* (Florence, 1988), 255-57; Adriano Prosperi, *Tra Evangelismo e Controriforma: G. M. Giberti* (Rome, 1969), 285-6, 314.

[6] See my "On the Nature of Italian Evangelism: Scholarship, 1953-1978", *SCJ* 9 (1978): 3-25.

[7] "De Lutheranorum haeresi reprimenda et ecclesia reformanda ad Clementem VII [4. octobris 1532]", *Concilium Tridentinum. Diariorum Actorum Epistularum Tractatuum nova collectio*, vol. 12 (Freiburg i. Br., 1929), 67-77. English translation in Elisabeth G. Gleason, ed. and transl., *Reform Thought in Sixteenth-Century Italy* (Chico, Calif., 1981), 55-80.

military knighthoods of crusading times. But in his sharply worded *Memorial* there was not even a hint of reservations about the extant ecclesiastical structures; only their imperfect functioning is scathingly criticized. Carafa, who was to part company with the *spirituali* by the end of the decade and later become their persecutor, here separated the areas of doctrine and tradition, which were not open to discussion, from disciplinary matters which did need reform. His unquestioning acceptance of clerical power and papal supremacy in the church foreshadowed that of the later Counter-Reformation.

Similar ideas concerning clerical abuses are found in a much more famous document, the *Consilium de emendanda ecclesia* of 1537, drawn up by a committee of nine prelates under the presidency of Contarini.[8] With the exception of Aleander, all of its members were *spirituali*. Its importance has frequently been overstated; despite proposals to tighten supervision over secular and regular clergy, in actuality the *Consilium* broke no new theoretical ground when dealing with clerical abuses. But when addressing the question of papal power, it pointed to a different concept than that which was then prevalent at the papal court.

Cardinal Sadoleto's speech at the beginning of the committee's deliberations sounded an urgent note of alarm at the state of the clergy. Reverting to the topos of the pure church of the first centuries, and contrasting it with the iniquities of the present, he spoke with passion of the hatred with which the clergy was regarded, and even accused its members of causing the troubles in Germany by their ruthless exploitation of the people through the sale of indulgences. Sadoleto's most recent biographer detects in this oration "a quality of bitter reproach ... that is almost vengeful in its implicit judgments of the Medici popes, if not of the entire papal succession of his own era."[9]

The committee's final document echoed Sadoleto's oration when it compared the church with a foundering ship about to sink. The report singled out what its authors considered to be the basic evil in the church: exaggerated claims for papal power made by false counsellors who had assured the popes that they were absolute masters — "domini" — over all the goods of the church and lords of all benefices. Further, the *Consilium* charged that the popes, by listening to these counsellors, were personally responsible for the ills besetting the church. The *spirituali* prelates envisioned the pope's office as that of a faithful steward rather than of a ruler with unlimited dominion.

---

[8] "Consilium delectorum cardinalium et aliorum praelatorum de emendanda ecclesia S. D. N. Paulo III iubente conscriptum et exhibitum", *Concilium Tridentinum*, 12: 131-45. English translation in Gleason, *Reform Thought*, 81-100.

[9] Richard M. Douglas, *Jacopo Sadoleto, 1477-1547: Humanist and Reformer* (Cambridge, Mass., 1959), 103.

Predictably, Paul III was impassive before these ideas, and ultimately came to share the fear of conservative cardinals that the *Consilium*, if made public, would backfire in the same way as Adrian VI's confession of guilt had done before the Diet of Nürnberg. This fear was justified, since the document was in fact leaked to wider circles, and soon reached Luther, who seized upon its recommendations with derision and scorn because he considered them merely cosmetic rather than substantive.[10] He showed no comprehension or sympathy for the men whose criticism of papal power was explicit and certainly courageous, given their position as papal appointees.

The most important result of the document was to make its presentor Contarini the recognized spokesman and center of a party of reform at the papal court. This group tried to formulate a theory of reform reaching beyond criticism of curial maladministration, sale of offices, papal fiscal policy and political entanglements, to the vision of a purified papacy which would begin the process of reform by breaking radically with the practices of the past. Their vision was presented as a challenge to Paul III who, however, stonewalled. He was much too political to seriously initiate radical measures that would rock the entire Roman establishment. Preferring to proceed cautiously, he defused the proposals of the *spirituali* by noncommittal words rather than action.

The most significant rethinking of the whole question concerning clerical and especially papal power among the *spirituali* was found in three brief and unsystematic tracts by Contarini. His views were first voiced when as Venetian ambassador to Clement VII he had ample occasion to compare the nature of papal power with that of secular rulers. In a long conversation with Clement in 1529, Contarini explained his vision of papal power as qualitatively different from that of other princes because of the pope's spiritual authority in the *respublica Christiana*. The pope's main task was to be a peacemaker and to give an example of unselfish behavior, Contarini argued, adding that papal spiritual power should be divorced from papal temporal power if that was necessary for the good of Christendom. The papal state was not an asset, he maintained: "Even before this state there was a church, and a most excellent one. This state is like that of an Italian prince, joined to the church."[11]

Clement VII discounted these words since they were spoken by a loyal Venetian ambassador who was trying to justify Venice's occupation of two papal cities. But Contarini meant his ideas seriously, taking them up again during his later career as statesman and cardinal. In his *De potestate pontificis quod divinitus sit tradita* of the early 1530s, he based his support

---

[10] *Luther's Works*. American Edition, vol. 34 (Philadelphia, 1960), 231-67.

[11] Franz Dittrich, *Regesten und Briefe des Cardinals Gasparo Contarini* (Braunsberg, 1881), 43 (No. 126).

for the authority of the pope on Scripture, reason, and history.[12] To the Lutheran idea that Christ leads the church directly, he countered with the assertion that given human nature, a visible head was necessary in every human group lest chaos ensue. Just as man, who depends on his senses, needs the visible signs of God's grace in the sacraments, he argued, so the church needs a visible leader to whom divine power is given. His own strong belief in the necessity of upholding a political hierarchy, so typical of his Venetian patrician class, made him attach exceptional importance to order in every organization. As an Aristotelian, he saw in the divine institution of the papacy the logical corollary to God's supreme rationality in structuring his church with the pope as its head. At no point did he doubt the divine institution of the papacy.

Contarini later wrote about papal power in the context of his work on commissions for the reform of curial offices, first the *dataria* and then the *poenitentiaria*. Each time he reiterated that all church reform would have to begin with the pope himself, and echoed ideas expressed in the *Consilium*. In fact, he called on Paul III to assert his independence of the curia and his authority over it by denouncing extreme papalism and exaggerated ideas of his power. In the tract *De usu potestatis clavium*,[13] he summarized his belief that holders of ecclesiastical dignities were servants of God, unable to grant any favors for money without being guilty of sin. In *De potestate pontificis in compositionibus epistola*,[14] Contarini repeated once again that curial jurists were responsible for wrong and pernicious theories of papal power. Precisely because no power on earth was superior to that of the pope, he argued, his authority should never be allowed to become tyrannical or arbitrary, expressing the will of only one man. It was founded on the light of reason, the precepts of God and Christian charity. The relation of the pope and the Christian people was that of a father and his children for whose spiritual welfare his office was instituted by Christ.

Contarini and other *spirituali* consistently called for an emphasis on the spiritual essence of papal power, but left unclear how this was to be achieved. So did another eminent member of their group, Reginald Pole, in his book on the papal office. His posthumously published *De summo pontifice*[15] envisioned papal power as reasonable, paternal, and spiritual but did not discuss any concrete issues concerning its exercise. Here we reach one of the fundamental problems in the ideology of many *spirituali*, sharply posed by Cardinal Ercole Gonzaga of Mantua, who was one of their marginal members. Upon hearing of proposals by Contarini and other

---

[12] Gasparo Contarini, *Gegenreformatorische Schriften (1530-1542)*, ed. Friedrich Hünermann (Münster i.W., 1923), 35-43.

[13] *Concilium Tridentinum*, 12: 151-3.

[14] Jodocus Le Plat, *Monumentorum ad historiam Concilii Tridentini potissimum illustrandam spectantium amplissima collectio*, vol. 2 (Louvain, 1783), 608-15.

[15] Louvain, 1569.

spirituali to reform curial offices, and of their attack on compositions and the payment by petitioners for spiritual graces like dispensations, Gonzaga coolly inquired what would happen to all the papal bureaucrats who in good faith had invested in a venal office. Could the papacy simply renege on its obligations to the purchasers of various curial positions without committing an injustice as great as accepting money for spiritual favors? The livelihood of hundreds of people and their families was involved. How could any reform effort extricate the popes from the economic network that had been spun ever since the late fifteenth century, and where would the money to pay all claims of dismissed officeholders be raised?[16]

There were no good answers to Gonzaga's questions other than an entirely imaginary ruthless cutting of the Gordian knot of papal finances. But here the *spirituali* prelates equivocated. The income of some of their leaders was at risk with any serious reform of the curia. A number of so-called poor cardinals — meaning not rich by Roman standards for cardinals of the time — received pensions from the very offices they wanted to reform. The registers of the *Dataria*, the *libri mastri*, show that eleven cardinals were paid regular pensions from the income of the *Dataria apostolica*, including Contarini and Carafa at the very time when they were calling upon the pope to stop the entrenched fiscal practices of that office.[17] These facts leave the modern historian face to face with jarring and disturbing inconsistencies.

One well-known explanation for the failure of the *spirituali* to accept the full implications of their criticism was that of Antonio Gramsci who in his *Notebooks from Prison* accused them and other leading Italian intellectuals at the time of cowardice.[18] He charged them with putting their economic security above their consciences, since many knew and agreed with ideas of Northern reformers yet allowed themselves to be "suffocated and domesticated" by the Catholic church which offered them positions and benefices as a reward for conformity. Gramsci's view acquired a certain radical chic. It accused members of the elite of selling out to the establishment, unlike the dissenters from the lower classes who clung to their beliefs and accepted the consequences. This accusation of the intellectuals lends another twist to the well-known Crocean idea that Italian free thought was driven under-

---

[16] Walter Friedensburg, "Der Briefwechsel Gasparo Contarini's mit Ercole Gonzaga", *Quellen und Forschungen aus italienischen Archiven und Bibliotheken* 7 (1904): 204-5.

[17] Barbara M. Hallman, *Italian Cardinals, Reform, and the Church as Property* (Berkeley, 1985), 61.

[18] Alessandro Pastore, *Marcantonio Flaminio: Fortune e sfortune di un chierico nell'Italia del Cinquecento* (Milan, 1981), 7-8, and note 1.

ground by the repressive mechanism of the church, not to emerge again until the *Risorgimento*.[19]

While a case in support of such views can be made, their reductionism ultimately makes them unsatisfactory as explanations for the failure of the *spirituali*. The supposition that an entire highly educated, religiously and morally serious group like the *spirituali* simply caved in when its economic status was threatened, and accepted the *status quo*, is too simplistic.

Maybe the most useful first step toward understanding their thought is to realize that they lived at the very end of an epoch in the history of the Italian church. The *spirituali* still belonged to the relatively open and tolerant church of the Renaissance. Their most conspicuous members formed part of its aristocratic elite of humanistically educated gentlemen who shared the same culture and played by the same rules. This elite freely criticized abuses of the clergy in private, but thought that the people should not participate in such criticism. Its members read and discussed Protestant works, and in many cases agreed with the idea that the Christian is justified before God by faith. While many assented to a "justificatio fide", they hesitated to embrace a "justificatio sola fide", and to advocate the dismantling of the ecclesiastical hierarchy and the sacramental system in consequence, as the Protestants had done. They stopped short not on account of cowardice, but out of conviction, because they still believed in the possibility of joining their revitalized personal and biblical Christian spirituality with reformed Catholic church structures and a spiritual pope at their apex.

At the heart of their position concerning the papacy was a profound inconsistency. While setting the same high value on peace and concord as Erasmus did, and calling for the pope to be a peacemaker, they left out of account the vexed question of how the pope's freedom to maneuver was to be assured in an Italy where Charles V's political hegemony became evident — and threatening — after the Peace of Bologna in 1530. By focusing on the failure of the clergy to observe its own laws and norms, the *spirituali* pointed to chaos in the church as a great evil. They believed that it was necessary to strengthen, not abolish the machinery connected to the juridical structure of the church because it assured internal order, just as good government made social order possible. The *spirituali* prelates wanted reform of curial offices, not their abolition: in a sense, they wanted to have it both ways.

Their rhetoric, so similar to that of preachers before the popes whose sermons John O'Malley has analyzed,[20] emphasized the pope's pastoral

---

[19] Benedetto Croce, "A Working Hypothesis: The Crisis of Italy in the Cinquecento and the Bond Between the Renaissance and the Risorgimento", in *The Late Italian Renaissance*, ed. by E. Cochrane (New York, 1970), 23-42.

[20] *Praise and Blame in Renaissance Rome: Rhetoric, Doctrine and Reform in the Sacred Orators of the Papal Court, ca. 1450-1521* (Durham, N.C., 1979).

role in the church. He was to be the "father", "shepherd", and intermediary between warring groups within the *respublica Christiana*. At the same time he was called upon to enforce canonical regulations and uphold extant laws. The *spirituali* knew that the papacy of their time was in essence the creation of the Gregorian reform movement with its insistence on institutional order and juridical structures. Yet they never tackled the tensions between pastoral rhetoric and juridical reality. One of the distinctive contributions of Protestant reformers was precisely the stance they adopted on these issues, which they pursued to its logical conclusions.

These ambiguities in the thought of the Italian *spirituali* were ultimately resolved not by a theological or philosophical synthesis, but by the fragmentation of their group in 1541. Moderates clustered in one form or another around Contarini, and more radical thinkers became associated with the so-called *ecclesia Viterbiensis*, at the head of which was Pole.[21] The former clung to the dream of combining the doctrine of justification by faith as a personal matter with their continued membership in the Catholic church, whose doctrinal authority they explicitly acknowledged. In effect, they separated personal devotional life and public conformity. The men around Pole, on the other hand, understood the basic conflict implicit in this combination much more clearly. Several became Protestants, leaving Italy for Switzerland, while a number of the others ended before the Inquisition. Massimo Firpo's recent edition of the *Processo Morone* is a mine of information on the gradations of opinions among the *spirituali*, and on this part of their history.[22]

On August 28, 1542, a few days after the death of Contarini and the flight to Switzerland of Bernardino Ochino, the first general of the Capuchins, Gianmatteo Giberti, bishop of Verona, wrote to Cardinal Ercole Gonzaga: "Because our *spirituali* give us so little comfort by their dying and fleeing, I believe that it will be well to abandon their company."[23] These words are particularly poignant since their author had been one of the most visible *spirituali* prelates of the 1530s, a friend and convinced supporter of Contarini's policy of conciliation with the Protestants at Regensburg, and a fellow-critic of curial abuses and exaggerated papal claims to power. Giberti sensed that a new wind was blowing and that a more militant Catholic church was emerging which had no toleration for the criticism or the ambiguities of the intellectual elite of the *spirituali*. 1542 was a year of great changes, culminating in the reinstitution of the Roman Inquisition. Soon new men were to fill curial posts who were career bureaucrats of middle-class background concerned with administrative efficiency, the tightening of

---

[21] Tommaso Bozza, *Nuovi Studi sulla Riforma in Italia, I. Il Beneficio di Cristo* (Rome, 1976), esp. ch. 8; Simoncelli, *Evangelismo italiano* (n. 4 above), ch. 2.

[22] Massimo Firpo and Dario Marcatto, *Il Processo Inquisitoriale del Cardinal Giovanni Morone*, 5 vols. in 6 (Rome, 1981-89).

[23] Quoted in Fragnito, "Gli «spirituali» e la fuga", 777.

doctrinal uniformity, and the offensive against dissent and heresy. Among these new organization men there was no talk about a spiritual papacy: in fact, any such notion became suspect.

The *spirituali*, by contrast, were the last elite of the old church so deeply marked by the culture of the Renaissance.[24] Their proposals for reform of the papacy were an in-house affair, as it were. Taken out of context, some of their criticism of the clergy and the papacy could have been written by Protestant reformers. Their brand of anticlericalism, still possible during the 1530s, came to be suspect in the church of the Counter-Reformation, together with the *spirituali* themselves.[25] The time for drawing clear lines and making unequivocal choices had arrived.

---

[24] The term "il Rinascimento perduto" has recently been used for the period when Renaissance culture was at home at the papal court: Gigliola Fragnito, *In museo e in villa* (Venice, 1988), esp. essays 1 and 3.

[25] Paolo Simoncelli, "Inquisizione romana e riforma in Italia", *Rivista Storica Italiana* 100 (1988): 5-125, vigorously takes up the thesis that the Counter-Reformation repressed Italian culture, and includes very full bibliography. For the opposite view see Eric Cochrane, *Italy: 1530-1630* (London, 1988).

WRITING THE BOOK ON ITALIAN ANTICLERICALISM

DONALD WEINSTEIN

University of Arizona, Tucson

In 1515 Pope Leo X, the former Giovanni de' Medici, made a formal entry into Florence. The elaborate procession, with floats, arches, and tableaux, evoking an imperial triumph, brought the Florentines out *en masse* to welcome their native son. Among the spectators was a certain Jacopo Melocchi who came with two of his sons from Pistoia, some eighteen miles away. Melocchi recorded his admiration of the magnificent spectacle in his diary, but then reflected that the pomp and sumptuosity of the papal courtiers was detrimental to the piety of the Florentines, a people "formerly Catholic and very devout, who had believed in the holiness of the court of Rome and of the prelates."[1] Melocchi was a priest, a fact in itself that should occasion no surprise, since many of the severest critics of the Curia and of the moral failings of the clergy came from within the ranks. But Melocchi was also a non-resident canon, a pluralist, probably a simoniac, he was married and the father of several children.

If Melocchi felt uncomfortable about the pot calling the kettle black he gave no hint of it in his diary; neither his personal situation nor his anti-Roman sentiments were in any way exceptional in early sixteenth-century Italy where a deeply embedded patronage and benefice system held Italian clerics and laity in its morally corrosive embrace. Lay rights of patronage to clerical office, appropriation of benefices, alienation of ecclesiastical property, and interference in clerical elections were a few of the widespread practices in which many of the clergy's sharpest critics were themselves involved. However critics might deplore the worldliness and corruption of the Papal court, the abuses of office by prelates, or the unsuitability of

---

[1] "Si fere grandissimi triomphi et paramenti con archi trionfali per firenze et molte altre cerimonie con devotioni et honore di Iddio et con grandissimo concorso de populi circumstati et Io con bonifatio et Ipolito andai avedere tali & tanti trionfi et grande cose ... et sappi che moltissimi anni erano passati che mai papa era stato a firenze. Ma ancor sappi che la vita de cortigiani et le lor pompe & sumptuosita tolsseno assai di devotione nel [blotted word here] populo fiorentino quale era prima Chatolicho et devotissimo Stimando che la corte di Roma et li prelati fusseno una santismonia del che persono assai di devotione." Messer Jacopo di Niccolo Melocchi da Pistoia, *Ricordi* Ms Biblioteca Nazionale di Firenze Acquisti e Doni Rossi Melocchi filza 8, fol. 62 r [modern folio numbering, pencil]. On the elaborate pomp and circumstance of Pope Leo's entry into Florence see Ilaria Ciseri, *L'ingresso trionfale di Leone X in Firenze nel 1515* (Florence, 1990).

monks, nuns, and priests for their vocations, any serious possibility of
reform was choked off by thickly tangled strands of lay and ecclesiastical
interest.[2]

Yet it would be a mistake to conclude that Italian anticlericalism was
simply a conventional, and therefore inconsequential cliché whose chief
historical significance was its function as a safety valve for pressures of
conscience. No doubt it was that too, although there is little evidence that
Italian consciences were much disturbed by the disjunction between words
and deeds. In this respect, Melocchi's utter lack of self-awareness was
undoubtedly more typical than Guicciardini's honest self-appraisal.[3] Nor
should we regard Italian anticlericalism as all of a piece, a constant, timeless
feature of the Italian mind, as some historians of Italian religion seem
inclined to do.[4] Italian feelings about the Church were as complicated and
as varied as might be expected from a long history of intense relations
between laity and clergy.

If I were to write a book on this history, limiting myself for convenience
as well as coherence to the period between the late eleventh and early
sixteenth centuries, the era of Italian communal and intellectual efflores-
cence, I would begin with a chapter on the Great Awakening (to borrow a
term from American religious history) of the eleventh and twelfth centuries
with all its attendant expectations and disappointments among both clergy
and laity. I would examine the religious aspirations and frustrations of such
initially lay movements as the late twelfth-century Franciscans and
fourteenth-century Gesuati. The Guelf-Ghibelline struggles and their
ferocious impact on Italian political and social life would rate a chapter, and
in this context I would discuss Dante's attack on the temporal pretensions
of the Papacy in *De monarchia*. The triangular relationship that characterized relations between the communes, local clergy, and the Roman Curia,
with all its attendant fiscal, political, and legal problems, would require
extensive treatment, and gives me an Italian background for Marsilius of

---

[2] See "Characteristics of Italian Anticlericalism" by Dr. Silvana Seidel Menchi in
this volume. Her formulation of a "disjunction between words and actions" aptly fits
the situation. For some of the recent literature on Italian patronage practices see her
references, especially Giorgio Chittolini and Giovanni Miccoli, eds., *La Chiesa e il
potere politico dal Medioevo all'età contemporanea*, Storia d'Italia, Annali 9 (Turin,
1986) and Roberto Bizzocchi, *Chiesa e potere nell Toscana del Quattrocento*
(Bologna, 1987).

[3] For the safety valve metaphor applied to Francesco Guicciardini and others, see,
again, Dr. Seidel Menchi's paper in this volume.

[4] I do not mean to deny that viewpoints arising out of specific historical
circumstances can become traditional cultural and social attitudes more or less
independent of their original applications. But it seems to me that Italian anticlericalism is sometimes treated as a sort of Hegelian *Geist*. For some instances, see
the important but sometimes redundant chapters on religion in the Einaudi *Storia
d'Italia* vols. 1, 2.1, and 2.2 (Turin, 1972-4).

Padua's *Defensor Pacis*, with its subordination of clerical to lay authority. I would explore the relations between fourteenth-century religious and social radicalism as exemplified by the Fraticelli and the Ciompi and the role of the laity in the Observantist reforms of the mendicant orders in the fifteenth century. I would examine the clerical stereotypes of the great Italian story tellers, with their peculiar blend of affection, outrage, contempt, and patronizing irony, fruits of a society in which clerics and laity rubbed elbows too familiarly for the good of either. My book would contain at least a chapter on Italian humanists, notably Bruni for his criticism of clerical malfeasance, Poggio Bracciolini, not only for his exposure of scandalous clerical behavior at the Council of Constance but also for his attack on the mendicant ideal of poverty, and Valla's demonstration of the forgery of the Donation of Constantine.[5]

Savonarola's prophecies of the scourging of the Roman Church, of a purified clergy and an Angelic Pastor, and his identification of the New Jerusalem with a reformed Florentine republicanism would surely require a chapter; so would the activities of the post-Savonarolan Piagnoni radicals who, in the Florentine Republic of 1527-1530, wrote the epilogue to the history of Florentine civic religion.[6] No historian of the sixteenth century should be surprised that these efforts to establish a total sacral community with lay persons playing central roles were not founded upon modern secular models of society. Nevertheless they were as subversive of existing clerical-lay relations as any movements we are likely to see in their time. They look back to the lay religious initiatives of the eleventh and twelfth centuries on the one hand and north to the urban Reformation movements of the mid-and late sixteenth century on the other.

Readers of my imaginary book will rightly object that it is nothing less than a history of late medieval and Renaissance Italy. They will see that "Italian anticlericalism" is an abstraction for a diversity of attitudes and

---

[5] See George Holmes, "Florence and the Great Schism", *Proceedings of the British Academy* 75 (1989): 291, 309-10. He cites a diarist, Gino di Neri Capponi († 1420), who called priests "the scum of the earth" (291); Holmes also discusses the criticism of the curia by Salutati, Poggio Bracciolini and Valla.

[6] Treated in detail in a forthcoming book, *The Elect Nation*, by Lorenzo Polizzotto. In the meantime, see Cesare Vasoli, "La attesa della nuova èra in ambienti e gruppi fiorentini del Quattrocento", in *L'attesa del età nuova nella spiritualità della fine del medioevo*, Convegni del Centro di Studi sulla Spiritualità Medievale 3 (Todi, 1962), 370-432; Donald Weinstein, *Savonarola and Florence: Prophecy and Patriotism in the Renaissance* (Princeton, 1970), Chapter X; Lorenzo Polizzotto, "Domenico Benivieni and the Radicalisation of the Savonarola Movement", in *Altro Polo*, ed. C. Condren and R. Pesman Cooper (Sydney, 1982); Polizzotto, "Confraternities, Conventicles and Political Dissent: The Case of the Savonarolan *Capi Rossi*", *Memorie Domenicane* n.s. 16 (1985): 235-83.

situations,[7] and will point out that if it is to be usefully employed it is best done within specific historical situations and with due regard for the variety of its meanings. I would go such critics one further, since I believe that anticlerical expressions should be treated as part of the wider subject of clerical-lay relations, both theoretical and practical, rather than as an independent variable. To focus on the negative aspect of the relationship is to risk missing its diverse tonalities and contradictions.

Predictably, another objection to my book will be that a number of chapters deal with movements and ideas that were not exclusively Italian. Again, I would have to agree that the imaginary critics of my imaginary book have a point. Many of the significant issues between clergy and laity involved all or large parts of European Christendom, so did the anti-Roman and anti-clerical feeling that they generated. Guelf-Ghibelline competition, Franciscan poverty, and Conciliarism come immediately to mind. For these and other issues as well, an exclusively Italian perspective is of limited value. On the other hand, it is undeniable that a good deal of Italian anticlericalism had a characteristically national dimension. No one expressed this side of it better than Niccolò Machiavelli.

> Since many think that the well-being of Italian cities depends upon the Roman Church, I want to give my reasons for a contrary view, especially two that are irrefutable. The first is that because of the wicked example set by that Court this country has lost all its piety and religion ... Therefore, we Italians owe this first debt to the Church and the priests, that we have become wicked and impious. But we owe her an even greater debt, and this is the second cause of our ruin: the Church is the sole reason why Italy is not in the same situation as France and Spain and is not ruled by a single republic or a single prince. Having acquired and retained temporal power she has been neither powerful enough or bold enough to seize command and make herself the ruler of the entire country. On the other hand if she had been weaker, fear of losing her temporal dominion might have kept her from calling in a foreign power to defend her whenever anyone in Italy became too strong ... Thus, the Church has neither been powerful enough to dominate Italy herself, nor has she allowed anyone else to dominate it, so that [Italy] has not had a single ruler but many princes and lords instead. As a result she has become so weak and disunited as to be the prey not merely of powerful barbarians but of whoever attacked her. This is a debt we Italians owe to the Church and to no one else.[8]

Machiavelli was neither a cleric, an employee of the Church, nor a dealer in ecclesiastical benefices, so his identification of the Church as the sole

---

[7] Some of them, even, mutually exclusive, such as the contemporary criticism of poverty as an ideal of the mendicant movement and the criticism of the Conventuals for violating that ideal.

[8] Niccolò Machiavelli, *Discourses on the First Ten Books of Titus Livius* Bk. I, Chap. XII; my translation from Sergio Bertelli, ed., *Il Principe e Discorsi sopra la prima deca di Tito Livio* (Milan, 1961).

cause of Italy's moral and political ruin was no self-serving psychological mechanism, but the product of careful reflection on the Italian experience and unblinking realism.[9] In investigating the sources of Italian anticlericalism we may wish to avoid Machiavelli's reductivism, but like him we ought to pay close attention to the details of Italian history.

---

[9] Sebastian de Grazia maintains that "Strictly speaking, [Machiavelli's] position is not anticlerical", although he shared with most educated people of his time the hatred and scorn for priests to be found in any society where there is a hierarchical, privileged clergy. Beyond this de Grazia differentiates between an "indiscriminate anticlericalism" which rejects clerical privilege or power, and a "reform clericalism" which distinguishes good priests from bad and effective prelates from inept ones. He places Machiavelli in the second category. *Machiavelli in Hell* (Princeton, 1989), 90-91. Whether or not we agree that the strict sense of the term "anticlerical" does not apply to Machiavelli, de Grazia's point is exemplary: not all criticism of priests falls in the same category or has the same weight or tone.

III. REFORM AND REFORMATION:
THE CALL FOR CHANGE

ONUS ECCLESIAE:
LAST DER KIRCHE — REFORMATION DER KIRCHE

MANFRED SCHULZE

Universität Tübingen

Die Schrift *Onus ecclesiae* gehört zum Genus der spätmittelalterlichen 'Reformatio'-Literatur. Im Jahre 1524 in Landshut bei Johann Weißenburger zum ersten Male erschienen,[1] will sie die Augen öffnen für die Last des Unheils, das die Kirche niederdrückt, und will zugleich enthüllen, daß vor allem die Geistlichkeit solches Unheil über die Kirche bringt. Weil Gott die Schwere der klerikalen Sünden nicht mehr ertragen will, vollzieht er bereits jetzt sein Strafgericht, das er in naher Zukunft noch vernichtend steigern wird. Diese 'Reformatio'-Schrift über die verheerenden Zustände in der Kirche ist zugleich eine apokalyptische Schrift, deren Autor, der in Kürze mit dem Ende rechnet, der Christenheit, allem voran dem Klerikerstand, ein scharfes Gericht ansagt.

Nach dem Namen des Autors sucht man vergeblich in diesem umfangreichen, sorgfältig gearbeiteten und übersichtlich gedruckten Werk.[2] Das *Onus*

---

[1] *Onus ecclesiae* (Landshut, Johann Weißenburger, 1524). Zu Weißenburger siehe Josef Benzing, *Die Buchdrucker des 16. und 17. Jahrhunderts im deutschen Sprachgebiet*, Beiträge zum Buch- und Bibliothekswesen 12 (Wiesbaden, 1963), 256. Fortgeschrieben mit Blick auf die Reformation und auf die Türkengefahr erschien das Werk zweimal im Jahre 1531: in Augsburg (Alexander Weißenhorn), Benzing, 17; und in Köln (Peter Quentel), Benzing, 223. Die Türkengefahr machte das Werk auch noch im 17. Jahrhundert aktuell; es erschien zum letzten Male im Jahre 1620: *Onus ecclesiae temporibus hisce deplorandis Apocalypseos suis aeque conveniens, Turcarumque incursui iam grassanti accommodatum*, s.l. 1620. Siehe die bibliographischen Angaben in *VD 16*, 16: 126f.; *Bertholds, Bischofs von Chiemsee, Tewtsche Theologey*, ed. W. Reithmeier (München, 1852), XXIf. Alle bibliographischen Angaben zum *Onus ecclesiae* bedürfen der Überprüfung und vor allem, genaue Druckbeschreibungen sind vonnöten.

[2] Das *Onus ecclesiae* ist in 70 Kapitel gegliedert, die wiederum — außerordentlich übersichtlich und leicht zu zitieren — in gesondert gezählte Paragraphen eingeteilt sind. Dem Erstdruck steht ein eindrückliches und programmatisches Titelbild voran: Der Teufel ist losgelassen und schlägt wild auf die Kirche ein. Dem Titelbild folgt die Vorrede des Korrektors, um dem Leser das *Onus* ohne Verfassernamen vorzustellen. Es beginnt dann das Werk selber mit einem Prolog und einem Inhaltsverzeichnis der 70 Kapitel. Eine kurze 'conclusio', das 'Explicit' und eine Errataliste beschließen den 280 Seiten umfassenden Band. Wie bei allen Werken Pirstingers fällt auch im *Onus ecclesiae* die übersichtliche Gliederung und der

ecclesiae begründet diese Verschwiegenheit mit der Aussage, daß der Gehalt des Werkes nicht abhängig sei von dem Gewicht eines Namens.[3] In einem Teil der ersten Landshuter Ausgabe gibt sich wenigstens der Herausgeber zu erkennen: Er heißt Vincentius Viepeckius, ist Dominikaner, "sacrae theologiae professor" und wirkt in der Offizin des Johann Weißenburger als Korrektor.[4] So sehr der Korrektor die Anonymität des Verfassers auch wahren wollte,[5] blieb der Forschung dennoch nicht verborgen, wer für diese aufrüttelnde, unbequeme und im Ton teilweise aggressive Reformapokalypse verantwortlich zu zeichnen hat. Berthold Pirstinger (†1543), seit 1508 Bischof von Chiemsee,[6] hatte im Jahre 1519 zur Feder gegriffen, um die 'Last der Kirche' niederzuschreiben.[7] Es muß Spekulation bleiben, warum sich die Veröffentlichung bis zum Jahre 1524 hingezogen hat. Pirstinger mochte den Druck hinauszögern und seinen Namen erst recht nicht preisgeben wollen, als nach dem Tode des ihm vertrauten Salzburger Erzbischofs Leonhard von Keutschach (†8. Juni 1519) der bisherige (seit 1512) bischöfliche Koadjutor, Kardinal (seit 1511) Matthäus Lang die

---

sorgfältig ausgeführte, ästhetisch ansprechende Druck ins Auge. Zitiert wird hier die erste, die Landshuter Ausgabe, jeweils nach Kapiteln und Paragraphen.

[3] Vgl. *Onus ecclesiae*, Prolog, 4.

[4] Siehe Johannes Ficker, "Pürstinger (Pirstinger), Berthold", in *Realencyklopädie für protestantische Theologie und Kirche*, Bd. 16 (1905), 307-15, 309. Ficker berichtet von "drei Varianten" des Landshuter Erstdruckes. Hermann Klüver, *Onus ecclesiae. Das apokalyptische Werk Berthold Pürstingers, des Bischofs von Chiemsee, aus dem Jahre 1519* (Diss. phil. [masch.], Halle, o. J. [1924]), 31. *VD 16*, 16: 126 zählt drei Exemplare des Erstdrucks auf, die über die Namensnennung verfügen. In dem Tübinger Exemplar, das ich benutzt habe, sind alle Angaben über den Korrektor bereits getilgt.

[5] In einer Kölner bei Quentel erschienenen Ausgabe des Jahres 1531 wird der Verfasser fast identifiziert. Der Titel des Drucks lautet: "Reverendi in Christo Patris ac Domini D. *Joannis*, olim Episcopi Chemensis ... Onus ecclesiae." *VD 16*, 16: 127.

[6] Zu Pirstingers Biographie siehe den immer noch maßgeblichen Artikel von Ficker in der *Realenzyklopädie*, ferner Engelbert Wallner, "Berthold Pürstinger, Bischof von Chiemsee (1465 - 16. Juli 1543)", in *Bavaria sancta. Zeugen des christlichen Glaubens in Bayern*, Bd. 3, ed. G. Schwaiger (Regensburg, 1973), 293-302. Gerhard Marx, *Glaube, Werke und Sakramente im Dienste der Rechtfertigung in den Schriften von Berthold Pürstinger, Bischof von Chiemsee*, Erfurter Theologische Studien 45 (Leipzig, 1982), 5-56.

[7] Im Sommer 1519 ist das Werk in seinem Hauptbestand vollendet worden. Zur Abfassungszeit siehe Klüver, 31. Ebenfalls Josef Schmuck, *Die Prophetie 'Onus Ecclesiae' des Bischofs Berthold Pürstinger. Religiöse Kritik der Zustände in Kirche und Welt aus den ersten Jahren der Reformationszeit*, Dissertationen der Universität Graz 22 (Wien, 1973), 5. Josef Schmuck kennt Klüvers Dissertation nicht. Die Hallenser Arbeit ist in ihrer Gestaltung völlig veraltet und dennoch die inhaltlich gewichtigere Untersuchung.

Nachfolge antrat.[8] Pirstinger, der Chiemseebischof, residierte mitten in Salzburg, im sogenannten Chiemseehof, und war somit direkt vom Wandel der politischen Verhältnisse im Erzbistum betroffen.

Betrachtet man des Autors literarische Produktion, dann wird man ihn als Ausnahme unter den deutschen Bischöfen des späten Mittelalters und der Reformationszeit bezeichnen müssen: Er ist im Gegensatz zu den meisten seiner Amtskollegen sowohl zum geistlichen Urteil als auch zur literarischen Darstellung befähigt. Nach seinem Rücktritt vom Bischofsamt im Mai 1526 hat er sich theologisch aktiv in den Kampf um die neue Lehre gemengt und neben zwei Schriften zur Theologie und Gestalt der Messe[9] sogar eine umfangreiche deutschsprachige Laiendogmatik verfaßt, die den Anspruch erheben kann, die erste ihrer Art zu sein. In dieser 'Deutschen Theologie', wie er sie nennt,[10] verteidigt er nach seiner Überzeugung ohne Abstriche

---

[8] Vgl. Klüver, 40-2. Matthäus Lang hielt am 23. September 1519 seinen Einzug als Erzbischof in Salzburg.

[9] Berthold Pirstinger, *Tewtsch Rational über das Ambt heiliger Meß* (s.l. [Augsburg, Alexander Weißenhorn], 1535). Am Schluß dieses Werkes faßt Pirstinger sein Anliegen kurz zusammen: "Dieweil in gegenwärtiger betrübter zeit wider das aller heiligist ambt der meß grewlich windstoß durch die ketzer an vil orten teutscher nation seinn auffgeblasen, deßhalb hab ich dargegen die obangezogen fünnff und zwaintzig Capitl zusam getragen." Er hofft, seine Meßerläuterung werde "frummen lewten, die noch zu heyliger meß genaigt sein, ain vertröstung geben ..." *Tewtsch Rational*, fol. n3ra. Das zweite Werk zur Messe ist zugleich mit dem vorhergehenden erschienen und führt den Titel: *Keligpuchel. Ob der kelig ausserhalb der mess zeraichen sey.* Es geht um die Austeilung der Eucharistie unter beiderlei Gestalt: "Gegenbertiger zeit" so Pirstinger, "hat in teutsch landen angehebt einzewurtzen die alt irrung der Calixtiner, so vermueten das hochwirdigist sacrament ausserhalb der meß zuempfahen unter bederlay gestalt prots unn weins, auß falscher underweysung etlich betriglicher lerer." *Keligpuchel*, fol. a2ra.

[10] *Tewtsche Theologey* (München, Hans Schobser, 1528). Zu Schobser siehe Benzing (wie Anm. 1), 315. Zitiert wird hier die Ausgabe von Wolfgang Reithmeier (wie Anm. 1). Um der Deutschen Theologie größere Wirkung auch unter den Gelehrten zu verschaffen, übersetzte Pirstinger das Werk ins Lateinische, das 1531 in Augsburg erschienen ist: *Theologia germanica, in qua continentur articuli de fide, evangelio, virtutibus et sacramentis ...* (Augsburg, Alexander Weißenhorn, 1531). Siehe *VD 16*, 16: 126 und Reithmeier, XVIIf. Johann Ecks lateinisches 'Enchiridion' (*Enchiridion locorum communium adversus Lutherum et alios hostes ecclesiae (1525-1543)*, ed. P. Fraenkel, Corpus Catholicorum 34, Münster, 1979) in seiner deutschen Übersetzung kann mit Pirstingers Dogmatik nicht mithalten. Vom Genus her ist das 'Enchiridion' nicht eine Dogmatik, sondern ein Hand- und vor allem Streitbuch 'gegen die Feinde der Kirche'. Wie Pirstinger zielte allerdings auch Eck auf die Menge, doch ist seiner deutschen Fassung die Tatsache der Übersetzung spürbar anzumerken. Das deutsche Enchiridion (*Enchiridion, Handbüchlin gemeiner stell unnd Arrickel der jetzt schwebenden neuwen leeren* (Augsburg, 1533), Corpus Catholicorum 35, Münster, 1980) ist oft nur schwer verständlich. Anders die *Tewtsche Theologey*. Sie ist eine fortlaufende Dogmatik, die Pirstinger von Anfang an deutsch

die Lehre der römischen Kirche gegen jene bis dahin unbekannte Zusammenballung von Häresien, unter denen die deutsche Christenheit in 'diesen Zeiten' zu leiden hat.[11]

Wenn man das anonyme *Onus ecclesiae* mit der 'Deutschen Theologie' vergleicht, dann entstehen Zweifel an der Identität der Autoren.[12] Es erscheint kaum denkbar, daß der rigorose Unheilsprophet des Jahres 1519 zum kompromißlosen Verteidiger des Jahres 1528 werden konnte — es sei denn, die Geschehnisse der Reformation hätten ihn zu einer Wende bewegt. Doch aller naheliegenden Bedenken zum Trotz stößt man auf gewichtige formale Übereinstimmungen der Werke Pirstingers mit dem *Onus ecclesiae*,[13] die nur zu erklären sind, wenn der Kläger gegen die Kirche mit

---

geschrieben hat und die den dogmatischen Stoff auch verständlich in der Sprache des Volkes ausdrückt.

[11] Seit Jahrhunderten haben die Deutschen treu zum Glauben der Kirche gestanden. "Aber diser gevaerlichen zeit hat grewlicher tewfel etlich fals lere und allt Sect, die lang geschlaffen und in der helle begraben gewest, widerumb awferweckht unnd herfür gezogen, daneben viel poess zuosatz erfunden und eingefueert, mit denen dewfel schier gantz deütsch land übergangen." *Tewtsche Theologey*, 2.

[12] Engelbert Wallner übergeht bei seiner Pirstingerdarstellung das *Onus ecclesiae*. Er hält es schlicht für unbewiesen, daß der Chiemseebischof diese Gerichtsschrift verfaßt habe. Vgl. Wallner (wie Anm. 6), 299. Nach Argumenten, warum die bisher vorgebrachten Gründe für Pirstingers Verfasserschaft nicht stichhaltig seien, sucht man bei Wallner vergebens.

[13] Formal ist vor allem auf die Gleichheit der Gliederungsweise aufmerksam zu machen. Alle Werke Pirstingers zeichnen sich genau wie das *Onus ecclesiae* dadurch aus, daß ihr Autor Wert legt auf die exakte Angabe der Quellen, die er benutzt. Im *Onus ecclesiae* finden sich alle Angaben am Rande verzeichnet, die anderen Werke verfahren 'moderner' und drucken den 'Apparat' jeweils an das Ende eines Kapitels. Alle Werke sind außergewöhnlich übersichtlich gegliedert. Sie sind ohne Ausnahme gleich eingeteilt in Kapitel und Paragraphen, die wiederum die einzelnen Kapitel untergliedern. Noch eine andere Eigenart verbindet alle namentlich ausgewiesenen Werke mit dem *Onus ecclesiae*: Der Autor begründet die Anzahl seiner Kapitel jeweils geistlich-biblisch.

Onus ecclesiae: "Distinguo ... praesentem materiam et collecturam in ... septuaginta capitula quasi in septuaginta palmas, quae erant in Helim (Ex. 15,27)", Prolog, 7.

Tewtsche Theologey (nur in der lateinischen Version): "Congessi itaque libellum in centum capitula, quibus iuxta paradigma evangelicum centum ovibus pascua uberrima praestaretur" (Mt. 18,12-14, par). Siehe Reithmeier, XXIV.

Tewtsch Rational: Das Rational ist eingeteilt in 25 Kapitel. Diese sollen die Frommen dazu bewegen, daß sie "destsicherer ruedern und aufm ungestumen möhre dieser weld destliber faren die fünff und zwaintzig gwandten wegs, so des herren junger auffm möhre bey Capharnaum angehebt haben zefaren" (Joh. 6,19), fol. n3ra/b.

Keligpuchel: Das Keligpuchel ist in 30 Kapitel eingeteilt. Pirstinger hofft, "wir haben mit hilff Gottes im grossen ungestümen sturmwind der obangezogenen ketzereyen ... durch oberzelte dreyssig capitel geruedert die dreyssig gwandten wegs,

ihrem bischöflichen Verteidiger gegen die Häretiker identisch ist. Zugleich kann man inhaltlich deutlich machen, daß Pirstinger seine vorreformatorische Kirchenkritik durch die Wirren der neuen Zeit keineswegs widerlegt sieht. Die Kritik des Jahres 1519 wird zwar nicht erneut zum Gegenstand der 'Deutschen Theologie', doch kann von einer Wende und Rücknahme der vorangegangenen Angriffe keine Rede sein. Im Gegenteil: Auch den Einbruch der Häresie deutet er nicht einfach nur als Schicksal, sondern analog zum *Onus ecclesiae* als Strafe — "villeicht aus ursach goettlicher verhengnuss, umb das wir geistlich ungeschickt leben fueeren, unsere ampt nit wol ausrichten, poes exempel vortragen." Das "geistlich ungeschickt leben" war das Thema im *Onus ecclesiae*, das hier zwar nicht mehr ausgebreitet, aber zur Situationsanalyse dennoch aufgegriffen wird. Die Laien, so beschreibt Pirstinger in der 'Deutschen Theologie' den Gang der Entwicklung, waren des längeren schon der Kirche nur noch "unwilliklich" gehorsam und haben gegen alles Geistliche 'einen Haß gefaßt', den sie lange Zeit verborgen hielten. Jetzt aber hat der Teufel diesem Haß Luft geschaffen.[14] Daß also die Laien in ihrem Klerikerhaß der Häresie zufallen, trifft nicht eine unschuldige, sondern eine schuldig gewordene Geistlichkeit. Gerade diese 'antiklerikale' Deutung der reformatorischen Gegenwart — in seinem Sinne: der deformatorischen Gegenwart — spricht dafür, daß der Verfasser der 'Deutschen Theologie' auch der Verfasser des *Onus ecclesiae* ist. Sowohl in dieser Reformschrift als auch in seiner 'Deutschen Theologie' tritt er gegen jene ungeheuren Deformationen an, unter deren Last die Kirche zusammenbricht.

Auch die apokalyptische Naherwartung findet sich in der 'Deutschen Theologie' wieder: Die Jetztzeit ist die Endzeit.[15] Diese Endzeit, so erläutert Pirstinger, ist beschrieben in dem Buch "der kirchen purde": "Dieser ellenden zeit ist dewfel aws gottes verhengnuss, unns zuo plag, abermals ledig gelassen ... Von anweygung (Anreizung) unnd aufloesung (Freilassung) des dewfels beschiecht lange meldung im pueechlen der kirchen purde."[16] Somit ist auch deutlich, wie Pirstinger selber seinen lateinischen Titel ins Deutsche übersetzt sehen will: 'Der kirchen purde'.

Die formalen Gemeinsamkeiten und die sachliche Stimmigkeit der Kritik und der apokalyptischen Naherwartung einschließlich der Berufung auf "der kirchen purde" bestätigen den fast einhelligen Konsens in der Forschung: Das *Onus ecclesiae* ist Berthold Pirstingers Werk.

---

von denen meldung beschicht im Evangeli Johannis am sexten capitel" (Joh. 6,19), fol. n5va.

[14] *Tewtsche Theologey*, 2.

[15] "Zuo lessten tagen (naemlich yetzmals) werden einfallen grawssam zeytung und menschen aufsteen, die von jnen selbs vil hallten, und seinn geytzig, trutzig, stoltz, aygenwillig, halsstarck, jren elltern ungehorsam, ... ungueetig, fraessig und dergleichen." *Tewtsche Theologey*, 107.

[16] *Tewtsche Theologey*, 167.

Um dem sachlichen Gehalt dieser apokalyptischen Schrift auf die Spur zu kommen, wird man zunächst fragen müssen, was Pirstinger unter der von ihm so genannten 'Bürde' versteht und wie sich ihm im Jahre 1519, als er das *Onus ecclesiae* konzipierte, die Situation der Kirche darstellte.

Ferner ist nach den Quellen seiner Kirchenanalyse zu suchen, wenn man den Härtegrad seiner Kritik bestimmen will: Ist seine 'Lastschrift' nur das Ergebnis eines emotionsgeladenen Antiklerikalismus, der zum Ausbruch kommt, wenn ein 'geladener' Bischof zur Feder greift, um sich seine Enttäuschungen über die Kirche und ihre Geistlichkeit von der Seele zu schreiben, die, einmal im Zorn herausgeschleudert, dann aber auch vergangen sind? Oder will Pirstinger den Anspruch erheben, distanziert und sachlich die Lage der Kirche so zu erfassen und darzustellen, daß sein Werk auch künftigen Generationen als zuverlässige Quelle für die Beschreibung kirchlicher Mißstände dienen kann?

Und schließlich ist nach Pirstingers Zielen zu suchen — ob die Last der Kirche ihm nur zur Abrechnung gerät, oder ob er auch Heilmittel sichtet und anbietet, damit die Christenheit eine Reformation vollziehen und sich ihrer Last dadurch entledigen kann.

I. Die Last der Kirche

Pirstinger unterzieht die Kirche einer durchgehend scharfen Kritik ohne Ansehen von Rang und Stand des betroffenen Klerus. Genausowenig wie Propheten, Apostel und Heilige geschwiegen haben, will auch er nicht schweigen zu all dem Unrecht und Übel, das von der Geistlichkeit ausgegangen ist und immer noch ausgeht.[17] Die Last der Kirche offenzulegen, ist also nicht, wie Propheten- und Apostelworte beweisen sollen, ein unerhörtes Sakrileg, sondern die vielfach in der Kirchengeschichte ausgewiesene Redepflicht des wahren Dieners Gottes.

Auch jene Last ist aufzudecken, die Papst, Kurie und Kardinäle der Kirche aufbürden. "Non est tacendum super iniquitatem Babylonis", erfährt

---

[17] Den Prolog zum *Onus ecclesiae* benutzt Pirstinger zur Rechtfertigung der Pflicht, gerade den Verfall der Kirche zu enthüllen. Solche Enthüllungen haben Anspruch auf Gültigkeit, weil Gott die Mittel an die Hand gibt, um die Zeiten und ihre Schäden auch dann durchschauen zu können, wenn es menschlicherweise am eigenen Durchblick mangelt: "Etsi non est nostrum nosse tempora vel momenta (Mt. 24,42), tamen id non est usque adeo intelligendum, quod futura sint a nobis omnino incognoscibilia. Nimirum qui virtutem supervenientis Spiritus Sancti acceperint, possunt intelligere ac prophetizare ea, quae eis filius revelavit." Prolog, 1. Dann folgt Pirstingers Anwendung dieser göttlichen Unterweisung auf seine eigene Person: Mir obliegt die "necessitas contionandi" gemäß dem Apostelwort: "Vae mihi est, si non evangelizavero ... " (1. Kor. 9,16). Und er hat auch teil an der Prophetenfurcht vor der Straf- und Bußpredigt: A, a, a Domine Deus, ecce nescio loqui ... " (Jeremia 1,6). Prolog, 2.

der Leser gleich zu Beginn des Papstkapitels.[18] Diese Offenheit bedeutet nicht, daß Pirstinger an der Funktion des päpstlichen Amtes rütteln würde. Jene Kirche, die Petri Namen trägt, ist das Haupt aller Kirchen, und die Nachfolger Petri sind seine Nachfolger auch im Primat über die Kirche.[19] Doch eben weil die kirchliche Lehre vom Papsttum keine Zweifel leidet, gerät die Kirche um so mehr in Gefahr durch die Träger dieses unaufgebbaren, weil gottgewollten Amtes. Die Päpste nämlich verleugnen in ihrem Leben und Handeln den Petrusdienst. Statt arm und demütig ihr Leben im Geiste Petri zu verbringen, schmücken sie sich mit Gold und Edelsteinen, tragen kostbare Gewänder, sind von Soldaten umringt, reiten erlesene Schimmel oder lassen sich in Sänften tragen. Aufreizend öffentlich also verwechseln sie die Nachfolge Petri mit der Nachfolge Konstantins. Bei solchen Päpsten findet die Herde weder Hirten noch Weide, hier stoßen die Christen vielmehr auf Verachtung. Heute gilt vom Papsttum dieses: "non est pastus ovium sed fastus hominum."[20]

Wie der Papst, so auch die Kurie. Diese hat sich wie einst das römische Reich zum gefräßigen Geldschlund entwickelt, dort blüht der Geiz, während der Geist vergeht.[21] Des Kritikers Sprache ist scharf, und die Sprache seiner Zeugen, die er heranzieht, wird von ihm so aggressiv zurechtgeschnitten, daß sie von antiklerikalem Sentiment nicht frei ist. Birgitta von Schweden (†1373), im 14. Jahrhundert die Prophetin gegen das verworfene Rom und das zu verwerfende Avignon, ist als Kritikerin im *Onus ecclesiae* stets gegenwärtig. Rom, läßt Pirstinger sie klagen, ist eine Lasterhöhle, und seine Fürsten sind Mörder.[22] Rom und der Papst, sie hassen Christus, und

---

[18] Cap. 19 (De indispositione Romanae curiae), proem.

[19] " ... Romana ecclesia, quae est caput ac mater et magistra omnium aliarum ecclesiarum." Cap. 19, proem. "Sicut enim Petrus fuit principalis Apostolorum, ita ecclesia suo nomine consecrata prima est et caput ceterarum, maxime occidentalium ... Petri successor primatum obtinuit ex plurium conciliorum decretis." Alle nachfolgende Kritik hebt nicht den einen Grundsatz auf: "Dignitate igitur et auctoritate est prima Apostoli Petri sedes Romana ecclesia non habens maculam neque rugam ... " Cap. 19,1.

[20] Daß Christus dem Petrus und seinen Nachfolgern den Primat verliehen hat, geschah "ob Petri praecipuam fidem, humilitatem et caritatem". Und heutzutage? "Quid quod papa incedit deauratus, gemmatus, vario ornatu decoratus, milite stipatus, equo albo vectus aut a ministris in altum portatus? Haec sunt magis daemonum quam ovium pascua. Ubi non est pastus ovium sed fastus hominum, ibi non Petro sed Constantino succeditur." Cap. 19,3.

[21] "Heu sicut olim in Romano imperio, sic hodie in Romana curia est vorago divitiarum turpissima, crevit avaritia, periit lex a sacerdote ac visio de propheta et consilium a senioribus." Cap. 19,8.

[22] "Christus apud Birgittam loquitur de Roma inquiens: Olim habitavit in Roma iustitia et principes eius principes pacis, nunc autem versa est in scoriam et principes eius homicidae." Cap. 19,8.

die Kurie raubt Christi Kurie im Himmel aus,[23] das heißt doch wohl: Rom macht dem Himmel die Seelen abspenstig. Der Papst sollte die Menschen mit dem Frieden locken: 'Kommt her zu mir', so will man ihn rufen hören, 'und eure Seelen werden Ruhe finden'! Tatsächlich aber schreien römische Taten ganz anderes in die Welt hinaus: 'Kommt her und schaut auf mich in meinem Pomp und eitlem Streben. Kommt her zur Kurie, leert eure Geldbeutel, und ihr werdet eure Seelen verderben finden'![24]

Die 'cathedra Petri' ist eine Institution göttlichen Rechtes, so wird man Pirstingers Papsttheologie zu deuten haben, auch wenn er diese Begrifflichkeit, die in den Kämpfen der Reformatoren von so großer Bedeutung sein wird, nicht verwendet. Das bedeutet allerdings nicht, seine Theologie sei papalistisch ausgerichtet. Die Tatsache, daß der Primat von Gott gesetzt ist, beweist nicht schon die Irrtumsfreiheit der Amtsinhaber des Primats, wenn sie über die Lehre der Kirche entscheiden wollen. Von einer Unfehlbarkeit des Papstes kann keine Rede sein, solche Rede ist in Pirstingers Augen vielmehr ein "pestiferum dictum".[25] Die Kirche ist es, die vom Heiligen Geist gelenkt wird, ihre "rectores" aber sind fragil wie alle Menschen und werden manchmal sogar vom Geist des Bösen angetrieben. Er erinnert daran, daß auch römische Bischöfe der Häresie, konkret der arianischen Häresie anheimgefallen sind.[26] Eben deshalb lehrt die Schrift die Notwendigkeit des Widerspruchs, für dessen Recht sich Pirstinger, wie immer im Streit um die Infallibilität des römischen Bischofs, auf den Widerstand des Paulus beruft: "Ad hoc optime sacra scriptura affirmat Paulum primo Papae Petro reprehensibili in faciem restitisse" (Gal. 2,11)[27] — die Heilige Schrift bestätigt eindeutig, daß der Apostel Paulus dem ersten Papste, nämlich Petrus, ins Angesicht hinein widerstanden hat, als es ihm zu widerstehen galt.

---

[23] "Rursus ad Papam Christus ait [scil. apud Birgittam]: Cur tantum odis me? Quare tanta est audacia et praesumptio tua contra me? Nam curia tua mundana depraedatur caelestem curiam meam." Cap. 19,11.

[24] "Sequitur ex Birgitta: Papa qui clamare deberet: 'Venite et invenietis requiem animarum vestrarum', clamat: 'Venite et videte me in pompa et ambitione plusquam Salomonem. Venite ad curiam meam et exhaurite bursas vestras et invenietis perditionem animarum vestrarum'. Sic enim clamat exemplo et facto." Cap. 19,12.

[25] Cap. 15,34.

[26] "Verum quidem ecclesia a spiritu sancto regitur, sed eius rectores tamquam homines fragiles quandoque a spiritu maligno exagitantur. Ita Papa Liberius Arrianae haeresi consensit." Cap. 19,4. Auch in seiner 'Deutschen Theologie' führt Pirstinger aus, daß es die Kirche ist, die als Ganze in der Wahrheit bleiben wird. Er schließt dort nicht gänzlich aus, daß sie, wenigstens am Rande und zeitweilig, auch vom Irrtum betroffen werden könne: Der Kirche ist "zegelauben und trostlich zehoffen, daz got sein prawt die kirch nit verlasse, noch verhenge lang zejren oder weyt von der warheit zeweichen." *Tewtsche Theologey*, 81.

[27] Cap. 19,4.

So deutlich die Kirche des Papstes bedarf, so deutlich ist auch ihr Leiden an solchen Päpsten, die von Nachfolgern Christi zu Nachfolgern Konstantins verkommen sind. Sucht die Kirche gegen Papst und Kurie bei den Kardinälen Hilfe, dann muß sie jede Hoffnung fahren lassen. Einst sollten Kardinäle dem Papst als "collaterales" hilfreich zur Seite stehen, genauso wie die Apostel als "collaboratores Christi". In gleicher Weise wie bei der Beschreibung des Papstamtes äußert Pirstinger keinen Zweifel am ursprünglichen Sinn des Amtes, das mit blumigen und hochfliegenden Begriffen beschrieben wird. Kardinäle sind "domini Dei", die Gott über die streitende Kirche gesetzt hat. Er hat sie als "cardines orbis terrae" erkoren, damit er sein Himmelstor in ihnen als Türangeln drehe. Gott schreitet durch diese Türangeln hindurch: "Circa cardines quidem caeli Deus perambulat."[28] Die Lobesworte für das kardinale Amt greifen also außerordentlich hoch, wenn auch dessen Funktionsbeschreibung gänzlich unkonkret bleibt. Um so konkreter wird Pirstinger, wenn er auf die verworfenen Kardinäle einschlägt. Er prangert die Gesellschaft der 'cardines' unverhohlen als üble Gesellschaft plündernder Schmarotzer an: Ein Kardinal ist der, der zweihundert, gar dreihundert Pfründen zu okkupieren und deren Einkünfte hemmungslos zu verprassen wagt, mit dem Ergebnis, daß viele geistliche Institutionen brachliegen müssen. Kloster und Pfarrpfründen können unter der Besatzung durch Kardinäle oder Hofschranzen keinerlei geistlichen Ertrag mehr einbringen; sie dienen weder Gott noch nützen sie dem Volk.[29]

Mitarbeiter des Papstes, so kann man Pirstinger zusammenfassen, sind die Kardinäle in der Tat, Mitarbeiter nämlich am Ruin der Kirche.

Mit Spannung erwartet man das Urteil des Bischofs über die Bischöfe. Auch hier zeichnet Pirstinger das gleiche Urbild wie bei Papst und Kardinälen. Keines der kirchlichen Leitungsämter ist sinnlos. Das Amt, das die Bischöfe bekleiden, ist in seinen Augen sogar das wichtigste nach dem Papstamt. Bischöfe sind als Hirten direkt von Gott eingesetzt, und wenn sie

---

[28] Cap. 19,17.

[29] "Quae utique abominatio, quod unus [scil. Cardinalis] ducenta, alter trecenta beneficia ecclesiastica occupat ... Id quod miserabilius est, in monasteriis ac beneficiis per cardinales aut aulicos occupatis nihil deo servitur nec populo proficitur." Cap. 19,19 (mit Berufung auf Gerson). Zu den harten antiklerikalen Kritikern des späten Mittelalters gehört auch Nikolaus von Clemanges mit seiner Darstellung des Verfalls der Kirche, die er nach dem Konzil zu Pisa (1409) geschrieben hat. Pirstinger hat Nikolaus benutzt, und mancher Anwurf im *Onus ecclesiae* findet sich schon bei Nikolaus, wie etwa die Kritik an der schamlosen Ausbeutung der Kirche durch die Kardinäle: Sie besitzen Benefizien in unvorstellbarer Menge: "Non quidem duo vel tria, decem vel viginti, sed centena et ducentena et interdum usque ad quadringenta vel quingenta aut amplius." Nicolaus de Clemangis, *De corrupto ecclesiae statu liber*, in *Nicolai de Clemangis Opera omnia*, (Leiden, 1613 [Gregg, 1967]), lla/b. Wenn man daran gehen will, die Traditionen des spätmittelalterlichen Antiklerikalismus zu verfolgen, dann ist auch ein gründlicher Vergleich zwischen Pirstinger und Clemanges notwendig.

ihres Amtes wirklich walten, dann wirken sie als Botschafter Christi, dann sind sie geistliche Väter, des Papstes Brüder und Mitbischöfe.[30] Das ist polemisch gegen die Theorie des Papalismus eingesetzt, die das Amt des Bischofs strukurell in die Abhängigkeit des Papstes bringt. Pirstinger hält dagegen: Der Bischof empfängt seine Amtsgewalt nicht vom Papst, sondern wie der Papst allein von Gott. Die Ekklesiologie des Chiemseebischofs, sein Verständnis von der Kirche und ihren Ämtern, ist stimmig.

Wie der Papst verleugnen auch die Bischöfe ihre Herkunft von Gott. Anstatt sich amtsgemäß als Christi Sachwalter zu verhalten, treten sie auf als Herren in Diensten der Welt, kämpfen mit den Waffen der Welt statt mit den Waffen des Geistes und bauen ihre Gewalt auf Geld und Gut.[31] Wenn Bischöfe aber wahrhaftig Bischöfe sind, dann sind sie reich an Armut, erhaben in Demut und großartig in der Verachtung von Ruhm und Ehre.[32]

Wo aber sind solche Bischöfe, fragt Pirstinger, wo werden noch Bischöfe gewählt, die nicht Knaben sind und die weder fleischlich gesonnen noch unerfahren sind in der Erfüllung ihrer geistlichen Aufgaben?[33]

Eine boshafte Sentenz reiht er an die andere, um die 'Last der Kirche' durch die Bischöfe den Lesern einzuprägen:

Bischöfe sorgen sich heute mehr um die Einnahmen des Fiskus als um die Hingabe an Christus: " ... magis officia fisci quam opera Christi exequentes."

Sie schmücken ihre Leiber mit Gold, ihre Seelen aber mit Kot: "ornant corpora sua auro, animas autem luto."[34]

Sie geben leeres Geschwätz von sich statt überzeugende Wahrheit: "In ore ... episcoporum est lex vanitatis pro lege veritatis."[35]

---

[30] Cap. 20 (De excessibus episcoporum), proem: "Status episcopalis est immediate a Christo et supernaturaliter in Apostolis institutus ... Dignitati vero episcopali a solo Deo potestas concessa est et post Papam ordinata est ... Siquidem episcopi sanctissimi nuncupatur, qui exsistunt legati Christi, spirituales sunt patres, Papaeque fratres et coepiscopi ... "

[31] E contrario lautet das bei Pirstinger so: "Arma enim militiae nostrae non sunt carnalia ... Apostolis non fuit aurum et argentum, sed spiritualis thesaurus non deficiens." Cap. 20,1.

[32] "Episcopi etenim quondam fuerunt paupertate locupletes, humilitate sublimes et gloria neglecta gloriosi." Cap. 20,1.

[33] "Ubinam bonus et probatus opere et doctrina in episcopum eligitur, non puer, non carnalis, spiritualium ignarus?" Cap. 20,2.

[34] Cap. 20,3.

[35] Cap. 20,4. Die Liste der boshaften Sentenzen läßt sich fortsetzen. Cap. 20,3: "Episcopi ... incumbunt mensis pro altaribus. — Imprudentes in divinis, mundanam diligunt sapientiam. — Apud eos verecundia est exercere spiritualia, gloria tractare scurrilia." Cap. 20,4: "Labia sacerdotis custodiunt scientiam saecularem, non spiritualem. — Ventres episcoporum frequentius despumant merum, quam cibum verum." Cap. 20,5: " ... quidam episcopi promptius indicunt bellum quam mansuetum flagellum."

Nicht minder heftig mischt Pirstinger Sozialkritik in die Enthüllungen des Verfalls, wenn er den Bischöfen ihren gottlosen Umgang mit dem Geld vorwirft. Bischöfe verschleudern das Gut der Kirche, verschwenden es an Verwandte und an zwielichtiges Gesindel; sie verschieben sogar die liegenden Kirchengüter an ihre zweifelhafte Klientel, alles zum Nachteil ihrer Kirchen, zum Schaden des Rechts und allermeist zu Lasten der Armen.[36] Solch scharfe Kritik kann er voller Sarkasmus der gesamten höheren Geistlichkeit entgegenhalten: Prälaten sollen Wächter der Kirche sein. Tatsächlich sind sie wie Heuschrecken, die in der Kühle des Tages in das bestellte Feld einfallen und bei aufkommender Sonne davonfliegen[37] — die Ernte Gottes ist vernichtet von denen, die sich "custodes ecclesiae" nennen. Wegen seiner Verschwendung des Reichtums und seiner Schändung der Armen kann Pirstinger den Klerus nur noch beschämen: Haben sich die Geistlichen die Bäuche vollgeschlagen, dann glauben Sie, Gott zu gefallen und ein ausreichendes Almosen zu verteilen, wenn sie die Brocken und Reste von ihren Tischen, mit denen man Schweine und Hunde füttert, unter die Armen ausstreuen.[38]

Eines der offenkundigen Symptome für den Verfall des Klerus ist die unrechtmäßige, nämlich simonistische Art der Ämterbesetzung. Zu viele Bischöfe erlangen ihre Stühle durch Bestechung, zu viele sind es, auf die das Wort Jesu zutrifft: "Wer nicht zum Tor in den Schafstall eingeht, der ist ein Dieb und Räuber (Joh. 10,1)."[39] Das ist kein Urteil nur über die Bischöfe. Es ist vielmehr allgemein üblich geworden, daß Kleriker ihre Pfründen erschleichen, oder daß Fürsten und Könige Stellenbesetzungen vornehmen, die der Papst auch noch bestätigt, gegen alle Privilegien der Kirchen, gegen alle Konkordate mit der deutschen Nation. Und schließlich nutzen die Päpste die Gelegenheit, ihre Köche, Steuerpächter und Stallmeister mit deutschen Pfründen zu versehen.[40] Hier melden sich traditionelle

---

[36] Vgl. Cap. 20,10.

[37] Cap. 21 (De praelatorum aliorumque curatorum vita vitiosa),5: " ... custodes [scil. ecclesiae] ... sunt quasi locustae, quae considunt in saepibus in die frigoris et sole oriente avolant." Angespielt ist auf Nahum 3,15-17.

[38] Cap. 21,10: "Et postquam suos ventres impleverint, aestimant se Deo placere ac eleemosinam sufficientem praestare, quando ex mensis suis fragmenta seu reliquias, quae porcis vel canibus debentur, distribuunt pauperibus."

[39] "Demum horribilior sententia est de episcopis aliisve praelatis male intrantibus, quorum multi illegitime eliguntur. Immo pauci sunt, qui absque ambitionis labe in praelaturas intrat, quibus solis maledixit Salvator ... inquiens: 'Amen, amen, dico vobis, qui non intrat per ostium in ovile, sed ascendit aliunde, ille fur est et latro'." Cap. 20,14.

[40] "Modernis autem temporibus pauci [scil. sacerdotes] canonice et absque ambitione eliguntur, quin plures praelati aliique beneficiati per reges et principes illegitime constituuntur, immo vel ambitiose simoniaceque introducuntur et per pontifices confirmantur, contra pivilegia ecclesiarum et compactata Germanica contraque omnem iustitiam. Porro pontifices suos cocos, tributarios, stipendiarios et

Gravamina der deutschen Bischöfe zu Wort, die sich gegen das wachsende Hineinregieren der Kurie in die deutsche Kirche zur Wehr setzen.[41]

Wo findet in der Kirche überhaupt noch geistlicher Dienst statt? Die Klöster waren einst der Hort des rechten Gottesdienstes, und wenn die Kirche auf Reformen hoffen konnte, dann durfte sie auf diejenigen hoffen, die ihr Leben dem Gehorsam, der Armut und der Keuschheit geweiht hatten. Wo Mönche lebten und beteten, entstanden Orte der Heilung für eine verweltlichte Kirche.[42] Nicht Menschen, sondern der Heilige Geist selber hatte die Einrichtung von Ordensgemeinschaften besorgt[43], damit Mönche durch Gehorsam, Armut und Keuschheit den Zorn Gottes über die sündige Christenheit stillen sollten.[44] Gerade jetzt, wo die Zerrüttung der Hierarchie einen Höhpunkt erreicht hat, wäre ein solcher Dienst der stellvertretenden Heiligung von allergrößter Wichtigkeit.

Tatsächlich aber tragen seit vielen Jahrzehnten auch die Mönche in ungeahnter Weise zur Last der Kirche bei. Pirstinger setzt wie so oft die 'Offenbarungen' der Birgitta von Schweden ein, um die inzwischen eingetretene Verkehrung dessen aufzudecken, was Mönche gelobt und als Auftrag erhalten haben:

Mönche sollen arm und demütig sein. 'Sie ziehen heute jedoch hochmütig und habgierig durch die Welt'. Sie haben Christus und den Orden zu ihren Herren. 'Jetzt aber sind sie Herren ihrer selbst'. Sie töten ihren Leib und seine Gier. 'Tatsächlich aber trachten sie nach Lust für ihre Leiber'.[45] Einst Waffen gegen den Teufel, sind sie, so lautet das erschreckte Urteil, zu Waffen des Teufels geworden. Die Mönche zerstören allenthalben die

---

stabularios frequenter animarum curae ac dignitatibus praeficiunt." Cap. 21,3.

[41] Die klassische Formulierung hat dieses Gravamen durch den Reichstag zu Worms 1521 erhalten: "Es werden die pfronden Teutscher nation zu Rom etwan buchsenmaistern, falknern, pfistern, eselstreibern, stallknechten und andern untuglichen, ungelärten und ungeschigkten personen verlihen ..." *Deutsche Reichstagsakten unter Kaiser Karl V.*, Bd. 2, ed. A. Wrede (Gotha, 1896 [Göttingen, 1962]), 673,34-674,1.

[42] Cap. 22 (De perversione religiosorum et capitularium clericorum),1: "Nam etsi in clero primitivae ecclesiae non fuerint religiones institutae, tamen postquam in ecclesia succrevit superbia, avaritia, luxuria, quae acriter offendunt Deum. Contra eadem crimina pro remedio utendum fuit oboedientia, paupertate et continentia."

[43] "Sed quia non omnibus datum est illa remedia capere et in mundo versari ac illas diabolicas immissiones usquequaque cavere, ideo pro remedio ecclesiae firmo adversus eadem tria mala [scil. superbia, avaritia, luxuria] ex instinctu Spiritus Sancti plures ac diversae in ecclesia religiones sunt institutae ac approbatae." Cap. 22,1.

[44] "Quo triplici remedio [scil. oboedientia, paupertate, continentia] adversus praemissos tres insultus [vide notam 43] ecclesia in suis membris uti ac frui solet." Cap. 22,1.

[45] "... de ... perversis religiosis in Birgitta ulterius dicitur: Qui sunt in monasteriis, vadunt in mundum pro superbia et cupiditate, habentes propriam voluntatem, facientes corporis sui delectamenta." Cap. 22,3.

Hingabe an Gott, bei sich selber, bei ihren Brüdern und auch außerhalb der Klöster bei den Christen in der Welt.[46]

Die Last der Kirche sind also nicht einfach nur Mißstände und Mißbräuche, die gewiß ärgerlich und deshalb auch abzustellen sind, die strukturell den Wandel der Kirche aber nicht betreffen. Die Last besteht vielmehr darin, daß alle Stände der Geistlichkeit ihren von Gott gesetzten Dienst inzwischen ins Gegenteil verkehrt haben: Der Nachfolger Petri handelt als Nachfolger Konstantins. Bischöfliche Hirten sind zu Dieben und Räubern im Schafstall Christi verkommen. Arbeiter in Gottes Ernte vernichten Gottes Ernte. Mönche, die Waffen des Heiligen Geistes in den Klöstern, kämpfen als Waffen des Teufels in der Welt. Alles also, womit Gott seine Kirche in ihrer Geschichte ausgestattet hat, hat sich in dieser Geschichte gegen die Kirche gekehrt. Die Geistlichkeit, die auf Erden so sichtbar wie maßgeblich die streitende Kirche repräsentiert, hat sich gegen die Kirche erhoben. Nur das eine wird von Pirstinger nicht erwähnt und damit auch nicht in Zweifel gezogen: Die Lehre. Sie scheint ihm im Jahre 1519 genauso intakt zu sein wie im Jahre 1528, als er sich dogmatisch gegen die Reformation wendete.

Nicht die Lehre, sondern das Leben ist die Last der Kirche.

II. DIE QUELLEN DER KIRCHENKRITIK

Überblickt man die Kritik, die der Bischof von Chiemsee im Jahre 1519 gegen die Kirche vorbringt, dann führt der erste Eindruck dazu, sein Werk als Handbuch des Antiklerikalismus zu verwerten. Kein Klerikerstand bleibt unbetroffen, und die Kritik, die der Autor vorbringt, ist so formuliert, daß sie auch betroffen macht. Sein Latein ist gewiß kein elegantes Humanistenlatein, und doch weiß er schmerzhaft mit Worten und Sentenzen zu stechen. Auch die Zitate, die er wählt, verleihen seinen Angriffen Aggressivität und Schwung. Bevor man dieses Werk aber allein unter den Stichworten 'Antiklerikalismus' und 'Kirchenkritik' ablegt, ist nach den Quellen dieser Kritik zu fragen. Erst dann wird man sich Klarheit darüber verschaffen können, ob das unstreitig in Fülle vorhandene antiklerikale Material bereits das Programm des *Onus ecclesiae* ausmacht. Falls das Material mit dem Programm identisch wäre, müßte man davon ausgehen, daß Pirstinger als antiklerikalem Kleriker nur daran gelegen wäre, "religiöse Kritik der Zustände in Kirche und Welt"[47] auszusprechen und zu verbreiten.

---

[46] "Religiosi facti sunt arma diaboli, corrumpentes religionem intus in se et fratribus ac extra circa saeculares." Cap. 22,6.

[47] Josef Schmuck (wie Anm. 7) legt im Untertitel seiner Dissertation eine solche Begrenzung nahe: "Religiöse Kritik der Zustände in Kirche und Welt aus den ersten Jahren der Reformationszeit." Tatsächlich hat aber auch Schmuck gesehen, daß man allein mit dem Begriff 'Kritik' bei Pirstinger zu kurz greift.

Es liegt nahe, als erste und entscheidende Quelle der Kritik Pirstingers die eigene bischöfliche Amtserfahrung zu benennen. In der Tat trifft man auf solche Erfahrungen, wenn er die Bürokratie der Kurie anprangert, die einen Erlaß mit dem anderen jagt und damit den Frieden zermürbt, ohne sich um Recht und Gerechtigkeit zu bekümmern.[48] Ebenso gehört der Umgang mit seinen Mitbischöfen zu seinen Amtserfahrungen. Er kenne persönlich, so berichtet er einmal, zwei Bischöfe — einer weile noch unter den Lebenden —, die als Heerführer aufgetreten seien. Fachgerecht haben sie logistische Dispositionen getroffen und im Felde sogar Mann gegen Mann gefochten. Sie hätten aber eines anderen Amtes walten sollen, hätten nämlich beten müssen, daß die Christenheit vom Blutvergießen verschont bleibe und vom Feinde befreit werde.[49] Auch die Kritik, daß die Bischöfe fahrlässig auf das Reformmittel der Provinzialsynoden verzichten, dürfte durch eigene Erfahrungen begründet sein.[50]

Dennoch, soweit man auch berechtigt ist, aus der Lebendigkeit und Treffsicherheit vieler Beschreibungen das eigene Erleben zu erschließen, so ist doch festzuhalten, daß Pirstinger selber den Eindruck des nur subjektiven emotionalen Ausbruchs zu vermeiden sucht. Die vorgetragenen Angriffe beziehen ihre Legitimation wie auch das Recht für ihre schneidende Schärfe und Zielrichtung aus anderen Quellen als aus den Quellen der persönlichen Erfahrung. Was das *Onus ecclesiae* prägt, ist die durchgehende Berufung auf

---

[48] Cap. 14 (De statu ecclesiae remissivo, qui est quintus in ordine),7: "Enimvero lex evangelica, quam Spiritus Sanctus promulgavit, est efficacissima et ad omnes causas salutis nostrae necessarias sufficientissima ... Ultra praedicta denique antiqua seu decretalia iura cotidie Romae eduntur novae constitutiones, quas cancellariae regulas nuncupant et pro *uberrima litium materia* ad unguem observari iubent. ... Ob tales similesque adinventiones Deus iustus aliquando nos perdat, quia: 'Vae illis, qui condunt leges iniquas'" (Jes. 10,1). Die Wahrscheinlichkeit, daß diese Klage sich mit der eigenen Erfahrung deckt, schließt nicht aus, daß sie längst vorformuliert worden ist, so etwa bei Nikolaus von Clemanges: "Nam quid hae tot novae regulae et constitutiones per unumquemque Pontificem editae, ultraque antiqua iura et paternas sanctiones observari iussae, nisi quidam captiosi laquei sunt atque *uberrima litium materia* ... " Nicolaus de Clemangis (wie Anm. 29), Cap. 9,2; S. 10b. Daß diese Kritik verbreitet ist, beweisen die Gravamina des Jahres 1521: "Die regel der canzlei zu Rom werden nach der cordissanen nutz und vortail gesatzt und oft geandert, damit die gaistlich lehen, sonderlich Teutscher nation, in ir Romisch hend kommen ..." *Reichstagsakten*, Bd. 2, 675,32-676,3.

[49] "Novi episcopos duos, quorum alter adhuc in humanis est, qui velut duces et capitanei exercitus, cappis, rochetis, librisque postergatis gladium super brachium suum et arma sumpserunt, metati sunt castra, in campis digladiati usque ad hostium pugnam, quos pro debito officio potissimum orare decuerat, ut populus Christianus a sanguinis effusione ab hostibusque malignis liberaretur." Cap. 20,5.

[50] "Concilia provincialia per archiepiscopos vel synodalia per diocesanos iuxta patrum aeditiones minime celebrantur. Unde multae res ecclesiasticae, quae opus habent correctione, negliguntur." Cap. 20,11.

Autoritäten sowohl innerhalb als auch außerhalb der Schrift, von denen Pirstinger überzeugt ist, sie seien durch göttliche Geistbegabung ausgewiesen, auch wenn sie nicht kanonisch sind.[51] Er begnügt sich also weder mit einem Erlebnisbericht über seine Erfahrungen mit Klerikern, noch mit der Abfassung eines 'objektiven' Sachreports über Klerikerskandale zur Information für künftige Generationen. Sein Verständnis von Realität und Sachlichkeit ist im Falle des *Onus ecclesiae* ein anderes als das von Historikern heute anerkannte. Pirstinger stützt sich vielmehr auf jene in seinem Sinne echten Realitäten, die ausgewiesene Propheten des alten und neuen Bundes sowie der Kirchengeschichte ans Licht des Tages gebracht haben. Die Gabe der Prophetie, erfaßt vom Geiste Gottes die Zeiten bis auf ihre Hintergründe durchschauen zu können, endet für Pirstinger nicht mit dem apostolischen Zeitalter. Eine Begrenzung dieser für alle Christen verbindlichen Prophetie auf die Schrift kennt er also nicht, und damit wird bereits im Jahre 1519 sichtbar, wie wenig Pirstinger und Luther in ihren theologischen Grundlagen miteinander gemein haben,[52] auch wenn sie die

---

[51] Cap. 1 ist der biblischen Prophetie gewidmet: "De auctoritate approbatarum prophetiarum Veteris et Novi Testamenti". Im zweiten Kapitel geht es um die nichtbiblische Prophetie: "De novis prophetis ac modernis revelationibus". Dort heißt es unter anderem: "Dedit quippe Deus Apocalypsim, id est revelationem secretorum palam facere servis suis, quae oportet fieri cito, et significavit mittens per angelum suum Joanni et aliis suis servis, quorum Dei servorum Thelosphorus Eremita in suo tractatu meminit nominatim Joachim Abbatis, Merlini, Cyrilli, Dandali, Rhabani, Rainerii, Vincentii, Francisci ac aliorum, inter quos Methodius Martyr magnae est auctoritatis, qui in carcere tentus a Deo per angelum revelationem futuri temporis usque ad finem huius mundi percepit." Cap. 2,3. Zu den hier angegebenen Namen siehe Klüver (wie Anm. 4), 69; zur Prophetie siehe auch J. Schmuck (wie Anm. 7) 184f.

[52] Dem entspricht die 'Deutsche Theologie', in der Pirstinger darstellt, daß es eine die Christen bindende Ergänzungstradition gibt, die neben und mit der Schrift besteht. Siehe *Tewtsche Theologey*, 120f. Vgl. Franz X. Remberger, "Die Lehre von der Kirche in der 'Tewtschen Theologey' Bertholds von Chiemsee", *Münchener Theologische Zeitschrift* 91 (1958): 97-109, 109.

apokalyptische Zeitdeutung miteinander teilen[53] — und ihre Reformations-
hoffnung auch, wie sich noch zeigen wird.[54]

Pirstinger sucht der durch Gott ausgewiesenen Prophetie seine Stimme zu
verleihen, weil diese zuverlässig über das Schicksal der Kirche in Geschichte, Gegenwart und Zukunft Auskunft zu geben vermag. Propheten, die einst
die Last Babylons offenbart haben, enthüllen jetzt die Last der Kirche. Von
allerhöchster Autorität ist Birgitta von Schweden, die so massiv und
unerschrocken den Zustand der Kirche im 14. Jahrhundert angeprangert und
vor deren Exil in Avignon gewarnt hat.[55] Christus hat sie, die schwache
Frau, so liest man bei Pirstinger, als Braut erwählt und ihr seine Klagen über
den Fall der Kirche offenbart.[56] Als Stimme des Bräutigams ist sie im *Onus
ecclesiae* stets gegenwärtig, um den Verfall der Kirche zu offenbaren. Neben
ihr stehen andere Propheten, der Franziskanerspirituale Ubertin von Casale

---

[53] Zu Luther vgl. Heiko A. Oberman, "Martin Luther. Vorläufer der Reformation",
in *Verifikationen. Festschrift für Gerhard Ebeling zum 70. Geburtstag*, hg. E. Jüngel
u.a. (Tübingen, 1982), 91-119. In diesem Aufsatz stellt Oberman jenen apokalyptisch
auf die Reformation schauenden Luther vor, den er in seinem Lutherbuch dann
ausgemalt hat: *Luther. Mensch zwischen Gott und Teufel*, 3. Aufl. (Berlin, 1987). Nur
am Rande behandelt Hans-Martin Barth die Antichristvorstellung bei Luther. Siehe
Barth, *Der Teufel und Jesus Christus in der Theologie Martin Luthers*, Forschungen
zur Kirchen- und Dogmengeschichte 19 (Göttingen, 1971), 106-11. Barth hat
immerhin gesehen, daß Luther den Antichrist nicht nur nach seiner Lehre bemißt,
sondern auch nach seinem Leben: Der Antichrist ist sowohl Häretiker als auch
Betrüger und Gewalthaber (107).

[54] Siehe unten S. 340.

[55] Zu Birgitta von Schweden siehe die Zusammenstellung der Literatur und der
Quellen durch Tore Nyberg, "Birgitta/Birgittenorden", in *Theologische Realenzyklopädie*, Bd. 6 (1980), 648-52. Birgittas Offenbarungen sind in Deutschland vielfach
gedruckt worden, zum ersten Male in Lübeck: *Revelationes. Vita abbreviata S.
Birgittae, Hymnus ad beatam Birgittam* (Lübeck, Bartholomäus Ghotan, 1492). Siehe
Gesamtkatalog der Wiegendrucke, Bd. 4 (Leipzig, 1930), Nr. 4391. Das erste und
zweite Buch der *Revelationes* liegt in einer Faksimile-Ausgabe vor: *Corpus
codicorum suecicorum medii aevi*, Bd. 13 und 14, ed. E. Wéssen (Kopenhagen, 1952-
1956). Eine zugängliche deutsche Übersetzung stammt von Ludwig Clarus, *Leben und
Offenbarungen der heiligen Brigitta*, 4 Bde., Sammlung der vorzüglichsten
mystischen Schriften aller katholischen Völker, 10-13 (Regensburg, 1856).

[56] Cap. 3 (De sanctitate et auctoritate Birgittae),4: Christus spricht zu Birgitta: "Ego
elegi te mihi in sponsam, ut ostendam tibi secreta mea, quia mihi sic placuit ... Ego
aperui tibi oculos spirituales, ut videas spiritualia; aperui aures, ut audias quae spiritus
sunt. Item talia loquor et tanta ostendi tibi, non propter te solam, sed propter aliorum
eruditionem et salutem." Warum eine schwache, dazu ungebildete Frau als Prophetin?
"... tibi Birgittae tamquam instrumento novo ostendere volo nova et vetera, ut superbi
humilientur et humiles glorificentur. Nam saepe Deus abscondit secreta a sapientibus
et prudentibus et revelat ea parvulis et humilibus, quibus dat gratiam resistendi
superbis." Cap. 3,7. Birgittas Aufzeichnungen der Offenbarungen sind also 'bewährte'
Schrift.

(† nach 1317) etwa,[57] die alle dem Bischof von Chiemsee das Belastungsmaterial und die Beweise liefern, daß die Mißstände in der Kirche mehr sind als nur Mißstände: Sie sind die 'Last' der Kirche. Der — zunehmende — Verfall der Kirche wird somit aufgeklärt und eingeordnet. Es waltet nicht ein unergründliches Schicksal, das Gottes Herrschaft in der Kirche verdrängt, sondern die Prophetie identifiziert den Fall der Kirche als Teil des Kampfes Gottes um sein Volk, das immer wieder mit neuen geistlichen Heilmitteln ausgestattet wird und immer wieder von seinem göttlichen Bewahrer abfällt. Die Fülle der prophetischen Autoritäten verhindert zudem, daß die persönliche Erfahrung des Autors zum entscheidenden, damit aber auch anfechtbaren Beweis werden muß. Pirstinger will göttliche Prophetie vortragen, nicht bischöfliche Meinung.

Entscheidend für die Zielsetzung des Werkes ist der geschichtstheologische Rahmen, der die Menge des Materials zusammenhält und der die Zielrichtung der harten Kritik bestimmt. Dieser Rahmen ist die apokalyptische Geschichtstheologie in der Tradition des Joachimitismus. Joachim, der Abt von Fiore (†1202), hat die Welt- und Kirchengeschichte eingeteilt in die drei Zeitalter des Vaters, des Sohnes und des Heiligen Geistes. Die Zeit des Sohnes ist die Zeit der Kirche, und deren Geschichte wird in der joachimitischen Tradition nach dem Modell der Siebenzahl der Johannesapokalypse in sieben 'status' gegliedert.[58] Als prophetische Autorität für diese Statuslehre steht Ubertin von Casale ein, dessen einschlägige Passagen von einem unbekannten Redaktor zu einem Tractatus "De septem statibus ecclesiae" kompiliert worden sind.[59] Diesen Traktat hat Pirstinger als geschichtstheologische Leitautorität für sein *Onus ecclesiae* benutzt.[60]

---

[57] Zu Ubertin von Casale siehe Johannes Chrysostomus Huck, *Ubertin von Casale und dessen Ideenkreis. Ein Beitrag zum Zeitalter Dantes* (Freiburg, 1903). Eine Zusammenstellung der 'prophetischen' und der nicht-prophetischen Quellen im *Onus ecclesiae* findet sich bei Hermann Klüver (wie Anm. 4), 44ff.; zu Ubertin vgl. 62-67.

[58] Vgl. *Onus ecclesiae*, Cap. 5, proem. Zur Tradition des Joachimitismus siehe Marjorie Reeves, *The Influence of Prophecy in the Later Middle Ages. A Study in Joachimism.* Oxford 1969; zu Pirstinger siehe dort 467f.

[59] Zum Traktat *De septem statibus ecclesiae iuxta septem visiones beati Joannis in Apocalypsim ... doctoris fratris Ubertini de Casali ordinis minorum* siehe Klüver, 76f. Dieser Traktat ist in dem wichtigen apokalyptischen Sammelwerk des Frater Rusticianus gedruckt worden, das Pirstinger ausgiebig benutzt hat. Der Titel des Sammelwerks: *Abbas Joachim magnus propheta* (Venedig, Lazarus de Soardis, 1516). Siehe Klüver, 67f. Der Traktat über die 'status' der Kirche ist ein Auszug aus Ubertins echtem Werk *Arbor vitae crucifixae* (Venedig, 1485), Klüver, 65; Reeves, 207-209.

[60] *Onus ecclesiae*, Cap. 5 (De septem statibus ecclesiae), proem: "Ad investigandum iudicium futurae calamitatis iam proximantis, intendo [scil. ego, Pirstinger] aliqua disserere de septem ecclesiae statibus, ut sciamus in quo statu huiuscemodi calamitas super nos sit eventura. Quamobrem quaedam excerpsi, quae ad hoc

In jedem ihrer 'status' widerfährt der Kirche sowohl Gutes wie Böses. Die Höhe eines Status ist seine gute Seite, der Tiefpunkt hingegen ist die Kehrseite des einstigen Guten. Je mehr ein Status sich seinem Ende zuneigt, desto mehr pervertiert die einstige Vollkommenheit zur Verwerflichkeit.[61] Die Zeit des ersten Status[62] umfaßt die Geschichte Jesu, als Gott seine Kirche pflanzte; das ist der 'status seminativus' (*Onus ecclesiae*, Cap. 10). Der zweite Abschnitt ist der 'status irrigativus' (Cap. 11), als Apostel und Märtyrer den Glauben durch die Welt trugen. Im darauf folgenden 'status illuminativus' (Cap. 12) verteidigen die 'doctores' ihre Kirche gegen die Angriffe von Häretikern. Der 'status ascensivus' (Cap. 13) ist die Zeit der Anachoreten mit ihrem Höhepunkt der großen Ordensgründungen durch Benediktiner oder Zisterzienser. Den fünften Status nennt Pirstinger den 'status remissivus' (Cap. 14). Das ist die Zeit der großzügigen Kirche, die weitherzig die harten Sündenstrafen nachläßt, mit denen sie in der Vergangenheit die Sünder beladen hatte. Die Perversion dieser Großzügigkeit ist der Mißbrauch des Ablasses, der im *Onus ecclesiae* mit Berufung auf Luthers "Resolutiones disputationum de indulgentiarum virtute" vom Jahre 1518 unnachsichtig angegriffen wird.[63] Pirstingers Gegenwart ist die Zeit des sechsten Status.[64] Dieser ist der 'status reformativus' (Cap. 16), in dem die Kirche ihre Reformation erfährt. Dieser Reformationsstatus war in seinen Anfängen die Zeit der Armen, vor allem der Bettelmönche, die den im fünften Status eingerissenen Schaden heilen sollten, den eine großzügige und reiche Kirche sich zugefügt hatte. Mit dem zunehmenden Ende des sechsten

---

necessaria esse duxi, ex documento, quod super Apocalypsi confecit Ubertinus de Casali ordinis minorum professus, de ecclesiae statibus septem ..."

[61] Vgl. Heinrich Werner, *Die Flugschrift "onus ecclesiae" (1519) mit einem Anhang über sozial- und kirchenpolitische Prophetien. Ein Beitrag zur Sitten- und Kulturgeschichte des ausgehenden Mittelalters* (Gießen, 1901), 15.

[62] Eine gedrängte Übersicht über diese 'status' findet sich bei Schmuck (wie Anm. 7), 197.

[63] "Ut autem indulgentiarum aliqua habeatur notitia, referam, qualiter Martinus Luther, etsi alias multa temerarie ac contumeliose scribere praetendit, tamen poenarum materiam per venias remittendarum in quinque membra acutissime distinxit." Cap. 15,1. Pirstinger bezieht sich auf Luthers Einteilung der Bußstrafen in fünf verschiedene *poenae*. Siehe Martin Luther, *Resolutiones disputationum*, WA 1. 534,25-536,5. Die Urteile über Luther, die sich im *Onus ecclesiae* finden, sind nicht einheitlich. Sie reichen von distanzierter Kritik bis zu unversöhnlicher Verwerfung. Heinrich Werners (wie Anm. 61) Vorschlag dürfte die Sachlage treffen, daß die Verschiedenheit der Urteile zeitlich zu erklären ist: Die distanzierte Kritik entstammt dem Abfassungsjahr 1519, als Luther und Eck von Pirstinger noch zusammengesehen werden als ehrgeizig-arrogante Gelehrte (siehe unten Anm. 77). Die Verwerfungen hingegen dürften — von wem auch immer — im Jahre 1524, dem Jahre des Druckes, in den Text eingefügt worden sein. Siehe Werner, 9; Klüver (wie Anm. 4), 33.

[64] Es heißt im *Onus ecclesiae*: "sextus nunc status", Cap. 16, proem.; "in praesenti sexto statu", Cap. 16,2; "in sexto nunc statu", Cap. 16,6.

Status verkehrt sich aber die ursprüngliche Reformation in jene ungeheuerliche Deformation, daß die Christenheit von einer flammenden Sündensucht befallen ist.[65] Der siebte 'status quietis temporalis' (Cap. 66) ist der Ruhestatus, den die Kirche mit dem Anbruch und Fortgang des Tausendjährigen Reiches erleben wird — und dann kommt Christus wieder, um Endgericht zu halten.

In allen sechs 'status' vor dem Anbruch des Friedensreiches ist der Antichrist durch seine Vorläufer in der Kirche stets gegenwärtig,[66] und je mehr die Zeit der Kirche sich ihrem Ende zuneigt, desto härter schlagen diese Vorläufer auf die Kirche ein. Ihren Höhepunkt erreicht die antichristliche Gewalt im sechsten Status, in jener gegenwärtigen Zeit also, in der es um die Reformation der Kirche geht. Spürbar wird dann die Gewalt des sogenannten 'Antichristus mixtus', der vor dem Anbruch des Tausendjährigen Reiches sein Wesen als falscher Papst treiben wird, während der unverhohlene Antichrist, der 'Antichristus purus' erst nach Ablauf der tausend Jahre über die Kirche herfällt. Als 'mixtus'[67] wird der vorläufige Antichrist bezeichnet, weil er die Gewalt des Betruges in frommer Papstgestalt ist, der unter dem Schein der Frömmigkeit die Christen von Gott abführen wird.[68] In dieser seiner Gegenwart, so Pirstinger, muß man bereits mit dem Erscheinen des 'Antichristus mixtus' rechnen.[69]

Diese Geschichtstheologie umrahmt die harsche Kleriker- und Kirchenkritik, die Pirstinger vorbringt. Sie macht deutlich, daß er sich nicht einfach mit der Enthüllung und Benennung von Mißständen begnügt. Er will vielmehr den Kirchenkampf aufzeigen, der immer schon die Geschichte der Kirche begleitet hat, der nun aber im gegenwärtigen Zeitalter des sechsten

---

[65] "In ... sexto ecclesiae statu nos Christiani sumus in ardentissimo peccandi desiderio." Cap. 16,6.

[66] Cap. 42 (De Idolo seu papa falso, qui dicitur Antichristus mixtus),3: " ... eiusdem idoli (scil. Antichristi) praecursores sunt omnes haeretici et falsi doctores, qui sacram scripturam pervertunt, unacum iniquis episcopis et perversis sacerdotibus, qui hoc idolum praecesserunt ..."

[67] Auf den merkwürdigen Begriff 'Antichristus mixtus' ist bereits J. Huck in seiner Studie über Ubertin von Casale (wie Anm. 57) gestoßen. Er schlägt eine Emendation vor: 'Antichristus mysticus' (Huck, 102). Ob diese Verbesserung für Ubertin gerechtfertigt ist, kann hier offenbleiben. Für Pirstinger darf man sie in keinem Falle aufgreifen, weil er mit dem Begriff 'mixtus' umgeht.

[68] "Duo Antichristi sunt futuri, prior mixtus, successor merus. Mixtus apparebit bonus Christianus et decipiet multos. Alter conabitur extinguere fidem Christianam, mixtus intrudetur in papatum ... Antichristus mixtus per fictam sanctitatem usurpabit sibi dignitates et divitias mundanas, unde omnes gentes vi vel sponte adhaerebunt eidem idolo." Cap. 42,9. Zusammenfassend zur Antichristvorstellung bei Pirstinger siehe Schmuck, 227-9.

[69] Die Zeit des 'Antichristus mixtus': " ... in fine quinti et in excursu sexti status ... " Cap. 42,10.

Status die tödliche Gefahr durch den antichristlichen falschen Papst heraufführt.

Aufgrund der Themen und der Sprachgebung möchte man 'Pfaffenhaß' bei Pirstinger vermuten. Es ist auch nicht zu bestreiten, daß er das antiklerikale Vokabular und Material des späten Mittelalters in einer Weise gesammelt hat, daß sich sein *Onus ecclesiae* als 'Handbuch des Antiklerikalismus' nutzen läßt. Aber: Wenn man die Intention seines Werkes auf den Antiklerikalismus begrenzt, hat man sein Anliegen, das er verbreiten will, verharmlost. Es geht längst nicht nur um den Ausbruch von Enttäuschungen und erst recht nicht um den Ausdruck der Gegnerschaft eines 'Aufklärers' gegenüber einem Klerus, der seine Privilegien nicht mehr rechtfertigen kann. Die Quellen der Kirchen- und Klerikerkritik, so wie Pirstinger sie vorträgt, sind entscheidend; es sind jene zumeist apokalyptischen Quellen, denen er prophetische Qualität und Autorität zuspricht. Das 'Handbuch des Antiklerikalismus' ist zugleich ein Kompendium der spätmittelalterlichen Apokalyptik.

Die Annahme, die Apokalyptik würde erst sekundär dem schon vorhandenen Antiklerikalismus Ausdruck verleihen, ist zwar nicht zu beweisen, aber doch wahrscheinlich. Wenn das der Fall ist, wird man sagen müßen, daß diese Quellen die Angriffe nicht gemindert, sondern die Kritik eher verschärft und zugleich die Zielrichtung des Antiklerikalismus bestimmt haben. Auf der Beweisgrundlage von enthüllenden Prophetien versieht Pirstinger seine schweren Beschuldigungen mit einer deutenden Vision, einer düsteren Vision zunächst, dann aber auch mit einer hellen, wie noch zu zeigen ist.[70] Das *Onus ecclesiae* soll allererst deutlich machen, daß die Zeiten vorbei sind, in denen heftige Kritik am Klerus noch grundlegende Änderungen bewirken könnte. Pirstingers Antiklerikalismus ist gewiß zorngeladen, er ist aber auch angstgeladen. Denn wer gegen die Perversionen in der Kirche anschreit, verwickelt sich nach seiner Darstellung nicht einfach nur in Auseinandersetzungen mit verworfenen Klerikern, sondern in Kämpfe mit dem Antichrist und seinen Vorläufern. Das ist ein Teil seiner düsteren Vision.

III. DIE REFORMATION DER KIRCHE

Es drängt sich zum Schluß die Frage auf, was das Ziel einer solchen dramatisch vorgetragenen Prophetie sein soll, die vom Kampf des Antichrist und seiner klerikalen Vorläufer gegen die Kirche berichtet. In der radikalen franziskanischen Tradition ist der sechste Status als Status der Reformation ausgemacht worden. In dieser Tradition waren es die Armen, speziell die armen Brüder des Franz von Assisi, auf denen die Reformhoffnungen ruhten. Diese franziskanische Tradition hat Pirstinger aufgegriffen, sie jedoch

---

[70] Siehe unten S. 340f.

umgeschrieben gemäß seiner Geschichtsdeutung vom Fortschritt des Antichrist. Die Bettelorden haben nach seiner Ansicht total versagt. Sie, die einst Reformhoffnung waren, sind 'onus ecclesiae' geworden: Sie halten sich weder an ihre 'via' noch an ihre 'vota' oder 'ceremoniae', "immo peiores quam ceteri sunt Christiani, malum exemplum praebentes et contra suam regulam nimium exorbitantes. Ecce religiosi, qui olim in observantia regulari erant via salvatoris, nunc sunt via perditionis"![71] Bettelmönche werden nichts mehr für die Reform der Kirche ausrichten, auch die Franziskaner nicht.[72] Damit fallen alle maßgeblichen geistlichen Kräfte und Institutionen der Kirche als Reformträger aus.

Man möchte nun annehmen, daß Pirstinger konsequenterweise auf neue Reformträger setzt, auf jene Bildungsschicht etwa, die in der Antike neue geistliche Kraftquellen auszumachen glaubt und die sich selber als Reformhoffnung für die Kirche ausgibt. Doch auch die Hoffnung auf das, was sich Bildung oder gar neue Bildung nennen mag, teilt er nicht.[73] Die Menschen sind zwar stolz auf ihre Kenntnisse über Himmel und Erde, über den Gang der Sterne und den Lauf der Welt, doch auf ihr eigenes Versagen haben sie nicht acht und wissen nicht, daß sie weder über die Erkenntnis des Heils noch über den Weg zum Himmel verfügen. Dahin ist es gekommen, daß für töricht gehalten wird, wer aus seinen Studien kein Kapital schlagen will. Der Studienbetrieb ist auf Gewinn und zweifelhaften Erwerb eingerichtet, es geht überhaupt nicht mehr um die Frage nach der Wahrheit: "Dulcius sapit nobis foetor mundi pessimus quam odor Dei suavissimus"[74] — das widerlichste Stinken dieser Welt dünkt uns verlockender als Gottes süßer Wohlgeruch. Die neuen Bildungsanstrengungen sind ihm ebenfalls ein Zeichen des geistlichen Zusammenbruchs der Zeit. Auch jene Köpfe, gerade jene, die soviel Aufhebens um sich machen, werden für die Kirche nichts erbringen. Einst waren Gelehrte die Leuchten der Kirche, weil sie von Gott erleuchtet waren;[75] heute tappen sie umher im Nebel ihrer Eigensucht und vermögen die Schrift nur noch buchstäblich, also ihrer äußeren Oberfläche nach zu verstehen:[76] "Sic hodie Luterani et Ecciani", die sich leichtfertig

---

[71] Cap. 22,5.

[72] Vgl. Cap. 16,4.

[73] Cap. 18 (De hominum caecitate),8: "Modo equidem cernimus omnia fere Germaniae gymnasia, ubi olim theologica tradebatur doctrina, poeticis figmentis, vanis nugis ac fabularum portentis esse impleta. Ubi est literatus? Ubi legis verba ponderans? Ubi est doctor parvulorum?"

[74] Cap. 18,4.

[75] "... olim sancti doctores a deo missi tamquam lucernae fuerunt illuminati lumine mystice intelligendi sacram scripturam." Cap. 12,7.

[76] "... lumen intellectus, quo sacra scriptura intelligitur, procedit a lumine supernaturali a Deo pendente, quo lumine superbi et flagitiosi carent ob amoris proprii nubem, quae excaecat spirituales oculos. Ideo isti intelligunt sacram paginam literaliter iuxta corticem exteriorem, non gustantes interiorem medullam scripturae."

und ehrgeizig im akademischen Kampf zanken, sich aber um ein rechtes geistliches Verstehen der Schrift nicht kümmern.[77] Den vielbeklagten Bildungsmangel, daß Geistliche und Gelehrte vom Wort des Geistes nichts mehr verstehen, den beklagt auch Pirstinger. Doch die Bildungsreform, die er in seiner Gegenwart sichtet, wird, so ist er überzeugt, nur zum weiteren Verfall der Kirche beitragen.

Ob vielleicht Hoffnung bei den weltlichen Ständen zu finden ist, daß sie der Kirche helfen könnten, da die Geistlichen und die Gelehrten versagen? Der künftige Kaiser Karl beflügelt die Reformphantasie, wie eine in Italien aufgetauchte Prophezeiung ausweist. Dieses 'praesagium Caroli', das Pirstinger in die Hände gefallen ist,[78] will von einer Zeitenwende wissen, die Karl durch seine Herrschaft heraufführen wird. Er wird Kaiser, wird den Erdkreis dem christlichen Glauben unterwerfen und dieses nun umfassende Weltreich an der Stätte des Kreuzes dem Himmelskönig übergeben.[79] Pirstinger aber ist skeptisch. Dieses 'praesagium', das in Karl den Friedens-kaiser preist, wird sich nur dann erfüllen können, wenn dieser sein Amt ohne Bestechung erlangen sollte. Gelingt das aber nicht, dann wird sich das 'praesagium' als Machwerk von Wichtigtuern oder Schmeichlern er-weisen.[80] Die Bedingung, die Pirstinger an die Erfüllung der Voraussage knüpft, wird man wohl als seine Kritik am Handel um die deutsche Königswahl verstehen können.

Den anderen weltlichen Ständen darf man erst recht keine Reformation der Christenheit zutrauen.[81] Die künftig in Fülle auftauchenden refor-

---

Cap. 12,7.

[77] "Sic hodie Luterani et Ecciani temeraria et ambitiosa disputatione mutuo altercantes pro sua audacia sacras litteras torquent, nil caritative sed omnia invective ad seditionem defenduntur ..." Cap. 12,7.

[78] "... mihi ... occurrit quoddam propheticum vel potius genethliacum inventum seu praesagium de potentissimo Rege Carolo, Genearcha Australi, editum." Prolog, proem. Er gibt auch an, wo und wann diese Nativität König Karls erschienen ist: "... accedit quaedam prophetia, si dici meretur, quae post natale dicti Karoli de eo fertur anno Domini 1505 in Italia apparuisse, cuius exemplar ... hoc anno [1505?] in manus meas pervenit ..." Cap. 48,7. Siehe dazu M. Reeves (wie Anm. 58), 361f.

[79] Vgl. Cap. 48,8.

[80] "Id [scil. praesagium Caroli] verificabitur, si Karolus iam in Caesarem utinam absque ambitione et avaritiae practica, legitime eligetur, Romani imperii coronam consecuturus. Tunc habebimus signum, quod praescripta revelatio a Deo emanaverit et non sit ab homine per tumorem vel adulationem excogitata." Cap. 48,9. Pirstinger hält die Erstellung solcher Nativitäten für nicht mehr gerechtfertigt: "Huius mathesis interpretatio olim concessa fuit tribus magis, ut natum annuntiarent Christum; quo nato neminem ulterius alicuius nativitatem de coelo interpretari decet, quoniam gentilium observationes tenere Christianis non licet." Cap. 48,9.

[81] Der Zustand des Reiches insgesamt ist bedrückend. Das Reich ist, wie er mit Augustin redet, ein 'magnum latrocinium', so daß zu fürchten ist, den Deutschen werde die Herrschaft genommen. Vgl. Cap. 48,10. Das macht die Hoffnung auf eine

matorischen Flugschriften propagieren den bibelfesten Bürger und sogar den Bauern, die so 'witzig' geworden sind, daß sie die Kleriker in ihrer arroganten Dummheit überführen. Pirstinger hingegen ist der festen Überzeugung, daß die Menschen in der Regel blind sind, gerade jetzt weit davon entfernt, witzig zu werden.[82] Das Selbstbewußtsein der Bürger, das sich im 16. Jahrhundert deutlich zu melden beginnt, teilt Pirstinger nicht. Sein Antiklerikalismus geht nicht mit einer Aufwertung des Weltchristen einher. Auch die Laien sind nicht anders als die Kleriker, denn auch sie sind der Welt, ihrem Trug, ihrem Unrecht und ihrer Gewalt verfallen.[83]

Diese Sicht hat zur Folge, daß im sechsten Status, dem Zeitalter der Reformation, von Klerikern oder Laien oder beiden eine Wende für die Kirche nicht zu erwarten ist. Was als nächstes geschichtlich zu überblickendes Zeitereignis bevorsteht, ist nicht die Reformation, sondern das Gericht. Über Bischöfe, die nicht Bischöfe, sondern Diebe und Räuber sind, wird die Strafe schrecklich hereinbrechen. Ihre Kirchen werden mit Feuer und Schwert gereinigt, werden so gewalttätig zerstört, daß lange Zeit niemand mehr da sein wird, der Trost spenden kann.[84] Jener gottvergessenen Prälaten wegen, die sich dadurch auszeichnen, daß sie Reichtümer anhäufen, den Gottesdienst aber außer acht lassen, ist der Teufel losgelassen, der gegen die Kirche anrennen und sie unterdrücken wird.[85] Die Verfallsgeschichte des Gottesvolkes in der Synagoge wiederholt sich in der Kirche: Ungetreue Priester gehen dem Verderber voraus und bereiten ihm den Weg. Zur Zeit des Alten Bundes hießen sie Jason, Menelaos oder Alkimos, die Hannas und Kaiphas den Weg bereiteten, die Synagoge zu zerstören. So auch jetzt:[86]

Wende durch Karl — den Deutschen — noch unwahrscheinlicher.

[82] "Porro omnes sumus excaecati, tam docti quam indocti, tam maiores quam minores, non cognoscentes tempus visitationis nostrae, in quo visitabit nos Deus maledictione sua; immo indies magis induramur." Cap. 18,5.

[83] Vgl. die Zusammenfassung von Schmuck (wie Anm. 7), 111-48. Siehe im *Onus ecclesiae*, Cap. 27 (De malitia communis populi),2 folgendes Urteil mit den Worten des Propheten Hosea (Hos. 4,1-3): "... non est veritas et non est misericordia et non est scientia Dei in terra, maledictum et mendacium et homicidium et furtum et adulterium inundaverunt et sanguis sanguinem tetigit."

[84] So die Strafankündigung gegenüber einem Bischof bei Birgitta von Schweden: "Convertat se citius episcopus ... alioquin sentiet manum iudicantis et ecclesia sua igne et gladio purgabitur, rapina et tribulatione affligetur intantum, quod in longa tempora non erit, qui consoletur eam." Cap. 20,14.

[85] Vgl. Cap. 21,3.

[86] "Sicut Jason et Menelaus, Alchiminus (1. Makk. 7; 2. Makk. 4) et ceteri simoniaci ac homicidae praecesserunt, antequam veniret Annas et Cayphas, sub quibus synagoga cecidit, sic et in ecclesia multi praelati vitiosi ... praecedunt ecclesiasticae dignitatis casum et ipsius ecclesiae Latinae ruinam, donec veniat mixtus Antichristus." Cap. 21,3.

Über bessernde Reformkuren ist die Zeit hinaus, denn die 'ruina ecclesiae' ist angesagt.[87]

Wird es je noch die Gelegenheit geben, daß durch eine Reformation die Kirche sich grundlegend wandeln kann? Zur Hoffnung auf die allenthalben ersehnte Reformation finden sich bei Pirstinger programmatische Aussagen, die er mit dem Verweis auf Birgitta von Schweden deckt: "[Ecclesia] maxime indiget reformatione, quemadmodum Birgitta exclamat ... Reformatio autem non erit unius hominis, utpote papae, nec multorum cardinalium officium, id est, sed totius Christianitatis, immo cunctipotentis Dei, qui solus sapit ac valet suam reformare ecclesiam" — die Kirche bedarf der Reformation. Reformation aber ist nicht Angelegenheit eines Menschen, des Papstes, auch nicht Sache vieler, der Kardinäle, sondern: Reformation ist Sache der ganzen Christenheit, vielmehr, sie ist Sache des allmächtigen Gottes, der allein seine Kirche zu reformieren weiß und dazu fähig ist.[88]

Unter der Autorität Birgittas ist Martin Luther verborgen. Wie in der Ablaßfrage stimmt Pirstinger mit diesem auch in der Erwartung überein, daß die Reformation der Gewalt der Hierarchie entnommen und Gott vorbehalten ist. In den Wittenberger "Resolutiones disputationum" vom Jahre 1518, die im *Onus ecclesiae* die Ablaßkritik untermauern sollen,[89] findet sich sachlich übereinstimmend und wörtlich ganz nahekommend jene Reformationsauffassung, die auch Pirstinger verbreitet. Bei Luther lautet der Text: "Ecclesia indiget reformatione, quod non est unius hominis Pontificis nec multorum Cardinalium officium, ... sed totius orbis, immo solius Dei."[90]

---

[87] "Christus equidem in sexto nunc statu censetur esse fatigatus, quasi non velit ulterius ecclesiae remedium habere aliud, quam sui ruinam ... Fatigatur igitur Jesus onere nostrorum peccatorum ..." Cap. 16,6, mit Berufung auf Joh. 4,6. Der Begriff 'ruina ecclesiae' ist ein vielfach von Pirstinger verwendetes Schlagwort, das zum kirchenkritischen Vokabular des späten Mittelalters gehört. Siehe Nicolaus de Clemangis (wie Anm. 29), Cap. 8,2 (9b); Cap. 12,1 (12a); Cap. 27,2 (25a/b).

[88] Cap. 19,15, mit Verweis auf Birgitta, *Quartus liber coelestium revelationum*, cap. 49. Dieses Kapitel ist in der Tat ein 'Reformationskapitel', doch der zitierte Pirstingertext is dort nicht enthalten.

[89] Siehe oben Anm. 63.

[90] *WA* 1. 627,27-30. Zu Luther siehe Heiko A. Oberman, "Martin Luther. Vorläufer der Reformation" (wie Anm. 53), 97. Noch näher rücken Pirstinger und Luther zusammen, wenn man beide mit einem Reformeiferer wie dem Erfurter Augustinereremiten Johannes von Paltz (†1511) vergleicht. Auch er fordert für eine Reformation das Eingreifen Gottes, doch das bedeutet nicht, die Kirche sei dem Fall preisgegeben. Nötig ist Gottes Eingreifen nur für die Reform des Weltklerus, während der geistliche Kern der Kirche, nämlich die Mönche, der Reform aus menschlichen Kräften zugänglich sind: "Multi mendicantes sunt irreformati, ergo merito reformandi. Quod est facile possibile in mendicantibus et fit cotidie." Durch wen? "per principes et civitates auctoritate summi pontificis". Das heißt: Fürsten und Stadträte wenden die sogenannten apostolischen Reformprivilegien auf die Klöster an. "Sed hoc est quasi impossibile in sacerdotibus saecularibus, quod reformentur stantibus rebus ut nunc,

Man muß feststellen, daß Pirstinger an dieser zentralen Stelle, an der er seine Reformationsauffassung niederlegt, Luther zwar nicht beim Namen nennt, sein Reformationsverständnis aber zitierend übernimmt.

Für Pirstinger ist deutlich, daß die Kirche keine der traditionellen 'reformationes' mehr zu erwarten hat, wie sie aus den anderen 'status ecclesiae' bekannt sind. Die Reformation geschieht am Ende des sechsten Status und ist allein Christus vorbehalten, auf dessen zweite, nämlich geistliche Wiederkunft sich deshalb alle Reformationshoffnungen richten.[91] Diese Hoffnung ist die helle Seite seiner Vision vom Schicksal der Kirche in der Endzeit des 'status reformationis'.

Der Reformation durch Christus wird das Strafgericht vorausgehen. Pirstinger konfrontiert die Kirche mit der Unumgänglichkeit des Gerichtes vor der Reformation, das die reiche, mächtige, verweltlichte Kirche zerschlagen wird.[92] Es geht zwar nicht jene wahre Kirche unter, die als 'navicula Petri' die recht lebenden Christen birgt, doch die Machtkirche wird fallen, muß fallen, denn ihr Untergang gehört zur Erneuerung unabdingbar hinzu. Es gibt keine Hoffnung auf den Erhalt oder die Restauration der weltlichen Machtstrukturen der Kirche. Geistliche, die von ihrer Macht nicht lassen wollen, erfinden die weltkluge Einrede, daß die Kirche der Macht bedürfe, um sich ihrer Feinde zu erwehren. Pirstinger trägt dementgegen die kompromißlose Antwort des Abtes von Fiore vor: Die Kirche wird sich ihrer Feinde nicht mit Macht, sondern mit Christus erwehren.[93]

Die 'ruina ecclesiae', der Zusammenbruch jener Kirche, wie 'wir' sie kennen, muß kommen. Das ist die Begründung dafür, daß Pirstinger seinem Antiklerikalismus so freien Lauf läßt. Es gilt neben der Tatsache der Klerikerkritik auch die Perspektive und die Intention des Kritikers zu berücksichtigen. Die Interessen des Bischofs sind kirchlich bestimmt. Er beschreibt nicht aus der Distanz des Chronisten, urteilt auch nicht aus der Sehweise des Bürgers und wird erst recht nicht von den kirchenpolitischen

---

nisi forte magna potentia dei descenderet et ecclesiae suae etiam in talibus subveniret." Johannes von Paltz, *Werke*, Bd. 2: *Supplementum Coelifodinae*, ed. B. Hamm, Spätmittelalter und Reformation 3 (Berlin, 1983), 282,19-24.

[91] "Quem [scil. Deum] in spiritu adventurum exspectamus, ut reformet corpus humilitatis nostrae. Nempe huiusmodi reformatio soli reservatur Christo, qui ecclesiam iam prope dilaceratam resarciet atque docebit in secundo suo adventu, qua die Filius Hominis revelabitur, hoc est in sexto praesenti ecclesiae statu." Cap. 19,15.

[92] Die Prälaten haben sich der Kirche bemächtigt. "Ideo in eosdem fertur sententia maledictionis." Dieses Verwerfungsurteil faßt Pirstinger in die Worte der Gerichtsrede über die ungetreuen Hirten Israels (Ezechiel 34,10): "Ecce ego ipse [scil. Deus] super pastores requiram gregem meum de manu eorum et cessare faciam, ut ultra non pascant gregem meum, ne pascant amplius pastores semetipsos." Cap. 21,11.

[93] "Aliqui [scil. praelati] autem se excusant quasi temporalibus indigeant bonis, quibus se adversus rebelles muniant. Contra quos Joachim invehit dicens: Praelati in suis adversitatibus non ad arma, sed ad Christum recurrere debent, qui eos liberaret ab omnibus tribulationibus." Cap. 21,10.

Interessen der weltlichen Führungsschicht im Reich gelenkt. Pirstinger schaut mitten aus der Kirche auf die Kirche; das ist die Perspektive des antiklerikalen Polemikers.

Seine in der Tat zornigen Verwerfungen verbindet Pirstinger mit einer apokalyptischen Vision über den Weg der Kirche in das Gericht und über die Rettung der Kirche aus dem Gericht heraus. Seine Vision ist seine Intention. Er warnt, daß sich mit dem Antichrist gemein mache, wer mit dem verworfenen Klerus gemeinsame Sache macht. Diese Kirche wird nicht bleiben, denn vor der Reformation wird — muß — das Gericht über sie hineinbrechen. Und er verheißt die Rettung aus dem Gericht: Christus wird kommen, um die Reformation zu vollziehen.

Dadurch, daß er apokalyptisch die Reformation dem Zugriff des Menschen entzieht, erscheint Pirstinger als Außenseiter in jener Zeit, die auch in Deutschland auf den Fortschritt setzt. Darin aber, daß er seinen Antiklerikalismus mit der Vision von der Erneuerung der Kirche verbindet, erweist er sich zugleich als typischer Zeuge der um 'Reformation' ringenden Kleriker- und Kirchenkritik seiner Zeit.

ANTIKLERIKALISMUS BEIM JUNGEN LUTHER?

MARTIN BRECHT

Universität Münster

In seinem provozierenden Buch *Pfaffenhaß und groß Geschrei. Die reformatorischen Bewegungen in Deutschland 1517-1529*[1] versucht Hans-Jürgen Goertz, den Antiklerikalismus als die gemeinsame gesellschaftliche Ursache der Reformation zu erweisen. Die These hat etwas Bestechendes. Sollte sie sich verifizieren lassen, ließe sich die Reformation recht einfach sozialgeschichtlich erklären. Man käme los von der alten Zentrierung auf Luther, die ohnedies schon für überwunden erklärt wird. Mißlich bleibt freilich die negative Bestimmtheit des Antiklerikalismus, die die positive Alternative vermissen läßt. Auch Goertz gesteht zu, Luther habe dem Antiklerikalismus ein theologisches Gerüst eingezogen (67), das dieser so nicht hatte. Die lutherische Deutung der Gerechtigkeit Gottes greife sehr viel tiefer als der Antiklerikalismus (84). Die Forderung nach der freien Evangeliumsverkündigung sei noch etwas anderes als der Antiklerikalismus, obwohl beide eine gemeinsame Wurzel hätten (87). Ganz wird man also auf den Faktor Theologie in der Reformationsgeschichte nicht verzichten können. Nach der Verbindung von Theologie oder Glauben mit den äußeren gesellschaftlichen Gegebenheiten wird weiter und energischer als bei Goertz gefragt werden müssen. Daß es der Reformation einfach um eine Abschaffung des Klerus gegangen sei (63ff.), ist zu bezweifeln. Das Festhalten der Reformation am kirchlichen Amt ist auch nicht erst eine Reaktion auf die Bedrohung durch Altgläubige und Radikale (78), sondern in Luthers Programm seit 1520 verankert. Gleichzeitig erfolgte die tiefgreifende Umformung des Amtsverständnisses.

Bei aller historischen Relativierung der Gestalt Luthers und ihrer Wirkung sollte sich die These von Goertz doch auch an ihm bewähren, will sie nicht von vornherein zweifelhaft sein. Mit der gewaltsamen Etikettierung bestimmter Gegenstände der Kirchen- und Theologiekritik als antiklerikal ist es dabei freilich nicht getan. Hier ist vielmehr Differenzierung geboten, damit das Syndrom Reformation genauer erkennbar und benennbar wird.

Wenn man sich intensiver mit Luther beschäftigt hat, fällt einem sogleich auf, daß Goertz auf einen Aufweis des Antiklerikalismus bei Luther vor 1517 verzichtet. Der Sachverhalt ist in der Tat komplex und für die These von Goertz sperrig. Dies dürfte übrigens auch für manchen anderen

---

[1] München, 1987. Die Seitenangaben in diesem Absatz beziehen sich auf Goertz, *Pfaffenhaß*.

Reformator zutreffen. Die theologischen und religiösen Ursachen für einen Paradigmenwechsel lagen nicht direkt auf diesem Gebiet. Dennoch lohnt es, sich die Problemfelder beim jungen Luther zu vergegenwärtigen, die sich zum Antiklerikalismus in Verbindung setzen lassen.

Luthers Vater hat offenbar die verbreitete kleruskritische Einstellung geteilt. Er soll Vermächtnisse an die Geistlichkeit abgelehnt und deren Berufung auf kirchliche Rechtsbestimmungen kritisiert haben.[2]

Aus Luthers Schulzeit sind andere Eindrücke überliefert: Die Begegnung mit dem asketischen Franziskaner Wilhelm von Anhalt in Magdeburg hat Luther beeindruckt.[3] In Eisenach gehörte Luther dem frommen Schülerkreis um den Vikar Johannes Braun an und dürfte dadurch nachhaltig geprägt worden sein.[4] Luthers Eintritt ins Kloster einschließlich seiner Weihe zum Priester lassen sich naturgemäß mit Antiklerikalismus nicht in Verbindung bringen. Dies dürfte übrigens ursprünglich für nicht wenige Mönche und Nonnen gegolten haben, die später zur Reformation übergegangen sind. Das Gewahrwerden kirchlicher Mißstände bei seiner Romreise hat Luther zunächst nicht irritiert.[5]

In Luthers frühem Schrifttum werden gelegentlich, aber nicht eben häufig Schäden der Kirche erwähnt. Besonders geboten schien ihm der Gehorsam gegen die kirchlichen Oberen, die Prälaten. Deshalb wandte er sich ausgerechnet gegen die Eigenmächtigkeiten der Observanten.[6] Dahinter standen Erfahrungen im eigenen Orden. Von den Prälaten wird umgekehrt erwartet, daß sie ihre Leitungsfunktion wahrnehmen.[7] Gegenüber Rebellen haben sie mit Härte vorzugehen.[8] Offenbar vorhandene Kritik an der Gehorsamsforderung der Prälaten wird zurückgewiesen.[9] Der Prälat ist der Exponent für die Einheit der Kirche, der ihrem Zerfall in Sekten und Häresien wehrt.[10] Daß es unter Bischöfen, Priestern und Doktoren sexuelle Verfehlungen ebenso wie theologische Irrtümer gab, war Luther bekannt, und er gab sich keinen Illusionen darüber hin, wie folgenschwer ein solches Fehlverhalten der "geistlichen Eltern" der Kirche sein mußte. Seinen Glauben an den Fortbestand der Kirche ließ er sich dadurch jedoch nicht in Frage stellen.[11]

Um die damalige an sich gesicherte Kirche stand es nach Luther bedrohlich: "Nulla tentatio omnis tentatio". Ein Symptom dafür war ihm die

---

[2] Martin Brecht, *Martin Luther*, Bd. 1 (3. Aufl., Stuttgart, 1990), 22f.
[3] Brecht, *Luther*, 28.
[4] Brecht, *Luther*, 31f.
[5] Brecht, *Luther*, 109.
[6] *WA* 3. 165,5-23; 579,8-10.
[7] *WA* 3. 405,23-29.
[8] *WA* 4. 573,8-10.
[9] *WA* 3. 572,1-5.
[10] *WA* 4. 186,23-25.
[11] *WA* 3. 216,6-32; 217,18-24.

Verschleuderung des durch Christus und die Heiligen erworbenen Schatzes der Kirche durch die Ablässe, wo doch dieser Schatz eigentlich gemehrt werden mußte. Aber deswegen wird keine totale Krise angenommen: "Non quod thezaurus Ecclesiae sit consumptiblis, sed nobis dico consumptiblis".[12] Angeprangert wird der Greuel der Gelage und des Luxus. Besonders anstößig ist er bei Klerikern und Ordensangehörigen.[13] Geistliche Überheblichkeit, wie sie in vielen Klöstern vorkam, war Luther zutiefst zuwider.[14] Klösterliches Leben durfte, anders als viele es sich damals wünschten, nicht bequem und ruhig sein.[15] Die Armenfürsorge der ganzen Geistlichkeit schien Luther nicht ausreichend zu sein. Sie komme gegenüber dem Aufwand für Bauten und Altäre zu kurz. Aber Gott hasse das ebenso wie die auf Kosten der Almosen erfolgende Zahlung von Ablaßgeldern.[16] Daß Papst und Kardinäle im Krieg gegen die Türken auf militärische Mittel setzten, die die Armen zu bezahlen hatten, anstatt auf Gottes Hilfe, wird kritisiert.[17] Daß sich die "Pontifices" so sehr ihren weltlichen Angelegenheiten widmen und darüber ihre geistlichen Aufgaben vergessen, gilt als heimliche Strafe Gottes.[18] Eine Reform durch die kirchlichen Oberen erwartete Luther nicht. Sie waren uneinsichtig. Er setzte seine Hoffnung bereits auf die politische Gewalt. "Nullum restat remedium, nisi seculares hunc nostrum torporem conspexerint".[19]

Den Plänen Friedrichs des Weisen und Spalatins, Staupitz auf ein Bistum zu bringen, hat sich Luther 1516 energisch und entschieden widersetzt. Nach seiner Ansicht war das Leitungsamt nunmehr ein ganz elendes Geschäft, in dem man sich auf alle römische Verkommenheit einlassen mußte. Mit dem alten Bischofsamt hatte es nichts mehr gemein. Gewaltausübung und Vermögensmehrung seien gefragt. In diese Wirrnis und Stürme bischöflicher Curien wollte Luther gerade Staupitz nicht verwickelt sehen.[20] Der Brief verrät eine äußerst negative Sicht des Bischofsamtes, weil Luther die Ernennung von Staupitz verhindern wollte. Fast gleichzeitig konnte er sich jedoch in Abgrenzung gegenüber den Böhmen gegen die Aufhebung kirchlicher Ordnungen und Ämter, einschließlich des Bischofsamtes, aussprechen.[21]

Überblickt man die aus der Zeit bis 1516, vor allem aus den *Dictata super Psalterium* und der *Praelectio in librum Iudicum* beigebrachten Belege, so

---

[12] *WA* 3. 424,11-425,6; 433,14-18.
[13] *WA* 3. 436,13-22; 509,25.
[14] *WA* 4. 131,15-21.
[15] *WA* 4. 545,28-546,26.
[16] *WA* 4. 571,33-572,14.
[17] *WA* 4. 551,27-35.
[18] *WA* 4. 582,14-24.
[19] *WA* 4. 585,6-26.
[20] *WABr* 1. 44,7-45,43.
[21] *WA* 56. 494,9-17.

fällt auf, daß nicht wenige Punkte der gängigen Klerikerkritik vorkommen. Die monastische Gehorsamsforderung wirkt dabei systemstabilisierend. Eine totale Krise wird nicht angenommem, so bedrohlich und unhaltbar die akute Situation auch sein mag, zumal angesichts des Zornes Gottes. Auch schwere Mißstände werden lediglich moniert, ohne daß zu allgemeinen Aktionen aufgerufen wird. Ein Einschreiten wird allenfalls von der Obrigkeit erwartet. Über sein Lehramt oder sein Provinzialvikariat im Orden hinaus sieht sich Luther persönlich nicht gefordert. Man hat auch nicht den Eindruck, daß er von einer allgemeinen antiklerikalen Animosität bewegt war.

Um 1517 äußert sich Luther mehrfach über die Misere der Predigt. Diese Kritik hängt bereits mit der entstehenden reformatorischen Theologie zusammen. Beklagt wird, daß fast nur moralisch und nicht vom Glauben gepredigt wird, der doch die Voraussetzung für die Werke ist.[22] Die Predigt wird entweder unterlassen oder besteht aus menschlichen Lehren und Gesetzen anstatt des Evangeliums. Wenn das Volk wegbleibt, ist dies darum die Schuld der Prediger.[23] Angesichts der fabulösen Legenden- und Ablaßpredigten erhebt Luther die Forderung einer *maxima reformatio ecclesiae*, die sicherstellt, daß nur Authentisches und Kanonisiertes gepredigt wird. Legenden und Wunder sollen allerdings zugelassen bleiben, wenn sie nicht auf Kosten, sondern zur Illustration des Evangeliums vorgebracht werden.[24]

In diesen Zusammenhang dürfte auch der Sermon gehören, den Luther wohl 1518 dem Propst Georg Mascov entworfen hatte für die Synode des Archidiakonats Leitzkau, zu dem auch Wittenberg gehörte. Die größte Sünde der Priester besteht nicht in fleischlichen Verfehlungen oder Vernachlässigung des Gebets, sondern in der Unterlassung des Wortes der Wahrheit. Darauf müßten die *pontifices* achthaben, tun es jedoch nicht. Die Wurzel der Bosheit im Volk ist der *defectus verbi veritatis*.[25] Die Kritik an der Predigtpraxis ist recht prinzipiell und generell gegen Prediger und Priester gerichtet. Dennoch wird man die dringliche Reformforderung nicht als antiklerikal bezeichnen dürfen. Luther will eine Reform, und die Voraussetzung dafür müßte ein anderes Verhalten und eine andere Einstellung der Prediger sein. Die Standeskritik ist auf den richtigen Inhalt der Verkündigung ausgerichtet. Dies ist von einem pauschalen Antiklerikalismus zu unterscheiden, sonst bekommt man das Proprium dieser reformatorischen Kritik nicht in den Blick.

Im Streit der Kölner Theologen mit Johannes Reuchlin hat Luther schon 1514 für den Humanisten Partei ergriffen. Nach seiner Meinung waren die

---

[22] *WA* 1. 118,28-32.
[23] *WA* 1. 445,18-34.
[24] *WA* 1. 509,34-510,8.
[25] *WA* 1. 12,36-14,13. Die in *WA* vorgenommene Datierung des Sermons auf das Jahr 1512 halte ich für verfrüht. Am ehesten kommt die übernächste der im Dreijahresturnus stattfindenden Synoden in Frage.

Kölner durch menschliche Kritik oder Spott nicht zu belehren; dies vermöge nur Gott. Luther freute sich darüber, daß Rom den Fall an sich gezogen hatte, und hoffte auf die Gelehrsamkeit unter den Kardinälen.[26] Damals bestand also noch sein Vertrauen in die theologischen Qualitäten der Kirchenleitung. Ihn selbst veranlaßte das Fehlverhalten der Kölner Theologen keineswegs zu eigenen Initiativen. Die Misere der Kirche bleibt auch hier zunächst einmal Gott überlassen. Ein von den Erfurter Sympathisanten Reuchlins gegen dessen Gegner verfaßtes Pasquill fand 1516 nicht das Gefallen Luthers, weil es keine Tatsachen enthielt. Obwohl er die Parteinahme für Reuchlin teilte, lehnte er damals noch Streit- und Schmähschriften ab.[27] Noch 1517 hielt er den satirischen *Julius exclusus* des Erasmus für kein angemessenes Mittel, sich mit den Lastern und Miseren der Kirche zu befassen. Sie seien vielmehr mit tiefsten Seufzern zu beklagen.[28] Das Kampfmittel der Satire entdeckte Luther für sich erst im Verlauf des Ablaßstreites. Man kann zwar feststellen, daß Luther die verbreitete Kirchenkritik vielfach teilte. Aber darüber sollte man nicht vergessen, daß dies bei ihm eben zunächst nicht auf eine Antihaltung hinausläuft. Ausgerechnet Luther scheint also ursprünglich allenfalls ein recht reservierter Antiklerikalist gewesen zu sein. Dies nötigt umso mehr, auf die positiven Inhalte zu achten, um die es ihm ging, weil ihnen möglicherweise im reformatorischen Umbruch doch erheblicheres Gewicht zukommt.

Man könnte einwenden, an kräftiger Kritik habe es Luther daneben auch nicht fehlen lassen. Die Theologen, die einen eigenen menschlichen Beitrag zur Rechtfertigung annahmen, apostrophierte er in der Römerbriefvorlesung immerhin als "Sawtheologen". Den scholastischen Doktoren warf er vor, das Volk zu täuschen und nicht zur Wahrheit zu bekehren. Er forderte deshalb zum Gebet um heilige Doktoren auf, die Christus und das Kreuz lehren.[29] Die Auseinandersetzung mit der Scholastik war die erste Frontstellung, in die Luther geriet. Man wird sie aber schwerlich unter dem Antiklerikalismus verrechnen können. Luther ging es nicht um eine Abschaffung der Theologen, sondern um eine alternative Theologie. Letztlich hob er von daher das alte System aus den Angeln.

Aus dem bisher gezeichneten Bild fällt allerdings ein Text heraus, den man als eindeutig antiklerikal reklamieren könnte. In der Römerbriefvorlesung gibt es einen wenig beachteten Exkurs zu Kap. 13,1, der sich mit dem Verhältnis von Geistlichkeit und Laien befaßt und dabei auch das Phänomen des Antiklerikalismus berührt.[30] Luther hielt es für notwendig, *nostri temporis densissimas tenebras* zu beschreiben. Die Geistlichen

---

[26] *WABr* 1. 23f.; 28f.
[27] *WABr* 1. 61,11-16; 63f.
[28] *WABr* 1. 118,3-8.
[29] *WA* 56. 274,14; *WA* 4. 562,24-563,4.
[30] *WA* 56. 476,27-480,16.

verhalten sich wie ein weitgeöffneter, nach zeitlichen Dingen gierender
Schlund und halten nichts für beschwerlicher, als wenn die kirchlichen
Freiheiten, Rechte, Gebiete und Besitztümer verletzt werden. Dagegen gehen
sie mit dem Bannstrahl vor und proklamieren die Gegner als Häretiker sowie
Feinde Gottes und der Kirche. Ob sie selbst Freunde oder nicht viel mehr
Feinde der Kirche sind als jene, darum kümmern sie sich nicht. Frommes
Christsein geht darin auf, daß man die Rechte und Freiheiten der Kirche
schützt, andernfalls ist man kein treuer Sohn und Freund der Kirche.
Kritisiert wird also die Fixierung der Kirche auf ihren rechtlichen und
finanziellen Besitzstand. Die Kirche hat von den weltlichen Fürsten
Reichtümer und Freiheiten empfangen. Zur Zeit der Apostel, als die Priester
aller Gunst würdig waren, zahlten sie trotzdem Steuern und waren der
Obrigkeit untertan. Nunmehr hingegen führen sie nichts weniger als ein
priesterliches Leben, erfreuen sich aber trotzdem der rechtlichen Freistellung.
Für Luther ist das ein seltsamer Zustand. Was die einstigen Priester verdient
gehabt hätten, das genießen die jetzigen unverdientermaßen. Dabei werden
nicht die kirchlichen Sonderrechte kritisiert, sondern ihre Inanspruchnahme
durch böse und gottlose Menschen. Luther fragt deshalb: Was ist, wenn ein
Laie die Kleriker haßt? Er konstatiert ausdrücklich die allgemeine Klage
über den Antiklerikalismus der Laien, nach dessen Ursachen jedoch nicht
gefragt werde. Warum waren die Laien früher den Aposteln und Heiligen
nicht feind, die sie in Armut, Leiden und Tod geführt haben?

Luther erwähnt dann eine mögliche Begründung der geistlichen Besitztümer, mit der er freilich nicht einverstanden ist: Die geistlichen Benefizien
seien wegen der besonderen Pflichten, nämlich der kanonischen Gebete,
gegeben worden. Aber die apostolische Zeit wußte nichts von den priesterlichen Gebeten. Die Priester werden ihrem Beruf nur zum Schein gerecht
und besitzen auch die Güter nur zum Schein. Der Rechtsanspruch wäre
gedeckt, wenn einer sich als guter Priester erweisen würde, andernfalls kann
dies Recht nicht guten Gewissens verfochten werden. Beklagt wird, daß die
Priester den letzten Willen frommer Stifter nicht erfüllen und doch
unbehelligt bleiben. Luther räumt ein, die Kirche müsse arme Priester auf
jeden Fall versorgen. Aber was soll mit den Habgierigen und unersättlich
Reichen geschehen? Luther meint, daß sich auf die Dauer Ansprüche, die
nicht durch Leistungen gedeckt sind, nicht aufrechterhalten lassen. Ließen
sich bisher die ungebildeten Laien hinhalten, so gebe es nunmehr Leute, die
beginnen, die Geheimnisse der Bosheit des Klerus zu kennen und dessen
Pflichten zu unterscheiden.

Nur solche, die sich als wahre Kleriker erweisen, werden sich darum
künftig der Rechte und Freiheiten erfreuen. Luther scheint es, als ob die
weltlichen Machthaber derzeit ihren Pflichten besser nachkommen als die
kirchlichen. Die politische Gewalt übe das Strafamt aus, die kirchliche gehe
lediglich gegen die vor, die ihre Interessen verletzen, und strafe im übrigen
nicht. Ungeeignete Bewerber für kirchliche Stellen werden nicht etwa
abgewiesen, sondern machen sogar Karriere. Dadurch werde die Kirche

verdorben und zum Gegenstand des Hasses. Für Luther ist ein solches Verhalten, das wissentlich und willentlich Anlaß zum Ärgernis gibt, unentschuldbar. Das ganze Rechtssystem der Kirche ist korrumpiert. Die Richter sind selbst Übertreter. Erwähnt wird ein Straßburger Rechtsfall, in dem der Bischof der Rechtsforderung der Stadt gegen einen Kanoniker nicht nachkam. Auch hier kommt Luther auf das Problem zu sprechen, daß Gott derartige Übertretungen zulasse. Dies wird als Mahnung an die Amtsträger verstanden, ihrer Pflichten und der evangelischen Vorschriften eingedenk zu sein. Das Selbstgericht ist also gefordert und nicht die rechtliche Verfolgung anderer. Luther gebraucht hier schärfste Bezeichnungen: *Pharaonici, Satanici, Behemotici*. Eine derartige eigennützige Rechtspraxis möge Gott zerstören.

Luther selbst ist am Ende gewahr geworden, wie scharf er sich geäußert hatte. Beschwörend warnt er davor, ihn in dem nachzuahmen, was er aus Schmerz und Pflicht vorgebracht habe. Tatsächlich hat er den ganzen Passus dann nicht vorgetragen.[31] Aber an sich hielt er die aktuelle Applikation seines durch päpstliche Autorität bestätigten Lehramtes für richtig. Er sah es als seine Aufgabe an, erkanntes Unrecht selbst der Hochgestellten vorzubringen. Dafür bot er am Schluß noch ein Beispiel: Julius II. habe verdienstvollerweise um kleine Besitzansprüche (*facultatulis*), die Venedig der Kirche sündhaft entwendet hatte, einen blutigen Krieg geführt. Daß dies bitter ironisch gemeint ist, beweist vollends die Fortsetzung: Aber keine Sünde sei die ganz verdorbene Schande der Kurie und das außerordentliche Gemisch von allem Luxus, Pomp, Habgier, Ehrgeiz und Tempelschändung. Mit Bernhard weiß sich Luther darin einig, daß der Leitung der Kirche nicht mehr bewußt ist, was eigentlich Sünde ist.

Trotz aller Schärfe der Kritik geht es Luther nicht um die Destruktion, sondern um die Reform des Klerus. Dabei lehnt er eine Festlegung der Priester auf die Funktion des kanonischen Gebets ab. Ihr Besitz wird der Kirche nicht prinzipiell bestritten, auch wenn angedeutet wird, daß sie ursprünglich darauf nicht angewiesen war. Jedenfalls müssen Besitz und Leistung der Priester in einem angemessenen Verhältnis stehen. Die Amtsführung der politischen Gewalt wird der Kirche als Vorbild vorgehalten. Luther macht sich nicht einfach den gängigen Antiklerikalismus zu eigen, sondern äußert sich aus schmerzlicher Betroffenheit und vor allem von Amts wegen als theologischer Lehrer. In der Wahrnehmung dieses Amtes löste er ein Jahr später den Ablaßstreit aus.

Eine Schlüsselfrage ist, in welchem Verhältnis die die Reformation auslösende Ablaßkontroverse zum Antiklerikalismus steht. Man sollte sich darüber verständigen können, daß es Luther in seinen Ablaßthesen und dem Brief an Albrecht von Mainz vorrangig um die wahre Buße gegangen ist.[32]

---

[31] Vgl. *WA* 57. 225f.
[32] *WA* 1. 233-238; *WABr* 1. 108-113.

Der Protest gegen den Ablaß wurde u.a. begleitet von der Kritik an den Bischöfen, die den Ablaß zuließen und die Verkündigung des Evangeliums dadurch verhinderten. Die Kritik an der mit dem Ablaß verbundenen Geldmacherei des Papstes brachte Luther in den Thesen 81 bis 90 besonders vor, und zwar bezeichnenderweise als Anfragen der Laien.[33] Dennoch ist die Ablaßkontroverse ein gutes Beispiel dafür, daß es sich bei der beginnenden Reformation um ein Syndrom handelte, zu dem die persönliche Heilsfrage ebenso gehörte wie die gesellschaftliche Kirchenkritik und einiges andere mehr. Gerade die Kombination aller Motive ergab die kritische Masse. Zutreffend ist, daß die deutschen und römischen Gegner Luthers die Problematik alsbald dann einseitig auf die Frage der päpstlichen Autorität verschoben. Luther selbst hob in seinem (Kleinen) Galaterkommentar von 1519 den Gegensatz seiner Rechtfertigungslehre zur völlig vergesetzlichten römischen Kirche ständig hervor.[34] Ob die von Goertz vorgenommene Verortung der reformatorischen Entdeckung Luthers "im antiklerikalen Kampfmilieu" historisch haltbar und systematisch hilfreich ist, läßt sich bezweifeln. Ebenso ist es gerade angesichts der sich in der Auseinandersetzung entwickelnden Sprache Luthers fraglich, ob sein Haß gegen die Papstkirche "vor allem und zuerst die überpersönliche Sprachgestalt des Antiklerikalismus" gewesen sei, wie Goertz meint.[35] Vieles spricht dafür, daß die Aversion unmittelbarer in Luthers religiöser Erfahrung und Theologie verwurzelt war.

Was den Antiklerikalismus beim jungen Luther insgesamt anbetrifft, ist der Befund also komplex. Ursprünglich ist er gewiß nicht auf dieser Schiene angetreten, und manchmal hat er sich dagegen reserviert verhalten. Der Antiklerikalismus ist keineswegs ein Hauptthema des jungen Luther. Mit dem Ernst seiner frühen Theologie wurde er freilich auch der kirchlichen Mißstände gewahr, und so konnte auch er als Kritiker auftreten. Zum Wortführer der nationalen Rom- und Kirchenkritik ist er allerdings erst 1520 geworden, und sie machte immer nur einen Teil seines theologischen Wollens aus. Die Reformation wird auch sozialgeschichtlich nicht allein aus der Aversion des Antiklerikalismus zu erklären sein. Zu ihr gehören ebenso die Bibel als neue Autorität, die Überwindung der Leistungsfrömmigkeit durch den Rechtfertigungsglauben und, teilweise über Luther hinausgehend, der nicht einfach mit dem Antiklerikalismus gleichzusetzende Spiritualismus als Widerspruch gegen eine materialisierte Religiosität, um nur einige wesentliche Komplexe zu nennen. Äußeres und Inneres, Sozialverhalten und Theologie sowie Frömmigkeit müssen auch hier besser verbunden werden.

---

[33] *WA* 1. 237,19-238,11.

[34] Vgl. Martin Brecht, "Der Zusammenhang von Luthers reformatorischer Entdeckung und reformatorischem Programm als ökumenisches Problem", in *Luthers Sendung für Katholiken und Protestanten*, hg. von K. Lehmann (Freiburg, 1982), 11-30.

[35] Goertz, *Pfaffenhaß*, 87.

Die einseitige These von Goertz kann als Herausforderung zu besserer und genauerer Differenzierung hilfreich sein. Dabei wird dann auch nochmals der von Goertz so beflissen heruntergespielte kreative Beitrag Luthers neu zu gewichten sein.

KLERUS UND ANTIKLERIKALISMUS
IN LUTHERS SCHRIFT
AN DEN CHRISTLICHEN ADEL DEUTSCHER NATION
VON 1520

BERND MOELLER

Universität Göttingen

Fragt man sich, wo im literarischen Werk Martin Luthers ein besonders wichtiger Beitrag zu unserem Thema "Antiklerikalismus" zu erwarten ist, dann liegt es nahe, sich der Schrift *An den Christlichen Adel deutscher Nation* zuzuwenden. Ja, man möchte in diesem Buch einen Schlüsseltext zu unserem Thema vermuten, und zwar in doppelter Hinsicht: Einmal im Blick auf Luthers eigene Gedankenentwicklung und deren literarische Formulierung, zum anderen im Blick auf Luthers Wirkungsgeschichte, im Blick also auf die Leser und damit auf die Geschichte der Reformation.

Die Schrift war ja generell ein Schlüsseltext der Reformation. Sie verdankt das nicht zuletzt dem geschichtlichen Ort, an dem sie entstand und wirksam wurde. Die neuen Inhalte, die sie enthält, wurden in einem Moment formuliert und publiziert, an dem sich ein entscheidender geschichtlicher Umbruch abzeichnete.

Bekanntlich entstand die Schrift an den Adel im Sommer 1520 zwischen dem 7. Juni[1] und dem 20. Juli,[2] in ganz kurzen Wochen.[3] Diese Wochen aber waren eine Entscheidungszeit in Luthers Leben und in der Geschichte der Reformation: Am 15. Juni wurde in Rom die Bannandrohungsbulle unterzeichnet.[4] Das aber heißt: Der Moment, zu dem die Schrift geschrieben wurde, ist dadurch qualifiziert, daß Luther noch kein Ketzer war, noch unverurteilt; es war beinahe der letzte Moment, für den das galt. Dieser Synchronismus[5] ist ein Faktum, das der Historiker konstatiert, doch war er

---

[1] Erste, noch sehr vage Ankündigung gegenüber Spalatin: *WABr* 2. Nr. 298,13-15.

[2] Mitteilung an Linck, die Drucklegung habe begonnen: *WABr* 2. Nr. 314,14-17.

[3] Im Wesentlichen dürfte die Schrift bereits am 23.6. fertiggestellt gewesen sein, dem Tag, an dem die Vorrede an Amsdorff und damit die Ankündigung einer Manuskriptsendung an diesen datiert ist: *WA* 6. 405,7. Vielleicht hat Luther also tatsächlich nur "etwa zwei Wochen" an dem Text gearbeitet, wie Karlheinz Blaschke in der Einleitung seiner Ausgabe (bei H.-U. Delius [Hrsg.], *Martin Luther Studienausgabe* 2 [Berlin, 1982], 91) annimmt.

[4] *Bullarium Romanum*, Taurinensis editio 5 (1860), 757.

[5] Vgl. dazu die aufschlußreiche Tabelle bei Scott Hendrix, *Luther and the Papacy* (Philadelphia, 1981), 95ff.

auch Luther beim Schreiben bewußt, wie wir aus gleichzeitigen Briefzeugnissen wissen,[6] und so dürfte er Auswirkungen auf den Inhalt der Schrift gehabt haben. Vor allem jedoch hatte er, wie es scheint, Auswirkungen auf deren zeitgenössische Wirkungsgeschichte.

Zuerst hierzu: Diese zeitgenössische Wirkungsgeschichte ist, sieht man auf die Hauptzeugnisse, durchaus merkwürdig. Als das Buch Mitte August 1520 erschien,[7] hatte es einen explosionsartigen Erfolg, der, obgleich ja Luthers publizistische Wirkungen zumal in den frühen Jahren auch sonst explosionsartig waren, doch auch innerhalb seines Werkes kaum Analogien hat. Die Schrift wurde noch in den verbleibenden Monaten des Jahres 1520 14 Mal nachgedruckt (in Wittenberg, Leipzig, Augsburg, Basel, Straßburg, München und Halberstadt),[8] wobei wir von dem ursprünglichen Druck zufällig einmal die Auflagenzahl kennen — nicht weniger als 4.000 Exemplare.[9] Selbst wenn man für die Nachdrucke nur die gewöhnliche Auflagenzahl von 1.000 ansetzt, bedeutet dies einen außergewöhnlichen Erfolg. Nicht weniger außergewöhnlich war jedoch, daß er schon nach wenigen Monaten versiegt war. 1521 erschienen nur noch zwei Nachdrucke,[10] seither bis zu Luthers Tod kein einziger mehr — auch in Gesamtausgaben konnten die Zeitgenossen das Buch in späteren Jahren nicht lesen. Weiterhin fällt auf, daß die Schrift über die "deutsche Nation", die im Titel genannt und im Text so mannigfaltig angesprochen ist, publizistisch kaum hinausgewirkt hat. Sie wurde in ihrer Zeit nicht ins Lateinische übersetzt, wie es sonst bei den großen Schriften Luthers die Regel war, und sie erschien zu Luthers Lebzeiten auch nur einmal in einer nichtdeutschen Nationalsprache — 1533, weit entfernt von ihrer Entstehungszeit, auf italienisch, und zwar bei einem Straßburger Drucker und in einer Ausgabe, von der sich in italienischen Bibliotheken, soweit wir wissen, kein einziges Exemplar erhalten hat.[11]

Mir scheint, die in dieser Konfiguration ungewöhnliche Publikationsgeschichte der Schrift an den Adel deutet darauf hin, daß neben dem Text selbst auch dessen literarische Wirkung dadurch beeinflußt worden ist, daß

---

[6] Am deutlichsten der Brief an Spalatin vom 10.7. (*WABr* 2. Nr. 310,6f.): "Ceterum pene opto venire famosam illam e Roma bullam in meam doctrinam ferocientem." Vgl. auch ebd., 25-31. Der kursächsische Hof wurde in der ersten Jahreshälfte 1520 über den Fortgang des römischen Prozesses gegen Luther auf dem Laufenden gehalten, wie W. Borth, *Die Luthersache 1517-1524* (Lübeck, 1970), 72ff., zeigt.

[7] Am 5. 8. wird sein Erscheinen letztmalig als bevorstehend bezeichnet (*WABr* 2. Nr. 324,14), am 18. 8. erstmalig als zurückliegend (ebd. Nr. 327,10f.), am 23. 8. (ebd. Nr. 329,6f.) ist von der zweiten Auflage die Rede.

[8] J. Benzing, *Lutherbibliographie* (Baden-Baden, 1966), Nr. 683-92; 695-97. Dazu H. Claus und M. Pegg, *Ergänzungen zur Bibliographie der zeitgenössischen Lutherdrucke* (Gotha, 1982), 52.

[9] *WABr* 2. Nr. 327,10.

[10] Benzing (wie Anm. 8), Nr. 693f.

[11] Benzing, Nr. 698.

sie an der Scheidelinie der beiden Zeitalter, die durch Luthers Exkommunikation und das Öffentlichwerden seines römischen Prozesses markiert
war, entstand und herauskam. Ich möchte die Annahme wagen, daß viele
ihrer frühen Leser die Schrift noch in dem Bewußtsein kauften und lasen,
daß der Autor unverurteilt war, oder anders und besser gesagt: daß sie das
Buch noch nicht von vornherein in dem Bewußtsein kauften und lasen, es
mit einem ketzerischen Buch zu tun zu haben. Vielleicht stellt gerade die
Schrift an den Adel den Scheitelpunkt dar, an dem Luthers Sache umbrach
— im Sinne der kirchenrechtlichen und politischen Faktizität, nach seinem
eigenen Bewußtsein, aber eben auch für das Bewußtsein der Öffentlichkeit.

Nach diesen Vorbemerkungen zur Fixierung der geschichtlichen Situation
der Schrift *An den Christlichen Adel,* auf die wir zurückkommen werden,
wenden wir uns unter der im Titel des Referats genannten Fragerichtung nun
ihrem Inhalt zu. Jeder von uns weiß, daß auch dieser Inhalt außergewöhnlich
war. Man könnte dies in zwei Aussagen zusammenfassen: Es handelt sich
bei dieser Schrift um das erste ein Reformprogramm entwickelnde deutsche
Buch,das einen breiten publizistischen Erfolg hatte, und es handelte sich in
Luthers schriftstellerischem Werk um das erste und einzige, von dem dies
galt.

Die beiden Teile dieser Aussage weisen in unterschiedliche Richtung:
Einerseits besagt sie, daß keine der in Deutschland erschienenen Reform-
schriften des späteren Mittelalters, auch nicht eine so vielgenannte wie die
Reformatio Sigismundi,[12] an den publizistischen Erfolg von Luthers
Adelsschrift auch nur von ferne heranreicht. Keine hatte eine derart große
Publizität, erst recht hatte keine eine derart plötzliche Publizität. Man wird
hieraus den Schluß ziehen dürfen, daß die Adelsschrift alle früheren
Schriften vergleichbarer Art dadurch übertraf, daß sie ihre Leserschaft aus-
weiten konnte. Die Annahme liegt nahe, daß sie, deutlicher, als das etwa für
die *Reformatio Sigismundi* galt, auch unprofessionelle, unvorgebildete Leser
fand — vielleicht hat tatsächlich "jeder nur einigermaßen am geistigen
Leben interessierte Deutsche damals dieses Buch zur Kenntnis genommen".[13]

In Luthers literarischem Gesamtwerk hingegen bildet es, andererseits,
beinahe so etwas wie einen Fremdkörper. Zumindest findet man ein Buch
mit solcher Thematik dort nicht noch einmal. Zwar hat Luther literarisch
bekanntlich auch in späterer Zeit bei mehreren Gelegenheiten Reformpro-
gramme entwickelt, die über den im engeren Sinn kirchlichen Bereich
hinausgingen und an "weltliche" Adressaten gerichtet waren — am
deutlichsten gilt das für seine Schriften zur Reform des Schulwesens — ;

---

[12] Vg. H. Boockman, "Zu den Wirkungen der 'Reform Kaiser Siegmunds'", in B.
Moeller, H. Patze, K. Stackmann (Hrsg.), *Studien zum städtischen Bildungswesen des
späten Mittelalters und der frühen Neuzeit* (Göttingen, 1983), 112-35.
[13] H. Scheible, "Die Gravamina, Luther und der Wormser Reichstag 1521", *Blätter
für pfälzische Kirchengeschichte* 39 (1972): 58-74, 68.

jedoch hatten sie jeweils ein begrenztes Thema, niemals wieder stand, wie
1520, gewissermaßen das Ganze des bestehenden Kirchen- und Gesell-
schaftssystems zur Debatte.

Das aber war ja in der Schrift *An den Christlichen Adel* in der Tat der
Fall. Programmatisch adressiert an eine bestimmte Gruppe von Lesern, den
"Adel deutscher Nation", d.h. an die weltlichen Machtträger im Reich mit
dem jungen, zum Zeitpunkt der Entstehung und Veröffentlichung der Schrift
zwar gewählten, aber im Reich noch nicht erschienenen und noch nicht
gekrönten jungen Kaiser an der Spitze, war doch in Wahrheit eine viel
weitere Leserschaft angesprochen. Das brachte Luther an einigen Stellen im
Text in direkten Anreden zum Ausdruck — "lieben Christen"[14] oder
"lieben deutschen"[15] — , insbesondere aber dadurch, daß er sich selbst mit
diesen Lesern durchgängig in einem "Wir" zusammenschloß. Sieht man
genau hin, dann zeigt sich, daß die gesamte Schrift von diesem "Wir"
durchzogen ist, in dem der Autor sich mit seinen Lesern solidarisierte und
diese Leser dadurch zugleich in seine Sache hineinzog und gewissermaßen
für sie reklamierte. Denn dieses "Wir" hatte emphatischen Sinn: Die in ihm
Zusammengeschlossenen distanzierten sich zugleich von einer weiteren
Gruppe von Personen, die als "sie" oder "die" ins Abseits gerückt wurden.
Das "Wir" diente also als ein Mittel der Agitation, in ihm ging Parteibildung
vor sich, parteiliche Konfrontation — ein stilistisches und publizistisches
Verfahren, das Luther zwar in einigen deutschen Schriften, z.B. in *Von den
guten Werken*, bereits früher angewendet, jedoch noch nie derart konsequent
durchgeführt hatte.[16]

Es ist offenkundig, daß wir mit diesen Beobachtungen unser Thema
erreicht haben: In dieser die Schrift *An den Christlichen Adel* kennzeichnen-
den Konfrontationsstruktur haben wir das, was man gegebenenfalls als
Luthers "Antiklerikalismus" bezeichnen könnte, vor uns und damit auch den
Beitrag, den dieses so erfolgreiche Buch Luthers, dieser Schlüsseltext der
Reformation, zur Ausbildung des reformatorischen Antiklerikalismus
geleistet haben mag. Freilich ist nun genauer zu klären, wie diese Konfrontation denn angelegt war, wen man also unter dem "Wir" und dem "Sie"
von Luthers Schrift genauer zu verstehen hat. Ich beginne mit der zweiten
Gruppe.

Hier gibt es, wie zunächst einmal prinzipiell festzustellen ist, eines nicht,
nämlich einen pauschalen, undifferenzierten "Antiklerikalismus". An den
hunderten von Stellen, an denen Luther sich in der beschriebenen Weise
distanziert, geschieht dies niemals ohne eine Angabe oder Andeutung
darüber, wer konkret gemeint sei. "Die" Kleriker, "die" Geistlichen sind es

---

[14] *WA* 6. 445,3.

[15] *WA* 6. 415,13.

[16] Der in dieser Hinsicht am deutlichsten ausgearbeitete Textabschnitt ist der über
die "ander maur" (*WA* 6. 411,8-412,38), wo in 67 *WA*-Zeilen 12mal "wir" und 18mal
"sie" in dem im Text gemeinten Sinn begegnen.

nirgends. Im Gegenteil rückt "der Klerus" im engeren Sinn, d.h. die ganze weitläufige und bunte Gesellschaft der *Pfarrgeistlichen*, der Kleriker am einzelnen Ort, in Luthers Adelsschrift überhaupt nirgends in ein wirklich unvorteilhaftes Licht.[17]

Dort, wo man angesichts der zeitgenössischen Diskussionen vor allem einen Seitenhieb oder eine verächtliche Aussage erwarten müßte, in der Passage über den Zölibat,[18] hält sich Luther von Polemik gegenüber den sittlichen Zuständen im Klerus gänzlich fern. Er qualifiziert die Zölibatsbrecher vielmehr als Opfer jener Gesetzlichkeit und Willkür gegenüber den Weisungen der Bibel, die der Papst sich zu Schulden kommen läßt. "Manchen frommen pfarrer, dem sonst niemand kein tadel geben mag",[19] sieht er betroffen, "mancher armer pfaff" ist da in Not geraten.[20] Luther formuliert sein Urteil über die Sexualmoral der Kleriker also in Wendungen, die ein im Grunde positives Pfarrerbild zeigen, und das spiegelt sich in seiner Schrift auch sonst an nicht wenigen Stellen.

Dabei wird freilich Näheres nur über den *Pfarrer im eigentlichen Sinn* gesagt — die zumindest im städtischen Kirchenwesen der Zeit zahlenmäßig dominierende Klerikergruppe, die Inhaber von Meßpfründen, bleibt unerwähnt, sie kommt in der ganzen Schrift an den Adel nicht oder so gut wie nicht in den Blick. Den Pfarrerstand jedoch sieht Luther von Gott selbst eingesetzt,[21] und seine Angehörigen haben als 'Amtleute' in der Christenheit[22] eine Elementaraufgabe, nämlich "ein gemeyn / mit predigen vnnd

---

[17] Abgesehen vielleicht von einer einzigen Stelle, dem Abschnitt über die abgebrochene Kirchenreform in Straßburg (*WA* 6. 422,9-423,5), wo nach Luthers Darstellung der Versuch des Bischofs Wilhelm von Honstein, seine Diözese zu reformieren, "durch anlangen der priesterschafft" vereitelt worden ist und Luther diese Machenschaften der "priester widder yren eygen bischoff" ausdrücklich tadelt; freilich handelte es sich um die Präbendare der beiden Kanonikerstifte Alt- und Jung-St.Peter: F. Rapp, *Réformes et réformation à Strasbourg* (Paris, 1974), 371-93. Dieser Abschnitt von Luthers Schrift hat eine spezifische, in diesem Fall genau bestimmbare Entstehungsgeschichte. Die Kenntnis über die (auf das Jahr 1509 zurückgehenden) Straßburger Vorgänge verdankte Luther Spalatin, wie aus seinem Brief an diesen vom 25.6.1520 (*WABr* 2. Nr. 305,20) hervorgeht: "Argentinensis tragedi memor ero satis loco suo". Er hat aber seine in dieser Briefstelle angedeutete Absicht, sein Wissen im Verlauf seiner Arbeit an der Adelsschrift zu verwerten, in der Weise verwirklicht, daß er den betreffenden Abschnitt in eine bereits fertiggestellte Passage nachträglich einschob, wie aus der Anschlußstelle 423,6 eindeutig hervorgeht, die sich auf den dem Abschnitt über Straßburg vorausgehenden Zusammenhang zurückbezieht. Der Sachverhalt wurde bisher unrichtig gedeutet, z.B. bei K. Bauer, "Luthers Aufruf an den Adel, die Kirche zu reformieren", *ARG* 32 (1935): 167-217, 195ff.

[18] *WA* 6. 440,15-443,24.

[19] *WA* 6. 442,10f.

[20] *WA* 6. 440,16.

[21] *WA* 6. 441,24.

[22] *WA* 6. 408,19.

sacramenten (zu) regierenn".[23] So haben die Christen in ihrer jeweiligen Pfarrei alles, dessen sie für ihr Heil bedürfen,[24] und Luther erwägt — weit entfernt davon, den Aufgabenbereich und die Amtsgewalt der Pfarrer einzuschränken — vielmehr an mehreren Stellen eine Ausweitung: Warum sollen es nicht die Pfarrer sein, die von Ehehindernissen zu dispensieren[25] und über die Validität von Ablaßbriefen, Butterbriefen und Meßbriefen zu entscheiden haben,[26] warum soll ihre Vollmacht der Sündenvergebung durch Reservatsrechte von Oberhirten beschnitten sein?[27] Einen Grund, ihnen das Vermögen oder die Eignung zur Übernahme solcher Aufgaben abzusprechen, scheint Luther nicht zu sehen. Kurzum: *Im Blick auf den Pfarrklerus sind in der Schrift an den Adel antiklerikale Tendenzen nicht zu bemerken.*[28]

Ähnliches aber gilt, wie ich im Vorbeigehen feststelle, in gewisser Hinsicht auch für *Mönche und Nonnen.* Zwar finden sich in der Schrift von 1520 bekanntlich erstmals bei Luther weitreichende Reformforderungen in Bezug auf den Ordensstand. Ein Jahr vor seiner grundsätzlichen Auseinandersetzung mit den Klostergelübden in *De votis monasticis* zieht er bereits eine ganze Reihe von Sachverhalten, die das Mönchtum fundamental prägen, in Zweifel — die Aufteilung in Orden, die Mitwirkung an der Pfarrseelsorge, den Bettel, ja die Beständigkeit der Gelübde[29] — , und er spielt mit der Möglichkeit, Stifter und Klöster in das zurückzuverwandeln, was er für ihren Ursprung hält, in "Christliche schulenn".[30] Deutlich (und anders als im Fall der Pfarrer) beschreibt Luther also diesen geistlichen Stand im defizienten Modus; nicht oder kaum jedoch, indem er ihn total verwirft[31]

---

[23] *WA* 6. 441,24f.

[24] *WA* 6. 450,6f.

[25] *WA* 6. 446,30f.

[26] *WA* 6. 446,31-5.

[27] *WA* 6. 432,14ff.

[28] Sollte Luther damals wirklich, wie H.-J. Goertz schreibt, ein "vitales Interesse" gehabt haben, "sich mit aller Kraft an die Spitze des antiklerikalen Kampfes zu stellen" (H.-J. Goertz, "Antiklerikalismus und Reformation", in H. Bartel u.a. [Hrsg.], *Martin Luther — Leistung und Erbe* [Berlin, 1986], 182-87, 184; ähnlich ders., *Pfaffenhaß und groß Geschrei* [München, 1987], 85f.), dann hätte er hierbei den Pfarrklerus jedenfalls gänzlich geschont.

[29] *WA* 6. 438,14ff.

[30] *WA* 6. 439,37f.

[31] Nur von den "newen Stifften" wird gesagt, sie seien "kein nutz ... odder gar wenig", da ohne *cura animarum* (*WA* 6. 452,11f.) — ein Urteil, das Luther in merkwürdiger Weise den "alten stifftenn vnnd thumen" mit Adelsprivileg erspart (ebd. 5ff.). Dies ist eine der Stellen, an denen eine unmittelbare Rücksichtnahme des Autors auf die adligen Adressaten der Schrift erkennbar wird.

und ihm die christliche Legitimation gänzlich abspricht.[32] Auch die
Mönche gehören in Luthers Schrift im Grunde nicht zu den "Die", von
denen die "Wir" sich distanzieren und mit denen sie sich konfrontiert sehen.
Und dies gilt nun endlich, wenn man genau zusieht, auch für die *Bischöfe*
nicht. Unter den gegebenen Voraussetzungen ist dies geradezu eine
überraschende Beobachtung: Luthers Schrift an den Adel hat im Gegenteil,
so könnte man sagen, episkopalistische Tendenzen, und zwar gleichfalls als
ein durchgehendes Merkmal. Im Grunde findet sich nirgends — wenn man
von einer isolierten und in unserem Zusammenhang uneindeutigen Stelle
absieht[33] — Polemik gegen Bischöfe. Eine Reform der Einsetzung ins
Bischofsamt — Wahl durch "die Christen",[34] Bestätigung durch Mitbischöfe,[35] Investitur durch den Kaiser[36] — wird zwar propagiert; auch konstatiert Luther gelegentlich die Wandlungen, die der Aufgabenbereich der
Bischöfe seit dem Urchristentum erfahren hat, übrigens ohne sie zu
kritisieren.[37] Doch kann ein Bischof auch einmal in freundlichem Licht
erscheinen,[38] vor allem aber geht es Luther in seinen zahlreichen Aussagen
zur Sache darum, die Bischöfe in ihrem Amt zu stützen und zu sichern. Das
soll geschehen, indem der Einfluß des Papstes auf sie vermindert, derjenige
der weltlichen Obrigkeit verstärkt wird. Denn der Papst hat sich — so sieht
es Luther — in den letzten Jahrhunderten die Bischöfe unterworfen, indem
er sie finanziell und zumal rechtlich entmachtete. Bloße "cifren" (d.h.
Nullen),[39] "Ciferen vnd olgotzen"[40] hat er aus ihnen gemacht, das eigenständige Amt ist ihnen genommen, "eytel pfarrer" sind sie geworden, damit
"der Bapst allein sey vbir sie".[41] Demgegenüber wäre nunmehr ein
kaiserliches Gesetz erforderlich, das die Abholung des Palliums aus Rom
untersagte,[42] die eidlichen Verpflichtungen der Bischöfe dem Papst
gegenüber wären aufzuheben,[43] alle Lehens- und Pfründangelegenheiten
ihnen zuzuweisen.[44] Ja, das Amt des Primas Germaniae sähe Luther gern

---

[32] Erst mit dreißig Jahren sollen in Zukunft die Gelübde abgelegt werden (*WA* 6.
468,10); als "ein sondere gnad" bleiben sie jedoch im Sinn des Paulus gültige
Ordnung (ebd. sowie 441,34ff.).
[33] *WA* 6. 430,17ff.; der Widerspruch gegen die "grewlich schinderey der Oficiel".
Der Absatz dürfte ebenfalls eine nachträgliche Einfügung sein.
[34] *WA* 6. 408,5; 455,36.
[35] *WA* 6. 429,11f.
[36] *WA* 6. 433,22-25.
[37] *WA* 6. 440,26-29.
[38] *WA* 6. 422,9ff.
[39] *WA* 6. 422,9ff.
[40] *WA* 6. 428,18.
[41] *WA* 6. 429,16.
[42] *WA* 6. 429,8f. Wie es in Frankreich in der Pragmatischen Sanktion von Bourges
vorlag!
[43] *WA* 6. 433,10f.
[44] *WA* 6. 431,3f.

ausgebaut.[45] Gerade nur als Appellations- oder Schiedsinstanz will er den
Papst den Bischöfen noch vorordnen[46] — das Ganze läuft also auf ein
sowohl nationalkirchliches[47] als auch episkopalistisches, man könnte sagen:
ein germanikanisches Programm von Reformen hinaus.

Unsere Untersuchung der antiklerikalen Elemente in Luthers Schrift an
den Adel führt uns auf ein eindeutiges, freilich zugleich sonderbares Resultat
zu: Es gibt im Grunde nur *ein* klerikales Amt und eine Institution, gegen die
Luther streitet — *den Papst und die päpstliche Kurie*, wobei die für gänzlich
unnütz erklärten Kardinäle nicht zu vergessen sind.[48] Das sind jene
"Romanisten",[49] die überall in der Schrift apostrophiert werden, "der Bapst
vnd die seinen",[50] "die Bepste vnd Romer"[51] — jenes Institut, das sich als
"stathelter des erhebten Christi ym hymel"[52] und als "der allerheyligst"[53]
ausgibt, in Wahrheit jedoch "ein vorstorer der Christenheit vnd abetheter"[54]
ist, ein Feind der Christenheit[55] und somit "der aller sundigst",[56] der
sowohl die weltliche wie die geistliche Ordnung zerstört und den Luther
daher unverblümt als Werkzeug des Teufels ansieht,[57] während er seine
volle Identifizierung mit dem Antichrist in einem leisen Vorbehalt gerade
eben noch vermeidet: "Er solt schier der widderchrist sein".[58]

Luthers *Antiklerikalismus* läuft in der Schrift an den Adel also, so könnte
man unsere bisherige Untersuchung zusammenfassen, auf *Antipapalismus*
hinaus, wobei allerdings *diese* Konfrontation nahezu nicht mehr zu steigern
ist und absolute, universale Züge trägt. An einer Stelle[59] kommt diese
Zuordnung und Verteilung der Fronten geradezu darin zum Ausdruck, daß
er den Bischöfen, Priestern und Doktoren die Aufgabe zuschreibt, sich gegen
Papst und Kurie zu wenden, sie also zumindest potentiell auf seiner eigenen
Seite sieht. Es verunklärt diesen eindeutigen Befund nur wenig, wenn man
feststellt, daß Luther freilich auch für den Papst und dessen Amt einen Platz
in der Christenheit sieht — es gäbe wohl Geschäfte für ihn: Als oberster

---

[45] *WA* 6. 431,6f.
[46] *WA* 6. 429,29-31.
[47] A. Adam, "Die Nationalkirche bei Luther", *ARG* 35 (1938): 39-62, 48ff.
[48] *WA* 6. 416,17ff.
[49] *WA* 6. 414,36; 406,21.
[50] *WA* 6. 459,17. Vgl. 410,24; 454,32; 457,22.
[51] *WA* 6. 406,18.
[52] *WA* 6. 416,13.
[53] *WA* 6. 453,12.
[54] *WA* 6. 423,28.
[55] *WA* 6. 428,24.
[56] *WA* 6. 453,12.
[57] *WA* 6. 410,24; 411,19f.; 426,13.
[58] *WA* 6. 434,15. Vgl. 411,6f.; 425,22; 429,23; 434,4; 453,19.
[59] *WA* 6. 426,21-3.

Bischof könnte er in der Kirche schlichten,[60] den Kaiser krönen,[61] "studieren vnd beetten", um "antwort zugeben / in des glaubens sachen";[62] insbesondere aber hätte er, wie alle anderen Geistlichen, "das wort gottis vnnd die sacrament (zu) handeln"[63] und wäre da, "in geistlichen ampten / als do sein predigen vnnd absoluieren", auch der weltlichen Gewalt vorgeordnet.[64] Doch sind das angesichts der Realität des Amtsmißbrauchs und der Preisgabe des göttlichen Wortes bloß theoretische Erwägungen — faktisch ist "der Bapst mit seinen Romischen prackticken"[65] unscheidbar vereinigt.[66]

Soviel zu den konkreten Aussagen Luthers über den Klerus in diesem Schlüsseltext des Jahres 1520. Es fehlt ihnen, so darf man sie vielleicht zusammenfassen, weder an Drastik noch an Eindeutigkeit — nur eines fehlt ihnen so ziemlich, der Antiklerikalismus, jedenfalls im üblichen Sinn des Begriffs.

Nun sind wir freilich mit unserer Untersuchung der Schrift noch nicht am Ende. Wir haben vielmehr eine Passage bisher ausgespart und umgangen, die recht verstanden maßgeblich zur Sache gehört — den Abschnitt über das *Priestertum aller Glaubenden*, der die ganze Schrift eröffnet und das eigentlich neue Element in ihr darstellt. Also jene berühmte Darlegung, in der Luther nachzuweisen suchte, daß die in der Kirche üblich gewordene Scheidung von Klerus und Laien als zweier "Stände" in der Christenheit im Blick auf das maßgebliche Kriterium des Christseins, die Zugehörigkeit zum Leibe Christi, untergeordnete Bedeutung habe. Von hier aus gesehen sind alle Christen "eyn Corper" und "warhafftig geystlichs stands".[67] Die bleibende Differenz zwischen Geistlichen und Laien ist eine solche des Amtes, und auch da sind die Scheidungen aufzuheben, da die Geistlichen aus der Gemeinde heraus (Luther sagt: aus "der gantzen samlung"[68]) zu wählen und gegebenenfalls auch wieder abzuwählen, also wieder in Laien zu verwandeln sind.[69]

---

[60] *WA* 6. 429,28ff.

[61] *WA* 6. 433,26f.

[62] *WA* 6. 433,6; 417,23f.

[63] *WA* 6. 409,3.

[64] *WA* 6. 434,6f.

[65] *WA* 6. 428,12.

[66] *WA* 6. 419,31ff.: Die Erwägung einer Divergenz zwischen Papst und Kurie bleibt isoliert und beiläufig und wird sogleich beiseitegeschoben.

[67] *WA* 6. 407,13-15.

[68] *WA* 6. 407,30.

[69] *WA* 6. 408,23f. Das Satzfragment "Es mug ein priester nymmer mehr anders den priester odder ein ley werden" ist entgegen der Angabe in der Studienausgabe (wie Anm. 3) 2, 101 Anm. 53 folgendermaßen aufzulösen: "Es könne ein Priester niemals mehr etwas anderes als ein Priester und niemals wieder ein Laie werden".

Dies wurde im Argumentationszusammenhang der Schrift an den Adel mit einer begrenzten Absicht dargelegt. Luther wollte beweisen, daß die unmittelbaren Adressaten des Buches, der "Adel", die "weltlich hirschafft", als "mitglid ... des christlichen Corpers"[70] Eingriffs- und Notstandsrechte im geistlichen Bereich besäßen. Doch begründete er seine Behauptung umfassend, mit fundamentalen Bibelzitaten, und in ganz knapper Form, auf wenigen Seiten, ohne weitläufige Deduktionen, als evidente, unwiderlegbare Erkenntnis. So war dies ohne Zweifel die eigentliche Sensation in Luthers Buch, und sie war es auch in der Geschichte von Luthers eigenem Denken. Eine ganz neue Vision von der christlichen Gesellschaft leuchtete hier auf.

Zwar war die Idee des allgemeinen Priestertums der Glaubenden (oder wie er in der Schrift an den Adel sagte: der Getauften) in Luthers bisheriger theologischer Entwicklung angelegt und in deren Zusammenhang konsequent. Auch hatte er das Motiv gelegentlich schon angedeutet,[71] freilich noch nie derart deutlich herausgehoben und noch nie in einen kirchlich-politischen Zusammenhang gestellt. Insoweit war es auch für ihn neu. Das läßt sich in der Schrift selbst daran erkennen, daß deren Gedankengang keineswegs durchgehend von der neuen Erkenntnis organisiert wird. Es gibt vor allem in den späteren Passagen, dort wo von den Einzelmaßnahmen der Kirchenreform die Rede ist, Stellen, an denen ein heutiger Leser sich wundern muß, wie wenig Luther seine große Vision selbst im Kopf zu haben schien. Nur ganz selten wird sie noch einmal erwähnt,[72] und es finden sich Vorschläge, die mit ihr kaum in Einklang zu bringen sind, wie etwa der zur Reform der Domstifte.[73]

Aber wie es nun mit Luthers eigener Stellung zu dieser Idee auch immer aussehen mochte — daß sie für die *Leser* sensationell neu war, liegt auf der Hand. Jeden von ihnen, in welchem Stand er sich auch befinden mochte, ging sie unmittelbar und persönlich an. Jeder wurde da als Christ gewissermaßen neu definiert, in seiner Gottesbeziehung ebenso wie in seiner sozialen Position. Alle, Laien wie Kleriker, fanden sich in diese neue Gemeinschaft der "Wir" versetzt, die sich von der in Wahrheit ganz kleinen Gruppe von "Die" im fernen Rom abgrenzte. Auch hier wurde zwar im Grunde kein Antiklerikalismus propagiert, wohl aber die Beseitigung herkömmlicher klerikaler Sonderrechte begründet und damit ein neues Verhältnis von Klerikern und Laien beschrieben. Luther führte damit allen Lesern ein neues

---

[70] *WA* 6. 410,3f.

[71] Erstmals, soweit ich sehe, in dem Brief an Spalatin vom 18.12.1519 (*WABr* 1. Nr. 231,28-42); ferner im Sermon von dem Neuen Testament, *WA* 6. 370f. Vgl. auch den Brief an J. Heß vom 27.4.1520, *WABr* 2. Nr.280,10-12.

[72] Immerhin *WA* 6. 449,26ff.

[73] *WA* 6. 452,19ff. Luther vertritt hier zwar mit dem Prinzip "ein Mann — eine Stelle" eine Neuerung, doch hält er an den Kategorien des Pfründenwesens und an den geistlichen Ämtern sine cura animarum fest und damit an bestimmenden Einrichtungen der mittelalterlichen Priesterkirche.

Selbstverständnis, ein neues Gemeinschaftsbewußtsein und eine neue Aufgabenstellung vor Augen und brachte ihnen dies alles nahe. Und zwar in einer leicht lesbaren Sprache und mit literarischer Kunst und als ein Autor, der sich Interesse und Vertrauen seiner Leser bereits früher erworben hatte. So wurde die Glaubwürdigkeit des Buches durch die Neuheit seiner Inhalte nicht belastet, die lange Liste aktueller Reformforderungen steigerte seine Attraktivität, und auch der kühne und erstmalige Schritt Luthers, sich nunmehr gewissermaßen selbst auf die höchste Ebene der Gesellschaft, die Ebene der Regierenden — Kaiser, Papst, Fürsten — zu stellen und sich ihnen als Gesprächspartner, ja als Ratgeber und Zensor aufzudrängen, mußte die Leser nicht notwendigerweise befremden und abschrecken.

Der literarische Erfolg der Schrift an den Adel läßt sich so also, denke ich, ohne große Mühe nachvollziehen. Jedoch spielte der geschichtliche Moment ihrer Entstehung dabei eine gewichtige Rolle. Um das anfangs hierzu Gesagte noch einmal aufzunehmen: Es war dies gewissermaßen das letzte Buch Luthers vor dem großen Bruch, dieser zeichnete sich für den Autor bereits ab, als er es schrieb, während er vielen zeitgenössischen Lesern erst nach der Lektüre bekannt und bewußt geworden sein dürfte. Wie hat man dies zu bewerten?

Was Luther angeht, so dürfte unsere Beobachtung, daß sich der Antiklerikalismus der Schrift auf Antipapalismus reduziert und konzentriert, durchaus in einen Zusammenhang mit dieser Entstehungsgeschichte zu bringen sein, ebenso Luthers kühner Schritt in die große Politik. Luther hatte, so darf man auch auf Grund anderer Quellenzeugnisse annehmen,[74] erkannt, daß in Sachen Papst die Akten geschlossen waren oder daß dies jedenfalls unmittelbar bevorstand; daß die innerkirchliche Reform, wie sie ihm bisher vorgeschwebt hatte, nicht zustande kommen würde, schien ihm, wenn er gebannt war, entschieden. In Sachen Kaiser und Reich dagegen war noch alles offen, der junge Kaiser noch außerhalb Deutschlands und gewissermaßen noch nicht im Amt. Hoffnungen, er werde eine wahrhaft "kaiserliche" Politik einschlagen, machten sich viele, Chancen und Anzeichen dafür schien es zu geben. So lag es für Luther, den der kursächsische Hof in der einen oder anderen Form beriet, nahe, die Dinge nunmehr "auf den Punkt" zu bringen, und auch die enorme Eile, in der das geschah, mochte gefordert erscheinen.

Soviel zur Situation und den Intentionen Luthers. Aber wie mußte die Schrift zu diesem Zeitpunkt auf die Leser wirken? Hierzu zunächst einige Vorbehalte: Es ist klar, daß diese Frage weder pauschal noch zuverlässig zu beantworten ist; es fehlt an Quellen, und "die" Leser sind eine fiktive Größe. Mehr als begründete Spekulationen sind nicht möglich.

Hierfür allerdings gibt es Anhaltspunkte. Die Plötzlichkeit des Erfolgs ist eine wichtige Gegebenheit. Und es ist auffällig und zu beachten, daß die

---

[74] S.o., 353-4.

Schrift sofort ganze Ketten von Gegenschriften veranlaßt hat. Es folgte ein Streitschriftenkrieg, wie ihn Luther in solcher Ausdehnung und Heftigkeit bis dahin noch nie erlebt hatte und an dem er sich selbst mit dem lebhaftesten Engagement beteiligte.[75]

Diese Geschehnisse würden eine eigene Untersuchung erfordern. Im vorliegenden Rahmen muß ich mich auf eine Feststellung beschränken, die freilich ihr Gewicht hat: Die Gegner, die in der Folgezeit mit literarischen Bestreitungen von Luthers Buch auf den Markt traten — Eck, Emser, Murner und Wulffer — , wendeten sich bis auf den Erstgenannten allesamt gegen das allgemeine Priestertum und traten für die Scheidung von Klerus und Laien und die Sonderstellung der Kleriker ein; dies war in jedem Fall der entscheidende Angriffspunkt, während die Papstfrage in den Hintergrund trat. Mit anderen Worten: Zumindest diese literarisch auftretenden Gegner nahmen das eigentlich Sensationelle an Luthers Buch auf und würdigten dessen Sprengwirkung, freilich ohne alle Bereitschaft, seiner neuen Vision einer christlichen Gesellschaft zu folgen.

Auch wenn man in Rechnung stellt, daß der publizistische Erfolg dieser Gegenschriften bescheiden und mit demjenigen Luthers nicht zu vergleichen war,[76] erlaubt der Sachverhalt doch wohl allgemeinere Schlußfolgerungen. Durch diesen Streitschriftenkrieg wurde dem interessierten Publikum, falls daran ein Zweifel bestand, vor Augen geführt, daß Luthers Vision nicht ohne weiteres in die Wirklichkeit umzusetzen war, und zwar geschah dies durch Kleriker. Diese selbst also waren es, die die Fronten, die Luther eher zu vermeiden oder zu verschleiern gesucht hatte, aufrissen. Damit bestätigten und verstärkten sie, daß zu derselben Zeit die Zugehörigkeit Luthers zur verfaßten Kirche durch die Exkommunikation beendet und das Gespräch mit ihm offiziell abgebrochen wurde. Es erwies sich gewissermaßen, daß ein auf Antipapalismus sich beschränkender Antiklerikalismus unter den gegebenen Umständen keine realistische Möglichkeit mehr war.

---

[75] Bereits im Herbst 1520 lag eine Streitschrift Johann Ecks gegen Luthers Adelsschrift vor (abgedr. in Corpus Cath. 14 [Münster, 1928], 1-18), auf die Luther sogleich antwortete (WA 6. 579-594). Es folgte vor und nach dem Jahreswechsel 1520/21 der "Streitschriftenkrieg" Luthers mit Emser, in dem sich beide Autoren viermal literarisch äußerten (L. Enders [Hrsg.], Luther und Emser. Ihre Streitschriften aus dem Jahre 1521 1-2 [Halle, 1890-92]; WA 7. 259-265; 266-283; 614-688; 8. 241-254). In der dritten seiner Antwortschriften an Emser reagierte Luther auch auf die am Jahresanfang 1521 erschienene Streitschrift Thomas Murners (W. Pfeiffer-Belli [Hrsg.], Thomas Murners deutsche Schriften, Bd. 7 [Berlin, 1928], 59-117). Eine letzte Bestreitung der Adelsschrift endlich erschien Anfang 1522 aus der Feder von Wolfgang Wulffer (vgl. W. Klaiber [Hrsg.], Katholische Kontroverstheologen und Reformer des 16.Jahrhunderts, RGST 116 [Münster, 1978], Nr. 3444).

[76] Keine von ihnen erfuhr einen Nachdruck. Vgl. Klaiber (wie Anm. 75), Nr. 974; 977-79; 2648; 3444.

Sehe ich recht, dann hat dies die Geschichte des reformatorischen Antiklerikalismus beeinflußt. Es ließe sich m.E. im einzelnen zeigen und sollte einmal untersucht werden, wie in Luthers Schriften von nun an der Ton gegenüber Klerikern, Bischöfen und Mönchen schärfer wurde[77] — die Zustimmung zum Priestertum der Glaubenden wurde in Zukunft zu einem Maßstab für sein Urteil über den Klerus. In der reformatorischen Flugschriftenliteratur aber, die seit 1521 anzuschwellen begann, spielte die Behauptung Luthers, daß alle Glaubenden Priester seien, sogleich und permanent eine wichtige Rolle, zumal mit dem Akzent, daß dies für alle *Laien* gelte.[78] Die Abgrenzung gegenüber Geistlichen jeglichen Standes, also Antiklerikalismus im eigentlichen Sinn, wurde seither zu einem reformatorischen Programmpunkt.

---

[77] In der im März 1521 abgefaßten 3. Streitschrift gegen Emser (*WA* 7. 679,6-12) liest man: "Ich hab meynß dunckens den Adell und welt mehr strafft denn euch geystlichen, nemlich yn dem buch von den gutten wercken, zehen geboten und an den deutschen Adel hab ich doch noch nie keyn mall die geystliche laster recht antastett, als unkeuscheyt, geytz, haß, fraß, hoffart, tracheit, on yn dißem einigen buch an deutschen Adell, da ich doch nie yn gemeyn der geystlichen, sondern des Bapsts und Römischen hoffs geytz unnd eyn kleyn teyll seynes grewlichen weßens antzeygt."
[78] Auch hierzu wären in Zukunft umfassende Untersuchungen wünschenswert. Einen ersten Schritt bedeutet: M. Arnold, *Handwerker als theologische Schriftsteller. Studien zu Flugschriften der frühen Reformation (1523-1525)* (Göttingen, 1990).

JE GEISTLICHER ... JE BLINDER:
ANTICLERICALISM, THE LAW, AND SOCIAL ETHICS IN LUTHER'S SERMONS ON MATTHEW 22:34-41

ROBERT J. BAST

University of Arizona, Tucson

Material aplenty exists in the major treatises for conducting an investigation into what the term anticlericalism means in relation to Luther.[1] Often overlooked in this regard, however, are the sermons, which contain a rich harvest of information. This investigation will concentrate on one little-known series of sermons preached by Luther on a single biblical text almost annually between the years of 1522 and 1537. I intend to demonstrate both the interdependance and the importance of three central concepts in these sermons: anticlericalism, the doctrine of the Law, and social ethics.

In the years between 1521 and 1537 Luther preached thirteen times on Jesus' summary of the Law of Moses as recorded in the gospel of Matthew, chapter 22, verses 34-41. While the majority of these sermons were preached before the congregation of the Wittenberg Stadtkirche, several of them reached a far wider audience through the printed press.[2] The evidence derived from Luther's interpretation of this one text over a period of some fifteen years leads us to the following conclusions:

First: when we speak of Luther's 'Kleruskritik', a basic distinction must be made between two phases of his career. Through 1521, Luther's critique is 'reformist'.[3] Though his rhetoric can be harsh indeed, Luther wields his scalpel to heal, not to kill, working to excise malignant growths from the body of what may yet become a healthy institution. This phase reaches its peak in 1521, with the publication of *De votis monasticis Martini Lutheri iudicium*. Shortly thereafter, however, we can document a shift in Luther's

---

[1] Heinz-Meinolf Stamm examines 24 treatises, 6 letters, and 3 sermons — though none of the latter from the series here under consideration — in *Luthers Stellung zum Ordensleben*, Veröffentlichungen des Instituts für Europäische Geschichte Mainz 101 (Wiesbaden, 1980).

[2] The sermon of 1526, for example, went through four editions; copies have been found in thirteen different cities, from Wittenberg to Munich, Berlin to London. The sermon of 1537 was also widely disseminated under the title *Ein Newe predigt von dem Gesetz und Euangelio*. For details of publication, see *WA* 45. xxvii-xxix.

[3] For a similar conclusion see Bernhard Lohse, "Die Kritik am Mönchtum bei Luther und Melanchthon", in Vilmos Viljas, ed., *Luther und Melanchthon* (Göttingen, 1961), 129-45.

attitude. As our sermons demonstrate, after 1522 Luther becomes far more radical, and his position can best be termed 'abolitionist'.[4] From here on, Luther begins to call with increasing clarity for the abolition of the doctrinally and socially privileged clerical estate: the 'geistliche Stand'. It is in this second phase that Luther develops an argument which we may justly term *anti*clerical, in as far as his energies are directed against the Roman clergy, and aimed at their dissolution.

Second: the transition from 'reform' to 'abolition' is fueled by a fundamental and incessant appeal to the Law of God as the standard against which all human institutions and relationships must be measured. It is not the doctrine of grace, but the doctrine of the Law which ultimately propels Luther from a reformist to an abolitionist stance vis à vis the Roman clergy.

Third: these sermons chart the confluence of two major streams of Luther's condemnation of the traditional clergy. In the wake of his so-called Reformation breakthrough, Luther quickly spoke out against what he saw as the various abuses of the office of priest: the Mass mumbled without understanding, for example, and performed privately and arithmetically for the souls of the dead, or as a necessary reenactment of the sacrifice of Christ. In *De votis monasticis* we encounter another current, as Luther attacks the monastic life for falling short of Jesus' command to love God and the neighbor rightly. In the sermons on Matthew 22:34-41, these two streams flow together to create a raging river of denunciation which can accurately be called anticlerical, as it seeks to wash away not simply the abuses, but the existence of the 'geistliche Stand'.

Finally, the anticlericalism characteristic of this abolitionist phase of Luther's career has a special function. It is no mere polemic, but serves rather as a foil against which Luther develops an ambitious ideal for social reform: an evangelical social ethic.[5] Here again, it is the Law which serves Luther's purpose. The injunction to practice love for God and neighbor gradually develops into the lens through which Luther reads the Ten Commandments. These function both as the source from which he sketches

---

[4] Cf. *De votis monasticis*: "Ita Bernhardus sub voto sine voto, ceu Apostolus sub lege sine lege, agebat, sed non ideo votum aut lex in doctrinam et formam vitae redigi, imo aboleri debet." *WA* 8. 617,32-35. Nevertheless I will argue that this text as a whole is not abolitionist, but marks a point of transition between Luther's hope for reform and his call for abolition. For a different view see Hans-Jürgen Goertz, n. 34, below.

[5] The extent to which Luther's social ethic is new must await a comparative study of the ethical principles evident in late medieval sermonic literature on the Ten Commandments. While a wealth of such sources exists, to my knowledge there has been no comprehensive analysis of them since the appearance of Johannes Geffcken's *Bildercatechismus des fünfzehnten Jahrhunderts*, vol. 1, *Die zehn Gebote* (Leipzig, 1855).

his concepts for social reform, and as the divine authority which compels him to do so.

I. LUTHER'S ANTICLERICALISM

The significance of Luther's shift from 'reform' to 'abolition' can best be grasped after we briefly consider two treatises which fall within the former phase. The first of these is *Eine Kurze Erklärung der Zehn Gebote*, written in 1518. Within this simple treatise for the instruction of the laity, Luther lists examples of sins which violate the divine mandates. According to his interpretation, the fourth commandment ("Honor your father and your mother") specifically condemns those who scorn or criticise the 'Priester-stand'.[6] This treatise, published verbatim in 1520, suggests that long after Luther 'discovered' the gospel, he continued to appeal to the Ten Commandments in an effort to encourage lay subservience toward the clerical estate.

A strikingly different picture emerges from the treatise of 1521 which marks the culmination of Luther's reformist phase. In *De Votis Monasticis*, Luther applies the standard of the Law to the monastic orders in a sharp and furious fashion. His decision to do so merits careful attention.

In the introductory letter addressed to his father, Luther claims that he has only recently discovered the importance of the Law of God.[7] This discovery, he says, sprouted from a seed planted sixteen years earlier during the conflict which followed upon young Martin's announcement that, despite his father's objections, he intended to become a monk. Luther recalls:

> ... you suddenly responded with a reply so fitting and so much to the point that in all my life I have hardly ever heard any man say anything which struck me so deeply and stayed with me so long. You said 'Have you not also heard that fathers must be obeyed?'[8]

Though shaken by this retort, says Luther, he persevered in his decision, confident that he followed the better course. Now, however — that is, in 1521, as he writes this treatise — he is equally as sure that he was wrong.

And so Luther changes course. His interpretation of the fourth commandment in 1518 and again in 1520 stands firmly within the tradition of

---

[6] "Wer briester standt unehret, nach redet und beleidigt." *WA* 1. 252,36-37.

[7] "Scire te volo, filium tuum eo promovisse, ut iam persuasissimus sit, nihil esse sanctius, nihil prius, nihil religiousus observandum, quam divinum mandatum. 'Infoeliciter (inquies) scilicet de hac re unquam dubitasti et nunc tandem haec ita habere didicisti?' Imo foelicissime, non solum enim dubitavi, sed plane ignoravi haec ita habere." *WA* 8. 573,12-17.

[8] "... repente tu me reverberas et retundis tam opportune et apte, ut in tota vita mea ex homine vix audierem verbum, quod potentius in me sonuerit et heserit. 'Et non etiam (dicebas) audisti tu parentibus esse obediendum?'" *WA* 8. 574,4-8.

the medieval Church: the clergy are to enjoy a position of honor since they
stand 'in loco parentis'. In *De votis monasticis*, however, it is precisely this
command which becomes the basis for a substantial part of Luther's attack
on monasticism.[9] To pledge allegiance to a clerical superior as ersatz father
is to subject oneself to a human office which usurps the command of the
Law of God. Therefore, Luther rebukes both monks and priests for
withdrawing themselves from obedience to their parents under the pretence
of serving God, "as though there were any other service to God except the
keeping of his commandments, which includes obedience to parents."[10]

It is clear, then, that during his months on the Wartburg Luther's views
on monasticism began to undergo fundamental change.[11] Existential
struggle commonly drove Luther to theological reflection on biblical texts
— this was the scenario behind the Reformation breakthrough, in which
'Anfechtung' drove him to the book of Romans, and to the rediscovery of
the doctrine of grace 'sola fide'. And this is also the scenario behind
Luther's critique of monastic vows. This time, however, Luther's personal
drama was resolved not by the doctrine of grace, on which scholarship has
generally concentrated, but by new insights into the significance of God's
law. With this new understanding, Luther retreats from his earlier position
on the honor due to the 'Priesterstand', and modifies it to the detriment of
his contemporaries: true spiritual fathers are not the traditional clergy, but
those who teach us to obey God's commandments before all else.[12]

As Luther employs the standard of the Law, his argument in *De votis
monasticis* spills over the boundaries of vows alone to become a far broader
critique. In short, Luther determines that in practice, monasticism violates
the Law at every turn: the first three commandments teach that God must
be honored and obeyed — yet monks want to honor themselves by earning
salvation through their own merits. The last seven commandments require
that one love and serve the neighbor — yet monks flee from the larger circle
of human relationships which God has established and take refuge in

---

[9] Despite the narrow scope of Luther's attack suggested by the title of his treatise,
he does not limit himself to the denunciation of monastic vows alone. Rather, in
many places his critique spills over and covers the institution of monasticism per se.
See for example *WA* 8. 621,9-11: "Quare quocunque te veteris, invenies institutum
impium, sacrilegum, blasphemum, adversarium Christo esse natura sua. ..."

[10] "... monachos et sacerdotes ... qui specie pietatis et titulo servitutis dei parentum
autoritati se subtrahunt, quasi ulla sit servitus dei alia, quam mandatus eius obedire,
inter quae est et obedientia parentum." *WA* 8. 576,10-13.

[11] Cf. Martin Brecht, *Martin Luther*, vol. 1, *Ordnung und Abgrenzung der
Reformation 1521-1532* (Stuttgart, 1986), 30-34.

[12] "Spirituales patres sunt, qui nos docent ante omnia mandatis dei obedire. ..." *WA*
8. 627,8. From this position, of course, Luther and other protestant reformers would
later insist that the fourth commandment required one to honor *pastors* who preached
according to the Word of God.

cloisters, where they are of no use to anyone. So goes the tenor of Luther's attack.[13]

Nevertheless, *De votis monasticis* is a reformist work. Just as Luther seems ready to consign monasticism to the dustbin of history, he stops short of calling for its wholesale dissolution. Toward the end of the treatise he proposes the radical cure that could yet save the patient's life: the monastery might be salvaged as a short-term abode for the voluntary schooling of adolescents "in faith and Christian discipline".[14]

The sermons on Matthew 22:34-41, however, mark a shift in Luther's thinking which began shortly after the publication of the treatise on monastic vows. Seen across the historical spectrum, this shift may be understood as Luther's growing conviction that the clerical estate per se — not just wrong thinking about the Mass, nor the improper practice of the monastic life — is nothing less than a nefarious human innovation based on human teaching; not simply a benign alternative lifestyle, but an audacious and diabolical affront to the structures of society which God ordained, and to the divine laws which God decreed.

These sermons allow us to chart this development with some precision. Beginning already in the sermon of October 19, 1522 — just five months after the publication of *De votis monasticis* — Luther again measures the clergy against the standard of the Law. Here, however, the target is not merely the monastery: Luther expands his critique to include nuns as well as all monks, and priests who would rather fast, pray the seven hours and be faithful to the Pope than obey Christ's command to feed and console the neighbor.[15] As one would expect, Luther is hardly silent about the basic disjunction he senses between the gospel of grace and the system of works-righteousness. Yet there is more to it than that. We find in this series an equally devastating attack on clerical morality, though not the sort of popular complaints which focused on the alleged drunkenness and whoring of the clergy. Rather, Luther assaults the failure of the clerical estate to observe Jesus' command to love the neighbor in socially useful acts of charity.

---

[13] This argument is carried out in two sections of the text. The first table of the Law is considered under IIII. "Vota Adversari Praeceptis Dei", *WA* 8. 617,17ff; the second table is treated as a subsection following directly under the heading, "Adversari Vota Caritati", *WA* 8. 623,4ff.

[14] "Et monasteria ad priscum ritum deo nihil aliud habere, quam Christianas scholas pro aetate iuvenili et ardente instituenda in fide et pia disciplina usque ad annos maturioris aetatis." *WA* 8. 641,7-9. See also *WA* 8. 646,39-647,6; 648,31-35; 649,23-26.

[15] "Ein pfaff der hatt ein gebott, von gott nicht suendern vom Papst, als die Septem horas betten, fasten die langen fasten, das und dis thun: er hengt dem mer an, des Papsts gehorsam zu erfuellen, den das er das zu lieb Christo tutt, Er leiß er seinen nechsten hunger und nott leyden." *WA* 10 III. 344,3-7.

On these grounds alone Luther uses his sermon of 1522, preached at the court in Weimar, to call upon the monks to leave the monasteries. His verdict could not be more conclusive: "the monastic life is completely wicked, for it does not help the neighbor."[16] Luther claims that the special status accorded the clergy has dazzled their perception; so enchanted are they with their own useless works that they have lost sight of the commandments of Christ. Nevertheless, they boast they they are the most spiritual of all. Hence Luther's punning verdict against the 'geistliche Stand': *je geistlicher, ... je blinder* — the more spiritual (or clerical), the more blind.[17]

We encounter this theme again and again, each time Luther takes up the subject of the summary of the Law, until in 1531 we find the clearest exposition of Luther's conviction that the entire clerical estate is a diabolical human construct, set both apart from and against the social orders of magistrate, pastor and family which God has ordained. "If the Pope and the Carthusians do not leave their orders and enter God's orders, they are of the devil."[18] This is the fundamental manifest of what we must call Luther's anticlericalism.

II. LUTHER'S ANTICLERICALISM AND THE LAW

Ernst Wolff has called Luther's doctrine of Law and Gospel an 'Irrgarten', a labyrinth, which defies a simple or perhaps even a definitive clarification.[19] The doctrine of the Law has been a theological battleground as well, and from the sixteenth century to the present, confessional struggles have been fought upon it, with various sides calling on Luther as their champion. The present study is neither the place to try the labyrinth nor to leap into the fray. Instead, I intend to focus primarily upon how Luther uses the Law in

---

[16] "Nun wen ich gleich ein Cartheuser ader muench wer, so ich dan befuendt das ich meynem nechsten nit hulff darinnen, so soel ich den orden frey zubrechen und dem nechsten helffen, got will ia kein werck an die lieb haben, da richt dich nach. Darumb ist der muenchen leben alles boeß, dan es hilfft dem nechsten nit." *WA* 10 III. 344,32-36.

[17] "... die selben menschen wissen wider vom cleinsten noch groesten gebott Christi. Also ie geistlicher und gleisnern, ie blinder. Aber dennoch ruemen sie sich die geistlichen die fruemsten zu sein." *WA* 10 III. 344,37-40.

[18] "Papa, Carthusianus, trit er nicht erauß und in disen orden, ßo ist er ouch des teuffels." *WA* 34 II. 313,28-29.

[19] "'Habere Christum Omnia Mosi', Bemerkungen zum Problem 'Gesetz und Evangelium'," *Peregrinatio II, Studien zur reformatorischen Theologie, zum Kirchenrecht und zur Sozialethik* (Munich, 1965), 22.

these sermons in an effort to better understand the relation of that theme to the others evident in these sources.[20]

First, it is clear that Luther appeals to the Law as the divine authority which permits him to criticize the institutional principles and the pious praxis of the established clergy. This belief, evident already in *De votis monasticis*, is apparent in each of the thirteen sermons on the summary of the Law as well. In essence, this can be understood as Luther's search for a divine law with which to replace canon law.[21]

Second, Luther's appeal to the Law in these sources is not one-dimensional, but presents several faces. In the sermons from 1522-1526, Luther is careful to treat the "gesetz und gebott Christi" — love God and your neighbor — as the standard and master over over all other laws, including the Ten Commandments.[22] Yet as the series progresses (especially from 1528 onward) this distinction fades away, and Luther focuses more and more insistently on obedience to the Decalogue itself.[23] One explanation for this phenomenon seems to be a change of emphasis best understood by recourse to the famous paradox so central to Luther's 1520 treatise, *Von der Freiheit eines Christenmenschen*. For in the early sermons, Luther's concern is primarily with Christan freedom; in the latter, with Christian servanthood. The early emphasis makes sense if, as I have been arguing, this sermon series is to be seen as an extension of Luther's theses in *De Votis Monasticis*, which ends with the plea that in the name Christian love and Christian freedom, conscience-stricken monks must be permitted to break their vows and leave the monastaries. Luther emphasizes freedom in an attempt to restrain the human impulse to emulate the clerical estate by trusting in works which, ultimately, cannot satisfy the God who requires perfect love toward himself and the neighbor.

---

[20] While I have not yet encountered a broad survey of these sermons in the secondary literature, there are several excellent studies of Luther's preaching on the Law in general. See Gerhard Heintze, *Luthers Predigt von Gesetz und Evangelium* (Munich, 1958), and Martin Schloemann, *Natürliches und Gepredigtes Gesetz bei Luther, Eine Studie zur Frage nach der Einheit der Gesetzesauffassung Luthers mit besonderer Berücksichtigung seiner Auseinandersetzung mit den Antinomern* (Berlin, 1961).

[21] See for example Luther's reinterpretation of the traditional maxim, "Kyrchen gutter syndt unsers hergots gutter", *WA* 34 II. 328,7-329,2.

[22] "Dis gebot der liebe ist gezogen durch alle gesetz und alle gesetz muessen lencken nach der liebe. Denn sie ist ein regel und meisterin aller gesetz. ..." *WA* 20. 510,29-30.

[23] In the sermon of 1533, the distinction between the law of love and the Ten Commandments disappears completely. There Luther compares the monastic orders to the Jews, and accuses both groups of having forgotten the Ten Commandments, 'which even our boys know': "nempe Timere et amare deum u. deinde honorem habere parentibus, Non occidere u. Et hoc possunt pueri dicere: Ey das thue, Ama deum et proximum." *WA* 37. 172,2-4.

Luther would discover, however, that Christian freedom can be heady stuff: easily misunderstood and easily abused.[24] His increasing preoccupation with the Ten Commandments can thus be seen as a response to problems which arose from the introduction of evangelical doctrine itself. Even among those sympathetic toward Luther — often with widely different levels of understanding, and for widely diverse reasons — the magnitude of his reform program fostered uncertainty. Luther's reinterpretation of the Christian faith undermined a centuries-old consensus on the social guidelines for recognizing good and evil. At the heart of his theology stood the message that the most notorious sinner could become a saint — and not by the public manifestation of repentance (that is, good works), but through faith alone. The other side of the coin proved equally unsettling: the most exemplary good works might be nothing less than the guilded mask behind which lurks a diabolical sinner.

One need not have possessed a great deal of theological sophistication to grasp the revolutionary nature of this message. Almost overnight new preachers were vilifying ancient expressions of piety like the pilgrimage, the Mass, and the monastic life, while lauding such scandals as the marriage of monks, nuns and priests. The new theology provoked at least bewilderment; often uproar.[25] In a second phase, then, Luther was forced to justify his reinterpretation of the daily business of the Christian life. And as our sermons demonstrate, Luther appealed to the Law of God as the source which revealed the structures and institutions which God had ordained for human society, and the guidelines by which human relationships must actually be lived.

By using the commmandments like this, Luther himself bursts the narrow bonds of interpretation which have been placed upon that abstraction commonly referred to as his 'doctrine of the Law'. Admittedly, Luther himself provided grist for the mill of the systematic theologians, most notably in his Galatians commentary of 1535. There he clearly spells out two uses of the Law, and two only: its theological use is to drive the sinner to seek grace; its civil use is to restrain sin and punish sinners temporally, through coercive force.

In our sermons, however, Luther's use of the Law cannot be forced into this simple schema. The 'usus theologicus' is readily apparent on nearly every page. Yet when Luther appeals to the Ten Commandments to teach

---

[24] On the shift from 'freedom' to 'discipline' in the Reformation see Steven Ozment, *The Reformation in the Cities* (New Haven, 1975), 151ff.

[25] Luther was not unaware of this problem. In the second sermon preached on October 19, 1522, he caricatures the response with which many must have greeted his message of grace 'sola fide': "Ey soellen wir nit gute werck thun? sein doch vorzeitten auch frum leutt gewest die soelchs gethan haben. Mein vatter und mutter haben also glaubt, wu die hin sein gefaren, da wil ich auch hin faren: die predigen wider gott und thun unrecht." *WA* 10 III. 347,31-348,1.

what *true* good works are, or to define the godly social orders, then we go far beyond the traditional understanding of the civil use of the Law. Indeed after 1528 we find Luther frequently insisting with ever greater intensity that obedience to the Law must be a normative part of the Christian life for the believer who has been justified by Christ. We have not been forgiven so that we can disregard the Law, he says in 1537. We do not teach that faith means you no longer need to love God and your neighbor. Instead,

> we were forgiven so that we might begin to keep the Law. This is the eternal, immoveable, unchanging will of God. ... Christ promises also to give the Holy Spirit, with which the heart begins to love God and to keep his Law.[26]

This later approach to the Law probably owes something both to the so-called antinomian controversy within the evangelical camp, and to the disappointing results of the Church Visitations of 1529; the former is explicitly mentioned in the later sermons, while the latter may be perceived behind some of Luther's pessimistic rumblings. Yet Luther's appeal to the Law began much earlier as the matrix for his anticlericalism, and arose from his conviction that the clerical estate had failed not only the Gospel but also the Law; not in its doctrinal responsibilities alone, but in its social responsibilities as well. His attack on the clergy after the publication of *De votis monasticis* stems therefore from the conviction that the works performed by the clergy are human fabrications which serve no social good; the works which God requires are revealed in the Ten Commandments and serve the neighbor. And as we shall see in the next section, this anticlericalism in turn served as the backdrop against which Luther could proceed to develop his own vision for a new, godly society.

III. THE EVANGELICAL SOCIAL ETHIC

Intimately connected with Luther's attack on the clerical estate per se is his attack on the nature of the piety it engendered. With a mixture of scorn, ridicule, and thundering admonition he assaults in these sermons the whole range of traditional pious praxis: pilgrimages, devotion to the saints, confraternities, private masses, endowed altars, images, the rosary, the monastic life itself — all are dismissed as unacceptable expressions of piety, as selfish attempts to secure personal salvation. The fault, he says, lies with

---

[26] "Also wird uns erstlich durch Christum geschencket, das wir das Gesetz nicht erfuellen, und die sunde ganz und gar vergeben, Aber doch nicht also oder dazu geschencket, das wir forthin nicht solten das Gesetz halten ... oder das man solt also leren: Wenn du den glauben hast, so darffstu nicht mehr Gott und den Nehesten lieben, Sonder das das Gesetz nu erst moege angefangen und gehalten werden, welches ist der ewige, unverrueckliche, unwandelbarer wille Gottes. ... Darnach verhaisset er auch den heiligen Geist zu geben, damit das herz anfahe Gott zu lieben und sein Gebott zu halten." *WA* 45. 149,15-21; 25-26.

the example set by the clerical estate, among whom the monks in particular are guilty of drawing the common folk away from the Ten Commandments, which reveal the works truly pleasing to God.[27]

Therefore Luther sets out on an ambitious program to reorient the piety of believers. He castigates those who think to serve God by withdrawing from the world: scholars and lawyers, for example, who say to themselves, "Until now I have served the world; now I shall serve God", and thereafter enter a cloister. "To creep into a corner? To help and advise no one? What does God need with such service?"[28]

For Luther, two essential characteristics serve to distinguish the false good works of the clerical estate from the true good works required by God. They must be socially useful, directed toward the neighbor for the betterment of his or her physical and spiritual wellbeing. But they must not be performed as if they were necessary for salvation. Rather, they should flow from love for God, and gratitude for grace. These new emphases in Protestant thought have been described by Heiko A. Oberman as the 'radical horizontalization' of social ethics: the believer, saved by faith alone, is freed from a self-centered concentration on personal salvation, and can thus do good works toward the neighbor for the neighbor's sake alone.[29]

That, at any rate, is how Luther would like it to work. Yet an abundance of evidence, from visitation records to Luther's personal observations, suggests that progress was slow at best.[30] This explains the third major theme developed in these sermons. Luther attempts to impel his audience to an evangelical form of piety. Individualistic works aimed at earning grace

---

[27] "Sic quando quaeris Monachum de bonis operibus, hellt er dir nicht fur 10 praecepta. Du must ein Munch werden, walfart aufrichten, da weisst er dich hin inn schlauraffen land a praeceptis dei, das ist das lohn der menschen leren, die solche werck auffwerffen und mutzen, das die leute da durch verblendet werden und sehen die decem praecepta nicht mehr." WA 37. 172,17-22.

[28] "Sic doctores et iuristae, so sie lang der welt gedienet hatten, dicebant: hab ich bis her der welt gedienet, iam deo serviam. ... ynn ein winckel kriechen, neimand helffen, raten, was darf unser herr Gott des diensts, den du yhm thusts?" WA 36. 339,29-34.

[29] The implications of this important theme for the various representatives of the Protestant movement are discussed by Oberman in *Masters of the Reformation: The emergence of a new intellectual climate in Europe* (Cambridge, 1981), 276; 294.

[30] For evidence from the visitation records see Gerald Strauss, *Luther's House of Learning: Indoctrination of the Young in the German Reformation* (Baltimore, 1978), 249-67, and Susan C. Karant-Nunn, *Luther's Pastors: The Reformation in the Ernestine Countryside* (Philadelphia, 1979), 21-7. Luther himself complains of the slow pace of moral reform in Wittenberg: "Saepe monui, ut haberetis charitatem invicem, sed peiores fitis, quam prius eratis. ..." WA 10 III. 190,3ff. Such statements must be used with caution, however. As the rest of this passage shows, Luther considered the moral problems of his congregation to be relative: the new standards of the gospel revealed sin which had previously gone unnoticed.

must be replaced by good works which focus on the needs of the neighbor; psalms must give way to service. Not heaven, but "herunter": this world is the scene of action, the place where God commands that faith find expression. In order to redirect popular piety, Luther employs a striking rhetorical device, adopting the voice of Christ himself. "Down here! Down here! says Christ. You find me in the poor. I am too lofty for you in heaven, you will lose your way in the heights."[31]

This attempt to redirect the practice of piety might be understood by borrowing a term from literary criticism. Luther's admonitions can be interpreted as the 'defamiliarisation' of the neighbor; the search for a device with which to stir the believer into seeing the neighbor in a new light.[32] "The world is full of God", Luther says; "in every lane, in front of your very door you find Christ."[33]

The call for faith active in service — so strong in these sermons — leads Luther to recast his famous concept of the priesthood of all believers. In *Von der Freiheit eines Christenmenschen* it is of course faith which functions as the great equalizer.[34] In the sermon of 1531, however, this concept is daringly reformulated: "Love makes us the greatest priests, greater than the Pope."[35]

The evangelical social guidelines articulated in these sermons were not intended to serve one particular social class, or to function exclusively in one social setting. Indeed, Luther repeatedly condemns the social separatism of the clerical estate: by withdrawing into cloister and convent, they narrowly restrict the community in which faith must be practiced. In contrast, Luther seeks to establish a communal ethical principle which can be applied across the social spectrum without limitation.[36] Nevertheless, certain themes within these sermons would have been of particular interest

---

[31] "... 'herundter, herundter', sagt Christus, 'du findest mich yn den armen, ich bin dir zuhoch ym hymel, du verstygest dich sonst'." *WA* 20. 517,31-518,1. For similar statements on this theme in this series see *WA* 29. 560,18; *WA* 32. 128,20-21; *WA* 36. 339,1ff.

[32] The term comes from Viktor Shklovsky; see Raman Selden, *A Readers Guide to Contemporary Literary Theory*, 2nd ed. (Lexington, 1989), 10ff.

[33] "Also ist die welt vol vol Gottes. In allem gassen, fur diener thur findest du Christum." *WA* 20. 514,27-28.

[34] Hans-Jürgen Goertz sees this concept itself as the foundation for the argument to abolish the clerical estate: *Pfaffenhaß und groß Geschrei* (Munich, 1987), 66. Yet while the doctrine undercuts the role of priest as mediator, it does not address the existence of monasticism as a legitimate form of Christian life: Luther launches that attack in the sermons under consideration here.

[35] "Nam dileccio macht uns die hohesten pfaffen ultra Papam." *WA* 34 II. 321,25-26.

[36] Peter Blickle discusses the communal nature of the entire Protestant movement in *Gemeindereformation. Die Menschen des 16. Jahrhunderts auf dem Weg zum Heil* (Munich, 1987), 122.

in the cities. To city governments already intent upon circumscribing the social and legal privileges of the local clergy, these sermons on the summary of the Law, so critical of the social uselessness of the clerical estate, offered a powerful theological weapon.

From our modern perspective, Luther's evangelical social program cannot be regarded as exemplary. It is strongly colored by a paternalism and an authoritarianism which have not withstood the course of time. Yet within their historical context, the sermons on Matthew 22:34-41 help to establish the role of anticlericalism in the progress of the Reformation movement. Luther's appeal to the Law of God against the clerical estate encouraged a strain of anticlericalism with which lay people could justify their rejection of clerical dominance in society.

GEISTBEGABTE GEGEN GEISTLOSE:
TYPEN DES PNEUMATOLOGISCHEN ANTIKLERIKALISMUS —
ZUR VIELFALT DER LUTHER-REZEPTION IN DER FRÜHEN REFORMATIONSBEWEGUNG (VOR 1525)

BERNDT HAMM[*]

Universität Erlangen-Nürnberg

I. DER INTERPRETATIONSANSATZ DES 'ANTIKLERIKALISMUS'-BEGRIFFS

Das Phänomen des Antiklerikalismus eignet sich zwar nicht als Zugangsweg zu einer Gesamtdeutung der Reformation, doch bietet es einen der wichtigsten Schlüssel zum Verständnis des sprunghaften Anwachsens der Reformationsbewegung nach Luthers Thesenanschlag. Freilich ist zu betonen, daß zunächst einmal (zumal beim gegenwärtigen Stand der Forschung) der allgemeine Begriff 'Antiklerikalismus' weniger erklärend als vielmehr erklärungsbedürftig ist. Als Begriff bietet er keine Erklärung für spätmittelalterliche und reformatorische Kirchenkritik, sondern bedarf er der Erklärung von den vielfältigen und z.T. gegenläufigen Ansätzen der Polemik, des Erneuerungsverlangens, der Reform- und Reformationsansätze her. So läßt die gegenwärtige Verwendung des Antiklerikalismus-Begriffs ein grundlegendes terminologisches Problem in der Schwebe: Wann wird Kritik am Klerus zum Antiklerikalismus? Gehört bereits eine partielle Kritik an bestimmten Gruppen des spätmittelalterlichen Klerus und an bestimmten Zuständen, die als provokative Mißstände empfunden werden, zum Phänomen des Antiklerikalismus (in einem weiteren Sinne), auch wenn sich mit dieser Kritik höchste Verehrung der priesterlichen Gnadenvermittlung, spezieller Kleriker-Gemeinschaften und vorbildhafter priesterlicher Leitgestalten, ja massivste Kirchenfrömmigkeit verbinden kann? Oder versteht man — in einem engeren Sinne — unter Antiklerikalismus eine ins Prinzipielle und Generelle gehende feindliche Haltung gegen den Klerus insgesamt und eine Abwendung vom hierarchischen System der spätmittelalterlichen Kirche überhaupt?

---

[*] Bei Zitaten aus frühneuhochdeutschen Quellen, auch aus kritischen Editionen, wurden die Groß- und Kleinschreibung, die Getrennt- und Zusammenschreibung sowie der vokalische und konsonantische Gebrauch von u und v bzw. i und j normalisiert. Auch wählte ich dort, wo es mir grammatikalisch korrekter bzw. zur Erhellung des Sinns nützlich erschien, eine eigene Interpunktion.

So fragwürdig der Antiklerikalismus-Begriff als schillerndes und tückisches Konstrukt geschichtswissenschaftlicher Terminologie ist, so hat er doch den Vorzug, daß er, behutsam verwendet, den Blick des Historikers auf vier Aspekte der reformatorischen Polemik gegen den katholischen Klerus lenkt, genauer gesagt auf zwei Aspekt-Paare: einerseits auf die *Kontinuität* zu spätmittelalterlichen Erscheinungsformen der Kritik an Klerus und Hierarchie; andererseits auf den systemsprengenden *Umbruch* gegenüber jenem Pfaffenhaß und jenen Reformbemühungen, die sich systemimmanent innerhalb der spätmittelalterlichen Koordinaten einer selbstverständlichen Kirchlichkeit und grundlegenden Anerkennung hierarchischer Strukturen bewegen; einerseits weist die Untersuchung des reformatorischen Antiklerikalismus auf eine innere thematische *Kohärenz* der reformatorischen Bewegung in ihrer antihierarchischen, antipapalen, antikurialen, antiepiskopalen, antimonastischen, antisacerdotalen Frontstellung[1] — eine Kohärenz, die um so deutlicher wird, wenn man (durchaus sachgemäß) die Spielarten des frühen reformatorischen Antiklerikalismus als Variationen der Luther-Rezeption begreift; andererseits zeigt gerade die Beachtung des Antiklerikalismus in paradigmatischer Weise eine *Vielfalt* der reformatorischen Ansätze, die schon vor 1525 auffallend ist und zu sorgfältigen Differenzierungen, gerade auch innerhalb der Luther-Rezeption, nötigt.

II. "WILDWUCHS" ODER "LUTHERISCHE ENGFÜHRUNG"?

Im folgenden wende ich mich besonders dem zuletzt genannten Paar 'Kohärenz und Vielfalt' und dabei speziell dem Phänomen der Vielstimmigkeit, Multiformität und Typenvielfalt im reformatorischen Antiklerikalismus zu. Von da her fällt auch neues Licht auf die Frage, ob man die frühe Reformation bis 1525 mit Franz Lau als "Wildwuchs" oder eher mit Bernd Moeller als eine "lutherische Engführung" charakterisieren will. "Wildwuchs" steht für Vielgestaltigkeit, für das Ungenormte und Ungeklärte, für eine fehlende einheitliche Ausrichtung und für ein unkontrolliertes Wuchern verschiedener Lehrweisen und Formen des Gemeindelebens.[2] "Lutherische

---

[1] Auf den Antiklerikalismus als Schlüssel zum Verständnis der Kohärenz des vielfältigen reformatorischen Umbruchs weist Hans-Jürgen Goertz, *Pfaffenhaß und groß Geschrei. Die reformatorischen Bewegungen in Deutschland 1517-1529* (München, 1987), 59 und 68.

[2] Franz Lau/Ernst Bizer, *Reformationsgeschichte Deutschlands bis 1555,* = *Die Kirche in ihrer Geschichte* Bd. 3 Lief. K (Göttingen, 1964; 2. Aufl., 1969), darin: Franz Lau, "Reformationsgeschichte bis 1532 (Manuskript 1962 abgeschlossen)", K 32f. und 43. Der gesamte § 2 (K 17-43) trägt die Überschrift: "Anbruch und Wildwuchs der Reformation". Es folgt § 3: "Die Entstehung reformatorischen Kirchentums" (K 43-65). Der Übergang vom Wildwuchs zum "geordneten evangelischen Kirchenwesen" wird so beschrieben: "Die im Bauernkrieg gesammelten Erfahrungen machten es aber unmöglich, die reformatorische Bewegung einfach wild

Engführung" hingegen steht in kritischer Wendung gegen Laus These für einen "theologischen Grundkonsens", der "sich in überraschendem Maße in Übereinstimmung mit den theologischen Grundaussagen Luthers" befinde, für ein "bemerkenswertes Ausmaß" an Einheitlichkeit der Doktrin und Programmatik in der frühreformatorischen Bewegung bis zum Bauernkriegsjahr.[3]

---

weiterwachsen zu lassen. Es wurde notwendig, Sicherungen gegen antiautoritäre Ausbrüche zu schaffen und klarzustellen, daß die von Luther u.a. im Bauernkrieg vertretenen Grundsätze (Obrigkeitsgehorsam) Geltung behielten. Das zwang zur Einführung klarer kirchlicher Ordnungen, auch zur Klarstellung über die Lehre, die die Geistlichen ihrer Predigt zugrunde zu legen hatten." (K 43)

[3] Bernd Moeller, "Was wurde in der Frühzeit der Reformation in den deutschen Städten gepredigt?", ARG 75 (1984): 176-93; 192f. Moeller untersucht in diesem Aufsatz eine bestimmte Quellengruppe: "die bisher übersehene Quellengattung der 'Predigtsummarien' in reformatorischen Flugschriften" (177f.), doch bezieht er dann am Ende die zitierten zusammenfassenden Bemerkungen über die "lutherische Engführung" allgemein auf "die frühe Reformation bis etwa zum Bauernkriegsjahr 1525 jedenfalls auf dem städtischen Kampffeld" (193). In einem Vortrag auf dem 7. Internationalen Kongreß für Lutherforschung, Oslo August 1988, hat Moeller die These unterstrichen, daß "die Jahre vor 1525 als eine Phase der 'lutherischen Engführung' zu charakterisieren" seien. Er bestimmt diesen Zeitraum der reformatorischen Bewegung als "eine Phase der Integration unter dem Vorzeichen und bestimmenden Einfluß Luthers". Die "Gemeinsamkeit" habe "seit dem Spätjahr 1524 in Diffusion umzuschlagen" begonnen. Ders., "Die Rezeption Luthers in der frühen Reformation", LuJ 57 (1990): 57-71; 65f. und besonders Anm. 13. Moellers These hat Widerspruch erfahren durch Susan C. Karant-Nunn, "What Was Preached in German Cities in the Early Years of the Reformation? Wildwuchs Versus Lutheran Unity", in P. N. Bebb, S. Marshall (Hgg.), The Process of Change in Early Modern Europe. Essays in Honor of Miriam Usher Chrisman (Athens, Ohio, 1988), 81-96. Im Blick auf Predigergestalten der frühen Reformationszeit in Sachsen und Thüringen (wie Johann Sylvius Egranus, Thomas Müntzer, Paul Lindenau, Andreas Bodenstein von Karlstadt, Gabriel Zwilling, Georg Amandus und Jakob Strauss) kommt die Verfasserin zu dem Ergebnis, daß Lau mit seiner Wildwuchs-These Recht hat — wobei sie 'Wildwuchs' definiert als "the rapid and disorderly growth of the evangelical movement" und als "spontaneous religious individualism". Aus den folgenden Ausführungen wird deutlich werden, warum ich mich einer so rückhaltlosen Zustimmung zu Lau und einer so generellen Ablehnung der Moellerschen Auffassung nicht anschließen kann. Vgl. neuerdings auch einen Vortrag von Miriam U. Chrisman, der unter sozialem Aspekt die Verschiedenartigkeit der Laien-Flugschriften in der frühen Reformationszeit herausstellt und von dieser Quellenbasis her die Suche nach Einheit in der Reformation — auch für die Jahre 1520-1525 — scharf kritisiert. Frau Prof. Chrisman hat diesen Vortrag über "The Reformation of the Laity" auf dem Kongreß "The Reformation in Germany and Europe: Interpretations and Issues", Washington, D.C. 25.-30. Sept. 1990 gehalten und mir freundlicherweise ihr Typoskript zur Verfügung gestellt.

III. ANTIKLERIKALISMUS UND PNEUMATOLOGIE

Bei den innerreformatorischen Konflikten zwischen Luther (bzw. den ihm
nahestehenden Theologen) und den sog. "Schwärmern", also Spiritualisten
und Täufern, aber auch im Abendmahlsstreit zwischen der lutherischen
Gruppe und den Schweizern sowie Oberdeutschen spielte bekanntlich die
Lehre vom Hl. Geist, besonders die Verhältnisbestimmung von Geist und
Kreatur (d.h. Wort, Schrift, Brot und Wein), eine zentrale Rolle: Die
Notwendigkeit des Geistbesitzes und einer so gegebenen inneren Unmittelbarkeit der geisterfüllten Seele wird ausgespielt gegen die angeblich
Geistlosen und 'Schriftgelehrten', die einen eingebildeten ('gedichteten')
Glauben an geistferne, 'tote' Kreaturen binden;[4] die Weltüberlegenheit des
göttlichen Geistes und des von ihm bewirkten lebendigen Glaubens wird
geltend gemacht gegen eine sich an äußere Heilsmittel hängende 'Kreatur-
vergötzung', die den Kampf gegen die mittelalterlich-katholische Veräußerlichung der Religion und für eine Erneuerung der Gottesverehrung 'im Geist
und in der Wahrheit' nicht konsequent weiterführe.[5] In diese Richtung geht
die antilutherische Polemik von so unterschiedlichen Theologen wie Andreas
Karlstadt, Hans Denck und Thomas Müntzer einerseits und Zwingli und
seinen Anhängern andererseits. Die Namen dieser Theologen weisen
zugleich darauf hin, daß diese fundamentalen pneumatologischen, mit der
Christologie unlösbar verwobenen Gegensätze schon vor 1525 bestehen, z.T.
bereits in offener Auseinandersetzung ausgetragen, z.T. (wie im Falle
Dencks und Zwinglis) latent den späteren Konflikt vorbereitend.
   Man darf aber die Vielgestaltigkeit, die sich in der frühreformatorischen
Auffassung vom Hl. Geist und in pneumatologisch begründeten Argumen-
tationsformen zeigt, nicht auf die scharfen Kontraste und Konflikte zwischen
Luther, Karlstadt, Müntzer, Zwingli und ihren jeweiligen Schülerschaften
reduzieren (wobei Zwingli aufgrund weit fundamentalerer Gemeinsamkeiten
mit Luther eigentlich nicht in einem Atemzug mit Karlstadt und noch
weniger mit Müntzer genannt werden kann[6]). Gerade der Antiklerikalismus
in den ersten Jahren der Reformation zeigt ein vielfältiges Spektrum
pneumatologischer Ansätze und Argumentationsebenen zwischen den Polen
Luther und Müntzer oder Luther und Karlstadt, so wie umgekehrt gerade die
Berücksichtigung des Argumentierens mit dem Hl. Geist die Differenziertheit des reformatorischen Antiklerikalismus und seiner Artikulationsweisen
erkennen läßt. Ich verwende daher Aussagen über den Hl. Geist als
thematischen Schlüssel, um in exemplarischer Weise die Vielfalt des
reformatorischen Antiklerikalismus der Jahre 1520 bis 1525 und damit

---

[4] So die Argumentation im Einflußbereich Müntzers und Karlstadts.
[5] So besonders die Argumentation im Einflußbereich Zwinglis.
[6] Vgl. Berndt Hamm, *Zwinglis Reformation der Freiheit* (Neukirchen-Vluyn, 1988),
besonders 53-62.

überhaupt die theologische Vielgestaltigkeit der frühen Reformation zu verdeutlichen.

Die pneumatologische Problemstellung bietet sich als exemplarischer Ansatz besonders aus zwei Gründen an: 1. Mit der Frage der Geistmitteilung und des Geistbesitzes verbindet sich nach allgemeinreformatorischer Auffassung elementar das persönliche Gewissensproblem der Gnaden- und Heilsgewißheit des Glaubens, das ethische Problem des neuen Lebens und das ekklesiologische Problem der Vollmacht und Legitimität wahrer Kirche und ihres geistlichen Amtes. In der Geistthematik laufen also alle Fäden des reformatorischen Umbruchs zusammen; hier konkretisieren sich Gotteslehre und Christologie in der Frage, was im einzelnen Gläubigen und in der christlichen Gemeinde geistlich 'ankommt' und wie es ankommt. Immer dann, wenn es im antiklerikalen Kampf um Begründung neuer Gewißheit und Sicherheit und neuer Vollmacht und Legitimität gegen falsche Sicherheiten, verweigerte Gewißheiten, Scheinvollmacht und angemaßte Legitimität geht, ist explizit oder implizit die Frage nach dem Ort des Heiligen Geistes und der Art seines Wirkens gestellt. 2. Eines der zentralen Probleme bereits des spätmittelalterlichen und erst recht des reformatorischen Antiklerikalismus ist das Verhältnis zwischen Klerus und Laien. Vielfältige Aspekte prägen diese Verhältnisbestimmung, besonders (a) der kirchenrechtliche Gegensatz (der Laie als der minder Privilegierte und Unterdrückte), (b) die Bildungsproblematik (der Laie als der — zumindest theologisch — nicht Gebildete und Ungelehrte, der Verdummte und Verführte), vor allem aber, mit dem kirchenrechtlichen Legitimitätsproblem eng verbunden, (c) die Frage des Geistbesitzes und der Geistvermittlung, d.h. die Bindung des Geistes an Institution und Amt: den 'Geistlichen', d.h. den in der Priesterweihe durch den Hl. Geist Versiegelten und zu besonderer, unverlierbarer Sakralität Emporgehobenen, stehen nach katholischem Verständnis die nicht geheiligten, nicht ausgesonderten Laien gegenüber. Sie können zwar individuell den Hl. Geist empfangen und persönlich geister-füllter sein als ein Priester, sind aber als Stand (*ordo*) prinzipiell geistferner, so wie nach verbreitetem mittelalterlichem Urteil der Mönchspriester von seinem Status her geistnäher ist als der Weltpriester. Der mittelalterliche Klerikalismus ist in mehr oder weniger massiver Form pneumatologischer Klerikalismus, und dies in abgestufter Weise — der Stellung in der klerikalen Hierarchie und damit der abgestuften Fähigkeit zur Vermittlung von Geistwirkungen entsprechend.

Innerhalb der Ordenskongregation, der Luther angehörte, begegnet uns unmittelbar vor der Reformation dieser pneumatologische Klerikalismus oder diese auf die kirchliche Sakralinstitution bezogene Pneumatologie in besonders gesteigerter Form z.B. bei seinem Erfurter Mitbruder Johannes von Paltz († 1511). Im Blick auf die hierarchische Spitze der *ecclesia universalis* betont er die Unfehlbarkeit des geistgeleiteten päpstlichen Lehramtes: Der Papst und die Kardinäle werden nämlich, wenn sie als Konsistorium versammelt sind, mit größter Gewißheit (*certissime*) durch den

Hl. Geist geführt.[7] Von der priesterlichen Gnadenvermittlung sagt Paltz, daß
Gott barmherziger durch den Priester als durch sich selbst ist.[8] Und der
antiklerikalen Haltung der Laien tritt er mit den Worten entgegen: "Warum
also haßt du den Priester so, setzt ihn herab, achtest ihn gering und fügst
ihm Schaden zu, der dir von seiten Gottes solch große Güter verschaffen
kann? Ja, Gott würde das durch sich selbst nicht gewähren, weil du allzu
unwürdig bist, aber er hat beschlossen, daß dir durch ihn (scil. den Priester)
solch große Güter dargeboten werden, durch die du zum Heil gelangen
kannst."[9] Entscheidend für diese Mittlerstellung der Priester zwischen Gott
und Laien ist, wie Paltz ganz traditionell betont, nicht die Heiligkeit der
Lebensführung, sondern die Heiligkeit aufgrund der Weihe: der Priester ist
"sanctus quoad consecrationem".[10]

Diese standesbezogene, sakralhierarchisch orientierte Pneumatologie
beantwortet die Reformation mit einem pneumatologischen Antiklerikalismus. Der Unterschied (die "Mauer") zwischen Priestern und Laien wird
beseitigt, indem einerseits die heiligende Wirkung einer besonderen Weihe
negiert und andererseits die Geistnähe der Laien akzentuiert wird. Die sog.
'Geistlichen', d.h. die Geweihten, Privilegierten und Gelehrten, werden als
Geistlose attackiert, während im Gegensatz dazu den angeblich Geistfernen,
den ungelehrten, verdummten und verführten Laien, die Belehrung durch den
Hl. Geist zugesprochen wird. Diese Umpolung, die bei allen Kontinuitäten
zu spätmittelalterlichen Formen antiklerikaler und institutionskritischer
Pneumatologie einen radikalen Umbruch zum mittelalterlichen Ordo-Denken
und Vorstellungsbereich von Spiritualität und Temporalität, von Sakralität
und Profanität bedeutet, diese Umkehrung artikuliert sich nun, wenn man
etwas genauer hinschaut, auf charakteristisch verschiedenartige Weise. Hier
zeigt sich jene Vielfalt der pneumatologischen Ansätze im Antiklerikalismus,
von der bereits die Rede war.

---

[7] Vgl. Berndt Hamm, *Frömmigkeitstheologie am Anfang des 16. Jahrhunderts.*
Studien zu Johannes von Paltz und seinem Umkreis, Beiträge zur Historischen
Theologie 65 (Tübingen, 1982), 268f. In ganz andere (nicht gerade papst- und
kardinalsorientierte) Richtung weist in der gleichen augustinischen Reformkongrega-
tion die Pneumatologie eines Johannes von Staupitz. In einer Sammlung von
Tischreden des Augustinervikars ist folgende launige Geschichte über das Konzil von
Konstanz überliefert: Als die Kardinäle zur Papstwahl versammelt waren, erschien
plötzlich der Hofnarr des Kaisers mit folgender Botschaft: "Der hailig gaist hab ine
zu der versamlung geschickt und laß ine sagen, das er yzo mit sovil geschefften
beladen sey, das er bey inen nit erscheinen kon; und dorumb so sollen sie nun on ine
welen." *Johann von Staupitzens sämmtliche Werke*, hg. von Joachim Karl Friedrich
Knaake, Bd. 1: *Deutsche Schriften* (Potsdam, 1867), 47.

[8] Hamm, *Frömmigkeitstheologie*, 269.

[9] Hamm, *Frömmigkeitstheologie*, 269f.

[10] Hamm, *Frömmigkeitstheologie*, 271f.

IV. THEMATIK UND QUELLENAUSWAHL: DAS BEISPIEL NÜRNBERG

Ich versuche im folgenden, diese pneumatologische Vielstimmigkeit an einer eng begrenzten Thematik und Quellengruppe darzustellen. Thematisch wende ich mich der Frage zu, wie das Verhältnis der *Laien* zum Hl. Geist gesehen und wie dabei das Problem des Lehrens und Lernens, des Belehrtwerdens, der Urteilsfähigkeit und der Gelehrsamkeit, besonders im Blick auf Bibel und Predigt, angegangen wird. Quellenmäßig beschränke ich mich auf Flugschriftenverfasser, die zwischen 1520 und 1525 in *Nürnberg* wirkten. Der gleiche lokale Bezug erhöht die Vergleichbarkeit (z.B. im Blick auf theologische Einflüsse, zugängliche Schriften, gehörte Predigten, Bildungsniveau der Laien, Sozialstruktur); zudem wird so deutlich, daß die Vielfalt im Spektrum des pneumatologischen Antiklerikalismus nicht künstlich und mühsam aus verschiedenen Orten (und womöglich aus einem großen Zeitraum) zusammengesucht ist, sondern sich am gleichen Ort zur gleichen Zeit (1523/24) in völlig naheliegender Weise zeigt.

Nürnberg ist sicherlich kein Sonderfall, sondern dürfte mit seiner theologischen Vielstimmigkeit exemplarisch für die Typenvielfalt reformatorischer Theologie in den städtischen Bildungszentren sein. Freilich ist Nürnberg ein besonders ergiebiges Beispiel, weil sich hier Vertreter der verschiedenen Rezeptions- und Artikulationsebenen reformatorischer Theologie zum genannten Themenbereich äußern: drei humanistisch gebildete Gelehrte, die eine Universitätsschulung haben: der Prediger von St. Lorenz und Reformator Andreas Osiander, der Schulmeister der Lateinschule von St. Sebald Hans Denck (erst seit Sept. 1523 in Nürnberg) und der Ratsschreiber Lazarus Spengler (im Unterschied zu Osiander sind Denck und Spengler kirchenrechtlich Laien); weiter der "Bauer von Wöhrd" Diepold Peringer, der sich bezeichnenderweise als grobschlächtiger, einfältiger Laie gibt, "der nicht schreiben und lesen kann", in Wirklichkeit aber ein durchaus gebildeter Geistlicher ist (er tritt in Nürnberg nur von Ende 1523 bis Mai 1524 in Erscheinung); schließlich zwei Handwerkertheologen: der Schuhmacher Hans Sachs, der einen gewissen humanistischen Bildungshorizont besitzt, und der deutlich weniger gebildete, aber gleichwohl durch zahlreiche Flugschriften hervortretende Maler Hans Greiffenberger.

Der Flugschriftenautor, der in Nürnberg am meisten gelesen wurde und auch alle genannten Autoren wesentlich geprägt hat, war selbstverständlich Luther. Und Luther war es auch, der mit seiner pneumatologischen Begründung des Angriffs auf die römische Hierarchie und Schulgelehrsamkeit und der Aufwertung des einfachen, ungelehrten Laien für die Nürnberger maßgeblich wurde.

V. Luthers pneumatologischer Antiklerikalismus (1520-1524)

In seiner Adelsschrift von 1520 greift Luther den pneumatologischen
Klerikalismus der römischen Kirche an und stellt ihm das allgemeine
Priestertum der Christen gegenüber,[11] die "gleich tauff, glaubenn, geyst und
alle ding haben"[12] und darum alle "warhafftig geystlichs stands" seien.[13]
Da für Luther wahre Geistlichkeit immer mit rechtem Schriftverständnis in
eins geht, wendet er sich dann konsequenterweise speziell gegen den
pneumatologischen Anspruch der Papstkirche, die Bibel in der Vollmacht
des Geistbesitzes unfehlbar auslegen zu können: "sie allein wollen meister
der schrifft sein, ob sie schon yhr leblang nichts drynnen lernenn";[14] "dan
dieweil sie es achten, der heylig geist lasz sie nit, sie sein szo ungeleret und
bosze wie sie kunden, werden sie kune, zu setzen, was sie nur wollen".[15]
Geistlose Ungelehrtheit in der Schrift und Bosheit stehen in Luthers Augen
gegen das Belehrtwerden der frommen Gläubigen, die durch den Hl. Geist
zum Verständnis der Schrift geführt werden. Gegen die päpstliche 'Bosheit'
betont Luther, daß der Geist nur "frume hertzen" innehaben kann;[16] gegen
das Lehrmonopol des Papstes und 'der Seinen' und ihr tatsächliches
Ungelehrtsein hebt er hervor, daß — nach Joh. 6,45 — "alle Christen sollen
geleret werden von got" — mit der Schlußfolgerung, daß gerade die
angeblich 'Geistlichen' und 'Gelehrten' an der Spitze der Hierarchie als
Geistverlassene und Ungelehrte irren, während gerade "ein geringer mensch
den rechten vorstand", d.h. das rechte Schriftverständnis, haben kann.[17]
Außer Joh. 6,45, dem *locus classicus* einer pneumatologischen Aufwertung
der Laien, zitiert Luther im gleichen Zusammenhang noch 1. Kor. 2,15 ("ein
geistlicher mensch richtet alle ding unnd wirt von niemants gerichtet")[18]
und 2. Kor. 4,13 ("wir haben alle eynen geyst des glaubens").[19] Da alle
Glaubenden den Geist haben, ist auch, wie Luther betont, der "gantzen
gemein" der Glaubenden die geistliche Vollmacht gegeben, nach dem
Maßstab ihres Schriftverständnisses über Wahrheit und Irrtum von Glaube
und Lehre zu urteilen ("zu schmecken und urteylen").[20]

---

[11] Der gesamte Textzusammenhang aus der Schrift *An den christlichen Adel
deutscher Nation von des christlichen Standes Besserung*, auf den ich mich im
folgenden beziehe, umfaßt *WA* 6. 407,9-412,38 (erste und zweite Mauer).

[12] *WA* 6. 410,16.

[13] *WA* 6. 407,13f.

[14] Zur zweiten Mauer: *WA* 6. 411,8f.

[15] *WA* 6. 411,14-16.

[16] *WA* 6. 411,18f.

[17] *WA* 6. 411,26-32.

[18] *WA* 6. 412,23f.

[19] *WA* 6. 412,24f.

[20] *WA* 6. 412,1.20-23.

Das Gewicht in diesem antiklerikal-pneumatologischen Gedankenduktus liegt also auf zwei Aspekten: 1. daß die Vollmacht, über alle Fragen der Schrift und des Glaubens zu urteilen, *jedem* Christen zukommt; 2. daß Gottes Geist gerade aus den *gering Geachteten* sprechen kann. Um zu zeigen, daß Gott tatsächlich die Höhergestellten und als gelehrt Geltenden durch die Stimme der Geringen belehren kann, beruft sich Luther auf zwei biblische Beispiele: Abraham-Sara (Gen. 21,12): "Muste doch vortzeytenn Abraham seine Sara horen, die doch yhm hertter unterworffen war, den wir yemant auff erden";[21] Bileam-Eselin (Num. 22,22-30): "szo war die eselynne Balaam auch kluger denn der Propheta selbs. Hat got da durch ein eselinne redet gegen einem Propheten, warumb solt er nit noch reden kunnen durch ein frum mensch gegen dem Babst?"[22]

An späterer Stelle der Adelsschrift, beim Punkt der Universitätsreform, nimmt Luther diesen Argumentationsfaden der allgemeinen Geistbelehrung aller Gläubigen und gerade auch derjenigen, die nicht durch äußeres Ansehen 'prangen', wieder auf — wieder mit Berufung auf Joh. 6,45 und wieder mit dem Beispiel der Eselin Bileams: "Aber sey nur gewiß: eynen Doctorn der heyligenn schrifft wirt dir niemandt machenn, denn allein der heilig geyst vom hymel, wie Christus sagt Johan. vi.: 'Sie mussen alle von got selber geleret sein.' Nu fragt der heylig geyst nit nach rodt, brawn parrethen [Doktorhüten] odder was des prangen ist, auch nit, ob einer jung odder alt, ley odder pfaff, munch odder weltlich, junpfraw [jungfräulich, unverheiratet] odder ehlich sey, ja ehr redt vortzeitten durch ein eselyn widder den propheten, der drauff reyt. Wolt got, wir weren sein wirdig, das uns solch doctores geben wurden, sie weren ja leyen oder priester, ehlich oder junpfrawen! wie wol man nu den heyligen geyst zwingen wil in den bapst, bischoff und doctores, szo doch kein zeychen noch schein ist, das er bey yhnen sey."[23]

Auch wenn in der Adelsschrift Luthers Argumentation darauf hinausläuft, daß er auf der Grundlage des allgemeinen Priestertums dem Laien-Adel die geistliche Vollmacht zuspricht, sein herausgehobenes obrigkeitliches Amt zugunsten der 'Besserung' des christlichen Standes einzusetzen, so hat doch Luther in den zitierten Passagen (wie besonders die Akzentuierung des "geringen menschen", der auch von Gott gelehrt sein kann, und des gleichmachenden Geistes, der sich nicht um weltliche Pracht und irdische Unterschiede kümmert, zeigt) nicht nur den Adel im Blick, sondern tatsächlich die Vollmacht und Legitimierung aller Christen. Luthers

---

[21] *WA* 6. 412,31-33.

[22] *WA* 6. 412,33-36. Luther fügt als drittes biblisches Beispiel noch die Belehrung des Petrus durch Paulus Gal. 2,11-14 hinzu: "Item sanct Paul strafft sanct Peter als einen yrrigen, Gal. ij. Darumb geburt einem yglichen Christen, das er sich des glaubens annehm, zu vorstehen und vorfechten, und alle yrtumb zu vordammen." Ebd. 412,36-38.

[23] *WA* 6. 460,30-40.

"Hinwendung zu jedermann im Glaubensstreit" vollzog sich also nicht erst Ende 1520, wie Junghans Luthers Entwicklung deutet,[24] sondern zeigt sich voll ausgebildet bereits im August 1520, als die Schrift *An den christlichen Adel deutscher Nation* erschien.[25]

Richtig ist allerdings, daß Luther diese pneumatologisch (und zugleich immer christologisch und rechtfertigungstheologisch) begründete Abwendung vom Monopolanspruch des Papstes, der römischen Geistlichkeit und der scholastischen Gelehrsamkeit und seine Hinwendung zur geistlichen Vollmacht und Gottesgelehrtheit der gering Geachteten und Ungelehrten in seinen 1521 erschienenen Schriften weiter entfaltet. Auch dabei ist vorauszusetzen, zumal nach den Wittenberger Unruhen vom Winter 1521/22, daß Luther bei konkreten Reformmaßnahmen immer vorrangig die Initiative oder Beteiligung der weltlichen Obrigkeit und besonders der gelehrten Räte in den fürstlichen Residenzen und städtischen Magistraten vor Augen hat.[26] Man hat bei den folgenden Passagen stets zu berücksichtigen, daß sich Luthers Stoßrichtung in den Jahren 1520-1525 zu keinem Zeitpunkt gegen die weltlich Hochgestellten und gegen Gelehrsamkeit und literarische Kompetenz an sich richtet. Im Gegenteil! Sie wendet sich ausschließlich gegen das herrschende Oben und Unten im klerikalen Gefüge, gegen eine (in seinen Augen) angemaßte Obrigkeit und Geistmächtigkeit der Hierarchie und gegen eine perverse Schulgelehrsamkeit, die nicht nur ohne den Hl. Geist ist und nicht nur einer wirklichen Sprachgelehrsamkeit, sondern auch dem allgemeinen vernünftigen Menschenverstand (wie er aus einem unverbildeten Bauern und Kind reden kann) widerspricht.

In diesem polemischen Kontext sind Luthers Invektiven in seiner "allen frumen christen" gewidmeten, im Januar 1521 erschienenen Vorrede zu seiner Schrift *Grund und Ursach aller Artikel D. M. Luthers, so durch römische Bulle unrechtlich verdammt sind* zu verstehen.[27] Er hebt hier

---

[24] Helmar Junghans, "Der Laie als Richter im Glaubensstreit der Reformationszeit", *LuJ* 39 (1972): 31-54; 51.

[25] In einer handschriftlichen Fassung (bereits die Endfassung?) war die Adelsschrift bereits am 23. Juni fertiggestellt; vgl. *Martin Luther Studienausgabe*, hg. von Hans-Ulrich Delius, Bd. 2, (Berlin, DDR, 1982), 91-93.

[26] Luther unterscheidet — vor und nach 1521 — stets zwischen der prinzipiellen Vollmacht und Legitimierung, die allen gläubigen Christen in gleicher Weise zukommt, und dem ius executionis, d.h. dem Recht zu konkreten Kirchenordnungsmaßnahmen, wie es innerhalb der Gemeinde vorrangig der Obrigkeit zusteht. Situationsbedingt kann eher der eine oder der andere Aspekt hervortreten. Das gleiche gilt für seine Unterscheidung zwischen dem allgemeinen Priestertum der Gläubigen und der besonderen Beauftragung befähigter Personen mit dem Amt der Wortverkündigung.

[27] Die Vorrede (*WA* 7. 309,4-317,24) beginnt mit den Worten: "Jhesus. Allen frumen Christen, die disz buchlin leszen odder horen, gnad und frid von got. Amen." *WA* 7. 309,4-6. Die auf den 1. Dez. 1520 datierte Vorrede zur vorher erschienenen lateinischen Fassung *Assertio omnium articulorum M. Lutheri per bullam Leonis X.*

hervor, daß Gott seit den alttestamentlichen Zeiten nicht "die großen hanßen", sondern "gemeyniglich nyderige, vorachte person aufferweckt" und durch sie gesprochen habe — so wie durch den Hirten Amos und die Eselin Bileams.[28] Bei den Angesehenen dagegen, bei Päpsten, Bischöfen und Gelehrten, sei die christliche Wahrheit untergegangen. Sie, die den wahren Glauben hätten schützen sollen, seien zur Quelle und zum Hort aller Ketzerei geworden, während die Wahrheit in den Herzen einiger Frommer weiterlebte — und seien es auch nur "kind in der wigen" gewesen.[29] So sei auch das geistliche Verständnis des Gesetzes (die Verbindung von Geist und Schriftverständnis) im Alten Testament "bey etlichen geringen" erhalten geblieben, es "ging aber unter bey den hohen priestern und gelereten". "Also spricht Hiere. v. [Jer. 5,4f], das er bey den ubirsten weniger vorstandt unnd recht funden habe den bey den leyen unnd gemeynem volck. Alszo ists auch itzt, das arm pawrn unnd kinder baß Christum vorstan den bapst, bischoff unnd doctores, und ist alles umbkeret."[30]

Luther gibt hier gleichsam die Parole aus, die dann stereotyp die Flugschriftenliteratur der frühen Reformationszeit durchzieht: 'die Gelehrten

---

novissimam damnatorum hatte Luther an den kursächsischen Rat Fabian v. Feilitzsch (der noch im gleichen Monat starb — nicht zu verwechseln mit dem Rat Philipp v. Feilitzsch) gerichtet. In seinen Augen ist Fabian, wie es in der Vorrede heißt, ein Musterbeispiel dafür, "daß auch in den Laien — damit ich es mit Jesaja sage [4,4] — der Geist des Urteilens und Entflammens ist" (*WA* 7. 94,6f); vgl. auch *WA* 7. 95,1-5. Daß Luther dann, nachdem Fabian gestorben war, die deutschsprachige Fassung allen frommen Christen widmete und dabei an das geistliche Urteilsvermögen der einfachen Laien appellierte, ist — nach allem, was er bereits 1520 gesagt hatte — völlig verständlich und naheliegend. Keineswegs wird damit ein Positionswechsel signalisiert, wie ihn Junghans (wie Anm. 24, S. 50) mit den Worten beschreibt: "Doch diese Unterscheidung zwischen jedermann und dem Adel im Laienstand in bezug auf das Richten im Glaubensstreit begann Luther Ende 1520 zu verwischen; denn als die ersten sechs Bogen der deutschen Ausgabe am 21. Januar 1521 verschickt wurden, war bereits die Hinwendung zu den frommen Christen erfolgt." Der besonderen Stellung, die der adligen Obrigkeit innerhalb der christlichen Gemeinde nach Luthers Auffassung zukommt, wird vielmehr durch die allgemeine Widmung an alle Christen und die sich daran anschließenden Ausführungen der deutschen Vorrede überhaupt nichts genommen (vgl. Anm. 26). Zur Entstehung der lat. und dt. Fassung und ihrer Vorreden vgl. *Luthers Werke in Auswahl*, hg. von Otto Clemen, Bd. 2, 6. Aufl. (Berlin, 1967), 60; *Martin Luther Studienausgabe*, Bd. 2 (wie Anm. 25), 311f. und 314 Anm. 1. Zu Fabian v. Feilitzsch vgl. Dieter Stievermann, "Sozial- und verfassungsgeschichtliche Voraussetzungen Martin Luthers und der Reformation — der landesherrliche Rat in Kursachsen, Kurmainz und Mansfeld", in V. Press/ders., *Martin Luther: Probleme seiner Zeit*, Spätmittelalter und Frühe Neuzeit 16 (Stuttgart, 1986), 137-76; 163 mit Anm. 120; vgl. auch 162 Anm. 110.

[28] *WA* 7. 311,30-313,5 und 313,25-29.
[29] *WA* 7. 313,12-16 und 313,37-315,2.
[30] *WA* 7. 315,2-7.

die Verkehrten'.[31] Wie sehr solche Aussagen bei Luther pneumatologisch
gefüllt sind — im Sinne eines unmittelbaren, nicht hierarchisch vermittelten
Belehrtwerdens aller gläubigen Christen durch Gottes Geist — zeigt eine
Passage aus der ebenfalls 1521 erschienenen Schrift *De abroganda missa
privata* (auch in deutscher Übersetzung: *Vom Mißbrauch der Messe*).[32] Mit
dem satanischen "sacerdotium visibile et externum" der Papstkirche, das
zwischen Priestern und Laien scheidet, konfrontiert Luther hier das durch
Christi Priestertum begründete "sacerdotium spirituale", das allen Christen
gemeinsam sei.[33] Der rote Faden des Textes wird durch den Gesichtspunkt
des rechten Belehrtwerdens und der wahren christlichen Gelehrsamkeit aus
Christus und seinem Geist allein (*spiritu solo*) gebildet[34] — eine spirituell-
biblische Umkehrung der Begriffe *docere, doctus, docibilis, doctor, doctrina*.
In klassischer Kombination tauchen hier auch die einschlägigen Bibelstellen
auf, die dann den reformatorischen Spiritualisten als *dicta probantia* für ihre
Auffassung von der unvermittelten Geistbelehrung der Gläubigen dienen
werden:[35] die bereits in der Adelsschrift zitierte Stelle Joh. 6,45 ("Et erunt
omnes docibiles dei")[36] und die beiden Prophetenstellen Jes. 54,13 ("Et
dabo universos filios tuos doctos a domino")[37] und Jer. 31,34 ("Non
docebit unusquisque fratrem suum et unusquisque proximum suum dicens:
Cognosce dominum. Omnes enim scient me a minore usque ad maxi-
mum").[38] Die Geistbelehrung ist also Gemeinbesitz der glaubenden
Gemeinde (*doctrina omnibus communis*).[39] Es bedarf dazu nicht eines
klerikalen Mittler- und Doktorenamtes, da der mediator und doctor der
Christen allein Christus ist. Durch seinen Geist ermächtigt er sie, als von

---

[31] Vgl. Heiko A. Oberman, "*Die Gelehrten die Verkehrten*: Popular Response to
Learned Culture in the Renaissance and Reformation", in S. E. Ozment (Hg.),
Religion and Culture in the Renaissance and Reformation, Sixteenth Century Essays
and Studies 10 (Kirksville, Mo., 1989), 43-62, mit dem Motto am Anfang des
Aufsatzes aus *Eynn Dialogus ader gesprech ...* (Erfurt 1523): "... du soltt inen nit
glauben, so sie sprechen: ja, die bawrenn verstehen die sach nit. Meint ich doch, weil
die verkerrten gelerrten die Schrifft verstünden, sie würden am ersten Selig."
Oberman geht insbesondere auf den spätmittelalterlichen Hintergrund der Parole in
der niederländischen Devotio moderna ein.

[32] Abschnitt *WA* 8. 415,15-416,4 (lat.) bzw. 486,18-487,14 (dt.).

[33] *WA* 8. 415,15-23.

[34] *WA* 8. 416,1f.: "ita sacerdotium novi testamenti prorsus sine personarum respectu
regnat communiter in omnibus spiritu solo".

[35] Vgl. Reinhard Schwarz, *Die apokalyptische Theologie Thomas Müntzers und der
Taboriten*, Beiträge zur historischen Theologie 55 (Tübingen, 1977), 10-34; zum
Abschnitt aus Luthers *De abroganda missa privata*: 21f.

[36] *WA* 8. 415,34-36.

[37] *WA* 8. 415,30f., von Luther eingeleitet mit den Worten: "Sic et per se ipsos a
deo docentur ..."

[38] *WA* 8. 415,31-33.

[39] *WA* 8. 415,37.

Gott Belehrte für diejenigen Mittler und Lehrer des Glaubens zu sein, die noch nicht Christen sind.[40] Dieser letzte Satz weist darauf hin, daß die Unmittelbarkeit der Christen zu Gottes Geist (d.h. die Unabhängigkeit von einem gnaden- und wahrheitsvermittelnden hierarchischen Priester- und Lehramt) bei Luther gerade nicht unvermittelte Unterrichtung bedeutet; sie ist vielmehr eine Unmittelbarkeit zu Gottes biblischem und gepredigtem Wort, wie es durch menschliche Schrift und Sprache geschichtlich vermittelt wird. Die Unmittelbarkeit ist ein unmittelbares Betroffenwerden (Belehrt- und Begnadetwerden) von biblischer Schrift und Verkündigung des biblischen Wortes;[41] und sie bedeutet unmittelbare Vollmacht zur Beurteilung der Predigt und Lehre und zum Selber-Lehren nach dem Maßstab des biblischen Wortes.

In diesem Sinn muß man auch andere Passagen in Luthers frühen Schriften vor der Konfrontation mit einem innerreformatorischen Spiritualismus verstehen, in denen er ungeschützt von einer Unmittelbarkeit der Geistbelehrung spricht — so etwa in seiner Magnificat-Auslegung aus dem gleichen Jahr 1521: "Dießen heiligen lobesang ordenlich zu vorstehen, ist zu merckenn, das die hochgelobte junckfraw Maria auß eygner erfarung redet, darynnen sie durch den heyligen geist ist erleucht unnd geleret worden. Denn es mag niemant got noch gottes wort recht vorstehen, er habs denn on mittel von dem heyligen geyst. Niemant kanß aber von dem heiligenn geist habenn, er erfareß, vorsuchs und empfinds denn, unnd yn der selben erfarung leret der heylig geyst alß yn seiner eygenen schule, außer wilcher wirt nichts geleret denn nur scheinwort unnd geschwetz."[42] Als Kontrast erkennt man im Hintergrund Luthers Polemik gegen den bibel- und geistfernen Lehrbetrieb der hohen Schulen und ihre Anhäufung von scholastischem Wissensballast,[43] gegen die "Doctores, Predicatores, Magistros, Pfaffen und Müniche, das ist grosse, grobe, fette esel mit rotten und braunen parreten geschmuckt wie die saw mit eyner gülden keten und perlen ..., die uns nichts guts lereten, sondern nur ymer mehr blinder und

---

[40] *WA* 8. 415,38-42: "Quid enim opus est sacerdote, dum non est opus mediatore et doctore? An sacerdotem sine opere constituemus? At mediator et doctor Christianorum praeter Christum nullus est. Quin ipsi per sese accedunt a deo docti, deinceps mediare et docere potentes eos, qui nondum sacerdotes, id est nondum Christiani sunt."

[41] Vgl. Schwarz (wie Anm. 35), 21: "Unmittelbar Betroffene sind sie als Begnadete, obwohl sie nicht unvermittelt davon unterrichtet werden" — im Unterschied zum Spiritualismus (etwa Müntzers), der Unmittelbarkeit der Geistbelehrung als Unvermitteltheit versteht.

[42] *WA* 7. 546,21-29.

[43] Eine klassische Textpassage bietet z.B. Luthers Schrift *An die Ratsherren aller Städte deutschen Landes, daß sie christliche Schulen aufrichten und halten sollen*, *WA* 15. 50,4-51,22. Vgl. Luthers Polemik in *An den christlichen Adel deutscher Nation* ..., *WA* 6. 457,28-460,40.

toller machten".[44] Dem scholastischen "eselsmist", der "vom Teuffel
eyngefurt ist",[45] der die Menschen verdummt und zutiefst ungelehrt
gelassen habe, steht die Schule des belehrenden Hl. Geistes gegenüber, der
allein das Wort Gottes erschließt und in die authentische Eigen-Erfahrung
mit dem Wort hineinführt.

Nach dem Gesagten ist es verständlich, daß Luther auch in seiner
Flugschrift von 1523 *Daß eine christliche Versammlung oder Gemeine Recht
und Macht habe, alle Lehre zu beurteilen und Lehrer zu berufen, ein- und
abzusetzen* diese Legitimierung und Vollmacht der Gemeinde mit dem
allgemeinen Priestertum der durch Gottes Geist belehrten Gläubigen
begründet — wieder unter Berufung auf Joh. 6,45: "Denn das kan niemant
leucken, das eyn iglicher Christen gottis wort hatt und von gott gelert und
gesalbet ist tzum priester; wie Christus spricht Johan. 6: 'Sie werden alle
von gott geleret seyn."[46] Wie in der Adelsschrift verknüpft Luther mit der
Johannesstelle die Zitation von 2. Kor. 4,13: "Wyr haben auch den selben
geyst des glaubens, darumb reden wyr auch."[47] Er begründet so die
geistliche Vollmacht aller Christen, die Lehre ihrer Lehrer zu beurteilen, und
ihre Ermächtigung, ja Schuldigkeit, selber das Wort Gottes "zu bekennen,
leren und ausbreytten".[48]

Wir haben nun eine gegen den traditionellen pneumatologisch begründeten
Klerikalismus gerichtete Argumentationslinie Luthers kennengelernt, die
bereits vor 1520 einsetzt und auch 1523 nicht einfach abbricht. Es ist die
Argumentation mit dem 'Geist allein', der unabhängig von allen Ansprüchen
hierarchisch-klerikaler Lehr- und Gnadenvermittlung die Herzen in seine
Schule nimmt, allein den Glauben lehrt und so auch die gering geachteten
Laien — unabhängig von Unterschieden des Geschlechts, Alters, Bil-
dungsgrades und sozialen Status' — zur Beurteilung der Lehre und zur
Verkündigung des Gotteswortes legitimiert. Es ist freilich bereits angeklun-
gen, daß man diese Akzentuierung des *solus spiritus* (im Gegensatz zu
angemaßter Menschenlehre, Menschensatzung und Menschenmacht) nicht
isolieren darf, sondern zu bestimmten — für Luther zentral wichtigen —
Einbettungen und Differenzierungen in Beziehung setzen muß. Nur dann
wird deutlich, wie wenig Luthers pneumatologische Argumentation gegen
Papst, Bischöfe, Geistliche und Schulgelehrte mit einer spiritualistischen
Verinnerlichung zu tun hat, die das innere Belehrt- und Versichertwerden
durch den Geist von einer Wirksamkeit der äußeren Sprachebene löst.

Beim Thema 'Unmittelbarkeit' habe ich schon darauf hingewiesen, daß
Luther das Wirken des Hl. Geistes immer eingebettet sieht in die sprachliche

---

[44] *WA* 15. 51,2-5.
[45] *WA* 15. 50,11.
[46] *WA* 11. 411,31-33.
[47] *WA* 11. 412,7f.
[48] "Ists aber also, das sie gottis wort haben und von yhm gesalbet sind, so sind sie
auch schuldig, dasselb zu bekennen, leren und ausbreytten." *WA* 11. 412,5f.

Vermittlung durch das biblische Wort und die Predigt dieses Wortes, also immer in Beziehung setzt zu jener Unmittelbarkeit, mit der jeder Christ — am Klerus vorbei — Gottes Wort lesen, hören und geistlich damit umgehen kann. Zum 'solo spiritu' gehört also das 'sola scriptura' und 'solo verbo'. Nur der Hl. Geist öffnet das verstockte Herz für Gottes Wort, und er allein erschließt dem Ausleger den Sinn des biblischen Wortes; aber der Geist erschließt sich auch nur über das Aufnehmen des biblischen 'verbum externum', d.h. nur durch das gehörte und gelesene Gotteswort findet der Mensch Zugang zum Geist, der den Glauben weckt — den Glauben an das, was er hört und liest. In diesen Zusammenhang gehören auch alle Aussagen Luthers darüber, daß das Herz oder Gewissen in Gottes Wort und seiner Wahrheit gefangen ist.[49] Wenn es im Blick auf 1. Kor. 2,15 heißt, daß der *homo spiritualis* alles beurteilen kann, dann heißt das daher nichts anderes, als daß er sich dem Urteil und der gewißmachenden Klarheit des biblischen Wortes unterwirft. Weiß er doch, daß er unfehlbare Gewißheit (*certitudo infallibilis*) über die Wahrheit der Lehre und die Zueignung von Gnade und Heil nicht an einer inneren Geisterfahrung festmachen kann (so grundlegend wichtig dieses Widerfahrnis des Geistes auch ist), sondern allein an der Klarheit des einleuchtenden und zueignenden äußeren Wortes. Ist doch dieses Wort selbst Wirkung von Gottes Geist und als Zeugnis des Geistes darum auch geistmächtiges, geist-mitteilendes und nur darum 'einleuchtendes' Wort. Nur wenn man beachtet, wie sich für den von tiefster Anfechtung herkommenden Luther alles auf die Gewißheitsproblematik und daher auch auf die Frage nach den Kriterien des Geistwirkens zuspitzt, kann man verstehen, warum die Klarheit des äußeren Bibelwortes für ihn so entscheidend wichtig ist — eine äußere Klarheit, die der inneren Klarheit des erleuchtenden Geistes entspricht, ja das Instrument seines klärenden Wirkens ist.

Diese gewißmachende Klarheit hängt nun unlösbar mit sprachlicher Vermittlung und darum mit der Verstehbarkeit der biblischen Sprachen, mit der Kenntnis von Begriffen, Grammatik, Sprachduktus und Skopos zusammen. Nur so kann die Schrift in ihrem sprachlichen Zusammenhang zur klärenden Auslegerin ihrer selbst werden und jene Gewißheit und Urteilsfähigkeit geben, die die Geister und ihre Lehren daraufhin prüfen kann, ob sie aus dem Hl. Geist kommen. Luther betont, daß sich Gottes Geist diesen und keinen anderen Weg der Mitteilung und Klärung gewählt hat.

---

[49] Vgl. das berühmte Ende des Berichts über die Rede Luthers vor dem Wormser Reichstag am 18. April 1521, *WA* 7. 838,6f.: "victus sum scripturis a me adductis et capta conscientia in verbis dei". Zum folgenden vgl. *WA* 6. 561,3-18 (*De captivitate Babylonica*) und dazu (speziell zu Luthers Auslegung von 1. Kor. 2,15) Wolfgang Rochler, *Martin Luther und die Reformation als Laienbewegung*, Institut für Europäische Geschichte Mainz: Vorträge Nr. 75 (Wiesbaden, 1981), 48-52.

Deutlich artikuliert er das in seiner Anfang 1524 erschienenen Schrift *An die Ratsherrn aller Städte deutschen Landes, daß sie christliche Schulen aufrichten und halten sollen.*[50] Nicht als ob Luther in den Jahren vorher diese Verbindung von Geist und Schriftwort, von innerer und äußerer Klärung, von Geistbelehrung und Sprachkompetenz, von Schule des Geistes und reformorientierter Schulbildung nicht bereits vor Augen gehabt und formuliert hätte, aber nun — in kritischer Auseinandersetzung mit einer spiritualistischen Geringschätzung äußerer Sprachvermittlung und einer laizistischen Verachtung der hebräisch-griechischen Sprachbildung[51] — akzentuiert er diesen Punkt in zusammenfassender Prägnanz. Programmatisch stellt er die Devise 'solus spiritus' in den Rahmen sprachlicher Vermittlung: "Wiewol das Euangelion alleyn durch den heyligen geyst ist kômen und teglich kompt, so ists doch durch mittel der sprachen komen und

---

[50] Der gesamte Textzusammenhang aus dieser Schrift, auf den ich mich im folgenden beziehe, umfaßt *WA* 15. 36,6-43,18.

[51] Ausdrücklich wendet er sich gegen diese Einstellungen zu Schrift und Sprache mit den Worten: "Es soll uns auch nicht yrren, das ettliche sich des geysts rhûmen und die schrifft geringe achten, ettliche auch wie die brûder Valdenses die sprachen nicht nûtzlich achten." *WA* 15. 42,15-17. "So kan ich auch die brûder Valdenses darynnen gar nichts loben, das sie die sprachen verachten." Ebd. 43,7f. Man muß bei diesen kritischen Abgrenzungen Luthers deutlich unterscheiden zwischen seiner Polemik gegen die (etwa von Müntzer und Karlstadt vertretene) spiritualistische Position — gegen solche, die "sich des geysts rhûmen und die schrifft geringe achten" — und seiner relativ zurückhaltenden und behutsamen Kritik an den "brûder Valdenses" und ihrer Geringschätzung der Sprachgelehrsamkeit (vgl. den ganzen Abschnitt ebd. 43,7-18). Mit 'Waldenserbrüdern' sind die Böhmischen Brüder gemeint, an die er im Frühjahr 1523 seine Schrift *Vom Anbeten des Sakraments des heiligen Leichnams Christi* gerichtet hatte: "Meynen lieben herrn und freunden, den Brudern genant Valdenses ynn Behemen und Mehren Gnad und frid ynn Christo." *WA* 11. 431,1f. Bereits in dieser Schrift befaßt sich Luther auch mit der Sprachproblematik. Er bittet die Böhmen, "das yhr die sprachen nicht alßo verachtet", und weist darauf hin, wie leicht man ohne die Hilfe der lateinischen, griechischen und hebräischen Sprache bei der Schriftauslegung und Predigt irren kann. "Denn ich erfare, wie die sprachen uber die maß helffen tzum lauttern verstandt gotlicher schrifft." Und er betont schließlich auch — ganz in der Weise seiner Schulschrift von 1524 (vgl. die folgende Darstellung) — den Konnex zwischen Hl. Geist und alten Sprachen: "denn der heylig geyst hatt ynn dißen zwo sprachen das allt und new testament geschrieben." *WA* 11. 455,27-456,3. Man sieht an dieser Passage deutlich, daß Luther 1524 eine Sicht entfaltet, die er schon lange vorher gewonnen und literarisch vertreten hat. Vgl. z.B. auch Luthers Brief an Eobanus Hessus vom 29. 3. 1523: "Ego persuasus sum, sine literarum peritia prorsus stare non posse sinceram theologiam, sicut hactenus ruentibus et iacentibus literis miserrime et cecidit et iacuit. Quin video, nunquam fuisse insignem factam verbi dei revelationem, nisi primo, velut praecursoribus Baptistis, viam pararit surgentibus et florentibus linguis et literis." *WABr* 3. 50,21-25. Zur Beziehung zwischen Luther und den Böhmen vgl. Martin Brecht, *Martin Luther*, Bd. 2 (Stuttgart, 1986), 78-82.

hat auch dadurch zugenomen, mus auch dadurch behallten werden."[52] Es
ist, so betont Luther mit Schärfe,[53] nicht der Geist-'Besitz' an sich, nicht
der Blick auf den *homo spiritualis*, der aus der Ungewißheit und Unsicher-
heit heraushilft — so unzweifelhaft es auch feststeht, daß "der geyst alles
alleyne thut". Eine sich von der Schrift und den Sprachen distanzierende,
selbstbezogene (auf Besitz fixierte) Berufung auf den Geist führt in den
Selbstruhm, der sich aufbläht. Nur der sich von der eigenen Innerlichkeit
lösende Blick auf die Außendimension sprachlicher Klärung macht "mich
der schrift sicher und gewiss". So will es der Geist selbst. Denn er selbst
hat, wie Luther ausführt, die Sprachen geschenkt,[54] sie vom Himmel auf
die Erde gebracht und Gottes Wort in hebräische und griechische Sprache
gekleidet.[55] Darum sind diese Sprachen die 'Scheiden, in denen das Messer
des Geistes steckt' (d.h. das Evangelium — nach Eph. 6,17: "das Schwert
des Geistes, welches das Wort Gottes ist"); die biblischen Sprachen sind das
'Schmuckkästchen', in dem man dieses Kleinod des Geistes und seines
Wortes besitzt, das 'Gefäß' für diesen Trank, die 'Kammer' für diese Speise,
die 'Körbe' für Brote, Fische und Brocken, die 'heilige Lade', um das
Evangelium 'sicher' zu verwahren und der verwirrenden Unordnung der
'Gesinnungen, Meinungen und Lehren' (also der diversen Berufungen auf
den Geist) zu entreißen.[56] Weil der Geist selbst die Sprachen gegeben und
sein Evangelium an sie gebunden hat, darum bringt die Beschäftigung mit
den biblischen Sprachen klärendes Licht,[56a] jene — der inneren Klarheit
des Geistes entsprechende — äußere Klarheit, die das Evangelium in seiner
Gewißheit verbürgenden Reinheit zum Leuchten bringt.

In der Konsequenz dieser Verbindung von Geistwirken und *verbum
externum* liegt es, daß Luther mit Leidenschaft den Aufbau, die Reform und
Pflege von Schulen fordert, in denen die alten Sprachen gelehrt werden und
alles gelernt wird, was der Auslegungskunst der biblischen Schrift dient.
Man sieht hier deutlich, welch hohen Rang in Luthers Augen Schulbildung
und Gelehrsamkeit besitzen, und zwar nicht nur in Hinsicht auf den
weltlichen Bereich von *politica* und *oeconomia*, sondern gerade auch in
geistlicher Hinsicht: "das sey gesagt von nutz und not der sprachen und

---

[52] *WA* 15. 37,4-6.
[53] Zum folgenden vgl. den Abschnitt *WA* 15. 42,15-43,1.
[54] *WA* 15. 37,1-38,6.
[55] *WA* 15. 39,9-14: "Und summa: Der heylige geyst ist keyn narre, gehet auch
nicht mit leichtfertigen, unnötigen sachen umb. Der hat die sprachen so nütz und not
geacht ynn der Christenheyt, das er sie offtmals von hymel mit sich bracht hat.
Wilchs uns alleyne sollt gnugsam bewegen, die selben mit fleys und ehren zu suchen
und nicht zu verachten, weyl er sie nu selbs widder auff erden erweckt."
[56] *WA* 15. 38,7-31. Vgl. Anm. 67.
[56a] *WA* 15. 39,4-9: "weyl itzt die sprachen erfur komen sind, bringen sie eyn solich
liecht mit sich ..."

christlichen schulen für das geystlich wesen und zur seelen heyl".[57] Luthers Polemik gegen Schulgelehrsamkeit ist immer, auch in den Jahren vorher, nur zu verstehen als Kritik an einer in seinen Augen perversen, den Schatz der Sprachen verschüttenden und daher verdummenden, von der biblischen Schrift weg in die Irre führenden scholastisch-klerikalen Gelehrsamkeit — eine Kritik, die getragen ist von größter Hochschätzung schulischer Bildung und gelehrter Sprachkompetenz. Die Wittenberger Universitätsreform und die Schlüsselrolle, die dabei von Luther Melanchthon zugedacht wird, sprechen für sich.

Mit Luthers Begeisterung für Sprachgelehrsamkeit und die hermeneutische Schlüsselfunktion der Grammatik — sozusagen die Grammatik des Hl. Geistes — hängt unmittelbar zusammen, wie er innerhalb der christlichen Gemeinde zwischen verschiedenen Stufen des Urteils- und Lehrvermögens unterscheidet. Nicht erst 1524, sondern schon in den Jahren vorher differenziert Luther zwischen der Vollmacht und Legitimierung ('Macht' und 'Recht') aller gläubigen Christen und der besonderen Befähigung für die Beauftragung mit einem herausgehobenen 'Amt' in der Gemeinde. Die Legitimierung durch das allgemeine Priestertum ist die Grundlage für die besondere Beauftragung von Lehrern und Predigern, "die das wortt treyben".[58] In seiner einflußreichen Schrift *Daß eine christliche Versammlung oder Gemeine ...* von 1523 sagt Luther, daß die christliche Gemeinde, die insgesamt die geistliche Bevollmächtigung zur Lehre und Beurteilung der Lehre hat, solche zu Lehrern und Predigern berufen soll, "so man geschickt datzu findet und die gott mit verstand erleucht und mit gaben datzu getziret hat".[59] 'Verstand' meint die Befähigung zum Schriftverständnis, der Begriff 'getziert' bezieht sich, wenn man von der traditionellen humanistischen Terminologie ausgeht, besonders auf den ornatus der Sprachbefähigung.[60]

Geisterleuchtung, Schriftverständnis und Sprachkompetenz sind, wie dann die zitierte Schulschrift von 1524 ausführlich entfaltet, aufeinander bezogen. In dieser Schrift geht Luther dann auch näher auf die notwendigen Differenzierungen zwischen allgemeiner Vollmacht und besonderer Befähigung und Beauftragung in der Gemeinde ein. Er unterscheidet hier allerdings nicht wie in der Schrift von 1523 zwischen der Legitimierung aller Christen und der Berufung von Predigern, sondern auf der Ebene der

---

[57] *WA* 15. 43,19f.

[58] *WA* 11. 411,22-24 (*Daß eine christliche Versammlung ...*, 1523).

[59] *WA* 11. 411,29f.

[60] Vgl. Berndt Hamm, "Hieronymus-Begeisterung und Augustinismus vor der Reformation. Beobachtungen zur Beziehung zwischen Humanismus und Frömmigkeitstheologie (am Beispiel Nürnbergs)", in K. Hagen (Hg.), *Augustine, the Harvest, and Theology (1300-1650): Essays Dedicated to Heiko Augustinus Oberman in Honor of his Sixtieth Birthday* (Leiden, 1990), 127-235; 165, 178 Anm. 156, 192.

Prediger zwischen zwei Gruppen:[61] Es gibt zum einen die einfachen
Prediger des Glaubens, die keine Kenntnis der alten Sprachen haben. Sie
können zwar, aus Übersetzungen schöpfend, "Christum verstehen, leren und
heyliglich leben und andern predigen", aber sie können die Schrift nicht
selbständig auslegen und gegen Irrtum schützen.[62] Anders dagegen die in
den biblischen Sprachen versierten "ausleger der schrifft",[63] die nicht mehr
oder weniger zufällig, sondern zielgerichtet durch ihren hermeneutischen
Zugangsweg der sprachlichen Erschließung den Sinn des biblischen Textes
treffen.[64] Die "kunst der sprachen"[65] löst den Ausleger von seinem 'sensus
proprius' und führt ihn hinein in die Selbsttätigkeit der Schrift, in ihren
Selbstauslegungs- und Vergewisserungsprozeß, der die Schule des Geistes
ist.

Kennzeichnend für Luthers pneumatologischen Antiklerikalismus in seiner
Auseinandersetzung mit hierarchisch-klerikaler Monopolisierung der
geistgeleiteten Schriftauslegung und mit scholastischer Schulgelehrsamkeit
ist somit zweierlei: ein zugleich integratives und differenzierendes Verständnis des Geistwirkens und der geistlichen Auslegungs-, Lehr- und Beur-
teilungskompetenz. Integrativ ist seine Sicht deshalb, weil er sprachliche
Vermittlung und philologische Gelehrsamkeit in die Tätigkeit des Hl. Geistes
integriert und weil er damit Geist und sinnlich-sprachliches Wort wechselseitig aufeinander bezieht: der Geist erschließt das Wort, das Wort erschließt
den Geist; und nur in dieser Wechselbeziehung entsteht Auslegungs- und
Glaubensgewißheit. Differenzierend ist sein Geistverständnis deshalb, weil
die Bindung des Geistes an sprachliche Vermittlung Differenzierungen
ermöglicht und notwendig macht: die Unterscheidung zwischen geistlicher
Vollmacht und kirchlichem Amt und die Unterscheidung zwischen
verschiedenen Stufen sprachlich-philologischer Annäherung an den Sinn der
Schrift, also zwischen Vollmacht/Legitimität und Befähigung. Da für Luther
der geistliche Sinn der Schrift gerade im Wortsinn liegt (so schon betont in
der Römerbriefvorlesung 1515/16), ist deutlich, daß die Fähigkeit des
gelehrten Schriftauslegers, sich auf die 'Grammatik' der Schrift einzulassen,
geistlichen Charakters ist — aber eben eine Fähigkeit, die nicht alle

---

[61] Textabschnitte: *WA* 15. 40,14-26 und 42,1-14.

[62] *WA* 15. 40,16-20.

[63] *WA* 15. 40,15.

[64] *WA* 15. 42,3-14. Zu dieser Unterscheidung Luthers vgl. Gersons Differenzierung
zwischen den einfachen, ungelehrten Christen, die im Geist affektiver *contemplatio*
leben, und den Fachtheologen, die nicht nur fromm, sondern auch in der Kenntnis der
Hl. Schrift und im Gebrauch der Vernunft geschult sind und denen daher das
Wächteramt, das in strittigen theologischen Fragen Klärung bringt und die
Glaubenswahrheit schützt, zusteht; vgl. Christoph Burger, *Aedificatio, Fructus,
Utilitas. Johannes Gerson als Professor der Theologie und Kanzler der Universität
Paris*, Beiträge zur historischen Theologie 70 (Tübingen, 1986), 192f.

[65] *WA* 15. 42,6.

Gläubigen der Gemeinde haben, sondern nur wenige, die mit diesem Schmuck 'geziert' sind.[66] So will es der Geist, dessen Evangelium wie ein "kleinod" im Schmuckkästchen ("schreyn") der hebräischen und griechischen Sprache ruht.[67]

VI. Zur Frage der Luther-Rezeption

Mit der pneumatologischen Begründung seines Angriffs auf Hierarchie, Klerus und irreführende, verdummende Schulgelehrsamkeit der Kleriker hat Luther in der frühen Reformationsbewegung vor dem Bauernkrieg eine enorme Wirkung ausgeübt. Ich sagte bereits, daß auch die Nürnberger Autoren in diesem Rahmen einer dominierenden Luther-Rezeption zu sehen sind. Die Frage ist freilich, *wie* Luther aufgenommen wird. Wird mit seiner 'solus-spiritus-Linie' (allein der Geist belehrt die Gläubigen und schenkt ihnen mit dem Glauben auch die Vollmacht, die Schrift zu verstehen, zu predigen und zu lehren und alle Lehre zu beurteilen), wird mit dieser Akzentuierung des Geistes zugleich seine integrative und differenzierende Sicht des Geistwirkens übernommen, oder zeigen sich ganz andere Gewichtungen, Argumentationszusammenhänge und Einzelbegründungen? Auch ganz abgesehen von der 'Wildwuchs'-These Laus wäre eine gewisse Eigendynamik und Verselbständigungstendenz der Luther-Rezeption nicht überraschend, sondern geradezu selbstverständlich, wenn man den alten Erfahrungssatz zugrundelegt: "Quidquid recipitur, secundum modum recipientis recipitur." (What is received, is received according to the conditions of the recipiant).

Der Blick auf die erwähnten Nürnberger Theologen, deren literarische Tätigkeit sich in den Jahren 1523/24 verdichtet und überlagert, zeigt verschiedene Typen der Rezeption von Luthers pneumatologischem Antiklerikalismus. Man kann dabei — je nachdem, wie pneumatologische Belehrung, Schriftverständnis und Lehrbefähigung der Gläubigen gesehen und begründet werden — zwischen drei Grundtypen unterscheiden. Am Rande tritt noch ein vierter Typ in Erscheinung. Auch ein Vergleich mit anderen Quellen außerhalb Nürnbergs zeigt, daß innerhalb der Lutherrezeption immer wieder diese drei bzw. vier Typen in Erscheinung treten.

---

[66] Vgl. oben 396 bei Anm. 59 und 60.

[67] *WA* 15. 38,9: "Sie [scil. die hebräische und griechische Sprache] sind der schreyn, darynnen man dis kleinod tregt." Nach dem Kontext (vorausgegangen ist die Mahnung "das wyr das euangelion nicht wol werden erhallten on die sprachen" und der Vergleich: "Die sprachen sind die scheyden, darynn dis messer des geysts stickt") ist das Kleinod das durch den Hl. Geist gesprochene Wort des Evangeliums. Das Evangelium ist das Schwert des Geistes (bzw. das Kleinod des Geistes), das in der Schwertscheide (bzw. dem Schmuckkästchen) der biblischen Sprache ruht. In diesem Textabschnitt zeigt sich bei Luther besonders schön der integrative Zusammenhang von Hl. Geist, zueignendem Wort und vermittelnder Sprache.

Auffallend ist, daß sich in den einzelnen Typen des Antiklerikalismus jeweils Kleriker und Laien zusammenfinden.

VII. Der erste (integrative) Typ des pneumatologischen Antiklerikalismus

Eine erste Gruppe bilden Andreas Osiander und Lazarus Spengler. Sie stehen mit ihrem antiklerikalen Geistverständnis sehr nahe bei Luther — auch wenn Osiander mit seiner stark pneumatologisch akzentuierten Rechtfertigungslehre schon in diesen Jahren eine ganz andere Richtung einschlägt als Luther und auch wenn Spengler als Laie den Fachtheologen, auch den evangelischen, zeitlebens mit einem gewissen Mißtrauen begegnet. Beide haben eine sehr selbständige Argumentationsweise. Nähe zu Luther und Selbständigkeit schließen sich bei ihnen nicht aus.

7.1 Andreas Osiander d.Ä.

Osiander, seit 1522 Prediger an St. Lorenz,[68] ist wahrscheinlich der Verfasser einer Vorrede zum Sendbrief Argulas von Grumbach an Rektor und Universität von Ingolstadt.[69] Zusammen mit dem Sendbrief erschien die Vorrede erstmals 1523 in Nürnberg im Druck. Die Polemik des Verfassers richtet sich gegen die "verplenten, plinden, wůtenden phariseier"[70] und "schrifftgelerten der hohenschůl zů Ingoldstat".[71] Ihrem geistfeindlichen Wüten[72] wird das Wirken Christi gegenübergestellt, der jetzt, in der anbrechenden Endzeit ("in diesen letzten tagen") nicht nur durch Gelehrte der Schrift, sondern auch durch viele andere Menschen, jung und alt, Männer und Frauen, seinem Wort Gehör schafft.[73] Die Formulierung "nit allein durch gelerte der schrift" weist darauf hin, daß die Argumentation nicht einen Gegensatz zur literarischen Gelehrsamkeit enthält, sondern gegenüber den scholastischen Theologen Ingolstadts, den Feinden des Hl. Geistes und Gotteswortes, die Allgemeinheit der Geistausgießung und Wortverkündigung betont. Darum wird Joel 3,1-4 mit seinen Aussagen über die Geistausgießung auf alles Fleisch, auf Söhne und Töchter, Knechte

---

[68] Überblick über die Quellenlage und Literatur zu Osiander bei Berndt Hamm, "Wort Gottes und Menschensatzung. Notizen zur Osiander-Gesamtausgabe und zu Osianders Theologie", *Zeitschrift für bayerische Kirchengeschichte* 51 (1982): 54-72.

[69] Ediert von Jürgen Lorz in *Andreas Osiander d.Ä. Gesamtausgabe*, Bd. 1, hg. von Gerhard Müller/Gottfried Seebaß, (Gütersloh, 1975), Nr. 6, 88-92; zur vermuteten Verfasserschaft Osianders ("mit einiger Wahrscheinlichkeit"), 89; Text, 91f.

[70] Ebd., 91,7f.

[71] Ebd., 92,9.

[72] Ebd., 91,8: "die ir alwegen dem heyligen Gaist widerstanden habt".

[73] Ebd., 91,11-15.

und Mägde zitiert[74] — mit der Pointe, daß erstaunlicherweise auch das
weibliche Geschlecht das verfolgte Evangelium in Schutz nimmt.[75] Argula
erscheint so als Paradigma dafür, daß nun, in der Endzeit, die Verheißung
von Joel 3 in Erfüllung geht. Die Weise, wie sie in ihrem Sendbrief aus der
Bibel argumentiert, vor allem aber die Tatsache, daß sie sich einer
Disputation mit den Ingolstädter Professoren zu stellen bereit ist, läßt nach
Meinung des Verfassers nur den Schluß zu, daß sie ihr Schreiben nicht unter
Anleitung anderer, sondern selbständig — "allein vom geist Gottes" getrie-
ben — verfaßt hat.[76] Das 'solus spiritus', wie es uns in diesem Zusammen-
hang begegnet, ist ganz im Sinne Luthers auf Schriftstudium und sprachliche
Vermittlung bezogen.

Was in den oben zitierten Passagen Luthers nicht vorkam, ist der
eschatologische Bezug auf Joel 3. Dieses Endzeitbewußtsein, das mit der
Akzentuierung der geistlichen Vollmacht der ungelehrten Laien eine enge
Verbindung eingeht, ist charakteristisch für den pneumatologischen
Antiklerikalismus vieler Flugschriftenverfasser: Die anbrechende Endzeit ist
mit der Anfangszeit der Apostel verknüpft und ihr gleichzeitig und
ebenbürtig durch das unmittelbare Wirken des Geistes, der das Wort des
Evangeliums freisetzt.

Die Vorrede, falls sie wirklich von Osiander stammt, fügt sich problemlos
in sein integratives Geistverständnis ein, wie es uns aus anderen Schriften
der frühen zwanziger Jahre bekannt ist. Gerade der exzellente Hebräisch-
spezialist Osiander betont sehr stark die Vermittlung des erleuchtenden und
begnadenden Geistwirkens durch das äußere Wort von Schrift und
Predigt.[77] Und von Anfang an betont er, wie wichtig das hermeneutische
Instrumentarium der Sprachkenntnisse für die Schriftauslegung eines
christlichen Predigers sei. Interessant ist in diesem Zusammenhang ein im
September 1522 entstandenes Gutachten Osianders über Johann Winzler, den
Prediger des Nürnberger Franziskanerkonvents.[78] Winzler hatte in einer
Predigt gesagt, daß Hebräisch- und Griechischkenntnisse zum Verständnis
der Schrift nicht ausreichen.[79] Osiander gibt dazu den Kommentar, daß das
zwar stimmt, weil Gottes Geist den Prediger belehren muß, daß andererseits
aber die Sprachkenntnisse durchaus etwas zum Schriftverständnis beitragen.
Denn Gottes Geist erfüllt — nach Weish. 1,7 — den gesamten Erdkreis, und
der alle Dinge in sich enthält (d.h. der Geist), besitzt immer die 'erkantnus

---

[74] Ebd., 92,3-7.

[75] Ebd., 92,7-13.

[76] Ebd., 92,13-17.

[77] Vgl. z.B. *Osiander Gesamtausgabe*, Bd. 1, 263,13-264,5 und 266,14f. (Nr. 21:
Gutachten über Heinrich Schwertfeger 1524); 413,5-32 (Nr. 32: Gutachten über Hans
Denck 1525).

[78] Ediert von Dietrich Wünsch in *Osiander Gesamtausgabe*, Bd. 1 (wie Anm. 69),
Nr. 2, 47-63; Text, 54-63.

[79] Ebd., 52.

der stim und sprach'. Dieses Bibelwort bedeutet für Osiander, daß der Geist sprachliche (lautliche und verbal-artikulierte) Qualität und umgekehrt die Sprache geistliche Dimension besitzt: "Die erkantnus der sprach schliest alle ding in sich."[80] Die Kenntnis des geistlichen Sinns der Bibel erschließt sich somit über die Kenntnis der biblischen Sprachen. Der integrative ('einschlie-ßende') Charakter von Osianders Geist- und Sprachverständnis — daß das Geistwirken die Sprache und das Lautwerden der Sprache den Geist einschließt — kommt in diesem dichten Text sehr deutlich zum Ausdruck.

7.2 Lazarus Spengler

Auch bei Lazarus Spengler, der nicht nur einer der fleißigsten Luther-Leser war, sondern auch in persönlicher Beziehung zu Luther stand, daneben aber auch durch Osiander beeinflußt wurde,[81] zeigt sich sehr deutlich diese wechselseitig integrative Beziehung von Geistwirken und Predigt- bzw. Schriftwort. Überblickt man Spenglers reformatorisches Schrifttum seit seiner Schutzrede für Luther von 1519, so wird man hervorheben müssen, daß er — verglichen mit anderen Flugschriftenautoren der frühen Refor-mationsbewegung — eher zurückhaltend vom Hl. Geist spricht, kaum in betonter Weise, sondern gelegentlich, wenn er in gut lutherischer Weise den Zusammenhang von Wort, Glaube, Geist und Wiedergeburt zur Sprache bringt. In Spenglers Sicht ist Gottes Geist so stark in die äußeren Bezüge von Bibelwort und Evangeliumsverkündigung hineingebunden und hat Gottes Wort als Zeugnis des Glaubens und glaubenschaffendes Wort so selbstverständlich geistlichen (geistgestifteten und geistvermittelnden) Charakter, daß er selten Anlaß sieht, eigens die Geistdimension des göttlichen Redens und Handelns hervorzuheben. Bisweilen freilich artikuliert er sehr deutlich seine Auffassung von der engen Beziehung zwischen *verbum externum* und Geist, sein integratives Verständnis von Geist und Wort. So verbindet er in zwei Flugschriften von 1522 jeweils die antihierar-chische Gegenüberstellung von Menschenwort, -lehre oder -satzung und Gotteswort mit der Erläuterung: "Dann gottes wortt und leer sind nymer on

---

[80] "Zum ailften spricht er, es sei nicht gnug etc. Ist war. Wir sagen auch frei, das ein christlicher prediger muß Gottis gelert sein. Das aber nichts darzuthun [Subjekt: die Sprachkenntnisse], glauben wir nicht. Die geschrift spricht: 'Der gaist Gottis hat erfullt den umkrayß des erdreichs, und das alle ding in sich beschliest, hat je erkantnus der stim und sprach etc.' [Weish. 1,7]. Die erkantnus der sprach schliest alle ding in sich." Ebd., 63,4-9.

[81] Vgl. Berndt Hamm, "Lazarus Spengler und Martin Luthers Theologie", in *Martin Luther. Probleme seiner Zeit* (wie Anm. 27), 124-36; die wichtigsten Arbeiten zu Spengler sind genannt in meinem Aufsatz, "Stadt und Kirche unter dem Wort Gottes: das reformatorische Einheitsmodell des Nürnberger Ratsschreibers Lazarus Spengler (1479-1534)", in L. Grenzmann, K. Stackmann (Hgg.), *Literatur und Laienbildung im Spätmittelalter und in der Reformationszeit* (Stuttgart, 1984), 710-29.

geyst, menschen wortt und leer haben nymer keynen geyst."⁸² Der Geist-
losigkeit der Papstkirche und ihrer nicht biblisch begründeten Satzungen
wird nicht die Geisterfülltheit von glaubenden Menschen, sondern der
Geistcharakter des biblischen Gotteswortes gegenübergestellt (obwohl für
Spengler selbstverständlich auch gilt, daß kein Glaubender ohne Geist ist).

Noch deutlicher wird der Wortbezug des Geistes bei Spengler in einer
Flugschrift von 1523,⁸³ in der er sich mit dem gegnerischen Argument
auseinandersetzt, Luther und seinesgleichen wollten die Hl. Schrift nach
"irem gefallen" auslegen.⁸⁴ Der Ratsschreiber entgegnet mit einer *solus-
spiritus*-Argumentation, die aber sofort in eine *solo-verbo-* und *sola-
scriptura*-Argumentation mündet. Gegenüber dem Auslegungsanspruch der
Papstkirche mit ihrem Arsenal der Väter-Autoritäten betont er: Es steht
überhaupt nicht in irgendeines Menschen "macht und urteil", die Schrift
auszulegen, denn nicht der Mensch, sondern der Hl. Geist allein ist der
Ausleger: "so doch der heylig geist keinen andern außleger dann sich selbs
leydenn kan. Es hat ye nit die weyse, das jme [sich] der Bapst, die Concilia,
heyligen lerer, doctores der kirchen oder andere menschen einichen gewalt
nemen mögen, das wort gottes (in der heyligen schrifft begriffen) inn dem
wenigstenn zů endern, darüber zů urteilen oder zu schliessen, dann das ist
alein das ampt des heyligenn geysts."⁸⁵ Daß Gottes Geist allein der
Ausleger ist, daß somit — wie Spengler im gleichen Zusammenhang auch
formulieren kann — Gott allein sein Wort in unser Herz hineinsagen
muß,⁸⁶ das bedeutet (mit Luther) für ihn, daß der auslegende Mensch durch
den Geist aus seinem Eigensinn herausgeholt und in die Selbstauslegung der

---

⁸² *Die haubt // artickel durch // welche gemeyne Chri // stenheyt byßhere // verfuret
wor= // den ist. [...]* (Wittenberg: Nickel Schirlentz, 1522), fol. E4v. *Ain kurtzer
begriff vnd // vnderrichtung aines gantzen // warhafften Christenlichen // wesens. [...]*
(o.O., o.Dr. 1522), Exemplar: UB München 4° Theol. 5333, fol. B5r: "Gotes wort
seind nimmer on gaist, menschen wort haben nimmer kainen gaist."
⁸³ *Verantwortung und auflösung etlicher vermeinter argument ...*, hg. von Alfred
Götze, in Otto Clemen (Hg.), *Flugschriften aus den ersten Jahren der Reformation*,
Bd. 2 (Leipzig, 1908; Nachdruck: Nieuwkoop, 1967), 339-413 (als Schrift von
Christoph Schappeler). Zur Verfasserschaft Spenglers s. Hans v. Schubert, *Lazarus
Spengler und die Reformation in Nürnberg*, QFRG 17 (Leipzig, 1934; Nachdruck:
New York, 1971), 401-6; ferner Oskar Tyszko, *Beiträge zu den Flugschriften Lazarus
Spenglers*, Diss. phil. (Gießen, 1939), 34 und 143-58.
⁸⁴ *Verantwortung und auflösung ...* (wie Anm. 83), 366,1-5.
⁸⁵ *Verantwortung und auflösung ...*, 366,7-16.
⁸⁶ *Verantwortung und auflösung ...*, 368,13-17: "Gottes wort muß uns allein got in
das hertz sagen, sonst ist es unbeschlossen und alles ungewyß, wie David sagt am 84.
psalm [zit. nach Vulgata Ps. 84,9 = 85,9]: 'Ich wil hören, was got in mir redt' und
mir eingibt, dann wann der schweygt, so ist es ungesprochen."

geistlichen (und darum hellen, klaren, erleuchtenden) Schrift hineingezogen wird.[87]

Es ist bemerkenswert, wie bei Spengler der Gesichtspunkt des auslegenden Menschen und damit der Aspekt der geistbegabten Person völlig zurücktritt hinter die Perspektive der sich selbst auslegenden, in sich klaren und verständlichen Schrift.[88] Nicht der geisterfüllte Mensch erklärt, sondern die geistliche Schrift und die Predigt des Gotteswortes klären.[89]

Damit hängt es zusammen, daß, soweit ich sehe, bei Spengler die verbreitete antiklerikale Gegenüberstellung von geistbegabten Laien und Ungelehrten einerseits und geistlosen Geistlichen und Gelehrten andererseits[90] fehlt, obwohl sie ihm durch Luther und Osiander durchaus vorgegeben ist. Der ganze Komplex der unmittelbaren Geistbelehrung des Gläubigen mit den entsprechenden Bibelstellen aus Johannes, Jesaja, Jeremia und Joel und der Spitze gegen die sterile scholastische Menschengelehrsamkeit ist bei ihm offensichtlich nicht aufgenommen, obwohl ihm als Laien durchaus die Frage auf den Nägeln brennt: Ist es auch den Laien, den Nicht-Geweihten und Ungelehrten, erlaubt, "sich in dem wort gottes unnd heyligen Euangelio zů underrichten, davon zů reden und zů disputirn"?[91] Ist es wirklich so, "das den leyen oder ungelerten das wort gottes mit den vermeinten geistlichen unnd gelerten nit solt gemein sein"?[92] Diese Frage behandelt Spengler eingehend in der gerade zitierten Flugschrift von

---

[87] "Darumb hat es gar nit die weyse, das yemand das wort gottes und die heiligen schrift zů seynem vermeinten, menschlichen synn zihe oder außlege, sonder ein yeder spruch der heyligen schrifft soll mit einem andern hellen spruch der schrifft ercleret unnd außgelegt werdenn." *Verantwortung und auflösung* ..., 366,24-28; vgl. 367,12-14 und 367,25-368,13.

[88] Vgl. besonders *Verantwortung und auflösung* ..., 368,1f.: "das wort gotes ist allen glaubigen gantz klar und verstendlich".

[89] Vgl. besonders *Verantwortung und auflösung* ..., 367,4-17: gegen diejenigen, die sagen, die Schrift sei an vielen Stellen "verborgen und tunckel", weshalb man sie "ercleren" müsse. "Das ist ein grosser irrsal, dann kein klarer wort unter dem hymel ist dann das wort gottes" — verbunden mit der Aussage: "allein der geist und das wort gottes das liecht ist, das uns allein lernt alle warheit". Vgl. auch 390,24-311,6: "... Wir aber glauben, das der heilig geyst, der vom vater gesandt ist, die junger Christi erleucht und erinnert hab alles das, ßo Christus gelernt [gelehrt], geredt und gethan hab, unnd sovil uns zu wissen not. Und ist derhalben in Euangelien die selb lere so clar unnd lautter außgedruckt, das es gantz nit not, ja got dem heyligen geist die hochst schmach unnd uneer were, wo sein leer durch irgent einen menschen solt verclert und außgelegt werden."

[90] Man vergleiche den unten dargestellten polarisierenden Typ des pneumatologischen Antiklerikalismus.

[91] *Verantwortung und auflösung* ... (wie Anm. 83), 385,8-10.

[92] *Verantwortung und auflösung* ..., 383,23-26.

1523.[93] Das so thematisierte Problem der Legitimität eines selbständigen Umgangs der Laien mit der Bibel zählt zu den wichtigsten antiklerikal zugespitzten Fragestellungen der frühen Reformationszeit. In Flugschriften für und von Laien wird die Frage stereotyp aufgeworfen und oft programmatisch formuliert. Die Antworten aber gehen, obwohl sie in Frage- und Lösungsansatz alle von Luther herkommen, in verschiedene Richtungen.

Spengler akzentuiert im Zusammenhang dieser Frage nicht die Rolle des Hl. Geistes, geschweige denn ein exklusives Geistwirken, sondern in einseitiger Weise den Öffentlichkeitscharakter und die Universalität des biblischen Wortes: Das Evangelium soll nach Christi Aussendungsbefehl der ganzen Welt und allen Kreaturen gepredigt werden. Somit soll es allen zugänglich und in aller Mund sein: "Christus sprach zů seinen jungern: 'Geet in die gantzen welt und predigt das Euangelion allen creaturn' (Mk. 16,15) — unnd diser gotloß hauffen wil arguirn [beweisen], als ob es nit zymlich und darzů farlich sey, das der gemein mann das Euangelion wissen soll. Dann ist das Euangelion ein genadenreiche potschafft, ein wort der frewden, des heyls und frydens — warumb solt es nit auch einem yeden offenbar werden und gemein sein, der dadurch muß geseliget werden, ja so gemein, das auch alle ir reden, disputation, gemeinschafft unnd wandel darinnen stee?"[94] Diese Argumentation, die nicht die Allgemeinheit der Geistausgießung oder die Exklusivität der inneren Geistbelehrung hervorhebt, sondern die Allgemeinheit und das äußere Offenbarwerden der Evangeliumsverkündigung, ist für Spengler typisch. Es ist eine Vorliebe von ihm, den Öffentlichkeitscharakter des Evangeliums und die Notwendigkeit einer allgemeinen, öffentlichen Diskussion über das Evangelium und Luthers Lehre zu unterstreichen — eine Öffentlichkeit außerhalb derjenigen Bereiche, wo die theologischen Fachgelehrten unter sich sind.[95] In dieser Forderung nach Öffentlichkeit und Allgemeinheit zeigt sich nicht nur der Laie, sondern auch der Ratsschreiber, der Mann des öffentlichen städtischen Lebens.

Spengler steht selbstverständlich ganz im Strom der antiklerikalen Polemik gegen die scholastische Schulgelehrsamkeit (gegen ihre bibelfernen 'Spitzfindigkeiten' und 'Menschenlehren'), doch ist dem literarisch hochgebildeten und versierten Ratsschreiber jeder Angriff auf gelehrte Bildung oder jede Relativierung schulischer Bildungsbemühungen fern. Ganz

---

[93] In der Auseinandersetzung mit dem antireformatorischen Argument: "Es sey darzů kummen, das auch schneyder, schůster, pawrn, alte weyber und kinder vom euangelio reden und disputirn wollen. Das sey färlich, verfůr vil lewt oder mach zum wenigsten allerley zweyfels, bring auch dem heyligenn euangelio verachtung." *Verantwortung und auflösung ...*, 383,17-21.

[94] *Verantwortung und auflösung ...*, 383,26-384,5.

[95] Vgl. seine *Schutzrede für Doktor Martin Luthers Lehre*, ediert in Laube 1: 501-16; besonders 508,25-509,6 und 510,2-13. Vgl. dazu Hamm, "Stadt und Kirche" (wie Anm. 81), 710.

im Gegenteil ist er wie Luther und Osiander ein leidenschaftlicher Verfech-
ter der grundlegenden Wichtigkeit einer neu gestalteten und auf die
Bedürfnisse eines evangelischen Kirchen- und Gemeinwesens hinorientierten
Schulbildung und Gelehrsamkeit. Schon in seiner ersten reformatorischen
Flugschrift von 1519 wendet sich Spengler gegen die Vorstellung, als seien
alle großen Kirchenlehrer und "alle ingenia und schickligkaiten [geistigen
Befähigungen]" in der Kirche ausgestorben, als gebe es nicht auch heute
noch "verstendig, gelert und hochgeschickt leüt, auß denen nit minder dann
vor [als zuvor] der geyst Gottes reden mag".[96] Schon in dieser Schrift zeigt
sich der integrative Charakter von Spenglers Geistverständnis,[97] in das die
äußeren Bezüge der sprachlichen Vermittlung und die Gelehrsamkeit der
Sprachbildung integriert sind — so wie umgekehrt in Spenglers Schrift-,
Predigt- und Gelehrsamkeitsverständnis seine Vorstellung von Gottes
Geistwirken integriert ist.

Den ersten Typ des pneumatologischen Antiklerikalismus, wie ihn
Osiander und Spengler vertreten, kann man somit als integrativen Typ
bezeichnen: Geistbelehrung steht nicht gegen sprachliche (schriftlich-
mündliche) und äußere Vermittlung, so wie sie auch nicht gegen Sprachbildung, Sprachgelehrsamkeit und Schule an sich gestellt wird. Im Gegenteil:
Beide sind davon überzeugt, daß sich das Wirken des Geistes mit Sprachgelehrsamkeit verbindet. Es ist bezeichnend, daß Luther seine Schulschrift
von 1530 *Daß man Kinder zur Schulen halten solle* Lazarus Spengler
gewidmet hat, seinem "besondern lieben herrn und freunde".[98]

VIII. DER ZWEITE (POLARISIERENDE) TYP
DES PNEUMATOLOGISCHEN ANTIKLERIKALISMUS

Einen sehr andersartigen Charakter zeigt die Verbindung von Antiklerikalismus, Aufwertung der kirchlichen Vollmacht von Laien und Argumentation
mit dem Geistwirken bei den Nürnberger Flugschriftenautoren Diepold
Peringer (dem 'Bauern von Wöhrd')[99] und Hans Sachs,[100] dem ehemali-

---

[96] *Schutzrede* (wie Anm. 95), 505,10-15.

[97] Man achte etwa auf die Weise, wie Spengler vom "geyst der schrifft" spricht:
Schutzrede, 503,32.

[98] *WA* 30/II. 517,1-3.

[99] Vgl. Günter Vogler, *Nürnberg 1524/25. Studien zur Geschichte der reformatorischen und sozialen Bewegung in der Reichsstadt* (Berlin, DDR, 1982), 135-51
(Literatur). Der Priester Diepold Peringer, der sich als ungelehrten Bauern ausgab und
entsprechend grob bäurisch aufführte (z.B. die Stiefel auf den Tisch legte und Bücher,
die man ihm gab, verkehrt herum hielt), trat in Nürnberg von Ende 1523 bis Mai
1524 als Laienprediger auf und ging dann nach Kitzingen. Treffend bemerkt Vogler
(140), daß uns in Peringer eine Gestalt begegnet, "die den Brückenschlag von der
reformatorischen Predigt in der Stadt zur Verbreitung des Evangeliums in den
Dörfern des Landgebiets gefördert hat", ohne daß man sein Wirken zu den Mitte Mai

gen Kleriker und dem Laien. Sowohl sozial als auch bildungsmäßig befinden
wir uns hier auf einer tieferen Ebene. Während Osiander und Spengler auf
dem Niveau der 'ehrbaren' Oberschicht stehen, gehören die folgenden
Verfasser zum Bereich der nicht ehrbaren Mittelschicht.[101] Anders als
Osiander und Spengler haben sie keine akademische Bildung genossen
(einen Universitätsbesuch Peringers halte ich für sehr unwahrscheinlich).

Ihren pneumatologischen Antiklerikalismus kann man als polarisierenden
Typ bezeichnen — polarisierend deshalb, weil das Wirken des Hl. Geistes,
des *solus spiritus*, prinzipiell gegen schulische Belehrung und Bildung
gestellt wird. Zwar muß man selbstverständlich davon ausgehen, daß
Peringer, Sachs und ähnlich argumentierende Autoren in anderen Städten,
wie etwa Sebastian Lotzer in Memmingen,[102] nichts gegen Schulbildung
von Christen einzuwenden haben; doch lassen sie den Standpunkt erkennen,
daß Gelehrsamkeit und Sprachbildung nichts zum Verständnis der Hl. Schrift
beitragen, daß sie in der Gemeinschaft der Glaubenden nicht zählen, sondern
daß hier — wenn es um die Hermeneutik des Gotteswortes, die Begründung
von Glauben und die geistliche Kompetenz zu lehren, zu predigen und zu
beurteilen geht — ganz andere Gaben gefordert sind. Begreiflicherweise
fehlen dann bei diesen Flugschriftenautoren auch die lutherischen Differenzierungen zwischen der allgemeinen geistlichen Vollmacht aller Christen und

---

1524 im Nürnberger Landgebiet einsetzenden ersten Zehntverweigerungen direkt in
Beziehung setzen kann. Als Quelle verwende ich im folgenden einen Sermon, der
zwar erst nach Peringers Weggang aus Nürnberg publiziert wurde, dem aber nach
Aussage Peringers eine Predigt zugrundeliegt, die er bereits in Wöhrd bei Nürnberg
gehalten habe und dann, am Fronleichnamstag (26. Mai 1524), wieder in Kitzingen
und die — die Fiktion der literarischen Unbildung des Autors soll ja aufrechterhalten
werden — von Zuhörern aufgeschrieben worden sei: *Ein Sermon // von der
Abgötterey / durch den // Pawern / der weder schreyben // noch lesen kan /
geprediget zů // Kitzing im Francken= // land auff vnsers // Herren // Fronleychnams
tag. // M.D.XXiiij.* [Nürnberg: Hans Hergot] 1524, Köhler, Fiche 1493 Nr. 3922. Zu
dieser Flugschrift vgl. Vogler, 146-150.

[100] Vgl. Vogler, *Nürnberg 1524/25*, 151-76 (Literatur); Martin Arnold, *Handwerker
als theologische Schriftsteller. Studien zu Flugschriften der frühen Reformation (1523-
1525)*, Göttinger theologische Arbeiten 42 (Göttingen, 1990), 56-105 (Literatur). Die
Reformationsdialoge (alle 1524) des Schuhmachermeisters zitiere ich im folgenden
nach der Ausgabe von Gerald H. Seufert, *Hans Sachs: Die Wittenbergisch Nachtigall.
Spruchgedicht, vier Reformationsdialoge und das Meisterlied Das Walt got* (Stuttgart,
1974; Reclam-Universal-Bibliothek Nr. 9737 [3], 1984).

[101] Zur Frage der Ehrbarkeit in Nürnberg und ihrer Kriterien vgl. Berndt Hamm,
"Humanistische Ethik und reichsstädtische Ehrbarkeit in Nürnberg", *Mitteilungen des
Vereins für Geschichte der Stadt Nürnberg* 76 (1989): 65-147; 73-95.

[102] Zum Kürschner Sebastian Lotzer, der als Redaktor der 'Zwölf Artikel' der
Bauernschaft in Schwaben (1525) gilt und 1523/24 fünf Flugschriften verfaßt hat, vgl.
neuerdings Arnold (wie Anm. 100), 145-193 (Literatur); die Flugschriften liegen vor
in der Edition von Alfred Goetze, *Sebastian Lotzers Schriften* (Leipzig, 1902).

dem besonderen Amt der Lehre, Predigt und Sakramentenspendung, zwischen allgemeiner Legitimierung und konkreter Befähigung oder zwischen der schlichten Predigt und der eigentlichen Schriftauslegung. Dagegen fällt das ganze Gewicht der Argumentation auf das Geistwirken und die Geistbegabung gerade solcher Menschen, die in keine Schule gegangen und keine Universität besucht haben: Allein der Geist belehrt. Er allein ist der Lehrer der Herzen, der ihnen Schriftverständnis schenkt — ganz unabhängig von Schulen und literarischer Bildung. Darum auch betont der 'Bauer von Wöhrd', daß er "weder schreyben noch lesen kan",[103] während z.B. der Kürschner Sebastian Lotzer mit einer sehr bezeichnenden Formulierung sagen kann: "er [Gott] ist der recht schůlmeister, kan ain in ainer stund meer lernen [lehren], dann ob ainer fünfftzig iar auff der hohen schůl stiend".[104] Die Relativierung der Schulbildung und die Aufwertung des Geistwirkens stellt die Laien den Gelehrten und Fachtheologen gleich, ja es wird betont, daß die Geistgelehrsamkeit den Laien eine Überlegenheit über die verbildende Schulgelehrsamkeit der Kleriker verleiht: "Dieweil nun alle die, die den rechten Glauben hahn, den Geist Christi hahn und vom Geist gelehrt werden, so sind sie auch wahrlich recht und göttlich gelehrt, und acht auch viel gelehrter, denn hätten sie Magistrum sententiarum gestudiert und Langröck an."[105]

Es handelt sich also um eine Argumentationsweise, die im pneumatologischen Kontext schulische Belehrung und Bildung völlig relativiert, um so 1. die allein belehrende Wirkung des Geistes, 2. die unmittelbare Beziehung zwischen Geistbelehrung und Kompetenz zur Schriftauslegung und mit all dem 3. die Laienvollmacht in der christlichen Gemeinde hervorzuheben. Stereotyp kehren in den verschiedenen Flugschriften immer wieder die gleichen Argumentationspunkte wieder. Die wichtigsten Argumente stelle ich im folgenden zusammen, indem ich außer Peringer und Sachs ergänzend auch andere Flugschriften des gleichen Argumentationstyps heranziehe:

1. Vorrangig werden als Belege für die nicht schulvermittelte Geistbelehrung der Laien die Bibelstellen aufgeboten, die uns bereits bei Luther bzw. in der (Osiandrischen?) Vorrede zu Argula von Grumbach begegnet sind: Joh. 6,45, Jes. 54,13, Jer. 31,33f und Joel 3,1-4.

---

[103] Vgl. Titelblatt seines Sermons von der Abgötterei: Anm. 99. Gleich zu Beginn des Textes (fol. A1v) wird diese Aussage noch zweimal wiederholt.

[104] Ausgabe Goetze (wie Anm. 102), 33,24-26 (*Ain hailsame ermanunge*, 1523).

[105] Zitat aus der anonymen Flugschrift, *Ein schöner Dialogus von einem Schneider und von einem Pfarrer* ... (1524), ediert in Rudolf Bentzinger (Hg.), *Die Wahrheit muß ans Licht! Dialoge aus der Zeit der Reformation* (Leipzig, 1982), 381-401; 382f. (Vorrede). Das Thema der Vorrede ("ob die Leyen auch sollen mit der Gschrift umbgahn") wird mit folgenden Worten eingeführt: "Dieweil dies Gespräch von einem Priester und einem Leyen geschehen und etlich sich hören lassen, als sollten die Leyen nit mit diesem umbgahn und sich des nit annehmen (als ob sie nit auch in dies Himmelreych gehörten), sondern allein die Gelehrten ..."

Das Beispiel einer derartigen Argumentation findet sich in Sachs'
Reformationsdialog *Disputation zwischen einem Chorherren und Schuhmacher* von 1524:

> Chorherr: Wo wolts ir leyen gelernt haben? Kan ewer mancher kein bûchstaben.
> Schuster: Christus spricht Joannis am vi. [6,45]: "Sy werden all von got geleert."
> Chorherr: Es muß kunst [Kenntnis, Wissen] auch da seinn. Wofür wern die
> hohenschûl?
> Schuster: Uff welcher hohenschûl ist Joannes gestanden, der so hoch geschrie-
> ben hat ("Im anfang was das wort, und das wort was bey got etc." Joan. i.)?
> War doch nur ein fischer, wie Marci i. steet.
> Chorherr: Lieber, diser hett den heyligen geist wie Actuum am ii.
> Schuster: Steet doch Johelis ii. [Joel 3,1-4]: "Unnd es soll geschehen in den
> letzten tagen, spricht got, ich wil außgiessen von meinem geist auff alles fleisch
> etc." Wie, wenn es von uns [Laien] gesagt wer?[106]

2. Weitere Bibelstellen treten nun hinzu, die uns bei Luther, Osiander und
Spengler in diesem Kontext des pneumatologischen Antiklerikalismus nicht
begegnen und die bei Autoren wie Peringer und Sachs mit besonderer
Zuspitzung die geistliche Auslegungskompetenz der nicht akademisch
gebildeten oder völlig leseunkundigen Laien hervorheben.[107] Eine große

---

[106] Ausgabe Seufert (wie Anm. 100), 52,231-53,246. Vgl. z.B. auch Diepold
Peringers *Sermon von der Abgötterei* (wie Anm. 99), fol. A1v: Joh. 6,42.45, Jes.
54,13, Jer. 31,33f.

[107] Peringer (ebd.) zitiert gemeinsam mit den genannten Bibelstellen Matth. 25,25
(von dem nicht zu vergrabenden anvertrauten Pfund), Luk. 10,2 (von den Arbeitern
in der Ernte des Herrn, die sein Wort verkündigen) und Matth. 15,14 (über die Schulgelehrten: die blinden Blindenführer). Sachs zitiert in dem Abschnitt seiner
Flugschrift *Disputation zwischen einem Chorherrn und Schuhmacher*, der von der
geistlichen Vollmacht der ungelehrten Laien, selbständig mit der Hl. Schrift
umzugehen, handelt (Ausgabe Seufert, 49,114-54,278), eine Fülle von Bibelstellen,
z.B. Joh. 5,39 (Durchsucht die Schrift, die gibt Zeugnis von mir), Ps. 1,2 (Selig ist
der Mann, der sich Tag und Nacht übet im Gesetz des Herrn), Luk. 10,2 (wie
Peringer), mehrere paulinische Stellen von der Geisterfülltheit der Gläubigen (Seufert,
53,256-265 und 54,277f.). Vgl. auch die Flugschrift *Ein schöner Dialogus ...* (wie
Anm. 105), Vorrede (zur gleichen Thematik), 382f.: Auf die klassischen Stellen Joh.
6,45, Jes. 54,13 und Jer. 31,33f. folgt die Zitation von Hebr. 8,10f (= Zitat der
Jeremia-Stelle), 1. Thess. 4,9 (Es ist nicht nötig, daß ich euch schreibe, denn ihr seid
von Gott gelehrt), 1. Joh. 2,27 (Es ist nicht nötig, daß euch jemand belehrt, sondern
wie euch der Geist Gottes lehrt, dabei bleibet). Der Verfasser gibt dieser Johannes-
Stelle die Deutung: "Da redet er [Johannes] von dem Geist, den alle Christen haben,
welcher Geist alle Christen gelehrt macht" (382). Es folgen zahlreiche weitere Bibel-
Zitate, die in die conclusio münden: "Damit acht ich nun gnugsam bewehrt sein, daß
alle Christen mit dem Gottswort mügen umbgahn, darvon reden, einander unterweisen
und lehren, wie oder was ein jeglicher kann oder vermag" (383). Diese Beispiele
zeigen, wie die kleineren Flugschriftenverfasser aufgrund eigener Beschäftigung mit
dem Bibeltext die biblischen Argumentationsketten anwachsen lassen und verändern
und wie sie innerhalb der Luther-Rezeption bereits darin ihre Selbständigkeit

Bedeutung spielt die Stelle Matth. 11,25 (bzw. die Parallelstelle: Luk. 10,21), wo davon die Rede ist, daß Jesus seinen Vater dafür preist, daß er "dies vor Weisen und Verständigen verborgen und es Unmündigen geoffenbart" hat. In Diepold Peringers *Sermon von der Abgötterei* wird diese Stelle in antiklerikaler Umformulierung (aus den Weisen und Verständigen werden die Stolzen und Hochmütigen) so in den Argumentationsduktus eingefügt: "Es thůt in [ihnen, d.h. den Schultheologen] wol zôrner [es erzürnt sie], das in eyn pawer die warheyt sagt, der nie auff keyner hohenschůll gewesen ist. Denn so ins eyn doctor sagt, so sprechen sie: Er ist auff eyner hohenschůl gestanden. Aber got macht solch blind, tôricht und unsinnig volck zů schanden, wie wir Matthei am 11., Luce 10. haben, da er dem vatter danckt, das er die weyßheyt verborgen hat den stoltzen und hochmůtigen unnd geoffenbart den kleynen; wie auch der David sagt am 8. psalm [Ps. 8,3]: 'Du hast vollbracht das lob von dem mund der kinder etc.'"[108]

Diese Laienautoren der Reformationszeit argumentieren nicht nur damit, daß sie und jeder einfache Laienchrist aufgrund des allgemeinen Priestertums und der damit gegebenen Gabe des Geistes prinzipiell das Recht und die Fähigkeit haben, zu Fragen der rechten Schriftauslegung das Wort zu ergreifen; sie sehen auch angesichts der Not der Kirche eine Nötigung und Verpflichtung zum Reden, da die vornehmlich zur Schriftauslegung Berufenen, die gelehrten Priester, in die Irre gehen und in die Irre führen[109] (klassisches antiklerikales Bibelargument in den Flugschriften: die

---

gegenüber Luther und anderen Reformatoren erweisen.

[108] *Sermon von der Abgötterei* (wie Anm. 99), fol. A2r. Diese Matth./Luk.-Stelle ist z.B. auch zitiert bei Hans Sachs: Ausgabe Seufert (wie Anm. 100), 63,554-558 (*Disputation zwischen einem Chorherren und Schuhmacher*, 1524); Sebastian Lotzer: Ausgabe Goetze (wie Anm. 102), 40,36-39 (*Ain christlicher Sendbrief*, 1523); Lotzer zitiert im Anschluß an dieses Zitat nicht wie Diepold Peringer Ps. 8,3, sondern Jes. 29,14: "wann die weißhait verdirbt von seinen weysen, und die vernunfft seiner witzigen wyrt verporgen" und 1. Kor. 1,19f.: vom Zuschandenwerden der Weisheit dieser Welt. Vgl. auch die 1523 erschienene Flugschrift von Balthasar Stanberger: *Dialogus zwischen Petro und einem Bauern ...*, in *Die Wahrheit muß ans Licht!* (wie Anm. 105), 296-315; 300: "Mich wundert, es ist aber Gottes Wille, daß die armen Bauern so viel vom Wort Gottes und mehr denn die Pfaffen wissen. Gott sei gebenedeit und gelobt in Ewigkeit, daß du deine heimliche Dinge den Großen verborgen und den Cleinen geoffenbart hast, als Matth. am 11., Luce am 10. steht." Hier wird ausdrücklich mit dem Aspekt von Bildung und Unbildung der ebenfalls antiklerikale Gesichtspunkt des sozialen Gegensatzes von Großen und Kleinen/Armen verbunden.

[109] Zu dieser Nötigung vgl. z.B. die Flugschrift, *Ein schöner Dialogus von einem Schneider und von einem Pfarrer* (wie Anm. 105), 389. Der Schneider sagt: "O ich glaub, daß wir am Jüngsten Tag alle Prediger geheißen sein müssen, welcher mehr denn ein andrer weiß und seinen Nächsten nit unterweist, daß Gott von ihm fordern wird das Blut von seiner Hand am Jüngsten Tag." In einer anderen Flugschrift wird

Blinden als Blindenführer, Matth. 15,14/Luk. 6,39).[110] Diese Verpflichtung wird stereotyp immer wieder mit Luk. 19,40 begründet: daß nämlich dann, wenn jetzt auch noch die Laien die Wahrheit verschweigen, die Steine schreien werden. So schreibt der Kürschner Sebastian Lotzer 1523 in einer an die Bürger seiner Heimatstadt Horb gerichteten Flugschrift: "Wiewoll sich vil gaistlichs und weltlichs standts darwider hefftig legen, yedoch hilffts alles nichts: das wort gottes wil eyn fürgang hon, zûvor under dem gmainen man; unnd ob wir schweygen wurden, mûßten die stain zûletst reden, auff das das wort gottes nit undergetruckt wurd."[111] Hans Sachs läßt am Ende der bereits ausführlich zitierten Flugschrift den Diener des Chorherrn zu seinem Herrn sagen: "Es thut euch and [Es beleidigt euch], das euch der schûster das rot piret [Barett] gesmâcht [geschmäht] hat. Laßt euchs nit wundern! Wann [denn] im alten gesetz hat got die hyrtten sein wort lassen verkündenn; also auch yetz mûssen (euch phariseyer) die schûster leren. Ja es werden euch noch die stein in die oren schreyen."[112] Den gesamten Dialog hatte Sachs auf dem Titelblatt unter das Motto gestellt: "Ich sage euch, wo dise schweygen, so werden die stein schreyen."[113]

---

betont, daß die Laien — etwa die Bauern — nicht predigen müßten, sondern ganz ihrer Arbeit nachgehen könnten, wenn die Geistlichen ihre Predigtaufgabe erfüllten. Aber leider ist es eben anders: "Aber yetzunnd layder ist die demût verwandelt und haist hochmût. Auch sag ich, daz ain yeglicher mag leeren ain andern, unnd uns ist allen geboten bey unser sel hail, das ainer den anndern sol gûts leeren, dann wann unser faist beüch, junckherren, thûm [Dom-] pfaffen predigetten, uns die warhait sagten, so dorfft [bräuchte, müßte] es kain baur thûn als ich bin, so wartet ich meyner arbaitt." Vorausgegangen ist die übliche Fragestellung: "Wie darff ain baur büecher schreyben oder machen, oder leeren ain anndern, so er kain priester ist unnd hat des nicht gewalt?" Aus: *Beklagung eines Laien, genannt Hans Schwalb, über viel Mißbräuche christlichen Lebens* (1521), ediert in Laube 1: 63-74; 65,41-66,10.

[110] Zu Peringer vgl. Anm. 107; vgl. Sachs, Ausgabe Seufert (wie Anm. 100), 86,306-308 (*Ein gesprech von den Scheinwercken der Gaystlichen*, 1524).

[111] Ausgabe Goetze (wie Anm. 102), 27,27-31.

[112] Ausgabe Seufert (wie Anm. 100), 70,794-71,799 (*Disputation zwischen einem Chorherren und Schuhmacher*, 1524).

[113] Ausgabe Seufert (wie Anm. 100), 43. Zur Verwendung dieser Luk.-Stelle vgl. z.B. auch die oben zitierte (von Osiander verfaßte?) Vorrede zum Sendbrief Argulas von Grumbach (wie Anm. 69), 92,2f.; ferner die 'Schirmred' des Konstanzer Stadtschreibers Jörg Vögeli von 1524, deren Vorrede abschließend und programmatisch den Laienstatus des Verfassers so zur Sprache bringt: "Verlach (das bit ich) nit mich layen, dann nit wer rede, besunder was man red, ze erwegen ist; es erschint die zit jetzo, so die menschen schwigen welten, das d'stain das lob gots reden wurden (Lu 19), die stain uß den muren werdent schryen und das holtz, das in fuogen der gebüwen ligt, würt antwort geben (Abacu 2[11])." Alfred Vögeli (Hg.), *Jörg Vögeli: Schriften zur Reformation in Konstanz 1519-1538*, Schriften zur Kirchen- und Rechtsgeschichte 39, Bd. 1 (Tübingen, 1972), 481.

3. Ein Argument, das uns bereits — bezogen auf den Evangelisten Johannes — bei Hans Sachs begegnet ist[114] und ebenfalls typisch ist für diesen gesamten Argumentationstypus, lautet: Auch die Apostel genossen keine Schulbildung und sind doch die Autoren des Neuen Testaments (also kann auch ein Ungebildeter das Neue Testament verstehen und auslegen); mit den Worten Peringers: "Seyn ye die Apostel auff keyner hohenschůl gestanden, dann die grundsuppen [Bodensatz, Grundübel] sind noch nit gewesen, mit welchen sie [die 'papistischen' Schulgelehrten] die gantzen welt betrogen haben."[115]

4. Das Apostel-Argument muß man in einen weiteren Argumentationszusammenhang einordnen, den man mit den Stichworten 'Endzeit', 'Allmacht Gottes' und 'Geistausgießung noch heute' umreißen kann. Die Endzeit, die 'letzten Zeiten' vor der Wiederkunft Christi,[116] stellen die Christenheit in eine unmittelbare Beziehung zur Anfangszeit der ersten Christen;[117] denn für diese Endzeit gilt die prophetische Verheißung der Geistausgießung, die das jetzige Zeitalter der Ursprungszeit mit ihrer Fülle der Geistwirkungen gleichstellt, die die jetzigen Christen den geisterfüllten Christen der Urgemeinde über die Jahrhunderte des kirchlichen Verfalls hinweg gleichzeitig sein läßt. Jetzt ist wieder die Zeit, in der durch Gottes endzeitliche Geistbelehrung einfache, ungelehrte Menschen gottgelehrt und schriftkundig sind — so wie damals, als ungebildete Hirten sein Wort verkündigten[118] und einfache Fischer und Handwerker Apostel wurden und die neutestamentlichen Schriften verfaßten. Und darin erweist sich Gott als der Allmächtige, daß sein Geistwirken nicht auf die Anfangszeit der Christenheit beschränkt blieb, sondern heute noch lebendig und wirkkräftig ist. So schreibt Diepold Peringer über die schulgelehrten Kleriker: "Nun last sie faren, sie seyn blynd unnd blyndenlaytter [Mt. 15,14], dann sie haben

---

[114] Oben 408 bei Anm. 106.

[115] *Sermon von der Abgötterei* (wie Anm. 99), fol. A2r. Vgl. z.B. auch Sebastian Lotzer: Ausgabe Goetze (wie Anm. 102), 33,26-36 (*Ain hailsame ermanunge*, 1523).

[116] Vgl. z.B. Lotzer, *Ain hailsame ermanunge* (wie Anm. 115), 27,25-29: "Dann got der almechtig sicht zů disen unsern letsten zeytten wunderbarlich herab in diß Jamertal, und wie woll sich vil gaistlichs und weltlichs standts darwider hefftig legen, yedoch hilffts alles nichts: das wort gottes wil eyn fürgang hon, zůvor under dem gmainen man."

[117] Vgl. die oben (399) zitierte (von Osiander verfaßte?) Vorrede zum Sendbrief Argulas von Grumbach (wie Anm. 69), 91,12f.: "in diesen letzten tagen (als im anfang seiner kirchen auch beschach)" wirkt Christus nicht allein durch "gelerte der schrift", sondern — was mit der allgemeinen Geistausgießung (Verheißung von Joel 3,1-4!) zusammenhängt — auch durch Ungelehrte.

[118] Vgl. z.B. Hans Sachs: Ausgabe Seufert (wie Anm. 100), 71,795-798 (*Disputation zwischen einem Chorherren und Schuhmacher*, 1524): "Laßt euchs nit wundern! Wann [denn] im alten gesetz hat got die hyrtten sein wort lassen verkündenn; also auch yetz müssen (euch phariseyer) die schůster leren." Sebastian Lotzer: Ausgabe Goetze (wie Anm. 102), 33,14-17 (*Ain hailsame ermanunge*, 1523).

keyn glauben, lassen got nicht almechtig seyn, das er seynen geist noch als
wol kûndt außgiessen als zû der zeyt der apostel. Ist ye eben der eynig got,
der alle ding regirt."[119] Zur Heiligenverehrung sagt er an späterer Stelle
der gleichen Schrift: "Sagstu: sie [die verstorbenen Heiligen] haben den
heyligen geyst gehabt, ich sag: Glaubstu an got, der noch lebt wie er alweg
gelebt hat, so kan er dir den geyst als volkumen geben als inen. [...]
Hierumb der so Petrum gesterckt und geheiligt hat, kan dirs auch thûn, doch
nach seynem willen."[120] Es ist auffallend, wie stark sich gerade solche
Flugschriften, die Recht, Vollmacht und Befähigung der einfachen Laien zur
Schriftauslegung unterstreichen, in dieser Weise auf Gottes Allmacht berufen
— auf die geistwirkende Allmacht, die menschliche Bildungsunterschiede
hinfällig werden läßt.[121]

5. Dieser Betonung der göttlichen Gabe entspricht es, daß die Bitte der
ungelehrten Laien zu Gott um das rechte Schriftverständnis eine zentrale
Rolle spielt. Nicht die Sprachgelehrsamkeit, sondern die Bitte um den Geist
bietet den Laien den hermeneutischen Schlüssel zum Schriftverständnis.
Ausgehend von der Zusage der Gebetserhörung in Mt. 7,7f (Luk. 11,9f)
kann geradezu die hermeneutische Regel formuliert werden: Wer Gott (auch
als einfacher, ungelehrter Laie) mit unablässigem Eifer um das rechte
Verständnis der Hl. Schrift bittet, dem wird Gott die Belehrung durch den

---

[119] *Sermon von der Abgötterei* (wie Anm. 99), fol. A1v-2r.

[120] *Sermon von der Abgötterei*, fol. C3r.

[121] Vgl. z.B. Sebastian Lotzer: Ausgabe Goetze (wie Anm. 102), 27,25-29 (zit. in
Anm. 116) und 33,14-17 (*Ain hailsame ermanunge*, 1523). Zur Verbindung von
Allmacht Gottes und Laienthematik vgl. auch das *Gespräch-Büchlein Neu Karsthans*
(1521), ediert von Herbert Demmer in *Martin Bucers Deutsche Schriften*, Bd. 1,
Frühschriften 1520-1524, hg. von Robert Stupperich (Gütersloh, 1960), 406-444;
415,33-35 und 416,23-25. Auf die Frage des Karsthans, woher (der Laie) Franz von
Sickingen "sollich ding" (d.h. den kundigen und gegen die Papstkirche gerichteten
Umgang mit der Hl. Schrift) gelernt habe, verweist dieser auf die Schriften Luthers
und die Vermittlung Huttens und dankt "dem almechtigen gott, das er mich zû
erkantnüß seiner rechten ler hat kommen lassen und von den falschen predigern und
Endchristischen lerern abgefordert". Die Berufung auf Gottes Allmacht ist zwar, wie
diese Flugschriften zeigen, implizit oder explizit mit der Vorstellung von der
Geisterleuchtung und -belehrung der Ungelehrten verbunden, doch fehlt (was unten
noch ausführlicher begründet wird) jede spiritualistische Färbung. Andererseits ist es
naheliegend, daß spiritualistisch geprägte Texte gerade auch den Allmachtsaspekt
besonders akzentuieren: daß der allmächtige Gott sein Geistwirken nicht an
kreatürliche Vermittlungen bindet — eben weil er der Allmächtige ist, der nicht der
äußerlichen Vermittler bedarf und sich auch nicht an sie bindet. Eine Flugschrift, die
in paradigmatischer Weise die durchgängige Berufung auf Gottes Allmacht mit einem
ausgeprägten Spiritualismus verbindet, ist die des Augsburger Täufers Jakob Dachser,
*Ein Göttlich vnnd gründt= // lich offenbarung: von den // warhafftigen wider= //
teuffern: mit Göt= // licher warhait // angezaigt. // M.D.XXVII.* [Augsburg: Philipp
Ulhart d.Ä.] 1527, Köhler, Fiche 1465 Nr. 3861.

Geist nicht versagen, den wird er so ausreichend belehren, daß er keiner weiteren schulgelehrten Belehrung durch die Gebildeten mehr bedarf. Man stößt hier gleichsam auf eine laientheologische, bibelhermeneutische Umprägung des alten spätmittelalterlichen Axioms: "Homini facienti quod in se est deus non denegat gratiam." Dem Menschen, der tut, was er kann, dem wird, ja dem kann Gott seine Gnadenzuwendung nicht versagen.[122]

In Nürnberg ist diese Umprägung am deutlichsten bei dem Maler Hans Greiffenberger zu fassen.[123] Bei Sebastian Lotzer in Memmingen begegnet

---

[122] Vgl. Heiko A. Oberman, "Facientibus quod in se est deus non denegat gratiam. Robert Holcot, O.P. and the Beginnings of Luther's Theology", *Harvard Theological Review* 55 (1962): 317-342; Berndt Hamm, *Frömmigkeitstheologie* (wie Anm. 7), 252-9 u.ö. (siehe Register s.v. 'facere quod in se est'). Die Analogie zum Lehrsatz "Homini facienti quod in se est deus non denegat gratiam" (auch in der Formulierung: "... deus infallibiliter dat gratiam") ist freilich nur eine vordergründig-formale, da es in unserem Zusammenhang nicht um den Erwerb der rechtfertigenden Gnade (gratia gratum faciens) und ein quasi-verdienstliches Tun des Menschen geht, sondern in selbstverständlicher Weise die grundlegende Gnadenzuwendung Gottes vorausgesetzt wird.

[123] Seine Flugschriften sind im Anhang bibliographisch aufgelistet. Ich rechne Greiffenberger zum dritten (spiritualistischen) Typ des pneumatologischen Antiklerikalismus und behandle ihn daher erst an späterer Stelle. Doch läßt sich feststellen, daß er offensichtlich in seinen ersten Flugschriften von 1523 (*Die Falschen Propheten* [Nr. 1], *Unsere maister der geschrifft* [Nr. 2]) noch keinen spiritualistischen Einschlag zeigt, sondern sehr nahe beim Argumentationstyp eines Hans Sachs, Diepold Peringer oder Sebastian Lotzer steht. In einer dieser frühen Schriften, der 'Meister'-Schrift (Nr. 2), wird der hermeneutische Schlüssel des Gebets so zur Sprache gebracht (fol. D3v): "Unnd habt vleiss, das ir vleyssig acht nempt der warheyt des wort gottes des heyligen Ewangelium und der heyligen geschrifft. Und pittet got den herren umb ain waren glauben und rechten verstanndt; derselbig ist, der den rechten verstanndt gibt unnd sonnßt khainer. Aber die schůlfatzen sagen, man lern es in der schůl [...] unnd sagen, man lern es in der schůl und schreyen: du versteet [verstehst] es nit. Aber du lay und ainfalltiger mensch kere dich nicht daran unnd schaw, das du das Ewangely lernest, und pitt got den herren mit vleyss; verstant [Verständnis der Schrift] wirt dir got gern geben und wirt dir es nit versagen, dann er spricht Mathei am vii. [V. 7]: 'Bitt, so wirt eüch geben, klopfft an, so wirt eüch aufgethan, sůcht, so vindt ir.' Und so ir den hymelischen vater pitet, so wirt er eüch geben sein heyligen geyst oder gůte gaben, Mathei am vi. [V. 5ff.?]. Man můeß den hymelischen vatter pitten umb solich gaben; man kanns sonnßt nicht lernen in der schůl, zůvor wo man nit Christum den herren lernet erkennen und vor augen hat." (fol. e1r): "Der pfaff oder münch ist nit dein mayster, sonnder Christus ist dein mayster. Das wiss gewiß! — unnd wirt nicht anndern in ewigkait. Darumb kere dich nicht daran, wann man sagt oder wann sy schreyen: Du versteest die geschrifft nit. Das ist des Sathans stymm. Ich sage dir in der warheyt: Ain yeder mensch, der die gnad von got dem allmăchtigen empfacht, das er geren die warheyt wissen wolt, damit das got der ewig glorificiert werde, so ist es unmüglichenn, das im got der herr versagt, so er pitt umb verstand der geschrifft des wort gottes, so er nicht das sein sůcht wie unnsere mayster, das man sag 'mayster', 'doctor', 'herr' etc." Vgl. auch

sie uns in folgender Form: "Christus sagt: 'Bittet, so wirtt euch geben, sûcht, so werden ir finden, klopft an, so wirt euch auffthon. Wer bitt, der empfacht, wer sûcht, der findtt, wer annklopfft, dem wirt auffthon etc.' [Mt. 7,7f] Hie vernempt ir, das uns Cristus nichts versagen wil, wa wir in nun hertzlich in festem glauben bitten. Lassent uns den gûtigen herren bitten, er wirt uns gnûg zû verston geben. Er mûß uns allain leeren, sunst wirt es wol ungeleernet bleiben."[124] Grundsätzlich gibt Lotzer den ungelehrten Laien den Rat: Kauft euch das Neue Testament, lest es oder laßt es euch vorlesen und "bitt got umb gnad: er wirt dir gnûg zû verston geben, was dir notwendig zûr seligkait ist"![125] Stellt das rechte Schriftverständnis nicht den Gelehrten anheim[126] und auch nicht einem künftigen Konzil![127] Denn Gelehrte und Konzilien haben geirrt; und jeder muß vor Gott für sich selbst Rechenschaft ablegen.

6. Der Grundsatz, wie er in dem Zitat aus Lotzers *Christlichem Sendbrief* von 1523 formuliert ist, daß Christus allein lehren muß,[128] daß er allein der Lehrer des Bibelverständnisses ist, ist auch für Nürnbergs Flugschriftenverfasser aus dem Laienbereich kennzeichnend. Um zu verdeutlichen, daß man sich nicht auf menschliche *magistri* und *doctores* verlassen soll, sondern nur auf den Meister Christus, zitiert man, wie etwa Hans Sachs, mit Vorliebe Mt. 23,10: "Ihr sollt euch nicht Meister nennen lassen, denn einer ist euer Meister: Christus."[129]

Noch weitere Argumente aus diesem Komplex der Geistbelehrung der Laien könnte man nennen. Dabei sind — aufs Ganze gesehen — bei diesem Typ des pneumatologischen Antiklerikalismus, wie er in Nürnberg durch Sachs und Peringer repräsentiert wird, folgende zusammenfassende Beobachtungen zu machen:

---

fol. f2r (die Bitte zu Gott dem Allmächtigen eröffnet das wahre Schriftverständnis).

[124] Ausgabe Goetze (wie Anm. 102), 40,25-31 (*Ain christlicher sendbrief*, 1523). Vgl. ebd. 33,23-26 (*Ain hailsame ermanunge*, 1523): "Ain mensch, wie schlecht [einfältig, gering] er ist, wan er got umb gnad bit, wil er im geben, was im not ist. Er ist der recht schûlmaister, kan ain in ainer stund meer lernen [lehren], dann ob ainer fünfftzig iar auff der hohen schûl stiend, zûvor in seynen gôtlichen wort."

[125] Ausgabe Goetze, 45,45-46,1 (*Ain christlicher sendbrief*); vgl. 27,31-33 (*Ain hailsame ermanunge*).

[126] Ausgabe Goetze, 40,32-36 (*Ain christlicher sendbrief*).

[127] Ausgabe Goetze, 45,43-46,3 (*Ain christlicher sendbrief*).

[128] Siehe oben im Text vor Anm. 124.

[129] Ausgabe Seufert (wie Anm. 100), 77,30-32 (*Ein gesprech von den Scheinwercken der Gaystlichen*, 1524). Vgl. auch die ganz dieser Meisterthematik gewidmete Flugschrift des Hans Greiffenberger von 1523 *Diss biechlin zaygt an, was uns lernen und gelernet haben unsere maister der geschrifft, darvor unns Cristus offt gewarnet hat* ... (Anhang Nr. 2), ferner Karlstadts Kritik an den Doktorpromotionen: Am 3. Febr. 1523 kam es in Wittenberg "zu einem Eklat, als Karlstadt solche Graduierungen für ein gottloses Unterfangen erklärte, weil Christus seinen Jüngern verboten habe, sich Meister zu nennen"; Brecht (wie Anm. 51) 158.

Die Polarisierung zwischen geisterfüllter Ungelehrsamkeit und geistloser Gelehrsamkeit führt in ihrer Radikalität, Generalisierung (ohne Differenzierungen) und in der Argumentationsweise deutlich über Luther und die Äußerungen anderer gelehrter reformatorischer Autoren hinaus: Man stellt nicht nur fest, daß *auch* Ungelehrte einen Zugang zum Schriftverständnis haben können, sondern man akzentuiert einseitig den Gedanken, daß Gott gerade durch die Ungelehrten und für die Ungelehrten die Wahrheit ans Licht bringt und daß das Schriftverständnis nicht auf seiten der gelehrten Kleriker, sondern der ungelehrten Laien ist. Es wird ein generelles Ressentiment gegen akademische Gelehrsamkeit, Sprachbildung und Schule sichtbar, wie es bei gelehrten Autoren der Reformationsbewegung kaum zu beobachten ist.[130] Dementsprechend führt auch die argumentative Verwendung bestimmter Bibelstellen und der Einsatz bestimmter Einzelargumente (z.B. die Gestaltung des Apostelarguments [Nr. 3], die Verknüpfung von Allmacht Gottes, endzeitlichem Geistwirken und Schriftverständnis [Nr. 4] oder die Verbindung von Gebetsbitte und ausreichendem Bibelverständnis [Nr. 5]) über Luther hinaus.

Andererseits aber ist zugleich die Nähe zu Luther bemerkenswert. Man sieht deutlich, wie die wesentlichen Impulse von Luthers Verständnis des allgemeinen Priestertums herkommen und von seiner Art, dem traditionellen

---

[130] In dieser Weise möchte ich meine sehr begrenzten Beobachtungen in die Form einer verallgemeinernden These kleiden, die freilich der Überprüfung bedarf. Selbstverständlich gibt es auf dem spiritualistischen Flügel der Reformation gelegentlich gelehrte Autoren, die der gelehrten Sprachbildung jede Bedeutung für den theologisch-geistlichen Erkenntnis- und Auslegungsprozeß absprechen. Doch bleibt diese Konstellation (so wohl zeitweilig Karlstadts Position, auch bei Thomas Müntzer breit zu belegen) die Ausnahme. Die Regel unter den gelehrten Autoren dürfte z.B. Martin Bucer mit seinen Aussagen über Geistempfang und Bibelverständnis einfacher, ungelehrter, nicht lateinkundiger Laien (sofern sie Gott mit 'begierigem und gläubigem Gemüt' darum bitten) repräsentieren — Aussagen, die in den Bereich des ersten (integrativen) Typs des pneumatologischen Antiklerikalismus gehören; *Martin Bucers Deutsche Schriften* (wie Anm. 121), 1: 85,1-86,12 (aus 'Summary' 1523). Der Gegensatz ist hier nicht Ungelehrte-Gelehrte, sondern Einfältige, die demütig sind, gegen Kluge, die stolz sind. Es ist bezeichnend, daß sich bereits Erasmus von Rotterdam, fern einer antigelehrten Haltung, 1515 gegen die Vorstellung wendet, die Lehre Christi könne nur von wenigen Theologen verstanden werden. "Erasmus faßt seine Meinung mit den Worten zusammen: 'Immo ut ipso Christo nihil fuit communius, ita doctrina illius nihil popularius'. Gegen den Einwand, daß der 'vulgus' die Schrift nicht verstehen könne, argumentiert er: 'Postremo non tam ingenio quam pietate percipiuntur'. Der Geist lehre sie, nicht Aristoteles, die Gnade, nicht die 'ratio', die Inspiration (afflatus), nicht der Syllogismus. Warum, so meint Erasmus, schließen wir das ganze christliche Volk aus?" Darum müsse die Bibel der christlichen Allgemeinheit durch Übersetzung in die Volkssprache zugänglich gemacht werden. Nach: *D. Martin Luther. Operationes in psalmos 1519-1521*, Teil 1, Gerhard Hammer, *Historisch-kritische Einleitung* (Köln, 1991), 63.

pneumatologischen Klerikalismus eine antiklerikale Pneumatologie entgegenzusetzen. Wichtig ist vor allem, daß mit Luther die pneumatologische Argumentation nie spiritualistische Züge gewinnt; d.h. die Dimension des göttlichen Geistwirkens wird nie als inneres Geschehen gegen eine Kraftlosigkeit, Insuffizienz und ungenügende Wirkungsfähigkeit des äußeren Schrift- und Predigtwortes gestellt. Immer besteht eine selbstverständliche, nicht problematisierte Verbindung von Innerem und Äußerem;[131] das Wirken des Geistes wird immer in Bezug gesetzt zum Lesen und Hören des Bibelwortes. Es fehlt jede innerreformatorische Polemik gegen die 'Schriftgelehrten', die ihr Vertrauen auf die gewißheitswirkende Kraft äußerer Worte und Buchstaben setzen. Das Gewißheitsproblem wird nicht auf einen inneren Bereich der Vergewisserung durch den Hl. Geist verlagert; es wird nicht von der Vorstellung her artikuliert, daß äußere Bibelworte und zugesprochene Vergebungsworte nicht innere Heilsgewißheit schaffen können. So ist es auch nicht verwunderlich, daß in dieser Gruppe von Flugschriften Anklänge an mystische Gedanken und Begriffe völlig fehlen. Wo rechtfertigungstheologische Passagen vorkommen, decken sie sich in ihrer vereinfachenden Form durchaus mit den Intentionen Luthers.

IX. Der dritte (spiritualistische) Typ
des pneumatologischen Antiklerikalismus

9.1 Hans Greiffenberger

Im Unterschied zu den beiden bisher vorgestellten Quellengruppen kann man einen dritten Typ des pneumatologischen Antiklerikalismus als spiritualistisch bezeichnen.[131a] In Nürnberg zeigt sich der spiritualistische Typ deutlich in Flugschriften des Handwerkertheologen Hans Greiffenberger.[132]

---

[131] Die bei Peringer und Sachs übliche Polemik gegen die Veräußerlichung des Kirchenwesens und der sog. 'guten Werke' im Gegensatz zur inneren Geisterfülltheit wahrer Frömmigkeit ist damit nicht gemeint.

[131a] Zur Terminologie: Spiritualismus ist ein Spezialfall der Pneumatologie (der Lehre vom Hl. Geist). Von Spiritualismus in seinen verschiedenen Schattierungen spricht man sinnvollerweise überall dort, wo, verglichen mit dem hebräisch-biblischen Wortverständnis, eine gewisse Entkopplung oder Distanzierung von sinnlich wahrnehmbarem (d.h. hör- oder lesbarem) Wort und innerseelischem Geistwirken stattfindet.

[132] Zur Person vgl. Vogler (wie Anm. 99) 176-194 (Literatur); vgl. auch Paul A. Russell, *Lay Theology in the Reformation. Popular Pamphleteers in Southwest Germany 1521-1525* (Cambridge, 1986), 159-165 und 266 (mit vielen Fehlern). Da die bisherige Literatur die Flugschriften Greiffenbergers nicht in bibliographischer Vollständigkeit verzeichnet hat, seien im Anhang unten (437) die sieben unter seinem Namen publizierten und die zwei anonymen (und in der Literatur ihm zugeschriebenen) Flugschriften von 1523/24 aufgelistet. Ob die anonymen Schriften tatsächlich von Greiffenberger stammen, müßte durch eine sorgfältige Analyse erst noch

Bei diesem Maler, der vermutlich erst im Laufe des Jahres 1523 nach Nürnberg kam,[133] wird eine Entwicklung und Steigerung über den zweiten Typ hinaus erkennbar. In einigen seiner Flugschriften, offensichtlich in seinen ersten, die 1523 erschienen,[134] liegt er ganz auf der Argumentationsebene eines Diepold Peringer oder Hans Sachs, so wie er ja auch sozial auf der Ebene dieser Autoren steht. Fast alle Argumente, die wir als kennzeichnend für den polarisierenden Typ zusammengestellt haben, finden sich bei ihm in prägnanten und scharfen Formulierungen.[135] Sowohl die Beeinflussung durch Luther als auch die Selbständigkeit des gegen die 'Meister' polemisierenden und alle Gelehrsamkeit und Bildung völlig

---

überprüft werden. Ich beschränke meine Untersuchung auf die zweifelsfrei authentischen Flugschriften des Malers. Sie werden im folgenden nach den Nummern des Anhangs zitiert.

[133] Aus der Zeit vor Greiffenbergers literarischer Wirksamkeit im Zusammenhang der reformatorischen Bewegung ist uns keine biographische Nachricht überliefert (auch von seiner Tätigkeit als Maler ist nichts bekannt, kein Werk ist unter seinem Namen überliefert). In einer Flugschrift, die in Augsburg — mit großer Wahrscheinlichkeit im Jahr 1523 — gedruckt wurde (Anhang Nr. 1), wird auf dem Titelblatt der Autor "Hanns Greyffenberger zů Pfortzhaym" genannt, und diese Angabe wird am Ende wiederholt: "Von mir Johann Greiffenberger zů Pfortzhaym". Die Art der Formulierung läßt darauf schließen, daß Greiffenberger damals noch in Pforzheim weilte. Irgendwann, wohl im Laufe des Jahres 1523, wird er von Pforzheim nach Nürnberg übergesiedelt sein. Darauf weist auch die Wahl der Druckorte: Die Flugschriften des Jahres 1523 wurden bis auf eine nicht in Nürnberg, sondern — wenn man die beiden anonymen auch Greiffenberger zurechnet — in Augsburg (Nr. 1 und 9.2) und vor allem in München bei Hans Schobser (Nr. 2, 8, 9.1) gedruckt. Diejenige Schrift von 1523, die als einzige in Nürnberg — bei Jobst Gutknecht — gedruckt wurde (Nr. 3.1), ist auch aus inhaltlichen Gründen als letzte der 1523 entstandenen Greiffenberger-Schriften zu bestimmen. Denn erst in dieser Schrift zeigen sich spiritualistische Züge. Alle weiteren Schriften, die in das Jahr 1524 fallen, weisen jeweils eine bei Jobst Gutknecht in Nürnberg gedruckte Ausgabe auf (Nr. 3.1, 4.1, 6, 7.1) — mit einer Ausnahme, die freilich in die räumliche Nachbarschaft Nürnbergs führt: Die Flugschrift Nr. 5 wurde in Bamberg bei Georg Erlinger (5.1) und dann in einer weiteren Ausgabe, bezeichnenderweise zusammen mit einer Schrift des Nürnbergers Hans Sachs, in Straßburg (5.2) gedruckt. Aufgrund dieses Befundes darf man vermuten: 1. Erst nachdem Greiffenberger in Nürnberg seßhaft geworden war, wurde der Nürnberger Drucker Jobst Gutknecht sein bevorzugter Drucker. 2. Spätestens die Schrift über die christliche "besserung" (Nr. 3) ist in Nürnberg entstanden (darauf weist auch die Anspielung auf die *Wittenbergisch Nachtigall* von Hans Sachs [1523] am Ende der Schrift). 3. Erst in Nürnberg, möglicherweise im Kreis um Hans Denck, geriet Greiffenberger in den Einflußbereich spiritualistisch-mystischen Denkens (vgl. dazu weiter unten).

[134] Es sind diejenigen Flugschriften von 1523 (einschließlich der beiden anonymen, deren Zuschreibung an Greiffenberger noch zu prüfen bleibt), die nicht in Nürnberg gedruckt wurden: Anhang Nr. 1, 2, 8, 9.

[135] Vgl. Anm. 123 und 129.

relativierenden Laientheologen werden so deutlich. Auch Greiffenberger versteht das allgemeine Priestertum der Gläubigen und die durch Gottes Geistwirken verliehene Gleichheit nicht nur als Gleichheit des 'Standes' in der Gemeinde Jesu Christi, als kultische Gleichheit und prinzipielle Gleichheit des Rechts und der Vollmacht, sondern vorrangig hinsichtlich der biblischen Schrift als Gleichheit der konkreten Auslegungsfähigkeit aller Christen und als radikale Entwertung ihrer Bildungsunterschiede.

Die Schärfe, mit der Greiffenberger gerade diese Seite des reformatorischen Antiklerikalismus akzentuiert, wird nun in seiner (vermutlich) letzten Flugschrift von 1523[136] und in seinen folgenden vier Flugschriften des Jahres 1524[137] noch weitergeführt: Das gleichmachende Wirken des Hl. Geistes, der dem einfachen Laien Unabhängigkeit von den Bildungsprivilegien der Fachtheologen schenkt, wird nun noch stärker betont; vor allem aber nimmt Greiffenbergers Geisttheologie spiritualistische und mystische Züge auf. Damit tritt der Gegensatz oder jedenfalls eine gewisse Spannung zwischen Innerem und Äußerem, zwischen innerem Geistwirken in den Herzen der Gläubigen und äußerer Wortebene, ins Zentrum. Das Innere wird vom Äußeren abgegrenzt; dessen Insuffizienz wird betont.

Diese spiritualistische, über die Argumentationsweise des zweiten Typs hinausführende Seite der Greiffenbergerschen Flugschriften von 1523/1524 sei etwas verdeutlicht. Die Vollmacht der Geistbelehrung wird exklusiv gegen das Unvermögen aller äußerlich-sinnlichen Worte gewendet.[138] Der Geist wirkt nicht wie bei Luther unmittelbar durch das Wort — unmittelbar deshalb, weil *er selbst* im Wort auf letztgültige Weise und *mich selbst* unmittelbar betreffend[139] spricht —, sondern er wirkt unvermittelt ohne Wort, oder präziser formuliert: zwar in Verbindung *mit* dem biblischen Wort Gottes, aber nicht *durch* das Wort. Diese eindeutig exklusive Wendung gibt Greiffenberger nun auch den drei klassischen Schriftzitaten des Spiritualismus Jes. 54,13, Jer. 31,33f und Joh. 6,45.[140] Geistliche Belehrung wird uns, wie Greiffenberger ausführt, nicht durch menschliche Worte, die von außen an unser Ohr dringen, zuteil, sondern nur im Herzen durch die Erleuchtung des Hl. Geistes. So schreibt er im Anschluß an Jer. 31,33f: "Hie hören wir, das got sein gesetz selbs in die herzenn der menschen schreiben wil unnd sy selbs leren, das keiner bedarf von menschen lernen. Dann ob

---

[136] Anhang Nr. 3; vgl. Anm. 133.

[137] Anhang Nr. 4-7.

[138] Zum ersten Mal und noch sehr knapp in der (vermutlich) letzten Flugschrift von 1523, der Schrift über die "besserung" des Christen: Anhang Nr. 3.1, S. 1 (die Besserung des Menschen "kumbt on mittel durch den geyst der warhait") und S. 3 (man kann die Besserung "auch mit nicht den menschen leren, sunder gottes geyst muß thun"); = Ausgabe Laube 1: 265,24f. und 266,27f.

[139] Vgl. oben 391 mit Anm. 41.

[140] Bezeichnenderweise zitiert Greiffenberger diese drei Schriftstellen in seinen früheren Flugschriften von 1523 überhaupt nicht, sondern erst 1524.

wol der mensch das wort dar thut, so schafft er doch nichts, gott erleücht dann das hertz. Derhalben sagt Christus, die ewig warheit: 'Wer es hôrt von meinem vatter, der lernt es und kumpt zů mir', Joan. 6 [45]."[141] Oder an einer anderen Stelle heißt es: "Hôren wir nit alltag, das geschriben ist Esaie 54 [13]: 'Si werden alle von got gelert werden', und Christus sagt Johannis 6 [45]: 'Wer es hôrt von meinem vater, der lernt es und der kumbt zů mir.' Es darff [braucht] niemant seinen nechsten lernen beichten oder bitten; der geyst gottes wirts in [ihn] warlich wol lernen."[142] Ausdrücklich sagt Greiffenberger, daß die Besserung des Menschen "on mittel durch den geyst der warhait" kommt,[143] und immer wieder stellt er dem gesamten Bereich äußerer Lehren und Worte, der 'äußerlichen Larve',[144] das innere 'Treiben' des Geistes[145] gegenüber: "es můß inwendig zůgeen, darvon die welt nichts waiß";[146] nur so entsteht ein "warhaffter, lebendiger glaube, der nit gedicht ist".[147]

So intensiv diese Gedanken aus der Bibel schöpfen, besonders aus der johanneischen und paulinischen Pneumatologie, so deutlich zeigt sich doch in dem Kontrast von Innen und Außen auch das Erbe der neuplatonisch-augustinischen Hermeneutik.[148] Gut augustinisch ist es, wenn Greiffen-berger zwischen Ermahnen und Lehren unterscheidet:[149] "Man mag [kann] ein[en] wol ermanen, aber leern ist nit ins menschen gwalt; sie müssen 'alle von got gelert sein' [Jes. 54,13, Joh. 6,45]."[150] In diesen Bereich des Ermahnens (des *admonere*) bezieht er auch das Evangelium ein, das völlig anders als bei Luther aus der Perspektive des Gesetzes gesehen wird (wie überhaupt Luthers Unterscheidung von Gesetz und Evangelium in rechtfer-

---

[141] Anhang Nr. 5.1, fol. A3r.

[142] Anhang Nr. 6, S. 4; vgl. ebd. S. 6: "Das ist klar gesagt, das gottes geyst allain leermaister wil sein in den sachen, die zur selen dienen, zwischen ir und got zů handeln; kurtz: 'und bedarff [braucht] niemant zů seinem nechsten sagen: Erkenn got!', Esaie 54 [V. 13; richtig: Jer. 31,34.33]. 'Dann sie werden in kennen' durch gottes treyben und offenbarung 'vom klainesten biß zum grôsten', dann got 'schreybt in [ihnen] in ir hertz', das sie kains leermaisters bedurffen, dann got můß thůn."

[143] Siehe Anm. 138.

[144] Vgl. besonders Anhang Nr. 6, passim, z.B. S. 2: "eüsserlich larffe"; vgl. unten Anm. 151 und 191.

[145] Vgl. Anhang Nr. 6, passim, z.B. S. 10: "der geyst wil treyber sein"; mit Verweis auf Röm. 8,14. Vgl. auch unten Anm. 165.

[146] Anhang Nr. 6, S. 9.

[147] Anhang Nr. 6, S. 10; vgl. Anhang Nr. 2, fol. e2v: "der recht ungedicht glaub".

[148] Vgl. Berndt Hamm, "Unmittelbarkeit des göttlichen Gnadenwirkens und kirchliche Heilsvermittlung bei Augustin", *Zeitschrift für Theologie und Kirche* 78 (1981): 409-41 (vgl. besonders auch die S. 412 Anm. 17 genannte Literatur).

[149] Zu Augustin (speziell zur anregenden Funktion der äußeren admonitio durch die Sinne, der die geistliche Erleuchtung durch den inneren Lehrer Christus gegenüber-gestellt wird) vgl. ebd., 412 und 435f.

[150] Anhang Nr. 7.1, fol. A3r.

tigungstheologischen Passagen der frühreformatorischen Flugschriftenliteratur oft nicht rezipiert wird). Das Evangelium als äußeres Wort sagt mir, "was ich für mangel hab" und "wie ich sein soll".[151] Das neue Sein selbst, die Wiedergeburt aus dem Glauben, der mir die Lust am Gesetz erschließt, ist eine Gabe des Gottesgeistes. Immer wieder unterscheidet Greiffenberger diese zwei Ebenen der äußeren Predigt des Gotteswortes und der unvermittelten, innerlich belehrenden und so erneuernden Tätigkeit des Gottesgeistes 'selbst': "Wann der maister, got selbs,[152] nit da ist und lernets, so ist es umsunst. Aber solchs hat er verordnet durch sein wort und leere und predig, das mans treiben sol[153] unnd got die wachssung gebe [vgl. 1. Kor. 3,6]; die menschen mügen [können] wol gottes wort sâen [sähen] und außtailn, aber got mûß ins hertz lernen."[154] "Man sol das wort gottes lauter und rain verkündigen und darnach dem geyst gottes sein raum lassen und sein werck lassen außrichten; dann er will maister sein in des menschen hertzen."[155] Verkündigung des Gotteswortes und Geistwirken sind als zwei prinzipiell getrennte Bereiche aufeinander bezogen.

Die beiden letzten Zitate lassen auch deutlich werden, wie eng das spiritualistische Wortverständnis Greiffenbergers mit der bereits erwähnten

---

[151] "Dann do Christus sagt Matthei 6 [V. 8.6]: 'Ee und ir bittet, so waiß ewer vater', was ir wôlt und 'was euch not ist'; 'er sicht ins verborgen', ins hertz. Er wil nit schône wôrtlein haben und eüsserlich larffen, es gefelt im nit, wils auch nit hôren, dann er sagt Johannis 4 [V. 24]: 'Mein vater ist ein geyst', und die er hôret, die sollen und 'mûssen in im geyst bitten und anrûffen'. Es geet nit mit solcher erdichtung zû, das man dichte und lerne [lehre] andere, wie man bitten und beichten sol. Das wort sol man treyben, das lert, wie und was unns not ist, das ich bitte zû got; dann durchs ewangelion wirt nûr erkündigt, was ich für mangel hab, wie ich sein sol, wie dann das gesetz mir anzaygt; und solchs sol man treyben und nit lernen [lehren], wie man sich stellen sol zûr bekantnuß und zum bitten." Anhang Nr. 6, S. 4f.

[152] Vgl. das augustinische "deus ipse": Hamm (wie Anm. 148), 410 (bei Augustin bedeutet das "deus ipse" immer zugleich ein "per se ipsum").

[153] Zu dieser äußerlich-sinnlichen Tätigkeit des Wort-Treibens (im Unterschied zum inneren Treiben des Hl. Geistes) vgl. Anm. 151.

[154] Anhang Nr. 7.1, fol. A3r.

[155] Anhang Nr. 6, S. 6. Ähnliche Formulierungen lassen sich auch in Schriften Luthers — besonders des jüngeren — finden: vgl. z.B. WA 10/III. 260,20 (Predigten des Jahres 1522) und WA 17/II. 174,19-21 (Fastenpostille 1525); dazu Paul Althaus, Die Theologie Martin Luthers, 5. Aufl. (Gütersloh, 1980), 45f., besonders Anm. 14 und 15; Regin Prenter, Spiritus Creator. Studien zu Luthers Theologie, Forschungen zur Geschichte und Lehre des Protestantismus 10/6 (München, 1954), 107-9. Greiffenberger kann — wie auch andere Flugschriftenautoren — an solchen Aussagen Luthers anknüpfen, die eine spiritualistische Tendenz zu fördern scheinen, d.h. an Aussagen der solus-spiritus-Linie, die die Souveränität des schöpferischen Geistes unterstreicht. Die andere Linie bei Luther, die der Bindung des Geistes an das äußere Wort und die Sprachbildung gilt, wird dagegen nicht rezipiert. Zur Zusammengehörigkeit beider Linien bei Luther vgl. Prenter, ebd., 109-32.

antiklerikalen Meisterthematik[156] verbunden ist. Ausgehend von Mt. 23,10 (Jesu Rede gegen die Pharisäer, die sich Meister und Lehrer nennen) richtet sich seine Polemik immer wieder gegen die selbsternannten 'Meister' der Kirche, die Fachtheologen, die sich mit ihren Lehren an die Stelle Gottes und Jesu Christi setzen. Er ist durch sein Geistwirken der einzige Meister, der die Seele heilvoll belehren kann: "Das ist klar gesagt, das gottes geyst allain leermaister wil sein in den sachen, die zur selen dienen, zwischen ir und got zů handeln."[157] Durch den Spiritualismus, durch die Akzentverlagerung auf das innere Geistwirken gegenüber der nur äußerlich an die Hörer und Leser herankommenden Menschenlehre, wird die Ablehnung der Meister noch verschärft: Die einfachen Laien werden nun erst recht in völliger Unabhängigkeit von der Instanz theologischer Gelehrsamkeit und Sprachbildung gesehen. Die Bildungsunterschiede, die als etwas nur Äußerliches gelten, werden vor der Meisterschaft Christi in den Herzen der Gläubigen vollends gleichgültig. So ist es kein Zufall, daß der reformatorische Spiritualismus besonders unter Handwerkern seine Anhänger gefunden hat — unter solchen Handwerkern, die gebildet genug waren, um ihre Unabhängigkeit von den Gebildeten und ihre 'geistliche' Autarkie des Schriftverständnisses zu proklamieren.

Greiffenbergers Attacke auf die theologischen 'Meister', die *magistri* und *doctores*, richtet sich zunächst gegen den katholischen Klerus. Diese Stoßrichtung zeigt sich besonders in einer Flugschrift von 1523, die den Titel trägt: *Diss biechlin zaygt an, was uns lernen und gelernet haben unsere maister der geschrifft, darvor unns Cristus offt gewarnet hat [...]*".[158] Ein Jahr später allerdings werden von diesem — nun spiritualistisch radikalisierten — Angriff nicht nur die alten Meister, sondern auch bereits die neuen Meister der evangelischen Bewegung getroffen. Dies zeigt besonders eine Flugschrift von 1524, die nun eine rein innerreformatorische Kritik vorträgt (und auch darin über den pneumatologischen Antiklerikalismus des zweiten Typs hinausführt): *Ein warnung vor dem teüffel, der sich wider [wieder] ůbt mit seinem dendelmarckt ...*[159] Als Tand, den der Teufel auf seinem 'Tändelmarkt'[160] feilbietet — jetzt wieder, nachdem die Zeremonien der alten Kirche als Tand entlarvt worden sind —, bezeichnet Greiffenberger die 1524 beginnenden Versuche der reformatorischen Prädikanten Nürnbergs, neue gottesdienstliche Formen für ein evangelisches Kirchenwesen zu

---

[156] Vgl. oben S. 414, Nr. 6.

[157] Anhang Nr. 6, S. 6; vgl. Anm. 142.

[158] Anhang Nr. 2.

[159] Anhang Nr. 6.

[160] Vgl. Jakob und Wilhelm Grimm, *Deutsches Wörterbuch*, Bd. XI/I,1, 105 s.v. 'Tändelmarkt'.

finden.[161] Habe man früher die Leute mit vorformulierten Gebeten geblendet, die an Maria und die Heiligen gerichtet waren, so falle man jetzt "auff die andern seyten und wil ein dendelmarckt auffrichten auff Christum".[162] Für Greiffenberger gehört der ganze Bereich des Sündenbekenntnisses und Gebets zum unmittelbaren Wirkungsraum des Hl. Geistes, wo er allein Meister und Lehrer sein will;[163] er selbst 'treibt'[164] die Herzen der Gläubigen zu einem Bekennen und Bitten, das keiner äußeren sprachregelnden Ordnung bedarf.[165] Wer die Sprache der Gemeinde zu regulieren versucht, indem er sie bestimmte vorformulierte und schriftlich fixierte Worte nachzusprechen heißt,[166] der stellt sich dem freien Wirken des Geistes entgegen: "das haißt dem geyst gottes seine werck versperren und in ein eüsserlich larffen ziehen".[167]

Kennzeichnend für den pneumatologischen Antiklerikalismus, wie ihn Greiffenberger gegen die alten und neuen Magistri vertritt, ist nicht nur die spiritualistische Zuspitzung der allgemeinen Geistbelehrung, sondern, was damit eng zusammenhängt, die Rezeption mystischer Terminologie und eine Akzentverschiebung im Rechtfertigungsverständnis, die von Luther wegführt. Von dieser Veränderung, wie sie sich in der Verhältnisbestimmung von Gesetz und Evangelium zeigt, war bereits die Rede.[168] Das rechtfertigende Gnadenhandeln Gottes erscheint in den späteren Flugschriften Greiffenbergers nicht als forensischer Freispruch *extra nos*, wie er durch Gottes vergebende Zusage zugeeignet wird, sondern (darin Osianders Lehre verwandt) als das erneuernde Heiligungsgeschehen, das Gottes Geist in den Herzen der Gläubigen wirkt. Rechtfertigung vollzieht sich "gantz haimlich

---

[161] Vgl. Gerhard Pfeiffer, "Die Einführung der Reformation in Nürnberg als kirchenrechtliches und bekenntniskundliches Problem", *Blätter für deutsche Landesgeschichte* 89 (1952): 112-33; Gottfried Seebaß, *Das reformatorische Werk des Andreas Osiander*, Einzelarbeiten aus der Kirchengeschichte Bayerns 44 (Nürnberg, 1967), 217f.; *Osiander Gesamtausgabe* Bd. 1 (wie Anm. 69), Einleitungen zu Nr. 18-20: 143-254.

[162] Anhang Nr. 6, S. 7.

[163] Anhang Nr. 6, S. 4, 6, 12.

[164] Vgl. oben S. 419 mit Anm. 145.

[165] Anhang Nr. 6, S. 5: "Dises aber hab ich nicht anzaygt, das mans aber [abermals] in ein larffen ziehe und machs nacheinander in ein ordnung, sunder es müß vom geyst getriben werden und nit von menschen in ein dichte oder zall gestelt; es ist sunst falsch." Ebd., S. 4: "Dann der geyst treybt in zů bitten. [...] Dises kan man nit mit schönen und geordneten wörtlein bitten oder lernen."

[166] Z.B. Anhang Nr. 6, S. 4: "Dann sobald man sagt: 'Sprecht mir nach, und ein yegklicher andechtiger mensch sol all tag also und also sagen und bekennen', so ist es des teüffels und des fleysch und der vernunfft dendelmarckt."

[167] Anhang Nr. 6, S. 3f.

[168] Siehe oben 419f.

und still" im Inneren,[169] wo der belehrende Geist zur Gesetzeserfüllung anleitet und antreibt. Dieses innerliche Geschehen der "besserung des menschen"[170] beschreibt Greiffenberger mit mystischen Begriffen als Passivität des Gott-(Er)leidens, als Gelassenheit und Sabbat der Seele, als Zerstörung des Eigenwillens, als Wiedergeburt durch den Geist und Vergottung des Menschen.[171]

Man kann vermuten, wie Greiffenberger in Nürnberg zu einer derartigen Konzeption antiklerikaler, gegen die Schultheologen gerichteter, spiritualistisch zugespitzter und mystisch gefärbter Geisttheologie gekommen ist. Man muß dabei vor allem an den Einfluß von Karlstadts und Müntzers Schriften, die in Nürnberg verbreitet waren,[172] denken. Möglicherweise stand der Maler im Überschneidungsbereich der Wirkungen Karlstadts, Müntzers und ihrer Schüler.

Daß er bei der Ausbildung seines spiritualistischen Ansatzes partiell von Müntzer beeinflußt wurde, halte ich — besonders im Blick auf die Präsenz Müntzerscher Theologie in Nürnberg 1524 — für wahrscheinlich. Gerade der ganze (bei Greiffenberger so akzentuierte) Komplex der Schule Gottes, des Hl. Geistes als alleinigen Schulmeisters des Glaubens, der unvermittelten Geistbelehrung, des Belehrtwerdens durch Gott und nicht durch menschliche Worte und Schriften samt den entsprechend spiritualistisch eingesetzten Bibelstellen Joh. 6,45 usw. ist besonders charakteristisch für Thomas

---

[169] Anhang Nr. 3.1, S. 1; = Ausgabe Laube, 1: 265,17f. (man beachte auch den Kontext dieser Stelle).

[170] Anhang Nr. 3.1, S. 1 (bei Laube der Abschnitt 1: 265,16-29); im Begriff der "besserung", wie ihn Greiffenberger versteht, fallen (lutherisch bzw. melanchthonisch formuliert) *iustificatio* und *sanctificatio/renovatio*, *fides* und *caritas* sowie *evangelium* und *lex* zusammen.

[171] Ansätze zur Rezeption der mystischen Terminologie zeigen sich bereits in der (vermutlich) letzten Schrift des Jahres 1523: Anhang Nr. 3 (Wiedergeburt aus dem Geist, Geisterleuchtung, das verkehrte Licht des 'Eigenwillens', die Notwendigkeit des Leidens). Vgl. Theodor Kolde, "Hans Denck und die gottlosen Maler von Nürnberg", *Beiträge zur bayerischen Kirchengeschichte* 8 (1902): 1-31, 49-72; 14 ("leise Anklänge", die "seine Bekanntschaft mit der Mystik erkennen lassen"). In sehr dichter Weise begegnet dann das mystische Gedankengut und Vokabular vor allem in einer Flugschrift von 1524: Anhang Nr. 7.

[172] Zu Karlstadt vgl. *Osiander Gesamtausgabe* Bd. 1 (wie Anm. 69), 407; Vogler (wie Anm. 99), 298. Schriften Karlstadts, die in Nürnberg 1523/24 gedruckt wurden: E. Freys/H. Barge, *Verzeichnis der gedruckten Schriften des Andreas Bodenstein von Karlstadt* (Nieuwkoop, 1965; Nachdruck der Erstausgabe 1904), Nr. 101 (*Ein Sermon vom Stand der christgläubigen Seelen ...*, 1523 [Nürnberg: Jobst Gutknecht?]); Nr. 107 (*Eine Frage, ob auch jemand möge selig werden ohne die Fürbitte Mariae* [Nürnberg: Hieronymus Höltzel, 1524]) = Erstdruck (Auskunft von Ulrich Bubenheimer). Zu Müntzer vgl. Anm. 193.

Müntzer.[172a] Auch einzelne terminologische Anklänge weisen auf Müntzer, ohne freilich ausschließen zu können, daß Greiffenberger diese Gedanken und Begriffe von anderer Seite empfangen hat. So sehr man nämlich mit Müntzers Einfluß rechnen muß, so deutlich ist auch, daß der Maler insgesamt dem Karlstadtschen Typ von Theologie, Frömmigkeit und Antiklerikalismus weit näher stand als dem Müntzerschen — davon später mehr. Wenn man ihn einer Anhängerschaft zurechnen will, dann jedenfalls nicht der Müntzers, sondern eher der Karlstadts.

Deutlich erkennbar ist die Nähe zu Karlstadt nicht nur in den beschriebenen spiritualistisch-mystischen Zügen der Greiffenbergerschen Flugschriften,[173] sondern auch an seiner Abendmahlsauffassung.[174] Sie wurde im

---

[172a] Vgl. Dieter Fauth, *Thomas Müntzer in bildungsgeschichtlicher Sicht*, pädagog. Diss./Pädagogische Hochschule Heidelberg 1989 (Privatdruck: Ostfildern 1990), besonders 66-88. Vgl. auch Georg Born, "Geist, Wissen und Bildung bei Thomas Müntzer und Valentin Icklsamer" (Diss. phil. [masch.], Erlangen, 1952).

[173] Vgl. z.B. aus den Flugschriften Karlstadts von 1523 zwei stark mystisch geprägte Schriften, auf deren Titelblatt er seinen Status als eines 'neuen Laien' hervorhebt: 1. *Uon manigfeltigkeit // des eynfeltigen ey // nigen willen // gottes. // was sundt sey. // Andres Bodensteyn // von Carolstat // eyn newer // Ley. // Anno. M.D.xxiij.* [Straßburg?, 13. März 1523]; Köhler, Fiche 1123 Nr. 2887 = Freys/Barge (wie Anm. 172) Nr. 102; Überschriften: fol. G2r/v: "Eusserliche zeichen vereynen gott nicht"; fol. G2v/3r: "Durch eusserliche dingk kan sich nymand mit gott vereynenn"; G4v/H1r: "Der inner mensch hat eyn ding und der eusser vil". 2. *was gesagt ist / Sich // gelassen / vnd was das wort // gelassenhait bedeüt / vnd // wa es in hailiger ge= // schrifft begriffen. // Andres Bodenstain von Ca= // rolstat / ain neüwer Lay.* [Augsburg: Sylvan Otmar] o.J. (Vorrede datiert auf 20. April 1523); Köhler, Fiche 1500 Nr. 3949 = Freys/Barge Nr. 105; fol. D3r/v: "Allhie solt ich auch sagen, wie ain rechtgelaßner mensch die hailig schrifft müß gelassen [hinter sich lassen] und nicht umb büchstaben wissen, sonder eingeen in die macht des herren (als David spricht) unnd got den herren on ablassen bitten, das er im waren verstand wöl eingeben; als wenn ainer etwas nit versteet oder ain urtail gern wölt vernemen, so sol er in der gelassenhait steen, das ist auß im geen unnd mit seiner vernunfft still halten unnd gestrencklich von got begern sein kunst und hören, was im got wöl sagen. [...] Liß die teütschen Theologiam; bist du nitt zůfriden, so warte, biß mein büchlin von der schůl gotes außgee." Diese Schrift 'Von der Schule Gottes', die wohl von der unmittelbaren Geistbelehrung der Gläubigen durch den 'Schulmeister' Christus handeln sollte, ist — falls Karlstadt sie tatsächlich zu Papier brachte — bisher nicht aufgefunden worden. Vgl. Fauth (wie Anm. 172a), 67 Anm. 97 und 85. Zum antiklerikalen und antiuniversitären Charakter des Themas der Gottesbelehrung der Laien vgl. z.B. die Karlstadt-Schrift über die Fürbitte Mariens (zum Nürnberger Erstdruck vgl. Anm. 172): *Eyn frage / ob auch // yemandt möge selig wer= // den / on dye fur= // bitt Ma= // rie. // Andres Carolstat. // Anno. M.D.XXiiij.* (o.O., u. Dr., 1524); Köhler, Fiche 829 Nr. 2073 = Freys/Barge Nr. 106; fol. B2r/v: daß die Laien die Prediger nach der Begründung ihrer Predigten aus der Schrift fragen dürfen und sollen; besonders fol. B2v: "Ich weyß, das vil handtwerker in gottes leer mehr wissen dann pfaffen, so die boßkugel und kegel werffen. Got leret die leyen, das sy den

'Fall Greiffenberger' verhandelt:[175] Der Nürnberger Rat wurde Ende
Oktober 1524 auf Greiffenberger aufmerksam und verlangte von ihm eine
'Antwort':[176] seine Verteidigungsschrift wurde dann von Osiander begut-
achtet, woraufhin es der Rat bei einer Verwarnung (10. Nov.) beließ. Die
Verantwortung Greiffenbergers von Anfang November[177] zeigt deutliche
Parallelen zur spiritualisierenden Abendmahlslehre Karlstadts. Mit ihrer
Gegenüberstellung von Äußerem und Innerlich-Geistlichem beim Abendmahl
läßt sie erkennen, daß die Ablehnung der Realpräsenz und die Betonung des
geistlichen Essens und Trinkens eben jener Entwertung des Äußeren
entspricht, die uns in den Flugschriften begegnet ist. Und auch in der
Verbindung mit der Abendmahlsthematik tritt wieder das Interesse
Greiffenbergers an der Unabhängigkeit der Laien hervor; denn mit der
Vorstellung von der Realpräsenz, dem Hangen an äußeren Zeichen und
Worten, habe sich, wie Greiffenberger ausführt, der Wahn der Priester

---

gekrönten doctorn und meystern vorgant." Vgl. Ronald R. Sider, "Karlstadt's
Orlamünde Theology. A Theology of Regeneration", *MennQR* 45 (1971): 191-218,
352-376; ders., *Andreas Bodenstein von Karlstadt: The Development of his Thought*,
SMRT 11 (Leiden, 1974), 202-303.

[174] Dietrich Wünsch kommt in der *Osiander Gesamtausgabe* Bd. 1 (wie Anm. 69),
272 zum Resultat: "Diese Parallelen [scil. zwischen Greiffenbergers 'Antwort' an den
Rat und Karlstadts 'Dialogus'; B.H.] kann man kaum als zufällig erklären.
Greiffenberger ist — was die Abendmahlsfrage betrifft — der erste Karlstadtschüler
in Nürnberg, von dem wir wissen." Ich möchte die Frage der literarischen Abhängig-
keit Greiffenbergers von Karlstadt (die mit der Datierung der Abendmahlstraktate
Karlstadts und der Beurteilung der Parallelen zusammenhängt) in der Schwebe lassen.
Sehr wahrscheinlich allerdings dürfte sein, daß die Flugschriften Greiffenbergers von
1524 (die sich noch nicht zur Abendmahlsthematik äußern) und dann die Verantwortung seiner Abendmahlsauffassung vom November 1524 (dazu gleich im Text) im
Wirkungsfeld Karlstadtscher Schriften und im Rezeptionsbereich des Karlstadtschen
Gedankengutes zu sehen sind — ganz unabhängig von der Frage, auf welchem Wege
Greiffenberger mit diesem Gedankengut in Berührung kam (vgl. auch Anm. 192).
[175] Zum Fall Greiffenberger (Okt./Nov. 1524) vgl. *Osiander Gesamtausgabe* Bd.
1, 267-82.
[176] Wie man aus den Ratsverlässen (31. Okt. und 10. Nov. 1524, zitiert *Osiander
Gesamtausgabe* Bd. 1, 268f.) erfahren kann, ging der Rat aus zwei Gründen gegen
Greiffenberger vor: wegen seiner "ungeschickten" (d.h. zu drastisch antipäpstlichen)
Gemälde und wegen seiner Abendmahlsauffassung ("der sonderlichen secten,
darinnen er des sacraments halb ytzo geirret hab"). Vgl. ebd., 269: "Für den Rat
scheint jedenfalls die Sache mit den 'Schandgemälden' der wichtigste Punkt gewesen
zu sein. Für Greiffenberger waren die Gewichte gerade entgegengesetzt verteilt. In
seiner angeforderten Verantwortung geht er nur nebenher auf 'seine Arbeit, die er
bisher gemalt hat', ein, stellt aber in einer längeren Ausführung seine Abendmahlsan-
schauung dar."
[177] Gedruckt bei Gerhard Pfeiffer, *Quellen zur Nürnberger Reformationsgeschichte*,
Einzelarbeiten aus der Kirchengeschichte Bayerns 45 (Nürnberg, 1968), 295-299 Br.
66.

verbunden, "sie seyen die, die alayn soliche wort reden solen, die lüt darmit gefangen zu nemen",[178] "sie alayn synd die, die das abentmal Cristi wirdig und recht handeln".[179] Auch der zweite Konflikt Greiffenbergers mit dem Rat im August 1526,[180] der zu seiner vorübergehenden Ausweisung aus Nürnberg führte,[181] steht in einer gewissen Kontinuität zum Geist seiner Flugschriften. Es wird ihm der Vorwurf gemacht, er habe seiner Frau selbst das Abendmahl gereicht.[182] Greiffenberger hat hier offensichtlich eine Konsequenz aus seiner Geisttheologie, seiner Überzeugung von der geistgewirkten Autarkie des Laienchristentums[183] und seiner Entwertung kirchlicher Ordnung gezogen.

9.2 Hans Denck

So berechtigt es wohl ist, sowohl die Flugschriften Greiffenbergers als auch sein Abendmahlsverständnis im Wirkungsbereich Karlstadtschen — und partiell auch Müntzerschen — Denkens zu sehen, so problematisch ist es doch, die spiritualistischen Einflüsse, wie sie in den Flugschriften des Jahres 1524 so deutlich greifbar sind, auf den literarischen Rezeptionsweg zu begrenzen. Persönliche Kontakte in Nürnberg werden diese spiritualistische Prägung und damit wohl auch den Einfluß Karlstadts und Müntzers vermittelt haben. Wahrscheinlich ist, daß der Maler kein theologischer Einzelgänger war, sondern in Verbindung zu einem Personenkreis stand, der ähnlich dachte wie er und dessen Kontakte besonders über den St. Sebalder Schulmeister Hans Denck gelaufen sein dürften.[184] Offensichtlich war

---

[178] Pfeiffer, 297.

[179] Pfeiffer, 298.

[180] Vgl. dazu Günther Bauer, *Anfänge täuferischer Gemeindebildungen in Franken*, Einzelarbeiten aus der Kirchengeschichte Bayerns 43 (Nürnberg, 1966), 127; *Andreas Osiander d.Ä. Gesamtausgabe*, Bd. 2, hg. von Gerhard Müller/Gottfried Seebaß (Gütersloh, 1977), Einleitung zu Nr. 75, 337-339.

[181] Am 16. August 1526. Greiffenberger durfte bereits einen Monat später wieder in die Stadt zurückkehren. Über sein weiteres Leben sind keine Zeugnisse bekannt.

[182] Ratsverlaß vom 9. Aug. 1526, zitiert in *Osiander Gesamtausgabe* Bd. 2 (wie Anm. 180), 337 Anm. 1. Der Vorfall selbst hatte schon geraume Zeit vorher (bereits im Herbst 1524?) stattgefunden, war aber erst jetzt dem Rat bekannt geworden; vgl. ebd., 338f. Vermutlich hatte der Maler seiner Frau vor ihrem Tode das Sterbeabendmahl gereicht; vgl. ebd., 339 und 342,22, kombiniert mit 341,1.

[183] Vgl. den Ratschlag des juristischen Ratskonsulenten Dr. Johann Hepstein vom 13. Aug. 1526: Er nehme an, "der Greyffennberger muge das aus dem grund thun haben, das im anfang etliche prediger angezeigt: wir seind alle priester, und hat ein ytlicher das und jhens macht etc." *Osiander Gesamtausgabe* Bd. 2, 342,22-25.

[184] Zu Hans Denck in Nürnberg (von Sept. 1523 bis zu seiner Ausweisung aus der Stadt am 21. Jan. 1525) vgl. Vogler (wie Anm. 99) 263-289 (Literatur zu Denck ist zusammengestellt S. 263 Anm. 2). Wie der Prozeß gegen Denck und die drei ('gottlosen') Maler Sebald Beham, Barthel Beham und Georg Pencz im Januar 1525 zeigt, stand Denck in engem Kontakt zu Malerkreisen. Über die Beziehungen

Denck eine wichtige Leitgestalt in jenem Nürnberger Beziehungsnetz, in dem sich die Einflüsse Karlstadts und Müntzers überlagerten; und aufs Ganze gesehen tendierte er mit seiner verinnerlichenden Geisttheologie wie Greiffenberger eher in die Richtung Karlstadts. Die spiritualistische und mystisch gestimmte Geistigkeit mag dem Maler vor allem im persönlichen Umgang mit dem universitär geschulten und humanistisch gebildeten Sebalder Schulmeister nahegebracht worden sein — möglicherweise auf diesem Wege sowohl aus Karlstadtscher als auch aus Müntzerscher Quelle. Doch kommt man bei diesem gesamten Fragenkomplex der Quellen und ihrer Vermittlung über Vermutungen nicht hinaus.

Zieht man Dencks Verteidigungsschrift ('Bekenntnis') an den Nürnberger Rat vom Jan. 1525 zu Rate,[185] so sieht man hier genau jene spiritualistisch verinnerlichende Pneumatologie entfaltet, wie sie sich ansatzweise in Greiffenbergers Flugschriften findet. Ganz in der Weise Karlstadts (und der darin verwandten spiritualistischen Theologie Müntzers) stellt Denck der äußeren Zeugnisebene von Schrift, Predigt, Taufe und Abendmahl die innere Wirkebene des Heiligen Geistes gegenüber. Die Entstehung von Gewißheit wird völlig von der sinnlichen Sprachebene abgekoppelt und in die innere Geisterfahrung des erleuchteten Menschen verlagert.[186] Allein durch das innere Wirken des 'allmächtigen Wortes' (des göttlichen verbum internum) entsteht Glaubens-, Berufungs- und Auslegungsgewißheit.[187] Aus begreiflichen Gründen — da jede Polemik in seiner bedrängten Situation von Anfang 1525 nur hätte schaden können — fehlt in Dencks Bekenntnis die antiklerikale Zuspitzung. Doch sind die ruhig darlegenden Sätze nur verständlich vor dem Hintergrund der Kritik an den alten und neuen 'Meistern', die der

---

zwischen dem Schulmeister und den drei Malern sagt Vogler (ebd. 299f.): "Den größten Einfluß auf die Maler wird jedoch Hans Denck ausgeübt haben. ... Denck wurde mit ihnen also nicht zufällig im Prozeß zusammengeführt. Ihre geistige Verwandtschaft datiert vielmehr aus der vorhergehenden Zeit, als sie sich zum Gespräch zusammenfanden und als Gesinnungsgenossen näherkamen." (Zum Prozeßverlauf vgl. ebd. 270-310). Ein geistiger Austausch Greiffenbergers mit seinen Malerkollegen und in diesem Zusammenhang eine engere Beziehung zu Denck während des Jahres 1524 ist m.E. wahrscheinlich. Zu anderen möglichen persönlichen Einflüssen außer Denck vgl. Anm. 192.

[185] Das 'Bekenntnis' Dencks ist ediert in *Hans Denck: Schriften*, 2. Teil: *Religiöse Schriften*, hg. von Walter Fellmann, QFRG 24/2 (Gütersloh, 1956), 20-26. Die beiden Teile des Bekenntnisses entstanden zwischen dem 10. und 16. Jan. 1525. Vgl. *Osiander Gesamtausgabe* Bd. 1 (wie Anm. 69), Einleitung zu Nr. 32 ("Gutachten über das Bekenntnis Hans Dencks"), 407-410. Die Frage der Einflüsse auf das Bekenntnis ist diskutiert bei Vogler (wie Anm. 99), 283f. (Literatur). M.E. hat sich diese Frage bisher viel zu einseitig auf die umstrittene Abhängigkeit von Müntzer konzentriert, statt die große Nähe zu Karlstadt zur Grundlage der Diskussion zu machen.

[186] Bekenntnis Dencks (wie Anm. 185), 22,18-23; vgl. 21,26-22,3 und 20,9-12.

[187] Bekenntnis Dencks, 23,25-30; vgl. 25,13-18.27-31 und 26,16-19.

Vorwurf trifft, sie würden an den äußeren Larven[188] hängenbleiben und
nicht ernst machen mit der Erkenntnis, daß Gottes Reich "inwendig in euch"
ist (Lk. 17,21).[189]

Jedenfalls wird bei der Lektüre dieser Ausführungen Dencks verständlich,
wie Greiffenberger in Nürnberg zu seiner spiritualistisch-pneumatologischen
Ausprägung des Antiklerikalismus, der sich nun — 1524 — auch gegen
Entwicklungen in der Reformation wandte, gekommen sein könnte. Es waren
offensichtlich die Denkrichtung Karlstadts und Dencks und dabei auch
Einflüsse Müntzers, die den Maler zunehmend in ihren Bann zogen und so
eine organische Weiterführung seines Antiklerikalismus bewirkten. Auch
direkte Einflüsse mystischen Schrifttums, insbesondere der "Theologia
Deutsch" und Taulers, sind denkbar. Überblickt man seine Flugschriften der
Jahre 1523/24, so sieht man, wie er vermutlich zunächst einen pneumatologischen Antiklerikalismus des zweiten Typs (etwa von der Art eines Diepold
Peringer, Hans Sachs oder Sebastian Lotzer) vertrat[190] und dann allmählich
auf die spiritualistische und mystisch beeinflußte Ebene des dritten Typs
geriet.[191] Schließlich mündet auch bei Greiffenberger — wie bei Karlstadt
und Denck — diese spiritualisierende Tendenz in eine entsprechende
Abendmahlsauffassung, die Inneres gegen Äußeres stellt.

Die Schere zwischen der Theologie des Malers und der Luthers, seines
wichtigsten Vorbildes, hat sich so im Zeitraum 1523/24 immer mehr
geöffnet.[192] Doch blieb auch der spiritualistische Typ des mit dem Hl.

---

[188] So Greiffenberger, oben 419 mit Anm. 144.

[189] Vgl. Greiffenberger, Anhang Nr. 3.1, S. 1; = Ausgabe Laube 1: 265,12-15.

[190] Am deutlichsten entfaltet in seiner Flugschrift von 1523 gegen "unsere maister
der geschrifft": Anhang Nr. 2.

[191] Mit polemischer Zuspitzung in seiner Flugschrift von 1524 gegen den "teüffel,
der sich wider übt mit seinem dendelmarckt unter einem gleissenden schein": Anhang
Nr. 6. Die polemische Weiterentwicklung, wie sie mit der spiritualistischen
Radikalisierung gegeben ist, zeigt sich z.B. darin, wie der Begriff der 'Larve'
verändert wird: In der Schrift gegen die Meister nennt Greiffenberger die Schultheologen stereotyp "schüllarfen": Anhang Nr. 2, passim (auch "schülaffen",
"schülfatzen", "schülesel" oder einfach "larffen"). In der Schrift gegen den
'Tändelmarkt' wendet er sich dann generell gegen die "eüsserlich larffen", d.h. gegen
die Fixierung auf den Umgang mit "schönen und geordneten wörtlein" in der Kirche:
Anhang Nr. 6, S. 2-4; vgl. oben 419 mit Anm. 144.

[192] Bei der Vermittlung der Karlstadtschen Abendmahlsauffassung an Greiffenberger mag der Prediger Martin Reinhart, ein Anhänger Karlstadts, der im Herbst
1524 für kurze Zeit (maximal zehn Wochen, wahrscheinlich aber wesentlich kürzer)
in Nürnberg weilte und am 17. Dezember ausgewiesen wurde, beteiligt gewesen sein.
Zu Reinhart vgl. Vogler (wie Anm. 99), 232-250, besonders 249 (über sein Wirken
in Nürnberg): "Manches deutet darauf hin, daß Reinharts Wirken Früchte trug.
Immerhin war der Maler Greiffenberger wegen seines abweichenden Abendmahls-
verständnisses in der ersten Novemberdekade belangt worden, zu einem Zeitpunkt
also, zu dem Reinhart sich offensichtlich in Nürnberg aufhielt." Die Flugschriften

Geist argumentierenden Antiklerikalismus in grundlegender Weise Luther verpflichtet. Schließlich war es Luther selbst, der den Blick auf die mystische Tradition, auf Tauler und die "Theologia Deutsch", lenkt und in ihr Verwandtes entdeckt hatte. Der spiritualistische Typ führt die *solus-spiritus*-Linie Luthers, seine Aussagen über die Souveränität des belehrenden Geistes, weiter, indem er sie von der anderen Aussagelinie Luthers abkoppelt: von der Linie des eingebundenen Geistes, der sich an das äußere Wort und Zeichen bindet.[192a] Es gibt wohl nur wenige Formulierungen Greiffenbergers in seinen Flugschriften, die sich nicht irgendwo auch bei Luther nachweisen lassen; doch hat sich der Gesamtduktus der Aussageintention verschoben, indem die lutherische Komposition des Ineinanders von Innerem (Geistwirken) und Äußerem (Wort- und Sakramentswirken) nicht aufgenommen wird.

X. Der vierte (Müntzersche) Typ
des pneumatologischen Antiklerikalismus

Wenigstens kurz erwähnt sei noch, daß in Nürnberg während des Spätjahres 1524 auch der Müntzersche Typ des pneumatologischen Antiklerikalismus mit seinen zugleich spiritualisierenden und zur gewaltsamen Reinigung drängenden Zügen präsent war — nicht nur durch den Druck von Müntzers Schriften, sondern auch durch seinen (vermuteten) eigenen Aufenthalt in der Reichsstadt[193] und die kurzen Wirksamkeiten seiner Schüler Hans Hut[194]

Greiffenbergers zeigen eine Entwicklung, die verständlich macht, warum er dann im November 1524 ein spiritualistisches Abendmahlsverständnis vertritt. Reinharts Einfluß kann, wenn überhaupt, nur auf das Ende dieser Entwicklung eingewirkt haben, nicht aber auf die Ausbildung des spiritualistischen Ansatzes, wie er sich in den Flugschriften zeigt. Vgl. auch Gottfried Seebaß, "Zur Geschichte der reformatorischen und sozialen Bewegung in der Reichsstadt Nürnberg im Jahre 1524/25", *Mitteilungen des Vereins für Geschichte der Stadt Nürnberg* 71 (1984): 269-276; 274; Seebaß vermutet einen noch kürzeren Aufenthalt Reinharts in Nürnberg als Vogler.

[192a] Siehe Anm. 155.

[193] Vgl. zusammenfassend Vogler (wie Anm. 99), 213-32: Müntzer und der Druck seiner Schriften in Nürnberg. Der Nürnberger Rat befaßte sich am 29. Okt. 1524 mit den "neugemachten und hie gedruckten Thomans Muntzers puchlein" (ebd., 215). Für einen Aufenthalt Müntzers in Nürnberg und/oder im Nürnberger Landgebiet gibt es zwar keine zweifelsfrei sicheren Belege, doch kann man einen kurzen Aufenthalt erschließen. "Dafür kommt die Zeit zwischen Ende Oktober und Mitte Dezember in Frage, am ehesten einige Tage im November oder Anfang Dezember." (Ebd., 230). Zum Kontakt Müntzers mit dem Nürnberger Montanunternehmer und Handelsherr Christoph Fürer vgl. Ulrich Bubenheimer, *Thomas Müntzer. Herkunft und Bildung*, SMRT 46 (Leiden, 1989), 39, 143, 268-276 (Edition von Fragartikeln Fürers mit Antworten Müntzers).

und Heinrich Schwertfeger (gen. Pfeiffer).[195] Dies ist ein vierter Typ des pneumatologischen Antiklerikalismus. Man kann ihn den aktivistisch-revolutionären und gewaltsamen Typ nennen. Er hat zwar in seiner spiritualistischen Kontrastierung von Innen und Außen, von toter Schrift-gelehrsamkeit und lebendigem Geistchristentum, von 'gedichtetem' und wahrem Glauben sehr viel mit dem dritten Typ gemeinsam[196] (so wie der dritte sehr viel mit dem zweiten und der zweite sehr viel mit dem ersten); doch muß — wie der Gegensatz zwischen Karlstadt und Müntzer zeigt — der Typ der antiklerikalen Pneumatologie, wie sie Müntzer und seine Schüler vertreten, deutlich von der Richtung Dencks und Greiffenbergers unterschieden werden. Letztere wollten die obrigkeitliche Ordnung und die traditionelle Sozialstruktur nicht antasten[197] und teilten nicht die apokalyp-

---

[194] Hans Hut weilte vermutlich Oktober/November 1524, vielleicht auch noch in der ersten Dezemberhälfte in Nürnberg. Vgl. Gottfried Seebaß, "Müntzers Erbe. Werk, Leben und Theologie des Hans Hut († 1527)" (Habil.-schrift [masch.], Erlangen/ Theol. Fakultät, 1972), 169-174.

[195] Pfeiffers Nürnberger Aufenthalt währte vermutlich nur wenige Tage. Nachdem der Rat der Reichsstadt seine Anwesenheit bemerkt hatte, wies er ihn am 29. Okt. 1524 aus. Vgl. Vogler (wie Anm. 99), 203 und 212. Aus dem Ende Oktober verfaßten Gutachten Osianders über zwei beschlagnahmte Manuskripte Pfeiffers (das Gutachten ist ediert in *Osiander Gesamtausgabe* Bd. 1 [wie Anm. 69], 255-66) kann man schließen, daß sich die Äußerungen des ehemaligen Zisterziensers vollständig mit denen seines Mentors Müntzer deckten — auch hinsichtlich des gewalttätigen Antiklerikalismus; vgl. dazu ebd. 262,25 (die falschen Propheten zu Tode schlagen), 263,2-4 (alle Prediger, die nicht mit Gottes Geist "umbgeen", erwürgen), 263,5f. ("mit der faust hinwider schlagen"), 265,1f. (man soll die verführerischen Prediger erwürgen).

[196] Vgl. Hans-Jürgen Goertz, "Zu Thomas Müntzers Geistverständnis", in S. Bräuer, H. Junghans (Hgg.), *Der Theologe Thomas Müntzer. Untersuchungen zu seiner Entwicklung und Lehre* (Berlin, DDR, 1989), 84-99.

[197] Zu Greiffenberger vgl. Vogler (wie Anm. 99) 188f: "Greiffenberger war ohne soziale Ambitionen. Natürlich klingt in der Verwerfung von Opfergeldern, Totenmessen und anderen Gebräuchen eine soziale Komponente an. Aber er formuliert niemals die sich daraus ergebenden Konsequenzen." "... er fordert seine Leser auf, der Obrigkeit gehorsam zu sein, spricht sich für Duldung und Leiden aus und propagiert den Grundsatz, zur Verteidigung des Glaubens nur das Wort zu gebrauchen." Dies macht auch verständlich, warum Greiffenberger seine Flugschriften in Nürnberg ungehindert verfassen und drucken lassen konnte. Vgl. auch Wenzeslaus Lincks Urteil über Greiffenberger vom 13. Aug. 1526: "... das diser Greuffennberger ein frum man, der nit zu unfrid oder auffrurn ursach gebe und sich bisher wol gehalten hab"; *Osiander Gesamtausgabe* Bd. 2 (wie Anm. 180), 340,13-341,1; dazu der Kommentar S. 340 Anm. 21: "Damit setzt Linck Greiffenberger zu Recht von den Anhängern Müntzers in Nürnberg ab". Auch Denck wollte die politische und soziale Ordnung nicht infrage stellen. Dementsprechend tauchen auch im Verfahren des Rats gegen ihn (Jan. 1525) solche Vorwürfe nicht auf, so wie er während des Prozesses auch nie mit der Müntzerschen Lehre in Verbindung gebracht wurde. Vgl. Vogler

tische Vision einer gewaltsamen Ausrottung der falschen Hirten. Daß beide partiell von Müntzers Theologie beeinflußt sein dürften, ändert nichts an dieser fundamentalen Verschiedenheit gegenüber Müntzers Anhängerschaft. Auf den vierten Typ soll nun nicht weiter eingegangen werden, weil das Quellenmaterial von Nürnberger Autoren fehlt.

XI. Weder "Wildwuchs" noch "lutherische Engführung"

Abschließend sei noch einmal jene anfangs angesprochene Fragestellung aufgenommen, die sich mit den Stichworten "Wildwuchs" (Lau) und "lutherische Engführung" (Moeller) verbindet.[198] Unser von Luther ausgehender und schwerpunktmäßig auf die Nürnberger Quellen eingehender Überblick hat gezeigt, daß beide Interpretationsansätze ihr Recht haben, aber auch zu korrigieren sind.

Mit großem Recht wendet sich Moeller gegen die verbreitete These von der angeblichen Isolierung Luthers, der von seinen Zeitgenossen kaum verstanden worden sei. Das von Moeller beigebrachte Quellenmaterial (Predigtsummarien in reformatorischen Flugschriften) widerlegt tatsächlich die Ansicht, "im Grunde sei Luther in der frühen Reformation nicht wirklich zur Geltung gekommen, sein Erfolg beruhe eher auf Mißverständnissen".[199] Die theologische Vielstimmigkeit der frühen Predigt- und Flugschriftenbewegung der Reformation vor 1525 ereignet sich im Rahmen einer dominierenden Luther-Rezeption — was noch klarer wird, wenn man berücksichtigt, wie nahe auch Zwingli in den Grundlinien seiner Rechtfertigungstheologie bei Luther steht und wie wichtig die Impulse waren, die er durch Luthers Schriften empfangen hat.[200] Diese breite, vielstimmige Rezeption Luthers zeigt tatsächlich in überraschendem Ausmaß Übereinstimmung mit theologischen Grundaussagen Luthers: etwa in der Auffassung von der sündhaften Unreinheit allen menschlichen Wesens und Tuns, in der Ablehnung von Verdienst und Genugtuung, in der Betonung der allgenugsamen Heilsmittlerschaft Jesu Christi allein — gegen die Mittlerschaft der Heiligen, gegen eine heilsbezogene Relevanz menschlicher Werke und die Möglichkeit einer integren Gesetzeserfüllung des Menschen, in der Gegenüberstellung von heilsempfangendem Glauben und selbstsüchtigen Werken, in der Akzentuierung des allgemeinen Priestertums der Gläubigen

---

ebd., 287f. und das Gutachten Osianders über Dencks Bekenntnis: *Osiander Gesamtausgabe* Bd. 1 (wie Anm. 69), 411-417.

[198] Siehe 380f. mit Anm. 2 und 3.

[199] Moeller, "Was wurde in der Frühzeit ... gepredigt?" (wie Anm. 3), 192; vgl. ders., "Die Rezeption Luthers" (wie Anm. 3), 58f. und 69.

[200] Vgl. Hamm (wie Anm. 6), besonders 53 Anm. 237 und 62. Zugleich hebe ich hervor (62): Es "ist nicht nachdrücklich genug zu betonen, daß die Wirkung Luthers auf Zwingli immer eine ungemein starke Eigenprägung des Leutpriesters und eine sehr selbständige Entwicklung seines Denkens einschloß."

und der christlichen Freiheit als Freiheit von frommer Leistung und als
Befreiung zu wahrhaft guten Werken. Aus dem Protokoll einer vom
Nürnberger Rat im März 1524 durchgeführten Befragung von Predigthörern
kann man in exemplarischer Weise erfahren, daß nicht nur die evangelischen
Prediger vor Ort, sondern auch ihre Hörer unter der einfachen Handwerker-
schaft wesentliche (vor allem auch rechtfertigungstheologische) Unterschiede
zwischen der traditionellen Kirchenlehre und der aus Luther schöpfenden
reformatorischen Verkündigung treffsicher und sehr pointiert erfaßt
haben.[201]

Verständnisvolle Rezeption bedeutet freilich nicht Gleichförmigkeit und
Einheitlichkeit, denn Maßstab ist für die Rezipienten gerade nicht Luther-
treue, nicht möglichst große Annäherung an Luther, sondern Evange-
liumstreue, d.h. möglichst wahrheitsgetreue Predigt und schriftliche
Verbreitung des Gottesworts. So ist es nur selbstverständlich, daß mit der
Aufnahme von Luthers Theologie eine selbständige Verarbeitung dieser
Impulse Hand in Hand geht. Man will Luther nicht kopieren, sondern sieht
sich durch ihn angeregt, mit der Bibel in der Hand selbst das Wort Gottes
zu entdecken und — je nach persönlicher, lokaler und regionaler Situation
und sozialer Stellung — andere Aspekte hervorzuheben und manches, wie
man gelegentlich meinen kann, klarer und unmißverständlicher auf eine
bestimmte Problemstellung hin zu formulieren. Die verschiedenen Typen des
pneumatologischen Antiklerikalismus, wie wir sie in Nürnberg gefunden
haben und wie sie wohl auch über Nürnberg hinaus für die frühe Reformationsbewegung charakteristisch sind, zeigen genau dieses zweiseitige
Phänomen: einerseits die starke Prägung durch Luther, die Aufnahme seiner
antiklerikal-pneumatologischen Gedanken, die man durchaus versteht;
andererseits die Selbständigkeit des Weiterdenkens und Argumentierens: wie
man bestimmte Aspektfelder Luthers wegläßt, wie man mit anderen
Bibelstellen argumentiert und andere Konsequenzen zieht — nicht weil man
Luther nicht verstehen kann (weil Luthers Lehre zu kompliziert und man zu
dumm wäre, um seine hohen, gedankenreichen Differenzierungen nach-

---

[201] Der Text der Höreraussagen (von 18 Personen, mehrheitlich Handwerkern,
besonders Messerern) ist ediert bei Gunter Zimmermann, "Die Rezeption der
reformatorischen Botschaft: Laienaussagen zu Predigten des Franziskanerpaters
Jeremias Mülich in der Fastenzeit 1524", *Zeitschrift für bayerische Kirchengeschichte*
58 (1989): 51-70 (Text: 65-70). Die Laien äußerten sich zu folgenden Themen (in
ablehnender Haltung gegenüber den altgläubigen Predigten des Franziskaners): Christi
genugtuendes Leiden, Erbsünde und Aktualsünden, die Bedeutung der guten Werke
für die Seligkeit, die genügende Gesetzeserfüllung, Rechtfertigung allein aus Glauben,
Vergiftung der Natur des Menschen und Unreinheit seiner Werke, Beichte vor dem
Priester oder vor dem Nachbarn u.a. Interessant ist, daß sich manche Hörer, z.B. der
Messerer Michel Ketzmann, den Inhalt der Predigten schriftlich notiert haben (68).
Zur Rezeption der reformatorischen Rechtfertigungslehre in Handwerkerflugschriften
vgl. Arnold (wie Anm. 100), 330.

zuvollziehen), sondern weil Leute wie Osiander, Spengler, Diepold Peringer, Hans Sachs, Hans Greiffenberger und Hans Denck aus einer anderen Lebenssituation heraus Theologie treiben, weil ihnen andere Seiten der Bibel wichtig sind und weil sie, aus verschiedensten Gründen, mit evangelischer Reformation partiell andere Zielsetzungen verbinden als Luther.

Die Typenvielfalt des pneumatologischen Antiklerikalismus vor dem Bauernkrieg zeigt exemplarisch die Grenze von Moellers Interpretationsansatz. Schon seine Begrenzung auf die Gattung der 'Predigtsummarien', d.h. auf die Aussageebene der Prediger, die zugleich eine bestimmte soziale und intellektuelle Ebene repräsentiert, ist, verglichen mit seinen allgemeinen Schlußfolgerungen über 'die' frühe Reformation, methodisch fragwürdig. Zu beachten ist ja nicht nur, was von den Predigern gepredigt wurde, sondern auch, wie ihre Predigten von Menschen ganz anderer sozialer Verortung und anderer Bildungsvoraussetzungen vernommen und verarbeitet wurden: von Rittern, Patriziern, gelehrten Juristen und Ratsschreibern, Handwerkern, Bauern usw. Miriam Usher Chrisman ist genau dieser Frage erst jüngst in einer Analyse der Laien-Flugschriften vor 1525 nachgegangen und hat zeigen können, wie erst der Blick auf dieses breite soziale Spektrum die ganze divergierende Vielfalt der Luther-Rezeption erschließt: die Verschiedenartigkeit der thematisierten Probleme, der Argumentationsweisen, der zitierten Quellen, des Umgangs mit der Bibel und des Sprachstils.[201a]

So berechtigt also Moellers Anliegen ist, die Dominanz der Luther-Rezeption und in ihr das Ausmaß an Luther-Verständnis zu unterstreichen, so problematisch und mißverständlich ist der Ausdruck "lutherische Engführung", so angreifbar ist es, wenn er von "einheitlicher Doktrin", "einheitlichen Lehren und Schlagworten" und einer "Partei-Gesinnung" spricht.[202] Einheitlichkeit im Sinne von Gleichförmigkeit ist gerade nicht das Kennzeichen der in der frühen Reformationsbewegung gepredigten und in Flugschriften verbreiteten Theologie. Mit der Kohärenz der reformatorischen Bewegung, die Moeller betont, ist ihre Multiformität und Differenziertheit verbunden. Das eine ist nicht gegen das andere auszuspielen.[203]

[201a] Zu Chrismans Vortrag siehe oben Anm. 3.

[202] Moeller, "Was wurde in der Frühzeit ... gepredigt?" (wie Anm. 3), 193.

[203] Anders Moeller, "Die Rezeption Luthers" (wie Anm. 3), 70: "Wie Sie sehen, bin ich der Meinung, ... die Reformation sei in ihren Ursprüngen nicht in erster Linie als ein multiformer, sondern als ein kohärenter Vorgang einzuschätzen." Ebd., 69 (über den "Konsens in der Phase der 'lutherischen Engführung'"): "Nach meiner Meinung wird das historische Urteil über diese Zusammenhänge durch das Bemühen von Theologen, in diesem Konsens die Differenzen aufzuspüren, irregeführt ..." Das muß nicht sein, wenn man sich durch die Wahrnehmung der tatsächlich vorhandenen Unterschiede, Vielstimmigkeiten und Dissense den Blick für die Kohärenz und den Konsens nicht trüben läßt. Es ist allerdings festzuhalten, daß Moeller zwar vom "Einheitlichen" der frühen Reformation und von "Engführung" spricht, nicht aber von Gleichförmigkeit. Er weiß sehr wohl um die Vielgestaltigkeit der Reformations-

Insofern hat Franz Lau recht, wenn er sagt: "Die vielen Prediger und Schriftsteller der Zeit vor 1525 problemlos als 'Lutheraner' anzusehen, wäre sehr voreilig."[204] Laus Bemühen, die Differenziertheit[205] und Ungenormtheit[206] der reformatorischen Predigt bis zum Ende des Bauernkriegs hervorzuheben, entspricht durchaus der Vielstimmigkeit und Vielgestaltigkeit der Quellen. Allerdings führt der Schlüsselbegriff "Wildwuchs", den er als Phasenbezeichnung für die Zeit vor der obrigkeitlichen Einführung reformatorischen Kirchentums verwendet,[207] in die Irre — als sei die reformatorische Vielstimmigkeit hypertroph, hemmungslos und willkürlich ins Kraut geschossen. In Wirklichkeit ist der theologische Variationsspielraum der reformatorischen Flugschriftenliteratur durch eine extensive Dominanz der Luther-Rezeption und eine erstaunliche Intensität des Angesprochenseins von Luthers Neubegründung des frommen Lebens bestimmt.[208] Auch den reformatorischen Spiritualismus eines Karlstadt,

---

bewegung vor 1525. Doch versucht er, Forschungstendenzen entgegenzuwirken, die vor lauter Bäumen den Wald aus den Augen verlieren, die nur noch sorgfältig analysieren und in Partikularinteressen auseinanderdividieren, statt auch das Verbindende und eine gemeinsame Gesamtrichtung der Reformation zu sehen. Tatsächlich besteht ja die Gefahr, daß man — fasziniert durch die divergierende Vielfalt der reformatorischen Strömungen und Individualitäten — das Gemeinsam-Reformatorische und die Reformation als großen, zusammenhängenden Systembruch atomisiert und so aus der Geschichte herausanalysiert. Dazu gehört auch die theologiegeschichtliche Isolierung Luthers. Deshalb nehme ich sehr zustimmend von Moeller das Interpretament der 'Kohärenz' auf, das ich selbst auf rechtfertigungs-theologischer Ebene in einem früheren Aufsatz (siehe Anm. 208) akzentuiert habe. Aus sachlichen und terminologischen Gründen halte ich es freilich für irreführend oder jedenfalls für mißverständlich, wenn man das Kohärente, d.h. das miteinander Verbundene und Kommunizierende, als "einheitlich" bezeichnet. Denn mit dem Begriff 'Einheitlichkeit', zumal in der Kombination mit 'Engführung', assoziiert man im gängigen Sprachgebrauch die Vorstellung von Gleichförmigkeit; damit aber bekommt die Beschreibung der Reformation, die sich ständig zwischen den Kategorien Kohärenz und Multiformität bewegen muß, eine falsche Schlagseite.

[204] Lau (wie Anm. 2), K 33.

[205] Lau, K 32f.: "In der Tat gab es vorerst nur differenzierte reformatorische Predigt und z.T. entsprechendes Gemeindeleben."

[206] Lau, K 33: "Die reformatorischen Prediger der Zeit vor 1525 waren eine vielgestaltige Gesellschaft; ihre Predigt war noch ungenormt."

[207] Vgl. Anm. 2.

[208] Dies gilt auch dann, wenn man den Begriff des 'Reformatorischen' nicht zu eng bestimmt. Im Blick auf den Antiklerikalismus möchte ich von 'reformatorisch' dann sprechen, wenn die spätmittelalterliche Klerus-Kritik umschlägt in einen Systembruch mit dem hierarchischen System und damit in einen generellen Angriff auf den römischen Klerus insgesamt — wobei für die reformatorische Begründung des Angriffs die normative Rückbindung an das biblische Gotteswort charakteristisch ist. Vgl. Goertz (wie Anm. 1), 113 und Berndt Hamm, "Was ist reformatorische Rechtfertigungslehre?", *Zeitschrift für Theologie und Kirche* 83 (1986): 1-38; 3f. Die

Denck oder Greiffenberger sehe ich noch im Rahmen einer dominierenden Luther-Rezeption. Ferner entstanden diese Variationen, diese Typenvielfalt, die ich am Beispiel des pneumatologischen Antiklerikalismus dargestellt habe, nicht in wildem Wachstum, sondern in sehr naheliegenden und selbstverständlichen Entwicklungen. Man muß nur das breite Spektrum der spätmittelalterlichen Frömmigkeitsprogramme, Reformkonzeptionen und kirchlich-gesellschaftlichen Idealvorstellungen vor Augen haben, um zu verstehen, daß und warum Luthers Gedanken in entsprechender Vielfalt weitergedacht wurden. So führten spätmittelalterliche Spiritualismen in naheliegende Formen eines reformatorischen Spiritualismus hinüber;[209] so wurden spätmittelalterliche Parolen von der Verkehrtheit der Gelehrten[210] in entsprechenden (nun reformatorisch radikalisierten) Formen eines antigelehrten Antiklerikalismus und einer Geringschätzung von Sprachgelehrsamkeit weitergeführt. In sehr naheliegender Weise also verbanden sich antiklerikale und kirchenkritische Impulse des Spätmittelalters mit reformatorischen Ideen antihierarchischer Zuspitzung. Die Ausdifferenzierung innerhalb der Luther-Rezeption war also nicht Wildwuchs, kein hypertrophes Wachstum, sondern eine naheliegende Konsequenz. Die Entwicklung zeigt — a posteriori betrachtet — eine innere Logik und Folgerichtigkeit. Überraschend und erklärungsbedürftig ist weniger die Typenvielfalt, sondern weit eher die breite Dominanz der Anziehungskraft von Luthers Theologie.

---

dort gegebene Definition von 'reformatorisch' möchte ich allerdings erweiternd modifizieren: Reformatorisch ist, was — im Hinblick auf die mittelalterliche Theologie, Kirche und Gesellschaft — systemsprengend ist in der Weise der Rückbindung an die Bibel und was nicht mehr als eine ausgefallene Position innerhalb der Variationsbreite mittelalterlicher Theologien und Reformmodelle erklärbar ist. Dieser weit gefaßte, vielgestaltige Bereich des Reformatorischen ist seit dem Ablaßstreit bis in die Mitte der zwanziger Jahre (und darüber hinaus) durch die überwältigende Dominanz der Luther-Rezeption und eines Ergriffenwerdens durch Luthers seelsorgerliche Theologie gekennzeichnet.

[209] Zur Kontinuität zwischen spätmittelalterlicher Mystik und reformatorischen Formen mystischer Denkweise vgl. Steven E. Ozment, *Mysticism and Dissent. Religious Ideology and Social Protest in the Sixteenth Century* (New Haven, 1973); vgl. auch Werner O. Packull, *Mysticism and the Early South German-Austrian Anabaptist Movement 1525-1531*, Studies in Anabaptist and Mennonite History 19 (Scottdale, Penn., 1977). Den Zusammenhang der Laien-Flugschriftenverfasser (wie Sachs und Greiffenberger) und ihrer Forderungen mit dem Strom der häretischen Bewegungen des Mittelalters und ihrer Laienfrömmigkeit seit dem 12. Jahrhundert betont — mit allerdings problematischer Argumentation — Russell (wie Anm. 132), 180-4.

[210] Vgl. Oberman (wie Anm. 31), über den spätmittelalterlichen Hintergrund in Gestalt der Devotio moderna.

Im übrigen waren am Nürnberger Material zwei weitere Beobachtungen zu machen, die das Bild von der Vielstimmigkeit der reformatorischen Bewegung noch etwas präzisieren:

1. Die Differenzierung nimmt (wie man an der Entwicklung Greiffenbergers exemplarisch sehen kann) im Jahr 1524 mit einem deutlichen Schub zu, und zwar in der Weise, daß sich nun die Klerus-Kritik auch massiv als innerreformatorische Polemik artikuliert. Es zeigt sich Unzufriedenheit und Enttäuschung über die Haltung der maßgeblichen Reformatoren, deren Haltung man als geist- und fruchtlos empfindet.

2. Mit der weitergehenden Polarisierung der folgenden Jahre, z.B. durch das Auseinanderdriften der reformatorischen Bewegung in obrigkeitliche Reformation und Täufertum, verschwinden Erscheinungsformen pneumatologischer Klerus-Kritik, die 1523/24 in der Flugschriftenliteratur präsent waren. So wird der zweite Typus (eines Peringer, Sachs oder Lotzer) zwischen dem ersten (bildungsbezogenen) und dem dritten (spiritualistischen) gleichsam zerrieben, während der vierte (Müntzers und seiner Anhänger) durch den Ausgang des Bauernkriegs eliminiert bzw. in Kanäle des Kryptodissidentismus abgedrängt wird. Die reformatorische Bewegung ist daher in gewisser Hinsicht — auch im Abendmahlsverständnis — vor 1525 differenzierter und nuancenreicher als danach, weil die Situation noch offener ist. Vor allem gewisse Zwischentypen verlieren in einer Phase der Abgrenzung, Polarisierung und Konfessionsbildung ihre Existenzgrundlage. Das gleiche Phänomen ist ja auch im Verhältnis zwischen der altgläubigen und der evangelischen Richtung zu beobachten. Gerade die spätere Entwicklung kann 'Engführungen' schaffen, wo zunächst ein stärker gefächertes Spektrum von Positionen möglich war. Zwar gibt es nach 1525 wieder neue, vielfältige Differenzierungen und Typen in der reformatorischen Theologie und Frömmigkeit, aber eben auch das Verschwinden vorher vorhandener Vielstimmigkeit und Zwischentöne.

Ich fasse zusammen: Weder Laus Wildwuchsthese — die als Kontrast die Gärtnerkunst der lutherischen *pura doctrina* postuliert[211] — noch Moellers

---

[211] Man muß sich ja verdeutlichen, daß Laus Begriff des 'Wildwuchses' nicht etwa im positiven Sinne urwüchsiger Kreativität lebendigen Gemeindechristentums gemeint ist, sondern — auf der Grundlage des konfessionellen Luthertums — als Negativbegriff, der etwas höchst Gefährliches bezeichnet, das unbedingt der Eindämmung und Klärung bedarf; vgl. Anm. 2.

Nachtrag: Erst nach Abschluß meines Aufsatzes ist ein vorzüglicher Beitrag zum Thema 'Die Gelehrten die Verkehrten' (vgl. oben bei Anm. 31 und 210) erschienen, der durch eine Fülle zitierter Quellen den von mir am Ende des Aufsatzes angesprochenen spätmittelalterlichen Hintergrund ausleuchtet und — ohne auf Antiklerikalismus und Pneumatologie einzugehen — Material für meine These beisteuert, daß die verschiedenen Typen des pneumatologischen Antiklerikalismus, wie ich sie für Nürnberg herausgearbeitet habe, auch über Nürnberg hinaus für die frühe Reformationsbewegung charakteristisch sind: Carlos Gilly, "Das Sprichwort

These von der "lutherischen Engführung" — die als Kontrast die späteren Lehrgegensätze im Protestantismus voraussetzt — ist ohne Bedenken zu übernehmen. Ich denke, man wird Lau, Moeller und den Quellen selbst gerecht, wenn man die frühen Reformationsjahre vor 1525 und ihre gepredigte bzw. in Flugschriften dokumentierte Theologie so charakterisiert: Dominanz und Kohärenz der Luther-Rezeption in der Typenvielfalt ihrer Ausprägungen.

ANHANG

Bibliographie der unter dem Namen Hans Greiffenbergers
publizierten und der ihm zugeschriebenen Flugschriften

Die unter Greiffenbergers Namen gedruckten Schriften:

1 *Diß biechlin zaigt an die Falschen // Propheten / vor den vnß gewarnet hat Christus / Paulus // vñ Petrus / vñ findt darin / was vñ wie wir vns Chri // sten halten sollen / yetz in diser geferlichen // zeyt / auff das kûrtzest begriffen /// gemacht durch Hanns // Greyffenberger zů // Pfortzhaym.*
[Augsburg: Philipp Ulhart d.Ä., 1523?].
Expl.: Köhler, Fiche 255 Nr. 715.
Lit.: Arnold Kuczyński, *Thesaurus libellorum historiam reformationis illustrantium* (Leipzig, 1870-1874; Nieuwkoop, 1960), 934; Karl Schottenloher, *Philipp Ulhart, ein Augsburger Winkeldrucker und Helfershelfer der 'Schwärmer' und 'Wiedertäufer' 1523-1529* (München, 1921), 152f. Nr. 6; Michael Pegg, *A Catalogue of German Reformation Pamphlets (1516-1546) in Libraries of Great Britain and Ireland* (Baden-Baden, 1973), 1273; *VD 16*: G 3150.

2 *Diss biechlin zaygt an // was vns lernen vñ gelernet ha= // ben vnsere maister der ge= // schrifft / dar vor vnns // cristus offt gewar // net hat / die aus= // sen scheyn wie // sy gerecht sind // jñen voller // hüchlerey // vnnd // lüg. // Anno &c. M.D.XXiij. // Hanns Greyffenberger.*
[München: Hans Schobser], 1523.
Expl.: Köhler, Fiche 313 Nr. 897.
Lit.: Karl Schottenloher, *Der Münchner Buchdrucker Hans Schobser 1500-1530* (München, 1925; Nieuwkoop, 1967), 75; Pegg 1274; *VD 16*: G 3159.

'Die Gelehrten die Verkehrten' oder der Verrat der Intellektuellen im Zeitalter der Glaubensspaltung", in Antonio Rotondò (Hg.), *Forme e destinazione del messaggio religioso. Aspetti della propaganda religiosa nel cinquecento*, Band der Studi e testi per la storia religiosa del cinquecento (Florenz, 1991), 229-375.

3.1 *Die welt sagt sy sehe // kain besserung vonn den / // die sy Luterisch*
    nennet // was besserung sey / // ein wenig hierin // begriffen. // Hans
    Greyffenberger. // M.D.XXiij.
    [Nürnberg: Jobst Gutknecht], 1523.
    Expl.: Köhler, Fiche 107 Nr. 277.
    Lit.: Emil Weller, *Repertorium typographicum* (Nördlingen, 1864;
    Hildesheim, 1961), 2444; Kuczyński 932; *VD 16*: G 3163.
    Edition: Laube 1: 265-70.

3.2 *Die welt sagt Sy sehe // kain besserung vō den // die sy Luterisch nen=*
    // net / was besserung // sey / ain wenig // hieriñ be= // griffen. // Hans
    Greiffenberger. // M.D.XXIII.
    [Augsburg: Silvan Otmar?], 1523.
    Expl.: Köhler, Fiche 1293 Nr. 3330.
    Lit.: Weller 2446; Kuczyński 933; *VD 16*: G 3160.

3.3 *Die Weltt // sagt sy sehe kain besse // rung von den / die sy // Luthe-*
    risch nenn // et wz besserung // sey / ein wenig // hierinn be // griffen.
    // Hans greiffenberger // Jm Jar. M D XXIII. //
    [Augsburg: Melchior Ramminger], 1523.
    Expl.: München Staatsbibliothek 4° Asc. 418.
    Lit.: *VD 16*: G 3162.

3.4 *Die Weltt // sagt sy sehe kain besse // rung von den / die sy // Luthe-*
    risch nen= // net wz besserüg // sey / ein wenig // hierinn be // griffen.
    // Hans greiffenberger // Jm Jar. M D XXIII.
    [Augsburg: Melchior Ramminger], 1523.
    Expl.: München Universitätsbibliothek 4° Theol. 2998:2
    Lit.: Weller 2445; *VD 16*: G 3161.

3.5 *DJe welt sagt Sy // sehe keyn besserung vō // den die sy Lûterisch nē=*
    // net / was besserung sy / // eyn wenig hierinn be= // griffen // Hans
    Grieffen // berger.
    Expl.: Berlin Staatsbibliothek, Cu 2806 R.
    In der Literatur fand ich keine Beschreibung dieser Ausgabe.

4.1 *Ein trostliche ermanüg / // den angefochten im gewissen / // von wegen*
    gethaner sündt / // wie vnnd wo mit / sie ge= // trôst werden / Den //
    Sathan / sich nit // erschrecken // lassen. // Hans Greyffenberger. // Den
    armen wirdt das Ewan= // geli gepredigt / Selig ist / der sich // nit
    ergert an mir. Mat. xj. Lu. vij. // M.D.XXiiij.
    [Nürnberg: Jobst Gutknecht], 1524.
    Expl.: Köhler, Fiche 1198 Nr. 3020.
    Lit.: Weller 2892; Kuczyński 938; *VD 16*: G 3154.

4.2 *Ein trostliche ermanung // den angefochtñ im gewissen / võ we- // gen
gethoner sünd / wye vñ wa // mitt / Sye getrôst werdenn / // Den Sathan
/ sich nit // erschrecken las- // senn. &c̄. // Hanns Greyffenberger. //
Den armen würdt das Ewann- // geli gepredigt / Selig ist / der // sich
nitt ergerdt an mir. // Math.xj. Luce vii. // M.D.XX.iiij.*
[Augsburg: Melchior Ramminger], 1524.
Expl.: Köhler, Fiche 1083 Nr. 2742.
Lit.: Weller 2893; Kuczyński 939; Pegg 1276; *VD 16*: G 3155.

5.1 *Ein Christenliche Antwordt // denen / die da sprechen / das Euangeliõ
// hab sein krafft võ der kirchen (Ver= // legt) mit gôtlicher geschrift /
auff // das kürtzist / zů trost den Chri= // sten / inn Christo. // Hanns
Greyffenberger. // M.D.XXiiij. // 1. Timotheon. 5. // Die da sündigen /
die straff vor allen / // auff das auch die andern // forcht habenn.*
[Bamberg: Georg Erlinger], 1524.
Expl.: Köhler, Fiche 254 Nr. 712.
Lit.: Weller 2889 (und Suppl. 1, 35); Karl Schottenloher, *Die Buch-
druckertätigkeit Georg Erlingers in Bamberg von 1522 bis 1541 (1543)*
(Leipzig, 1907), 91 Nr. 26; *VD 16*: G 3149.

5.2 [Zusammen mit Hans Sachs:] *Underweysung. // der vngeschickten /
vermeinten // Lutherischen / so in eüsserlichen sachen / zů // ergernüß
jres nechsten / freüntlich handlē. // Hans Sachß. // Item. // Ob das
Euangelium sein krafft // von der kirchen hab. // Hans Greiffenberger.
// M D xxiiij. // Secunda Corinth. vj. // Last vns niemant jrgent ein
ergernüß geben / auff // das vnser ampt nit verlestert werd / sunder in
allē // dingen last vns beweysen / wie die diener Gottes.*
[Straßburg: Wolfgang Köpfel], 1524.
Expl.: Köhler, Fiche 1199 Nr. 3022.
Lit.: Weller 3149; Kuczyński 2311; *Short-Title Catalogue of books
printed in the German-speaking countries and German books printed in
other countries from 1455 to 1600 now in the British Museum* (=BM
STC), 770; Pegg 3564; Josef Benzing, *Bibliographie Strasbourgeoise*
(Baden-Baden, 1981), 1622; *VD 16*: G 3153.

6 *Ein warnũg vor // dem Teüffel / der sich wider // ûbt mit seinem
dendelmarckt / vnter // einem gleissenden schein / in merck= // lichen
stückenn / des Christen= // lichen lebens betreffen. // Hans Greyffenberger // 1524*
[Nürnberg: Jobst Gutknecht], 1524.
Expl.: Köhler, Fiche 1198 Nr. 3019.
Lit.: Weller 2894; BM STC, 370; *VD 16*: G 3158.

7.1 *Ein kurtzer begriff võ // gůten wercken / die got behagē / // vñ der welt
ein spot seind / yetzt // ein grosse klag / wie niemandt // mer gůts thů*

/ vnnd aller gots // dinst vnter gee / wie sie gedŭckt // in jrem syn / Ein antwort was // gŭtte werck seind. // Hans Greyffenberger. // M.D.XXiiij.
[Nürnberg: Jobst Gutknecht], 1524.
Expl.: Köhler, Fiche 343 Nr. 967.
Lit.: BM STC, 370; *VD 16*: G 3152.

7.2 *Ein kurtzer begrif // von gŭtteñ werckenn / dye // gott behagen / vñ der welt // ain spot seynd / yetz ein gro // se klag / wye nyemāt mer // gŭts thŭ / vnd aller Gots // dyenst vndergee / wie sy // gedunckt in jrem syñ // Eyn antwurtt wz // gŭtte werck // seynd. // Hanns Greyffenberger. // M.D.XXiiij.*
[Augsburg: Melchior Ramminger], 1524.
Expl.: Köhler, Fiche 750 Nr. 1916.
Lit.: Weller 2890; Kuczyński 937; Pegg 1275; *VD 16*: G 3151.

Die Greiffenberger zugeschriebenen anonymen Druckschriften:

8 *Diss buechel zaygt an // wie wir allso weyt gefŭert sind von // der lere vnnsers maysters Cristo // j̄m gepet / vñ andern sachñ vast // nützlich zŭwissen eym der da // begert sŭlig zŭ werdñ / vñ // zŭ erkennē die falschē ver // fŭerer des widercristen / // vñ von der heylige ere // vñ anrŭeffung vñ // glaubē cristo dē // haylmacher dē // sun gottes zŭ // glory. // M.D.XXiij.*
[München: Hans Schobser], 1523.
Expl.: Köhler, Fiche 1079 Nr. 2736.
Lit.: Schottenloher, *Schobser*, 73; *VD 16*: G 3164.

9.1 *Diss biechlin sagt von // den falschen Kamesierern / die sich auß // thŭnd vil gŭts mit fasten / peeten / // meßlesen für anndre / auff das // jn der sack / tasch vol werd // achten nit wo die // seelen hinfarē. // Jr bauch jr got // spricht Paulus // Anno &c. M.D.XXiij.*
[München: Hans Schobser], 1523.
Expl.: Köhler, Fiche 314 Nr. 899.
Lit.: Kuczyński 255; Schottenloher, *Schobser*, 74; *VD 16*: G 3157.

9.2 *Disz biechlin sagt von // den falschen Kamisierern die sich auß // thŭnd vil gŭts mit fasten / peten / me= // ße leßen für andere / auff dz in der // sack / tasch vol werd / achten // nit wo die seelen hinfa= // renn. // Jr bauch ir got // spricht Paulus. // Anno. &c. M.D.XXiij.*
[Augsburg: Jörg Nadler], 1523.
Expl.: München Staatsbibliothek 4° Polem. 481/10.
Lit.: Weller 2375; vgl. bei Schottenloher, *Schobser*, 74; *VD 16*: G 3156.

ANTICLERICALISM IN THOMAS MÜNTZER'S PRAGUE MANIFESTO

HANS J. HILLERBRAND

Duke University

Thomas Müntzer, who said of himself "qui veritate militat in mundo",[1] entered the literary arena of Reformation controversy in November, 1521 with linguistic vehemence and theological flair. What has been called his *Prague Manifesto* was to be his pronouncement of reform.[2] The document denounced a church that had become a whore, a gospel that had been obscured, and a clergy that was misleading the people. Clearly it was crucial for Müntzer, in a time of exuberant pursuit of reform and renewal, to make sure that the authentic meaning of the gospel was rightly understood. His journey to Prague, that old Hussite stamping ground, had begun at Zwickau, where his message of reform and renewal was swallowed up in controversy. Indeed, as has been argued, Müntzer may well have wished to express misgivings in the *Manifesto* about Martin Luther's new interpretation of the gospel.[3] Be that as it may, the basic theme of the *Manifesto* was one of reform — since the people had been led astray.[4] And, he, Thomas Müntzer, had been called to set things straight and do so in a setting of intense urgency: "Dye zceyt der ernde ist do! Drumb hat mich Gott selbern gemit in seyn ernde."[5]

Accordingly, the overriding concern of the *Manifesto* was the religious renewal of Christendom.[6] Müntzer claimed to understand the nature of God's "order", and the *Manifesto* was his vehicle for outlining his convictions. We will probe the *Manifesto* for its anticlericalism. The garden I propose to till is quite small — no sweep of a century or two — just a simple document, unpublished at the time, of some eight pages.[7]

---

[1] *SUB*, 564.

[2] The most comprehensive introduction to the document, replete with extensive polemical asides, is H. J. Goertz, "'Lebendiges Word' und 'totes Ding'. Zum Schriftverständnis Thomas Müntzers im Prager Manifest," *ARG* 67 (1976): 153-78.

[3] A. Lohmann, *Zur Geistigen Entwicklung Thomas Müntzers*, (Leipzig, 1931), 22.

[4] Later on Müntzer charged that the reformers soothingly told the people "du must dich mit solchen hochen dingen nicht bekommern", *SUB*, 238.

[5] *SUB*, 504.

[6] W. Elliger, *Thomas Müntzer, Leben und Werk* (Göttingen, 1975), 191.

[7] H. J. Goertz, *Thomas Müntzer. Mystiker. Apokalyptiker. Revolutionär* (Munich, 1989), 75. "So gesehen war die Kritik am Klerus mehr als eine vordergründige

The very first sentence of the *Manifesto* recorded Müntzer's conviction. It was a profound, if somewhat dramatic expression of deep existential agony. His had been ignorance, total ignorance, for neither monks nor theologians had conveyed to him "dye rechte ubungk des glaubens" nor had the "vormaledeygthn pfaffen" allowed him to see the true meaning of faith.[8] They — all priests and monks and theologians — bore the responsibility for obscuring the true Gospel.

This theme of false leaders and shepherds reverberates throughout the *Manifesto*. "Woe, woe, woe, unto the hellish and fiendish clergy who demonstrably mislead the people."[9] Theologians and clergy claim to understand the Bible — to have "eaten" it — when in fact they locked it up.[10] They use the Bible to advance erroneous claims. They "steal" the true Scripture, the living word of God, from the Bible like murderers and thieves.[11]

Müntzer argued that the true knowledge of God has been obscured so that an understanding of faith no longer exists. We need not ponder the controversial issue of the precise nature of Müntzer's message or its specific late medieval sources.[12] Far more important for understanding the *Manifesto* is the agony of spirit that bespeaks Müntzer's message. Müntzer's soul is in anguish, he is deeply burdened by the perversion of the church. "Ich habe mich bitterlich seher erbarmet", he says[13] and he speaks of the "poor, poor, poor little people".[14]

The perversion of the church, the absence of a proper understanding of the faith, the prevalence of false teaching have a reason. It is the clergy, who are responsible for the despicable state of affairs. However, "clergy" is for Müntzer a complex term in two ways. First of all, its meaning has nothing to do with the morality of individual priests, nothing with the societal role of the clergy. "Clergy" means those who, in the postapostolic age, have perverted the true faith, turning the immaculate bride of Christ

---

Kritik, die Müntzer mit dem *Prager Manifest* verfolgte. Sie war das Milieu, in dem er zu seiner reformatorischen Grunderkenntnis fand, und der Stoff, aus dem eine neue Theologie entstand." See also Goertz's earlier pronouncement, "Aufstand gegen die Priester. Antiklerikalismus und reformatorische Bewegungen", in *Bauer, Reich und Reformation*, ed. P. Blickle (Stuttgart, 1982), 190, "sein Prager Manifest ist mit antiklerikalen Ausfällen geradezu gespickt."

[8] *SUB*, 491.

[9] *SUB*, 503.

[10] *SUB*, 498.

[11] *SUB*, 492; see also 498, "das dye pfaffen den slussel von dissem buche, das geslossen ist, stelen, sie slissen dye schrifft zcu."

[12] The best guide to Müntzer's sources, derived from a creative reading of the relevant documents is A. Friesen, *Thomas Muentzer, a Destroyer of the Godless: The Making of a Sixteenth-Century Religious Revolutionary* (Berkeley, 1990).

[13] *SUB*, 503; see also 495, "bezceuge ich und clage jemmerlich".

[14] *SUB*, 500.

into a harlot and this means the priests and monks, as well as theologians and church leaders, including the pope. Müntzer is against the "church", against its teachings and its principles. Some themes of the anticlerical expression of his time — criticism of luxurious living, claims to political power, moral depravity, financial involvement — are absent from the *Manifesto*.[15] Prominent is the call to move from perversion to purity, and to understand the gospel aright.

The fact that the "clergy" thus become a code word for perversion of the gospel takes me to the second aspect of the complex term. It is highly important that Müntzer uses several interchangeable terms — all referring to the same phenomenon. He talks about the "priests", about the "popes", but also about "those greedy fellows" — "geltdorstigen buben"[16] — and especially focuses on the "glerthen", the learned ones, the scribes, as those responsible for the fall of the church.[17] The fateful role of the clergy has been to have perpetuated through the centuries the intellectuals' and leaders' misunderstanding of the Scriptures.

It follows that Müntzer's preoccupation is not so much with the clergy and church of his own time, but with a broader view of history. The current state of affairs, which is so despicable, has long antecedents. What is in place now must be put against what has been the case for centuries, indeed, ever since "dem tode der apostln schuler".[18] Müntzer's opposition against the clergy is not existential, nor is it focused on the notion of a recent deterioration of the church. His own generation is neither different nor worse than the long stretch of generations before him. Müntzer unfolds a sweeping understanding of history, which is a history of perversion of the gospel and true faith, rather than on particular clerical shortcomings in his time. Indeed, as we have noted, the "fall" of the church occurred more on account of the "glerthen" than of the clergy.[19] But the clergy perpetuated it.

The clergy were indicted for their complicity in the perversion of the gospel.[20] "sie vorleucken das gruntlich heyl des glaubens."[21] Thus, the priests of his time were to be pitied rather than hated, persuaded rather than persecuted.

Conceptually, of course, Müntzer's message of reform was not possible without the presupposition of the repudiation of the ecclesiastical status quo.

---

[15] As an exception, note *SUB*, 504, "Dan dye pfaffen haben allzceyt wollen obenansitzen."

[16] *SUB*, 500.

[17] See *SUB*, 494; see also 501, "unser nerrischen, hodenseckysschen doctores".

[18] *SUB*, 494.

[19] *SUB*, 494.

[20] *SUB*, 496, "Ufft und dicke habe ich von yhn gehoret dye blosse schrifft, welche sie schalkhafftig gestalten haben ... wie dye tukyssen diebe unde grausamen mordere."

[21] *SUB*, 497.

It is crucially important, all the same, to understand that Müntzer superimposed a vision of history on that status quo. This vision of history presupposed acquaintance with, and study of it.

Of utmost importance was the purity of the church. Reform was necessary, because the church had lost its purity. The voice of the living God was ignored. And, horror of horrors, wheat and tares, the elect and the ungodly, were both found in the church. The clergy came in for chastisement only as willful perpetuators of the perverted status quo.

Something else must be noted. It is known that differences exist between the four versions of the *Manifesto*. In particular, the extended German version contains references to clergy that are absent in the Latin version which, after all, was addressed to intellectuals, to the clergy.[22] We may be disposed to see this difference of the versions as an exquisite measure of strategic subterfuge. But there is another point of view as well. Thomas Müntzer was able to vary the versions because he saw his indictments, abusive and vehement as they were, as peripheral to his paramount concern: to portray the meaning of true faith. Accordingly, he could address even the clergy in his Latin version, because, after all, they, too, were victims as much as victimizers.

Underlying the arguments of the *Manifesto* is, of course, the plea for new authority, even more radical, perhaps, than had been the case with Luther. I would doubt, however, if this entailed the repudiation of existing forms of governance.[23] The issue — after all, it is late in 1521 and not as yet 1524 — was the acceptance of a new understanding of the faith by all — German and Czech, clergy and laity alike. "Dise schrifft künnen alle auserwelten menschen lesen."[24] It is the new principle of authority, the priesthood of all believers, which is enunciated here, and which, of course, is anticlerical par excellence in that the direct access to the living word renders superfluous all clerical mediators.

Our thesis that Müntzer was primarily concerned about the larger sweep of things, about God's salvation history, finds its confirmation in the closing passages of the *Manifesto*.[25] The reading of the eschatological signs is clear for Müntzer. Things — "confusum cahes" — will not continue indefinitely as they have in the past.[26] God has a plan; divine patience will not last

---

[22] *SUB*, 498, "Dorrumbme weil hymel unde erden stehet, vermügent dyeselbigen bosewichtisschen, verretherischen pfaffen." See also Elliger (n. 6 above), 193ff. for additional comments. By the same token, the "buben" of the German version became the "pastores" of the Latin version, *SUB*, 500 vs. 508.

[23] This is the argument of H. J. Goertz, "'Lebendiges Wort' und 'totes Ding'" (n. 2 above), 153ff.

[24] *SUB*, 498.

[25] *SUB*, 494ff.

[26] *SUB*, 510.

forever. Changes are in the making. "Hyr wirdt dye new kirche anghen."[27] Then will come the reign of the Antichrist. Finally, at long last, Christ will turn over the rule of this world to his elect "in secula seculorum".[28] As one steeped in the world of the Bible and the medieval underground of divining its history of salvation, Müntzer concluded that the end was near.[29] Anticlericalism narrowly defined pales against such a grandiose view of human affairs.

The anticlericalism in Thomas Müntzer's *Prague Manifesto* offers interesting perspectives. For one, the scathing criticism of the clergy seems to be a rhetorical device, an attention-getting device, rather than the heart of the argument. Müntzer's reaction against the wordliness, the immorality, the fiscal and political involvement of the clergy found expression in strings of abusive modifiers.[30] But, neither the demeanor of individual clergy nor that of the clergy as a class nor clerical exercise of societal power seemed worth doing more than that.

But, having said this, I must add that Müntzer indicts the clergy at precisely the point of their crucial claim to be mediators between God and man. They *are* mediators, Müntzer tells his readers, but mediators of a false gospel, of a perverted faith, of a fallen church. Thus, he opposes them for the very role they play. They must be rejected, for they have no place in the new church that is to arise.

Tellingly, Müntzer employs a different term, already in the *Manifesto*, but as time went on, ever more pointedly, say in his *Von dem getichten glawben*. This was the category of "Christendom", the "arme, elende, erbermliche, jamerliche cristenheit". This "cristenheit" had to be emancipated, take charge of its own destiny. It dare no longer accept the clergy as mediators of a phony faith.

Finally, Müntzer's anticlericalism in the *Manifesto* is a fusion of antipapalism and antiintellectualism as well. He is, plainly and simple, against all perverters of the faith. This is surely the meaning of the arrogant and yet agonizing opening passages of the *Manifesto* — that no one to whom he had turned had been able to convey to him the meaning of the true exercise of faith. It is Thomas Müntzer, if not *contra mundum* then surely

---

[27] The Latin version renders it, "Hic incipiet renovata ecclesia apostolica in universum orbem profectura", *SUB*, 510.

[28] *SUB*, 505.

[29] G. Maron, "Thomas Müntzer als Theologe des Gericht", *ZKG* 83 (1972): 195-225.

[30] I note but a few: "Dye unbeflecte jungfrawliche kirche ist dorch den geystlichen ebruch czur hurn worden der glerthen halben"; "pechgesalbeter pfaffe"; "geystscheynender münich"; "hellegruntfesten pfaffen"; "neronischer, heiliger, allerhultzeister bapst und pruntztopf zcu Rome", the latter with the addition in the Latin version "in babilonico lupanari", *SUB*, 494ff.

contra totam ecclesiam. No wonder that he seems, at the end of the *Manifesto*, to wish for allies, that is, the invasion of the Turks.

After Prague Müntzer disappeared from the public limelight until he surfaced, two years later, in Alstedt. What he published from then on, for two more years, gave him prominence as a pivotal figure of the 1520s, something the *Prague Manifesto* had failed to do. On the face of things the theme of anticlericalism seems to disappear. But does it really?

In Alstedt, reform and renewal meant for Müntzer something quite different from what it had meant in the *Manifesto*. Gone is the concern with monks and priests and popes. The concern is with only *one* of the "glerthen", with Martin Luther. Now, the task is the unmasking of Luther. *If* nothing else, Müntzer's tracts of 1523/1524 were tell-tale evidence for Luther's overpowering influence on events. *If* Müntzer wanted to impact the direction of reform, Luther had to be attacked, and Müntzer did so with skillful determination and theological insight. The "soft-living" flesh in Wittenberg and his "honey-sweet Christ" (a phrase found already in the *Manifesto*) became the epitome of an erroneous faith, the object of vehement attack. Thus, it seems, there was no room for anticlerical polemic, because the issue was Luther and his distorted view of the Christian faith.[31] But the basic theme of the *Manifesto* is still present: Martin Luther acts as erroneous mediator, as perverted "priest", between the true gospel and "poor Christendom".

Finally, in the context of the uprising of 1524/25, Thomas Müntzer seems to have undergone yet another shift. Now, say in his *Daniel Sermon*, even Luther appears to be left behind. A new concern has arisen — the relationship of structures of political power to the gospel. But, demonstrably, the old themes very much persist. The separation of the wheat from the tares, the purification of the church into that virginal bride which she had been in the days of the Apostles — this is still Müntzer's overriding passion. Accordingly, he continued to denounce, revile, ridicule, and reject those who misinterpreted the true gospel.

But now the identity of the perverters is defined anew. Müntzer must have concluded that the priests and even Luther were unimportant in comparison with the real culprits — the princes. And they are the ones who are exposed to his biting and scathing accusations.

The themes are still very much the old themes. The rulers do essentially what the priests and what Luther had done. They prevent access to the true gospel. They are mediators, but mediators not of Christ, but of the Antichrist. The rulers not only thwart the proclamation of the true gospel — which is abominable enough — but also, by suppressing the common

---

[31] Understandably, there is no anticlerical sentiment at all in Müntzer's *ernster sendebrieff an seine lieben bruder zu Stolberg, SUB*, 21-24.

people, enforce societal conditions of injustice and inequity which render a meaningful proclamation of the gospel impossible. They all are the godless.

As in the *Manifesto* the theme of judgment is still very much present, except the Turks have now been forgotten, and the common people have taken their place. And not just potentially so either — their very rising up in arms is proof positive that the larger views of human history espoused by Müntzer is beginning to unfold before everyone's eyes.

Finally, from the Müntzer of the *Manifesto* to the Müntzer of the letters of the spring of 1525, there runs the common thread of the argument that you will know them by their fruit. To be sure, I sought earlier to argue that in the *Manifesto* the themes of sexual debauchery, fiscal immorality, or political license are peripheral. But they are present, of course, very much so as a matter of fact, except that these themes are to demonstrate, as we have seen, a more basic point. The reality that priests are immoral and worldly only proves the point that they preach a perverted gospel. The same applies to Martin Luther, whose Christ is not the Christ of the "gospel of all creatures". No wonder then, that he is that soft-living flesh, Dr. Liar. The princes are very much cut from the same cloth.

But back to the *Prague Manifesto*. That document shows, when Müntzer first stepped forward to share his vision of a renewed Christendom, his was already a system that required the categorical repudiation of the theological, but also historical, role of the clergy. Still, the melodramatic flair of his characterizations was done with an eye to the gallery. The *sitz-im-Leben* was the specific situation of 1521 when Luther's excommunication and ban had petrified the parameters within which reform and renewal might take place.

When, after Frankenhausen, Thomas Müntzer awaited his execution and penned his sensitive reflection on what had just happened, he did not retract the validity of his vision. But one part of this vision — the eschatological reading of his own time — had demonstrably proved to be wrong.

He paid for that mistake with his life, and with much infamy thereafter.

CONSIDERING THE CLERGY'S SIDE:
A MULTILATERAL VIEW OF ANTICLERICALISM

SCOTT H. HENDRIX

Blue Bell, Pennsylvania

My approach to the topic of anticlericalism is, as far as I know, different from those which have been applied heretofore to the sources of the Protestant Reformation in Germany. By "a multilateral view" I mean an approach to anticlericalism that tries to see and to appreciate the different sides of the parties involved in anticlerical disputes. Since anticlericalism is a social form of blame, the sources usually present grievances or charges against the clergy that arise out of anger or disappointment. For that reason, we cannot assume that the sources present a fair view of the clergy's side or, for that matter, an accurate picture of what motivates the attacks. By "multilateral", therefore, I mean an approach to the sources that will utilize them to construct a fairer and more balanced picture of the two (or more) sides in controversy.

The specific identities of these sides change as the Reformation unfolds. In particular, I am interested more in the *target* of early Reformation attacks than in the attackers, i.e., I want to investigate the side of the Catholic clergy who were attacked by early Protestants, whether lay or clerical. By the "side" of Catholic clergy I mean three things: 1) to what extent the attacks upon them were fair or unfair; 2) how they would defend themselves against those attacks which they felt were unjust; and especially 3) what were the frustrations, disappointments and resentments that the clergy suffered and that caused them to feel unfairly treated?

Several kinds of sources provide insight into the side of early sixteenth-century Catholic clergy. First are the records that enable us to reconstruct the actual historical context of late medieval clergy. Second are treatises of Catholic theologians which defend the case of the clergy and reveal some of their motives. And, third, are the Protestant pamphlets that disclose, sometimes inadvertently, the frustrations of the clergy that led to the very behavior which Protestants were attacking. In the following I will offer samples of each kind of source and show, in a preliminary way, how they can contribute to a more balanced historical understanding of anticlericalism.

The prerequisite for representing fairly the side of any party is to understand as accurately as possible who belonged to that party and what circumstances governed their thinking and their actions. Applied strictly to the clerical context, this prerequisite would require a comprehensive history of the late medieval clergy — an enormous task which has yet to be accomplished. Two ways of focusing the sources, however, make the task more manageable: studies of the clergy in one local area and portraits of the clergy that are sketched from a cross section of similar records. One example of each — neither the most recent nor necessarily the most intensive such study — will illustrate the relevance of such work to the evaluation of anticlericalism.

The first example is the examination by Rolf Kießling of church and society in pre-Reformation Augsburg.[1] Clerical privileges were a prominent source of the laity's resentment in German cities. Prior to the Reformation in Augsburg, however, Kießling demonstrates that the city council was able to make inroads into the special rights and benefits of the clergy. The council adopted measures that reduced clerical advantages in matters of taxation, business competition, and juridical competence — all matters that were of utmost importance to Augsburg's citizens.[2] Later, therefore, when Protestant laity in Augsburg expressed resentment of clerical immunity in their town, the clergy scarcely needed to feel guilty since they had already lost some of their significant privileges. They were entitled to protest further infringement of their historic rights and benefits, as Bishop Christoph of Stadion did on their behalf in 1537.[3]

A second example comes from the German Protestant church orders of the sixteenth century as analyzed and summarized by Ernst Walter Zeeden.[4] Zeeden's intent was to point out the continuity between late medieval and sixteenth-century Lutheran worship and practice. Given the nature of church orders and visitation records, the continuities which he found accentuated the inadequacies and hardships of the clergy. Instead of blaming them, however, Zeeden was able to recognize and to credit the burdens under which the late medieval and Reformation clergy both labored. For example, in North Germany, out of economic necessity the pastors had to tend their own fields in spite of the fact that church orders prohibited such labor or at least tried to save Saturday for the clergy to carry out their pastoral duties. Zeeden concluded that poor remuneration, which was carried over from the Middle Ages into the Reformation, continued to be a liability for the clergy, both

---

[1] Rolf Kießling, *Bürgerliche Gesellschaft und Kirche in Augsburg im Spätmittelalter. Ein Beitrag zur Strukturanalyse der oberdeutschen Reichsstadt* (Augsburg, 1971).

[2] Kießling, 97-8.

[3] Herbert Immenkötter, "Die katholische Kirche in Augsburg in der ersten Hälfte des 16. Jahrhunderts", in *Die Augsburger Kirchenordnung von 1537 und ihr Umfeld. Wissenschaftliches Kolloquium*, ed. R. Schwarz (Gütersloh, 1988), 9-31, here 31. Without acknowledging the losses suffered by the Catholic clergy in the city, Immenkötter is quick to criticize Bishop Christoph for ignoring the legitimate need for reform of the church.

[4] Ernst Walter Zeeden, *Katholische Überlieferungen in den lutherischen Kirchenordnungen des 16. Jahrhunderts* (Münster, 1959).

for their pastoral work and for the reputation of their office.[5] Underpaid Catholic and Protestant clergy justifiably felt resentment when they were attacked for not being good pastors, for reading their sermons out of the *postilla*, or for selling beer in the village to make additional money. Why should they work harder for nothing?

A second kind of source that raises the side of clergy are the tracts of the Catholic controversialists. Their theological replies to Protestant works on such topics as ordination and celibacy do not necessarily yield the most relevant material. As a rule, they provide arguments from Scripture and tradition that defend Catholic practice or engage in polemic against Protestant authors.[6] On occasion, however, these Catholic theologians express dissatisfaction with their own clergy. In so doing, they reveal motives that led people to become priests and confirm the ill-preparedness of the clergy which Protestants criticized.

For example, in his reply to Luther's *Schmalkald Articles*, the Colmar Augustinian prior Johann Hoffmeister (ca. 1510-1547) agreed that the negligence of the bishops was responsible for what he called the "jamer der secten".[7] Their main failure consisted of not regulating the caliber and motives of candidates for the priesthood. As a result, laments Hoffmeister, men are transferred directly from the plow to the altar and the coarsest wild asses (*waldesel*) occupy the richest benefices, while those who could and would best serve the church are left to go begging. Even worse, he continues, the priesthood has become a career opportunity; those who cannot earn a living for themselves become priests even though they are not dedicated to the ministry. When teachers notice a lazy student who will not study, they say: "He will make a fine priest."[8]

It is not surprising to find an Augustinian prior expressing criticism of the secular clergy. His own standards aside, however, these non-polemical remarks identify some of the burdens which were imposed on Catholic clergy. They confirm, first of all, what we already suspect and in some cases know: the lack of preparation and the poor academic qualification of many priests. But, second, they also testify indirectly to the professional injustice and resentment that many qualified priests must have experienced, when they saw less qualified colleagues — even upstarts and newcomers —

---

[5] Zeeden, 69-70.

[6] For example, Johann Eck in his *Enchiridion* [German edition: Augsburg, 1530], ed. Erwin Iserloh (Münster, 1980), 28-31, 59-62.

[7] Johann Hoffmeister, *Warhafftige endeckung unnd widerlegung deren artickel, die M. Luther auff das concilium zu schicken und darauff beharren furgenummen*, in *Drei Schriften gegen Luthers Schmaldkaldische Artikel von Cochläus, Witzel und Hoffmeister (1538 und 1539)*, ed. Hans Volz (Münster, 1932), 116-187, here 175,22-24: "Ich halt warlich dafür, das dise hinlessigkeit nit die kleinest ursach sey, das wir in solchen jamer der secten kummen sind."

[8] Hoffmeister, 175,24-176,3.

receive the best-paid and more prestigious positions. Add to this resentment the poor reputation that the priesthood enjoyed with teachers and educated laypeople, and it becomes more understandable why the priesthood neither attracted more qualified candidates nor inspired those who did serve to perform their duties with zeal and devotion. As Hoffmeister himself asks: "When such circumstances force one into the priesthood and the regular authorities do not provide better oversight, what good can finally come out of that?"[9]

The writings of the controversialists further illuminate the side of the clergy when they challenge directly the anticlericalism of Protestants or reflect the experience of their authors. Even that toughened opponent of Protestantism, Johann Cochlaeus (1479-1552), allows attacks against Catholics and their clergy to get under his skin. In his reply to the articles of the Münster Anabaptists (1534), Cochlaeus bristles at the notion that Catholics along with Protestants should be addressed as "the godless". If, says Cochlaeus, "you include among the 'godless' also those Christians who have stayed with the old faith and with the pope, then you talk like other faithless heretics; [you] have learned it from that rowdy Lutheran crowd which haughtily and maliciously label us such, against all Scripture, justice, honor, and propriety." Even though he blames it on the Lutherans, we can hear in the indignation of Cochlaeus the injury and insult that the unjust label "godless" also inflicted on him and on other Catholic clergy.[10]

In his response to Johann Bugenhagen's epistle to the English people (1526), Cochlaeus shows specific sensitivity to the charges against Catholic clergy. He accuses Bugenhagen of stirring up the Catholic laity against their clergy by attributing to the priests what Christ said about the scribes and the Pharisees "as if the clergy of the church were not a Christian but a Jewish people." When by such slander, he continues, the people have been inflamed with envy and hatred against the priests, the evangelicals serve up their own impious teachings while the people cheer them on.[11] Cochlaeus not only argues that Catholic clergy are different from the scribes and Pharisees; he

---

[9] Hoffmeister, 176,4-6: "Wo dan einen ein solche ursach zu dem preisterthumb zwingt unnd die ordentliche obergkeit nicht bass sorget, was solt dan entlich guts darauss erwachsen?"

[10] Johann Cochlaeus, *XXI Artickel der Widderteuffer zu Munster durch Doctor Johan Cocleum widerlegt*, in *Die Schriften der Münsterischen Täufer und ihrer Gegner*, vol. 2: *Schriften von katholischer Seite gegen die Täufer*, ed. Robert Stupperich (Münster, 1980), 101: "Wo sie aber durch die gottlosen wöllen versteen die gemeinen christen, die es im alten glauben der kirchen mit dem babst halten, so reden sie wie andere abtrünnige ketzer und habens auch vom Lutherischen hauffen gelernt, die uns also heissen wider alle schrifft, recht, eher, und zucht aus ubermessiger hoffart und eigenwilliger bossheit."

[11] Johannes Cochlaeus, *Responsio ad Johannem Bugenhagium Pomeranum*, ed. Ralph Keen (Nieuwkoop, 1988), 107,1-8.

also testifies to the investment that he and other clergy had made in the Church as the guarantor of the old (and still for them) true faith: "So you will not scare us away from our ancient faith, even if ten thousand times over you call us hypocrites, Pharisees, apostles of the Antichrist, the kingdom of Satan, and the like."[12] The anger of Cochlaeus is not the detached polemic of a theological debate, but personal hurt and indignation aroused by the criticism of his own allegiance to the "ancient faith". His anger also stems from the Protestant dismissal of himself and of other Catholic clergy as (to use a word of the young Luther) *antichristiani*.

Another interesting insight into the side of the clergy can be gleaned from the blame which Cochlaeus places upon the laity. Although he holds both secular authorities and evangelical preachers responsible for the laity's defection, he also faults the people for so easily falling away from the old faith. They too readily believed the strange itinerant preachers rather than adhering to their regular bishops and pastors.[13] Cochlaeus' blame extends to the way the laity treat their clergy after they have become Lutheran. They refuse to pay their pastors what they owe them, deny them the customary tithe, contribute no offerings or anything else that is justly required of them.[14] Cochlaeus' defense of the clergy exposes the loss of secure income which pastors and priests might suddenly suffer. His criticism of the laity, I suspect, also exposes a kind of *clerical anti-laicism* that crossed confessional lines and arose from a common resentment of the laity's disrespect and disregard for clerical sustenance.

A third kind of source which reveals the side of the Catholic clergy is the Protestant pamphlet. It may seem an unlikely source from which to learn more about the Catholic side, since it will often contain just the opposite —

---

[12] Cochlaeus, *Responsio ad Johannem Bugenhagium*, 107,34-109,1. Cf. the translation on 106 and 108.

[13] Cochlaeus, *XXI Artickel der Widderteuffer zu Munster*, in *Die Schriften der Münsterischen Täufer und ihrer Gegner*, 2: 97: "Das volck aber darumb, das sie so leichtfertig sind und von altem glauben so liederlich abfallen und gleuben mehr den losen frembden landtleuffern dann yren ordentlichen bischoffen und pfarherrn und lassen sich äffen und umbher führen von itzlichem winde newer leere wider manigfeltige warnung Christi, Pauli und aller heyligen väter."

[14] Cochlaeus, *Responsio ad Johannem Bugenhagium*, 109,9-11: " ... non reddentes Clero census debitos, non decimas consuetas, non oblationes, non alia quae iuste ab eis exiguntur." A similar complaint about the support of evangelical preachers is offered in 1538 by Urbanus Rhegius, *Wie man die falschen Propheten* ... (n. 15 below), D^v-Dii: " ... da hat man wider korn noch gelt/ das die armen prediger vor hunger entrinnen müssen/ und da die undanckbar welt zuvor hat mit aller volle/ mehr denn 400. Baals Propheten können erneeren/ Da kann und wil man itzt schwerlich wenig rechte Propheten/ mit wasser und brot erhalten." Rhegius claims that the monasteries which formerly could support forty or sixty monks now cannot support one evangelical preacher. Why? Because God's Word does not appeal to the "old Adam" (ibid.).

a strong polemic against the old clergy. But consider an obvious example of such a pamphlet: *Wie man die falschen Propheten erkennen ia greiffen mag*, based on a sermon delivered in Minden in 1538 by the Protestant preacher Urbanus Rhegius.[15] The false prophets are the cathedral clergy in Minden who, together with the rest of the clergy, receive a bitter scolding from Rhegius. The keynote of his polemic is the charge that the Catholic clergy are responsible for the terrible state of the church. Instead of being our faithful fathers and pastors, the bishops and the priests [*seelsorger*] are now our greatest enemies and slayers of souls [*seelmörder*].[16] "Summa summarum", he concludes, "if you examine the clerical estate inside and outside, you will find nothing but a facade with nothing behind it."[17]

The same polemic, however, contains evidence of Rhegius' own disappointment in that clergy to which he too once belonged. Several times he flashes back two decades, to the year prior to his own ordination (1518), and expresses his amazement that the clergy could have turned out so badly. "Twenty years ago who would have believed that monks and nuns would deny Christ. . . . [or] that our clergy and pastors would be such devouring wolves?"[18] Yet, of all people, Rhegius should have believed it; for in this same pamphlet he recalls the time when "I was one of your preachers."[19] Rhegius agreed to the printing of his sermon so that the angry canons of Minden would become even angrier at their apostate Rhegius, who fifteen years earlier in Augsburg had been a member of their order. He hopes, however, that their anger will force them to realize the error of their ways. If Urbanus passed up the opportunity to become a rich canon and a prominent papist, and fled in the nick of time out of Sodom and Gomorrah, then they too might recognize the danger of their estate and turn to Christ.[20]

More evident here than the anger of the Minden canons is the anger of Rhegius himself, which arises out of his disappointment at the profession

---

[15] It is extant in three printed editions: 1) s.l., 1538; 2) Wittenberg: Hans Frischmut, 1539; 3) Brunswick: Anders Goldbeck, 1539.

[16] *Wie man die falschen Propheten* ... (Brunswick, 1539), Eiv[v]: "Die Bischoff und geistlichen die unsere trewen Veter und seelsorger sein solten/ die sind itzt unsere grösten feind und seelmörder."

[17] Ibid., Fiii: "Summa summarum/ ersuch den geistlichen stand inwendig und auswendig/ so findstu nichts anders denn einen schein/ und nichts darhinter."

[18] Ibid., Giv[v]: "Wer hete fur 20 jar gleubt/ das pfaffen/ Mönch und Nonnen solten Christum verlaugnen?" Cf. ibid., H: "Wer hett aber vor zwentzig jaren geglaubt? Das unsere Geistlichen und Hirten solch reissend Wolff weren?"

[19] Ibid., Jiii: "Ich bin ewer prediger auch gewesen/ aber es wolt mir mein Bisschoff zu Brixen fur xiiij jaren einbinden/ Ich solt menschen lehr predigen und bekennen/ das menschen lehr die conscientz möge billich verstricken/ do ichs nicht einrümen wolt/ richt er mir ein solche persecution an bey der Oberkheit/ das ich meins lebens weder tag noch nacht sicher was."

[20] Ibid., Aii-Aii[v].

that he chose and wanted to improve. That disappointment must have deeply penetrated the soul of this illegitimate son of a priest whom Johann Eck once called a "priestly whore's son".[21] From the time of his ordination, whether as Catholic priest or as Protestant preacher, Rhegius sought to improve the quality of the clergy; it was the leitmotif of his career. When, in 1538, Rhegius wonders who could have believed that the clergy would become such ravenous wolves, he is still wrestling with his own disappointment. At the same time, I think, he exposes the frustration of the very Catholic clergy whom he was attacking. Why should the canons of Minden have shared the ideals of Rhegius? Why should they not have expected to become guardians of the church's assets and to live comfortably in exchange for their vows? They certainly had a right to be angry at Rhegius, because he threatened their wealth and prominence and because they felt just as betrayed by him as he still felt by them. The canons of Minden may also have felt unfairly treated by being lumped together with the monks and all the secular clergy. Seventeen years earlier Rhegius did not make that mistake. Instead, he singled out for recognition the clergy whom he called "die frummen priester", who would be better off, he said, if it were not for the Roman clergy and the courtesans.[22]

In the early Reformation, Rhegius was not the only evangelical author to remind his readers that devoted Catholic priests did exist. On the title page of his 1522 pamphlet written in Wittenberg, Johann Eberlin von Günzburg placed the following admonition: "There are still many pious priests, and for their sake the laity should refrain from undertaking anything against the clergy, so that the innocent do not have to *pay* for the guilty."[23] This pamphlet, entitled *Seven Pious But Disconsolate Priests Bewail their Distress* ... , is one of a pair which present the conflicts that beset the Catholic clergy in the early stage of the reform movement. Its companion, which offers consolation to the priests through Eberlin's spokespersons, the

---

[21] Maximilian Liebmann, *Urbanus Rhegius und die Anfänge der Reformation* (Münster, 1980), 70.

[22] In the context of denying that Luther was simply against the priesthood; *Anzaygung/ dasz die Romisch Bull mercklichen schaden in gewissin manicher menschen gebracht hab/ und nit Doctor Luthers leer* (s.l., 1522), Aiv[v]: "Do schryen etlich der Luther sy gar wider de priesterschafft/ das thond allain die/ die nitt verston wellen/ was mainung der Luther von semlichen dingen redt. Er hat wol wider die Romischen gytigkait und die Kurtisanen geredt/ denen niemantz hold ist dann jr brotmaister der teüfel/ wann die selben nit weren/ die frummen Priester kemen basz herfür/ er beriert niendert anders/ dann allain die böse myszbreijch und zaigt an die rechten wirdigkait der priester/ ..."

[23] *Syben frumm aber trostloss pfaffen klagen ire not, einer dem anderen, und ist niemant der sye tröste, Gott erbarme sich jre*, in Ludwig Enders, ed., *Johann Eberlin von Günzburg*, vol. 1: *Ausgewählte Schriften*, vols. 2-3: *Sämtliche Schriften*, Flugschriften aus der Reformationszeit 11, 15, 18 (Halle, 1896, 1900, 1902), 2: 57-77, here 2: 57.

Fünfzehn Bundesgenossen, also adds insight into the mentality of the priests, even though it offers mainly, as expected, evangelical solutions.[24] Together the pamphlets form a remarkable expression of what I have called the *side* of the Catholic clergy, which Eberlin, a former Franciscan monk and preacher, knew from experience and, despite his sympathy for the Wittenberg movement, was still able to credit.[25]

Each of the seven *Pfaffen* describes the dilemma which faces him. These descriptions are not without comic elements and they certainly have an edge that is critical of the clergy and of the hierarchy in particular. But Eberlin is not sarcastic, and the dilemmas contain a genuine element which many a priest must have faced. The general tone is set by the first priest who has to ask a layperson which book of the Bible he should read first. The layman replies that he will find everything a priest needs to know in the three letters to Timothy and Titus. After having read and reread them, the priest exclaims in frustration: "If a pastor has to be like what is taught there, then God help me!"[26]

As portrayed by Eberlin, however, the challenge to the clergy is greater than living up to the ideal described in Scripture. They are also caught in real dilemmas which seem insoluble. For example, the priest who struggles with the requirement of celibacy describes his dilemma this way:

> So I am caught [*Also binn ich verwickelt*]. I cannot be without a wife. If I am not permitted to have a wife, then I am forced to lead publicly a disgraceful life, which damages my soul and honor and leads other people, who are offended by me, to damnation. How can I preach about chastity and unchastity, adultery and depravity, when my whore comes openly to church and my bastards sit right in front of me? How shall I conduct mass in this state?[27]

His options are either to remain chaste as well as celibate or to leave the priesthood, both of which he considers. If he tries to be chaste, then he fears that God will give him up to the desire of his heart and he will fall into even worse sins, as described in the first chapter of Romans. If he leaves the priesthood, he says, he cannot support himself, and if he stays [with a

---

[24] *Der frummen pfaffen trost. Ein getrewer glaubhaffter underricht unnd antwort uff der syben trostlossen pfaffen klagen, Newlich durch die Fünfftzehen Bundsgnossen beschriben, uff die hye vertzeychneten artickel*, in Enders (n. 23 above), 2: 79-93.

[25] For a summary of his Wittenberg pamphlets and commentary on his place among the Wittenbergers, see Martin Brecht, "Johann Eberlin von Günzburg in Wittenberg 1522-1524", *Wertheimer Jahrbuch 1983* (1985): 47-54.

[26] *Syben frumm aber trostloss pfaffen*, in Enders 2: 59.

[27] Ibid., 2: 63: "Also binn ich verwickelt, ich kan on weyb nitt sein, so lässt man mir kein eeweib, also würd ich gezwungen zu eim offentlichem schandtlichem [*sic*] leben, zu schaden meiner seelen und eeren, ja zu verdamnüss viler menschen, die sich an mir ergeren, wie soll ich predigen von unkeüscheit unnd keüscheit, von Eebruch, von buberey etc. so mein hur zu kirchen und strass gat, so meine bastart mir vor augen sitzen, wie soll ich messs lesen in diesm standt."

concubine], he will be caught as described.[28] The dilemma is enough, he concedes, finally to make him believe that the pope and the bishops are the Antichrist. And he concludes: "No state in Christendom is so scandalous and desolate as the priesthood."[29]

While the first priest deplores the current frustration of the Catholic clergy, the second and third priests illuminate the disappointment that must have sprouted among clergy when they realized that a career in the priesthood would not fulfill their expectations. The second priest is disturbed by the fact that clergy do not have to earn their support but receive it from the tithes and donations of the laity. They are hungry, he says, while we sit around full, they are busy while we play, they have worries, while we whistle a merry tune and make love to our mistresses. And this sin [of not working], he continues, is so ingrained and callous that people think it is right, and parents raise their children to become priests so that they will have a good life.[30] The career of this priest, however, and perhaps for the Franciscan Eberlin and colleagues whom he knew, was not the good life which they had been raised to expect. The sixth priest calls anyone an archfool who believes that priests have a good life. Even though he became a priest unawares and now cannot escape, he warns other young men to avoid this life of misery.[31]

The conscience of the third priest is bothered by the superficiality, deceit, and pompousness of the vigils and masses at which he presides. He voices a theme that commonly appears in the literature of reform: the longing for the way things used to be. I would like to be a priest, he says, if the priestly office were godly as it was in earlier times, when a priest would preach, administer the sacraments, and consecrate.[32] The fifth priest, who fears an uprising of the laity, mourns the loss of his honor and reputation with God and with the people: "Before God, in my conscience, I am ashamed of my soulless, godless life; I lack the knowledge and honor of God in myself, and people will add me to that godless crowd which they are now calling *pfaffen*

---

[28] Ibid., 2: 64.

[29] Ibid., 2: 64: "So ist kein standt der christenheit ergerlicher und wüster dann pfaffenstandt."

[30] Ibid., 2: 65: "Und ist dise unser sünd so tieff und hart worden, das sye für gut und recht wird geachtet, also, das die elteren ire kind darumb uff pfaffheit ziehen, das sye gut tag haben, und man für ubel achtet, wann ein pfaff solt arbeiten."

[31] Ibid., 2: 75: "Aber wiewol ich in die pfaffheit binn kommen, wie Contz hinder das vyhe, und nit wol mag davon kommen, so wolt ich doch gerne andere junge knaben wären trewlich gewarnet, das sye nit in diezen jamer kämend. Man sagt, wir pfaffen haben gut leben, ja einer ist ein ertznarr, welicher unser leben für gut haltet."

[32] Ibid., 2: 68: "Ich wolt gern priester sein, wann priester ampt göttlich were als vorzeiten, do ein priester predigt, sacrament reicht, und consecriert, etc."

und münch."[33] Eberlin does not blame Luther for the loss of priestly status, but Luther is blamed in another document which voices the same regret. In a pamphlet, called bluntly *Lamentation of the Priests*, Haug Marschalck has the clergy intone:

> Vor waren wir all inn grossen ehren,
> das thustu, Luther al[le]s verkeren
> mit deinem schreyben und auch leren.[34]

Much is being exaggerated here — the prestige which a career in the priesthood allegedly used to carry, and the ideal of the priesthood as a ministry of Word and sacrament. Despite this exaggeration and its anti-clerical tone, and regardless of who receives the blame, I still suspect that a genuine loss for the clergy is being mourned. That loss is not just the loss of respect and prestige, but it is also the loss of an ideal, the disappointment of hopes, and the realization that expectations of what the priesthood would be cannot be fulfilled. That loss and disappointment had been accumulating over generations. The sixth priest claims that his great uncle, who was a priest himself, told his father: "If you were to drown your son, it would be better for him and for you than if he became a priest."[35]

When all that loss is combined with the dilemmas facing the priesthood, then the burden borne by conscientious priests must have been heavy. The consolation offered by Eberlin, I doubt, could scarcely have offset the weight of that burden. The consequences of turning evangelical do not appear especially attractive. If he preaches God's Word, the pastor will be a "man of death", who has to risk everything he has and can expect to lose his friends and his life. And even death would be better than being locked up, forced to recant, or sent into exile.[36] The compensation for such a risk might seem inadequate. Eberlin argues that God has not made a mistake by calling them to the priesthood. Although they are lumped together with their scurrilous brethren, there are still many good priests and pious, insightful

---

[33] Ibid., 2: 72: "Ich klage sonderlich den verlust meiner eeren und rhum vor gott unnd den menschen, ich schäme mich vor gott in meinem gewissen, meines seelosen gottlosen lebens, das ich in mir selbs mangel Gottes erkantnisz und eere, auch vor den menschen erkannt würd als ein zusatz des gottlosen hauffen, welche man yetzund pfaffen und münch nennet."

[34] Marschalck, *Der Pfaffen Klage*, in Laube 1: 570,5-7.

[35] *Syben frumm aber trostloss pfaffen*, in Enders (n. 23 above), 2: 75.

[36] Ibid., 2: 71: "Soll ich aber sagen gottes wort, so binn ich ein mann des tods, wie will ich blyben vor pfaffen, münchen, fürsten, ja vor bischoffen, Babst, Keyser, deren aller bann, Acht, gebott, verbott, in allen landen, stetten, kirchen gezeigt und gelesen werden, ich muss eer und gut dran wagen, ja aller meiner freund verlust. zuletzt grifft man mir nach dem leib und erwürgt mich, das ich nit so gross achte, als ob man mich würff in einen thurn, wie vilen geschehen ist, oder zwüng mich zu einem wideruff, oder vertrib mich vom land."

laypeople who recognize that no field is without its weeds. They should preach the truth and suffer for it, and God will sustain them.[37]

Observed from the side of the laity, early Reformation anticlericalism might look like an issue of power, as Bob Scribner proposes.[38] Seen from the side of the Catholic clergy, however, it was more an issue of justice. For urban clergy it was unjust to be asked to surrender more privileges when they had already been eroded by the city. For rural clergy, it was unfair to labor all week for practically nothing and then have to work on Sunday as well, and even worse to be told you could not earn a few extra pfennig. It was insulting for your allegiance to the ancient faith of the church to be despised and to be labeled godless as well. It was disappointing to sacrifice family for a good benefice and then be told you had no right to a comfortable life. It was even more painful to wake up one day with an enlightened but stabbing conscience that would not let you enjoy the benefits to which you thought you were entitled by your sacrifices. You received no credit for what you did. And it was most distressful of all to realize that, instead of seeing your expectations fulfilled, you confronted a dilemma with no simple solution and faced massive losses. I imagine that the clergy felt just as angry and cheated as the laity; and, consequently, some of the clergy did abuse their power. But, as often happens in cases of abuse, the sources recount the injuries of the abused more readily than they reveal the side of the abusers.

---

[37] Ibid., 2: 90, 91.

[38] "Anticlericalism and the Reformation in Germany", in R. W. Scribner, *Popular Culture and Popular Movements in Reformation Germany* (London, 1987), 243-256, here 244.

ANTICLERICALISM
IN GERMAN REFORMATION PAMPHLETS

HANS-CHRISTOPH RUBLACK

Universität Tübingen

I

Beginning with a brief overview of the medieval anticlerical tradition, this lecture will endeavor to demonstrate the variety of adaptations which this tradition underwent as it was incorporated into reformation pamphlet literature. This will be followed by a section in which I relate the criticism of the clergy to the dominant theme or code of the pamphlets, from which it is possible to deduce the reformation understanding of the Word of God. My perspective may be seen as a differentiation of the concept of anticlericalism which A. G. Dickens has cited as "unduly capacious".[1] What has emerged from my investigation of some 400 reformation pamphlets[2] is,

---

[1] A. G. Dickens, "The Shape of Anti-clericalism and the English Reformation", in E. I. Kouri, Tom Scott, eds., *Politics and Society in Reformation Europe* (London 1987), 379-410, 379.

[2] The ca. 400 texts selected do not provide a "sample". Pamphlets addressing a popular level have been given preference, such as dialogues to sermons and thematic tracts, polemic texts to teaching, as well as prognostica. Research for this paper is based, apart from the pamphlet editions in print — Adolf Laube, ed., *Flugschriften der frühen Reformationsbewegung*, 2 vols. (Berlin, 1983), henceforth cited as Laube; Oskar Schade, ed., *Satiren und Pasquille aus der Reformationszeit*, 3 vols. (Hannover, 1863; reprint Hildesheim, 1966), henceforth Schade; Otto Clemen, ed., *Flugschriften aus den ersten Jahren der Reformation*, 4 vols. (Leipzig, 1906-1911; reprint Nieukoop, 1967), henceforth Clemen — on the 10 series of microfiches (Köhler et al., eds., *Flugschriften des frühen 16. Jahrhunderts* [Zug, 1978ff.], henceforth cited as Köhler, Fiche), which I was able to use thanks to the generous kindness of Dr. Hans-Joachim Köhler, who provided information available to him as well, and copies and excerpts from my own research in the libraries of Augsburg Stadt- und Staatsbibliothek, München Staatsbibliothek, Wien Nationalbibliothek, and Wolfenbüttel Herzog August Bibliothek. For the assistance provided by the staff of these libraries I am grateful. The publication of the first volume of Hans-Joachim Köhler's *Bibliographie der Flugschriften des 16. Jahrhunderts* (Tübingen, 1991), has made valuable additions possible as to the pamphlets listed from A - G. It is referred to as Köhler, *Bibliographie*, followed by the number of the pamphlet cited. I acknowledge critical reading of a draft by Pete Dykema, Tucson, Arizona, as well as I am grateful for an English version of my second draft by Elizabeth Rublack-Diamond.

in addition to an appreciation of the great variety of texts in this corpus, a recognition of the decided emphasis and weighting throughout on the concept of the Word of God.

II.1

Accusations of avarice, negligence and depravity directed against individual clerics, the clergy as a whole, and the church as an institution, in addition to the exploitation of laymen by ecclesiastical recourse to secular power, are recurrent themes in the medieval apocalyptic tradition.[3] They remained prevalent as this tradition underwent redefinition in direct contextual applications.[4] The institutional ecclesiastical powers endeavored to subdue these elements within the church and indeed integration proved possible as in the case of St. Bridget.[5] In an analogous context, the monastic reform movements were also assimilated into the ecclesiastical structure, yet — most notably in the Franciscan order — preaching continued to reflect a critical attitude towards the parochial clergy.[6]

---

[3] Horst Dieter Rauh, *Das Bild des Antichrist im Mittelalter: Von Tyconius zum Deutschen Symbolismus*, Beiträge zur Geschichte der Philosophie und Theologie des Mittelalters, Neue Folge 9 (Münster, 1973); for a shorter account Marjorie Reeves, *The Influence of Prophecy in the Later Middle Ages: A Study in Joachimism* (Oxford, 1969), 295-305; Robert Konrad, *De ortu et tempore Antichristi. Antichristvorstellung und Geschichtsbild des Abtes Adso von Montier-en-Der*, Münchener Historische Studien Abteilung mittelalterliche Geschichte 1 (Kallmünz, 1964); Karin Boveland, Christoph Peter Burger, Ruth Steffen, *Der Antichrist und Die Fünfzehn Zeichen vor dem Jüngsten Gericht. Kommentarband* (Hamburg, 1979); Gustav Adolf Benrath, "Antichrist: Mittelalter", and Gottfried Seebass, "Antichrist: Neuzeit", both in *Theologische Realenzyklopädie* 3 (Berlin, 1978), 24-43. For an overview and source material cf. Bernard McGinn, *Visions of the End: Apocalyptic Visions in the Middle Ages* (New York, 1979); Robin Bruce Barnes, *Prophecy and Gnosis: Apocalypticism in the Wake of the Lutheran Reformation* (Stanford, 1988).

[4] Reeves, *The Influence of Prophecy in the Later Middle Ages*, 306: "Political hopes and rivalries soon entered eschatological history"; Franz Kampers, *Die deutsche Kaiseridee in Prophetie und Sage* (Munich, 1896).

[5] *Revelationes* (Nuremberg, 1500): Staatsbibliothek München Rar. 424a, 424b (Ludwig Hain, *Repertorium bibliographicum, in quo libri omnes ab arte typographica inventa ad annum 1500 typis expressi ordine alphabetico vel simpliciter enumerantur vel accuratius recensentur*, 4 vols. [Paris, 1826-1838; reprint Milan, 1966], 3205); *disz biechlin* (Augsburg: Hans Schoensperger, 1522): Staatsbibliothek München P.lat. 251d; Elias Wessén, ed., *Revelationes S. Birgittae a codice*, Bibl. Universitatis Lundunensis: Corpus Suevicorum medii aevi 13, 14 (Hafniae, 1952); L. Clarus, *Leben und Offenbarungen* ... 1-4, Sammlungen der vorzüglichsten mystischen Schriften 10-13 (Regensburg, 1856).

[6] G. R. Owst, *Preaching in Medieval England* (Cambridge, 1926).

Particular emphasis was placed throughout on the figure of the "Antichrist", which is typified in a 1486 Augsburg tract,[7] rendering the apocalyptic ideas of Vincent Ferrer, an early fifteenth century Dominican papalist and apocalyptic preacher.[8] Ferrer characterized the clergy as follows:

> Sy seind worden ein weg der sel verdamnusz die da solten sein der weg des heyles, sy stellent nach eren aber nit nach sitten. Die priester seind vnwissend, fürnämisch vnd spotter, vngelert, gleichszner, den weisen übelredend, geitig, symoneyer, böser dann dye juden, vnkeüsch, neydig vnd vnlauter dye ganczen welt zerstörent, sy laffend bald nach den pfenning, sy seind aber langsam zu den laff der tugent, sy seynd hört on all barmherczikeyt, Sj haben vil waffen vnd wenige bücher, Sj seind vnweisz claffer vnd vnwarhaft. Die cristenheit freüet sich wenn sy einen andechtigen vnder tausenten funde.

We note that the criticism directed against the clergy focused on three main issues:
1. The attitude of the clergy to worldly goods and power
2. Their life style
3. Their understanding of the clerical office

The range of criticism incorporated into Ferrer's prophetic tradition made it easily adaptable and applicable to varying contexts.

Though messianic ideas never seemed to have been more than one element of Christian teaching, it proved possible at the end of the fifteenth century, to rally a number of parties behind a mystic leader, as demonstrated by the case of Savonarola.[9] This tradition provided a framework of reference for reformation teaching, which we find applied by Andreas Osiander in his 1527 tract, *Sant Hildegardten Weissagung vber die Papisten vnd genanten Geystlichen Welcher erfullung zu vnsern zeytten hat angefangen vnd volzogen sol werden*,[10] or by Luther in his preface to Lichten-

---

[7] *Hienach hebt an ein wunderberlicher tractat des heyligen sant Vincency prediger ordens von dem ende der weltt* [Augsburg, 1486]. See Hain, *Repertorium bibliographicum*, 7022; Sigismund Brettle, *San Vincent Ferrer und sein Literarischer Nachlass* (Münster, 1924), 163.

[8] Francis Oakley, *The Western Church in the Later Middle Ages* (Ithaca, 1979), 261-70.

[9] Donald Weinstein, *Savonarola and Florence: Prophecy and Patriotism in the Renaissance* (Princeton, 1970).

[10] *Sant Hildegardten Weis= // sagung / vber die Papisten / vnd genanten // Geystlichen / Welcher erfullung / zu vn= // sern zeytten hat angefangen vnd vol // zogen sol werden. // Eyn Vorred durch Andrean Osiander. // ym M.D.xxvij. Jar. //*, Köhler, Fiche 886/2235; Gerhard Müller, Gottfried Seebass, ed., *Andreas Osiander d.Ä. Gesamtausgabe* (Gütersloh, 1977), 2: 485-501; Gottfried Seebass, *Das reformatorische Werk des Andreas Osiander*, Einzelarbeiten aus der Kirchengeschichte Bayerns 44 (Nuremberg, 1967), 99; Marjorie E. Reeves, "Some Popular Prophecies from the Fourteenth to the Seventeenth Centuries", in *Popular Belief and Practice*, ed. G. J. Cuming, D. Baker, Studies in Church History 8 (London, 1972), 107-34,

berger's prophecy,[11] and in his citing of Thomas Müntzer as a false prophet.[12]

II.2

A positive ideal of the clerical function can be found in a translation by Heinrich Steinhöwel[13] of Rodrigo Sanchez de Arévalo's *Der Spiegel des menschlichen Lebens*,[14] which details the layman's concept of this function in hierarchical order. It was expected that a good pastor take responsibility for the souls of the laymen and that he should care for the poor and comfort the bereaved and lonely. Although the metaphor of the shepherd caring for his sheep was seen as part of canon law, the tract noted that the priests wished to be honored for a mere aura of sainthood, though there was neither virtue nor truth in them. Essentially they were pastors by name only, who exploited the laymen by means of confession and penitence. They did not preach, "their belly is their God", being as merchants, robbers and idlers. This text is construed as an advice or instruction to the varying estates, and displays no apocalyptic context. As such it cannot be considered as purely anticlerical, since positive clerical values are presented in detail.

122.

[11] *WA* 23. 1-12, where he testifies that at least the clergy knew Lichtenberger (7,6-10): "Nach dem aus diesem buch ein fast gemeine rede ist entstanden gewest: Es wurde ein mal uber die pfaffen gehen, und darnach widder gut werden, Und meinen [scil. die Geistlichen], es sey nun geschehen, sie seyen hindurch"; Dietrich Kurze, *Johannes Lichtenberger (†1503). Eine Studie zur Geschichte der Prophetie und Astrologie*, Historische Studien 379 (Lübeck, 1960).

[12] Kurze, *Johannes Lichtenberger*, 33, n. 199. Theologically orientated scholarship has recently rediscovered Müntzer's affinities to Joachim von Fiore, cf. Reinhard Schwarz, "Thomas Müntzer und die Mystik", in S. Bräuer, H. Junghans, eds., *Der Theologe Thomas Müntzer. Untersuchungen zu seiner Entwicklung und Lehre* (Göttingen, 1989), 292.

[13] Hans Rupprich, *Die deutsche Literatur vom späten Mittelalter bis zum Barock. Das Ausgehende Mittelalter, Humanismus und Renaissance, 1370-1520*, vol. 4/1 of *Geschichte der deutschen Literatur*, ed. H. de Boor and R. Newald (Munich, 1970), 573ff.

[14] *DJses buechlin genannt der spiegel des menschlichen lebens von dem hochwirdigen Rodorico von hyspania byschoffen Zamorensi gemachet ... In dem sich all toetliche menschen. sy seyend geystlich oder weltlich eynes yetlichen wesens nach irem gelucke oder widerwärtigkait gesehen mugent ...*, Stadt- und Staatsbibliothek Augsburg, fol. Inc. 230. Barbara Weinmayer, *Studien zur Gebrauchssituation früher deutscher Druckprosa. Literarische Öffentlichkeit in Vorreden zu Augsburger Frühdrucken*, MTU 77 (Munich, 1982), 120, lists three editions (1475 [?], 1479, 1488) by the Augsburg printer Zainer, who published the Latin original *Speculum vitae humanae* in 1471.

Revival of the true church was a catchword not only of apocalyptic and Joachimite manuscripts, or the Wyclifite[15] and Hussite movements, but also part of a disciplining propaganda from above. Since the Cluniac reform criticism of the clergy was not exclusively a movement from below. Lazarus Spengler collected passages from canon law in his *Ein kurtzer auszuge aus den Bebstlichen rechten der Decret vnd Decretalen Ynn den artickeln die vngeferlich Gottes wort vnd dem Euangelio gemes sind odder zum wenigsten nicht widderstreben* of 1530, which supported the charges which reformation pamphlets levelled against the clergy.[16]

Other late medieval traditions of interest in this context include the antijudaic[17] and astrological.[18] Local conflicts of city magistrates with ecclesiastical hierarchs, as in the cities of Strasbourg and Constance, shortly before the Reformation, provide a contextual framework for late medieval criticism of the clergy, which was later incorporated into local pamphleteering.[19]

---

[15] Rudolf Buddensieg, *Johann Wiclif's De Christo et adversario suo Antichristo, zum ersten Mal aus den Wiener und Prager Handschriften herausgegeben*, Programm des Vitzthumschen Gymnasiums 19 (Dresden, 1880).

[16] Lazarus Spengler, *Ein kurtzer // auszuge / aus den // Bebstlichen rechten der De= // cret vnd Decretalen / Ynn den // artickeln / die vngeferlich Got // tes wort vnd dem Euangelio // gemes sind / odder zum we // nigsten nicht widder // streben. // Mit einer schoenen Vorrhede. // Mart. Luth. // Wittenberg. 1530. //* (Wittenberg: Josef Klug, 1530), Köhler, Fiche 206/586.

[17] As summed up by Carlo Ginzburg, *Hexensabbat. Entzifferung einer nächtlichen Geschichte* (Berlin, 1990), 43.

[18] Hans Copp, *Doctor Joannes Copp // Was auff disz dreyundtzweyntzigist // vnd tzum teyl vierundtzweyntzigist iar // des hymmels lauff kuennfftig sein auszweysz Do // ctoris Joannis Copp vrteyl. //* (Leipzig: Wolfgang Stöckel [1523]), Köhler, *Bibliographie*, Nr. 603: Köhler, Fiche 1103/2806, A4r-v, B2r. Helga Robinson-Hammerstein, "The Battle of the Booklets: Prognostic Tradition and Proclamation of the Word in early sixteenth-century Germany", in P. Zambelli, ed., *'Astrologi hallucinati': Stars and the End of the World in Luther's Time* (Berlin, 1986), 129-51; Aby Warburg, *Heidnisch-antike Weissagung in Wort und Bild zu Luthers Zeiten*, Sitzungsberichte der Heidelberger Akademie der Wissenschaften, Phils.-hist. Klasse 1919, 26 (Heidelberg, 1920): = Aby M. Warburg, *Ausgewählte Schriften und Würdigungen*, ed. D. Wuttke, Saecula Spiritvalia 1 (Baden-Baden, 1979), 199-304.

[19] Francis Rapp, *Réformes et réformation à Strasbourg. Eglise et société dans le diocèse de Strasbourg (1450-1525)* (Paris, 1974), 435ff.; Jean Rott, "Pfaffenfehden und Anfänge der Reformation in Strassburg. Die Streitigkeiten des Johannes Murner mit den Brüdern Wolff und dem Jung Sankt Peter-Stift daselbst (1519-1522)", in *Landesgeschichte und Geistesgeschichte. Festschrift für Otto Herding zum 65. Geburtstag*, ed. K. Elm, E. Gönner, E. Hildenbrand (Stuttgart, 1977), 279-94; Hans-Christoph Rublack, *Die Einführung der Reformation in Konstanz*, QFRG 40 (Gütersloh, 1971), 138f.

II.3

Erasmus' *Praise of Folly*[20] reflects a similar critical attitude heightened by satirical bitterness, which is, however, substantially congruent with traditional criticism. Over against a popular anticlericalism,[21] Erasmus upheld true Christian love, Scriptural knowledge and inwardness of faith,[22] but criticized papal and theological arrogance, and monastic ceremonialism.[23] He demanded a truly spiritual pope who would imitate Christ, his poverty and work, his cross and teaching,[24] in contrast to the mechanisms of the transfer of responsibility for piety and pastoral care which characterized the ecclesiastical system.[25] Erasmus' pacificism led him to object strongly to warring popes and bishops,[26] but he also criticized monks for their routinized ceremonialism.[27] This is to be understood in the Erasmian context of folly which also extends to popular religion.[28] Erasmus' pamphlets published in the early 1520s elaborated this criticism of the clergy and monks, but did not radicalize it — he never termed the pope an Antichrist.[29] The unity of Christianity as well as the vision of ecclesiastical

---

[20] Clarence H. Miller, ed., *Moriae Encomium id est Stvltitiae Laus*, in *Opera Omnia Desiderii Erasmi Roterodami* IV/3 (Amsterdam, 1979); citations to Erasmus von Rotterdam, *Moriae Encomion sive Laus Stultitiae*, in Werner Welzig, ed., *Erasmus von Rotterdam: Ausgewählte Schriften*, vol. 2 (Darmstadt, 1975), 1-211; cited as *Laus Stultitiae*. Christine Christ-von Wedel, "Das 'Lob der Torheit' des Erasmus von Rotterdam im Spiegel der spätmittelalterlichen Narrenbilder und die Einheit des Werkes", *ARG* 78 (1987): 24-36; Léon E. Halkin, *Erasmus von Rotterdam. Eine Biographie* (Zurich, 1989), 91-108, 325-34; Cornelis Augustijn, *Erasmus von Rotterdam. Leben-Werk-Wirkung* (Munich, 1986), 54-65.

[21] "An non audis cotidie ab iratis laicis atrocis convicii loco nobis in os iaci clerici, sacerdotis et monachi vocabula, idque prorsus non alio animo ac voce, quam si incestum aut sacrilegium exprobrarent?", Erasmus von Rotterdam, *Enchiridion*, 284. Quoted from Werner Welzig, ed., *Erasmus von Rotterdam: Ausgewählte Schriften*, vol. 1 (Darmstadt, 1968), 55-375; cited as *Enchiridion*.

[22] "Intus acceptum est vulnus, intus pharmacum admoveatur necesse est." *Enchiridion*, 236.

[23] " ... nonne videmus arctissimum quodque monachorum genus fastigium religionis aut in caerimoniis aut in certa lege psalmorum aut in corpore labore ponere?" *Enchiridion*, 220.

[24] *Laus Stultitiae*, 164-66.

[25] *Laus Stultitiae*, 172.

[26] *Laus Stultitiae*, 168-70.

[27] *Laus Stultitiae*, 146.

[28] *Laus Stultitiae*, 98.

[29] Heinz Holeczek, *Erasmus Deutsch*, vol. 1, *Die volkssprachliche Rezeption des Erasmus von Rotterdam in der reformatorischen Öffentlichkeit 1519-1536* (Stuttgart, 1983); id., "Die Haltung des Erasmus zu Luther nach dem Scheitern seiner Vermittlungspolitik 1520/21", *ARG* 64 (1973): 85-112. For the late Erasmus, Karl

reform by merging *bonae litterae* and spiritual thinking[30] and a purifying renovation[31] kept him from covering a fuller spectrum of anticlericalism.[32]

The more radical vein was represented by Ulrich von Hutten,[33] who continued the critical tradition of the gravamina by citing papal abuse of jurisdictional rights and interference in the German prebendary system, as well as the bishops' and priests' neglect of pastoral care.[34] The gravamina had devised an ecclesiastical organization which was congruent with vested social interest. Thus anticlericalism gained specific application in attacks on the prebendary system,[35] or the appeal to restore ecclesiastical possessions to the aristocracy.[36]

II.4

Anticlericalism was not a purely reformation phenomenon, nor did it terminate with the Reformation, as can be seen with reference to the continuing accusations levied against Lutheran clergymen throughout the early modern period.[37] Anticlericalism appears as an element of the

---

Heinz Oelrich, *Der späte Erasmus und die Reformation*, RGST 86 (Münster i.W., 1961), 63-7.

[30] Cornelis Augustijn, "Erasmus, Desiderius", in *Theologische Realenzyklopädie* 10 (Berlin, 1982), 1-18.

[31] Heinz Holeczek, "Erasmische Reform und Reformation", in *Erasmus von Rotterdam. Vorkämpfer für Frieden und Toleranz*, Ausstellung zum 450. Todestag ... veranstaltet vom Historischen Museum Basel (Basel, 1986), 58-62, 58.

[32] Georg Gebhardt, *Die Stellung des Erasmus von Rotterdam zur Römischen Kirche* (Marburg, 1966), 332-59.

[33] Ulrich von Hutten, *Clag vnd vor= // manung gegen dem über // maessigen vnchristlichen gewalt des // Bapstes zuo Rom / vnd der vngeist= // lichen geistlichen. Durch herrn Vl // richen von Hutten / Poeten / vnd Orator der gantzen // Christenheit / vnd zuouoran dem Vatterland Teüt= // scher Nation zuo nutz vnd guot / Von wegen ge= // meiner beschwernüsz / vnd auch seiner eig= // nen notdurfft / In reimens weie be // schriben. Iacta est alea. Ich // habs gewagt. //* [Straßburg: Knoblouch, 1520], Köhler, Fiche 115/307.

[34] Heinz Scheible, "Die Gravamina, Luther und der Wormser Reichstag 1521", *Blätter für pfälzische Kirchengeschichte* 39 (1972): 167-83; Hans-Christoph Rublack, "Gravamina und Reformation", in I. Batori, ed., *Städtische Gesellschaft und Reformation*, Spätmittelalter und Frühe Neuzeit 12, Kleine Schriften 2 (Stuttgart, 1980), 292-313.

[35] *Von dem pfründ // marckt der Curtisanen // vnd Tempelkne // chten* (Basel: Adam Petri, o.J.), Laube 1: 90-100.

[36] *Der güt frum Lu= // therisch Pfaffen narr haysz ich // Der mich kaufft der lesze mich. //* [Augsburg: Erhard Oeglin, 1521], Köhler, *Bibliographie*, Nr. 1456: Köhler, Fiche 49/138.

[37] Robert W. Scribner, "Anticlericalism and the Reformation in Germany", in *Popular Culture and Popular Movements*, 243-56. So it did in the Roman Catholic

Reformation, which related it to its medieval past, provided a certain impetus, but cannot be seen as the primary agent in effecting the Reformation.

III.1

The elements of criticism outlined above were not only incorporated into reformation pamphlets but formed the basis of purely anticlerical tracts, such as the dialogue of a *Schultheiss and the Pfarrer of Gaisdorf*,[38] or the anonymous *Evangelium Pascuilli*.[39]

It is possible to construe nine different types of criticism directed against the clergy in reformation pamphlets.[40] These types are not mutually exclusive but are rather interrelated and can be co-related. There is at least a three-dimensional interpretation possible, i.e., socio-religious, scriptural and apocalyptic-demonic. In the texts these dimensions are found as overlapping themes.

The first type emerges when pamphlet authors distinguish the varying types of clergy, beginning at the bottom of the social scale. The image which is depicted is that of the priest, who is relient on a mass prebend for his living,[41] as a "poor ass",[42] whom Hutten described as follows: "Dy

---

Church, as indicated by an incident, reported by Barbara Goy, *Aufklärung und Volksfrömmigkeit in den Bistümern Würzburg und Bamberg*, Diss. phil. (Würzburg, 1968), 70, when in the Bamberg diocese in 1770 the number of holy days was reduced. There was a tumult in Auerbach when the decree was read: "die ganze Kirche bewegte sich, Weibs-persohnen und männer stunden auf in voller Furie, Sie murreten überlaut: eine Kugel vor den Kopf solte mann dem pfaffen schiesen, weiset ihn von der Canzel, jetzt werden die Sieben Sacramenten auch gar aufgehoben, und in diesen Wuth liefen sie aus der Kirch....". [In the inns one said] "Der Bischof zu bamberg hat uns einen ... [!] zu befehlen, der Pabst ist ein Kezer, ja ein Erz-Ketzer ist er, der Teufel hat es ihm eingegeben, kein guter geist, wir werden Lutherisch, und was braucht es viel, kein mensch ist schuld daran, als unsere verdammte bamberger Pfaffen, diese mögen nicht mehr predigen, noch beicht sitzen, ..."

[38] *Ain schoener dialogus vnd // straffred von dem Schulthaysz von gaysz // dorff / mit seinem schuoler / wider den Pfarrer da selbst vnd seinen // helffer in beyweszen der fierer vnd etlich nachbauren des // dorffs / antreffendt allen mangel vnnd geytz // gaystlich vnd weltlichs Stands etc. //* (o.O, o.Dr., o.J.,), Köhler, Fiche 264/744.

[39] *Ain Euange= // lium Pascuilli / Darinnen das // Roemisch / ja Phylargirisch / Geytzig // leben gegründet vnnd bestet- // tiget würdt. Getruckt vnd auszgangen zuo Rom / // durch den Phylauton. //* (o.O., o.Dr., o.J.), Köhler, Fiche 966/2422.

[40] These types are not ideal types, they have been selected from the texts (n. 2 above) and constituted according to frequency, the broadness of interpretation they offer, and centrality of their criticism.

[41] *Klag // vnd ant= // wort von // Lutherischen // vnd Bebstischenn // pfaffen vber die Refor // macion so neulich zu Reg= // enspurg der priester halben // auszgangen ist im Jar. MDxxiiij //* (Nuremberg, o.Dr., o.J.), Köhler, Fiche 342/964, Aijr: "Dann

armen pfaffen arbeit han. / dy reichen sicht man muessig gon."[43] He sees himself endangered by the reformation's rejection of endowed masses.[44] The scriptural epithet which is applied here is that of the "mute dog",[45] since the simple cleric is unable to respond to the challenges posed by the Reformation.[46] This apparent sympathy is counterbalanced by Caspar Güttel, who sees the simple clergy as distorting religious truth, as serving the creature, not the creator, and focussing their attention on securing their own comfort through exploitation of their congregation.[47]

Linked to this first type is the second, which portrays the priest as "Tempelknecht".[48] His role in the church is more diversified since he is

---

wir seind arm priester / wir haben der Bibel nit gewont / vnd haben mit dem beten zuoschaffen."

[42] *Klag // vnd ant= // wort* (n. 41 above), A ijr.

[43] Ulrich von Hutten (n. 33 above), dijr.

[44] *Der Curtisan und Pfründenfresser*, Schade 1: 7-12, 10: "Eim armen pfaffen der nit kan / ... / Der fro ist dasz er möge han / Ein bleibens, darzuo sich erneren / Des hungers oder betels erweren."

[45] Matthias Wurm, *Balaams // Eselin. // Von dem bann: das er // vmb geltschuld / vnd andre geringe sa= // chen nit mag Christlich gefelt werden. // Vnd das aller geystlicher standt / // schuldig ist / der weltlichen ober // keit zuo gehorsamen / ob sie // Christen woellen sin / durch // Mathis Wurm // von Geydert // heim. //* (o.O., o.Dr., 1522), Köhler, Fiche 1497/3940, K ijr; Johannes Hus, *Das die Secten vnd // Menschenleren in der // Christenheyt sollen auszgetilget // werden. // Joannis Husz. // Verdeütscht durch Wen- // tzelsaum Linck. Ecclesiasten // zuo Aldenburgk. // Anno:M.D.XXV //* (Altenburg: Gabriel Kantz, 1525), Köhler, Fiche 446/1193, Biijr; Caspar Güttel, *Dialogus oder ge= // sprechbuechleyn wie Christlich // vnd Euan-gelisch zuo leben / Nach dem vnd // lustig / Also auch in hayliger schrifft gegrundt fast // nutzlich. // Vill ruemen sich Ewangelisch // Der leben doch gantz ist Teüffelisch // Wilt guot Euangelisch leben // Disz buechleyn mag dirsz klar geben. // Allen vnd yetlichen Christglaubigen // menschen / die da gern guot Euangelisch sein woel // len wünschet vnnd begert Caspar Guethel / // jm Augustiner Kloster vber Eysz= // leben gelegenn. // Gnad etc. // 1522. //* ([Augsburg: Philipp Ulhart d.Ä.], 1522), Köhler, *Bibliographie*, Nr. 1439: Köhler, Fiche 265/747, F iijr, referring to Isaiah 56: 10; *Eynn Dialogus ader ge // sprech zwischen einem // Vatter vnnd Sun dye // Lere Martini Luthers vnd sunst an // dere sachen des Cristlichen glaub // ens belangende. //* (Erfurt: Michael Buchfürer, [1523]), Köhler, *Bibliographie*, Nr. 701: Köhler, Fiche 266/748, Ai v; Hans Staigmayer, *Ain Schoner Dialogus oder // Gesprech / von aynem Münch vnd // Becken / woelcher die Oster // ayer Samlen // wollt. Hanns Staygmayer / Beck zuo Reytlingen. //* (o.O., o.Dr., o.J., [1524]), Köhler, Fiche 4/17, Bir.

[46] *Dialogus von Zweyen pfaffen // koechin / Belangendt den abbruoch des opffers / vnnd // nyderlegung der vorgengknis. // Im Jar M.DXXiij. //* (o.O., o.Dr., 1523), Köhler, Fiche 567/1451.

[47] Güttel, *Dialogus oder gesprechbuechleyn ...* (n. 45 above), F iijr.

[48] *Von dem pfründ // marckt* (n. 35 above); Johann Sonnentaler, *Ursache, warum der vermeintlich geistliche Haufen das Evangelium nicht annimmt* ([Strassburg: Johann Prüss d.J.], 1524), Laube 1: 397-421, 397. Johannes Oecolampadius described

involved not merely in reading the mass[49] but is also active in the collection, purchase and sale of mass prebends. The pamphleteer considers him from a social perspective a mass dealer or trader (*Messkrämer*),[50] and from a scriptural viewpoint, a hypocrit (*Gleisner*),[51] whose pretence at piety[52]

---

this "Tempelpfaffen" in *WAs Misz= // breuch im wych= // bischofflichem // ampt. //* (Basel: Thomas Wolff, 1527), Köhler, Fiche 1166/2944, Ci v.

[49] *Ain new Ge= // dicht wie die gaystlich // ait zuo Erffordt in Dhüringen // gesturmbt ist worden // kurtzweylig // zuo lesen // Anno.M D XXI. //* (o.O., o.Dr., 1521), Köhler, Fiche 221/616: "Und kan nit mer dann zelen geldt / jm kor heülen wie die eszel im veldt / Sein horas schnattern wie ain gansz / die wort versteen als kyttelhansz / Wo man vom Euangeli sagt / so hat man in gar bald veriagt." See also Sonnentaler (n. 48 above), 401.

[50] Georg Fener, *Sturm wider ain laymen thurn // ains Roemischen predigers / der ausz der hayligen // Mesz gern ain opffer mächte. // Durch Georgium Fener von weyl. // Bel / Beelphegor / Moloch / Baal. // Die standen noch im alten stal. // Der starck irsal ist schon vor hand. // Woelff goend herein in schaffs gewand. //* [Augsburg: Sigmund Grimm and Marx Wirsung, 1521], Köhler, *Bibliographie*, Nr. 1133: Köhler, Fiche 1/6, Ai v.

[51] Erasmus von Rotterdam, *Herr Erasmus von Ro= // terdam verteutschte auszlegung über // disen spruch Christi vnsers Herrnn // Matthei am dreyundzweintzigsten // Capittel / vonn den Phariseyernn / // Sie thun alle jre werck / // das sie von den menschen // gesehen werden / Vnd breyten // jr gebottzedeln ausz. // Vom heyltumb etc. //* ([Mainz: Johann Schöffer], 1521), Köhler, *Bibliographie*, Nr. 1043: Köhler, Fiche 558/1421, Aijr; Ulrich von Hutten (n. 33 above), Aij v; *Ernstliche ermanung des Fridens // vnd Christenlicher einigkeit des durch= // lüchtigen Fürsten vnnd genädigen // herren / Hugonis von Landenberg // Bischoff tzu Costantz mitt // Schoener vszlegung vnnd // erklaerung / vast trost= // lich vnd nutzlich // zuo laeszen / nüw= // lich vszgan= // gen. //* [Augsburg: Uhlhart, 1523], München StBibl. 4° Polem. 1093a, Aivr.; [Martin Bucer], *Gesprechbiechlin neüw // Karsthans. // Zuo dem Leser. // Ein neüwer Karsthans komm ich her // Vol guotter manung / rechter ler. // Mit Edlen bin ich worden eins // Als was ich weisz / do schweyg ich keins // Vnd würd mit henden greyffen zuo // Ein ander auch sein bestes thuo. //,* Ernst Lehmann, ed., *Gesprechbiechlin neüw Karsthans*, Neudrucke deutscher Literaturwerke des XVI. und XVII. Jahrhunderts 282-284 (Halle, 1930), 53; referring to monks, as in *KLagred eins jungen Münchs // über sein Kutten. //* (o.O., o.Dr., o.J.), Köhler, Fiche 1315/3421, Aijr.; placed in an apocalyptic perspective by Balthasar Wilhelm, *Practica Deütsch ausz der // Goetlichen heyligen geschrifft / darinn zuo // vernemen die grausamen Coniunction der fin // sternüsz / wie lange zeyt her / durch die // Gotlosen widerchristen / wider das // Heylig Wort Gottes eyn= // gefuert. //* (o.O., o.Dr., o.J.), Köhler, Fiche 1435/3811, Aivr; *Die Deudsche // Vigilig / der gotlosen // Papisten / Münch // vnd Pfaffen etc. // Vigilig Buch bin ich genant / // In viel landen gar wol bekand // Gehe nicht fuer vber kauff mich / // Der geistlichen betrug leer ich. //* [Zwickau: Wolfgang Meyerpeck, ca. 1535], Köhler, *Bibliographie*, Nr. 687: Köhler, Fiche 1506/3961, Aijr; Eberhard Weidensee and Johannes Fritzhans, *Wie Doctor Cubito Bo= // nifacius / vnd der sontags prediger // yhm thum zu Magdeburg / / Gottes wort schenden // vnd lestern. // Dyalogus. // Anno 1 5 2 6. Jar //* (o.O., o.Dr., 1526), Köhler, Fiche 831/2081, Biv v; *Klag // vnd ant= // wort von // Lutherischen*

cannot conceal his concern to secure and expand his living. This social element may be linked to medieval eschatological notions of the Antichrist.

Clerical ignorance of scripture,[53] one of the central criticism of reformation pamphlets, gained particularly poignancy when applied to a third type. The priest's ability to convey the gospel message found comparison in the metaphor of the blind leading the blind.[54] This biblical analogy implied less a sense of helplessness on behalf of the priest but rather his unwillingness to comprehend the true gospel, which gained him the title of false preacher (*Lugenprediger*).[55] The social dimension of this type was enriched with terms such as the fantastic masked preacher,[56] and the

---

// *vnd Bebstischenn* // *pfaffen* (n. 41 above), Di v; Wenzeslaus Linck, *Ob die Geyst=* // *lichen Auch schuldig* // *sein Zinsze* / *geschosz etc. zuogeben vnd* // *andere gemeyne bürde mit* // *zuotragen.* // *Eyn Sermon* // *Auffs Euangelion Mat. 22. Ob* // *sich getzymme dem Keyser* // *Zinsz geben etc.* // *Wentzeslaus Linck.* // (o.O., o.Dr., o.J.: [At the End: Altenburg: Gabriel Kantz]), Köhler, Fiche 132/355, Aiij v.

[52] *Ein bannbrieff des* // *Bapsts* / *vnd gantzen Endt=* // *christischen reichs.* // *Darbey ein gnaden* // *brieff des goettlichen vnd him=* // *melschen ablasz* / *allen Christ=* // *glaeubigen troestlich.* // *Wee eüch schrifftgelerten* / *denn* // *ir habt den schlüssel der erkant=* // *nüsz entpfangen* / *ir seyt nit hyn=* // *ein kumen* / *vnd habt gewoert* // *denen die hynein wolten.* // *Luce. xj.* // [Straßburg: Johannes Schwan, 1524], Köhler, *Bibliographie*, Nr. 219: Köhler, Fiche 1251/3189, Aiij v.

[53] E.g. *Beclagung aines ley=* // *ens genant Hanns schwalb*, Laube 1: 63-70, 67; Georg Fener, *Sturm* (n. 50 above), Aijr, the clergy is "inn iren koepffen zerrüt / kennen die warhait nit / vermainen vnser glawb sey ain geltgewin vnd kauffmanschatz"; Ulrich von Hutten, *Clag vnd vor=* // *manung* (n. 33 above), Bir; Hans Staigmayer, *Ain Schoner Dialogus* (n. 45 above), Aijr: "jr wend nun der geschrifft maister seyn / vnnd wisset doch nichts vmb kain geschrifft".

[54] Hans Staigmayer, *Ain Schoner Dialogus* (n. 45 above), Aiv v; *Der recht weg* // *Zuom Ewigen leben* // *Vil nutzer halysamer leer vnd* // *sprüch vnsers herrnn Jesu Cristi* // *ausz den vier Ewangelien vnd* // *Episteln des hailigen Sannt* // *Pauli* / *kurtzlich begriffen vnd* // *auszgezogen zuo vnderweysung* // *dem gemaynen layen dann da* // *werdent angezaygt gar nach.* // *alle gebot vnd leer Jhesu* // *Christi die allen Chri* // *sten menschen not sind zuo wis=* // *sen.* // [Augsburg: Heinrich Steiner, 1524], München StBibl 8° Asc 4656 d/1, Bijr, also in Emil Weller, *Repertorium typographicum* (Nördlingen, 1864), 3212; Wolfgang Zierer, *Ein Christenlich Ge=* // *sprech* / *von ainem Waldbruoder* / *vnd ainem waysen der* // *von seinen vorgengern verlassen ist* / *die in solten le* // *ren vnd speisen* / *mit dem goettlichen wort des dann* // *ist ain speisz der seel* / *gemacht durch Wolff-* // *gang zierer* / *ain frommer Lantzknecht wie* // *ers von in gehert hat* / *also hat ers* // *auff geschriben.* // (o.O., o.Dr., o.J. [At the End: 1522]), Köhler, Fiche 7/31; Aiijr.

[55] *Ain schoener dialo* // *gus von zwayen gutten ge* // *sellen genant Hanns Tholl. vnnd Claus* // *Lamp. sagendt vom Antechrist* // *vnd seynen jungern.* // *Sytzende peym weyn* // *guots muots vnuer=* // *holen ausz der* // *Epistel* // *Pauli* // (o.O., o.Dr., o.J.), Köhler, Fiche 264/746, Aiijr.

[56] Cunrad Distelmair, *Ain trewe erma* // *nung* / *das ain yeder Christ selbs zuo seiner seel* // *hail sehe* / *vnd das schwert (das ist die hai* // *lig geschrifft) auch selbs*

babbling preacher of dreams,[57] whose sermons contained only that which was pleasing to the ear.[58]

The image of the devil's fattened pig (*Teufels Mastschwein*),[59] was another type which evoked rich social connotations. The traditional notion of *plenus venter*[60] was transposed into the Pauline dictum: their belly is their God,[61] hence the term "Bauchprediger".[62] This type is based on the medieval tradition, which figuratively applied the base, sensual nature of the animal to the members of the clergy. Thus we find sexual analogy of the clergy in the terms "mating horse" (*brünstiges Pferd*)[63] or "lewd bull" (*geiler Stier*).[64] Similarly their avarice and greed earned them the title of

---

zuo seinen // handen neme / sich der feind // damit were / auff das er // nit mit falscher leer // überwunden vnd // verfueret // werde // Durch ainn layen Cunrad Distelmair // von Arberg gethon. // 1523. // ([Augsburg: Heinrich Steiner], 1523), Köhler, *Bibliographie*, Nr. 755: Köhler, Fiche 223/625, Bij v.

[57] Johann Locher (Pseudonym?), *Ernstlicher ver= // standt guter vnd falscher // Prediger / mit erklerung des // Pfaffenschoeffel / Zehen= // den vnd opffers mit // ettlichen artickeln // zuo warnung // dem Leser. // Anno. M.D.xxiiii. // Karsthans // Die Papisten thuont hoch pochen // Von Christo wirt es als gerochen. //* (Zwickau: Jörg Gastel, 1524), Köhler, Fiche 583/1517, Bi v.

[58] Hans Staigmayer, *Ain Schoner Dialogus* (n. 45 above), Bir.

[59] [Jörg Modschidler], *Eyn newer Dialo= // gus oder gesprech / zwischen // einem verprenten / vertrib= // nem Edelman / vnd ey= // nem Münch / welchen // am vnrechstenn ge= // schech / wann die // selben bey= // de ver= // triben / vnd // dy Münch cloester // auch verbrant wurden. // M.D.XXv. //* (o.O., o.Dr., 1525), Köhler, Fiche 1196/3009, Bi v; The image is a fattened sow (*Mastsäue*) in *Figur des Antichristlichen // Bapsts vnd seiner Synagog //* (o.O., o.Dr., o.J.), Köhler, Fiche 1048/2649.

[60] Johann Sonnentaler, *Ursache* (n. 48 above), 399.

[61] Nicolaus Cattelspurger, *Ain Missive (oder Sendtbrieff) // Nicolai Cattelspurger / darinn klarlich // durch hailig geschrift angezaygt wirt // von den falschen leeren / auch Abgoet // terey / byszher gehalten / wie sy // auffgericht / vnd verstanden // werden sollen / seiner Schwe // ster zuo Bamberg wo= // nend / vmb rechtes // glaubens verstand // geschriben. // 1.5.2.4. //* ([Augsburg: Philip Ulhart d.Ä.], 1524), München StBibl. 4° Polem 584, Aij v; *Ain schöner Dialogus // wie ain Baur mit aim Frauenbruoder Münich // redt dasz er die Kutten von im wirfft. // Lustbarlich und lieblich zuo lesen. // 1525. //*, Schade 2: 155-59, 157.

[62] *Disz biechlin sagt von // den falschen Kamisierern die sich ausz // thuond vil guots mit fasten / peten / me= // sze lesen für andere / auff dz in der // sack / tasch vol werd / achten // nit wo die seelen hinfa= // renn. // Ir bauch ir got // spricht Paulus. // Anno. etc. M.D.XXiij. //* (o.O., o.Dr., 1523), Augsburg StBibl. 4° ThH 469, Aivr.

[63] Johann Sonnentaler, *Vrsach* (n. 48 above), Biijr.

[64] *Ain schoener dialogus ... von dem Schulthaysz von gaysz // dorff* (n. 38 above), Aij v.

gluttonous folk (*Fressvolk*).[65] When applied to the clerical estate these analogies inferred a particularly discreditable perversion of the holy order: "was gut ist das mach ich boesz / vnd was boesz ist mach ich gut / vnd ich kan es wenden wie ich wil", ran the satirical version in a pamphlet.[66] The same is true of the most common type, termed "avaricious buck",[67] and its associated social metaphors.[68] Greater weight is placed on the

---

[65] Johann Bader, Georg Mussbach, *ARtickel vnd clagstuck* / // *wider Johan Bader pfarher zu Landaw von geyst* // *lichen Fiscal zu Speyer* / *des Euangelij halben* / *in=* // *brocht vff dornstag nach Letare. M.D.XXiiii.* // *Antwort Johan Baders* // *vff gemelte artickel.* // *Banbrieff so vber genan=* // *ten Johan Bader auszgangen vnd zu Speyer an* // *die grosz küerchthür anngeschlagen vff Sonntag* // *Cantate. M.D.XXiiii. Mit anzeygung der* // *falseten* / *So darin begriffen sein.* // *Appellation Johan Ba=* // *ders vonn vermeyntem vnnchristlichen Bann vff* // *Mitwoch noch Cantate. M.D.XXiiii.* // [Speyer: Johann Eckhart, 1524], Köhler, *Bibliographie*, Nr. 213: Köhler, Fiche 1115/2848, Aivr: "farlosigen vnd das freszfolck (die nicht dan des bauch achten)."

[66] A satirical version in *Ein Predig vom* // *Wolff zu den Gen* // *sen kuortzweylig zu lesen.* // *M.D.XXiiij.* // (o.O., o.Dr., 1524), Köhler, Fiche 1078/2729, Aij v. A "practica"-version, *Practica* // *Auszgezogen von Sybilla* / *Brigitta* / *Ci* // *rilli* / *Joachim* / *Methodij* / *vnnd Bruoder Reinharts* / // *Wirt weerenn noch ettliche Jar* / *Vnd sagt von wunnder=* // *lichen dingen* / *Vormals gertuckt im 18. Jar etc.* // (o.O., o.Dr., 1521), Köhler, Fiche 1248/3175, Biij v: "Alle stendt der welt haben sich verkert. / Darumb wirt mit plagen sie grosz gemert. ... ". A descriptive version in Heinrich Summenhart, *Ain hüpsche frag von ainem iüngling* // *an ainen altten Carthüser* / *wie die Epistel ad Titum* // *zu versteen sey* / *vnnd wie der Carteüser in vn* // *derweyszt* / *vnd im darleget* / *wie yetz vnnsere* // *chefflin von den hürten so übel versorgt* // *seind* / *darbey ist ain Lantzknecht ge-* // *standen* / *hat solchs auffgeschriben* // *mit namen hainrich Summer* // *hart von Colmar. Im* // *Jar. M D* // *XXIIII.* //, ed. Helga Robinson-Hammerstein, *Heinrich Summenhart: Ain Hüpsche Frag. A Polite Inquiry* (Dublin, 1980), Aij vff. *Ich kan nit vil Neues denken* // *Ich musz der Katzen dschellen anhenken* //, Schade 1: 13-18, 14: "die welt ist also ganz verkert."

[67] Caspar Güttel, *Dialogus oder ge=* // *sprechbuechleyn* (n. 45 above), C1r. Those pretending to be priests, are the most lacking a spiritual quality, they are "ungeistlichste, stinkende Böcke": "ye groesser jr samlung / ye reicher die stifftung / ye mer gotlosz volcks"; Thomas Stör, *Von dem christlichen Weingarten*, [Bamberg: Georg Erlinger, 1524], Laube 1: 357-96, 364, 369.

[68] Simon Reuter, *Anntwort Symonis* // *Reuthers von Schleytz* / // *wider die Baals pfaffen vnd pre=* // *diger welche* / *die fest Marie vnnd* // *aller heyligen* / *auch das gebet vnd* // *guotte wergk für die lieben seelen so* // *fleysiglich vnd ernstlich hantha=* // *ben verteydigen* / *vff den spruch* // *Jo. xij. (so sich Judas vmb* // *die vergossene salbe von* // *wegen der armeleüt be=* // *kümmert) lauter vnd* // *kurtz gegründt vnd* // *der loeblichen ober=* // *keit teütscher* // *Nation zuo* // *handenn* // *gestellet.* // (o.O., o.Dr., o.J.), Köhler, Fiche 225/633, Aiijr: "O dw geytziger hundt / Odw geltsuchtiger Judas / O dw falsch hertz / Dw gybst mir radt auff deinenn nutz gestellet." For the similar metaphor, "cook of avarice", see Erasmus Amann, *All welt die fragt nach neüer mer* // *So kumpt ain baur von Wurms her* // *Der ist sein tag gewandert weytter* // *Sagt newe mer auch disem reytter* // *Zuo lob vnd eer dem newen küng* // *So lesent*

biblical reference to Judas as the priests' advocate,[69] with one pamphlet even pointing out that the sum for which Judas betrayed Christ was minimal in comparison to the sums the clergy had invested in their greedy accumulation of positions.[70] Gengenbach contrasted the biblical fisher of men to this "fisher of pennies" *(Pfennigfischer)*,[71] that capitalist parasite,[72] who infringed upon other people's means of living. Avarice and usury both had particulary negative overtones in this period and are treated extensively in anticlerical pamphlets of the reformation period.[73]

Also recurrent are the images of the ravaging wolf,[74] robber[75] and

---

disen spruch gering // (Augsburg: [Melchior Ramminger], 1521), Köhler, *Bibliographie*, Nr. 113: Köhler, Fiche 1310/3396, Aij v.

[69] Simon Reuter, *Anntwort Symonis // Reuthers* (n. 68 above), Aijr: "der pfaffen aduocat oder wortreder"; *Ain straffred vnd ain vnderricht // Wie es des bapsts junger auff geytz hond zuo gericht // Darwider ist auff erstanden ain baur vnd ain reitter // Leeszt fürbas so wert jr hoeren weyter //* (o.O., o.Dr., o.J.), Köhler, Fiche 624/1618, o.p.; Johannes Oecolampadius, *WAs Misz= // breuch* (n. 48 above), Cvi v; *Die Deudsche // Vigilig* (n. 51 above), Aiijr.

[70] *Ain schöner Dialogus. // (Cuntz und Fritz)*, Schade 2: 119-27, 125; Eckhart zum Drübel, *Ein demütige ermanung an // Ein gantze gemeine Christen // heit. Von Eckhart zuom // Drübel. etc. // Da. Gloriam deo. // Mann soll. In der. Kirchen // nitt mitt. Gelt vmb gon. //* (Straßburg: Martin Flach, [1523]), Köhler, *Bibliographie*, Nr. 769: Köhler, Fiche 1946/4960, o.p.

[71] Pamphilus Gengenbach, *Ein kurtzer begriff wie // der Schultheisz vnd die gemein desz dorffs Frid // husen vff dem gnoden baerg / gemeinlich erkant // vnd erwelt haben ein schoeffel irs dorffs mit na= // men Hans Knüchel / dz der selbig an stat ires // Pfarrers sol verkünden vnd predigen die Ewan= // gelische leer vnd den waeg der saeligkeit / bisz zuo der // zuo kunfft irers Pfarrers. //* [Basel: Pamphilus Gengenbach, 1523], Köhler, *Bibliographie*, Nr. 1275: Köhler, Fiche 1548/4015, Bir.

[72] Eckhart zum Drübel, *Ein demütige ermanung* (n. 70 above) is devoted to such a critique; Jacob Strauss, *Hauptstücke und Artikel christlicher Lehre wider den unchristlichen Wucher*, Laube 2: 1073-77, 1073: "Der wuecher ist ein starker grundt des unersettlichen geitz der pfaffen und munichen", contrary to the gospel (ibid. 1074); usurers will not possess the kingdom of God (ibid., 1075). Strauss relates a lay usurer to Antichrist (ibid., 1074); *Hie kompt ein Beüerlein zu // einem reichen Burger von der güldt / den wucher // betreffen / so kumpt ein Pfaff auch darzu // vnd dar nach ein münch / gar kurtz= // weylich zu lesen. //* (o.O., o.Dr., o.J.), Schade 2: 73 and Köhler, Fiche 165/448.

[73] Matthias Wurm, *Balaams // Eselin* (n. 45 above), Bij v.

[74] Martin Bucer, *Gesprechbiechlin neüw // Karsthans* (n. 51 above), 7; *Ein Predig vom // Wolff zu den Gen // sen* (n. 66 above), Aivr; *Ayn freundlich gesprech / zwyschen ainem // Barfuosser Münch / ausz der Prouyntz Oster= // reych / der Obseruantz / vnd ainen Loeffel // macher / mit namen Hans Stoesser // gar lustig zuo leesen / vnnd ist // der recht grundt. //* [Augsburg: Heinrich Steiner, 1524], Köhler, *Bibliographie*, Nr. 1199: Köhler, Fiche 626/1625, Aiij v; Caspar Güttel, *Dialogus oder ge= // sprechbuechleyn* (n. 45 above), Fiij v; Wolfgang Zierer, *Ein Christenlich Ge= // sprech / von ainem Waldbruoder* (n. 54 above), Aiijr, uses "zuckende Wölfe",

thief.[76] While in social terms the emphasis is on the clerical exploitation of the laymen,[77] in biblical terms the reference is to the wolf in sheep's clothing. The latter can be developed into an image of murderer of souls (*Seelmörder*)[78] or demonized further as a thief escaped from hell.[79]

---

also referring to Matthew 7: 15.

[75] Ulrich von Hutten, *Clag vnd vor= // manung* (n. 33 above), Bir; *Von dem pfründ // marckt der Curtisanen* (n. 35 above), 92; *Ein Spruch // von dem bösen Misbrauch // in der heiligen Christenheit entstanden //*, Schade 1: 27-37, 28: "Das macht alein des pfennings lieb, / Hat ausz uns gmacht rauber und dieb. Der geiz und unser eigner nutz / Macht manigen seltsam fasnachtbutz."

[76] [Jörg Modschidler], *Eyn newer Dialo= // gus* (n. 59 above), Bi v: "jr dieb / wo habt jr den gemaynen man betrogen."

[77] *15.Dyalogus.24. // Andaechtigs volck kumpt sehet mich an // Ob ich nicht sey ain haylig man // Mit namen bruoder Goetzer genant // Der schier zuo Pern ward verbrandt // An marterer schar billich wurd gesetzt // Vmb mein fünff wundeu* [!] *die mir seind geetzt // Von den München Prediger orden // Wie dann von uns gedruckt ist worden // Darumb kumpt her vnd rüefft mich an // Dann ich wol Hosen flicken kan. //* ([Augsburg: Heinrich Steiner], 1524), Köhler, *Bibliographie*, Nr. 696: Köhler, Fiche 9/35, Aiij v; [Jörg Modschidler], *Eyn newer Dialo= // gus* (n. 59 above), Biijv, in which the speakers form a gang with a courtisan.

[78] Cunrad Distelmair, *Ain trewe erma // nun* (n. 56 above), Bir; Christoff Gerung, *Ain kurtze vnderweysung // wie man Got allain Beychten sol / vnd // dz die Orenbeycht nur in den yrrdischen // satzungen von des hayligen beycht pfen= // ings wegen wider die geschrift vnd gebot // gots auffgesetzt. Auch das die selb // Beycht vnd die oelung damit bey vnsern // zeytten die krancken gesalbt werdenn // kaine Sacrament seyen / Ausz der Epi= // stel Jacobi am Fünfften Capitel // allen Christen menschen zuo guot // Durch Christoffen Gerung // vonn Memmingen ge= // zogenn. Im jar. // M.D.XXiij. // quinto Sept= // tembris. //* ([Augsburg: Heinrich Steiner], 1523), Köhler, *Bibliographie*, Nr. 1327: Köhler, Fiche 293/850, Aiv v; *Geistlicher Bluothandel // Johannis Hussz / zuo Costentz // verbrannt Anno Domini // M.CCCC.xv. // am sechsten tag Julij. // Mit gegen vergleichung goettlicher schrifft / vnd Baepstlicher satzungen. // Dabey von dem krefftigen // syg Christi / // vnd des Endtchrists prachts / // abgang vnd zerstoerung. // Mit zeügnüssz seiner zeit art // gemaelde vnd figuren. //* [Straßburg: Johann Schott, 1525], Köhler, *Bibliographie*, Nr. 1242: Köhler, Fiche 1184/2971, Bi v; *Der recht weg // Zuom Ewigen leben // Vil nutzer halysamer leer vnd // sprüch vnsers herrnn Jesu Cristi // ausz den vier Ewangelien vnd // Episteln des hailigen Sannt // Pauli / kurtzlich begriffen vnd // auszgezogen zuo vnderweysung // dem gemaynen layen dann da // werdent angezaygt gar nach. // alle gebot vnd leer Jhesu // Christi die allen Chri // sten menschen not sind zuo wis= // sen. //* [Augsburg: Heinrich Steiner, 1524], München StBibl 8° Asc 4656 d/1, Avr, see Weller, *Repertorium Bibliographicum*, 3212; Thomas Stör, *Von dem christlichen Weingarten* (n. 67 above), 371.

[79] *Eyn Clag vnd bitt der deutschen // Nation an den almechtigen // gott vmb erloszung ausz // dem gefecknis des // Antichrist. //* [Wittenberg, 1520: handwritten], Köhler, Fiche 1315/3419, Aijr.

A more distinguished position is held by what Blarer called the ecclesiastical lord (*Kirchenjunker*),[80] who other pamphleteers portray astride a high horse.[81] Socially he can be termed a tyrant,[82] an extension of the concept of the "ruthless villain" (*Wüterich*).[83] In a demonic perspective he is then

---

[80] Ambrosius Blarer, *Ir gwalt ist veracht // ir kunst wirt verlacht // Irs liegens nit gacht // gschwecht ist jr bracht // Recht ists wiesz Gott // macht. // Ambrosius Blaurer. // M.D. xxiiij. //* ([Augsburg: Philipp Ulhart d.Ä.], 1524), Köhler, *Bibliographie*, Nr. 294: Köhler, Fiche 746/1909, Bir; *Eyn Dialogus / das ist eyn gesprech // zweyer personen / Christus zuo eynem / vnd // Christianus zum andern teyl / in wel= // chem von dem Edict / vnd Re= // formation / so zuo Regenspurg // durch die Herrschafft // allda versamlet / auszgegan= // gen vnd // gemacht / eyn // kurtzer vnderricht // begriffen kurtzweylig zuolesen. //* [Nürnberg: Hieronymus Höltzel, 1524], Köhler, *Bibliographie*, Nr. 691: Köhler, Fiche 268/754, Aiij v, attributes this title "Junker" to bishops.

[81] *Ein Spruch // von dem bösen Misbrauch* (n. 75 above), Bir; Pamphilus Gengenbach, *Ein kurtzer begriff* (n. 71 above), Aiv v; *Von der Finsternüsz die zu // Rhom geschehen ist Im. M.D. vnd 22. Jar. // Rhom sich für dich zuo disser frist // Disz Finnsternus dir zaigen ist // Ain straff von got dir ist vorhanndt // Hat dich drey tag darumb vorblanndt // Eyl baldt zum herren Jesu Christ // Der kompt dir zuo hülff in kurtzer frist // Disz Finnsternus ist anderst nit bedeütten // Dann Rhom hab Rew mit ander leütten // Folg leer / dir ist gesanndt von Got // Vnnd treib ausz Christo nitt meer spot. //* (o.O., o.Dr., o.J.), Köhler, Fiche 1435/3809.

[82] *Eyn Dialogus / das ist eyn gesprech // zweyer personen / Christus zuo eynem / vnd // Christianus* (n. 81 above), Aij v; *Eyn Clag vnd bitt der deutschen // Nation an den almechtigen // gott vmb erloszung ausz // dem gefencknuss des // Antichrist. //* (o.O., o.Dr., o.J.), Köhler, Fiche 534/1370, Aijr; Hans Copp, *Doctor Joannes Copp ... vrteyl* (n. 18 above), Aiv v; *Ein bannbrieff des // Bapsts* (n. 52 above), Köhler, *Bibliographie*, Nr. 219: Köhler, Fiche 1251/3189, Aivr; *Ain grosser Preisz so der Fürst der // hellen genant Lucifer yetzt den gaystlichen als // Baepst / Bischoff / Cardinel / vnnd der // gleychen zuo weyszt vnd empeüt. etc. //* [Straßburg: Johann Prüss d.J., 1521?], Köhler, *Bibliographie*, Nr. 1394: Köhler, Fiche 1818/4662, o.p.; *Dyses buchlein wirdt genent der // Leyen Spiegell. Darjnnen die frommen vn= // gelerten eynfeltigen christen menschen ersehen vnd lernen sol= // len / was jne nach den wortten Christi vnnsers lieben // herren / seiner heyligen apostell vnd Ewannge= // listen / zuo glauben vnd zuo thuon sey. Welches // mitt den Propheceyen ausz dem alten ge= // setzs gezogenn / bewert Ist. //* (o.O., o.Dr., 1522), Augsburg Stbibl 4° ThH 1598, Biijr,v; [Martin Bucer], *Gesprechbiechlin neüw // Karsthans* (n. 51 above), 24; *Ernstliche ermanung des Fridens ... Hugonis von Landenberg* (n. 51 above), Ci v.

[83] *Beclagung Teutscher Nation. / // Disz zeychen bedeut den text des Propheten Hieremie. // Disz zeychen bedeut die auszlegung des texts. [Weiser] //* [Erfurt: Matthes Maler, 1521?], Köhler, *Bibliographie*, Nr. 249: Köhler, Fiche 1106/2821, Aiijr, where the successor of St. Peter is also Nero's successor; *Das deutsche Requiem der verbrannten Bullen und päpstlichen Rechte* (Basel: Valentin Curio, 1520?), Laube 1: 58-60, 58; *15.Dyalogus.24.* (n. 77 above), Aiij v: "darmit die wueterey des thyrannischenn wuetrichs vnd Endtchrists" would be recognized, the poor oppressed people and Christ's sheep be liberated and confirmed, in order to heal weakness and pest (Bijr).

presented as a devilish lord (*teuflischer Herr*),[84] which of course implies a perverted usurpation of God's lordship, and a life style directly contrary to Christ's commandment.[85] The analogy of the "seducer" provides the biblical dimension of a feudal lord who belongs to the devil's inner circle.[86]

The most severe comparison is the type of the Pharisee[87] and the subsequent association with Pilate,[88] who ultimately ordered the crucifixion of Christ.[89]

---

[84] *Beclagung aines ley= // ens genant Hanns schwalb* (n. 53 above), 68, here referring to the pope.

[85] *Eyn Dialogus / das ist eyn gesprech // zweyer personen / Christus zuo eynem / vnd // Christianus* (n. 80 above), Aiv v.

[86] Balthasar Wilhelm, *Practica Deütsch* (n. 51 above), Aiijr, referring to apocalyptic passages Matthew 24:4, Luke 21:8, Mark 13:21f. and Isaiah 24.

[87] Erasmus von Rotterdam, *Herr Erasmus von Ro= // terdam verteutschte auszlegung über // disen spruch Christi vnsers Herrnn // Matthei am dreyundzwein- tzigsten // Capittel* (n. 51 above); *Das Wolfsgesang*, Schade 3: 1-35, 30; *Ain schöner Dialogus // wie ain Baur mit aim Frauenbruoder Münich* (n. 61 above), 157; *Die Deudsche // Vigilig* (n. 51 above), Avir; Mathis Wurm, *Christlicher bericht vnd // vermanung Mathis wur= // men von Geydertheim // Anden würdigen // vnd gelerten herr Ja= // cob kornkauff pfarherren zuo // Geydertheim auch an= // dre seins genossen. // Die kirch Christi / den // newen glauben (als sye // in nennen) vnd // langem ge= // brauch be= // treffen // etc. //* (o.O., o.Dr., 1524), Köhler, Fiche 797/2005, Aivr; Explicitly so in the pamphlet *In disem buchlein // wirt klerlich angezeigt / grundt // vnd vrsach / warumb der Geistliche stant // Nemlich die Bischoff vnd Priester zuo // Jheruschem / Christum vnd seyne glidmes // sen ausz hasz / als Ketzer vnd verfurer // des volcks / getodt vnd verfulget haben. // Zuo trost alle den ghenen / so von // wegen des Gotlichen wortes // von den boesen Geist / // lichen verfulgt // werden. // Nicolaus Symmen // dem newen Leyen zuo Wormsz // ym elendt / zuo geschriben // wurden. Anno.M.ccccc.xxiiij. //* (o.O., o.Dr., 1524), Köhler, Fiche 283/812; *Ain Christenliches lustigs gesprech / das // besser / Gotgefelliger / vnd des menschen sel haylsamer seye / // ausz den Kloestern zuokommen / vnd Eelich zuowerden / dan dar // innen zuobeleyben / vnd zuouerharren / Woellichs gesprech / nit // mit menschen thandt / oder derselbigen yrrigen gesatzen / // sonder allain inn der hayligen / goetlichen / Biblischen / // vnd Ewangelischen geschrifft gegründt / gemacht // vnnd darausz gezogen ist / Im jar 1524. auff // den vj tag Januarij. //* [Augsburg: Heinrich Steiner, 1524], Köhler, *Bibliographie*, Nr. 532: Köhler, Fiche 268/756, Aiijr; Hans Staigmayer, *Ain Schoner Dialogus* (n. 45 above), Aij v; Wolfgang Zierer, *Ein Christenlich Ge= // sprech / von ainem Waldbruoder* (n. 54 above), Aijr.

[88] Caspar Güttel, *Dialogus oder ge= // sprechbuechleyn* (n. 45 above), Fiijr: "Ir fragt von Euangelischen Prelaten / ich kenn vil Teüffelischer Pilaten."

[89] *Hab Gott lieb // vnnd diene // jm al= // lein //* (o.O., o.Dr., o.J.), Köhler, Fiche 612/1576; Wenzeslaus Linck, *Ob die Geyst= // lichen Auch schuldig // sein Zinsze / geschosz etc. zuogeben vnd // andere gemeyne bürde mit // zuotragen. // Eyn Sermon // Auffs Euangelion Mat. 22. Ob // sich getzymme dem Keyser // Zinsz geben etc. // Wenzeslaus Linck. //* (o.O., o.Dr., o.J.: [At the End: Altenburg: Gabriel Kantz]),

This type approximates also to the ninth type which is most frequently treated in the pamphlets, the concept of the false prophet.[90] Here we note a marked absence of social attributions and find instead a singularly rich range of apocalyptical terminology applied, i.e. Baal's prophets,[91] the apostles and disciples of the Antichrist.[92]

Köhler, Fiche 132/355, Aiijr. This is generalized to the Jew by Dieterich (a Franciscan), *Ain practica oder weyssa // gung eins bruoders / Barfuosser ordenns / mit namen Die= // terich / beschehen zuo Zeug in Granatenn / Nach der // geburt Christi ym 1420. Jar / woelche sich ver= // gleycht mitt den wunderbarn vnd froembden // geschichten / etlicher new verschynen // jar her / Vnd yetzs disen vnsern // Schwebendenn / zeyten.* // (o.O., o.Dr., o.J.), Köhler, Fiche 613/1579, Aiijr.

[90] E.g. [Bucer], *Dialogus das // ist ein gesprech oder rede / zwischen // zweien. Einem Pfarrer vnd ei // nen Schultheisz / antzeigende // geistliches vnnd weltli= // ches stands übel han // dlung / war zuo allein // geytzigkeit sie // zwinget.* // (Basel: Thomas Wolff, 1521), Köhler, Fiche 264/742. [Martin Bucer], *Eyn schoner Dialogus vnd ge= // sprech Zwischen eym Pfarrer vnd eym // Schultheysz / betreffend allen uebelstand der geyst= // lichen / vnd boeszhandlung der weltlichen.* // Alles mit geytzigkeyt beladen.* // [Nürnberg: Johann Stuchs, 1521], Köhler, *Bibliographie*, Nr. 391; Schade 2: 135ff.; Köhler, Fiche 138/377, Avir; *Ain schoner Dialogus von Martino // Luther vnd der geschickten pottschafft ausz der helle die falsche // gaystligkayt vnd das wortt gots belangen // gantz hubsch zu lesen.* // *Anno. 1523.* // (o.O., o.Dr., 1523), Köhler, Fiche 87/239, Aijr; *Ain Epistel.* // *meinen lieben bruedern inn // Christo Jhesu zuogeschriben / Die da // begeren das Euangelion / vnd // hoffnung haben in Christo jhe // su / Dieweil ich jnen nichtt // mag mit lebendiger // stimme offenbaren / // So wil ich ausz // bruederlycher // liebe in zuo // schrey // ben. Damit sy // nicht auffnemen die falschen wiessagen vmb dz // wir nit von jnen werden betrogen.* // *Im jar. MDXXiij.* // (o.O., o.Dr., 1523), Köhler, Fiche 211/622, Ai v, Aiij v, Aiv v; Hans Greiffenberger, *Disz biechlin zaigt an die Falschen // Propheten / vor den vnsz gewarnet hat Christus / Paulus // vnd Petrus / vnd findt darin / was vnd wie wir vns Chri // sten halten sollen / yetz in diser geferlichen // zeyt / auff das kuortzest begriffen / gemacht durch Hanns // Greyffenberger zuo // Pforzhaym.* // [Augsburg: Philipp Ulhart d.Ä. 1523?], Köhler, *Bibliographie*, Nr. 1360: Köhler, Fiche 255/715, Aij v.

[91] Heinrich Kettenbach, *Ein new Apologia vnnd ver= // antworttung Martini Lut= // thers wyder der Papisten // Mortgeschrey / die zehen // klage wyder in usz // blasieniren so // wyt die // Christenn= // heyt ist / dann // sy toben vnnd wut= // tendt recht wie die vnsin // nige hundt thondt.* // (o.O., o.Dr., 1523), Köhler, Fiche 13/54, Ai v: God has "aber einmal zuo dyser zyt vns geben etlich hochgeleert Christlich lerer / die vns das wort gots lawtter vnd reyn fürlegen / vnd die falschen propheten vnd dromprediger Baal / des bauchs mit dem swert des worts gots schlagen"; Simon Reuter, *Anntwort Symonis // Reuthers* (n. 68 above), Aiijr: "O dw Baals vnnd Babylonischer Pfaffe / des Teuffels vnnd Enchristenn thumherr"; Heinrich Vogtherr d.Ä., *Eine christliche Anrede* ([Augsburg: Heinrich Steiner], 1524), Laube 1: 480-90, 400f.

[92] Heinrich Kettenbach, *Ein new Apologia vnnd ver= // antworttung Martini Lut= // thers* (n. 91 above), Ai v; Heinrich Kettenbach, *Eyn gesprech Bruoder Hainrich von // Kettenbach mit aim frommen altemuot // terlin von Vlm von etlichen zuofellen*

From this survey we see that adaptation of the apocalyptic tradition was a prevalent motif in reformation pamphlets. The clergy as a whole are depicted as the servants of the Antichrist, as they are seen as adherents of the Pope.[93]

This apocalyptical tradition was, however, not simply transposed from a late medieval to a reformation context. A decided shift in emphasis and tone in the language employed in the reformation period is detectable. This is particularly notable in the broader range of metaphors and analogies which were employed. These had been developed and generated by the continued propagation of the coming of the Antichrist and now gained their fullest expression in reformation pamphlets.

Pamphlets such as those of Johannes Eckart,[94] who defended the church against early Lutheranism, could point at the undifferentiated critical generalisations about the clergy, despite the continuing tradition of clerical self-criticism. This is exemplified in a pamphlet outlining a dialogue between an Augustinian and a Dominican monk, which ended in the latter's conversion to the gospel. The Augustinian spelled the anticlerical catalogue out in terms of monastic garments: cowl — "Das man dich dester bas erkenn das du ain abgetretner vom glauben seyest"; gown — "Dz es vor den menschen eüwerer grossenn schalckhayt byeberey vnd neyds vnd hasz ain bedeckung seye"; white shirt — "Das man vnnder dem scheyn aynes frumb

---

// *vnd anfechtung des altmuoterlin auf* // *wellyche anttwurt gegeben von Bruo* [sic] // *Hainrich.* // *Dasselb altmueterlin hat begert jr anzuoschreiben / des* // *sy gewert ist worden von obgemeltem bruoder /* // *Darnach weytter kommen in ander mensch* // *en hend zuolesen vnd ytzund zuolettst* // *in den druck / als man sagt.* // *zuo Eer gott.* // *Im Jar M D xxiij.* // (o.O., o.Dr., 1523), Köhler, Fiche 266/749, Aiijr; Hans Greiffenberger, *Disz biechlin zaigt an die Falschen* // *Propheten* (n. 90 above), Aivr; *Hüpsch ar* // *gument red Frag=* // *en vnd anntwurt Drey* // *er personen Nemlichen* // *ains Curtisanen ain-* // *es Edelmans vnd* // *aines Burgers* // *Nit allain kürtzwey=* // *lig Sunder vast nutzlich zuo* // *lesen vnd zuo heren Alles* // *D.M.L.leer betref-* // *fent.* // (o.O., o.Dr., 1522), Köhler, Fiche 267/752: München StBibl. 4° Polem 3341, Ci v.

[93] Hans Greiffenberger, *Disz biechlin zaigt an die Falschen* // *Propheten* (n. 90 above), Aiij: the cattle of Antichrist have good fattening food from the confession, their God is their belly.

[94] Johannes Eckart, *Ain Dialogus zwischenn* // *Doctor Martin Luthers Au* // *gustiners vnd Joann Eckartz* // *pfarher zue Bobenhausen /* // *Augspurger Bistumbs /* // *Christum das Hoechst* // *goldtrain opfer der* // *heyligen Mesz* // *betreffent.* // [Ingolstadt: Andreas Lutz, ca. 1521], Köhler, *Bibliographie*, Nr. 867: Köhler, Fiche 730/1861, A4v: "Das mancherlay geferbter geystlichait in dem aingen volck Cristi erwaxen sey / mit wollicher mer die priederlich lieb vntergetruckt / dann ergrainet vnnd scheinet, ist ann dem tag ... Das aber soliche gleyssnerey / distel vnnd boes frucht des gesatz sey / ist nit zu glaben / die weil das gesatz albeg vil orden / stendt / vnd wirdickait gehabt hat / die teglich mit pruderlich lieb / im rechten glauben / iber ain kumen sind."

geachten menschen ainen grossenn schalck so darynn steckt nit erkenne."[95] Another form of monastic self-criticism is seen in a dialogue between a Franciscan and a spoon maker, where the former outlines in detail the corrupt life in his monastery.[96]

III.2

Eberlin von Günzburg[97] tended to gear his preaching and writings to a level at which lay people could relate their own experiences of clerical vice. His criticism focussed less on the parish clergy than on the Franciscan order, of which he was a member. He suggested that there was a conspiracy between Rome and the monastic orders to systematically exploit the German nation.[98] Although he shared the general verdict on the clergy,[99] he brought some refreshing touches to his portrayal. He not only pointed to the dilemma of priests who wished to teach God's word but hesitated for fear of losing their living,[100] which he ironically commented generally afforded a comfortable life-style.[101] This dilemma was most obvious in the nunneries, where parents had placed their daughters less for reasons of piety than simply to avoid payment of a dowry.[102] It was shown how nuns who wished to live a pious life were impeded by tyrannical statutes.[103] Eberlin not only highlights the laymen's share in clerical greed,[104] but also the acceptance of age old abuses by the peasantry.[105] In both groups he allows for differentiation: Some priests were honorable, pious and anxious to improve.[106] In trespassing God's commandments laymen were equal to priests.[107] Eberlin thus criticised the indiscriminate use of anticlericalism, especially if it was devised to support material ends. He also drew attention to a latent anticlerical tradition among the clergy themselves, exemplified by the great uncle who told his nephew, he had better drown his son than allow

---

[95] *Ain Christenliches lustigs gesprech* (n. 87 above), Bi v.

[96] *Ayn freuntlich gesprech / zwyschen ainem // Barfuosser Münch* (n. 74 above).

[97] Ludwig Enders, ed., *Johann Eberlin von Günzburg*, vol. 1: *Ausgewählte Schriften*, vols 2-3: *Sämtliche Schriften*, Flugschriften aus der Reformationszeit 11, 15, 18 (Halle 1896, 1900, 1902).

[98] Enders (n. 97 above) 1: 7.

[99] Enders 1: 40-1, 52, 77, 146-8, 176.

[100] Enders 2: 72f.

[101] Enders 2: 75.

[102] Enders 1: 24.

[103] Enders 1: 92.

[104] Enders 1: 37, 75f.

[105] Enders 1: 68.

[106] Enders 1: 77, 94.

[107] Enders 1: 197.

him to be a priest, but the son later succeeded his great uncle in his prebend.[108]

III.3

Luther's polemic pamphlet against the pope formulated his appeal to the authorities to initiate the reform of the Roman church of 1520.[109] Compared with his more popular sermons and devotional pamphlets both before and after 1520,[110] there is a marked change in accent and tone. In violent and aggressive terms Luther depicts the papalists as the agents of Satan and Antichrist. The papal court's devilish practices were specified in terms of the gravamina[111] which introduced a national element, not found in the earlier Luther. Despite the predominance of a polemical style the pamphlet contained constructive elements as well. Luther saw the ministry and the parish as the basis from which a possible reformed church could be rebuilt. Luther took exception at the clergy's arrogance and avarice, suppression of the laity, exploitation of the prebendary system, as well as willful tyranny. These traits were best summarized by referring to the pope and all papalists as the servants of Antichrist. In contrast, the gravamina tradition allowed concessions to social interest as in the case of chapters, where children of the nobility were to devote their lives to serving God. Luther, in a strange blindness, conceded this abuse to vested interest.

Luther had moved swiftly towards this change in his pamphleteering in 1520. Two years previously he had considered dishonoring priests to be contrary to the fourth commandment.[112] In 1519, his letters reveal a growing distance to Rome,[113] yet he attributed the ignorance of priests to an absence of fervour among the laymen. He added that if the clerical estate and the word of God were reformed, Christianity would flourish.[114] Of

---

[108] Enders 2: 75.

[109] *An den christlichen Adel*, quoted according to *Martin Luther: Studienausgabe*, ed. Hans-Ulrich Delius, vol. 2 (Berlin, 1982), 89-167. For the context cf. Martin Brecht, *Martin Luther: Sein Weg zur Reformation. 1483-1521* (Stuttgart, 1981), 352-61; Remigius Bäumer, *Martin Luther und der Papst*, Katholisches Leben und Kirchenreform 30 (Münster i.W., 1970), 57ff.

[110] Hans-Christoph Rublack, "Martin Luther und die städtische soziale Erfahrung", in V. Press, D. Stievermann, eds., *Martin Luther. Probleme seiner Zeit*, Spätmittelalter und Frühe Neuzeit 16 (Stuttgart, 1986), 88-123, 103ff., 121-23.

[111] Heinz Scheible, "Reform, Reformation, Revolution. Grundsätze zur Beurteilung von Flugschriften", *ARG* 65 (1974): 108-34, 119.

[112] *Eine kurze Erklärung der zehn Gebote* (1518), *WA* 1. 247-56; 252,36-7: "Wer briester standt unehret, nachredet und beleidigt."

[113] Bäumer (n. 109 above), 49ff.

[114] *Auslegung deutsch des Vaterunsers für die einfältigen Laien* (1519), *WA* 2. 80-130; 110,15ff.; 114,13ff.

course, as in his academic lectures,[115] he had publicly blamed arrogance, tyranny and ignorance, but the more evils there were in the Roman church, he stated in 1519, the more one should rally to assist the church.[116]

It seems that Luther waived such subtle distinctions after 1520. Now it was not only the pope, but also monasteries which were built on the devil's excrement.[117] Monastic orders and chapters he held to be "sects of damnation".[118] Luther joined the front of wholesale condemnation: priests were compared to those in the temple of Baal,[119] they were described as whores and criminals.[120] It was only from physical violence that Luther warned people to distance themselves.[121]

Another surprising fact about the pamphlet to the nobility, which Luther termed a fool's work, is that there were few references to Luther's essential theological doctrine, apart from the necessity of preaching the word of God, obedience to his commandments, the priesthood of all believers and christian charity.[122] Again these references are in contrast to the elaborate stress on inward faith in his more devotional tracts which had gained greatest popularity. This suggests that Luther not merely provided a theoretical foundation for popular anticlericalism, but became intensely involved in its public propagation. The shift from an essentially pious position prior to 1520, to a stereotyped aggressive stance would seem to indicate on the one hand that he was influenced by prevailing public opinion, which may be reflected in his adaptation of the gravamina, or alternatively that his own personal experience prompted him to assume a leading role in public opinion which led him to generalized statements of aggression, without any clear concept of the possible effects of his actions. The most popular tracts of the early 1520s demonstrate, however, that Luther's polemics against the clergy were marginal. The orientation towards an internalized concept of faith remained dominant.

---

[115] Brecht (n. 109 above), 144-49; Bäumer (n. 109 above), 13.

[116] *Unterricht auf etliche Artikel, die ihm von seinen Abgönnern aufgelegt und zugemessen werden* (1519), *WA* 2. 69-73; 72.

[117] *WA* 10 III. 227,5. This sermon and two others from the summer of 1522 (*WA* 10 III. 170-5 and 228-34) were included in the pamphlet, *Drei schöne Sermon.*

[118] *Von Menschenlehre zu meiden* (1522), *WA* 10 II. 72-92; 85,10.

[119] *Doctor Martinus Lutthers verteutschte schrifft an das Capitel zuo Wittenberg,* Köhler, Fiche 416/1141 (= *WABr* 3. Nr.648), Aiij; *Ain sermon von der hoechsten gottszlesterung, WA* 15. 764-774, here at 759 (Preface of Philip Melhofer).

[120] *Tröstung an die Christen zu Halle* (1527), *WA* 23. 401-31; 407,24: "hurenbelge und bubenbeuche".

[121] *Epistel oder Unterricht von den Heiligen an die Kirche zu Erfurt* (1522), *WA* 10 II. 164-68; 167,16-20.

[122] *An den christlichen Adel* (n. 109 above), 129.

III.4

Pamphlets reflect a variety of anticlerical attitudes. In pamphlets we find peasants most commonly referred to in the context of withholding tithes to the clergy. "Got geb den bawrn die beul vnd ryth / Yr keiner schyr auff pfaffen gyt."[123] A monk commented as follows on the layman's reception of the new doctrine: Luther "macht die groben bawren auff hohen bergen vnd taelern also gelert / wa ich zuo aim bawren hausz kumm / bitt jn vmb ain almusen / ist das erstwort / der Luther verbewt / man soll kaym münch ain almusen geben / sy soellen arbaiten vnd sich mit harter arbayt ernoeren."[124] The layman thus considered himself equal to the clergy and as well anointed as any priest when they were drunk. They also felt no longer obliged to support the clergy since Luther as God's prophet had uncovered the pope and his adherents as the Antichrist and his followers.[125] With an ironic touch Lazarus Spengler pointed out, that even peasants, this rude and unknowledgable folk, had been enlightened by evangelical truth.[126] So they drove monks away, as if they were wolves.[127] The devil's comment on this changing of sides was: "Sy wollen den pfaffen nit meer geben vnnd gend den armen gar nutz."[128] The peasants may have lived up to their true Karsthans image in relation to their pastors: Gengenbach tells how they gathered in a commune to appoint a lay preacher who was taught by the spirit only.[129] As early as 1524 Lutheran pastors are reported to complain, that they obtained no support from the peasants at all.[130]

Caspar Güttel presents another brand of anticlericalism, which seems to have been merely polemical.[131] Papist pamphleteers argued that the new

---

[123] *Dialogus von Zweyen pfaffen // koechin* (n. 46 above), Bir.

[124] *Ayn freuntlich gesprech / zwyschen ainem // Barfuosser Münch* (n. 74 above), A2rf.

[125] *Klag // vnd ant= // wort* (n. 41 above), 156.

[126] Lazarus Spengler, *Die Hauptartikel, durch welche die gemeine Christenheit bisher verführt worden ist* (Wittenberg: Nickel Schirlentz, 1522), Laube 1: 156-85, 157.

[127] Caspar Güttel, *Dialogus* (n. 45 above), Kiv v.

[128] Pamphilus Gengenbach, *Eyn Dialogus wie der heylig vatter babst // Adrianus eyngeritten ist zcu Rom auff den xxviij. // tag des Monats Augusti. Im iar. // M.D.xxij. // Dar von ein gesprech von // dreyen personen. // Curtison Teuffel Aptt //* [Erfurt: Matthes Maler, 1522], Köhler, *Bibliographie*, Nr. 1263: Köhler, Fiche 171/471, Aiijv.

[129] Pamphilus Gengenbach, *Ein kurtzer begriff wie // der Schultheisz vnd die gemein desz dorffs Frid // husen* (n. 71 above), Aijr-Aiijv.

[130] *Klag // vnd ant= // wort* (n. 41 above), Diij v: "die pawren wollen nit mer opffern / auch dasz jr pracht vnd huererey desterbasz erhalten werden"; the tract continues by demanding for sufficient support of pastors.

[131] Caspar Güttel, *Dialogus* (n. 45 above), Hijr. Princes, nobility and peasants soon learned to scold monks, their avarice and their perverted life: "nicht mer vil mer

doctrine and adherence thereto was morally reprehensible.[132] Sebastian
Lotzer maintained that it was the ignorant and violent who turned against
both Papists and Lutherans.[133] The most pronounced criticism on the
absence of moral reform came from Haug Marschalk of Augsburg, who also
noted that with the elimination of the rites of sacrifice and confession, the
laymen could construe their unwillingness to give alms as reflecting their
desire to be truly evangelical.[134] Pious authors tended to take a critical
stance against mere anticlericalism.

<h2 style="text-align:center">III.5</h2>

The clergy were not treated in isolation but were brought into play with the
common man, who was equally subject to accusations of vice. Erasmus
found the common man to be generally crude and ignorant,[135] and to

---

beten / nicht fasten / nicht vil mer opffern / so haben etlich münch lernen schnell die
kappen von sich werffen / künnen sampt ander holtzen goetzen verbrennen / am
freytag flaysch fressen / vil vnfuegs vor den armen baufeldigen Christen ueben alles
vnder dem scheyn (das ist ir suenden deckel) Sy schreyen vnd sagen / wie das sy
seyndt guett Euangelisch."

[132] Petrus Sylvius, *Eyn erschreglicher // vnd doch widderumb kurtzweylliger vnd
nutzlich gesangk // der Lutziferischen vnd Luttrischen kirchen / auff dy // nachfolgend
weyse durch eyn Euangelischen vnd // Apostolischen Prister ytzt zum nawen Jar //
der Christenheyt tzu heyl vnd seligkeyt // ausz gegangen. // [Melodie] // Martinus hat
gerathen Das Ri Rum Ritz. // Man sal die pfaffen brathen Das Ri rum Ritz etc. // M.
P. Syl. // M.D. xxvj. // (o.O., o.Dr., 1526), Köhler, Fiche 990/2509, Ai v, Aijr:*
      Mann sal dy pfaffen braten
      Dy mönchen vnttirschuren
      Die nonnen yns freyhausz furen
      Das gefelt wol vnserm Lutzfer
      Des gleychen vnsern Luthrer.
[133] Sebastian Lotzer, *Entschuldigung ain // er Frummen Christlichen // Gemain zu
Memmingen // mit sampt jrem Bischoff / vnd // trewen Botten des Herren // Christoff
schappeler Pre- // diger alda. Von wegen der em- // poerungen so sich bey vns be=
// geben. etc. Im jar 1525. // Sebastian Lotzer der jünger // von Horb jetz in
Memmingen. // Psalm am. 1.17 // Der Herr ist mit mir ich fuerchte // mich nit waz
mit der mensch thuot //* (o.O., o.Dr., [1525]), Köhler, Fiche 464/1257, Aij v.
[134] Haug Marschalk, *Der Spiegel der Blinden* ([Augsburg: Melchior Ramminger],
1522), Laube 1: 128-155, 146, cf. ibid. 136, 149.
[135] Erasmus, *Ein schoen Epistel // Erasmi von Ro- // terdam / das die Euangelisch
// ler von yederman sol ge= // lesen vnd verstanden // werden.* (Basel: Adam Petri,
1522), Köhler, *Bibliographie,* Nr. 1016: Köhler, Fiche 181/505, Ciijv: "Es sind yetzt
on zal vil / auch fünffzig iaerig menschen / die do nit wissen was sy im tauff
versprochen vnd gelobt haben / denen es noch nie getreumt hat was die artickel desz
glaubens vermoegen vnd vszweisen / wie sy desz herren gebett / das ist / das
paternoster / vestan sollen / was die sacrament bedeuten / das hab ich offt erfarn vsz
teglich gesprech vnd bywonen / auch etwan ausz der heimlichen beicht"; Civ v: "Der

support both superstition and avarice.[136] Some dialogues pointed to instances of solidarity between greedy citizen merchants and priests who joined together in defence of their usurious practices.[137] An instance is reported where a monk in search of a prebend conspired with a Franconian nobleman to rob merchants. Wenzeslaus Linck described this feudal coalition as one of common interest based on honor and money.[138] A dialogue of 1522,[139] clearly stated that the poor standard of the clergy was fostered by the unwillingness of the nobility and citizens to encourage their most able offspring to pursue a clerical career.[140]

IV

Greater emphasis was placed however on the transition to evangelical freedom:

> Wiewol der leyb layder mit ainer schmutzigenn kutten vnnd brayttten gürtel verwickelt vnd bedeckt ist / so hab ich doch in Christo meynen herren vnd got vnd in seyn hayligs Ewangelion ain freyes gemuet / des weder kutten platten personen wercken Kloster gelübdt vnd genoettigter keüschayt mit nichten vnderworffenn ist / dann die Euangelisch freyhayt kayn gebot oder schweres joch sonder leycht vnnd suesz ist.[141]

New contextual frameworks arose from this process of transition such as the case of the son who outlined the evangelical message to his father prompting him to convert[142] and a citizen of Basel who, despite his

---

gemein hauff hat auch seine woelff / füchs / lüchs / vnd andre schedliche thier undersich vermüscht / aber gemeinklich ist der grosz hauff vsz den schaefflin / sy sind wol grob / einfeltig vnd vngelert / aber got nützlich / wann sy allein mit eim truwen hirten versorgt sind."

[136] Erasmus von Rotterdam, *Herr Erasmus von Ro= // terdam verteutschte auszlegung* (n. 51 above), A3r: " ... der pfaffen geitz / vnnd etlicher münchen gleysznerey / welche durch die torheit des gemeinen folcks ernert."

[137] *Hie kompt ein Beüerlein* (n. 72 above).

[138] As did Caspar Güttel, *Dialogus*, (n. 45 above), 3v: "Aber mit Fürsten / Herren / Graffen Prelatten jar vnnd tag / jm sausz leben / Ist eyttel frumm vnd nutz der Styfftunng / also mag man Schlosz Stett / vnnd so vil Doerffer / in getrewlicher besitzung erhalten."

[139] *Hüpsch ar // gument* (n. 92 above), C2r.

[140] *Hüpsch ar // gument* (n. 92 above), C2v: "es wer schad dz er gaistlich wurd."

[141] *Ayn freuntlich gesprech / zwyschen ainem // Barfuosser Münch* (n. 74 above), Aiv v-Bir.

[142] *Eynn Dialogus ader ge // sprech zwischen einem // Vatter vnnd Sun* (n. 45 above).

identification with family tradition, became convinced of the evangelical truth.[143]

Divine truth was the focal point of reformation pamphlets and its breakthrough was cited as a most significant moment in history. The metaphor of the darkness being overcome by the light signified the breakthrough from a tradition of decay.[144] This did not exclude eschatological notions. The apocalyptic code could be assimilated to the light-darkness code: It was the darkness of human laws which had kept consciences imprisoned,[145] and as such they were Antichristian.[146] The word of God had been suppressed[147] and the world filled with vice,[148] but could now become purified through the gospel.[149] Luther, cited as a true light of Christian faith, could be depicted as the teacher[150] and prophet sent by

---

[143] *Ain guotter // grober dyalogus // Teütsch / zwschen zwayen // guoten gesellen / mit namen // Hans Schoepfer / Peter // Schabenhuot // bayd von Basel die auh nit noet // tiger gschaefft sunst // auszzuorichten hab // ent angericht von // aim wirt. //* [Augsburg: Melchior Ramminger, ca. 1521], Köhler, *Bibliographie,* Nr. 1458: Köhler, Fiche 264/743.

[144] *Von dem pfründ // marckt der Curtisanen* (n. 35 above), 90; *Ain schoner Dialogus von Martino // Luther* (n. 90 above), Aijv; *Eyn Dialogus / das ist eyn gesprech // zweyer personen / Christus zuo eynem / vnd // Christianus* (n. 80 above), A2r; *Klag // vnd ant= // wort* (n. 41 above), A2r; Bader and Mussbach, *Artickel vnd clagstuck* (n. 65 above), Aivr; Symphorian Pollio, *Wes man sich ge= // gen newen meren: so teglich // von den predigern des Euangelij werden // auszgeben / halten sollen. // Was zu Straszburg der // schrifft nach von der Ee gepredigt würt. // Verantwortung Simpho= // riani Pollionis / von etlicher lugen wegen / // auff jn erdacht die Ee belangend. //* (Strassburg: Wolfgang Köpfel, 1525), Köhler, Fiche 1485/3894, Aij v; Erasmus Alber, *Ein schoener Dialogus / von // Martino Luther / vnd der geschickten Bot= // schafft ausz der Helle die falsche gayst- // ligkait vnd das wort Gots belan- // gen / gantz hüpsch zuo leeszen. // Anno. M D xxxiij. //* (o.O., o.Dr., 1523), München StBibl 4° Polem 871, Aiij v; *Triumphus veritatis // Sik der warheit // mit dem Schwert des Geists // durch die Wittenbergische Nachtigall // erobert. //,* Schade 2: 198-251.

[145] Lazarus Spengler, *Die Hauptartikel* (n. 126 above), 157; *15.Dyalogus.24.* (n. 77 above), Aij v; *Ain Christenliches lustigs gesprech* (n. 87 above), Cij v.

[146] Hans Greiffenberger, *Disz biechlin zaigt an die Falschen // Propheten* (n. 90 above), A4r.

[147] Balthasar Wilhelm, *Practica Deütsch* (n. 51 above), Ci v.

[148] *Ain new Ge= // dicht wie die gaystlich // ait zuo Erffordt* (n. 49 above).

[149] *Der schlüssel Dauid. // Ich schleüsz auff die finsternisz Egypt // Troest meine freündt / nach dem sichs begibt // Zuo den die Sonne ir krafft mag han // Mit PHaraon anderst vmb gan // Im sein narren kolben zeygen // Doch / die froesch mag nyemant geschweigen. //* (o.O., o.Dr., 1523), Augsburg StBibl 4° ThH 2363, Ai v.

[150] Heinrich Kettenbach, *Ein new Apologia vnnd ver= // antworttung Martini Lut= // thers* (n. 91 above), Ai v: God has "aber einmal zuo dyser zyt vns geben etlich hochgeleert Christlich lerer / die vns das wort gots lawtter vnd reyn fürlegen / vnd die falschen propheten vnd dromprediger Baal / des bauchs mit dem swert des worts

God to reveal truth, as well as to overcome the darkness of the age of Antichrist.[151]

The appeal to the word of God and to Christ's commandments moved anticlericalism into a context of a new polarization, which did not allow it to be marginalized. It was now possible to present the "word of God" in positive terminology as a motor of change and to counterpose the clergy in their negative stance to the evangelical message. The evangelical courtier's initial hostility to Luther, prompted by the latter's criticism of the clergy, was transformed after he had heard readings from scripture.[152] A detailed interpretation of a dialogue, published in 1524, which outlines a conversation between a highly knowledgable Reutlingen baker and a monk provides us with valuable insights.[153] The initial conversation covered aspects of practical religion — fasting, confession, communion — but soon the topics gained in abstraction and complexity. The monk was queried why he called his brethren lords, how he would describe a heretic and what he would define as the church. In addition he was questioned about his motives for joining a monastic community which isolated him from the world and his fellow christians. From the dialogue it emerges that the baker was exceedingly well versed in his subject and in contrast to the monk could refer with ease to scriptural evidence. This allowed various negative spiritual terms, such as blindmen, mute dogs, wolves, magicians, etc., to be applied to the clergy and ensured that anticlerical terminology derived from a spiritual context.

> Lieber bruder dz aller noetigest ist / dz wir der zusagung Christi gelauben miessen / darinn stat vnser selikait als Christus spricht Johan. Ich bin der weg / vnd die warhait vnd dz leben / wan lyeber bruoder so ich die gschrifft lisz / so find ich so vil trost vnd verhaissung / das ich mich weder bapst bischoff / pfarrer lay priester münch noch Curtisonen daruon lasz treyben / wan durch dz wort gotes wirt vns geholffen.[154]

---

gots schlagen."

[151] Heinrich Pastoris, *Practica Teütsch // von vergangen vnd zuokünffti= // gen dingen / Ausz der Heyligen // // geschrifft gegründt vnd // gezogen // Auff das // 1524. // Jar. // Christus Jhesus // eyn Herr vnd Meyster disz Jars // vnnd alle tzeyt. Matthei am xxiij. //* (o.O., o.Dr., o.J.), Helga Robinson-Hammerstein, ed., *Heinrich Pastoris: Practica Teütsch. Casting a German Horoscope* (Dublin, 1980), Aijr: God has the "auszerwöleten Heliam / Martin Luther / inn diser letsten ferlichen zeyt erwecket", who is to open the "Buoch Gottes im Tempel Gottes", in order to proclaim it to the world against the Antichristians.

[152] *Ain Nützliches Ge= // sprech vnd vnderweisung / zu notturfft der bekümertten // menschen vrsach der zwispaltigen leer so wider // ain anndern von den hochgeleertten ein= // gebracht wirtt / die frummen prediger // vnangefochten etc. M D xxv. // Hoffman. Bawr. //* (o.O., o.Dr., 1525), Köhler, Fiche 268/757, Aijr.

[153] Hans Staigmayer, *Ain Schoner Dialogus* (n. 45 above).

[154] Wolfgang Zierer, *Ein Christenlich Ge= // sprech* (n. 54 above), Aivr.

It is interesting to note that although apocalyptic notions appear in this context, they did not play a major role.

V. CONCLUSIONS

What this campaign against the clergy represents is more than "geistespolitische(r) Tendenzliteratur",[155] although a certain journalistic approach is detectable. An attempt to describe its importance from an evolutionary perspective[156] would distinguish the role of the primary Christian code, the gospel or scripture, from secondary ones, such as canon law, apocalypticism, etc. In the middle ages these codes were incorporated into the ecclesiastical system and controlled either by being integrated — as in case of the Franciscans and Dominicans — or used as a means of discipline or control from the centre. Criticism of the clergy was part of moral teaching or of an apocalyptic theology and religion. It is as yet unclear why the ecclesiastical system abandoned its practice of a flexible response to criticism by the beginning of the sixteenth century. Its complexity had grown, but this did not necessarily mean that the church had to be depicted as a system of corrupt disorder. The reactions which the pamphlets generated indicate an awareness among the clergy and laymen of the need to concern themselves with the church and the issues which made the state of the church untenable. Another prime mover was, of course, what can be described as the abstraction of the primary code from ecclesiastical control. This allowed the church to be viewed no longer just from within but at a distance. The concept of truth was placed outside or in opposition to the ecclesiastical system, as represented by its clerical institutions. Scripture then was the prime mover towards aggressive polemics, or criticism, as well as the attempts to redefine the church. The variations and orientations of the pamphlet discourse point to the differentiations that had been achieved within society.

It is evident from the charges levelled against the clergy, as well as from the primary code, that the religious code had not moved to entirely new frontiers. It was medieval moral criticism complaining of usurous clerics or the figure of Antichrist which had been moved to the front line of battle. The evangelical campaign reduced the complexity of the ecclesiastical system. In a perspective which attributes complexity to modernity, the church in the late middle ages was certainly more modern than any segmentary structures suggest. At the same time it was the word of God,

---

[155] Aby Warburg, *Heidnisch-antike Weissagung* (n. 18 above), 201.

[156] Niklas Luhmann, *Soziale Systeme. Grundriss einer allgemeinen Theorie* (2nd ed., Frankfurt, 1985), esp. 191ff., 488ff.; idem, *Gesellschaftsstruktur und Semantik. Studien zur Wissenssoziologie der modernen Gesellschaft* (Frankfurt, 1989), vol. 3, 259ff.

transmitted by communication, that pointed to a more modern concept of organizing society. But this medium could not be implemented as an ecclesiastical (institutional) model. What seems to have shaken the foundations was a new delineation of the sacred and the secular as a consequence of abstracting the gospel. Priests were no longer held to be sacred per se as the spiritual demands of an ascetic elite were included within the fold of laypeople. The re-entry of the grace/sin dualism testifies to the traditional note of the religious system: God and devil were still held to be the prime movers of this world.

ANTICLERICALISM
IN GERMAN REFORMATION PAMPHLETS:
A RESPONSE*

R. PO-CHIA HSIA

New York University

The pamphlets of the early evangelical movement offer a rich source for the study of anticlericalism in Reformation Germany. But before we can evaluate the nature of this source material, we need to ask questions about the genre of *Flugschriften*.[1] In other words, the question of anticlericalism in the pamphlet literature cannot simply be answered by a thorough textual study of all available pamphlets. Such a literal approach will no doubt yield a rich taxonomy of theological and propagandistic commonplaces; Hans-Christoph Rublack's paper represents an impressive research effort that has given us a preliminary classification of the themes and images of this anticlerical discourse in the pamphlet literature. But as Rublack himself has pointed out, very little of this anticlerical discourse was new to the evangelical movement. Indeed, one can go further back than the Lollard and Hussite movements, with their apocalyptic language of lay anticlericalism, to seek the origins of the long established anticlerical discourse. The medieval cities were a hotbed of anticlericalism.[2] To be sure, much of the language of urban gravamina against the clergy was economic and not apocalyptic in tone, concentrating on denouncing the tax-exemption of the clergy, their wealth, their privilege, and their economic competition. Occasionally, however, the economic anticlericalism of the cities adopted the millenarian pose of more radical critique; witness the examples of the fraticelli or the central criticism of Savonarola and his followers in late fifteenth-century Florence.

---

* This paper was written as a dialogue to the paper presented by Hans-Christoph Rublack. Please refer to his paper in this volume for specific discussions. I am indebted to Heiko A. Oberman for the invitation to speak and to H.-C. Rublack for his always stimulating discussions.

[1] For an introduction to Reformation pamphlets, see Steven Ozment, "Pamphlet Literature of the German Reformation", in *Reformation Europe: A Guide to Research*, ed. Steven Ozment (St. Louis, 1985), 85-105. For a summary of recent research see the 1980 conference volume, *Flugschriften als Massenmedium der Reformationszeit*, ed. Hans-Joachim Köhler (Stuttgart, 1981).

[2] Anton Störmann, *Die städtischen Gravamina gegen den Klerus am Ausgange des Mittelalters und in der Reformationszeit*, RGST 24-26 (Münster, 1916).

Clearly, the pamphlets do not constitute a single category of source material generated by a single historical context, in spite of their appearance in the *Sturmjahre* of the Reformation. The fact that Hans-Joachim Köhler has assembled five thousand pamphlets published between 1517 and 1530, an heroic scholarly effort undertaken under tremendous duress, should not mislead us into thinking of the pamphlets as an uniform category of sources, comparable, let us say, to city council minutes or visitation records. The pamphlets brought together in the Tübingen project represent, in fact, a highly disparate set of source material, produced under very different historical contexts.[3] And we must turn our attention to the differences in the source material before we can ask more meaningful questions about the relationship between anticlericalism and the pamphlet literature.

Let us start with the obvious. Textual differences: Some pamphlets were short, erudite theological treatises, demonstrating detailed knowledge of the Scriptures and Canon Law, such as the anonymous *Von dem Pfründenmarkt der Kurtisanen und Tempelknechte*, in which the author, who calls himself a layman, shows knowledge of Latin and Canon Law.[4] Or take the example of the pamphlet, *Beklagung eines Laien, genannt Hans Schwalb, über viel Mißbräuche christlichen Lebens*, with citations from the Vulgate.[5] Alongside these discursive pamphlets of anticlericalism, others were composed in dialogue form, or as illustrated broadsheets, or, more rarely, as songs, including two cited in the paper by Rublack: The song by Petrus Sylvius, *Eyn erschreglicher ... gesangk*, with the melody "Martinus hat gerathen Das Ri Rum Ritz / man sal die pfaffen brathen Das Ri rum Ritz etc" ("Brother Martin well boasts, the clergy are ready to roast.").[6] And secondly *Ein neues Gedicht, wie die Geistlichkeit zu Erfurt gestürmt worden ist.*[7] Therefore, in regard to the modes of communication, the pamphlets represent

---

[3] See the microfiche series edited by Hans-Joachim Köhler, *Flugschriften des frühen 16. Jahrhunderts* (Zug, 1978-87). Hereafter cited as Köhler, Fiche.

[4] *Von dem pfründt // marckt der Curtisanen // vnd Tempelkne // chten* ([Basel: Adam Petri], 1521), Laube 1: 90-104.

[5] *Beclagung aines ley= // ens genant Hanns schwalb über // vil mißbreüch Christliches lebens / vnd dariñ be // griffen kürtzlich von Johannes Huß- // sen* ([Augsburg: Melchior Ramminger], 1521), Laube 1: 63-74.

[6] *Eyn erschreglicher // vnd doch widderumb kurtzweylliger vnd nutzlich gesangk // der Lutziferischen vnd Luttrischen kirchen / auff dy // nachfolgend weyse durch eyn Euangelischen vnd // Apostolischen Prister ytzt zum nawen Jar // der Christenheyt tzu heyl vnd seligkeyt // ausz gegangen. // [Melodie] // Martinus hat gerathen Das Ri Rum Ritz. // Man sal die pfaffen brathen Das Ri rum Ritz etc. // M. P. Syl. // M.D. xxvj. //* (o.O., o.Dr., 1526), Köhler, Fiche 990/2509.

[7] *Ain new Ge= // dicht wie die gaystlich // ait zu Erffordt in Dhüringen // Gesturmbt ist worden // kurtzweylig // zu lesen.* ([Augsburg: Melchior Ramminger], 1521), Laube 2: 1316-22.

diverse forms of literary, visual, musical and dialogical forms, appealing to a wide spectrum of audiences.

A second point of difference in the pamphlets is their relationship to historical events: in other words the fictive or realistic nature of the pamphlets. I would admit, the line between fiction or reality is perhaps not a strict one because the pamphlets combined these two narrative characteristics in their function as propaganda. Some scholars have pointed to the pamphlets as early newssheets, notably the nineteenth-century publicist Gustav Freytag, who avidly collected sixteenth-century Flugschriften.[8] But Reformation Flugschriften were very different from the *Newe Zeitungen*, although examples in both categories contain elements of what we would recognize as journalism. A pamphlet which I have already cited, *Ein neues Gedicht* (n. 7 above), described an actual historical event, the anticlerical riot in Erfurt between 11-13 June, 1521, when students at the University, joined by townspeople, demolished many houses that belonged to the clergy of the collegiate churches of St. Severin and St. Marie. Exploiting the situation, the city council blackmailed the clergy into paying 10,000 gulden as protection money, extracted an agreement to tax their houses as well as to force them to pay an excise tax, in addition to reducing interest on annuities owned by the clergy from 6% to 4% per annum. Only then did the magistrates send in the militia to restore order. This is perhaps the most telling example of the illustrative function of anticlerical pamphlets. As Ulman Weiss's monograph demonstrates, incidents of anticlericalism in Erfurt can be documented with great precision all the way back to the Hussite Wars; and the riot of 1521 represented a prelude to the adoption of evangelical worship in the city.[9]

If the pamphlet *Ein neues Gedicht* can be situated within its historical context, the task of historical contextualization is more difficult for the other pamphlets. Take this pamphlet as an example: *Ain guotter/grober dyalogus/ Teutsch/ zwischen zwayen/ guoten gesellen/ mit namen/ Hans Schoepfer/ Peter/ Schabenhuot/ bayd von Basel die auh nit noet/tiger geschaefft sunst/ auszzuorichten hab/ent angericht von aim wirt*, with no author, place, or year of publication.[10]

Can one take this dialogue as a faithful representation and publication of an actual conversation in Basel, during which an old believer was convinced of the truth of the new evangelical movement? Surely, from the purported detailed title, with its suggestions of verisimilitude of a real event, one might give it more credence than say the dialogue, *Eynn Dialogus ader ge/sprech*

---

[8] For a catalogue of the Gustav Freytag pamphlet collection, see Paul Hohenemser, ed., *Flugschriftensammlung Gustav Freytag* (Frankfurt, 1925). The collection is deposited in the Universitätsbibliothek Frankfurt.

[9] Ulman Weiss, *Die frommen Bürger von Erfurt. Die Stadt und ihre Kirche im Spätmittelalter und in der Reformationszeit* (Weimar, 1988), 124-32.

[10] Köhler, Fiche 264/743.

zwischen einem/ vatter vnnd Sun dye/ lere Martini Luthers vnd sunst an/dere sachen des Christlichen Glaub/ens belangende, which seems to be an obvious literary invention.[11] Or can one really take on faith that the two burghers Hans Schoepfer and Peter Schabenhuot were really citizens of Basel and not the invented names of the anonymous pamphleteer? Clearly, the dialogues between supposedly real persons were not more real than obviously fictive ones. The pamphlet *Ayn freuntlich gesprech/ zwyschen ainem/ Barfuosser Munch/ ausz der Prouyntz Öster/reych/ der Obseruantz/ vnd ainen Loeffel/macher/ mit namen Hans Stoesser/ gar lustig zuo lessen* represents a literary conceit, but a common trope in the rhetoric of the evangelical movement, namely, that the simple truth of the gospel was understood by the common people, who could confound the friars and monks, ignorant and perverse in their errors.[12] One can no more interpret these dialogues as true representations of the evangelical movement than one can read as anything but evangelical propaganda the dialogues composed during the 1520's showing Jewish rabbis convinced by the truth of the Gospel.[13]

Yet, one cannot simply dismiss these dialogues as mere literary representations. Some of the scenes of theological discussions in the pamphlets were corroborated by other sources in city archives. Witness the following description in the pamphlet by Haug Marschalck, *Der Pfaffen Klage*.[14] The priest complains:

> Oh Luther, you have done evil! You have misled the common folk. ... When we go into an inn, they come around asking questions and want to dispute with us. The German books have aroused hatred and envy against us: everyone now wants to write books against monks and priests, in order that people may despise us.

These satirical verses sound a ring of truth. Numerous reports of the early evangelical movement documented the extraordinary religious ferment among the common people who discussed theology and politics in inns, which served as centers of dissemination of rumors and agitation. To that extent, the anticlerical discourse of the pamphlets was both a representation

---

[11] Köhler, Fiche 266/748.

[12] Köhler, Fiche 626/1625.

[13] See for examples: *Ein Gespräch zwischen einem Christen und Juden auch einem Wirte samt seinem Hausknecht, den Eckstein Christum betreffend* (1524) and *Ein Unterredung vom Glauben durch Herr Micheln Kromer, Pfarrherr zu Kunitz, und einen jüdischen Rabbiner* (1523), both in Otto Clemen, ed., *Flugschriften aus den ersten Jahren der Reformation*, vol. 1 (Leipzig, 1907), 373-440.

[14] *Pfaffenklag // Der Pfaffen Klag heyß ich/ // Wer mich find der kauff mich // Vber den Luther schrey ich/ // Wen ich tryff der ker sich* ([Altenburg: Gabriel Kantz], 1525), Laube 1: 569-74.

of these agitations as well as propagandistic material for promoting anticlericalism.

It would be inaccurate, however, to speak only of one kind of anticlerical discourse. Two distinct voices are present in the pamphlets, one representing clerical self-criticism, and the other a far more radical rejection of the clerical estate. In the first category of self-critical pamphlets, one finds both evangelical clergy and defenders of the old faith. The pamphlets of Erasmus are good examples of the kind of ecclesiastical self-criticism that Rublack cites in his paper. They hold out the promise of reform within the Roman Church. But even for reformers who had renounced monasticism and the religious orders, the criticism of the clerical estate was within limits. The ex-Franciscan Johann Eberlin von Günzburg was dismissed from his cloister in Ulm in February 1521 for his criticism of the church. Yet, in his *Der zehnte Bundesgenosse*, his anticlericalism is limited to antipapalism and antimonasticism.[15] In his words, "Nobody shall leave our land for Rome, whether out of business or on pilgrimage, lest our people may become minions of the Antichrist and our land worse than Sodom and Gomorrah." He had no use for monks and nuns (they were forbidden to wear habits and their numbers were to be circumscribed), yet Eberlin had a clear vision of an evangelical clergy. The parish priest, elected by the bailiff and the local village community, was allowed to marry and live from a salary; he could not charge titles or fees for rituals, and must be a local person. As a citizen, the parish priest enjoyed the same rights and shared the same burdens as others but could not be elected to public office. The bishop, responsible for twenty priests, drew a lower salary; his main task was to examine the priests for doctrine and conduct and he was subject to the authority of the local magistrate. The evangelical clergy in Eberlin's *Bundesgenosse* in fact closely resembled the protestant clergy after the establishment of the territorial and urban churches. Eberlin's pamphlet is a reminder that the majority of the anticlerical pamphlets were much more circumscribed in their objects of attack: not the clerical estate as such, but the papacy, the episcopacy, and monasticism represented the objects of scorn and apocalyptic anger. This clerical anticlericalism was best illustrated by the many pamphlets of Martin Luther, who dominated the Flugschriften literature. A preliminary examination of Köhler's collection reveals that close to half of all pamphlets preserved were works of Martin Luther.

The existence of two kinds of anticlerical discourse raises the question of the relationship between author and text: Were lay authors more critical of the clergy than clerical reformers? Can one establish any relationship

---

[15] *New statutē // die Psitacus gebracht hat // vß dem lād Wolfaria wel // che betrǎffendt reformie= // rung geystlichen stand. // Wañ man annǎm diß re= // formatz/ // So gschweigt man man= // che kloster katz/ // Die vornen lǎckt vnd hin // den kratzt. // Der .X. bǔdt // gnoß* [Basel: Pamphilius Gengenbach, 1521], Laube 1: 75-89.

between social class and anticlerical discourse? Is there a correlation between theological learning and social radicalism? In the pamphlets studied by Rublack, forty-five names are given as authors or interlocutors in the pamphlet, whereas some thirty-nine or close to one-half of the pamphlets were anonymously published. The list of forty-five names includes well-known figures in the evangelical movement, beginning, of course, with Luther himself, and including, among others, Andreas Osiander, Wenzelaus Linck, Lazarus Spengler, Erasmus, Ulrich von Hutten, Martin Bucer, Johannes Oecolampadius, Jacob Strauss, Ambrosius Blaurer, Sebastian Lotzer, and Pamphilius Gengenbach. Of the 84 pamphlets cited by Rublack, 39 are anonymous; 21 are published with authors whose biographies remain obscure — a number of these explicitly naming themselves laymen; and of the remaining 24 pamphlets, fourteen were written by clerics, three by knights, two by city secretaries, and one each by a soldier, printer, furrier and painter. In other words, we know next to nothing about most of the authors or the circumstances of the writing and publication of the vast majority of these pamphlets. A desideratum of Reformation research would be the reconstruction, to the extent possible, of the social background of pamphlet authors. The very limited research which has been undertaken so far, such as Paul Russell's *Lay Theology in the Reformation*, is a small beginning in the right direction.[16] One would need to break down themes in anticlerical discourse and try to establish correlations with particular categories of pamphlet writers, such as whether attacking clerics as "Jews" or "Antichrist" was particular to the vocabulary of urban artisanal anticlericalism; and whether economic grievances seem important in clerical anticlericalism.

Obviously the agenda for future research is a long one, even though certain difficulties with interpretation of the Flugschriften will, I suspect, be impossible to solve. The reconstruction of a prosopography of lay pamphlet-eers may be beyond the resources of any one individual, since the documentation, of it exists at all, is scattered in numerous local archives, in notarial and tax lists. I shall simply conclude my paper by pointing out two fruitful areas of textual investigation which the pamphlets have opened up for us: one of these has already been pointed out by Rublack, namely, the similarity of discourse in anticlericalism and antisemitism. Both the clergy and the Jews were attacked for usury, sloth, seducing women, and for being demonic minions of the Antichrist. The language is particularly striking when one compares this anticlerical/anti-Jewish discourse to the philo-Semitic pamphlets, or at least to the pamphlets that called for Jewish conversions in the early evangelical movement. One must try to reconstruct the very different social and intellectual milieu that produced these two vastly

---

[16] Paul A. Russell, *Lay Theology in the Reformation: Popular Pamphleteers in Southwest Germany 1521-1525* (Cambridge, 1986).

different and in fact opposing positions. The second avenue of future research that the pamphlets open up is a possible relationship between anticlericalism and anti-feminism. Many pamphlets associated "Roman superstitions" with female support for the clergy. In the pamphlet *Eine demütige Ermahnung an die Christenheit, in der Kirche nicht mit Geld umzugehen*,[17] Eckhart zum Drübel attacks the corruption of the Roman rituals when all ceremonies became venal: "Therefore, take heed, see how the priest stands at the altar and runs to the old women who are standing around the altar for their money, just like geese going to the stream... ."[18] Or listen to Haug Marschalk in his *Der Pfaffen Klage*, lamenting that nowadays nobody gave alms to the clergy: "Only the old mothers are shuffling along with their pennies."[19]

No pamphlet was more explicit in its anticlericalism, antisemitism, and misogyny than Heinrich von Kettenbach's *Ein Gespräch mit einem frommen Altmütterlein*.[20] Kettenbach, who succeeded Eberlin von Günzburg as preacher in the Ulm Franciscan cloister, claimed that his pamphlet was based on an actual conversation. The old woman was angry that the evangelical preacher in the cathedral, Martin Edelhauser, preached against superstitious practices, especially against burning candles. Kettenbach used the occasion to attack the cult of saints, pilgrimage, Latin mass, and the general wealth of the clergy: "The clergy are as blind as the Jews at the time of Christ; their end will be the same as that of the Jews." The old woman was gradually brought around to his viewpoint and confessed: "How is it, brother Heinrich, that you monks and clerks are free from excise, tax, tolls, and guard money, etc. and I am an old woman, who spins at the wheel in moonlight until midnight, and I am not free?"[21]

To this, the evangelical preacher only repeated his condemnation of monks and nuns and evaded the crucial question determining the relationship between the laity and clergy: the perception and reality of economic exploitation. The pamphlet literature did not provide an answer to the difficult question it raised for the common people. Yet they answered their own query with massive rent strikes, and ultimately in anticlerical uprisings during the Peasants War. But the defeat of the peasants also signaled the

---

[17] *Ein demütige ermanung an // Ein gantze gemeine Christen // heit. Von Eckhart zům // Drübel. ... // Da. Gloriam deo. // Mann soll. In der. Kirchen // nitt mitt. Gelt vmb gon.* (Strassburg: Martin Flach, [1523]), Laube 1: 218-21.

[18] "Item so nemen acht, so der priester ob dem altar stot und im die alten weiber mitt dem gelt um den altar lauffen, wie die gens zu der bach... ."

[19] "Allein die alten mütterlein/ zotten umbher mit eym heller ... ", Laube 1: 574.

[20] *Eyn gesprech Brůder Hainrich von // Kettenbach mit aim frommen alte můt // terlin von Vlm von etlichen zůfellen // vnd anfechtung des altmůterlin auf // wellyche anttwurt gegeben von Brů // Hainrich... .* ([Augsburg: Melchior Ramminger], 1523), Laube 1: 201-17.

[21] Laube 1: 211.

decline of the pamphlets, which had served their purpose in rousing and channeling popular resentment and anger against the Roman clergy.

"WHAT A TANGLED AND TENUOUS MESS THE CLERGY IS!" CLERICAL ANTICLERICALISM IN THE REFORMATION PERIOD

HANS-JÜRGEN GOERTZ

Universität Hamburg

I

In the Christmas days of 1523 burghers chased the parson of St. Blasius in Mühlhausen through the streets and "women, girls and men ran into the rectory and took what they wanted in food and drink."[1] This scene occurred after the priest of the church at one of the town's market squares had refused to install an evangelical preacher at the chapel of St. Kilian. Nothing could keep the aroused crowd from venting their anger about the miserable state of the church and society upon a priest and, as can be learned from another source, threatening him with knives while he read the mass at the altar. The priest assumed that he was in mortal danger and hid himself in the vestry. Only with the coming of evening was he accompanied home by the burgomaster; the next day the priest left town.[2] The preaching of runaway monks, who earlier denounced the clergy,[3] had fallen on fertile soil.

Earlier incidents in Mühlhausen had already occasioned the complaint that "the clergy were troubled with great persecution."[4] Similar episodes were reported in numerous towns which were on their way to the Reformation. In Erfurt in 1521 the houses of the clergy were plundered and wrecked; here a regular "priest riot" swept over the town: a "first tumult of the Lutherans against the clergy."[5] Elsewhere militiamen with guns had to be called up to

---

[1] Reinhard Jordan, ed., *Chronik der Stadt Mühlhausen/Thür.* (Mühlhausen, 1900), 175; cf. Walter Peter Fuchs, ed., *Akten zur Geschichte des Bauernkriegs in Mitteldeutschland*, vol. 2 (Jena, 1942), 23f.

[2] Jordan, *Chronik*, 176.

[3] Jordan, *Chronik*, 166.

[4] Felician Gess, ed., *Akten und Briefe zur Kirchenpolitik Herzog Georgs von Sachsen*, vol. 1 (Leipzig, 1905), 546.

[5] Cf. Ulman Weiss, "Das Erfurter Pfaffenstürmen 1521: 'Haec prima Lutheranorum adversus Clericos seditio ...'", *Jahrbuch für die Geschichte des Feudalismus* 3 (1979): 233-79; Ulman Weiss, *Die frommen Bürger von Erfurt. Die Stadt und ihre Kirche im Spätmittelalter und in der Reformationszeit* (Weimar, 1988), 124-32. Latin citation in subtitle of essay: P. Lange, *Chronicon Numburgense*, in J. B. Mencken, *Scriptores rerum Germanicarum*, vol. 1 (Leipzig, 1726), 65 (cited from Weiss, ibid., 126).

protect the worship service against interruption by enraged burghers. In Ittingen Cloister peasants broke in and stripped a monk of his clothes in a demeaning manner. They tore off his habit, starting with his cowl, and mocked the naked monk with derisive laughter, until a pro-Reformation preacher took mercy on his Catholic colleague and threw his own robe over him.[6] Nuns and canonesses, too, had to put up with a lot of offense.[7] Heinrich Richard Schmidt wrote of Nuremberg:

> Everywhere the ceremonies of the Old Church were insulted, Catholic sermons interrupted. Clergymen had to submit to scorn and mockery. The greater number of these episodes occurred in 1523. At the time of the Corpus Christi feast of that year the town council was afraid of violent attacks from the congregations upon representatives of the church. The council felt, so it declared, "much upset and displeasure" at the townspeople's expressions of anticlericalism. Even council employees joined in the mockery of the clergy.[8]

However in this imperial city a politically strong council succeeded to a degree in holding anticlerical excesses in check. In other towns, by contrast, the situation was more difficult. Here there were spectacular riots, and as in Mühlhausen many clergy feared for their lives.

The clergy had attracted the anger of the people, who were not only powerfully incited by Reformation propaganda but also systematically used to advance the implementation of the Reformation. So, for instance, the Erfurt Council skillfully directed the "priest riots" in the town in order to bring the clergy under the jurisdiction of its taxation;[9] and so Ulrich Zwingli tolerated and used the sermon interruptions of his followers in order to bring the Zurich Council into negotiations for the introduction of the Reformation.[10] This happened, moreover, at a period when Martin Luther had already begun to warn against such excesses. In his writing, *A Faithful Admonition to all Christians to be on Guard against Riot and Rebellion* (1522), the Wittenberg Reformer sought to cool down the anticlerical anger that he himself had heated up.[11] But it didn't help. Wherever the evangelical preachers built up a following, wherever genuine social movements

---

[6] From the documents of the Ittingen Cloister riot. See Peter Kamber, "Die Reformation auf der Zürcher Landschaft am Beispiel des Dorfes Marthalen. Fallstudie zur Struktur bäuerlicher Reformation", in *Zugänge zur bäuerlichen Reformation*, ed. P. Blickle, Bauer und Reformation 1 (Zurich, 1987), 108, n. 68.

[7] E.g., Gess, *Akten und Briefe*, 1: 222, 546.

[8] Heinrich Richard Schmidt, *Reichsstädte, Reich und Reformation. Korporative Religionspolitik 1521-1529/30* (Stuttgart, 1986), 52.

[9] Weiss, *Die frommen Bürger von Erfurt*, 127f. On the contextual link of riots against priests and the Reformation, cf. 129ff.

[10] Heinold Fast, "Reformation durch Provokation. Predigtstörungen in den ersten Jahren der Reformation in der Schweiz", in *Umstrittenes Täufertum 1525-1975. Neue Forschungen*, ed. H.-J. Goertz (Göttingen, 2nd ed., 1977), 85-9.

[11] *WA* 8. 673-87.

for the Reformation came into existence, whether in Hersfeld, Hamburg or
Stralsund, Augsburg, Kitzingen or Colmar, everywhere anticlericalism
belonged to the scenario of the outbreak of the Reformation. What other
possibilities did the lay people have to participate in the course of the
Reformation? They must involve themselves, reject the hated priests and
drive them away. In this way the slogan of "the priesthood of all believers"
found its tangible consequence.

It is often asserted that although anticlerical tumults accompanied the
process of the Reformation, they had nothing to do with the Reformation
itself. When it is taken into account how consciously anticlerical actions
were employed to create symbols and to start negotiations — that they were
often staged with cunning and premeditation at appropriate times and with
the best interests of the Reformers in view — the question arises of what
role evangelical clergy played in awakening emotions and stirring up
tempers against the Catholic clergy. In Mühlhausen, for example, the
following preliminary preceded the incident already described: A "runaway
monk with a great crowd of people" broke into the chapel, seized the chalice
out of the hand of the priest and afterward "gave communion to many
people in both kinds in the Lutheran manner."[12] One can focus the problem
in an extreme way and ask whether anticlericalism was not generated by the
clergy itself — as the argument of the "priesthood of all believers" certainly
was — and only gradually transmitted to the populace. The matter could
naturally be interpreted differently, namely, that the learned theologians
conceptualized with their arguments an inarticulate popular desire that was
seeking to express itself: the desire to jump over the chasm between clergy
and laity and to struggle for their own closeness to God undeterred by
priests. Finally, there would still be a third possibility to consider: that
evangelical preaching incited resistance from the Catholic clergy, which the
populace for its part would no longer tolerate and which it sought to break
with defiant conduct. There are examples to be found of each of these
various possibilities, but one thing is clear: the clergy were as much
involved in anticlericalism as the laity. Often the clergy were even leading
the way, and in general they gave the anticlericalism of the early Reformation era a particular stamp. The theme of this paper is the anticlericalism
that was developed by erstwhile clergy of the Roman church. Nevertheless,
this anticlericalism can only be appropriately presented in the context of the
attitude that numerous lay-people took to the clergy.

II

"Anticlericalism" is a concept that originated from political controversies in
the wake of the Enlightenment and the *Kulturkampf* of the nineteenth

---

[12] Fuchs, *Akten zur Geschichte des Bauernkriegs*, 2: 24.

century. It referred to the objective of checking clerical influence in politics and public life, on the basis of a standpoint of enmity to the church or a general turning away from Christianity. More current than anticlericalism in this context is the concept of "laicism". At first glance it would seem that these concepts apply only indirectly to the situation of the Reformation era, because it was not then the objective to remove clerical influence from public life so as to restrict religion to the private sphere. Rather, in the Reformation era criticism was directed at the officials of the church, and not only at them but in general at the first estate in the social structure of the period. This occurred not from a weariness with piety but from a need for original religiosity. Often more than mere criticism occurred. The clergy was mocked and scolded, opposed, threatened, occasionally pursued and physically attacked. Under the term anticlericalism should be understood all those attacks on the clergy that arose from disappointment at the neglect of duty and moral misbehavior by an estate that allowed the discrepancy between its pretensions and reality to become too great and that was no longer capable of satisfying people's religious needs.

It does not make much sense to talk of anticlericalism if there are only occasional attacks on the clergy. Rather it must permeate the whole atmosphere and the discredited clergy must have fully forfeited their authority. One can properly speak of an atmosphere of insubordination, of rebelliousness and of a fight against the priests. In the Reformation period this fight turned out negatively for the Catholic clergy. It was liquidated; the pinnacle was broken off the medieval social pyramid.[13]

Anticlericalism is not identical with criticism of the church. The latter is directed against an institution, the former against persons. Of course these persons represent the church to the highest degree; indeed, the church defined itself as the clerical hierarchy. To that extent criticism of the clergy also applies to the church, and conversely the laity in particular presented their criticism of the church as an institution through criticism of its officials. The lay people encountered the church in the person of pope, bishop or priest. Indeed the clergy mediated salvation; nevertheless in the eyes of the laity their misbehavior casts dark shadows on the church and is responsible for its desolate condition. There was great fear that the church's ship might founder in the storm; and how often can one read in the pamphlets that the clergy have neglected their real duties and caused great damage to the church: Hence they should "attend only to spiritual things and give up the worldly entirely."[14] This was written by Ulrich von Hutten, still

---

[13] Cf. Hans-Jürgen Goertz, *Pfaffenhaß und groß Geschrei. Die reformatorischen Bewegungen in Deutschland 1517-1529* (Munich, 1987), 52-68.

[14] Ulrich von Hutten, *Deutsche Schriften*, ed. Heinz Mettke, vol. 1 (Leipzig, 1972), 46f. Cf. Joseph Grünpeck, *Ein spiegel der naturlichen himlischen vnd prophetischen sehungen* (Nuremberg, 1508). There are numerous references to the anticlerical orientation of Grünpeck in Heike Talkenberger, *Sintflut, Prophetie und Zeitgeschehen*

completely in the spirit of late medieval humanist criticism of the clergy. "The blessed light of Christian truth" was "suppressed before this by the pope and his following" — in this manner Luther underscored the personal aspect of the decay of the church.[15] A basic and vital reaction to this situation is properly called anticlericalism rather than criticism of the church. No new church was called for but only the improvement of the spiritual estate, and ultimately its abolition. Criticism of this sort had a visible, tangible object — particularly for ordinary people who could not cope with theological teachings and anonymous ecclesiastical structures but only with persons whom they encountered daily. They chose agitation rather than disputation, tangible signs rather than learned words. The background experience for anticlericalism is close contact with the clergy.

Anticlericalism has many faces, depending upon whether the pope, the bishops, canons and prelates (the higher clergy) or secular priests, nuns and monks (the "ordinary priesthood") are the targets of criticism. Its faces also change depending upon who voices the criticism and in which life situations the clergy encounter the laity: whether a peasant complains about oppressive ecclesiastical financial burdens (tithes and rents) and deficient religious service; a handworker about competition from the cloisters in craft production; a council member about clerical resistance to taxation and opposition to incorporation into the civil community of the town; whether a burgher finds himself no longer willing to tolerate the legal immunity of the clergy; or the members of the Imperial estates in the Reichstag, by means of the *Gravamina nationis germanicae*, seek to resist the outflow of money to Rome.

Anticlericalism is a complex phenomenon that calls for a carefully differentiated analysis. However, it is also a phenomenon that is widespread and diffuse, or in any case that is the way contemporaries experienced it. It included mutually entangled moral-religious, legal-fiscal and economic characteristics. For the clergy was not only a religious but also a temporal estate and it encountered the people in this combination. This phenomenon of anticlericalism was also diffuse particularly because the spiritual estate was omnipresent in people's lives from the cradle to the grave and its services were by no means cheap. Any analysis of anticlericalism has to take account of this diffuse complexity. The anticlericalism of the clergy is embedded in this complexity. Although it will be set apart for the purposes of this paper, it is and remains an inextricable element of the general anticlerical milieu of the time. In what follows I want to emphasize three aspects of this complex subject: (1) anticlericalism polarized religious and

---

in *Texten und Holzschnitten astrologischer Flugschriften 1488-1528* (Tübingen, 1990), 110-45.

[15] *WA* 8. 676.

political controversy; (2) it produced spectacular deeds; and (3) it was anchored in the center of Reformation thought.

III

In canon law a sharp distinction is drawn between clergy and laity.[16] The former have the purpose of leading the church, and the latter are called upon to entrust themselves to this leadership for the sake of their souls' salvation. The difference between the spiritual and temporal estates originates in the sacrament of ordination, which stamps upon the future cleric an indestructible quality (*character indelebilis*) and raises him to a level of participation in the divine essence to which a layman cannot attain. Only the clergyman is able to offer a sacrifice of Christ in the mass. This repeated performance of the sacrifice legitimates his special spiritual estate. As long as clergy and laity conducted themselves peaceably with each other the difference of the two estates was a matter of course. As soon, however, as tensions arose and the laity had grounds to doubt the integrity and question the leadership of the clergy, the traditionally established differences could develop into an antagonism that burdened Christendom. The reaction of the laity changed over the course of time. At times people turned their backs on the clergy and created movements that were declared to be heretical. At other times criticism rained down, the clergy were mocked, scolded or otherwise put under pressure, but the laity still relied upon them for the mediation of salvation. The laity could even intensify their piety so as to compensate in this way for their deficient spiritual nurture.[17] In the most extreme cases, it was even possible to suppress the clergy entirely and for the laity to assume their place. That is exactly what happened with the Reformation slogan of the "priesthood of all believers". People were no longer dependent on priest, bishop and pope, "for the infant who crawls out of the baptismal font may boast that it has already been consecrated priest, bishop and

---

[16] C. 12, q. 1, c. 7, *Corpus iuris canonici*, ed. Emil Friedberg (Graz, 1959), 1: 678; *Dictionnaire de Droit Canonique* (Paris, 1935ff.), 6: 328ff. Georges Duby presents the division of estates from a social history perspective in this way: "Originally the initiative to create a juristic division between ecclesiastics and laity, and in the process to fuse clerics and monks into a unity, began with the legislation of the peace movement ("the peace of God") of the eleventh century." "Die Laien und der Gottesfrieden", in *Wirklichkeit und höfischer Traum. Zur Kultur des Mittelalters*, ed. G. Duby (Berlin, 1986), 121.

[17] Cf. Bernd Moeller, "Frömmigkeit in Deutschland um 1500", *ARG* 56 (1965): 5-31. Moeller, however, does not stress the compensatory character of this piety and accordingly refers repeatedly to his findings as reason not to accept that there was a late medieval anticlericalism. Most recently , cf. Moeller, "Die Rezeption Luthers in der frühen Reformation", *LuJ* 57 (1990): 67f.

pope."[18] Luther, to be sure, added the qualifier that it was not suitable for everyone to exercise such an office, but it was still fundamentally the case that the spiritual mission of the church was not anchored in the clerical hierarchy but rather in the baptismal grace in which each Christian participated.

What first strikes the eye is the polarization between clergy and laity. Whether this polarization was so extensive before the Reformation era can remain unanswered here; we are concerned only to ascertain the part played in it by the various Reformers, themselves persons of clerical origin.

At the beginning of *The Address to the Christian Nobility of the German Nation*, which was just cited, Luther says unmistakably that the clerical estate has failed, that it "has become entirely inattentive to its duties", and that only the laity are in a position to rescue Christendom.[19] The pope is in the center of the attacks on the clergy. He is the "destroyer of Christendom". At first the expression is that he "almost seems to be an Antichrist", but then Luther speaks clearly: the pope is the "Antichrist" who reigns in the "Devil's nest at Rome".[20] But the pope is not the only object of this devastating condemnation. Luther's target is "the pope and his following", or as he says ironically: "Therefore, let them carry on in their lively way, whether it be pope, bishop, priest, monk or academic, they are the right people, they should persecute the truth, as they have always done."[21] *To the Christian Nobility* incited emotions against the clergy and certainly did not lack an impact among the people.

Luther's attacks against monasticism also had important consequences. Here the "disruptive effect of the Reformation" showed itself particularly clearly.[22] In 1521 he authored the ground-breaking *Judgement on Monastic Vows*, which encouraged numerous cloistered people to break their vows and to leave their orders with good conscience. Later his German paraphrase of this tract, which he presented in the Epiphany sermon of the church postils for 1522, assured a broader reception of his criticism of "the Devil's slimepools and whore houses".[23] Most recently Hans-Christoph Rublack referred to this and to "the catalogue of anticlerical exposes", a veritable catalogue of vices with detailed examples and arguments that could hardly have been more forcible and massive. He shows that the theological grounding of the critique of monasticism, and particularly the anticlerical

---

[18] *WA* 6. 408.
[19] *WA* 6. 404.
[20] *WA* 6. 423, 434, 453.
[21] *WA* 6. 469.
[22] Cf. Bernhard Lohse, "Luthers Kritik am Mönchtum", *Evangelische Theologie* 20 (1960): 413.
[23] *WA* 8. 325.

sallies, were taken up and underscored in the reception process.[24] "Thus we have what belongs to Herod and Christ, two spiritual governments, one unbelieving, the other believing."[25] The polarization of the clerical and lay estates — Rublack registers even an "aggressively anticlerical and anti-monastic" attitude on the part of the Reformer[26] — is not of a merely incidental but of a fundamental nature. "[The monks] are the ones through whose works the kingdom of the Antichrist is fortified."[27]

This polarization was also advanced by others. Franz Günther and Thomas Müntzer became engaged in an anticlerical struggle against the Franciscan monks in Jüterbog in 1519, and Sylvius Egranus and Müntzer picked a fight with the mendicants in Zwickau in 1520-21.[28] The *Prague Manifesto* of 1521 is a document saturated with anticlericalism, in which Müntzer proclaims the apocalyptic division between the damned priests and the elect.[29] Simon Reuter, whose clerical origin is likely but not absolutely proven, expressed the polarization in another manner. In his pamphlet, *Against the Priests of Baal* (1523), he wrote as follows: "In brief, we want to present this great multitude of so very careful priests as of the same party with Judas the betrayer of the Lord. And we, as the other party, want to look freely into the hearts of these esteemed, faithful children, drenched in the gospel."[30] Judas Iscariot becomes the "advocate and spokesman" of the clerical party, which passes up no opportunity to delude the laity and to make a big profit from the cult of Mary and the saints. Opposed to the clerical party stands the evangelical party which sees through all this. As a total antithesis to the monastic ethic, the ex-Dominican Jakob Strauss developed a fraternal ethic which could not be equaled for decisiveness. In the early course of his turn to the Reformation in Hall in Tyrol, he attacked expressions of clericalism, including that of the semi-clerical confraternities, which, he said, were "created and established by misled priests and monks." To these confraternities he opposed the "great brotherhood" taught and led by Christ. By this he meant the worshipping congregation or the community of daily living, in which everything takes place according to the principle of "brotherly love" and all goods are "common" to all: clerical hierarchy

---

[24] Hans-Christoph Rublack, "Zur Rezeption von Luthers De votis monasticis iudicium", in *Reformation und Revolution*, ed. R. Postel, F. Kopitzsch (Stuttgart, 1989): 224-37, esp. 233ff.

[25] *WA* 10 I. 625.

[26] Rublack, "Rezeption", 230.

[27] *WA* 8. 329.

[28] Gerhard Brendler, ed., *Der Lutheraner Müntzer. Erster Bericht über sein Auftreten in Jüterbog. Verfaßt von Franziskanern anno 1519* (Berlin, 1989).

[29] *SUB*, 491-511.

[30] Simon Reuter, *Wider die Baalspfaffen*, in Laube 2: 793.

and tutelage (by a "patron or guardian") are set in opposition to fraternal community and mutual responsibility.[31]

Ulrich Zwingli, too, in his *Exposition and Principles of the Articles* (1523), spoke out clearly against the clerical "estate", that opposed God "for the sake of cowls, special status, misuse of wealth and power".[32] The clergy's claim to dominance was energetically rejected. Wherever this occurs the opposing fronts are particularly clear and the Reformation can take off. Besides that, one also finds with Zwingli a disparaging judgement about monasticism. So it soon became clear to all Zurich burghers that Zwingli, a one-time papal pensioner, had transformed himself into a Reformer.

The biting, satirical criticism of Eberlin von Günzburg also was kindled by his sense that the clergy was always grabbing for power. "All priests are just as smart as their ancestors, the apes", mocked the run-away Franciscan Observant:

> The manner of the ape still attaches itself to them; they want to present themselves as normal people but it ill suits them, just as human gestures are badly suited for an ape. The apes want to associate with princes and noblemen and through them attain higher status, and it worked out successfully for them as one sees at the present.[33]

For Eberlin, too, it was no casual inspiration to single out the clergy for such strong attack, since he was also convinced that two "parties" confronted each other: the papist and the evangelical.[34]

The above are only some of the examples that could have been cited. Basically all former clerics who crossed over to the side of the Reformation participated in the process of polarization: from Martin Bucer, Andreas Karlstadt and Sebastian Franck through the Swiss and South German Anabaptists to the Anabaptist leaders in the Netherlands. If Bucer once contrasted the "apostles of the Antichrist" with the "apostles of Christ", Menno Simons, too, later juxtaposed in an elaborate contrast the characteris-

---

[31] *Ein kurtz christenlich untherricht von dem besondern erdichten pruderschafften denen von hal im inthal von doctor Jacob Straus tzu gesant, in dem du leichtlich vernemen magst, wie unchristenlich in denen bruderschafften wider got und den nechtsten geirt wirt* (1522), Köhler, Fiche 171/469, unpaginated: 2, 3. Recently Strauss' anticlericalism has been referred to as "the center point that organizes [his] network of arguments" by Christoph Wiebe, "Die Stellung des Jacob Strauss innerhalb der reformatorischen Bewegung", unpublished academic paper, Heidelberg, 1988, 56.

[32] Ulrich Zwingli, *Auslegen und Gründe der Schlussreden*, Laube 2: 876 (article 34).

[33] Eberlin von Günzburg, *Mich wundert, dass kein Geld im Land ist*, Laube 2: 1127f. Cf. Geoffrey L. Dipple, "Woe unto you, Stomachpreachers, Cheesbeggars and Hypocrites: Antifraternalism and Reformation Anticlericalism", Ph.D. Diss. Queens Univ., Kingston, 1991.

[34] Ibid., 1133.

tics of the "church of the Antichrist" and those of the "church of Christ".[35] He used what amounted to a negative ecclesiology in order to develop a positive one and present it with conviction. The polarization of clergy and laity was developed in its complete logic.

IV

The process of polarizing clergy and laity meant more than only a clarification of the opposing fronts in the battle for the renewal of Christendom. Polarization also brings about an effect: motion, gestures, deeds. When reproaches are formulated so sharply and relentlessly, they not only contribute to the clarification of ideas and feelings, they compel action and often they provoke violence.

Luther gave the decisive impetus to the flight from the cloister of many monks and nuns even before the appearance of his writing, *Judgement on Monastic Vows,*[36] although with that publication he accelerated the desertion of the monasteries. He advised numerous regular clergy to renounce obedience to their superiors, to break their vows and to shape their lives anew. Here polarization produced its first fruit. It was even recommended to parents to remove their children from the cloisters.[37] Possibly Luther instigated three burghers of Torgau to free the nuns from a neighboring Cistercian cloister. He sheltered some of them temporarily in his Wittenberg cloister and defended the deed of freeing them with the writing *Cause and Reply, that Maidens May Forsake the Cloister in a Godly Manner* (1523): "that they should be advised and helped to escape the cloisters; that their souls should be torn away, led, stolen and robbed from [the cloisters] in any way possible, regardless of whether a thousand oaths and vows were sworn."[38] A report by the abbess Caritas Pirckheimer shows what dramatic consequences such a quickly circulated writing could have. She describes how in 1525 some townswomen broke into the Clares cloister in Nuremberg in order to take their daughters who resided there back home against their wills. Like "fierce wolves and she-wolves", they invaded the

---

[35] Martin Bucer, *Dass sich selbst niemand, sondern anderen leben soll,* Laube 2: 914; Hans-Jürgen Goertz, "Der fremde Menno Simons. Antiklerikale Argumentation im Werk eines melchioritischen Täufers", *MGB* 42 (1985): 24-42, esp. 36.

[36] Helmar Junghans, "Die Ausbreitung der Reformation von 1517 bis 1539", in *Das Jahrhundert der Reformation in Sachsen. Festgabe zum 450jährigen Bestehen der Evangelisch-Lutherischen Landeskirche Sachsens,* ed. H. Junghans (Berlin, 1989), 41.

[37] *WA* 10 I. 641.

[38] *WA* 11. 396f. Cf. Heinz-Meinholf Stamm, *Luthers Stellung zum Ordensleben* (Wiesbaden, 1980), 61f.

cloister and moved among the "dear lambs".[39] She wrote in a letter that she "almost cried her eyes out as the children were taken away from her by violence. And it affected her especially that the mothers behaved so violently."[40] The women achieved their purpose with agitation followed by direct action.

Usually refusal was one consequence of polarization: refusal to participate in the mass or refusal to follow commands of the clergy such as performing auricular penance or observing fasts. In many localities the breaking of fast regulations expanded to become a calculated provocation of the Catholic clergy; likewise the refusal to render tithes to the cloisters.[41] The attack on celibacy was also a provocation against the Catholic clergy. Karlstadt was the first who committed himself to the marriage of priests, as early as 1521 in his writing *That Priests May and Should Take Wives*. Others followed him. The first cleric to marry was Bartholomäus Bernhard, the Provost at Kemberg.

In Luther's own case it may be observed that the transition from refusal of obedience to demonstrative agitation was a fluid one. When he went with students and colleagues out the Elster Gate and threw the papal bull threatening excommunication, together with the canon law, into the flames of a hastily constructed bonfire, that could surely be understood as an anticlerical act: in contempt of the authority of the pope and the whole hierarchy of the church of Rome. The book of the Antichrist was rejected, the book of Christ on the contrary held in honor.

This polarization had direct consequences for the behavior and action of many people. The authority of the Catholic clergy was undermined and the convention of having always to approach them respectfully was broken down. They were laughed at and mocked, scolded and physically attacked. Before it came to the most extreme step of violence against persons, action was often at first only taken against "things". In this way the departing monks wrecked the chapel in the Wittenberg Augustinian cloister, and the burghers in numerous other places smashed images, plundered cloisters or torched chapels. The magic spell that attached itself to the rites of the church was broken. The images, the sacraments and the spiritual persons were demystified. Once the magic was lost there was no longer a need for priests. As Müntzer wrote, no more tricks would be played "under the little

---

[39] *Caritas Pirckheimer — Quellensammlung*, vol. 2, *Die "Denkwürdigkeiten" der Caritas Pirckheimer (aus den Jahren 1524-1528)*, ed. Josef Pfanner (Landshut, 1962), 80. The description of violent actions appears on p. 83.

[40] Caritas Pirckheimer, *Ein Lebensbild aus der Zeit der Reformation*, introduction by E. Iserloh, 5th ed. (Münster, 1982), 165; cf. Gerhard Pfeiffer, ed., *Quellen zur Nürnberger Reformationsgeschichte* (Nuremberg, 1968), 430, 432.

[41] Fast, "Reformation durch Provokation" (n. 10 above), 86; James M. Stayer, "Anfänge des Täufertums im reformierten Kongregationalismus", in Goertz, *Umstrittenes Täufertum*, 27-33.

hat".[42] Now the priests received a final blow. When it came to attacks on spiritual persons, occasionally everything proceeded with a strange logic: in connection with a worship service in Zwickau — on St. Stephen's Day — the congregation chased a Catholic priest from the church and threw dung and stones at him (this priest had previously denounced Müntzer and he was now in church, probably seeking new incriminating material or as a challenge to his colleagues).[43] Obviously stirred up about the wicked stoning of the apostle by the godless heathen — that is what would have been spoken about on this day — they spotted one of the godless in their own church and took revenge on him in exactly the same way. Whether Müntzer called on them to do this, or whether it was a spontaneous actualization of a biblical narrative which came to the worshippers by itself, can no longer be ascertained. In any case this incident shows how much pressure there was for the word to become deed — in a truly ritualized manner. The biblical account was carried over into the present and dramatically acted out. There were other episodes of the same sort. Anabaptists in Zurich, Münster and Amsterdam rioted, ran through the alleys and into the squares and cried out "woe, woe" over the unrepentant cities.[44] Shortly before Lent, during carnival time, a pro-Reformation priest rode into church on an ass, just like Jesus into Jerusalem, very probably catching the priest and congregation at the altar by surprise.[45] And in still another case Peter Flötner depicted the "new" passion of Christ in a woodcut: the suffering of the Lord under the contemporary clergy;[46] indeed, even earlier Luther's journey to Worms had been presented in analogy to the stations of Jesus' passion on the Mount of Olives.[47] In this manner Reformation history was dramatized and transfigured as salvation history. Remembering the history of salvation as described in the Bible unleashed Reformation energies.

However, there were not only creeping transitions from word to deed. Physical acts of aggression were retrospectively justified, also by the

---

[42] *SUB*, 208.

[43] Hans-Jürgen Goertz, *Thomas Müntzer. Mystiker, Apokalyptiker, Revolutionär* (Munich, 1989), 62f.

[44] Cf. Fritz Blanke, "Die Propheten von Zollikon (1525). Eine vergessene Szene aus der Täufergeschichte", *MGB* 9 (1952): 2-10.

[45] Gess, *Akten und Briefe*, 1: 294, no. 321 (21 March 1522).

[46] Peter Flötner, "Die neue Passion Christi, Holzschnitt um 1530/35", in M. Geisberg, *The Single-Leaf Woodcut 1500-1550*, rev. and ed. W. L. Strauss (New York, 1974), vol. 3, no. G 823-24. Hans-Jürgen Goertz, "'Bannwerfer des Antichrist' und 'Hetzhunde des Teufels'. Die antiklerikale Spitze der Bildpropaganda in der Reformation", *ARG* 82 (1991): 5-38.

[47] *Passion D. Martin Luthers durch Marcelleum beschrieben* (Augsburg, 1521), Köhler, Fiche 1566/4061. Bob Scribner, "Luther-Legenden des 16. Jahrhunderts", in *Martin Luther. Leben-Werk-Wirkung*, ed. G. Vogler, et al. (Berlin, 1983), 380f.

Reformers, and this in its turn encouraged or incited new aggressions. This happened, for example, in Karlstadt's writing *On Getting Rid of Images* (1522), in Zwingli's defense of the fast violators, *On Choice and Freedom of Foods* (1522), and in the Anabaptists' reference to the biblical model upon which they grounded their commission for missionary preaching in alleys, corners and squares. They imagined themselves following in the footsteps of the apostles and biblical messengers. Neither consecration nor installation into an office but the consciousness of standing in the succession of Christ and the apostles was the decisive thing for them. When it came to establishing a foundation for a new connection with the sacraments, one also could call upon biblical patterns. The communion was no longer received in front of the altar from the hand of the priest, instead people passed bread and wine to one another at a table. And infants were not carried to baptism by a priest, but instead adults were baptized on confession of faith in private houses, in the river or by the lake: these were anticlerical signs stimulated by bible reading. The "priest-ridden customs of the Antichrist" were abhorred and the "customs of the apostles" were restored.[48]

These examples, which could easily be multiplied, show that the verbal polarization of clergy and laity was not a self-contained phenomenon but unleashed a dynamic that led to concrete changes. Hardly a place where evangelical preachers appeared failed to witness anticlerical actions. It can be said that anticlericalism belonged to the etiology of the Reformation. In this way in a short time a climate developed that not only brought the Catholic clergy more and more into discussion — one could literally talk of an anticlerical public opinion[49] — but at the same time brought about the mobilization of movements that struggled for a renewal of Christendom. Anticlericalism was an important hinge that made possible the transition from the Reformation word to the Reformation deed. If the Reformation is to be regarded not only as a theological phenomenon but above all and primarily as a historical phenomenon, then anticlericalism contributed decisively to the mobilization of Reformation movements and to the Reformation's taking on a historical shape.

V

In the Epiphany sermon from the church postils of 1522 Luther remarked, "What a tangled and tenuous mess the clergy is!"[50] Here he not only

---

[48] Leonhard von Muralt and Walter Schmid, eds., *Quellen zur Geschichte der Täufer in der Schweiz*, vol. 1, *Zürich* (Zurich, 1952), 16: "brüch der apostlen" — "dess entchristen pfäffischen bruch".

[49] On the Reformation and public opinion, cf. Rainer Wohlfeil, *Einführung in die Geschichte der deutschen Reformation* (Munich, 1982), 123-33.

[50] " ... wie gantz vorwyrrett, bodenloß ding das geystlich weßen ist." WA 10 I. 700,22.

produced a theological judgement on the clergy generally but also contended with his own monastic past. The attack on the clergy was among other things — and perhaps first of all — a settling of accounts with the false orientation towards life that he had now overcome, an attack on the strenuous, exhausting piety of works. In contrast to the anticlericalism of the laity, this anticlericalism did not grow out of experience with other clergy (for instance, drunken and immoral monastic brothers) but from horror at his own failures before God and men. It was the product of a painful but redemptive metamorphosis: "my tribulations have brought me to this point."[51] This anticlericalism, like Luther's theology generally, had an existential starting point.

When Karlstadt exchanged his clerical vestments for the gray garb of the peasant and went into the countryside as "Brother Andreas", it was more than a mere anticlerical insult against those who continued to display their clerical habit.[52] It was an act in which he freed himself from the image of the cleric and experienced himself in a new environment as something different, as a brother among brothers. Karlstadt was not an isolated instance. For example, a pro-Reformation priest at Döbeln in Thuringia was reported to have said that "bishops, priests, monks and others in long robes are all rogues; vestments and official robes don't count for anything; it is a completely indifferent matter what sort of dress one wears." The account continues: "He always went about in a gray riding coat with a long knife that reached to the ground; but when he wanted to preach the organist lent him a long robe."[53] That was his way of ordering his life anew out of an existential need. Balthasar Hubmaier, once the renowned pilgrimage preacher at the "Beautiful Mary" in Regensburg, emphatically directed anticlerical reproach against his own previous life in the Old Church:

> I confess honestly that I have sinned against heaven and against God, not only with my sinful life which I led among you full of arrogance, whoring and worldly luxury contrary to the teaching of Christ, but also with false, unfounded and godless teaching, in which I instructed, nurtured and initiated you outside of the Word of God, particularly, as I still very well remember, that I have spoken a lot of useless trifles about infant baptism, vigils, saints' days, purgatory, masses, idols, bells, organs, pipes, indulgences, processions, confraternities, sacrifices, singing and chanting.[54]

---

[51] *WATR* 1. no. 352.

[52] Cf. Ulrich Bubenheimer, "Andreas Rudolff Bodenstein von Karlstadt: sein Leben, seine Herkunft und seine innere Entwicklung", in *Andreas Bodenstein von Karlstadt 1480-1541. Festschrift der Stadt Karlstadt zum Jubiläumsjahr 1980*, ed. W. Merklein (Karlstadt, 1980), 5-58. Cf. Calvin A. Pater, *Karlstadt as the Father of the Baptist Movements: The Emergence of Lay Protestantism* (Toronto, 1984), 64-8.

[53] Gess, *Akten und Briefe*, 1: 220, no. 267 (4 Dec. 1521).

[54] Heinold Fast, ed. *Der linke Flügel der Reformation. Glaubenszeugnisse der Täufer, Spiritualisten und Antitrinitarier* (Bremen, 1962), 37f.; *Quellen zur*

And later Menno Simons, too, expressed himself in the same sense: "I thought back over my own impure, fleshly life, as well as over my hypocritical teaching and idolatry, that I carried on daily for the sake of appearances without inner inclination and to the vexation of my soul."[55] The "old creature" was dissolved by the "new creature". Anticlericalism is a remembrance of a fundamental biographical rupture.

The existential anchoring of anticlericalism accounts for the special engagement with which the former clergyman worked for an "improvement of life" and a renewal of Christendom. The laity were engaged, too. Still, the sharpness, the relentlessness, the wealth of verbal inspiration and the theological depth that the former clergy brought to anticlericalism were hardly attained by the laity. In concluding we shall take a short look at the theological assimilation of anticlericalism, looking at the cases of Luther, Müntzer and Michael Sattler.

There can be no doubt that Luther's anticlericalism grew out of the center of his Reformation theology. The justice which God imputes to a man annuls any mediation of salvation through a priest. Christ is the priest who has sacrificed himself for the salvation of mankind and further sacrifices are not necessary.[56] All other detailed foundations that Luther cited in order to undergird his attack on the priests and monks are tributary to this Christological argument which rings out as early as his lecture on the Epistle to the Hebrews of 1517/18: the true priest is on one side and the false priests on the other.[57] When we take into account that anticlericalism is anchored in the center of his theology, it is understandable why Luther could not forego his public attack on the clergy.

> Many say, one ought to spare the clergy, not scold or chastise, but honor and excuse them. Yes, I ought better to be silent if they were only very bad on their own account and destroyed only themselves. But their government destroys the whole world. Whoever keeps silent and does not risk his body and life in this matter is no proper Christian, does not love his neighbor's salvation as his own. If I could only tear the souls from hell's judgement, I would indeed be more moderate in my scolding.[58]

The works righteousness of cloister people opposes the righteousness of faith: "They are the ones through whose works the kingdom of the

---

Geschichte der Täufer, vol. 9, *Balthasar Hubmaier. Schriften*, ed. Gunnar Westin, Torsten Bergsten (Gütersloh, 1962), 108; cf. English trans. in H. Wayne Pipkin, John H. Yoder, eds., *Balthasar Hubmaier: Theologian of Anabaptism* (Scottdale, Penn., 1989), 83. Cf. Hans-Jürgen Goertz, *Die Täufer. Geschichte und Deutung*, 2nd ed. (Munich, 1988), 43-75, esp. 47-51.

[55] Fast, *Der linke Flügel*, 154f.

[56] *WA* 10 I. 720.

[57] Martin Brecht, *Martin Luther. Sein Weg zur Reformation 1483-1521* (Stuttgart, 1981), 217.

[58] *WA* 10 I. 665f.

Antichrist is fortified", or again, "The priests hurl the ban for the Antichrist; they are the devil's bloodhounds."[59] From the standpoint of anti-clericalism's connection with his theological center it can be explained why Luther took such a deep fright after the priest riots in Erfurt; when he had to recognize that the anticlerical agitation would end in rebellion and uprising. Hence he could likewise warn against the practical consequences of anticlericalism on the basis of justification by faith, the center of his Reformation theology. He rejected the works which were supposed to achieve a renewal with force. He said that as early as his Erfurt sermon on his way to Worms and he repeated it in his *Faithful Admonition* of 1522.[60] To repeat, he turned against acts of anticlerical violence but not against an anticlerical standpoint. To be sure that was difficult for the laity to understand. Rather, for them the practical consequences of verbal agitation became paramount; nuanced theological arguments did not want to stay in their heads. For them Luther actually was the club-swinging *Hercules Germanicus*, as he was depicted in the woodcut of Hans Holbein the Younger (1522), in which he had not only felled Aristotle, Thomas Aquinas, Duns Scotus and others but was also about to slay a monk. He had already enchained the pope and hung him from his own nose, as a trophy. This woodcut did not express Luther's self-understanding — or if it did, then only in a very figurative sense.[61] So the critique which was possibly expressed in this woodcut cannot really touch him. Luther rather trusted that Christian faith would annihilate the pious appearance with which the clergy had misleadingly surrounded itself, and believed that under the impression of evangelical preaching the clergy would soon entirely disappear without added human assistance.[62] Luther reckoned upon the loss of credibility of the first estate and its self-dissolution, perhaps under governmental supervision.

In his own way Thomas Müntzer, too, anchored anticlericalism in the center of his theological thought. Already in 1521 in Prague he confessed to having exerted himself with particular diligence from his youth onward to know "how the holy, invincible Christian faith was founded." But no "pitch-smeared priest" or "spirit-feigning monk" had spoken about that. The clergy have failed and have led no one properly to the "practice of faith".[63] In the situation of anticlerical controversy Müntzer appropriated mystical ideas in order to construct from them the counter-type to that of the priest:

---

[59] *WA* 8. 329; *WA* 19. 11.

[60] *Ein Sermon auf dem Hinwege gen Worms zu Erfurt gethan* (1521), *WA* 7. 803-13; *Eine Treue Vermahnung zu allen Christen, sich zu hüten vor Aufruhr und Empörung* (1522), *WA* 8. 670-87.

[61] Cf. Werner Hofmann, ed., *Luther und die Folgen für die Kunst* (Munich, 1982), 158f.

[62] *WA* 10 I. 666, 672.

[63] *SUB*, 491, 495.

the layman who was seized by the divine Spirit and restored into the "order of God".[64] The priest no longer has divine authority at his disposal, rather now only the layman, who has suffered through the work of God in his innards, is filled with the divine Spirit after painful purification and now can go on to take over the lordship of this world in harmony with the Creator. The elect person, deliberately conceived in opposition to the damned priest, is the fundamental content of Müntzer's theology. The construction of this theology follows the style of anticlerical struggle with its image and counter-image, type and counter-type. Still, Müntzer used not only the mystical tradition but also the apocalyptic mood of the time to interpret and to advance the anticlerical controversy of his days — so much so that soon the Wittenberg Reformers and the temporal princes were added by him to the clerical front and consigned to the judgement of God. Hence a great deal about Müntzer is explainable from the anticlerical situation: the laicist theology, extraordinarily oriented to religious subjectivity; the sharp dualisms that put the godless and damned on the one side, the laity and the elect on the other; and the revolutionary undertaking to fight for and win the lordship over this world for the elect. Müntzer had shaped anticlericalism into a theologically grounded reform program and thus in a special way lent his voice to the revolutionary movement of the "common man".

Michael Sattler, onetime prior of the Benedictine monastery, St. Peter in the Black Forest, probably went over to the early Anabaptists after rebellious peasants defied the canons who ran his cloister and the monks left it.[65] He later described his turning away from monasticism in his trial at Rottenburg:

> When God called me to testify to his Word, and I read Paul, I considered the unchristian and dangerous estate in which I had been, in view of the pomp, pride, usury and great whoring of the monks and priests, with one of them making a whore of his wife, another of his daughter, the third of a maid. I therefore was converted and took a wife according to the command of God (I Cor. 7:2). For Paul prophesies on the subject to Timothy (I Tim. 4:3): "In the last days it shall come to pass that they will forbid marriage and food, which God has created that they might be enjoyed with thanksgiving."[66]

Not a whole lot is known about Sattler. He is accepted however as the author of the "Fraternal Union" of Schleitheim (1527). At Schleitheim Anabaptists assembled, seeking a new way out of the crisis into which they had come due to the forced suppression of the peasant uprisings; and they tried to solve their problems through a consistent separatism. They wanted

---

[64] *SUB*, 496.

[65] C. Arnold Snyder, *The Life and Thought of Michael Sattler* (Scottdale, Penn., 1984), 59ff. Cf. the critical discussion of Snyder in Klaus Deppermann, "Michael Sattler. Radikaler Reformator, Pazifist, Märtyrer", *MGB* 47-8 (1990-91): 21f.

[66] Otto Clemen, ed., *Flugschriften aus den ersten Jahren der Reformation*, vol. 2 (Leipzig, 1908), 328f.; cf. English trans. in John H. Yoder, ed., *The Legacy of Michael Sattler* (Scottdale, Penn., 1973), 72, 82-3.

to separate themselves from everything "that has not been united with our God and Christ." Meant were "all popish and new popish works and idolatry, gatherings, church attendance", hence the worship services of the Catholic clergy as well as the sermons of the Reformed ministers.[67] Meant also was immoral life in public houses and inns, as well as the "guarantees and commitments of unbelief". Whatever may have been referred to in detail with those expressions, the Anabaptists set up a rigorous dualism. They imagined themselves within the "perfection of Christ", and everyone else in their opinion stood "outside" of this perfection.[68] Not the clergy, who advertised that they possessed perfection (in Luther's opinion, too[69]), but the baptized brothers who had entered into the "obedience of faith" were situated in the "perfection of Christ". Not the "segregation", that Zwingli criticized in the monastic clergy, but the "separation" of the brothers was willed by God. Here it is apparent that Wolfgang Capito was not on a false scent when he believed himself to observe in the activities of Sattler the "beginning of a new monkery".[70]

Arnold Snyder has pointed to the connection between the Benedictine Rule and Anabaptist separatism. This connection appears not only in the significance attributed to baptism as the gate of entry into a new community, analogous to the monastic vows. It shows itself also in moral rigorism and understanding of community.[71] Very important is the voluntary union of the brothers, who subject themselves to the power of the ban and choose a "shepherd" from their midst, who provides them with spiritual leadership and edification but does not tower above, much less oppose, their community, since he continues to be bound into it.[72] The congregations were more important than the congregational leaders. That was one consequence of the original anticlerical impulse, a radical form of the "priesthood of all believers". A similar dualism to the one developed at Schleitheim also emerged in Dutch or North German Anabaptism following the suppression of the Anabaptist kingdom in Münster. However, here the stress was not on community but on the prophetic, charismatic leading role of the elders. Therefore an "oligarchy of elders" could be spoken of, which had put itself in the place of the Catholic hierarchy.[73] So the original anticlerical impulse of Anabaptism could be developed in various directions: on one side it

---

[67] Heinold Fast, ed., *Quellen zur Geschichte der Täufer in der Schweiz*, vol. 2, *Ostschweiz* (Zurich, 1973), 30; cf. English trans. in Yoder, *Sattler*, 38.

[68] Fast, *Ostschweiz*, 31; cf. English trans. in Yoder, *Sattler*, 38-9.

[69] Lohse, "Luthers Kritik am Mönchtum" (n. 22 above), 413.

[70] *Quellen zur Geschichte der Täufer*, vol. 7, *Elsass*, 1, *Strassburg 1522-32*, ed. Manfred Krebs and Hans Georg Rott (Gütersloh, 1959), 82.

[71] Snyder, *Sattler*, 170ff. (ch. 9) and 184ff. (ch. 10).

[72] Fast, *Ostschweiz*, 31.

[73] Christoph Bornhäuser, *Leben und Lehre Menno Simons'. Ein Kampf um das Fundament des Glaubens* (Neukirchen, 1973), 104-12.

strengthened the laity, and on the other it gave rise to an elite charisma of leadership. For a time in the beginning among the Hutterites in Moravia there was a distinctive synthesis of both these aspects: laicist community of goods recreated essential traits of the atmosphere of monasticism, under charismatic leadership.

Anticlericalism was the common concern of the Reformers and the movements that they called into existence, or which originated spontaneous-ly with the help of the Reformers' impulse. Various were the ways in which this anticlericalism was theologically grounded, the intensity that it assumed and the outcomes to which it led. Luther represented a moderate anti-clericalism, Müntzer a radical or revolutionary type. Michael Sattler developed a peaceful anticlericalism that in any case did not submit itself to political norms in the manner of Luther. All of them worked not only to get rid of particular grievances but to break the domination of the Catholic clergy and to dissolve that estate entirely (here we have the distinction between the anticlericalism of the Reformation and the anticlericalism of the late Middle Ages). They also worked to take advantage of the gradual loss of clerical function that came with the tendency to demystify ceremonial religiosity and with the interiorization and spiritualization of individual piety; furthermore they sought to direct the corrosive force of this functional loss into courses leading to a renewal of all Christendom. This was a process that began before the Reformation but that was given a new direction by it, and in many respects received its decisive impetus from the Reformation.

All the Reformers exerted themselves to fill the gaps created by the abolition of the clergy. Luther dissolved the identification between person and office in the understanding of the clergy of the Roman church and made a sharp distinction between person and office. In this way a greater space could be opened up for the unfolding of the priestly personality. Eugen Drewermann recently referred to this matter with particular emphasis.[74] Other Reformers, like Müntzer, Karlstadt and the Anabaptists, sought another solution. They did not divide the person and the office, but rather totally laicized the office: not only was each devout Christian theoretically a priest, this was the case as a matter of practice. This could lead to the clericalization of the laity; but it could also create an environment in which the congregation secured its independence over against religious and civil authorities, and was able to maintain it as long as it possibly could. Both the Lutheran and the nonconformist solutions left pre-Reformation anti-clericalism far behind.

Pre-Reformation anticlericalism was not the "powder keg" to which Luther, effective as he was, only needed to light a match in order to explode

---

[74] Eugen Drewermann, *Kleriker. Psychogramm eines Ideals* (Olten, 1989), 745ff.

the medieval church into the air.[75] Not at all! Pre-Reformation anticlericalism was absorbed and surpassed by Luther and numerous allies. The real transformation was effected not by pre-Reformation anticlericalism but by Reformation anticlericalism. Earlier, in his essay "Piety in Germany around 1500", Bernd Moeller wrote of the "diastase" that emerged between clergy and lay people, but he did not employ the concept of anticlericalism in order to describe the reaction of the laity.[76] Nevertheless the diastase that was taking shape was one source of the increasingly allergic attitude of the laity towards clerics of all sorts. Geiler von Kaysersberg spoke of hatred toward priests, and this attitude can certainly be characterized by the concept of "anticlericalism".[77] It is not necessary that this oppositional stance should have had the goal of totally abolishing the clergy. In the framework of a type of religious thought that could conceive of salvation only inside and not outside of the church but which at times could treat the clergy quite disrespectfully (although, or perhaps even because, it relied upon the clergy for mediating help) the concept of anticlericalism certainly makes sense. Here a remark about the use of academic concepts that Paul Veyne has recently introduced into the discussion about historical theory is helpful:

> Historical concepts are [thus] not concepts in a precise sense of the term. They are not complexes of necessarily interconnected elements; instead they are collections of ideas that indeed convey the illusion of conceptual knowledge but are in reality something like generic images.[78]

The concept of "anticlericalism" ought also to be used in this sense of generic images: ideas of a long struggle of the laity against the clergy — sometimes concealed, sometimes open, sometimes expressing itself in criticism, mockery and abuse, at other times in agitation or in acts of violence. Often the motive was only to release pent-up anger, or to call priests and monks to reflection upon themselves in this way. Often anxiety about the laity's own salvation awakened the violent reactions against the clergy, or left flight into excessive religious activity as their only escape.

---

[75] Moeller, "Die Rezeption Luthers" (n. 17 above), 60. One of Moeller's important arguments is that the spiritual function of the pre-Reformation priest did not offer serious cause for criticism. To see how, on the contrary, it was virtually impossible to separate financial and juristic problems from the needs of citizens and rulers for regular cure of souls, and how precisely this spiritual dimension came into the forefront of criticism, cf. Heinz Noflatscher, "Gesellpriester und Kapläne in der Reformation. Das deutsche Haus in Sterzing", in *St. Elisabeth im Deutschhaus zu Sterzing*, ed. Messerschmitt Stiftung (Innsbruck, 1989), 110f.

[76] Moeller, "Frömmigkeit" (n. 17 above), 29.

[77] John Geiler of Kaysersberg, *Die Emeis. Dis ist das buch von der Omeissen vnnd auch Herr der Könnig ich diente gern* (Strasbourg, 1516), 28b.

[78] Paul Veyne, *Geschichtsschreibung — Und was sie nicht ist* (Frankfurt, 1990), 96.

And finally there was the demand to abolish totally the useless but nevertheless pernicious estate.

Historically the movement that was permeated by moderate anticlericalism had the greatest success. It led to the dissolution of the monasteries and the ecclesiastical principalities, initiated the secularization of church property and dissolved the clerical "estate". This anticlericalism, however, did not achieve its original goal of putting into practice the "priesthood of all believers". Ultimately the church was placed under the command of the temporal authorities, which were concerned with peace and order. Confronting the laity a new spiritual elite soon developed that had given up the autonomy of the clerical estate and that had found its way to a different self-understanding, but in many respects had fallen back into the old structures. The laity were led once more, and soon disciplined as well; they were deprived of the opportunities tested in anticlerical struggle to give their own shape to religious life (and to an extent political life as well). A shaping which had been based on primary moral resources originating in anticlerical struggle.[79]

Translated by James M. Stayer

---

[79] Robert Scribner distinguishes three historical phases of anticlericalism: a pre-Reformation, a Reformation and a post-Reformation (intra-Protestant) anticlericalism. "Anticlericalism and the German Reformation", *Popular Culture and Popular Movements in Reformation Germany* (London, 1987), 243-56.

CLERICAL ANTICLERICALISM
IN THE EARLY GERMAN REFORMATION:
AN OXYMORON?

SUSAN C. KARANT-NUNN

Portland State University

Throughout the many and multiplying accounts of the local arrival of Reformation preaching in Germany runs the fact that the earliest bearers of the evangelical tidings often used their positions and rhetorical powers to lambast the clergy. No one seems to have found it astonishing that these clergymen should have attacked their brethren in the profession. Perhaps it is because we historians, having sat in academe for varying numbers of decades, have long since realized that even within a university or a single department, feuds may be carried on among colleagues in an unfortunately vocal and prolonged manner. Perhaps at the human level, clerical anticlericalism need not be questioned. Nevertheless, as part of my assignment for this conference, I am going to question it. I shall confine my treatment to the years of *Wildwuchs* or "wild growth", a label introduced by Franz Lau to designate the high individualism and disorder of the years from 1517 to 1525, a concept that both Professor Goertz and I have defended in print.[1] The preachers were part of that disorder, feeling called on by the same spirit that Martin Luther invoked to speak out, until the so-called "new papists" put a damper on their utterances and enlisted the civil authorities in an effort to obtain quiescence and conformity.[2] As much as possible, I shall avoid radical mystics like Thomas Müntzer and Andreas Bodenstein von Karlstadt,

---

[1] Franz Lau, "Reformationsgeschichte bis 1532", in F. Lau, E. Bizer, *Reformationsgeschichte Deutschlands bis 1555. Ein Handbuch* (Göttingen, 1964), 3-66. Hans-Jürgen Goertz, "Aufstand gegen den Priester. Antiklerikalismus und reformatorische Bewegungen", in *Bauer, Reich und Reformation*, ed. P. Blickle (Stuttgart, 1982), 182-209. In this context, however, Goertz is not specifically treating clerical anticlericalism. Susan C. Karant-Nunn, "What Was Preached in German Cities in the Early Years of the Reformation? *Wildwuchs* Versus Lutheran Unity", in *The Process of Change in Early Modern Europe*, ed. P. N. Bebb, S. Marshall (Athens, Ohio, 1988), 81-96. I am aware of Franz Lau's critical attitude toward the period of *Wildwuchs*; nevertheless, I wish to retain the term as an apt description of the high individualism of the years 1518-1525.

[2] On the concept of "new papists", see Steven E. Ozment, *The Reformation in the Cities* (New Haven, 1975), 151-66.

although whatever their beliefs, both *acted* in ways that supported the pastoral office.[3]

It is a commonplace, accurate and much recited at this conference already, that by 1517 anticlerical traditions ran long and deep. The laity again and again drew a distinction between Christian standards of piety and the lives of many clergymen and nuns. Few people profess difficulty in labeling this lay activity anticlerical. But what if the critics were clerics? I should like to ask whether either during the Middle Ages or during the Reformation era, when clergy made scathing remarks about other clergy, they too were anticlerical. When the Cistercians accused the Cluniacs of self-indulgent departure from the rule of St. Benedict, were they anticlerical? When the theologians of Paris objected to the presence and privileges of the friars, were they anticlerical? Was John Geiler von Kaisersberg (†1510) anticlerical when he frequently lamented the corruption of the clergy?[4] Or Erasmus in his biting satires? When John Colet preached his famous Convocation sermon of 1511, was he anticlerical? Were the august authors of *De emendanda ecclesia*, in their depiction of prelates' immorality, being anticlerical? Were those secular clergy who opposed the incursions of the Jesuits anticlerical?

It is not as helpful as one might think to draw a distinction between clerical office (*Amt*) and incumbent (*Besitzer*). Medieval critics sometimes did demand the eradication of certain clerical offices and not merely the correction of their occupants. The Church labeled the popular critics heretics, however, and succeeded in marginalizing them. This contrasts with much of Germany in the sixteenth century in that it proved impossible to move the dissidents to the periphery of society. In the end, historians, resistant as they are to the blandishments of models, will probably regard categorical conclusions with skepticism and judge each outburst as anticlerical or not based on its particulars and the circumstances that produced it.

All of the examples given stand within a venerable medieval tradition of opposing blatant clerical transgression and exploitation of the laity,[5] and, of resisting innovation that seemed to curtail the perquisites of established parties within the clergy. Is nothing qualitatively different, and thus a departure from this tradition, when we encounter men who took part in the

---

[3] As Goertz notes, Müntzer disputed the need for clergy: "Träume, Offenbarungen und Visionen in der Reformation", in *Reformation und Revolution. Beiträge zum politischen Wandel und den sozialen Kräften am Beginn der Neuzeit*, ed. R. Postel, F. Kopitzsch (Stuttgart, 1989), 179-82.

[4] Jane Dempsey Douglass, *Justification in Late Medieval Preaching*, SMRT 1 (Leiden, 1966; 2nd ed., 1989), 62, 79-80, 94-95, 97-98.

[5] See, for example, "The Reformation of the Emperor Sigismund", in Gerald Strauss, ed. and trans., *Manifestations of Discontent in Germany on the Eve of the Reformation* (Bloomington, Ind., 1971), 3-31, here 8-18, 24.

evangelical movement of which Luther was a paramount exponent? As we well know, much of "To the Christian Nobility of the German Nation" is an attack on one rank or another of the Catholic clergy.[6] What about Johann Eberlin von Günzburg's treatment of the mendicant orders in *Die 15 Bundgenossen 1521*? Similar sentiments permeate his writings:

> The life and profession of monks, priests, nuns, and [faculty of the] universities is in so many respects opposed to God's will, that not even the simplest person on reading the Bible could fail to see how ungodly the [clerical] estate is; and even human reason tells us that this estate is an abomination in the world. ... I want to be your faithful Eckhart and warn you.[7]

When Johann Brenz called monks the monkeys [*Affen*] of the apostles — and by this I think he meant mere imitations, or even worse, caricatures — and the devil's relatives, how was he to be distinguished from earlier critics of monastic deportment?[8] What about Matthias Zell's resolute preaching against the clergy, summarized in his *Christeliche Verantwortung 1523*?[9] William Stafford correctly observes that this summary of Zell's early sermons is "seldom free from bitter anticlerical polemic".[10] Professor Goertz has provided further copious examples in his article, "Aufstand gegen den Priester: Antiklerikalismus und reformatorische Bewegungen".[11]

There is a good deal in the sermons of the *Wildwuchs* preachers that is clearly similar to those of their pre-Reformation counterparts, above all the generously documented recounting of clerical abuse. These catalogs of corruption were an important bridge between the old message and the new. The old message did not simply end and a new begin. Reformation preachers inserted new notes and accents into old songs.

---

[6] *WA* 6. 404-69.

[7] *Alle und yetlichs was stands er ist, sey gewarnet das er keynen pfaffen hindere am ehelichen standt.* (Nuremberg, 1523), no pagination but near the beginning.

[8] Martin Brecht, "Brenz als Zeitgenosse", in *Johannes Brenz 1499-1570. Beiträge zu seinem Leben und Wirken*, ed. G. Schäfer, M. Brecht, *BWKG* 70 (Stuttgart, 1970), 31.

[9] *Christeliche verantwortung ... über Artickel jm vom Bischöfflichem Fiscal daselbs entgegen gesetzt ... MD XXIII* (Strasbourg: Wolfgang Köpfel, for example; other printers also brought it out).

[10] *Domesticating the Clergy: The Inception of the Reformation in Strasbourg 1522-1524* (Missoula, Mont., 1976), 12, see also 5-12, 55. Of interest, too, are the accounts in Miriam Usher Chrisman, *Strasbourg and the Reform* (New Haven, 1967), esp. 81-130; and Marc Lienhard and Jean Rott, "Die Anfänge der evangelischen Predigten in Strassburg und ihr erstes Manifest: Der Aufruf der Karmeliter Tilmann von Lyn (Anfang 1522)", in *Bucer und seine Zeit. Forschungsbericht und Bibliographie*, ed. M. de Kroon, W. Kruger (Wiesbaden, 1976), 54-73.

[11] n. 1 above.

I

One of the characteristic shifts audible before the outbreak of reform is a consequence of the return to original texts, including but not confined to the Bible. Religious humanists had a broader attraction to the works of antiquity before the Reformation than after, when the focus of those who became evangelically committed came to lie more exclusively on Holy Writ. Now preachers justified their harangues with the rediscovered central text, the Word of God. Johann Eberlin raged, "When a person uses the word *pfaff*, he refers to a soulless, godless person, drunk, lazy, greedy, cantankerous and quarrelsome, rascally [*schirmig*], whoring, adulterous, ... for the common man is all heated up against the priests. ... it is a wonder that the people don't stone us to death."[12] In "The Tenth Confederate", Eberlin declared, "All mendicants should be outlawed [*soll man gar abthun*] on pain of death."[13] But before such drastic action could be taken, God's approval was required. In drawing on the Gospel as evidence of divine approval, the preachers stressed what was *not* there more than what was. Zwickau burgomaster Laurentius Bärensprung knew that few Franciscans had existed three hundred years before and that the Bible gave them no validity.[14] Bärensprung had an M.A. from the University of Paris. For others it was enough that nowhere in God's Word was there any evidence of priests, friars, monks, or nuns. These categories of the religious were human inventions and thus departures from God's ordinance. Luther may have launched this line of offense in "To the Nobility of the German Nation", though the conviction existed before. Still, subsequent evangelical preachers often took their cue from him, and many were persuaded of the paramountcy of the Word by Luther's early treatises.[15] The people found scriptural arguments an appealing rationalization of what they had seen more in moral and economic terms before.

The primacy of Scripture need hardly be further discussed here; it extended far beyond the matter of a proper clergy to all areas of human life and belief. Yet year after year, Luther relentlessly applied this fundamental principle to questions concerning clerical propriety. In *De votis monasticis Martini Lutheri iudicium. 1521*, the reformer's basic argument was that

---

[12] *Syben frumm aber trostloss pfaffen klagen ire not, einer dem anderen, vnd ist niemant der sye troste* ... , cited by Heger, *Johann Eberlin von Günzburg* (n. 24 below), 88, n. 38.

[13] Actual title: *Ein klagliche klag an den christlichen Römischen Keyser Karolum von wegen Doctor Luters vnd Vlrich von Hutten. Auch von wegen der Curtisanen vnd Bettel Münch. Das Kayserliche Maiestät sich nit lass sollich leut verfüren* (Speyer: Johann Eckhart, 1521), Mii, known as *Die 15 Bundgenossen*.

[14] Zwickau Stadtarchiv, Ratsprotokolle 1511-15, *1525*, fol. 56.

[15] See Stafford, *Domesticating the Clergy*, 15-16, for Matthias Zell's use of Scripture in his sermons against Catholic clergy in Strasbourg.

"vows do not depend on the Word of God but, on the contrary, oppose the Word of God."[16] In a parallel argument, Martin Bucer stated, "The pope, bishops, abbots, priests, and monks have moved away from the Word of God, which they should serve exclusively."[17] Wenceslaus Linck while still in Altenburg preached that the clergy were obligated to help bear the civic financial burden. He pointed out the clergy's disregard of scriptural directive; indeed he accused them of trying to suppress the Gospel for their private gain.[18] Caspar Guethel, in his Augustinian cowl and cloister in Eisleben, preached against his clerical opponents, "We must observe exclusively the Word and work of God's son, our own master."[19] Such preachers inspired leading citizens of Lutheran towns from 1525 on to carve into the street-side beams and lintels of their half-timbered houses, "Verbum dei manet in aeternum", or simply, "VDMIA".[20]

II

A manifestation of *Wildwuchs* preachers' awareness of their broad lay audience was their publishing of sermons in German. Whereas before the Reformation ecclesiastical opinion censorious of other men of the cloth had been cast in Latin phrases and thereby shielded from public scrutiny and reaction, Luther set a new tone in 1520 when he wrote, albeit necessarily, to the ruling class in the vernacular. Prudence would earlier have dictated restraint. Whether Luther took the decision to appeal to the public, or whether he naively, unreflectingly trod an unknown path, the die was cast, and the masses consumed his anticlerical German treatises as voraciously as those on other topics. The next year, *De votis monasticis* appeared in Latin,

---

[16] *WA* 8. 578; on p. 578 alone, the word *Evangelium* occurs thirteen times. Consult also Hans-Christoph Rublack, "Zur Rezeption von Luthers De votis monasticis iudicium", in *Reformation und Revolution*, ed. Postel and Kopitzsch (n. 3 above), 224-38. Rublack, citing Josef Benzing's *Luther-bibliographie*, 980-84, mentions five German editions in 1521. Curiously none are shown in *VD 16*, 12: 518.

[17] *Martin Bucers deutsche Schriften*, ed. Robert Stupperich, vol. 1: *Frühschriften, 1520-1524* (Gütersloh, 1960), 102. Bucer's works from this period are filled with similar statements.

[18] *Ob die Geystlichen Auch schuldig sein Zinsse, geschoss etc. zu geben und andere gemeyne bürde mit zutragen* (Altenburg, probably 1525), Aii-Aiv.

[19] *Schuczrede widder eczliche ungetzembdte freche Clamanten, wilche die Euangelischen lerer schuldigen, wie das sie eynen newen Glawben predigen. ...* (Wittenberg, 1522), Aii.

[20] Burgomaster Hermann Mühlpfort did this in Zwickau before 1527, as did numerous home owners in Freiberg/Saxony after the introduction of reform there in 1537. Carl C. Christensen discusses this motif, which became a slogan of the Reformation, in his forthcoming book, "Princes and Propaganda: Electoral Saxon Art of the Reformation".

but Justus Jonas immediately set out to translate it.[21] From 1522, Luther's every major statement against the clergy was composed in German and quickly printed. There can no longer have been any doubt about the laity's ready access to these works.[22] That these diatribes were addressed to clergymen, yet written and published in German reveals Luther's thorough awareness of his true audience, the laity.

This rapid shift to German represents nothing less, then, than the preachers' desire to communicate with the laity. The purpose was no longer simply to lament and to inspire sinful clergy to repent; it was also to enlist the laity in the process of compulsion. This was a significant break with earlier critique. The preachers revealed to their public another facet of the Word of God: not alone that which reposes in the sacred Book, available for the perusal of the initiate; but the Word preached aloud and unambiguously for the entire citizenry, the Word put to use remolding human society. I agree with Professor Goertz that "in anticlericalism the Reformation prepared the ground for its own reception and dissemination" among the people.[23]

III

Humanism may have prepared some preachers to accept the authority of texts, above all of the Bible, but the Bible did not absolutely require an attack on clergy. The fervent lay — including magisterial and princely — hatred of clerical exemption and abuse gave the preachers a theme with which to appeal to the populace. Eberlin's biographer, Günther Heger, perceives this link when he says, "Eberlin's pamphlets are genuinely people's pamphlets, written from the people's point of view and for the people. In them the common man finds a voice... ."[24] Many preachers came from an urban middling class and knew full well what was in the minds of their listeners. We must look as much to the laity as to the preachers for an

---

[21] *VD 16*, 12: 518, L7322-L7328.

[22] *Wider den falsch genannten geistlichen stand des Pabsts und der Bischöfe. 1522*, WA 10 II. 105-58, addressed to the bishops themselves; *An die Herren deutsches Ordens, dass sie falsche Keuschheit meiden und zur rechten ehelichen Keuschheit greifen, Ermahnung. 1523*, WA 12. 232-44; *Vom Greuel der Stillmesse. 1525*, WA 18. 22-36; and the later *Von der Winkelmesse und Pfaffenweihe. 1533*, WA 38. 195-256, which Luther drafted in Latin but published in German.

[23] "Aufstand gegen den Priester", 207. See also Loretta Turner Johnson's unpublished Ph.D. dissertation, "An Infinite Clamor: Clerical Anticlericalism in Pre-Reformation England", (University of Nebraska, 1979). Although the setting is somewhat different, Johnson is confident of the role of late medieval sermons critical of the clergy in preparing the populace to accept the Reformation.

[24] *Johann Eberlin von Günzburg und seine Vorstellungen über eine Reform in Reich und Kirche*, Schriften zur Rechtsgeschichte 35 (Berlin, 1985), 45.

explanation of anticlerical topics. Where attendance is voluntary, sermons on all subjects must reflect an interaction between popular concerns and clerical values.[25] Without such reciprocity, preachers' audiences would have vanished in this period before state compulsion was in place.

In a recent article, Bob Scribner has attributed to the early Reformation sermon "an explosive effect" when joined to the widespread hatred of the clergy. He suggests a three-step model of the progression from sermon to action: First, the preacher reveals (*Offenbarung*) to the people the ways and extent to which they have been swindled and betrayed by the clerics. Second, the clergy come to represent to the laity the "personification and concretisation" of the cosmic battle between God and the devil. Third, under homiletic inspiration, the populace rises against the clergy.[26] Other than the possibility that the word *Offenbarung* is too strong — suggesting that but for the preachers, the people would have been unaware of clerical predations — I find this a useful schema, one that can be tested against each detailed concrete setting of popular anticlerical outburst that we are able to document.

In Zwickau prior to the Reformation, the city council tried repeatedly, with limited success, to curtail the jurisdictions and privileges of clerical corporations. Its principal triumph was the acquisition of patronage over the pastorate early in the century. The craftsmen themselves in 1516-1517, in what was essentially a revolt against restrictions on brewing, revealed in their grievances resentment at the vicar's and the Cistercians' serving up beer on their premises, which set them in competition with local taverners.[27] On this particular score, the city councillors were in sympathy with the people but could not curtail the clerics' rights. The main evidence of anticlerical activity in the immediately following years lies in Stephan Roth's notes on preacher Johann Sylvius Egranus's sermons in both Zwickau and Joachimsthal between 1519 and 1522. In 1519 Egranus assailed clerical abuses but defended the role of the priest and the (seven) sacraments. He severely criticized indulgences. During December 1520, just when his hostile colleague Thomas Müntzer occupied the chancel in the other city church, Egranus salted his homilies with anticlerical remarks.[28]

---

[25] Goertz has commented on Luther's response to widespread popular anticlericalism in *Pfaffenhaß und groß Geschrei* (Munich, 1987), 69. This interaction with the people applies to other preachers as well.

[26] R. W. Scribner, "Anticlericalism and the Reformation in Germany", in *Popular Culture and Popular Movements in Reformation Germany* (London, 1987), 243-56, here esp. 250-52. Scribner has written extensively on various aspects of anticlericalism. Among others, see "Preachers and People in the German Towns", in *Popular Culture and Popular Movements*, 122-43.

[27] Zwickau Stadtarchiv, Ax AII 7, Nr. 11.

[28] *Ungedruckte Predigten des Johann Sylvius Egranus (gehalten in Zwickau und Joachimsthal 1519-1522)*, ed. Georg Buchwald (Leipzig, 1911), sermon 1, 1-19;

Thomas Müntzer's arrival in the spring of 1520 shattered the pattern of restraint that had prevailed till then. The councillors were aware of his anticlerical tendencies when they hired him as a temporary preacher. By this date, Martin Luther's opinions on the clergy were in circulation and finding a receptive hearing among the councillors themselves. It is likely that men like the burgomasters Laurentius Bärensprung and Hermann Mühlpfort wanted Müntzer to foment popular antipathy to the clerical establishment, and we know that he did so. He hurled his invective against monastic persons in general, very likely creating open opposition to the powerful Zwickau Franciscans where it had been latent before. Certainly, there is no mention of the Franciscans in the grievances of 1516-1517. While Müntzer did not *cause* anticlerical feeling, he increased, focused, and legitimated it. He jeeringly abandoned Egranus's moderation. A duly examined and employed city preacher tacitly enjoyed official condonation and some prestige. During these months, the gentlemen of the council approved of his performance.

The unseen preacher, whose diatribes and authority reached Zwickau in written form, is, of course, Martin Luther; his impact must not be overlooked even if his most direct audience was the smaller body of literate citizens. We cannot reconstruct these relationships precisely nor depict states of mind with certainty; yet Luther was an "absent presence" who may have reinforced the councillor's broad tolerance of Müntzer's increasingly harsh teachings. Müntzer came to condemn *all* other clergymen in Zwickau, not merely monks and Egranus, and he quickly turned on the councillors themselves. The pastor was in absentia at the time, and there was as yet no vicar.

Surviving records indicate that even after his dismissal, Müntzer's power to move the artisan class continued to be felt. Dissident leaders, whether accurately or not, are nearly always referred to as followers of Müntzer, and not of Niclas Storch, for years afterward. When Scribner's "third moment", that of anticlerical action, arrived during *Fastnacht* 1522, it was surely the people's negative experiences; Luther's, Egranus's, and Müntzer's liberating ideology; and the council's Lutheran frame of mind and political self-interest that combined to promote the destruction of the local Cistercian outpost.

Similarly, in the Saxon silvermining town of Buchholz, we have evidence of very active pro-reform preaching by several dynamic figures in 1524: Friedrich Myconius (Mecum), Gabriel Zwilling, and Wenceslaus Linck.[29] As far as we know, none of their sermons were explicitly anticlerical, but we do not possess a record of the content of most of them; Buchholz is a more opaque case than Zwickau. Evangelical preaching had charged the at-

---

sermon 7, 36-8; sermon 9, 40-2.

[29] Felician Gess, *Akten und Briefe zur Kirchenpolitik Herzog Georgs von Sachsen*, vol. 1 (Leipzig, 1905), no. 692, pp. 699-702.

mosphere. It was evident that change was at hand; the Catholic pastor agreed to resign at about this time. Preaching, even if on other evangelical subjects, made it possible for a "very large number" of miners and young people ritually and rather elaborately to mock the official translation in Meissen of the bones of Bishop Benno. Good Catholic citizens in fact suspected that this ridicule had been inspired by a sermon.[30]

Every outburst of popular anticlerical furor would need to be evaluated to ascertain to what extent preconditioning sermons were to blame. Certainly, the populace was able to demonstrate its antipathy for some clerics and clerical institutions without benefit of preaching. But the interaction between preachers and listeners resembled that between fuel and fire, and authorities were understandably apprehensive even when they hoped that the ensuing blaze would advance their own anticlerical goals. In their origins, clerics', ordinary citizens', and rulers' dominant anticlerical motives differed. The preachers were concerned primarily with religious rectitude, the laity with the direct social and economic effects of clerical abuse, and the magistrates with the consolidation of power. None could have attained its ends without the others. An aspect of the era of *Wildwuchs* is the cooperation of all three groups. The preachers often provided a catalyst and a justification for action. Their willingness to take up the verbal cudgel against their brothers was often indispensable to the processes of reform.

IV

Evangelical preachers broke with their predecessors in the extent to which they demanded the outright *eradication* of all religious corporations that had a deleterious effect upon the common weal. Popular outrage, biblicism, political advantage, and economic pressure came together in the demand that above all, mendicant friars be outlawed, followed by the only somewhat less oppressive monks, excess priests, and nuns. Eberlin, an admirer of Thomas More, and in 1521 not yet moderated by an encounter with Martin Luther, was not unusual in calling for the abolition of mendicancy. The *Wildwuchs* preachers were close to agreement here. The cities may have felt the presence and pressure of the friars more than of the monks, but, as Henry Cohn has reminded us, the moment one left town, the most exploitive clerical presence was undoubtedly the traditional monks with their extensive

---

[30] L. Bartsch, "Kirchliche und schulische Verhältnisse der Stadt Buchholz während der ersten Hälfte des 16. Jahrhunderts", *Beiträge zur Geschichte der Stadt Buchholz* 3 (1897): 24-72; 4 (1899): 73-216, here esp. 62-87, 205-16. See Bob Scribner's analysis of this parody in "Reformation, Carnival and the World Turned Upside Down", *Social History* 3 (1978): 234-64, here 237-38; reprinted in Scribner, *Popular Culture and Popular Movements*, 70-101.

and far-flung estates.[31] In suburbs and countryside, people responded well to the inclusion of monks among those who should be dealt with harshly.[32]

When evangelical preachers advocated the abolition, not just the correction, of certain types of clergy, they were to that degree genuinely anticlerical; in this respect the concept of clerical anticlericalism is not an oxymoron.

Curiously, a number of these very preachers had been, and for a time remained, mendicants, the very sort of clergyman whose legitimacy, using the scriptural criterion, they challenged. How did they regard themselves during this period of disorder? Looking back later, Luther admitted to being horrified when he recalled how he and others had held private masses (*Winkel Messe*). He had done it, he said, out of ignorance.[33] Martin Bucer explained that despair had driven him to become a monk.[34] These years were ones of personal crisis and transformation for all our conscientious anticlerics. They sensed the incompatibility of their new convictions with their old self-image. They heard Luther, examined the Gospel, and could not refrain from applying what they found there to themselves as well as to society. Their redefinition of self was not complete before they mounted the chancel. In the course of preaching, they drew themselves toward a private turning point, with all its discomfiture, from which there was no going back.

In urging upon their hearers and readers an earthly future cleansed and reordered by the Word of God, they were not characteristically moderate. Luther asked in 1522, "Tell me, isn't that a strict command from the high Majesty that a preacher is duty bound, at the risk of his soul's salvation, to punish the godless?"[35] People expected a certain amount of hyperbole when they listened to sermons, and they got it. The preachers saw themselves as small Jeremiahs, as the mouthpieces of God in a needy world, as the articulators of his Word and the agents of the Holy Spirit, by whose working the Word took root in people's hearts. They were indispensable. So central does the preaching function become within the reformed church that we historians have to look closely at the terms of appointment of some clerics to determine whether they were officially pastors or preachers. The distinction between the two was much smaller after the Reformation than

---

[31] Henry J. Cohn, "Anticlericalism in the German Peasants' War 1525", *PaP* 83 (1979): 3-31, here esp. 17-9; refer also to H. J. Cohn, "Reformatorische Bewegungen und Antiklerikalismus in Deutschland und England", in *Stadtbürgertum und Adel in der Reformation*, ed. W. J. Mommsen et al. (Stuttgart, 1979), 309-29.

[32] Karl Czok, "Zur sozialökonomischen Struktur und politischen Rolle der Vorstädte in Sachsen und Thüringen im Zeitalter der deutschen frühbürgerlichen Revolution", *Wissenschaftliche Zeitschrift der Karl-Marx-Universität Leipzig, Gesellschafts- und Sprachwissenschaftliche Reihe* 24 (1975), 53-68.

[33] *Von der Winkelmesse*, WA 38. 249.

[34] *Martin Bucers deutsche Schriften*, 1: 160.

[35] *Wider den falsch genannten geistlichen Stand*, WA 10 II. 108.

before it.[36] Before 1518 many pastors per se were absent from their parishes and employed vicars — often weak, irresolute, and non-preaching vicars — to fulfill their pastoral obligations. Both mendicants and official preachers were able to take advantage of this weakness at the ecclesiastical center of the parish.

Our *Wildwuchs* evangelical activists rarely envisioned doing away with either preaching positions or pastorates. They did not generally advocate a Christian polity led by inspired and self-appointed laity. They were never categorically anticlerical. To be sure, the thought of Martin Luther on this subject underwent a distinct evolution during the 1520s, hastened along by popular enthusiasm for men like Müntzer and Karlstadt as well as by the Peasants' War. But certain early, utopian, and untried utterances aside, the most sweeping anticlerics desired the retention of a recognizable, tradition-defined clergy.[37] Despite his initial over-sanguine statements in favor of each congregation selecting freely from its midst its own spiritual leader, and despite his opposition to a formal rite of ordination until in the mid-1530s Elector Johann Friedrich compelled him to change at least his public mind, Luther enthusiastically supported the pastorate. Neither early nor late in his career was he an unqualified anticlerical. In "On the Freedom of a Christian" he wrote,

> What is the difference, you ask, between priests and laymen in the Christian religion if all are priests? The answer is that an injustice has occurred in connection with the little words *priest*, *parson*, *cleric*, and the like: they have been removed from the common masses into a small group that today is called the clerical estate. The Holy Scriptures make no other distinction than to call those learned or ordained individuals who are meant to preach Christ, faith, and Christian freedom to others, by the name of *ministros*, *servos*, or *oeconomos*,

---

[36] It is astonishing, for example, how often Thomas Müntzer is identified as having been a pastor in Zwickau, as, in recent years, in Steven E. Ozment, *Mysticism and Dissent: Religious Ideology and Social Protest in the Sixteenth Century* (New Haven, 1973), 61; Eric W. Gritsch, *Thomas Müntzer, a Tragedy of Errors* (Minneapolis, 1989), 24; and Abraham Friesen, *Thomas Muentzer, a Destroyer of the Godless: The Making of a Sixteenth-Century Religious Revolutionary* (Berkeley, 1990), 3, 73.

[37] Luther wrote in 1539 in *Von den Concilijs vnd Kirchen*, "One has got to have bishops, pastors, or preachers who publicly and as their special duty preside over, distribute, and practice the aforementioned four pieces or sacred tasks [preaching God's word, baptising, administering the Eucharist, and having the power to ban] on behalf of and in the name of the church, but even more because Christ so ordained. ... He made some men apostles, some prophets, evangelists, teachers, rulers, etc. For the masses can't do such things but must direct someone else or have someone else directed to do them. What would become of us if each person wanted to speak or distribute [the sacraments] and no one would yield to another? It must be given to one person alone to preach, baptise, absolve, and dispense the sacrament; the others must be satisfied and give their consent." *WA* 50. 632-33.

that is, servant, attendant, and steward. For even though we are all priests alike, we could not all serve or be stewards and preach.[38]

Or let us consider the minutely detailed, if somewhat fanciful, list of the clerical ungodly compiled by Franz Lambert. Lambert referred specifically to Luther's *De votis monasticis*.[39] He proceeded to list ninety-four classes of religious, the habits of which he described when labels failed him. He began with "the sect of the popes", which over time had perverted itself into "an anti-Christ".[40] He moved on to the cardinals, "false patriarchs", "false archbishops", "false bishops", canons, "false priests" ("namely, those anointed and tonsured"), "the sect of non-evangelical deacons", "the sect of subdeacons", "the sect of acolytes", and he continued on to every type of monk, friar, and nun he had ever heard of.[41] As inclusive as his condemnation was, major gaps remained: non-false, which was to say *genuine* patriarchs, *genuine* archbishops, *genuine* bishops, *true* priests, and *evangelical* deacons. Besides this, Lambert did not refer to the office of pastor at all. By the process of elimination, we see that Lambert looked forward to the retention of a reformed — New-Testament-oriented and simplified — ecclesiastical hierarchy, in East as West.

In the period of *Wildwuchs*, not every evangelically-convinced preacher desired precisely this scheme. Lambert even implied that if the Franciscans themselves were to have a change of heart, they still might be tolerated, evidence, perhaps, of his own inner struggle. But as things stood, they were intolerably greedy, desired to gather all things of value on earth into their own private heap, and thus in the end remained "the roaches in the clothing, the mice and worms in the fleece, the caterpillars, beetles, and locusts in the garden, the rust of metal... ."[42] Like most of his fellows, Lambert pointed to the Gospel as the source of human knowledge concerning God's will.

As a group, nonetheless, early Reformation preachers wholeheartedly supported the reinstatement of the pastorate as the center of parish religious life. Their verbal attacks on pastors had invariably to do with individual occupants of the office and with local circumstances, not with the office itself. Luther insisted on a distinction between the person and the office:

> Don't be led into error, whether he [your pastor] has been called in an orderly manner or has bought or forced his way into [his position] ... whether he is Judas or Saint Peter. ... Separate the office from the person who holds it, and that which is holy from that which is abominable.

---

[38] *Von der freiheit eines Christenmenschen. 1520, WA* 7. 20-38, here 28.

[39] *Ein Evangelischer beschreibung über der Barfüsser Regel, dahär offenbar würd, nit allein was von jre sunder auch von anderer münchen Regeln und satzungen zuhalten sey 1524* (n. p.), Bii.

[40] Lambert, Bii.

[41] Lambert, Bii-Biv.

[42] Lambert, Ci.

Go ahead. He is the pastor, and even under the horror of popery, Christ preserved his holy and dear pastoral office. If he should not preach the pure text of the Gospel, say to yourselves, "It is the atrocity of the devil that distorts the Word."[43]

Reformation preachers realized that in many parishes, one pastor would not be able to carry the entire cure of souls himself. The assistance of preachers and deacons would be needed. Johann Eberlin wrote that each parish would need a pastor and a deacon, who should be paid the same amount. Nevertheless, the deacon should obey the pastor. Both would preach every week. Larger parishes might have two deacons, but no more. He proposed that bishops be in charge of exactly twenty parishes and consult regularly with their subordinates.[44]

V

The clerical anticlericalism of the early German Reformation was, then, not simply a continuation of that medieval anticlericalism that was ubiquitous from the eleventh century on — virtually from the moment when Catholicism triumphed over public paganism in western Europe. Preachers of the sixteenth century added their own ingredients to oft-tried recipes. The question of whether the Reformation produced the kind of clergy that either evangelical preachers or people hoped for is probably tangential to the present discussion. I agree with Scribner when he writes of the severe new clericalism of the Reformation.[45] A period of time elapsed, however, between the official exclusion of the old regime and the institution and effective control of the new. In the cities of Saxony, this period was about a decade, and never more than fifteen years, in length; outside the towns it was twice as long. But the brief hour of clerical anticlericalism in the service of reform was over in 1525. From that date on, princes and magistrates strove to harness the preachers and subordinate them to the state. There was little room in the increasingly authoritarian atmosphere for advocates even of spiritual revolution. During the second half of the sixteenth century, the pastorate would become a scion of the state bureaucracy, against which, ironically, a newly disenchanted laity would react with passion.[46]

---

[43] *Von der Winkelmesse, WA* 38. 243.

[44] *Die 15 Bundgenossen*, "Die X. bund genos", Liv-Mi.

[45] "Antiklerikalismus in Deutschland um 1500", in *Europa 1500. Integrationsprozesse im Widerstreit*, ed. F. Seibt, W. Eberhard (Stuttgart, 1987), 368-82, here esp. 374-75.

[46] See in this volume the essay by Gerald Strauss on late sixteenth-century anticlericalism in the vicinity of Weimar. Coincidentially, in May 1990 I presented a paper on a closely related subject, "Rural Morality and the Second Reformation: The

Renewal of Anticlericalism in Saxony", at the meetings of the Society for Reformation Research in Kalamazoo. Also pertinent are Hans-Christoph Rublack, "'Der
wohlgeplagte Priester'. Vom Selbstverständnis lutherischer Geistlichkeit im Zeitalter
der Orthodoxie", *ZHF* 16 (1989): 1-30; and another excellent essay by Rublack on
the continuation of anticlerical feeling in the seventeenth and eighteenth centuries,
"Success and Failure of the Reformation: Popular 'Apologies' from the Seventeenth
and Eighteenth Centuries", forthcoming in *Germania Illustrata: Essays on Early
Modern Germany*, ed. A. Fix, S. Karant-Nunn (Kirksville, Mo., 1992), 141-65.

ANTIKLERIKALISMUS
IN DEN FORDERUNGEN UND AKTIONEN
DER AUFSTÄNDISCHEN VON 1524-1525

SIEGFRIED HOYER

Universität Leipzig

In den revolutionären Ereignissen von 1524/25 komprimierte sich die in den vorhergegangenen Jahren vereinzelt aufgetretene städtische und bäuerliche Kritik am Klerus als kirchliche und als feudale Institution: verbal sowie in Angriffen Bewaffneter. Beide Erscheinungsformen gehören zum Gesamtbild eines 'Aufstandes des gemeinen Mannes', in dem sich, gemäß der sozialen Zusammensetzung seiner Träger, antiklerikale Forderungen aus dem städtischen und aus dem ländlichen Bereich vermischten.

Unverkennbar sind Programme und Ordnungen der Aufständischen in vielfältiger Weise mit der reformatorischen Theologie Wittenberger und Züricher Prägung verbunden. Das in ihr vorgestellte neue Modell der christlichen Freiheit[1] stimulierte nicht nur soziale Sehnsucht, es profilierte den Protest gegen wirtschaftliche Belastung, juristische Unfreiheit und die Aversion gegen Träger und geistliche Praxis der alten Kirche.

H. J. Hillerbrand hatte versucht, durch eine Quantifizierung der bekannten Artikel der Aufständischen von 1524/25 die Frage zu beantworten, welche Rolle religiöse Forderungen im weiteren und antiklerikale Kritik im engeren Sinne in ihnen spielten.[2] Kritisch wurde dagegen eingewandt, daß solche Aussagen nicht nur gezählt, sondern auch gewichtet werden müßten,[3] hinzuzufügen wäre, auch spezifiziert, auf das, was gefordert wurde oder auf den Zielpunkt der Kritik.

Läßt man die Anwendung von Gewalt gegen die Einrichtung der Kirche zunächst beiseite, so haben wir recht unterschiedliche Forderungen und Klagen gegen den Klerus vor uns und auch ein unterschiedlich dichtes Vorkommen. Deshalb bleibt zu untersuchen, wo die antiklerikale Kritik

---

[1] H. A. Oberman, "Tumultus rusticorum. Vom 'Klosterkrieg' zum Fürstensieg", in *Deutscher Bauernkrieg 1525*, hg. von H. A. Oberman, 160f. (= *ZKG* 85 [1974]: 304f.).

[2] H. J. Hillerbrand, "The German Reformation and the Peasants' War", in *The Social History of the Reformation*, hg. von L. B. Buck, J. W. Zophy (Columbus, 1972), 122ff.

[3] H. J. Cohn, "Anticlericalism in the German Peasants' War 1525", *PaP* 83 (1979): bes. 29f.

besonders massiv in Erscheinung tritt und wo sie weniger stark verbreitet war.

Bei einer Summierung der unterschiedlichen Artikel gegen den Klerus in allen Programmen von 1524/25 sind 3 besonders häufig vertreten: das Verlangen nach freier Predigt des unverfälschten Wort Gottes, womit die bisher unzulängliche Vermittlung der christlichen Botschaft kritisiert wird, die Forderung nach Wahl der Pfarrer und die Weigerung, in Zukunft den kleinen Zehnten zu zahlen.[4] Dies wird mit dem Verlangen verknüpft, die Verwendung des großen Zehnten zu kontrollieren und ihn für die Besoldung des eigenen Pfarrers zu verwenden.

Die Wahl eigener Geistlicher negierte bisher gehandhabte Rechte klerikaler und weltlicher Patrone, wandte sich damit gegen die alten Strukturen bzw. den obrigkeitlichen Einfluß generell und stärkte in erster Linie kommunale Selbstverwaltung. Wenn eine solche Wahl Voraussetzung sein sollte, durch die Predigt dem göttlichen Recht als Norm sozialer Verhältnisse Geltung zu verschaffen,[5] dann wurden Prädikanten gebraucht, die diese Auffassung vertraten, was bekanntermaßen nicht überall der Fall war. Auch Martin Luther verlangte bereits 1522 die Wahl der Pfarrer und verband dies im folgenden Jahr (1523) in der Schrift "Daß eine christliche Versammlung oder Gemeinde Recht und Macht habe, alle Lehre zu verurteilen und Lehrer zu berufen, ein- und abzusetzen" mit der Forderung, diejenigen zu nehmen, die man geschickt dazu fände und die Gott mit Verstand erleuchtet habe.[6] Insofern wird der reformatorische Einfluß in dieser bäuerlichen Forderung besonders deutlich.

Als die Memminger Bauern Ende Februar 1525 die Pfarrerwahl und eine Predigt "rain, lauter und clar nach rechtem Verstand ... on allem Menschenzusatz"[7] forderten, ging der Rat der Reichsstadt sofort darauf ein, da in ihren Mauern der Einfluß evangelischer Prediger stark war.

Bereits in der älteren Bauernkriegsforschung wurde nachgewiesen, daß die Pfarrerwahl durch den Einfluß von Prädikanten, in erster Linie wohl des Sebastian Lotzer, in den ersten der Zwölf Artikel kam, nicht als Summe lokaler Beschwerden.[8] Nur sechs der 71 überlieferten lokalen Beschwerden,

---

[4] Hillerbrand, "German Reformation", 123; Cohn, "Anticlericalism", 7f.

[5] G. Vogler, "Der revolutionäre Gehalt und die räumliche Verbreitung der oberschwäbischen Zwölf Artikel", in *Revolte und Revolution in Europa. Referate und Protokolle des Internationalen Symposiums zur Erinnerung an den Bauernkrieg 1525 (Memmingen 24.-27. März 1975)*, hg. von P. Blickle, *HZ* Beiheft 4 (München, 1975), 216.

[6] *Martin Luther, Studienausgabe*, Bd. 3, hrsg. von H. U. Delius (Berlin, 1983), 79.

[7] *Quellen zur Geschichte des Bauernkrieges*, ges. und hg. von G. Franz, Ausgewählte Quellen zur deutschen Geschichte der Neuzeit. Freiherr vom Stein-Gedächtnisausgabe 2 (München, 1963), 169.

[8] G. Franz, "Die Entstehung der 'Zwölf Artikel' der deutschen Bauernschaft", *ARG* 36 (1939): 201ff.

aus denen die Zwölf Artikel komprimiert wurden, fordern die Pfarrerwahl. Die lokalen Beschwerden von Rettenberg im Allgäu enthalten dazu weitere interessante antiklerikale Passagen, auf die zurückzukommen sein wird.[9] Infolge ihrer Verbreitung durch Druck und Abschrift erhielten aber die Zwölf Artikel ein ungleich größeres Gewicht für die Profilierung der bäuerlichen Forderungen insgesamt als lokale Beschwerden.

Das gleiche Mißverständnis zwischen einem Artikel über freie Pfarrerwahl in dem Meraner Programm vom 30. November 1525, ergänzt durch die Zusätze, als Kandidat dürfe kein Mönch oder Angehöriger des Deutschen Ordens angenommen werden und der Gewählte solle nur eine Pfründe innehaben, besteht zu den zahlreichen (insgesamt 136) Beschwerden Tiroler Gerichte bzw. kleiner Städte.[10] Von der Stadt Meran abgesehen, ist in diesen die Pfarrerwahl nur zweimal enthalten, allerdings mit einer Begründung des alten Herkommens. So berufen sich die Bewohner des Sarntales auf das frühere Recht unter Herzog Sigmund, das 1468 durch die Verpachtung der Pfarrei an den Deutschen Ritterorden verlorenging; das Salurner Gericht begründete die Forderung mit dem "Mißbrauch" dieses Rechtes durch den Propst von St. Michael.[11]

Wahrscheinlich erfolgte die Redaktion der lokalen Beschwerden auf dem Landtag in der Südtiroler Stadt ebenfalls durch Geistliche oder unter deren Mithilfe, doch wurden hier reformatorisches Gedankengut und altes Recht eingebracht. Nun sind die Meraner Artikel nicht gedruckt worden, gingen aber als Innsbruck-Meraner-Artikel in die Materialien des Tiroler Landtages vom Juli-September 1525 in Innsbruck ein und erreichten auf diese Weise ebenfalls eine hohe Publizität. Allein im Vertrag von Renchen wird die Einschränkung, daß der Prediger kein Ordensangehöriger sein dürfe, auch auf Frauen ausgedehnt.[12]

Das Verlangen nach der freien Predigt des unverfälschten Wort Gottes verband sich häufig mit der Forderung, daß diejenigen abgesetzt werden

---

[9] Tabellarische Übersicht der einzelnen Forderungen: P. Blickle, *Die Revolution von 1525*, 2. Aufl. (München, 1982), 296-301.

[10] *Quellen Bauernkrieg*, 274; H. Wopfner, *Quellen zur Geschichte des Bauernkrieges in Deutschland 1525*, Acta Tirolensia III, T. 1 (Innsbruck, 1908), 1ff.

[11] Wopfner, *Quellen*, 107, 146. Die Berufung auf solche Traditionen war auch anderswo schon vor dem Bauernkrieg verbreitet. Zum Beispiel Wendelstein: R. Endres, "Die Reformation im fränkischen Wendelstein", in *Zugänge zur bäuerlichen Reformation*, hg. von P. Blickle (Zürich, 1987), 139ff; Wendelstein gehört in die Reihe jener Orte, in denen im 14./15. Jh. wegen besonderer Bedingungen eine Pfarrerwahl erfolgen konnte (vgl. D. Kurze, *Pfarrerwahlen im Mittelalter* (Köln, 1966), 250-323.

[12] *Quellen Bauernkrieg*, 563; Martin Luther bekräftigte zwar das paulinische Verbot der Predigt von Frauen, gestand sie ihnen aber in Ausnahmefällen ebenso zu wie die Taufe (I. Ludolphy, "Die Frau in der Sicht Martin Luthers", in *450 Jahre lutherische Reformation. Festschrift für Fr. Lau* (Berlin, 1967), 212ff.

sollten, die dem widerstrebten. In diesem Sinne steht es in der ebenfalls mehrfach gedruckten Memminger Bundesordnung, in Weigands Reichs-reformentwurf, den genannten Meraner-Innsbrucker Artikeln und in Gaismairs Landesordnung.[13]

Ähnlich wie Luther geschickte und mit Verstand erleuchtete Priester verlangt hatte, wandten sich die Salzburger Artikel gegen die "schalkhaften Buben", die nie eine Predigt taten, einen Vikar auf die Pfarrstelle setzten, der auch nichts konnte, und forderten einen gelehrten, wohlbeleum(unde)ten, geschickten Mann. Ergänzend wird die auch in anderen Programmen angesprochene Residenzpflicht des Pfarrers am Ort seiner Pfarre genannt. Von der Herrschaft wegen reformatorischer Predigt gefangengenommene Priester sollen freigelassen, evangelische Schriften fürderhin nicht mehr verboten werden.[14]

Wenn Herrschaften unter dem Druck des Aufstandes gezwungen waren, auf das Verlangen nach freier Predigt einzugehen, versuchten sie, ihre Interessen dabei mit ins Spiel zu bringen. So gestand der erzbischöfliche mainzische Stadthalter in Bingen (Rheingau) den Aufständischen zu, das Evangelium frei zu predigen, ergänzte aber, "ohne uffrur und empörung".[15] Eine ähnliche Formulierung findet sich in den lokalen Tiroler Beschwerden von Thauer und Rettenberg,[16] was wohl auf das Spannungsverhältnis innerhalb des Gerichts bei der Durchsetzung dieser Grundforderung, möglicherweise auch auf den Einfluß lutherischer Gedanken über das Verhältnis zur Obrigkeit zurückzuführen ist.

Nicht nur regionale Verbreitung, die Häufigkeit einiger Anliegen in der Vielzahl von Einzelartikeln, auch die Fähigkeit, antiklerikale Argumente bildhaft und pointiert zu formulieren, sind für die breite Wirkung in Rechnung zu stellen. Wenige Programme ragen hier aus der Vielzahl meist knapp formulierter Forderungen heraus, u. a. die von dem Bauernhauptmann Leonhard Schwär verfaßten Artikel der Landschaft Gastein. Auf dem politischen Hintergrund des alle Stände umfassenden Bündnisses im Erzbistum Salzburg gegen die geistliche Landesherrschaft, die in den Jahren vor der großen Empörung evangelische Prediger verfolgen ließ, den Ständen ihre Privilegien entzog u. a., entstand ein sprachliches Meisterwerk, das freie Predigt, die Wahl der Pfarrer verlangte und, das weist auf einen neuen Themenkreis hin, den Geistlichen verbot, weltliche Rechtshandlungen

---

[13] *Quellen Bauernkrieg*, 194, 264, 286, 372.

[14] *Quellen Bauernkrieg*, 292f.; Zu den "24 Artikeln" H. Dopsch, "Bauernkrieg und Glaubensspaltung", *Geschichte Salzburgs. Stadt und Land*, Bd. 2,1 (Salzburg, 1988), 45f.

[15] W. H. Struck, *Bauernkrieg am Mittelrhein und in Hessen* (Wiesbaden, 1975), 156.

[16] Wopfner, *Quellen*, 71. In den Artikeln wird auch gefordert, gefangene Prediger freizulassen; wo aber Prediger Aufruhr predigen, solle die Herrschaft eingreifen.

verschiedener Art auszuführen. Ein feuriger Aufruf gegen die Unterdrückung des göttlichen Wortes leitet die konkreten Forderungen ein.[17]

Das Verlangen nach der Predigt des reinen Evangeliums dürfte sich zwar in den meisten Fällen an den Gedanken der Reformation orientiert haben. Allerdings ließen auch altgläubige Herrschaften ihr Interesse an einer besseren Wortverkündigung vor dem Bauernkrieg deutlich werden, so der Würzburger Bischof oder der Regensburger Konvent vom Juli 1524.[18] Inwieweit dem Folge geleistet wurde, auch altgläubige Prediger sich in diesem Sinne bemühten, läßt sich aus den Quellen nicht beantworten.

Die drastische Beschränkung der Anzahl der Klöster sowie ein Verbot, neue Mönche aufzunehmen, findet sich vorzugsweise in jenen Artikeln, die von Aufständischen in Klostergrundherrschaften formuliert wurden,[19] in Städten, die sich der Gesamterhebung 1524/25 anschlossen oder in denen es ebenfalls zu Unruhen kam. Die Bürgerschaften von Würzburg, Mainz und Fulda wollen die geistlichen Güter, im Einzelfall (Fulda) auch die Kleinodien, in Verwahrung nehmen.[20] Die Meraner Artikel sehen eine drastische Beschränkung, keine vollständige Beseitigung der Klöster vor; unter den verbliebenen dürfen allerdings keine Nonnenklöster und keine von Bettelorden sein. Betteln wurde, ganz im Sinne der Reformation, generell untersagt,[21] Pfarren in klösterlichem Besitz sollten der lokalen Zuständigkeit zurückgeführt, (Grund-)Zinsen den Klöstern nicht mehr gezahlt werden. Die Beispiele ließen sich fortsetzen und auf Spitäler unter geistlicher Verwaltung ausdehnen.

Aus den städtischen Artikeln ist zu ersehen, daß es aus unterschiedlichen Motiven unter dem Druck des Aufstandes um eine friedliche Beseitigung der Ordensniederlassungen ging.[22] Ein Übereinkommen, das im Rheingau zwischen den Aufständischen und Konventen, z. B. dem Kloster Aulhausen, geschlossen wurde, sieht eine finanzielle Unterstützung (200 fl.) für Austretende vor.[23] In einigen Gebieten wollten die Bauern sich von der weltlichen Herrschaft der Geistlichkeit vollständig trennen.[24] Das Anliegen dürfte häufiger gewesen sein als dies verbal formuliert worden ist; manche

---

[17] *Quellen Bauernkrieg*, 290ff.; Dopsch, *Bauernkrieg und Glaubensspaltung*. 43f.

[18] J. Maurer, *Prediger im Bauernkrieg* (Stuttgart, 1979), 29.

[19] Z. B. im thüringischen Ichtershausen, gerichtet an den Landesherren, Herzog Johann: *Akten zur Geschichte des Bauernkrieges in Mitteldeutschland*, Bd. 2, hg. von G. Franz, W. P. Fuchs (Jena, 1942), 144f.; Gleiches wurde im "Bauerneid" des fränkischen Adels vorgesehen (*Quellen Bauernkrieg*, 369).

[20] *Quellen Bauernkrieg*, 353, 456, 466; zu Mainz F. X. Kraus, "Beiträge zur Geschichte des deutschen Bauernkrieges", *Archiv des Vereins für Nassauische Geschichte* 12 (1873): 65.

[21] *Quellen Bauernkrieg*, 274.

[22] Wopfner, *Quellen*, 68.

[23] Struck, *Bauernkrieg*, 216.

[24] Maurer, *Prediger*, 186f.

Teilforderungen liefen auch praktisch auf eine Beseitigung der weltlichen Macht hinaus. Die "24 Artikel gemeiner Landschaft in Salzburg" forderten die Beseitigung der geistlichen Gerichtsbarkeit und eine Gebührenfreiheit aller geistlichen Dienste. Sehr anschaulich wenden sie sich gegen die Ausübung der Grundherrschaft durch Pfarrer und Vikar und forderten, daß sie vielmehr Diener sein sollen.[25] Die Artikel von Rettenberg verwerfen generell die geistliche Blutgerichtsbarkeit und alle weltlichen Handlungen des Klerus, der in Zukunft wie andere Stände besteuert werden soll.[26] In lokalen Forderungen werden einzelne Personen oder Vorfälle direkt angesprochen, etwa unberechtigte Abgabenforderungen des Komturs von Beuggen in der Grafschaft Rheinfelden[27] oder die widerrechtliche Aneignung des von einem Bauern gepachteten Pfarrhofs in Unterroth (Baltringer Haufen).[28]

Die Abgabe des zehnten Teiles der Ernte erörterten die Reformatoren schon vor 1525 kontrovers. Ein Teil von ihnen sah diese Abgabe als überflüssig an, andere, wie M. Luther und H. Zwingli, plädierten für ihre Beibehaltung, doch sollte ihre Verwendung kontrolliert werden.[29] Im Unterschied zur begrenzten Basis in den lokalen Beschwerden der Gemeinden, die der Artikel über die Pfarrerwahl in den Zwölf Artikeln besaß, war diese bei dem über die vollständige Abschaffung des kleinen Zehnten und die Umwandlung des großen in eine staatliche Steuer wesentlich umfassender.[30] Auch in anderen Programmen des Aufstandes ist die Ablehnung des Zehnten sehr stark vertreten. In jedem Fall schwächte dies den Klerus wirtschaftlich, bedrohte unter Umständen sogar sein Existenzminimum.

Gab es einen Zusammenhang zwischen radikalen Äußerungen und Gewalt gegen die Geistlichkeit oder geistliche Einrichtungen im Bauernkrieg?[31] Wie kam es angesichts der häufig angestrebten friedlichen Lösung der bäuerlichen Forderungen zu den zahlreichen Klosterstürmen, der Zerstörung von Konventen und der Austreibung von Mönchen und Nonnen? Waren es vor allem militärische Ziele, die Aneignung von Proviant und eventuell von Kleinodien zur Finanzierung der Kriegsführung?[32] Die Chroniken über den Aufstand sind voller Berichte über gewaltsame Angriffe gegen Ordenskonvente, ihr Inventar, gegen Pfarrhöfe etc. Aussagen von Geistlichen und Adligen ergänzen das Bild. Im Einzelfall dürfte die Differenz zwischen Androhung und Tat zu beachten sein. Übertreibungen sind nicht auszuschließen, etwa, wenn der Kaplan des Klosters Eschbach bereits im Mai

---

[25] *Quellen Bauernkrieg*, 298f.
[26] *Quellen Bauernkrieg*, 163f.
[27] *Quellen Bauernkrieg*, 224.
[28] *Quellen Bauernkrieg*, 156.
[29] Maurer, *Prediger*, 66f.
[30] Blickle, *Revolution*, 38ff., 296ff.
[31] Maurer, *Prediger*, 38f.
[32] So Cohn, "Anticlericalism", 17f.

1524 dem Landvogt im Oberelsaß mitteilt, "sie (die Bauern) wollten den Adel erwürgen und die Pfaffen alle".[33]

Befragen wir noch einmal die zahlreichen Artikel und lokalen Forderungen. Dem sogenannten Schlösserartikel des Artikelbriefs der Schwarzwälder Bauern zufolge sollen Schlösser, Klöster und Pfaffenstiftungen in den weltlichen Bann getan werden, es sei denn, ihre Bewohner räumen die bisherigen Unterkünfte freiwillig. G. Seebaß präzisierte neuerdings: weltlicher Bann ist Meidung, Ausschluß aus der menschlichen Gemeinschaft, nicht Zerstörung.[34] Nun finden wir den sogenannten "Schlösserartikel" auch in der Memminger Bundesordnung, dem Taubertaler Programm und den Artikeln der Frankenhäuser Bauern vom Mai 1525, aber ausschließlich auf die Bastionen des weltlichen Adels bezogen, d.h. ohne Erwähnung der Klöster, Stifter etc., andererseits mit dem weiter gehenden Gewaltaspekt: Mauern abbrechen, Gebäude ausbrennen.[35]

Über das Verdikt des Artikelbriefes kommen wir also nicht zur Begründung eines gewaltsamen Vorgehens. Zu beachten wäre in der zugespitzten Situation nach dem Ausbruch bewaffneter Auseinandersetzungen 1524/25, daß der Artikel gegenüber den geistlichen Einrichtungen eigene Ziele verfolgte. Das wird im sogenannten Bauerneid des fränkischen Adels vom Mai 1525 deutlich, in dem sich der den Eid Leistende auf der Grundlage der Zwölf Artikel und des Taubertaler Programms verpflichtete, Mönche und Nonnen, die bei ihm Zuflucht fanden, zu veranlassen, weltliche Kleider anzuziehen, und im übrigen für ein Absterben der Ordensniederlassungen zu sorgen.[36] Und sollte nicht auch eine Bemerkung Wilhelm von Hennebergs an den ehemaligen Ordenshochmeister der Deutschritter und späteren Herzog von Preußen, Albrecht, von Belang sein: "Und wir (d.h. der Adel) sahen in der erst (zunächst) alle zu, gefiel es uns auch wohl, daß es über Pfaffen und Mönche ging, wußten aber nicht, daß uns das Unglück auch als nahend war".[37]

Das gewaltsame Vorgehen gegen die Klöster und Stifter begann mit den ersten militärischen Handlungen im Herbst 1524 und endete in der Niedergangsphase des Aufstandes. Keine Landschaft war davon ausgenommen. Studiert man die zahlreichen Aussagen dazu, so ist von Zerstörung, Plünderung der Vorratslager, eventuell auch der Kleinodien, Zerschlagung

---

[33] *Quellen Bauernkrieg*, 85.

[34] G. Seebaß, *Artikelbrief, Bundesordnung und Verfassungsentwurf. Studien zu zentralen Dokumenten des südwestdeutschen Bauernkrieges*, Abhandlungen der Heidelberger Akademie der Wissenschaften, phil. hist. Klasse, Jg. 1988, 1 (Heidelberg, 1988), 153f.

[35] G. Vogler, "Schlösserartikel und weltlicher Bann im deutschen Bauernkrieg", in *Der deutsche Bauernkrieg 1524/25. Geschichte. Tradition. Lehren*, hg. von G. Brendler, A. Laube (Berlin, 1977), 115f.

[36] *Quellen Bauernkrieg*, 369f.

[37] *Quellen Bauernkrieg*, 471.

der Altäre, Kruzifixe, Bilder etc. die Rede, von einer Austreibung der Mönche und Nonnen, aber kaum von Mord und Totschlag. Wenn dies geschieht, dann im allgemeinen durch altgläubige Chronisten und mit sehr vagen Angaben. Die komplizierten sozio-psychologischen Hintergründe der Klosterstürme stellte R. Endres 1975 am Beispiel der beiden fränkischen Hochstifte Würzburg und Bamberg dar.[38] Ehe wir kurz auf die Argumente eingehen, die Vorbemerkung, daß gewaltsame Angriffe auf Klöster bereits in der frühen Reformation begannen; bekanntermaßen 1521 in Erfurt,[39] und es eine große Anzahl solcher Stürme gab, bevor der Bauernkrieg ausbrach, ebenso wie Antiklerikalismus in den ländlichen und städtischen Gemeinden längere Zeit vor 1524 in den Quellen faßbar ist. Beide zunächst getrennte Phänomene—Klosterstürme waren bis 1524 ein ausschließlich städtisches Ereignis—flossen mit dem Ausbruch der bewaffneten Auseinandersetzungen zusammen.

Notwendigkeiten und Begleiterscheinungen der Kriegsführung sind dafür sicher eine wichtige Ursache. Die in zahlreichen Programmen und Artikeln geforderten reformatorischen Veränderungen wurden nun durch Gewalt ergänzt. Nicht nur die Verpflegung der Haufen, auch schlicht das Plündern, die Gier nach Beute, die Angst, eventuell leer auszugehen, sind nicht zu unterschätzen. Als wichtigste Erscheinung des sozio-psychologischen Hintergrundes verbanden sich Haß auf die privilegierten Einrichtungen, die ja im Unterschied zu den meisten Adelsburgen militärisch ungeschützt waren, mit Widerstand gegen die wirtschaftliche Konkurrenz und reformatorischem Eifer. Dieser wurde sicher durch Prädikanten, nicht zum geringen Teil ehemalige Mönche, geschürt und vom Adel wohlwollend geduldet. Adlige waren, wenn sie auf ihre Privilegien verzichteten, willkommene Mitglieder der christlichen Gemeinschaft. Mönchen und Nonnen blieb nur der Austritt aus dem Kloster und danach die Wahl, als Prediger für die Reformation zu wirken oder sich einen Beruf zu suchen.

Welche Rolle spielten die antiklerikalen Forderungen im Gesamtcorpus der bäuerlichen Beschwerden, wie fügte sich der Antiklerikalismus in die Ziele der Aufständischen ein? Standen den insgesamt gemäßigten sozialen wesentlich radikalere antiklerikale Artikel und Taten gegenüber?[40]

Forderungen gegen die alte Kirche, den Klerus und gegen die Erhebung bzw. Verwendung des Zehnten waren in den lokalen Beschwerden, auch in den weiter verbreiteten Programmen wie den Zwölf Artikeln in der Minderheit. Hier bildeten sie einen von 4 Themenbereichen. Das ist keine neue Erkenntnis. Betrachtet man die qualitative Bedeutung der antiklerikalen

---

[38] R. Endres, "Zur sozialökonomischen Lage und zur sozialpsychologischen Einstellung des 'gemeinen Mannes'", in *Der deutsche Bauernkrieg 1524/25*, hg. von H. U. Wehler, *Geschichte und Gesellschaft*, Sonderheft 1 (Göttingen, 1975), 63ff.

[39] U. Weiß, "Das Erfurter Pfaffenstürmen 1521", *Jahrbuch für Geschichte des Feudalismus* 3 (1979): 233-89.

[40] Maurer, *Prediger*, 36.

Artikel im Vergleich zu den übrigen, so verschieben sich die Gewichte allerdings. Die Forderungen nach freier Pfarrerwahl und die Ablehnung des kleinen Zehnten stärkten die kommunale Selbstverwaltung (administrativer Bereich) und trugen zur Minderung der wirtschaftlichen Lasten bei. Insofern besaßen sie eine größere Bedeutung als die einfache zahlenmäßige Addition ergäbe. Während der Aktionen der bewaffneten Bauernhaufen waren die Klosterstürme durchweg erfolgreicher als die Einnahme von Adelssitzen. Die Wahl der Pfarrer und die Beseitigung des kleinen Zehnten wurde in fast allen Landschaften des Reiches gefordert, was sich von sozialen Anliegen, z.B. der Beseitigung der Leibeigenschaft, nicht sagen läßt, da diese in einigen Gebieten nicht verbreitet war. Die vermeintliche Differenz zwischen antiklerikaler Radikalität und gemäßigter sozialer Absicht löst sich auf, wenn man gewaltsames Vorgehen gegen die Grundherrschaft einerseits und die reformatorische (deshalb reformerische) Absicht des Antiklerikalismus im deutschen Bauernkrieg beachtet. Die "Ablehnung des Priesterstandes"[41] begann in breitem Maße mit der Reformation, wurde nun stärker sozial motiviert und zu einem Angriff auf die Kirche als feudale Institution ausgeweitet. Der Antiklerikalismus aber bleibt ein Bindeglied zwischen allen regionalen Aufständischen und auch zwischen unterschiedlichen sozialen Teilnehmern.

---

[41] Maurer, *Prediger*, 40.

CHANGING PLACES: PEASANTS AND CLERGY 1525

HENRY J. COHN

University of Warwick, Coventry

The rural population, unlike more literate elements in early sixteenth-century Germany, left only scant and ambiguous evidence of how they viewed the social order, and in particular the place of the clergy within it. Historians have naturally turned to the many lists of grievances presented by "peasant" rebels during the conflicts of 1524-1526 and to their correspondence with lords and rulers. Many recent commentators have emphasized the anticlerical edge to most of these articles and demands,[1] a few have given greater weight to the common features in attacks on both clerical and lay lords.[2] Future, more exhaustive analysis of the surviving gravamina may well push this debate further. However, a parallel, if subsidiary, approach to the problem is not only to examine what peasants, rural artisans and day labourers wrote, or what was written on their behalf or about them in reform proposals and pamphlets, but to consider the actions they committed and the words they were reported to have uttered in the heat of the moment.

Two types of activity in the Peasants' War, alongside others, shed light on rural resentment against the clergy, especially clerical lords. Whereas the well-known sacking and destruction of hundreds of monasteries and ecclesiastical houses spring first to mind, attention should also be paid to the smaller number of recorded incidents — previously often overlooked — in which peasants declared their wish, directly or symbolically, to exchange places with clerics, others in which townsmen or nobles were the butt of this view of the world-upside-down or reversed.

---

[1] H. J. Cohn, "Anticlericalism in the German Peasants' War 1525", *PaP* 83 (1979): 3-31; P. Blickle, *The Revolution of 1525* (Baltimore, 1981), 57; S. Lombardini, "La guerra dei contadini in Germania", *Archivio Storico Italiano* 140 (1982): 403-31; H.-J. Goertz, "Aufstand gegen den Priester. Antiklerikalismus und reformatorische Bewegung", in *Bauer, Reich und Reformation*, ed. P. Blickle (Stuttgart, 1982), 193-201; H. Buszello et al., eds., *Der deutsche Bauernkrieg* (Paderborn, 1984), Index s.v. Antiklerikalismus; K.-H. Ludwig, "Thesen und Antithesen zum Bauernkrieg in Salzburg", *Veröffentlichungen des Verbandes Österreichischer Geschichtsvereine* 23 (1984): 17-19, 23; K.-H. Ludwig and F. Gruber, *Gold- und Silberbergbau im Übergang vom Mittelalter zur Neuzeit* (Cologne, 1987), 215-17, 219.

[2] H. J. Hillerbrand, "The German Reformation and the Peasants War", in *The Social History of the Reformation*, ed. L. P. Buck, J. W. Zophy (Columbus, 1972), 121-5; A. Laube, G. Vogler, eds., *Die Epoche des Übergangs vom Feudalismus zum Kapitalismus*, vol. 3 of *Deutsche Geschichte* (Cologne, 1983), 35-37, 185.

The problems of assessing the evidence for anticlericalism are especially severe in the case of its rural manifestations. Already the reports of attacks on monastic houses need care in their evaluation. The almost universal tearing up and burning of rent-rolls and documents was part of the attempt to destroy the existing legal basis for oppressive lordship and not limited to clerical lords. The buildings of rural monasteries sometimes had a strategic value which could account for their occupation or destruction during the campaigns of 1525. Large insurgent forces far from home also had practical reasons for requisitioning the especially abundant grain and food stocks of many monastic landlords and tithe lords; other valuables taken as booty were often sold to buy provisions for the rebel armies and even to pay a weekly wage to their members, whether mercenaries or not. Yet the numerous accounts of more "wanton" destruction, extending sometimes to the ritual appurtenances of the faith, suggest strong elements not only of sheer hatred of the monks and clerics who were usually expelled but even of evangelical influences. Although descriptions of images smashed and the host being trampled underfoot or defiled are with few exceptions written by embittered regular and secular clergy and may well have been exaggerated, they can hardly all have been pure invention.

In August 1525 the humanist Nikolaus Ellenbog wrote to his sister, Barbara, abbess of Heggbach,[3] that in his absence from Ottobeuren in April the peasants had made that abbey's buildings uninhabitable, violated and broken all but three altars, hacked feet and hands off the statue of St. Salvator, and strewn the relics of saints on the ground and dishonoured them. "Our peasants and their pseudo-prophets and their accomplices" had decapitated and mutilated images of the saints and the Virgin Mary. The archives, newly-built library and printing presses were destroyed; one peasant took a large world map home, which his wife washed until it was clean enough for her to use the linen.[4] The connection which such accounts suggest between the plundering of monasteries and priests' houses, anticlericalism, and the rebel adoption of the Gospel could hardly be more clearly demonstrated than in the narrative of a Lutheran nobleman, Count Ulrich von Rappoltstein, the son of the Landvogt of Upper Alsace. The Ebersheimmünster troop, some 5,000 strong, had already taken half a dozen monasteries and the property of priests and Jews in the vicinity when they appeared before Rappoltsweiler on 13th May to tell the young count that

---

[3] From Isny, retailing information which the prior had brought from Ottobeuren a few days previously; Nikolaus Ellenbog, *Briefwechsel*, ed. A. Bigelmair, F. Zoepfl (Münster, 1938), 201-2; A. Weitnauer, *Allgäuer Chronik. Daten und Ereignisse*, vol. 2 (Kempten, 1971), 31.

[4] 18 May 1534; Ellenbog, *Briefwechsel*, 329.

> They wanted neither castle nor town, but only to help protect the pure Gospel, so that it be preached plainly and clearly; they were also enemy to no one but priests, monks, nuns and Jews, whom they intended to punish.

Clergy and Jews together were now to experience the fruits of economic, social and religious resentments which fired both popular anticlericalism and popular antisemitism. With the aid of the burghers, who had rebelled against Count Ulrich three weeks earlier, the peasant troop entered the market town, spent the night eating and drinking provisions taken from priests' houses, and on Sunday morning ransacked and emptied the monastery, broke its windows, removed or destroyed several painted images, and used the banner from a chapel to make themselves garters. At their next port of call they told the inhabitants of the small town of Gemar to continue paying the tithe to their lords but to make their priests marry and say the mass in German.[5] These instances of collective action are matched by those of individual rebels who, while plundering ecclesiastical institutions, expressed Reformation sentiments shot through with anticlericalism. In the see of Bamberg Fritz Meissner of Seibelsdorf tore up the indulgence letters of the pilgrimage church of Vierzehnheiligen at Lichtenfels; he took a chalice in his hand, saying "formerly peasants could not touch the chalice, now they take it entirely."[6]

For some the ceremony of the mass was a target alongside the physical contents of churches and chapels. At the height of the devastation at Kempten in Upper Swabia on Easter Friday, the peasants destroyed what remained in the abbey after their previous visitations: pictures of the saints and Virgin, the sacrament house, pulpit, font and organs. At the hour when mass was normally celebrated, they held a mock procession round the abbey with pikes, lances and bows.[7] Another mock mass was held in the peasant camp before Bamberg, and at the Augustinian priory of Anhausen in Franconia a rebel peasant dressed as a priest mocked the mass. The later confession of a village priest, Andreas Metzger, implied that when taking part in the sack of Munzingen castle in the Breisgau he had seen his task as to remove the wealth with which the Church financed its ritual: on transferring successive sacks of corn from barn to cart, he had recited "this is the early mass, this is the second mass, this high mass."[8]

---

[5] L. Baillet, "La Guerre des Paysans: un cas de conscience dans la famille de Ribeaupierre", *Bulletin Philologique et Historique (jusqu'à 1610) du Comité des Travaux Historiques et Scientifiques (Année 1967)* 1 (1969): 361-4, 406-7, 412-23; K. Hartfelder, *Zur Geschichte des Bauernkriegs in Südwestdeutschland* (Stuttgart, 1884), 78-87.

[6] B. Dietz, *Der Bauernkrieg im Obermaintal* (Lichtenfels, 1925), 45.

[7] J. B. Haggenmüller, *Geschichte der Stadt und der gefürsteten Grafschaft Kempten*, vol. 1 (Kempten, 1840), 526.

[8] J. H. Maurer, *Prediger im Bauernkrieg* (Stuttgart, 1979), 191, 193, 343, 563.

The question remains whether incidents of this kind, assuming the reportage to be more or less accurate, may be taken as clear proof of strong rural anticlericalism. Firstly, the line between urban and rural manifestations of anticlericalism is hard to draw, especially as many of the attacks occurred in or near towns, and most peasant troops included volunteers from towns both small and large. Indeed, vinedressers who lived in the Franconian towns but worked outside the walls or travelled to find labour in more distant country districts could not be clearly classified as either townsmen or peasants.[9] Equally difficult to read is the fact that the rebels had often drunk copiously of the clergy's wine when they committed their outrages; the Ebersheimmünster troop consumed or destroyed over 100 *Fuder* on passing through the small territories of Rappoltstein, without paying, as the count ruefully complained.[10] It is a matter of fine judgment whether to conclude that wine led peasants to actions they would otherwise never have contemplated, or, perhaps more likely, that drink loosened inhibitions and gave free rein to the expression of deeply-felt resentments. Even so, the destruction of churches and misuse of ceremonial objects need not necessarily signify Reformation influences. Desecrations of churches were such common occurrences for military forces, both before and after the development of the *Landsknechte*, that military regulations contained provisions against them.[11] During the Soest Feud of the mid-fifteenth century the archbishop of Cologne's troops, including Bohemian Hussite mercenaries, had done violence to "virgins, women, monasteries, churches, hermitages, religious persons and priests ..., they took the chalices ... [and] monstrances, [and] threw the holy sacrament on the ground ...."[12] A popular song described the destruction of the monastery of Waldsassen by troops of Margrave Frederick of Brandenburg-Ansbach during the Bavarian Succession War of 1504:

... das closter thäten sie verbrennen
sie raubten das heilig sacrament
und wolltens nicht erkennen.

---

[9] R. L. Vice, "Vineyards, Vinedressers and the Peasants' War in Franconia", *ARG* 79 (1988): 147.

[10] Baillet, "Ribeaupierre", 424-5.

[11] However, whereas regulations for the *Landsknechte* allowed attacks on ecclesiastical buildings used by the enemy for defence or storing provisions, ordinances for the peasant armies of Franconia and the Palatinate in 1525 permitted only the troop captains to order an onslaught on church property; G. Franz, ed., *Quellen zur Geschichte des Bauernkriegs* (Darmstadt, 1963), 352, 442; S. Hoyer, *Das Militärwesen im deutschen Bauernkrieg 1524-1526* (Berlin, 1975), 101-2.

[12] *Die Chroniken der westfälischen und niederrheinischen Städte*, vol. 2, *Soest*, vol. 21 of *Die Chroniken der deutschen Städte* (Leipzig, 1889), 150-1; W. Janssen, "Der Bischof, Reichsfürst und Landesherr (14. und 15. Jahrhundert)", in *Der Bischof in seiner Zeit*, ed. P. Berglar, O. Engels (Cologne, 1986), 211.

Sie haben unser lieben frauen bild
mit füßen getreten also wild,
das geschah wol in der heidenschaft nicht,
sie lebten gar ungeheure.
    Hauptmann Bibrizsch war ein freudiger mann,
er leget priesters kleider an,
darinnen thät er tanzen und springen.[13]

Violation of the sacraments and images of the Virgin, as well as the captain's adoption of clerical garb, were to recur in the armies of 1525, manned as they largely were by *Landsknechte*, former *Landsknechte*, and peasants with experience in the territorial levies. The rough ways of the soldiery probably played a part alongside anticlericalism and evangelical sentiment in the forms taken by violence against clerics in 1525.

However, neither drunkenness nor the recreational habits of soldiers fully account for those instances of agitation in which rebels expressed towards clergy and others their view of the world-upside-down, or reversed. The nun who chronicled the tribulations of the convent at Heggbach in Upper Swabia reported that, after the peasants had taken away their corn,

> ... wicked women came and accused the abbess and other nuns who held office of having called in the [army of the Swabian] League to attack their husbands. If their husbands were killed, they would enter the convent and scratch out their eyes; they must come out and milk the cows and wear shabby clothes, while the women would enter the convent and wear clean furs. They would drive us into the common herd and tie our habits above our heads. We would also have to have children and allow ourselves to be hurt, as they were ...[14]

Previously, the women added, the nuns had consorted carnally with their two confessors and the convent's secular administrator (*Hofmeister*). Gossip here laced an already heady cocktail of anticlericalism, role reversal, and female envy.

Male peasants seem to have been more immediately concerned with the role of monks as oppressive lords than with their superior lifestyle. Vinedressers living in the suburbs of Würzburg expressed a mixture of urban and rural concerns in a demonstration outside the town's abbey of St. Stephen:

> ... the monks had long enough lived free of all taxes, but they, the day labourers, had to render taxes, field labour, watch duties, digging and other

---

[13] "Vom treffen bei Ebnet", in *Die historischen Volkslieder der Deutschen vom 13. bis 16. Jahrhunderts*, ed. R. von Liliencron, vol. 2 (Leipzig, 1866), 527. For further details, including the theft of vestments and altar cloths, see "Wie Waldsassen zerstört ward", ibid., 523-6.

[14] Franz, *Quellen*, 142; cf. M. Kobelt-Groch, "Von 'armen frowen' und 'bösen wibern' — Frauen im Bauernkrieg, zwischen Anpassung und Auflehnung", *ARG* 79 (1988): 103.

services. They intended in future to tolerate it no longer, but wanted to turn over the leaf, take the monasteries, houses and properties of monks and priests into their own hands, and also for once be lords and free ...[15]

When monasteries were actually occupied, it was possible to put this reversal of roles into practice. At Roggenburg in Upper Swabia the peasant leader, a smith, appointed himself abbot and put on habit and mitre.[16] At Anhausen the prior's subjects in the village of Volkertshausen were told by the mass-priest and a peasant from neighbouring Ellrichshausen that they were now prior at Anhausen; farms, fishponds and woods were theirs and the tenants must receive their holdings from them.[17] In some houses it was not just one or two individuals who acted out their fantasies, but a whole group of peasants, who moreover kept up the masquerade for a considerable time. Hans Kumli of Sundheim, a former *Landsknecht* on double pay but of peasant stock, acted as ruling abbot of Ottobeuren. He occupied the abbot's rooms, appointed his own servants, hung the abbot's keys on his leather mercenary's belt, and underdook daily tours of the abbey with liberal dispensation of wine in true carnival fashion.[18] The abbot of Weißenau fled when the Rappertsweiler troop, including his own subjects, asked him to join them and to instruct his priests to preach the pure gospel, but he probably saved his house from destruction by leaving behind four monks, who were also parish priests, with orders to take an oath to the rebels and feed them. The peasants elected one of their number, Johann Ule, as abbot. Perhaps the best-known scene in Jakob Murer's illustrated chronicle of the abbey depicts drunken peasants in the courtyard, some fighting, others breaking into the chancery, taking bread and grain sacks from the store-house, fishing in one pond, and letting water out of another. Indoors, flanked by five other peasants and the four hostage monks, sits Johann Ule in the abbot's place, drinking out of a large cup.[19]

Other peasants were content merely to take the places of servants to clerical lords. The cook at the house of the Teutonic Order in Sterzing, in the Tyrol, had his jug for pouring wine seized by a peasant who reprimanded him: "You have been servant to clerics long enough and enjoyed a good

---

[15] Recounted in a biography of the abbot by Lorenz Fries, see C. Heffner, "Michael Leyser, Abt zu St. Stephan in Würzburg, eine Episode aus dem Bauernkrieg", *Archiv des Historischen Vereins von Unterfranken und Aschaffenburg* 12 (1853): 277-8.

[16] F. L. Baumann, ed., *Quellen zur Geschichte des Bauernkrieges in Oberschwaben* (Tübingen, 1876), 81, 83, 669; A. Kanz, *Chronik von Tüssen* (Illertissen, 1911), 63.

[17] G. Bossert, "Beiträge zur Geschichte des Bauernkriegs in Franken", *Württembergisch-Franken* N.S. 1 (1882): 19.

[18] M. Feyerabend, *Des ehemaligen Reichsstifts Ottobeuren Benediktiner-Ordens in Schwaben sämtliche Jahrbücher*, vol. 3 (Ottobeuren, 1815), 49-52; H. W. Bensen, *Geschichte des Bauernkrieges in Ostfranken* (Erlangen, 1840), 287, 560.

[19] Jakob Murer, *Weißenauer Chronik des Bauernkrieges von 1525*, ed. G. Franz, W. Fleischhauer, vol. 2 (Sigmaringen, 1977), 21, 28-30, 49.

life for long, let us also live well for once." Claiming now to be a cellarer, he filled utensils of every kind, including chamber pots eagerly cleaned by the women, with wine for both men and boys. The cook made the mistake of laughing the incident off as a joke; when he tried to join in the spirit of the occasion and asked for some wine, the reply came, "you must drink water; the Gospel is now fulfilled without clerics and their servants."[20] Higher within the rebel ranks, the two booty masters of the army which governed Württemberg called themselves "officials", since they taxed the clergy just as had previously the holder of the judicial post with that title.[21]

One way to humiliate clerics was not merely to eat their food and drink their wine, which happened widely, but to make them stand by and watch. A vicar-choral of the Bamberg cathedral chapter was held captive by nine peasants in his own house while his maid was forced to roast fowl for them.[22] Peasants carousing in the house of the Teutonic Order at Heilbronn made those knights who had not fled stand bareheaded by the table. To one a peasant called, "Today little Junker, we are the knights", and struck him on his fat paunch so that he fell over.[23] The symbolism of such acts reversed the image of the clergy (or indeed nobles, which the knights also were) eating sumptuously at the expense of the peasantry. This was explained by the women who occupied a convent in Schlettstadt, a town in Alsace where over half the population was engaged in agriculture, "You have long eaten our bread, now it is our turn to eat at your table."[24] The removal of grain and wine from ecclesiastical institutions was likewise justified as the recovery of rents and tithes which the peasants themselves had rendered.[25]

The nature of rural anticlericalism has however to be seen in the perspective of popular attitudes in the countryside towards other social classes. Interestingly, two of the attested cases of peasants wanting to become townees involved women. One called out to the wife of an

---

[20] K. Fischnaler, *Geschichts-, Kultur- und Naturbilder aus Alttirol* (Innsbruck, 1936), 234-6.

[21] G. Bossert, "Aus der Zeit der Fremdherrschaft, 1519-1534", *Württembergische Jahrbücher für Statistik und Landeskunde* (1911), part 1: 62.

[22] J. Looshorn, *Die Geschichte des Bisthums Bamberg*, vol. 4 (Bamberg, 1900), 579.

[23] Bensen, *Ostfranken*, 158.

[24] 8 Feb. 1525; G. Heumann, *La Guerre des Paysans d'Alsace et de Moselle (Avril-Mai 1525)* (Paris, 1976), 59; similarly at Heilbronn, " ... dieweyll die pfaffen lang mit uns gessen und druncken, wellen wir auch ein weill mit inen fressen und sauffen ...", *Urkundenbuch der Stadt Heilbronn*, vol. 4, ed. M. von Rauch (Stuttgart, 1922), 299; cf. S. Nitz, "Handlungsfähigkeit im Deutschen Bauernkrieg", dissertation (Frankfurt am Main, 1979), 179-81.

[25] E.g., *Urkundenbuch ... Heilbronn*, 4: 285, 287; M. Thomann, "Mentalités et révolution dans une petite ville d'Alsace: 'Pauvres gens' et seigneurs à Marmoutier en 1525", in *La Guerre des Paysans 1525*, ed. A. Wollbrett (Saverne, 1975), 75.

innkeeper at Bozen in the Tyrol: "I will come and be mistress in your house; you must go up into the hills and be a peasant wife."[26] Women villagers subject to the Teutonic Order sacked its house in Heilbronn, saying that they wanted to live for a while in the city and its burghers must go and live in the villages.[27] A villager in the Rothenburg troop confessed under torture that their intention had been to take the houses of the town's burghers and let the burghers be peasants for a while; he himself would occupy the front room in the house of his Junker, while the Junker would have to stay in the back; as the torture continued, though still without weights, he admitted, more improbably, that he and the peasant leaders had intended to drive all lords and princes out of both the town and the land, and murder them.[28] Two old peasants subject to the imperial city of Schwäbisch-Hall claimed, "we have long been lying under the bench, now we want to get on it",[29] by which they presumably meant the bench near the stove. Such instances suggest that at least some peasants were aware of the clear differences between townsmen and countryfolk, whatever the common features everywhere of the "revolt of the common man".

Egalitarianism and some forms of role reversal extended also to nobles and the occasional prince. The humiliation most often inflicted on nobles, as on some other lords as well, was to be called "brother" and be made to go on foot with the peasant army, which happened as far apart as Württemberg, Franconia, southern Thuringia, and East Prussia.[30] The egalitarian streak in such demands mingled with hatred of mounted soldiers who had damaged peasant property and were feared in battle. For this reason, after the Weinsberg bloodbath of Württemberg nobles the local official (*Amtmann*) at Krautheim was advised by a leader of the peasant troop to disguise his mounted men in the clothes of foot soldiers.[31] When on Easter Day

---

[26] H. Wopfner, "Bozen im Bauernkriege von 1525", *Der Schlern* 5 (1924): 179.

[27] *Urkundenbuch ... Heilbronn*, 4: 291.

[28] G. Franz, ed., *Der Deutsche Bauernkrieg. Aktenband*, 2nd ed. (Darmstadt, 1968), 358-9; Nitz, "Handlungsfähigkeit", 241-2.

[29] C. Kolb, ed., *Geschichtsquellen der Stadt Hall*, vol. 1, Württembergische Geschichtsquellen 1 (Stuttgart, 1894), 200.

[30] H.-M. Maurer, "Der Bauernkrieg als Massenerhebung. Dynamik einer revolutionären Bewegung", in *Bausteine zur geschichtlichen Landeskunde von Baden-Württemberg*, ed. G. Haselier (Stuttgart, 1979), 283; K.-H. Schmöger, *Der Bauernkrieg im oberen Werratal* (Suhl, [1958]), 32; F. L. Carsten, "The Peasants' War of 1525 in East Prussia", in idem, *Essays in German History* (London, 1985), 65. Peasants forced the representatives of Schwäbisch-Hall to dismount before their camp, but others called in vain on Margrave Casimir of Brandenburg-Ansbach to appear before them on foot with his nobles and councillors; H. Prescher, *Geschichte und Beschreibung der Reichsgraffschaft Limpurg*, vol. 1 (Stuttgart, 1789), 258; C. Jäger, "Markgraf Casimir und der Bauernkrieg", *Mitteilungen des Vereins für die Geschichte der Stadt Nürnberg* 9 (1892): 122.

[31] *Urkundenbuch ... Heilbronn*, 4: 68.

1525 the hated count of Helfenstein ran a gauntlet of pikes through the ranks of the rebel troops at Weinsberg, his former piper, Melchior Nonnenmacher, played a death march and said, "once I often piped you to dinner, now it is right that I summon you to another dance."[32] Jakob Wirt, a subject of the count who had given the first pike thrust, put on the count's doublet and mocked the countess, who had been made to watch the massacre, "Lady, how do I please you in this costume?"[33] Clothes were a powerful symbol of status. Many a rebel soldier imitated the *Landsknechte* in wearing a slashed white doublet with blue lining, short slashed breeches, and a hat with a feather.[34] Since *Landsknecht* dress was also fashionable among nobles, to discard the plain peasant smock for these garish and shocking garments symbolized the sloughing off of servile and subordinate status.

Oaths, as the highest form of obligation, served well as signs that the old authority had given way to new forms. In April 1525 a peasant in the assembled Neckar valley-Odenwald troop addressed the counts of Hohenlohe:

> Brother Albert and brother George, come here and swear to remain with the peasants as brethren and do nothing against them. For you are no longer lords but peasants, and we are the lords of Hohenlohe; the opinion of our whole army is that you shall swear to our Twelve Articles ... and sign a treaty with us for 101 years.[35]

When the counts raised their hands to swear to the treaty, they had to take off their gloves, which were a sign of lordship,[36] whereas the peasants kept theirs on; they also scratched out the counts' coats of arms. By the end of May, however, the captains of the same troop addressed a letter to the counts as "the well-born lords, lords Albert and George, counts of Hohenlohe, brothers, our gracious lords" before expressing their "brotherly service" and asking for troops and cannon.[37] It was difficult to shake off the habits of deference.

---

[32] A. Scarbath, "Bischof Konrad III. von Würzburg und der Bauernkrieg in Franken", dissertation (Würzburg, 1935), 44.

[33] J. Vochezer, *Geschichte des fürstlichen Hauses Waldburg in Schwaben*, vol. 2 (Kempten, 1900), 567.

[34] Baumann, *Quellen* (n. 16 above), 250, 256; Nitz, "Handlungsfähigkeit", 249.

[35] *Geschichtsquellen der Stadt Hall*, 1: 207; J. C. Wibel, *Hohenlohische Kirchen- und Reformations-Historie*, 4 vols. (Onolzbach, 1752-55), 1: 238; 4: 78; T. Robisheaux, *Rural Society and the Search for Order in Early Modern Germany* (Cambridge, 1989), 59-60.

[36] B. Schwineköper, *Der Handschuh im Recht, Ämterwesen, Brauch and Volksglauben*, 2nd ed. (Sigmaringen, 1981), 106, 110-14.

[37] Maurer, "Massenerhebung", 283; F. F. Oechsle, *Beiträge zur Geschichte des Bauernkrieges in den schwäbisch-fränkischen Grenzlanden* (Heilbronn, 1830), 187, 300.

Margrave Ernst of Baden was threatened with the ultimate degradation, short of deposition, for a secular prince, when the rebel captains and assembly in his lordships of Badenweiler, Rötteln, and Sausenberg would acknowledge him as lord only as representative of the Emperor and on condition that he promised to observe the Twelve Articles, become a peasant himself, and take the advice of a council consisting solely of peasants appointed by them.[38] In Thuringia both princes and nobles, if not regarded as opponents of the Gospel, were still expected to submit themselves to election in order to resume their former posts.[39] Elsewhere princes were usually accepted as rulers, although bishops might be required to become secular princes.

Through role reversal and other symbolic devices peasants voiced the desire to escape from the sway of other classes no less than from clerical rule. Artificial fishponds, a source of supply mainly for monasteries but also for the duke of Württemberg and other secular lords, were fished out or destroyed;[40] similarly, the hunting and occasional festive eating of game were directed mainly against secular lords. The demand for abandonment or destruction of garrisoned castles, made of nobles and prelates alike in Swabia, Franconia, the Black Forest and Thuringia, ran in tandem with the attack on monasteries.[41] In areas which rebel troops controlled for a time, they taxed both clergy and nobles and gave individuals from the two privileged estates letters of protection or safe conduct. All these actions reversed the normal order of authority. The letter of protection for Bishop George of Spires allowed him to hunt in forests and fish in waters, a right which he can only have regarded as his own prerogative.[42]

Two questions remain. Where did these levelling ideas come from? and was their edge greater towards the clergy than towards others?

---

[38] H. Schreiber, ed., *Der deutsche Bauernkrieg*, vol. 2 (Freiburg im B., 1864), 86; H. Buszello, *Der deutsche Bauernkrieg von 1525 als politische Bewegung* (Berlin, 1969), 70.

[39] W. P. Fuchs, ed., *Akten zur Geschichte des Bauernkriegs in Mitteldeutschland*, vol. 2 (Aalen, 1964), 202-3.

[40] H. Heimpel, "Fischerei und Bauernkrieg", in *Festschrift Percy Ernst Schramm*, ed. P. Classen, P. Scheibert, vol. 1 (Wiesbaden, 1964), 363-9; Bossert, "Fremdherrschaft" (n. 21 above), 62.

[41] G. Vogler, "Schlösserartikel und weltlicher Bann im deutschen Bauernkrieg", in *Der deutsche Bauernkrieg 1524/25*, ed. G. Brendler, A. Laube (Berlin, 1977), 113-21; Buszello, *Der deutsche Bauernkrieg von 1525* (n. 38 above), 39, 68; G. Vogler, *Die Gewalt soll gegeben werden dem gemeinen Volk*, 2nd ed. (Berlin, 1983), 98-100.

[42] F. J. Mone, ed., *Quellensammlung zur badischen Landesgeschichte*, vol. 3 (Karlsruhe, 1863), 22. The Schmalkalden troop rejected Count William of Henneberg's offer of a safe conduct on the grounds that they already had one from Christ and needed no other, but granted the count himself safe conduct for their meeting; O. Merx, G. Franz, eds., *Akten zur Geschichte des Bauernkriegs in Mitteldeutschland*, vol. 1 (Aalen, 1964), 347.

The couplet

> When Adam delved and Eve span
> Who was then the gentleman?

was by this time better known in German lands than elsewhere in Europe. The German version, contained in *The Peasants' Praise (Der Bauernlob)*, also called *The Poem of the First Gentleman (Das Gedicht vom ersten Edelmann)*, ran through three printed editions between 1493 and 1497; it went as far as to claim explicitly that the peasant was not merely equal, but superior to the nobleman. The couplet appeared in many German proverb collections of the early sixteenth century and earned no less than seven pages of commentary in Agricola's collection of 1529.[43] Since its diffusion as a proverb would not depend on literacy, it is somewhat surprising to find no trace of it in the chronicles, confessions and other records of what peasants said during their revolt. Only afterwards, at Neumarkt in Bavaria, did one peasant openly ask, in June 1526, "Who had created the first prince or nobleman? did he [the peasant] not have the same five fingers on his hand as any one of them?"[44]

However, already by 1525 peasants may have had access to alternative visual representations of the world-upside-down. An illustration to the first chapter in the 1508 and 1522 editions of Joseph Grünbeck's *Spiegel der naturlichen himlischen und prophetischen sehungen* presents the frightening image of a village church standing on its spire; inside, a peasant celebrates mass at the altar, while outside a monk and a priest work with plough and team.[45] Nevertheless, the most striking and explicit representations of an inverted social order, like the woodcut illustration for the pamphlet *To the Assembly of the Common Peasantry* or those of the anonymous Petrarch master, were not published until the revolt had begun or even later. Astrologers in the early 1520s had predicted a peasant rebellion, especially against the Church hierarchy, and illustrated their theme with portentous fish in the sky and other topsy-turvy topoi, but again peasants only very rarely

---

[43] Johannes Agricola, *Die Sprichwörtersammlungen*, ed. S. L. Gilman, vol. 1 (Berlin, 1971), 207-12; S. Resnikon, "The Cultural History of a Democratic Proverb", *Journal of English and German Philology* 36 (1937): 394-400, 404.

[44] J. E. Jörg, *Deutschland in der Revolutions-Periode von 1522 bis 1526* (Freiburg im B., 1851), 297-8.

[45] Reproduced by R. W. Scribner, *For the Sake of Simple Folk* (Cambridge, 1981), 169. The illustration is also in the Latin edition of 1508 (*Speculum naturalis, coelestis et propheticae visionis*), but not the German one of 1515. Scribner gives a good introduction (164-9) to themes related to the world-upside-down in early Reformation pamphlet illustrations. Whereas Scribner assumed that Grünbeck "predicted an upturning of the social order", it can be argued that he intended his dreadful vision merely as a warning to the clergy to mend their ways; see N. Jørgensen, *Bauer, Narr und Pfaffe* (Leiden, 1988), 36, 114-5, 173. Even so, such representations may have had a subversive effect on some of those who saw them.

allude to Sybilline and other prophecies in 1525.[46] On the other hand, the reversible world was a feature of carnival, and although carnival was primarily an urban and not a rural popular festival, peasants may have gone to the nearby towns on such occasions. Explanations, if any are given in 1525 for changing places with social superiors, are usually some form of allusion to the Gospel and indirectly to the priesthood of all believers. Count George of Tübingen was told peremptorily by a peasant near Freiburg: "Brother George, your body is my body, my body is your body; your property is my property, my property is your property; we are all equal brethren in Christ."[47] Evangelical influences may be accepted as the most likely trigger to have brought out into the open what were anyway probably deep-seated resentments and dreams among the rural population.

Anticlericalism was more in evidence against large clerical landowners and lords, as the greater oppressors, than against the lesser clergy, but the latter also suffered plundering and were forced to join the peasant troops if they were not already willing. Moreover, in another form of role reversal, and of integrating the clergy into the community, it was made clear to the priests in the Franconian villages Wendelstein in 1524 and Wallhausen in 1525 that the community, not the patron of the benefice, was now their lord.[48] Yet peasants rarely treated clerics as less than fellow humans. Threats to kill the clergy were probably far less frequent than the confessions later made to that effect; even when uttered, death-threats were not to be taken literally, as the Würzburg clergy realised.[49] Very few clergy were killed and, although nuns were insulted by rude remarks or exposure to naked peasants bathing in their fishponds, there were no reliable reports of rapes, in which *Landsknechte* were known to indulge when on campaign.[50]

Many forms of action against the clergy had their counterparts in measures against nobles. The Eichsfeld peasants called in the Mühlhausen forces of Müntzer and Pfeiffer to help to destroy the large number of monasteries in their region, but the castles and estates of some twenty-one nobles also succumbed.[51] In the sees of Bamberg and Würzburg the looting of castles which had often been bases for lawlessness was highly systematic.

---

[46] Nitz, "Handlungsfähigkeit" (n. 24 above), 82-7; Maurer, *Prediger* (n. 8 above), 196-7.

[47] F. Schaub, "Der Bauernkrieg um Freiburg 1525", *Zeitschrift des Freiburger Geschichtsvereins* 46 (1935): 94.

[48] The margrave of Brandenburg-Ansbach presented to the benefice at Wendelstein, the prior of Anhausen to that at Wallhausen; R. Endres, "Die Reformation im fränkischen Wendelstein", in *Zugänge zur bäuerlichen Reformation*, ed. P. Blickle (Zurich, 1987), 141-2; Jäger, "Markgraf Casimir" (n. 30 above), 98.

[49] Nitz, "Handlungsfähigkeit" (n. 24 above), 84-5.

[50] Ibid., 106-7.

[51] R. Stempel, "Der Bauernkrieg auf dem Eichsfelde", *Zeitschrift des Historischen Vereins für Niedersachsen* 76 (1911), part 4: 44-5.

It would require a detailed catalogue to make anything more than a subjective judgment as to whether attacks on the clergy were more venomous and more universal than those on nobles. This certainly appears to have been the case in regions like Alsace, the Black Forest, Upper Swabia and the Austrian lands, but not everywhere. Nobles who were abbots or Teutonic knights had additional privileges which made them especially hated and the victims of a disproportionate number of the few instances of role reversal.

The significance of role reversal lies in that it went beyond mere egalitarianism, at least in the short term, in seeking to humiliate and to exact revenge. Its perpetrators aimed not merely to mitigate or even abolish the relationship between lord and peasant, but to reverse it. The exaggerations and mockery inherent in role reversal were the strongest means available for conveying to the lords the full force of peasant anger at the injustice of their oppression.

In this context anticlericalism was only one factor among many in the consciousness of the rural population. Once the historian has isolated anticlericalism, dissected and described it, the means must be found to reintegrate it into the entire explanatory matrix for social attitudes. Overwhelmingly, both the attacks on ecclesiastical houses by peasants and their recourse to devices expressing an inverted social order towards the clergy gave vent to economic and social grievances, but from time to time they also reflected the other forms of anticlerical resentment — political, legal, sacral and sexual. In the peculiar form of role reversal, moreover, anticlericalism helped to remove inhibitions about obedience to authority. It thereby opened the door to a wider egalitarianism and made peasants more receptive to the new visions of the social order broadcast by some of the less restrained evangelical preachers and pamphleteers.

REFORMATION, PEASANTS, ANABAPTISTS: NORTHEASTERN SWISS ANTICLERICALISM

JAMES M. STAYER

Queen's University, Kingston

There are several ways to approach the topic of anticlericalism in the radical wing of the Swiss Reformation. Recently Arnold Snyder has shown the frequency among Anabaptist leaders of allusions to John 10, which portrayed the clergy of the Reformed established church as thieves, murderers, hirelings and wolves. Among the Anabaptist rank and file the epithet of "false prophets" was thrown at the clergy, with clear reference to Matthew 7:15-16.[1]

The focus of this paper will be upon the attack on the system of clerical benefices and the tithes apportioned to finance them. As Martin Haas has shown, the clergy loved their livings, apparently even more than their doctrines, for in the territories of Zurich eighty percent of the clerics stayed in their places by changing from the Old Faith to the new, and almost all the rest found new posts in Catholic territories.[2] To radical adherents of the Reformation they were "hirelings" and the Reformation could not amount to much as long as they presided over it. Opposition to the system of benefices was anticlerical in two respects — it expressed economic anti-clericalism as a demand for "cheap religion", and it rejected the status the benefice gave to its holder as a "lord" integrated into a hierarchy to which commoners were expected to defer. The aim of Reformation radicals and resisting villagers was to turn the beneficed "lord" into an unbeneficed servant of his parishioners, completely dependent upon their good will for his livelihood and his continued employment. (Similar proposals were made some years ago to strip academics of tenure and to put them at the mercy of their students. If we can remember those days, perhaps we can begin to grasp the enormity of the attack on benefices.) Everything to be related here took place in the adjoining Swiss cantons of Zurich and Schaffhausen, although had the scope of the paper been expanded to St. Gallen and Appenzell the picture would have been the same.

---

[1] Arnold Snyder, "Biblical Text and Social Context: Anabaptist Anticlericalism in Reformation Zurich", *MennQR* 65 (1991): 169-91.

[2] Martin Haas, "Der Weg der Täufer in die Absonderung. Zur Interdependenz von Theologie und sozialem Verhalten", in *Umstrittenes Täufertum 1525-1975. Neue Forschungen*, ed. H.-J. Goertz (Göttingen, 1975), 60.

Simon Stumpf, the priest of Höngg just outside Zurich, told Ulrich Zwingli in 1523 that the Reformation could not succeed "if the priests were not slain", in compliance with Deuteronomy 13:5 which commanded the killing of prophets who led Israel to worship other gods. Zwingli, apparently shocked, said that he gave Stumpf a "good answer".[3]

Stumpf, our archetype of clerical anticlericalism, was a student of Beatus Rhenanus in Basel. Zwingli helped him very shortly after his own call to Zurich in 1519 to get the benefice in Höngg in succession to his uncle, after which Stumpf became a regular member of Zwingli's Greek study group.[4] Such combinations of nepotism and Erasmianism were normal at the time. Stumpf was a very zealous champion of the early Zwinglian Reformation. His troubles with his collator, the Abbot of Wettingen, were one of several factors that prompted the calling of the First Zurich Disputation (29 January 1523);[5] and in the Second Disputation (26-28 October 1523) it was he who denied the Zurich councils the right to regulate the pace of the abolition of the mass and images, crying out: "The decision is already made: the Spirit of God decides."[6] Stumpf formally abandoned his benefice and lived from the financial support of his flock.[7] He tried to carry through the purification of his parish church, together with his congregation removing and breaking religious images, without the authorization of the Zurich government. Before the end of 1523 he was first discharged from his pastorate and then banished from Zurich territories.[8] He was the only member of the Zurich clergy to resign his benefice because of his radical beliefs.[9]

Stumpf became associated in the first years of the Zurich Reformation, 1522 and 1523, with the causes and leaders of its radical vanguard. The refusal of clerical tithes and the associated attack on clerical benefices were the first such issues to drive a wedge between radical and moderate Reformers in Zurich. Stumpf's pulpit denunciation of the monks in Wettingen called them "good-for-nothing clerics before God and the world

---

[3] Leonhard von Muralt, Walter Schmid, eds., *Quellen zur Geschichte der Täufer in der Schweiz*, vol. 1, *Zürich* (Zurich, 1952) [hereafter *QGTS*, 1: *Zürich*], 121; Leland Harder, ed., *The Sources of Swiss Anabaptism: The Grebel Letters and Related Documents* (Scottdale, Penn., 1985) [hereafter *Grebel Letters*], 437.

[4] *Grebel Letters*, 565-7; Z 7: 195-6.

[5] J. F. Gerhard Goeters, "Die Vorgeschichte des Täufertums in Zürich", in *Studien zur Geschichte und Theologie der Reformation. Festschrift für Ernst Bizer*, ed. L. Abramowski, J. F. G. Goeters (Neukirchen, 1969), 249-52; Robert Hoppeler, "Zur Charakteristik des Leutpriesters Simon Stumpf von Höngg", *Zwingliana* 4 (1926): 321-9.

[6] Z 2: 783-4.

[7] Goeters, "Vorgeschichte", 273.

[8] Emil Egli, ed., *Actensammlung zur Geschichte der Zürcher Reformation in den Jahren 1519-1533* (Zurich, 1879), 165-7, 178-9, 190.

[9] Haas, "Weg in die Absonderung", 60.

for their robbing and stealing from the poor".[10] The government of Zurich had its own jurisdictional quarrels with the Wettingen cloister and gave it only luke-warm support against Stumpf; but when in 1523 the refugee priest Wilhelm Reublin organized the refusal by six peasant parishes of the tithes owed to the Grossmünster Chapter, Zurich's chief religious foundation, the Zurich magistrates perceived this as a serious threat to their authority. The villagers petitioned that they were "now informed and instructed by the holy Gospel that the tithe was nothing else but an alms, yet it is common knowledge that some of the canons misuse it for useless and frivolous purposes."[11] Reublin, who travelled around these villages, including the future Anabaptist centre of Zollikon, preached against "murdering, heretical and thieving priests, tonsured and damned scoundrels and priests". He told salacious stories about masturbating nuns who would better be decently married, and then extended the discussion to the lay orders: "You stinking burgomaster, you sit there in your official chair, and while he sits there he is feared. You pious peasant, you should know how good you are — but then it would not be well for him to find out."[12] These attacks on the tithes were the occasion for Zwingli to write his tract *On Divine and Human Righteousness*, in which he declared that, although tithes were not justified under divine law (that is, they were not an obligation to God), they could properly be levied by human authorities.[13] This issue was the watershed of division between moderates and radicals in the Zurich Reformation. Zwingli's erstwhile radical adherent, the young patrician Conrad Grebel, sided with Stumpf, Reublin and the peasant resistance against the Zurich government and preachers.[14]

Writing to Thomas Müntzer in September 1524, Grebel declared that he and his friends had long been in serious error about baptism and the Lord's Supper, "despising the divine word, and revering the papal word, or the anti-papal preacher's word, which does not confirm and accord with the divine word either." They remained in confusion, he wrote, "as long as we were content to be listeners and readers of the evangelical preachers", and were freed from it only after they read the Bible on their own.[15] Their object was to restore the New Testament practice of the Lord's Supper and baptism, which in the latter case, they thought, pointed clearly to the baptism of adult believers. They also wanted to reorganize the support of

---

[10] Egli, *Actensammlung*, 93, 899.

[11] Egli, *Actensammlung*, 81, 132-3.

[12] Egli, *Actensammlung*, 137.

[13] Z 2: 458-525; Hans Nabholz, *Die Bauernbewegung in der Ostschweiz* (Bülach, 1898), 52-6; Ulrich Gäbler, *Huldrych Zwingli: Eine Einführung in sein Leben und sein Werk* (Munich, 1983), 71-2.

[14] *QGTS*, 1: *Zürich*, 2-4.

[15] *QGTS*, 1: *Zürich*, 14; trans. Peter Matheson, ed., *The Collected Works of Thomas Müntzer* (Edinburgh, 1988), 122.

preachers according to the New Testament model. As they told Müntzer: "If your benefices are funded from interest and tithes, which are both usurious, as is the case with us, and the whole congregation does not nourish you, you, too, should divest yourself of the benefices."[16] Since Christmas Day 1522 Reublin had been enjoying this kind of direct support in the village of Witikon.[17] Later, either in 1523 or 1524, Johannes Brötli, another priest like Reublin originally a fugitive because of his support of the Reformation, set himself up as the preacher in Zollikon.[18] Like St. Paul he supported himself by his trade, afterward writing to his congregation: "You know how I had the courage to live among you, to work with my hands and to be a burden to no one."[19] As mentioned previously, Stumpf resigned his benefice in 1523 and relied on congregational support.

When the dispute over baptism came to a head in January 1525, the native Zurich radicals led by Grebel and Feliz Mantz were ordered to stop meeting together, but the four most prominent radicals whose home was outside Zurich territories were banished.[20] Two of these four were the unbeneficed priests Reublin and Brötli. Before they left they were almost certainly participants in the first adult baptisms of January 21, 1525.[21]

As it happened, the beginning of Anabaptism in Zurich coincided almost exactly with the outbreak of the main phase of the Peasants' War in Upper Swabia. The rural uprising was very closely connected with the Reformation.[22] Its program, in the first two of the Twelve Articles, continued the themes of Reformation radicalism in Zurich: the abolition of the traditional system of benefices and the appointment, dismissal and support of their own pastors by village congregations.[23] Throughout 1525 in the whole region of northeastern Switzerland — Zurich, Schaffhausen, St. Gallen and Appenzell — there was a thorough intermingling of Anabaptism and rural resistance to authority. In Switzerland, unlike the Empire, there was no large-scale military suppression of rural resistance, hence, in a strict sense, no Peasants' War.

---

[16] *QGTS*, 1: *Zürich*, 16; trans. Matheson, *Collected Works of Müntzer*, 126.

[17] Egli, *Actensammlung*, 101-2, 125, 179-80, 901.

[18] Egli, *Actensammlung*, 266.

[19] *QGTS*, 1: *Zürich*, 44-5.

[20] *QGTS*, 1: *Zürich*, 35-6.

[21] A. F. K. Zieglschmid, ed., *Die älteste Chronik der Huterischen Brüder* (Ithaca, 1943), 47.

[22] James M. Stayer, *The German Peasants' War and Anabaptist Community of Goods* (Montreal, 1991).

[23] Alfred Götze, ed., "Die Zwölf Artikel der Bauern 1525: Kritisch herausgegeben", *Historische Vierteljahrschrift* 5 (1902): 1-33; trans. in Peter Blickle, *The Revolution of 1525: The German Peasants' War from a New Perspective*, trans. T. A. Brady, Jr., H. C. E. Midelfort (Baltimore, 1981), 196-7.

Grüningen, an important dependency of Zurich, experienced the sacking of monasteries, a characteristic anticlerical episode in 1525. When the abbot of Rüti, widely known to be an enemy of the Reformation, fled with valuables from his monastery, twelve hundred villagers devoted two days to consuming the food and wine supplies of the monasteries of Rüti and neighbouring Bubikon. This carnival-like happening was the prelude to Grüningen's making extensive demands upon the government of Zurich for increased local independence.[24] Jörg Berger, Zurich's governor in Grüningen during this troubled period, noted how the ringleaders of the peasant uprising later turned out to be Anabaptists. This was true of the innkeeper, Hans Girenbader, regarded as the leader of the Rüti assembly.[25] Berger was particularly wrought up about a man he called "Bad Uli" (probably Uli Seiler), who led a prison breakout of Grüningen Anabaptists in February 1526, and who staged one of the area's noisier acts of anticlerical guerilla theatre. "Bad Uli" conducted a pigeon shoot directed at the church tower, "while the priest was proclaiming God's Word, ... which was a terrible shame and disgrace!", according to Berger.[26]

The rural disturbances did not help the reputations of the Grüningen priests — especially six radicals (half of the beneficed clergy of the district) who at first supported peasant resistance to tithes and in some cases also opposed infant baptism. The laity accused them of stirring up unrest in their sermons and then quickly making their political accommodations with Zurich and theological accommodations with Zwingli.[27] This loss of prestige by the local clergy was made to order for the leading Zurich Anabaptists, Grebel and Mantz, and a newcomer, the priest from Chur Georg Blaurock, each of whom successfully recruited Anabaptists in Grüningen in the months following the uprising. In various places Blaurock would attempt to usurp the pulpits of the regular pastors, saying: "Not you, but I have been sent to preach."[28]

Jörg Berger and his bailiffs always maintained some Zurich authority in Grüningen and they eventually arrested the Anabaptist missionaries. Brötli and Reublin, on the other hand, went to a place where all authority had broken down, the village of Hallau that organized the resistance of the rural

---

[24] Gustav Strickler, *Geschichte der Herrschaft Grüningen. Das ist Geschichte des Züricher Oberlandes und seine Beziehungen zur Stadt Zürich und dem See* (Zurich, 1908), 139-54.

[25] Strickler, *Geschichte der Herrschaft Grüningen*, 144-5; *QGTS*, 1: *Zürich*, 158, 172-3; Matthias Hui, "Vom Bauernaufstand zur Täuferbewegung", *MGB* 46 (1989): 120-3, 141-2.

[26] *QGTS*, 1: *Zürich*, 171-2.

[27] Hui, "Vom Bauernaufstand", 125-31.

[28] Hui, "Vom Bauernaufstand", 131-5; Fritz Blanke, *Brüder in Christo. Die Geschichte der älteste Täufergemeinde (Zollikon 1525)* (Zurich, 1955), 33.

subjects of Schaffhausen.[29] The Schaffhausen government did send an armed contingent to arrest them, but complained that the villagers "kept the priests away from our men with violence and weapons."[30]

Shortly after the arrival of Reublin and Brötli, probably in February 1525, Hallau took the initiative in convening a general assembly of the rural subjects of Schaffhausen, to draw up demands on the town government. These demands attacked serfdom, compulsory labour services and, of course, tithes. All tithes were to be spent from henceforth in the parishes where they were collected for the "servant of the congregation" and the support of the poor.[31] About the same time Brötli wrote back to Zollikon that he had been preaching regularly at Hallau: "I found a great harvest there but few cutters. The people earnestly desired to hear me and still do." The beneficed pastor at Hallau, he continued, was a miser and a womanizer and Antichrist was still powerfully entrenched there.[32] By April this pastor, Hans Ziegler, was expelled from the village[33] and replaced by Brötli and Reublin, who, according to Hallau's next Reformed pastor, "baptized virtually the whole population."[34] Reublin won the nearby Austrian town of Waldshut, then involved in the Peasants' War, for an Anabaptist Reformation and baptized some Schaffhausen burghers, trying to introduce a radical Reformation there, too.[35] On at least one occasion in 1525 an armed action against Schaffhausen joined Anabaptist villagers from Hallau and Anabaptist townsmen from Waldshut.[36] The breakdown of authority during the Peasants' War created circumstances in rural Schaffhausen in which unbeneficed Anabaptist preachers served rebellious villagers as replacements for the clergy.

The neighbouring village of Schleitheim refused to pay tithes in 1525 under Hallau's leadership. Almost certainly the first adult baptisms there

---

[29] James M. Stayer, "Reublin and Brötli: The Revolutionary Beginnings of Swiss Anabaptism", in *The Origins and Characteristics of Anabaptism / Les debuts et les caracteristiques de l'anabaptisme*, ed. M. Lienhard (The Hague, 1977), 89-102.

[30] Heinold Fast, ed., *Quellen zur Geschichte der Täufer in der Schweiz*, vol. 2, *Ostschweiz* (Zurich, 1973) [hereafter *QGTS*, 2: *Ostschweiz*], 23.

[31] Paul Herzog, *Die Bauernunruhen im Schaffhauser Gebiet 1524-25* (Aarau, 1965), 41; Nabholz, *Bauernbewegung* (n. 13 above), 64-5; Karl Schib, *Geschichte der Stadt und Landschaft Schaffhausen* (Schaffhausen, 1972), 247-9, 265-7; Reinhard Meyer, Hans Reinhard Meyer, *Heimatkunde und Geschichte von Hallau* (Bern, 1938), 394-5.

[32] *QGTS*, 1: *Zürich*, 45-6, 54-5.

[33] *QGTS*, 2: *Ostschweiz*, 22, n. 3; Staatsarchiv Schaffhausen, Justiz, Bl 1527 (*sic* — although the date of the document is 16 May 1525), 27-30; Ratsprotokolle, vol. 6 (1522-1526), 256, 264.

[34] *QGTS*, 2: *Ostschweiz*, 49.

[35] *QGTS*, 1: *Zürich*, 391-2; *QGTS*, 2: *Ostschweiz*, 48-9.

[36] Karl Schib, ed., *Quellen zur neueren Geschichte Schaffhausens* (Thayngen, 1948), 24; J. Huber, ed., "Heinrich Küssenbergs Chronik", *Archiv für schweizerische Reformations-Geschichte* 3 (1876): 423.

were conducted by Brötli and Reublin.[37] Both preachers had to flee the area at the end of 1525 when peasant resistance collapsed everywhere and Hallau formally submitted to the government of Schaffhausen. In February 1527 Reublin returned to his former centre of activity with Michael Sattler and other Anabaptist leaders to draw up the Seven Articles of Schleitheim, the major foundational document of early Swiss Anabaptism.

The central principle of the Seven Articles was separation from the world, the subject of Article 4. First among the things mentioned to be shunned were "all popish and new popish works and idolatry, gatherings and church attendance."[38] Replacing the Catholic and the Reformed clergy, there were to be "shepherds in the church of God" ("hirten in der gemein gottes", the same terminology used by Zwingli). These leaders were to have "a good report of those who are outside the faith. The office of such a person shall be to read and exhort and teach, warn, admonish or ban in the congregation, and properly to preside among the brothers and sisters in prayer and in the breaking of bread." They were to be supported by the congregations and promptly replaced when they were banished or killed. However, the banning of a sinful shepherd by the congregation was also provided for.[39]

In the practice of the Swiss Brethren the Schleitheim Articles' stress on the unity and equality of the congregation prevailed over the leadership of the pastor. The evangelical ideal of the priesthood of all believers was put into practice by wide congregational participation in bible reading, teaching and administration of the ban.[40] When the prominent Anabaptist lay theologian, Pilgram Marpeck, encountered northeastern Swiss Anabaptists in Appenzell in the 1540s, his opinion was that they had carried laicism to destructive extremes: "There are very few leaders among you, who, if they haven't been excommunicated twice by you and your congregations, then at least once! ... It is contrary to the manner of Christ that the flock should punish the shepherd, rather than the shepherd pasture the flock."[41]

Evidence for Marpeck's assessment comes from the case of Martin Weninger, one of the last prominent leaders of the Swiss Anabaptists to survive from the immediate associates of Conrad Grebel and Michael Sattler.[42] Weninger was a native of the Schaffhausen area; some evidence suggests that he came from the village of Schleitheim itself.[43] In the early

---

[37] Herzog, *Bauernunruhen*, 55, 135; *QGTS*, 2: *Ostschweiz*, 48-9.

[38] *QGTS*, 2: *Ostschweiz*, 30; trans. John H. Yoder, ed., *The Legacy of Michael Sattler* (Scottdale, Penn., 1973), 38, n. 61. I accept the sense of Yoder's translation of "widerbäpstich", but substitute "new popish" for his unclear "repopish".

[39] *QGTS*, 2: *Ostschweiz*, 31; trans. Yoder, *Sattler*, 38-9.

[40] Haas, "Weg in die Absonderung" (n. 2 above), 66-7: "Das Gewicht der Gemeinde was grösser als jenes des Amtes."

[41] *QGTS*, 2: *Ostschweiz*, 226.

[42] *Grebel Letters* (n. 3 above), 557.

[43] *QGTS*, 2: *Ostschweiz*, 40-1.

1530s he circulated a document called the *Vindication*, justifying the refusal of the Anabaptists to attend Reformed church services. It voices the sectarians' rejection of the new clergy, most of whom were in place before the Reformation, and some of whom had returned to the Old Faith when Catholic Swiss conquered their territory in the Second Kappel War: "When such hirelings, such shepherds who have bargained for their wage, see the wolf coming, they flee and do not lay down their lives for the sheep (John 10)." "The rulers of the world have chosen the priests and commissioned them for a specified wage. Therefore it is of the world and the world hears them (I John 4)." "The preaching of the priests is also an unfruitful work ... Their preaching does not help; people are getting worse all the time; no one is improving."[44] Weninger's anticlerical message seems to have been thoroughly absorbed by his congregations. When he breached the prescriptions of the Seven Articles of Schleitheim by swearing an oath in order to secure his release from prison, he lost his followers' trust and was removed from his position as a teacher.[45]

It can be doubted whether Simon Stumpf really wanted to slay priests, any more than did Andreas Karlstadt, who made similar references to Deuteronomy. But the Reformation radicals in Zurich and Schaffhausen wanted to liquidate the long-established clerical system of tithes and benefices, and to turn the preacher into a servant of local congregations instead of being an agent of a church or state hierarchy whose authority pressed down upon the common laity. Whether or not priests, monks and nuns were dissolute luxury-lovers or untrustworthy hirelings, these formulas of denunciation were thrown at them, often by anticlerical members of the clergy. The Anabaptists, who claimed that direct access to the Bible revealed the deceptions both of the old papists and the new popes, found favour in rebellious villages that had lost their Old Faith and had become disillusioned by Reformers who allied so smoothly with those in authority. Pressed by the governments after 1525 into an illegal, often hunted, sectarian existence, they tried to maintain shepherds for their scattered flocks. But the flocks had grown allergic to authority, and sometimes it appeared that the norm was for the flock to punish the shepherd rather than for the shepherd to pasture the flock.

---

[44] *QGTS*, 2: *Ostschweiz*, 108-13; trans. John C. Wenger, "Martin Weninger's Vindication of Anabaptism, 1535", *MennQR* 22 (1948): 180-7.

[45] *QGTS*, 2: *Ostschweiz*, 116.

IV. TOWARD THE CONFESSIONAL AGE

ENGLISH ANTICLERICALISM:
A PROGRAMMATIC ASSESSMENT

RICHARD A. COSGROVE

University of Arizona, Tucson

According to the orthodox version of anticlericalism in English history, it appeared first at some indeterminate date in the fourteenth century. Whether from Chaucer's often unflattering representations of the clergy, or from the theology of John Wyclif with its doubts about the intermediary role of a cleric between God and an individual, or from the philosophical sallies of William of Ockham, a spirit of anticlericalism arose that remained a permanent undercurrent in English life throughout the fifteenth century in the guise of Lollardy. Anticlericalism was a latent force in English society until it erupted in full fury at the time of the reformation. Significant manifestations of anticlerical feeling included designs on church wealth, resentment of clerical hypocrisy about issues of personal morality, and the hatred of clerical arrogance best exemplified by Cardinal Wolsey. The triumph of the reformation, indeed the recognition of England's fundamentally Protestant national identity, emphasized those abuses associated solely with the Catholic church. To this day, for example, some dictionaries define anticlericalism as a phenomenon directed specifically against the Catholic clergy. Once exposed and excised, these vices disappeared amidst the final Protestant settlement of religion.

This depiction of English history has a long pedigree. From the publication of John Foxe's *Book of Martyrs* in 1563, the progressive unfolding of England's Protestant destiny pushed the topic of anticlericalism into an intellectual box labeled Catholic only. The use of anticlericalism as an organizing concept in the nineteenth century reinforced this simplistic vision of Tudor history. Popular prejudice against Catholicism retained a substantial hold on the Victorian imagination. Application of anticlericalism as an analytical tool to events and personalities of the sixteenth century raises the question: To what extent have concerns central to Victorian values affected the formulation of the original concept? An examination of anticlericalism has something to tell us of the way the recent past interpreted the distant past. Such a review must consider its place in that patriotic English history that has fused national consciousness with the virtues (and victories) of Protestantism.

The Victorian definition of anticlericalism proved a self-fulfilling prophecy derived from its own experience of clerical privileges, whether the tithe wars in the Ireland of the 1830s, the long and ultimately successful campaign against the religious tests for matriculation at Oxford and Cambridge, or even Protestant England's fundamental assumption that Irish Catholics depended too heavily on their priestly caste. The Irish political situation of the late nineteenth century provided an excellent contemporary model by which anticlericalism became equated with Protestant liberty and subservience to clericalism marked Catholic despotism. This identification stretched back to the early years of the reformation when Sir Francis Bigod had written in 1535 that "we be delivered from the hard, sharp and ten thousand times more than judicial captivity of that Babylonical man of Rome, to the sweet and soft service, yea, rather liberty of the gospel."[1] The deliverance of the English nation from papal tyranny became a prominent motif of historical writing.

If the basic explanation of anticlericalism derived from the pieties of national assertion, then it seems appropriate, after a century's interval, to reassess the concept and its origins. John Guy has written recently about the state of Elizabethan religious divisions:

> Attitudes to parish clergy and Protestant preachers sometimes divided on confessional lines, but anticlericalism was sparked by financial and jurisdictional grievances especially tithe disputes. In fact, when lay-clerical relations are examined in terms of litigation, clerical recruitment, and religious benefactions, it becomes clear that anticlericalism was a consequence, rather than a cause, of the English Reformation.[2]

Guy's assertion makes a striking contradiction to the traditional story familiar to historians of Tudor England. It is now clear that a revision to the use of anticlericalism is in full swing; its usefulness in historical explanation has implications for other interpretations of important reformation issues.

By the beginning of the sixteenth century the fundamental profile of anticlericalism was plain: many of the faithful had accumulated grievances against the church in its human and institutional manifestations, yet simultaneously they proclaimed a continuing allegiance to doctrinal orthodoxy. The people of England, long noted for their loyalty to Rome, loved their church but in a fashion that permitted criticism of its most glaring defects. These complaints against the church were real. Most historians would still concede that legal, financial and moral objections to aspects of church actions helped create a popular image, no matter how infrequent the instance, that promoted a culture of hostility to the clergy.

This story of a cumulative anticlericalism building to 1529 must be carefully distinguished. The romantic history of anticlericalism from Chaucer onwards as a progressive realization of the nascent Protestant spirit of the nation has little meaning apart from basic popular perceptions of a clergy

---

[1] Sir Francis Bigod, *A Treatise Concernynge Impropriations of Benefices*, in A. G. Dickens, ed., *Tudor Treatises* (York, 1959), 42.

[2] John Guy, *Tudor England* (Oxford, 1988), 293-4.

that failed sufficiently to heed its own exhortations. Do the concrete examples of hostility to the clergy after 1500 give a better insight into the range of complaints that allegedly constituted an influential atmosphere of anticlericalism? Each part of the anticlerical puzzle might not on its own have sufficed to generate resistance to the old order, as one line of argument holds, but taken together the accumulated dislike of disparate actions combined to form a popular prejudice waiting for deployment by state authorities. J. J. Scarisbrick has argued against this convenient idea:

> We have hitherto been content with the image of the Tudor regime unleashing and then riding the back of the tiger of popular anticlericalism, anti-papalism, patriotism and so on. If that is now suspect, this is because one can no longer find much of a tiger.[3]

If these traditional accounts of anticlericalism need revision, then it must start with the reinterpretation of evidence familiar to historians.

I. THE SIXTEENTH-CENTURY EVIDENCE

Debate about the sources of anticlericalism is over; controversy about their significance has dominated recent discussions. The most obvious, because the most sensational, involved sexual misconduct by the clergy. That such transgressions of official church morality occurred is indisputable; how frequently and with what consequences makes for greater difficulty. The sexual exploitation of women constituted a major part of a standard litany. Belief in widespread homosexual activity, particularly in the monasteries where recruitment often focused on adolescents, added a dimension of unnatural vice to these stories. Yet it remains difficult to conclude specifically how extensive these actions actually were. Peter Heath's book on the parish clergy has done much to revise the stereotype of a clergy mired in immorality.[4] Most historians have acknowledged that the charges of Simon Fish in the 1528 *Supplication of the Beggars*, with its extended metaphor of clerical wolves and lay sheep, were highly exaggerated. His assertion that a hundred thousand women had suffered sexually must be taken symbolically, not as a literal description of prevailing conditions. Indeed, one argument (especially by Scarisbrick) suggests that the English laity had fashioned a clergy in its own image. Clerical shortcomings were part of the world, not worth getting too excited about, particularly if a cleric did not tax his own parishioners too keenly about their own peccadillos. Evidence from monastic visitations examined by G. W. O. Woodward and Joyce Youings has

---

[3] J. J. Scarisbrick, *The Reformation and the English People* (Oxford, 1988), 2.

[4] Peter Heath, *The English Parish Clergy on the Eve of the Reformation* (London, 1969).

supported a finding of the limited extent of clerical misconduct in this area.[5] A sexually corrupt clergy, while not exonerated, nevertheless has been given its proper proportion.

The next genesis of anticlerical sentiment arose from the bewildering maze of church courts and the actions of church lawyers. Many daily activities now thought secular came under the jurisdiction of the church in the later middle ages. The *Supplication unto the Most Gracyous Prynce Henry VIII* (1534) by Robert Barnes argued that the clergy had usurped many temporal powers, whose legitimate authority was the crown. The most obvious examples of clerical regulation in this regard were marriages and wills, both highly personal and with financial ramifications as well. Church lawyers received the same abuse as their lay brethren, whether accusations of excessive litigation to promote financial interests, dragging out suits to delay justice, or using their forensic skills to prevent exposure of clerical misdeeds. Immediate supervision of personal conduct followed by entanglement in church courts undoubtedly promoted popular antagonism, yet it is not clear to what extent involvement with the courts was necessary for the expression of this complaint. Few suitors in England, whatever the century or the cause, have relished the prospect of becoming enmeshed in protracted court proceedings. Nor were litigants pleased when they lost their cases. The hatred of church jurisdiction may well have reflected anticlerical attitudes only as a response to broader concerns.

In this context there also existed another source of resentment against church courts. Common law courts and church courts historically had competed with each other to extend control over lucrative classes of cases. Criticism of the traditional relationship between the two court systems, as in Christopher St. German's *A Treatise Concerning the Division Between the Spirituality and Temporality* (1532), may do little more than express jealousy on the part of one interest group directed against a competent adversary; it mirrored the same sort of internecine warfare that the common law courts waged among themselves.[6] Thus this criticism did not necessarily indicate a popular sense of grievance against the pre-reformation church.

Another major part of anticlericalism stemmed from the church's undoubted financial strength. That the wealth of the pre-reformation church, especially when measured against ideals of apostolic poverty, aroused envy needs little elaboration. Statutory exactions of the kind that provoked the Richard Hunne affair from 1511 to 1514 no doubt caused harsh feelings against the church precisely because the laity could sympathize with Hunne's resistance to mortuary fees. In addition, tithe payments affected

---

[5] G. W. O. Woodward, *The Dissolution of the Monasteries* (London, 1966); Joyce A. Youings, *The Dissolution of the Monasteries* (London, 1971).

[6] Christopher Haigh, "Anticlericalism and the English Reformation", *History* 68 (1983): 391-406, here 398.

laypeople in good times and bad. Large monastic estates and the role of monks as landlords gave rise to the stereotype of an idle clergy living off the labors of the faithful. Perhaps even more scandalous was the inequitable division of clerical income such that some major prelates enjoyed a fabulous income, while ordinary clergy carried out their ministry in poverty. Unlike some of the other sources of anticlericalism, the wealth of the church was immediate, evident to all ranks of society and a significant catalyst to lay envy and greed.

Despite these outward signs, however, it has become clear that the overall wealth of the church in proportion to the nation at large had declined in the later middle ages. Many monasteries labored with inadequate incomes, and parish clergy suffered from insufficient financial support. Despite the popular perception, the church was actually slipping in its economic position, a ripe target for the attacks of an increasingly prosperous landowning class. As Felicity Heal has shown, the spirit to plunder the church remained alive and well throughout the century; it was not an attitude unique to the period before 1529.[7]

In the sphere of theology the persistence of Lollardy, a contentious issue in itself, kept alive a tradition of clerical criticism that stressed the direct relationship between the individual and God that rendered unnecessary the mediation of a special clerical caste. If the clergy did not provide special spiritual services, how could their privileges be justified? Older accounts depicted the Lollards as the first Protestant heroes of the nation who kept alive the spirit of reformation through the perils of the fifteenth century. The Lollards were a living testament to the existence of anticlericalism itself.

Often seen as the forerunners of the reformation and a link between Wyclif and Luther, the exact importance of the Lollard tradition has remained difficult to gauge. In 1977 Geoffrey Elton characterized the Lollards as "a barely surviving underground movement".[8] Questions about social composition, regional strength and sophistication of theological thought have not found easy answers. Indeed the church had a stake in the existence of Lollardy if only to flex periodically its power against suspected heretics. The extent and tenacity of Lollard beliefs remain in dispute and perhaps forever beyond exact calculation.[9] Anticlericalism did not necessarily entail heretical positions, although the church found it convenient to allege that criticism represented heresy. The first session of the Reformation Parliament in 1529 exemplified this scenario when bishop John Fisher charged that reform schemes smacked of Hussite principles; the members of

---

[7] Felicity Heal, *Of Prelates and Princes: A Study of the Social and Economic Position of the Tudor Episcopate* (Cambridge, 1980), 215.

[8] Geoffrey Elton, *Reform and Reformation: England, 1509-1558* (Cambridge, Mass., 1977), 10.

[9] See Anne Hudson, *The Premature Reformation: Wycliffite Texts and Lollard History* (Oxford, 1988).

the Commons angrily asserted their orthodoxy while maintaining their purpose of church reform. The existence of Lollardry as a factor in anticlericalism cannot be gauged precisely.

Finally, anticlericalism stemmed in part from the church's long involvement with secular politics. The church had struggled for a millennium in balancing its world-rejecting tendencies against the necessity to function in the real world. Medieval monarchs had long depended for able servants on an educated clergy. That this situation led to vocations based upon secular ambition rather than spiritual commitment was a continuing problem. Churchmen in high political office became the most visible representatives of the church for the laity. One Wolsey, for example, offset the daily labors of the parish clergy. The failure to provide spiritual leadership added to the agenda of reform; Wolsey never set foot in the province of York until fleeing the wrath of Henry VIII, even though he had been archbishop for fifteen years. Wolsey's pluralism and indifference to moral standards added to the image of a corrupt clergy that required dramatic renewal. It is little wonder, therefore, that anticlericalism has long provided such a basic explanation for the context and ultimate success of the English reformation.

In the last decade these standard charges have become subject to sharp revision. While conceding the validity of these sources of anticlerical sentiment, Scarisbrick has assembled an impressive body of evidence to question the extent of anticlericalism among the general population. The growth of lay confraternities indicated a piety that far outstripped isolated cells of Lollardy. Writings such as the *Supplication of the Beggars* could have reached a limited audience at best because of low literacy rates. While certainly important, Scarisbrick has argued, the Hunne case was isolated and cannot bear the interpretive weight placed upon it.[10] Careerism, pluralism and absenteeism did not match the sorry record of the continental church. This evidence, while notable for demonstrating that the church did not oppress the laity as traditional accounts held, still does not explain the acquiescence in religious change so central to the English reformation. Widespread hostility to the clergy did not exist, but this does not explain the absence of affection that might have altered the outcome of events. Even the reformation enforced from above does not explain why so few, especially from the clergy, resisted the course of events.

Christopher Haigh went even further and has consigned anticlericalism to oblivion, calling it a convenient fiction without basis in the historical record.[11] The usual manifestations of anticlericalism on closer inspection turn out to be a limited number of interest group statutes, a minority of reformist clamor and losers in church court suits. These categories provide

---

[10] Scarisbrick, *The Reformation and the English People*, 45.

[11] Haigh, "Anticlericalism and the English Reformation", 391. Haigh's position was scrutinized carefully by Rosemary O'Day and found unpersuasive. See Rosemary O'Day, *The Debate on the English Reformation* (New York, 1986), 141-2.

little of importance to explain the onset of reformation. Haigh continues by arguing that anticlericalism was an Elizabethan consequence of the reformation, citing increased resistance to the regulation of daily conduct, the loss of vocations, and the decline of benefactions. As a basis for the reformation itself, anticlericalism simply has no value in explaining its origins or the events of 1529 and after.

The key factor in the success of the reformation, according to Haigh, was the enforcement by the state, a task notoriously difficult because of a recalcitrant population.[12] This conclusion contradicts directly the more traditional view of the reformation as "the gradual, exacerbating growth of anticlerical and erastian opinion among Englishmen".[13] Anticlericalism did not cause the reformation in any meaningful sense; it arose from the much sterner measures of the Elizabethan church: "The single orthodoxy of late Tudor England, a religion of spartan services and long, moralizing sermons, provoked the popular anticlericalism which even mortuaries had not caused — Richard Hunne notwithstanding."[14] The state of the question among historians thus could not be more polarized between an explanation of long standing and recent accounts that have questioned the fundamental validity of their predecessors.

The definition of anticlericalism that permeates this volume neatly addresses the many problems that have arisen from the traditional perception of anticlericalism as a unique feeling occasioned by the Catholic clergy. It is now clear, for instance, that tithes caused resentment whether in support of a Catholic or Protestant clergy. A religion backed by the power of the state increased personal regulation in the cause of godliness and the financial tribute that an established church required. The control of the state over social misconduct, such as capital punishment for sexual deviance in place of more lenient ecclesiastical discipline, gave to the Protestant clergy a fiercer instrument of guidance for the laity. The advent of Puritanism made these demands even stronger. The connection between religious leadership and asserting greater social control over an expanding population has frequently been noted. Resistance to this by the poor often resulted in their depiction as stiff-necked in their unwillingness to follow the gospel. Lay grievances in the sixteenth century did not respect religious changes.

My reassessment of anticlericalism examines two problems suggested by the trenchant criticism of the concept itself. The first concerns the general acceptance of religious change in Tudor England, even when allowance is made for the increased coercion of the state. Refusal to adhere to the Catholic clergy, I would argue, resulted in part from the ambiguities of popular culture. On the eve of the English reformation the clergy suffered

---

[12] Geoffrey Elton, *Policy and Police: The Enforcement of the Reformation in the Age of Thomas Cromwell* (Cambridge, 1972).

[13] A. G. Dickens, *The English Reformation* (London, 1964), 83.

[14] Haigh, "Anticlericalism and the English Reformation", 406.

from the antagonism associated with what modern society would term their 'profession'. In today's world harsh criticism of doctors and lawyers has become commonplace. The catalogue of complaints has become standard: they are aloof, greedy and oblivious to the needs of patients and clients. These charges are capable of almost infinite elaboration. Yet the person who voices these accusations often makes a significant reservation about his or her own doctor or lawyer. That individual is usually credited with the virtues of compassion, technical mastery and a generous attitude. It is always someone else's experience that creates the negative image to which a person gives assent. A hostility to lawyers and doctors in general has become part of popular attitudes even though individual cases remain judged on a more impartial basis.

This model provides insight into the culture of anticlericalism, a set of beliefs that gained a life of their own to which individuals responded even while they admitted that local examples did not apply. In the *Dialogue Concerning Heresies*, for instance, Thomas More wrote that most clergymen lived up to their calling, with only a few who did not; but, as Richard Marius has written: "People would always prefer to believe the evil than to speak of the good in their priests."[15] Many who harbored no specific anticlerical feelings nevertheless joined the general chorus of approval when unspecified clergy were denounced. Such behavior would help explain the phenomenon of little overt anticlericalism simultaneously with a failure to react positively in support of the clergy when they came under attack at the reformation. While an individual might abstain from attacking a particular cleric, adherence to a general culture of anticlericalism might also prevent dissent when the clergy in general attracted criticism. With respect to the variable evidence on anticlericalism, this model explains how an individual might straddle opinion, at once devoted to the local cleric and yet accepting society's constellation of popular beliefs. It explains the sense of comfort about the clergy felt by many on the eve of the reformation, but also accounts for the undercurrent of hostility to which many contributed.

II. THE NINETEENTH-CENTURY EVIDENCE

The second problem I would address is the Victorian genesis of the role that anticlericalism has played as a convenient explanation of the reformation. The word anticlerical was first used in 1845, and thus its application to the sixteenth century also reveals something about the nineteenth century. The traditional account of the English reformation, with its emphasis on the part played by popular consensus and the vices of an unreformed clergy, has survived through the dominance of one historian, James Anthony Froude (1818-1894). His twelve volume *History of England from the Fall of Wolsey*

---

[15] Richard Marius, *Thomas More: A Biography* (New York, 1984), 384.

to the Defeat of the Spanish Armada became the standard interpretation of this period, and its hegemony has only a century later come under a renewed scrutiny. The reassessment of anticlericalism and its place in the English reformation must begin with a review of Froude: his purposes and the intellectual context in which he formulated his influential arguments.[16]

Three elements of mid-Victorian life contributed to the making of Froude's *History*: the popular view of religious change as political patriotism, the reaction against the "clerical resurgence" of the 1850s and 1860s, and the continuing preoccupation of Froude with events in Ireland. The synthesis of these elements provided Froude with an imaginative context congenial to the assumptions of Victorian society. The reformation, Froude contended, "sprung up spontaneously, unguided, unexcited, by the vital necessity of its nature, among the masses of the nation."[17] Froude's depiction of popular anticlericalism has colored subsequent histories of the reformation; to understand that portrait, the Tudor historian must turn to Victorian England.

Although Froude never qualified as a political Whig, his history illustrates some (not all) of the characteristics associated with the Whig interpretation, the most famous general account of English history. In summary the underlying assumption of Whig historiography stressed that God invariably sided with parliament and Protestantism in the unfolding of English history. The basic fallacy of the Whig theory, of course, was its historical teleology — the presentist bias that the final purpose of English history was whatever existed at the time of writing. It made the division of heroes and villains an easy task, with the latter role usually played by royalists and Catholics. Whig history stressed the essential continuity, the fundamental absence of conflict that allegedly characterized English history. In the face of these values, how could the English people have embarked on such a major departure from their history as the reformation without irreparable damage to the national consensus? Froude answered this question with the argument that the church, by its long decline into vice, had actually broken the consensus. The events of the reformation actually reaffirmed the national sense of purpose: "Protestantism, although it may have become an intellectual system and Church establishment, was first of all a protest against the moral corruption of the old system."[18] The appearance of the concept anticlericalism, the indignant wrath of the English people, became

---

[16] About Froude's influence there can be little debate: "His books sold in hundreds of thousands; he was read all over the English-speaking world; he was a public figure." See A. L. Rowse, *Froude the Historian: Victorian Man of Letters* (Gloucester, 1987), 1.

[17] James Anthony Froude, *History of England from the Fall of Wolsey to the Defeat of the Spanish Armada*, 12 vols. (London, 1856-70), 2: 26.

[18] Jeffrey P. Von Arx, *Progress and Pessimism: Religion, Politics, and History in Late Nineteenth Century Britain* (Cambridge, Mass., 1985), 188-9.

the theme that Froude utilized to tie national consensus to older traditions of historical explanation.

By the middle of the nineteenth century the polemics of earlier centuries had given way to more sophisticated analyses of religious reform. Yet so essential was the reformation to national identity that any account of the Tudor age invariably became a reprise of English patriotism. The Victorian spirit of national assertion expressed itself in those historians, like Froude, who regarded anticlericalism as a necessary precursor to political unity. By this path the people fulfilled the historic role of exemplifying the nation's destiny. In this fashion, therefore, Froude gave a prominence to anti-clericalism that remained unquestioned until the past decade: "Froude's portrayal of the English Reformation as a lay revolt against a corrupt and self-interested clerical caste explains the relatively minor place he assigned to theology in bringing about what was, after all, a religious reform."[19] Richard Hunne was important; William Tyndale was not. Once the reformation meant a process steered by special interest groups empowered by the state, however, Froude's elaboration of anticlericalism has sounded increasingly hollow.

In the second instance, Froude's use of anticlericalism reflected significant aspects of Victorian religious history. In his youth Froude had been a close friend of John Henry Newman and other members of the Oxford Movement. When Newman 'returned' to Rome, Froude found that he could not follow his mentor back to Catholicism. Newman precipitated the final break when he asked Froude for historical research on the lives of the saints in Britain to illuminate the divine mission of the Catholic church. Froude found little evidence to support Newman's hopes, only a hopeless collection of legends and other unverifiable stories. This situation became ironic when Froude, so skeptical of the lives of the saints, remained so credulous about the allegations of widespread sexual misconduct by the pre-reformation clergy. No charge could have aroused indignation more than this affront to Victorian values. Froude came to the defense of the English reformation because the Oxford Movement had denigrated its importance and impugned its leaders.[20] Froude, whose own religious belief waned after this flirtation with the Tractarians, regarded the Anglican church "not as a divinely guaranteed dogmatic system ... but as a national institution: the embodiment of a long process of historical development, still valid because it preserved and fostered the best and the highest in the religious sensibilities of the English people."[21] The emphasis on anticlericalism provided one means to put distance between the Anglican and Roman Catholic churches. It also entitled the reformation to rank as a major determinant of national identity.

---

[19] Von Arx, *Progress and Pessimism*, 185.

[20] Rowse, *Froude the Historian*, 13.

[21] Von Arx, *Progress and Pessimism*, 185.

Moreover, Froude reacted against the "clerical resurgence" in mid-Victorian England. This phrase covers the strengthening of the Church of England by the high church party, particularly with reference to its institutional and organizational reform. By extension it also included the growth of the Catholic church after the restoration of the hierarchy in 1850, the so-called "papal aggression". For Froude these changes indicated that the Anglican clergy stood in danger of becoming too Catholic, that they might repeat the mistakes of the pre-reformation era: "too much of a priestly caste — without spirit yet insistent of dignities and privileges."[22] The use of anticlericalism as an explanatory category served as a warning of what might befall the Anglican church if it persisted in pride and complacency.

The ambiguities of sixteenth-century anticlericalism stood as a convenient proxy for the hopes and fears of Froude's Victorian liberalism. On the one hand, one great goal of liberalism was the elimination of clerical privilege in whatever guise it appeared. The demands for Irish and Welsh disestablishment, with the Irish cause successful in 1869, symbolized one line of attack on Anglican supremacy. The Anglican monopoly on education also attracted criticism on the ground that the established church ought to compete with other religions on an equal basis, a touchstone of liberal faith. Religious tests for matriculation and the holding of fellowships at Oxford and Cambridge were eventually abolished. The Forster Education Act of 1870 signaled the demise of Anglican control over much elementary and secondary education. Dissenters resented their inability to conduct marriage and funeral services on the same terms as the established church, and they regarded the mandatory payment of rates for maintenance of the Anglican church as a particular injustice. With these various causes Froude sympathized.

On the other hand, Froude never abandoned his attachment to the established church for its secular achievements. The counterattack against evangelical pressures led to high church claims that threatened to fasten upon the national church precisely those attitudes that had led to the original reformation. Froude prized the Church of England for its temporal achievements more than its spiritual victories and thus, despite his anxieties about its direction, he desired that the church continue its work as a source of national character. The symbiotic relationship between Froude's own distrust of the contemporary clergy and his faith in the historic mission of the church as a vehicle of national identity permitted him to admire anticlericalism as a foundation of national greatness and yet not fall prey to the clericalism of the 1860s.

The third influence on Froude's construction of anticlericalism was his perception of the Catholic church as it existed in Ireland. The pernicious effects of clerical power still were manifest in the image of an Irish political

---

[22] Von Arx, *Progress and Pessimism*, 189.

and cultural life dominated by the parish priests. Unlike the majority of his contemporaries who voiced opinions about Irish affairs, Froude could claim special qualification by virtue of frequent residence in various parts of Ireland. This led him, however, to reflect rather than analyze the prevailing prejudices of Victorian public opinion about the Irish: "It was rather an impatience of control, a deliberate preference for disorder, a determination in each individual man to go his own way, whether it was a good way or a bad, and a reckless hatred of industry. The result was the inevitable one — oppression, misery, and wrong."[23] This listing of defects of Irish character makes a classic example of blaming the victim in the consideration of a troubled relationship. So hostile did Froude's writings become against the Irish that historian W. E. H. Lecky felt compelled to right the wrong by a more judicious appraisal of the Anglo-Irish connection.[24] Like many another Unionist publicist, Froude claimed a personal sympathy for the Irish people; their tragedy lay in continuing subordination to their priests.

The Catholic church in nineteenth-century Ireland remained so central that it made the worst fears of the Protestant fortress mentality imminent. From the Catholic emancipation campaign directed by Daniel O'Connell in the first decades of the nineteenth century to the home rule movement begun in the 1870s, the potential of the Catholic church to influence Irish politics made a constant refrain. After 1867 the scenario became more insidious because political democracy guided by priests had the capacity to affect the fate of governments at Westminster. For Froude, who wrote a three-volume history of *The English in Ireland* to vindicate the role of Protestantism in Irish history, political turmoil in Ireland illustrated the pernicious effects of an overmighty clergy. Froude never recognized, apparently, that the Catholic church for Ireland played the same part that he praised so highly when taken by the Anglican church. The difference still remained that the Catholic church represented papal tyranny and individual dependence whereas Protestantism meant national liberty and individual freedom for England, a motif that has resonated through much subsequent historiography. Anti-clericalism fit neatly into Froude's Victorian concerns as well as serving as a new instrument of historical analysis.

III. Conclusion

Froude's formulation of anticlericalism and the primary place he assigned it bequeathed an interpretation that has, until recently, dominated most discussions of reformation origins. The strong critiques of anticlericalism offered by Haigh and Scarisbrick with the ancillary contention that it applies

---

[23] Froude, *History of England*, 2: 258.
[24] W. E. H. Lecky, *History of England in the Eighteenth Century*, 8 vols. (London, 1878-92).

only to the post-1529 church, represents a complete break with the patriotic heritage initiated by Froude. If anticlericalism is to survive in the English context as a useful analytical tool, it must provide a more vigorous vision than Froude supplied. He ignored that reform of the clergy before 1529 turned into reform of the laity afterwards, now augmented by the power of the state. It did not result in a happy outcome for many laypeople.[25] On any future agenda issues about which Froude has proved inadequate must receive a high priority: the reformation from above or below, anticlericalism as an Elizabethan phenomenon, the Catholic church on the eve of the reformation. It may well transpire that anticlericalism has hindered rather than enhanced the ability of the historian to reconstruct the past. A considerable amount of research on Tudor religious history has appeared, especially in the last two decades; but it also appears that much remains to be done, especially in the rectification of conclusions made under the influence of Froude's anticlericalism. A fresh study of English anticlericalism from 1529-1603 would make a welcome addition to the reassessment of a basic problem.

---

[25] See Robert von Friedeburg, "Reformation of Manners and the Social Composition of Offenders in an East Anglian Cloth Village: Earls Colne, Essex, 1531-1642", *Journal of British Studies* 29 (1990): 347-85.

ANTISACERDOTALISM AND THE YOUNG CALVIN

CARLOS M. N. EIRE

University of Virginia, Charlottesville

I. Introduction

Many reformers and would-be reformers in the late fifteenth and early sixteenth century complained about the failings of the clergy, not because they sought to displace them from their privileged position, but rather because they sought to increase the clergy's influence over society. Clerical reformers who were very proclerical often shared a common contempt for corruption and abuse with anticlerical social reformers, and even agreed on some grievances, but their rhetoric was aimed towards very different ends. Clerical self-criticism could focus attention on the failings of the clergy, but was not usually inclined to deny the power and privilege of the clerical state, or question the intercessory nature of the Christian ministry. With the advent of the Reformation, this grievance rhetoric aimed against the corruption of the clergy assumed another configuration: some critics began calling for a change in the very nature of the Christian clergy, from a sacerdotal, or priestly ministry, into a disciplinary and pedagogical ministry. This "antisacerdotalism" was as varied as the Reformation itself, but one type in particular became dominant in the Reformed tradition, and eventually came to exert a powerful influence on the development of many European societies: this was the strain preferred by John Calvin, the clerical reformer who transformed Geneva into the Protestant Rome.

It has been argued that the Reformation in Geneva began as an anticlerical revolution.[1] Nothing confirms this thesis more convincingly or dramatically than simple numbers. In pre-Reformation Geneva, a city of ten thousand inhabitants, there were roughly four hundred clerics.[2] After 1536, in contrast, these numbers shrank by an astounding 97.5%, when the clergy within the city walls were reduced to a paltry ten ministers.[3] This quan-

---

[1] Robert M. Kingdon, "Calvin and the Government of Geneva", in *Calvinus Ecclesiae Genevensis Custos, Proceedings of the International Congress for Calvin Research*, ed. W. H. Neuser (Frankfurt, 1984), 51.

[2] Henri Naef, *Les origines de la réforme à Genève*, 2 vols. (Geneva, 1936, 1968), 1: 22-35.

[3] Kingdon cautions against taking these figures literally. The four hundred pre-Reformation clerics were not all priests, or involved in the "cure of souls". Also, the ten Reformation ministers were assisted by presbyters and lay deacons. Still, he

titative fact is confirmed in a more symbolic manner by a contemporary chronicler, Antoine Fromment. When the final riot that ushered in the Reformation took place in Geneva on Sunday, 8 August 1535, it seemed that even youths and children knew that they were struggling against the clergy. "Here we have the gods of the priests", a group of youths (*enfans*) chanted in triumph as they carried out into the streets bits and pieces of the images they had just demolished inside St. Peter's Cathedral. "Would you like some?", they asked curious onlookers.[4]

Oddly enough, however, this anticlerical revolt eventually evolved into Calvin's Geneva, the godly city-state dominated by the clergy, the Protestant Rome, the training ground and exporting center of hundreds of well-trained missionaries who sought to create and lead similar societies throughout France and the rest of Europe. As Robert Kingdon has pointed out, the status of the Genevan clergy changed dramatically between 1536 and 1555. Immediately after the Reformation, the clergy became "powerless civil servants ... employees of the state, completely subject to the government". After 1555, the clergy not only exercised leadership in Genevan society, but had also "made themselves indispensible to the Genevan governing class."[5]

How did this metamorphosis take place? How did an anticlerical revolt transform itself into a clerical theocracy? Much of the credit (or blame, depending on one's perspective) can be assigned to John Calvin, and to the proclerical antisacerdotalism which he had adopted in France as a budding humanist, and brought with him to Geneva as a young reformer. In this paper, I will analyze one of Calvin's earliest publications, "On the Duty of the Christian Man in Administering or Rejecting the Priesthood of the Papal Church", a treatise in which he attacked the sacerdotal priesthood of the Roman Catholic Church and juxtaposed against it an ideal conception of the "true" Christian ministry.[6] By studying what the twenty-seven-year-old Calvin had to say about the clergy before he became the Reformer of

---

concludes, "there was a very drastic decline" in the total number of clergy; "Calvin and the Government of Geneva", 53-4.

[4] "Nous avons les dieux des Prebstres, en voulles vous?" Antoine Fromment, *Les actes et gestes merveilleux de la cité de Genève* (1544), reissued by J. G. Fick (Geneva, 1954), 144-5.

[5] Kingdon, 58. See also Harro Höpfl, *The Christian Polity of John Calvin* (Cambridge, 1982), esp. 128-51.

[6] "De christiani hominis officio in sacerdotiis papalis ecclesiae vel administrandis vel abiiciendis." Issued together with another letter addressed to Nicholas Duchemin, also on the subject of compromise with Catholicism, "De fugiendis impiourum illicitis sacris, et puritate christianae religionis observanda." Both epistles were published under the single title *Epistolae duae de rebus hoc saeculo cognitu apprime necesariis* (Basel, 1537). A second edition appeared in 1550, this time from a Genevan press. Subsequent anthologies of Calvin's writings included the *Duae epistolae* (1552, 1576, 1597). An inexact French translation first appeared in Theodore Beza's *Recueil des Opuscules* (Geneva, 1566).

Geneva it should be possible to better understand how a certain kind of anticlerical rhetoric gave rise to the most aggressive sort of proclericalism. It should also be possible to better understand the development of Calvin's break with Catholicism, and what would become his life-long battle against those "temporizers" and "Nicodemites" who thought it possible to remain in the Roman Catholic Church and still work for a reform of Christendom.

II. CALVIN AND HUMANIST "ANTICLERICALISM"

When John Calvin censured certain abuses committed by the Roman Catholic clergy, he drew upon personal experience: throughout his adolescence and early adulthood he had been an absentee unordained beneficed "cleric" who performed none of the duties ostensibly required of him. In May 1521, a few weeks shy of his twelfth birthday, Calvin had obtained his first ecclesiastical benefice, a portion of the income from a chaplaincy at the cathedral of Noyon. At the age of eighteen, he had also been assigned the relatively more substantial post of curate at Marteville, a village near Noyon. Both benefices were obtained through the influence of his father, Gerard Calvin, secretary to the cathedral chapter of Noyon. Though he was most probably tonsured as a formality in 1521, and began to prepare for the priesthood, John Calvin was not ordained. When he dutifuly obeyed his father's command to take up the law instead of theology, the young Calvin continued to fund his education with the income from these benefices.[7]

Since Calvin never gave a specific date for his "conversion" from Catholicism, many biographers have assigned great significance to that moment in May of 1534 when he returned to his native Noyon in spite of the threat of persecution, and officially relinquished the income he had been drawing from these benefices for half of his life.[8] From this point forward, Calvin's commitment to the Reformed cause only intensified. Before long, he was advising other benefice holders to imitate him. Shortly after finishing the first version of the *Institutes* in 1536, during his stay in Ferrara, Calvin wrote an impassioned letter to a close friend, Gerard Roussel, newly appointed Bishop of Oleron, and Abbot of Clairac, in which he warned him

---

[7] As was customary under such circumstances, Calvin apparently used part of the income to pay someone else to carry out his duties. See Emile Doumergue, *Jean Calvin. Les hommes et les choses de son temps* (Lausanne, 1899-1928), 1: 37-40.

[8] For a discussion of past attempts to date Calvin's conversion see Paul Sprengler, *Das Rätsel um die Bekehrung Calvins* (Neukirchen, 1960), and Alexandre Ganoczy, *Le jeune Calvin: genèse et évolution de sa vocation réformatrice* (Wiesbaden, 1966). See also Doumergue, *Jean Calvin*, 1: 424, 336-55. William Bouwsma has recently agreed with Ganoczy in saying that Calvin most probably experienced a gradual conversion, and that no attempt should be made to fix a single specific date. *John Calvin, A Sixteenth Century Portrait* (New York, 1988), 10-11.

not to accept the income from his two posts.[9] Calvin told Roussel that his "nearly fraternal" affection would not allow him to see his friend take a "fatal fall" into the error and deception involved in the Roman Catholic priesthood:

> All of this great income of the Roman Church, from the papacy on down, even to the poorest chaplaincy ... is so crammed full of deceptions, thefts, depredations, sacrileges, and the most wretched practices, that one cannot even handle the smallest coin without incurring guilt for a thousand misdeeds.[10]

Calvin's sense of revulsion was no doubt stimulated by guilt over his own misuse of benefices. This remorse, however, was only part of a much larger sense of discontent: a profound abhorrence of the behavior of the Catholic clergy as a whole, a disillusionment shared by many of his contemporaries.[11] Consequently, this letter to Roussel not only mirrors Calvin's unique reflections, but also those of the vast reservoir of late medieval and early Reformation anticlericalism. Calvin, it seems, was especially affected by the grievance rhetoric of reform minded clerics, particularly those of the Erasmian humanist stripe.

William Bouwsma has recently observed that "Calvinism was the creation of a devout sixteenth-century French Catholic." He has also convincingly argued that Calvin was deeply indebted to Erasmus.[12] Alexandre Ganoczy has maintained that Calvin was deeply influenced by clerics ("hommes d'Eglise") as a youth, and that he remained gripped by churchliness ("esprit d'Eglise") throughout his life.[13] The young Calvin undoubtedly shared much with other young devout humanist Catholics throughout Europe in the sixteenth century. Like many of his well educated and religiously inclined contemporaries, Calvin adhered to an elitist conception of the *corpus christianorum* according to which the clergy were considered to be the head of the body of the faithful. Those who shared this view consequently believed that the health of the Christian religion depended on the behavior of the clergy. If Christendom had strayed far from its ideal form during the

---

[9] Calvin never named his "friend". It was Theodore Beza who first disclosed Roussel's identity in his *Vita Calvini* (*CO* 21. 127). No one has questioned Beza's credibility on this point. See Doumergue, *Jean Calvin*, 2: 25-8.

[10] *CO* 5. 281. I have also consulted the French version, "Quel est l'office de l'homme chrestien en administrant ou reiettant les benefices de l'eglise papale", *Recueil des Opuscules* (Geneva, 1565), 98.

[11] John Viénot briefly outlines "le mouvement littéraire et anticlérical" from 1530 to 1547, paying special attention to Rabelais, Clement Marot, and Ettienne Dolet: *Histoire de la réforme française des origines à l'Edit de Nantes* (Paris, 1926), 131-47.

[12] Bouwsma, *John Calvin*, 11. "Calvin inhabited the Erasmian world of thought and breathed its spiritual atmosphere, he remained in major ways always a humanist of the late Renaissance.", 13.

[13] Ganoczy, *Jeune Calvin*, 130.

middle ages, the clergy were to blame; conversely, if Christendom were to be restored to its original purity, the clergy must not only be reformed, but also take the initiative in the process of change. There is much more than a trace of proclerical "anticlericalism" in the young Calvin, if one may use such seemingly oxymoronic terminology. Like many other reforming humanist clergy in sixteenth century Europe, Calvin exalted the status of the ideal Christian ministry, and it was often through a juxtaposition of this ideal exalted state against all perceived abuse, negligence, and corruption that Calvin called for reform.[14]

At this point, another sort of juxtaposion may serve to shed additional light on this Erasmian pro-clerical grievance rhetoric. It would be difficult to think of a sharper contrast to Calvinist Christianity than Spanish Catholicism. Yet, it is not altogether misleading to say that the grievance rhetoric of the founder of Calvinism was in many respects similar to that of St. John of Avila, a Spanish priest who had no small influence upon Ignatius Loyola and the Council of Trent, and who is revered as the patron saint of the Spanish clergy.

Juan de Avila (1499-1569) was almost an exact contemporary of Calvin.[15] He was an Erasmian who had imbibed his humanism at at the University of Alcalá, the new school founded by the clerical reformer Cardinal Ximenez de Cisneros in the second decade of the sixteenth century.[16] Like other Erasmians, Juan de Avila blamed the clergy for much that had gone wrong in Christendom, and he longed for a renewal of Christianity which would be led by the clergy.[17] As he said to the fathers of the Council of Trent:

---

[14] Within the Reformed tradition, Ulrich Zwingli, another Erasmian, had set the tone in 1524 with his vernacular treatise *Der Hirt* ("The Shepherd"), Z 3. 1-68, esp. 45-65.

[15] The most complete biography of the "Maestro de Avila", as he is commonly known in Spain, is that of Luis Sala Balust, in *Obras Completas del Santo Maestro Juan de Avila*, edited by him and Francisco Martin Hernandez (Madrid, 1970), 1: 3-392.

[16] See Jose Luis Abellán, *El Erasmismo Español* (Madrid, 1976), esp. 229-36; and José Garcia Oro, *Cisneros y la reforma del clero español en tiempo de los Reyes Catolicos* (Madrid, 1971).

[17] Florencio Sanchez Bella, *La reforma del clero en San Juan de Avila* (Madrid, 1981). Outside of Spain, Juan de Avila has attracted some attention. See Marcel Bataillon, *Erasmo y España*, 2nd. ed. (Mexico, 1950), first published in French (Paris, 1937). Also by Marcel Bataillon, "Jean d'Avila retrouvé", *Bulletin Hispanique* 57 (1955): 5-44. Hubert Jedin, "Juan de Avila als Kirchenreformer", *Zeitschrift für Askese und Mystik* 11 (1936): 124-38. For a recent assessment of his influence on other reform movements in Spain see Jodi Bilinkof, *The Avila of Saint Teresa: Religious Reform in a Sixteenth Century City* (Ithaca, 1989), esp. 80-7.

> It is ordained by God that the harm or benefit of the people depends upon the diligence and care of the ecclesiastical state, much as the earth depends on the influences of heaven.[18]

Like the young Calvin, this Spanish reformer was greatly displeased by the behavior of much of the clergy. Juan de Avila despised the way in which the ministry had become trivialized by insincere, uneducated men of privilege, especially through the abuse of benefices. As a remedy, he proposed that ordination be restricted only to those who felt a genuine calling: those who merely wanted to enjoy the income from benefices, the honor due to clerics, or the juridical privileges of the priestly class would be necessarily excluded. Although this would produce fewer priests, he thought, it would create a more effective and dedicated clergy. Moreover, Juan de Avila also criticized chaplaincies, principally because they tied down the clergy to a single duty and prevented them from ministering in other ways to the faithful. As he saw it, chaplaincies were an exploitative system: the few rich donors who could afford chaplaincies demanded that the clergy spend their time saying masses for them. "In many places", he observed, "there is a sufficient number of masses and extreme poverty among the poor."[19]

Like many other Erasmian reformers in Spain, Juan de Avila encountered resistance and hostility. In 1531 he was denounced for "dangerous" preaching and brought before the Inquisition. His accusers, members of the privileged families of La Mancha, considered him a heretical revolutionary, and reported him as having said that "heaven had been made for the poor and those who worked the land and ... [that] it was impossible for the rich to find salvation." In spite of the power and influence of his opponents, Juan de Avila defended himself successfully, and earned an acquittal two years later.[20] During the remainder of his life he continued to devote himself to the reform of the clergy, and by the time of his death in 1569 he had

---

[18] "Memorial segundo al concilio de Trento", 1561, *Obras*, 6: 86. This sentiment was not the exclusive property of Erasmians. Numerous examples can be cited in anticlerical literature which express similar ideas. One especially poignant complaint was voiced by the German layman Hans Schwalb: "Das ist uns armen unverstendingen bauren ain gut exempel oder beyspil; bey söllichen beyspilen leren mir Eebrechery, büberey, ketzery." *Flugschriften aus den ersten jahren der Reformation*, ed. Otto Clemen (Nieuwkoop, 1967), 1: 350, *Beklagung eines Laien, gennant Hans Schwalb, über viel Misbräuche Christlichen Lebens* (1521).

[19] *Obras*, 1: 31-63. For examples of his complaints against beneficed clergy, see *Obras*, 6: 40, 55, 222-5. St. Ignatius Loyola must be counted among those who took this criticism seriously, since he prohibited the Society of Jesus from saying masses in exchange for alms, so that its members could devote their undivided attention to preaching and teaching.

[20] See *Obras*, 1: 39-63.

established numerous schools throughout Spain, including several seminaries for the training of priests.[21]

Though they shared a common Erasmian heritage, the two Johns — John Calvin and John of Avila — reached very different conclusions. Whereas John of Avila worked for the reform of the priesthood as a faithful Catholic, John Calvin rejected the Roman Catholic Church and worked for the creation of a non-sacerdotal ministry in a purified, "Reformed" church.

The young Calvin's rejection of the sacerdotal Catholic priesthood provides us with a glimpse into an epochal parting of the ways among humanist reformers of the Erasmian stripe within France — one group bound to tradition and the sacerdotal ministry, the other hostile to tradition and committed to a non-sacerdotal ministry. This parting of the ways is most clearly evident in a document that has received scant attention since the sixteenth century, Calvin's letter to his friend, Gerard Roussel.[22]

While a student at Paris, Calvin became an associate of the "Fabrician" circle, a group of reform minded followers of the humanist Jacques Lefèvre D'Etaples and Erasmus.[23] One of the close acquaintances Calvin made among this circle was a beneficed cleric, Gerard Roussel.[24] There can be little doubt that Roussel was strongly inclined toward the Reformed evangelical cause. During his stay at Meaux in the early 1520's, where he actively participated in the reforms of bishop Guillaume Briçonnet,[25] and later during a brief exile in Strasbourg in 1525, he corresponded with Zwingli and Oecolampadius, and openly admitted his admiration for them. In addition, he praised the reforms carried out by Martin Bucer in Stras-

---

[21] Sanchez Bella, *La reforma del clero*, 143-72.

[22] Roussel's only biographer, Charles Schmidt, devotes no more than three pages to Calvin's letter: *Gerard Roussel, prédicateur de la Reine Marguerite de Navarre* (Strassbourg, 1845; Geneva, 1970), 114-17. Alexandre Ganoczy devotes a scant three pages (315-17) to this letter in *Jeune Calvin* and only one (388) in his earlier *Calvin, théologien de l'église et du ministère* (Paris, 1964).

[23] See Richard Stauffer, "Lefévre D'Etaples: Artisan ou spectateur de la réforme?", *Bulletin de la Societé de l'Histoire du Protestantisme Français*, 113 (1967): 405-23; P. Imbart de la Tour, *Les origines de la réforme* (2nd ed., Melun, 1944), 2: 488-523, 3: 109-53, 288-303; J. Barnaud, *Jacques Lefévre D'Etaples, son influence sur les origines de la réformation française* (Paris, 1900); Margaret Mann, *Erasme et les débuts de la réforme française* (Paris, 1933), esp. 23-112; and Henry Heller, "Reform and Reformers of Meaux" (Ph.D. diss., Cornell University, 1969).

[24] Roussel himself has been ignored by modern scholars. Charles Schmidt's sketchy *Gérard Roussel* (n. 22 above), is still the only available biography.

[25] See Lucien Febvre, "Idée d'une recherche d'histoire comparée: le cas Briçonnet", *Au coeur religieux du xvie siècle*, 2nd ed. (Paris, 1968), 145-61.

bourg, and at the same time expressed remorse about his own inability to openly break with the Roman Catholic Church.[26]

In his position as preacher to Princess Marguerite of Navarre, sister to King Francis I, Roussel had the opportunity to carry the reformist message to high places. He also had the opportunity to obtain favors from his employer and patron. After first granting him the abbacy of Clairac, in Béarn, near the Pyrenees, Marguerite of Navarre rewarded Roussel in 1536 with the bishopric of Oleron, in the same region. Much to the disappointment of his Reformed friends, Roussel took up residence in Oleron, and began to devote himself to church reform as a Catholic bishop.[27]

When Calvin learned of Roussel's decision, he wrote him a lengthy letter, in which he tried to draw Roussel away from his bishopric through rhetoric and emotion, as well as by reasoned argumentation. This letter was intended for a wide audience. Calvin admitted that he was not concerned solely with this case, but with all such cases, and that it was not his intention to speak only against one specific kind of benefice, but against all benefices.[28] Less than a year later, when he was beginning his ministry in Geneva, this letter was the first thing that Calvin published.

III. THE ABUSES OF THE ROMAN CATHOLIC CLERGY

In order to convince Roussel that he had acted wrongly in accepting the bishopric of Oleron, Calvin outlined what was wrong with the Roman Catholic priesthood. The resulting catalogue of abuses is filled with many traditional anticlerical complaints — theological, economic, and political — but as shall be seen, Calvin's antisacerdotalism is strongly proclerical.

Calvin's argument in this impassioned letter against the priesthood of the Roman Catholic Church begins with a denunciation of the corruption of the Roman Catholic Church in general, then follows through with a condemnation of the "Roman" priesthood, and finally empties out into a turbulent censure of Roussel himself. Calvin's argument rests on the conviction that

---

[26] Roussel's letters can be found in A. L. Herminjard, *Correspondence des réformateurs dans les pays de langue française* (Paris-Geneva, 1866-97; Nieuwkoop, 1965), numbers 104, 117, 118, 162, 167, 168, 184. Also, along with other relevant correspondence, as "pièces justificatives" in Schmidt, *Gerard Roussel*, 169-222. I have analyzed the reformism of the Fabrician circle and Roussel in my *War Against the Idols: The Reformation of Worship from Erasmus to Calvin* (New York, 1986), 166-94.

[27] Theodore Beza, *Vita Calvini*, CO 21. 127, held Roussel responsible for steering Marguerite de Navarre away from Protestantism. Maurice Causse has recently analyzed the Nicodemite learnings of Roussel's patron: "La dissimulation de Marguerite de Navarre", *Bulletin de la Société de l'Histoire du Protestantisme Français* 132 (1986).

[28] *CO* 5. 280-81; *Recueil* (n. 6 above), 97.

the Roman Catholic priesthood is evil for two reasons: first, because it promotes all sorts of impious worship, and thus offends God; second, because it mistreats the laity, and thus offends one's neighbor. As Calvin put it; "There is neither one single impious act against God, nor one single injustice against men that they will not fail to commit as long as they simply carry out their duties."[29] By not leading their people away from error, these so-called pastors had become traitors, and were worse than wolves. In Calvin's opinion, no punishment could be harsh enough for such clerics. "What word shall we find to properly express such treachery?", he asks, "or what torment shall prove sufficient to punish it as it deserves?"[30]

3.1 Practical Abuses

The negligence of the Roman Catholic clergy is singled out by Calvin as one of their worst abuses. Bishops, for instance, were supposed to be models of frugality, modesty, and sobriety. Instead of laboring diligently at the task assigned to them by God, they ignored their duties and lived sumptuously.

> Why all this grand opulence without limit and measure? ... Is this not above all an intolerable excess, better suited for some royal magnificence, or tyrannical luxury? ... It is a great villainy on your part, to draw great profits without doing a lick of work. I say plainly, that it is overt cheating and scrounging: I say that it is the most audacious robbery imaginable (and this word is difficult to swallow for you and all bishops like you), that those who have never lifted a finger should demand payment, and even take it by force of authority.[31]

Instead of focusing attention on their duties, complained Calvin, bishops had become negligently self-absorbed in the trappings of wealth and power.[32]

So much for the bishops. What about the lower clergy? According to Calvin, the *curez* were no better, since many did not even take up residence in the churches assigned to them. Occasionally, one would find them there on a feast day, when they mounted the pulpit to preach a bad sermon. All that the best among them ever accomplished was to "sprinkle the people with some seeds of piety."[33]

---

[29] *CO* 5. 288-9; *Recueil*, 106.

[30] *CO* 5. 296; *Recueil*, 114. See also *CO* 5. 289; *Recueil*, 106.

[31] *CO* 5. 291; *Recueil*, 109. Juan de Avila also attacked the negligence and excessive "luxury" of bishops: *Obras*, 6: 89ff., 177, 232-3.

[32] *CO* 5. 282-3; *Recueil*, 99. "In mitra partim, et lituo, et pallio, et annulo, reliquaque eiusmodi supellectile defixae sunt omnium mentes: partim vero, et quidem altius, in illis facultatibus, quibus et domesticus splendor, et populosa familia, et mensae elegantia, et omne deliciarum magnificentiaeque genus continetur."

[33] *CO* 5. 292; *Recueil*, 110. See also *CO* 5. 299; *Recueil*, 117.

3.2 Financial Abuses

Throughout this letter to Roussel, Calvin repeatedly accuses the Roman Catholic clergy of the worst sort of venality and greed, and he did so with the vitriol of a sensationalist pamphleteer. Beginning at the top of the church hierarchy, Rome extorts the greatest "booty" from Christendom. The name *Roma* itself is an acronym for corruption. "O Roma", curses Calvin, the root of all evil and avarice contained in one word: "ut uno verbo Radicem Omnium Malorum Avaritiam complectar." The pope himself is the "romanus archipirata".[34] Calvin assaults Roussel with a barrage of charges against the clergy, speaking of *rapina* (pillage), *exactio* (extortion), *depopulatio* (plunder), *latrocinium* (piracy), and *furtum* (theft). These abuses, he complains, "claw at the substance of the people and torment them, and are cruel and full of inhumanity."[35] At the bottom of the hierarchy, the parish priests engage in the same sort of behavior. What Calvin says about the vicarages of the *curez* summarizes his attack against the economic abuses of the clergy:

> They use these [vicarages] for petty villainy, thievery, and piracy, and through them they commit an infinite number of depredations, extortions, plunders, pillagings, and highway robberies. It would take a very large book to discuss all of this in detail.[36]

The practice of tithing is cited by Calvin as one of the most common of the numerous "violent and coercive extortions" carried on by the Catholic clergy. Although tithing was an ancient practice that dated back to Old Testament times (and thus could be supported by scripture), Calvin argues that it was part of the Mosaic Law, and was thus no longer appropriate for Christians. Since the Old Covenant had been effaced by the New Covenant, the Roman Catholic clergy could not rightly claim anything that had pertained to the Levitical priesthood.[37]

Here one finds a practical application of the priesthood of all believers: Calvin argues that the sacrificial Levitical priesthood had been replaced by Christ's priesthood, and that this new priesthood belongs universally to all

---

[34] *CO* 5. 305; *Recueil*, 124. The "Roman archpirate" is omitted from the French translation.

[35] *CO* 5. 305; *Recueil*, 125. This was a recurrent complaint against the clergy. See J.-G. Baum, ed., *Le Sommaire de Guillaume Farel, reimprimé d'après l'edition de 1534* (Geneva, 1867), 62; also *Triumphus Veritatis (Sik der Warheit)* (1525), in Oscar Schade, ed., *Satiren und Pasquille aus der Reformationszeit* (Hannover, 1856-8), 2: 231-2.

[36] " ... furacissimos praedones, rapinas, direptiones, populationes, latrocinia omne genus ..." *CO* 5. 299; *Recueil*, 117.

[37] *CO* 5. 303; *Recueil*, 122.

of Christ's faithful, not just to the ordained clergy.[38] Furthermore, the Catholic priests are inconsistent in their arguments. Although the Levitical priests were not allowed to use their tithes toward the purchase of any land, the beneficed clergy of Rome choose to ignore this part of the Mosaic Law, according to their own interest. "Why do they swallow up so much land?", asks Calvin; "Why do they seize everything they can lay their hands on?" His sense of outrage is undeniable.

> The priests and beneficed clergy exact tithes from the people which they cannot justly claim according to divine or human law, and thus violate the rights of their neighbors as thieves and brigands.[39]

According to Calvin, these abuses were also a reversal of Christian charity. Instead of alleviating the condition of the poor, the Roman Catholic clergy made it worse. Calvin tells Roussel: "The honorable title of Prelate ... will also bring you a great income ... with which you will not only maintain a high style of living, but also drive many people into poverty and indigence."[40] Nothing else points this out as clearly as the fact that the word "bishop" has become synomymous with "thief" or "plunderer", concludes Calvin.[41]

Calvin goes further, accusing his old friend Roussel of thievery and demanding his punishment. "You go robbing and pillaging from house to house", he charges. Where did you find a license to steal? Do you think God's judgment will be anything but terrible?, he asks Roussel.

> The Lord prounounces loud and clear that you are a thief, and He takes you to task over your misdeeds ... you and all those other horned bishops, because there is not one in the whole gang who is not guilty of thievery and sacrilege.[42]

3.3 Corruption of Faith and Piety

In Calvin's eyes, benefice money is coinage from hell, and the income collected by the beneficed clergy is doubly tainted. First, because it is illicitly and unfairly extracted from the laity. Second, because it is inextricably associated with idolatry and superstition. What Calvin seems to have difficulty understanding is why Roussel did not also see it the same way.[43]

---

[38] See A. Ganoczy, *Jeune Calvin*, 249-53 for a detailed analysis of Calvin's opposition to the sacrificial priesthood and his preference for a ministry of service.

[39] *CO* 5. 304; *Recueil*, 123.

[40] *CO* 5. 282; *Recueil*, 99.

[41] *CO* 5. 305; *Recueil*, 124.

[42] *CO* 5. 292; *Recueil*, 110.

[43] "Sic anathemate referta sunt omnia, ut ad ipsum contactum vos non exhorrescere valde mirer. Quibus idolis, quanta cum Dei contumelia, qua superstitione offerantur, vobis clam non est." *CO* 5. 305; *Recueil*, 124.

The Roman Catholic clergy are not only indolent thieves, charges Calvin, they are bad theologians who mix truth with error and lead the laity into blindness and darkness.[44] Moreover, on those rare occasions when they actually try to teach their flocks, they do it so poorly as to leave the people in a fog. Even trained theologians have difficulty understanding their prattle.[45] Calvin tells Roussel that the work carried on by the parish clergy in the Roman Catholic Church is better suited for pagan sorcerers than for Christians. By compromising with false worship, these so-called pastors do not try to accomodate the truth to their flocks, but rather go over directly to the devil's camp.[46] Calvin further protests that these priests do not only *passively* allow errors to persist, but also *actively* encourage false piety, "by administering with their own hands all the instruments of error and superstition."[47] The fact that the Roman Catholic parish clergy sink the people further into error could be clearly seen in the church buildings themselves. At the entrance, for instance, one could find Holy Water. At the other end of the nave, the focal point of the church building, one could see a sacrificial altar. Did not the Catholic clergy approach the altar in order to offer "a sacrifice replete with horrible blasphemies"? Did they not invite the people to worship "the execrable idol" of the consecrated host?[48]

Calvin continues: theological and devotional error is inseparably linked to financial abuse in the case of annual rents, another common source of benefice income. Calvin tells Roussel that annual rents would not exist if it were not for belief in Purgatory. After all, was not rental income most often bequeathed to the Church in civil wills and testaments in order to fund masses and prayers for the dead? The beneficed clergy build their financial empire on the fable ("fausse imagination") of purgatory, and scare the laity into thinking that they can escape the flames of Purgatory if they pay for masses and prayers, and continue "stuffing the fat bellies of the priests and monks."[49] Thus, it has come to pass that so much land and so much rental income is in the hands of the Roman Catholic clergy. "It is indeed fair to

---

[44] *CO* 5. 293; *Recueil*, 111.

[45] *CO* 5. 293; *Recueil*, 111. Juan de Avila also condemned "defective preaching" as a major fault among the clergy. *Obras* 6: 93ff.

[46] Calvin also disparaged Roussel's other title, that of Abbot of Clairac: "Quid autem est abbas, nisi monasticae superstitionis praeses atque assertor?" *CO* 5. 299; *Recueil*, 118. An abbot such as Roussel, then, was responsible for all the sacrilege, impiety, and idolatry that took place in his monastery.

[47] *CO* 5. 296; *Recueil*, 115.

[48] *CO* 5. 296; *Recueil*, 115. For Calvin, the corruption of Roman Catholicism was most clearly evidenced in the abuse of the Mass, and this could be blamed on the bishops. "Quod est sacrilegium sub coelo missa exsecrabilius? ... Missis ergo suis, quibus nulla est in terris nocentior lues, quoties populum fascinant, acceptum abs te venenum porrigunt." *CO* 5. 288; *Recueil*, 106.

[49] *CO* 5. 304; *Recueil*, 123.

say", Calvin tells Roussel, "that you do not own any piece of land that has not been placed in your hands by Purgatory." Calvin's argument assumes the form of a personal challenge against Roussel: "Tell me now before God, if you think that you own these aforementioned properties justly and in good conscience."[50]

It makes no difference to Calvin that such bequests are often made willingly and according to correct legal procedures. The fact that these transactions are based on a fiction makes them unethical, and also illegal. Calvin the young law student does not fail to point out that in civil law any donation based on an "illicit condition" could be declared null and void.[51] Doctrinal and financial fraud were inextricably linked in every benefice, but it was chiefly because of theological error, said Calvin, that such "villainy" and "illicit gain" could never be justified, and that Roussel could be called "thief" and "plunderer". As Calvin put it, "your food cannot be cooked on that side unless the fire of Purgatory is lit."[52]

3.4 Abuses of Power

Doctrinal and devotional error combined with ambition and lust for power to produce yet another evil among the Roman Catholic clergy, according to Calvin. As if it were not bad enough to lead their flocks into perdition through false worship, the Catholic clergy also abused them politically, exercising "sheer tyranny" over their lives.[53]

One of the worst examples of this for Calvin is the case of confession, which he sees as inseparably linked to the fear of Purgatory.

> What should we say? ... Do they not put the poor people through the flames with this wretched torture of auricular confession? Do they not abuse the people with these fables about satisfactions and absolutions invented by men? Do they

---

[50] CO 5. 304; Recueil, 123. This was one of the most common charges levelled against the Catholic clergy in the early years of the Reformation. A good example is the play Die Totenfresser. Von Papst und seiner Priesterschaft (1523) by the Swiss painter Nicholas Manuel: F. Vetter, ed., Niklaus Manuels Spiel Evangelischer Freiheit (Leipzig, 1923).

[51] "Donationes autem istas solo errore niti, bona etiam ex parte impostura non carrere scitis. Iisdem legibus, quae illicitam conditionem habet donatio, irrita esse pronunciatur." CO 5. 304-5; Recueil, 124.

[52] CO 5. 304-5; Recueil, 124. Calvin also argued that all "extraordinary oblations" (all other contributions which were made voluntarily by the faithful in church, such as offertory donations and gifts) were based on doctrinal error and could not be accepted in good conscience by a true Christian.

[53] CO 5. 288; Recueil, 106 reads "tyrannie outrageuse".

not establish and confirm all of their banter about Purgatory with solemn prayers, from which then issues the greatest heap of impiety?[54]

According to Calvin, the Roman Catholic clergy were principally motivated by ambition, and in their ferocious lust for power they left "the entire flock of Christ wounded and mutilated". Even the parish clergy, the *curez*, were more interested in their own status than in the well-being of the church, and wanted to be considered as better than other human beings.[55]

To what could this behavior be compared?, Calvin asks Roussel. It is as if a surgeon would try to heal a patient by first cutting his throat, or as if a physician would advise someone with a stomach malady to drink poison.[56]

IV. The Alternative to the Roman Catholic Priesthood: Calvin's Aggressive "True Ministry"

In his letter to Roussel, Calvin does not for a moment argue against the episcopal office itself; on the contrary, he accepts it as divinely ordained. Calvin, in fact, seeks to contrast all superficial and selfish abuses of the episcopal office against the exalted and rigorous duties God had in mind for His bishops. By juxtaposing Roman Catholic abuses and the "true" duties of the episcopal office, Calvin attempts to make Roussel see that he has placed himself in a most difficult position.

The true ministry of bishops, according to Calvin, is entirely the opposite of that practiced by the rapacious, self-interested prelates of the Roman Catholic Church. "It is not for your own profit that you are a bishop", he says to Roussel, "but for the benefit and service of others". To be a bishop is to be a pastor, or shepherd. "Those ordained by the Lord as pastors in His church, have been established by Him as guardians and sentries for the defense of His people" (*custores, speculatores*). It is an arduous duty that should never be taken lightly.[57]

Calvin's conception of the bishop as pastor, or shepherd becomes crucial in his argument against the "Roman" episcopacy, and his attempt to shake

---

[54] *CO* 5. 297; *Recueil*, 115. This, too, was a common complaint against the Catholic clergy. Guillaume Farel had made the same complaint in his *Sommaire* (n. 35 above), 67-72. See also *Triumphus Veritatis*, Schade (n. 35 above), 2: 217-18. Calvin would continue to assail confession throughout his life. In the 1559 *Institutes* III. 4. 17-18, he said "the requirement of complete confession is a measureless torment" that can only "destroy, condemn, confound, and cast into ruin and despair."

[55] *CO* 5. 294; *Recueil*, 112. Yet another common complaint in pamphlet literature. For two examples see: Heinrichs von Kettenbach, *Eyn Sermon über das Ewangelium Matthei*" (1525) in Clemen (n. 18 above), 2: 217; and *Triumphus Veritatis*, Schade 2: 229.

[56] *CO* 5. 298; *Recueil*, 117.

[57] *CO* 5. 283; *Recueil*, 100.

Roussel from complacency.[58] According to Calvin, the office of bishop involves two responsibilities: guiding and policing. In this very early document, it is already possible to recognize the well developed embryo of Geneva's consistory.

> All of those who are ordained for the government of the churches, then, are set up as guardians over the people of God ... They have certainly not been appointed to some vile and sordid ministry, but have rather been installed to dispense the mysteries of celestial wisdom, and to work as laborers and directors in the construction of the house of God.[59]

Those called to *govern* (Calvin's term) the people of God are called to a state "full of difficulties, labor, and solicitude".[60] What could they do to reform the people? First, they could teach them to pray.[61] Then they could also reproach the people for being so attached to idols and superstitious ceremonies, and they could combat the idolatrous tendencies of the people, instead of giving in to them.[62]

For Calvin, the ministry should be an office that requires constant vigilance, both night and day. The ultimate paradigm for the pastor is the "good shepherd" mentioned by Jesus, who will lay down his life for his sheep.[63] Yet, Calvin's vision of the "true" pastor is not passive, but rather aggressive. The "true" shepherd takes charge of his flock, sees to it that it is well nourished with the Word of God, and well protected from the possible ravages of the Enemy, Satan. The "true" bishop, or pastor, is one who constantly teaches by word and example, and who vigilantly guards against all threats.[64]

Those who shepherd the flock of God's people, moreover, have an even more difficult duty than those who watch over real sheep. Whereas sheep are only threatened by predators from the outside, God's people are imperiled from both within and without. Within the church itself there are possible predators. "There are two kinds of people", Calvin warns Roussel,

---

[58] Calvin seems to intensify and enhance the responsibility of pastors from that described by Zwingli in "The Shepherd" (*Der Hirt*), Z 3. 23, 32, 37ff., and Farel in his *Sommaire*, 86-93.

[59] (I Cor. 3.10) "ad ipsam Dei domum exaedificandam et constituendam destinantur" *CO* 5. 283. The French translation seems to have the consistory very much in mind, saying instead: "pour travailler à l'edifice et police spirituelle de la maison de Dieu." *Recueil*, 100.

[60] "at quos Dominos ad regendam ecclesiam suam vocat" *CO* 5. 284; *Recueil*, 101.

[61] *CO* 5. 294; *Recueil*, 113.

[62] *CO* 5. 295 *Recueil*, 113. Calvin believed that the clergy had led the laity into a labyrinth of error through their accomodation to human traditions.

[63] *CO* 5. 284; *Recueil*, 101.

[64] *CO* 5. 285; *Recueil*, 102.

"One sort can learn from admonitions and exhortations; the other has to be struggled against, and must have its obstinacy broken."[65]

In drawing for Roussel this vivid picture of the "true" ministry, Calvin reveals that his antisacerdotal rhetoric is in fact intensely proclerical. The reason Calvin finds so much to dislike in the Roman Catholic clergy is not the fact that he opposes them as a class, or rejects their place in society, but rather the opposite: he has a very elevated view of the ministry and its role in society, and it is precisely because they have failed in their role as leaders that the Catholic clergy are blameworthy. Throughout his letter to Roussel, one can see a clear foreshadowing of the consistory and of the aggressive calvinist ministry. "Certainly", he said, the true pastors "will not have fully performed their duties unless they have been on guard hour after hour, reproving, warning, and exhorting with great kindness and sound learning."[66]

V. BENEFICES AS SOURCES OF POLLUTION

Calvin's conclusion regarding Roussel's dilemma is as clear as it is severe: It is impossible for any true Christian to hold a benefice in the Roman Catholic Church.

> It is impossible to hold one [benefice] that does not carry in itself two abominable sacrileges, neither of which any good Christian would want to commit, even for all the wealth in the world ... Even though there are different kinds of duties [in a benefice], there is one that is always found in all benefices every day: this is that one must say mass for the souls of the departed: which is considered as satisfaction for their sins. Here you have, I say, one duty which must be somehow fulfilled by all those who hold benefices. There is no Abbacy so rich, or chaplaincy so poor that is not linked to this duty. It is all the same if they [the benefice holders] perform this chief duty themselves, or if they pass it on to a vicar, putting someone else in their place.[67]

No one can take the money and run. It does not matter if one does not actually say mass: merely to collect such revenue is to implicitly participate in the sacrilege of the mass. Whether the masses are said by proxy or go unsaid is all the same to Calvin. Mass money is blood money, and there is no benefice that is free from this pollution.

But why is the mass such an abomination? Calvin has a clear answer: it is an affront to the true priesthood of Christ and to his sacrifice on the cross.

> Thus it is that the Priesthood of Christ, which is eternal, is degraded by the Mass: it abolishes the one sacrifice through which He once and for all erased

---

[65] *CO* 5. 285-6; *Recueil*, p. 103.

[66] "arguendo, increpando, exhortando cum onia lenitate et doctrina" *CO* 5. 292-3. The French adds "patience", *Recueil*, 110.

[67] *CO* 5. 300-301; *Recueil*, 120.

all our sins; it mocks and trods underfoot the blood through which we are all cleansed; it overturns the redemption which he acquired for us through his death; it profanes the sacred meal in which he consecrated for us the remembrance of his death; it overturns the majesty of God, and seeks to place a detestable idol in His place.[68]

Anyone who says mass, or even implicitly agrees to say mass is guilty of every one of the crimes mentioned above. It is a mockery to Christ and to God, the very work of Satan, and it would be a thousand times better to die than to be responsible for such an affront to the majesty of the Son of God.

> How can any man hope to be cleansed of his own filth by the blood of Christ, if he has forsaken it and allowed himself to be trampled by swine? ... With what assurance of conscience will he be able to appear before the jugdgement seat of God, when he has daily been responsible for attributing to an idol the glory which should properly be reserved for His Sovereign Majesty?[69]

Can any true Christian, then, accept the income from a benefice? "O accursed and most detestable wealth", Calvin cries out against Roussel, "there is not even a single coin that is not besmirched with theft, or sacrilege, or piracy."[70] No compromise is acceptable, no excuse appropriate. Even if Roussel were to claim that he uses his income frugally, and that he contributes generously to charity, he would still be acting in a reprehensible manner. Should robbers and looters be forgiven for their crimes if they claim to aid the poor with their ill-gotten gain?, asks Calvin. Certainly not: the bread with which a true Christian feeds the poor must be his own, not that of his neighbor.[71]

Calvin would brook no excuse from Roussel, or any other beneficed cleric. Roussel may want to argue that it is impossible to force the people to make a clean break with tradition, speculates Calvin, and that it is best to reform slowly and piecemeal, accomodating the process of change to the intellectual and spiritual capacities of one's flock. "This is an excuse that does not deserve to be taken seriously", counters Calvin. In matters of life and death, such as questions of belief and worship, there can be no compromise with error: truth is never to be mingled with error, or light with darkness, or the Gospel with "execrable things", or Christ with Belial.[72] Accomodation and treason are two very different things.[73] For Calvin,

---

[68] *CO* 5. 301-2; *Recueil*, 121.

[69] *CO* 5. 302; *Recueil*, 121.

[70] *CO* 5. 305-6; *Recueil*, 125.

[71] *CO* 5. 306; *Recueil*, 126. Calvin admonished Roussel: "Immanis autem illa profusio, quae domi vestrae visitur, quid cum hac regula simile habet?"

[72] *CO* 5. 297; *Recueil*, 116.

[73] *CO* 5. 298; *Recueil*, 116.

every Mass is evil because it is tainted with the "falsehood" of Purgatory.[74] Calvin dismisses the conciliatory and accomodating arguments of all Nicodemites and would-be temporizers, Roussel included. "O moyenneurs", he warns, "you are guilty of heinous idolatry and sacrilege a thousand times over."[75]

VI. CALVIN'S ULTIMATUM TO ROUSSEL

According to Calvin, only a fool could fail to see the contrast between the "true" ministry and the beneficed clergy of the Roman Catholic Church. How, then, he asked Roussel, could anyone rejoice over an episcopal appointment in the Roman Catholic Church? Calvin does more than doubt the intelligence of his old friend Roussel, he also repeatedly accuses him of implicit participation in the corruption common to all contemporary Roman Catholic bishops.[76]

Hoping that Roussel would change his mind and openly join the Reformed cause, Calvin continues to hammer away at him with further questions. How can he ever hope to become a "true" pastor in a church that was totally disordered? How can he reform and restore that which is thoroughly decadent? Since corruption is inseparable from his new office, how can he avoid guilt?

> With one hand, the entire true religion of God is sullied, mocked, trampled underfoot, contaminated, and even overturned and completely ruined. With the other hand ... the poor people are villanously deceived, abused, and robbed through a thousand deceptions ... and ... all of this is done right before your eyes ... It is not only a question of saying that you close your eyes and allow such things to happen, because all this wickedness is the work of your own hands.[77]

For Calvin, it was not only the sheer number of different abuses that makes pollution inescapable, but also the magnitude of some of them. "Is there any sacrilege under heaven more execrable than the Mass?", asks Calvin. "Yet ... it is you who consecrate and ordain the priests who perform this abominable sacrifice."[78] Since the "infection" is unavoidable, it would thus seem impossible, concludes Calvin, that any Roman Catholic bishop can escape being blamed for the worst crimes imaginable against God and his

---

[74] "Quod vero, ut alia multa ommitamus, missaticum sacrificium paragere, nisi uno simul exitio et populum dare, et ipsam quoque religionem?" *CO* 5. 298; *Recueil*, 117.

[75] *CO* 5. 298-9; *Recueil*, 117.

[76] *CO* 5. 287; *Recueil*, 104.

[77] *CO* 5. 288; *Recueil*, 105.

[78] *CO* 5. 288; *Recueil*, 105.

people.[79] Through such accusations, Calvin calls on his old friend to become a true reformer:

> Sound the trumpet, you sentry: to arms, you pastor. Why do you delay? Why are you sluggish? Why do you sleep? As long as you turn away your spirit from your duties, to surround it with things that do not at all belong to you, then all is filled with piracy. Oh, wretch, you will have to account for the death of so many before the Lord! You are a murderer many times over, and are accountable for that blood many times over; there is not one single drop that the Lord will not require from your hand.[80]

Calvin further sharpens the edge of his polemic against his old friend. Why this "disordered cupidity" on the part of Roussel?, he asks. Has he lost his mind? Does he want to join the "flock of horned beasts", that is, the bishops, abbots, and priors who subject themselves to the pope?[81] Calvin concludes that Roussel has been led by Satan to accept his bishopric,[82] and reprimands him for his willingness to compromise: "I am not unacquainted with those pitiful complaints you are wont to make, in which, if anyone is not inclined to grant you forgiveness, you then judge them as unfeeling and incontinent."[83]

Calvin reserves his harshest comments for the end of the letter. Why not give up your benefice and flee into exile?, he asks Roussel. Are you afraid of giving up your wealth and of really having to work for a living?[84] You are mistaken if you think you can be a good Christian and a Catholic bishop at the same time, Calvin concludes.

> You deceive yourself if you think you have a place among the people of God, when, in fact, you are a soldier in the army of the Antichrist. You deceive yourself if you hope to partake in the Kingdom of Heaven with the Son of God, when, in fact, you keep company with wretched brigands and take part in their robberies and depredations.[85]

It is difficult to find any trace of Calvin's "almost fraternal" affection for Roussel in his closing remarks.

---

[79] Even the most banal of all deceptions, false relics, could also be attributed to bishops: *CO* 5. 288; *Recueil*, 106.

[80] *CO* 5. 290; *Recueil*, 108.

[81] *CO* 5. 308; *Recueil*, 127.

[82] *CO* 5. 309; *Recueil*, 129.

[83] *CO* 5. 309; *Recueil*, 129.

[84] This was another common anticlerical complaint. For examples see Hans Schwalb, *Beklagung*, Clemen 1: 352; *Triumphus Veritatis*, Schade 2: 230; and *Ain schöner dialogus wie ain Bauer mit aim Frauenbruder Münich redt dasz er die Kutten von im wirft* (1525), Schade 2: 158.

[85] *CO* 5. 310; *Recueil*, 130.

You will be counted as one of that gang whom Christ calls robbers, brigands, and murderers of his Church. Think whatever you want about yourself: I, at the very least, will never consider you a Christian, or a good man. Farewell.[86]

VII. CONCLUSION

The legacy of the young Calvin's antisacerdotalism is twofold: first, Calvin helped to vanquish the spirit of compromise that still lingered in the hearts of some humanist reformers, particularly in France; second, Calvin provided the Reformed Church with an ideology that helped to transform anticlerical sentiment into a kind of proclerical reformism. The impact of these contributions may perhaps be more clearly seen through narrative, in the symbolic dimensions suggested by the fate of two men who did not share Calvin's views on the ministry.

The first of these men is Gerard Roussel himself. Roussel's friendship with Calvin came to an abrupt end in 1536. Instead of heeding Calvin's advice, Roussel remained at Oleron and dedicated himself to the reform of his diocese. Contrary to Calvin's expectations, Roussel did not grow indolently fat or surround himself in luxury. In one sense he proved Calvin wrong, living frugally, working tirelessly for change, inspiring clergy and laity alike through his own exemplary behavior.[87] Nonetheless, he proved Calvin right in another sense: for the sake of his own peace of mind, and his personal safety, perhaps Roussel should have fled from Oleron to Geneva.

In 1550 the Sorbonne condemned some of his writings for "false propositions" and prevented their publication.[88] Not long after this censure Roussel paid with his life for his Reformed evangelical leanings. Sometime in the early in 1550's, while preaching a sermon at Mauléon, in nearby Gascony, in which he criticized the observance of saint's feast days, an enraged local noble attacked the pulpit with a hatchet and caused it to collapse. According to accepted tradition, Roussel died a day later from the injuries he sustained in this fall, a martyr to his lingering Reformed sympathies. Tradition also has it that the see of Oleron was immediately

---

[86] *CO* 5. 312; *Recueil*, 131. In spite of statements such as this, Alexandre Ganoczy still thinks Calvin was not against the Roman Catholic episcopacy per se. See *Jeune Calvin* (n. 8 above), 315; *Ministère* (n. 22 above), 388.

[87] Schmidt, *Gerard Roussel*, 121ff. Doumergue, *Jean Calvin*, 1: 420 ff., cites evidence that suggests that the bishopric of Oleron provided Roussel with a meager income.

[88] Schmidt, *Gerard Roussel*, 160-3. These manuscripts were entitled "Forme de visite de diocèse" and "Exposition familière en forme de colloque sur le Symbole, Decalogue et Oraison Dominicale". Schmidt reproduces the "Forme de visite", 226-39; the preface to the "Exposition familiére", 223-26; and the condemnation by the Sorbonne, 240-43.

passed on to the son of this noble, as a reward for his "pious and beautiful gesture".[89]

Calvin's condemnation of the Roman Catholic priesthood and his break with Roussel marked the beginning of a life-long battle against compromise, in which the Genevan Reformer would prove most inflexible. Roussel's ignominious end might have been interpreted by Calvin as a confirmation of his worst suspicions about compromise and Nicodemism, and he would not have been mistaken in seeing it as a foreshadowing of future conflict in his native France.[90] Four centuries later, we are perhaps entitled to interpret it as a testament to the death of one strain of Erasmian humanist reformism. After about 1550, the only progeny of Erasmus who could prevail would be those who shirked compromise and committed themselves to reform within one confession: men who would be acclaimed as saints by one church, but reviled as traitors to Christ by another, men such as Juan de Avila or John Calvin.

Amy Perrin was a Genevan noble, a leader in the revolt of 1535-36, who helped instigate the final iconoclastic riot, and afterwards continued to express his anticlericalism through words and actions. Perrin and his supporters proved themselves to be the most painful thorn in Calvin's side at Geneva.[91] Calvin waged a protracted battle against these so-called "libertines" who favored a less intrusive clergy and believed that control of behavior should be a civil rather than ecclesiastical matter. In 1555 this political struggle was finally settled in Calvin's favor, and Perrin was expelled from Geneva.[92] Ironically, Perrin's confiscated property helped pay for the establishment of Calvin's Academy, the school in which the Calvinist clergy were to be trained.[93] Thus it is that the ideas of the young Calvin were finally implemented in Geneva, and that anticlericalism was eventually overcome by an aggressive ministry.

---

[89] Schmidt, *Gerard Roussel*, 164. Though Schmidt dates Roussel's death as early 1550, Emile Doumergue (*Jean Calvin*, 1: 421-2) cites documentary evidence proving that Roussel lived until at least 1552, when he made some complex arrangements regarding his benefice at Clairac in order to help two of his nephews gain other benefices of their own.

[90] See my *War Against the Idols*, chapters 7 and 8. For a slightly different interpretation, see Perez Zagorin, *Ways of Lying: Dissimulation, Persecution, and Conformity in Early Modern Europe* (Cambridge, Mass., 1990), 63-82.

[91] R. W. Collins, *Calvin and the Libertines of Geneva* (Toronto, 1968).

[92] Kingdon speaks of two revolutions in Geneva, one in 1536, which ushered in Protestantism, and the other in 1555, which marked the triumph of Calvin over his local opponents; "Calvin and the Government of Geneva" (n. 1 above), 52.

[93] E. William Monter, *Calvin's Geneva* (New York, 1967), 113. Kingdon, 51, says "I would argue further that the main social result of the Reformation was the creation of a new clerical class, an elite of a very different type."

CALVIN AND THE MONASTIC IDEAL

DAVID C. STEINMETZ

Duke University

> Let my readers accordingly remember that I have spoken rather of monasticism than of monks, and noted not those faults which inhere in the life of a few, but those which cannot be separated from the order of living itself.[1]

With these words Calvin indicates that his criticisms of monasticism are not primarily directed against the failure of individual monks to live up to the ideals they profess, but against the institution and ideology of monasticism as such. That does not mean, of course, that Calvin is reluctant to criticize the faults of individual monks. "No order of men", he complains, "is more polluted by all sorts of foul vices."[2] "You will scarcely find one [monastery] in ten which is not a brothel rather than a sanctuary of chastity."[3] Monks are "ignorant asses", plagued by Pharasaical pride and hypocrisy, who lay claim to a learning they do not have.[4] They are false prophets who obscure the clarity of the gospel with specious arguments sprung from the human brain.[5] They are idlers who regard themselves as a regular order, but who are regarded by God as irregular and disorderly.[6] Although Calvin concedes that there may be some good monks left in the various houses, they form a scattered and hidden band, a *vestigium purioris ecclesiae* in an institution which is otherwise hopelessly corrupt.[7]

Nevertheless, in spite of Calvin's energetic criticism of monastic abuses (a criticism which does not in the main distinguish between communities of monks and friars), his principal energies are concentrated in an assault on the institution itself, especially on its intellectual foundations. In order to understand the force of Calvin's critique of monasticism, it may be useful to place his criticism in the context of medieval debates over the status of the religious life.

---

[1] *Inst.* IV. xiii. 15. Translations into English are from *Calvin: Institutes of the Christian Religion*, Library of Christian Classics 20-21, ed. John T. McNeill and trans. Ford Lewis Battles (Philadelphia, 1960).

[2] *Inst.* IV. xiii. 15.

[3] *Inst.* IV. xiii. 15.

[4] Comm. on Acts 15:5; II Corinthians 10:12.

[5] Comm. on Jeremiah 5:30-31.

[6] *Inst.* IV. xiii. 10; Comm. on II Thessalonians 3:11.

[7] *Inst.* IV. xiii. 15.

I

The thirteenth-century theologian, Thomas Aquinas (†1274), argued vigorously for the monastic life as a state of perfection. Thomas did not mean to assert that all monks are in fact perfect or that it is impossible for secular priests or laity to attain perfection. Monks are in a state of perfection only because they have put themselves under obligation by their vows to strive for perfection in love.[8] It is the vow and the obligation which it entails that marks the crucial difference between the status of a monk and the status of a secular priest or layperson.[9]

Monks do not tread the only path to perfection, but they do walk a better way. Fundamental to this belief is Thomas's understanding of the distinction between commands and counsels.[10] The old law, the law of Moses, which the Church now recognizes after the advent of Christ to be a law of bondage, contained only commands, such as the prohibition of theft or murder. The new law, however, the law of liberty, contains both commands and counsels, including the counsels to embrace celibacy and voluntary poverty. While all Christians are summoned to obey the commands, the religious have obligated themselves by a vow to follow the evangelical counsels as well. The counsels make it easier to attain perfection; therefore mendicant friars (like the Dominicans in Thomas's own order) find themselves in a more advantageous position in the quest for holiness.

There is, of course, another sense in which one may be in a state of perfection. Bishops are in a state of perfection as well as monks, not because they are obligated by their vows to the quest for sanctity, but because they are obligated by their ordination to a perpetual cure of souls.[11] Bishops are in a state of perfection by virtue of their *cura animarum perpetua*. Their task is to lead others to perfection.[12] Ordinary priests, who for Thomas are only bailiffs of the bishop, are not obligated to a perpetual cure of souls and are therefore not in a state of perfection.[13] The very fact that they may be released from the care of souls without the permission of their bishop to become monks — as a bishop may not without the permission of the pope — is proof for Thomas that the state of perfection is a status for monks and bishops only.[14]

---

[8] Thomas Aquinas, *Summa Theologiae* II-IIae, q. 186, a. 1, ad 3. Cf. q. 184, a. 5, ad 2; q. 184, a. 4 concl.

[9] Thomas Aquinas, *Summa Theologiae* II-IIae, q. 184, a. 4.

[10] Thomas Aquinas, *Summa Theologiae* I-IIae, q. 108, a. 4.

[11] Thomas Aquinas, *Summa Theologiae* II-IIae, q. 184, a. 5.

[12] Thomas Aquinas, *Summa Theologiae* II-IIae, q. 184, a. 7.

[13] Thomas Aquinas, *Summa Theologiae* II-IIae, q. 184, a. 6, ad 2.

[14] Thomas Aquinas, *Summa Theologiae* II-IIae, q. 184, a. 6 concl.

Theoretically Thomas gives preeminence to bishops when he concludes that "the state of perfection is more potent and perfect in prelates and bishops than in the religious."[15] Against this theoretical preeminence of bishops must be set such practical monastic advantages as the greater meritoriousness of their good works. Thomas affirms, and that affirmation is hotly contested by Goch, that good works performed because of a vow are higher and more meritorious than other works.[16] He holds this view because he believes that a vow is an *actus latriae*, the highest of the moral virtues, and can therefore confer an additional dignity on good works which result from it.[17]

Furthermore, monks who profess vows undergo a second baptism.[18] Thomas does not go as far as some later theorists who press the analogy of baptism and monastic vows to the extent of believing that the monk has been forgiven both the guilt and penalty of his post-baptismal sin. Vows only alleviate the penalty of sin through the obligation of a perpetual satisfaction. But profession of a monastic vow places monks in a higher spiritual state than priests and laity. All Christians have died to sin through baptism. Monks have died through the second baptism of their vows, not only to sin, but also to the world. Since only a few secular priests become bishops while all monks by reason of their vows are in a state of perfection, the overall impact of Thomas's argument is to stress the advantages enjoyed by the mendicant orders in comparison with the secular priesthood.

II

While the fifteenth-century theologian, Jean Gerson (†1429), draws the same distinction between commands and counsels as does Thomas Aquinas, he is led to a quite different set of conclusions.[19] The essence of the commands may be summarized for Gerson in the dual commandment of love of God and neighbor. Perfection is found, therefore, in the commands, in perfect charity, and not in the counsels which are added to the commands.[20] Counsels contribute instrumentally and accidentally to perfection, but not essentially.[21]

---

[15] Thomas Aquinas, *Summa Theologiae* II-IIae, q. 184, a. 7 concl.

[16] Thomas Aquinas, *Summa Theologiae* II-IIae, q. 189, a. 2.

[17] Thomas Aquinas, *Summa Theologiae* II-IIae, q. 88, a. 6.

[18] Thomas Aquinas, *Summa Theologiae* II-IIae, q. 189, a. 3, ad 3.

[19] For a discussion of Gerson's criticism of Thomas see D. Catherine Brown, *Pastor and Laity in the Theology of Jean Gerson* (Cambridge, 1987), 73-78.

[20] Jean Gerson, "De consiliis evangelicis et statu perfectionis", *Oeuvres Complétes*, III: *L'Oeuvre Magistrale*, ed. P. Glorieux (Paris, 1962), 10-11. The treatise covers pages 10-26.

[21] Gerson, 14.

Vows, which have a central important for Thomas, are downgraded by Gerson. The monastic vow only has an instrumental character.[22] Perfection can be reached without it, and *perfecti* can be found among the faithful in every *status*, *gradus*, and *sexus*. Gerson agrees with Thomas that a vow increases merit, since the offering of fruit and tree is worth more than the offering of the fruit alone.[23] Still he does not press the point and even observes that "many works completed without a vow are more perfect and better than some others that take their origin from a vow."[24]

The real attack on Thomas's thought is concentrated in Gerson's view that the state of the secular clergy is more perfect than the state of the religious. While the monk is obligated by his vow to acquire perfection, the bishop is obligated to exercise it in the Church.[25] The task of the secular clergy is higher because it is directed toward the common good, while the monk's quest for sanctity is directed to his own private good.[26] Gerson can thus conclude that the status of a priest is higher than the status of the religious because of the greater proximity of the office of a priest to the office of a bishop.[27]

Gerson buttresses his argument by affirming that the priesthood was founded by Christ and therefore has its own independent dignity.[28] The priest is not the bailiff of the bishop but a minister in his own right. Indeed, the sanctity of ordination to priesthood is higher than the sanctity of monastic vows. Whereas a monk may be released from his religious vows, no power on earth can dissolve ordination to priesthood.

The locus of the state of perfection is found for Gerson above all in the office of a bishop and secondarily in the office of a priest.[29] The churchly dimension, which is also stressed in Thomas, receives greater attention at the hands of Jean Gerson. At the same time, Gerson is less interested in a spiritual elite than Thomas. He wishes to take mystical theology out of the hands of a favored few and make it the concern of the whole people of God. Perfection is found essentially in the commands, in the call to perfect love of God and neighbor that summarizes the whole law and prophets.

---

[22] Gerson, 20-21.
[23] Gerson, 20-21.
[24] Gerson, 21.
[25] Gerson, 22.
[26] Gerson, 25.
[27] Gerson, 23-24.
[28] Gerson, 25.
[29] Gerson, 22.

III

Very little is known for certain about John Pupper of Goch (†1475), one of the severest critics of Thomas's understanding of the religious life before the Reformation. He appears to have been a priest of the archdiocese of Utrecht, who founded a house of Augustinian canonesses in Malines in 1459 and who had previously been a rector in Sluis. He may have studied in Cologne, though that is subject to some doubt, or even in Paris, though that remains to be proven. His historical importance rests on four theological treatises he composed which attacked scholastic theology and monastic theory in the name of Christian liberty.[30]

Perfection consists for Goch in the perfect conformity of the will of the Christian to the will of God.[31] Goch resists both the Thomistic tendency to locate perfection in the intellect and the Franciscan propensity to equate it with poverty.[32] He finds no bar to perfection in the legal ownership of material goods, provided that the heart is not attached to its possessions.[33] To the degree that the will is conformed to the will of God, to that degree the believing man or woman is perfect.

Goch rejects the Thomistic understanding of the distinction between commands and counsels, though he does not reject the distinction as such or affirm with Gerson that one should seek perfection in the commands.[34] He argues, rather, that both commands and counsels belong to the one perfection of evangelical law and that both contribute to perfection in charity.[35] What Goch rejects is the notion that commands are for ordinary Christians while counsels are for the religious, who have bound themselves by a vow to seek perfection in love. All Christians stand under the claim of the whole law of God, which embraces both commands and counsels. If it is objected that married couples are barred by that understanding from the higher degree of perfection that virginity confers, it may be responded that most monks are similarly barred from the higher perfection granted to

---

[30] Goch's works include the following: *De quatuor erroribus circa legem evangelicam exortis et de votis et religionibus factitiis dialogus* [Abbreviated: *Dial.*], ed. C. G. F. Walch, *Monumenta medii aevi*, vol. 1.4 (Goettingen, 1760), 74-239; *De scholasticorum scriptis et religiosorum votis epistola apologetica* [Abbreviated: *Epist. Apol.*]. ed. C. G. F. Walch, *Monumenta medii aevi*, vol. 2.1 (Goettingen, 1761), 1-24; *De libertate christiana* [Abbreviated: *De lib. chr.*], ed. F. Pijper, *Bibliotheca Reformatoria Neerlandica*, vol. 6 (Hague, 1910), 1-263; *Fragmenta* [Abbreviated: *Frag.*], ed. F. Pijper, *Bibliotheca Reformatoria Neerlandica*, vol. 6 (Hague, 1910), 267-347.

[31] *Dial.* X. 132, 138; XII. 158; XVIII. 186; XIX. 196.

[32] *Dial.* X. 132, 135; XIX. 191-192.

[33] *Dial.* XXII. 234-235.

[34] *De lib. chr.* IV. 10. 247.

[35] *De lib. chr.* IV. 11. 251.

martyrs.[36] All the faithful are called to conform their wills to the will of God so far as the special circumstances of their own vocation and situation allow. All the faithful can merit beatitude, but not all can attain the same degree of perfection *in via*.[37] Some of the faithful embody more perfectly than others the apostolic life.

Goch does not, in other words, deny that there is a state of perfection. What he does find unacceptable is Thomas's contention that mendicant friars are in it. Goch's attack on the Thomistic understanding of the state of perfection concentrates on three points: (1) the meaning and importance of the religious vow; (2) the notion that the vow is a second baptism; and (3) the conception of ministry and ordination implicit in monastic theology.

Goch denies that the profession of vows has any warrant in the New Testament.[38] The exegetical evidence traditionally cited by monks and friars to buttress their claims is weighed briefly by Goch and found wanting.[39] Indeed, vows are incompatible with Christian freedom since they introduce an element of compulsion and constraint that is foreign to it.[40] The gospel is the message of the restoration of freedom to sinners to perform the will of God through charity. Whoever has been liberated by the Spirit to do God's will does not need the compulsion and constraint of vows and rules to elicit a grudging consent.

Goch dismisses with undisguised contempt Thomas's idea that a vow increases merit.[41] On the contrary, since vows are incompatible with Christian freedom, they tend to undercut merit.[42] Does that mean that a vow can never be meritorious? Goch is unwilling to go that far. A vow can be meritorious if it springs spontaneously from the activity of the indwelling Spirit and is accepted by God.[43] It is meritorious, not because it is a vow, but because God has accepted it.[44] The dignity of a vow is distinguished in no special way from the dignity of any good act of whatever sort.

If a vow is not automatically meritorious and even tends to undercut the merit of other acts performed because of it, of what use is a vow? Goch holds that monasticism and monastic vows are a positive constitution of the

---

[36] *Dial.* XIX. 194-195. Thomas Aquinas regards martyrdom as the *actus maximae perfectionis* (*Summa Theologiae* II-IIae, q. 124, a. 3 and q. 184, a. 5, ad 3).

[37] *Dial.* XIX. 192.

[38] *De lib. chr.* IV. 1. 226.

[39] *De lib. chr.* I. 6. 53; *Epist. Apol.* 15.

[40] *De lib. chr.* I. 7. 55.

[41] *Dial.* XVII. 181; *De lib. chr.* III. 4. 190-191, 5. 193.

[42] *Epist. Apol.* 19; *Dial.* XVII. 181, XVIII. 183; *De lib. chr.* IV. 3. 229, 4. 231-232, 6. 238.

[43] *Dial.* XVIII. 184.

[44] *Frag.* 309. Cf. *Frag.* 307; *De lib. chr.* I. 22. 83, 23. 85, 24. 89, 24. 90; II. 23. 128; III. 4. 191, 5. 195.

Church.[45] Monasticism is not grounded in natural law nor in an explicit teaching of revelation, but in a tactical decision of the Church to establish certain structures to gain certain ends. Monasticism was founded, not as the most exemplary form of the state of perfection, but as a hospital where the spiritually weak can be supervised and assisted to make at least some small progress in the spiritual life.[46] The mendicant orders are the home of the spiritually infirm rather than an encampment of the spiritually elite.

Goch does not appear to dispute the contention that monasticism is a state of penance.[47] The idea that the monk is one who performs perpetual satisfaction for his sins is not in itself an objectionable idea. Goch does not, however, accept the view of Thomas that monasticism is a second baptism in which monks who had previously died to sin now die to the world. Such a viewpoint tends to exalt the status of monks over the status of priests and laity. Goch rejects it by denying that it is in any sense possible to draw an analogy with baptism. It is not a vow but an intention that is required of the candidate for baptism.[48] Nor is baptism, which is necessary for salvation, in any sense comparable with religious vows, which are not.[49]

If Christian perfection is possible without a vow, does Goch reject altogether the notion of a spiritual elite? The answer, clearly, is no. The highest status in the Church is the status of a priest, whose dignity derives from his ordination to celebrate the sacraments, above all, the sacrament of the eucharist.[50] The bishop does not differ from the priest in order but solely in jurisdiction.[51] Just as ordination to the priesthood is the highest order in the Church militant, so, too, the state of a priest is the state of highest perfection.[52] Bishop and presbyter share the same order because each has an equal right to confect a valid eucharist. The priesthood as such is the state of perfection. With respect to jurisdiction, the bishop is a unique successor of the apostles; with respect to order, the bishop is only a priest among priests.[53]

While Goch rejects the notion that monasticism is a state of perfection and only admits in a very limited sense that it is a state of penance, he does not reject altogether the ideal of a common life. The best expression of the apostolic life is a community of Augustinian canons — i.e., a community of secular priests — who live a common life with their bishop in obedience

---

[45] *Dial.* XVII. 178; XVIII. 183.
[46] *Dial.* XII. 159; XIV. 164-165; XV. 167.
[47] *Dial.* XXII. 211.
[48] *De lib. chris.* IV. 1. 228.
[49] *Dial.* XII. 153.
[50] *Dial.* XX. 199, 201, 205, 206.
[51] *Dial.* XX. 209-210.
[52] *Dial.* XX. 199, 201, 205, 206.
[53] *Dial.* XX. 209-210.

to both commands and counsels.[54] The pattern of life established by St. Augustine with his cathedral clergy and maintained by the Augustinian canons perpetuates the pattern of life taught by the apostles and given its highest expression in the relationship of Jesus to his disciples. While the mendicant orders have a foundation in the positive law of the Church, the Augustinian canons can claim legitimation for their societies in revelation itself. The priesthood, Goch concludes, is the *status perfectionis* and the communal societies of priests the best embodiment of the apostolic life. On the whole, it is not surprising that the founder of a house of Augustinian canonesses should find in the Augustinian pattern a corrective for the less authentic life of the mendicants.

IV

Calvin shares with Goch a respect for the moderate monasticism practiced by Augustine and uses Augustine's description of early monastic practice as a norm by which to judge the defects of contemporary monasticism.[55] It is clear, for example, that early monks thought of themselves as a community in aid of piety, whose rule was tempered by the goal of brotherly love.[56] Monks who could not live a celibate life were released from the community and allowed to marry.[57] Unlike modern monks who are constrained by rigid rules, ancient monks followed a flexible discipline moderated by the practical rule of charity.

Furthermore, ancient monks were more fully integrated into the life of ordinary Christian congregations.[58] They had no separate chapels of their own and worshipped in the parish church. While some monks were chosen to be clergy or bishops, most monks were not.[59] As monks they were not regarded by early Church fathers as a separate order, but were ruled by priests. Jerome lists five Church orders: bishops, presbyters, deacons, believers, and catechumens: "he gives no special place to the remaining clergy and monks."[60]

Indeed, Calvin wonders whether on Catholic principles priesthood and monasticism are not mutually exclusive.[61] A priest is ordained to a service of Word and sacrament in the world; a monk is called to a life of prayer and contemplation withdrawn from it. Gregory the Great had ordered abbots to

---

[54] *Dial.* XX. 212.
[55] John Calvin, *Inst.* IV. xiii. 9.
[56] *Inst.* IV. xiii. 10.
[57] *Inst.* IV. xiii. 17.
[58] *Inst.* IV. xiii. 14.
[59] *Inst.* IV. xiii. 8.
[60] *Inst.* IV. iv. 1.
[61] *Inst.* IV. v. 8.

withdraw from the clergy "on the ground that no one can properly be both a monk and a cleric."[62] To be sure, Calvin concedes, "some of the mendicants preach;" but "all the rest ... either chant or mutter masses in their dens."[63]

Of course, monastic theologians may appeal to the decrees of Innocent and Boniface, which support the ordination of cloistered monks. But Calvin is unimpressed by innovations introduced into Church life by medieval popes. "What sort of reason is this," he demands, "that every ignorant ass, as soon as he has occupied the see of Rome, may overthrow all antiquity with one little word?"[64] Calvin is far more impressed by the example of the early Church that considered it "a great absurdity for a monk to function in the priesthood. ... For when they are ordained they are expressly forbidden to do those things that God has enjoined on all the presbyters."[65]

The appeal of Catholic defenders of monastic life to antiquity is regarded by Calvin as a formal appeal devoid of content. The role of monks in early Christianity is strikingly different from their role in sixteenth-century society. "By this comparison of ancient and present-day monasticism," concludes Calvin, "I trust I have accomplished my purpose: to show that our hooded friends falsely claim the example of the first church in defense of their profession — since they differ from them as much as apes from men."[66]

Although Calvin prefers ancient monasticism to modern, he does not regard ancient monasticism as beyond criticism. Even ancient monks were not exempt from "immoderate affectation and perverse zeal" in the exercise of outward discipline.[67] While it is a beautiful act to abandon one's possessions for the sake of Christ, it is an even more beautiful act to rule one's household in the love and fear of God. Calvin rejects the ancient vision of voluntary poverty: *nudus nudum Christum sequens*.[68] Poverty is worthless if love is lacking. The story of the rich young ruler must be read in the context of 1 Corinthians 13. God calls us to perform the duties he has commanded. Withdrawal from the world to a contemplative life is finally for Calvin a lesser calling than an active life of obedient love in society.

Among the principal criticisms Calvin levels against modern monasticism is the charge that it is schismatic.[69] "All those who enter into the monastic life break with the Church" and every cloister and monastic house is a

---

[62] *Inst.* IV. v. 8.
[63] *Inst.* IV. v. 8.
[64] *Inst.* IV. v. 8.
[65] *Inst.* IV. v. 8.
[66] *Inst.* IV. xiii. 16.
[67] *Inst.* IV. xiii. 16.
[68] *Inst.* IV. xiii. 13.
[69] *Inst.* IV. xiii. 10.

"conventicle of schismatics".[70] The schismatic character of monasticism is evident in the monastic understanding of the vow as a second baptism. A second baptism lacks biblical support and establishes "a double Christianity" that separates monks from the whole body of the Church.[71]

The advocates of such a double Christianity claim to follow the counsels as well as the commands, but Christ's rule of life embraces both commands and counsels and is intended for all Christians.[72] All Christians, not merely the religious, are enjoined to love their enemies; all Christians, not merely monks and nuns, are forbidden to seek revenge. The Sermon on the Mount is not restricted to a monastic elite within the Church. Indeed, the distinction between commands and counsels "never entered the minds of the ancients" at all. Every early Christian writer declares "with one voice that men must of necessity obey every little word uttered by Christ."[73]

Monks have set themselves further apart from ordinary Christians by claiming to be in a state of perfection. Calvin is well aware that to claim to be in a state of perfection is not to be confused with the claim that one is already perfect. "I am not ignorant", he observes, "of their sophistical solution: that monasticism is not to be called perfect because it contains perfection within itself, but because it is the best way of all to attain perfection."[74] This "intolerable mockery" deceives "untutored and ignorant youths". Moreover, it gives great honor to an institution nowhere approved by God and makes all other callings seem "unworthy by comparison". "How great an injury, I beg of you, is done to God when some such forgery is preferred to all the kinds of life ordained by him and praised by his own testimony?"[75]

Of the vows taken by religious orders the vow on which Calvin comments most extensively is the promise of perpetual virginity. Calvin shares the widely held Protestant viewpoint that celibacy is a gift and cannot be made a law for every person.[76] When Catholic defenders of celibacy point to the ancient order of widows as an example of a celibate community in the early Church, Calvin replies that these widows were celibate, not as something religious in itself, but "because they could not carry on their function without being their own masters and free of the marriage yoke."[77] In order to avoid as much as possible a conflict between the calling of widow and

---

[70] *Inst.* IV. xiii. 14.
[71] *Inst.* IV. xiii. 14.
[72] *Inst.* IV. xiii. 12.
[73] *Inst.* IV. xiii. 12.
[74] *Inst.* IV. xiii. 11.
[75] *Inst.* IV. xiii. 11.
[76] *Inst.* IV. xiii. 17.
[77] *Inst.* IV. xiii. 18.

the normal desire for sexual fulfillment, Paul set an age commonly beyond danger for entrance into this group.[78]

At any rate, widows were never nuns.[79] Nuns offer their celibacy to God as some kind of service. Unlike widows who gave up family life in order to devote themselves to a life of strenuous activity for sake of the gospel, modern nuns are all too frequently idlers, who attempt to appease God with their songs and mumblings. Many take their vows too young and find themselves in difficulty, when they are no longer able to reconcile their vow of celibacy with their sexual longings.

The good news, however, is that monastic vows are not indissoluble.[80] Men and women who feel that they must keep on as celibate monks and nuns simply because at an early age they made a solemn promise to God should know that unlawful vows are not binding.[81] Otherwise Christians would be bound to what God does not require.

V

In the movement from Thomas Aquinas to John Calvin the argument over the status of monks has come full circle. Thomas regarded both bishops and monks as participants in the state of perfection on earth, bishops by virtue of their perpetual cure of souls and monks by virtue of their vows. Secular priests and laity, who had no such perpetual care, were excluded from the state of perfection. What marked monks off from other Christians was the obligation they had incurred to keep the counsels as well as the commands.

Gerson agreed with Thomas that both monks and bishops were in a state of perfection, but emphasized that perfection was to be found in the commands rather than the counsels. Counsels play an instrumental rather than an essential role in the quest for perfection. Moreover, bishops were not only in a higher state of perfection than monks (a point admitted by Thomas), but even shared their dignity with secular priests (a point that Thomas explicitly denied).

Goch pushed the argument still further by stressing the sacramental equality of priests and bishops, who differ only in jurisdiction. The *status perfectionis* is the state of the priesthood as such, in which bishops share by virtue of their ordination to celebrate the eucharist. Goch rejected the Thomistic theology of the vow as a second baptism that added an additional dignity to good works and excluded monks from the state of perfection. Monasteries are institutions the Church has created to assist the spiritually infirm.

---

[78] *Inst.* IV. xiii. 18.
[79] *Inst.* IV. xiii. 19.
[80] *Inst.* IV. xiii. 21.
[81] *Inst.* IV. xiii. 20.

Calvin took the argument to yet another stage when he suggested that the state of perfection is the state of every Christian, clerical and lay, who is discharging a lawful vocation. All Christians are bound to follow the rule of Christ whose final end is the perfection of the elect. The notion of a *status perfectionis* is, in a certain sense, broadened to include all the faithful, with the exception of monks and nuns, who are pursuing a vocation not authorized by Scripture. They, too, may be included in the state of perfection, rightly understood, if they will renounce their dissoluble vows, abandon their schismatic conventicles, and reintegrate themselves into community of the faithful. The distinction between commands and counsels dissolves into a general obligation to keep every word of Christ and the celibate ethic into a reaffirmation of marriage as the normal state of the Christian man and woman.

If there is a distinctive note in Calvin's criticism of monasticism, it may lay in his emphasis on Christian unity. Calvin found no place for the monastic ideal, which he regarded as unavoidably schismatic, in a Church that is one, holy, catholic and apostolic. To tolerate monasticism is to admit a double Christianity, a second baptism, a dual path to the heavenly Jerusalem, and a spiritual elite. Whatever other faults monasticism might have had in Calvin's eyes, this fault alone was sufficient to condemn it.

ANTICLERICALISM IN THE REGISTERS
OF THE GENEVA CONSISTORY 1542-1564

ROBERT M. KINGDON

University of Wisconsin, Madison

Anticlericalism was a major force in the city-state of Geneva during the sixteenth century. In one form it helped cause the Protestant Reformation there. That Reformation began as a revolution against the power of the ruling prince-bishop and his ally, the duchy of Savoy. It led to the dismissal of almost all of the several hundred clergy then active in Geneva and to the expulsion of most of them from the city and its associated territory. In another form, anticlericalism bedeviled John Calvin and his associates among the handful of Protestant clergymen appointed to replace the expelled priests as ministers of the newly reformed church of Geneva. It is this second form of anticlericalism that I wish to discuss in this paper.

The main target of the leaders of this second wave of Genevan anti-clericalism was an institution called the consistory. It had been established by John Calvin himself, as a part of the bargain that brought him back to Geneva from exile in Strasbourg, in ecclesiastical ordinances he drafted in 1541. This Consistory was made up of two benches. On one bench sat all of the salaried pastors of the republic, headed by Calvin. On the other sat twelve lay elders, elected for this duty every February, in the elections in which the entire Genevan government was reconstituted each year. The presiding officer was a syndic, one of the four magistrates elected as chief executives for the year. The Consistory met once a week to cross-examine local residents suspected of misbehavior. It thus became the most important ecclesiastical institution charged with shaping behavior, as distinguished from belief. Its chief weapon in controlling behavior was simply verbal. It administered "admonitions" and "remonstrances", some of considerable vehemence, mostly to unruly teen-agers or to elderly men and women obviously confused by the considerable changes imposed upon them. Most of these people meekly accepted their reprimands and agreed to mend their ways. The Consistory could also excommunicate people called before it, if their misbehavior was serious or if they were unrepentant. The sanction of excommunication became extremely effective in Calvin's Geneva, driving most of those who received such a sentence into either frantic attempts at reconciliation or into permanent exile. The Consistory also could and did refer those who misbehaved to the Small Council, which effectively controlled the city government, for other forms of punishment.

Important though the Consistory is for an understanding of the history of
Geneva and of Calvinism, it has never received the sustained scholarly
attention it deserves. This is not for a lack of relevant sources. Manuscript
registers of its weekly meetings, with remarkably few gaps, do survive and
are carefully preserved in the Geneva State Archives. But they have never
been properly utilized. Generations of scholars have been frightened away
by the bad handwriting of the Consistory's secretaries. All previous
scholarly work on the Consistory, with only a few minor exceptions, has
been based on a set of transcripts prepared in 1853 by a Genevan antiquary
named Cramer.[1] But Cramer transcribed only about five percent of the
cases, often with gaps and erroneous readings. And he chose for transcription largely the more lurid and sensational cases. As a result all previous
work on the Consistory is, in varying degrees, distorted and misleading.

To remedy this defect in studies of the Calvinist Reformation, I organized
in 1987 a team of amateur paleographers in this country and in Switzerland,
under the sponsorship of the Meeter Center for Calvin Studies at Calvin
College and Seminary. We have transcribed all the surviving twenty-one
volumes covering the period of Calvin's ministry, from 1542 to 1564. If we
can obtain additional funds, we would also like to begin editing this
material.

These registers, when available, will provide an extremely rich source for
study of anticlericalism in Calvin's Geneva, particularly as it was directed
against the Calvinist pastorate. It will provide a source that is sympathetic
to Calvin and his supporters, of course, but it will be a source that is so
detailed that sensitive scholars should be able to reconstruct the anticlerical
position fairly.

I would now like to present to you some examples of expressions of
anticlericalism in the registers of the Geneva Consistory. The particular
examples I chose are not from among the more common and run-of-the-mill
expressions one finds in these registers. They are rather examples already
known in part to local specialists through the Cramer transcripts. I choose
them because they express anticlericalism in a particularly strong and locally
influential way. My analysis is based, furthermore, on a fresh check of the
original manuscripts kept in Geneva.

The examples I present were expressed by members of the family of
François Favre. Favre was a wealthy merchant who had been one of the
leaders in the city's earlier fight for independence from the prince-bishop,

---

[1] [Frédéric-Auguste Cramer], *Notes extraites des registres du Consistoire de
l'église de Genève, 1541-1814* (Geneva, 1853, in lithograph). For influential uses of
these transcripts, see Baum, Cunitz, and Reuss, eds., "Annales calviniani", in *CO* 21;
Emile Doumergue, *Jean Calvin, les hommes et les choses de son temps* (Lausanne,
1899-1927), 5: 189ff.; Walther Köhler, *Zürcher Ehegericht und Genfer Konsistorium*,
10 in the *Quellen und Abhandlungen zur Schweizerischen Reformationsgeschichte*,
vol. 2 (Leipzig, 1942), ch. 14, "Johann Calvin und Genf", 505-652.

leading diplomatic missions and military expeditions in that cause. He had been an active member of the city's governing Small Council during the crucial decade, 1526-1537, in which the Catholic clergy were ejected and a Protestant regime installed. Between 1545 and 1547, the years in which he and his family got into trouble with the Consistory, he was an old man, in his 60's, no longer active in government, no doubt tapering off in business. Members of his large family, however, remained very active. One of his daughters was then married to Ami Perrin, Captain-General of the republic, member of the Small Council, repeatedly elected syndic. Another daughter was married to another prominent member of the Small Council, and yet another was married to the Procurator-General of the republic. François Favre was also joined in business by a younger brother, Jean, and an unmarried son, Gaspard.[2]

It is this son Gaspard who provides the most striking expressions of the type of anticlericalism that here interests me. In the fall of 1545 he was summoned to appear before the Consistory for questioning about scandalous and disrespectful remarks he had made in public.[3] For several months he ignored the summons and simply refused to appear. The Consistory appealed to the Small Council for help in enforcing these and other summons. Finally the Council ordered that Gaspard be thrown into jail for his disobedience and be released only on the day of the next Consistory meeting with the expectation that he would go straight to that meeting.[4] He duly appeared before that body on 4 March 1546, and the usual tough cross-examination began.[5] He was informed that he had been summoned for disobedience. He was then questioned about various public statements that he was alleged to have made. The first was that he had said that when he became a ruling syndic, a reasonable if distant prospect given the prominence of his family, he would reintroduce bordellos into Geneva. This alleged brazen defence of

---

[2] For a useful genealogy of the family, see Albert Choisy, *Généalogies genevoises* (Geneva, 1947), 118-38, especially 120-22. On Gaspard, see also Edouard Favre, "Gaspard Favre et sa donation aux fugitifs (1556), un épisode de l'opposition à Calvin dans Genève", in *Mémoires et documents publiés par la Société d'histoire et d'archéologie de Genève*, t. 31 (1908-1909), 209-341. On François Favre, see also Henri Fazy, "Procès et démêlés à propos de la compétence disciplinaire du Consistoire (1546-1547)", in *Procédures et documents du XVIe siècle (1546-1547)* (Geneva, 1886), reprinted from t. 16 of the *Mémoires de l'Institut National Genevois*, hereafter cited as Fazy, *Procès*.

[3] Archives d'Etat de Genève (hereafter A.E.G.), Registres du Consistoire (hereafter R.Consistoire), II, fol. 11v., 19 November 1545, and fol. 14, 3 December 1545, notices that Gaspard was not responding to summonses to appear.

[4] A.E.G., Registres du Conseil (hereafter R.C.), t. 41, fols. 33 and 36, 1 and 4 March 1546. Cf. t. 40, fol. 324, 11 December 1545, for an earlier order that he be imprisoned for this offense, apparently not enforced.

[5] A.E.G., R.Consistoire, II, fol. 37v., 4 March 1546. For a partial transcription, see *CO* 21. 371.

prostitution obviously shocked Calvin and his fellow ministers and elders. Gaspard denied making the statement. The presiding syndic than asked Calvin to administer the usual "remonstrance", a scolding, usually of some vehemence. If Gaspard had simply sat still and listened, that might have been the end of the matter. Instead he counterattacked. He said he would not answer to Calvin. Nor would he answer to any of the other ministers. He did not recognize their authority as judges of his behavior. He would answer questions only if put by the presiding syndic or by those members of the Consistory who were, like him, citizens and bourgeois of Geneva. That meant the lay elders. To be a citizen of Geneva one had to be born there of a bourgeois family. Calvin and all of his fellow ministers present that day were not and could not ever be citizens. They were all recent immigrants from France. This reaction of Gaspard's infuriated the Consistory. He was immediately peppered with questions about other blasphemous things he had allegedly said and done. The Consistory clearly had a long list of questions they wanted to put to him. In the end he was ordered to return to the Small Council for punishment.

There is no evidence that Gaspard obeyed this order. Calvin and other Consistory members neglected to mention it the very next day when they attended the Council in connection with another case, of a local merchant who had gone so far as to accuse Calvin of preaching false doctrine.[6] In the uproar provoked by this other case, Gaspard Favre seems to have been temporarily forgotten. But not for long. Gaspard continued to misbehave. On Easter day he got involved in a noisy bowling game during services at the parish church of St. Gervais. He and his companions insulted the minister and others who came to reprove them.[7] After a further delay, Gaspard finally appeared once more at a meeting of the Consistory of 17 June 1546.[8] He behaved much as he had before, again insisting that he would not answer to Calvin. He nevertheless had a rather violent exchange with Calvin. Calvin told him: "Here we are above you." Gaspard retorted: "You are above everyone." This so infuriated Calvin that he stormed out of the room, shouting that he meant to resign from the Consistory. Others said that they would also resign unless Gaspard was punished. He was immediately thrown into jail. Not even a personal appeal later that same day to the Consistory from his brother-in-law, the Captain-General Ami Perrin, asking that Gaspard be released from jail into the custody of family members, could calm them down.[9]

---

[6] A.E.G., R.C., t. 41, fol. 37v., 5 March 1546; transcribed in *CO* 21. 372-73.

[7] A.E.G., R.C., t. 41, fols. 80v., 26 April 1546; 82, 27 April 1546; 84, 30 April 1546.

[8] A.E.G., R.Consistoire, II, fol. 65v., 17 June 1546; partially transcribed in *CO* 21. 382-83.

[9] A.E.G., R.Consistoire, II, fol. 66v.

The next day Calvin and all the other members of the Consistory appeared before the Small Council to complain about Gaspard Favre. They complained specifically about his failures to answer Calvin and his insistence that he would answer only to questions put by the presiding syndic and the citizen-members of the Consistory. It was ordered that Gaspard be jailed and placed in solitary confinement.[10] He was held in jail for ten days, then finally released after being administered "remonstrances".[11] He then left the city for about two years, going into military service elsewhere, most probably with Geneva's ally Bern.[12]

A further step in the Favre family's anticlerical campaign came a year later when Gaspard's father François decided to use his son's tactics. François was in much more serious trouble than his son. This over-sixty-year-old retiree was accused and convicted of multiple fornication, with two or more servant girls, one of whom he had gotten pregnant and who had then moved to a village in France to give birth to her child. He had admitted the charges quite freely, perhaps even with pride, arguing that these were simple sins of the "flesh" (his actual word was somewhat more crude) and that many of them had occurred when he was temporarily widowed, between legitimate wives. He was nevertheless punished in the usual manner, sentenced by the city government to a short term of imprisonment on bread and water. But he was then sent on to the Consistory to see if he merited additional punishment, no doubt further "remonstrances", perhaps even excommunication if he did not seem sufficiently repentant.[13]

At the next meeting of the Consistory, on 3 February 1547, Calvin was not present, so it fell to his colleague, Abel Poupin, to administer the usual "remonstrances". But François Favre refused to recognize Poupin and at first would speak only to the presiding syndic. In effect he was following his son in denying the right of the ordained ministers to sit in judgment in the Consistory and in insisting that the administration of justice of any kind must be reserved to duly elected citizens. Finally, however, François turned to the bench of ministers and cried out: "I have nothing to do with you. I do not know who you are. I do not recognize you at all." And then he repeated this manifesto several times. The ministers were so angry that they shouted back, with one of them, apparently Poupin, going so far as to say that François was behaving like a dog. The Consistory as a whole then decided to send François back to the Small Council for further punishment and to appear before the Council themselves as a body in order to demand more respect for their form of discipline.[14]

---

[10] A.E.G., R.C., t. 41, fol. 116v., 18 June 1546; transcribed in *CO* 21. 383.

[11] A.E.G., R.C., t. 41, fol. 133v., 28 June 1546.

[12] Edouard Favre (n. 2 above), 224-5.

[13] For a full study, with relevant documents, see Fazy, *Procès*.

[14] A.E.G., R.Consistoire, III, 14, 3 February 1547. There is a transcription of a somewhat different and longer account in *CO* 21. 395-6.

There followed a lengthy series of formal trials, in which François Favre, his daughter Mme. Perrin,[15] and his brother Jean[16] were called in and subjected to intensive cross-examination on charges of displaying disrespect for authority. François was treated with particular harshness and was kept in jail for long periods of time. Finally the affair was brought to a close on 6 October 1547, with a final appearance before the Consistory of François Favre and his daughter, Mme. Perrin. This time the old man, no doubt broken by months in prison, was in a much more subdued mood. He explained that he had always respected the authority of the ministers as preachers and did not want to diminish that authority in any way. He had been upset only by their personal attacks on him as a sinner whom even God should forgive and by their treatment of his son. He then listened patiently to a series of remonstrances administered to him by John Calvin on behalf of the entire Consistory. He then said that if Calvin had always treated him as gently as he had that day, things would never have gone as far as they did. He shook hands with all the ministers. He and his daughter, who also had to listen to remonstrances intended specifically for her, were both forgiven.[17] But François had been so thoroughly upset by these experiences that he had already announced a decision to leave Geneva for good. He spent the rest of his life on family properties within the territories of Bern, beyond the jurisdiction of Genevan courts.

The attempts by the Favre family to argue that the Consistory should be an entirely secular institution, that salaried ministers should not be active members of it, thus failed. The Favres had insisted throughout that they were good Protestant Christians, that they accepted the right and duty of ministers to preach the Word of God from the pulpit. But they denied that ministers should ever serve as judges, or exercise any political or judicial powers outside their pulpits. That was the form their anticlericalism took. Their point of view failed in the short run. It has taken up by others in the years immediately following their trials, specifically by a party within Geneva called the libertines, led by Favre's son-in-law, Ami Perrin. That party was crushed with some brutality in 1555. The faction supporting Calvin triumphed completely and for decades its views prevailed. Their triumph was not permanent, however. Over the decades clerical power was gradually eroded, so that by the seventeenth century the political and judicial

---

[15] For full texts of the dossiers prepared for these two trials, see Fazy, *Procès*, 37-48 and 49-54. The originals are to be found in A.E.G., P.C., Ière série, nos. 424 (Favre) and 447 (Mme. Perrin).

[16] A.E.G., P.C., Ière série, no. 429.

[17] A.E.G., R.Consistoire, III, 147, 6 October 1547; partially transcribed in *CO* 21. 414-15.

powers of the Genevan clergy were considerable reduced.[18] By the nineteenth century they were gone. This particular form of anticlericalism had triumphed. A full understanding of the shape it took at its origins in the sixteenth century, however, in all its varieties and nuances, must wait upon a full examination of the registers of the Geneva Consistory.

---

[18] There is considerable freshly available evidence of this reduction in the *Registres de la Compagnie des Pasteurs de Genève*, t. 9 (1604-1606), edited by Matteo Campagnolo, Micheline Louis-Courvoisier, and Gabriella Cahier, vol. 236 in the *Travaux d'Humanisme et Renaissance* (Geneva, 1989).

LOCAL ANTICLERICALISM IN REFORMATION GERMANY

GERALD STRAUSS

Indiana University, Bloomington

I give the title "Local Anticlericalism" to the following observations because I want to call attention to their source in the mundane give-and-take of everyday communal life in Reformation Germany. Although "anti-clericalism", with the largely nineteenth-century associations this word carries in the general literature on the subject,[1] may seem too heavily weighted a term to fit the modest phenomena we discover in this commonplace setting, "anticlerical" as a descriptive label does seem to characterize accurately the effects, if not also the intentions, of expressed, and presumably felt, resentment of and opposition to clerical office, status, and practice — after the Reformation in Lutheran regions as much as before.

My example is taken from the record of a visitation conducted in 1569 and 1570 in the superintendency of Weimar as part of a general tour of inspection then being carried on in Ernestine Saxony under the auspices of Duke Johann Wilhelm. This was the fifth visitation in Ernestine lands since the inauguration of the Reformation there, and the first since Johann Wilhelm's installation as sovereign of all Ernestine territories in 1566 during the course of political and religious troubles that were pitting the Wettin inheritors against one another at that time. In addition to the usual agenda of a general visitation undertaken on the principles laid down by Luther and Melanchthon in the late 1520s, the visitation of 1569-70 had one overriding concern, and this was the re-establishment of the orthodox doctrines contained in the Weimar Book of Confutation against Victorinus Strigel's synergistic position on free will and justification. Strigel, a Philippist theologian who had come to short-lived influence under Johann Wilhelm's predecessor, his brother Johann Friedrich, had drawn up a formal statement of his views in 1562, and a number of Saxon clerics had signed their names to this so-called *Declaratio Victorini*, most of them under duress.[2] With the

---

[1] E.g., José Sánchez, *Anticlericalism: A Brief History* (Notre Dame, 1972); J. Salwyn Schapiro, *Anticlericalism: Conflict Between Church and State in France, Italy, and Spain* (Princeton, 1967); article "Clericalism and Anticlericalism" in *Encyclopedia of Religion and Ethics* (n.d.).

[2] On this controversy, see the detailed account given in August Beck, *Johann Friedrich der Mittlere, Herzog zu Sachsen. Ein Beitrag zur Geschichte des sechszehnten Jahrhunderts* (Weimar, 1858), 1: 279-403, especially 375-94. On the Book of Confutation, see ibid., 307-13.

accession of Johann Wilhelm the doctrinal winds shifted. Recantation was now made obligatory for the signatories if they wanted to hold on to their livings and continue to reside in the country.[3] Appointed to oversee this campaign were the two most conservative Lutheran theologians in the land, the Jena professors Johann Wigand and Tilemann Heshusius, who were joined by the Weimar superintendent Bartholomäus Rosinus (who had refused to sign Strigel's declaration in 1562 and lost his job for it) and three secular officials, one of them a jurist.

A lengthy ducal "Instruction" informed the visitors, and through them the pastors, what the real issue was. It was nothing less than the restoration of pure religion in the land, the evangelical faith of the days of Luther, Frederick the Wise, John the Steadfast, and John Frederick. This restoration had to be preceded by a rooting out of all "adiophisterei, widerteuferischen schwenkfeldischen, zwinglischen, antinomischen, Osianders, synergistischen und majoristischen oder andern dergleichen in unsern confutationibus begriffen vorfuerischen secten und coruptelen",[4] and this, in turn, was to be accomplished in the first instance by an inquisition of each pastor and pastor's assistant in every parish and affiliated congregation in Duke Johann Wilhelm's realm, together with an interrogation of all patrons residing in the territory, all church elders and curators (*Altarleute*), the leading citizens in each town, and the governing elders (*Heimburgen*) of every village. Authority was given to the visitors to compel these dignitaries to appear before them for examination, and to submit their books and registers for inspection. Eighty-nine parishes and forty-eight *Filialen* were visited in the Weimar superintendency in this manner during the late winter and early spring of 1569-70.

Along with to the problem of orthodoxy, what engaged the ducal officials as they made their way through the region were the following tasks, which I list here in the order of their apparent importance as reflected in the documents. 1: Find the funds to assure an adequate and reliable income for pastors, teachers, and other ecclesiastical staff, and do this without drawing on the state's resources, except in cases of hopeless local impoverishment;

---

[3] The visitation protocol cited in note 5 below, contains six such recantations (35r-36v), as do many other protocols. The most voluminous record of written recantations I have seen is Staatsarchiv Coburg B 2461, fols. 31-140, containing identical statements of revocation by pastors in the superintendency of Coburg who, seven years earlier, in 1562, had been compelled by the Coburg superintendent Maximilian Mörlin to sign the *Declaratio Victorini*.

[4] Johann Wilhelm's Instruction is printed in Emil Sehling, ed., *Die evangelischen Kirchenordnungen des XVI. Jahrhunderts* Volume 1, Part 1 (Leipzig, 1902), 242-5 (hereafter cited as Sehling). Verbatim repetitions from the 1554 instruction: ibid., 222-8. Quoted passage on 243-4. On visitations generally, see ibid., 70-1. Also Gerald Strauss, *Luther's House of Learning: Indoctrination of the Young in the German Reformation* (Baltimore, 1978), chapter 12.

instruct pastors to keep orderly books and registers of who should pay, and who has or has not paid, when, and how much. 2: Convince parish folk that it is their duty to provide materials and labor to keep church structures, including the pastor's and schoolmaster's dwellings, in decent repair. 3: Ascertain that pastors and teachers are able and respectable; replace incompetents and suspects. And 4: Probe the causes of local disharmony, and do what can be done to neutralize them; identify offenses and delin- quencies — *Gebrechen*, things that are amiss — and make sure they are noted, reported through channels, and punished. Most of the information obtained by the visitors on these and related matters came from *Klagen*, complaints and accusations brought forward by local informants. As nearly everyone who appeared had something to divulge, there was plenty of opportunity for the reciprocal airing of grudges and recriminations. The visitation protocols, compiled from notes taken at the site by professional scribes, record these grievances in detail.[5]

Sorting out the anticlerical elements in this compilation of local lore draws us some distance into the realm of inference. What, for our purposes, we may want to call "anticlericalism" was, at the time, a bundle of unorganized perceptions on the part of ordinary people, perceptions expressed in attitudes and externalized as a certain kind of behavior, but never asserted as principled opposition to a sacerdotal presence in the community. Whether a particular word or deed is "anticlerical" or not is therefore a function of *our* judgment, not of theirs. Perceptions and attitudes being rooted in experience, in this case in people's interactions with the church and its agents in the routine circumstances of their lives, what we must decide is whether enough ill will was generated by these relations, and with sufficient regularity, to have produced, or at least reinforced, a mindset we may legitimately tag "anticlerical". The visitation reports, I believe, provide us with the data for making a decision on this point.

Obviously the Reformation produced a substantial change in the structuring of relations between laity and clergy. The number of clerics with whom the layperson had contact was sharply reduced; the propaganda barrage that had imbued the public with stereotypical images of priestly duplicity and corruption gave way to admonitions that respect was due the good pastor and curate. *Sola fide* and *sola scriptura* may well — to the extent they were understood and internalized — have lessened the laity's sense of minority vis-à-vis the clergy, and thus narrowed the grounds for antagonism. At the same time, the events of 1525, despite their outcome, probably strengthened the claims of secular and material interests, and thus gave fresh impetus to the criticism of the clergy's implication in these interests. The idea of the community as an authentic form of the church,

---

[5] The protocol of the 1569-70 visitation in the superintendency of Weimar is in Staatsarchiv Weimar, Reg N, 506.

possibly as an alternative to the existing church, must have gained great force as a result of the ideology of the revolution.[6]

These consequences of the Reformation, disparate though they are, can plausibly be judged to have moved the balance between laity and clergy toward greater autonomy for the former, a shift that should have brought with it a reduction of tensions between the two groups. Other factors, however, clearly resisted a major change in this direction, as several scholars — Bob Scribner and Hans-Christoph Rublack most recently[7] — have argued, and as I shall try to demonstrate in detail in this paper. Should we then, in the light of this lag, suppose that clericalism survived the Reformation in Germany and that anticlericalism was the response to it? My answer is yes, we should. Clericalism[8] may be said to refer to a situation in which churchmen are perceived as a group apart, poorly integrated into society, possessing privileges not available to most others, exercising arbitrary power and using it in a way that strikes many observers as self-serving, interfering in people's lives but hypocritical in advancing the moral claims on which their right to meddle rests, grasping and avid for gain, especially for money, a burden on society. Certain other objectionable features commonly attributed to clericalism in its later, mainly ultramontane, form, were obviously absent from the sixteenth-century scene. But as defined in the terms I have just given, clericalism, and anticlericalism as a reaction to it, can, I think, be demonstrated to have been palpably present in Reformation Germany.

Such a global statement means little by itself. What is the evidence for it? I turn to the 1569-70 reports from the Weimar parishes. They suggest that two direct and constant sources of antagonism between laity and clergy existed in small towns and villages, along with several other sources breeding resentment somewhat less immediately and unremittingly. It will not occasion surprise to learn that the church's demands on people's money, goods, and labor head my list of public irritations. Given the prevailing concepts of revenue assessment, this was an unavoidable cost of parish rebuilding in the age of the Reformation, for securing the local church's economic base was, after doctrinal reliability, the chief priority of ecclesiastical administrators, in Saxony as elsewhere, especially in the countryside,

---

[6] This point is emphasized by Hans-Jürgen Goertz, "Aufstand gegen den Priester. Antiklerikalismus und reformatorische Bewegungen", in *Bauer, Reich und Reformation*, ed. P. Blickle (Stuttgart, 1982), 193ff.

[7] Bob Scribner, "Antiklerikalismus in Deutschland um 1500", in *Europa 1500. Integrationsprozesse im Widerstreit: Staaten, Regionen, Personenverbände, Christenheit*, ed. F. Seibt, W. Eberhard (Stuttgart, 1987), 368-82; Hans-Christoph Rublack, "'Der wohlgeplagte Priester'. Vom Selbstverständnis lutherischer Geistlichkeit im Zeitalter der Orthodoxie", ZHF 16 (1989): 1-30.

[8] For the history of "clericalism" as a term, see the (very anticlerical) article "Clericalism and Anticlericalism", in the *Encyclopaedia of Religion and Ethics* (n.d.).

where the previous regime's neglect was most keenly felt. Custom as well as financial prudence dictated that the wherewithal for a well-functioning parish be supplied locally; no matter how well off and willing the patron, therefore, local people were always expected to help provide the means. Lay contribution to the upkeep of clerical personnel seems to have fallen off in the early decades of the Reformation, no doubt owing to the circulation of so many ugly stories about exploitative priests and a Roman curia fairly drowning in its riches.[9] Nearly everywhere in the land the visitors noted slackness, penny-pinching, and a grudging spirit in meeting obligations. A plaintive reproach in an earlier visitation instruction (1554) had reminded people of how willingly they used, in the old days, to give their hard-earned money to the papacy; now, the Instruction noted sadly, Christian preachers and pastors are shown only "niggardliness and shameful ingratitude".[10] Transmitted to people via the parish pulpit, this reproach was turned into nagging admonitions, backed up by new regulations transforming the old voluntary or customary payments of cash and *naturalia* into compulsory contributions.[11]

Persuading people to make these payments and grants-in-kind on time and in full was a ceaseless chore for visitors. Their aim was to place this task as an administrative responsibility on town councillors and village elders (Staatsarchiv Weimar, Reg N 506, 59v, 60r. All references in the text are to this document). But the job was a labor of Sisyphus, as is revealed in innumerable complaints by pastors and other clergy concerning unpaid, or short, or laggard remittance of tithes and other fees "nicht volkommlich gereicht", or given "gar seumlich" (e.g., 127r, 70v). The usual remedy was to issue stern reminders to pay "ohne abbruch und zu gebürlicher Zeit" (69v), with the threat of a fine of one gulden into the *Gotteskasten* — the poor relief box — hanging over the offender. The evidence is overwhelming that people were unenthusiastic about supporting the church, and sullen in submitting to what they were compelled to do. They reduced money payments (74r), measured short what they owed in kind (90v), handed "mit

---

[9] Henry J. Cohn cites the sense of the Roman Church's enormous wealth as one of the four chief sources of late medieval anticlericalism: "Reformatorische Bewegungen und Antiklerikalismus in Deutschland und England" in *Stadtbürgertum und Adel in der Reformation. Studien zur Sozialgeschichte der Reformation in England und Deutschland*, ed. W. J. Mommsen (Stuttgart, 1979), 309-27, especially 314-5.

[10] *Instruction ... Johans Friderichen des mitlern, Johans Wilhelm und Johans Friderichen des jungern ... die neue visitation belangende ...* (1554), in Sehling 1.1: 225.

[11] Sehling 1.1: 225: "... das an denen örtern, so die leut albereit gegen dem alten zugengen oder opferpfennige nichts zugeben pflegen, ein ieder wirt und wirtin ein quartal iren selsorgern drei pfennig und die andern, so über zwölf jar alt drei heller geben sollen."

widerwillen und abbruch" (134r) a small, stale, or mouldy loaf of bread, instead of the requisite "gute hausbackene brot" (87v) to the sexton or the schoolmaster when they came to the door on their *Umgang* (92v), refused the *Zinshuhn* or similar dues owed from time immemorial (99r and v),[12] and kept back the compulsory school fee (69r and v), thus making clear their view of formal education as a wasteful luxury. The visitors, in their attempts to arrange for the adequate support of church and school, generally tried to shift the burden from individual householders to the community, but this was a move that could not have pleased the well-to-do, whose share increased in proportion to the numbers of poor in their respective parishes (136r and v). From these poor folk, the church demanded labor, a not insubstantial drain on people's time and energy. In nearly every parish the visitors assigned tasks and set deadlines for restoring neglected church structures (70v): patching roofs, putting up a study room or a bed chamber in the pastor's dwelling, building a pig sty or an outhouse, laying a wooden floor, making long overdue repairs (98v, 176v, 126r, 156v). The reports leave no doubt that parishoners rarely, if ever, undertook these jobs on their own initiative, and even when prodded by officials they acted "gar seumig und ungehorsam" (126r), and with unconcealed distaste for the work.

Indeed, it seems evident that the church was a heavy burden on the ordinary person and the community. Parishioners were told, for example, that, as a quid pro quo for hearing the gospel preached, they "must plow the pastor's field or else give him a sum of money out of the common chest, and not out of the poor box."[13] They must also harvest and thresh the pastor's and the schoolmaster's crops (83v, 136v). When the weather was bad, the residents of a *Filiale* — an affiliated, or branch congregation without a minister of its own — were expected to send a wagon or at least a horse to fetch the pastor for the sermon, for a funeral, a baptism, or a sick visit, and then take him home again.[14] Clerics often brought up complaints about *widerwillige* compliance with, or outright refusal of this service (164v), even though the visitors set fines and other penalties for the *undankbare* who were guilty of such recalcitrance (83r, 170r). Carting duties of this and a similar kind seem to have been especially unwelcome, perhaps because they were classified as a *frohn* (161v), perhaps because they involved, as well, the transport of firewood for the pastor, the sexton, and the school teacher (113v, 154v).

---

[12] For an exhaustive survey of the tradition of payments and contributions owed to the Church, see Anton Störmann, *Die städtischen Gravamina gegen den Klerus am Ausgange des Mittelalters und in der Reformationszeit* (Münster, 1916).

[13] Staatsarchiv Weimar, Reg. N, 506, 72r: "Dagegen müssen die Eingepfarrten dem pfarrer seinen acker bestellen ... ."

[14] Staatsarchiv Weimar, Reg. N, 506, 75r. Elsewhere this obligation fell on the people of the parish: ibid., 83r.

Another object of frequent contention was the custom of charging the cost of the altar wine to the community. Where the church had sufficient income, the visitors lifted this burden (137r); but more often they decided that the commune must bear it (229r). Treating the school teacher to a full meal on the occasion of a baptism in the family was a further source of protest. Because they recognized that this usage fell disproportionately on the poor, the visitors sometimes allowed substitution of the small sum of one groschen (101v), but this seems to have been no less grudgingly given. The same was true of the contributions of food or other *naturalia* required of people too poor to pay the modest school fee (136r and v). In this and similar instances, what impresses the modern reader of these documents is the disputatious resistance aroused by even petty sums and trivial liabilities: a pound of wax annually from the communal beehives (219r), the right to cut and use grass growing in the churchyard (226r), access to a watering pond (100v-101r), a few pennies to pay the village herdsman (123r). Over more substantial figures than these the wrangling was interminable. Disbursements from the *Gotteskasten* were fought over so vehemently that, according to the townspeople in one place, "irem selbst bericht nach [er] *vulgo* der Hader Casten genannt wirdet" (255r). And for a typical dispute, to suggest the flavor and texture of lay-clerical relations at the time, let me quote the following passage from a note added a couple of years later to the 1570 visitation report:

> On June 28, Anno domini 1572, the community of Ottmanshausen lodged a complaint against its pastor Peter Kniden, as follows. Item: that he sells the straw from the parish field for his own profit. ... Item: that he carts an acre and a half worth of parish manure to a field he owns in the village of Stetten while allowing the parish field to go to waste. Upon hearing this complaint, the visitors declared to the pastor that he must henceforth winter and summer his two cows and five sheep within the parish, that he must feed them the parish straw, let them make manure of it, and then use this manure to fertilize the parish field. ... And he must never again sell the straw.

For his part, the Ottmanshausen pastor protested that the house, the barn, and the stable belonging to the church were so tumbledown and leaky that neither beasts nor grain could be sheltered in them. The townspeople, he said, had never made a move to repair them, despite his requests and pleas (205r).

Elsewhere, deep frustration surfaced at times over incompetent pastoral stewardship of natural resources attached to the church. In one place, an earlier incumbent had so depleted the parish wood that not enough was left for the present pastor to heat his house and the school. This neglect cost the community five gulden annually, the price of purchasing firewood (79r, 20r, 31v). Even more apt to lead to ill will was the threat of clerical competition in profit-making activities, especially brewing beer and selling it by the pitcher. This was an ancient but forever current source of discord between laity and clergy,[15] and the visitation reports include many descriptions of it (63r).

Economically, then, the clergy weighed on people with demands for cash, products, and services that most of them could ill afford to render, especially in a time of rising prices — about which many pointed complaints are reported in the visitation protocols (e.g., 51r, 54r and v). But in another way, too, the church was a heavy burden to bear. Its situation in the midst of communal and family life meant more or less constant interference: prying, meddling, censorious disapproval, prompting, moralizing, and — not infrequently — intimidation. Just as the church's material requirements made inroads on people's working time, its ideological objectives invaded their leisure,[16] most exactingly — and no doubt most irritatingly — in the form of the catechism, the memorizing of which was made mandatory for old and young. In this task, too, the visitors enlisted the agency of town councillors and village elders. Following the visitation, the *Obrigkeit* of each place was instructed to summon all the residents and proclaim to them the main points laid down for their correction and improvement — fifteen such items in the aftermath of the 1569-70 visitation (42r-45v).[17] Attendance at the Sunday sermon and regular participation in catechism practice were the chief religious duties laid on parishioners, especially the catechism, for this was the teaching tool relied on most confidently by Lutheran churchmen. Everyone, of all ages, faced the catechism three times a week: recitation and explanation, one article at a time, every Thursday or Friday; repetition of this as part of the service on Sundays; and an examination, with additional instruction, on another day (41r-v).[18] Absentees were noted and the pastor told to "proceed" (*procediren*) against them (57r). Taverns had to remain closed to travellers as well as to locals during weekday catechism and Sunday sermons.

While the catechism was doing its — agonizingly slow — work of individual reform, the church, acting under the auspices of the state, and in accordance with confessional Protestantism's agenda for moralizing secular life, moved against habits and customs it deemed injurious to people's spiritual condition. *Abgöttische* and *abergläubische* practices were being discovered in nearly every parish, and these were now ordered *verboten und abgeschafft*:[19] pictures, bell-ringing, Hail Marys, "idolatrous altars" (44v), and so on. Spinning bees were forbidden on Sundays, as were other types of social gatherings labelled "ergerliche böse missbräuche" (98r). Wedding

---

[15] Cf. Störmann, *Die städtischen Gravamina gegen den Klerus*, 150ff., esp. 153ff.

[16] A point made for the English Reformation by A. G. Dickens, "The Shape of Anti-clericalism and the English Reformation", in *Politics and Society in Reformation Europe*, ed. E. I. Kouri, T. Scott (Houndsmills, Basingstoke, 1987), 402.

[17] Also printed in Sehling 1.1: 688-90.

[18] Sehling 1.1: 688.

[19] Sehling 1.1: 689, 225.

dances had to be chaperoned by village elders so as to discourage "unzüchtig drehen und herumbwerffen" (92v). When one pastor complained of a tavern keeper who ignored the closing hours set by the *Landesordnung*, the visitors directed that one or two of the elders walk about the village at night to spy out "lästern, fluchen und gross geschrey", and identify the noise makers (77v-78r). A stop was ordered put to the long-standing and near universal custom of selling, buying, and talking business (all referred to as *wuchern*) outside the church on Sundays and during catechism.[20] Violations cost offenders one gulden each, a heavy forfeit, and councillors and elders who failed to report delinquents were themselves fined.

In all these moves, the Lutheran pastorate employed measures that — in intent if not necessarily in effect — would seem to justify Bob Scribner's finding that a "new clericalism" was a prominent feature of the post-Reformation Lutheran church.[21] Amidst the legal and other changes that had been altering the clerical status in regions turned Protestant, the church establishment's deployment of spiritual weapons seems to have been left largely undiminished by the transformation — certainly it must have seemed so to the laity, regardless of the actual effectiveness of this arsenal. So deep was the sense of mistrust with which clerics observed their flocks that the latter's delinquencies, including such minor lapses as taking God's name in vain, were always assumed to be committed "deliberately" (*mutwillig*)[22] and out of contempt (*verachtung*) or hatred (*hass*) for God's word, even for the Christian faith itself.[23] The clergy seems to have considered it axiomatic that — as the visitation instruction puts it — only "furcht und scheu", fear and trembling, could motivate people to their religious duties.[24] Clerics were therefore authorized to refuse the sacrament to the dying if they had neglected it in health, and to give due *vorwarnung und bedräuung* from the pulpit of this prospect.[25] But they could also withhold the sacraments for lesser infractions: for obtuseness to pastoral correction, for example, or for persistence in carrying on neighborly quarrels (94v). In cases of hardened resistance, they had the power to "excommunicate [offenders] and separate them from the Christian community."[26]

Pastors could also prevent offenders from serving as godparents (42v).[27] They could call fathers and mothers to account for failing to bring up their children in the fear of God.[28] Contrite wrong-doers were subjected to open

---

[20] Sehling 1.1: 690.
[21] Scribner, "Antiklerikalismus", 377.
[22] Sehling 1.1: 246, 689.
[23] Sehling 1.1: 224, 225.
[24] Sehling 1.1: 224, from the 1569 (1554) Instruction.
[25] Sehling 1.1: 224, 244.
[26] Sehling 1.1: 224, 689.
[27] Sehling 1.1: 689.
[28] Sehling 1.1: 247.

humiliation — "publica poenitentia und öffentliche abbittung" — before they were rehabilitated (44v).[29] The church's engagement in searching out and castigating secular offenses along with religious ones[30] must have considerably broadened the base of popular resentment against clergymen acting, if they were doing their job, as thought police. This duty placed pastors in a very difficult role: how could they win their people's trust as ministers if, at the same time, they functioned against them as censors and informants? The Saxon state seems to have recognized this predicament, for Duke Johann Wilhelm's instructions to his pastors, conveyed to them by the visitors, favored them with the conscience-clearing assumption that the many faults and short-comings they were bound to observe at their posts must trouble them so sorely that "in the oppression of their spirit they cannot do otherwise" than to report offenders to the authorities.[31]

There was a fundamental ambiguity in the Lutheran pastor's relationship to his congregation. He was intended to "improve" — *bessern* — his flock; but he could do it only by ensuring that they were *gebürlich gestraft*, "blamed and chastised, as they deserve".[32] He was a functionary delegated to ascertain conformity, but he was expected to succeed by overseeing a flock with strongly independent views on religion, church, and pastoral conduct. He must assert the spiritual and moral authority appropriate to his position as God's representative, but he was placed in a condition of material dependency upon those asked to respect him. This ambiguity epitomizes, I think, the lack of effective integration which some scholars have identified as a significant cause of the difficulties faced by the Protestant church in undertaking its job of reform.[33] But the social and cultural assimilation of clergy to populace was never an object of Lutheran ecclesiastics. Quite the contrary; the rules laid down for pastors pushed them decisively in the direction of separation and difference. In the view of Lutheran church administrators, such "building and improving" — *bauen und bessern* — as pastors were expected to accomplish through preaching and curatorial work[34] presupposed hierarchical distinction in their interaction with common folk. Social distance resulted naturally from the fact that few pastors, if any, served in their native places, and from the virtual

---

[29] Sehling 1.1: 689.

[30] See the list of "öffentliche grobe laster", for the discovery and punishment of which pastors were made responsible, in Duke Wilhelm's Instruction for the 1569-70 visitation, in Sehling 1.1: 225. The passage was taken over verbatim from the 1554 Instruction.

[31] " ... da sie es aus bedringung ires gewissen nicht umbgehen können, anzaigen, ..." Sehling 1.1: 225.

[32] Sehling 1.1: 224, 223.

[33] Scribner, "Antiklerikalismus", 368-9; Rublack, "'Der wohlgeplagte Priester'", 2-3, 29-30.

[34] Sehling 1.1: 223.

absence of intermarriage: pastors' wives rarely came from villages where their husbands ministered, nor did their children marry locals. Instead, Lutheran ministers formed what Heide Wunder has called "eigene Heirats-kreise".[35] The criteria laid down for correct pastoral conduct accomplished the rest. At least in rural parishes, close association with local people was frowned upon. Sitting with them at beer or wine was forbidden. Pastors could not play at cards or dice and were, of course, expected to condemn gambling wherever they saw it. They must avoid gossip. Joining in a carousal after a baptism or wedding could bring disciplinary action against them.[36] Given this enforced posture of censorious distance, mutual suspicion and latent hostility were normal. In fact, the ever-presence of such antagonistic feelings was formally recognized by church officials when they drafted rules for dealing with situations in which pastors and people were so riven by *zwitracht*, *abgonst*, and *hass* that transfer seemed the only solution.[37]

Antagonism was exacerbated, on occasion, by unneighborly behavior on the part of clerics, by their failure, especially, and as we have seen, to treat with prudent foresight the woods, fields, and ponds entrusted to their care as part of their living. Such irresponsibility, which the 1569-70 protocol acknowledges as a *gemeine clage* (31v), may well have convinced the locals that the clergy was not a fully accountable part of the community. There were times, as well, when a sexton or a schoolmaster refused to perform a community service — writing a clean copy of the annual chest register, for instance. The visitation reports of such incidents clearly reflect popular resentment (81v). Add to this the laity's awareness of the tensions dividing the clerical ranks at times, and occasionally breaking into the open when bickering pastors and schoolteachers competed with one another to gain allies in the parish (122r). Such *gezenck*, as it was dismissively called, undermined respect, and so — it seems plausible to assume — did the embarrassing recantations extracted in 1569 and 1570 by the visitors from those of the superintendency's pastors who had earlier signed the *Declaratio Victorini*, and the official proceedings toward the removal of *contumaces* and *deficientes* (37r, 19r). That parish people were drawn into these internal altercations we know from the, sometimes desperate, attempts of accused pastors to call on their congregations to bear witness to their orthodoxy, competence, and probity.[38] All this may well have left people with a sense

---

[35] Heide Wunder, *Die bäuerliche Gemeinde in Deutschland* (Göttingen, 1986), 105. Wunder points out (106) that godparentage occasionally bridged the gap between villagers and the pastor's family.

[36] In the 1554 and 1569 Visitation Instruction: Sehling 1.1: 225. On this point, see Rublack, "'Der wohlgeplagte Priester'", 23.

[37] From the 1569 (1554) Instruction: Sehling 1.1: 223.

[38] E.g., the case of Johann Langepeter, pastor in Kapellendorf; see Staatsarchiv Weimar, Reg N, 506, 31v-32v.

of the Lutheran church as a foreign element in the collective body whose members had long since, in their attitudes and actions, blurred any clear distinction between community and congregation.[39]

In light of the conditions suggested by the 1569-70 report from Weimar, then, it seems appropriate to conclude that, in this one district certainly, and most likely elsewhere as well, anticlericalism survived into the Reformation and continued to take the traditional populist form of resentment against economic, social, and behavioral pressures exerted upon the commons by a privileged clergy.[40] This resentment was clearly much less virulent than the rabid anti-sacerdotalism of the years just before the Reformation, fanned as this had been by the ferocious verbal attacks aimed against Rome. But one cannot, I think, doubt that old anti-priestly prejudices remained active among people who had been so relentlessly propagandized only half a century before.[41] And this carry-over must have helped sustain the old notion of an entrenched church, politically powerful, far from above reproach on moral grounds, above all interfering, and of its ministers as costly intruders.[42]

If these were the common perceptions, they must have formed a frame of reference in which the often vexatious daily experiences with church and clerics were noted, judged, and reacted to, and the modern historian's protest that at no time was the Lutheran church nearly as powerful in action as its declarations suggest, that it saw itself as beleaguered and weak, that it took its preaching and civilizing mission with the utmost seriousness, and that its pastors were for the most part hard-working, honest, and dedicated, is, therefore, beside the point. To people whose overriding concern it always was to gain a little ground in the struggle for material security and comfort, the church — Lutheran or Catholic — with its very different set of priorities, was, as often as not, a hindrance.[43] An enduring anticlericalism

---

[39] On the general relationship between community and congregation, see Karl Siegfried Bader, *Dorfgenossenschaft und Dorfgemeinde* (Weimar, 1962), 182-234. Also Dietrich Kurze, *Pfarrerwahlen im Mittelalter. Ein Beitrag zur Geschichte der Gemeinde und des Niederkirchenwesens* (Cologne, 1966).

[40] The economic causes of anticlericalism are emphasized by Henry J. Cohn, "Anticlericalism in the German Peasants' War 1525", *PaP* 83 (1979): 3-31, especially 12-14.

[41] On the effect of this propaganda, cf. Hans-Jürgen Goertz, "Aufstand gegen den Priester", 185-6, 208.

[42] Using the terminology suggested by José Sánchez, *Anticlericalism*, 8, the phenomena I have enumerated might be called "pragmatic", as opposed to "ideological", anticlericalism.

[43] This point is also made by Hans-Christoph Rublack in "'Der wohlgeplagte Priester'", 29-30. The widening gap between ordinary people and the confessional churches of the late sixteenth and the seventeenth centuries is pointed to by Richard van Dülmen in the conclusion to his "Volksfrömmigkeit und konfessionelles Christentum im 16. und 17. Jahrhundert", in *Volksreligiosität in der modernen Sozialgeschichte*, ed. T. Schieder (Göttingen, 1986), 28.

would thus seem to have been an inevitable product of a deeply problematic, if not fundamentally incongruous, relationship.

THE COUNTER-REFORMATION
IMPACT ON ANTICLERICAL PROPAGANDA

PHILIP M. SOERGEL

Arizona State University, Tempe

In January 1570, the Jesuit Peter Canisius travelled to the Marian shrine Altötting with an entourage that included members of the highest ranks of Bavarian society. The purpose of this soon-to-be notorious pilgrimage was to exorcize a young Bavarian noble woman named Anna von Bernhausen. A lady-in-waiting to the Baronness Sybilla Fugger, Bernhausen had been afflicted by multiple demons for several years before her journey to the shrine of Our Lady in Altötting. During a series of public ceremonies in the Augsburg Cathedral, the Jesuit Canisius had been able to expel six demons from the young woman, but a seventh stubbornly remained. One night the Virgin appeared to Anna with the message that the final spirit would only be made to flee through a journey to the famous Bavarian shrine. Canisius, Anna, and members of the Fugger household soon set out on their pilgrimage and during three days of pious observances in the chapel, the priest was able to force the recalcitrant, seventh spirit from the woman's body.

One year later, the Catholic convert and theologian Martin Eisengrein published an account of the exorcism in a book entitled *Our Lady at Altötting*, a work intended to revive this once popular shrine.[1] Eisengrein used the incident polemically to prove the greater effectiveness of Catholicism and its priests and saints in fighting the devil. Immediately controversial among Protestant theologians, Canisius's exorcism and Martin Eisengrein's pilgrimage book precipitated a battle of polemic and counter polemic that lasted more than four years. At Strasbourg, Johannes Marbach, President of the Lutheran Church, hastily wrote and published a 400-page reply entitled *On Miracles and Miraculous Signs* that denounced Canisius

---

[1] Martin Eisengrein, *Unser liebe Fraw zu Alten Oetting: Das ist Von der Uralten heligen Capellen unser lieben Frawen unnd dem Fuerstlichen Stifft ...* (Ingolstadt: Wolfgang Eder, 1571), 248-93. On the life of this controversial Counter-Reformation theologian see "Eisengrein, Martin", *ADB*, s.v.; and Luzian Pfleger, "Martin Eisengrein (1535-1578). Ein Lebensbild aus der Zeit der katholischen Restauration in Bayern", in *Erläuterungen und Ergänzungen zu Janssens Geschichte des deutschen Volkes* 6,2 (1908).

as a sorcerer.[2] By virtue of his alliance with the devil, Marbach charged, Canisius was able to conjure up spirits not only to inhabit the young Anna's body, but to assume the form of the Virgin to tell the woman of the "false" exorcistic power that resided at Altötting. Further, the Strasbourg theologian denounced all the miracles Eisengrein attributed to Our Lady in his pilgrimage book as cases of priestly and diabolic magic. To inoculate his readers against these false idolatries, Marbach recommended they console themselves with the great miracles of faith revealed in the Lutheran Reformation. He extolled the success of Luther's attack against the Roman Church, the translation of the Bible into vernacular languages, and the propagation of the doctrine of faith in the world as the "true" godly miracles of the sixteenth century.[3]

The charge that Catholic exorcism, thaumaturgy, and miracles were a form of priestly and diabolic magic was becoming increasingly common in the late sixteenth century. The early Protestant reformers had attacked devotions like Altötting as visible embodiments of a false and sometimes even diabolic religion. They had not blackened the clergy who promoted these sites with the charge of practicing sorcery and magic. Most often, they insisted that the clergy was deceived by Satan and blinded by their greed into promoting false miracles and pilgrimages.[4] In the years following the

---

[2] Johannes Marbach, *Von Mirackeln und Wunderzeichen* ... (Strasbourg, 1571). In Bavaria, the Catholic convert and Wittelsbach court preacher replied with *Christlicher und wohlgegruendter Gegenbericht von Mirackeln und Wunderzeichen* ... (Dillingen, 1572, 1573). At Strasbourg, Lutherans countered yet again with a staged disputation that debated the claims of Eisengrein and Rabus. The text of this event was printed as *Propositiones DE DONO MIRACULORUM: contra MIRABILIARIOS Papistos* ... (Strasbourg: Nicolaus Wyriot, 1574). Rabus responded with a reply to this disputation in *Adversus theses a° 1574 publice disputatas contra sacrarum reliquiarum miracula velitatio succincta* (Strasbourg, 1574; Munich, 1575). Martin von Chemnitz also attacked the use of the Altötting exorcism as propaganda, see *Examination of the Council of Trent*, trans. F. Kramer, 4 vols. (St. Louis, 1971-86), 3: 404.

[3] Johannes Marbach, *Von Mirackeln und Wunderzeichen*, passim, but see especially kii, where the author draws parallels between the Old Testament Witch of Endor story and Canisius's sorcery. He writes, "Das aber die Papisten unnd sonderlich Eysengrein dieses Mirckels zu alten Oetting scriben anzeucht die Hystoriam I. Samuelis 28. Cap. von dem König. auß dem der H. Samuel soll erschinen sein reimet sich gleich wol zu erweisen das dise Maria von deren er redet nicht die Heilig Jungfraw Maria Christi unsers Herren Muter gewesen sey sonder ein falsche die die Abergleubische Jesuiten in der Gestalt und Form der H. Jungfraw Maria durch jhr Zauberen und gemeinschafft so sie mit den teuffeln haben herfür bracht haben. Gleich wie die teuffels Hure und Warsagerin mit jrem beschweren und zauberen nicht Samuelem sonder den teuffeln selber in der gestalt Samuelis auß der Hellen herauff bracht."

[4] On the early Reformation counter-offensive against shrines and pilgrimage, see Carlos M. N. Eire, *War Against the Idols: The Reform of Worship from Erasmus to*

conclusion of the Council of Trent, however, a renewed Roman priesthood became increasingly active publicizing the miracles of the Roman Church's shrines throughout south Germany. The scope of this resurgence was by any standard enormous and the revival of miraculous publicity was often directly posed as a challenge to Protestantism. Concentrating their efforts in Protestant-Catholic border regions and in areas where Lutheran and Calvinist sympathizers were common, the Catholic Reformers hoped in part to achieve a renewed confessional allegiance through demonstrating the greater supernatural power of their tradition. At Neukirchen bei Heilig Blut, a shrine located in a Protestant-Catholic border region between Bohemia and Bavaria, more than 12,500 miracles were to be recorded and pronounced from the late sixteenth through the mid-eighteenth centuries. At Bettbrunn, a similarly situated bridgehead of the Counter Reformation on the border between Catholic Bavaria and the Protestant Upper Palatinate, this number totalled almost 17,000.[5]

The renewed efforts of the Catholic Reformers was to be met with equally persistent Protestant propagandistic denunciations. In his study of the Lutheran propaganda of the early Reformation, Robert Scribner once noted the strongly visual and symbolic techniques the early Protestants used to popularize their reforms and to denounce the traditional clerical caste.[6] Visual imagery and symbols continued to be forcefully employed in the propaganda of the late sixteenth century, but with an essential difference. These elements were now increasingly submerged into a narrative that often resonated with the most extreme kinds of scatological and magical imagery. Instead of identifying a distant Roman "Antichrist", targeting an abstract Satan, or denouncing "idolatry", late Reformation propagandists relied more persistently on tales that objectified and concretized the charges they made against a now-reviving Catholic Church. By directing their efforts at counter-reforming leaders like Canisius and at priests working domestically on the local scene, this storytelling propaganda attempted to prove that a diabolically inspired and aided priestly caste was working to destroy the gospel of faith. Filled with villifying and often filthy imagery, narrative propaganda addressed itself to a popular audience with a strong appetite for fantastic tales.

While the Reformation had called traditional saintly thaumaturgy into question, it had not destroyed the widely held belief that the world was a place filled with signs of God's intervention. A theologian like Johann Marbach might recommend to his readers that they satisfy their longing for

---

Calvin (Cambridge, 1986).

[5] See Philip M. Soergel, "Spiritual Medicine for Heretical Poison: the Propagandistic Uses of Legends and Miracles in the Counter Reformation", *Historical Reflections* 17 (1991): 125-49.

[6] R. W. Scribner, *For the Sake of Simple Folk: Popular Propaganda for the German Reformation* (Cambridge, 1981).

divine confirmation by looking to the "wonders" that the gospel of faith had produced in the world. Yet clearly among those living in late sixteenth-century Protestant territories, a deep longing persisted to find more concrete and tangible signs of God's approval. Since the 1520s, Luther had often been presented to the popular audience in images that repeated the stock symbols and attributes of the medieval saints. Stories of his miracles and prophecies circulated within the new confession until at least the eighteenth century. And cults of his images which wept or were preserved inviolate from fire and attack survived as a focus for Lutheran piety long after the early Reformers had attempted to expunge traditional thaumaturgy and pilgrimage.[7]

Beyond the bounds of this sometimes officially sanctioned Luther cult, a lush undergrowth of stories about God's direct intervention in the world persisted throughout Germany. The sixteenth-century world knew not only the miracles of the saints and the magic of the devil. Its supernatural theory also admitted natural events which were otherwise inexplicable according to the parameters of its science as instances of divine intervention. Comets, earthquakes, floods, visions seen in the clouds, deformed births, and strange, unknown creatures were a part of a tertiary category of miracles, which Jacques Le Goff has termed the "marvelous", and which German scholars have often categorized as "prodigies".[8]

Accounts of bizarre and sometimes horrifying tales had circulated orally for centuries, been retold in the sermons of medieval preachers, and set down in collections of exempla.[9] By the late fifteenth century, the press was beginning to fulfill an important function in recording and circulating these stories, satisfying the appetite for news of events that were perceived as both sensational and miraculous. While oral modes of communicating these tales remained dominant throughout the sixteenth century, the printed broadside allows us a glimpse upon the ways in which the laity interpreted the inexplicable events that occurred around them.

Unlike the refined theological polemics of an Eisengrein or Marbach, the illustrated prodigy had humbler origins in the early modern city. At Augsburg, for example, more than fifty small printers plied the trade in broadsides during the period from 1550 to 1750, and three quarters of their shops were located within one of the city's poorer suburbs. Often the

---

[7] R. W. Scribner, "Luther Myth: A Popular Historiography of the Reformer", in *Popular Culture and Popular Movements in Reformation Germany* (London, 1987), 301-22; and idem, "Incombustible Luther: The Image of the Reformer in Early Modern Germany", 323-55. See also Scribner's *For the Sake of Simple Folk*, 14-36.

[8] See Jacques Le Goff, "The Marvelous in the Medieval West", *The Medieval Imagination* (Chicago, 1988), 27-46; and the catalogue of folktale motifs produced in Wolfgang Brückner, ed. *Volkserzählung und Reformation* (Berlin, 1971).

[9] See Aron Gurevich, *Medieval Popular Culture: Problems of Belief and Perception* (Cambridge, 1988), 39-77.

purveyors and producers of these works clustered around a city's gates, where they could sell their wares not only to the poorer artisans who lived in a town's suburbs, but to travelling peddlars and merchants. Cheaply produced in editions ranging from several hundred to about 2,500, the modest cost of these broadsides — about four to six pfennigs — remained constant throughout the late sixteenth and early seventeenth centuries.[10]

Prodigies were consequently a product of market forces with printers competing against one another to produce the accounts that would most excite curiosity and generate sales. Their efforts often followed formulas, with illustrations sometimes being copied from those that appeared in more polished and expensive chronicles.[11] Entire accounts published in other cities could also be plagiarized. But while they were often formulaic, the vast profusion of this literature vividly reveals that many both in Protestant and Catholic territories retained their intense curiosity to learn and communicate cases of divine intervention. Scholars have long noted the dramatic increase in this literature's production that occurred during the second half of the sixteenth century. During this period, it was in Protestant centers — where traditional saintly thaumaturgy had been denounced for more than a generation — where prodigies multiplied most profusely. In combination with the huge upswing in apocalyptic works and "devil books", the popularity of these prodigies points to a general explanatory crisis that afflicted Lutheranism in the wake of its attempts to do away with the traditional functionalism of the medieval Church. While Protestant theologians and preachers often anxiously attributed the woes of their Church and the successes of a resurgent Catholic priesthood to the devil, the miraculous beliefs recorded in the prodigies reveals a legacy of storytelling that ran counter to their aims.

More than four-fifths of the prodigies that survive from the late sixteenth century retold stories about apparitions, comets, meteors, or related incidents of abnormal births, the appearance of strange new species of animals, and the discovery of freakish grain, plants, and animals. The remaining cases told of floods, storms, and other natural disasters, while a small number reported a variety of strange incidents, i.e., inexplicable murders, cases of women who survived without food, and various other kinds of events that ran counter to the normal or expected course of nature.[12]

---

[10] Wolfgang Seitz, "The Addresses of Augsburg Broadsheet Makers", in D. Alexander, W. L. Strauss, eds., *The German Single-Leaf Woodcut, 1600-1700* (New York, 1977) 3: 827; and Walter L. Strauss, ed., *The German Single-Leaf Woodcut, 1550-1600* (New York, 1975) 1: 1-9.

[11] One important source in codifying the illustrations produced in these broadsheets was Conrad Lykosthenes' *Prodigiorum ac Ostentorum Chronicon* (Basel, 1557). It included more than 670 illustrations of comets, abnormal births, and metereological phenomena.

[12] Alexander and Strauss, *The German Single-Leaf Woodcut, 1600-1700* 1: 20-1.

How did artists, writers, and printers explain these extraordinary events to their audience? Although more numerous in Protestant, especially Lutheran territories, the prodigy appeared in all German confessional regions. Whether published in Lutheran, Calvinist, or Catholic territories and cities, these accounts bear an almost textbook similarity. The following examples are typical of those that were in circulation around the time that theologians and preachers like Johann Marbach were campaigning against the resurgence of Catholic miracles. In 1570, a printer in Protestant Augsburg told of a "miraculous" shower of grain that had occurred in several places in Bavaria and Austria.[13] A four-footed hare discovered in the Calvinist Palatinate provided the subject of a Heidelberg printer's account in 1583.[14] And in Catholic Cologne, a 1578 prodigy relayed the story of the strange birth of a Dutch boy with the multiple heads of a Cyclops and the legs and feet of a centaur.[15] The message of these three typical cases was essentially the same. The "miraculous" shower of grain, the four-footed hare, and the cyclopean Dutch boy were all, their promoters proclaimed, "wondrous signs" sent by God as both a warning and a testimony to his mercy. They were intended to call people to repentance and to live pious lives. The persistent diabolism and apocalypticism that was often such a cogent feature of late Lutheran theological pamphlets and books is notably absent from most of these accounts. While the prodigy sometimes included a vague eschatological observation that a comet, celestial apparition, strange plant or animal were signs of the "last times", the tendency toward explicit reckoning or astrological forecasting that were often typical features of late Lutheran theology is not present.[16] Perhaps more important, however, is the relatively small explanatory role that Satan played in these accounts; in only a very few cases do the late sixteenth-century prodigies attribute some contemporary event to the devil.[17]

The prodigy then reflected an enduring religious mentality that was in part resistant to the attempts of Protestant reformers to attribute contemporary woes, horrors, and the clerically-promoted miracles of the Catholic

---

[13] *Ein warhafftige doch wunderseltzame geschicht so gesehen ist worden ... in dem Ländlein ob der Ens dem Hauß Osterreich zugehörig ...* . Reproduced in Strauss, *The German Single-Leaf Woodcut, 1550-1600* 2: 666.

[14] *Dieser Hase hierunder contersey ist im Jar M.D.lxxxiii. zu Türckheim an der Hardt LS. Aprillen gefangen ...* . Reproduced in Strauss, *The German Single-leaf Woodcut 1550-1600* 2: 771.

[15] *Warhafftige Contrafactur einer erschrecklichen Wundergeburt eines Knebleins Welches recht am newen Jarstage dieses jetztlauffendern 1578. Jars. ...* Reproduced in Strauss, *The German Single-Leaf Woodcut 1550-1600* 3: 892.

[16] See Robin Barnes, *Prophecy and Gnosis: Apocalypticism in the Wake of the Lutheran Reformation* (Stanford, 1989).

[17] Alexander and Strauss, eds. *The German Single-Leaf Woodcut, 1600-1700* 1: 20-1.

Reformation to Satan. For both the purveyors and readers of this literature, the earth was like a vast book in which God, not the devil, was continuously writing things that were horrific and strange in order to call the faithful to live pious lives. These were not the miracles of faith that a theologian like Johann Marbach recommended to his readers as the true wonders of the contemporary world. They were cases where God intervened directly in the natural order to produce some visible testimony of his anger and mercy. The resilience of this tradition throughout Germany helps explain the increasingly demonic attacks that Lutheran propagandists advanced against the Catholic Reformers. It required no more credulity to believe that God could work miracles at the Altötting shrine than it did to accept the widely held belief that four-footed hares or malformed human births were signs of his merciful warnings. Moreover, the miracles that the Counter Reformers were promoting were even more appealing than these tales since rather than being a pronouncement of divine authority or a call to repentance, Catholic thaumaturgy actually helped people.

In an attempt to prevent a Catholic resurgence among their laity, Protestant propagandists produced their own kinds of anti-prodigies designed to prove that the Counter Reformers were engaged in sorcerous and diabolic activities. In their sermons and printed works, Lutherans endeavored to set into circulation tales about the deceits and trickery of the Roman priesthood. Stories had always played an important role in Reformation propaganda. One thinks immediately of the publication of Luther's *Table Talk*, filled as it was with numerous tales that fulfilled the didactic, pedagogic, and apologetic needs of the Lutheran movement. Both Catholic and Protestant theologians and preachers were assiduous collectors of tales that denigrated their opponents. In France, Jesuits gathered some of the most remarkable, far-fetched stories about Protestant crimes of ritual murder and bizarre sacrilege.[18] The anti-Catholic polemic of Johann Marbach had also placed instances of deceits and trickery before its readers. But in this kind of theological polemic, tales performed a primarily corroborative role for a rationally conceived and argued theological position. When appealing to the laity en masse, the popular propagandist often crafted attacks on the Counter-Reformation priesthood in which the story assumed an autonomous role. Retold in sermons, modest broadsides, and pamphlets, black tales about the Counter Reformers had become one frequently used tool in the late Reformation armory of propagandistic techniques.[19]

Unlike other kinds of arguments that theologians and preachers could adduce — the appeal to scripture, to an abstract tradition, or to logically-fashioned principles like the *sola fide* — stories offered a unique opportunity because they alleged that something had actually happened. By recounting

---

[18] A. Lynn Martin, *The Jesuit Mind* (Ithaca, N.Y., 1988), 95.

[19] See J. Janssen, *A History of the German People* (New York, 1963), vol. 16.

tales about Catholic priests, the propagandists of the late Reformation yearned to set in motion among both their literate and oral audiences, stories that would tarnish the allure of a resurgent Catholicism. Allegations of crimes like ritual murder and diabolic sorcery — which both Catholics and Protestants exchanged during the period — certainly appear extreme from the modern scholar's perspective. But they were not beyond the bounds of sixteenth-century credulity. For more than two centuries, many had been conditioned to hate the Jews by appeals to fantastic tales of ritual human sacrifice and host desecration. The sexual crimes attributed to the beguines and the Brethren of the Free Spirit may also have been colosssal, but for many, no less believable. Even as monstrous polemical tales about the crimes of Protestant and Catholics circulated, much of Northern Europe was also being successfully taught to fear the onslaught of witches, which one inquisitor warned numbered in "the thousands everywhere", and were "multiplying upon the earth even as worms in a garden."[20]

The accusations that Protestants made against the Counter Reformers often repeated the same charges long associated with the Jews, witches, and other heretical groups. This demonization of the Roman Church and its priesthood had certainly been underway since the early years of the Reformation. But as the sixteenth century drew to its conclusion, the creation of a kind of black legend in Lutheran propaganda concerning the Roman priesthood now achieved its fullest expression. In this regard, the Lutheran preacher, Hieronymus Rauscher had shown the way. During the early 1560s, he had published five "centuries" of pamphlets that each transformed one hundred traditional saints' legends into lies. For Rauscher, the lives the Church had long circulated were none other than ploys created by the devil "to damn simple people and lead them to the abyss of hell." Widely distributed in numerous editions, these pamphlets were to provide a source of inspiration for later storytellers.[21]

Rauscher had concentrated his venom largely on discrediting the historical exempla and saintly legends promoted through such late medieval devotional classics as Jacopa da Voragine's *Golden Legend*. Those who followed him

---

[20] Henri Boguet, *An Examen of Witches*, ed. Montague Summers, trans. E. A. Ashwin (London, 1929), xxxiv. Cited in Alison P. Coudert, "The Myth of the Improved Status of Protestant Women: The Case of the Witchcraze", in *The Politics of Gender in Early Modern Europe*, ed. J. R. Brink, A. P. Coudert, M. C. Horowitz, Sixteenth Century Essays and Studies 12 (Kirksville, Mo., 1989), 61, n. 3.

[21] Hieronymus Rauscher, *Hundert Außerwelte groß, unverschempte, feiste Papistische Lügen* (n. p., 1562). This was the first of five books that each recounted a hundred "popish" lies. The impact of this remarkable collection is examined in greater detail in Rudolf Schenda, "Hieronymus Rauscher und die protestantisch-katholische Legendenpolemik", in *Volkserzählung und Reformation*, 179-259; and idem, "Die protestantisch-katholische Legendenpolemik", *Archiv für Kulturgeschichte* 52 (1970): 28-48.

demonized more completely and viciously the contemporary missionary activities of the Catholic Church. In a pamphlet published in 1566, a Lutheran minister explained that the Jesuits were able to work their numerous conversions through the aid of magical salves which they smeared on their pulpits to attract the young and simple. He concluded with the plea that these Catholic magicians be burnt at the stake, rather than merely being expelled from Protestant territories, because it was the only way possible to end their black magic.[22] In 1576, a pastor in Württemberg fabricated the story of an imaginary Jesuit named Georg Ziegler, who allied himself with a witch to be able to conjure up demons. After capturing one of these spirits in a jar, the Jesuit then used it to perform his dark prodigies. One day his demon escaped. Flying across the Protestant territories along the Neckar and Main rivers and across Alsace, the spirit had wreaked havoc with the weather and destroyed crops. The writer of the pamphlet used the incident to explain a bout of bad weather that had afflicted these regions in 1576.[23]

Allegations of priestly sorcery worked in the Roman Church abounded in Protestant Germany during the late sixteenth century. In 1600, the Regensburg chronicler Enoch Widmann retold the legend that he alleged had grown up in Regensburg around that city's notorious pilgrimage to the "Fair Mary". Whether or not the tale was actually repeated and retold, can never be determined. But Protestant preachers working in the city likely drew upon it as they endeavored to prevent a Catholic resurgence. In Widmann's chronicle, the famous pilgrimage to the town's anti-Jewish shrine emerges as a case of priestly black magic. To lure the insane and senseless to the site, Widmann related, the city's Cathedral preacher, Balthasar Hubmayer had pronounced incantations over a human heart and enclosed it as a talisman inside the church's altar. Thereafter, the accursed object had functioned to draw frequently hysterical pilgrims to the site, producing the sensational events that occurred at the shrine during 1520 and 1521. While an early Reformation account had explained the shrine's popularity as a case of Jewish magic, Protestant propaganda now turned the charge toward the Roman clergy.[24]

Through their stories, Protestant propagandists charged that clerical sorcery was both a historical legacy and a continuing reality. Sometimes victoriously, their tales celebrated the exposing and defeat of some new case

---

[22] Johannes Janssen describes the work in his *History of the German People* 16: 457.

[23] Janssen 16: 456.

[24] Enoch Widmann, "Hofische Stadt Chronik", in *Fortgesetzte Sammlung von alten und neuen Theologischen Sachen* (Leipzig, 1735), 430-34. The earlier charge of Jewish magic appeared in the anonymous pamphlet, *Ein Gespräch Zwischen Vier Personnen, wie Sie ein Gezänk Haben von den Wallfahrt im Grimmental ...* (1523 or 1524). Reproduced in *Die Flugschriften aus den ersten Jahren der Reformation*, ed. Otto Clemen (Leipzig, 1906), 1: 147.

of Roman deceit. An illustrated broadside published in 1569 told how a Jesuit had costumed himself as a demon to frighten a Protestant girl into relinquishing her religion. "Through the Almighty's intervention", the story related, one of the family's male servants had come upon the deception and stabbed the Jesuit to death. The account proclaimed God's mercy and the servant's decisive action in preserving the young girl from the "monkish" devil.[25] Another anonymous broadside printed in the same year related how a Jesuit had attempted to set himself up as a false Messiah at Vienna. When his magic had been incapable of raising a dead man, the account noted approvingly, he had been permanently exiled from that city.[26]

There was almost no crime so hideous or fantastic that it could not be attributed to the Counter Reformers. One broadside published in 1570 recounted the birth of a child to a Jesuit at Vienna. From their exterior appearance, the narrative warned, the Jesuits appear to be the very model of a well ordered piety. Yet they conduct their lives in private luxury and sensuality. In Vienna, the maternal Jesuit had also carried a picture of a woman under his clothes and his seething, unrequited lust had produced this magical progeny. Having delivered this offspring, his fellow priests in the Society of Jesus had his child bed set up in a public place so that the locals could make pilgrimages to the site and direct their worship to him. The account concluded with a ringing condemnation of the practice of clerical celibacy, noting that it produced both impious devotions and magical progeny.[27]

The charge that the Jesuits were a kind of demonic progeny and that they could produce their own magical offspring appeared more than once in the Lutheran propaganda of the late Reformation. Protestant propagandists relied on it undoubtedly because of the widespread contemporary fascination with strange and horrific births that was so evident in the prodigy literature. No one ever quite matched the Strasburgher Johann Fischart's efforts in this vein. A close associate of Marbach, this Strasbourg poet's works presented a simpler, more immediate condemnation of Catholic sorcery than was to be found in his colleague's voluminous polemics. In a series of illustrated single-page prints completed in the 1570s, he related the history of the Jesuit Order. Adopting the pen name Jesuwalt Pickart, Fischart told how Lucifer had grown sick as a result of Luther and the Reformation's message. The Pope, saddened by his colleague's illness, smeared Satan's buttocks with a

---

[25] *Newe Zeytung unnd warhaffter Bericht eines Jesuiters welcher inn Teuffelsgestalt sich angethan* ... (Augsburg, 1569). Reproduced in *The German Single-Leaf Woodcut 1550-1600* 3: 1335.

[26] *Von Eynem Jesuwider wie der zu Wien inn Oesterreich die Todten lebendig zumachen* (n.p., 1569). Reproduced in *The German Single-Leaf Woodcut 1550-1600* 3: 1397.

[27] *Newezeitung von diesen M.D.Lxx. Jare welches uns ein recht fruchtbar und Fröhlich Jubel Jahr*, in *The German Single-Leaf Woodcut 1550-1600* 3: 1338.

magical salve, causing him to give birth to a child through defecation. The pope christened the child "Anti-Christus", but Lucifer, familiar with the German language, made the Holy Father change the name to Jesuwider (literally Anti-Jesus). It was this child who was the founder of the hateful Society of Jesus and who had sent his recruits into the Empire to work their diabolic miracles. In other poems, Fischart continued to demonize the Jesuits and other Counter Reformers at work in contemporary Germany, relying on equally grotesque physical and scatological imagery.[28]

The poet's characterization of the Society of Jesus as the devil's 'shit' drew upon imagery that enjoyed a distinguished lineage within Reformation propaganda. Themes of the diabolic defecation of monks and the Antichrist had enjoyed a perverse kind of popularity among the illustrated broadsides of the early Reformation.[29] But the imagery was given its broadest currency through Luther's own polemical efforts. In 1545, the year before his death, the reformer had published an illustrated pamphlet entitled "The Papacy at Rome, Founded by the Devil". The illustrations that Lucas Cranach the Elder supplied for the work gave visual expression to Luther's charges. The devil was shown squatting to relieve himself of his "devil's shit" — the pope and the Roman curia. In successive episodes throughout the woodcut, the papacy appeared as a child suckled and reared by demons. The additional illustrations for the pamphlet explored the relationship between bodily excrement, Satan, demons, and the Roman Church. They showed, for example, worshippers defecating in the papal tiara and German peasants baring their bottoms to fart defiantly at the pope.[30]

Luther took great pride in this work, referring to it as his *Testament*, and as one of his last publications it was widely distributed in the years following 1545.[31] But while this was one of his most extreme attacks on the papacy, it also represented a highly personal statement about his own struggle for salvation. A longtime sufferer from hermorrhoids and urine retention, the reformer had actually received his salvific breakthrough while in the monastery privy. More than three decades ago, Erik Erikson called

---

[28] Johann von Fischart, *Von Ursprung und wunderlichen Herkommen des Heyl. Ordens der Jesuiten* (Strasbourg, 1577). For a discussion of the author's anti-Roman poems, see Adolf von Haufen, *Johann Fischart. Ein Literaturbild aus der Zeit der Gegenreformation* (Berlin, 1921), 2: 98-135.

[29] See Scribner, *For the Sake of Simple Folk*, 84-8.

[30] On this extraordinary pamphlet see R. W. Scribner, "Demons, Defecation and Monsters: Popular Propaganda for the German Reformation", in *Popular Culture and Popular Movements*, 277-300; Mark Edwards, *Luther's Last Battles* (Ithaca, 1986), 182-200; and Heiko A. Oberman, *Luther. Mensch zwischen Gott und Teufel* (Berlin, 1982), 163-6.

[31] Besides Fischart's employment of the imagery, the polemical theologian Martin von Chemnitz also depicted the Roman Church as the "devil's shit". See Johannes Janssen, *History of the German People* 8: 239.

attention to the meaning that lurked in this precise location, noting that the realization of the *sola fide* was connected to a physical catharsis and cleansing. While the psychiatrist remained sensitive to the fact that sixteenth-century mores, customs and languages differed from those of the modern era, he nevertheless relied on the incident to indicate Luther's psychic distresses.[32]

Reformation historians have persistently attacked Erikson's attempts to psychoanalyze the dead Luther, but in the years since his work first appeared, they have also shed their reticence concerning Reformation-era scatology. Luther's "cloaca crisis", now appears less a sign of his emotional instability, than as an incident consonant with both the popular culture and the learned traditions of the late Middle Ages. In popular superstition, the privy was a place haunted with maleficent spirits, and the devil was believed to stink like human feces. Medieval monastic literature, too, warned of the dangers that lurked in the water closet.[33] Luther's reference to his break-through and his triumph over Satan as occurring in the monastery privy were consonant with a society in which defecation was both a sign of human humiliation and a precarious function exposing men and women to the dangers of evil spirits.

The Reformation's uses of scatological language, however, also derived from the numerous meanings that human waste possessed in sixteenth-century society. Everywhere there was little reserve about bodily functions or the use of scatological language, but those who have studied this phenomenon are agreed that the concentration on the polluting consequences of excrement and defecation was greater in sixteenth-century Germany than in other regions.[34] German cesspool cleaners were considered members of a "dishonorable profession", (*unehrliche Gewerbe*), a designation that marked them as a kind of marginal caste.[35] When seeking to redress libels and slanders, members of the nobility often sent "defamatory letters" that sometimes included depictions of their enemy's coats of arms being plunged into steaming dung.[36] The tendency to associate opposing opinions and enemies with feces was strong in every layer of German society. In the numerous medieval and early modern depictions of the "Jewish Sow",

---

[32] See Erik Erikson, *Young Man Luther: A Study in Psychoanalysis and History* (New York, 1958), 204-6.

[33] On popular superstition, Scribner, *For the Sake of Simple Folk*, 84, citing H. Bächtold Stäubli, *Handwörterburch des deutschen Aberglaubens* (Berlin, 1927), 1: 93. On monastic traditions concerning the privy, see Oberman, *Luther. Mensch zwischen Gott und Teufel*, 164, esp. n. 8.

[34] See Dieter and Jacqueline Rollfinke, *The Call of Human Nature* (Amherst, Mass., 1986); and Alan Dundes, *Life is Like a Chicken Coop Ladder* (New York, 1984).

[35] Michael Kunze, *Highroad to the Stake* (Chicago, 1987).

[36] Scribner, "Demons, Defecation, and Monsters", 293.

(*Judensau*), German artists often showed the animal eating feces.[37] Those who came in contact with human waste were deemed dishonored. Feces libelled and defamed, but the motif also served satiric and comic purposes. In the carnival plays that survive from fifteenth-century Nuremberg, references to defecation play a secondary role only to those concerning sex. In fact, sexual and scatological metaphor were often blended, forged into new kinds of imagery that like Luther and Fischart's, depicted reproductivity and regeneration arising from the degenerative act of defecation.[38]

The uses of this imagery evoke what Mikhail Bakhtin once termed "the material bodily" principle. References to feces, defecation, and urination humiliated by inverting an enemy's thoughts, deeds, and actions, associating them with the most primal human functions. In his now classic study of Rabelais's *Gargantua and Pantagruel*, Bakhtin argued that the origins and provenance of this language were in a "popular culture" that rejoiced in carnival and other ritualized forms of play that reversed normal patterns and conventions.[39] Rabelais's satire appealed both to a moral and comic sense, Bakhtin argued, which was fast disappearing in sixteenth-century Europe. It derided the late medieval schoolmen for their extremely intellectualized and routinized logic, degrading their efforts by connecting the realm of the intellect with the lower stratum of the body. In place of scholastic sterility, Rabelais exalted the popular culture of the marketplace whose rites celebrated the organically-based rituals of degeneration and regeneration.

While the French author's language and imagery may have derived from the popular culture of the marketplace as Bakhtin theorized,[40] German uses of scatology appear to have been far more universal. Rabelais had directed his attacks against what he judged a sterile intellectual culture, but Luther, Fischart, and the many "grobian" poets and propagandists of the late Reformation employed the material bodily principle in their attempts to destroy residual Catholic devotion. The use of physical imagery, demonized priests, and in general of literary "mudslinging" remained one of the most readily recognizable and easily understood ways that late sixteenth-century Protestants possessed to attack the Catholic clergy. Since the early Reformation, extreme charges like these had been advanced, but as the religious situation grew more tangled, propagandists like Fischart were to heighten the brew of diabolism and scatology to baroque proportions. In the

---

[37] Isaiah Schachar, *The Judensau: A Medieval Anti-Jewish Motif and Its History* (London, 1974).

[38] Johannes Müller, *Schwert und Scheide. Der sexuelle und skatologische Wortschatz im Nürnberger Fastnachtspiel des 15. Jahrhunderts* (Bern, 1988), 195-215, esp. 212.

[39] Mikhail Bakhtin, *Rabelais and His World*, trans. H. Iswolsky (Cambridge, Mass., 1968).

[40] For a dissenting evaluation of Bakhtin's work, see Aron Gurevich, *Medieval Popular Culture*, 177-9.

late Reformation's offensive against a renewed Catholic priesthood and its employment of miracles, Lutheran theologians and propagandists could only rarely venture that Catholicism was a merely deluded religion. Their jeremiads warned incessantly that it was a diabolic cult.

In tales of sorcerous priests and diabolically-produced miracles, late Reformation pastors, poets, and propagandists strained to destroy the enduring allures of Catholic thaumaturgy and the saints. That many in the Lutheran leadership believed these charges cannot be doubted, since they themselves were caught in an explanatory malaise in which Satan was playing an ever greater role. These extremely negative attacks could never have achieved a universal inoculation of the Protestant laity against the resurgence of clerically promoted miracles underway in many South German regions. For the negativism of late Lutheran anticlerical propaganda carried with it no way to inculcate and promote a "purified" Protestant doctrine of the supernatural. On just what such a theology should include, there was little agreement. Some like Marbach argued that the "true" miracles of the present were those that increased the gospel of faith. At the same time, however, Lutheran writers and pastors were often promoting the founder of their confession in ways that were virtually identical to the late medieval thaumaturgic and prophetic traditions. Revering his images and retelling his prophecies, they celebrated signs that confirmed his divine inspiration and message. Some searched the heavens for clues that would reveal the impending date for the conclusion of world history. While still others continued the trade in strange, prodigious tales about cases of divine interventions worked in the seas, grain fields, and child beds of Europe. While we cannot doubt that this last truly popular audience feared the onslaughts of Satan, they remained unwilling to credit him with everything inexplicable that was occurring around them.

In the limited confines of cities like Strasbourg, Augsburg, or Regensburg, the incessant jeremiads of Protestant propagandists against the Catholic priesthood may have helped prevent a resurgence of the traditional Church. In the environment of these cities, a renewal of the traditional Church also appeared as politically, socially, and economically threatening to burghers as it did religiously ominous to the Protestant clergy.[41] Beyond the boundaries of urban gates, in rural Alsace, Franconia, Bavaria, and in the other Catholic territories of South Germany, Lutherans remained incapable of stopping the intense missionary efforts of a resurgent Catholic clergy. As this revived group redoubled its efforts, miracles began to reverberate once again from the confines of pilgrimage chapels like Eberhardsklausen and Altötting. There hundreds and sometimes even tens of thousands of reports of healings and intercessions were to be assiduously recorded and circulated

---

[41] See Lorna Jane Abray, *The People's Reformation* (Ithaca, 1985), 83-7, and 116-41.

during the late sixteenth and seventeenth centuries.[42] There were clearly many Germans who after a half century of Protestantism were still inclined to agree with the Catholic Reformers when they argued: if the miracle's end result was good, it was surely a work of God.

---

[42] Abray, *The People's Reformation*; Paul Hoffmann and Peter Dohms, eds., *Die Mirakelbücher des Klosters Eberhardsklausen* (Düsseldorf, 1988); Louis Chatellier, *The Europe of the Devout* (Cambridge, 1989), 154; and R. Po-Chia Hsia, *Social Discipline in the Reformation* (London, 1989), esp. 154-9.

AFKEER VAN DOMINEESHEERSCHAPPIJ:
EIN NEUZEITLICHER TYPUS DES ANTIKLERIKALISMUS

HEINZ SCHILLING

Humboldt-Universität zu Berlin

I

Mein Beitrag führt wohl am weitesten weg von dem zeitlichen und sachlichen Kernbereich, den die Historiker in der Regel meinen, wenn sie von Antiklerikalismus reden. Ich berichte über die Auseinandersetzungen um die "domineesheerschappij" in der frühneuzeitlichen Republik der Vereinigten Niederlande,[1] der Gesellschaft also, die im späten 16. und im 17. Jahrhundert als europäische Vorreitergesellschaft galt, und zwar vor allem bei der hier interessierenden Beziehungsgeschichte zwischen Religion und Gesellschaft bzw. zwischen Kirche und Staat. So beachtlich die niederländische Lösung aber auch war, so ist doch unverkennbar, daß es immer aufs neue gewaltiger Anstrengungen bedurfte, um beide Größen im rechten Gleichgewicht zu halten, das heißt Staat und Gesellschaft die nötige und gewünschte Freiheit und Autonomie zu garantieren, aber nicht die religiösen Fundamente anzutasten, ohne die offensichtlich auch die am weitesten entfaltete Gesellschaft der frühen Neuzeit nicht auskommen konnte.[2]

---

[1] Allgemein zur Stellung der calvinistischen Prädikanten in den frühneuzeitlichen Niederlanden: G. Groenhuis, *De predikanten. De sociale positie van de gereformeerde predikanten in de Republiek der Verenigde Nederlanden voor 1700* (Groningen, 1977); M. Th. uit den Bogaard, *De Gereformeerden en Oranje tydens het eerste stadhouderloze tydperk* (Groningen, 1954); A. Th. van Deursen, *Bavianen en Slijkgeuzen. Kerk en kerkvolk ten tijde van Maurits en Olderbarnevelt* (Assen, 1974); ders., *Het kopergeld van de Gouden Eeuw*, Bd. 4, *Hel en hemel* (Assen, 1980); S. Cuperus, *Kerkelijk leven der Hervormden in Friesland tijdens de republiek*, Bd. 1, *De Predikanten* (Leeuwarden, 1916); M. van der Bijl, *Idee en Interest. Voorgeschiedenis, verloop en achtergronden van de politieke twisten in Zeeland en vooral in Middelburg tussen 1702 en 1715* (Groningen, 1981). Zu "domineesheerschappij" vgl. uit den Bogaard, *Gereformeerden en Oranje*, 79; Groenhuis, *De predikanten*, 117. Für Hilfe beim Verifizieren der Zitate danke ich Fräulein Henrike Clotz.

[2] Vgl. dazu H. Schilling, "Religion und Gesellschaft in der calvinistischen Republik der Vereinigten Niederlande — 'Öffentlichkeitskirche' und Säkularisation; Ehe und Hebammenwesen; Presbyterien und politische Partizipation", in F. Petri (Hrsg.), *Kirche und gesellschaftlicher Wandel in deutschen und niederländischen Städten der werdenden Neuzeit*, Städteforschung Reihe A, 10 (Köln, 1980)), 197-250; dort vor allem 201-22, engl. Fassung in: Heinz Schilling, *Religion, Political Culture and the*

"Domineesheerschappij" und dagegen ankämpfender Antiklerikalismus waren die beiden Extrempositionen, vor denen sich die tolerante niederländische Republik gleichermaßen hüten mußte, wollte sie sich nicht selbst aufgeben. Dessen ungeachtet gab es immer wieder Phasen, in denen beide eine reale Gefahr darstellten und politische Auseinandersetzungen darüber ausbrachen.

Das Problem begleitete die Republik von den Anfängen bis zu ihrem Niedergang in unterschiedlicher Dringlichkeit und in wechselnden politischen und gesellschaftlichen Konstellationen. Das gilt für Jahrzehnte des Aufstandes, als die laikale Losung "pro libertate" mit der klerikalen Losung "pro religio" in Einklang zu bringen war,[3] ebenso wie für den Konflikt zwischen Remonstranten und Kontraremonstranten zu Beginn des 16. Jahrhunderts und die verschiedenen Phasen innenpolitischer Auseinandersetzungen um die Macht in der Republik und um deren Verfassung, bei denen es immer auch um die Stellung der calvinistischen Öffentlichkeitskirche und ihrer Prädikanten ging, und schließlich gilt es auch noch für die Batavische Revolution zu Ende des 18. Jahrhunderts, als der neuzeitliche Laizismus endgültig über die Idee einer religiösen Fundierung des Gemeinwesens und entsprechend hervorgehobener Stellung der Kirchendiener triumphierte.[4] Die folgenden Ausführungen konzentrieren sich auf die mittlere Phase der 1650er und 1660er Jahre, als in den Konflikten zwischen Regenten- und Oranierpartei nicht nur zwei verschiedene Gesellschafts- und Staatsmodelle um die Vorherrschaft stritten, sondern auch zwei Vorstellungen über das rechte Verhältnis von Staat und Kirche bzw. zwischen laikalen und klerikalen Elementen innerhalb der gesellschaftlichen Ordnung. Ich gehe in drei Schichten vor: Zunächst skizziere ich die religiösen und staatskirchenrechtlichen Konfliktlinien (II.1). Dann beschreibe ich die hierin eingebetteten Auseinandersetzungen um die "domineesheerschappij" (II.2). Abschließend stelle ich einige allgemeine Schlußfolgerungen über den neuzeitlichen Antiklerikalismus zur Diskussion (II.3).

Emergence of Early Modern Society, SMRT 50 (Leiden, 1992), 353-412; A. C. Duke und C. A. Tamse (Hrsgg.), *Church and State since the Reformation* (Den Haag, 1981).

[3] H. A. E. van Gelder, *Revolutionnaire Reformatie. De vestiging van de Gereformeerde Kerk in de Nederlandse gewesten, gedurende de eerste jaren van de opstand tegen Filips II, 1575-1585*, Patria 31 (Amsterdam, 1943), 34f., 175-80. Der Gegensatz spielte noch im Pamphletenstreit der 1650er Jahre eine Rolle, der im folgenden analysiert wird. Es ist üblich, die Pamphlete nach dem Verzeichnis W. P. C. Knuttel, *Catalogus van de Pamflettenverzameling berustende in de Koninklijke Bibliotheek*, 9 Bde., Suppl.- und Registerband (Den Haag, 1889-1920), zu zitieren. Im folgenden abgekürzt mit Knuttel und fortlaufender Nummer. Zu dem genannten Gegensatz vgl. Knuttel Nr. 6851, fol. D 2 v; Nr. 6855, 20f.; Nr. 6900, B 3 v.

[4] Grundlegend J. Th. de Visser, *Kerk en Staat*, Bd. 3, *Nederland van 1796 tot op heden* (Leiden, 1927); O. J. de Jonge, *Nederlandse Kerkgeschiedenis* (Nijkerk, 1972), 296ff.

II.1

In den zwischen Regenten-Republikanern und Oranierpartei ausgetragenen Kontroversen der Jahre 1649 bis 1672 ging es um grundsätzliche Entscheidungen über Verfassung, Gesellschafts- und Militärordnung sowie über die Außenpolitik der jungen Republik und eben auch um die Rolle von Religion und die Stellung der calvinistischen Öffentlichkeitskirche in Staat und Gesellschaft.[5] Wie seit Gründung der Republik standen die rigiden Calvinisten, die ein Monopol für ihre Kirche verlangten, auf seiten der Oranier und unterstützten deren Kriegspolitik und die Forderung nach entsprechender Organisation von Staat und Gesellschaft. Demgegenüber waren die holländischen Regenten bereits Ende des 16. Jahrhunderts den Ansprüchen der Calvinisten entgegengetreten und hatten dafür gesorgt, daß den anderen Glaubensgemeinschaften, die mancherorts die Mehrheit hatten, geistig und institutionell ein weiter Spielraum eingeräumt wurde. In Fortsetzung dieser Tradition war auch zu Mitte des 17. Jahrhunderts im Programm der Regentenpartei das Streben nach politischer und ökonomischer Freiheit eng mit der Forderung nach religiöser Toleranz verbunden sowie mit dem Willen, die dem entgegenstehenden Ansprüche der calvinistischen Öffentlichkeitskirche bzw. ihrer führenden Theologen zu zähmen.

Allerdings ist festzuhalten, daß es anders als in den übrigen Streitpunkten in der Religionsfrage nicht mehr um eine Grundsatzentscheidung ging. Diese war 1618/19 auf der Synode von Dordrecht gefallen. Bei aller Entschlossenheit theokratischen und inquisitatorischen Ansprüchen einzelner calvinistischer Prädikanten entgegenzutreten, stellte die Regentenpartei diese staatskirchenrechtliche Basis nie ernsthaft in Frage. Unter den Beschlüssen der Großen Versammlung von 1651, mit denen die Regenten nach ihrem Sieg über die Oranier Staat und Gesellschaft nach ihren Vorstellungen umformten, fielen daher die über Religion und Kirche am wenigsten radikal aus. Die Calvinisten erhielten den Status einer bevorrechtigten Öffentlichkeitskirche bestätigt. Und auch in der praktischen Politik nahm Johan de Witt offenbar stärker als häufig vermutet auf die Wünsche der Calvinisten Rücksicht. Umgekehrt enthielt sich die Mehrheit der Calvinisten einer

---

[5] Ausführlich hierüber H. Schilling, "Der libertär-radikale Republikanismus der holländischen Regenten. Ein Beitrag zur Geschichte des politischen Radikalismus in der frühen Neuzeit", *Geschichte und Gesellschaft* 10 (1984): 498-533; dort ausführliche Literaturhinweise, veränderte engl. Fassung in: ders., *Religion* (wie Anm. 2), 413-28. Die nachfolgenden Erörterungen zum Antiklerikalismus, die auf ausgewählten Pamphleten mit meist großer Verbreitung basieren, behandeln einen wichtigen Teilaspekt der generellen Debatte über die Kirchen- und Religionsverfassung der Republik, die als einer der drei Grundsatzdebatten zwischen 1650 und 1672 geführt wurde. Vgl. Schilling, "Republikanismus", 514ff. mit Anm. 33. Guter Einstieg in englischer Sprache: H. H. Rowen, *Johan de Witt, Grand Pensionary of Holland, 1625-1672* (Princeton, 1978).

Stellungnahme zugunsten der entmachteten Oranier und akzeptierte die republikanischen Veränderungen.

Sahen die Regenten nach dem Sturz der Oranier 1650/51 somit zunächst wenig Anlaß, religiöse und staatskirchenrechtliche Fragen in der Öffentlichkeit zu erörtern, so änderte sich das rasch, als kurz hintereinander führende calvinistische Theologen sich leidenschaftlich auf die Seite der Oranier stellten und feurige Pamphlete veröffentlichten, die nicht nur die Kirchenpolitik der Regenten angriffen, sondern sogar deren persönliche Religiosität in Frage stellten und sie des Atheismus bezichtigten. Am weitesten gingen die beiden von monarchistischer Oranierverehrung durchtränkten Pamphlete "Lauweren-Krans"[6] und "Oogen-Salve",[7] die der Haager Prädikant Jacobus Stermont auf den Markt geworfen hatte. Mit eindringlichen Worten erheben sie die Religion, d.h. natürlich den Calvinismus, zum einzigen Garanten der staatlichen Einheit und Unabhängigkeit.[8] Den Regenten werfen sie vor, den Staat aufs Spiel zu setzen und die Gesellschaft im Kern auszuhöhlen "durch Zulassung des römisch-abgöttischen Aberglaubens und von allerlei Ketzerei und Irrglaube, sogar solche, die das Christentum leugnen, wie es kein Türke oder Heide in seiner Regierung dulden würde".[9] Der gesamte von den Regenten gegen die Oranier erzwungene Kurswechsel — der außenpolitische ebenso wie der innenpolitische — sei in letzter Konsequenz ein Angriff auf die wahre Religion. Schuld an der Krise seien "ghespangioliseerde Libertynen, Arminianen, die gheen Religie in het herte hebben".[10]

Vor allem der Atheismusvorwurf zwang die Regenten zur Gegenoffensive. Sie betonten ihre Zugehörigkeit zur calvinistischen Öffentlichkeitskirche und stellten ihre Verdienste für deren Aufbau und Erhalt heraus.[11] Diese Passagen sind zunächst ein Beleg für die propagandistische Gefährlichkeit des Atheismusvorwurfes, insbesondere im Hinblick auf die notorisch calvinistisch gesonnenen Unter- und Mittelschichten, deren Unterstützung die Regenten bei der republikanischen Neugründung nötig hatten. Neben diesem propagandistischen Gehalt entsprach das Bekenntnis zur religiösen Grundlegung des menschlichen Zusammenlebens im allgemeinen und der

---

[6] Knuttel Nr. 6851.

[7] Knuttel Nr. 6852.

[8] Knuttel Nr. 6851, fol. D 2 v. Zu Stermont vgl. unten Anm. 16.

[9] Knuttel Nr. 6851, fol. D 2 r.

[10] Knuttel Nr. 6852, fol. A 3. Selbst das "laikale" Oranier-Pamphlet *Bickerse Beroerten* (Knuttel Nr. 6843), das nach J. J. Poelhekke ("Kanttekeningen by enige pamfletten", in ders., *Geen blyder maer in tachtigh jaer. Verspreide studien over de crisisperiode 1648-1651* [Zutphen, 1973], 35-61) von einem Politiker des Oranierhofes und nicht von einem Prädikanten stammte, verzichtete nicht auf den Ketzervorwurf.

[11] Sie nannten insbesondere die Ratsherren und Bürgermeister Andries und Cornelius Bicker, die 1650 im Zentrum des oranischen Angriffes gestanden hatten. Knuttel Nr. 6848, fol. D 3 r und B 1 v; Knuttel Nr. 6855, 7.

niederländischen Gesellschaft im besonderen aber auch der persönlichen Einstellung der meisten Regenten. Sie waren sogar bereit, der calvinistischen Öffentlichkeitskirche Vorrechte einzuräumen. So hatten die holländischen Provinzialstände bereits Anfang Dezember 1650 bei der republikanischen Umbesetzung der Magistrate alle Amtsträger erneut formell auf die Mitgliedschaft in der calvinistischen Kirche festgelegt.

Die religiöse, allgemeinchristliche Grundlage des Regenten-Republikanismus zeigt sich auch in den eschatologischen Zügen seiner Gesellschafts- und Politiktheorie: Die Pamphlete und selbst die Traktate der de la Courts und Johan de Witts stellen immer wieder die biblische Fundierung der republikanischen Staatsform heraus.[12] Das Mißlingen des oranischen Anschlages auf Amsterdam deutete man als Zeichen der göttlichen Vorsehung und als Beweis dafür, daß die städtische Autonomie gottwohlgefällig sei.[13] In einer Passage des "Interest van Hollandt", die möglicherweise von Johan de Witt selbst stammt, heißt es, die Früchte der republikanischen Regierungsform seien "dergestalt, daß wir uns dem gelobten Land nun bereits merklich zu nähern beginnen. Der Rest des Zuges durch die Wüste wird schnell vonstatten gehen, sofern wir uns nicht durch Undankbarkeit und Murren gegen Gott den Herrn und gegen unseren Moses [d.h. die republikanischen Obrigkeiten, H. Sch.] wiederum der Sklaverei von Ägypten unterwerfen".[14] Auch die in ihrer Zeit in mancher Hinsicht radikalste und "modernste" Gesellschaftstheorie ging somit — zumindest in propagandistischer Absicht — eine Verbindung mit der christlichen Eschatologie ein. Nur so konnte sie jene Öffentlichkeitswirksamkeit und Dynamik erreichen, die sich auch Mitte des 17. Jahrhunderts nur aus dem religiösen Kontext gewinnen ließ, weil eine entsprechende säkulare Zukunftserwartung noch nicht voll entwickelt war.

Gravierende Unterschiede zwischen den konfessionellen und staatskirchenrechtlichen Vorstellungen der oranischen Calvinisten und der republikanischen Regenten setzten erst da ein, wo es um die politischen und gesellschaftlichen Konsequenzen dieser religiös-kirchlichen Fundierung des

---

[12] Knuttel Nr. 6900, fol. B 2 r; de Witt, *Deductie ofte Declaratie van de Staten van Holland ende West-Vrieslandt* (Den Haag, 1654), Teil 2, Kapitel 1, § 30-33.

[13] Knuttel Nr. 6848, fol. B 1 v; ähnlich de Witt, *Deductie*, 38: Gott selbst habe durch eine plötzlich einbrechende Finsternis und durch einen Platzregen den Erfolg Wilhelms II. vor Amsterdam verhindert; die Amsterdamer ließen eine Münze prägen mit der Aufschrift: "Godt Heeft Ons bewaert", abgebildet bei S. Groenveld, *De prins voor Amsterdam. Reacties uit pamfletten op de aanslag van 1650*, Fibulareeks 30 (Bussum, 1967), 102.

[14] [Pieter de la Court], *Interest van Hollandt* (Amsterdam, 1662), 127. Zu de la Court vgl. J. W. Wildenberg, *Johan en Pieter de la Court, Bibliografie en Receptiegeschiedenis*, with a summary in English (Amsterdam, 1986); H. W. Blom und J. W. Wildenberg (Hrsgg.), *Pieter de la Court in zijn tijd*, with a summary in English (Amsterdam, 1986).

Gemeinwesens ging. Ihrer Gesamteinstellung entsprechend vertraten die
Regenten auch in kirchenverfassungsrechtlicher Hinsicht die dezentralisierte
Lösung, ohne sich allerdings wie ihre englischen Gesinnungsgenossen auf
das independentistische Modell festzulegen, das jeden übergemeindlichen
Zusammenschluß ablehnte. Die calvinistischen Synoden konnten im
provinzialen Rahmen ungehindert zusammentreten, nicht aber auf der Ebene
des Gesamtstaates. Staatskirchenrechtlich propagierten die republikanischen
Pamphlete die erastianische Richtung innerhalb des Reformiertentums, d.h.
die Unterstellung der Kirche unter die weltlichen Obrigkeiten, konkret unter
die städtischen Magistrate und die Provinzialstände. Es war eine Folge dieser
Theorie, wenn die religiösen und kirchlichen Verhältnisse in der Republik
starke Unterschiede aufwiesen — von einem in den Pamphleten der
holländischen Regentenpartei wiederholt kritisierten calvinistischen
Klerikalismus in Friesland und Seeland[15] über eine gewisse Bevorzugung
der Calvinisten in einzelnen holländischen Städten, wie etwa in Leiden, bis
hin zu einem Zustand weitgehender Glaubensfreiheit, wie vor allem in
Amsterdam.

II.2

Der skizzierte republikanische Erastianismus war der staatskirchenrechtliche
Boden, auf dem sich der neuzeitliche Antiklerikalismus der Regenten
entfaltete. Denn jeder Versuch der calvinistischen Theologen, die Selbständigkeit der Kirche und deren eigenständige Verantwortung für die öffentlichen Dinge zu betonen, erhielt dadurch unweigerlich den Anschein der
Einmischung in politische und gesellschaftliche Angelegenheiten. Die
Vorwürfe zielten nämlich weniger auf die Presbyterien oder Synoden als auf
den Klerikalismus und die hierarchisch-autoritären Ansprüche einzelner
Prädikanten, zumal dann, wenn ihr Einfluß den Rahmen einer Stadt oder gar
der Provinz überstieg. Diese Wende ins Politische war der Kern des
neuzeitlichen Antiklerikalismus der niederländischen Regentenpartei.

In den 1650er und 1660er Jahren kam es zu teils erbitterten Kontroversen
um Schriften und Predigten von Prädikanten der Öffentlichkeitskirche, die
als Ausdruck klerikaler Haltung die leidenschaftliche Kritik der Regentenpartei hervorriefen. Von lokalem Ursprung erlangten diese Vorgänge
sogleich breite Resonanz in der Öffentlichkeit und erhielten dadurch
nationalen Rang: Im Fall des bereis erwähnten Prädikanten Jacobus Stermont
(1612-1665) ergab sich das nachgerade zwangsläufig. Denn als Diener der
calvinistischen Kirche zu Den Haag wirkte er unter den Augen der
Generalstaaten, und zudem war er ein talentierter Pamphletist, der den
wunden Punkt des Gegners zu treffen wußte. Als er 1652 seinen orangisti-
schen Parteienstandpunkt offen von der Kanzel der Haager Klosterkirche

---

[15] Knuttel Nr. 9587, 38.

verkündete, suspendierten ihn die angegriffenen Staten von Holland vom Dienst, konnten aber nicht verhindern, daß er bald wieder hohe Funktionen in der Öffentlichkeitskirche übertragen erhielt.[16] Bei Maximiliaan Teellinck (1606?-1652), von 1640 bis 1652 Erster Prädikant in Zierikzee, war die Reaktion der Regentenpartei deswegen so heftig, weil sich hier klerikale Opposition mit der traditionell starken Oraniergesinnung der Provinz Seeland verband.[17] Teellinck hatte 1650 gleich nach dem mißglückten Anschlag des ungestümen Wilhelm II. von Oranien auf Amsterdam eine Schrift seines Vaters mit dem Titel "Den Politijcken Christen ofte Instructie voor alle hooge en leege Staatspersonen" herausgegeben, und zwar mit einem Vorwort, dessen feurige Oranierverehrung eine klare Parteinahme für die Politik des Statthalters und gegen diejenige der Stände bedeutete.[18]

Ein weiterer Herd calvinistischer Opposition gegen das Regiment der Stände war Utrecht, wo 1658 Johannes Teellinck (1614-1674), ein jüngerer Bruder des Zierikzeer Teellinck, und Abraham van de Velde (1614-1677)[19] mit dem Stadtrat und den Provinzialständen ins Gericht gingen. Anlaß waren die 1651 von der Großen Versammlung beschlossene Aufhebung aller "unnützigen Kollegien und päpstlichen Sozietäten" sowie die Zuweisung "ihres Einkommens ad pios usus". Verwaltung und Nutznießung der Utrechter Kapitel-Präbenden waren daraufhin aus calvinistisch-kirchlicher Hand in diejenige der Stadt und der Stände überführt worden. Als die beiden genannten Prädikanten das öffentlich anprangerten, wurden sie im Juli 1660 aus Stadt und Provinz Utrecht verwiesen. Neben diesen prominenten, in vielen Pamphleten behandelten Fällen, kam es zu weiteren öffentlichen Parteinahmen von Prädikanten für Oranien und gegen die Regenten bzw. gegen die neue erastianischen staatskirchenrechtlichen Regelung, die nur beiläufig Erwähnung fanden. So etwa das öffentliche Gebet, das der Delfter Prädikant Johannes Goethals (1611-1673) anläßlich des plötzlichen Todes von Wilhelm II. für die Oranier gesprochen hatte.[20] Goethals war ehemaliger Hofprediger Prinz Friedrich Heinrichs und besaß in der Oranier-Partei hohes Ansehen, weil er dem Fürsten auf dem Sterbelager beigestanden und über dessen gottseliges Sterben berichtet hatte. Ähnlich der Fall des

---

[16] So *Nieuw Nederlandsch biografisch woordenboek* (*NNBWb*), hg. von P. C. Molhuysen, P. J. Blok, 10 Bde. (Leiden, 1911-37), 10: 973-5; *Biographisch woordenboek der Nederlanden*, hg. von A. J. van der Aa, 7 Bde. (Haarlem, 1852; ND Amsterdam, 1969), 6: 311f., wo der Vorfall für 1656 berichtet wird.

[17] *Biografisch lexicon voor de geschiedenis van het Nederlandse protestantisme*, Bd. 1 (Kampen, 1983²), 372f.; *NNBWb*, 5: 888f.; v. d. Aa, 7: 11.

[18] Bogaard, *Gereformeerden en Oranje*, 68-72.

[19] Zu Johannes Teellinck: *NNBWb*, 5: 885-7; v. d. Aa, 7: 10f.; *Biografisch lexicon*, 1: 371f. Zu Abraham van de Velde: *NNBWb*, 5: 996; v. d. Aa, 7: 20; *Biografisch lexicon*, 1: 392f.

[20] Knuttel Nr. 6899 und Nr. 7325, 23; zu Johannes Goethals: v. d. Aa, 3: 80; *NNBWb*, 8: 620f.

Prädikanten Lotius,[21] der zusammen mit seinem Kollegen Stermont im
Beisein von Mitgliedern der holländischen Stände ein öffentliches Gebet für
den Oranierprinzen gesprochen und ihm dabei die Stellung "van een
Souverain" und eines semimonarchischen Herrschers eingeräumt hatte[22]
und dessen monarchische Gesinnung auch in einer Predigt anläßlich der
Hinrichtung Karls I. von England zum Ausdruck kam.[23]

Die Auseinandersetzung mit diesen und anderen Mitgliedern der
orangistisch gesonnenen "dominees-Faktion" innerhalb der calvinistischen
Geistlichkeit zeigt bereits in der Semantik deutliche Züge des Antiklerikalismus. Die Theologen wurden bloßgestellt als "Haegsche Pausen of Bisschoppen";[24] als "hoofsche Flateur" oder "gehuyrde Hof-Kryter";[25] als "Oor-
logs-trompetten";[26] als "verkeerde Propheet" oder "verkeerde Evan-
gelist";[27] "Jesuiten ende Jesuitische Puritainen", die aller rechtmäßigen
Regierung Feind seien, vor allem den Regenten in Holland.[28]

An diesen Schimpfnamen läßt sich die inhaltliche Stoßrichtung des
regentenrepublikanischen Antiklerikalismus ablesen. Die Kritik zielt auf vier
eng verbundene Verhaltensweisen bzw. Motive der calvinistischen dominees
ab: Erstens auf die Einmischung in politische Angelegenheiten und den
Aufgabenbereich der weltlichen Gewalten sowie die damit verbundene
Herrschsucht; zweitens auf ihre Unduldsamkeit, die sich zu neuer Papisterei
und Inquisition verdichten; drittens auf ihre Selbstsucht, die Eitelkeit und
persönliche Interessen vor das Wohl der Kirche und der christlichen
Gesellschaft stellen; viertens schließlich, als integrativer Kern von alldem,
auf die Propagierung eines Staats- und Gesellschaftsmodells, das gleichermaßen gegen die Freiheitstraditionen der Niederlande wie gegen die Bibel
und den dort geoffenbarten Willen Gottes verstoße.

Der erste Vorwurf, sich in die Politik einzumischen — "die Nase in
politische Angelegenheiten zu stecken"[29] —, bezog sich zunächst auf die
Parteinahme als solche, nämlich für Oranien und gegen die Regenten. Er
bezog sich dann aber auch auf konkrete Einzelfragen, vor allem auf die
Forderung, den Krieg gegen Spanien fortzusetzen. Die Prädikanten, die sich

---

[21] Bogaard, *Gereformeerden en Oranje*, 64-6, 150.

[22] Knuttel Nr. 6899.

[23] H. A. Enno van Gelder, *Getemperde vryheid. Een verhandeling over de
verhouding van kerk en staat in de Republiek der Verenigde Nederlanden en de
vryheid van meningsuiting in zake godsdienst, drukpers en onderwys, gedurende de
17e eeuw*, Historische Studies 26 (Groningen, 1972), 35; Bogaard, *Gereformeerden
en Oranje*, 64f.

[24] Gemeint sind Stermont und Lotius; Knuttel Nr. 6899.

[25] Knuttel Nr. 7325, 12.

[26] Knuttel Nr. 7325, 18 und Nr. 7596.

[27] Knuttel Nr. 7325, 15, 21.

[28] Knuttel Nr. 7301, 4.

[29] Knuttel Nr. 7596.

selbst "Diener von Christus, dem Friedensfürst" nennen, entblödeten sich nicht, den Münsteraner Frieden anzugreifen und die Friedenspolitik der Regenten als "lästerlich, furchtbar, verderblich und betrügerisch zu brandmarken". "Prädikanten der reformierten Kirche, denen es zustünde Ausrufer und Verkünder des Friedens zu sein, werden zu Trompeten des Krieges, und die Kanzeln donnern und hallten wider von dem Gezeter, das einige im Volk über den Friedensschluß machen".[30]

Die Kritik weitete sich schließlich aus gegen politische Äußerungen von Prädikanten überhaupt, insbesondere, wenn sie von der Kanzel herab erfolgten. Vor allem die Stellungnahmen zur Hinrichtung Karls I. und zur innenpolitischen Situation in England wurden scharf kritisiert.[31] Schließlich kam es zu einem generellen Erlaß der holländischen Stände, der allen Theologen verbot, sich in die Außenpolitik einzumischen.[32] Entsprechendes galt natürlich auch für die Innenpolitik, etwa wenn die Prädikanten öffentlich von der Kanzel herab die Gefangennahme von sechs Führern der Regenten-partei durch Wilhelm II. und ihre Inhaftierung auf der Feste Loevenstein freudig begrüßten.[33] Als besonders ärgerlich empfanden es die Regenten, daß die Prädikanten die Publikation von staatlichen Verordnungen und Verlautbarungen, zu der sie die Magistrate verpflichteten, kommentierten und so die Politik der Obrigkeit kritisierten.[34] Der Teellinck-Konflikt in Seeland, das England-Problem und der Utrechter Disput um die Kirchen-güter zusammengenommen ließen auf seiten der Regentenpartei den Eindruck entstehen, die Prädikanten strebten die Herrschaft ("hoogheydt") in Kirche und Staat ("in het politijk") an. Das aber sei "ein unglückliches

---

[30] Knuttel Nr. 6862; Nr. 7596 u.a. Im Zentrum standen der Utrechter Theologe van der Velde, der den Münsteraner Friede als "vervloekt en goddeloos" verurteilt hatte (L. van Aitzema, *Saecken van staet en oorlogh, Den Haag 1621-1669*, 14 Bde., 9: 1054, zitiert bei P. Geyl, "Historische appreciaties van het 17de eeuwse Hollandse regenten regiem", in *Mededelingen van de koninklyke Vlaamse academie voor wetenschappen, letteren en schone kunsten van België — Klasse der Letteren* 16, Nr. 2: 3-20, dort 13f.), und Teellinck, für den die Friedenspolitik "een verdorven gordel, die nergens toe zal deugen" war (Knuttel Nr. 9675, 15 [= Jer. 13,7]).

[31] Bogaard, *Gereformeerden en Orange*, 67f.

[32] Resolution der Staten von Holland und West Friesland vom 26. 2. 1649, zitiert in Knuttel Nr. 7325; vorher schon in Utrecht am 24. 7. 1655, zitiert bei: Gelder, *Getempeerde vryheid*, 33f.

[33] Knuttel Nr. 7596.

[34] So wird 1665 angeordnet, daß Prädikanten sofort entlassen werden sollen, wenn sie "de deliberatiën en resolutiën van de regeeringe publiquelyk van den stoel voor de ghemeente mochte komen te traduceeren en de overheid by de onderdanen verdagt te maaken of andersins door het verhandelen van politieke saaken op den predikstoel ... te contravenieren de resolutie daarjegens ... genomen." *Kerkelyk Plakaatboek, behelzende de plakaten, ordonantiën en resolutiën over kerkelyke zaken*, gesammelt von N. Wiltens, N. Scheltus, 4 Bde. (s'Gravenhage, 1722-43), 2: 385, zitiert bei: Gelder, *Getemperde vryheid*, 33.

Land, in dem ihre Äußerungen auf dem Gebiet der Politik etwas bewirken und sie die Gemeinde so in der Hand haben, daß sie ihre Befehle ausführt".[35]

Aufs engste verbunden mit diesem Vorwurf der politischen Herrschsucht ist derjenige der Intoleranz — gegen andersgläubige Christen und deren Kirchen ebenso wie gegen Andersdenkende unter den Reformierten selbst. Letzteres bezog sich vor allem auf das erastianisch-arminianische Staatskirchenkonzept der Regenten, das den weltlichen Magistraten das Kontrollrecht über die Öffentlichkeitskirche einräumen sollte. Es wird geradezu als Skandal empfunden, daß die dominees die von der Obrigkeit in christlicher Absicht angeordneten Buß- und Bettage dazu mißbrauchten, "statt das Volk zu Gottesfurchtigkeit zu ermahnen und es mit Gott zu versöhnen, Dispute gegen Papisten, Mennoniten, Arminianer und vor allem Sozinianer auf die Kanzel zu bringen". Letztere kenne man in den Niederlanden überhaupt nur von den Greuelmärchen der Prädikanten, die sie so monströs machten, daß viele im Volk bereit wären, Eintrittsgeld zu zahlen, um einen Sozianer zu sehen. Hier werde das Predigtamt mißbraucht, um "gegen Menschen zu hetzen, die weder herrsch- noch staatssüchtig sind, jeden in Frieden lassen" und mannigfach zum Gemeinen Besten beitragen.[36] Wohl am bittersten wurde der neue, intolerante Klerikalismus der calvinistischen dominees in einem Gedicht gegeißelt, das der Katholik Vondel als Antwort auf Teellincks Angriffe verfaßte und in einer Flugschrift verbreitete. Mit kaum zu überbietender Ironie heißt es dort von dem Streben der Domines:

... Kon Burgerlijcke Tucht die Monsters[37] niet betemmen
Al't land zou tot de keel in bloet en tranen zwemmen:
Want als men steden ziet het onderste omgekeert,
Dan heeft men op zijn Schots den Staet gereformeert.[38]

All dies — und hier geht der Vorwurf der Intoleranz in denjenigen der Eitelkeit und Selbstsucht über — diene nicht dem Wohl der Kirche, sondern allein den egoistischen Interessen der Prädikanten selbst. So verfolgten sie die Dissidenten, weil deren abweichende Gesinnung ihrer Herrschsucht und

---

[35] Knuttel Nr. 7309: "Ja wel het is een ellendich Lant daer haer seggen in't stuck van de Politie yets vermach / en daer sy de Gemeente dan terstont op de handt hebben om hare bevelen uyt te voeren." Knuttel Nr. 6855, 7: "regeer-sucht der Predicanten".

[36] Knuttel Nr. 7596; ähnlich Knuttel Nr. 6862: Dort wird Teellinck vorgeworfen, er verbreite statt Nächstenliebe Bitternis und Haß gegen Mitchristen — gegen Katholiken, die doch gegen die Spanier mitgekämpft hätten, gegen Remonstranten, die doch derselben Religion angehörten, und selbst gegen die Wallonischen Gemeinden. Vgl. auch Knuttel Nr. 6848, fol. B 1 r; Nr. 6855, 11; Nr. 6900, fol. B 2 r; Nr. 6978, fol. A 2: Einführung einer "neuen schottischen Hierarchie".

[37] Nämlich die von den Prädikanten beschworenen Gefahren der Toleranz.

[38] Knuttel Nr. 6864.

ihren politischen Plänen im Wege stünden.[39] Die höfische, einschmeicheln-
de Unterwürfigkeit gegenüber den Oraniern und den Monarchen in Europa,
konkret der Stuart Dynastie in England, entspringe dem Verlangen nach
höfisch gesellschaftlichem Ansehen. Es sei — und hier sind die Anklänge
an den frühprotestantischen Antiklerikalismus besonders deutlich — "loutere
ambitie: sy sullen wel met de naem van Bisschoppen of Praelaten willen
hebben". Sie wollten die Gunst de Oranier Prinzen, um danach sowohl über
ihre Mitbrüder als auch über "het politijck" zu dominieren. Denn es ist nicht
die Religion, sondern es ist die Hoheit, der Teellinck und Stermont
nachjagen.[40]

Die Vorwürfe der Einmischung in Politik und Gesellschaft, der Unduldsamkeit und Herrschsucht sowie der höfischen Eitelkeit und des
Egoismus bündeln sich zu dem Kardinalvorwurf, ein Staats- und Gesellschaftsmodell zu vertreten und einführen zu wollen, das nicht nur die
herrschende ständische Verfassung umstürzen, sondern auch den Willen
Gottes verkehren würde. Kernpunkt des regentenrepublikanischen Antiklerikalismus ist somit die von den Prädikanten selbst implizit oder gar
explizit zur Schau gestellte Affinität zwischen "domineesheerschappij" und
fürstlichem Absolutismus. Es ist die berühmte Formel Jakobs I. von England
"no bishops, no king", die die niederländischen Regenten hier aufnahmen,
nur daß sie diese als negative Alternative zu ihrem eigenen republikanisch-
laikalen Staats- und Gesellschaftsmodell bekämpften.

Den beiden "Haagschen Pausen en Bishoppen ... Lotius en Stermont"
wirft der statisch-republikanisch gesonnene Heer van Blyenberg in einem der
beliebten Dialogpamphlete vor, daß ihre prooranischen Predigten und ihre
öffentlichen Fürbitten für die Oranierprinzen zu nichts anderem dienten, als
den Statthalter zum "Souverain" zu erklären und damit seine "absolute
Regeringe" zu fördern.[41] Dies sei aber — so das Pamphlet "Trouwhartige
Aenspraeck, Aen alle goede Patriotten"[42] in offenem Widerspruch zur
Bibel, deren "Text unmißverstandlich sage, daß Republiken Gott angenehmer
sind als Monarchien". Wenn einige Prädikanten, voran Stermont in den
Haag, gegen dieses staats- und verfassungsrechtliche Grundprinzip der Bibel
angehen, dann geschehe das nur um persönlicher, höfischer Ambitionen
willen. Es sei offenbar, daß dieser und alle anderen "schmeichelnden und zu
Hofe laufenden oder mit diesem korrespondierenden Prädikanten etwas
anderes suchen als das, was sie in der Bibel finden — nämlich, "daß sie wie
die Bischöfe in England ihre Erhebung in die Autorität wollen, um über ihre
Mitbrüder zu gebieten, auf daß diese fortan, ihre gesetzmäßige Berufung und
allen Aufstieg allein durch sie erhalten können". Um diese autoritäre
Verfassung in Kirche und Staat etablieren zu können, setzten die calvinisti-

---

[39] Knuttel Nr. 6848, fol. B 1 r; Nr. 6855, 7 ("hoogvaerdije"); Nr. 6900, fol. B 2 r.
[40] Knuttel Nr. 6900, fol. B 2 r.
[41] Knuttel Nr. 6899.
[42] Knuttel Nr. 6900, B 2 r und v. Dort auch die folgenden Zitate.

schen dominees in Schrift und Wort alles daran, alle "politische Obrigkeit, die den Frieden als heilsam, christlich und für den Staat nötig ansieht, suspekt zu machen". Den plötzlichen Tod Wilhelms II. habe Stermont als göttliches Zeichen deuten wollen, das den "bevorstehenden Fall dieses Landes" ankündige, während ein Blick in die Bibel offenbare, daß Gott für sein Volk die Freiheit vorgesehen habe. Wenn die Niederländer den dominees folgten und diese Freiheit aufs Spiel setzten, werde Gott sagen, "sie haben mich verworfen und uns danach in seinem Zorn einen König" geben.

II.3

Auf der Basis der ausgewerteten Pamphlete, deren Aussagen über Öffentlichkeitskirche und Prädikanten als repräsentativ für die Meinung der Regentenpartei gelten können, lassen sich einige allgemeine Schlußfolgerungen über den Antiklerikalismus der nachreformatorischen Phase formulieren:

1. Auch die offene und multikonfessionelle Gesellschaft der nördlichen Niederlande bot in der frühen Neuzeit genügend Ansatzpunkte für die Entstehung klerikaler Ideologien und Strukturen sowie, im Gegenschlag dazu, für einen frühneuzeitlichen Antiklerikalismus.

2. Der politischen Ausrichtung und der sozialen Trägergruppe nach handelte es sich konkret um einen regentenrepublikanischen Antiklerikalismus, der sich gegen semi-absolutistische und klerikale Tendenzen in der Allianz zwischen Oranierpartei und den rigid calvinistischen Kreisen der Öffentlichkeitskirche richtete.

3. Dieser frühneuzeitliche Typus des Antiklerikalismus stand einerseits in der Tradition des spätmittelalterlichen und vor allem des frühreformatorischen Antiklerikalismus: Es war kein atheistischer Antiklerikalismus, streng genommen war es nicht einmal ein laizistischer Antiklerikalismus. Denn Ausgangspunkt war stets gerade das richtige, biblische, christliche Verhalten, gegen das sich nach Ansicht der Regentenpartei einige Prädikanten versündigten, indem sie Eigeninteressen oder weltliche Zielsetzungen vor den göttlichen Auftrag und das Wohl der Kirche stellten. Sie wurden zu "falschen Propheten" und verderblichen Seelenhirten, denen das Handwerk zu legen war. Dagegen war die Nützlichkeit, ja Notwendigkeit guter und frommer Geistlicher nicht in Frage gestellt.

Diese alteuropäische Form des Antiklerikalismus, die mittelalterliche und frühneuzeitliche Spielarten einschließt, verschwand erst in dem Moment, in dem mit Aufklärung und gesellschaftlich-politischer Transformation seit dem ausgehenden 18. Jahrhundert die strukturelle und theoretische Verzahnung von Religion und Gesellschaft, von Staat und Kirche prinzipiell in Frage gestellt und schießlich auch tatsächlich aufgehoben wurde. Erst danach konnte sich der atheistische Antiklerikalismus herausbilden, der das Bild im 19. und 20. Jahrhundert beherrscht.

4. Innerhalb des alteuropäischen Antiklerikalismus zeigt der frühneuzeitliche andererseits aber auch eigenständige Züge, jedenfalls der hier beschriebene Antiklerikalismus der niederländischen Regentenpartei. Drei Punkte erscheinen mir zentral:

a) Läßt sich der Antiklerikalismus des 15. und frühen 16. Jahrhunderts mit Professor Scribner als "mentality" und "behavior" begreifen,[43] so war er ein Jahrhundert später in den Niederlanden im Kern politisches Programm. Wie weit das typisch für die nachreformatorische bzw. nachkonfessionelle Phase der europäischen Frühneuzeit ist, wäre durch vergleichende Untersuchungen zu prüfen. Die von Robert Kingdon beschriebenen Verhältnisse in Genf[44] deuten jedenfalls in dieselbe Richtung.

b) Der Antiklerikalismus der niederländischen Regentenpartei richtete sich dezidiert gegen klerikale Wortverwaltung und damit gegen den Kernbereich des neuen protestantischen Verständnisses des geistlichen Amtes in der Kirche. Im vorliegenden Fall kann dieses aber eindeutig nicht als Kampf gegen eine auf protestantischem Boden neu etablierte Sakralkaste von Wortverwaltern gedeutet werden. Denn die Vorwürfe richteten sich nicht gegen eine sakrale oder gar magische Umbiegung des Wortes oder gar gegen dessen Mißbrauch im angegebenen Sinne. Im Gegenteil, es war gerade die rationale und funktionale Verwendung des Kanzelwortes und der Predigt für außerkirchliche, politische Zwecke, die den Unmut der Regentenpartei hervorrief. Ähnlich verhielt es sich mit dem Vorwurf, die calvinistischen Prädikanten wollten einen neuen Episkopalismus und Papalismus begründen. Auch dies war politisch gemeint, richtete sich gegen den für die altkirchliche Hierarchie in den Augen der Protestanten charakteristischen politischen Herrschaftsanspruch. Aus dem beschriebenen Antiklerikalismus der niederländischen Regenten läßt sich somit nicht auf eine Erneuerung der mittelalterlichen "Sakralkaste" im Zeichen des evangelischen Wortchristentums schließen. Der Geistliche als herrschsüchtiger Politiker und Interessenvertreter, nicht als sacerdos war die Zielscheibe. Damit gibt sich der Antiklerikalismus der niederländischen Regenten als neuzeitlich-protestantisch zu erkennen. Die Kritik richtet sich nicht gegen ein Fehlverhalten bei Sakralpflichten, sondern gegen den Mißbrauch des Wortes.

c) Wahrscheinlich war auch die Trägergruppe und das kulturelle Substrat ein anders als im Mittelalter und in der Reformationszeit — nicht breite Bevölkerungsschichten, sondern eher Intellektuelle und die Politikelite. Hierzu läßt sich aus dem untersuchten Korpus der Pamphlete wenig sagen. Sicherlich war es nicht so, daß — wie bisweilen zu lesen ist — der Antiklerikalismus der Regenten wie deren Staatsprogramm überhaupt keine

---

[43] Vgl. "Anticlericalism and the Cities" in diesem Band.
[44] Vgl. "Anticlericalism in the Registers of the Geneva Consistory, 1542-1564" in diesem Band.

Resonanz in breiteren Bevölkerungsschichten fanden. Unbestreitbar ist aber, daß sich über die Jahrhunderte hinweg die Oranier auf die städtischen Mittel- und Unterschichten stützten — auf das berühmt-berüchtigte "Oranje gepeupel", wie es die Gegner nannten. Diese orangistische Massenbasis war vor allem dem Einfluß der calvinistischen "dominees" zugeschrieben, die somit Einfluß und Ansehen bei den Mittel- und Unterschichten gehabt haben müssen. Das schließt natürlich nicht aus, daß es daneben auch in den Niederlanden im lokalen Umfeld noch den älteren Typus des popularen Antiklerikalismus gab, wie ihn Gerald Strauss für das späte 16. Jahrhundert beschrieben hat.[45]

5. Betrachtet man, wie eingangs von Herrn Oberman vorgeschlagen, Antiklerikalismus als Agent oder besser Indikator von sozialem Wandel, so läßt sich an dem vorgetragenen Beispiel eine fundamentale Verschiebung zwischen Mittelalter und Neuzeit markieren. Sie betrifft die veränderte Struktur und Funktion der Massenbasis von sozialen Bewegungen wie dem Antiklerikalismus. Die "breiten Schichten", das "einfache Volk", der "gemeine Mann", oder wie man die Trägerschicht auch immer bezeichnen will, erscheint Mitte des 17. Jahrhunderts in den Auseinandersetzungen zwischen Regenten- und Oranierpartei nicht als Substrat alteuropäischen Protestverhaltens, das letztlich systemstabilisierend war, sondern als Massenbasis für parteienähnliche Organisationen.[46] Diese war auch und nicht zuletzt durch den Klerus politisch mobilisierbar, woraus sich ganz neue Konstellationen ergaben. Im Parteienstreit zwischen Oraniern und Regenten, der das innenpolitische Feld der nördlichen Niederlande auf weiten Strecken des 17. und 18. Jahrhunderts prägte, waren calvinistische dominees wichtige Agenten politischer Meinungs- und Parteienbildung. Der von ihnen unterstützten Oranierpartei stand die Regentenpartei gegenüber, die eine solche Einflußnahme bekämpfte und somit einen neuen, politischen Antiklerikalismus vertrat, der ebenfalls auf breite Unterstützung in der sich herausbildenden öffentlichen Meinung angewiesen war. Im Streit um die Stellung der calvinistischen Prädikanten innerhalb der politischen Auseinandersetzungen der alteuropäischen Republik deutete sich bereits jener große Antagonismus zwischen liberalen und christlich-konservativen Parteien an, der in der modernen Welt des 19. Jahrhunderts aufziehen sollte.

---

[45] Vgl. "Local Anticlericalism in Reformation Germany" in diesem Band.

[46] Ausführlich diskutiert in H. Schilling, "Die Geschichte der nördlichen Niederlande und die Modernisierungstheorie", *Geschichte und Gesellschaft* 8 (1982): 475-517, besonders 493-505; engl. Fassung in ders., *Religion* (wie Anm. 2), besonders 322-38.

ABBREVIATIONS

The following list contains sigla commonly used throughout the volume. Generally they are in keeping with those given in the *Theologische Realenzyklopädie—Abkürzungsverzeichnis* (Berlin, 1976). Abbreviations specific to a single chapter are explained in a footnote at or near the beginning of that chapter.

AFH	*Archivum Franciscanum Historicum*
AGKKN	*Archief voor de Geschiedenis van de Katholieke Kerk in Nederland*
AGU	*Archief voor de Geschiedenis van het Aartsbisdom Utrecht*
AHR	*American Historical Review*
AKeG	*Archief voor Kerkelijke Geschiedenis van Nederland*
Annales ESC	*Annales. Economies, sociétés, civilisations*
ARG	*Archiv für Reformationsgeschichte*
ATB	Altdeutsche Textbibliothek
BIHR	*Bulletin of the Institute for Historical Research*
Bijdr.	*Bijdragen. Tijdschrift voor Filosofie en Theologie*
BWKG	*Blätter für württembergische Kirchengeschichte*
ChH	*Church History*
CO	*Corpus Reformatorum. Ioannis Calvini Opera quae supersunt omnia.* 59 vols. Brunswick and Berlin, 1863-1900; reprint, New York and Frankfurt, 1964.
EHR	*English Historical Review*
GAG	Göppinger Arbeiten zur Germanistik
HJ	*Historisches Jahrbuch*
HSA	Hauptstaatsarchiv
HZ	*Historische Zeitschrift*
JEH	*Journal of Ecclesiastical History*
Köhler, Fiche	*Flugschriften des frühen 16. Jahrhunderts (1501-1530) auf Microfiche*, ed. Hans-Joachim Köhler, Hildegard Hebenstreit-Wilfert, Christoph Weismann. Zug, 1978-1987.
Laube	*Flugschriften der frühen Reformationsbewegung (1518-1524)*, ed. Adolf Laube, Sigrid Looß, Annerose Schneider. 2 vols. Berlin, 1983.
LÜAMA	Leipziger Übersetzungen und Abhandlungen zum Mittelalter
LuJ	*Lutherjahrbuch*
MennQR	*Mennonite Quarterly Review*
MGB	*Mennonitische Geschichtsblätter*
MGH	Monumenta Germaniae Historica
MGH.QG	Monumenta Germaniae Historica. Quellen zur Geistesgeschichte des Mittelalters
MGH.SS	Monumenta Germaniae Historica. Scriptores
MTU	Münchener Texte und Untersuchungen zur deutschen Literatur des Mittelalters
NAKG	*Nederlands Archief voor Kerkgeschiedenis*
OGE	*Ons Geestelijk Erf*
PaP	*Past and Present*
QFRG	Quellen und Forschungen zur Reformationsgeschichte
RGST	Reformationsgeschichtliche Studien und Texte
RHE	*Revue d'histoire ecclésiastique*
RHPhR	*Revue d'histoire et de philosophie religieuses*

SCJ	*Sixteenth Century Journal*
SMRT	Studies in Medieval and Reformation Thought
SUB	Thomas Müntzer, *Schriften und Briefe*, ed. Günther Franz. Gütersloh, 1968.
SVRG	Schriften des Vereins für Reformationsgeschichte
VD 16	*Verzeichnis der im deutschen Sprachgebiet erschienenen Drucke des XVI. Jahrhunderts.* Stuttgart, 1983ff.
WA	*D. Martin Luthers Werke. Kritische Gesamtausgabe. Abteilung Schriften.* Weimar, 1883ff.
WABr	*D. Martin Luthers Werke. Kritische Gesamtausgabe. Abteilung Briefwechsel.* 18 vols. Weimar, 1930-85.
WATR	*D. Martin Luthers Werke. Kritische Gesamtausgabe. Abteilung Tischreden.* 6 vols. Weimar, 1912-21.
Z	*Corpus Reformatorum. Huldreich Zwinglis sämtliche Werke.* 14 vols. Berlin, Leipzig and Zurich, 1905-90.
ZHF	*Zeitschrift für Historische Forschung*
ZKG	*Zeitschrift für Kirchengeschichte*

THEMATIC BIBLIOGRAPHY

PETER A. DYKEMA

This bibliography is intended to assist and guide the reader in the study of European anticlericalism, 1300-1700. Included are monographs, journal articles and chapters in books which have as a central theme anticlerical sentiments and actions. Some of the works listed are comprehensive in scope, while others are specific case studies. General surveys or works which deal only tangentially with the stated theme are not included. An emphasis has been placed on recent literature with complete bibliography. While focusing on the forms and carriers of anticlerical sentiment in late medieval and early modern Germany, the bibliography seeks to encompass studies investigating this phenomenon throughout Europe during the entire period in question.

Abray, Lorna Jane. *The People's Reformation: Magistrates, Clergy, and Commons in Strasbourg, 1520-1599*. Ithaca, 1985.

Arnold, Klaus. *Niklashausen 1476. Quellen und Untersuchungen zur sozialreligiösen Bewegung des Hans Behem und zur Agrarstruktur eines spätmittelalterlichen Dorfes*. Saecula Spiritalia 3. Baden-Baden, 1980.

Arnold, Martin. *Handwerker als theologische Schriftsteller. Studien zu Flugschriften der frühen Reformation (1523-1525)*, Göttinger Theologische Arbeiten 42. Göttingen, 1990.

Aston, Margaret. "Lollardy and Sedition." *PaP* 17 (1960): 1-44.

———. *England's Iconoclasts: Laws Against Images*. Oxford, 1988.

Bäumer, Remigius. *Martin Luther und der Papst*. Katholisches Leben und Kirchenreform im Zeitalter der Glaubensspaltung 30. Münster, 1971; rev. 5th ed., 1987.

Beck, Rainer. "Der Pfarrer und das Dorf. Konformismus und Eigensinn im katholischen Bayern des 17./18. Jahrhunderts." In *Armut, Liebe, Ehre. Studien zur historischen Kulturforschung*, ed. R. van Dülmen. Frankfurt, 1988. 107-43.

Bennassar, Bartolomé. *The Spanish Character: Attitudes and Mentalities from the Sixteenth to the Nineteenth Centuries*. Berkeley, 1979.

Berthold, Otto, et al., ed. *Kaiser, Volk und Avignon. Ausgewählte Quellen zur antikurialen Bewegung in Deutschland in der ersten Hälfte des 14. Jahrhunderts*. LÜAMA A 3. Berlin, 1960.

Beutin, Wolfgang. "Zur Problematik des Antiklerikalismus in der europäischen Erzählliteratur um 1400." *Jahrbuch der Oswald-von-Wolkenstein-Gesellschaft* 4 (1986/87): 81-94.

Bierlaire, Franz. "Erasme et Rabelais: d'un anticléricalisme l'autre?" In *Aspects de l'anticléricalisme du Moyen Age à nos jours. Hommage à Robert Joly*, ed. J. Marx. Problèmes d'histoire du christianisme 18. Brussels, 1988. 35-46.

Bizzocchi, Roberto. *Chiesa e potere nell Toscana del Quattrocento*. Bologna, 1987.

Blickle, Peter. *Gemeindereformation. Die Menschen des 16. Jahrhunderts auf dem Weg zum Heil*. Munich, 1985.

Blochwitz, Gottfried. "Die antirömischen deutschen Flugschriften der frühen Reformationszeit (bis 1522) in ihrer religiös-sittlichen Eigenart." *ARG* 27 (1930): 145-246.

Boockmann, Hartmut. "Zu den Wirkungen der 'Reform Kaiser Siegmunds'." In *Studien zum städtischen Bildungswesen des späten Mittelalters und der frühen Neuzeit*, ed. B. Moeller, H. Patze, K. Stackmann. Göttingen, 1983. 112-35.

Boor, Friedrich de. *Wyclifs Simoniebegriff. Die theologischen und kirchenpolitischen Grundlagen der Kirchenkritik John Wyclifs*. Halle, 1970.

Bowker, Margaret. *Secular Clergy in the Diocese of Lincoln 1495-1520*. Cambridge, 1968.
——. *The Henrician Reformation: The Diocese of Lincoln under John Longland 1521-1547*. Cambridge, 1981.
Brigden, Susan. "Tithe Controversy in Reformation London." *JEH* 32 (1981): 285-301.
——. "Youth and the English Reformation." *PaP* 95 (1982): 37-67.
Burger, Christoph. "Huttens Erfahrungen mit Kirche und Frömmigkeit und seine Kritik." In *Ulrich von Hutten in seiner Zeit. Schlüchterner Vorträge zu seinem 500. Geburtstag*, ed. J. Schilling, E. Giese. Kassel, 1988. 35-59.
Burleigh, Michael. "Anticlericalism in Fifteenth-Century Prussia: The Clerical Contribution Reconsidered." In *The Church in Pre-Reformation Society*, ed. C. M. Barron, C. Harper-Bill. Woodbridge, Suffolk, 1985. 38-47.
Caro Baroja, Julio. *Introducción a una historia contemporánea del anticlericalismo español*. Madrid, 1980.
Chittolini, Giorgio and Giovanni Miccoli, ed. *La Chiesa e il potere politico dal Medioevo all' età contemporanea*. Storia d'Italia, Annali 9. Turin, 1986.
Chrisman, Miriam Usher. "Lay Response to the Protestant Reformation in Germany, 1520-1528." In *Reformation Practice and Principle: Essays in Honour of Arthur Geoffrey Dickens*, ed. P. N. Brooks. London, 1986. 33-52.
Cohn, Henry J. "Anticlericalism in the German Peasants' War 1525." *PaP* 83 (1979): 3-31.
——. "Reformatorische Bewegungen und Antiklerikalismus in Deutschland und England." In *Stadtbürgertum und Adel in der Reformation. Studien zur Sozialgeschichte der Reformation in England und Deutschland*, ed. W. J. Mommsen. Veröffentlichungen des Deutschen Historischen Instituts London 5. Stuttgart, 1979. 309-29.
Coleman, Janet. "FitzRalph's Antimendicant 'Proposicio' (1350) and the Politics of the Papal Court at Avignon." *JEH* 35 (1984): 376-90.
Coville, Alfred. *Le traité de la ruine de l'église de Nicolas de Clémanges et la traduction française de 1564*. Paris, 1936.
Davis, Natalie Zemon. "The Rites of Violence." *Society and Culture in Early Modern France*. Stanford, 1975.
Deetjen, Werner-Ulrich. "Die Reformation der Benediktinerklöster Lorch und Murrhardt unter Herzog Ulrich und das 'Judicium de votis monasticis' vom Dezember 1535." *BWKG* 76 (1976): 62-115.
Demandt, Dieter. *Stadtherrschaft und Stadtfreiheit im Spannungsfeld von Geistlichkeit und Bürgerschaft in Mainz (11.-15. Jahrhundert)*. Wiesbaden, 1977.
——. "Konflikte um die geistlichen Standesprivilegien im spätmittelalterlichen Colmar." In *Städtische Gesellschaft und Reformation*, ed. I. Bátori. Spätmittelalter und Frühe Neuzeit 12, Kleine Schriften 2. Stuttgart, 1980. 136-54.
Despey, Georges. "Hérétiques ou anticléricaux? Les 'Cathares' dans nos régions avant 1300." In *Aspects de l'anticléricalisme du Moyen Age à nos jours. Hommage à Robert Joly*, ed. J. Marx. Problèmes d'histoire du christianisme 18. Brussels, 1988. 23-34.
Dickens, Arthur G. "Intellectual and Social Forces in the German Reformation." In *Stadtbürgertum und Adel in der Reformation. Studien zur Sozialgeschichte der Reformation in England und Deutschland*, ed. W. J. Mommsen. Veröffentlichungen des Deutschen Historischen Instituts London 5. Stuttgart, 1979. 11-24.
——. "The Shape of Anti-clericalism and the English Reformation." In *Politics and Society in Reformation Europe: Essays for Sir Geoffrey Elton*, ed. E. I. Kouri, T. Scott. Houndmills, Basingstoke, 1987. 379-410.
——. *The English Reformation*. London, 1964; rev. 2nd ed., 1989. See esp. new ch. 13 in 2nd ed., "Three Retrospective Enquiries", 316-38.
Dionisotti, Carlo. "Chierici e laici." *Geografia e storia della letteratura italiana*. Turin, 1967; 3rd ed., 1977.
Doelle, P. Ferdinand. *Der Klostersturm von Torgau im Jahre 1525*. Franziskanische Studien Beiheft 14. Münster, 1931.

Duggan, Lawrence G. "Fear and Confession on the Eve of the Reformation." *ARG* 75 (1984): 153-75.

——. "The Unresponsiveness of the Late Medieval Church: A Reconsideration." *SCJ* 9 (1978): 2-26.

Edwards, John. "Religious Faith and Doubt in Late Medieval Spain: Soria circa 1450-1500." *PaP* 120 (1988): 3-25.

Eire, Carlos. *War Against the Idols: The Reformation of Worship from Erasmus to Calvin.* Cambridge, 1986.

Elm, Kaspar. "Verfall und Erneuerung des Ordenswesens im Spätmittelalter. Forschung und Forschungsaufgaben." In *Untersuchungen zu Kloster und Stift.* Veröffentlichungen des Max-Planck-Instituts für Geschichte 68, Studien zur Germania Sacra 14. Göttingen, 1980. 188-238.

——. "Die Brüderschaft vom gemeinsamen Leben. Eine geistliche Lebensform zwischen Kloster und Welt, Mittelalter und Neuzeit." *OGE* 59 (1985): 470-96.

Elsener, Ferdinand. "Der eidgenössische Pfaffenbrief von 1370. Ein Beitrag zur Geschichte der geistlichen Gerichtsbarkeit." *Zeitschrift der Savigny-Stiftung für Rechtsgeschichte* 75, Kanonistische Abteilung 44 (1958): 104-80.

Elton, Geoffrey R. "Tithe and Trouble: An Anticlerical Story." *Star Chamber Stories.* London, 1958. 174-220.

Endres, Rudolf. "Zur sozialökonomischen Einstellung des 'gemeinen Mannes'. Der Kloster- und Burgensturm in Franken 1525." In *Der deutsche Bauernkrieg 1524-1526*, ed. H. U. Wehler. *Geschichte und Gesellschaft* Sonderheft 1. Göttingen, 1975. 61-78.

Erickson, C. "The Fourteenth-Century Franciscans and Their Critics." *Franciscan Studies* 35 (1975): 107-35; 36 (1976): 108-47.

Fast, Heinold. "Reformation durch Provokation. Predigtstörungen in den ersten Jahren der Reformation in der Schweiz." In *Umstrittenes Täufertum 1525-1975. Neue Forschungen*, ed. H.-J. Goertz. Göttingen, 1975; 2nd ed., 1977. 79-110.

Firpo, Massimo. "Pasquinate Romane del Cinquecento." *Rivista Storica Italiana* 96 (1984): 600-21.

Fleming, J. V. "Anticlerical Satire as Theological Essay: Chaucer's *Summoner's Tale*." *Thalia* 6 (1983): 5-22.

Franz, Günther, ed. *Beamtentum und Pfarrstand 1400-1800.* Deutsche Führungsschichten der Neuzeit 5. Limburg, 1972.

Franzen, August. *Zölibat und Priesterehe in der Auseinandersetzung der Reformationszeit und der katholischen Reform des 16. Jahrhunderts.* Katholisches Leben und Kirchenreform im Zeitalter der Glaubensspaltung 29. Münster, 1968.

Frölich, Karl. "Kirche und städtisches Verfassungsleben im Mittelalter." *Zeitschrift der Savigny-Stiftung für Rechtsgeschichte* 53, Kanonistische Abteilung 22 (1933): 188-287.

Fubini, Riccardo. *Umanesimo e secolarizzazione da Petrarca a Valla.* Rome, 1990.

Fuhrmann, Rosi. "Die Kirche im Dorf. Kommunale Initiativen zur Organisation von Seelsorge vor der Reformation." In *Zugänge zur bäuerlichen Reformation*, ed. P. Blickle, P. Bierbrauer. Bauer und Reformation 1. Zurich, 1987. 147-86.

——. "Dorfgemeinde und Pfründstiftung vor der Reformation. Kommunale Selbstbestimmungschancen zwischen Religion und Recht." In *Kommunalisierung und Christianisierung. Voraussetzungen und Folgen der Reformation 1400-1600*, ed. P. Blickle, J. Kunisch. ZHF Beiheft 9. Berlin, 1989. 77-112.

Gebhardt, Bruno. *Die Gravamina der deutschen Nation gegen den römischen Hof.* Breslau, 1884; 2nd ed., 1895.

Gilly, Carlos. "Das Sprichwort 'Die Gelehrten, die Verkehrten' in der Toleranzliteratur des 16. Jahrhunderts." In *Anabaptistes et dissidents au XVIᵉ siècle*, ed. J.-G. Rott, S. L. Verheus. Bibliotheca Dissidentium Scripta et Studia 3. Baden-Baden, 1987. 159-75.

Gilman, Sander L. *The Parodic Sermon in European Perspective: Aspects of Liturgical Parody from the Middle Ages to the Twentieth Century.* Beiträge zur Literatur des XV. bis XVIII. Jahrhunderts 6. Wiesbaden, 1974.

Goertz, Hans-Jürgen. "Aufstand gegen den Priester. Antiklerikalismus und reformatorische Bewegungen." In *Bauer, Reich und Reformation. Festschrift für Günther Franz*, ed. P. Blickle. Stuttgart, 1982. 182-209.

———. "Der fremde Menno Simons. Antiklerikale Argumentation im Werk eines melchioritischen Täufers." *MGB* 42 (1985): 24-42.

———. "Antiklerikalismus und Reformation." In *Martin Luther—Leistung und Erbe*, ed. H. Bartel, et al. Berlin, 1986. 182-7.

———. *Pfaffenhaß und groß Geschrei. Die reformatorischen Bewegungen in Deutschland 1517-1529*. Munich, 1987.

———. "'Bannwerfer des Antichrist' und 'Hetzhunde des Teufels'. Die antiklerikale Spitze der Bildpropaganda in der Reformation." *ARG* 82 (1991): 5-38.

Goring, Jenny. "The Reformation of the Ministry in Elizabethan Sussex." *JEH* 34 (1983): 345-66.

Gradon, Pamela. "Langland and the Ideology of Dissent." *Proceedings of the British Academy* 66 (1980): 179-205.

Graus, František. *Pest—Geissler—Judenmorde. Das 14. Jahrhundert als Krisenzeit*. Veröffentlichungen des Max-Planck-Instituts für Geschichte 86. Göttingen, 1987; rev. 2nd ed., 1988.

Green, Ian. "The Persecution of 'Scandalous' and 'Malignant' Parish Clergy during the English Civil War." *EHR* 94 (1979): 507-31.

———. "Career Prospects and Clerical Conformity in the Early Stuart Church." *PaP* 25 (1981): 71-115.

Greiffenhagen, Martin, ed. *Das evangelische Pfarrhaus. Eine Kultur- und Sozialgeschichte*. Stuttgart, 1984.

Gugerli, David. *Zwischen Pfrund und Predigt. Die protestantische Pfarrfamilie auf der Zürcher Landschaft im ausgehenden 18. Jahrhundert*. Zurich, 1988.

Haigh, Christopher. "From Monopoly to Minority: Catholicism in Early Modern England." *Transactions of the Royal Historical Society* 31 (1981): 129-47.

———. "Anticlericalism and the English Reformation." *History* 68 (1983): 391-406.

Harper-Bill, Christopher. "Dean Colet's Convocation Sermon and the Pre-Reformation Church in England." *History* 73 (1988): 191-210.

Harvey, A. E. "Economic Self-Interest in the German Anti-Clericalism of the Fifteenth and Sixteenth Centuries." *American Journal of Theology* 19 (1915): 509-28.

Hashagen, Justus. "Zur Charakteristik der geistlichen Gerichtsbarkeit vornehmlich im späteren Mittelalter." *Zeitschrift der Savigny-Stiftung für Rechtsgeschichte* 37, Kanonistische Abteilung 6 (1916): 205-92.

Heal, Felicity. "Economic Problems of the Clergy." In *Church and Society in England: Henry VIII to James I*, ed. F. Heal, R. O'Day. London, 1977. 99-118.

———. *Of Prelates and Princes: A Study on the Economic and Social Position of the Tudor Episcopate*. Cambridge, 1980.

Heath, Peter. *The English Parish Clergy on the Eve of the Reformation*. London, 1969.

Hecker, Norbert. *Bettelorden und Bürgertum. Konflikt und Kooperation in den deutschen Städten des Spätmittelalters*. Frankfurt, 1981.

Hendrix, Scott. "In Quest of the *Vera Ecclesia*: The Crises of Late Medieval Ecclesiology." *Viator* 7 (1976): 347-78.

———. *Luther and the Papacy*. Philadelphia, 1981.

Hergemöller, Bernd-Ulrich. *"Pfaffenkriege" im spätmittelalterlichen Hanseraum. Quellen und Studien zu Braunschweig, Osnabrück, Lüneburg und Rostock*. Städteforschung, Reihe C: Quellen 2, 1-2. Cologne, 1989.

Herzig, Arno. "Die Beziehungen der Minoriten zum Bürgertum im Mittelalter. Zur Kirchenpolitik der Städte im Zeitalter des Feudalismus." *Die alte Stadt* 6 (1979): 21-53.

Hoffmann, Konrad. "Typologie, Exemplarik und reformatorische Bildsatire." In *Kontinuität und Umbruch. Theologie und Frömmigkeit in Flugschriften und Kleinliteratur an der*

Wende vom 15. zum 16. Jahrhundert, ed. J. Nolte, H. Tompert, C. Windhorst. Spätmittelalter und Frühe Neuzeit 2. Stuttgart, 1978. 189-210.

Hofmann, Konrad. *Die engere Immunität in deutschen Bischofsstädten im Mittelalter.* Paderborn, 1914.

Houlbrooke, Ralph. *Church Courts and The People During the English Reformation, 1520-1570.* Oxford, 1979.

Hoyer, Siegfried. "Lay Preaching and Radicalism in the Early Reformation." In *Radical Tendencies in the Reformation—Divergent Perspectives*, ed. H. J. Hillerbrand. Sixteenth Century Essays & Studies 9. Kirksville, Mo., 1988. 85-97.

Hsia, R. Po-chia. *Social Discipline in the Reformation: Central Europe 1550-1750.* New York, 1989.

Hudson, Anne. *The Premature Reformation: Wycliffite Texts and Lollard History.* Oxford, 1988.

Ingram, Martin. *Church Courts, Sex and Marriage in England 1570-1640.* Cambridge, 1987.

Isenmann, Eberhard. *Die deutsche Stadt im Spätmittelalter 1250-1500. Stadtgestalt, Recht, Stadtregiment, Kirche, Gesellschaft, Wirtschaft.* Stuttgart, 1988.

Janssen, Wilhelm. "'Under dem volk verhast': Zum Episkopat des Kölner Erzbischofs Wilhelm von Gennep (1349-62)." *Annalen des Historischen Vereins für den Niederrhein* 177 (1975): 41-61.

Jedin, Hubert. "Mittelalterliche Wurzeln des Klerikalismus." *Kirche des Glaubens—Kirche der Geschichte. Ausgewählte Aufsätze und Vorträge.* 2 vols. Freiburg, 1966. 1: 331-45.

——. "Das Bishofsideal der Katholischen Reformation. Eine Studie über die Bischofsspiegel vornehmlich des 16. Jahrhunderts." *Kirche des Glaubens—Kirche der Geschichte. Ausgewählte Aufsätze und Vorträge.* 2 vols. Freiburg, 1966. 2: 75-117.

Johnson, Loretta Turner. "An Infinite Clamor: Clerical Anticlericalism in Pre-Reformation England." Ph.D. Diss., University of Nebraska, Lincoln, 1985.

Jørgenson, Ninna. *Bauer, Narr und Pfaffe. Prototypische Figuren und ihre Funktion in der Reformationsliteratur.* Leiden, 1988.

Kaminsky, Howard. "Peter Chelčický: Treatises on Christianity and the Social Order." *Studies in Medieval and Renaissance History* 1 (1964): 104-79.

——, et al., ed. *Master Nicholas of Dresden—The Old Color and the New: Selected Works Contrasting the Primitive Church and the Roman Church.* Transactions of the American Philosophical Society 55/1. Philadelphia, 1965.

——. *A History of the Hussite Revolution.* Berkeley, 1967.

Karant-Nunn, Susan C. *Luther's Pastors: The Reformation in the Ernestine Countryside.* Transactions of the American Philosophical Society 69/8. Philadelphia, 1979.

——. "What was Preached in German Cities in the Early Years of the Reformation?" In *The Process of Change in Early Modern Europe: Essays in Honor of Miriam Usher Chrisman*, ed. P. N. Bebb, S. Marshall. Athens, Ohio, 1988. 81-96.

Kaufman, Peter Iver. "John Colet's *Opus de sacramentis* and Clerical Anticlericalism: The Limitations of 'Ordinary Wayes'." *Journal of British Studies* 22 (1982): 1-22.

——. *The "Polytyque Churche": Religion and Early Tudor Political Culture 1485-1516.* Macon, Ga., 1986.

Kießling, Rolf. *Bürgerliche Gesellschaft und Kirche in Augsburg im Spätmittelalter. Ein Beitrag zur Strukturanalyse der oberdeutschen Reichsstadt.* Augsburg, 1971.

Kingdon, Robert M. "Was the Protestant Reformation a Revolution? The Case of Geneva." In *Transition and Revolution: Problems and Issues of European Renaissance and Reformation History*, ed. R. M. Kingdon. Minneapolis, 1974. 53-76.

——. "Calvin and the Government of Geneva." In *Calvinus Ecclesiae Genevensis Custos*, ed. W. H. Neuser. Frankfurt, 1984. 49-67.

Kintz, Jean-Pierre. "Eglise et société strasbourgeoise du milieu du XVI⁰ siècle au milieu de XVII⁰ siècle." *Annuaire de la Société des Amis du Vieux-Strasbourg* 11 (1983): 33-69.

Kolb, Christian. "Zur Geschichte des Pfarrstandes in Altwürttemberg." *BWKG* 57-8 (1957-8): 69-190.

Kopelke, Otto. *Beiträge zur Geschichte der öffentlichen Meinung über die Kirche in den deutschen Städten von 1420-1460.* Halle, 1910.

Künstle, Franz Xaver. *Die deutsche Pfarrei und ihr Recht zu Ausgang des Mittelalters.* Kirchenrechtliche Abhandlungen 20. Stuttgart, 1905.

Kurze, Dietrich. *Pfarrerwahlen im Mittelalter. Ein Beitrag zur Geschichte der Gemeinde und des Niederkirchenwesens.* Forschungen zur kirchlichen Rechtsgeschichte und zum Kirchenrecht 6. Cologne, 1966.

Lagarde, Georges. *La naissance de l'ésprit laïque au déclin du Moyen Age.* 5 vols. Paris, 1934-46; rev. 2nd. ed., 1956-63.

Lau, Franz. "Reformationsgeschichte bis 1532." In F. Lau, E. Bizer, *Reformationsgeschichte Deutschlands bis 1555,* 3-66. Vol. 3, Lief. K of *Die Kirche in ihrer Geschichte,* ed. K. D. Schmidt, E. Wolf. Göttingen, 1964; 2nd ed., 1969.

Laube, Adolf. "Social Arguments in Early Reformation Pamphlets." *Social History* 12 (1987): 361-78.

Laudage, Johannes. *Priesterbild und Reformpapsttum im 11. Jahrhundert.* Cologne, 1984.

Lehmann, Paul. *Die Parodie im Mittelalter.* Munich, 1922; 2nd ed., Stuttgart, 1963.

Lehmberg, Stanford E. *The Reformation Parliament 1529-1536.* Cambridge, 1970. See esp. ch. 5, "The First Session, 1529: The Anti-Clerical Commons", 76-104.

Lenk, Werner. *"Ketzer" lehren und Kampfprogramme. Ideologieentwicklung im Zeichen der frühbürgerlichen Revolution.* Berlin, 1976.

Lips, E. J. G. "De Brabantse geestelijkheid en de andere sekse." *Tijdschrift voor Geschiedenis* 102 (1989): 1-29.

Löhr, Joseph. *Methodisch-kritische Beiträge zur Geschichte der Sittlichkeit des Klerus besonders der Erzdiözese Köln am Ausgang des Mittelalters.* RGST 17. Münster, 1910.

Lohse, Bernhard. "Luthers Kritik am Mönchtum." *Evangelische Theologie* 20 (1960): 413-32.

———. "Die Kritik am Mönchtum bei Luther und Melanchthon." In *Luther und Melanchthon,* ed. V. Vajta. Göttingen, 1961. 129-45.

———. *Mönchtum und Reformation. Luthers Auseinandersetzung mit dem Mönchsideal des Mittelalters.* Forschungen zur Kirchen- und Dogmengeschichte 12. Göttingen, 1963.

———. "Zu Thomas Müntzers früher Kirchenkritik." *MGB* 46 (1989): 23-9.

Lortz, Joseph. "Zur Problematik der kirchlichen Mißstände im Spätmittelalter." *Trierer theologische Zeitschrift* 58 (1949): 1-26, 212-27, 257-79, 347-57.

Mack, Eugen. *Die kirchliche Steuerfreiheit in Deutschland seit der Dekretalengesetzgebung.* Kirchenrechtliche Abhandlungen 88. Stuttgart, 1916; repr., Amsterdam, 1965.

McCready, William D. "Papalists and Antipapalists: Aspects of the Church/State Controversy in the Later Middle Ages." *Viator* 6 (1975): 241-73.

McDonald, William W. "Anticlericalism, Protestantism, and the English Reformation." *Journal of Church and State* 15 (1973): 21-30.

Meersssemann, Gérard-Gilles. "Groppers Enchiridion und das tridentinische Pfarrerideal." In *Reformata Reformanda. Festgabe für Hubert Jedin,* ed. E. Iserloh, K. Repgen. 2 vols. Münster, 1965. 2: 19-29.

Meier, Johannes. *Der priesterliche Dienst nach Johannes Gropper (1503-1559). Der Beitrag eines deutschen Theologen zur Erneuerung des Priesterbildes im Rahmen eines vortridentinischen Reformkonzeptes für die kirchliche Praxis.* RGST 113. Münster, 1977.

Miedel, J. "Zur Memminger Reformationsgeschichte. Der Tumult in der Frauenkirche." *Beiträge zur bayerischen Kirchengeschichte* 1 (1895).

Moeller, Bernd. "Frömmigkeit in Deutschland um 1500." *ARG* 56 (1965): 5-31.

———. *Pfarrer als Bürger.* Göttinger Universitätsreden 56. Göttingen, 1972.

———. "Kleriker als Bürger." In *Festschrift für Hermann Heimpel.* Veröffentlichungen des Max-Planck-Instituts für Geschichte 36. 3 vols. Göttingen, 1972. 2: 195-224.

———. "Was wurde in der Frühzeit der Reformation in den deutschen Städten gepredigt?" *ARG* 75 (1984): 176-93.

———. "Die Rezeption Luthers in der frühen Reformation." *LuJ* 57 (1990): 57-71.

Moss, Howard K. "A Reevaluation of Masuccio's Anticlericalism." *Italian Quarterly* 19 (1975-76): 43-61.

Mostert, Walter. "Die theologische Bedeutung von Luthers antirömischer Polemik." *LuJ* 57 (1990): 72-92.

Müller, Wolfgang. "Der Beitrag der Pfarrergeschichte zur Stadtgeschichte." *HJ* 94 (1974): 69-88.

Neidiger, Bernhard. *Mendikanten zwischen Ordensideal und städtischer Realität.* Berlin, 1981.

Oakley, Francis. "Religious and Ecclesiastical Life on the Eve of the Reformation." In *Reformation Europe: A Guide to Research*, ed. S. Ozment. St. Louis, 1982. 5-32.

Oberman, Heiko A. *Forerunners of the Reformation: The Shape of Late Medieval Thought Illustrated by Key Documents.* New York, 1966; 2nd ed., Philadelphia, 1981.

——. "Tumultus Rusticorum: Vom 'Klosterkrieg' zum Fürstensieg. Beobachtungen zum Bauernkrieg unter besonderer Berücksichtigung zeitgenössischer Beurteilungen." In *Deutscher Bauernkrieg 1525*, ed. H. A. Oberman, 157-72; = *ZKG* 85 (1974): 301-16. Engl. trans. with appendix, "The Gospel of Social Unrest: 450 Years After the So-Called 'German Peasants' War' of 1525." *The Dawn of the Reformation.* Edinburgh, 1986. 155-78.

——. *Werden und Wertung der Reformation. Vom Wegestreit zum Glaubenskampf.* Tübingen, 1977; 3rd edition, 1989. See esp. discussion on tithes and edition of Summenhart's treatise. Engl. trans. *Masters of the Reformation: The Emergence of a New Intellectual Climate in Europe.* Cambridge, 1983.

——. "The Impact of the Reformation: Problems and Perspectives." In *Politics and Society in Reformation Europe: Essays for Sir Geoffrey Elton*, ed. E. I. Kouri, T. Scott. Houndmills, Basingstoke, 1987. 3-31.

——. "Captivitas Babylonica: Die Kirchenkritik des Johann von Staupitz." In *Reformatio et reformationes. Festschrift für Lothar Graf zu Dohna*, ed. A. Mehl, W. C. Schneider. THD-Schriftenreihe Wissenschaft und Technik 47. Darmstadt, 1989. 97-106.

——. "Duplex misericordia: Der Teufel und die Kirche in der Theologie des jungen Johann von Staupitz." Festschrift für Martin Anton Schmidt, *Theologische Zeitschrift* 45 (1989): 231-43.

O'Day, Rosemary, Felicity Heal, ed. *Princes and Paupers in the English Church 1500-1800.* Leicester, 1981.

Oehmig, Stefan. "Mönchtum—Reformation—Säkularisation. Zu den demographischen und sozialen Folgen des Verfalls des Klosterwesens in Mitteldeutschland." *Jahrbuch für Geschichte des Feudalismus* 10 (1986): 209-50.

Ozment, Steven E. *The Reformation in the Cities: The Appeal of Protestantism to Sixteenth-Century Germany and Switzerland.* New Haven, 1975.

Packull, Werner O. "The Image of the 'Common Man' in the Early Pamphlets of the Reformation (1520-1525)." *Historical Reflections/Réflexions Historiques* 12 (1985): 253-77.

Pfaff, Carl. "Pfarrei und Pfarreileben. Ein Beitrag zur spätmittelalterlichen Kirchengeschichte." In *Innerschweiz und frühe Eidgenossenschaft.* Olten, 1990. 203-82.

Pfrunder, Peter. *Pfaffen, Ketzer, Totenfresser. Fastnachtskultur der Reformationszeit—Die Berner Spiele von Niklaus Manuel.* Zurich, 1989.

Postel, Rainer. "Horenjegers und Kökschen. Zölibat und Priesterehe in der hamburgischen Reformation." In *Städtische Gesellschaft und Reformation*, ed. I. Bátori. Spätmittelalter und Frühe Neuzeit 12, Kleine Schriften 2. Stuttgart, 1980. 221-33.

Rapp, Francis. *Réformes et reformation à Strasbourg. Eglise et société dans le diocèse de Strasbourg (1450-1525).* Collection de l'Institut des Hautes Etudes Alsaciennes 23. Paris, 1974.

——. "Jean Geiler de Kaysersberg (1445-1510), le prédicateur de la cathédrale de Strasbourg." In *Grandes figures de l'humanisme alsacien. Courants, milieux, destins*, ed. F. Rapp and G. Livet. Strasbourg, 1978. 25-32.

Ritter, Susanne. "Die kirchenkritische Tendenz in den deutschsprachigen Flugschriften der frühen Reformationszeit." Diss. Phil., Universität Tübingen, 1970.

Rodes, Robert E., Jr. *Lay Authority and Reformation in the English Church: Edward I to the Civil War*. Notre Dame, 1982.

Rott, Jean. "Pfaffenfehden und Anfänge der Reformation in Straßburg. Die Streitigkeiten des Johannes Murner mit den Brüdern Wolff und dem Jung Sankt Peter-Stift daselbst (1519-1522)." In *Landesgeschichte und Geistesgeschichte*, ed. K. Elm, E. Gönner, E. Hildenbrand. Stuttgart, 1977. 279-94.

Rublack, Hans-Christoph. "Forschungsbericht Stadt und Reformation." In *Stadt und Kirche im 16. Jahrhundert*, ed. B. Moeller. SVRG 190. Gütersloh, 1978. 9-26.

——. "Gravamina und Reformation." In *Städtische Gesellschaft und Reformation*, ed. I. Bátori. Spätmittelalter und Frühe Neuzeit 12, Kleine Schriften 2. Stuttgart, 1980. 292-313.

——. "Zur Rezeption von Luthers De votis monasticis iudicium." In *Reformation und Revolution. Beiträge zum politischen Wandel und den sozialen Kräften am Beginn der Neuzeit. Festschrift für Rainer Wohlfeil*, ed. R. Postel, F. Kopitzsch. Stuttgart, 1989. 224-37.

——. "'Der wohlgeplagte Priester'. Vom Selbstverständnis lutherischer Geistlichkeit im Zeitalter der Orthodoxie." *ZHF* 16 (1989): 1-30.

Russell, Paul A. *Lay Theology in the Reformation: Popular Pamphleteers in Southwest Germany, 1521-25*. Cambridge, 1986.

Sabean, David W. *Power in the Blood: Popular Culture and Village Discourse in Early Modern Germany*. Cambridge, 1984.

Sánchez, José. *Anticlericalism: A Brief History*. Notre Dame, 1972.

Sanchez Bella, Florencio. *La reforma del clero en San Juan de Avila*. Madrid, 1981.

Scarisbrick, John J. *The Reformation and the English People*. Oxford, 1988.

Scase, Wendy. *"Piers Plowman" and the New Anticlericalism*. Cambridge Studies in Medieval Literature 4. Cambridge, 1989.

Schnabel-Schüle, Helga. "Distanz und Nähe. Zum Verhältnis von Pfarrern und Gemeinden im Herzogtum Württemberg vor und nach der Reformation." *Rottenburger Jahrbuch für Kirchengeschichte* 5 (1986): 339-48.

Schorn-Schütte, Luise. "'Papocaesarismus' der Theologen? Vom Amt des evangelischen Pfarrers in der frühneuzeitlichen Stadtgesellschaft bei Bugenhagen." *ARG* 79 (1988): 230-61.

Schüppert, Helga. *Kirchenkritik in der lateinischen Lyrik des 12. und 13. Jahrhunderts*. Medium Aevum 23. Munich, 1972.

Schultze, Alfred. *Stadtgemeinde und Reformation*. Recht und Staat in Geschichte und Gegenwart 11. Tübingen, 1918.

Schulze, Manfred. *Fürsten und Reformation. Geistliche Reformpolitik weltlicher Fürsten vor der Reformation*. Spätmittelalter und Reformation, Neue Reihe 2. Tübingen, 1991.

Scribner, Robert W. "Memorandum on the Appointment of a Preacher in Speyer." *BIHR* 48 (1975): 248-55.

——. *For the Sake of Simple Folk: Popular Propaganda for the German Reformation*. Cambridge Studies in Oral and Literate Culture 2. Cambridge, 1981.

——. "Practice and Principle in the German Towns: Preachers and People." In *Reformation Practice and Principle: Essays in Honour of Arthur Geoffrey Dickens*, ed. P. N. Brooks. London, 1986. 95-117.

——. "Antiklerikalismus in Deutschland um 1500." In *Europa um 1500. Integrationsprozesse im Widerstreit. Staaten, Regionen, Personenverbände, Christenheit*, ed. F. Seibt, W. Eberhard. Stuttgart, 1987. 368-82.

——. "Anticlericalism and the Reformation in Germany." *Popular Culture and Popular Movements in Reformation Germany*. London, 1987. 243-56.

——, ed. *Bilder und Bildersturm im Spätmittelalter und in der frühen Neuzeit*. Wolfenbütteler Forschungen 46. Wiesbaden, 1990.

——. "Luther's Anti-Roman Polemik and Popular Belief." *LuJ* 57 (1990): 93-113.

Seidenberger, Johannes B. "Die Kämpfe der Mainzer Zünfte gegen Geistlichkeit und Geschlechter im 15. Jahrhundert." *HJ* 8 (1887): 430-53.

Šmahel, František. *La révolution hussite, une anomalie historique*. Paris, 1985.

Snyder, Arnold. "Biblical Text and Social Context: Anabaptist Anticlericalism in Reformation Zürich." *MennQR* 65 (1991): 169-91.

Spaeth, Donald. "Parsons and Parishioners: Lay-Clerical Conflict and Popular Piety in Wiltshire Villages, 1660-1740." Ph.D. Diss., Brown University, 1985.

Stafford, William. *Domesticating the Clergy: The Inception of the Reformation in Strasbourg 1522-1524*. Missoula, Mont., 1976.

———. "Anticléricalisme et mouvement évangélique." In *Strasbourg au coeur religieux du XVIe siècle. Hommage à Lucien Febvre*, ed. G. Livet, F. Rapp. Strasbourg, 1977. 63-74.

Stamm, Heinz-Meinolf. *Luthers Stellung zum Ordensleben*. Veröffentlichungen des Instituts für Europäische Geschichte Mainz 101. Wiesbaden, 1980.

Stayer, James. "The Swiss Brethren: An Exercise in Historical Definition." *ChH* 47 (1978): 174-95.

Störmann, Anton. *Die städtischen Gravamina gegen den Klerus am Ausgange des Mittelalters und in der Reformationszeit*. RGST 24-26. Münster, 1916.

Strauss, Gerald, ed. *Manifestations of Discontent in Germany on the Eve of the Reformation*. Bloomington, Ind., 1971.

———. *Luther's House of Learning: Indoctrination of the Young in the German Reformation*. Baltimore, 1978.

Sydow, Jürgen. "Bürgerschaft und Kirche im Mittelalter. Probleme und Aufgaben der Forschung." In *Bürgerschaft und Kirche*, ed. J. Sydow. Stadt in der Geschichte 7. Sigmaringen, 1980. 9-25.

Szittya, Penn R. *The Antifraternal Tradition in Medieval Literature*. Princeton, 1986.

Thomson, John A. F. *The Later Lollards 1414-1520*. London, 1965.

———. "Tithe Disputes in Later Medieval London." *EHR* 78 (1963): 1-17.

Trüdinger, Karl. *Stadt und Kirche im spätmittelalterlichen Würzburg*. Spätmittelalter und Frühe Neuzeit 1. Stuttgart, 1978.

Urban, Hans J. "Der reformatorische Protest gegen das Papsttum. Eine theologiegeschichtliche Skizze." *Catholica* 30 (1976): 295-319.

Vasella, Oscar. "Der Ittinger Sturm im Lichte österreichischer Berichte (1524)." In *Reformata Reformanda. Festgabe für Hubert Jedin*, ed. E. Iserloh and K. Repgen. 2 vols. Münster, 1965. 1: 365-91.

Venard, Marc. "Pour une sociologie du clergé au XVIe siècle: Recherche sur le recrutement sacerdotal dans la province d'Avignon." *Annales ESC* 23 (1968): 987-1016.

Vice, Roy L. "The Village Clergy near Rothenburg ob der Tauber and the Peasants' War." *ARG* 82 (1991): 123-46.

Viénot, John. *Histoire de la réforme française des origines à l'Edit de Nantes*. Paris, 1926.

Vogler, Bernard. "Recrutement et carrière des pasteurs strasbourgeois au XVIe siècle." *RHPhR* 48 (1968): 151-74.

———. *Le clergé protestant rhénan au siècle de la réforme (1555-1619)*. Paris, 1976.

Vogler, Günther. "Imperial City Nuremberg, 1524-25: The Reform Movement in Transition." In *The German People and the Reformation*, ed. R. Po-chia Hsia. Ithaca, 1988. 33-49.

Voigt, Johannes. "Über Pasquille, Spottlieder und Schmähschriften aus der ersten Hälfte des 16. Jahrhunderts." In *Historisches Taschenbuch*, ed. F. von Raumer. Vol. 9. Leipzig, 1838. 321-524.

Vose, Heather M. "A Sixteenth-century Assessment of the French Church in the Years 1521-4 by Bishop Guillaume Briçonnet of Meaux." *JEH* 39 (1988): 509-19.

Walsh, Katherine. *A Fourteenth-Century Scholar and Primate: Richard FitzRalph in Oxford, Avignon and Armagh*. Oxford, 1981.

Weiler, A. G. "Recent Historiography on the Modern Devotion: Some Debated Questions." *AGKKN* 27 (1985): 161-75.

Weinhold, Rudolf. "'Wer waiß wers recht verstanden hat!' Das Erfurter Pfaffenstürmen im Spiegel zweier zeitgenössischer Lieder." In *Der arm man 1525. Volkskundliche Studien*, ed. H. Strobach. Berlin, 1975. 219-36.

Weiss, Ulman. "Das Erfurter Pfaffenstürmen 1521: 'Haec Lutheranorum adversus Clericos seditio'." *Jahrbuch für Geschichte des Feudalismus* 3 (1979): 233-79.

———. *Die frommen Bürger von Erfurt. Die Stadt und ihre Kirche im Spätmittelalter und in der Reformationszeit.* Weimar, 1988.

Werner, Heinrich. "Die Reformation des Kaisers Sigmund. Die erste deutsche Reformschrift eines Laien vor Luther." *Archiv für Kulturgeschichte* 3 (1903): 1-113.

Wilks, Michael. "*Reformatio regni*: Wyclif and Hus as Leaders of Religious Protest Movements." In *Schism, Heresy and Religious Protest*, ed. D. Baker. Studies in Church History 9. Cambridge, 1972. 109-30.

Wolter, Hans, S.J. "Die Gravamina des Klerus gegen den Rat von Frankfurt am Main im Jahre 1526." *Archiv für mittelrheinische Kirchengeschichte* 25 (1973): 203-26.

Wunderli, Richard M. *London Church Courts and Society on the Eve of the Reformation.* Cambridge, Mass., 1981.

Yunck, John A. *The Lineage of Lady Meed.* Publications in Medieval Studies 17. Notre Dame, 1963.

Zeeden, Ernst Walter and Peter T. Lang, ed. *Kirche und Visitation. Beiträge zur Erforschung des frühneuzeitlichen Visitationswesens in Europa.* Spätmittelalter und Frühe Neuzeit 14. Stuttgart, 1984.

INDEX OF SUBJECTS

INDEX OF PERSONAL AND PLACE NAMES

INDEX OF MODERN AUTHORS

STUDIES IN MEDIEVAL
AND REFORMATION THOUGHT
EDITED BY HEIKO A. OBERMAN

1. DOUGLASS, E.J. Dempsey. *Justification in Late Medieval Preaching.* 2nd ed. 1989
2. WILLIS, E.D. *Calvin's Catholic Christology.* 1966 *out of print*
3. POST, R.R. *The Modern Devotion.* 1968
4. STEINMETZ, D.C. *Misericordia Dei.* The Theology of Johannes von Staupitz. 1968 *out of print*
5. O'MALLEY, J.W. *Giles of Viterbo on Church and Reform.* 1968 *out of print*
6. OZMENT, S.E. *Homo spiritualis.* The Anthropology of Tauler, Gerson and Luther. 1969
7. PASCOE, L.B. *Jean Gerson: Principles of Church Reform.* 1973
8. HENDRIX, S.H. *Ecclesia in Via.* Medieval Psalms Exegesis and the *Dictata super Psalterium* (1513-1515) of Martin Luther. 1974
9. TREXLER, R.C. *The Spiritual Power.* Republican Florence under Interdict. 1974
10. TRINKAUS, Ch. with OBERMAN, H.A. (eds.) *The Pursuit of Holiness.* 1974 *out of print*
11. SIDER, R.J. *Andreas Bodenstein von Karlstadt.* 1974
12. HAGEN, K. *A Theology of Testament in the Young Luther.* 1974
13. MOORE, Jr., W.L. *Annotatiunculae D. Iohanne Eckio Praelectore.* 1976
14. OBERMAN, H.A. with BRADY, Jr., Th. A. (eds.) *Itinerarium Italicum.* Dedicated to Paul Oskar Kristeller. 1975
15. KEMPFF, D. *A Bibliography of Calviniana.* 1959-1974. 1975 *out of print*
16. WINDHORST, C. *Täuferisches Taufverständnis.* 1976
17. KITTELSON, J.M. *Wolfgang Capito.* 1975
18. DONNELLY, J.P. *Calvinism and Scholasticism in Vermigli's Doctrine of Man and Grace.* 1976
19. LAMPING, A.J. *Ulrichus Velenus (Oldřich Velenský) and his Treatise against the Papacy.* 1976
20. BAYLOR, M.G. *Action and Person.* Conscience in Late Scholasticism and the Young Luther. 1977
21. COURTENAY, W.J. *Adam Wodeham.* 1978
22. BRADY, Jr., Th. A. *Ruling Class, Regime and Reformation at Strasbourg, 1520-1555.* 1978
23. KLAASSEN, W. *Michael Gaismair.* 1978
24. BERNSTEIN, A.E. *Pierre d'Ailly and the Blanchard Affair.* 1978
25. BUCER, Martin. *Correspondance.* Tome I (Jusqu'en 1524). Publié par J. Rott. 1979
26. POSTHUMUS MEYJES, G.H.M. *Jean Gerson et l'Assemblée de Vincennes (1329).* 1978
27. VIVES, Juan Luis. *In Pseudodialecticos.* Ed. by Ch. Fantazzi. 1979
28. BORNERT, R. *La Réforme Protestante du Culte à Strasbourg au XVIe siècle (1523-1598).* 1981
29. SEBASTIAN CASTELLIO. *De Arte Dubitandi.* Ed. by E. Feist Hirsch. 1981
30. BUCER, Martin. *Opera Latina.* Vol. I. Publié par C. Augustijn, P. Fraenkel, M. Lienhard. 1982
31. BÜSSER, F. *Wurzeln der Reformation in Zürich.* 1985
32. FARGE, J.K. *Orthodoxy and Reform in Early Reformation France.* 1985
33, 34. BUCER, Martin. *Etudes sur les relations de Bucer avec les Pays-Bas.* I. Etudes; II. Documents. Par J.V. Pollet. 1985
35. HELLER, H. *The Conquest of Poverty.* The Calvinist Revolt in Sixteenth Century France. 1986
36. MEERHOFF, K. *Rhétorique et poétique au XVIe siècle en France.* 1986
37. GERRITS, G.H. *Inter timorem et spem.* Gerard Zerbolt of Zutphen. 1986
38. ANGELO POLIZIANO. *Lamia.* Ed. by A. Wesseling. 1986
39. BRAW, C. *Bücher im Staube.* Die Theologie Johann Arndts in ihrem Verhältnis zur Mystik. 1986
40. BUCER, Martin. *Opera Latina.* Vol. II. Enarratio in Evangelion Iohannis (1528, 1530, 1536). Publié par I. Backus. 1988
41. BUCER, Martin. *Opera Latina.* Vol. III. Martin Bucer et Matthew Parker: Florilegium Patristicum. Edition critique. Publié par P. Fraenkel. 1988
42. BUCER, Martin. *Opera Latina.* Vol. IV. Consilium Theologicum Privatim Conscriptum. Publié par P. Fraenkel. 1988
43. BUCER, Martin. *Correspondance.* Tome II (1524-1526). Publié par J. Rott. 1989
44. RASMUSSEN, T. *Inimici Ecclesiae.* Das ekklesiologische Feindbild in Luthers »Dictata super Psalterium« (1513-1515) im Horizont der theologischen Tradition. 1989
45. POLLET, J. *Julius Pflug et la crise religieuse dans l'Allemagne du XVIe siècle.* Essai de synthèse biographique et théologique. 1990
46. BUBENHEIMER, U. *Thomas Müntzer.* Herkunft und Bildung. 1989

47. BAUMAN, C. *The spiritual legacy of Hans Denck*. Interpretation and Translation of Key Texts. 1991
48. OBERMAN, H.A. and JAMES, F.A., III (eds.) in cooperation with SAAK, E.L. *Via Augustini*. Augustine in the Later Middle Ages, Renaissance and Reformation: essays in honor of Damasus Trapp. 1991
49. SEIDEL MENCHI, S. *Erasmus als Ketzer*. Reformation und Inquisition im Italien des 16. Jahrhunderts. 1993
50. SCHILLING, H. *Religion, Political Culture, and the Emergence of Early Modern Society*. Essays in German and Dutch History. 1992
51. DYKEMA, P.A. and OBERMAN, H.A. (eds.) *Anticlericalism in Late Medieval and Early Modern Europe*. 1993

Prospectus available on request

E.J. BRILL — P.O.B. 9000 — 2300 PA LEIDEN — THE NETHERLANDS

DATE DUE
